ASHE Reader Series

ASSESSMENT AND PROGRAM EVALUATION

Second Edition

Edited by
Wynetta Y. Lee
Dillard University

ASHE Reader Series Editor
Lenoar Foster, Washington State University

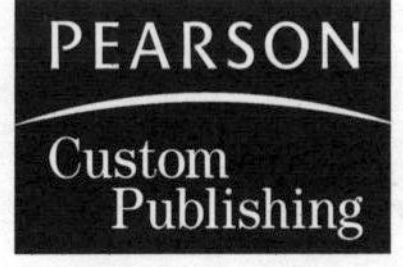

Cover art by Bernadette Levasseur.

Printed in the United States of America

10 9 8 7 6 5 4 3 2 1

ISBN 0-536-75350-4

BA 997789

JA/NN

Please visit our web site at *www.pearsoncustom.com*

PEARSON CUSTOM PUBLISHING
75 Arlington Street, Suite 300, Boston, MA 02116
A Pearson Education Company

CONTENTS

SECTION II. ADMINISTRATION AND INSTITUTIONAL PERFORMANCE

SECTION III. TEACHING AND LEARNING

Current Readings

ACKNOWLEDGMENTS

The support and patience of the ASHE Reader Series Board is greatly appreciated. The plans for proceeding with the reader were deterred and revised for several reasons, as plans often are. However, frustrations regarding the unexpected did have a benefit; several lessons were learned that will be invaluable in future iterations of effort to contribute to knowledge in the field. The editor of this reader has extensive training and an established recorded in the assessment and evaluation field, including ten years of teaching at the graduate level. Nonetheless, it is impossible for a project of this magnitude to be a solitary venture. In the spirit of the African proverb that says "no matter how big the eye, two are better," several established and emerging scholars were invited to lend their wisdom to the development of this reader via participation on an Advisory Committee. This group is credited with considerable help regarding focus, content and the identification of literature for the reader; errors (commission or omission) rest with the editor. The level of support and professionalism from colleagues involved with the project can never be repaid nor will it be forgotten. The advisory committee members include

Duane Akroyd
Jo Allen
Guadalupe Anaya
James Anderson
Trudy Banta
Jeannette Barker
Christopher Brown
Thomas Conway
James Earl Davis
Latrice Eggleton
Kassie Freeman
Lenoar Foster
Millie Garcia
Janet Guyden
Stephanie Helms
Joseph Hoey
Bruce Jones
Frankie Laanan
Michael T. Nettles
Cheryl Presley
Laura Rendon
Carolyn Thompson
Cora Salzburg
Ephraim Schechter
Darryl Smith
Nannette Smith
Linda Susskie
Gayle Harris Watkins

Special thanks goes to Ronyelle D. Bertrand, doctoral student and research assistant at The Pennsylvania State University, for the countless hours spent in organizing the content of the reader. Hopefully the experience will not discourage her future productivity in the field. Special thanks are also extended to Zena Ezeb, administrative assistant at Dillard University, for her willingness to go beyond the call of duty in the production of the reader.

PREFACE

WYNETTA Y. LEE
PROFESSOR & ASSISTANT PROVOST FOR CURRICULUM AND UNDERGRADUATE RESEARCH
DILLARD UNIVERSITY

The drive to be globally competitive diminishes the wisdom of conducting business as usual. Savvy powerbrokers and 21st century leaders tend to favor evidence-based decisions over "shooting from the hip" strategies. The connection of assessment and evaluation to the increasing demands for accountability is a double edged sword. Calls for accountability carry expectations for improvement over time, which fuels the momentum for the positive utility of assessment and evaluation in the decision-making process. However, accountability demands also carry the potential for punitive consequences via assessment and evaluation (Stark & Thomas, 1994).

Evolution of the Field

The high visibility of assessment/evaluation gives the impression of being a new development but quite the opposite is true (Madus, Stufflebeam & Scriven, 1987). Assessment/evaluation has undergone several iterations of development with identifiable eras, beginning with the age of reform in the 1800s when assessment/evaluation was the kingpin for reforming education and social programs. Since that time, many other "ages" of evaluation evolved, each with various economic, political or technical drivers that anchored the period.

The prevailing influence on the field, initially, was that of measurement, which most often occurred in schools in the form of testing. The evaluator's role was strictly technical, responsible for measuring various variables upon request. This approach, especially by today's standards, was one-dimensional. Focusing on the technical nature of measurement precluded the ability to put measurement into context relative to the stated objectives of planned efforts. This lead to the next influence on the development of the field which was the "description of patterns of strengths and weaknesses with respect to certain stated objectives… measurement was no longer treated as the equivalent of evaluation but was redefined as one of several tools that might be used in its service"(Guba & Lincoln, 1989, p. 28). The role of the evaluator expanded to be both technical skill for measurement and that of describer. Over time, measurement and description was not enough. During the late 1960s judgment became a trait of evaluation, evidenced by the emergence of various decision based evaluation models. Thus the role of the evaluator was technical, describer and judge. The growing pains of the field generated considerable (and sometimes heated) debate over the appropriateness of these roles.

The transition of leadership practice from a top-down decision making process to a collaborative, consensus building process paved the way for another milestone in the development of evaluation field. Responsive constructivist evaluation (Guba & Lincoln, 1989) uses the claims and concerns of stakeholders as a foundation for identifying what information is needed. One of the benefits of this approach is that it empowers stakeholders to be meaningfully involved in the evaluation planning process. It is important to note that this approach to evaluation is different from, not easier than, the traditional social science methods that prevailed during the early years. Involving stakeholders is a large investment of the evaluator's time and energy on the front end of the process. Nonetheless, stakeholders tend to have different perspectives and values. Reconciling stakeholders' differences could slow down the process; timeliness in presenting findings is a continuous challenge for those conducting evaluations. However, the time investment is well worth the effort since it promotes a multi-dimensional evaluation and enhances the utility of the final product.

Assessment and Evaluation: Two sides of the same coin?

Scriven (1995) argues that "evaluation has to be distinguished from near-synonyms such as assessment . . . , on the one hand, and from substantially different concepts such as monitoring . . . on the other . . . (p.51). There are varying perspectives regarding the difference between assessment and evaluation. The terms "assessment and evaluation" appear in some literature as an amalgamated concept, synonymous in meaning. Yet, other literature approaches the terms as distinctively different—the main difference being the value of one over the other. At the risk of oversimplification, assessment generally means to measure (e.g. usually individuals) while "evaluation," as a term in the literature, frequently means to attach value (e.g. usually to programs or organizational entities) (Davis, 1989). In other words, the distinction between the two is that assessment is a numerical value while evaluation is a subjective judgment. To further confuse matters, the broad field of assessment and evaluation has related terms and the lines of distinction are often blurred. Students of assessment and evaluation should become familiar with related terms (such as self-study, program review, formative assessment, summative assessment, evaluation research) since there is much to be learned from literature regarding related concepts. Michael Scriven's (1991) book, *The Evaluation Thesaurus,* is a useful reference for defining terms in the field.

The dialogue on assessment and evaluation is voluminous and eclectic in the literature. However, clarity in understanding assessment and evaluation as concepts could be enhanced by distinguishing *what* is done from *how* it is done. For example, assessment is an action that measures, or determines boundaries in a way that makes the unknown known or the intangible tangible. This task could be accomplished mathematically (e.g. a numerical value) or verbally (e.g. description in proper context). Evaluation can be thought of as what happens after assessment, the process of determining merit or value based on what was measured. From this point of view, assessment could happen without evaluation but evaluation should not occur without assessment at its foundation. Each term (what) should be accomplished via adherence to the rules of rigor for investigative paradigms (how). Applying this logic means that both processes and outcomes can be assessed and in each case a judgment regarding value can be made.

In addition to what and how, it is important to note when the assessment and evaluation activities occur. The process, whether formative or summative, is the same—distinguished by timing. Formative assessments/evaluations occur when an activity (e.g. program, instructional strategy, treatment, etc.) is still developing, or "forming." Arguably, the value of formative assessments/evaluations is the opportunity to fine tune strategies early such that the likelihood of positive effects are enhanced and the inefficient use of resources are minimized; formative assessments/evaluations are most helpful to program planners, teachers, and others who are responsible for implementation of policies or planned interventions/strategies. Summative assessments/evaluations occur when the implementation of the activity is repetitive and consistent, or when the activity terminates. Summative assessments/evaluations are most useful to those who focus on outcomes and the lessons learned in the process.

The Assessment/Evaluation Process

Inquiry that adheres to the rules of rigor for research, regardless of paradigm, is the foundation for assessment and evaluation. The process is continuous and consists of identifying the focus, data acquisition and analysis, drawing conclusions and making recommendations. At this point, as far as the evaluator is concerned, the assessment/evaluation process cycle ends since evaluators usually have no control over making decisions (i.e. using evaluation findings). As for stakeholders, the recommendations should "complete the loop," making evaluation and assessment a continuous process. Strategies for completing this process are virtually limitless. Planning the process is an essential element for quality in the resulting product. The process is rooted in research procedures and even under ideal circumstances the best made plans can go awry. However, lack of planning leads to missed opportunities for data collection that could result in inconclusive findings. Even worse, the lack of planning could result in wrong conclusions that form a basis for future decisions.

The discussion here might lead readers to conclude that evaluation is a simple process that can be accomplished with a minimum amount of effort. Actually, the process for assessment and evaluation must be viewed as a form of applied, action, basic or field research and should undergo the same diligence in planning and execution as that of any credible process of systematic inquiry.

Assessment/Evaluation Standards

The Joint Committee on Standards for Educational Evaluation (JCSEE) was founded to develop standards for educational evaluation. Professional organizations such as The American Psychological Association, the National Council on Measurement in Education, and the American Educational Research Association initiated the JCSEE and membership has grown to include several other organizations. Currently the standards include program evaluation standards, personnel evaluation standards and student evaluation standards. The standards are useful guides for quality and appropriateness in the evaluation process.

The Program Evaluation Standards focus on utility, feasibility, propriety and accuracy. The utility standard has seven points that address issues such as stakeholder identification, values identification, report clarity and evaluation impact. The utility standards focuses on assuring that an evaluation will serve the information needs of intended users. The feasibility standards address practical procedures, political viability and cost effectiveness. This standard focuses on the extent to which the evaluation will be frugal, diplomatic and realistic. The propriety standards have eight points that address issues such as rights of human subjects, human interactions, complete and fair assessment and fiscal responsibility. The purpose of the propriety standards is to ensure that an evaluation will conducted ethically with regard for the wellbeing of those involved in or affected by the evaluation. The accuracy standard has 12 points and addresses issues such as context analysis, defensible information sources, valid and reliable information data analysis and impartial reporting. The accuracy standards ensure that an evaluation will determine and disseminate technically adequate information about the factors that establish worth or merit of the program.

The Student Evaluation Standards include propriety standards, utility standards, feasibility standards and accuracy standards. The propriety standards have seven point such as appropriate policies and procedures, access to evaluation information, treatment of students and balanced evaluation. The propriety standards focus on the legal and ethical conduct of evaluations with regard for the welfare of the students being evaluated as well as others affected by the evaluation findings. The utility standards have 7 items that address items such as defining users and uses, evaluator qualifications, and effective reporting. The utility standards focus on factors that will make evaluations useful for enhancing student learning. The feasibility standards include practical orientation, political viability and evaluation support. The feasibility standards address factors that affect the implementation of planned evaluation. The accuracy standards have 11 points such as defined expectations for students, documented procedures, bias identification and management, and justified conclusions. The purpose of the accuracy standards is to assure the production of sound information about students' learning and performance.

The Personnel Evaluation Standards include propriety standards, utility standards, feasibility standards and accuracy standards. The propriety standards have five points that assess issues such as formal evaluation guidelines, conflict of interest and interactions with those being evaluated. The point of the standard is to conduct evaluations that are legally and ethically sound and are conducted in a manner that regards the wellbeing of the person being evaluated and the clients who authorized the evaluation. The utility standards have five points such as defined uses and follow-up/impact. The utility standards are guides for evaluations that will result in informative, timely and influential reporting. The feasibility standards consist of practical procedures, political viability and fiscal viability. These standards support the notion of evaluations that are reasonably easy to implement, efficient in the use of time and human resources and are sufficiently funded to assure complete implementation. The accuracy standards have eight points such as work environment, documentation procedures, data validity and reliability, systematic data control and monitoring evaluation systems. The accuracy standards in personnel evaluation, just as in program evaluation and student evaluation, addresses the extent to which data used is technically accurate and that conclusions have a logical link to appropriate information.

The previous passages were short, compressed summaries of the standards for program, student and personnel evaluations. A full review and discussion of the standards merit attention. For additional information about the work of the JCSEE and reprints of essential documents contact: The Joint Committee on Standards for Educational Evaluation, The Evaluation Center, Western Michigan University, Kalamazoo, MI 49008-5178.

References

Davis, B.G. (1989). Demystifying assessment: learning from the field of evaluation. In Gray, P.J. (ed.). *Achieving Assessment Goals Using Evaluation Techniques. New Directions for Higher Education* n. 67. Jossey-Bass: San Francisco.

Guba, E. G. & Lincoln, Y.S. (1989). *Fourth Generation Evaluation.* Sage Publications: Newbury Park.

Madus,G.F., Stufflebeam, D.L., and Scriven, M.S. (1987). Program evaluation: a historical overview. *Evaluation Models.* Kluwer Academic Publishers: Norwell.

Patton, M. Q. (1986). *Utilization-Focused Evaluation. Second Edition.* Sage Publications: Newbury Park.

Scriven, M. S. (1995). The logic of evaluation and evaluation practice. In Fournier, D. M. (ed.) *New Directions for Evaluation. Reasoning in Evaluation: Inferential Links and Leaps.* n68.

Scriven, M. S. (1991). *Evaluation Thesaurus.* Sage Publications: Thousand Oaks.

Stark, J.S. and Thomas, A. (1994). *Assessment & Program Evaluation.* ASHE Reader Series. Simon & Schuster Custom Publishing:Needham Heights.

Assessment/Evaluation Resources

Publishers. Books on the topic of assessment and evaluation are sprinkled among many publishers. Two of the major publishers in the field, in terms of volume of production on the topic, are Sage Publications and Jossey Bass Publishers.

Organizations. Several organizations address assessment and evaluation topics in education and their websites are helpful for timely access to salient information. A list of organizations to monitor include (but not limited to)

- Department of Education
- The College Board
- American Evaluation Association (AEA)
- Association for Institutional Research (AIR)

- American Association of Community Colleges (AACC)
- American Association of Higher Education (AAHE)
- American Council on Education (ACE)
- American Association of Colleges and Universities (AAC&U)
- National Science Foundation (NSF)

Organization of the Reader

The reader consists of five major sections, each beginning with a brief introduction that sets the stage for the section but does not annotate the content of the section. The first section addresses conceptual issues relating to evaluation and assessment such as underlying principles of evaluation and dialogue regarding the quantitative and qualitative research paradigms. Subsequent sections address assessment and evaluation issues regarding (a) administration and institutional performance, (b) teaching and learning, (c) student performance and outcomes and (d) measurement issues. Each section has four parts. The first part of each section has literature that is considered to be a classic in the field. Part two of each section presents assessment/evaluation literature considered to be exemplary and was produced since the previous reader on this topic. There is a tremendous amount of knowledge regarding assessment and evaluation which made it difficult to balance the quantity of selections with the cost of reprinting selected literature. Therefore, the third part of each section is a recommended reading list that identifies additional literature that merit the attention of students, scholars and other professionals who are interested in assessment and evaluation. The fourth part of each section is a list of questions that are intended to fuel discussion and learning.

Readings were selected based on prevailing practice, impact on higher education, emerging trends and educational equity from an institutional diversity perspective. Selections address process as well as outcomes over a wide spectrum of assessment and evaluation issues in higher education. Placement of the literature into section is purely for organizational purposes since many of the selected items fit multiple topics. The introduction to each section is intentionally kept brief; a description of each selection was omitted for space reasons without sacrificing quality since the selections generally include abstracts or conclusions that highlight major points.

Section I

Conceptual Overview of Assessment & Evaluation

CONCEPTUAL OVERVIEW OF ASSESSMENT & EVALUATION

Introduction

The literature in this section provides a foundation for understanding assessment and evaluation activities. The selections here focus more on concepts than techniques and they address some of the continuing debate regarding different research paradigms. The intent of this section is not to persuade readers to take any specific position, but rather to illustrate that assessment and evaluation is a complex field that is fueled by social and political realities from multiple perspectives. Thus, frameworks, or models are useful tools for reflecting on the purpose of assessment and evaluation. Consequently, the multipurpose nature of the field mandates that there is no one best way to conduct assessment and evaluation activities. Literature in this section, included or identified, focuses on evaluation frameworks and their utility for organizing evaluation objectives as well as the discourse on various research paradigms.

Classic Readings

Five Evaluation Frameworks: Implications for Decision Making in Higher Education

Don E. Gardner*

The author identifies a need for greater understanding of alternative evaluation approaches available in higher education. Five basic definitions of evaluation are identified: (1) evaluation as measurement, (2) evaluation as professional judgment, (3) evaluation as the assessment of congruence between performance and objectives (or standards of performance), (4) decision-oriented evaluation, and (5) goal-free/responsive evaluation. Their basic assumptions, distinguishing characteristics, principal advantages, and disadvantages are presented. Criteria for selecting an evaluation methodology appropriate to specific circumstances, are summarized in the concluding paragraphs.

The accountability crisis has had profound effects on the implementation of evaluative studies in higher education. In the not too distant past, decisions affecting all phases of university operations were routinely made on the basis of unchallenged assumptions regarding benefits (the "assumed good") or the unquestioned judgments of key administrators. Today, those same administrators are often constrained to produce evaluative data to support even the most basic kinds of decisions—to the extent that the cost of collecting the required information is often suspected of rivaling the cost of the course of action ultimately chosen.

The effects of the clamor for evaluative data have been pervasive. For example, in the first issue of the Jossey-Bass *New Directions for Institutional Research* series, *Evaluating Institutions for Accountability* [4] the authors discussed the need for evaluation as it relates to: the ultimate benefits of higher education to society, institutional goals, educational cost-effectiveness, measurement of educational outcomes, the development of management information systems, the implementation of "quantitative fixed effectiveness models," evaluating student performance, evaluating resources and processes, evaluating faculty performance, program review, and evaluations by external agencies. Other examples of current evaluation topics include hiring practices, salary determination and tenure policies, and program cost/benefit.

Correspondingly, there is a rapidly expanding body of literature on different theories, models, and techniques in educational evaluation. Although there have been several notable attempts at categorizing and defining the array of evaluation models and methodologies that has emerged (of particular importance are the works by Stufflebeam, et al. [15], Worthen and Sanders [19], and Anderson, et al. [3]), these are generally unfamiliar to individuals outside the ranks of the "expert" evaluator. Unfortunately, it is most often "nonexpert" evaluators—higher education administrators—who are ultimately responsible for the implementation of evaluation studies and their consequences.

Reprinted from *Journal of Higher Education* 58, no. 5 (September–October 1977).

In many situations, lack of familiarity with the basic options available for structuring an evaluation is not a key issue. For example, the kinds of evaluative data needed to satisfy the requirements of an affirmative action report are generally dictated by the requesting agency. Even where the type of evaluation to be conducted is not mandated, common practice or a conspicuous precedent may determine the type of methodology employed, as for example, when the accrediting team approach is used by a college or department for purposes of internal program review. However, where an administrator has a choice with regard to the type of evaluation to be conducted—even if that choice will be expressed only in the selection of the particular expert evaluator who will conduct the study—that individual should be fully aware of the fundamentally different assumptions and outcomes that obtain when a particular type of strategy is selected.

The most prominent educational evaluation models, methodologies, or techniques can be generally classified within five major frameworks corresponding to five different basic definitions of evaluation. Stufflebeam, et al., identified three of these before introducing a fourth, new definition [15, pp. 9–16, 40]; a fifth category is required to accommodate the goal-free type of evaluation proposed by Scriven [12, 13]. In real life situations it would appear that distinctions between the five definitions of evaluation are often blurred by practical considerations. However, the principal focus of any particular evaluation effort—from evaluation of student progress in the classroom to the evaluation of competing academic programs by statewide governing boards—is almost always identifiable as falling within the boundaries of one or another of the frameworks described below.

The premise of this paper is that because the selection of an evaluation methodology is so often determined by latent political or convenience factors, many evaluations are destined to fail before they begin. The selection of a particular evaluation framework always entails certain consequences and constraints. In this light, the administrator faced with the responsibility to evaluate should carefully consider the following question: "Is the selected methodology appropriate to the circumstances?" or, put another way, "What is the probability that this type of strategy will produce results effectively serving the need that prompted the evaluation?"

This article is divided into three main sections: (1) a brief review and analysis of the five basic frameworks or definitions of evaluation (summarized in chart form in Figure 1), (2) discussion of some of the negative and positive consequences that are likely to result from application of the frameworks (summarized in chart form in Figure 2), and (3) a summarization of basic criteria for selecting a methodology appropriate to specific circumstances.

Five Definitions of Evaluation

The five definitions of evaluation that establish the general framework for most evaluations in education today are: (1) evaluation as professional judgment, (2) evaluation as measurement, (3) evaluation as the assessment of congruence between performance and objectives (or standards of performance), (4) decision-oriented evaluation, and (5) goal-free/responsive evaluation. As was noted earlier, in actual practice hybrid types are abundant, but the principal *emphasis* or *focus* of a particular effort will almost always be identifiable as belonging to one of these categories.

The review and description of the five frameworks is presented using the following outline as a guide:[1]

(a) Statement and explanation of the principal focus of the definition

(b) Examples of the definition in current practice

(c) Basic premises and assumptions

(d) "Advance organizers"—variables that structure the evaluation process:

1. Basic value perspective of the approach
2. Nature of typical evaluation designs
3. Typical evaluator roles
4. Nature of typical methodologies
5. Types of communication and feedback

(e) Nature of expected outcomes and mode of interpretation.

Evaluation as Professional Judgment

Evaluation as professional judgment is a well-known concept requiring only a brief description here. The utility of this definition is evidenced in the numerous situations where a qualified professional is asked to examine the thing to be evaluated and then render an expert opinion regarding its quality, effectiveness, or efficiency. In this case, the resulting statement of relative worth *is* the evaluation.

Examples of the use of this model in education include reliance on the judgment of teams of professionals by the various accrediting associations, the use of peer review panels to evaluate funding proposals, use of expert referees in the process of selecting manuscripts for publication, and the passing of judgment on candidates for promotion or tenure by faculty committees [19, pp. 126–27; 15, pp. 13–16].

This approach is obviously based on the assumption that the best judge of worth is an expert in the area of the thing to be evaluated. Values or criteria which form the basis for judgment of the professional is accepted on the basis of that individual's assumed association with a commonly shared value system, or on the basis of assumed superior knowledge which accompanies stature in the particular field in question. In other cases, some type of compromise mechanism is used to deal with differences in point of view, as, for example, in the case where committee meetings are held to arrive at a consensus before a group judgment is delivered.

Basically, the evaluation design based on this definition provides for some type of personal contact between the evaluator and the thing to be evaluated (or its products or effects) structured in accordance with the expectations of the individuals to be served by the evaluation. The outcome may be of little personal concern if the evaluator is an outsider called in to evaluate some aspect of a program or institution; in this case, the values brought to bear might be said to be relatively objective. On the other hand, if the evaluator has a personal stake in the process—as, for example, in the case of the fellow faculty member on the tenure review committee—the needs of the department, college, and personalities involved (as perceived by that individual) will undoubtedly have a bearing on the values that are applied in the evaluation process.

In this type, the evaluator is seen as an information processor whose job is to assimilate and judge relevant data. Skill in synthesizing and weighing facts is assumed, in addition to expertise in the domain of the thing being evaluated. The evaluator's methodology may include personal observation, interviews, component tests, and review of documentation; in short, whatever kind of experiential contact is deemed necessary and agrees with client expectations. However, the assimilation of the data collected is internal—i.e., the final report (whether formal or informal) will emanate from the evaluator's thought processes. The desired outcome is, of course, the educated opinion of the evaluator/judge; interpretation is expressed generally in the form of a pronouncement.

Evaluation as Measurement

This definition is based on a commonly recognized traditional (but narrow) view which simply equates evaluation with measurement. To evaluate means to measure results, effects, or performance using some type of formalized instrument which produces data that can be compared to some sort of standardized scale.

Examples of this definition in practice include such varied applications as the use of SAT or GRE scores to evaluate academic aptitude, and instructional cost analysis studies based on data collected from faculty activity analysis questionnaires.

Measurement experts such as Thorndike [16] and Ebel [6, 7] admit that true evaluation involves a judgment of merit which extends beyond the collection of measurement data, but the focus of this approach is clearly on those data and the instruments used to collect them [15, pp. 9–10]. The instrumental focus of this definition is not difficult to understand since it is based on observations and practices which are common throughout our experience. For example, to evaluate the merits of one metal alloy relative to another, experts *measure* various attributes (strength, flexibility, etc.) using the sophisticated instruments which are available for that purpose, and then compare the resulting figures.

The basic constructs of this approach include assumptions that phenomena to be evaluated have significant measurable attributes, and that instruments can be designed which are capable of measuring them. Misapplication of this type of evaluation—and resulting failures—can generally be traced to the violation of these assumptions: either the thing to be evaluated does not possess significant measurable attributes, or the design of application of the instrument (test, questionnaire, etc.) does not effectively measure the attribute desired. The continuing debate over measurement of the outcomes of higher education is a conspicuous example of the controversy which has resulted, at least in part, from attempts at applying this type of evaluation technique in the field of higher education.

Values in this type of evaluation approach are established in reference to standardized scales, or on the basis of comparability of the results of multiple applications of the same instrument or test under controlled conditions on like objects. The use of SAT or GRE percentile scores is a good example of such norm-referenced values, while the comparison of numbers of degrees granted as an institutional outcome measure is a crude example on a larger scale.

Although some test and measurement technology is highly complex and sophisticated, an evaluation design based on this definition is conceptually quite simple: first, the attributes to be measured are identified; second, an appropriate instrument is designed and tested (validated); third, the instrument is applied to the thing to be evaluated (under controlled conditions to insure reliability); and, fourth, the results are compared to a standard (which may be the results of a pretest specific to the particular person or thing or established norms for groups of that kind of person or thing).

The evaluator in this type of effort must be, of necessity, an expert in the design and/or use of the measurement instruments which are to be employed, including an understanding of how results should be analyzed and interpreted. Measurement methodologies are almost as varied as the phenomena people attempt to measure, ranging from the use of the previously mentioned standardized tests for evaluating academic aptitude to simple information systems in the registrar's office that routinely collect data on students; the latter are generally not thought of as being instruments of evaluation, but where the resulting information is taken as measures of institutional success or failure, the analogy applies.

Measurement technology is formal and systematic, and focuses on the use of instruments that provide results which can be replicated. In an evaluation project, communication between the evaluator and a "client" administrator is likely to be limited to a discussion of the measurement goal; for example, the desired outcome of a questionnaire on faculty attitudes toward tenure policies. Being the expert, the evaluator is generally responsible for selecting or designing an appropriate instrument. Feedback to the administrator will probably come in the nature of a formal report which may even be limited to a simple display of the results of the application of the instrument; e.g., the number of responses in each of the various question categories.

The expected outcome from the measurement type of evaluation is a number or set of numbers which can be compared and interpreted with reference to another number or set of numbers, or a generally accepted standard scale. The number of professors or assistant professors who favor or disagree with a proposed change in tenure policy would be one example—although care must be exercised to insure that the questions were phrased in such a way that they actually measured the attitude intended.

The Assessment of Congruence Between Performance and Objectives

Theories or methodologies that fall into this category basically define evaluation as the process of specifying or identifying goals, objectives, or standards of performance; identifying or developing tools to measure performance; and comparing the measurement data collected with the previously identified objectives or standards to determine the degree of discrepancy or congruence which exists.

Perhaps no other type of evaluation has received more attention in recent higher education literature; competency-based teacher education, the success of institutions in meeting the goal of equal educational opportunity or in preparing students for meaningful careers are familiar goal-oriented evaluation topics.

Evaluation models based on this definition assume that the most important decisions regarding the thing to be evaluated are contingent on its objectives and the criteria established for judging relative success or failure in the attainment of those objectives. The Provus [10] model emphasizes that evaluations of this type are not solely interested in whether or not an objective has been met (i.e., the attainment of a level of performance equal to a minimum standard) but in describing performance whatever the level reached and in determining the reasons for relative success or failure. Furthermore, Scriven has pointed out that this type of evaluation process can play two basic kinds of roles: a *formative* role (evaluation used to improve an ongoing process or project by providing feedback to the administrator in charge), and a *summative* role (evaluation of a completed product) [19, pp. 61–65]. In any case, formal evaluation methodologies are required if rational decisions are to be made as to whether the program or thing should be maintained, improved, expanded, or terminated [10, pp. 183–92].

Evaluation designs based on the congruence between performance and objectives definition may vary from the simple application of a pretest-treatment-posttest technique (as is commonly used to evaluate student learning) to a wide range of more complicated processes and techniques. However, a generalized approach would undoubtedly contain the following elements: (1) identification of goals or objectives of the project, program, or thing to be evaluated; (2) clarification of the variables which affect performance; (3) identification of the criteria (standards) by which performance will be judged; (4) development or identification of tools, techniques, and procedures for collecting information regarding performance; (5) collection of the performance data; (6) comparison of the information regarding performance with the pre-established standards (resulting in a judgment of worth); and (7) communication of the results of the comparison to appropriate audiences.

Several important distinctions between evaluator roles are proposed by the authors of evaluation models falling into this general framework. For example, Scriven argues that in a formative (process oriented) evaluation the evaluator should be prepared not only to clarify or identify objectives, but should make an assessment of the worth of the objectives themselves. Stake carries this a step further by suggesting that expert evaluators should be involved from the beginning of any program or project and should be instrumental in defining its objectives—thereby *insuring* their worth and the feasibility of collecting relevant performance data. Where a summative (end-product oriented) evaluation is desired, the evaluator's primary function will most likely be an after-the-fact determination of the previously defined goals of the project (and pertinent criteria of performance) through interaction with participants and a review of documentation.

In addition to the evaluator's interactive role with administrators in identifying, developing, or judging objectives, this type of evaluation demands that the evaluator be expert in measurement methodology relative to the performance of the thing to be evaluated, the analysis of the performance data, and the formulation of meaningful descriptive reports. Both Scriven and Stake have added that the evaluator should be a capable judge, able to provide educated professional opinion regarding the worth or effectiveness of the thing evaluated in addition to the descriptive information upon which the judgment is based [19, pp. 83–86, 103, 109].

The methodologies used in the implementation of an evaluation design such as the one described above will contain the following specific elements: examination of documentation which describes the thing to be evaluated in detail; small group interaction between evaluation staff and key personnel to further define variables, objectives, and performance standards; rigorous analysis of processes and relationships; identification of the tools or instruments which will be used to obtain performance data; collection and processing of performance data; analysis of the performance data compared to objectives and standards; formulation of judgments and reports; and, finally, communication of reports.

The nature of the outcome expected from this type of evaluation has been alluded to several times in the preceding discussion. To summarize, the intended results of an evaluation of this sort are *judgments of worth* regarding the institution, program, process, or thing based on interpreted comparisons between performance data and objectives (or standards of performance). The judgments themselves may be arrived at by the evaluator, or by administrators based on information supplied by the evaluator. If the evaluation conducted is of the formative type, judgments may be made on an ongoing basis to control and shape performance (as for example, where intermediate results are reviewed in the light of the stated goals of a residential learning project in the early stages of implementation). If the evaluation is summative only, it will focus on products or end results as compared to intended outcomes (i.e., the final impact of the residential-learning project on a group of students who just completed the program as compared to stated objectives).

Decision-Oriented Evaluation

There are currently two major evaluation models which are primarily decision oriented in nature: The CIPP [Context, Input, Process, Product] Evaluation Model developed by the Phi Delta Kappa (PDK) National Study Committee on Evaluation and a model developed at the University of California at Los Angeles Center for the Study of Evaluation. The two models are practically identical in their essential characteristics; the CIPP model is based on a definition of evaluation as, "the process of delineating, obtaining, and providing useful information for judging decision alternatives," [15, p. 40] whereas the UCLA definition is stated as, "Evaluation is the process of ascertaining the decision areas of concern, selecting appropriate information, and collecting and analyzing information in order to report summary data useful to decision-makers in selecting among alternatives" [1, p. 107]. Building on the work of the PDK committee, Dressel has recently proposed a definition of evaluation in the service of decision making that focuses primarily on assumptions and values as they relate to anticipated procedures and goals compared to actual processes and results [5, p. 12].

The essence of the CIPP model is an institutionalized feedback mechanism which provides for a continuous assessment of decision-information needs and the obtaining and providing of information to meet those needs. Efforts at implementing PPBS and Integrated MIS principles in higher education are examples of attempts to institutionalize systematic, decision-oriented, evaluation mechanisms. Also, the WICHE/NCHEMS Costing and Data Management System, and the Higher Education Planning System (HEPS) marketed by Education and Economic Systems, Inc. (EES) are examples of packaged systems (including procedures, input documents, and report producing computer software) which support CIPP-like institutionalized decision-oriented evaluation with at least one important difference: the initial determination of decision-information need has been made by NCHEMS and EES—although admittedly with input from the higher education community—and individual user institutions are constrained to accept and live with assumptions about institutional goals and processes which may or may not be totally appropriate in a particular setting. Also, these systems are more or less rigid in terms of their ability to produce new types of decision information based on feedback from administrators. In contrast, the CIPP model proposes maximum flexibility as an essential ingredient.

Four of the basic assumptions underlying the CIPP model have been stated by Stufflebeam [19, pp. 129–30]: (1) Evaluation is performed in the service of decision making, hence, it should provide information which is useful to decision makers; (2) Evaluation is a cyclic, continuing process and, therefore, must be implemented through a systematic program; (3) The evaluation process includes the three main steps of delineating, obtaining, and providing. These steps provide the basis for a methodology of evaluation; (4) The delineating and providing steps in the evaluation process are interface activities requiring collaboration between evaluator and decision maker, while the obtaining step is largely a technical activity which is executed mainly by the evaluator.

Another basic concept underlying the CIPP model is that different types of decisions require different types of informational inputs. Four basic types of decisions are identified and discussed at length in the PDK book [15, pp. 80–84; 5, pp. 12–15]. Fulfillment of information needs of the four types of decisions is the principal value orientation of the approach. To accomplish the goal of service to decision makers, the CIPP model proposes four different kinds of evaluation activities: *context evaluation* (to assist decision makers in the determination of objectives); *input evaluation* (to clarify decisions regarding the different ways resources might be used to achieve project goals); *process evaluation* (to provide periodic feedback to the persons responsible for decisions during implementation); and *product evaluation* (for the purpose of assessing and interpreting project attainments, whether at the end of a project cycle or at intermediate points through its life, as they relate to decisions regarding whether the activity should be continued, modified, terminated, or repeated). The UCLA model was conceived along the same general lines although the terminology used is different [1, p. 109].

Stufflebeam has provided a logical structure of evaluation design which he has asserted is the same for all of the four primary evaluation activities (context, input, process, and product) encompassed by the CIPP model [19, p. 144]. The proposed design structure includes the following basic elements: focusing the evaluation (identifying the specific decision situations to be served and defining the criteria to be used in the judgment of alternatives), and the collection, organization, analysis, and reporting of information.

With regard to evaluator roles, on a large scale, Guba and Stufflebeam [9, pp. 7–13] have proposed the creation of an evaluation unit within the organization, which might include the following: individuals engaged in research aimed at providing a "dynamic baseline" of descriptive information about the "decision arena" of the institution; persons skilled in identifying alternative ways of determining institutional needs and the criteria by which processes and outcomes will later be judged; a unit which systematically maintains records of the process or thing to be evaluated and measures and interprets attainments relative to both intermediate and final objectives; individuals engaged in the development and implementation of instruments for collecting data; an information office comprised of persons skilled in data reduction, storage, retrieval, and analysis techniques; and a reports section containing individuals skilled at highlighting information in terms of its "relevance, scope, and importance to the decision process."

In real life, the functions described above are typically carried out by offices of institutional research, MIS development teams, systems analysts and programmers, and research and evaluation units—with varying degrees of coordination depending on the situation. The CIPP model provides a useful framework for structuring the tasks that must be assigned to someone if systematic decision-oriented evaluation is to occur.

Regarding evaluation methodology, the authors of the CIPP model stated that, "The methodology of evaluation is the methodology of an information system designed to provide information for project, program, and system decisions" [15, p. 136]. As was pointed out earlier, the general evaluation design of the CIPP model includes three major areas: delineation of information needs, a plan for obtaining the information, and a plan for providing the information. Within those general categories, examples of specific methodological tasks and techniques include: systems analysis, construction of a model of decision paths within the organization, identification or report requirements, identification of policies with regard to data access, identification of information sources, selection of appropriate instruments, and designing an effective combination of media and personal resources for presenting information to decision makers in timely and meaningful ways.

In summary, the desired outcomes of an evaluation of this kind are a continual exchange between evaluators and administrators regarding information needs associated with critical decisions, and a continuous flow of systematically collected, timely, and relevant information to satisfy those needs. Final interpretation of data is generally assumed to be the responsibility of the administrator(s) served, as, for example, when the final report on grade statistics is placed in the hands of the academic vice-president who is looking for evidence of grade inflation. The evaluator's interpretive skills are brought to bear more on issues related to data reduction and extraction (synthesis) than on meaning as it relates to decisions affecting institutional policy.

Goal-Free/Responsive Evaluation

The goal-free concept is a relatively recent definition of evaluation which has been proposed and developed by Scriven [12]. The central theme of this approach is critical examination of the institution, project, program, or thing irrespective of its goals. In other words, the intent of goal-free evaluation (GFE) is to discover and judge actual effects without regard to what the effects were supposed to be. All of the evaluation approaches discussed earlier depend on some kind of preordained establishment of goals, standards, or decision information needs. However, it is often the case that an evaluator turns up information about unintended side effects of the project or program which may be more important in some regard than the information relative to project goals or preidentified decisions.

For example, an evaluator may find that an educational program designed to improve employment opportunities for underprivileged minorities (by providing free special training to persons who meet certain criteria) has succeeded admirably in its efforts to achieve that goal, but has unintentionally resulted in an undesirable intensification of racial hostilities among persons who do not qualify for the program. Many evaluative reports include information about this kind of side effect along with the information regarding intended effects. However, the side effect information may have been acquired merely by accident, and other important information of this type may have been overlooked completely. Scriven has argued [13] that if the main objective of the evaluation is to assess the worth of the outcomes, why make any distinction at all between those that were intended, as opposed to those that were not?

In addition to the concept of GFE proposed by Scriven, an evaluation approach called "responsive evaluation" has recently been proposed by Stake [14]. Responsive evaluation is an iterative process of acquiring information about an institution, program, or project; defining issues of importance to constituencies; and describing strengths and weaknesses relative to those issues. Stated objectives may or may not be centrally important to the issues identified; all aspects of the thing being evaluated are taken into consideration initially, but no single element (whether goals, resources, processes, or participants) is preconceived as being necessarily more important to the evaluator than another.

As mentioned, one of the basic premises of GFE is that an evaluation effort may produce valuable results if it is unencumbered by preordained linkages to goals or standards. However, GFE is not goal free in an absolute sense; an evaluation involving a judgment of merit involves some kind of comparison with a standard, and the evaluator must have some basis for selecting only certain information about a project or program out of the total information pool. What is proposed in GFE is allowing the evaluator to select wider-context goals as opposed to only those prespecified in mission statements, statements of objectives, or the project design [2]. In other words, the evaluator may collect information relevant to project effects as they relate to accepted societal norms (e.g., the evidence of increased racial hostilities produced by the hypothetical employment opportunity program described above is important because of a generally accepted need for decreasing antagonisms of this kind in our society) or some other type of generally recognized standard. In the responsive evaluation model these standards emerge in the identification of the issues that the evaluator has discovered are important to concerned constituencies.

The Scriven concept of GFE calls for an evaluation design centered around the collection of information with regard to actual outcomes or performance. At some point the evaluator will undoubtedly make some assumptions regarding standards by which an outcome or effect might be judged, but Scriven has emphasized that the evaluator should be free to choose those standards for comparison from a wide range of possibilities. Once the information has been collected and analyzed the evaluator then makes the report.

Stake has been more explicit in providing a guiding framework for conducting a responsive evaluation. He has proposed the following cycle of prominent events to guide the evaluation process: (1) talk with clients, staff, and audiences; (2) identify program scope; (3) overview program activities; (4) discover purposes and concerns; (5) conceptualize issues and problems; (6) identify data needs (according to identified issues); (7) select observers, judges, and formal instruments (if any); (8) observe selected antecedents, transactions, and outcomes; (9) "thematize"—prepare portrayals and case studies; (10) match issues to audiences; and (11) prepare and deliver presentations and formal reports (if any) [14, p. 12]. These events do not necessarily occur in sequence, but take place as the result of a series of negotiations and interactions which proceed more or less informally.

In GFE the evaluator is conceptualized as an investigator skilled in identifying important relationships and outcomes. Stake has called for the responsive evaluator to operate informally (though systematically) in the environment of continual interaction with people, drawing conclusions and descriptive information out of the observations and reactions of the persons involved. Obviously, this requires that the evaluator be skilled in social interaction, eliciting honest comments and opinions, and in capturing and recording conversations. Stake further suggests that although a formal report may be a part of a responsive evaluation, much might be accomplished through the use of portrayal and holistic communication techniques [14, pp. 15–19] which may be entirely communicated through verbal means, for example, in informal discussion settings.

The final outcome of GFE should be accurate descriptive and interpretive information relative to the most important aspects of the actual performance, effects, and attainments of the institution, program, or thing evaluated. Interpretation of results by the evaluator should be responsive to the concerns of the individuals affected whether they are simply program participants or those who commissioned the study. While it is probably not yet possible to identify many specific situations where this approach to evaluation has been formally applied, it has potential appeal to a wide range of individuals who have long felt that other methods of evaluation were inappropriate to their particular area, such as evaluating educational programs in the arts. In effect, by including informal investigation and personal testimony as valid tools for evaluation, this approach may help legitimize methods that have had intuitive appeal in many circumstances but have previously received little formal support.

Implications for Decision Making

The basic assumptions and distinguishing characteristics of the five evaluation frameworks described above are summarized in chart form in Figure 1. The chart suggests several implications that might affect decisions to evaluate based on the different approaches.

For example, when the five definitions are arrayed as in Figure 1, a more or less well-defined outline of evolution in educational evaluation thought is apparent: the professional judgment approach being a legacy from earlier times; followed by the appearance of measurement technology in the wake of empiricism; focused after World War II on performance vs. objectives by the work of Tyler [17] and others; further enhanced in the sixties by the application of the system approach and computer technology to the problems of educational decision making; and, most recently, expanded by individuals such as Scriven [12, 13] and Stake [14] as they have attempted to responsively evaluate in situations where earlier approaches have been less than successful.

In view of this evolutionary pattern, administrators concerned with taking advantage of new developments might be tempted to look toward the goal-free/responsive approach as being the most up-to-date solution to their evaluation problems. Obviously, such an assumption could be dangerously misleading. As displayed in Figure 1, each of the frameworks has distinguishing characteristics that make it potentially useful depending on the circumstances. Stufflebeam et al. [15, pp. 9–16] provided a point of departure for determining potential utility in their discussion of the advantages and disadvantages of three of the five approaches. A brief summary of just a few positive and negative aspects, expanded to include all five of the evaluation definitions, is presented in Figure 2.

Advantages vs. Disadvantages

An administrator faced with the question, "Will an evaluation study based on the 'professional judgment' approach effectively serve the need?" will undoubtedly be aware that the results of such studies are often criticized on the basis of their subjectivity and noncomparability. In matters of high constituent interest such as, "Should X department be abolished because its programs no longer serve valid educational purposes?" if one expert in the field says "yes," it is almost always possible to find another who will return an emphatic "no"—often after reviewing the same body of evidence. That politicians (both on and off campus) use this situation to advantage is certainly no secret.

On the other hand, it is common knowledge that the simplest method, at least conceptually, of evaluating an activity or thing is to hire a consultant, a definite advantage where time is of the essence and the nature of the problem does not require a more objective approach. Furthermore, the worship of objectivity should not obscure the fact that individuals "uniquely qualified to judge" (because of their experience and expertise) do exist, and that the human mind can function as a complex mechanism for assimilating and integrating rich bodies of data.

The negative aspects of measurement evaluations are familiar topics. Two common questions related to this subject are: "Did the student achievement test really measure the knowledge or skills supposedly taught in the course?" and, "Are 'student credit hour production' and 'number of degrees granted' valid surrogate measures of the true outputs of higher education?" Measurement experts are frequently accused of measuring only those attributes for which an instrument (test, questionnaire, computerized system, etc.) is readily available and which produces results that are easily quantifiable. As a result, variables that are not easily measured, such as the personal enrichment a person may receive from going to college, continue to be treated by measurement experts as intangibles and/or relatively unimportant.

On the positive side, if a particular measurement instrument has demonstrated some reliability or validity, for example, as is claimed for the SAT, GRE, and certain IQ tests, comparability for certain purposes may be assumed. Also, if procedures are consistently applied, results may be legitimately termed "objective," and may be generalizable in the sense that what is true for one group is probably true for a similar group under identical (or nearly identical) conditions. For administrators who are comfortable with quantitative methods, another advantage of this approach is that results generally will be mathematically manipulable and may be conducive to sophisticated statistical analysis.

The congruence between performance and objectives approach has been criticized as being too narrow in focus in many educational situations. Detractors point out that goal clarification may be a useful exercise where a mission is well defined and where effectiveness and efficiency in pursuit of that mission are primary concerns. But they are quick to point out that academicians are concerned with highly complex activities with ambivalent goals and standards of performance. Also, servicing a pluralistic society makes simple goal statements relatively hard to come by and, in some cases, perhaps even counterproductive. Furthermore, proponents are often accused of focusing on those goals for which measurement data are readily available while disregarding more important objectives in areas where performance is more difficult to assess. Another major criticism is its frequent focus on end results, i.e., after the program, project, class, or cycle of activity (on an institutional scale) is terminated. Where this is the case, intermediate benefits which might have accrued from an evaluation in process would not be realized.

The disadvantages described above represent only a few of the problems that are often associated with the goal-oriented approach to evaluation. Dressel has provided a much more detailed account in his *Handbook of Academic Evaluation* [5, pp. 27–52]. However, he also has highlighted some of the advantages of goal-oriented evaluation. For one, where it is possible to identify clear, stated goals, an objective base is automatically established for the purposes of evaluation; assuming that the goals are generally accepted, it becomes only necessary to devise measures of performance relating to those goals, instruments to collect data, and procedures for comparing the results with the previously established standards of performance. Obviously, this can be a very difficult task in some situations, but—conceptually, at least—the task is relatively well defined. Also, criteria for making value judgments regarding the actual performance of the persons or thing evaluated will be suggested by the nature of the goals and the measurement data collected.

One of the major disadvantages of the decision-oriented approach is its assumption of rationality in decision-making, and that systematically produced decision information will be used, at least to the extent of justifying the cost of collection. Unfortunately, this does not seem to be the case. For example, on the basis of extensive work in this area, Weathersby has recently affirmed what many institutional researchers and systems analysts have long suspected: "The application of rational analysis in public decision making appears to be rather limited" [18, p. 98]. The assumption that a great many important decisions are so cyclic in nature that they can be supported by programmed algorithms and systematic processes appears to be open to question as well.

One of the main advantages of the decision-oriented approach is the impetus it provides for institutional self-study, and analysis of decision processes. Further, by focusing on the specific decisions to be served by evaluation, the decision-oriented-approach assures that whatever data are collected will be relevant to specific issues and questions. Also, in the case of the CIPP model (discussed earlier), all aspects of the decision setting may be appropriate for analysis, including administrative relationships, decision types, objectives, processes, and outcomes.

One of the disadvantages of the goal-free and responsive models is their lack of emphasis on formal measurement techniques, which may result in relatively subjective outcomes. However, in contrast with the professional judgment approach, in goal-free/responsive evaluations more emphasis is placed on the evaluator's expertise as an *evaluator* (skilled in goal-free/responsive techniques) as opposed to superior knowledge in the discipline of the thing to be evaluated.

The positive appeal of the goal-free/responsive frameworks lies clearly in their flexible, open-minded approach to the identification and assessment of human concerns. By accepting the potential relevance, at least initially, of all outcomes, effects, and participant attitudes, evaluators may come closer to assessing the true worth of an educational program or activity in some cases than if they were tied to the necessity of finding measurable effects that relate to narrowly defined goals or objectives. Also, if the evaluator is truly responsive, potential acceptance of the evaluation results should be relatively high.

Conclusion

While this review and analysis has been relatively brief, it is designed to highlight some of the principal differences between the major evaluation frameworks in higher education today. Based on this discussion, a number of basic criteria can be identified for selecting an evaluation approach appropriate to specific circumstances. These might be expressed as follows: in situations where a high degree of objectivity is not required, where time is short, where a relatively simple evaluation design is desired and an expert human resource is available, the professional judgment approach may be most appropriate. In situations where high objectivity and reliability/comparability are required, where mathematically manipulable results are desired, where relevant measurable attributes can be identified and valid instruments can be designed and implemented to measure them, the measurement approach is probably indicated. If goals are a primary concern, if specific objectives or standards of performance can be identified, if valid ways to assess performance can be devised and applied, and effects unrelated to stated goals are of little or no importance, then a goal-oriented evaluation framework should be selected. Where systematic evaluation is desired in a relatively cyclic decision environment, where information is likely to be used as an important input to policy decision making, and where a dynamic understanding of decision processes is desired, a decision-oriented information systems approach may be successful. Finally, if all observable effects are potentially relevant, if human concerns are uppermost, if a relatively high degree of objectivity is not required, and if the situation is highly fluid and lacking well-defined goals and/or traditional measurement data, a goal-free or responsive approach may be beneficial.

Literature Cited

1. Alkin, Marvin G. "Evaluation Theory Development." In *Evaluating Action Programs: Readings in Social Action and Education*, by Carol H. Weiss. Boston: Allyn and Bacon, 1972.
2. _____. "Wider Context Goals and Goal-Based Evaluators." *Evaluation Comment*, 3 (December 1972), 5–6.
3. Anderson, Scarvia B., et al. *Encyclopedia of Educational Evaluation*. San Francisco: Jossey-Bass, 1975.
4. Bowen, Howard R., ed., *Evaluating Institutions for Accountability*. New Directions for Institutional Research, No. 1. San Francisco: Jossey-Bass, 1974.
5. Dressel, Paul L. *Handbook of Academic Evaluation*. San Francisco: Jossey-Bass, 1976.
6. Ebel, Robert L. "Educational Tests: Valid? Biased? Useful? *Phi Delta Kappan*. 57 (October 1975), 83–88.
7. _____. *Measuring Educational Achievement*. Englewood Cliffs, N.J.: Prentice Hall, 1965.
8. Guba, Egon G. "The Failure of Educational Evaluation." In *Evaluating Action Programs: Readings in Social Action and Education*, by Carol H. Weiss. Boston: Allyn and Bacon, 1972.
9. Guba, Egon G., and Daniel L. Stufflebeam. "Strategies for the Institutionalization of the CIPP Evaluation Model." Paper presented at the Eleventh Annual PDK Symposium on Educational Research, June 24, 1970, at Ohio State University. Mimeographed.
10. Provus, Malcolm. *Discrepancy Evaluation*. Berkeley, Calif.: McCutchan Publishing Corp., 1973.
11. Salasin, Susan. "Exploring Goal-Free Evaluation: An Interview with Michael Scriven." *Evaluation*. 2 (1974), 9–16.
12. Scriven, Michael. "Goal-Free Evaluation." In *School Evaluation: The Politics and Process*. edited by Ernest R. House. Berkeley, Calif.: McCutchan Publishing Corp., 1973.
13. _____. "Prose and Cons about Goal-Free Evaluation." *Evaluation Comment*, 3 (December 1972), 1–4.
14. Stake, Robert E. "Responsive Evaluation in the Arts and Humanities: To Evaluate an Arts Program." Xeroxed. Urbana, Ill. August 26, 1974.
15. Stufflebeam, Daniel L. et al., *Educational Evaluation and Decision Making*. Itasca, Ill.: F. E. Peacock Publishers, 1971.

16. Thorndike, Robert L., ed. *Educational Measurement*, 2nd Ed. New York: John Wiley & Sons, 1971.

17. Tyler, Ralph W. *Basic Principles of Curriculum and Instruction: Syllabus for Education 360.* Chicago: The University of Chicago Press, 1950.

18. Weathersby, George B. "The Potentials of Analytical Approaches to Educational Planning and Decision Making." In *Proceedings of the 1976 National Assembly* of the National Center for Higher Education Management Systems, edited by William Johnston. Boulder, Colorado: NCHEMS/WICHE, 1976.

19. Worthen, Blaine R., and James R. Sanders. *Educational Evaluation: Theory and Practice.* Worthington, Ohio: Charles A. Jones Publishing Co., 1973

* The author wishes to express special appreciation to Egon G. Guba for thoughtful criticism and insights offered during the preparation of this article.

1. The categories of the outline represent a combination of considerations suggested by Worthen and Sanders [19], and a framework developed by Guba, "Comparison of Preordinate with Responsive Evaluation (after Stake)," presented at the American Educational. Research Association convention, Chicago, April 16, 1974.

Figure 1 Basic Assumptions and Distinguishing Characteristics

	"Professional Judgment"	"Measurement"	"Congruence Between Performance and Objectives"	"Decision Oriented"	"Goal-Free Responsive"
Principal Focus	Expert opinion of qualified professional(s)	Measurement of results, effects, or performance, using some type of formal instrument (test, questionnaire, etc.).	Comparison of performance or product with previously stated standards of performance, goals or objectives.	"Delineating, obtaining and providing useful information for judging decision alternatives."	Identification and judgment of actual outcomes (irrespective of goals, standards, etc.) and/or the "concerns of constituents."
Examples	Accreditation teams. Doctoral Committees. Peer review of grant proposals. Referees for selection of manuscripts for publication/promotion/Tenure decisions.	GRE scores. Faculty activity questionnaires. Attitude surveys. Teaching effectiveness questionnaires.	Teacher certification based on achievement of prescribed competencies. Evaluation of academic departments on the basis of stated goals. Behavioral objectives. Contract learning.	Management Information Systems. NCHEMS Costing and Data Management System. HEPS (Higher Education Planning System).	Evaluation reports of "program side effects." "Holistic" evaluation of educational programs in the arts.
Basic Assumptions	Best evaluation is the expert opinion of a qualified professional. There is a commonly shared value system in the "arena" of the program or thing to be evaluated and/or, A "compromise mechanism" exists for accommodating differences in professional opinion.	Best evaluation is obtained from measurement data. Thing to be evaluated has measurable attributes. Instrument effectively measures attributes selected.	Best evaluation is based on an examination of achievement in light of goals or objectives. Goals or objectives exist and are identifiable. Attributes exist (and can be measured) that indicate relative success in achieving goals.	Best evaluation is one that serves decision makers in specific decision situations. Decision making processes are rational. Different types of decisions require different information. Many decisions are cyclic; systematic processes can be devised to support them.	Best evaluation highlights actual outcomes and/or concerns of constituents and sponsors. The "real" effects of a program or thing can be identified (as can the concerns of affected individuals). The most effective approach is "openminded" and "sensitive."
"Advance Organizers"	Values may or may not be explicitly defined. Evaluator expected to be an information collector, synthesizer and judge.	"Norm-referenced," quantitative values. Formal setting required for application of the measurement instrument. Instrument must be validated, reliable, etc. Evaluator must be a measurement expert.	"Criterion-referenced" (goal oriented) values. Measurement technology commonly used within the context of performance vs. goal assessment. Evaluator may be expected to "judge" as well as measure.	"Decision-oriented" values. Information system methodology. Evaluator should be an information system specialist.	"Wider-context" values (selected by evaluator). "Holistic approach" (all contributive elements, etc. considered as they relate to each other). Evaluator must be skilled in human interaction and identification of concerns.
Nature of Outcome/Interpretation	Educated, personalized opinion (judgment of worth) of a qualified judge or panel of judges. Interpretation in form of a "pronouncement."	Number of set of numbers which can be compared to other numbers or a standardized scale; data; descriptive statictics. Interpretation in reference to norms.	Judgment of worth based on comparisons between performance data and objectives or standards of performance. Interpretation based on relative discrepancy or congruence.	"Continuous," timely, and relevant information for administrators to assist in judging decision alternatives. Interpretation an administrative function; evaluator concerned with extraction and reduction of data.	Descriptive information regarding "actual" outcomes. Interpretation responsive to constituent concerns.

Figure 2 Advantages vs. Disadvantages

	"Professional Judgment"	"Measurement"	"Congruence Between Performance and Objectives"	"Decision Oriented"	"Goal-Free Responsive"
Advantages	Easily implemented. Uses assimilative and integrative capabilities of human intellect. Recognizes outstanding expertise.	Proper validation and consistent application results in high comparability and replicability. Data mathematically manipulable. Generalizable results.	"Goal-orientation" provides objective basis for evaluation. Judgment criteria pre-established by objectives vs. performance measures selected. Relevant to current societal concerns.	Increased understanding of decision setting and information requirements. Focus on decision information needs assures relevancy of data. Encourages analysis of all factors affecting important decisions.	Flexible, adaptive approach. Useful in complex, relatively unstructured situations. All outcomes, etc. potentially relevant. "People-oriented"—high acceptance potential.
Disadvantages	Results criticized as non—replicable, non-comparable and overly subjective. Generalizability diffic ult or impossible.	Many variable difficult or impossible to measure. Often anappropriate and/or inflexible—serving available measurement tools instead of the problem. Measurement attributes often irrelevant.	Focus may be too limited—not worthy goals easily identified. important side-effects may be overlooked. Tendency toward over-emphasis on end-product evaluation.	"Rational decision making" not predominant model in most real-life situations. In practice, frequent inability to cope with changing decision information needs. Inflexibility of "packaged" systems.	Relatively unstructured approach may be difficult to focus an manage. Results criticized as non-replicable, non-comparable and overly subjective. Questionable credibility if an evaluator non-expert in area of thing evaluated.

Program Evaluation: A Historical Overview

George F. Madaus, Daniel Stufflebeam, and Michael S. Scriven

Program evaluation is often mistakenly, viewed as a recent phenomenon. People date its beginning from the late 1960s with the infusion by the federal government of large sums of money into a wide range of human service programs, including education. However, program evaluation has an interesting history that predates by at least 150 years the explosion of evaluation during the era of President Johnson's Great Society and the emergence of evaluation as a maturing profession since the sixties. A definitive history of program evaluation has yet to be written and in the space available to us we can do little more than offer a modest outline, broad brush strokes of the landscape that constitutes that history. It is important that people interested in the conceptualization of evaluation are aware of the field's roots and origins. Such an awareness of the history of program evaluation should lead to a better understanding of how and why this maturing field has developed as it did. As Boulding (1980) has observed, one of the factors that distinguishes a mature and secure profession from one that is immature and insecure is that only the former systematically records and analyzes its history. Therefore since program evaluation continues to mature as a profession, its origins and roots need to be documented.

Where to begin? For convenience we shall describe six periods in the life of program evaluation. The first is the period prior to 1900, which we call the *Age of Reform*; the second, from 1900 until 1930, we call the *Age of Efficiency and Testing*; the third, from 1930 to 1945, may be called the *Tylerian Age*; the fourth, from 1946 to about 1957, we call the *Age of Innocence*; the fifth, from 1958 to 1972, is the *Age of Expansion* and finally the sixth, from 1973 to the present, the *Age of Professionalization*.

The Age of Reform 1800–1900

This period in the history of program evaluation encompasses the nineteenth century. It was the Industrial Revolution with all of its attendant economic and technological changes, which transformed the very structure of society. It was a period of major social changes, of cautious revisionism and reform (Pinker, 1971). It was a time of drastic change in mental health and outlook, in social life and social conscience, and in the structures of social agencies. It was when the laissez-faire philosophy of Bentham and the humanitarian philosophy of the philanthropists was heard (Thompson, 1950). It was a period marked by continued but often drawn out attempts to reform educational and social programs and agencies in both Great Britain and the United States.

In Great Britain throughout the nineteenth century there were continuing attempts to reform education, the poor laws, hospitals, orphanages, and public health. Evaluations of these social agencies and functions were informal and impressionistic in nature. Often they took the form of government-appointed commissions set up to investigate aspects of the area under consideration. For example,

Reprinted from *Evaluation Models,* (1987), by permission of Kluwer Academic Publishers.

the Royal Commission of Inquiry into Primary Education in Ireland under the Earl of Powis, after receiving testimony and examining evidence, concluded that "the progress of the children in the national schools of Ireland is very much less than it ought to be."[1] As a remedy, the Powis Commission then recommended the adoption of a scheme known as "payment by results" already being used in England, whereby teachers' salaries would be dependent in part on the results of annual examinations in reading, spelling, writing, and arithmetic (Kellaghan & Madaus, 1982). Another example of this approach to evaluation was the 1882 Royal Commission on Small Pox and Fever Hospitals which recommended after study that infectious-disease hospitals ought to be open and free to all citizens (Pinker, 1971).

Royal commissions are still used today in Great Britain to evaluate areas of concern. A rough counterpart in the United States to these commissions are presidential commissions (for example, the President's Commission on School Finance), White House panels (e.g., the White House Panel on Non Public Education), and congressional hearings. Throughout their history royal commissions, presidential commissions and congressional hearings have served as a means of evaluating human services programs of various kinds through the examination of evidence either gathered by the Commission or presented to it in testimony by concerned parties. However, this approach to evaluation was sometimes merely emblematic or symbolic in nature. N.J. Crisp (1982) captures the pseudo nature of such evaluations in a work of fiction when one of his characters discusses a royal commission this way: "Appoint it, feel that you've accomplished something, and forget about it, in the hope that by the time it's reported, the problem will have disappeared or been overtaken by events."[2]

In Great Britain during this period when reform programs were put in place, it was not unusual to demand yearly evaluations through a system of annual reports submitted by an inspectorate. For example, in education there were schools inspectors that visited each school annually and submitted reports on their condition and on pupil attainments (Kellaghan & Madaus, 1982). Similarly the Poor Law commissioner had a small, paid inspectorate to oversee compliance with the Poor Law Amendment Act of 1834 (Pinker, 1971). The system of maintaining an external inspectorate to examine and evaluate the work of the schools exists today in Great Britain and Ireland. In the United States, external inspectors are employed by some state and federal agencies. For example, the Occupational Safety and Health Administration (OSHA) employs inspectors to monitor health hazards in the workplace. Interestingly, the system of external inspectors as a model for evaluation has received scant attention in the evaluation literature. The educational evaluation field could benefit from a closer look at the system of formal inspectorates.

Two other developments in Great Britain during this period are worthy of note in the history of evaluation. First, during the middle of the nineteenth century a number of associations dedicated to social inquiry came into existence. These societies conducted and publicized findings on a number of social problems which were very influential in stimulating discussion (for example, Chadwick's Report on the Sanitary Condition of the Laboring Population of Great Britain in 1842 [Pinker, 1971]). Second, often in response to these private reports, bureaucracies that were established to manage social programs sometimes set up committees of enquiry. These were official, government sponsored investigations of various social programs, such as provincial workhouses (Pinker, 1971). Both these examples are important in that they constitute the beginnings of an empirical approach to the evaluation of programs.

In the United States perhaps the earliest formal attempt to evaluate the performance on schools took place in Boston in 1845. This event is important in the history of evaluation because it began a long tradition of using pupil test scores as a principal source of data to evaluate the effectiveness of a school or instructional program. Then, at the urging of Samuel Gridley Howe, written essay examinations were introduced into the Boston grammar schools by Horace Mann and the Board of Education. Ostensibly the essay exam, modeled after those used in Europe at the time, was introduced to replace the *viva voce* or oral examinations. The latter mode of examination had become administratively awkward with increased numbers of pupils and was also seen as unfair because it could not be standardized for all pupils. The interesting point in terms of program evaluation was the hidden policy agenda behind the move to written examinations: namely, it was the gathering of data for inter-school comparisons that could be used in decisions concerning the annual appointment of headmasters. Howe and Mann attempted to establish differential school effects and used these data to eliminate headmasters who opposed them on the abolition of corporal punishment. This is an interesting early example of politicization of evaluation data.

Between 1887 and 1898, Joseph Rice conducted what is generally recognized as the first formal educational-program evaluation in America. He carried out a comparative study on the value of drill in spelling instruction across a number of school districts. Rice (1897), like Mann and Howe before him, used test scores as his criteria measures in his evaluation of spelling instruction. He found no significant learning gains between systems which spent up to 200 minutes a week studying spelling and those which spent as little as ten minutes per week. Rice's results led educators to re-examine and eventually revise their approach to the teaching of spelling. More important from the point of view of this history of program evaluation is his argument that educators had to become experimentalists and quantitative thinkers and his use of comparative research design to study student achievement (Rice, 1914). Rice was a harbinger of the experimental design approach to evaluation first advanced by Lindquist (1953) and extended and championed by Campbell (Campbell & Stanley, 1963; Campbell, 1969) and others in the 1960s and 1970s.

Before leaving this very brief treatment of what has been characterized as the age of reform, another development should be mentioned. The foundation of the accreditation or professional judgment approach to evaluation can be traced directly to the establishment of the North Central Association of Colleges and Secondary Schools in the late 1800s. The accreditation movement did not, however, gain great stature until the 1930s when six additional regional accrediting associations were established across the nation. Since then the accrediting movement has expanded tremendously and gained great strength and credibility as a major means of evaluating the adequacy of educational institutions. (Cf. chapter 15 by Floden for a treatment of the accreditation approach to evaluation.)

The Age of Efficiency and Testing 1900–1930

During the early part of the twentieth century the idea of scientific management became a powerful force in administrative theory in educational as well as in industrial circles (Biddle & Ellena, 1964; Callahan, 1962; Cremin, 1962). The emphasis of this movement was on systemization; standardization; and, most importantly, efficiency. Typifying this emphasis on efficiency were the titles of the fourteenth and fifteenth yearbooks of the National Society for the Study of Education (NSSE), which were, respectively, *Methods for Measuring Teachers' Efficiency* and the *Standards and Tests for the Measurement of the Efficiency of Schools and School Systems*.

Surveys done in a number of large school systems during this period focused on school and/or teacher efficiency and used various criteria (for example, expenditures, pupil dropout rate, promotion rates, etc.). By 1915, thirty to forty large school systems had completed or were working on comprehensive surveys on all phases of educational life (Kengall, 1915; Smith & Judd, 1914). A number of these surveys employed the newly developed "objective" tests in arithmetic, spelling, handwriting, and English composition to determine the quality of teaching. These tests were often developed in large districts by a bureau or department set up specifically to improve the efficiency of the district. For example, the Department of Educational Investigation and Measurement in the Boston public schools developed a number of tests that today would be described as objective references (Ballou, 1916). Eventually tests like those in Boston took on a norm-referenced character as the percentage of students passing became a standard by which teachers could judge whether their classes were above or below the general standard for the city (Ballou, 1916). In addition to these locally developed tests there were a number of tests developed by researchers like Courtis, Ayers, Thorndike, and others, which were geared to measuring a very precise set of instructional objectives. These tests by famous researchers of the day had normative data that enabled one system to compare itself with another (Tyack & Hansot, 1982).

Many of these early twentieth-century surveys were classic examples of muckraking, "*often* initiated by a few local people who invited outside experts to expose defects and propose remedies."[3] Another problem associated with these early surveys—a problem not unknown to evaluators today—was that the "objective" results obtained were often used as propaganda "to build dikes of data against rising tides of public criticism."[4] However, researchers at the time did recognize that such surveys could and should avoid muckraking and public relations use and should indeed be constructive, be done in cooperation with local advisors, and be designed to produce public support for unrecognized but needed change (Tyack & Hansot, 1982).

With the growth of standardized achievement tests after World War I, school districts used these tests to make inferences about program effectiveness. For example, May (1971) in an unpublished paper on the history of standardized testing in Philadelphia from 1916 to 1938 found that commercially available achievement tests, along with tests built by research bureaus of large school districts, were used to diagnose specific system weaknesses and to evaluate the curriculum and overall system performance, in addition to being used to make decisions about individuals. Throughout its history, the field of evaluation has been closely linked to the field of testing. Test data have often been the principal data source in evaluations; this use of tests has been a mixed blessing as we shall see presently.

During the late 1920s and 1930s, university institutes specializing in field studies were formed and conducted surveys for local districts. The most famous of these institutes was the one headed by George Stayer at Teachers College (Tyack & Hansot, 1982). These institutes could be considered the precursors of the university centers dedicated to evaluation that grew up in the 1960s and 1970s.

It is important to point out that studies of efficiency and testing were for the most part initiated by, and confined to, local school districts. In contrast to the national curriculum development projects of the late 1950s and early 1960s, curriculum development before the 1930s was largely in the hands of a teacher or committee of teachers. It was natural, therefore, that evaluations of that period were addressed to localized questions. This focus or emphasis on local evaluation questions continued into the 1960s despite the fact that the audience for the evaluations was statewide or nationwide; this resulted in many useless educational evaluations being carried out during the 1960s. It was only in the 1970s that educators and evaluators recognized and began to deal with this problem of generalizability.

The Tylerian Age 1930–1945

Ralph W. Tyler has had enormous influence on education in general and educational evaluation and testing in particular. He is often referred to, quite properly we feel, as the father of educational evaluation. Tyler began by conceptualizing a broad and innovative view of both curriculum and evaluation. This view saw curriculum as a set of broadly planned school-experiences designed and to implemented to help students achieve specified behavior outcomes. Tyler coined the term "educational evaluation," which meant assessing the extent that valued objectives had been achieved as part of an instructional program. During the early and mid-1930s, he applied his conceptualization of evaluation to helping instructors at Ohio State improve their courses and the tests that they used in their courses.

During the depths of the Great Depression, schools as well as other public institutions, had stagnated from a lack of resources and, perhaps just as importantly, from a lack of optimism. Just as Roosevelt tried through his New Deal programs to lead the economy out of the abyss, so too John Dewey and others tried to renew education. The renewal in education came to be known as the Progressive Education Movement, and it reflected the philosophy of pragmatism and employed tools from behavioristic psychology.

Tyler became directly involved in the Progressive Education Movement when he was called upon to direct the research component of the now-famous Eight-Year Study (Smith & Tyler, 1942). The Eight-Year Study (1932–1940), funded by the Carnegie Corporation, was the first and last large study of the differential effectiveness of various types of schooling until well after World War II. The study came about when questions were asked in the early 1930s about the efficacy of the traditional high school experience relative to the progressive secondary school experience. As a result of these questions, leading colleges began to refuse progressive-school graduates admittance because they lacked credits in certain specific subjects. To settle the debate, an experiment was proposed in 1932 in which over 300 colleges agreed to waive their traditional entrance requirements for graduates from about 30 progressive secondary schools. The high school and college performance of students from these secondary schools would be compared to the high school and college performance of students from a group of traditional secondary schools.

The Eight-Year Study introduced educators throughout America to a new and broader view of educational evaluation than that which had been in vogue during the age of efficiency and testing. Evaluation was conceptualized by Tyler as a comparison of intended outcomes with actual outcomes. His view of evaluation was seen by advocates as having a clear-cut advantage over previous approaches. Since a Tylerian evaluation involves internal comparisons of outcomes with objectives, it need not provide for costly and disruptive comparisons between experimental and control groups, as were required in the comparative experimental approach that Rice had used. Since the approach calls for the measurement of behaviorally defined objectives, it concentrates on learning *outcomes* instead of organizational and teaching *inputs*, thereby avoiding the subjectivity of the professional judgment or accreditation approach; and, since its measures reflect defined objectives, there was no need to be heavily concerned with the reliability of differences between the scores of individual students. Further, the measures typically cover a much wider range of outcome variables than those associated with standardized norm-referenced tests.

Clearly by the middle of the 1940s Tyler had, through his work and writing, laid the foundation for his enormous influence on the educational scene in general and on testing and evaluation in particular during the next 25 years. (A more detailed treatment by Tyler of his rationale for program evaluation can be found in chapter 4.)

The Age of Innocence 1946–1957

We have labeled the period 1946–1957 as the *Age of Innocence*, although we might just as well have called it the *Age of Ignorance*. It was a time of poverty and despair in the inner cities and in rural areas, but almost no one except the victims seemed to notice. It was a period of extreme racial prejudice and segregation, but most white people seemed oblivious to the disease. It was when exorbitant consumption and widespread waste of natural resources were practiced without any apparent concern that one day these resources would be depleted. It was a period of vast development of industry and military capabilities with little provision for safeguards against damage to the environment and to future generations.

More to the point of this review, there was expansion of educational offerings, personnel, and facilities. New buildings were erected. New kinds of educational institutions, such as experimental colleges and community colleges, emerged. Small school districts consolidated with others in order to be able to provide the wide range of educational services that were common in the larger school systems, including: mental and physical health services, guidance, food services, music instruction, expanded sports programs, business and technical education, and community education. Enrollments in teacher-education programs ballooned, and, in general, college enrollments increased dramatically. Throughout American society, the late 1940s and 1950s were a time to forget the war, to leave the depression behind, to build and expand capabilities, to acquire resources, and to engineer and enjoy a "good life."

This general scene in society and education was reflected in educational evaluation. While there was great expansion of education, optimism, plenty of tax money, and little worry over husbanding resources, there was no particular interest on the part of society in holding educators accountable. There was little call for educators to demonstrate the efficiency and effectiveness of any developmental efforts. Educators did talk and write about evaluation, and they did collect considerable amounts of data (usually to justify the need for expansion or for broad, new programs). However, there is little evidence that these data were used to judge and improve the quality of programs or even that they could have been useful for such a purpose. During this period there was considerable development of some of the technical aspects of evaluation; this was consistent with the then prevalent expansion of all sorts of technologies. This was especially true of the testing approach to evaluation, but was also true of the comparative experimental and "congruence between objectives and outcomes" approaches. Chief among these developments was the growth in standardized testing. Many new nationally standardized tests were published during this period. Schools purchased these tests by the thousands and also subscribed heavily to machine scoring and analysis services that the new technology made available. The testing movement received another boost in 1947 when E.F. Lindquist, Ralph Tyler, and others helped establish the Educational Testing Service.

By the 1950s, the practice of standardized testing had expanded tremendously, and the professional organizations concerned with testing initiated a series of steps designed to regulate the test related activities of their members. In 1954, a committee of the American Psychological Association prepared *Technical Recommendations for Psychological Tests and Diagnostic Techniques* (APA, 1954). In 1955, committees of the American Educational Research Association and the National Council on Measurements Used in Education prepared *Technical Recommendations for Achievement Tests* (AERA and NCMUE, 1955). These two reports provided the basis for the 1966 edition of the joint AERA/APA/NCME *Standards for Educational and Psychological Tests and Manuals* (APA, 1966) and the 1974 revision entitled, *Standards for Educational and Psychological Tests* (APA, 1974). The latter report recognized the need for separate standards dealing with program evaluation. (At this writing a joint committee is at work revising the 1974 Standards.)

This rapid expansion of testing was not the only technical development related to program evaluation during this period. Lindquist (1953) extended and delineated the statistical principles of experimental design. Years later, many evaluators and educators found that the problems of trying to meet simultaneously all of the required assumptions of experimental design (for example, constant treatment, uncontaminated treatment, randomly assigned subjects, stable study samples, and unitary success criteria) in the school setting were insurmountable.

During the 1950s and early 1960s there was also considerable technical development related to the Tylerian view of evaluation. Since implementing the Tyler approach in an evaluation required that objectives be stated explicitly, there was a need to help educators and other professionals to do a better job articulating their objectives. Techniques to help program staffs make their objectives explicit, along with taxonomies of possible educational objectives (Bloom et al., 1956; Krathwohl, 1964), were developed to fill this need. The Tyler rationale was also used extensively during this period to train teachers in test development.

During this period evaluations were, as before, primarily within the purview of local agencies. Federal and state agencies had not yet become deeply involved in the evaluation of programs. Funds for evaluation that were done came from either local coffers, foundations, voluntary associations such as the community chest, or professional organizations. This lack of dependence on taxpayer money for evaluation would end with the dawn of the next period in the history of evaluation.

The Age of Expansion 1958–1972

The age of innocence in evaluation came to an abrupt end with the call in the late 1950s and early 1960s for evaluations of large-scale curriculum development projects funded by federal monies. This marked the end of an era in evaluation and the beginning of profound changes that would see evaluation expand as an industry and into a profession dependent on taxpayer monies for support.

As a result of the Russian launch of Sputnik I in 1957, the federal government enacted the National Defense Education Act of 1958. Among other things, this act provided for new educational programs in mathematics, science, and foreign language; and expanded counseling and guidance services and testing programs in school districts. A number of new national curriculum development projects, especially in the areas of science and mathematics, were established. Eventually funds were made available to evaluate these curriculum development efforts.

All four of the approaches to evaluation discussed so far were represented in the evaluations done during this period. First, the Tyler approach was used to help define objectives for the new curricula and to assess the degree to which the objectives were later realized. Second, new nationally standardized tests were created to better reflect the objectives and content of the new curricula. Third, the professional judgment approach was used to rate proposals and to check periodically on the efforts of contractors. Finally, many evaluators evaluated curriculum development efforts through the use of field experiments.

In the early 1960s it became apparent to some leaders in educational evaluation that their work and their results were neither particularly helpful to curriculum developers nor responsive to the questions being raised by those who wanted to know about the programs' effectiveness. The best and the brightest of the educational evaluation community were involved in these efforts to evaluate these new curricula; they were adequately financed, and they carefully applied the technology that had been developed during the past decade or more. Despite all this, they began to realize that their efforts were not succeeding.

This negative assessment was reflected best in a landmark article by Cronbach (1963; cf. chapter 6). In looking at the evaluation efforts of the recent past, he sharply criticized the guiding conceptualizations of evaluations for their lack of relevance and utility, and advised evaluators to turn away from their penchant for post hoc evaluations based on comparisons of the normreferenced test scores of experimental and control groups. Instead, Cronbach counseled evaluators to reconceptualize evaluation—not in terms of a horse race between competing programs but as a process of gathering and reporting information that could help guide curriculum development. Cronbach was the first person to argue that analysis and reporting of test item scores would be likely to prove more useful to teachers than the reporting of average total scores. When first published, Cronbach's counsel and recommendations went largely unnoticed, except by a small circle of evaluation specialists. Nonetheless, the article was seminal, containing hypotheses about the conceptualization and conduct of evaluations that were to be tested and found valid within a few years.

In 1965, guided by the vision of Senator Hubert Humphrey, the charismatic leadership of President John Kennedy, and the great political skill of President Lyndon Johnson, the War on Poverty was launched. These programs poured billions of dollars into reforms aimed at equalizing and upgrading opportunities for all citizens across a broad array of health, social and educational services. The expanding economy enabled the federal government to finance these programs, and there was widespread national support for developing what President Johnson termed the Great Society.

Accompanying this massive effort to help the needy came concern in some quarters that the money invested in these programs might be wasted if appropriate accountability requirements were not imposed. In response to this concern, Senator Robert Kennedy and some of his colleagues in the Congress amended the Elementary and Secondary Education Act of 1964 (ESEA) to include specific evaluation requirements. As a result, Title I of that Act, which was aimed at providing compensatory education to disadvantaged children, specifically required each school district receiving funds under its terms to evaluate annually—using appropriate standardized test data—the extent to which its Title I projects had achieved their objectives. This requirement, with its specific references to standardized-test data and an assessment of congruence between outcomes and objectives, reflects the state-of-the-art in program evaluation at that time. More importantly, the requirement forced educators to shift their concern for educational evaluation from the realm of theory and supposition into the realm of practice and implementation.

When school districts began to respond to the evaluation requirement of Title I, they quickly found that the existing tools and strategies employed by their evaluators were largely inappropriate to the task. Available standardized tests had been designed to rank order students of average ability; they were of little use in diagnosing needs and assessing any achievement gains of disadvantaged children whose educational development lagged far behind that of their middle-class peers. Further, these tests were found to be relatively insensitive to differences between schools and/or programs, mainly because of their psychometric properties and content coverage. Instead of measuring outcomes directly related to the school or to a particular program, these tests were at best indirect measures of learning, measuring much the same traits as general ability tests (Madaus, Airasian & Kellaghan, 1980).

There was another problem with using standardized tests: such an approach to evaluation conflicted with the precepts of the Tylerian approach. Because Tyler recognized and encouraged differences in objectives from locale to locale it became difficult to adapt this model to nationwide standardized-testing programs. In order to be commercially viable, these standardized-testing programs had to overlook to some extent objectives stressed by particular locales in favor of objectives stressed by the majority of districts. Further, there was a dearth of information about the needs and achievement levels of disadvantaged children that could guide teachers in developing meaningful behavioral objectives for this population of learners.

The failure of attempts to isolate the effects of Title I projects through the use of experimental/control group designs was due primarily to an inability to meet the assumptions required of such designs. Further, project-site visitation by experts—while extensively employed by governmental sponsors—was not acceptable as a primary evaluation strategy because this approach was seen as lacking the objectivity and rigor stipulated in the ESEA legislation. When the finding of "no results" was reported, as was generally the case, there were no data on the degree to which the "treatment" had in fact been implemented; the evaluator had overlooked the messy "black box" that constituted the "treatment." Further, we encased the word treatment in quotes advisedly since the actual nature of the treatment rendered to subjects was generally unknown. The technical description was nothing more than a vague description of the project. For example, the term Title I itself was often used to describe an amorphous general treatment. In any event, the emphasis on test scores diverted attention from consideration of the treatment or of treatment implementation.

As a result of the growing disquiet with evaluation efforts and with the consistent negative findings, the professional honorary fraternity Phi Delta Kappa set up a National Study Committee on Evaluation (P.D.K., 1971). After surveying the scene, this committee concluded that educational evaluation was "seized with a great illness"; and called for the development of new theories and methods of evaluation as well as for new training programs for evaluators. At about this same time many new conceptualizations of evaluations began to emerge. Provus (1969 & 1971), Hammond (1967), Eisner (1967), and Metfessel & Michael (1967) proposed reformation of the Tyler model. Glaser (1963), Tyler (1967), and Popham (1971) pointed to criterion-referenced testing as an alternative to norm-referenced testing. Cook (1966) called for the use of the systems-analysis approach to evaluate programs. Scriven (1967), Stufflebeam (1967 & 1971, with others), and Stake (1967) introduced new models of evaluation that departed radically from prior approaches. These conceptualizations recognized the need to evaluate goals, look at inputs, examine implementation and delivery of services, as well as measure intended and unintended outcomes of the program. They also emphasized the need to make judgments about the merit or worth of the object being evaluated. (Overviews of these developments can be found in chapters 2 and 3.) The late 1960s and early 1970s were vibrant with descriptions, discussions, and debates concerning how evaluation should be conceived; however, this period in the history of program evaluation ended on a down note. A number of important evaluations resulted in negative findings. First, Coleman's famous study, *Equality of Educational Opportunity* (1966, with others), received considerable notice. Particular attention went to his famous conclusion that "schools bring little influence to bear on a child's achievement that is independent of his background and general social context."[5] Title I evaluations (Picariello, 1968; Glass et al., 1970; U.S. Office of Education, 1970) argued against the efficacy of those programs. The Westinghouse/Ohio University Head Start investigation (Cicirelli et al., 1969) turned up discouraging results. Likewise, the results of the evaluation of *Sesame Street* (Ball & Bogatz, 1970; Bogatz & Ball, 1971)—when critically analyzed (Cook)—were discouraging. These disheartening findings raised serious questions about evaluation in general and certain methodologies in particular. For many supporters of these programs, this set the stage for our next period which we call the Age of Professionalization.

The Age of Professionalization 1973–Present

Beginning about 1973 the field of evaluation began to crystallize and emerge as a distinct profession related to, but quite distinct from, its forebears of research and testing. While the field of evaluation has advanced considerably as a profession, it is instructive to consider this development in the context of the field in the previous period.

At that time, evaluators faced an identity crisis. They were not sure whether they should try to be researchers, testers, administrators, teachers, or philosophers. It was unclear what special qualifications, if any, they should possess.

There was no professional organization dedicated to evaluation as a field, nor were there specialized journals through which evaluators could exchange information about their work. There was essentially no literature about program evaluation except unpublished papers that circulated through an underground network of practitioners. There was a paucity of pre-service and in-service training opportunities in evaluation. Articulated standards of good practice were confined to educational and psychological tests. The field of evaluation was amorphous and fragmented—many evaluations were carried out by untrained personnel; others by research methodologists who tried unsuccessfully to fit their methods to program evaluations (Guba, 1966). Evaluation studies were fraught with confusion, anxiety, and animosity. Evaluation as a field had little stature and no political clout.

Against this backdrop, the progress made by educational evaluators to professionalize their field during the 1970s is quite remarkable indeed. A number of journals, including *Educational Evaluation and Policy Analysis, Studies in Evaluation, CEDR Quarterly, Evaluation Review, New Directions for Program Evaluation, Evaluation and Program Planning*, and *Evaluation News* were begun; and these journals have proved to be excellent vehicles for recording and disseminating information about the various facets of program evaluation. Unlike 15 years ago, there are now numerous books and monographs that deal exclusively with evaluation. In fact, the problem today is not trying to find literature in evaluation but to keep up with it. The May 12th Group,[6] Division H of the AERA, the Evaluation Network, and the Evaluation Research Society have afforded excellent opportunities for professional exchange among persons concerned with the evaluation of education and other human service programs.

Many universities have begun to offer at least one course in evaluation methodology (as distinct from research methodology); a few universities—such as the University of Illinois, Stanford University, Boston College, UCLA, the University of Minnesota, and Western Michigan University—have developed graduate programs in evaluation. Nova University was perhaps the first to require an evaluation course in a doctoral program. For seven years the U.S. Office of Education has sponsored a national program of inservice training in evaluation for special educators (Brinkerhoff et al., in press), and several professional organizations have offered workshops and institutes on various evaluation topics. Centers have been established for research and development related to evaluation; these include the evaluation unit of the Northeast Regional Educational Laboratory, the Center for the Study of Evaluation at UCLA, the Stanford Evaluation Consortium, the Center for Instructional Research and Curriculum Evaluation at the University of Illinois, The Evaluation Center at Western Michigan University, and the Center for the Study of Testing, Evaluation and Educational Policy at Boston College. The Evaluation Institute of the University of San Francisco briefly expanded evaluation out into the product and personal areas. The state of Louisiana has established a policy and program for certifying evaluators (Peck, 1981), and Massachusetts is currently working on a similar certification program for evaluation. Recently Dick Johnson (1980) issued a first draft of a directory of evaluators and evaluation agencies.

Increasingly, the field has looked to meta evaluation (Scriven, 1975; Stufflebeam, 1978) as a means of assuring and checking the quality of evaluations. A joint committee (Joint Committee, 1981*a*), appointed by 12 professional organizations, has issued a comprehensive set of standards for judging evaluations of educational programs, and materials Joint Committee, 1981a), and has established a mechanism (Joint Committee, 1981b) by which to review and revise the Standards and assist the field to use them. (Cf. chapter 23 for an overview of these standards.) In addition, several other sets of standards with relevance for educational evaluation have been issued (cf. Evaluation *News*, May 1981).

During this period, evaluators increasingly realized that the techniques of evaluation must achieve results previously seen as peripheral to serious research; serve the information needs of the clients of evaluation; address the central value issues; deal with situational realities; meet the requirements of probity; and satisfy needs for veracity. While the field has yet to develop a fully functional methodology that meets all these requirements, there have been some promising developments, including: goal-free evaluation (Scriven, 1974; Evers, 1980); adversary-advocate teams (Stake & Gjerde, 1974; cf. chapters 11-13); advocate teams (Reinhard, 1972); meta analysis (Glass, 1976; Krol, 1978); responsive evaluation

(Stake, 1975; cf. chapter 17); and naturalistic evaluation (Guba & Lincoln, 1981; cf. chapter 18). Under the leadership of Nick Smith (1981a; 1981b), a large number of writers have examined the applicability to evaluation of a wide range of investigatory techniques drawn from a variety of fields (cf. chapter 22). Eisner (1975) and his students have explored and developed techniques for applying the techniques used by critics in evaluating materials from the arts (cf. chapter 19). Webster (1975) and his colleagues have operationalized Stufflebeam's CIPP model within the context of a school district (cf. chapter 7). Stake (1978; cf. chapter 17), has adapted case study methods for use in evaluation. Roth (1977; 1978), Suarez (1980), Scriven & Roth (1978), Stufflebeam (1977) and others have begun to make both conceptual and operational sense of the crucial yet elusive concept of needs assessment. Personnel of the Toledo Public Schools, in collaboration with Bunda (1980) and Ridings (1980), have devised catalogs of evaluative criteria and associated instruments to help teachers and administrators tailor their data collection efforts to meet their information requirements. Finally, a great deal of work has been done to encourage the use of objective-referenced tests in evaluation studies. A particularly fruitful application of this latter technique is seen in curriculum-embedded evaluations, which provide teachers and students with an ongoing assessment of attainment in relation to the sequential objectives of a curriculum (Chase, 1980; Bloom, Madaus, & Hastings, 1981).

This substantial professional development in evaluation has produced mixed results. First, while there is undoubtedly more, and certainly better, communication in the field, there has also been an enormous amount of chatter (Cronbach, 1980). Second, while progress has been made in improving the training and certification of evaluators to ensure that institutions obtain services from qualified persons, some observers worry that this development may result in a narrow and exclusive club (Stake, 1981). Third, the cooperation among professional organizations concerned with educational evaluation, fostered by the Joint Committee on Standards for Educational Evaluation, is a promising but fragile arrangement for promoting the conduct and use of high-quality evaluation work. Finally, while the creation of new professional organizations has increased communication and reduced fragmentation in the evaluation field, there, unfortunately, remains a fairly sharp division between Division H of the AERA, the Evaluation Network, and the Evaluation Research Society of America.

Even though there has been increased communication between those advocating positivistic/quantitative approaches to evaluation and proponents of phenomenological/qualitative approaches, there is a present danger of a polarization developing between those camps. The roots of this polarization are not primarily methodological, but instead reflect ideological differences. Madaus & McDonagh (1982) describe the dangers of this polarization:

In both cases, the evaluator, if not careful, could become a priest class which gives warning and advice, but does not take it, a class which practices on the one hand in the name of science and on the other through charismatic personality.[7]

Finally, in spite of growing search for appropriate methods, increased communication and understanding among the leading methodologists, and the development of new techniques, the actual practice of evaluation has changed very little in the great majority of settings. Clearly, there is a need for expanded efforts to educate evaluators to the availability of new techniques, to try out and report the results of using the new techniques, and to develop additional techniques. In all of these efforts, the emphasis must be on making the methodology fit the needs of society, its institutions, and its citizens, rather than vice versa (Kaplan, 1964).

Conclusion

Evaluators need to be aware of both contemporary and historical aspects of their emerging profession—including its philosophical underpinnings and conceptual orientations. Without this background, evaluators are doomed to repeat past mistakes and, equally debilitating, will fail to sustain and build on past successes.

We have portrayed program evaluation as a dynamic, yet immature, profession. While the profession is still immature, there can be no doubt that it has become increasingly an identifiable component of the broader governmental and professional establishment of education, health, and welfare. The prediction commonly heard in the 1960s that formalized program evaluation was a fad and soon would disappear proved false, and there are strong indications that this field will continue to grow in importance, sophistication, and stature. The gains over the past 15 years are impressive, but there are many obvious deficiencies, and we still lack sufficient evidence about the impact of evaluations on education and human services. There is a need to improve research, training, and financial support for program evaluation. Leaders of the evaluation profession must ensure that efforts to improve their profession are geared to the service needs of their clients, not merely designed to serve their private or corporate needs. Ultimately the value of program evaluation must be judged in terms of its actual and potential contributions to improving learning, teaching and administration, health care and health, and in general the quality of life in our society. All of us in the program evaluation business would do well to remember and use this basic principle to guide and examine our work.

Notes

1. Ireland. Royal Commission of Inquiry into Primary Education, 1870.
2. N.J. Crisp, 1982, p. 148
3. D. Tyack and E. Hansot, 1982, p. 161.
4. D. Tyack and E. Hansot, 1982, p. 155.
5. J.S. Coleman, E.Q. Campbell, C.J. Hobson et al., 1966, p. 325
6. In the early 1970s a group of evaluators met on May 12th to discuss issues in evaluation. The group, with added members continues in existence and meets annually to discuss current issues and problems in the field.
7. G.F. Madaus and J.T. McDonagh, 1982, p. 36.

References

American Educational Research Association and National Council on Measurements Used in Education. *Technical Recommendations for Achievement Tests*. Washington, D.C.: Author, 1955.

American Psychological Association. *Technical Recommendations for Psychological Tests and Diagnostic Techniques*. Washington, D.C.: Author, 1954.

American Psychological Association. *Standards for Educational and Psychological Tests. and Manuals* Washington, D.C.: Author, 1966.

American Psychological Association. Standards for Educational and Psychological Tests. Washington, D.C.: Author, 1974.

Ball, S., and Bogatz, G.A. *The First Year of Sesame Street: An Evaluation*. Princeton, New Jersey Educational Testing Service, 1970.

Ballou, F.A. "Work of the Department of Educational Investigation and Measurement, Boston, Massachusetts." In G.M. Whipple, (ed.), *Standards and Tests for the Measurement of the Efficiency of Schools and School Systems*. National Society for the Study of Education, Fifteenth Yearbook Part I. Chicago: University of Chicago Press, 1916.

Biddle, B.J., and Ellena, W.J. (eds.) *Contemporary Research on Teacher Effectiveness*. New York: Holt, Rinehart & Winston, 1964.

Bloom, B.S.; Englehart, M.D.; Furst, E.J.; Hill, W.H.; and Krathwohl, D.R. *Taxonomy of Educational Objectives Handbook 1: The Cognitive Domain*. New York: David McKay Co., 1956.

Bloom, B.S.; Madaus, G.F.; and Hastings, J.T. *Evaluation to Improve Learning*. New York: McGraw-Hill Book Co., 1981.

Bogatz, G.A., and Ball, S. *The Second Year of Sesame Street: A Continuing Education*. 2 vols. Princeton, New Jersey: Educational Testing Service, 1971.

Boulding, K.E. "Science, Our Common Heritage." *Science*, no. 4433, 207 (1980), 831-36.

Brinkerhoff, R. "Evaluation Technical Assistance: Reflections on a National Effort." *CEDR Journal*, forthcoming Assessment and Program Evaluation: Defining the Need and the Scope 33.

Bunda, M.A. *Catalog of Criteria for Evaluating Student Growth and Development*. Toledo: Toledo, Ohio Public Schools and the Western Michigan University Evaluation Center, 1980.

Callahan, R.E. *Education and the Cult of Efficiency*. Chicago: University of Chicago Press, 1962.

Campbell, D.T. "Reforms as Experiments." *American Psychologist*, no. 4, 24 (1969), 409-29.

Campbell, D.T., and Stanley, J.C. "Experimental and Quasi-Experimental Designs for Research on Teaching." In: N.L. Gage (ed.) *Handbook of Research on Teaching*, Chicago: Rand McNally, 1963.

Chase, F. *Educational Quandries and Opportunities*. Dallas, Texas: Urban Education Studies, 1980.

Cicirelli, V.G.. et al. *The Impact of Head Start: An Evaluation of the Effects of Head Start on Children's Cognitive and Affective Development*. Study by Westinghouse Learning Corporation and Ohio University. Washington, D.C.: Office of Economic Opportunity, 1969.

Coleman, J.S.; Campbell, E.Q.; Hobson, C.J. et al. *Equality of Educational Opportunity*. Washington, D.C.: Office of Education, U.S. Department of Health, Education, and Welfare, 1966.

Cook, D.L. *Program Evaluation and Review Technique Applications in Education*. Washington, D.C.: Government Printing Office, 1966.

Cremin, L.A. *The Transformation of the School*. New York: Knopf, 1962.

Crisp, J.J. *The Brink*. New York: Viking Press, 1982. Cronbach, L.J. "Course Improvement through Evaluation." *Teachers College Record*. 64 (1963): 672-83.

Cronbach, L.J. *Toward Reform of Program Evaluation*. San Francisco: Jossey-Bass Publishers, 1980.

Eisner, E.W. "Educational Objectives: Help or Hindrance?" *The School Review*. 75 (1967): 250-60.

Eisner, E.W. *The Perceptive Eye: Toward the Reformation of Educational Evaluation*. Stanford, California: Stanford Evaluation Consortium, December 1975.

Evaluation News. Sponsored by the Evaluation Network, Sage Publications, no. 2, 2 (1981).

Evers, J.W. "A Field Study of Goal-Based and Goal-Free Evaluation Techniques." Unpublished doctoral dissertation, Western Michigan University, 1980.

Glaser, R. "Instructional Technology and the Measurement of Learning Outcomes: Some Questions." *American Psychologist 18* (1963): 519-21.

Glass, G.V. "Primary, Secondary, and Meta Analysis of Research." *Educational Researcher*, no. 10, 5 (1976), 3-8.

Glass, G.V. et al. *Data Analysis of the 1968-69 Survey of Compensatory Education, Title 1. Final Report on Grant No. OEG8-8-961860 4003 (058)*. Washington, D.C.: Office of Education, 1970.

Guba, E.G. *A Study of Title III Activities: Report on Evaluation*. Indiana University, National Institute for the Study of Educational Change, October 1966.

Guba, E.G. and Lincoln, Y.S. *Effective Evaluation*. San Francisco: Jossey-Bass Publishers, 1981.

Hammond, R.L. "Evaluation at the Local Level." Address to the Miller Committee for the National Study of ESEA Title III, 1967.Ireland, Royal Commission of Inquiry into Primary Education. *Report of the Commissioners*. (H.C. 1870, xxviii, part i).

Johnson, R. *Directory of Evaluators and Evaluation Agencies*. New York: Exxon Corporation 1980.

Joint Committee on Standards for Educational Evaluation. *Standards for Evaluations of Educational Programs, Projects, and Materials*. New York: McGraw-Hill Book Co., 1981a.

Joint Committee on Standards for Educational Evaluation. *Principles and By-Laws*. Western Michigan University Evaluation Center, 1981b.

Kaplan, A. *The Conduct of Inquiry*. San Francisco: Chandler, 1964.

Kellaghan, T. and Madaus, G.F. Trends in Educational Standards in Great Britain and Ireland. In G.R. Austin & H. Garber (eds.), *The Rise and Fall of National Test Scores*. New York: Academic Press, 1982.

Kendall, C.N. "Efficiency of School and School Systems." In *Proceedings and Addresses of the Fifty-third Annual Meeting of the National Education Association*, 389–95, 1915.

Krathwohl, D.R.; Bloom, B.S.; and Masia, B.B. *Taxonomy of Educational Objectives: the Classification of Educational Goals. Handbook 11: Affective Domain*. New York: David McKay Co., 1964.

Krol, R.A. "A Meta Analysis of Comparative Research on the Effects of Desegregation on Academic Achievement." Unpublished doctoral dissertation, Western Michigan University, 1978.

Lindquist, E.F. *Design and Analysis of Experiments in Psychology and Education*. Boston: Houghton-Mifflin, 1953.

Madaus, G.F.; Airasian, P.W.; and Kellaghan, T. *School Effectiveness*. New York: McGraw-Hill Book Co., 1980.

Madaus, G.F., and McDonagh, J.T. "As I Roved Out: Folksong Collecting as a Metaphor for Evaluation. In N.L. Smith (ed.), *Communicating in Evaluation: Alternative Forms of Representation*. Beverly Hills, California: Sage Publications, 1982.

May, P. "Standardized Testing in Philadelphia, 1916–1938" Unpublished manuscript, 1971.

Metfessel, N.S. and Michael, W.B. "A Paradigm Involving Multiple Criterion Measures for the Evaluation of the Effectiveness of School

Programs." *Educational and Psychological Measurement* 27 (1967):931–43.

National Society for the Study of Education. *Methods for Measuring Teachers' Efficiency*. Fourteenth Yearbook. Part II. Chicago: University of Chicago Press, 1916.

Peck, H. "Report on the Certification of Evaluators in Louisiana." Paper presented at the meeting of the Southern Educational Research Association, Lexington, Kentucky, Fall 1981.

Phi Delta Kappa Commission on Evaluation. *Educational Evaluation and Decision Making*. Itasca, Illinois: Peacock Publishers, 1971.

Picariello, H. *Evaluation of Title 1*. Washington, D.C.: American Institute for the Advancement of Science, 1968.

Pinker, R. *Social Theory and Social Policy*. London: Heinemann Educational Books, 1971.

Popham, W.J. *Criterion-referenced Measurement*. Englewood Cliffs, New Jersey: Educational Technology Publications, 1971.

Provus, M. *Discrepancy Evaluation Model, 1969*. Pittsburgh, Pennsylvania: Pittsburgh Public Schools, 1969.

Provus, M. *Discrepancy Evaluation*. Berkeley, California: McCutcheon Publishing Co., 1971.

Reinhard, D. "Methodology Development for Input Evaluation Using Advocate and Design Teams." Unpublished doctoral dissertation, Ohio State University, 1972.

Rice, J.M. "The Futility of the Spelling Grind." *The Forum* 23 (1897):163-72.

Rice, J.M. *Scientific Management in Education*. New York: Hinds, Noble & Eldredge, 1914.

Ridings, J. *Catalog of Criteria for Evaluating Administrative Concerns in School Districts*. Toledo: Toledo, Ohio Public Schools and the Western Michigan University Evalua

Roth, J. "Needs and the Needs Assessment Process." *Evaluation News* 5 (1977):15-17.

Roth, J.E. "Theory and Practice of Needs Assessment With Special Application to Institutions of Higher Learning." Unpublished doctoral dissertation, University of California, Berkeley, 1978.

Scriven, M.S. "The Methodology of Evaluation." In *Perspective of Curriculum Evaluation*. AERA Monograph Series on Curriculum Evaluation, no. 1. Chicago: Rand McNally, 1967.

Scriven, M.S. "Pros and Cons about Goal-Free Evaluation." *Evaluation Comment* 3 (1974):1-4.

Scriven, M.S. *Evaluation Bias and its Control*. Occasional Paper Series no. 4. Western Michigan University Evaluation Center, 1975.

Scriven, M. and Roth, J.E. "Needs Assessment." *Evaluation News* 2 (1977):25-28.

Scriven, M. and Roth, J.E. "Needs Assessment: Concept and Practice." *New Directions for Program Evaluation* 1 (1978):1-11.

Smith, E.R., and Tyler, R.W. *Appraising and Recording Student Progress*. New York: Harper, 1942.

Smith, H.L., and Judd, C.H. *Plans for Organizing School Surveys*. National Society for the Study of Education, Thirteenth Yearbook, Part II. Bloomington, Illinois: Public School Publishing Co., 1914.

Smith, N.L. *Metaphors for Evaluation: Sources of New Methods*. Beverly Hills, California: Sage Publications, 1981a.

Smith, N.L. *New Techniques for Evaluation*. Beverly Hills, California: Sage Publications, 1981b.

Stake, R.E. "The Countenance of Educational Evaluation." *Teachers College Record* 68 (1967):523–40.

Stake, R.E. "Setting Standards for Educational Evaluators." *Evaluation News* no. 2, 2 (1981), 148–52.

Stake, R.E. "The Case-Study Method in Social Inquiry." *Evaluation Researcher* 7 (1978):5–8.

Stake, R.E. "Setting Standards for Educational Evaluators." *Evaluator News* no. 2, 2 (1981), 148–52.

Stake, R.E., and Gjerde, C. *An Evaluation of T-City, the Twin City Institute for Talented Youth*. AERA Monograph Series in Curriculum Evaluation, no. 7. Chicago: Rand McNally, 1974.

Stufflebeam, D.L. "The Use and Abuse of Evaluation in Title III." *Theory into Practice* 6 (1967):126-33.

Stufflebeam, D.L. *Needs Assessment in Evaluation*. Audio-tape of presentation at the American Educational Research Association Meeting, San Francisco, September 1977. Published by the American Educational Research Association.

Stufflebeam, D.L. "Meta Evaluation: An Overview." *Evaluation and the Health Professions*, no. 2.1. (1978).

Stufflebeam, D.L. et al. *Educational Evaluation and Decision-Making*. Ithaca, Illinois: Peacock Publishing.

Suarez, T. "Needs Assessments for Technical Assistance: A Conceptual Overview and

Comparison of Three Strategies." Unpublished doctoral dissertation. Western Michigan University, 1980.

Thompson, D. *England in the Nineteenth Century (1815–1914)*. Baltimore: Penguin Books, Inc., 1950.

Tyack, D., and Hansot, E. *Managers of Virtue*. New York: Basic Books, Inc., 1982.

Tyler, R.W. "Changing Concepts of Educational Evaluation." In R.E. Stake (ed.), *Perspectives of Curriculum Evaluation. vol. 1*, New York: Rand McNally, 1967.

U.S. Office of Education. *Education of the Disadvantaged: An Evaluation Reporton Title: Elementary and Secondary Education Act of 1965. Fiscal Year 1968*. Washington, D.C.; Author, 1970.

Webster, W.J. *The Organization and Functions of Research and Evaluation Units in a Large Urban School District*. Dallas, Texas: Dallas Independent School District, 1975.

DEMYSTIFYING ASSESSMENT: LEARNING FROM THE FIELD OF EVALUATION

BARBARA GROSS DAVIS

The challenge confronting those undertaking assessment efforts is to make use of the extensive body of knowledge and good practices developed within the field of evaluation.

In the last four years since the assessment movement began, the following developments have occurred: (1) All but fourteen state legislatures have taken action to consider or begin campus assessment programs (National Governors' Association, 1988). Some forty states now require assessment by state law or policy (Blumenstyk, 1988). (2) Accreditation agencies are requesting assessments of student achievement as critical elements in the accrediting process. (3) The Fund for the Improvement of Postsecondary Education (FIPSE) has awarded assessment-related grants to over twenty institutions and organizations. (4) Three national conferences have been held on assessment, the most recent attracting over 1,000 people. (5) Special issues of professional journals have been devoted to assessment; in the last three years, four Jossey-Bass sourcebooks have appeared on this topic (Banta 1988; Bray and Belcher, 1987; Ewell, 1985; Halpern, 1987). (6) Offices of assessment have sprung up at colleges and universities across the country. (7) The testing industry has been aggressively developing new instruments to measure students' cognitive growth and personal development.

As others have pointed out (Ewell, 1988), there is nothing terribly new about higher education's attempt to assess itself. For decades, higher education has assessed student learning and demonstrated institutional effectiveness to external agencies. So, why the flurry of activity at this time?

Observers (Rossman and El-Khawas, 1987; Westling, 1988) have speculated on how economic, social, and political concerns have converged to create a welcome climate for assessment. First, the public perceives that college students often lack basic skills on entry and at graduation. New demands in the workplace for greater sophistication in writing, reading, and computing may have magnified college graduates' weakness. Second, the perceived failings of higher education, as documented by several books and national reports, have credited a crisis of confidence and led to calls for improving the educational system. And education, critics argue, should be judged by assessment; traditional measures of student achievement, such as course grades and retention and graduation rates, do not satisfy these critics' standards for reliability and interpretability across programs and institutions.

Political pressures have also played a role. State legislators know that "creating better schools" is a popular campaign theme, and tight budgets lead public officials to demand accountability and proof of cost effectiveness. Assessment thus becomes the lever helping states to meet their economic and social goals: "It is essential that states maintain the pressure to access despite the many vocal arguments against it" (National Governors' Association, 1988, p. 42).

In the rush to meet external demands for assessment, those involved in assessment have overlooked what the field of evaluation can contribute to their endeavors. To bring some order to the

Reprinted from *New Directions for Higher Education* 16, no. 67, by permission of Jossey-Bass Publishers, Inc. This material is used by permission of John Wiley & Sons, Inc.

diverse literature of the assessment, this chapter analyzes assessment using the conceptualization of educational evaluation put forth by Stufflebeam (1974) and expanded by Nevo (1986). Ten questions provided the framework for this analysis:

1. What does the term *assessment* mean?
2. What is the purpose of assessment?
3. What can be assessed?
4. What kinds of questions can be asked in assessment?
5. What criteria can be used to judge the merit or worth of what has been assessed?
6. Who should be served by assessment?
7. What are the procedures for conducting an assessment?
8. What methods of inquiry can be used in assessment?
9. Who should do an assessment?
10. By what standards is assessment judged?

What Does the Term Assessment Mean?

Despite increasing nationwide attention to the topic of assessment, there is not consensus on exactly what topics and processes assessment comprises. Is the primary concern to be assessment of the performance of individual students or groups of students, the effectiveness of instructional practices, or the functioning of departments or the institution itself? Various definitions are in widespread use.

Some writers (Boyer and Ewell, 1988; Bray and Belcher, 1987; Eison and Palladino, 1988) approach assessment broadly, describing it as encompassing general activities of testing, evaluation, and documentation. For example, Boyer and Ewell (1988) define assessment as "processes that provide information about individual students, about curricula or programs, about institutions, or about entire systems of institutions." Others equate *assessment* and *evaluation*, using the terms interchangeably.

Still others view assessment narrowly, as specifically tied to student learning, knowledge, skill, and outcomes (Marchese, 1987; Jacobi, Astin, and Ayala, 1987; National Governors' Association, 1988). For this group, assessment encompasses various procedures that determine the extent to which students have met curricular goals, mastered the prescribed subject matter, and acquired the skills and characteristics essential to an educated person (Chandler, 1986). Recognizing the confusion in terminology, some researchers speak about outcomes assessment (Banta, 1988) or assessment of student learning (Adelman, 1988) when referring to assessment and student performance. But many writers simply use the term *assessment* as shorthand notation for measuring student achievement and development.

The problems in defining assessment are similar to those encountered in defining evaluation in the early years of the development of the field. Many definitions of evaluation have been proposed and used (Nevo, 1986). For example, in the 1950s evaluation was defined as the process of determining the extent to which educational objectives are being met. (Note the similarity to Chandler's definition of assessment as the extent to which individual students meet curricular goals.) In the 1960s and early 1970s, evaluation was defined as the process of providing information for decision makers. (Note the similarity to Boyer's and Ewell's definition of assessment as the process of providing information about students, curricula, programs, and institutions.) More recently, a broader definition has been adopted by evaluators: Evaluation is the process of determining the worth or merit of an activity, program, person, or product (Joint Committee, 1981). The special features of evaluation, as a particular kind of investigation, include concerns with needs, description, context, outcomes, comparisons, costs, audience, utilization, and the supporting and making of sound value judgments.

It may be that the field of assessment will evolve in much the same manner. But the assessment movement seems to be making little use of what is known about evaluation. For example, a glossary of assessment terminology (Boyer and Ewell, 1988) does not include an entry for "evaluation," and few writers in assessment make reference to the body of evaluation theory and practice.

Given the lack of consensus on what constitutes assessment, we cannot be surprised that there is little agreement on the relationship between the terms *assessment* and *evaluation*. Prior to the growth of the assessment movement, those in the evaluation field sometimes used assessment as a synonym for evaluation. Even then, however, there was a sense that the two were not completely interchangeable. As Scriven (1981) points out, assessment tends to focus more on quantitative or testing approaches, as exemplified by the National Assessment of Educational Progress.

Today, one finds three stances: that evaluation is a subset of assessment, that assessment is a subset of evaluation, that evaluation and assessment are converging. The first is proffered by some in the assessment movement who consider evaluation to be the program or curricular evaluation component of assessment. But this is an inaccurate view, since evaluation encompasses more than programs and curricula.

The second view relies on a narrow definition of assessment focusing on student achievement and development. In fact, "outcome evaluation," or "impact assessment," is an accepted component of evaluation (Rossi and Freeman, 1985; Posavac and Carey, 1985), investigating the results, impact, or outcomes of a program or intervention.

If a broad definition of assessment is adopted, then assessment and evaluation begin to merge into a common effort to understand and judge the merit and worth of teaching and learning within a course, curriculum, educational program, sequence of study, department, unit, or institution.

What Is the Purpose of Assessment?

In the assessment literature, one tends to find statements of wide ranging purposes. For example, Ewell (1988) cites the following: to evaluate curricula, to demonstrate external accountability, to recruit students, to raise funds for institutions, and to change the way teaching and learning occur in individual classrooms. Jacobi, Astin, and Ayala (1987) identify these purposes of assessment: to provide information about students' change and development, to establish accountability for external agencies, to evaluate programs, to analyze cost-effectiveness, and to set goals.

From the field of evaluation comes a more meaningful, less complex, conceptually clearer way to think about the purposes of assessment. A major distinction is made between formative and summative evaluation. Formative evaluation is undertaken for the purpose of improving and developing an activity, program, person, or product. Summative evaluation is undertaken for the purposes of accountability or resource allocation (in the case of programs), for certification, selection, and placement (in the case of students), or for decisions about merit increases and promotions (in the case of faculty). Similarly, we can say that institutions undertake assessments to improve what they are doing (formative) or to make decisions about resources, institutions, programs, faculty, or students (summative). Some writers (Ewell and Boyer, 1988) have grasped the importance of the distinction, but others have overlooked it and therefore have also ignored how the purpose of an assessment influences aspects of its design and analysis.

By borrowing concepts from evaluation, we have highlighted key differences between formative and summative assessment in Figure 1.

What Can Be Assessed?

Those who adopt a broad view of assessment see all aspects of higher education as subjects for assessment: students, educational and administrative personnel, curricula, programs, departments, and institutions. Under this broad definition, assessment includes the many program reviews, self-studies, faculty evaluations, special-project evaluations, and so on that institutions routinely conduct to gather data about their effectiveness. Here are examples of such regularly scheduled activities at the University of California at Berkeley:

- Peer reviews (including student and faculty surveys as well as interview data) of all undergraduate and graduate programs conducted on a regular review cycle
- Peer reviews of the quality of teaching of every faculty member as part of the regular merit and promotion process
- Annual surveys of entering freshmen regarding students' backgrounds, interests, aspirations, and attitudes
- Placement tests in mathematics and composition used to determine students' skill levels
- Surveys of students in every class each semester about the effectiveness of the course and the teaching performance of the instructor

Figure 1 Formative Versus Summative Assessment

Feature	Formative Assessment	Summative Assessment
Purpose	Improvement or development of activities, programs, products, people	Accountability, resource allocation; selection, placement, certification; pay and promotion decisions
Audience	Internal decision maker: program or department administrators; individual faculty	External decision maker: central administrators; government officials; accrediting bodies; public
Scope	Diagnostic, detailed, specific assessments	Global assessments
Procedures	Informal; narrow; specialized	Formal; comprehensive
Timing	Ongoing or during a program or sequence of study	Before and after or simply at the completion of a program or sequence of study
Sources of Information	One or more	Multiple and diverse
Emphasis	Suggestions for improvement	Overall judgments

- Department, college, and campuswide surveys conducted periodically of graduating seniors and alumni regarding their opinion of the education they have received
- Occasional surveys of employers of graduates conducted by individual departments
- Exit interviews with students who leave the campus before graduation
- Review of ethnic diversity of applicants, enrollees, graduates, and dropouts
- Review and analysis of retention rates for students in aggregate and by various subgroups
- Formative and summative evaluation of individual support units and student services, such as the counseling center.

One would think that such information would interest public and state legislatures concerned about assessment. But these data are often overlooked, and special assessment reports are sought instead. The institutions are partly to blame in that they sometimes provide so much data in such detail, without a framework for interpreting their significance, that legislators dismiss the information as just another numbing report. There is also the problem with self-reports: If an institution prepares a negative report, its credibility is usually not questioned. But, for many external audiences, positive self-reports are highly suspect or simply not believed. The final blow against data from routine reviews and surveys is precisely that they are routine. Legislators and the public want to know what is new. The same high levels of accomplishment, reported year after year, may not satisfy external audiences. This demand for news challenges institutions that have been regularly reporting routine data to recast the information and present it as special assessment data.

Those who adopt a narrow view of assessment focus on the student outcomes of higher education. Even with such a view, there are still many possible outcomes. Virtually every human characteristic can be assessed (Baird, 1988a): knowledge, skills, attitudes, values, and behaviors. The problem, then, is not deciding what to assess but deciding how to select the outcomes to be examined. These choices depend on the values and priorities of those commissioning the assessment and those who will actually or potentially use the results (called "stakeholders" in evaluation terminology), as well as on the practical constraints of time, resources, and tools to measure outcomes.

What Kinds of Questions Can Be Asked in Assessment?

The best place to begin any investigation is to define the questions of most interest to the stakeholders—the potential users and audience. In evaluation, emphasis is placed on identifying and asking questions of most interest to decision makers, program participants, and the audiences for the evaluation. A wide range of questions are generated, refined, and narrowed down to those that can be answered given the resource constraints, the interest of the stakeholders, and the circumstances for the evaluation.

This same approach can be used to generate assessment questions. Here are some examples of questions generated, in part, by faculty members of the University of California at a conference called "Assessing the Lower Division," held at the University of California at Los Angeles, in February 1989:

1. *Who applies to and enrolls in the university, and how well prepared are these students?* For summative assessment, information about applicants and new students is a measure of an institution's quality—whether it can recruit and enroll high-ability students—and also a measure of how well the institution is enrolling underrepresented minority students. For formative assessment, information about new enrollments is critical in giving faculty an understanding of the abilities and preparation of the students they will be teaching. Measures that help answer this question include demographic characteristics of students' standardized test scores and high school performance, percentage of students in the upper 5 percent or 10 percent of their graduating class who apply and enroll in the university, number of valedictorians and number of National Merit Scholars, and pass rates on campus freshmen placement exams in composition and mathematics.
2. *What do students learn?* The specific aspects of learning to be investigated will depend on the values and priorities of individual institutions. Here are some components of student learning, with an indication of data sources for answering the question:
   - *What type of education is represented by the courses students take?* Do the courses students take exemplify the university's concept of a good education? Source: analysis of students' transcripts to identify course-taking patterns.
   - *Does the undergraduate experience develop qualities valued in educated persons?* Such qualities might include critical thinking, problem solving, mastery of general skills, and an understanding of the contemporary world. Sources: transcript analysis; review of course syllabuses; senior theses or projects; comprehensive exams, if available; survey of faculty and students.
   - *Have students developed aesthetic interests and an appreciation of the arts?* Sources: transcript analysis; student attendance at campus museums and performing art events; number of submissions to campus arts award programs; use of campus arts facilities such as darkrooms and pottery studios; student participation in arts clubs.
   - *To what extent can students communicate in writing with clarity and style?* Sources: transcript analysis; junior-level writing exams, if offered; portfolios or collections of students' written work; student journals.
   - *What is the course withdrawal rate?* Measures: percentage of total course registrations that result in withdrawals; percentage of individual student with at least one withdrawal.
   - *How knowledgeable are graduating seniors?* Sources: Graduate Record Examination (GRE), Law School Admission Test (LSAT), and Medical College Admission Test (MCAT) test scores; senior theses, projects, comprehensive exams; external awards and recognition of students.
3. *What do students value?* Again, the priorities and values of each college and university will determine what is measured within this area. Here are some examples:
   - *To what extent do students show interest in and respect for different cultures and different points of view?* Measures: analysis of racial, ethnic, and religious incidents that indicate bias, prejudice, or stereotyping;

enrollments in courses dealing with ethnic, gender, and cultural diversity; number of applicants and enrollments in study-abroad programs.

- *To what extent are students socially responsible and involved in the community?* Measures: student participation in volunteer groups, charitable work, and the like; transcript analysis of field study courses and internships.

4. *Who is dropping out?* Through exit interviews or surveys, one can identify the reasons students withdraw: transfer to another institution, involuntary withdrawal (health or financial reasons), voluntary withdrawal (job, marriage), or academic dismissal. Rates of attrition and retention can be calculated by major, gender, ethnicity, grade point average, and transfer status.
5. *What is the quality of undergraduate teaching?*
    - *Who teaches undergraduate courses, particularly in the lower division?* Measures: percentage of faculty who teach at least one undergraduate course per term; percentage of lower-division courses taught by faculty at each rank; percentage of undergraduate students by year in school who have had at least three regular faculty members during each term; differences among departments in allocating faculty to the lower division.
    - *How effective is undergraduate teaching?* Sources: student ratings by size of course, discipline, instructional method; alumni surveys; peer judgments of deans and faculty committees reviewing personnel cases.
    - *To what extent are faculty interested in undergraduate teaching?* Sources: course assignments by faculty teaching load and rank; faculty survey; faculty participation in instructional improvement activities.
    - *To what extent do lower-division students have opportunity for quality contact with professors?* Sources: student and faculty surveys; transcript analysis; use of office hours; number of faculty involved in advising.
    - *What is the level, nature, and quality of attention given by departments to the training of teaching assistants (TAs)?* Sources: percentages of departments that offer training for TAs; surveys of faculty and TAs.
    - *How effective are services provided to faculty and TAs for teaching improvement?* Source: evaluation of support services.
6. *What is the quality of the curriculum?*
    - *What reform efforts have taken place or are under way?* Sources: task force reports; changes in policy; comparison of catalogues before and after curriculum revision.
    - *How accessible are lower-division courses? Can students get into the courses that they need or want?* Sources: demands for enrollment; transcript analysis; student surveys.
    - *What is the effectiveness of the lower-division curriculum in satisfying students' needs to explore a diversity of subjects and to pursue a major?* Sources: materials available describing different through transcript analysis; length of drift before declaring a major; number of students who change majors; student performance in upper-division courses; student surveys.
    - *What is the quality of departments with large undergraduate enrollments?* Sources: academic program reviews; alumni surveys; surveys of faculty and current students.
    - *What are the class-size experiences of students?* Measures: percentage of lower-division students who have had at least one course each term that enrolled fifty or fewer students; percentages of lower-division students who have had all courses in their first year enrollment 100 or fewer students; percentage of lower-division students who have had at least one seminar class.
7. *How effective is the advising that students receive?* Who advises students about academic issues (selecting courses and programs of study), career options (career choices and opportunity for further education and training), and personal development (participation in extracurricular activities or job experiences)? Sources: stu-

dent and alumni surveys on advisers' knowledge, availability, and rapport.

8. *How do students feel about their undergraduate experiences?* Sources: surveys of junior or seniors; counseling reports on student problems; and ombudsman reports of students' experiences and complaints.
9. *How effective are support services?* Sources: surveys of students and faculty who use particular services.
10. *What happens to students after they graduate?* Sources: alumni surveys; graduate school admissions; job placements; follow-up surveys of employers of graduates.

What Criteria Can Be Used to Judge the Merit or Worth of What Has Been Assessed?

The assessment literature is largely silent on judging worth or merit. In contrast, in evaluation a variety of criteria has been offered for judging merit, and the evaluation literature stresses the importance of using multiple criteria for judging any program, activity, service, person or object. Criteria may include the extent to which the entity being evaluated responds to identified needs of actual and potential clients; achieves national goals, ideals, or social values; meets agreed on standards and norms; outdoes or outperforms alternative objects; or achieves important stated goals (Nevo, 1986).

Judging merit does surface in discussion of value-added or talent-development assessment, which attempts, through pre- and post-testing, to estimate the portion of students' growth or development that can be reasonably attributed to specific educational experiences (the value added by particular in higher education). The assessment asks how a college education has changed students' knowledge, skills, and values, and those institutions that report greater changes are considered more successful. As Ewell (1988) points out, however, students may change greatly but still fall below acceptable standards: Are institutions to be judged primarily in terms of the amount of change or the levels students finally attain? Too, the pre- and post-test model betrays a reductive premise, the education is "addictive" rather than synergistic, multifaceted, and multicausal.

At heart, value-added and talent-development assessments are new terminology for an old fundamental issue in educational research: What are the net effects of an educational experience on students' cognitive and noncognitive development? This question has also been phrased more complexly as "What kinds of students change in what ways when exposed to what kinds of educational experiences?" (Pascarella, 1986). Yet, as the literature shows (Halpern, 1987; Pascarella, 1986; Warren, 1984; McMillan, 1988; Hanson, 1988; Baird, 1988b), reliable, meaningful value-added assessment is difficult to implement. The technical problems include the difficulties (such as regression effects, maturation effects, cohort incomparability, and so on) of measuring change and of unbundling the influence of education from other influences on student growth; the absence of reliable, valid, standardized instruments to measure meaningful educational outcomes beyond content knowledge; and the challenge of developing instruments sensitive enough to measure subtle changes in noncognitive areas.

Finally, even if we had the measures, there are the difficulties of attributing changes to the institution, its students' aptitude or prior achievements, or the quality of students' learning efforts. Research indicates that the largest effects on student growth and change are due to maturation, followed by, in order, effects due to attendance at any college, effects due to attendance at a particular college, and specific college experiences (Baird, 1988b).

Given these conceptual and technical problems, those in the assessment movement may wish to adapt the criteria used in evaluation to judge merit and worth (Nevo, 1986): fills a critical need; achieves universally recognized goals, ideals, or values; meets agreed-on standards and norms; outperforms competitors; achieves important stated goals.

Who Should Be Served by Assessment?

Many in the field of evaluation have adopted Guba and Lincoln's (1981) term *stakeholders* to refer to all the groups of persons having some actual or potential stake in the performance of the entity being evaluated. Stakeholders for an assessment might include the decision makers commissioning the investigation, policy makers with some interest in the result, state and federal officials, campus administrators, program participants, faculty, students, parents, taxpayers, and the public at large.

Baird (1988a) lists examples of the kinds of assessment questions different audiences might post about a college or university:

1. *Parents:* How likely is my child to be admitted? What is the curriculum like? What programs or facilities are available to meet my child's interests? What are the chances a student will drop out, get A's, or go on to graduate school? What is the daily experience of this college like? Is there a sense of community and a strong intellectual climate?
2. *Taxpayers:* What are the costs to the taxpayers of this institution? Is this college meeting the current and future needs of the state in the training it is providing students? Are there provisions for excellence and equity? Can students from families with limited means attend and graduate from this college? Does this college make a difference to the economy and culture of the state?
3. *Faculty:* What are the implications for the curriculum and for students of a rise in student careerism and concern for wealth? What conditions promote research among the faculty? How good is the teaching?

Baird's examples reinforce three important points stressed in the evaluation literature (Nevo, 1986) that are directly applicable to assessment: (1) An investigation can have more than one client, audience, or stakeholder; (2) different audiences may have different information needs; (3) since the questions important to different audience will affect the kind of information collected, the level of data analysis, and the form of reporting the results, the specific audiences and their specific needs must be identified at the early stages of planning the study.

What Are the Procedures for Conducting an Assessment?

Case studies of how to conduct an assessment are widely reported in the literature (Bray and Belcher, 1987; Banta, 1988; Ewell, 1985; Halpern, 1987). Typical advice includes: start small, develop incrementally, use existing data when possible, use multiple measures rather than single test scores, stress formative aspects, ensure support of top leadership, involve faculty during all phases of development and implementation, recognize and incorporate the institution's unique mission and history. In addition, descriptions of activities at the University of Tennessee, Alverno College, and Northeast Missouri State University are available (Halpern, 1987). But the assessment movement as a whole lacks a specific methodology, models, or theoretical perspectives to inform practice.

In contrast, over the last four decades the field of evaluation has evolved detailed methodologies and various models that describe processes for conducting evaluations. Though the specific steps in an evaluation may depend on the evaluator's theoretical bent, evaluators agree on the following general steps:

1. Focus the evaluation problem by defining the charge from the client and the constraints.
2. Identify various stakeholders and audiences.
3. Generate questions of interest to stakeholders.
4. Refine and limit questions through negotiation with vested parties so the questions can be addressed.
5. Determine the methodology: Specify for each question the instrument or data source (new or existing), the sample from whom data have been or need to be collected, the time frame for data collection (if gathering new date), the methods of analysis, and the intended use of the results.
6. Communicate the findings to stakeholders in ways that they can use the results.

What Methods of Inquiry Can Be Used in Assessment?

Both the evaluation field and the assessment movement make use of traditional educational research methods: tests, surveys, interviews, and observations using experimental and quasi-experimental designs. The assessment movement has concentrated primarily on these methods. In contrast, the evaluation field has developed and popularized a range of naturalistic methods and qualitative approaches (Guba and Lincoln, 1981; Lincoln and Guba, 1986; Patton, 1987) and has explored unusual methods of inquiry: jury trials, art criticism applied to educational evaluations, and modus operandi (Smith, 1981a, 1981b).

As Hutchings (1988) notes, there is a growing interest in assessment methods that give more qualitative and complete pictures of what students learn under what conditions. Here, the vitality in evaluations methodology can provide useful models.

Who Should Do an Assessment?

The assessment literature (Ewell, 1988; Mentkowski, 1988; Miller, 1988) stresses the importance of faculty involvement in each step of the assessment process. Researchers also recommended that assessment activities elicit the support and advocacy of influential opinion makers on campus. For conducting an assessment, Ewell recommends that a small separate office of assessment be set up, reporting to high-level policy makers.

Appelbaum (1988) advocates a team approach to assessment. The team must be collectively knowledgeable about relevant instructional goals, current directions in the area under study, and basic evaluation principles and practices. From the evaluation literature, one might add that the team should also include collective expertise in administration to plan and manage the effort, as well as strong interpersonal and communication skills (Davis, 1986).

By What Standard Is Assessment Judged?

The literature on evaluation utilization and evaluation standards has direct implications for assessment, but the findings have not been widely applied. For example, evaluators have developed a set of thirty standards for judging an evaluation (Joint Committee, 1981). These standards are divided into four major categories: utility (does the evaluation serve practical information needs?), feasibility (is the evaluation realistic and prudent?), propriety (does the evaluation conform to legal and ethical standards?), and accuracy (is the evaluation technically adequate?).

Regarding the utilization of evaluation, the literature (Alkin, Daillak, and White, 1979; Braskamp and Brow, 1980; Patton, 1985) identifies general conditions that promote the use of evaluation results. These include involving potential audiences in the process from the beginning; providing opportunities for ongoing discussion of findings between client and evaluator; garnering support of key administrators; ensuring that the data are valid, reliable, and credible; offering explicit recommendations; preparing brief reports that address the client's concerns; releasing results in a timely manner; and identifying one or more concerned individuals who will provide the leadership to ensure that the findings are acted on.

Conclusion

As this review has shown, evaluation has much to offer assessment. The challenges confronting those in assessment is to become familiar with and make use of the extensive body of knowledge and good practices developed within the field of evaluation. For example, from work in evaluation utilization, those facing assessment can learn how to gather information that is likely to be used, and evaluation methodology can provide models for expanding the repertoire of assessment methods in order to gain richer insights and greater understanding of the workings of higher education.

In addition, by reference to evaluation, the assessment movement may be able to defuse some of its critics who tend to view assessment as focusing solely on student outcomes. By linking evaluation and assessment, the two may merge into a common broad-based effort to understand and judge the merit and worth of higher education.

References

Adelman, C. (ed.). *Performance and Judgment.* Washington, D.C.: Superintendent of Documents, U.S. Government Printing Office, 1988.

Alkin, M. C., Daillak, R., and White, P. *Using Evaluations: Does Evaluation Make a Difference?* Newbury Park, Calif.: Sage, 1979.

Appelbaum, M. I. "Assessment Through the Major." In C. Adelman (ed.), *Performance and Judgment.* Washington, D.C.: Superintendent of Documents, U.S. Government Printing Office, 1988.

Baird, L. L. "A Map of Postsecondary Assessment." *Research in Higher Education,* 1988a, 28(2), 99–115.

Baird, L. L. "Value-Added: Using Student Gains as Yardsticks of Learning." In C. Adelman (ed.), *Performance and Judgment.* Washington, D.C.: Superintendent of Documents, U.S. Government Printing Office, 1988b.

Banta, T. W. (ed.). *Implementing Outcomes Assessment: Promise and Perils.* New Directions for Institutional Research, no. 59. San Francisco: Jossey-Bass, 1988.

Blumenstyk, G. "Diversity Is Keynote of States' Efforts to Assess Students' Learning." *Chronicle of Higher Education,* July 20, 1988, pp. A17, A25–A26.

Boyer, C. M. and Ewell, P. T. *State-Based Approaches to Assessment in Undergraduate Education: A Glossary and Selected References.* Denver, Colo.: Education Commission of the States, 1988.

Braskamp, L. A., and Brown, R. D (eds.). *Utilization of Evaluative Information.* New Directions for Program Evaluation, no. 5. San Francisco: Jossey-Bass, 1980.

Bray, D., and Belcher, M. J. (eds.). *Issues in Student Assessment.* New Directions for Community Colleges, no. 59. San Francisco: Jossey-Bass, 1987.

Chandler, J. W. "The Why, What, and Who of Assessment: The College Perspective." In Educational Testing Service, *Assessing the Outcomes of Higher Education.* Princeton, N.J.: Educational Testing Service, 1986.

David, B. G. (ed.). *Teaching of Evaluation Across the Disciplines.* New Directions in Program Evaluation, no. 29. San Francisco: Jossey-Bass, 1986.

Eison, J., and Palladino, J. "Psychology's Role in Assessment." *APA Monitor,* September 1988, p. 31.

Ewell, P. T. (ed.). *Assessing Educational Outcomes.* New Directions for Institutional Research, no. 47. San Francisco: Jossey-Bass, 1985.

Ewell, P. T. "Implementing Assessment: Some Organizational Issues." In T. W. Banta (ed.), *Implementing Outcomes Assessment: Promise and Perils.* New Directions for Institutional Research, no. 59. San Francisco: Jossey-Bass, 1988.

Ewell, P. T., and Boyer, C. M. "Acting Out State-Mandated Assessment." *Change,* July / August 1988, pp. 40–47.

Guba, E.G., and Lincoln, Y. S. *Effective Evaluation: Improving the Usefulness of Evaluation Results Through Responsive and Naturalistic Approaches.* San Francisco: Jossey-Bass, 1981.

Halpern, D. F. (ed.). *Student Outcomes Assessment: What Institutions Stand to Gain.* New Directions for Higher Education, no. 59. San Francisco: Jossey-Bass, 1987.

Hanson, G. R. "Critical Issues in the Assessment of Value Added in Education." In T. W. Banta (ed.), *Implementing Outcomes Assessment: Promise and Perils.* New Directions for Institutional Research, no. 59. San Francisco: Jossey-Bass, 1988.

Hutchings, P. "Report on Third National Conference on Assessment in Higher Education." *AAHE Bulletin,* October 1988, pp. 3–5.

Jacobi, M. Astin, A., and Ayala, F. *College Student Outcomes Assessment: A Talent Development Perspective.* ASHE-ERIC Higher Education Report, no. 7. Washington D.C.: Association for the Study of Higher Education, 1987.

Joint Committee on Standards for Educational Evaluation. *Standards for Evaluations of Educational Programs, Projects, and Materials.* New York: McGraw-Hill, 1981.

Lincoln, Y. S. and Guba, E.G. *Naturalistic Inquiry.* Newbury Park, Calif.: Stage, 1985.

McMillan, J. H. "Beyond Value-Added Education." *Journal of Higher Education,* 1988, 59 (5), 564–579.

Marchese, T. J. "Third Down, Ten Years to Go." *AAHE Bulletin,* December 1987, pp. 3–8.

Mentkowski, M. "Faculty and Student Involvement in Institutional Assessment." Paper presented at the American Evaluation Association meeting, New Orleans, October 1988.

Miller, R. I. "Using Change Strategies to Implement Assessment Programs." In T. W. Banta (ed.). *Implementing Outcomes Assessment: Promise and Perils.* New Directions for Institutional Research, no. 59. San Francisco: Jossey-Bass, 1988.

National Governors' Association. *Results in Education: 1988.* Washington, D.C.: National Governors' Association, 1988.

Nevo, D. "The Conceptualiztion of Educational Evaluation: An Analytic Review of the Literature." In E.R. House (ed.), *New Directions in Educational Evaluation.* Philadelphia: Falmer Press, Taylor and Francis, 1986.

Pascarella, E. T. "Are Value-Added Analyses Valuable?" In Educational Testing Service, *Assessing the Outcomes of Higher Education.* Princeton, N.J.: Educational Testing Service, 1986.

Patton, M. Q. *Utilization-Focused Evaluation.* (2nd ed.) Newbury Park, Calif.: Sage, 1986.

Patton, M. Q. *Creative Evaluation.* (2nd ed.) Newbury Park, Calif.: Sage, 1987.

Posavac, E. J., and Carey, R. G. *Program Evaluation Methods and Case Studies.* (2nd ed.) Englewood Cliffs, N.J.: Prentice-Hall, 1985.

Rossi, P. H. and Freeman, H. E. *Evaluation: A Systematic Approach.* (3rd ed.) Newbury Park, Calif.: Sage, 1985.

Rossman, J. E., and El-Khawas, E. *Thinking About Assessment.* Washington, D.C.: American Council on Education and the American Association for Higher Education, 1987.

Scriven, M. *Evaluation Thesaurus.* Pt. Reyes, Calif.: Edgepress, 1981.

Smith, N. L. (ed.) *Metaphors for Evaluation.* Newbury Park, Calif.: Sage, 1981a.

Smith, N. L. (ed.) *New Techniques for Evaluation.* Newbury Park, Calif.: Sage, 1981b.

Stufflebeam, D. L. "Metaevaluation." Occasional paper, no. 3. Kalamazoo: Evaluation Center, Western Michigan University, 1974.

Warren, J. "The Blind Alley of Value-Added." *AAHE Bulletin,* September 1984, pp. 10–13.

Westling, J. "The Assessment Movement Is Based on a Misdiagnosis of the Malaise Afflicting American Higher Education" *Chronicle of Higher Education,* October 19, 1988, pp. B1–B2.

CURRENT READINGS

THE CHANGING FACE OF HIGHER EDUCATION ASSESSMENT

SAMUEL MESSICK

For most of this century, the face of higher education assessment has displayed a singular countenance. Admissions testing was its salient feature because student selection was the primary function that assessment served. However, as we enter the 21st century, the face of higher education assessment is progressively changing. The lines of character associated with validity and equity will be deepened, but many of the age spots and wrinkles will be rejuvenated by technology. The intent of this change is not merely cosmetic but, rather, regenerative.

We are not simply contemplating a technological face-lift to better serve the old function of selection but, instead, the reconstruction of a genuinely new face to serve new and expanded functions and purposes. For years the main function of assessment in the academy was selection to maximize the level of talent as an outcome of higher education: Then around mid-century there began a growing concern for selection to broaden the range of talent, which brought with it a concomitant concern for cultural and group diversity. Now the twin goals of high levels and broad ranges of talent are coming to be addressed more and more not only through selection but also through student growth and development, which greatly expands the role of assessment in higher education. Admissions testing becomes less salient as more emphasis is placed on assessment for instructional guidance and placement, for career guidance and decision making, for the improvement of instruction and student performance, for the certification of learning and competence, and for the evaluation of program quality.

The expanded purposes of higher education assessment constitute the main topics of this volume, but they are addressed not just in functional terms but also in terms of a number of cross-cutting issues that entail competing social values and consequent tensions and tradeoffs. These include the issues of access, quality, diversity, and accountability, all of which feed into higher-order concerns about public policy with respect to higher education goals and outcomes. An integrating thread that weaves through all of these issues is the concept of equity, especially as it bears on social justice in education and on fairness in assessment.

From the perspective of equity, the main issue with respect to access is the ethical defensibility of any limits, especially the need to isolate ideologically based barriers from the practical constraints of distributing scarce resources. With respect to the quality of higher education, a central concern is the ethical basis of the criteria of excellence, in particular whether excellence constitutes the achievement of institutional and faculty repute or of student growth and development. With respect to diversity, an important issue is the balancing of concern for group parity with individual as well as institutional and societal benefits. With respect to social justice in education, which for many is the ultimate

Reprinted from *Assessment in Higher Education: Issues of Access, Quality, Student Development and Public Policy,* (1999), by permission of Lawrence Erlbaum Associates, Inc.

basis for accountability, the equity issues are often phrased in terms of equal access and treatment as well as equal opportunity to learn. However, as will be seen throughout this volume, the diverse value bases for social justice are more complex than this (see also, Deutsch, 1975; Messick, 1989; Nozick, 1974; Okun, 1075; Rawls, 1971). The plain fact is that not all inequalities are inequities (e.g., see Heller, Holtzman, & Messick, 1982). In education, for example, equitable treatment may not be equal treatment but, rather, treatment sufficient to the need.

This complexity stems from a pluralism of social values that creates tensions and the need for tradeoffs both in pursuing educational goals and in establishing the fairness of assessments that support those pursuits. In effect if not in original intent, this volume attempts to clarify the nature of this complexity, especially as it bears on the fairness, validity, and usefulness of higher education assessment.

Another integrative thread is the role of computer and audiovisual technology not only in improving the efficiency and power of all the functions of higher education assessment, but also in revolutionizing the delivery of higher education itself. Indeed, technology and equity are joined, not in battle but as warp and woof of the social fabric of higher education. The two are difficult to disentangle without severely damaging that fabric. Technology has enormous potential to improve equity in education and assessment if its availability becomes widespread, but also to exacerbate inequity if its effective availability is uneven.

Hence the application of technology in education is itself an equity issue, but it is not a new equity issue. In essence, it is another instance of a long-standing and profound social problem, namely, equity in the availability and distribution of effective educational resources, which is at the heart of the problem of inequitable opportunities to learn. One of the thrusts of this volume is that technology is only superficially part of the ***problem*** of equity in education and assessment. Rather, it is a basic and perhaps inevitable part of the ***solution***.

In summary, Part I of this volume has outlined the topical content to be addressed; namely, assessment for admissions, placement, guidance, student development, instructional improvement, the certification of learning and competence, and the evaluation of institutional excellence. These assessment topics are treated not just in the functional terms of their contributions to higher education, but also in terms of the cross-cutting policy issues that they perennially evoke. These are primarily issues of access, diversity, quality, and accountability. A more fundamental policy concern permeates all of these issues, namely, a concern for equity and fairness. Finally, computer and audiovisual technology is viewed as a promissory means of improving equity by, among many other things, enhancing network access to a variety of self-directed learning resources in ways that circumvent many institutional, social, and financial barriers.

Part II focuses on assessment for student development, for the improvement of instruction, and for credentialling experiential learning that occurs outside the academy. Emphasis is placed on the development not only of the knowledge, skills, and personal qualities constituting the aims of liberal education, but also of those required for career success and for mature adult functioning. This section also introduces a theme to be reprised in several later sections. This recurrent theme is that developed competence should be revealed in performance and not just knowledge, thereby sounding an incipient call not only for performance assessment but for performance-based pedagogy in higher education.

Part III argues that admissions testing in higher education needs to be revamped. In part, this is a recognition of the fact that as the purposes of assessment in higher education are expanded, some of them, especially those bearing on placement and guidance, might be well-served by enhanced testing in the admissions process. The press to transform admissions testing also stems from the need to keep pace with the standards-based reform movement in elementary and secondary education, with its reliance on performance assessment as the primary instrument for changing teaching practices and modes of student learning. If student learning of complex skills becomes performance-based (as well as often being computer-based), then admissions testing also needs to become performance-based so that students can demonstrate their competence in the same form in which it was learned. This raises questions of the relevance of the assessment mode to the learning mode and of fairness in affording students a congenial means of expressing their competence. Other factors facilitating the reconstruction of admissions testing are recent advances in computer technology, psychometric modeling, and cognitive psychology. These advances should lead to the assessment of a broader array of constructs validly interpretable in terms of cognitive processes relative to standards and not just performance levels relative to norms.

Part IV addresses issues of public policy that arise when the assessment of higher education quality becomes enmeshed in the politics of accountability. A key issue is what the criteria of excellence ought to be. Should the criteria reflect high quality faculty and students or institutional reputation or successful student development? The current political consensus appears to call for a new accountability in terms of return on investment to society as a whole, which translates in part to a demand for value-added outcomes of higher education in the form of student growth in knowledge, skills, and character over and above what students entered college with. It also translates in part to a demand for societal input into what the outcomes of higher education ought to be. However, it turns out that the substance of desired outcomes politically relevant to the new accountability differs little from traditional goals of liberal education, except for a heightened emphasis on affective and motivational as well as cognitive aspects of competence. And once again, there is an insistence that developed competence be demonstrable in performance and action, not just in knowledge and theory.

Part V examines the social values of equity and fairness as they bear on the validity and usefulness of higher education assessment. Equity issues are addressed in terms of the appropriateness and effectiveness of educational practices for serving the needs of disabled, linguistic minority, and culturally diverse students. Fairness issues are addressed in terms of the comparability of score meaning and action implications in assessing the knowledge, skills, and other competencies of individuals from diverse educational, linguistic, and cultural backgrounds. The issues of both equity and fairness are framed in the context of human diversity broadly conceived, which goes far beyond a concern for accommodating group differences to a concern for appropriately assessing individual differences. Because the range of within-group individual differences consistently dwarfs any between-group differences, it is felt that the problems of equity and fairness will not be ultimately resolved without understanding and accommodating the major sources of individual differences in learning and performance. Until that happy time, however, Part V concludes with practical recommendations for increasing test fairness as comparable validity across all stages of the assessment process as applied to diverse individuals, groups, and contexts.

Part VI focuses on the technological future of higher education assessment as well as of higher education itself. The advent of computer and audiovisual technology introduces the prospect of alternative self-directed modes of learning that will lead to a widening and deepening of individual differences in learning and thinking styles. Technology also instigates both a rapidly changing environment requiring enhanced flexibility in learning and problem solving as well as the development of new information-processing skills for capitalizing on the new media. These and other consequences of technology will need to be addressed by higher education and its supporting assessment system as the academy attempts to prepare students for a technology-dominated society. Part VI concludes by broaching the possibility that as the academy confronts these new educational needs, its whole mode of operation may itself be technologically transformed by the advent of the virtual university.

Thus the face of higher education assessment is changing because the needs of higher education are changing. These needs are changing because technology is dramatically transforming not only modes of assessment but also modes of learning and problem solving. The overarching concerns for equity in education and fairness in assessment become paramount in this era of societal flux, especially as they intersect with issues of access, quality, diversity, and accountability in higher education. These are the themes of the present volume, as they are also major themes in the work of Warren Willingham, whose career contributions to research on higher education this volume celebrates.

References

Deutsch, M. (1975). Equity, equality and need: What determines which value will be used as the basis of distributive justice? *Journal of Social Issues, 31*(3), 137–149.

Heller, K. A., Holtzman, W. H., & Messick, S. (Eds.). (1982). *Placing children in special education: A strategy for equity.* Washington, DC: National Academy Press.

Messick, S. (1989). Validity. In R. L. Linn (Ed.), *Educational measurement* (3rd ed., pp. 13–103). New York: Macmillan.

Nozick, R. (1974). *Anarchy, state, and utopia.* New York: Basic Books.

Okun, A. (1975). *Equality and efficiency: The big trade-off.* Washington, DC: The Brookings Institute.

Rawls, J. A. (1971). *A theory of justice.* Cambridge, MA: Harvard University Press.

Complementary, Not Contradictory: The Spurious Conflict Between Qualitative and Quantitative Research Methodologies

Azam Mashhadi

Abstract

Zubir and Pope (1984), and Howe (1985, 1988) have both argued against the 'tyranny of methodological dogma' and that the division between quantitative psychometric and qualitative phenomenological and anthropological traditions is unnecessary. The post-modern self-consciousness of educational research has resulted in the realization that there is an unavoidable interaction between the researcher and the researched. Likewise modern physics acknowledges that it is not a mirror of nature but a 'myth' about it (Rorty, 1989). The history of science is arguably not a history of discovery but a history of metaphoric construction (Sutton, 1992). Niels Bohr's framework of *complementarity* provides a powerful metaphoric conceptual viewpoint for resolving the paradigm war between quantitative and qualitative methodologies. The reductionist-mechanistic and holistic-anthropomorphic methodologies or paradigms are not contradictory but complementary. Both quantitative and qualitative methodologies provide insight into differing aspects of a constructed reality that is too complex to be comprehended from only one view-point.

Introduction

Research into students' acquisition of, say, scientific concepts is usually allocated to one of two different types of paradigm: one is traditional, scientific, experimental, reductionist, prescriptive, quantitative and nomotechnical, and the other is nontraditional, artistic, naturalistic, holistic, descriptive, qualitative and idiographic. Zubir and Pope (1984), and Howe (1985, 1988) have both argued against the 'tyranny of methodological dogma' and that the division between quantitative psychometric and qualitative phenomenological and anthropological traditions is unnecessary.

Complementary

Underlying much of the contention that quantitative and qualitative methods are incompatible is the outmoded identification of positivism with science, and the positivistic notion that scientific inference consists of building quantitative laws in a mechanistic fashion. As Howe (1985: 16) points out:

Paper presented at the Conference on Educational Research, November 25-29, 1996, Singapore.

> ... the contention that quantitative and qualitative methods are incompatible is an upshot of the positivistic notion that scientific inference consists in building quantitative laws in a mechanistic fashion.

Research into the history of science, and the actual practice of scientists argues against this identification (Barnes, 1974; Feyerabend, 1978; Nader, 1996).

In addition King (1987) has argued that there is 'no best method' and that the methodology adopted should be suited to the topic being explored. Researchers should proceed on the pragmatic basis of 'what works' (see Broadfoot, 1988; Bryman, 1984; Hammersley, 1992; Osborne, 1995).

The post-modern self-consciousness of educational research has resulted in the realization that there is an unavoidable interaction between the researcher and the researched. Likewise modern physics acknowledges that it is not a mirror of nature but a 'myth' about it (Rorty, 1989: 16). The history of science is arguably not a history of discovery but a history of metaphoric construction (Sutton, 1992). The physicist Niels Bohr's framework of *complementarity* provides a powerful metaphoric conceptual viewpoint for resolving the 'paradigm war' between quantitative and qualitative methodologies. Lewis Elton (1977) has drawn on Bohr's complementarity principle and has argued that the reductionist-mechanistic and holistic-anthropomorphic methodologies are not contradictory but complementary. Each methodology provides insight into differing aspects of a reality that is too complex to be comprehended from only one viewpoint. As Elton (1977: 38) points out:

> The choice between opposing methodologies is not therefore between right and wrong, but between appropriate and inappropriate. The crucial judgement that a researcher must make at the very beginning of his research is which methodology is appropriate for the research which he wishes to pursue. If he chooses an inappropriate one, he will still get results—research is like that—but they will be meaningless.

'Complementarity' of research paradigms

The 'tyranny of methodological dogma' and the division between quantitative psychometric and qualitative phenomenological and anthropological traditions is unnecessary. Both quantitative and qualitative methodologies provide insight into differing aspects of a constructed reality that is too complex to be comprehended from only one view-point.

For a given study, the researcher's conception of the 'nature' of what is being investigated influences the choice of method (Hashweh, 1988). The choice will depend upon a number of factors: the nature of the study, the type of information required (e.g. factual data, 'understanding', thought processes), the purpose of the study, the outcomes for the data (e.g. predictions, generalisations), research skills of the researcher, time and resource constraints, and the sample population (e.g. availability and access). The key factor for the choice of methods for data collection and analysis is the nature of the research questions. As Elton (1977: 38) points out:

> The choice between opposing methodologies is not therefore between right and wrong, but between appropriate and inappropriate. The crucial judgement that a researcher must make at the very beginning of his research is which methodology is appropriate for the research which he wishes to pursue. If he chooses an inappropriate one, he will still get results—research is like that—but they will be meaningless.

Qualitative understanding through quantitative methodology

> Elementary particles seem to be waves on Mondays, Wednesdays and Fridays, and particles on Tuesdays, Thursdays and Saturdays.
>
> Sir William Bragg

A study recently completed on students' understanding of the concept of 'wave-particle duality' will be used to illustrate the complementary of quantitative and qualitative (see Mashhadi, 1995, 1996). Students experience considerable conceptual difficulties in trying to incorporate the ideas of quantum physics into their overall conceptual framework (Faucher, 1987; Gil and Solbes, 1993).

In this study the powerful metaphor of the map is used to construct graphic representations of A-level students' 'understanding' of quantum physics. The aim of the study is to try and go behind students' overt performance and describe the organisation of knowledge that underpins overt performance, and define understanding in terms of elements of memory and the pattern of association of these elements (White, 1988). The study has adopted an operational definition or limited 'measure' of understanding at the level of the population group in which understanding is represented by the relationships or groupings of ideas (conceptions). The nature of students' understanding being represented by their construction of groupings of ideas in a personal psychological space, with underlying dimensions providing a coordinate system for their conceptions. Kelly (1955) suggested the idea of a 'psychological space' as a term for a region in which an individual can place and classify elements of his/her experience.

Cognitive structure or the metaphor of the map

This research study utilises the powerful heuristic 'metaphor of the map' to reflect the psychological structure of knowledge in the area of quantum physics as perceived by the sample population of A-level physics students. The act of mapping involves the combination of a reduction of reality and the construction of an analogical space (Robinson, 1982). It also enables structures to be constructed or discovered that would remain unknown if not 'mapped'. Maps constructed by different population samples can be used to research differences in 'understanding' between, say, first and second year A-level students. All maps are approximations and involve distortions of perceived reality, as they inherently involve the use of a projection, and a systematic reference frame. However the 'metaphor of the map' is a powerful means for the holistic representation of knowledge (Wandersee, 1990).

Data gathering methodology

The definition of understanding adopted in terms of the structural relations between conceptions immediately raises the methodological question of how to access and represent such a conceptual structure if it is present. As students progress through a physics course they do get better at 'playing the game of physics'. Students in maintaining a separation between 'physics' and 'the real world' avoid the need for making basic conceptual changes. Students may however give the impression that by 'learning' the material they have made such changes. To use the type and style of questions to which they are used to would be to 'trigger' reproductive memory techniques. In physics courses students typically solve problems by 'rote equation cranking'.

Problems test more than understanding. The elicitation of conceptions in a problem solving situation brings in problems related to metacognitive skills, and a mastery of knowledge that is not strictly within the domain of the subject. It also has the disadvantage of tending to cue school science knowledge. The research instrument, therefore, should not utilise definitions and mathematical manipulations that feature so heavily in an A-level physics syllabus and course. The students' written work is also ruled out as class notes may well be tightly structured by the teacher or be heavily influenced by text in books. This would sharply limit their usefulness, and any insight obtained on students' understanding.

The general strategy was, therefore, to develop specific statements which represent a range of conceptions, and then ask students to respond to them. Since it is the students' perceptions that are sought for in response to particular statements then the use of an attitude scale is appropriate. The simplest method of response scaling is the five-point scale, where the subjects are, essentially, being asked to 'agree' to 'strongly disagree'. Responses on five-point scales are ordinal-level, as the psychological distance between each of the points may not be equal. The scale is discontinuous, and an individual's response will be subjective. The use of a response scale enables students to indicate the degree of uncertainty in their answers. The unit of analysis in this study is taken as the group, and not the individual. The results, therefore, reflect the tendencies of the group's responses to the statements, and not necessarily the perceptions of individuals.

The quantification of a categorical measurement does not fundamentally change its nature. When a student is asked to rate his/her feelings or respond to statements by using a response scale the data obtained has been quantified. However, despite quantification, the data still reflects the student's subjective viewpoint.

A questionnaire, therefore, appeared to be the most suitable research instrument to address my research question, and it enabled access to be gained to fairly large sample population(s) from two different year groups, and across a variety of schools. Previously most work on students' conceptions has been carried out using homogenous population samples. The investigation of differences between groups is then only possible by comparing the outcomes of several studies.

Data analysis methodology

The research question is based on the hypothesis that there might be regularities and similarities in forms of reasoning or understanding shared by groups of individuals. The forms of reasoning may emerge as non-random patterns in the relationships between responses to specific statements, rather than individual responses to individual questions.

The aim of data reduction is to reduce as much as possible the large amount of information obtained to a small number of factors or dimensions, while preserving its essential characteristics and provide an accurate summary. Also to abstract from the data any hidden structure that results from some basic typology (using cluster analysis), or any latent dimensions (using multidimensional scaling and factor analysis). It should be pointed out that although quantitative methods are employed the aim is not to arrive at or build quantitative laws.

The essential aim of this study with respect to students' conceptions of quantum physics is the same as the aim of any map which is to construct a bounded graphic representation that corresponds to a perceived reality. Just as a map cannot be reduced to strings of text, student understanding of science concepts is usually nonlinear, hierarchical and web like. The methodology enables a graphic representation of the students' scientific knowledge to be constructed. A pictorial representation of underlying dimensions and clusters of statements or propositions is 'visually efficient' and easy to understand. For instance, as in the diagram below:

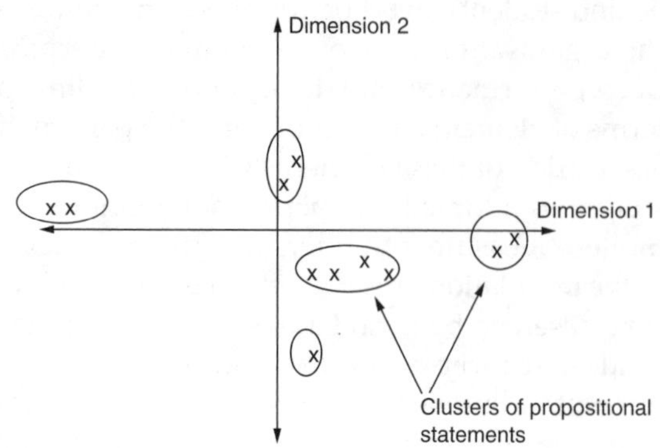

The responses by students were entered into an EXCEL spreadsheet, and the essentials of the structure of the underlying reasoning, in terms of fundamental factors or dimensions, were obtained using multivariate statistical techniques (multidimensional scaling, factor analysis and cluster analysis) on SPSS (Statistical Package for the Social Sciences). Multidimensional scaling (MDS) can be used to determine if there are any underlying dimensions. Factor analysis is very similar to multidimensional scaling, and since the principal factors are equivalent to the dimensions from MDS confidence in their interpretation is enhanced. Cluster analysis can be used to further define and help interpret any groupings. The validity, reliability and plausibility of any structure and its interpretation is established and enhanced using 'triangulation' between three different analytical techniques.

Multidimensional scaling

Multidimensional scaling is designed to analyse data that indicates the degree of dissimilarity (or similarity) of two things in such a way as to display the structure of the distance-like data as a geometrical picture. Each object (or variable) is represented by a point in a multidimensional space. Two similar objects are represented by two points that are close together, and two dissimilar objects by two points that are far apart. The space is usually a two- or three-dimensional Euclidean space but may have more dimensions. The five point response scale provides ordinal data, which means that the space is generated with very few assumptions about the distribution of the data. Since the data is ordinal level non-metric multidimensional scaling using the ALSCAL program in SPSS is used. The 'goodness-of-fit' of the data to the model increases each time another dimension is added as the additional dimension allows more freedom to arrange the points. The number of dimensions is determined through considerations of 'goodness-of-fit', parsimony and interpretability of the dimensions generated.

The model generated by the multidimensional scaling software (ALSCAL) provides coordinate axis that can be interpreted as perceptual dimensions. The label given to the dimensions or axis of the map are the result of an interpretation depending on the nature and location of specific statements. The dimensions are orthogonal, and their interpretation can be considered independently of each other.

Factor analysis

Suppose there are no particular groupings of conceptions or statements in the questionnaire. If this supposition were valid then, say, factor analysis of student responses to the statements should reveal that they do not fall significantly into particular groupings. The factors generated are rotated, to simplify the structure as much as possible and thereby aid the process of interpretation, using Varimax rotation. Varimax rotation was used based on its general usefulness with orthogonally rotated factors, and it gave the most easily interpretable factors. The rotated factor matrix highlights significant loadings of variables (statements) which contribute to a factor. The process of interpreting and naming the factors has to be done in such a way that it represents the essence of the variables loading on it. Each variable has ideally a large loading on just one factor and low loadings on the other factors. Since a variable has loadings on the other factors an interpretation of a factor solution should not be regarded as definite or 'correct', but the most likely possible interpretation from a set of possibilities.

Cluster analysis

Cluster analysis was used to investigate the grouping of conceptions. The clustering technique used is an Agglomerative Hierarchical method: the Complete Linkage method. In this method the individual statements or variables (and not the respondents or cases) are classified into groups, and the process repeated at different levels to form a tree (dendogram graph) through a series of successive fusions of the variables into groups. The groups which initially consist of single variables are fused according to the distance between their nearest members. The distance between groups being defined as the distance between their most remote pair of statements. Each fusion decreases by one the number of groups, and proceeds until all the statements are clustered. The Complete Linkage method is used as the values attributed to the statements are ordinal, and it avoids having too many small clusters.

A 'conventional' viewpoint might regard the use of multivariate statistical techniques as inadequate for eliciting any deep or significant aspects of thought, especially as the statements utilised a fixed (five-point) response scale. Answers to statements might seem to need more subtlety of response. However, as Da Silva (1994: 262) expresses it:

> People can be directly asked about things they are conscious of thinking or feeling, but deeper and less conscious patterns of thought are less directly accessible, and are to be identified not in individual responses to particular questions, but in patterns of responses to many related situations or questions.

Conclusion

In this study quantitative techniques are being used to arrive at a qualitative appreciation of underlying dimensions of reasoning employed by students when faced with questions on quantum phenomena. The method of analysis provides a pictorial or graphical representation of the structure or relationships between ideas. However this representation inherently involves the researcher's interpretation of data. All studies, whether employing qualitative or quantitative methodologies, are inherently interpretive. The principal 'problem' of all studies is still that of the epistemological question of the hermeneutic circle—the researcher's knowledge of students' conceptions is dependent on the researcher's constructions, which are based on the researcher's conceptions.

References

Barnes, B. (1974): *Scientific Knowledge and Sociological Theory* (Routledge and Kegan Paul: Boston).

Broadfoot, P. (1988): 'Educational research: two cultures and three estates', *British Educational Research Journal*, Vol. 14, pp. 3–15.

Bryman, A. (1984): 'The debate about quantitative and qualitative research: A question of method or epistemology?', *British Journal of Sociology*, Vol. 35, No. 1, pp. 75–92.

Da Silva, L.E.F. (1994): *Commonsense reasoning about processes: a study of ideas about reversibility*, unpublished Ph D thesis (University of London Institute of Education).

Elton, L.R.B. (1977): 'Methodological themata in educational research', *Research Intelligence*, Vol. 3. No. 2, pp. 36–39.

Faucher, G. (1987): 'Pragmatical Conceptions in the Atomic Domain', in J. Novak (Ed.), *Proceedings of 2nd International Seminar on Misconceptions and Educational Strategies in Science and Mathematics* (July 26–29 1987, Cornell University).

Feyerabend, P. (1978): *Science in a Free Society* (NLB Press: London).

Gil, D. and Solbes, J. (1993): 'The introduction of modern physics: overcoming a deformed vision of science', *International Journal of Science Education*, Vol. 15, No. 3. pp. 255–260.

Hammersley, M. (1992): *What's wrong with Ethnography?* (Routledge: London).

Hashweh, M. (1988): 'Descriptive studies of students' conceptions in science', *Journal of Research in Science Teaching*, Vol. 25, No. 2, pp. 121–134.

Howe, K. (1985): 'Two dogmas of educational research', *Educational Researcher*, Vol. 14, No. 8, pp. 10–18.

Howe, K. (1988) 'Against the quantitative-qualitative incompatibility thesis (or, dogmas die hard)', *Educational Researcher*, Vol. 17, No. 8, pp. 10–16.

Kelly. G.A. (1955): *The Psychology of Personal Constructs* (Norton: New York).

King, R.A. (1987): 'No best method: qualitative and quantitative research in the sociology of education', in G. Walford (Ed.), *Doing Sociology of Education* (Falmer Press: Lewes).

Mashhadi, A. (1995): 'Students' conceptions of Quantum Physics', in C. Bernardini, C. Tarsitani and M. Vicentini (Eds.), *Thinking Physics for Teaching* (Plenum Press: New York), pp. 313–328.

Mashhadi, A. (1996): *What is the nature of the understanding of the concept of 'wave-particle duality' among Advanced level Physics students?*, unpublished D Phil-thesis (St Cross College/University of Oxford).

Nader, L. (Ed.) (1996): *Naked Science: Anthropological Inquiry into Boundaries, Power, and Knowledge* (Routledge: London)

Osborne, J. (1995): *Young children's understanding of science in four domains*, unpublished Ph D thesis (King's College, University of London).

Robinson, A.H (1982): *Early Thematic Mapping in the History of Cartography* (University of Chicago Press: Chicago).

Rorty, R. (1989): *Contingency, Irony, and Solidarity* (Cambridge University Press: Cambridge).

Sutton, C. (1992): *Words, Science and Learning* (Open University Press: Buckingham).

Wandersee. J.H. (1990): 'Concept mapping and the cartography of cognition', *Journal of Research in Science Teaching*, Vol. 27, No. 10. pp. 923–936.

White, R. (1988): *Learning Science* (Blackwell: Oxford).

Zubir, R. and Pope, M. (1984): 'A meeting of paradigms: The use of triangulation method in an investigation into student learning', *Research Intelligence*, Vol. 17, pp. 7–10.

The Qualitative Method of Impact Analysis

Lawrence B. Mohr

Abstract

Consider the qualitative approach to evaluation design (as opposed to measurement) to be typified by a case study with a sample of just one. Although there have certainly been elaborate and emphatic defenses of the qualitative approach to program evaluation, such defenses rarely attempt to qualify the approach explicitly and rigorously as a method of impact analysis. The present paper makes that attempt. The problem with seeking to advance a qualitative method of impact analysis is that impact is a matter of causation and a non-quantitative approach to design is apparently not well suited to the task of establishing causal relations. The root of the difficulty is located in the counterfactual definition of causality, which is our only broadly accepted formal definition of causality for social science. It is not, however, the only definition we use informally. Another definition, labeled "physical causality," is widely used in practice and has recently been formalized. Physical causality can be applied to the present problem. For example, it explains the persuasiveness of Scriven's "Modus Operandi" approach to causal inference in evaluation. Under this conceptualization, a tailored case study design with a sample size of one becomes in principle as strong a basis for making inferences about program impact as a randomized experiment. Crucial for the application of the method to program evaluation is the finding that people's "operative reasons" for doing what they do are the physical causes of their actions. Lastly, it is shown that external validity using this qualitative approach would have exceptional strengths.

Introduction

Qualitative designs for program evaluation have become widely accepted and practiced (Greene, 1994; Goddard & Powell, 1994). The idea has also generated a good deal of controversy (summarized in part in Chen, 1990) wherein each side in the debate—qualitative vs. quantitative—finds its own method to be clearly superior and the other to be woefully inadequate. Many authorities take what they see as a middle ground, advocating that both approaches may be used in concert (Reichardt & Cook, 1979; Chen, 1990; Greene & Caracelli, 1997). It has begun to be increasingly clear, however, that although both approaches may well have something to contribute to program evaluation, their areas of contribution are not identical. Although there is undoubtedly overlap between the two approaches in what they seek to accomplish, they are not substitutes for one another.

Quantitative designs or approaches have been seen by their advocates as being especially good for impact analysis. Qualitative designs, on the other hand, have been advocated primarily in

Reprinted from *The American Journal of Evaluation* 20, no.1 (Winter 1999), pages 69–84, by permission of Elsevier.

conjunction with other evaluative functions such as implementation analysis, process analysis, community self-analysis, the empowerment of staff, and the interpretation and understanding of experience. The functions in this latter list will not be reviewed here because they are not germane to the present purpose, which focuses on impact analysis. Maxwell and a small number of additional scholars (summarized in Maxwell, 1996) have begun to explore a role for qualitative work in the assessing of impacts. More typical, perhaps, the defense of the case study method by one of its most outspoken proponents in program evaluation does not credit it with efficacy in the assessment of impacts and distinguishes it from quantitative research in part on that basis (Stake, 1981). Of course, some proponents of the qualitative approach suggest that it is better than the quantitative approach precisely because its particular goals or functions have greater value than the goal of impact analysis (see, for example, Guba & Lincoln, 1981), but that debate is also outside of the present scope.

Let us assume, recognizing that some might deny it, that there often is some value to impact analysis in program evaluation. If one were concerned with impact analysis and if there were a qualitative approach that did indeed have clear relevance for that function, then it would be reasonable to bring it to light and discuss it. The purpose of this paper is to advance the idea of one such qualitative approach and to provide an introductory treatment of it. This idea must of necessity be viewed against a backdrop composed of concepts that, while familiar to the evaluator, are here combined in a nontraditional picture that will help bring clarity to the issue at hand.

Causation

Impact analysis deals with causation. While some may take the position that program evaluation as a discipline should rid itself of the preoccupation with causation (or equivalently here, causality), let us also assume tentatively that causal analysis is suitable for at least some purposes in program evaluation and therefore question how qualitative designs might contribute to such analyses.

For the present discussion, it will be helpful to define the quantitative approach to impact analysis as one that relies on the counterfactual definition of causality (a more defensible version of this species of definition is called "factual causation" and will be elaborated below). The counterfactual definition states that *X* was a cause of *Y* if and only if *X* and *Y* both occurred and, in the circumstances, if *X* had not occurred, then neither would *Y*. It is the final "if" clause ("if *X* had not occurred . . .") that we call "the counterfactual." We will see momentarily that this conceptualization leads naturally to what we usually think of as quantitative research designs. It is also the source of the well known principle (whose validity will nevertheless be disputed, below) that comparison is necessary to establish causality, the comparison being between evidence for the "result" on the one hand, that is, the occurrence of *Y* after *X*, and evidence for the counterfactual claim on the other. Classically, we get our result from observing a group to which a treatment has been applied and our estimate of the counterfactual from a similar group (or a "before" measure) to which the treatment has not been applied. Putting these two sets of observations together so that we have variance on the proposed causal or treatment variable makes the whole amenable to statistical analysis. Design and analysis together yield the classic quantitative package. Note that without data on the counterfactual, a statistical technique such as regression or correlation analysis would not be applicable, even if there were thousands of cases, because there would be no variance on the variable denoting whether or to what extent the treatment was received.

Accordingly, we may provide a specialized definition of the term "qualitative," as well as "quantitative," as they both apply to the idea of design (as opposed, for example, to measurement). A design whose purpose is to determine impact will be considered *qualitative* if it relies on something other than evidence for the counterfactual to make a causal inference. It is qualitative first in the positive sense that it rests on demonstrating a quality—in the present treatment the quality will be a physical connection in the natural world between the proposed cause and effect—and second in the negative sense that it is not quantitative, that is, it does not rely on a treatment *variable*, or on comparing what is with an estimate of what would otherwise have been. A vast number of observations may be and usually are made in a qualitative evaluation, but when it comes to the core of causal inference there is only one *kind* of observation in the perspective of the counterfactual definition, that showing the co-occurrence of *X* and *Y*. Conversely, even if a study has only two empirical observations—one showing that the proposed cause and effect occurred together and the other showing that when the cause did not occur, then neither did the effect—it is clearly based on *variables* and counterfactual reasoning and will therefore be considered quantitative.

These two approaches would seem to present an interesting and viable picture except for one matter. The qualitative approach does not fulfill the requirements of the counterfactual definition since it does not deal in variables and does not incorporate evidence on the no-treatment condition, but, apparently, no other rigorous definition of causality is accepted in social science (King et al., 1994). If it is indeed true that there is no other, then it would simply be impossible to infer causation based on a qualitative design. Criticisms of the case study as being based on a sample of only one case make exactly this point. On the other hand, there has been at least one approach to causality in the literature on program evaluation that seems on the surface to be both legitimate and to have nothing to do with counterfactuals or quantitative analysis. It may be found in Scriven (1976), where it is called the "modus operandi" method of demonstrating causality. An explicit alternative definition is not provided there, but the method proceeds as follows:

Y has occurred and the task is to demonstrate that the treatment T caused Y. This is done in part by the process of elimination. That is, there are several other possible causes of Y, such as U, V, and W, and these must be eliminated as contenders in order to settle on T. The process also depends critically on the idea that each possible cause has a known "signature, and if the signatures of U, V, and W can be shown to have been absent while that of T was present, then it may be concluded that T was the cause. The signature may contain events of two types: (a) a known causal chain of events by which T or U, etc., would lead to Y (George & McKeown, 1985); and (b) other events in addition to Y that are known to be associated with an active T, or U, and so on (Campbell, 1979). The elimination of other possible causes is of course a prominent tool in almost all causal inference but it is not enough by itself except in the rare circumstance, such as in randomized experiments, when *all* other possible causes can be identified or controlled. Even then, a reservation remains, as will be shown in a later section. In short, we will see below that while the method of elimination can be extremely helpful in causal inference from qualitative designs, we must rely more on demonstrating that the signature of *T itself* was present and that this proves the causal point. For the present, it is important to see, as Scriven (1976) emphasizes, that the modus operandi scheme is extremely common in everyday causal inference. It is not an arcane, academic conceptualization, but a method of determining causality that is in constant use in the professions and in everyday life, such as in diagnosing what is wrong with a car, or in medical diagnosis, detective work, cause-of-death determination, and so forth. The auto mechanic can infer that a car is overheating because a thermostat is stuck by feeling the temperature of certain hoses. The physician can determine that a certain disease is at work by establishing the presence of two or three critical symptoms.

It is also important to emphasize that this common method is not at all the same as determining causality by counterfactuals. Suppose that a woman has had a heart attack and has died. Probably she would not have died at that time if she had not had the heart attack, but that is not certain. In fact, suppose we could demonstrate that she would have died then anyway from some other cause. Using the counterfactual definition, we would be forced to conclude that the heart attack was *not* the cause of her death because we could not claim the counterfactual (if no heart attack, then no death). But by examining the tissues and otherwise identifying the signature of a heart attack, we might be able to establish the truth, namely, that she did indeed die of a heart attack. Note that in making this determination we do not proceed by bringing forth evidence for the counterfactual—what would have happened had she not had a heart attack—which would in fact lead us completely astray in this case because she would have died anyway. We do not make a dichotomous *variable* out of heart attack, the supposed cause. We consider this to be a one-case study and determine causality by exposing the incontrovertible, physical signature of the heart attack. Finally, it may well be that the signature is known because of prior medical research and also that the prior research in question might possibly have employed counterfactuals, but that does not mean that our causal inference rests on the counterfactual definition. We are not doing that other research at present. We are researching the death of this woman, just as we might research the outcome of a program being evaluated, and we do not use counterfactuals to reach the particular causal conclusion in the specific instance of causality that links this heart attack with this death. To drive the point home, suppose that many impact studies have given us the knowledge that employment can definitely decrease criminal recidivism, just as heart attacks can cause death. If we now do a new study of recidivism and wish to explore a possible causal link with employment, we have two distinct choices of approach—the quantitative and the qualitative. It does not matter how the prior research was conducted. Both research options are real and independent in the present.

Other research in social science and program evaluation has shown a role for qualitative research in impact analysis, particularly Huberman and Miles (1985) and King et al. (1994). When pressed, however, the core determination of causality in these treatments depends ultimately on the counterfactual method. The best clue we have that a core determination may indeed be qualitative lies in the concept of the signature as it emerges under the various labels of "modus operandi" (Scriven, 1976), "process tracing" (George & McKeown, 1985), and "pattern matching" (Campbell, 1979). The possibility of a qualitative determination of causality, then, has been very strongly suggested and what remains to consider is how this general approach aspires to establish instances of causation without variance on a causal variable (Maxwell, 1996). A totally different definition of causality must necessarily be involved.

The working out of that definition, which is too lengthy to reproduce here in full, may be found in Mohr, 1996. There it is argued that it is appropriate in social science to employ a dual conceptualization of causality. Furthermore, there is abundant evidence that such a dual conceptualization actually is employed. The two facets of the concept are labeled *physical* and *factual* causality, respectively. The first is a relation between events in the natural world, as in "The car skidded sideways and toppled the lamp post on the corner." The second is a relation between statements, truths, or facts (Strawson, 1985), as in, "The fact that the ex-prisoner had steady employment caused the fact that he did not commit further crimes."

Of the two, *physical causation* is more important in terms of the present inquiry, although it is not necessarily the most commonly encountered in program evaluation and social science. Its importance lies in the fact that (a) it is fundamental within the dual approach (it is itself part of the definition of factual causation); and (b) it is the key to causal inference in qualitative research. Physical causality is the common, mechanical or Newtonian sense of causation that is familiar to all. Cause and effect are the relation between a force and a motion, respectively. It is the causation we recognize in the lifting, smashing, pulling, pushing, or tearing of something. The classic example in the Humean tradition is billiard balls on a table, but Hume (1955) sought to exclude this idea as a definition. It is argued elsewhere (Strawson, 1985; Mohr, 1996) that Hume put too much emphasis on the sense of vision and not enough on the sense of touch in reaching this conclusion, but it would be a lengthy and unwarranted digression to review the arguments here. We must proceed as though physical causation were not only intuitively appealing but philosophically sound and refer the interested reader to the cited works for a fuller treatment.

The counterfactual definition of causality, serviceable as it is for some purposes, is well known to be plagued with serious philosophical problems (Mackie, 1980; Mohr, 1996). *Factual causation* is a variant achieved through the interjection of physical causality that preserves the counterfactual definition in spirit while overcoming those problems. The definition is as follows: X was a factual cause of Y if and only if X and Y both occurred and X occupied a necessary slot in the physical causal scenario pertinent to Y. The interjection of physical cause is clear. The spirit of the counterfactual definition is preserved in the idea of a *necessary* slot: if *something* did not occupy that particular functional slot (and it happened in this case to be X), Y would not have occurred. For our purposes, we may treat factual causation as though it were the simpler, counterfactual definition without undue or misleading distortion. The two facets, then, though related, are quite distinct. Physical causation rests on the idea of a direct physical connection in the real world. Factual causation rests on a counterfactual claim and has no need to refer to a direct physical relation. (For example, in "Because the ex-prisoner was employed, he committed no further crimes," there is no direct physical connection referenced between events in the natural world.)

Reasons as Causes

We have seen that causation can be demonstrated through qualitative research when physical rather than factual causality is the guiding conceptualization. That is why we needed no variables or other quantitative paraphernalia to make an inference about the heart attack, the stuck thermostat, or the diagnosis of the disease. There would seem to be a problem in terms of our central purpose, however, in that the effects of interest in program evaluation and social science are so frequently human behaviors. This is overwhelmingly true in the case of program evaluation, in fact, where common outcomes of interest are behaviors such as self care in nursing homes, criminal recidivism, juvenile delinquency, teen pregnancy, preventive health behaviors, welfare-to-work, substance abuse, overcrowded housing, divorce, safe driving, and safe sex. What are the physical causes of intentional human behaviors? They are at any rate not so tangible or clearcut as hot and cold hoses, or sore throats and fevers. Many if not most who ponder this issue seem to feel that mental states or acts such as decisions, choices, and reasons—especially the latter—are the causes of behavior (Davidson, 1980). We will be guided here by the finding, based in the physiological rather than the philosophical literature, that reasons, in a special sense of the term, are indeed not only the causes but the physical causes of intentional human behaviors (see Mohr, 1996, and works cited there).

Before elaborating the special sense of reasons referred to, let us review the more general sense. Most definitions are similar and suggest two components: If you (1) want to accomplish Y; and (2) believe that action X will do it, then you have a reason for undertaking action X. For example, if you want to improve your agency's productivity and believe that privatizing some of the tasks will do it, then you have a reason for privatizing. So far, the general sense of the concept of a reason does not seem very physical, since wanting and believing are mental constructs. In addition, it is hard to see how reasons so construed can be the causes of behavior. We all have a great many reasons for doing a variety of things at a given time but we do not act on most of them at that time, and some of them are never implemented at all. One might have a good reason, for example, to go to the market for eggs this evening and also to replace a washer in a leaky faucet, but one might carry out only one of those activities, or none. Moreover, a student may see, and even keenly feel that getting good grades is a reason for studying long and hard, but never study very long or hard at all. What does it mean, then, to say that reasons are causes when so many of the reasons that were definitely "there" at a given time did not cause anything?

To answer, it is convenient to introduce the notion of "operative reason," i.e., the reason that actually operated to produce the behavior performed, and to stipulate that the operative reason was different from all of its contemporary reasons in that it was the strongest. If the person fixed the faucet, for example, instead of going to the market, it is because he wanted to stop the drip more than he wanted the eggs. If the student studies little (given a belief in the connection between studying and good grades), it is because she wants something else more, perhaps being accepted as one of an "in" crowd with whom she regularly associates. And if the Director is more interested in pleasing the public employees union than in productivity, the tasks in question may not be privatized this year, or perhaps ever. In this way, in short, one of the many reasons that may be active at a given time becomes an operative reason and the associated behavior ensues. As a footnote, we see that if a program aims at getting people to behave in certain ways—showing up for work regularly and on time, for example—the program must not only motivate them but motivate them strongly to carry this action out, and if the evaluator wishes to relate the presence or absence of a successful result to the program, it will be important to adduce evidence regarding the strength or weakness of the critical motivation.

The most important aspect of the special sense of "reason" referred to is that, as used here, a reason is an unaware physiological entity and not a mental construct. We all know that we frequently do things intentionally, but without being aware of any particular reason. On the other hand, we are often very much aware of particular reasons for doing things (which we may or may not do). These conscious reasons or thoughts, it is argued, do not cause behavior, although they may at times closely parallel the physiological elements that do. It is well known that for an experience to be stored in and recallable from long-term memory, it must be accompanied by a physical affect residue, a component that records the related affect, if any, at the time of the experience. The "want" part of what we think of as a reason, although we now speak of a "want" that is totally below the level of consciousness, is the positive or negative affect residue attached to some object in memory. The strength of the reason is the electrical or chemical strength of this affect residue. The "belief" part of a reason is the memory of having done some X to achieve Y or something similar in the past, or even of having heard of accomplishing something like Y by doing X. The X is selected and activated when the affect on the relevant Y becomes dominant by virtue of its strength. We see therefore, that operative reasons as rendered here are the *physical* causes of undertaking action X. Finally, it is important for the research implications to note that operative reasons, being unaware, are not necessarily obvious, either to the subject or the investigator. They may frequently be accompanied by a parallel reason or decision that is an aware, mental state, but they also may not, and even if they are, it is the physiological "reason" and not the mental one that is causal. Indeed, when we think sometimes that a certain conscious reason for our behavior was operating we may well be wrong, as we might find out, perhaps, only by careful introspection or with the help of a psychotherapist.

In sum, qualitative research to determine the causes of intentional human behaviors, such as whether or not those behaviors were induced by a program being evaluated, must involve a search for the operative reasons behind the behaviors. In most cases this would undoubtedly involve obtaining information from the subjects whose behavior is at issue. Given that operative reasons are unaware, however, that is not necessarily all that one must do. It might be necessary to obtain information from many other people, from documents, and from the histories of relevant events. These are methods, however, that are familiar in social science, especially in such areas as history, anthropology, and area studies.

Causal Reasoning

We have seen that there are two types or conceptualizations of causation, the factual and the physical. When research proceeds as sketched out just above, the causal inference will be based on an argument that makes a case for the operative reason and connects it with the behavior, perhaps with some reservations. The kind of argument involved in that case, as well as that involved in previous qualitative examples such as establishing the connection between the temperatures of hoses and the overheating of the car, will be called "physical causal reasoning." When the causal inference is to be an inference of factual causation, a different sort of research process is dictated, one that results in the ability to make the argument, again perhaps with reservations, that factual causation has been established. The form of that particular argument would be called "factual causal reasoning."

Factual causal reasoning must necessarily rely on a counterfactual claim. A good deal of energy and design ingenuity would be devoted to being able to argue persuasively that if X had not occurred, neither would Y. This might actually be done within the confines of a single case study, or when talking about a single event that is a minor part of a larger story. That is, one might show that X and Y occurred and argue as best one can on the basis of knowledge of past events, plus a careful and detailed examination of the context and circumstances surrounding the present event, that if X had not occurred here, neither would Y. One might not, that is, purposely make one or more empirical observations of a "control group"—a similar subject and context in which X did not occur. Still, this would be factual causal reasoning and, as the terms are used here, a quantitative design. Or, as featured prominently in the book by King et al. (1994), one might study in depth one or two cases in which X was present and one or two in which it was not. The authors tend to refer to such "small n" studies as qualitative because of the depth of exploration and the manner of data collection and measurement, but in design perspective, these are again quantitative. In most cases, however, factual causal reasoning is based on designs and sample sizes for which statistical methods of analysis become suitable. In that kind of case, it is important to remember from the counterfactual definition that the control group or comparison group or "before" measure, for example, is not of interest in its own right. It is not a matter of comparing what happens (present tense) when X does and does not occur. Rather, the control or similar group is of interest only as a basis of estimating what would have happened in the experimental group if X had not occurred *there*. That is the essence of factual causal reasoning.

Take the evaluation of health education efforts, for example. There we have statistical designs of various sorts in which investigators have concluded that *knowing about* certain risk factors leads to (i.e., causes) certain health related behavior, such as nutritionally sound eating practices (Edwards, 1985). Frequently, there is no thought that this knowledge about risk factors might be a physical cause. Being exposed to information about proper nutrition, for example, is not thought to have *made* the subjects eat property, but rather we can see that adequately *motivated* people (here is where the physical causation comes in) are much more likely to eat properly if they indeed know what is proper than if they do not—accurate knowledge is more auspicious than ignorance or misconception. In any case, the reasoning proceeds by showing that those who received and absorbed the health education materials tended to eat properly. Those who did not, however, or who did not understand it or remember it, tended not to eat property, thereby indicating that the knowledge in the first group was a necessary condition. (Mohr, 1995, p. 267)

Physical causal reasoning, on the other hand, is focused on demonstrating persuasively that a particular kind of physical connection took place between two events in the real world, in essence, the connection between a force and a motion. There is some basis for considering that it is this sort of reasoning, in contradistinction to factual causal reasoning, that gets at *real* causes. Frequently, in other words, we are not satisfied with evidence from observational studies or even randomized experiments because the real, that is, the physical causal mechanism remains a mystery. The physical evidence may frequently be required to support the statistical, and it will almost always contribute to a more convincing package if it can be obtained.

One excellent example is the long and persistent interest in the question of how, physiologically, smoking operates to cause lung cancer. We have been bothered, in other words, by the fact that the signature of smoking has remained obscure. In contrast, it took us less time to become convinced of the effect of fluorocarbons on the ozone layer because we not only had statistical time series relating the two, but an account of the chemical processes involved, as well.

To elaborate in the context of more standard program evaluation, consider that we might be trying to learn whether to attribute a lower fatality rate from motor vehicle accidents to a well-publicized police crackdown on speeding in one community. Application of the before-after or the interrupted time series design to the fatality rate is one option. Comparison to a community that is similar and that has had no crackdown is another. Both of these are in the classic, quantitative or factual-causal mode and both are weakened by the standard threats to the validity of quasi-experiments. An alternative to be pursued instead, or perhaps better yet in addition, would lead us to confine our attention to the one community and the one time period of concern—a case study insofar as this particular aspect of the design is concerned. We might use a survey to determine not only whether and to what extent but *how* the citizenry became aware of the existence of the crackdown. That is, we would *not* try to show that they would never have heard of the crackdown if not for the media used by the project (factual causal reasoning), but rather to document that they actually did read about it here, or did see it on TV there, or were told about it by a police officer, or by a friend who claimed to have seen the TV spot, and so forth—all physical processes. Furthermore, we would be interested in understanding the behavior itself—not only *whether* the citizens consciously drove more slowly, but why—was it a heightened sense of the dangers of speeding, for example, or a heightened subjective probability of getting caught? Note that the quantification involved in both of these links in the project, given the survey involved, would be just a matter of counting citizens to get an idea of the prevalence of the causal processes uncovered. The quantification would not in any way be part of a *design* to permit causal inference. The design is unmistakably qualitative. No evidence for the counterfactual would be brought forward because the survey would not contain any. On the contrary, whether one citizen is surveyed or a hundred, the design is critically dependent on persuasively establishing the occurrence of the two physical causal processes in the individuals concerned—learning about the crackdown because of project activities and modifying behavior because of strong motivations sparked by the project's messages.

Another brief example might be helpful in suggesting the kinds of roles available for physical causal reasoning. In the kind of research exemplified by eating practices and knowledge of good nutrition in the quoted paragraph above, the efforts to increase knowledge would necessarily be evaluated by factual causal reasoning alone. The nutritional knowledge simply was not a physical cause. As suggested, however, there would have to be separate motivations, or reasons, impelling the sound dietary behavior apparently advocated. A more thorough program would seek to inculcate these, as well. An impact analysis of the program might then proceed either by factual or by physical causal reasoning or both. There is no reason, in other words, why the two forms of logic or research design cannot both be brought to bear (a) within the same evaluation, as in evaluating the efforts to impart knowledge by factual and motivation by physical causal reasoning; or (b) on the same outcome, as long as we are concerned with a physical cause, as in employing two different designs to determine whether or not people changed their eating habits because of the program's efforts to persuade them of the benefits.

The purpose of this paper is in large part to identity the idea of physical causal reasoning and to suggest its functions. The details of successfully implementing such reasoning in evaluation and other research are beyond the scope of our efforts here and no doubt will only be accumulated over many trial projects. Something about the basic elements of implementation, however, rises out of the definitional logic of physical causation itself. This conceptualization of causality has to do with the relation between a force and a motion. With regard to human behavior, these components are bound up in the operative reason and the behavior itself, respectively, as in the relation between fear of getting caught by the police and keeping within the speed limit during the crackdown. To establish this relation persuasively, four elements are apparently important. One must show first that the person or group studied must have had the reason to which we want to attribute causality—sometimes whether they themselves claim it or not. Second, it is important to make the case that this reason was very strong relative to other considerations that could have been active at the time. Third, it is generally crucial to show by various other manifestations that it was indeed this reason that was operating—tracing out the "signature" of the reason in the style of the modus operandi approach. And last, it will generally be helpful to establish that it is proper to *interpret* the actors' behavior as intentionally keeping below the speed limit, for example, or following sound nutritional practice, and not just as driving at a certain speed or eating certain foods, as would be common in quantitative research.

It would be a digression to discuss at length the various other perspectives on causality and causal reasoning that have been suggested in relation to qualitative research, such as constructivism, neorealism, and so forth. It may be well, however, to emphasize one point, and that is that what is offered here are *definitions* of causation such as must normally support all such perspectives. If one takes a constructivist view of "causation," therefore, or emphasizes "webs of causation" rather than single, linear, cause and effect dyads, or aims with the neorealist at discovering "causal mechanisms" rather than causes, one can always be challenged to specify what one actually means by the root term "causation" or "causal" in one's own particular context. Exactly as was the case with the modus operandi method, these other perspectives do not obviate the need to conceptualize causality, nor do they automatically provide the required conceptual definition in themselves. They tend to use the term "cause" as though it were previously defined. It is suggested here that the response to this challenge to define can always be rendered in terms of one of the two conceptualizations proposed above. It is therefore suggested further that the two types of causal reasoning, physical and factual, will in that sense always be pertinent, whatever the philosophical framework, although they may not always be important enough to an author's point to warrant attention. Finally, although qualitative research is firmly established as a scholarly approach in social science and program evaluation, still, consideration of the notion of causality seems to be ruled by the counterfactual definition, which, from the standpoint of design, is basically quantitative in orientation. Thus, the possibility of thinking in physical causal terms should open up notably wider prospects for thought, particularly within the qualitative regime.

Internal and External Validity in the Qualitative Approach

Let us first accept the term *internal validity* to mean the validity of a causal inference based on the research, as was the case when the term was first used by Campbell and Stanley (1966). In this light, the concept has not been very relevant for qualitative evaluation in the past because qualitative evaluation has not been much preoccupied with causality. Given that the present paper has been vitally concerned with the marriage of "qualitative" and "causal," however, internal validity does become germane as an issue.

There are two components to the practice of establishing internal validity in quantitative research, and the same two will hold for qualitative research, as well. The first has to do with showing the fulfillment of the governing idea of causation through the *design* and the operations of the research. In the quantitative mode, this primarily means arranging to produce evidence for the counterfactual (since establishing that X and Y both occurred is generally not much of a challenge)—as for example by the device of a comparison group. In the qualitative mode, it means arranging to produce evidence for a certain sort of physical relation between X and Y. In both cases, however, the evidence will never be unassailable, so another important component of establishing internal validity becomes the attempt to rule out certain other, plausible causes. Even in the randomized experiment, the evidence for the counterfactual is only probabilistic, and not certain, so it is common to achieve greater certainty on at least some dimensions by introducing control variables. In both approaches, therefore, ruling out alternative causes occupies a prominent place in the quest for internal validity, but the deductive logic of the process of elimination does not obviate the role of the factual causal argument in the quantitative approach, nor does it eliminate the role of the physical causal argument in the qualitative approach.

In this light, we see that the elimination of other causes in the modus operandi method is not meant to be the same as establishing evidence for the counterfactual, which would be mixing the two forms of reasoning, and indeed it is not the same. First of all, one could in no way claim to prove the counterfactual by that method unless one eliminated *all* other causes, and it will always be impossible to make that claim legitimately. Second, even if we knew that nothing else caused Y, we would not necessarily know that nothing else *would have* caused Y. This is illustrated by our prior example of the woman and the heart attack. Recall that we assumed for the sake of argument that she would have died then anyway, even if she had not had the heart attack. Suppose that the woman had been found dead in her car, which had crashed into a tree. The question is whether she had a heart attack and died, crashing into the tree while the death was in process, or if she died of a concussion as a result of crashing into the tree. We might be able to tell by careful autopsy that she died of a heart attack, so that all other causes are categorically eliminated, but it may in fact be true that if she had not actually died of the heart attack, she would surely have died of the concussion or other injuries. To eliminate all other possible causes, therefore, as by finding the incontrovertible signature of the heart attack, does not establish the truth of the counterfactual—here, she actually would have died anyway. In quantitative research, the process of elimination is meant rather to strengthen a basic claim for the counterfactual that will generally have weaknesses. In qualitative research, it is meant to strengthen the basic claim of a certain physical connection—for example, in striving to rule out excess greenhouse gases resulting from forces independent of industrial and other human activities. In fact, it will by no means always be necessary to resort to the effort to identify and eliminate other plausible causes. The design-based claim for the counterfactual or the physical relation may suffice. Just as in a randomized experiment, and even in some quasi-experiments, we might frequently consider the case for the counterfactual to be strong without bothering to try to identify other plausible causes and enter them as control variables, so in a qualitative study we might consider the case for the physical relation to be strong, or obvious, without bothering to try to identify other plausible causes and show the absence of their signatures. For example, if we show that certain drivers became aware of the police crackdown because they got tickets and the officers told them about it, we do not necessarily have to speculate on how those particular drivers might have become aware of the crackdown otherwise, but did not.

Nevertheless, many will say that internal validity in the qualitative approach must be inherently weak. Usually, the claim that a certain reason was the operative reason for a behavior, for example, must in the end be speculative. In that approach, there is nothing like the laws of probability to give credence to an inference. This reservation is valid and important, but it needs to be put in perspective. The difficulty is relative. Other approaches have similar problems, and weak internal validity for a method has never been a good reason to reject it categorically. In particular, one cannot make an airtight case on the basis of factual causal reasoning, either. There is always a necessary residue of subjective assessment. In randomized experiments, the threat of contamination (impure treatment delivery or inadequate control of the environment) can never be extinguished altogether, nor can the reservation that the statistical causal inference carries a probability of error equal to the significance level. At the 5% level, we *will* make errors about 5% of the time. In quasi-experimental designs, which are extremely well represented in evaluation journals, the threat of selection bias is similarly persistent and is in fact notoriously troublesome. Furthermore, ex-post-facto or observational studies are well known to be pathetic in terms of internal validity, yet they are in constant use, probably because there is often much to be learned from them nevertheless. On the other hand, just as we have imperfect but substantial confidence at times in the conclusions of experiments, quasi-experiments, and observational studies, we may often have substantial confidence in the case made for a physical cause through the modus operandi method or other physical causal reasoning, whether the subject be the overheating of an engine, the penetration of a message by means of the mass media or a policeman, the controlling desire to avoid speeding tickets or, let us say, the controlling desire to avoid the inevitable future hassles with bureaucrats by immediately correcting violations noted on a safety inspection. Reasons and other physical causes that are not obvious may nevertheless frequently be demonstrated with considerable satisfaction and edification.

This is not to say that further constructive thought regarding internal validity is either futile or unnecessary in the context of qualitative designs for impact analysis. On the contrary, much should be done and there is in fact evidence that the issues are not intractable. For example, as will be reviewed momentarily, Lincoln and Guba (1986) have summarized much that has been done to conceptualize for qualitative research what would seem to be analogous to issues of validity in quantitative research. Much of the collective conceptualization has more to do with qualitative approaches to measurement or description rather than design, but some concepts, credibility for example, are clearly applicable to the present discussion and make a stimulating contribution. The whole idea is both new enough and challenging enough, however, that we should not expect definitive analyses to have been produced already. Finally, Mohr (1999) has suggested the criterion of a "consummate causal understanding" that should also be helpful in developing methods of achieving and testing for internal validity in the qualitative approach to impact analysis. A consummate causal understanding of the past behavior investigated is achieved when all pertinent challenges and questions regarding that past behavior and one's explanation of it are answerable from the data presented and their logical extensions.

The issue of *external validity* must also be considered, but the first observation to be made, it would seem, is that it is important to keep the two types of validity distinct. Because a sample size of just one case appears to threaten both types, there may be a tendency to blend them together when critiquing the case study as a design. "Let us accept," the critic might suggest, "that causality can be established with a sample of one, but is it not better to have a large sample? Is it not better to observe many causal instances rather than just one or two? The one or two might have been unique." Perhaps so. We proceed now to consider exactly that issue. But it is necessary to recognize at the outset that it is an issue of external validity and not internal. If causation is established then causation is established. The question whether it is better to establish it in more subjects rather than fewer is purely an issue of generalizability.

It is well known that external validity is critical (Cronbach, 1982). There is hardly a point in finding out for sure that T caused Y if we have no interest in applying the finding either to the same subjects in a subsequent time period or to other subjects. The strongest case for internal validity, however, guarantees nothing in regard to external validity. True, if the observed subjects were randomly sampled from a larger population we can generalize the results to that population, but (a) that pertains to internally valid physical as well as factual causal results; and (b) such a generalization is still limited to that particular larger population and, even more restrictive, to the past time period in which the subjects were observed. In particular, there is no basis for claiming that a result is theoretically valuable just because one can generalize it to a certain population that has been randomly sampled.

Since internal validity is in no sense an aid to establishing external validity, it follows that factual causal reasoning is no more auspicious for external validity than physical causal reasoning. Both are oriented toward causality, not generalizability. As noted previously, for example, if we used old or impressionistic evidence to reason for one individual subject that if *T* had not occurred, then neither would *Y*, the mode would definitely be one of factual causal reasoning (quantitative reasoning, that is, even in the single case), but it is hard to see that this would give us any particular basis for generalizing the results to other subjects. We see, therefore, that it is not the design that leads us to prefer quantitative research over case studies as a basis for generalization, but the mere fact of the number of subjects involved, whether people, schools, cities, or countries. It will usually be more comfortable to generalize when many subjects have been causally affected by a treatment than when only one or two have been affected. The one or two might be unusual, even unique. Of course, the many subjects observed in a large sample may also be quite different from others to which one would like to generalize, and in fact they generally are, as is evidenced by the fact that one can almost always find interacting variables of interest that qualify a relationship. There is therefore some advantage in numbers, but it should not be oversold. Conditions change over tune. One subculture is different from another. One school is even different from another within the same district, so that one may very well not observe the same regression coefficients as one replicates the analysis.

At the same time, qualitative studies have their own advantage with respect to external validity that has long been recognized. It is that the study in depth should enable one to *understand the process*, and there may be no factor as important as this for generalizability in social science. The more thoroughly we understand the causal process by which a treatment has affected an outcome in one case, the better the position we will be in to know when a similar outcome will result in another case (cf. "extrapolation" in Cronbach, 1982; see also Lincoln & Guba, 1986). Thus, the quantitative approach generally has an advantage in numbers and the qualitative approach generally has an advantage in understanding. It is unfortunately difficult to capture both simultaneously because they tend to work against each other in practical terms. There is no reason why quantitative studies cannot strive for depth, but limited resources will constrain the effort. Similarly, physical causal reasoning can be carried out on a large sample, as the example of the survey in connection with the crackdown on speeding was meant in part to show, but again resources constrain depth when numbers are large. We can conclude regarding external validity that it is well to be sensitive to both advantages—numbers and understanding—regardless of the approach one takes, but the primary point to be made in the present context, perhaps, is that by no means is the qualitative approach to impact analysis inherently inferior in terms of external validity.

In this section, physical causal reasoning has been scrutinized in terms of internal and external validity. One might well ask, in addition, how it would fare on criteria of appraisal that have been more specifically devised for qualitative evaluation research. This area does not have as long a history as internal and external validity and is not as well developed. We may briefly consider, however, the overview by Lincoln and Guba (1986) of some of the major suggestions and ideas. They are summarized into the two umbrella categories of "trustworthiness" and "authenticity."

It appears that some of these ideas, at least, are applicable to physical causal reasoning and that the latter can be expected to score high on such criteria in a well planned and executed study. Under trustworthiness, in particular, the category of transferability is suggested as a parallel criterion to external validity. As indicated above in the discussion of "understanding the process," the criterion of the capability of the transfer of results from an observed application to a potential one is a strong form of external validity and, perhaps, the strongest form that can be achieved in social science, where universal laws are dubious. Similarly, the whole idea of "audits" that has been developed in connection with qualitative research is fully applicable to physical causal reasoning and would seem to be an effective way to insure against any unavowed and unwelcome intrusions of personal values and biases. Finally, when applied to qualitative design, Lincoln and Guba's category of "credibility" would seem to have almost the same meaning as internal validity in more traditional contexts. The issues that are important to consider in this regard were summarized earlier in this section under the rubric of internal validity.

In the category of "authenticity," Lincoln and Guba (1986) discuss a number of criteria that are not meant to be parallel to the criteria traditionally applied to quantitative evaluation but grow rather out of the specific characteristics of qualitative evaluation. These criteria, such as fairness, educative authentication, and catalytic authentication are less applicable to the approach outlined here. The reason is that they are largely bound up with alternative goals for evaluation, beyond impact analysis. In some dimensions they should be important for all evaluation, including quantitative, as for example the importance of obtaining fully informed consent from human subjects and informants or of considering the values of all stakeholders rather than just a few when assessing the merit or worth of a program. For the most part, however, they are not only pertinent primarily to goals and functions of evaluation other than impact analysis, but at times they articulate those very goals. For example, according to Lincoln and Guba, "It is . . . essential that they come to appreciate . . . the constructions that are made by others and to understand how those constructions are rooted in the different value systems of those others" (p. 81). Authenticity, in sum, seems less applicable to the physical causal approach in qualitative evaluation than trustworthiness, but that is not surprising when the central role of causation is considered.

Conclusion

Physical causation as a way of explaining the world seems to come naturally. There is ample room in the practice of program evaluation for using it to demonstrate the causal nature of one or more links on an outcome line. In particular, in-depth study and interpretation are well suited to discovering the true or operative reason behind a behavior. In this introductory treatment, the purpose has not been to show how qualitative evaluation is done, but rather to show how awareness of an alternative causal epistemology may be coupled with current knowledge of qualitative methods of data collection and measurement to fashion a sound, independent approach to the analysis of impacts.

Acknowledgments

The text of this paper is based in part on Mohr (1995), Chapter 11. A prior version of the paper itself was delivered at the annual meeting of the American Evaluation Association, Vancouver, November 1–5, 1995. I wish to express my appreciation to the editor, to his editorial assistant, to Jennifer Greene, and to three anonymous reviewers for helpful comments and criticisms on an earlier draft—to which, no doubt, I have not done full justice.

References

Campbell, D. T., & Stanley, J. C. (1966). *Experimental and quasi-experimental designs for research*. Chicago, IL: Rand McNally.

Chen, H. T. (1990). *Theory-driven evaluations*. Newbury Park, CA: Sage.

Cook, T. D., & Reichardt, C. S. (Eds.). *Qualitative and quantitative methods in evaluation research* (pp. 49–67). Beverly Hills, CA: Sage.

Cronbach, L. J. (1982). *Designing evaluations of educational and social programs*. San Francisco, CA: Jossey-Bass.

Davidson, D. (1980). *Essays on actions and events*. Oxford: Clarendon Press.

Edwards, P. K., Acock, A. C., & Johnston, R. L. (1985). Nutrition behavior change: Outcomes of an educational approach. *Evaluation Review* 9(4), 441–460.

George, A. L., & McKeown, T. J. (1985). Case studies and theories of organizational decision making. In L. S. Sproull & P. D. Larkey (Eds.), *Advances in information processing in organizations*. R. F. Coulam & R. A. Smith (Eds.), *Research on public organizations*. Vol. 2. (pp. 21–58). Greenwich, CT: JAI Press.

Goddard, A., & Powell, J. (1994). Using naturalistic and economic evaluation to assist service planning. *Evaluation Review, 18*(4), 472–492.

Greene, J. C. (1994). Qualitative program evaluation: Practice and promise. In N. K. Denzin & Y. S. Lincoln (Eds.), *Handbook of qualitative research* (pp. 530–544). Thousand Oaks, CA: Sage.

Greene, J. C., & Caracelli, V. J. (Eds.). (1997). *Advances in mixed-method evaluation: The challenges and benefits of integrating diverse paradigms*. New Directions for Program Evaluation, No. 74. San Francisco, CA: Jossey-Bass.

Guba, E. G., & Lincoln, Y. S. (1981). *Effective evaluation: Improving the usefulness of evaluation results through responsive and naturalistic approaches*. San Francisco, CA: Jossey-Bass.

Huberman, A. M., & Miles, M. B. (1985). Assessing local causality in qualitative research. In D. N. Berg & K. K. Smith (Eds.), *The self in social inquiry* (pp. 351–381). Newbury Park, CA: Sage.

Hume, D. (1955). *An inquiry concerning human understanding*. C. W. Hendell (Ed.). New York, NY: Liberal Arts Press.

King, G., Keohane, R. O., & Verba, S. (1994). *Designing social inquiry: Scientific inference in qualitative research*. Princeton, NJ: Princeton University Press.

Lincoln, Y. S., & Guba, E. G. (1986). But is it rigorous? Trustworthiness and authenticity in naturalistic evaluation. In D. D. Williams (Ed.), *Naturalistic evaluation* (pp. 73–84). New Directions for Program Evaluation, No. 30. San Francisco, CA: Jossey-Bass.

Mackie, J. L. (1980). *The cement of the universe: A study of causation*. Oxford: Clarendon.

Maxwell, J. A. (1996). Using qualitative research to develop causal explanations. *Working Papers*. Cambridge, MA: Harvard project on schooling and children.

Mohr, L. B. (1995). *Impact analysis for program evaluation* (second ed.). Newbury Park, CA: Sage.

Mohr, L. B. (1996). *The causes of human behavior: Implications for theory and method in the social sciences*. Ann Arbor, MI: University of Michigan Press.

Mohr, L. B. (1999). One hundred theories of organizational change: The good, the bad, and the ugly. In H. G. Frederickson & J. M. Johnston (Eds.), *Public administration in a time of turbulence: The management of reform, reinvention, and innovation*. Birmingham, AL: University of Alabama Press, forthcoming.

Reichardt, C. S., & Cook, T. D. (1979). Beyond qualitative *versus* quantitative methods. In T. D. Cook & C. S. Reichardt (Eds.), *Qualitative and quantitative methods in evaluation research* (pp. 7–32). Beverly Hills, CA: Sage.

Scriven, M. (1976). Maximizing the power of causal investigations: The modus operandi method. In G. V. Glass (Ed.), *Evaluation studies review annual*, Vol. 1 (pp. 101–118). Beverly Hills, CA: Sage Publications.

Shadish, W. R., Jr., Cook, T. D., & Leviton, L. C. (1991). *Foundations of program evaluation: Theories of practice*. Newbury Park, CA: Sage.

Stake, R. E. (1981). Case study methodology: An epistemological advocacy. In W. Welch. (Ed.), *Case study methodology in educational evaluation*. Minneapolis, MN: Minnesota Research and Evaluation Center.

Strawson, P. F. (1985). Causation and explanation. In B. Vermazen & M. B. Hintikka (Eds.), *Essays on Davidson: Actions and events* (pp. 155–136). Oxford: Clarendon.

THE QUANTITATIVE–QUALITATIVE DEBATES: "DEKUHNIFYING" THE CONCEPTUAL CONTEXT

WILLIAM R. SHADISH
The University of Memphis

One of the milestone accomplishments of program evaluation has been the incorporation of qualitative methodologies into our repertoire of tools. These methods have been used in the social sciences for decades, but until recently they were limited largely to a few disciplines such as anthropology and qualitative sociology. But the 1970s saw the introduction of qualitative methods into program evaluations, sometimes as complements to quantitative methods and sometimes as the main or sole methodology. Today such methods are an accepted part of program evaluation methodology for many important tasks.

But this salutary outcome clearly oversimplifies the complex struggle it took to achieve. The rise of qualitative methods in program evaluation has been slow and controversial for many reasons, including but not limited to (a) issues of allocation of resources such as grant funding or journal space, (b) discussions of social recognition in the forms of professional awards or elected positions in professional associations, (c) differences of both fact and opinion about what different methods were able to contribute, (d) diverse conceptualizations of the philosophical underpinnings of methodology, and (e) the social psychological structure of intergroup competition in science. All these many reasons and controversies have become known by the shorthand phrase: "The Quantitative–Qualitative Debate" (QQD). What an over-simplification! Quite obviously, this isn't just one debate; hence the title of this special feature refers to debates in the plural. To paraphrase one reviewer of this special feature, *which* quantitative–qualitative debate? The one about using numbers or not? The one about methodology? The one about social recognition? Or the one about conceptual and philosophical issues?

In the present case, the answer to the question is that this special feature is mostly about the philosophical debates. Those debates seem to have lasted the longest, and in many respects to have been the least tractable. In its early years, during the initial barrage of philosophical material at the start of these debates, it was all that most evaluators could do to learn some of the basic terms of the philosophical debate such as logical positivism, constructivism, and paradigms; and to identify some of the key issues such as causation, realism, and the implications of quantum physics. These were not terms with which most evaluators had much familiarity; and even when they did, as with causation, there was a large gap between the methodological issues best known by evaluators and the philosophical and conceptual issues being raised in the QQD. So the learning curve has been steep. But much progress has been made over the last 20 years. For example, many fine, accessible scholarly works inform evaluators about the important philosophical positions that might bear on the

Reprinted from *Evaluation and Program Planning* 18, no. 1 (1995), pages 47–49, by permission of Elsevier.

QQD (Phillips, 1987, 1990; Reichardt & Rallis, 1994). Today, the philosophical aspects of the debate are sharper than before. In the early years, one could make a great variety of claims about philosophy and not much worry about being seriously challenged because few evaluators had the requisite philosophical background. That is now changing. Philosophers themselves have sometimes entered the fray (Phillips, 1990), and the participants to the debate have often become more knowledgeable. Consequently, philosophical claims that seemed compelling a decade ago are more often found inadequate, inaccurate, or just plain wrong today—on all sides of the QQD. This should not surprise us, nor dismay us, for this is how we learn to improve our philosophical claims.

But the progress of the debate has remained particularly contentious and controversial over the years. In part this may be due to the complexity and unfamiliarity of the topics to many evaluators—such matters as ontology, epistemology, ethics, the role of scientific information in our decision making, and the nature of social life. These issues are made even more controversial because they are so difficult—indeed, sometimes impossible—to resolve with empirical data of any sort. How can you prove that physical reality exists? How can you convince the skeptic that some kinds of knowledge are worth taking more seriously than others? How can you show what society would be like in a century if we all adopted a particular view of social justice? Consequently, different evaluators have taken widely different positions on the answers to these questions. So, for example, in epistemological debates one will find evaluators who advocate realism, constructivism, postpositivism, skepticism, feminism, and critical multiplism, to name just a few. Those who speak of ethics discuss social justice (in egalitarian and libertarian forms), liberty, and the role of descriptive values in a democracy. The range of positions on all these conceptual and philosophical issues is enormous.

Yet for some reason, the issues tend to be portrayed as falling neatly into two (and only two) paradigms (Kuhn, 1970)—the quantitative paradigm and qualitative paradigm—each complete with different methods, different concepts, different assumptions, and different philosophies. But there is little empirical evidence in support of such a Kuhnian paradigm portrayal. Hence, one common feature of the articles in this special feature is that, in one way or another, they each "deKuhnify" the QQD by showing that the relevant conceptual and philosophical issues are far more complex than the simple quantitative–qualitative dichotomy implies. As influential as Kuhn (1970) has rightly been, that work is no longer viewed as the vanguard of the science studies literature; and viewing the central issues of the world of science as revolving mostly around paradigms is no longer widely accepted in the science studies community. More recent developments in philosophy, sociology, and psychology of science "deKuhnify" science studies by painting a far more complicated picture of the world of science than the Kuhnian paradigm picture (Fuller. DeMey, Shinn, & Woolgar, 1989; Laudan, 1992; Shadish & Fuller, 1994; Woolgar, 1988, Ziman, 1984).

In this sense, the four articles in this special feature each contributes to "deKuhnifying" the QQD in evaluation—even though none were initially conceptualized with this goal in mind. The articles challenge simple distinctions and common stereotypes; they correct common errors, and they point to the many different ways these debates could be conceptualized. The first article is by James Heap: "Constructionism in the Rhetoric and Practice of *Fourth Generation Evaluation*." Heap's paper is an extended analysis of the philosophical and conceptual justification for using qualitative methods that is given in Guba and Lincoln's (1989) book *Fourth Generation Evaluation*. On the one hand, Heap describes himself as much taken with the methodological practices that those authors outline. But he also argues that Guba and Lincoln base their arguments on metaphysics that is neither necessary to nor consistent with those practices. He points out that their arguments confuse cognitive constructivism (everything is constructed in the mind) with social constructivism (everything is constructed through external social interactions). Their advocacy of cognitive constructivism involve certain assumptions that cannot support the methods they advocate. He argues that their methods have much merit if justified by moral arguments and outlines the kinds of moral arguments that accomplish this end. He concludes with the hope that Guba and Lincoln will drop the extreme relativist, subjectivist rhetoric, while keeping their exposition of their methodology. By breaking the link between philosophy and method that Guba and Lincoln pose, Heap shows that the "paradigm" is not a unitary thing at all.

The second article is by William Shadish: "Philosophy of Science and the Quantitative–Qualitative Debates: Thirteen Common Errors." Shadish starts with the notion that many philosophical arguments put forth in the QQD incorrectly portray the current state of affairs in philosophy of science and related topics. Examples of erroneous statements include (a) logical positivists are realists, (b) the concept of causation is no longer accepted in philosophy, (c) experiments must be quantitative, and (d) results from particle physics show that there is no reality. Using extensive examples and quotations, Shadish demonstrates the errors in each of these positions and outlines a more accurate portrayal in each case. Here the larger goal is to break the links among concepts that have been traditionally linked together and called a quantitative paradigm—for instance, realism, causation, logical positivism, and experimentation. These things do not clearly belong together; and the links among them are complex.

The third article is by Lee Sechrest and Souraya Sidana: "Quantitative and Qualitative Methods: Is There an Alternative?" These authors argue that all sciences use a combination of both quantitative and qualitative methods, citing examples from particle physics and from geology—without arguing over it, breaking into opposing camps, or making paradigms out of the methodologies. They then suggest that this ought to be the case in evaluation, too, and argue that it is not the case because of misstatements or misunderstandings of the positions involved. They provide a large number of examples of these. The authors then show how these methodologies could be reconceptualized under the two entirely different concepts of clinical research (personal, cognitive, and not constrained by external rules) and formulaic research (external, formal rules for proceeding). Both quantitative and qualitative methods can be either formulaic or clinical in nature; and both formulaic and clinical work have places in evaluation. But they end their article by advocating that we not teach our students to be either quantitative or qualitative, or either clinical or formulaic. Teach them to gather and report good, persuasive information, whatever the form.

The final article is by David Krantz: "The Dynamics of Controversy: The Quantitative–Qualitative Debate." He starts by noting that the QQD bears a striking resemblance to the far older debate in philosophy between romanticism and rationalism. A major lesson there has been that some aspects of the debate are simply not resolvable, so that a tolerance for pluralism is needed. He asks why it is that evaluation has seemed sometimes resistant to this tolerance, concluding that the QQD is maintained as much or more by the social psychological nature of scientific controversy as it is by the conceptual issues involved. He then addresses the possibility of integration of methodological diversity in evaluation. He proposes two alternative ways that this diversity can be integrated. One is technical eclecticism, which aims to integrate techniques by systematically combining methods in ways that empirical work shows work well in evaluation practice. The other is theoretical integration, which asks whether any superordinate theoretical concepts, such as the notion of evaluation as argument, can be used to develop points of unity into integrated approaches. He explores the advantages and disadvantages of each of these two integration techniques. Instead of accepting that the two paradigms are different, Krantz tries to find how to make them the same.

The articles in this special feature will not resolve the conceptual and philosophical controversies that we call the quantitative–qualitative debates. After all, debates about methods and philosophies are a part of scientific life. And it may well be inevitable that we sometimes get carried away somewhat by the power of the debates and the forces they marshal. After all, such debates can mobilize resources, arouse emotions, and lend themselves all to easy to stereotyping those with whom we might disagree. It is convenient to reduce all this to Kuhnian paradigms. But hopefully the articles in this special feature will convince readers that such a reductionism may be more the cause of the controversies than a description of them. The tendency to reduce one's opponents to stereotyped paradigms—paradigmism, if you will—is an intellectually lazy solution to an intellectually important set of problems. We can do better than that.

References

Cook, T.D., & Reichardt, C.S. (Eds.). (1979). *Qualitative and quantitative methods in evaluation research.* Newbury Park, CA: Sage Publications.

Fuller, S., Demey, M., Shinn, T., & Woolgar, S. (Eds.). (1989). *The cognitive turn: Sociological and psychological perspectives on science*. Dordrecht, Netherlands: Kluwer.

Guba, E.G., & Lincoln, Y.S. (1989). *Fourth generation evaluation*. Newbury Park CA: Sage Publications.

Kuhn, T.S. (1970). *The structure of scientific revolutions* (2nd ed.). Chicago: University of Chicago Press.

Laudan, L. (1992). *Science and relativism*. Chicago: University of Chicago Press.

Phillips, D.C. (1987). *Philosophy, science, and social inquiry*. Oxford, UK: Pergamon Press.

Phillips, D.C. (1990). Postpositivistic science: Myths and realities. In E.G. Guba (Ed.), *The paradigm dialog* (pp. 31–45). Newbury Park, CA: Sage Publications.

Reichardt, C.S., & Rallis, S.F. (Eds.). (1994). *The qualitative–quantitative debate: New perspectives.* San Francisco: Jossey-Bass.

Shadish, W.R., & Fuller, S. (Eds.). (1994). *The social psychology of science*. New York: Guilford Publications.

Woolgar, S. (Ed.). (1988). *Knowledge and reflexivity: New frontiers in the sociology of knowledge*. Newbury Park, CA: Sage Publications.

Ziman, J. (1984). *An introduction to science studies: The philosophical and social aspects of science and technology*. Cambridge, UK: Cambridge University Press.

RECOMMENDED READINGS

Brown, S. K., & Glasner, A. (eds.)(1999). *Assessment matters in higher education: choosing and using diverse approaches.* Philadelphia, PA: Open University Press.

Bickman, Leonard (2000). Summing Up Program Theory. *New Directions for Evalution. Program Theory in Evaluation.* N. 87, p. 103–112.

Chen, Huey (1997). Applying mixed methods under the framework of theory-driven evaluations. *New Directions for Evaluation* n74 p. 61–72.

Fournier, Deborah M. (1995). Establishing evaluative conclusions: a distinction between general and working logic. In Fournier, D.M. ed. (1995). *New Directions for Evalution. Reasoning in Evaluation: Inferential Links and Leaps* n.68 pp. 15–32.

Kirkhart, Karen E. (2000) Reconceptualizing evaluation use: an integrated theory of influence. New Directions for Evaluation n88, p. 5–23.

Rossi, Peter H., Freeman, Howard E., Lipsey, Mark W. (1999). *Evaluation: A Systematic Approach. Sixth edition.* Sage: Thousand Oaks, CA.

Ryan, Katherine E. and Johnson, Trav D. Democratizing evaluation: meanings and methods from practice. *New Directions in Evaluation. Evaluation as a Democratic Process: Promoting Inclusion, Dialogue, and Deliberation* n85, pp. 39–50.

Scriven, Michael (2001). Evaluation: future tenses. *American Journal of Evaluation* v22, n3 p. 301–307.

Scriven, Michael (1999). The nature of evaluation. Part II: training. ERIC/AE Digest. ED432711.

Shadish, William (1998). Some evaluation questions. *Practical Assessment, Research & Evaluation.* 6(3). Available online: http://ericae.net/pare/getvn.asp?v=6&n=3.

Shadish, William R., Newman, Diana L., Scheirer, Mary Ann, and Wye, Christopher eds. (1995). *New Directions for Program Evaluation: Guiding Principles for Evaluators* n60 Summer 1995.

Tierney, William G. (2002). Reflective evaluation: improving practice in College preparation programs. In Tierney W. G. & Hagedorn, L.S. (eds.). Increasing Access to College: Extending Possibilities for All Students. SUNY: Albany.

Worthen, Blaine R. (2001). Whither evaluation? That all depends. *American Journal of Evaluation.* V. 22 n.3 pp. 409–418.

Yin, Robert K. (1997) Case Study Evaluations: a decade of progress? *New Directions for Evaluation* n76, p. 69–78.

Discussion & Reflection

In what ways does the historical evolution of assessment/evaluation influence practice in the 21st century?

How does the qualitative paradigm contribute to the process of determining worth and merit?

How does using only quantitative methods limit what can be measured in the assessment/evaluation process?

How might using mixed methods (quantitative/qualitative) enhance the assessment/evaluation process? What are the pros and cons to using a mixed methods approach to assessment/evaluation?

SECTION II

ADMINISTRATION AND INSTITUTIONAL PERFORMANCE

Administration and Institutional Performance

Introduction

Mandates to demonstrate quality and the press to be accountable are tremendous influences on the perpetuation of assessment and evaluation in higher education. Some would argue that the effect of these influences is very much like the tail wagging the dog. However, one positive effect is that administrators are becoming evidence-based decision makers, which suggests that evaluations are more than bookcase ornaments; they are tools for improvement. Literature, included or identified, in this section addresses accreditation and institutional research in relationship to planning, mission and public accountability.

CLASSIC READINGS

ACADEMIC PROGRAM REVIEWS: INSTITUTIONAL APPROACHES, EXPECTATIONS, AND CONTROVERSIES

CLIFTON F. CONRAD AND RICHARD F. WILSON

Major Issues in Program Review

Six issues concern the individuals in colleges and universities who are involved in academic program review: (1) accommodating multiple purposes; (2) selecting an evaluation model; (3) assessing quality; (4) using external reviewers; (5) increasing use of evaluations; and (6) assessing the impact of evaluations. (The selection of these six issues was based on two considerations—the significance of the issue and the extent to which a review of the literature might aid in illuminating its dimensions.) This chapter defines and clarifies these issues and presents alternative perspectives regarding their resolution. Those engaged in program review need to address these issues regularly.

Accommodating Multiple Purposes

Because a number of reasons usually exist for establishing a program of review, institutions have developed a fairly lengthy list of purposes to guide their review efforts. The following list represents those adopted by many institutions:

- to assess program quality, productivity, need, and demand
- to improve the quality of academic offerings
- to ensure wise use of resources
- to determine the program's effectiveness and to consider possible modifications
- to facilitate academic planning and budgeting
- to satisfy state-level review requirements

The advantage of designing an evaluation system that incorporates all of these purposes is that it will appeal to several constituencies. Such support is often needed in the early stages of implementation, but it can become self-defeating. It is possible, however, to design an evaluation system in which information is collected and judgments made that respond to widely different expectations.

Serious questions can be raised about two accommodations of purposes. The first involves institutional efforts to combine program improvement and resource reallocation as major purposes of the review. The second concerns an institution's attempts to use a single review process to satisfy both its own review agenda and that of a state-level coordinating or governing board.

Combining Program Improvement with Resource Reallocation

Although many institutions conducting program reviews emphasize either the improvement of program quality or resource reallocation (including program discontinuance), a growing number of institutions combine both emphases into a single process. At first glance, the two purposes would seem compatible. Each requires an assessment of current quality to identify where strengths exist and where improvement is warranted. Most people also would agree that quality assessment is an important first step in deciding how to reallocate resources. The problem, however, is that it is difficult, if not impossible, for those responsible for the review process to achieve both objectives at once. "Quality assessment should not be ignored in a retrenchment process, but the two distinct motivations of improvement and reduction in resources will generally involve somewhat different processes and may produce quite different results" (George 1982, p. 45). Several distinct difficulties in merging these two purposes merit consideration.

A major problem in attempting to achieve both purposes in a single review system is that the underlying assumptions and ultimate objectives may not be easily reconciled, if at all. When an institution wishes to assess the quality of its programs and to improve programs where weaknesses appear, the emphasis of the evaluation will be on how to assess current performance, on what progress has been made over time, and on what institutional strategies might facilitate further improvement. At the University of North Carolina—Asheville, for example, program improvement, not resource allocation, was the principal incentive behind recent program reviews. After studying a range of data, nine department chairs rated the institution's programs on the basis of nine criteria. Future resources of the institution were earmarked for programs with low rankings to promote program improvement (Cochran and Hengstler 1984).

On the other hand, the approach to evaluation is likely to depart from this strategy if an institution concludes it must reduce the number of program offerings or reallocate resources away from low-priority or low-demand programs. In this case, evaluators must judge relative worth and value and often must act quickly in the face of immediate budget pressures. In this situation, quality is only one of several factors that gets considered.

In distinguishing between the two types of evaluations, it is useful to consider the "industrial" and "biological" models of evaluation (Pace 1972). The industrial model focuses on quantitative measures used to judge efficiency and productivity, and the biological model searches for ways to enrich experiences and to assess broader and more enduring program effects on students and society (Pace 1972). It is not stretching this analysis too far to suggest that most resource reallocation processes are frequently industrial in orientation, while program improvement processes are more biological. Others have questioned the compatibility of the two purposes, pointing out the great difference between a unit thinking it is being evaluated to identify areas needing additional strength and units thinking such an assessment serves to identify areas where quality is low and support should be diminished or even eliminated (Arns and Poland 1980).

The discussion of the review activities of the Select Committee on Academic Program Priorities at SUNY—Albany supports this view: "The Select Committee ... felt a certain frustration that the budget recommendations had created a climate that led to the implementation of its negative recommendations but not its positive ones" (Volkwein 1984, p. 393).

Yet another problem in merging these two purposes is a temporal one: The careful assessment of quality and the development of recommendations for improvement require considerable time. Most institutions are unable to conduct more than six or eight program reviews each year. Such a protracted schedule does not mesh well with resource reallocation reviews, which usually transpire within relatively short periods in response to anticipated budget problems. The latter reviews use extant information on quality but usually lack sufficient time to conduct detailed analysis of the quality of every program offered. Hence, a timing factor militates against efforts to combine the two types of reviews.

Accommodating Institutional and State-Level Purposes

A second accommodation of purposes concerns how institutional review processes relate to the expectations for review of state higher education agencies. State agencies' authority and activity in program review have increased dramatically in the last few years, and the proper role of state boards in institutional review processes continues to be debated.

A key issue in this debate is whether institutional and state-level interests converge or are sufficiently complementary so that a single review process can achieve the aims of both. Some believe that state-level interests can indeed mesh with those of institutions (Hines 1980). In Hines's view, the predominant institutional interest lies in assessing merit, while state agencies are most interested in statewide needs or plans. Although the primary objective of review differs for the two groups, the secondary objectives overlap considerably; that is, states have more than passing interest in merit, and institutions frequently want to know how programs could be more responsive to statewide needs.

An analysis of the relationship between program review for institutions and for state-level agencies identified eight purposes for undertaking program reviews and discussed how review responsibility varies by purpose (Wallhaus 1982) (see table 1). In this view, responsibility for review is vested in the state agency when the review serves to develop a statewide plan or overall programmatic priorities. Conversely, reviews focusing on curricular and personnel matters are the province of institutions. Between these two extremes exist a number of purposes where the assignment of responsibility is not so straight-forward. It is these purposes that institutions and state agencies frequently try to accomplish cooperatively through a single review process.

These cooperative efforts have been labeled "shared reviews" (Floyd 1983). Responsibilities in shared reviews are defined variously. Frequently, the institution conducts the review and endeavors to attend to matters of interest to both the institution and the state. On the surface, this plan would seem to be reasonable and efficient. The issue, again, is whether a single review process can have more than one driving purpose.

In the last few years, a number of states have adopted shared responsibilities for reviews. Illinois, Idaho, New Mexico, California, Oregon, and Ohio have adopted review processes in which the state agency, rather than conducting reviews itself, simply ensures that each institution is doing so (Barak 1982). In a comparable arrangement within the University of Wisconsin system, each institution is required to have a review process and must report its findings to the system office (Craven 1980b). Only in unusual circumstances, such as when enrollments are low or when unnecessary duplication seems to exist, does the system office conduct a review of its own.

In shared reviews, then, institutions attempt to accommodate institutional and state-level purposes by developing an evaluation process that satisfies both institutional and state board requirements. In theory, the institution designs an evaluation system to meet its own needs and, by making minor adjustments in, say, data collection or reporting lines, is able to satisfy state-level needs as well. Moreover, this strategy minimizes duplication of review activities.

Despite these positive features, the shared review approach has drawn criticism. While combining reviews appears to be a solid idea, theoretical and practical reasons militate against the success of such an approach (Barak 1982, p. 84). For example, whereas institutions frequently establish the need for a program on the basis of students' or faculty members' perspectives, state agencies usually look at program need from a societal or manpower perspective. Another example of potential conflict centers on efficiency. Institutions tend to assess efficiency by comparing similar departments on campus or by collecting data from peer departments. State agencies tend to look at efficiency from a statewide perspective, for example, how costs in a discipline vary among institutions in the state. Thus, separate reviews by institutions and state agencies may be the best solution (Barak 1982, pp. 84–88).

Under certain conditions, combined reviews may not be productive (Wilson 1984). If the system office or state-level board prescribed the review process in too much detail, local initiatives aimed at establishing an effective system may be stifled. Where the state agency insists upon close adherence to a prescribed format, it may be more useful for separate reviews to be conducted, one by the institution for its own use, another by the state agency.

Selecting an Evaluation Model

The key issue for evaluators is which model—goal-based, responsive, decision-making, and connoisseurship—should guide program reviews in higher education, and the decision is an important one:

> Where an administrator has a choice with regard to the type of evaluation to be conducted . . . that individual should be fully aware of the fundamentally different assumptions and outcomes that obtain when a particular type of strategy is selected (Gardner 1977, p. 572).

Goal-Based Model

The goal-based model focuses principally on assessing the extent to which a program's formal objectives are being achieved. As part of

Table 1
Purposes and Objectives of Program Review

	Tends to be more closely tied to state-level responsibilities	Tends to be more closely tied to institutional responsibilities
• Determination of statewide educational policies, long-range plans and programmatic priorities (that is, support development of statewide master plans)	X	
• Elimination of unnecessary program duplication or, conversely, identification of needs for newprograms	X	
• Determination of educational and economic priorities in terms of:		
1. consistency with role and mission	X	
2. need for improvement or expansion and additional resources necessary to accomplish (link to budget decisions)	X	
3. decisions to decrease or terminate (link to resource reallocation decisions)	X	
• Determination of relationship to established standards of quality, or preparation for entry into professions, and so on (link to accreditation, continuation of operating authority, or licensing authority)	X	
• Improvement of communications with constituents; assurance that information provided to students, prospective students, parents, alumni, governmental agencies, and others is consistent with actual practice	X	
• Determination of quality controls and policies (for example, admission policy, graduation requirements)		X
• Determination of curricular modifications, advisement procedures, institutional plans, and priorities relative to instructional, research, and service objectives		X
• Personnel and organizational decisions—faculty promotion and tenure, academic leadership, organizational structures, and philosophies		X

this effort, considerable attention is given to specifying program objectives, establishing standards of performance, identifying data to assess performance, and evaluating whether objectives have been achieved.

A goal-based approach to evaluation offers a number of positive features. First, the importance placed on objectives focuses attention on what those responsible for a program hope to accomplish. These goal statements become more than general statements of intent; they are specified as precisely as possible because of their significance to the subsequent assessment of performance. Second, a goal-based system can be used to make periodic checks of progress (formative evaluation) as well as to make consummate judgments of program worth (summative evaluation). Third, the approach encourages systematic attention not only to whether program goals have been reached but also to those features contributing to success or failure. For example, if the desired goal is to increase student retention and if certain actions are taken to achieve this goal, the goal-based design would require both an assessment of whether retention had improved and an understanding of the effect on retention of the actions themselves.

To be sure, the goal-based model has some limitations. The specification of goals can become an obsession resulting in lengthy lists covering every conceivable desire, significant as well as trivial, for a program. "Some people believe that when every objective is related to every other, the program is properly managed" (House 1982, p. 10). But "a major criticism of evaluation as congruence between performance and objectives is that a focusing on measurable products rather than processes occurs. This may permit the overlooking of important side effects" (Feasley 1980, p. 9). In essence, this criticism berates the propensity of evaluators to focus on whether goals have been accomplished while ignoring other, unintended contributions that goal statements have not captured.

On a related matter, the goal-based system has been criticized because of the inflexible way in which a priori goals drive the process (Guba and Lincoln 1981). Evaluators have a tendency to accept the goal statements and to pursue data relating to those goals in a very determined way. If, in mid-evaluation, it becomes apparent that some of the goal statements no longer apply or that those responsible for the program should change directions, the goal-based evaluator might not perceive the necessary changes or, more significantly, might not be inclined to suggest that plans be changed, even if the need is apparent. Thus, the goal-based model sometimes engenders a singleminded pursuit of information relating to goal statements while ignoring everything else.

Perhaps the major defect of the goal-based approach lies in its assumption that ways can be found to measure performance in relation to all goals. This observation is especially significant for those institutions of higher education in which goals, such as those of program quality or centrality, frequently are elusive. Attempts to "force" a goal-based model in a particular setting may result in redefining the goals in ways that can be measured (for example, number of publications equals research quality), thus trivializing what is being done.

Use of the goal-based model, therefore, offers the two advantages of a systematic attention to how a program has performed in relation to its intent and of a concern for the factors contributing to its success or failure. The model's chief limitations are the propensity to reduce everything to a goal statement, the insensitivity to outcomes that are unrelated to goal statements, and the assumption that valid measures can be found for all goals.

Responsive Model

The driving objective of the responsive model is to collect information to illuminate the concerns and issues of those who have a stake in an evaluation. Programs goals are not central. In essence, a responsive evaluation investigates what various constituents believe a program is accomplishing and their concerns about the program.

The strength of this model is that it can help those responsible for a program to understand both its actual achievements and where action is needed to reconcile results with plans. For this reason, a responsive approach can be especially helpful during the early and middle stages of program implementation.

One major criticism of the responsive model is that it is "unscientific and lacks an emphasis on formal measurement" (Gardner 1977). Critics suggest that the role of the evaluator is not to observe a program from afar and to make judgments based on the analysis of "objective" data but to become immersed in the program to the point of rendering an accurate description and interpretation of its accomplishments. Such immersion, however, may well sacrifice objectivity, and it certainly increases the time commitment to a review.

One particular type of responsive evaluation—the case study—has some definite shortcomings: the fact that the evaluator assumes enormous responsibility in trying to portray a program accurately; the difficulty for the evaluator to protect against bias; the requirement for a large number of subjective judgments (House 1982).

Decision-Making Model

The main purpose of the decision-making model is to conduct evaluations responsive to the informational needs of decision makers. The strength of this model derives from the explicit connection between evaluation and decision making, a link that focuses the evaluation and increases the likelihood that results will be used.

"The principal criticism of the decision-oriented approach is that the evaluator accepts the decision context and values/criteria that have been defined by the decision makers" (Feasley 1980, p. 10). This criticism implies that the evaluator is aligned with the decision makers and may find it difficult to remain objective. The evaluator collects data according to the questions defined by decision makers and accepts the values implicit in their questions. If those responsible for the program do not share such values or consider the questions unimportant, the evaluation will not be credible.

Another problem is that this model assumes rational decision making (Gardner 1977). The task of the evaluator is to identify the questions of interest, collect pertinent information, present findings, and wait for the results to be used. The evaluation therefore becomes a critical ingredient in decision making. This approach is likely to overemphasize the importance of evaluative information and to fail to recognize that evaluations provide only one source of data for decision makers. Further, to assume that all decision alternatives can be accurately anticipated and that Sufficient data can be collected in relation to these alternatives is to place unrealistic expectations on an evaluation.

Decision makers are frequently biased in their acquisition and processing of information (O'Reilly 1981, pp. 55–57), and this bias occurs in the search for information, in the preference for information that is easy to secure and supports preconceived ideas, in the transmission of information that distorts reality if it optimizes certain outcomes, in the selective use of available information, and in the preference for vivid examples, even if they are misleading.

A final criticism of this model relates to an evaluator's ability to identify decision makers. It is not easy to identify decision makers in many complex organizations (Guba and Lincoln 1981). Decisions are frequently made at several organizational levels, by various individuals. Most actions involve more than one decision maker and a number of key decision points. It is almost impossible to identify all of these individuals and to collect all of the data necessary to inform them.

Connoisseurship Model

The central tenet of the connoisseurship model is that an expert (a connoisseur) can use his experience and expertise to judge a problem. In essence, the human being is the measurement instrument.

The use of outside reviewers in higher education is a good example of the connoisseurship model. The strength of this model is that those who are most knowledgeable about a subject are asked to make the assessment. The connoisseurship model has high credibility because those within a discipline or profession are judged by peers who have a sound basis for understanding what is—or is not—being accomplished.

One problem is that the connoisseurship model frequently lacks evaluative guidelines, so that a premium is placed on the evaluator's judgment; it is hard to know whether the evaluator's perceptions are accurate (Guba and Lincoln 1981). Many institutions attempt to sidestep this problem by inviting more than one expert to participate in a review, a strategy introducing valuable "triangulation." At the same time, however, this strategy can yield as many different assessments as there are evaluators.

Another problem with this approach lies in the difficulty of generalizing across programs (Feasley 1980, p. 8). In rating different programs, no two experts will have the same value structure or will weigh criteria equally. One evaluator may rate a program weak because of difficulties in its graduate instructional program; another may overlook the graduate program entirely if the record of faculty research is strong.

The connoisseurship model is popular in higher education because most faculty members believe that only those within a discipline can adequately evaluate accomplishment. Certainly, a disciplinary background can greatly enhance an evaluation. At the same time, certain problems are inherent—the ability to generalize procedures across programs, the subjectivity of perceptions, and the emphasis placed on the person chosen to conduct the evaluation.

Assessing Quality

For those engaged in program review, the assessment of quality has generated more confusion and than any other issue. Pressure always has existed to define "quality" and to determine which types of information should be collected, but more recently, interest has burgeoned because of the emphasis on program review for reallocation and retrenchment. The problem is that no one has yet found a way to measure quality directly. The issue for evaluators is how to define this concept and how to determine what types of information (indicators) should be used to guide data collection.

The literature (cf. Astin 1980; Conrad and Blackburn In press b) and institutional documents identify four perspectives on how to define quality: a reputational view, a resources view, an outcomes view, and a value-added view. The particular view held affects the kind of information used to assess quality. The issue is which of these views of quality is most accurate and helpful (see Table 2).

Reputational View

This view of quality is derived from the connoisseurship model of evaluation and assumes that experts in the field make the best judgments on the criterion. In essence, the reputational view reflects a belief that the optimum way to assess quality is to seek a consensus of informed opinion. The typical indicator is some type of reputational survey. The past two decades have seen a number of surveys of this type (Carter 1966; Jones, Lindzey, and Coggeshall 1982; Roose and Anderson 1970).

The main strength of this view lies in the fact that the raters are those who supposedly know best what quality is. It also has an intuitive appeal to ratings, reflecting what most people believe is true (Webster 1981).

Reputational rankings are criticized, however, because, while the raters may have insight into the scholarly productivity and reputation of a department, they are not likely to know much about the instructional program. Surely a program assessment must include more than research and scholarship (Conrad and Blackburn

Table 2
Views of Quality and Representative Indicators

Reputational View
- Peer judgments of the quality of program, students, faculty, or resources

Resources View
- Student selectivity
- Student demand
- Faculty prestige
- Faculty training
- Faculty teaching loads
- Budget affluence
- Library holdings
- Equipment adequacy
- Size of endowment

Outcomes View
- Faculty scholarly productivity
- Faculty awards and honors
- Faculty research support
- Faculty teaching performances
- Student achievement following graduation
- Student placement
- Student achievement
- Alumni satisfaction

Value-added view
- Change in students' cognitive abilities
- Student personal development
- Student career development
- Social benefits

1985). The lack of national visibility for many programs suggests that even reputational ranking based on faculty members' scholarly productivity are not likely to be meaningful below the top 15 or 20 programs in the country (Webster 1981). Other problems are apparent—"reputational lag" (the ranking of programs based on their quality several years old) and "halo effects" (ranking a program a program high because the institution is held in high regard). These and other limitations are discussed extensively in the literature (Conrad and Blackburn 1985; Dolan 1976; Lawrence and Green 1980; Webster 1981).

Despite these limitations, such ratings have received support:

> In our view controversy over reputational studies should not deter researchers from conducting such studies in the future. If reputational studies are designed to respond to the criticisms . . . we are persuaded that they can make an important contribution to the evaluation of quality in higher education (Conrad and Blackburn 1985, p. 23).

Resources View

This particular view of quality emphasizes the human, financial, and physical resources that go into a program. According to this view, high quality exists where these resources—bright students, excellent faculty, adequate budgets, strong research support, strong libraries, and adequate facilities—are plentiful. The extent to which these resources are available to a particular program has been measured in various ways—for example, student test scores, proportion of the faculty with a doctorate, grant support, and number of volumes in the library. The advantages of using such measures of resources are that relevant data are readily available at most institutions, that the measures reflect what exists today, not what the situation was a decade ago, and that comparisons can be made across all colleges and universities, not just a few highly ranked institutions (Webster 1981).

Notwithstanding these benefits, the resources view suffers some serious limitations. Little evidence supports the view that more resources equate with increased student learning (Astin 1980). Further, and more important, the resources approach places a false ceiling on the amount of quality that can exist in higher education by asserting that "such resources as bright students and prestigious faculty are finite" (Astin 1980, p. 4).

Outcomes View

Another way to define and assess quality is to emphasize results—what the investment of resources produces. Here, attention is focused on the quality of the product. Typical indicators associated with this view are faculty productivity, students' accomplishments following graduation, employers' satisfaction with program graduates, and institutional contributions to the solution of local, state, or national problems. Specific outcome measures include the number of faculty publications in scholarly journals, the number of graduates admitted to leading graduate or professional schools, employer surveys, percentage of graduates finding employment soon after graduation, and lifetime earnings of graduates.

Collecting information on outcomes boasts a number of advantages. Chief among them is the emphasis on what is happening to those who are or have been part of a program; the focus of attention shifts from the resources invested to the results. Like the resource measures, many of the outcomes measures hold relevance for all institutions; all institutions, for example, are interested in the accomplishments of their alumni (Webster 1981).

Perhaps the most significant problem with the outcomes view is the difficulty of delineating the special institutional contribution to results. "Most output measures depend more on the quality of students admitted to the institution than on the functioning of the institution or the quality of its program" (Astin 1980, p. 3). Another disadvantage is that outcomes measures frequently limit themselves to the past. The period between graduation and inclusion in *Who's Who in America* obstructs the drawing of precise conclusions about the current quality of a program (Webster 1981).

Value-Added View

This view of quality focuses attention on program impact. "The basic argument underlying the value-added approach is that true quality resides in the institution's ability to affect its students favorably, to make a positive difference in their intellectual and personal development"

(Astin 1980, pp. 3–4). Consonant with this view, evaluation should attempt to identify what a program contributes to students' learning. One typical indicator is what students learn while enrolled, which is sometimes measured by administering an achievement test at the time of enrollment and at graduation.

The chief advantage of this view is that one takes into account the quality of students at entry. This approach is especially attractive to institutions seeking to respond to "the twin doctrines of entitlement and equal education opportunity" (Lawrence and Green 1980, p. 54). Thus, institutions are judged by how much they help students, by how much they "add" to students' knowledge and personal development.

Like the other views of quality, the value-added approach has limitations. First, it is expensive, both in time and money. Investigating a program's contribution requires extensive recordkeeping for a large number of students. Another problem is the difficulty of reaching consensus on what students should learn and on measuring such quantities, even if they are defined (Lawrence and Green 1980, p. 40). For example, significant measurement problems are associated with assessing how much a student has improved in critical thinking skills. Finally, it is no easy matter to determine what one program's contribution is to a student's learning or development. The effects of other variables, such as maturation, travel experiences, and summer employment are difficult to control.

Using External Reviewers

This review of current evaluation processes indicates that most institutions have incorporated the judgments of external reviewers into their program reviews. Most often, these reviewers are faculty members within the same discipline but at another institution or within the institution but outside the program under review. The issue faced by those designing an evaluation system is to decide which of these two types of reviewers to use. Knowledge of the possible strengths and limitations of each should prove helpful in making the choice.

Reviewers From Other Institutions

The use of peers from other institutions to help in institutional reviews is rapidly becoming the norm rather than the exception. The program review process at California State University at Long Beach illustrates the use of outside reviewers. That institution's review process consists of four phases: (1) a self-study prepared by those in the program under review; (2) a review by a subcommittee of faculty from other programs on campus; (3) an external review by disciplinary experts; and (4) a "response report" prepared by those in the program (Office of the Associate Vice President n.d.). The external review serves to provide a comparative perspective, which is balanced with the program's own view and that of colleagues on campus.

Like other approaches to assessing program quality, the use of external peers has its strengths and weaknesses. Characteristics of the problems are the following observations on experiences with outside reviewers at the University of Nebraska—Lincoln: The selection of a review team was frequently controversial; the review teams suffered because of lack of knowledge about the local context; too little time was available for the reviews; the review teams tended to focus on insignificant issues; the review teams often were asked to address problems they could not resolve; the review teams were provided with more information than they could comprehend; and the review teams tended to solve all problems by recommending additional resources (Seagren and Bean, 1981, pp. 20–24).

In a more positive vein, the use of external peers provides a perspective that is frequently helpful. In most program reviews, it is considered crucial to have some kind of disciplinary perspective on the quality of what is being done and to seek advice on future directions. In addition, reports from external peers are usually perceived as objective and therefore can stimulate change that might not otherwise be possible.

Reviewers From the Same Institution

A number of institutions choose to use on-campus (but outside the discipline) colleagues to help evaluate programs. At California State University at Long Beach, for example, faculty from within the institution conduct an internal review of a program to provide an assessment based on institutional (as opposed to disciplinary) standards of performance and quality (Office of the Associate Vice President n.d., Appendix B, p. 14). This strategy offers the advantages of familiarity with the local context and norms and a stake in the results. The recommendations will affect not only those evaluated but also the evaluators—they must live with what they recommend. On the other hand, such reviewers may frequently be unfamiliar with the discipline under study or, conversely, tend to allow previous familiarity with a program or its personnel to bias results.

Despite these criticisms, many believe that reviewers outside a particular discipline can recognize quality as long as enough information is available and enough opportunities exist to interact with program personnel. An interesting test of this idea examined results of faculty ratings of students' oral examinations (DiBiaso et al. 1981). A graduate school representative from outside the student's discipline was appointed to each of the review committees. A comparison of the ratings of the internal and external reviewers revealed

> no evidence of a significant difference between how graduate school representatives rate examinations conducted inside their own colleges compared to their ratings of examinations outside their own colleges. These results suggest that members have some common perceptions about the quality of doctoral examinations, regardless of discipline (DiBiaso et al. 1981, p. 10).

Thus, the issue is not whether to use reviewers in higher education, but whether to use on-campus colleagues or disciplinary peers.

Increasing Use of Evaluations

One of the most perplexing issues facing evaluators is how to increase the likelihood that others will employ the results of their efforts. Considerable time and attention is being given to evaluation these days, yet a frequent criticism is that the results of such efforts really have no effect on decisions. The perception is that evaluations are undertaken not because the results are expected to be used but because someone simply feels they "ought to be done." This criticism is so prevalent that it must be taken seriously.

To the uninitiated, it would seem that the issue of use should not even arise. Is not the basis of an evaluation the need for information to make a decision or to become more knowledgeable about a program or activity? If so, then every evaluation should be used. Nevertheless, utilization is a problem.

The results of program evaluations are not used for four general reason: (1) organizational inertia; (2) the state of evaluation practice, for example, the inability to define valid measures of important criteria; (3) the uncertainty about the need for some evaluations; and (4) the multiple sources of information competing for the attention of decision makers (Anderson and Ball 1978).

The conflicting information needs of people at different levels of an organization make it difficult to conduct a useful evaluation (Patton 1985, p. 13). Highly detailed discussion of a specific case is seldom of much use at higher organizational levels; aggregate comparisons are of little use at the unit level. One important reason for lack of use of an evaluation is the inadequate personal involvement and commitment of key people. The personal factor is more crucial than structural, organizational, or methodological variables (Patton 1981, pp. 15–16).

Use of evaluation is also hindered because institutions compartmentalize the function of evaluation. Typically, the responsibility for program review is assigned to a staff office or to a specific individual. The delegation of responsibility for program review by the executive officers of an institution relieves them of the responsibility for such activities and places distance between those conducting the reviews and those in a position to use the results.

Utilization is also impeded because the decisions frequently involve social, political, and financial considerations outside the task of evaluation. It should not be too disturbing to evaluators to know that occasionally these other considerations will outweigh the findings of an evaluation report (Dressel 1976; O'Reilly 1981).

Given that these problems exist, the issue of how to increase the likelihood that results will be used warrants special attention. This matter has engendered a number of views. Anderson and Ball (1978), for instance, recommend encouraging communication between those evaluated, those evaluating, and those responsible for the process; varying the modes for disseminating results according to audiences; identifying users early and finding ways to make sure that their questions are being addressed; finding ways to include those responsible for the evaluation in its planning; reporting results in a timely way;

and maximizing such virtues as brevity, timeliness, and responsiveness. Others suggest that utilization should become an immediate rather than a post-report concern, that reports relate to the concerns of decision makers, that credibility and rapport be maintained, and that all participants in the evaluation communicate among themselves (Brown and Braskamp 1980). "Evaluation is undertaken in a social and political environment in which various groups have vested interests in the evaluation process. . . If an evaluation is to be used by these groups in their deliberations, discussions, and policy making, the evaluation system must be designed to maximize communication between the audiences" (Braskamp 1982, p. 58).

A critical element in utilization relates to the approach of the evaluator (Alkin 1980). In particular, rapport established with program staff can enhance use of results. Use is not related to any particular evaluation model; the most important consideration is to adapt the strategy to the program and to the questions being asked.

One of the most important ways to increase utilization is for decision makers and information users to be clearly identified (Patton 1978). Decision makers cannot be treated as "abstract audiences" (p. 284). Decision makers should not delegate responsibility for an evaluation but should assume an active role in its implementation:

> There has been considerable discussion in the literature and among evaluators about how to make managers, clinicians, board members, and others better consumers of evaluations. . . . This effort is misplaced. For evaluations to be useful and to be used, the managers have to accept responsibility for owning and defining the evaluation function (Clifford and Sherman 1983, p. 32).

One way to increase use is to ensure that evaluators focus their efforts on three issues: (1) who the decision makers will be; (2) what information is needed; and (3) when the information is needed (Feasley 1980, p. 43). Perhaps the most important issue is to identify the evaluative question (Patton 1978).

A study of the characteristics of decision makers identifies six managerial characteristics relating to the issue of utilization:

1. Decision makers work at an unrelenting pace;
2. their daily routines are characterized by brevity, variety, and fragmentation;
3. they prefer active rather than passive use of time;
4. they prefer verbal as opposed to written communication;
5. they serve as active communication links;
6. they blend rights as well as duties so that personal objectives can be realized (Mintzberg 1973, chap. 3).

This list suggests that evaluations are more likely to be used if they relate to decision makers' concerns, are communicated clearly and concisely, and are presented both verbally and in written form.

In wrestling with the question of utilization, institutions have adopted several strategies to try to ensure that results of evaluations will somehow link to other decision-making processes. Ohio State University has developed the concept of a loosely coupled system, which means that all "parties to a review," including the college dean, the university's chief academic officers, the graduate dean, and those in the program, are consulted throughout the review process. At the conclusion of the review, a "memorandum of understanding is developed in which the parties agree on actions to be taken. These agreements are monitored and updated each year (Arms and Poland 1980).

At the University of North Carolina at Asheville, six aspects of the program review process contribute to its usefulness:

1. clarity of purpose
2. involvement of decision makers in all stages of the process
3. maximization of communication
4. understanding of the political nature of the environment
5. recognition of the subjectivity of evaluation
6. competence of the institutional research staff and confidence in the data collected (Cochran and Hengstler 1984, p. 184).

At the State University of New York at Albany, evaluations are an integral part of a planning process. The evaluations consist of both annual monitoring of programs and five-year in-depth reviews. This arrangement is useful because:

1. *it capitalizes on an annual, synoptic view all major university activities;*
2. *it is a goal-driven activity;*
3. *it is merged with resource allocation, thereby linking budgeting with evaluation*
4. *evaluation (both ongoing and annual monitoring as well as selected in-depth reviews) provides feedback for planning and resource allocation;*
5. *it more clearly integrates evaluation with existing decision-making structures and processes (Hartmark 1982, p. 16).*

Thus, a review of the literature on utilization reveals consensus on the objective of utilization but little agreement on how it is best accomplished, and suggestions vary from encouraging decision makers to participate more actively in evaluation to accounting for the managerial characteristics of decision makers to conducting evaluations in a manner responsive to those characteristics.

Assessing Impact

If results are used, another issue emerges—the impact of those results. The basic concern is whether the consequences of implementing an evaluation are positive or negative. First, however, one must distinguish between the outcomes and the effects of a review—a subtle but important distinction. Decisions to eliminate a program, to increase admissions requirements, to change department heads, or to establish consortia are outcomes, not effects, of program reviews. As defined here, "effect" refers to the consequences of actions taken. Concern about the effects therefore requires attention to the long-term effects of decisions, for example, whether the program is stronger, more efficient, or higher quality. Some believe the effects of program review are salutory; others are less optimistic. The question is which view is more correct.

How does one make such assessments? Efforts should focus on the question, "Does the system function better as a result of the evaluation effort?" (Cronbach 1977, p. 2). Explicit in this question is the principle that an evaluation must be beneficial.

The following kinds of consequences should be noted:

> The ideal held forth in the literature is one of major impact on concrete decisions. The image that emerged in our interviews is that there are few major, direction-changing, decisions in most programming . . . (Patton 1978, p. 32).

Most conceptions are too narrow (Alkin 1980). Consequences cannot be examined solely on the basis of immediate impact; longer-term implications must also be considered. Evaluations have unintended results that go beyond the formally stated recommendations. Further, the evaluation process often generates benefits beyond those chronicled in a report. Thus, the assessment of impact must be done in a naturalistic way, as in conducting case studies and recording participant observations. Finally, one should not confuse lack of implementation with lack of impact. An evaluation report frequently provides valuable information even though no specific recommendations are implemented (Alkin 1980, pp. 21–22).

The assessment of impact must not be limited to immediate and direct influences; indirect, catalytic, and inclusive results also demand attention (Braskamp and Brown 1980, p. viii). This approach requires special skill in analyzing multiple causes of specific actions as well as a willingness to view utilization broadly. Thus, those assessing impact must heed results that may be latent as well as immediate, incremental as well as radical, subtle as well as obvious. This view of impact is consistent with the admonition that "most change in education is incremental rather than radical, and advertising of this fact would improve the climate for evaluation" (Dressel 1976, p. 5).

Just as the advice on how to assess impact is far from uniform, so too is the evidence on impact far from definitive. Most campuses have critics who believe that the costs of program review outweigh the results. Several criticisms have been cited frequently:

- Time and effort are wasted because more data are collected than can be productively used.
- Viewed as inherently threatening and negative, the review process creates unwarranted anxiety.

- Leaders' credibility is diminished because the information requested is not used, or its use is not made visible enough.
- Distrust is created because the uses of the information are not conceived and articulated clearly enough from the outset, confidentiality of the report is not clarified, or the various roles in the process are not adequately determined.
- Inaccurate information causes unwarranted embarrassment or pride.
- Attention and time are diverted from the institution's teaching, research, and service functions.
- Resentment arises because the process is not designed to be useful at the program level as well as at higher organizational or system levels.
- The review leads to raised expectations for resources that are unavailable, which causes disappointment (Seeley 1981, p. 56).

On the other hand, program review—"if implemented properly and combined with other retrenchment strategies—can be a major tool for effectively reducing expenditures while maintaining essential program quality" (Barak 1981, p. 219). A study of program reviews in research universities found, not surprisingly, that the benefits were greatest at the program level and least at the institutional level (Poulton 1978). Table 3 displays the nature of the effects at three organizational levels.

The results of graduate program reviews at the University of California indicated several conclusions: (1) the institutions conducting reviews did not save money and, in fact, lost money (if the cost of the review process itself is taken into account); (2) reviews did not uncover previously unknown information; (3) reviews did stimulate change in some situations; (4) the reviews did tend to clarify impressions and develop a fair portrayal of programs; and (5) many of the reviews' recommendations were implemented (Smith 1979, pp. 2–3).

Table 3
Typical Effects of Program Reviews

Organizational Level	Relative Utility	Nature of Changes
Department/Program	Greatest Utility (primarily from single reviews)	• Increased introspection • Revised objectives for teaching and research • Better organized qualitative and quantitative information • Clarified unit/program goals, strengths, and deficiencies • Improved unit procedures • Improved contact among unit members • Improved rationale for resources • Potentially increased frustrations
School/College	Moderate Utility	• Improved information on unit trends and priorities, strengths, and weaknesses • Better indications of unit quality and responsiveness • Adjusted college policies and procedures • Adjusted resource decisions (occasional) • Adjusted organizational structures (occasional)
University Administration	Least Utility (requires accumulation of reviews)	• Revised institutional policies and procedures policies and procedures • Major organizational changes (rare) • Major budgetary commitments or cuts (rare)

Overall, the study concluded that the institution benefited from the reviews. A similar assessment at the University of Iowa took place in 1977, when an ad hoc committee of the faculty senate was appointed to evaluate the program review process on campus (Barak 1982). Through interviews with participants, the committee found that the reviews required a substantial commitment of time and effort but that many positive benefits accrued to the institution. The self-study process was found to benefit the units and to lead to improvements. The reviews also provided systematic information useful in keeping faculty and administrators knowledgeable about programs.

A survey of the program review authority and practices of 37 state-level higher education agencies, paying special attention to results in terms of resources, found:

> Despite the concern about resource savings, only one respondent supplied a dollar figure for resources saved. In fact, 95 percent of the 20 respondents who have discontinued programs do not know the amount of resources saved or reallocated and only 35 percent of those same 20 respondents believe that resources have been saved, even though they could not supply a dollar figure (Skubal 1979, p. 231).

On the basis of these results, one of three possible scenarios is taking place: (1) savings accrued at the institutional level, rather than at the state level; (2) it was impossible to attach a dollar amount to the savings; and (3) the review activity was purely cosmetic—programs being eliminated involved no resources (Skubal 1979). As far as the state boards were concerned, program discontinuance had not had a substantial impact on resources (p. 232).

A study of the effects of program reviews conducted by state-level higher education agencies gave careful attention to the effects of the Louisiana Board of Regents' program reviews involving Louisiana State University-Baton Rouge (LSU) and Northeast Louisiana University (Mingle 1978). At LSU, no cost savings were realized, but the belief persisted that the reviews facilitated cooperation among programs, provided a basis for judging programs' worth and for reallocating resources, stimulated personnel changes, and enhanced quality standards. By contrast, the reviews at Northeast were viewed as biased and as having fostered a "sense of declining prestige and fear for the future" (p. 64).

Reviews conducted by the Florida Board of Regents used outside consultants to review selected programs in the nine universities of the system (Hill, Lutterbie, and Stafford 1979). The consultants' task was to review a particular program at all of the institutions and to make recommendations on "program quality, duplication of programs, financial support, and the need for any additional programs or a shifting of programs in the discipline under review" (p. 3). These reviews provided better documentation of the need for new programs, resulted in a small number of programs' being eliminated, and controlled program growth. Further, the reviews led to the establishment of several cooperative programs among institutions within the system and between those institutions, and private colleges and universities in the state. For example, an engineering consortium was established, and contracts between the state and several private colleges and universities were developed. Further, the reviews helped the board identify underfunded areas and provided some systematic information that could serve as part of a recently initiated planning exercise (pp. 5–8).

While several problems with the review process were noted in Florida, the overall assessment was quite positive. The consultants' reports were believed to have aided greatly in identifying the strengths and weaknesses of programs in the system and in stimulating plans to strengthen some programs and to address important issues in others. "Some of the impact [of the reviews was] felt immediately by the universities, but the larger impact [was] more subtle as the intricate process of change in a multicampus system [was] initiated, developed, and brought to conclusion" (p. 9).

Although some evidence suggests that program reviews are helpful, the basis for this conclusion is weak, because only a few studies have examined effects systematically. Some evidence also suggests that such reviews do not achieve desired results. The stubborn fact is that not much is known about the effects of program review.

An Organizational Perspective for the Effective Practice of Assessment

G. Roger Sell

Although the current emphasis on assessment in higher education is the appraisal of student outcomes (Adelman, 1986, Ewell, 1985), colleges and universities engage in a wide variety of assessment activities. These activities focus not only on students but also on faculty, programs, and the institutions themselves. The treatment of assessment in this chapter reflects an organizational perspective that includes, but goes beyond, student assessment.

There is not a single organizational approach to the study of higher education institutions as organizations but rather several theoretical frameworks, such as bureaucratic (Blau, 1973), collegial (Millett, 1962, 1978), political (Baldridge, 1971), and organized anarchy (Cohen and March, 1974). While each of these approaches emphasizes particular features of and assumptions about colleges and universities, the essence of an organizational perspective is that it brings attention to collective concerns. These concerns include but are not limited to the acquisition of resources to maintain and develop the institution, the allocation of authority and the structure of decision-making processes, the design and performance of work, and the outcomes and impacts associated with an institution.

An organizational perspective on assessment can have a number of benefits. It can help reveal relationships among assessment activities and the use of scarce resources for them. It can help locate and diagnose competing purposes that assessment serves. It can help identify constraints as well as opportunities for assessment in the service of institutions. And it can help formulate actions to remove barriers and provide support for effective assessment practices.

This chapter begins with a broad description and critique of assessment activities in colleges and universities. The ideals of assessment are then discussed along with organizational realities that temper and restrain them. The chapter concludes with some suggested strategies for practicing assessment in such a way that its perils are reduced and its contributions are enhanced.

The Scope of Assessment in Higher Education Institutions

With the primary attention of assessment activities in higher education now focused on student outcomes, those who are calling for more and better assessment have emphasized approaches such as:

- Standardized tests of student knowledge, general as well as specialized
- Follow-up studies of graduates and their careers
- Student attrition and retention studies
- Surveys interviews of students to discuss their perceptions of the quality of their educational experiences, the climate of their institutions, and gains from their educational experiences.

Reprinted from *Achieving Assessment Goals Using Evaluation Techniques–New Directions for Higher Education,* edited by P.J. Gray, no. 67, Jossey-Bass Publishers, Inc. This material is used by permission of John Wiley & Sons, Inc.

One might conclude from listening to and reading the claimsof critics that colleges and universities are neglecting their assessment responsibilities—that little is done in the way of assessment in higher education. From an organizational perspective, however, higher education institutions have been and continue to be actively involved in a wide range of assessment activities. Often these activities are overlooked when assessment is limited to the appraisal of student outcomes using specific measures or techniques.

Most colleges and universities are already doing extensive work in assessment if we define the term *assessment* as a process for informing decisions and judgments through (1) framing questions; (2) designing or selecting instruments and procedures for collecting data; (3) collecting, analyzing, and interpreting data; and (4) reporting and using information that is derived from qualitative as well as quantitative data. Some might object to this broad definition (Hartle, 1986). However, in conversations as well as in the literature, the term *assessment* is often used interchangeably with terms such as *testing, evaluation,* and *appraisal.* While clarity and precision in the use of terminology is surely desirable, the purpose here is not to settle long-standing arguments about the proper domains of research, evaluation, assessment, and related concepts (for a discussion of these terms, see Shalock and Sell, 1971). Readers who are more comfortable with substituting *evaluation* or *appraisal* for the term *assessment* should do so.

The various assessment activities of higher education institutions can be grouped generally into four broad categories. These include student assessment, faculty assessment, program assessment, and institutional assessment.

Student Assessment. While the recent attention given to assessment has focused on measuring institution wide student outcomes, the most frequent and often overlooked form of student assessment occurs in courses and academic departments (McMillan, 1988). Student assessment at the course and department levels frequently serves the primary purpose of awarding grades and credits. However, institutions also conduct student testing for selection and placement before students enroll in courses and sometimes after they matriculate. In addition, some colleges and departments use senior exams, internships, and major projects as capstone experiences for assessing student performance.

Faculty Assessment. Most institutions have at least annual reviews of faculty performance, some for merit salary increases, and virtually all institutions have periodic reviews of faculty for tenure and promotion decisions (Centra, 1979). Some institutions have implemented assessment procedures for the posttenure evaluation of faculty (Bennett and Chater, 1984; Licata, 1986). Faculty are also nominated and judged for distinguished teaching, research, and/or service awards (Beidler, 1986). Each of these activities is an example of some form of assessment as that concept is developed here.

Program Assessment. In addition to accreditation reviewsof academic programs, many institutions have established procedures for internal reviews and self-studies of academic programs (Arns and Poland, 1980; Conrad and Wilson, 1985). Some institutional procedures and responses are linked to state-level program reviews (Barak, 1982; Ohio Board of Regents, 1979). Academic programs are also at times rated or ranked by external reviewers and peers at other institutions (Lawrence and Green, 1980).

Institutional Assessment. Each of the regional accrediting associations conducts periodic reviews of higher education institutions in their area. Self-studies and external visitors are usually part of these reviews. In addition, institutions respond to federal and/or state compliance reviews for affirmative action, auditing and data reporting, health and safety, and so forth. Colleges and universities have also initiated assessments associated with strategic planning and the annual budgeting process (Barak, 1986; Micek, 1980; Shirley and Volkwein, 1978).

A Critique of Assessment Practices

The claim of critics that most colleges and universities are ignoring or neglecting their assessment activities is simply off target. It is not that institutions fail to engage in assessment; rather, institutions may lack systematic and reflective examinations of the purposes that assessment serves and the compatibility of practices with realizing the selected purposes. It would appear that the large portion of assessment activities in universities and colleges is directed more at summary descriptions and periodic judgments about quality than at specific diagnoses for the improvement of performance. Examples of this counterclaim are provided for each of the major groupings of assessment activities.

Student Assessment. Even when we change our instructional objectives, materials, or procedures, it is not uncommon that we use the same tests or other performance measures of student achievement. Student assessment can be conducted on the basis of expediency, habit, or external pressure rather than for ensuring that what we try to assess is worthy of assessment, is related to our instruction and objectives, and is a trustworthy indicator of student learning and development. Student assessment more frequently serves the purpose of awarding credits and grades (Milton, Pollio, and Eison, 1986) than the purpose of providing students with feedback that can improve their learning or providing instructors with feedback that can improve their teaching and courses (Loacker, 1988). One consequence of an overemphasis on grading is that students tend to view academic work through the "grade point average perspective" (Becker, Geer, and Hughes, 1968).

Student assessment and learning can and should be integrally related. Learning, in the broad sense, is both a process and an outcome, resulting in some qualitative change in knowledge, skills, attitudes, and/or values. Feedback resulting from both informal and formal means of student assessment can aid the learning process if that feedback is specific, timely, and on target with clear performance expectations. A test score or grade without such diagnostic feedback or explanation lacks completeness for the learner. Furthermore, frequent opportunities to perform and practice with informed and diagnostic feedback are usually necessary for novice learners to become more expert. The formative use of student assessment can help learners to become more proficient in their own self-assessments and in learning how to learn, as well as in acquiring substantive knowledge and skills (Study Group, 1984).

Similarly, faculty can improve their instructional performance through student assessment. The construction and use of student assessment measures is one of the most critical, yet underemphasized, instructional responsibilities of faculty. No matter what we say our expectations are for student performance, the instruments, procedures, and interpretations we use in student assessment constitute the operational objectives of our instruction. Significant gains can occur in the quality of our instruction when we make changes in our student assessment practices that are consistent with the learning outcomes we wish our students to attain and when we modify our instruction based on what we learn from student assessment. Student performance on carefully selected and developed assessment measures can provide important indicators of instructional practices that are relatively weak or strong. Along with other information, assessment results can help locate particular aspects of instruction that can be improved. In these respects, the quality of student assessment is closely associated with the quality of instruction that students actually experience (Loacker, 1988).

Faculty Assessment. Our disposition toward counting things and quantifying performance is often reflected in decisions about faculty involving promotion, tenure, and merit salary increases (Tuckman, 1976). Examples of the propensity to quantify performance include such measures as the number of published articles in particular refereed journals (indicator of research productivity), student ratings of instructors using Likert-type scales (indicator of teaching productivity), and the number of professional association and university committees served on (indicator of service productivity). The problem is not with these quantitative measures themselves. The problem is that quantitative evidence of faculty performance is susceptible to use independent of the objectives, substance, context, or other circumstances surrounding the tasks that faculty actually perform (Seriven, 1987). Furthermore, an overemphasis on quantifying performance can result in "bottomline" calculations or comparisons that overlook the responsibilities, effort, and outcomes representing individual faculty members' contributions to their academic units.

With regard to formative feedback, faculty have reported generally receiving little (Davey and Sell, 1984, 1985). Prior to fourth-year or sixth-year reviews, new faculty may not have received any detailed and diagnostic feedback from colleagues or the department chairperson. Faculty claims that they are not sure of the basis on which their performance is judged or how their performance could be improved can sometimes be traced to omissions of sound personnel practices (Miller, 1987). Tenured faculty, especially full professors, sometimes do not seek or receive feedback that could improve their teaching, research, or service performance.

In most institutions, the front-line responsibilities for faculty assessment fall on the shoulders of department chairpersons, with faculty committees or the faculty at large contributing recommendations on which the chairpersons are expected to act. The role of the department chairperson in the assessment of faculty is reflected in two main responsibilities. One is to work with faculty in the assessment of colleagues (or prospective colleagues) and of their own performance. Another is to make judgments about the worth and merit of individual faculty for personnel decisions. A complicating factor is that chairpersons tend to walk a thin line between being a faculty colleague and being an administrator (Tucker, 1981).

The responsibilities of department chairpersons imply technical and interpersonal expertise, as well as legal savvy, associated with faculty assessment. Seldom are department chairpersons formally prepared or mentored for their complex roles in faculty development and evaluation. Acquiring knowledge and skills related to chairperson responsibilities for faculty assessment usually occurs on the job and through trial and error. Bennett (1983) illustrates some of these dilemmas and ambiguities faced by academic unit administrators.

Program Assessment. Program reviews may serve a wide range of purposes. When conducted for the purpose of external accreditation or recognition, they tend to be directed toward providing evidence of how well instruction, research, and/or service activities are performed, usually based on perceptions of quality (Conrad and Wilson, 1985). In this sense, not only is feedback for improvement underemphasized but also program weaknesses may be camouflaged or rationalized because of the sanctions they could bring.

External program reviews, similar to student and faculty assessments, often emphasize the quantitative aspects of performance. Examples of such quantitative measures of programs include: the number and high school background of students served; the standardized test scores of students who apply and are admitted; class size; the number of credit hours and grade point averages of students who take particular courses or who are majors in particular programs; the number or percent of undergraduates who are accepted to graduate school or who pass a certifying exam; the publication, citation, and grant record of faculty; the size and currency of physical facilities, equipment, and materials; and so forth. While important judgments about quality are embedded within these kinds of quantitative data, the underlying qualitative factors often must be unraveled and systematically examined in detail to reach a more profound understanding of program quality. Given these kinds of data normally collected and examined during program reviews, we should not be surprised that external program reviews lead to recommendations such as downsizing or eliminating programs, implementing or elevating selective admissions policies, expanding library holdings, updating physical facilities, and conducting more focused or larger research projects. Attention to the detailed and in-depth diagnosis of what and how programs could improve can be easily overlooked in assessments associated with program reviews.

When institutions establish their own form of internal program review, these reviews may be tied to budget decisions or designed to emphasize the improvement purpose of assessment. Using a combination of department and institution wide representatives who concentrate on understanding how a program works and why, internal program reviews can, with proper arrangements, lead to action plans for improving academic performance (Arns and Poland, 1980). Furthermore, internal program reviews can help prepare for external reviews and provide information beyond the quantitative and comparative features of programs.

Institutional Assessment. Many of the comments about external program reviews can also be applied to institutional accreditation reviews, which are usually conducted by one of the regional accrediting associations. The process usually includes an institutional self-study, documentation of evidence responding to several prescribed issues, an on-site visit by a team of external reviewers, and a written report by the review team (North Central Association of Colleges and Schools, 1984). Since there is a relatively long time between institutional accreditation reviews and since such reviews for a complex institution are so vast, they may be perceived more as a formal procedure than as an instrumental undertaking that can result in significant changes for improvement. The recent emphasis of accrediting associations on evidence of student outcomes as part of institutional self-studies has the potential to change some institutional assessment practices, but this development is in an early stage, and its role in using assessment to improve performance is yet to be demonstrated.

The most common form of institutionwide assessment occurs through data bases that are regularly collected and updated. Colleges and universities have a long history of collecting institutional data that can serve a number of useful purposes. Examples of these purposes include recruiting, selecting, and placing students; making judgments about students, faculty, and program performance; forecasting and controlling income and expenditures; scheduling and servicing classroom facilities; and so forth.

However, potential users of institutional data bases may not know they exist, may not have access to them, or may not know how to access them. In some cases, institutions may not be collecting data that would be useful. In other cases, existing institutional data bases may have structural or technical defects, such as the lack of relational properties for linking or comparing two sets of data or the lack of conceptually sound and discrete data categories with explicit definitions of data elements.

Then, too, data that could be useful for institutional assessment are often mindlessly (that is, in a mechanical or routine manner) collected, stored, retrieved, analyzed, and reported. Sometimes mindlessness extends to the use of institutional data because of the form in which they are reported, the lack of contextual information, inadequate preparation of those who use the data, and so forth. For the most part, institutional data are reported and used in a summary fashion—that is, in gross detail and from one time period to the next. Relatively little attention is given to the diagnostic value of institutional data—that is, their use as indicators of what could be improved and what could be looked at in greater detail. Data-rich institutions can still be information poor because (1) the proper data are not available to the relevant users in a timely or convenient fashion, (2) data are viewed as power and access to them is strictly limited, (3) capabilities are lacking for organizing and translating data into useful information for particular audiences, uses, and circumstances, or any combination of these.

When we consider the breadth of student, faculty, program, and institutional assessment activities that colleges and universities undertake, with concomitant commitments of human and financial resources, there appear to be serious shortcomings in realizing the promises of assessment for improvement and development. An institution that effectively practices assessment for both improvement and accountability (including demands originating from sources outside the institution as well as decisions involving resource allocation, personnel decisions, certification, and so forth within the institution) is an ideal that few have realized. After a description of this ideal, some of the organizational realities that confront the practice of assessment are addressed, followed by a discussion of some strategies that could enhance the benefits of assessment.

A Model of the Ideal Self-Assessing Institution

Wildavsky (1972) has given considerable thought to the characteristics of institutions that have strong commitments to assessment. Although Wildavsky did not concentrate on any particular type of organization, the model he describes could be applied to colleges and universities. The ideal college or university, slightly adapted from Wildavsky's description, would have the following characteristics that cut across student, faculty, program, and institutional assessment:

1. Activities would be continuously monitored so as to determine whether goals were being met or even whether those goals should continue to prevail.
2. When assessment suggests that a change in goals or in the means to achieve them is desirable, these proposals would be taken seriously by those in the institution who could effect changes.
3. Organizational members would not have undue vested interests in the continuation of current activities; they would steadily pursue new alternatives to better serve the latest desired outcomes.

4. In some meaningful way, the entire institution would be infused with the assessment ethic, both for accountability and for improvement.
5. Assessments would result in the alteration or abolition of activities when the analyses indicate that changes are desirable.
6. All knowledge would be contingent, because improvement is always possible and change for the better is always in view though not necessarily yet attained.
7. Assumptions would be continuously challenged and reinforced by an attitude of scientific doubt rather than dogmatic commitment.
8. New truth would be sought rather than the defense of old norms and errors, and testing hypotheses would be essential to the main work of the institution.
9. The costs and benefits of alternative strategies (approaches, programs, policies) would be analyzed as precisely as available knowledge permits.
10. Assessments would be open, truthful, and explicit; conclusions would be publicly stated, showing how they were determined and giving others the opportunity to refute them; everything would be aboveboard, nothing would be hidden.

These characteristics of the self-assessing organization would seem on the surface to be entirely compatible with and reinforcing of the nature of academic pursuits in higher education institutions. However, does this model of the ideal assessing organization square with the needs of institutions and their individual members? Assuming that assessment is desirable, to what extent can we reasonably expect that colleges and universities will fully practice it? Which organizational characteristics might account for varying degrees of success with assessment, and how might these characteristics be changed?

Organizational Realities

As Wildavsky (1972) points out, the concepts of organization and assessment may be contradictory notions. At the institutional and academic unit levels, organization provides a structure that, among other things, offers stability for its members, generates and supports long-term commitments to the academic enterprise, and relates existing activities and programs to clientele and sponsors external to the university. Assessment, on the other hand, is an intervention that suggests change or at least the potential for change, that promotes skepticism and criticism, and that seeks to establish (and question) relationships among needs, objectives, and actions.

At the level of the individual faculty member and administrator, the potential conflict between assessment and individual needs is also apparent. The change threshold for individuals is limited. If assessment is forever challenging cherished beliefs and seeking to promote changes on a continuing basis, faculty and administrators could experience disabling stress and anxiety, finding it difficult to get their bearings and being in a quandary about what they should be doing. Continuing assessment activities could lead to severe individual hesitation or random behavior designed to cover as many bases as possible. Widespread confusion among faculty and administrators would produce unacceptable inefficiencies and adversely affect a necessary degree of cohesiveness and stability in academic units and central administration.

Beyond these general considerations, other more specific conditions are encountered in the assessment activities of higher education institutions. Attention is given here to six such organizational conditions that are viewed as restraining or tempering the practice of assessment.

Required Effort and Expertise. If faculty and administrators were fully involved in all aspects of assessment, there would be little time available for other responsibilities related to teaching, research, service, student advising, administration, and external relations. Needs for assessment must be balanced somehow with other institutional responsibilities.

Then, too, not everyone is equally qualified to perform all aspects of assessment. Effective assessment requires a mix of conceptual, technical, and interpersonal skills for which individual faculty and administrators may not be adequately prepared or experienced. Yet my assertion is that, to make formative and summative assessment most useful, faculty and administrators should be involved as practitioners of assessment and not just as passive recipients of assessment information.

Some of the organizational issues related to required effort and expertise for assessment include: To what extent will faculty and administrators be involved in assessment? Are assessment responsibilities considered as part of, or in addition to, ongoing tasks? How will faculty and administrators be supported and rewarded in their continuing professional development of assessment capabilities? If other people besides faculty and administrators will be involved with assessment, what will they be expected to do, with what authority, and in which realms (student, faculty, program, institution) of assessment activities? How will the responsibilities for assessment be divided among faculty administrators and staff, and to what extent will assessment be decentralized?

Costs and Benefits. Resources used for assessment are part of institutional costs, and incremental assessment activities add to institutional costs. On the other hand, existing or new assessment practices can produce benefits not only for satisfying accountability requirements but also for meeting the continuing development needs of students, faculty, programs, and the institution itself.

There is little evidence in the literature that trade-offs between the costs and benefits of various kinds of assessment have been systematically examined (Halpern, 1987). For example, do institutions have a reasonable fix on the cost of student assessment that occurs as a regular part of testing and grading within courses? Have institutions examined what benefits are associated with current assessment practices? Do institutions have any baseline for comparing either the benefits or costs of assessment alternatives?

Ewell and Jones (1986) sidestep these issues in favor of exploring incremental or marginal costs associated with adding new assessment activities, primarily student assessment instruments (tests and surveys) administered at the institutionwide level. They consider the direct costs of instruments constructed locally or purchased from an outside vendor, of administration of the instruments, of instrument scoring and data analysis, and of coordination of the assessment effort. Taking four different types of institutions (private liberal arts college, major public university, comprehensive regional university, and community college), Ewell and Jones construct four sets of institutional cost estimates based on student samples within each kind of institution. Their cost estimates show a range of approximately $29,000 to $130,000 for an annual student assessment program limited to quantifiable indicators within relatively constricted measures of student development. Assuming for the moment the accuracy of these cost estimates, we can see that student assessment (not to mention other aspects of faculty, program, or institutional assessment) can add significantly to institutional costs. These incremental requirements for assessment compete with other institutional priorities for attention and, for most institutions, do so without reference to other ongoing assessment costs or the current and potential benefits from these investments.

In addition to direct and indirect costs for assessment, there are likely to be opportunity costs since attention to assessment could reduce or eliminate effort devoted to other productive activities. Perhaps equally or even more significant, there are additional costs of changes linked to the assessment process and its results. As with other initiatives, a university or college will be limited in the resources it can allocate for assessment and the changes associated with it.

The main point here is that the various costs of assessment should be carefully considered in relation to the actual and potential benefits. Assessment can have both positive and negative effects as well as intended, unintended, and unanticipated outcomes (see Conrad and Wilson, 1985, for a discussion of the possible differences between outcomes and effects). Just as not all change is for the better, not all assessment is for the better. A thorough and continuing examination of the costs and benefits of assessment (current and proposed practices) would seem to be an organizational imperative.

External Support. If the survival and vitality of institutions is dependent, in large part, on the supply of resources (financial, human, and so forth) from their environments (Pfeffer and Salancik, 1978) and if a college or university is not strongly committed to particular programs, clientele, and sponsors (one of the qualities of the self-assessing organization), it may be unreasonable to expect that assessments will lead to the building of external support (although assessment may be required as a condition for funding or accreditation). Furthermore, if one requirement of an organization is to adapt to its environment, it may also be unreasonable to expect that administrators and faculty will select priorities and programs that are based primarily on internal assessments and their justification. Faculty and administrators, for reasons of both self-interest and institutional interest, may interpret and use assessment results with a view toward receiving external support and achieving some relatively high degree of success. The ideals of a higher education institution as a self-assessing organization become suspect, however, if faculty and administrators (1) seek out problems that are easy to solve and changes that are easy to make because they do not require radical departures from the past, (2) hold back assessment information until the time is propitious for its release, or (3) seize an opportunity whether or not the assessments are completed or justified. All of these conditions limit the potential of assessment in colleges and universities.

Internal Politics. Assessments may be wielded as a weapon in institutional wars—that is, they may be used by one party against another or for one cause, policy, or program against another. When this happens, assessment becomes much less than an ideal organizational characteristic as described by Wildavsky (1972). The assessment enterprise depends on a common recognition and respect that the activity is being carried out in order to secure better programs and practices, whatever these may be, and not to support a predetermined position or decision.

Equilibrium and Stress. As with other organizations, higher education institutions require some balance between efforts that provide stability and those that induce changes. If those involved in assessments try to do too much—that is, undertake initiatives that lead to sustained and widespread organizational changes—they risk failure in maintaining a "vote of confidence." If they try to do too little, they risk abandoning their own beliefs and losing the support of their most dedicated followers. The strains of maintaining a balance between change and stability are not easy for those dedicated to assessment. Likewise, the dissemination of assessment information can cause negative side effects that create instability in the organization. If assessment information shows how badly off an institution, program, faculty, or student body is compared to what it ought to be, this can create (or accelerate) paranoia, distrust, or general dissatisfaction detrimental to the college or university and its constituencies.

Rewards and Disincentives. In the ideal situation, the assessment ethic would be infused throughout the institution and would be equitably rewarded. Other considerations (such as required effort, financial implications, external image, internal politics, and stability) can often prevail, however, over assessment initiatives and their results. Furthermore, if assessments are accepted when they lead to a reduction in required resources and rejected when they require increases in expenditures, individuals and organizational units are likely to withhold information or selectively offer information to protect themselves. As Wildavsky (1972) aptly summarizes, "it's the same the whole world over: The analytically virtuous are not necessarily rewarded nor are the wicked (who do not evaluate) punished" (p. 515).

Making Assessment Effective

In view of the organizational realities of most colleges and universities, it is possible to practice effective assessment within some reasonable constraints and expectations. Some actions that administrators and faculty could take are discussed next.

Involve Individuals and Offices with Recognized Authority, Leadership, and Expertise. Wildavsky (1972) observes: "If evaluation is not done at all, if it is done but not used, if used but twisted out of shape, the place to look first is not the technical apparatus but the organization itself" (p. 518). Two important features of college and university organization that are necessary for a viable assessment enterprise are recognized authority and leadership with expertise. Authority is legitimated power (French and Raven, 1968). One approach to attaining such, authority for the assessment function is to institutionalize it in some manner. While the ideal institutionalization of assessment is to diffuse and embed it in activities throughout a college or university, a more common approach is to establish one (centralized) or several (decentralized) units or offices within the institution to spearhead this function. The institutionalization of assessment requires resource commitments that involve a dependable flow of resources beyond one-shot studies. Adequate financial resources for assessment activities, with their associated accountability, might be allocated to established units, such as offices of institutional research, planning, evaluation, or program review; new offices or units charged with the specific mission of assessment or some subset of assessment activities; or external assessors or firms who conduct specific studies for the institution and report to a designated office, committee, or administrator. Whichever arrangements are made for the institutionalization of assessment, the works of Clark (1987) and others have underscored the importance of "organizational culture," especially faculty norms and values, in establishing and maintaining institutional support. The faculty role in staffing and governing the assessment function, wherever it is located, is a critical consideration for its legitimization. A blend of administrative, collegial, and individual authority (Bess, 1988) will probably be necessary for the effective performance of assessment activities in colleges and universities.

The leadership requirement for assessment has at least three dimensions. First, leadership is needed in the form of advocacy for assessment. Without strong and influential advocates for assessment, adequate resources and other forms of authority are not likely to be available. Second, leadership is required in the practice of assessment. If we assume that proper assessment requires both expertise and dedicated effort, relating assessment activities to the most important concerns of faculty, academic units, and central offices is a significant leadership task. Arrangements for the support and reward of those engaged in assessment is also associated with this leadership task. Third, leadership is needed in the allocation and use of computer technology for assessment. Two particular kinds of expertise for technology-related assessment activities are becoming more evident. These are the design and development of academic information systems that conveniently link data to the tasks that faculty and administrators perform and the translation of data into information and knowledge that is useful for particular audiences and purposes. The potential of assessment activities to support organizational inquiry is closely linked to the effective use of computer technology (Fincher, 1985; Rohrbaugh and McCartt, 1986).

Undertake Affordable Assessments That Demonstrate Effects. If one of the deficiencies of ineffective organizations is that they do not learn well from their experiences, an effective organization seeks to inquire into its experiences and to organize related information so that knowledge can be gained from these informations (Mandelbaum, 1979). The most important part of this process is to select organizational questions that are worthy of pursuit and that are susceptible to some form of disciplined inquiry within available resources. In other words, assessment activities must be affordable while addressing questions and issues of significance to the quality and effectiveness of the institution. Cameron (1987) provides a conceptual framework for examining literature on the quality and effectiveness of higher education institutions.

Assessments and their results should also be more than a set of good ideas without a notion of how they can be implemented. The proof of a good idea is that it works when tried, realizing that implementation may require a number of trials, errors, and their associated learnings. The implementation of new assessment practices, as well as changes resulting from assessment activities, may depend on the ability of those who produce the changes to make others (including those outside the institution and clients) pay for the associated costs. If the change makers are themselves forced to bear the financial brunt of their actions, they are likely to become conservative and try to stabilize their environment (Wildavsky 1972). This all suggests that some slack resources may be required within the institution for assessment practices to be effective.

In addition, the selection, design, and use of assessments should be informed by the diagnosis of costs and benefits of associated with current and alternative courses of action. An examination of the cost-effectiveness or cost-benefit of assessment alternatives should include the immediate resources and effects attributed to particular practices as well as the longer-term ones.

Maintain Discretion, Diversity, and Flexibility. Assessments that become public and reveal findings or promote changes that are perceived as detrimental to institutional constituencies are likely to be rejected by them. In addition, assessment information should be always treated with sensitivity and discretion.

Just as diversity of programs can enable institutions to be more responsive to a range of problems and clientele, a similar case could be built for the diversity of assessment practices. Placing all of the assessment eggs in one methodological basket—such as standardized instruments or informal ways of assessing student outcomes—is not a sound strategy for any institution. Neither is it sound practice for an institution to emphasize only one dimension of assessment (for example, the cognitive development of students in quantitative reasoning or the lecture performance of faculty in multimethod courses) to the exclusion of other dimensions that are necessary to understand and enrich the meaning of particular findings. Again, some reasonable balance should be sought between being spread too thinly across assessment methods and topics and concentrating attention on only one area. Teaching and learning and the environments that influence them are complex phenomena that require suitably matched approaches to assessment. Being wed to only one approach or area of assessment not only limits the realms of understanding but also constrains the ability of the institution to shift its assessment strategy.

Form Internal Coalitions to Cooperative Endeavors. Institutional assessment activities, in the broad view, are political in the sense of policy or program advocacy. "Without a steady source of political support . . . assessment will suffer the fate of abandoned children" (Wildavsky, 1972, p. 515). In addition, effective assessment is simply not possible without adequate data that can be turned into useful and timely information. To secure data from various sources, assessment activities require cooperation. The incentives (or potential gains) for cooperation must outweigh the disincentives (or potential losses).

Building support for assessment and related concerns in the institution usually requires some internal selling and, frequently, the formation of coalitions or special-interest groups. However, "political muscle" within colleges and universities must be exercised cautiously and within the rules for exercising power (more precisely, authority or legitimated power) with respect to particular decisions and decision-making processes. University policies, faculty rules, governance structures, and administrative procedures each play a part in shaping the arena in which decisions related to assessment are made and implemented. In addition, as noted earlier, the culture of colleges and universities often characterized by faculty autonomy, academic freedom, discipline affiliations and specializations, and decentralization of authority—plays a powerful role in shaping decisions and decision-making processes (Clark, 1987).

Attend to Institutional Characteristics and Readiness to Change in Assessment Design and Implementation. Assessments of student outcomes, general education curricula, or faculty performance can occur without regard to the particular characteristics of a college or university or its readiness to support assessment initiatives. However, unless key organizational factors are anticipated and accommodated or changed in assessment activities, it is highly unlikely that existing assessment practices will be altered or made more effective. Examples of organizational features of colleges and universities that should be examined for their changeability in relationship to assessment activities and findings include: institutional mission, priorities, and diversity of programs; course schedules and offerings; instructional formats and approaches; academic calendars; space and equipment restrictions; budgeting processes and financial resources available; faculty assignments and workloads; student selection, enrollment, and graduation requirements; collective bargaining agreements (if applicable); and so forth.

Assessment can be adapted to particular organizational characteristics as well as serve as an organizational change agent. Both individual and organizational changes are potentially involved in implementing assessment practices. The success of assessment may depend on readiness to change—that is, readiness to accept certain assessment practices or to implement recommendations growing out of assessment findings. When individual faculty members or administrators are the focus, readiness for change can involve a combination ofattitudes, values, beliefs, skills, and knowledge about assessment and its uses. When organizational units and the total organization are the focus, readiness for change can involve a combination of structures, rewards, norms, resources, and policies that bear on assessment (Abedor and Sachs, 1978).

Those involved in deliberation about undertaking new assessment initiatives could profitably address the following issues: Is the institution (faculty, students, administrators, support staff, trustees) prepared to undertake new assessment practices with reasonable expectations for success? What can be done to prepare individuals and organizational units for a proposed change in assessment? How can assessment practices accommodate needs for individual and organizational stability while providing evidence for changes that can lead to improvements?

Build Community That Values Assessment. One of the most fundamental steps for colleges and universities wishing to upgrade their assessment practices is to ascertain whether prevalent values in the institution support the notion of assessment and, if not, what can be done to develop support. Two shared values, in particular, are directly related to the effective practice of assessment.

One value is an orientation toward experimentation and reasonable risk taking. Experiments are necessary for testing hypotheses and relating goals and objectives to results in the context of limited resources. In this sense, a college or university is a natural laboratory for experimentation and for assessment aimed at the improvement of performance.

Cooperation and collaboration comprise a second shared value essential to an effective assessment program. If the primary orientation of faculty and administrators is that organizational members (and units) are competing for a fixed pie of limited resources and if information about individuals and units is a powerful source to be protected, then collaboration within and across groups is likely to be limited. If, however, the primary orientation is that the pie of organizational resources can expand and that the performance of individuals and units is interdependent, then there is a much more positive environment for cooperation in assessment activities. Astin (1985) discusses these and other issues related to values that underlie concepts of quality in higher education.

The sense of trust among individuals and groups underlies cooperative acts beneficial to assessment activities. The credibility and equitability of assessment activities can, in turn, build trust that promotes cooperation and an experimental attitude. However, more assessment information alone will not necessarily lead to greater agreement or collaboration if the institution is wracked by fundamental differences in values. Assessment need not create agreement, but it may presuppose agreement (Wildavsky, 1972).

Conclusion

I do not wish to play down the importance of student outcomes assessment. It is terribly important, is often not adequately attended to, and should be vigorously and thoughtfully pursued on each college and university campus. Beginning with work initiated almost two decades ago at the Western Interstate Commission for Higher Education (Lawrence, Weathersby, and Patterson, 1970) and extended through current work at the National Center for Higher Education Management Systems (NCHEMS) under the leadership of Peter Ewell and Dennis Jones, I have been both an observer and participant in the formative stages of the assessment movement. For example, the NCHEMS student outcomes structure was applied in my work on adult and continuing education with the late John Putnam at the National Center for Education Statistics (Putnam and Sell, 1983). I have also been fortunate for nearly the past ten years to be located at an institution that has provided "hands-on" experiences with student assessment as a teacher, researcher, consu tant, and administrator for an office of instructional development and evaluation. All of these experiences have enhanced, not reduced, my sense of the importance of student outcomes assessment.

What I have tried to emphasize in this chapter is the organizational context and forces within colleges and universities that inhibit as well as nurture assessment in its many forms. I have tried to say that student outcomes assessment is never separate from other institutional issues, is affected and used by other kinds of assessment activities, and should be carefully examined for its avowed purposes, actual uses, and consequences. Throughout this chapter I have pleaded a case for balance—of the purposes that assessment serves, of methodological approaches and foci for assessment, of effort given to assessment and other critical activities, and of response to external concerns while continuing to develop and improve individual and organizational performance.

I wish to conclude on an upbeat note. The outlook for the future of higher education and for the contribution of assessment to that future has never been brighter. With the possible exception of the late 1960s and early 1970s, higher education is more visible and more widely discussed today than in any preceding period. All kinds of audiences and stakeholders have high expectations for colleges and universities and the models and benefits that they provide for other segments of society.

I believe that most institutions are becoming highly sophisticated in dealing with a variety of assessment issues. Many of these assessment issues will continue into the next decade, but some new challenges and opportunities will also present themselves. If we are able to balance and meet the competing needs for our attention and to use assessment for enhancing the worth of individuals as well as our institutions, we will be on our way toward building strong colleges and universities for the twenty-first century.

References

Abedor, A. J., and Sachs, S. G. "The Relationship Between Faculty Development, Organizational Development, and Instructional Development: Readiness for Instructional Innovation in Higher Education. In R. K. Bass and D. B. Lumsden (eds.) *Instructional Development: The State of the Art.* Columbus, Ohio: Collegiate Publishing, 1978.

Adelman, C. *Assessment in Higher Education.* Washington, D.C.: Office of Educational Research and Improvement, U.S. Department of Education, 1986.

Arns, R. G., and Poland, W. "Changing the University Through Program Review." *Journal of Higher Education,* 1980, 51(3), 268–285.

Astin, A. W. *Achieving Educational Excellence: A Critical Assessment of Priorities and Practices in Higher Education.* San Francisco: Jossey-Bass, 1985.

Baldridge, J. V. *Power and Conflict in the University.* New York: Wiley, 1971.

Barak, R. J. *Program Review in Higher Education: Within and Without.* Boulder, Colo: National Center for Higher Education Management Systems, 1982.

Barak, R. J. "The Role of Program Review in Strategic Planning." *Association for Institutional Research Professional File,* 1986, 26, 4–7.

Becker, H.S., Geer, B., and Hughes, E. C. *Making the Grade: The Academic Side of College Life. New York:* Wiley, 1968. Beidler, P. G. (ed.). *Distinguished Teachers on Effective Teaching: Observation on Teaching by College Professors Recognized by the Council for Advancement and Support of Education.* New Direction for Teaching and Learning, no. 28. San Francisco: Jossey-Bass, 1986.

Bennett, J. B. *Managing the Academic Department: Cases and Notes.* New York: American Council on Education, 1983.

Bennett, J. B., and Chater, S. S. "Evaluating the Performance of Tenured Faculty Members." *Educational Record,* 1984, 65, 38–41.

Bess, J. L. *Collegiality and Bureaucracy in the Modern University.* New York: Teachers College, Columbia University, 1988.

Blau, P. M. *The Organization of Academic Work.* New York: Wiley, 1973.

Cameron, K. S. "Improving Academic Quality and Effectiveness." In M. W. Peterson (ed.), *Key Resources on Higher Education Governance, Management, and Leadership: A Guide to the Literature.* San Francisco: Jossey-Bass, 1987.

Centra, J. A. *Determining Faculty Effectiveness: Assessing Teaching, Research, and Service for Personnel Decisions and Improvement.* San Francisco: Jossey-Bass, 1979.

Clark, B. R. *The Academic Life: Small Worlds, Different Worlds.* Princeton, N.J.: Princeton University Press, 1987.

Cohen, M. D., and March, J. G. *Leadership and Ambiguity;* New York: McGraw-Hill, 1974.

Conrad, C. F., and Wilson, R. F. *Academic Program Review: Institutional Approaches, Expectations, and Controversies.* ASHE-ERIC Higher Education Report, no.5. Washington, D.C.: Association for the Study of Higher Education, 1985.

Davey, K. B., and Sell, G. R. "The Role Evaluation Could Play in Improving and Developing Instructional Excellence in a Doctoral-Granting University." Paper presented at the joint meeting of the Evaluation Research Society and Evaluation Network, San Francisco, October 11, 1984.

Davey, K. B., and Sell, G. R. "Instructional Evaluation for Development/Improvement: Fact or Fiction Based on a Case Study of Faculty Practices?" Paper presented at the annual meeting of the American Educational Research Association, Chicago, April 1, 1985.

Ewell, P. T. (ed.). *Assessing Educational Outcomes,* New Directions for Institutional Research, no. 47. San Francisco: Jossey-Bass, 1985.

Ewell, P. T., and Jones, D. P. "The Costs of Assessment." In C. Adelman (ed.), *Assessment in Higher Education.* Washington, D.C.: Office of Educational Research and Improvement, U.S. Department of Education, 1986.

Fincher, C. "The Art and Science of Institutional Research." In M.W. Peterson and M. Corcoran (eds.), *Institutional Research in Transition.* New Directions for Institutional Research, no. 46. San Francisco: Jossey-Bass, 1985.

French, R. P., and Raven, B. "The Bases of Social Power." In D. Cartwright and A. Zander (eds.), *Group Dynamics: Research and Theory.* (3rd ed.) New York: Harper & Row, 1968.

Helpern, D. F. (ed.) *Student Outcomes Assessment: What Institutions Stand to Gain.* New Directions for Higher Education, no. 59. San Francisco: Jossey-Bass, 1987.

Hartle, T. W. "The Growing Interest in Measuring the Educational Achievement of College Students." In C. Adelman (ed.), *Assessment in Higher Education.* Washington, D.C.: Office of Educational Research and Improvement, U.S. Department of Education, 1986.

Lawrence, B., Weathersby, G., and Patterson, V. W. *Outputs of Higher Education: Their Identification, Measurement, and Evaluation.* Boulder, Colo.: Western Interstate Commission for Higher Education, 1970.

Lawrence, J. K., and Green , K. C. *A Question of Quality: The Higher Education Ratings Game.* AAHE-ERIC Higher Education Report, no. 5, Washington, D.C.: American Association for Higher Education, 1980.

Licata, C. M. *Post-tenure Faculty Evaluation: Threat or Opportunity.* ASHE-ERIC Higher Education Report, no. 1. Washington, D.C.: Association for the Study of Higher Education, 1986.

Loacker, G. "Faculty as a Force to Improve Instruction Through Assessment." In H. McMillian (ed.), *Assessing Students' Learning.* New Directions for Teaching and Learning, no. 34. San Francisco: Jossey-Bass, 1988.

McMillan, J. H. (ed.), *Assessing Students' Learning.* New Directions for Teaching and Learning. no. 34. San Francisco: Jossey-Bass, 1988.

Mandelbaum, S.J. "The Intelligence of Universities." *Journal of Higher Education,* 1979, 50(6), 697–725.

Micek, S. S. (ed.). *Integrating Academic Planning and Budgeting in a Rapidly Changing Environment.* Boulder, Colo.: National Center for Higher Education Management Systems, 1980.

Miller, R. I. *Evaluating Faculty for Promotion and Tenure.* San Francisco: Jossey-Bass, 1987.

Millett, J. D. *The Academic Community.* New York: McGraw-Hill, 1962.

Millett, J. D. *New Structures of Campus Power. Success and Failures of Emerging Forms of Institutional Governance.* San Francisco: Jossey-Bass, 1978.

Milton, O., Pollio, H. R., and Eison, J.A. *Making Sense of College Grades: Why the Grading System Does Not Work and What Can Be Done About It.* San Francisco: Jossey-Bass, 1986.

North Central Association of Colleges and Schools. *A Handbook of Accreditation.* Chicago: Commission on Institutions of Higher Education, North Central Association of Colleges and Schools, 1984.

Ohio Board of Regents. *Developing a Process Model for Institutional and State-Level Review and Evaluation of Academic Programs.* Columbus: Ohio Board of Regents, 1979.

Pfeffer, J., and Salancik, G.R. *The External Control of Organizations: A Resource-Dependence Perspective.* New York: Harper & Row, 1978.

Putnam, J.F., and Sell, G. R. *Adult Learning Activities: A Handbook of Terminology for Classifying and Describing the Learning Activities of Adults.* Washington, D.C.: National Center for Education Statistics, 1983.

Rohrbaugh, J., and McCartt, A. T. (eds.). *Applying Decision Support Systems in Higher Education.* New Directions for Institutional Research, no. 49. San Francisco: Jossey-Bass, 1986.

Schalock, H. D., and Sell, G. R. "A Framework for the Analysis and Empirical Investigation of Educational RDD&E." In H. D. Schalock and G. R. Sell (eds.), *The Oregon Studies in Educatinal Research, Development, Diffusion, and Evaluation (RDD&E): Conceptual Framework.* Monmouth, Ore.: Teaching Research, A Division of the Oregon State System of Higher Education, 1971.

Scriven, M. "Validity in Personnel Evaluation." Journal of Personnel Evaluation in Education, 1987, 1(1), 9–23.

Shirley, R. C., and Volkwein, J. F. "Establishing Academic Program Priorities." *Journal of Higher Education,* 1978, 49 (5), 472–489.

Study Group on the Conditions of Excellence in American Higher Education. *Involvement in Learning: Realizing the Potential of American Higher Education.* Washington, D.C.: National Institute of Education, 1984.

Tucker, A. *Chairing the Academic Department: Leadership Among Peers.* Washington, D.C.: American Council on Education, 1981.

Tuckman, H. P. *Publication, Teaching, and the Academic Reward Structure.* Lexington, Mass.: Health, 1976.

Wildavsky, A. "The Self-Evaluating Organization." *Public Administration Review,* 1972, 32 (5), 509–520.

Involving Faculty Members in Assessment

Carol Schneider

Discourse

Daniel Resnick and Marc Goulden have argued recently that there is a close connection between periods of rapid expansion and innovation in American higher education and renewed attention to assessment. We saw such a connection in the first part of this century, when rapid curricular and institutional development gave way—in the late 1920s and 1930s—to comprehensive examinations. Comprehensives were seen as a way to redress both the loss of coherence and the erosion of standards in college and university education. American higher education has entered an analogous period of consolidation and review in the 1980s following the unprecedented expansion, both in scope and student numbers, of postsecondary education. The current interest in assessment serves both as index and strategy for our current self-examination.

The Consequences of Assessment

As many commentators have pointed out, however, the current assessment movement is beset by contradictory impulses. One impulse is a laudable concern for the substance and quality of student learning. As programs have become more fragmented, and as students have become more diverse in background and preparation, many proponents of assessment see the study of learning outcomes and "value added" as a way to focus attention on both fundamental educational goals and on the quality of learning in relation to those goals. AAC's own 1985 and 1988 reports on the baccalaureate degree and on general education each reflect this view of assessment. From this perspective, assessment is seen as diagnostic, providing a way to help focus students, faculty members, and institutional resources on common goals and on areas where additional effort is needed.

At the national level, in some state legislatures, and even on many campuses, however, assessment is demanded as evidence of higher education's willingness to be "accountable" to the constituencies it serves. The consequences of this accountability can be both unclear and intimidating. The outcomes of institutional and program assessment may have budgetary implications; they may have program implications. Does one penalize a program whose assessments show problems? Or endow it with extra resources? When a system is involved, how will its different elements fare comparatively once the assessment findings are compiled? The potential consequences of accountability can make institutions reluctant rather than eager to provide documentation about the quality of real learning on their campuses.

A further danger of this focus on assessment as a means of public accountability is that it can make data-based portraits of outcomes ends in themselves. This prospect has troubling implications both for the choice of assessment instruments and for questions about who will be actively

Reprinted from *Liberal Education* 74, no. 3, (May 1988), Association of American Colleges & Universities.

involved in implementing and interpreting the assessment. In terms of assessment instruments, assessors often face trade-offs concerning interinstitutional comparability versus local usability. When a program, department, or colleg develops assessment approaches and instruments that are highly responsive to its priorities and traditions, it generally yields ease of comparability with other institutions. Bobby Fong's article on external examiners and Clifford Adelman's report on an approach to assessing student learning in biology each reflect this difficulty. Conversely, as Ted Marchese's report on "The Uses of Assessment" makes clear, when a college concerned with showing how it compares to others selects available normed tests for its assessments, it often finds itself with a result that is hard to connect usefully to its programs and faculty priorities. Moreover, as both Fong and Stephen Ehrmann suggest, an institution—simply by choosing a standardized test for its assessments—may generate faculty incredulity that the findings measure anything either significant or important.

The Consequences of Bypassing Faculty

A related and even more basic concern is that assessment focused on the production of public portraits may become the primary responsibility of an office of research specialists producing reports that have no effect on the classroom. The assessment experts report findings, and some of the results may lead to the development of new program interventions: more tutoring in math, an expansion of the writing program, better student placements. The danger is that it is entirely possible to mount such assessment programs in ways that bypass almost completely the typical faculty member in the typical classroom. Yet to bypass faculty members is to bypass those interactions around teaching, learning, and classroom-level assessment that are fundamental to strengthening the quality of student learning and achievement.

The reality compounding this danger, unfortunately, is that many faculty members are very ready to be bypassed by the assessment movement. When I first began attending conference sessions on assessment five or six years ago, I observed that they typically attracted assessment specialists and academic administrators. The rare faculty member or two joining such a group was the exception who proved the rule. As either topic or process, assessment—especially assessment that leads to the possibility of formed comparisons—does not interest faculty members. In fact, many faculty members believe fervently, as one asserted to me, "The things I value in my teaching cannot be quantified with scores and numbers."

Although assessment has since become far more visible on the educational agenda, little or nothing has happened to alter such longstanding faculty attitudes. Faculty responses to the furor over assessing learning outcomes range from neutrality to active hostility. Some see assessment as make-work. One faculty member at a selective liberal arts college told me, "We work closely with our students. They go to Yale, Harvard, Columbia, and other top institutions for graduate school. We faculty members are very busy and we just don't see a need to spend our limited time finding new ways of asking questions about what they are learning. Others, in similar institutions, tie the whole assessment movement to William Bennett's administration in the U.S. Department of Education, and wait impatiently for the day that both Bennett and the assessment initiative will retire from view.

In other settings, where assessment is not a voluntary activity, faculty members are often similarly skeptical. Some departments are apprehensive about pending assessment initiatives, seeing their students' academic weaknesses as symptoms of longstanding and perhaps systemic problems that they cannot hope to redress in a single course. Other faculty members echo the skepticism of those who think that gathering numbers can never address the most important questions about teaching and learning.

Yet if the resources now being devoted to assessment of student learning are to make any difference at all in the quality of either student learning or educational programs, assessment initiatives must centrally involve faculty members. Faculty members need to be involved in the formulation of the important questions to be asked through assessment, in decisions about the strategies to be used in asking questions, and above all in the interpretation of the findings. Despite faculty apprehensions, there is no inherent need for assessment strategies to be crippling reductionist—excluding nuances and differences among students' patterns of development. Indeed, as the articles in this issue imply, assessment need not be primarily quantifiable. It can and should bring into play the qualities of judgment and interpretation that faculty possess in abundance.

The critical factor is that faculty need to become *collectively engaged* in the assessment of both programs and learning. Such engagement requires a shift in emphasis from technical decisions—about which instruments to use—to strategic questions about how to generate the widest possible institutional learning from the interpretation of the findings. If the ultimate objective of assessment is to find ways of strengthening students' learning, then it defeats the purpose to delegate assessment to an office—or even to a committee of faculty members—whose deliberations and activities only peripherally involve the majority of their colleagues.

Assessment can and should be an opportunity for faculty members responsible for departments and programs to come together to revisit the purposes of these programs and consider ways of learning from evidence that can be gathered and collectively interpreted at central points in those programs. In such a process, faculty members may well be interested in the results of standardized tests. But they might find it even more valuable to collect portfolios of students' analytic work during the course of a program and to assess the quality of that work over time. Clifford Adelman's article in this issue on a proposed strategy for assessing learning in biology describes a matrix of outcomes and evidence that could be used for gathering and assessing such portfolios. Faculty members working together can develop other effective approaches.

Reviewing such portfolios allows faculty members to see and evaluate both the kinds of challenges their programs are placing before students and students' development in meeting those challenges. Over time, such a review is likely to lead to something now absent on most college campuses: searching discussion of the kinds of challenges that should be put before students and of the differences between entry-level, intermediate, and genuinely advanced work in a program.

The articles in this issue and the several programs described in Praxis—describe approaches to assessment that can centrally involve faculty members. Ted Marchese's introduction to our Praxis section provides important suggestions about ways to link assessment to questions that faculty—and other members of the community—want to pursue. Stephen Ehrmann takes on the knotty and challenging question of how we assess the open-ended and unique uses that students ought to be making of their college experience. He stresses the importance of course assignments to assessment that is likely to influence learning, and he suggests ways that technology can improve both the quality of our assignments to students and our ability to learn—and help students learn—from their performance on those assignments. He points out, moreover, that students' unique uses of the curriculum can become a basis for program evaluation as well as for individual assessment and that technology can help us achieve that elusive synthesis.

Many of the campus attempts to assess learning outcomes have focused on general education. But for most students, and indeed for faculty members, the major is the most important element of the education experience. Bobby Fong and Clifford Adelman each address national projects to find ways of identifying and assessing the most important outcomes for learning in the major.

Finally, George Klemp's Perspective brings us full circle from assessment back to questions of goals. Our current assessment efforts are highly focused, as both Fong and Adelman indirectly illustrate, on content and cognitive process outcomes of undergraduate learning. But as Klemp's comments on assessment findings from the world of work suggest, there may be other outcomes from liberal learning that are also important and make a critical difference to the quality of a graduate's life beyond campus. Klemp introduces another dimension to the assessment question. We need to know not just how well we are doing with our educational priorities but whether the priorities themselves capture the full range of our students' learning needs.

Notes

1. Daniel P. Resnick and Marc Goulden, "Assessment, Curriculum, and Expansion: A Historical Perspective," in Student Outcomes Assessment: What Institutions Stand to Gain, ed. Diane F. Halpern, New

Directions for Education series, no. 59 (San Francisco: Jossey-Bass, 1987), 77–88. The Halpern volume is a helpful introduction to the whole topic of outcomes-based assessment. It contains informative reports on campus struggles to find assessment strategies appropriate to curricular objectives.

2. Select Committee on the Project on Redefining the Meaning and Purpose of Baccalaureate Degrees, *Integrity in the College Curriculum* (Washington, D.C.: Association of American Colleges, 1985); Task Force on General Education, *A New Vitality in General Education* (Washington, D.C.: Association of American Colleges, 1988).

CURRENT READINGS

ENCOURAGING INVOLVEMENT IN ASSESSMENT

CATHERINE A. PALOMBA AND TRUDY W. BANTA

INVOLVE (*v.*): to include or occupy

Of all the important factors in creating a successful assessment program, none matters more than widespread involvement of those who are affected by it. For this reason, it is vital that faculty have a strong role in the assessment process. Indeed, as one observer has said, "If administrators want faculty to shape the assessment process, then they need to turn assessment over to faculty" Pitts, Lowe, Ranieri, and Palomba, 1997). Students, too, need to be valued participants in the assessment process. In this chapter, we discuss several approaches for involving faculty and students in assessment. (Many of our suggestions apply equally well to involving professional staff who have responsibilities for educating students.)

Involving Faculty in Assessment

In this section of the chapter, we consider ways to ensure that faculty take the lead in carrying out assessment programs. We have organized our discussion around three Rs of faculty involvement: responsibility, resources, and rewards. Faculty need to have clearly defined roles, they need to have resources to learn about and understand assessment, and they need to receive rewards for their efforts such as recognition, stipends, or funds for assessment-related travel. If these three Rs are used wisely, they will help overcome another R of assessment, faculty resistance.

Faculty Responsibility

To ensure assessment is a faculty-driven activity, faculty must have responsibility for carrying it out. Initially, faculty should articulate the purposes of assessment for the campus or unit, select a comfortable definition of assessment, and identify the central questions or areas of inquiry that will drive assessment activities. Further, they should develop learning objectives, create assessment plans, select and design assessment tools, interpret results, and develop recommendations based on assessment findings. In other words, faculty need to be involved in all steps of the assessment process.

Carrying out these responsibilities will take several forms and will differ from individual to individual. Some faculty will serve as assessment coordinators in their departments. Some will serve on department, division, or campuswide committees that provide direction for assessment. Serving on assessment committees puts faculty in leadership roles with respect to assessment and often

Reprinted from *Assessment Essentials: Planning, Implementing and Improving Assessment in Higher Education*, (1999), Jossey-Bass Publishers, Inc. This material is used by permission of John Wiley & Sons, Inc.

becomes a major responsibility for them. Committee members generally are more knowledgeable about assessment matters and more involved in making decisions about assessment. Although the number of faculty members serving on assessment committees may be small, other faculty will participate in assessment by attending meetings, administering assessment instruments in their classes, providing comments, and responding to other requests with respect to assessment. Some faculty will have responsibility for analyzing data or writing reports. Where possible, their interests should drive how they contribute. For example, those who enjoy planning should plan, and those who enjoy working with data should conduct analysis. Ann Ferren warns assessment leaders to "set realistic goals for faculty involvement" (1993, p. 3) and to expect involvement to be "episodic" with faculty moving in and out of active roles (p. 5).

Certain approaches to assessment lead to more involvement than others. On some campuses, faculty who are teaching general studies courses are asked to demonstrate that these courses are meeting the learning goals of the program. Thus course instructors must work together as they develop and carry out a plan for assessing the course. In this approach, the responsibility for assessment is placed directly on individual classroom teachers, usually with a campuswide committee that acts as a review body for the reports it receives from faculty.

An explicit list of expectations about the roles of various groups involved in the assessment process can help clarify and establish responsibilities. After faculty on the graduate curriculum and assessment committee (GCAC) of Ball State's College of Business developed a draft assessment plan for the MBA program, they created a statement of responsibilities for all parties, including individual faculty members, students, and the GCAC. The plan and statement were then presented to the entire graduate faculty for approval. Sharing the statement with all faculty made it clear what was expected of them, as well as what they could expect of others (N. Palomba, 1997). Exhibit 5.1 displays this statement.

EXHIBIT 5.1
Participation in Assessment of the MBA Program

Faculty, Students, and the Graduate Curriculum
and Assessment Committee (GCAC)

MBA faculty are expected to provide the GCAC with

- A checklist of course coverage vis-à-vis MBA program objectives
- A copy of the course syllabus
- An assessment plan that indicates how program objectives addressed in the course will be assessed
- An assessment report with results and conclusions
- Exam questions for the MBA Core Competency examination

MBA students are expected to

- Participate in written assessment projects
- Maintain examples of their classroom assignments
- Complete a Core Competency Exam

The GCAC will

- Review faculty checklists to determine if program objectives are being met
- Review course assessment plans and reports
- Review selected examples of student work
- Review the results of the Core Competency Exam
- Provide faculty with feedback and opportunities for discussion at each stage of the assessment process

Assessment Resources for Faculty

The resources provided for faculty must mirror faculty responsibilities. Information about the reasons for undertaking assessment, strategies for formulating learning outcomes, and possible approaches for writing assessment plans are all important topics and well worth any time spent on them. Only after faculty are comfortable with the basics of assessment should time be spent on learning about methods. Here, we describe some of the assessment resources available to faculty.

Written Materials Developed on Campus

Many institutions have developed assessment materials for internal use. Some of these are meant for all faculty regardless of their disciplines; others have been developed within departments or colleges and are discipline specific. Examples include pamphlets describing assessment, question and answer documents, and loose-leaf binders containing assessment materials that can be supplemented as time passes. Several campuses use assessment newsletters that keep faculty up to date on what is happening locally as well as in the overall field of assessment. At Southern Illinois University Edwardsville (SIUE), assessment office staff have placed a number of faculty development resources on the Assessment Web Page (D. J. Eder, personal communication, Sept. 22, 1997). Some campuses have developed workbooks that contain comprehensive information about assessment (Rogers and Sando, 1996; Wolf, 1993; Palomba and others, 1992). Eastern Michigan University has created both a "Questions and Answers About Assessment in the Academic Major at EMU" brochure and a monthly newsletter with the title "Assessment Matters" (Bennion, Collins, and Work, 1994).

There are specific points in the assessment process where it is particularly helpful to provide faculty with resource materials that can facilitate their tasks. For example, the work of faculty who are asked to create plans to assess their programs can be greatly enhanced if they have an outline to follow. Other helpful materials include a list of characteristics of good assessment plans or a list of criteria that will be used to critique plans after they are submitted. At Ohio University such criteria include a clear statement of goals, faculty involvement, use of multiple measures from entry to exit, use of data collected centrally, and evidence that data are used to direct improvements (A. M. Williford, personal communication, Sept. 19, 1997). If faculty are expected to submit annual assessment reports, providing them with a report outline is helpful. Criteria for evaluating reports about assessment activities can also be developed and shared with faculty.

Written Materials from Other Sources

Several helpful books have been written about assessment (Banta and Associates, 1993; Banta, Lund, Black, and Oblander, 1996; Gainen and Locatelli, 1995; Nichols, 1995a, 1995b) that provide overviews of the process and specific examples about the experiences of many institutions and departments. *Assessment Update*, a bimonthly publication, is another valuable source, not only for examples of assessment in practice but also for more general discussions of assessment trends. The American Association for Higher Education Assessment Forum has published a helpful resource guide, *Learning Through Assessment* (Gardiner, Anderson, and Cambridge, 1997), that contains annotated bibliographies as well as descriptions of several assessment instruments. Another useful way to obtain written assessment materials is to request them from other institutions. The practice of assessment has been marked by a tremendous willingness of institutions to share with one another. For example, many campuses have developed Web sites containing assessment materials, including Montana State University and George Mason University (Connolly and Lambert, 1997).

National, Regional, and State Conferences

The American Association for Higher Education (AAHE) began its annual assessment conference more than a decade ago and continues to draw more than a thousand participants each year. This conference provides sessions that cover many areas of assessment, including examples from individual campuses and discussions of assessment issues. The annual assessment conference in Indianapolis is now in its eighth year, and for six years prior to the move to its present site it was held in Knoxville, Tennessee. Alverno

College regularly conducts one-day sessions that provide participants with information about ability-based curriculum design. Participants are invited to spend "A Day at Alverno College" focused on teaching and assessing student abilities. For more than a decade, a number of states, such as Virginia and South Carolina, have convened assessment practitioners from within their boundaries and beyond for annual conferences. The Virginia Community College System Group has presented workshops on assessment design and techniques through interactive video teleconferencing (Banks, 1996). Many discipline-specific conferences such as speech communication and physical education also highlight assessment issues.

These conferences give faculty a tremendous opportunity to learn about assessment. At the AAHE conference the sessions are tracked by subject matter and by level of expertise so that attendees can make good choices about which sessions to attend. At the Indianapolis conference, all participants have several opportunities to hear from national assessment leaders. Both of these conferences are preceded and followed by workshops that allow participants to study specific aspects of assessment in more detail. It is impossible to attend these conferences without becoming significantly more knowledgeable about assessment.

Campus Gatherings

In addition to sending faculty to national or regional conferences, strategies are available for faculty to learn about assessment on their own campuses. Many departments regularly offer lectures or symposia for faculty. External assessment experts can be invited to share general or specific information at these gatherings. Alternatively, experts on campus can share their knowledge with others, providing a real source of expertise. For example, faculty in teachers' colleges or English departments may have experience with portfolios or with developing learning goals and objectives they are willing to share with faculty in other units. Faculty at Ferris State University were invited to a series of sessions led by members of their own faculty and staff who are experienced in aspects of assessment. Each session included an overview of a particular topic followed by a question-and-answer period. The program was called the "This-Is-How-We-Do-It Series" and was well received by faculty (Outcomes Assessment Council, 1994, p. 49). Workshops can serve similar purposes but are usually designed to give participants a chance to actually work with the information they are receiving. For example, faculty can complete worksheets designed to help them state learning objectives.

At Northern Illinois University, several departments have scheduled full-day retreats to launch assessment planning. Faculty are asked to bring any materials developed by disciplinary associations and to think about desired student outcomes. At the retreat the campus assessment coordinator provides some background information about assessment and writing program-level objectives. Then faculty work in subject area groups to develop drafts of student learning objectives (R. Gold, M. Pritchard, and S. Miller, personal communication, Oct. 29, 1997).

Rather than conducting workshops that tend to last no longer than a day or two, another strategy is to create a "working group." Working groups tend to meet over a period of several weeks, generally with the goal of completing some task. This strategy has been used with classroom assessment where faculty meet once a week for two or three weeks to learn techniques and then meet several additional times to report on their experiences using these techniques in the classroom. Discussion groups are a similar strategy but tend to be more open-ended and less focused on completing a particular task.

Other ways to gather faculty together to learn about assessment include brown-bag lunches, round tables, town-hall style meetings, and development days. The latter might involve several presentations on a particular topic. The University of Indianapolis recently devoted its annual fall Faculty/Staff Institute to the topic of assessment, inviting faculty to present posters describing their assessment activities. Twenty-three faculty participated by creating posters and preparing abstracts that were included in a descriptive booklet. The poster session was well received by attendees who found it helpful in learning about assessment (Domholdt, 1996). Faculty at Eastern Michigan University and surrounding campuses were invited to display posters describing their assessment work at a one-day Assessment Expo held in spring 1998. In addition to professional colleagues, students were also invited to come and learn about assessment (Bennion and Work, 1998).

Institutional Support

Appropriate institutional and administrative support for assessment greatly enhances faculty efforts. Secretarial support is necessary for activities such as letter writing, data entry, logging surveys, and other tasks. Support from professional staff and administrators is also important. Some divisions have an undergraduate or graduate program coordinator who can facilitate the activities of the faculty and maintain an overall view of how assessment is proceeding. At campuses where there is no assessment office, there may be an institutional research office with responsibility for facilitating assessment. An alumni, career services, or student affairs office may engage in assessment-related activities or have expertise that can support assessment in other units. For example, career services may be collecting useful information about the short-term placement of graduates. At many campuses, computing center staff have expertise in designing research projects or in survey or test construction that can facilitate assessment.

Faculty Rewards

Faculty who participate in assessment should be rewarded for their efforts. Some of the rewards are intrinsic. A well-designed assessment program will result in interaction with other faculty that may have been lacking in the past. It will lead to improved clarity with respect to goals and objectives for learning and ultimately to improved teaching and learning. Faculty may also see a link between assessment and other important processes such as internal program review, planning, and budgeting. The latter is particularly rewarding if additional funding is made available to achieve departmental objectives. Faculty in units that are accredited by professional organizations often show strong support for assessment, reflecting the increased interest of accreditors.

What about more explicit rewards? In some units, faculty may receive release time to serve as assessment coordinators or to undertake projects. At Northern Illinois University, faculty involvement has been encouraged initially through release time for a single faculty member for one course for one semester (R. Gold, M. Pritchard, and S. Miller, personal communication, Oct. 29, 1997). This has provided time for the individual to study assessment, attend campus workshops and national conferences, and prepare to lead colleagues in identifying course and curriculum outcomes and selecting or designing assessment instruments.

Promotion and tenure processes should also recognize assessment efforts. In some units, faculty are encouraged to report assessment activities on their annual reports under the heading of teaching and teaching-related activities. Assessment may also be recognized as service to the department, division, or campus.

Recognition

At many institutions, participation in assessment leads to recognition on the local campus. Presenting posters, writing reviews of activities for local newsletters, or giving on-campus presentations provide recognition for assessment efforts. Faculty also have opportunities to publish articles about their assessment activities in journals that are related to the disciplines. Accounting, mathematics, economics, journalism, and other fields have journals that publish assessment-related studies. The bimonthly *Assessment Update* provides an opportunity for faculty to publish their work. These activities can be supported through release time for faculty research and should be recognized in the promotion and tenure process.

Grant Programs

These programs can take several forms. Some institutions provide substantial grants to a small number of faculty who are undertaking major projects. In this model, a team of faculty might receive release time to accomplish a large-scale assessment project during the academic year. At Ohio University $200,000 annually is set aside for awards to six units that propose to improve undergraduate education using assessment data to establish need and chart progress (A. M. Williford, personal communication, Sept. 19, 1997). At Northern Illinois University (NIU), four to six proposals are funded annually to accomplish substantial assessment projects. Initially the

NIU Assessment Committee awarded grants to faculty who were interested in student outcomes as a research area and had innovative project ideas. As departments became more involved, faculty proposals were required to demonstrate a relationship to the assessment plan for a degree program. Grants often fund the work of teams composed of faculty and graduate students (Gold and Hewitt, 1996).

Another approach is to give smaller grants for work that can be accomplished during the summer. Summer grants give faculty the opportunity to focus their energies on specific projects in a concentrated time frame. Rather than conducting routine assessment business, the summer can be used to undertake a task that is quite focused, such as developing an alumni survey. It is often easier to create faculty teams in the summer, when schedules are more flexible. The usual approach to awarding summer grants is to ask for proposals that are reviewed by a committee of peers. Guidelines for grants generally ask for a description of the project and a statement of how the project fits into department assessment plans. The proposal should also include a description of how results will be used.

Faculty may need some guidance in applying for assessment grants because they are not quite sure what a credible assessment project involves. To ensure that proposals focus on important tasks needed to move a department's overall assessment program forward, faculty should be encouraged to consult with deans, chairs; or assessment committee members about what might be included in a proposal.

Ball State University has had a very successful summer grant program in place for several years. Each summer, as many as forty faculty members work individually or on teams to undertake assessment projects. Stipends range from $300 to a maximum of $1,200 depending on the focus of the project and the number of individuals involved. Although many proposals arise from faculty members, the director of the Office of Academic Assessment also visits with deans and department chairs early in the spring semester to discuss assessment needs. After a plan for summer activities is developed, faculty are invited to work on the projects. This approach has brought more focus to summer activities and has helped colleges and departments make great strides in assessment.

Travel Funds

Because there are several conferences that focus on assessment, faculty have opportunities to give presentations about their assessment activities to audiences beyond their own campuses. Funding this travel is a way to reward faculty for their assessment activities. Providing funds for faculty who are new to assessment to attend conferences, perhaps with colleagues who are presenting there, is an effective way to encourage additional faculty involvement in assessment.

Maximizing the Role of Faculty and Faculty Acceptance

At most institutions there is a desire to maximize the role of faculty in assessment—to involve as many individuals as possible and to engage them in meaningful ways. In this section we share some hints about maximizing the role of faculty in assessment. These observations come from our own experiences working with faculty from many different disciplines. And because faculty can play a role in assessment without necessarily valuing it, we also address the issue of faculty acceptance.

Share Tasks Wisely

A number of strategies can increase the likelihood that many faculty will assume responsibility for assessment. First, involvement is maximized if each faculty member is given at least some role in the process. That role may be something easy to accomplish, such as reviewing a plan developed by a committee or ranking the importance of program goals. It may be much more extensive, such as developing an assessment plan to reflect the contributions of an individual course to an overall academic program or designing an assessment instrument. The important point is that faculty cannot be involved in assessment if they have no responsibility for its undertaking.

A second strategy is to put in place a plan that divides the assessment process into specific assignments. It is easier to involve faculty if they know the specific task at hand and if they can approach the assessment program as a series of steps rather than an overwhelming burden. As Ann Ferren states, "Assessment can be made up of many small projects, which, when integrated, give a fuller picture" (1993, p. 7). Taking an incremental approach is greatly facilitated by a plan with a clearly developed time line. For example, the initial step of developing statements about goals and objectives for learning can be followed by a careful consideration of assessment techniques that address them.

Next, make sure that faculty are involved in every step of the process. Too often, faculty are asked to articulate learning objectives for their courses, but the department chair writes the assessment plan. The assessment committee should be responsible for actually creating the assessment plan, not for providing comments on approaches proposed by administrators (Chaffee and Jacobson, 1997). A different pitfall occurs when a small committee takes so much control of the process that the typical faculty member has little role. Thus, broadly representative committees and shared tasks are preferred.

Use at Least Some Local Instruments

Assessment practitioners have learned from experience that the role of faculty can be maximized if local instruments are used rather than nationally available instruments. As John Muffo recently observed on the basis of his decade of experience in assessment, "faculty, like many others, will accept the results of studies most readily if they gather the data themselves. . . . It's far better to have less-than-perfect data gathered by departmental faculty than perfect data from some other source" (Muffo, 1996, p. 1). Integrating assessment activities into the classroom and drawing on what faculty are already doing increases faculty involvement.

Encourage Teamwork and Team Building

Educators understand the value of teamwork for students and frequently give group assignments in the classroom. Similarly, assessment flourishes when faculty, staff, and students work together. Not only the assessment committee but additional faculty members should have opportunities to work in teams. For instance, several faculty can be invited to design a portfolio project. One of the benefits of grant programs is the ability to get several individuals together to collaborate on specific projects.

Chaffee and Jacobson (1997) recommend team-building activities for groups that will be working together on planning. Strategies include brainstorming—that is, getting all the ideas out on the table for careful attention—and consensus taking to see if there is substantial agreement on essential points. Senge (1990) distinguishes between dialogue, where a group openly examines previously held assumptions and explores complex issues from many perspectives, and discussion, where different points of view are presented and defended. Teams that work well must use both as they seek to reach agreement. Brookfield (1995) suggests having ground rules for group conversations that might include such things as providing evidence for assertions; taking periodic breaks to allow those who have not spoken to do so; limiting the time any one person can speak; and including periods of mandated silence for reflection (allowing participants to think about their own thinking) at some point in each meeting. To be meaningful, each group must set up its own ground rules and, of course, follow them. Occasionally, inviting an outsider to help facilitate meetings is a good idea. An assessment specialist may be able to help faculty keep focused at meetings and make the progress needed to keep everyone engaged.

Meetings should be held only when there is a specific agenda. Although it is often helpful for faculty to get together, especially if they are trying to accomplish a specific task, they can contribute to assessment in many ways without attending meetings. Reactions, suggestions, and ideas can be solicited through campus mail or e-mail.

Foster Acceptance of Assessment

Maximizing the role of faculty may contribute to faculty acceptance, but it is only one of several ingredients. At the most basic level, it helps to concentrate on important questions—questions that faculty care about. Start with what matters most and, rather than trying to assess every possible program goal, concentrate on three or four major learning objectives.

Faculty often have concerns about the methods and instruments used to collect assessment data. They are not likely to accept results generated with instruments that are not of high quality, and they will not support decisions based on this information. Issues of reliability and validity need to be addressed, and campus experts on instrument design should review data collection instruments and procedures. Faculty acceptance of assessment is also enhanced if assessment information is used in appropriate ways. If information is collected but not acted on, faculty soon lose interest in continued participation.

Helpful Administrative Actions

Key administrators have an important role in the assessment process. The actions they take can hinder assessment or foster it. If administrators view assessment as an unpleasant burden, many faculty will as well. Likewise, administrators can impose unnecessary restrictions on how the program is carried out. For example, they may insist on a particular method, such as standardized testing.

Administrators need to be willing to express as well as reiterate a sincere commitment to assessment; allow adequate time for faculty to understand, accept, and carry out assessment; encourage and support use of assessment information; and be flexible in their approach. A college dean recently summarized some of the lessons he has learned after working with assessment for several years. In his view, faculty must design the assessment program themselves. However, "You have to let faculty know that assessment is a serious endeavor, and you have to be willing to repeat yourself." He also feels that, "While being flexible about time schedules helps faculty make progress, faculty need to see annual progress if they are to maintain interest" (N. Palomba, 1997).

View Faculty Development as a Continuing Process

Just as the student body changes from year to year, so do at least some members of the faculty. Thus faculty development related to assessment must be seen as a continuous process. On many campuses new faculty receive an introduction to outcomes assessment during the annual orientation for newcomers. According to D. Eder (personal communication, Sept. 22, 1997), new faculty at SIUE "are beginning to ask their departments to become more engaged in assessment."

Some Stumbling Blocks in Understanding Assessment

For assessment to be successful it must build on shared values. Some points of confusion create stumbling blocks in the way faculty view assessment and these are areas in which clarification is particularly important.

Entry-Level Placement

Many programs collect and use information about potential students to determine their qualifications for entering a program. In some cases, information is also used to select the appropriate level for students to begin their studies. Educators are comfortable making these decisions. They realize how important it is to select students who are qualified for their programs and to place new students at appropriate levels for learning. The information collected for entry-level decisions about individual students often provides a good starting point for assessing academic programs. Reviewing initial papers, performances, and portfolios provides valuable information about where students begin. Programmatic assessment requires faculty to collect information about the curriculum as a whole. Faculty need to know where students end up, as well as where they begin, and something about what happens along the way. Thus, although entry-level data collection might be part of an overall program of assessment, it can only be a beginning. Additional information needs to be collected during the time students are on campus.

Course Grades

Confusion often arises about the role of course grades in assessment. One of the primary functions of teachers is to grade individual students in their classes. Course grades tell students how they did in the class relative to other students and convey to students how well they have met their teachers' expectations. Grades also allow educators to compare groups of students across courses and over time using a common (although inconsistently applied) measure. Some faculty believe their grade distributions tell all there is to know about the performance of students in their classes. This belief is one of the biggest stumbling blocks in getting individual faculty involved in and excited about assessment.

Why aren't course grades enough? The assignment of a grade to an individual student provides a summary measure about the student's performance in the class and, perhaps, tells something about the standards of the teacher. It does not usually convey direct information about which of the course's goals and objectives for learning have been met or how well they have been met by the student. Likewise, the grade distribution for the class as a whole tells about the relative performance of the group of students but not about what or how much they have learned. Course grades alone do not necessarily help students improve. To be meaningful, assessment should provide both students and faculty with information for improvement at both course and program levels. A recent article by Barbara Wright (1997) contains a discussion of these issues. She notes the supportive and respectful spirit of assessment as compared to the often judgmental nature of assigning course grades. As Leon Gardiner (1994) reminds us, rather than generating improvement, the preeminent use of grades is for those outside the institution, such as employers and graduate schools, to use when selecting among graduates.

In a move that is all too rare in higher education, faculty at Rivier College are working to integrate goals described in the institution's mission statement and the standards on which grades are based (P. F. Cunningham, personal communication, Aug. 27,1997). That is, individual course grades should reflect that a student has achieved specific course objectives and collegewide general education goals and competences at a level considered appropriate for the course and subject matter.

Tests and activities on which grades are based can be useful for assessment. But educators must find ways to take what they have learned from these activities and make it meaningful for assessment purposes.

Faculty Evaluation

Many faculty fear the relationship between assessment and faculty evaluation, often thinking the two processes are the same. Thus it is important to make a clear distinction between them. The information collected through assessment strategies is collected for the purpose of evaluating programs, not faculty members. Yet many times assessment activities generate results that may reflect on individuals. This information can be made available to these instructors for purposes of improvement, but should not be included in their personnel folders nor used for making tenure, promotion, or salary decisions. An essential factor in making assessment work is building trust among faculty that the information collected through assessment activities will not be used for inappropriate purposes. A clear distinction must be made between rewarding assessment activities and using assessment findings. As we noted earlier, faculty should be rewarded for the time and energy they invest in assessment-related activities. Institutions should encourage the recognition of assessment activities in faculty review processes.

The Nature of Resistance

At least two recent national surveys have identified faculty resistance as among the most important challenges facing assessment (Ewell, 1996; Steele, 1996). Although we saved a description of the last R, faculty resistance, until the end of our discussion about faculty involvement, it is important to be aware of its nature. Some faculty, as well as administrators, resist assessment for a number of reasons. Some continue to believe that assessment is primarily for external audiences and fail to see its potential to improve programs. Some resent the cost of assessment in terms of time and resources. Others question the quality of the data collected. Some fear their efforts will be for naught if the information is not used; others fear that the information will actually be used but in some way that is harmful to their interests.

Some faculty view assessment as a threat to academic freedom. As several observers have pointed out, many faculty consider teaching to be a very private activity and they do not want to open themselves to judgment on the results of this endeavor. Assessment requires a sharing of information and a commonality of goals that can cause individuals to be uncomfortable at times. Assessment is a group activity that requires a great deal of openness.

Because of these issues, some faculty question the value of assessment. Fortunately, many who initially fear assessment come to accept it over time. This chapter has considered a variety of ways to support the role of faculty in assessment. If faculty have responsibility, resources, and rewards for participating in assessment, the chance they will come to appreciate its value greatly increases.

Involving Students in Assessment

Assessment must be seen as an activity done with and for students, rather than to them. Students need to be active partners in assessment. Here we discuss several ways to involve students in the assessment process. As with our discussion of involving faculty, we refer to three areas of importance: responsibility, resources, and rewards. Students need to know what is expected of them, have appropriate support and information to live up to these expectations, and have some incentive or reward for their participation. If educators are thoughtful about how they include students in the assessment process, they can help overcome motivation problems that can hinder assessment.

Student Responsibility

In order for assessment to work, students must be active participants. Questionnaires and focus groups can obtain information from other interested parties, but assessment information that directly demonstrates the learning of students originates with students themselves. Thus, the most basic responsibility of students is to participate in direct assessment activities such as tests, performance measures, and portfolios as well as indirect assessment activities such as interviews and focus groups. In addition to participating in activities, students can play a number of other roles in the assessment process.

Serving on Committees

Several campuses or units include students on their assessment committees. In this capacity, students play a very important role, helping to conceptualize and design the overall program. In addition, students may serve on task forces that are concerned with developing specific assessment instruments. For example, students can help plan activities such as portfolios or other performance projects. Some colleges or departments have student advisory boards that contribute advice on a variety of topics. Asking these boards to provide feedback and suggestions about the assessment process makes sense.

Providing Comments

Whether or not they are serving in an official advisory capacity, students should be encouraged to provide their comments about the activities in which they participate. This can happen in both formal and informal ways. Many assessment instruments ask students about the usefulness of what they are doing. For example, students who are completing portfolios are often asked to provide comments about what they have learned from their experiences and how valuable the activities have been for them. Students can also be asked to participate in focus groups that are concerned with various aspects of the assessment process, such as examining the value of a capstone experience.

Even without a specific request for comments, students can be quite vocal about an assessment activity that they do not feel is worthwhile. Educators need to consider these opinions very carefully. Students will ordinarily have great insight into the value of what they are asked to do. Listening to them does not mean faculty have to abandon what they are doing every time students voice criticisms. It may mean they need to make some modifications in their approach. For example, one university modified its writing competence examination for juniors after receiving a steady stream of negative comments from students. Many students felt the test duplicated assessment in their writing classes and was too general in the topics provided. The examination was changed so that students now sign up for specific test sessions in which they receive essay topics related to their majors. They also receive their writing topics at the test sessions rather than in advance. These changes have helped increase the motivation of students to do well on their essays.

Facilitating Assessment

At some institutions, students play yet another role with respect to assessment: acting as assessors themselves. One fairly common example of this is with respect to group work. Many group work projects ask students to evaluate the functioning of the group and the contributions of other students, as well as themselves, to the group. In fact, Jack McGourty (McGourty, Sebastian, and Swart, 1997) at the New Jersey Institute of Technology has designed software called Student Developer to enable these assessments to be recorded and summarized electronically. Students can also be asked to critique class projects or presentations of other students. They will need some instructions and practice to do this well.

At Alverno College, professional communication students in a junior-level course work in teams to devise a campaign theme and rationale, design a logo and other visual materials, and create an outline for a promotional event for a local nonprofit agency. In addition to evaluations by the instructor and the agency representative, students receive peer assessments of their contributions to their team's culminating presentation (A. J. Johnson, personal communication, Sept. 26, 1997).

Students can be trained to conduct telephone interviews or to take notes for focus groups. The University of Minnesota uses work-study students called "pulsers" to conduct regularly scheduled telephone surveys of undergraduate students. Project Pulse surveys are used to investigate needs of the institution and are requested by various units on campus including colleges, departments, and student affairs offices. Approximately twenty surveys are conducted each year (Upcraft and Schuh, 1996, p. 42).

Students can help interpret results from completed assessment projects. For example, focus groups of students can be useful if faculty want to gain insight about test or survey results that are surprising. Students can also help the assessment process by acting as mentors for other students. Juniors and seniors can be asked to help freshmen get started on portfolios. Students can be asked to work together or be available to help each other prepare for assessment activities that involve performances or products.

Resources for Students

Universities, colleges, and departments can provide information for students to help them fulfill their assessment responsibilities. These approaches include catalogue statements, flyers, brochures, project instructions, and examples of completed assessment activities. All of these approaches can help students understand what assessment is about, why they are asked to participate, what is expected of them, and how they will be evaluated. In particular, students must be made aware of the goals and objectives for learning that drive programs. If students are aware of what faculty want them to know, do, and value, they have a much better likelihood of achieving these objectives.

Catalogue Statements

A Web search reveals that many institutions include statements about assessment in their catalogues. Generally, these statements are relatively short but nevertheless describe the basic responsibility of students. Whereas many statements indicate that participation in assessment is *required* of all students, other statements indicate that participation in assessment is *expected*.

The 1995–97 catalogue at Bloomsburg University of Pennsylvania includes the following statement of expectations about student participation in assessment activities: "The university routinely conducts campus-based studies of student attitudes, student achievement, student satisfaction, and personal, professional and career development. These studies are grouped under the heading of student outcomes assessment. Participation in outcomes assessment activities is expected of all students. While every student is not selected for participation in every activity, it is likely that an individual student will be involved in one or more assessment activities during the college years. It is only through cooperative participation in the assessment process that the university can better understand itself and better serve its students" (p. 58).

In contrast, Jacksonville State University's 1996–97 catalogue includes the following statement requiring students to participate in assessment activities: "To assess and improve its academic programs, the University must obtain periodic measurements of student perceptions and intellectual growth. As a requirement for graduation, all seniors must take a general education achievement test (currently, the College BASE Examination) and complete a Graduating Senior Questionnaire. Additionally, some programs require that their majors take a comprehensive test of achievement in the discipline. Students may also be required to participate in other evaluations of University programs and services. The information obtained through these assessment procedures is used solely to improve the quality of the educational experience for future generations of JSU students" (p. 38).

Both of these catalogue statements are concerned with obtaining information for programmatic assessment. The first statement sets out an expectation, the second a requirement. Although participation in the same assessment activities is required of every student at JSU, graduation is not tied to any performance level. If students are required to achieve a satisfactory level of performance on an assessment activity as a condition for graduation or advancement within a program, they should be made aware of this in the catalogue. For example, a particular performance level on a test of writing or computer competence may be required. If this is the case, students need to know.

Statements such as those just reproduced contain information that is applicable to all students, but catalogues can also contain statements about assessment activities in particular majors. Several programs require students to complete standardized assessment tests such as the Educational Testing Service Major Field Tests prior to graduation. Some colleges require students to pass the general knowledge and communication skills sections of the National Teachers Examination prior to participation in student teaching. If so, the catalogue needs to include these requirements.

Brochures and Flyers

In addition to catalogue statements, some campuses have developed other materials to convey information about assessment activities. Truman State University has developed a small but effective brochure for students called "Assessment at Truman." Although the brochure is sixteen pages long, it is only four inches wide and six inches tall. The brochure opens with a letter from the university president expressing the hope that students will use assessment activities as tools for self-improvement as well as a means to provide feedback to faculty and staff at the university. It contains descriptions of the tests, surveys, writing experiences, and other assessment activities in which students at Truman State University participate. It estimates the amount of time students will spend on each activity and indicates that students will spend an average of sixteen total hours on assessment while at the university. The brochure ends with an invitation for students to help assess the assessment program. Students are told they can participate in this process by serving on the advisory panel, participating in focus groups and interviews, or simply providing their comments.

Some schools provide flyers or brochures when students begin classes; others provide them earlier, perhaps at orientation. In fact, some campuses provide flyers to both parents and students at orientation. This is particularly helpful if students are being asked to participate in testing at that time. These flyers can be used to describe the purposes of testing, how it will affect grades and placement in courses, how much time it and other assessment activities will take, and who will see results.

Brochures and flyers about assessment in particular programs can often be more specific than those provided to all students. For example, a brochure designed for majors can provide a rationale for each of the programs' learning goals, explain how goals are addressed in various courses, and describe how assessment activities will be used to determine if these goals are being achieved.

Project Instructions

Students need to have specific directions for all the assessment activities in which they participate. Instructions are particularly important with respect to comprehensive projects such as portfolios, where students are asked to accumulate materials for an extended time. As they begin their portfolios, students need to have enough information to understand the overall dimensions of the project. They need to know what is currently expected of them, as well as what they will be asked to provide in subsequent classes or time periods. They also need to be aware of the specific criteria that will be used to judge their portfolios. This is true for other types of performance assessment as well. Students need to know what is expected of them and how their performance will be scored. Some institutions provide written guidelines for creating portfolios and participating in performance assessment. Others ask their students to attend orientation sessions so any questions they have can be addressed. It is important as part of any instructions to indicate how information will be used and to assure students that their results will be treated confidentially.

Almost all institutions have policies regarding the use of human subjects in research that may be applicable for assessment projects.

Examples

Another helpful approach for providing assessment information to students is to let them examine past examples. Students who are being asked to develop portfolios can be provided examples that represent a range of work. Opportunities to examine average work as well as excellent work can be very useful. Such material can be helpful with respect to other performance projects as well, such as essays or art objects. Versions of assessment tests that are no longer in use can also be made available.

Student Rewards

Just as some faculty rewards from assessment are intrinsic and others extrinsic, the same is true for student rewards. Students can and should benefit from the assessment process in a variety of ways.

Improved Programs

Assessment frequently leads to changes in academic programs (Banta and Associates, 1993; Banta, Lund, Black, and Oblander, 1996). Although some improvements may be introduced after current students have left campus, many faculty have been able to introduce changes rather quickly so current students benefit as well. Improvements such as clearer syllabi, more fully articulated goals and objectives for learning, and more explicit evaluation standards are often introduced soon after assessment programs are initiated. In addition, improvements to instruction based on classroom assessment activities may occur immediately. Nevertheless, some change is slower in coming. Fortunately, as evidenced by their thankful comments on student surveys, we have observed that current students often welcome the opportunity to provide feedback about what they have experienced, even if it is future students who may benefit.

Feedback

Direct feedback to students about their own performances is an additional benefit of many assessment projects. Although some tests provide only group results, many assessment instruments provide results at the individual level. In these cases, it is recommended that students be given their scores. One of the primary advantages of performance assessment is the opportunity to give direct and immediate feedback to students. In some cases, feedback will be provided by professionals in the field as well as by departmental faculty. Peer review is also included in several assessment projects.

Grant Wiggins (1997) has argued strongly for the appropriate use of feedback. He notes, "You can't learn without feedback" (p. 33). Useful feedback lets students know what they did or did not do, without expressing approval or disapproval. It is "rich, clear, and direct enough to enable students and teachers to self-assess accurately and self-correct their own performances increasingly over time" (Wiggins, 1998, p. 12). Helpful feedback causes students to think about what they have or haven't done, and how they can improve. Wiggins argues for assessment strategies that "include the student's ability to use the feedback" (1997, p. 35). Because self-adjustment is more important than self-assessment, students learn best if they can respond to feedback, if they can decide which feedback to take and why, and if they can explain their choices. In Wiggins' view, the best assessment allows faculty to see if students can deal with feedback.

Survey projects can also be structured to provide feedback to students. In many cases, students are asked if they would like to receive a summary of results. Those who answer "yes" can be sent a short summary of highlights from the project. Alternatively, a page or two of results can be sent to all participants. Results can also be made available through department, college, or university Web pages.

Some schools have developed survey projects that provide individualized results for participants. These reports can be created using word-merge software. Ball State University's Making Achievement Possible Survey (MAP) is administered to entering freshmen each fall semester. Soon after they complete the survey, respondents receive a personalized report with specific messages based on their own responses to the survey. For example, students who indicate they plan to study only a few hours per week are reminded that faculty will expect them to study approximately two hours for each hour spent in class. Many students report that they find this feedback very valuable. The MAP project is a collaboration between the Learning Center, Academic Assessment, Housing and Residence Life, and Academic Advising.

Opportunities for Reflection and Self-Assessment

Although students often need time to develop self-assessment skills, among the greatest benefits from many assessment projects is the opportunity they provide students to reflect on their own learning and development. Kramp and Humphreys describe self-assessment as "a complex, multidimensional activity in which students observe and judge their own performances in ways that influence and inform future learning and performance" (1995, p. 10). In their view, self-assessment provides a valuable opportunity for students to think carefully about their learning activities.

Most portfolio projects include specific requests for expressions of self-reflection. In fact, the very act of creating portfolios requires students to think carefully about the materials they have developed and their performance on these items. In addition, students are generally asked to justify their choices explicitly and to reflect on their growth through written statements or essays contained in their portfolios. Other direct assessment methods can also be used for self-reflection, including journal entries and oral presentations. Several classroom assessment techniques provide opportunities for self-assessment as well.

Nona Lyons believes that reflection should include "making connections" through critical, collaborative conversations rather than be conducted as a "solitary, individual enterprise" (1998b, p. 254). Reflection benefits from a listener who participates in the dialogue. In this view, as in Wiggins' view, feedback and reflection need to occur together.

Indirect assessment methods provide additional opportunities for self-assessment. Many surveys include blocks of questions asking students to reflect on their learning and development. Students often comment on surveys that they appreciate the chance to think about what they have experienced and to provide their reactions. Focus groups, too, provide an opportunity for students to consider and react to various aspects of their education.

Self-assessment is one of the hallmarks of the master's-level program for practicing professionals at the School of New Learning at DePaul University. Marienau and Fiddler (1997) report the results of research conducted with students in the master's program on the role of self-assessment in their professional development. Almost two-thirds of a group of eighty adult students said they had become more goal oriented as a result of engaging in self-assessment; more than half reported that they were taking more responsibility for their own work. The greatest impact of self-assessment appears to be on interpersonal skills: 75 percent of the participants in the study said they had become more active listeners, more adept at giving and receiving constructive feedback. Self-acceptance, self-confidence, autonomy, and self-direction in one's career were other attributes influenced by experience in self-assessment.

Tangible Rewards

Some campuses provide incentives for students to participate in assessment projects. Rewards such as passes to movies, coupons for free food, or small payments of money are sometimes used to increase participation in projects. In some cases, coupons are included in mailings to all eligible students. In other cases, respondents are sent a coupon after they have returned their assessment instruments. Students who participate in focus groups may be treated to pizza and sodas.

Rather than providing all participating students with small tokens, some campuses use raffles for institution-wide projects. For example, the cover letter for a survey may tell all students who are invited to participate that a small number of respondents will be randomly selected to win prizes. Prizes can include such things as cash awards or free semesters of books. Local bookstores are often willing to cooperate in providing free books or books at cost. These raffles can increase the motivation of students to participate in assessment projects. As one respondent optimistically wrote with respect to a possible cash prize for completing a survey, "Show me the money!"

Maximizing Student Acceptance of Assessment

The most important element in enhancing student acceptance of assessment is the commitment shown by faculty to assessment. The messages given by faculty with regard to assessment are very powerful motivators. If faculty care about assessment, students are much more likely to care too. Alternatively, if students perceive from the way faculty introduce an assessment project that they are not interested or actually resent the time the project is taking from other activities, students will be resentful as well. Even the most enthusiastic faculty need to share information with students about the purposes of assessment and the way the information will be used. Tying assessment to classroom activities is also helpful. If assessment is seen as a natural part of the teaching and learning process, students are motivated to do well. Drawing on already existing classroom activities for assessment provides a way to utilize information that is tied to important consequences for students. Other consequences may exist as well; for example, at some institutions, participation in assessment has an impact on students' priority in registering for classes (Hyman, Beeler, and Benedict, 1994).

Practical concerns are also important. In cases where students are required to attend testing sessions, provisions should be made for their convenience. Offering alternate test days may be necessary. At the University of Wisconsin–Superior, no classes are scheduled on testing days. In addition, a temporary day-care center is set up to accommodate students with child care responsibilities (Katz, 1996).

Acting Ethically

M. Lee Upcraft and John H. Schuh (1996, pp. 298–305) provide several suggestions for ethical conduct with respect to all assessment activities. Among others, ethical behavior includes the following considerations.

1. Where possible, give students the right to decide whether they will participate in an assessment. For example, students who are tested in orientation should be excused if they object. Assessment done in classes is often required, but should be an important factor in course grades only if it is a natural part of class assignments.
2. Ensure that participation in assessment does no harm. Information that is collected should be treated confidentially. No information should be released publicly in such a way that individual students are identified. Notes or tapes from focus groups or interviews should never identify participants by name.
3. Explain the purposes of assessment projects to students and carry out projects as described. Researchers need to honor all promises for reports, feedback, and rewards. Overall, students need to be treated with respect, as valuable partners in assessment.

EFFECTIVE AND INEFFECTIVE ASSESSMENT PROGRAMS IN HIGHER EDUCATION

A PRESENTATION TO MSERA BY
ANGELA MAYNARD SEWALL, ED.D.AND
TOM E.C. SMITH, ED.D.
UNIVERSITY OF ARKANSAS, LITTLE ROCK

Abstract

Universities have long been in the business of assessment, particularly the assessment of students. Recently, several national and regional accreditation agencies have mandated that universities also engage in self-assessment programs. However, assessment is not clearly defined from campus to campus. Some of the issues in educational assessment in higher education are explored and illustrated with a discussion of the assessment process as it operates at the University of Arkansas at Little Rock. To be effective, college and university assessment plans must include more than simply assessing students through examinations. They must include a comprehensive approach to determine if, and how, skills learned in classes are actually applied later on. Developing assessment plans that evaluate ongoing students' achievement and long-term students-employer perceptions of the value and pertinence of the graduate's program of study allow faculty to review curricula and examine instructional practices. At the University of Arkansas, this sort of assessment has begun, with a plan developed for each faculty in a collegial, but stressful, process. The assessment process evolved to allow each faculty to evaluate assessment plans in its own college, resulting in a more positive attitude. Faculty members are more comfortable having their plans evaluated by colleagues, and the assessment process is becoming more likely to lead to program improvement. (Contains 11 references.) (SLD)

Universities have long been in the business of assessment, primarily assessment of students and, if requested, assessment of programs. In excess of 82% of the institutions of higher education in the United States are involved in assessment of programs for the purpose of measuring student outcomes (Mentkwoski, Astin, Ewell & Moran, 1991, p. i). Recently,several national and regional accreditation agencies have mandated that universities engage in self-assessment programs. These endeavors, which are mandated by law in at least eighteen states and by accrediting agencies such as the North Central Association (The Chronicle of Higher Education, 1995, p. 10.), are simply designed to ensure the provision of a quality educational experience and a value added education for students at the graduate and undergraduate levels.

Paper presented at the 27th Annual Meeting of the Mid-South Educational Research Association, November 4-6, 1998.

Unfortunately, assessment is not clearly defined from campus to campus. Rarely have universities traditionally engaged in self-assessment programs. The result of legislation and policy implemented by accrediting agencies has been a flurry of activity on most campuses to develop and implement required assessment programs. What has often been discovered is that university faculty who have long been engaged in assessing students have a very difficult time developing and implementing their own assessment programs.

It is on each campus that decisions are made regarding what assessment actually is and should do. This paper seeks to address the issues in educational assessment which have influenced and will continue to impact performance and performance evaluation, and some successful and some unsuccessful experiences in assessment at one institution. The session will review how the assessment program at the University of Arkansas at Little Rock (UALR) was implemented three years ago and how it has evolved from an activity that was initially met with a great deal of confusion and criticism from faculty to one that is finally being accepted as helpful in program improvement.

The decade of the 1990's is rightly called the decade of accountability. This has been the decade in which the concerns and questions which were raised relative to K-12 education in the 1980's have become issues for colleges and universities as well. For example, the Arkansas Policy Foundation, in late September of this year, published a study (The Murphy Report) funded by private industry at the request of the Governor. The report includes a set of 12 recommendations concerning K-12 education and a 13th for higher education. The 13th recommendation is for higher education in the state be studied to determine its effectiveness.

While the national goals have had far reaching implications for K-12 education and educators, changes in accreditation requirements and recent legislative activities, including such studies as the Murphy Report, have begun to deeply impact higher education. These issues will continue to have an effect on teaching, the admission and retention of students, and even on academic freedom. In fact, the traditional model of university peer review and faculty governance has already been examined as a direct result of external assessments imposed at the state and national levels. One result with far ranging impact has been post tenure review mandated by legislative action in several states.

Regardless of the difficulties experienced on some campuses to develop assessment programs, there are strong reasons to do so. Too often, faculty teach courses using the same content and methods that have been used for years. And, often there has never been an effective program assessment to determine if what students are taught in courses results in their abilities to accomplish specific actions later. Therefore, to be effective, assessment plans must include more than simply assessing students using a final examination or scores on a standardized test. They must include a comprehensive approach to determining if, and how, skills learned in courses are actually applied later.

Colleges and universities are obliged to develop assessment plans by which ongoing student achievement and long term student/employer perceptions of the value and the pertinence of the graduate's program of study are evaluated. The purpose is to allow program faculty to review curriculum in light of data, to examine instructional practices, and to consider programmatic additions and/or deletions in order to better serve the students and community of consumers.

In our own university, the review of programmatic goals and the identification of skills, conceptual sets, and knowledge bases have been ongoing during the past four years. Virtually all faculty members have been involved, some more willingly than others. During the first three years, the plan developed by faculty in each program was evaluated by members of an Assessment Planning Review Committee and the Assessment Review Groups (ARG). Although the process was collegial, it was also stressful. It often produced some competition and tension as certain plans were "rated" as excellent while others are merely acceptable in the eyes of readers who may or may not speak the same educational language as those who wrote the plan.

Additional tension has been associated with the concern about results of assessment. In fact, no one is really certain how outcomes, absent negative accreditation reports, will impact either programs or individual faculty members within them. Assessment can truly help higher educators learn about the curriculum, student performance and their own teaching, if properly used. The question in many minds, however, is whether these results will be employed for other purposes, particularly those related to decisions with regard to faculty tenure, promotion, and annual evaluations. Still other issues called productivity goals may factor into the determination of college or university funding. These include retention of students from year to year; passage rate of juniors on a standardized examination (the so-called rising junior exam), a writing sample; and graduation rates.

"High stakes testing is pervasive in education." (Phillips, 1993). Faculty governance has traditionally been the decision making base from which the parameters of faculty evaluation are derived; however, legislatively mandated testing of students adds new wrinkles to the usual evaluative criteria. Criteria for faculty evaluation traditionally has included teaching, as measured by student evaluations, peer visitation, and observation; scholarship, measured by the production of articles, monographs, texts, grants, and presentations at professional meetings; and service, including service to the university, community, and profession. Solomon (1993) noted that these areas have provided the basis for the awarding of tenure and promotion. The concern about assessment spills over into a generalized unease about the fundamental issues of tenure, promotion and, now, post-tenure review.

Lately, some cases based on (1) lack of competence, (*In the Matter of Dismissal Proceedings Against Dr. Barney K. Huang*, 1994); (2) unsatisfactory performance (*Mary Carroll Smith v. University of North Carolina at Chapel Hill*, 1980); (3) grading policies (*Levi v. University of Texas at San Antonio*, 1988); and (4) poor teaching ability (*Fields v. Clark University* (1991) have made their way to the courts. They reflect the reality of these concerns relative to assessment and to the entire evaluation process. These cases relate to the denial of tenure for faculty members predicated at least in part on student evaluations of teaching in the classroom.

The choice which we have is to take charge of and use assessment as a demonstrable tool for improvement and change. If we do not do this, there is a high probability that the results of such assessment, whether developed on campus or mandated by the legislature in the form of student retention, graduation rates, or a standardized instrument, may become the next legal battle ground for higher educators who have been denied tenure, promotion and/or employment. Even though such items as retention and graduation rates may be susceptible to economic trends, these standards when legislated become (1994) the law. Therefore, as Benjamin noted, in spite of inadequacies in new accreditation processes, higher educators should be active participants in reforming accreditation and continue to be involved in the process. As noted by Van Patten (1994), "the challenge of university department heads (and administrators of every stripe) is to use assessment (and other faculty productivity measures) with integrity and not to get entangled in a subtle web of political game playing . . ." (p. 6). If no one joins the game and all focus on our academic efforts and excellence, assessment is not a threat.

Although faculty at our institution have not engaged in this discussion of recent courts cases on a broad basis, the discomfort felt around the issue of assessment is reflected in the fact that in one college an entire program faculty refused to participate in the assessment process. In other colleges, anger at colleagues across campus was evident after the campus wide readers' panels completed their work each year. More than one faculty member has spoken of low morale directly related to the results of the assessment report review, not the results of the program assessment itself.

It was predicated on this skewed focus, i.e. report evaluation rather than assessment results, which led the Dean's Council on campus to recommend a change in the review process campus wide. The suggested change was that the readers for each college be primarily from the college itself and that only one member of the Readers' Panel be from another college. Additionally, colleges would rotate membership on the readers' panels of other colleges so that over a period of six years, at least one representative from each college would have served on every other college's readers' panel.

The idea behind this suggestion was that faculty might tend to take suggestions or criticism more positively when it came from a colleague in the same field and college. Secondly, by having one member of the panel from another college, capacity and understanding would be developed over time across campus of the terms, needs, assessment methodology and successes of other colleges in a less stressful environment. Finally, there was an incentive for college faculty to serve on the readers' panel since one would be working with colleagues known to them rather than on a campus wide panel comprised of representatives from multiple colleges. In other words, the competition changed. Programs, departments, and colleges began to compete with themselves and to focus on improvement rather than competing with other colleges.

As a result of the Dean's Council recommendations, the assessment process on campus was changed to enable college faculty to evaluate assessment plans in their own college. As noted above, this resulted in less paranoia and a more positive attitude. During the 1997–1998 academic year, the following process occurred in the College of Education.

The first activity was the appointment of the assessment committee. This was done by the Dean, who also appointed the assessment chairperson. The college assessment chairperson also served on the campus-wide assessment committee. Following appointment of the committee and chair, the committee convened to discuss the process that would be used. Individual programs developed and submitted their assessment progress reports, and in some cases, entire assessment plan revisions.

The assessment committee divided into two subcommittees. Each subcommittee was coordinated by a team member, and each subcommittee set its own work schedule. The program assessment plans were divided into two groups and assigned to an assessment subcommittee. Efforts were made to prevent individual committee members from reviewing their own assessment plans or plans from their own departments. The subcommittee members evaluated the assessment plans and progress reports independently and gave each plan a rating (1–3). Additionally, specific comments for improvement were provided for each plan. Overall ratings included acceptable, acceptable with minor revisions, and acceptable with major revisions. Strong efforts were made to provide positive feedback to faculty, especially in light of the negative feedback that some faculty had received from their assessment plan evaluations in previous years. This resulted in no plan being rated "unacceptable." which itself is a motivational and morale factor.

Following each subcommittee evaluation, the coordinators of the two subcommittees met and reconciled ratings. These final ratings were compiled and returned, along with suggestions, to individuals who developed their program assessment reports. A summary of the college assessment plans and their ratings was developed and shared with the campus-wide assessment committee. Each college developed such a summary. The campus-wide assessment committee then provided an overall summary of the assessment plan reports and their evaluations in a report to the Provost.

The revised assessment plan development and review process worked significantly better this past year as a result of the changes made by the Dean's Council. Faculty members were more comfortable having their plans evaluated by colleagues in their college than when this was done by individuals from other colleges who did not particularly understand programs in the College of Education. This change in faculty attitude has helped move the assessment process from a mandatory activity to one which is being used for program improvement. Flattening the layers has also caused faculty to feel more in control of their programs and the process, and reflected acknowledgment of program faculty and expertise.

References

Benjamin, E. (July–August, 1994). "From accreditation to regulation: The decline of academic autonomy in higher education," *Academe*.

Breneman, D.W. The Chronicle of Higher Education. September 8, 1995, p. B1, 2.

Diamond, R. M. "How to change the faculty reward system." *Trusteeship v1* n–5. (October, 1993) p. 17–21.

Longanecker, D.A. (July–August, 1994). "The new federal focus on accreditation." *Academe*.

Magner, D.K. "Beyond tenure." *The Chronicle of Higher Education*. (July 21, 1995), p. A13.

Mooney, C. "After lengthy hearings,. Rutgers faculty panel recommends dismissal of tenured professor." *The Chronicle of Higher Education*. (January 13, 1988). p. A 11, 12.

Solomon, R. & Solomon, J. (1993). *Up the University: Recreating Higher Education in America*, Reading, MA: Addison-Wesley.

Sowell, Thomas. (1994). "Tenure versus teaching." *Forbes* (November 21, 1994). p. 96.

Sowell, Thomas. (1995). *Forbes* "Good teachers need not apply." (June 19, 1995). p. 67.

"The nation." *The Chronicle of Higher Education*. September 1, 1995, p. 10.

Van Patten, J. J. (1994). "The politics of assessment of the professoriate in education: Reflections on challenges facing higher education." (unpublished manuscript).

Leadership in a Fishbowl: A New Accreditation Process

Janice Clinard and Lenoar Foster

Montana is piloting a five-step process that places control of state accreditation with local educators and communities

Imagine a hotel ballroom filled with teachers and administrators. They listen intently as three primary-level classroom teachers and their principal defend their school's mission, educational goals, assessment tools, and improvement plans. This staff is in the "fishbowl," a simulation activity through which 15 teams are being trained to interview staff, examine documents, and observe schools in Montana's new, voluntary accreditation process.

After nearly an hour of responding to probing questions, the defenders seek advice from their interviewers: How would you approach this problem? Would this assessment tool be useful at you school? Both sides gain new perspectives through the dialogue. Finally, the interviewers unveil a preposterous-looking trophy: the Super Mighty MISTA. The simulation ends with relief, laughter, and applause.

Empowering Schools

Montana Improving Schools Through Accreditation (MISTA) is a pilot program that empowers schools to attain accreditation through their own visions of improved student learning. The process itself is called "Performance-Based Accreditation" (PBA).

Montana is among several states that have tied state accreditation to school improvement. Lauree Harp of the National Study of School Evaluation estimates that nearly 1,000 schools nationwide are engaged in at least on step of a school improvement process tied to regional accreditation. Iowa, for example, has mandated a process similar to Montana's voluntary approach. In Oregon, about 100 schools are involved in the School Improvement Process for regional accreditation with the Northwest Association of Schools and Colleges. The Southern Association of Schools and Colleges is granting accreditation through the Tennessee School Improvement Planning Process, which was mandated by the Tennessee Board of Education.

Montana schools now have the option of either letting their accrediting agency tell them what is best or participating in a process that helps them discover their own ways to improve schools. Because PBA is optional, it may have the advantage of "flourishing in a sandwich, " Pascale's (1990) concept of striking the right balance between pressure from below and consensus from above. From the field,

Reprinted by permission from *Educational Leadership* 55, no. 7 (April 1998), by permission of the Association for Supervision and Curriculum Development.

Montana felt pressure to develop a more meaningful way to accredit schools, one that considered the quality of programs and processes instead of numbers of students, teachers, and administrators. From the top, PBA represents a consensus among the regional accrediting agency, the state education agency, and the board of education.

But as Michael Fullan (1993) says, "You can't mandate what matters." So Montana agencies are providing professional development to the 18 pilot schools and are turning leadership over to steering committees at each school.

Performance-Based Accreditation

Historically, Montana awarded accreditation based on a school's ability to meet uniform state standards, such as class-size limits, professional staff assignments, and program offerings. Such standards do not reveal what—or whether—students learn. Now, schools that choose performance-based accreditation must complete five steps over the course of three to five years:

- Develop a student/community profile.
- Develop a school mission statement that reflects a locally derived philosophy of education.
- Identify desired learner results (exit performance standards).
- Analyze instructional and organizational effectiveness.
- Develop and implement a school improvement plan.

In addition, each school is subject to a comprehensive on-site review. (Using the strategies demonstrated in the "fishbowl," teams are currently conducting on-site visits for one another.)

These five steps transfer the responsibility for accreditation review from the state education agency to school district and community representatives. The required on-site visit goes far beyond a paper-and-pencil report, engaging the school's entire staff and a team of peers. PBA also recognizes that each school's road to improvement may differ. By balancing the five-step process with on-site review, PBA offers both local control and statewide influence.

Launching MISTA

Initially, Montana's accreditation officials feared that PBA would open a floodgate of petitions to waive standards. As anticipated, the first inquiries focused on the last sentence of the standard: "Accredited schools electing this formative process may petition the Board of Public Education to waive existing standards except those that are required by law." Public meetings about performance-based accreditation and the user's manual (Montana Office of Public Instruction 1996) clarified the scope and rigor of the work. Only schools truly committed to improvement and ready to make substantive change joined MISTA.

MISTA schools began work in September 1996 with two days of training that focused on how to involve the public, conduct successful meetings, and develop the student/community profile. Participants found that developing a profile of the school and community generated pertinent, concrete, and often surprising information. After three months of work, they also reported a high level of community participation, some frustration with the slow nature of gathering and displaying data, and a new appreciation for the ideas and skills that students can contribute. For example, high school computer students were asked to compile data on the school/community profile and create information displays, giving their work authentic purpose (see fig. 1). The debate about how much data to collect and what is useful still arises, but participants agree on the key criterion: Can we use the information to improve student performance?

Profiling can involve the whole school community. According to Colstrip High School Principal Carol Wicker:

> Sharing the leadership with people outside your field is often a scary process—for you and for them. About halfway through the profiling step, one of the community representatives observed, "We would never think of allowing community members to come in and help us make decisions in my line of work. But if it worked as well as this has, it certainly would increase community buy-in; and it might make our jobs much easier."

As the profiling continued, MISTA schools held community meetings to explore their values and beliefs, which led to writing or revising their mission statements. These steps were extremely time-consuming, but without them, the schools could not have generated the "accurate picture of reality and compelling picture of the future" that Peter Senge (1990) deems essential to building creative tension and effecting change.

Standards and Strategies

Although state standards may be based on research and public consensus, the state education agency must learn to trust innovation from the local level. As MISTA schools look at current standards, they may be translated into strategies for a school improvement plan. For example, a standard limiting class size in a writing class might become a strategy for achieving the goal of improving students' written communication skills. At MISTA's Billings Senior High, Vice-Principal Barbara Ostrum explains part of the school's improvement plan:

> Our profiling revealed a general dissatisfaction with student tardies, which were robbing students of learning time. After much discussion, teachers suggested that increased passing time [between classes] in conjunction with not allowing students out of class during the hour [in class] might solve the problem. After a month of using a schedule with passing time increased by three minutes, the overwhelming response from faculty is complete satisfaction. Our teachers are making statements such as, "I'm able to start teaching when the bell rings. Last year I generally had to wait five minutes before I could begin." This effort has improved the climate at Billings Senior. . . . A feeling of hope pervades our school—hope that improvements are possible.

Professional Development

Under older accreditation models, neither regional agencies nor state departments offered much staff development. Training amounted to "orientations" on how to fill out forms and conduct visits. But an accreditation system based on school improvement requires focused professional development to succeed. The 18 MISTA schools shared a total of $25,000 per year from the state; plus they received help from the Northwest Regional Educational Laboratory, which provides about eight days of regional training each year.

MISTA schools have made connections with their communities, strengthened relationships among teachers, and formed a network across schools. The lively discussions that take place within each MISTA school committee are continued and expanded at training sessions. The development of these groups is a key to the change process. To quote Fullan again:

> [Teacher] isolation is a problem because it imposes a ceiling effect on inquiry and learning. Solutions are limited to the experiences

Figure 1
Respect: A School Community Profile

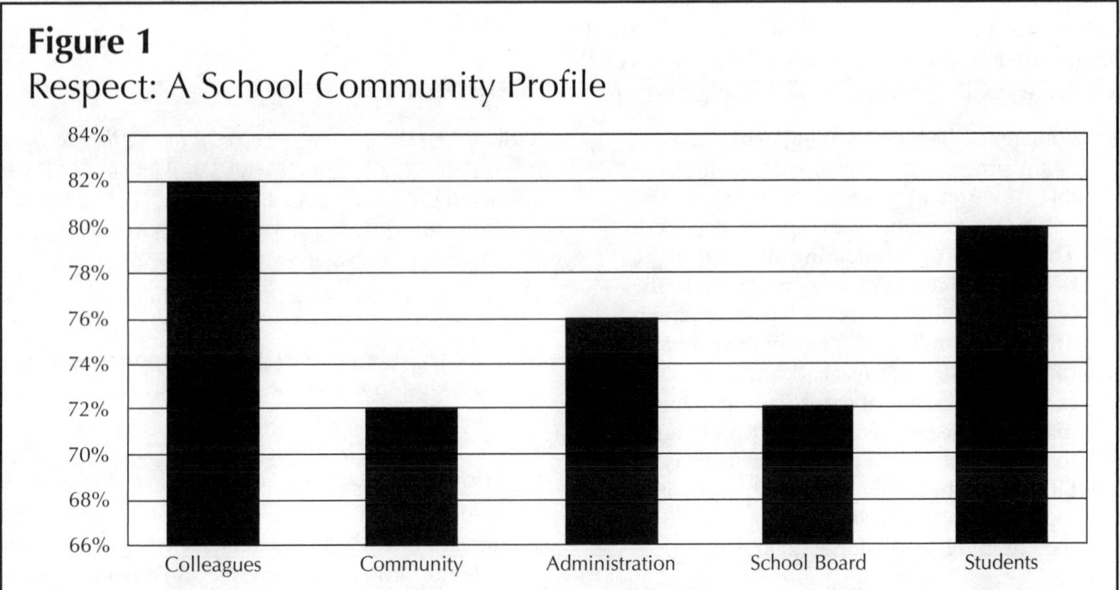

Students collected and entered data from surveys distributed to certified and classified staff at Colstrip High School in Montana. This graphic shows the responses to the question: Does the staff feel respected as professionals by colleagues, the community, the administration, the school board, and the students?

> of the individual. For complex change you need many people working insightfully on the solution and committing themselves to concentrated action together (1993, p. 34).

Currently, MISTA schools are analyzing what is preventing them from fully achieving their educational goals. In some cases, this analysis has become a painful experience. Discovering that deep-seated cultural beliefs may create barriers to student success has forced one school to explore new approaches to attendance problems. Teachers at another school believe they aren't meeting the needs of students with different learning styles. Yet another school will experiment with block scheduling in an attempt to foster more project-oriented instructional methods. With the support of information gathered through profiling, a shared mission, and educational goals identified by stakeholders, these groups are "getting to the heart of school improvement" (Sergiovanni 1992).

Studies promoting networking often point out the unfortunate truth "that people in schools don't talk to each other about serious educational matters very much: nuts and bolts—yes; educational issues—no" (Roberts 1992, p. 28). In the MISTA schools, conversations have shifted. At Havre High School, staff members say, "At meetings, we take time to talk about teaching and learning." At Billings Senior, "Discussions at lunch and in the faculty workroom indicate a heightened awareness of a school moving as one toward a goal." Principal Carol Wicker reports:

> Sometimes the most meaningful by-products of any process or project are not the most visible. As we have worked on our mission statement . . . a vocabulary change has occurred. The staff is understanding the critical tie between what and how they present to the learner and the results we have identified. Those who traditionally taught their content through lecture are saying, "We must become facilitators because there is too much information in the world of the '90s to ever hope to cover it all." . . . Some teachers have even talked of eliminating some of their favorite topics to teach because they cannot see where they fit into our mission with any clarity.

The Learning Community

Faculty, students, and parents who devote countless hours to performance-based accreditation are engaged in a rigorous process to do what is right for children. According to Thomas Sergiovanni, people are driven not only by self-interest but also by emotions, values, beliefs, and social bonds. Motivators include "a sense of achievement, recognition for good work, challenging and interesting work, and a sense of relationship on the job" (1992, p. 60). These characteristics of a learning community are evident in the MISTA schools. All share a sense of optimism about the futures they can create.

As MISTA schools move through the next steps of the process, they will be among the first in the nation to earn accreditation through a method that involves an entire school community, focuses on qualitative measures, and is based on an individual school's vision of how to help students reach higher levels of achievement. These schools and their accrediting agencies are rethinking leadership by turning responsibility over to those who see, firsthand, the results of their decisions. As one of the fishbowl participants put it, "We now have teachers actively learning about our school, making decisions about what students are learning and what needs improving. . . . We are empowered."

References

Fullan, M. (1993). *Change Forces: Probing the Depths of Educational Reform*. Bristol, Pa.: The Falmer Press.

Montana Office of Public Instruction. (1996). *The Performance-Based Alternative: Improving Schools Through Accreditation*. Helena, Mont.: Author.

Pascale, P. (1990). *Managing on the Edge*. New York: Touchstone.

Roberts, H. (February 1992). "The Importance of Networking in the Restructuring Process." *NASSP Bulletin* 76, 541: 25–29.

Senge, P. (1990). *The Fifth Discipline: The Art and Practice of the Learning Organization*. New York: Doubleday.

Sergiovanni, T. (1992). *Moral Leadership: Getting to the Heart of School Improvement*. San Francisco: Jossey-Bass.

TWO CONTINUUMS COLLIDE: ACCREDITATION AND ASSESSMENT

EDWARD S. LUBINESCU, JAMES L. RATCLIFF, MAUREEN A. GAFFNEY

Calls for accountability and improvement reverberate with higher education's internal and external constituencies today. The dialogue takes a variety of forms: cost and benefit, implementation of online learning, greater engagement with the communities the institution serves, program renewal, organizational transformation, and changing the accreditation process itself. Yet stakeholders have found common ground in the discussions and concerns focused on student learning outcomes. Increasingly they are becoming embedded in the accrediting process in a variety of ways. Regardless of whether the accreditation is programmatic, institutional, or virtual, colleges and universities are expected to show effective student learning outcomes. The Council for Higher Education Accreditation (CHEA), the body that brings together the various forms of higher education accreditation in the United States, recognizes the obligation that institutions and the accrediting bodies have in addressing continuing public pressure for evidence of student learning outcomes (Eggers, 2000).

Accreditation and student learning outcomes assessment have been discussed extensively. This volume examines contemporary dimensions of how accreditation and student outcomes assessment come together. Running through the dimensions explored in this volume are two key questions:

- How should student learning outcomes be demonstrated in the accreditation process?
- How should assessment information be used to show improvement in programs, services, and student learning?

In our discussions with faculty serving on self-study teams and with college administrators overseeing accreditation processes, we find that many involved do not reflect on or fully understand what accreditation is, what ends it serves, and what its connection to the assessment of student learning may be. This chapter thus provides a backdrop for the discussions that follow.

Accreditation Purposes and Processes

Accreditation may be "the most fully developed institutionalization of the idea of accountability in higher education" (van Vught, 1994, p. 42). Within the context of the United States, accreditation has the following purposes:

Fostering excellence through the development of criteria and guidelines for assessing effectiveness
Encouraging improvement through ongoing self-study and planning

Reprinted from *New Directions for Higher Education,* Spring 2001, by permission of Jossey-Bass Publishers, Inc.

Ensuring external constituents that a program has clearly defined goals and appropriate objectives, maintains faculty and facilities to attain them, demonstrates it is accomplishing them, and has the prospect for continuing to do so

Provides advice and counsel to new and established programs in the accrediting process

Ensures that programs receive sufficient support and are free from external influence that may impede their effectiveness and their freedom of inquiry

In the United States, regional bodies accredit institutions of higher education. These have separate and different standards and guidelines from program accrediting agencies (Ratcliff, 1998). Whereas a program review may serve as a basis for reallocation of resources toward a specific program, the institutional accreditation assists in achieving a balance of human and financial resources among the various programs.

Van Vught (1994) has presented a vision of a multidimensional system of accreditation wherein a number of accrediting organizations coexist, each using its own standards, guidelines, and review processes. These different accrediting bodies represent different constituencies external to the program and the university. Some serve to attest to institutional, program, or student quality to the government, while others may represent the needs and views of employers, students, or the specific field of study. Taken together, they provide multiple frames of reference in determining the quality of the institution, the program, and the student experience, forming a "market" in which institutions of higher education "compete" for students, research awards, and public recognition. In such a system, governments clearly have the right and responsibility to decide what constitutes an accrediting body. Governments may also wish to review accrediting procedures to ensure that there are adequate procedural safeguards and rigorous application of program standards. In such a vision, the accrediting body becomes a meta-level agent to the field of study, and the government makes procedural rather than substantive specification of the quality review process (Ratcliff, 1998).

What are the elements of a multidimensional system of evaluation that incorporates the evaluation of institutions, programs, and students? First, there needs to be a managing body that is legally empowered to recognize programs deemed legitimate and efficacious. This is the accrediting association, agency, or organization, which is most often empowered by the state and recognized by the federal government to determine quality for programs or institutions. Second, academics of the field need to have a substantive involvement in the development of standards and guidelines for conducting accreditation program reviews so that they may bear the credence desired with internal and external constituencies. Third, the process needs to provide for mechanisms by which a faculty of the program under review accepts the team of external peers assigned to the review process. If the team does not have the confidence of the faculty, it likely will not be persuasive in presenting its findings and recommendations. Fourth, the report of the site visitation team should be developed according to guidelines by which the process is approached as one of communication. That is, the utility of the evaluation of program strengths and weakness and of any recommendations or suggestions made by the site review team is diminished to the extent that it is not fully understood and deliberated by the program faculty and host institution. Fifth, the relationship between the program review process and the funding process needs to be clearly articulated. If funding decisions and the review are tied, then there needs to be clear criteria to determine at what point a weak program will receive enhancements or be subject to discontinuance. Several writers in the field of quality assurance believe it best to separate funding and review processes rather than to link them tightly (Barak, 1982; George, 1982; van Vught and Westerheijden, 1993).

The accreditation process has at least five steps (Kells, 1992, p. 32):

1. The accrediting body sets standards, produces guidelines, and often provides training to peers in the program review process.
2. The program describes its goals and objectives, its faculty, facilities, and courses of study, and evaluates its strengths and weaknesses relative to its goals.
3. An evaluation team of peers identified by the accrediting body visits the program, using the guidelines and standards to

examine faculty, facilities, students, and administrators. The team provides oral commentary followed by a written report to the accrediting body and to the institution housing the program under review.

4. The institution and its faculty respond to the report, providing supplemental evidence where questions remain, and indicating if and where they take exception with the findings of the report.
5. The accrediting body decides to grant, reaffirm, or deny accreditation to the program based on the self-study, the visiting team's findings, and the institutional reply. Frequently accreditation is reaffirmed with the accrediting body making specific recommendations or suggestions for improvement during the forthcoming accrediting period.

Program (or Specialized) Accreditation. Program accreditation, a quality assurance process based on program review, is a means to verify the quality of academic programs and of institutions to external stakeholders. The accreditation process most often involves a formal review, with self-study of a specific academic program, evaluations by peers and external constituents, and a report to the agency, association, or organization that will certify program quality. The accrediting process necessarily encompasses the judgment of peers, as well as some determination of the extent to which the program is needed—through formal needs assessment—or valued—through graduate follow-up or employer surveys. An external body judges the quality of the program using clearly defined standards for the review and a process of self-study where the program's goals and their fulfillment are judged according to the accrediting body's standards. Accrediting bodies assemble a group of peers to review the self-study report, conduct site visits, and render judgments used in the accrediting process (Young and others, 1983). However, there are no established bases for determining who are the relevant external stakeholders, how they are selected, and what program information should guide their judgment about program effectiveness.

Accreditation needs to fulfill two dimensions of program quality. First, there should be some evidence that the programs have clear goals and courses of study to attain them. Second, the process should demonstrate that responsibilities associated with the goals are being carried out (Ewell, 1987). For a typical academic program, it means showing that the program provides courses of study appropriate to the disciplinary field, conducts research in the bodies of knowledge within its purview, and engages in service activities appropriate to the university and the field. It is also increasingly incumbent on the program to portray its impact on students, the discipline and the advance of knowledge within it, and the university and the communities it serves.

In program accreditation, peers interpret quality within the context of the program's own aims and activities. Central to specialized accreditation is the program review conducted as a self-study process. The underlying assumption of the self-study is that evaluators from outside the field of study cannot credibly or effectively examine the quality of a program in depth unless those carrying out the program have first studied and reached a judgment about its quality (Kells, 1992).

Institutional (or Regional) Accreditation. Regional accreditation can be defined as "a quality assurance process based on the voluntary association of schools and colleges" (Ratcliff, 1996). As defined by the CHEA (1996), certain defining characteristics are symbolic of the regional accreditation process. Regional accreditation:

1. Is a process in which a set of criteria is used to evaluate the effectiveness of an institution
2. Is voluntary and is not required by the state or federal government
3. Is a process that reflects the mission, history, and purpose of an institution
4. Is a process that presents evidence to external constituents that an institution meets or surpasses the criteria used in the evaluation
5. Does not normally use comparison in its methods; rather, it treats each institution as a unique entity
6. Is orchestrated by an external, voluntary commission comprised of representatives from the region
7. Is a process wherein the involvement of faculty and staff is regarded as fundamental to its legitimacy

8. Is conducted each time on the basis of a typical ten-year time period
9. Is a process that acknowledges "student learning and development" as a central point for use in the criteria

Regional associations accredit entire institutions (Young and others, 1983). These associations are responsible for a specific geographical region, of which there are six throughout the United States. The associations are Middle States Association of Colleges and Schools, New England Association of Schools and Colleges, North Central Association of Colleges and Schools, Northwest Association of Schools and Colleges, Southern Association of Colleges and Schools, and Western Association of Schools and Colleges. Their purpose is to evaluate the quality of the institution as a whole. Normally they do not try to ascertain quality for individual academic programs within the institution; however, a significant weakness in an individual program can alter a regional accreditor's evaluation (Commission on Institutions of Higher Education, 1983). Regional accreditation is typically reviewed every ten years (Middle States Association of Colleges and Schools, Commission on Higher Education, 1997). Each regional association may give specific focus or character to its accreditation process. For example, the Commission for Senior Colleges and Universities of the Western Association of Schools and Colleges Accrediting seeks to foster a "culture of evidence" among its member institutions through the self-study process (Wolff and Astin, 1990). In such an environment, an institution is open to receiving critical comments on its performance and can use data to respond to such comments. Regional accreditation provides recognition to institutions that meet a minimum standard of quality. Institutions then must strive to maintain this level of quality while seeking to improve human, physical, and financial resources; programs and services; and impact on students and other constituents. In order to maintain accreditation, an institution must respond to any criticism or suggestions given and work to improve the problems identified. Through this process, regional accreditation provides opportunities for institutional improvement and accountability.

The regional accreditation process has three phases: institution self-study, external review, and final decision by the regional commission on accreditation (or reaccreditation). The first phase consists of a probe of the institution or specific programs for which accreditation is sought by a team drawn from within the institution under review (Young and others, 1983). Self-study is conducted through review guidelines established by the accrediting body conducting the review. The accrediting body uses the self-study to evaluate the strengths and weaknesses of the institution in the areas of goals, student composition, faculty qualifications, program structure and content, support services to students, and administrative services, which includes the physical plant, organization, governance, financial areas, research, public services, and outcomes (Young and others, 1983). The self-study aids in the improvement of institutions by helping to establish the foundation for planning, the expansion of research and self-analysis, a chance to review policies, increasing openness among the different factions of university, and helping staff to develop (Young and others, 1983). Accreditors assert that a well-developed and thorough self-study can give an institution a tool for planning and self-analysis (Middle States Association of Colleges and Schools, Commission on Higher Education, 1997). The first phase of self-study can provide valuable information that can serve to promote change.

The next phase brings the accrediting body, chosen by the accrediting association, to campus to conduct an on-site review. The team members are typically from the academic community of similar institutions who serve as peers of the institution under review. They can include various stakeholders and quality assurance agencies (Ewell, 1998). The team's final report is based on the review of the self-study presented by the institution, additional evidence gathered during their site visit, and their professional opinions. A constructive exit interview with institutional leadership and the self-study team allows the reviewers to provide appropriate advice to institutions on how they may improve their quality. The reviewers also make a recommendation to the association based on their findings. The external reviewers serve as a liaison between the institution and the accrediting body.

In the third phase, a committee of the accrediting association, whose members are most often professionals and faculty in the field, reviews the final report submitted by the external review team. It then makes a decision about whether accreditation (or reaccreditation) should be granted. The committee suggests specific areas in which the institution can improve its effectiveness and may pose a variety of institutional courses of action depending on the context and the issue addressed. The final decision made in this third phase completes the accreditation process.

Regional accreditation is a process intended to improve the quality of institutions. Society holds higher education accountable for providing evidence that students are receiving the maximum yield possible from their personal, financial, academic, and emotional investment. Higher education institutions are considered "vendors" in an economy in which the perspective of the consumer is central (Braskamp and Braskamp, 1997). Society demands "product guarantees," and accreditation provides the stamp of approval (Uehling, 1987). To receive this approval, institutions are subject to the three phases in the regional accreditation process. All phases demand adherence to quality and integrity (Uehling, 1987). They serve to identify potential problems within an institution or program and provide a statement of quality to external stakeholders.

Initiatives in Accreditation

The nature of accreditation as a voluntary process has changed over the years. A review of the recent evolution of regional accreditation reveals a transition from an initially voluntary nature to one that is increasingly mandatory.

Voluntary accreditation is a complex story of American institutions' seeking to maintain quality and integrity in education. When institutional eligibility for receipt of federal funding was attached to regional accreditation, the voluntary nature of such accreditation became largely involuntary. Today regional accreditation remains a nongovernmental pursuit, but tension remains between the federal government and higher education, particularly following the failed introduction of State Postsecondary Review Entities in 1965. Colleges and universities and their constituent associations have joined to form several voluntary agencies to coordinate regional and programmatic accreditation. Since 1995, the most recent of these, the CHEA has sought to restore the voluntary nature of the accreditation process to its original purpose: promoting quality. Along with CHEA, regional accrediting bodies have started initiatives aimed at creating a national agenda.

The U.S. Department of Education proposed changes in June 1999 to the 1998 Higher Education Act that directly affected accrediting agencies. Among the several key issues, agencies are expected to review distance-education programs using the same standards they use for evaluating other academic programs (Healy, 1999). If an institution were developing off-campus locations, the accreditors would be required to visit only the first three locations, after which they could use their own discretion. The U.S. secretary of education would take on a new role of setting deadlines for the improvement of accrediting agencies that are experiencing problems. "Unannounced campus visits" were no longer expected as part of the review process. Accreditors would be required to do a periodic review of their own standards to comply with issues of reliability and validity better. All of these changes are in the spirit of making the process of accreditation more flexible and, to some extent, more collegial. For example, the Middles States Association is currently concluding such a review. The proposed regulations seek to return to the traditional role of accreditation: assessing quality and helping institutions become better places of learning (Healy, 1999).

In order for institutions to become better places of learning, each of the regional accrediting associations has undertaken a variety of projects and activities. Under the aegis of the CHEA, the six regional accrediting bodies have sought to foster similar goals and practices. Each has identified its purpose and defined initiatives that serve to improve the process of regional accreditation, as well as improve the connection between regional accreditation and student outcomes assessment. These initiatives range from surveys concerning accreditation standards to new frameworks dealing with outcomes assessment. Each of the initiatives is unique, but its underpinnings adhere to similar ideals of Continuous Quality Improvement (CQI) and collegiality among institutions and their accrediting bodies.

Current Initiatives of the Regional Accrediting Bodies

In July 1999, the North Central Association of Colleges and Schools (NCACS) embarked on the development of a new framework for accredi-

tation. Its Academic Quality Improvement Project is based on helping higher-education institutions develop individual efforts at promoting systematic and continuous improvement. This new model maintains a focus on educational quality while preserving the ideas of institutional autonomy and distinctiveness. The project emphasizes the connection between assessment and accreditation standards. The NCACS is also involved in a project revising its mission and purpose.

The New England Association of Schools and Colleges (NEASC) conducted a survey of chief executive officers in 1998–1999 that sought to determine if the standards for accreditation were capable of assessing the effectiveness of their individual institutions. This initiative is aimed at involving institutions further in the standards that assess their educational quality. The NEASC has conducted an additional survey to learn more about its members' procedures for increasing institutional effectiveness through student outcomes assessment.

The Western Association of Schools and Colleges (WASC) has organized current initiatives around the word *dialogue,* defined as communication among institutions. Since 1997, WASC has recognized and promoted the importance of sharing and communicating best practices in assessing student learning outcomes and other areas of significance with institutions and other regional accrediting bodies. WASC also revised its standards along three dimensions: reducing the number of standards to simplify the regional accreditation process, shifting the stance of accreditation from compliance to collaboration, and giving emphasis to educational effectiveness and student learning.

The other regional accrediting bodies—the Commission on Colleges of the Southern Association of Colleges and Schools (SACS), the Northwest Association of Schools and Colleges (NASC), and the Commission on Higher Education of the Middle States Association of Schools and Colleges (MSASC)—also have stimulated initiatives aimed at enhancing educational quality, promoting greater collaboration among accrediting bodies and institutions, and emphasizing the assessment of student learning outcomes. SACS modified their criteria to allow members confident of meeting basic SACS standards to augment the self-study process with "strategic visits," which give external input and counsel to the institution on its chosen directions for future development of the institution. Institutions need to demonstrate educational quality continually in addition to doing so when they are granted accreditation. SACS is demonstrating the viability of continual visits to improve the process of accreditation, the institution's self-study, and the ability to transfer standards of quality to working examples of change.

In 1996, the MSA issued Framework for Outcomes Assessment, which emphasized that the goal of outcomes assessment is improvement of teaching and learning. The framework supports the idea that student outcomes assessment should attempt to determine the extent and quality of the learning students are receiving. This can be done through the nine steps in the framework assessment plan, which MSA has provided to its members. MSA also is concluding a review of its standards to sharpen the standards relative to the teaching and learning processes of institutions.

As we shall see in subsequent chapters, the six regional accrediting bodies, by adhering to a national agenda focused on improving the regional accreditation process, have created changes and programs and started initiatives that also affect the other regional accrediting bodies, specialized accrediting bodies, and institutions of higher education. These initiatives, along with a close adherence to collaboration among entities, will serve to improve the regional accreditation process by incorporating specific criteria relative to student outcomes assessment.

Student Outcomes Assessment

The shift toward more student-centered and learning-oriented accreditation standards that began in the mid-1980s links student outcomes assessment and accreditation.

In the mid-1980s, calls for reform in higher education were heeded by national reports. Reports such as *Involvement in Learning* (Study Group on the Conditions of Excellence in American Higher Education, 1984), *Integrity in the College Curriculum* (American Association of Colleges, 1985), and *Time for Results* (National Governors' Association, 1986) stimulated a conversation between government representatives about student learning outcomes and the preparation of college graduates (Banta and Moffett,

1987). Individual institutional pioneers in implementing student learning outcomes as a priority included Alverno College in Milwaukee, WI, Truman State University in Kirksville, MO, and the University of Tennessee, Knoxville (Banta, 1985; Palomba and Banta, 1999). Although these individual institutions implemented assessment programs in the 1980s, the majority of assessment programs began as a result of statewide initiatives. Since the early 1980s, states increasingly have mandated the documentation of student outcomes. Formal state-level interaction began with Tennessee and Virginia. In 1979, Tennessee adopted a policy that granted funding based on standardized testing and student outcome assessment results. A different model in Virginia emerged in 1985, where institutions choose their own assessment procedures to reflect individual institutional missions (National Center for Education Statistics, 1996). The institutional autonomy inherent in Virginia's model is a more accepted model of state-mandated student outcomes assessment. In 1984, Florida began a statewide student assessment program, the College Level Academic Skills Test. These examples portray very different state initiatives. In fact, no two states have identical policies regarding accreditation or assessment (Paulson, 1990). Nevertheless, since 1985, state mandates and regional accreditation criteria have required most colleges and universities to implement procedures for student outcomes assessment (Borden and Bottrill, 1994).

In the fall of 1988, William Bennett, the U.S. secretary of education, suggested that accreditation organizations incorporate criteria for institutional student outcomes into their accrediting criteria (U.S. Department of Education, 1988). Over the next few years, regional and programmatic accrediting bodies issued new guidelines for accreditation that included student outcomes assessment. The role of statewide initiatives was crucial to stimulating the kind of attention being paid to student outcomes. Today these initiatives are reinforced by the standards of the regional accreditation agencies (El-Khawas, 1993).

Rossman and El-Khawas (1987) suggest three reasons that assessment exists in higher education institutions: political, economic, and educational. Erwin (1991) proposes a fourth: societal. Political reasons include the need of government officials to ascertain that funds allocated to higher education are being used effectively for programs and services. Assessment is seen as a tool to ensure that colleges and universities produce graduates who constitute a well-trained, competent, and competitive workforce—the economic reason. Educational reasons for assessment often come from within higher education and are reflected in the various national reports. In these reports, quality is most often the primary educational reason for implementing assessment. The societal reason refers to the broader public aspect of higher education. Society needs to understand what higher education is offering and how it is meeting the needs of the public. Such social concerns extend beyond the immediate needs of government officials for attestation that public funds are being used wisely and are larger than the internal academic discourse over the quality of programs and services.

The reasons given for why assessment exists are closely related to why accreditation exists. Federal and state governments are interested in both assessment and regional accreditation because they have a vested interest in knowing how funding is spent. Given increasingly tight budget restrictions, the federal and state governments are forced to take a more active role in determining the outcomes and quality of institutions for the money invested. Economically, the issue is providing quality institutions that will produce quality learning to ensure a capable and proficient workforce. This translates into positive student outcomes, and these students become productive, contributing members to the economy. Educationally, the assessment of learning is important, and curricular reform may be necessary to produce a quality learning experience. Increasing tuition costs and parental concern provide reasons for the societal concerns relating to assessment (Erwin, 1991). The rationale for student outcomes assessment helps define its scope and the methods of implementation.

Assessing Student Learning Outcomes

Student learning outcomes are commonly defined as "any change or consequence occurring as a result of enrollment in a particular educational institution and involvement in its programs" (Ewell, 1983). Assessment is the process of defining, selecting, designing, collecting, analyzing, interpreting, and using information to increase students' learning and development (Marchese, 1987). A framework is often useful in organizing and coordinating the process. One such framework offers five dimensions (Rowntree, 1987).

The first dimension of Rowntree's framework addresses the question: Why assess? This involves deciding why assessment needs to be conducted and what can be expected as a result. There are many purposes of assessment. For example, assessment can be used in maintenance of standards, admissions, motivation of students, and feedback purposes for both teachers and students. The purposes of assessment may overlap and be reciprocal or can conflict. An example of where two purposes of assessment reciprocate can be found in selecting a group of candidates who score extremely high on standardized tests. An institution may be improving its standards because it will have a student body that entered at a higher level than in the past. An example where purposes may conflict is providing feedback to a student within the confines of a course. This may detrimentally affect that particular student's motivation. The above purposes of assessment do not exhaust possible reasons for conducting assessment. Other reasons for conducting assessment include demonstrating external accountability, recruiting, fundraising, and improving instruction (Ewell, 1998). It is very important that an institution or program decide on and state the purpose of assessment beyond that of fulfilling accreditation requirements. Most purposes of assessment revolve around improving performance in some aspect or demonstrating effectiveness. Both involve some aspect of evaluation that is making judgments about the efforts of assessment (Ratcliff, 1996). These two concepts are also related to the differentiation between formative and summative assessment.

The second dimension of Rowntree's framework focuses on the question: What to assess? Given the exploration of the variety of student outcomes, it is difficult to determine which are most important. Four types of outcomes emerge: cognitive-psychological, cognitive-behavioral, affective-psychological, and affective-behavioral (Astin, 1973). The variety of possible student outcomes makes the process of assessment difficult to implement. Given individual institutions, different populations of students, varying state regulations, and a variety of student learning taxonomies, what to assess has become an individual institutional decision based on mission and institutional goals.

The third dimension addresses the question: How to assess? This dimension entails selection of a way to describe student learning from the many possible choices. The methods and measures selected should describe and differentiate excellent, satisfactory, and unsatisfactory performance. The criteria and measures selected often imply a method of data collection as well as integrating assessments from out-of-class experiences and in-class experiences, which can yield better judgments about what a particular student is learning than relying on one measure (Ewell, 1983). Also, it may be useful to incorporate both traditional and nontraditional assessment measures, such as interviews, self-judgment of one's own learning, and practical skills tests.

The fourth dimension answers the question: How to interpret? After obtaining results from the selected measures, the next step is exploring the results. Understanding this aspect of the framework is extremely important for each person in the assessment process. Data do not render their own significance. A low undergraduate performance on a writing assessment may mean that the institution needs to give more attention to improving student abilities in that area. Or it may mean that the writing assessment chosen does not adequately reflect the type of writing skills taught. Or it may mean that students are not being asked to write and improve their writing in the first courses they select in college. The results of the writing assessment alone will not illuminate where the problem lies. Further inquiry is required for improvement to occur. This further inquiry provides the interpreters of the results with a yardstick by which to measure the outcomes in the future as well.

The fifth dimension considers the question: How to respond? This involves determining to whom to communicate the findings and through what medium. Rowntree (1987) presumes two important things to consider in how to respond: providing the information to the public and providing information that is accurate and detailed. The greater the amount of information that an institution can provide, the more valid and reliable the assessment procedure will be. Also, by using honest information, the institution can consider its assessment process a means to change and improve its practices.

This framework provides only a beginning. It allows programs and institutions to organize their thoughts and give a sense of direction to a complicated process. It is also useful to determine what goes into assessing. Banta, Lund, Black, and Oblander (1996) stated: "A general theme running throughout appeals for reform is the need for institutions to focus their assessment efforts on what matters most" (p. 4). Institutions can use this framework as a way to determine where and how assessment efforts would matter most based on mission, goals, outcomes, and expectations.

Putting Accreditation and Assessment Together: Some Conclusions

Assessment and accreditation are both premised on the importance of quality assurance. Everyone in the educational enterprise has responsibility for maintaining and improving the quality of services and programs. Equally important are regular reviews of the validity and viability of the systems for examining quality. Colleges and universities, which seriously value and undertake quality assurances (including peer reviews), normally engage in a self-critical and reflective process. This process includes all members of the community as they strive to contribute to and enhance the educational enterprise.

The formal self-study and review process relies on certain key attributes in order to formulate strong plans. First, it should be "clear to all parties concerned (government, parliament, higher education institutions—staff and students) what may be expected from such a review process (Vroeijenstijn, 1995, p. 39). Clear expectations defining the purposes and the outcomes to be achieved through review processes must be articulated and shared with all participants. Major purposes of evaluating quality can include contributing to decisions on planning or funding, validating, granting professional recognition to programs, accrediting, or making awards of degrees (Frazer, 1991). Reviews also need to define whether the focus is on teaching, student learning, or research.

Second, the review process should be directed toward either a summative or formative evaluation. Attempts to conduct both simultaneously may lead to less successful efforts. Formative evaluations are most useful in providing directions for programmatic improvements, which faculty and administrators most highly value.

Third, college and universities should have direct responsibility and active engagement in the review processes. Taking self-study and student assessments seriously as means to accountability and improvement helps faculty and administrators to gain commitment and ownership for both the process and the outcomes. The results are more likely to be viewed as useful and credible by faculty and will have more potential to lead to targeted enhancements. Fourth, these review processes are not ends in themselves but represent ongoing processes that should be constantly refined or adapted to changing conditions within and external to the institutional environment. Regular, systematic, and cyclical reviews help institutions to monitor the strengths of their system continuously, with a particular focus on the types of improvements made after each evaluation cycle.

There is a growing consensus that effective quality assurance methods such as accreditation and program review will depend on the history, traditions, and culture of the country, state, or territory concerned. Whatever these may be for a particular program or institution, an external element to the processes selected is necessary to attain a clear, objective, and credible outcome (Bethel, 1991). Increasingly, faculty and administrators value the views emanating from peer evaluations in crafting the course of reform.

Most countries recognize that the need to sustain or develop their economies requires an increasing population of skilled individuals to achieve stability and meet competitive challenges in the world. Escalating costs of higher education and increased student access have led to significant growth and complexity in U.S. colleges and universities. External constituencies, including employers and the public, will continue to want evidence that higher education is meeting the needs of the workplace and society in general.

The formal review processes discussed here outline the important roles that accreditation and program review have in aiding institutions to improve and inform their constituents. University alumni will assume expanded roles as citizens who must address complex issues in society and will assume leadership positions in industry and commerce. Also, sustaining basic and applied research is necessary if the skills needed by society and the global economy are to be reached.

The introduction of student outcomes assessment in the early 1980s with Tennessee and Virginia demonstrated a movement in higher education largely characterized by increased state intervention. Statewide mandates often brought about the need for student outcomes assessment plans. From the early 1980s through 1988, states increasingly became involved in mandating student outcomes assessment, and institutions felt an infringement on institutional autonomy. Beginning with the urgings of U.S. Secretary of Education William Bennett in 1988, accrediting bodies began to incorporate student outcomes assessment into the accreditation criteria.

The accountability movement in the 1990s followed the campus-based assessment movement of the 1980s (Gaither, 1995). Accountability put accreditation and assessment on a collision course. Two parallel continuums can be seen: one detailing the cycle of accreditation and the other student outcomes assessment. Now the two continuums have merged. The accountability movement is still an active issue in higher education. The chapters that follow illustrate how these can be positive forces in public accountability, the impetus for internal change, the extension of distance learning, and accreditation processes.

References

American Association of Colleges. *Integrity in the College Curriculum: A Report to the Academic Community*. Washington, D.C.: American Association of Colleges, 1985.

Astin, A. "Measurement and Determinants of the Outputs of Higher Education. In L. Solmon and P. Taubman, (eds.), *Does College Matter? Some Evidence on the Impacts of Higher Education*. Orlando, Fla.: Academic Press, 1973.

Banta, T. W. "Use of Outcomes Information at the University of Tennessee, Knoxville." In P. T. Ewell (ed.), *Assessing Educational Outcomes*. New Directions for Institutional Research, no. 47. San Francisco: Jossey-Bass, 1985.

Banta, T. W., Lund, J. P., Black, K. E., and Oblander, F. W. *Assessment in Practice: Putting Principles to Work on College Campuses.* San Francisco: Jossey-Bass, 1996.

Banta, T. W., and Moffett, M. S. "Performance Funding in Tennessee: Stimulus for Program Improvement." In D. F. Halpern, *Student Outcomes Assessment: What Institutions Stand to Gain*. New Directions for Higher Education, no. 59. San Francisco: Jossey-Bass, 1987.

Barak, R. J. *Program Review in Higher Education: Within and Without*. Boulder, Colo.: National Center on Higher Education Management Systems. ERIC Document Reproduction No. ED 246 829, 1982.

Bethel, D. "Conclusions." In Craft, A. (ed.), *Quality Assurance in Higher Education: Proceedings of an International Conference Hong Kong*. Washington, D. C: The Falmer Press, 1991.

Borden, V. M. H., and Bottrill, K. V. "Performance Indicators: History, Definitions, and Methods." In V. M. H. Borden and T. W. Banta (eds.), *Using Performance Indicators to Guide Strategic Decision Making*. New Directions for Institutional Research, no. 82. San Francisco: Jossey-Bass, 1994.

Braskamp, L. A., and Braskamp, D. C. "The Pendulum Swing of Standards and Evidence." *CHEA Chronicle,* July 1997, p. 5. [http://www.chea.org/Chronicle/vol1/no5/index.html].

Commission on Institutions of Higher Education, New England Association of Schools and Colleges. *Accreditation Handbook: 1983 Edition*. Winchester, Mass.: New England Association of Schools and Colleges, 1983.

Council for Higher Education Accreditation. "Why CHEA?" CHEA *Chronicle,* Nov. 1996, *1*(3). [http://www.chea.org/Chronicle/vol1/no3/index.html].

Eggers, W. "The Value of Accreditation in Planning." CHEA *Chronicle*, Jan. 2000, *(3)*1. [http://www.chea.org/Chronicle/vol3/nol/value.html].

El-Khawas, E. *Higher Education Panel Report No. 83*. Washington, D.C.: American Council on Education, 1993.

Erwin, T. D. *Assessing Student Learning and Development: A Guide to the Principles, Goals, and Methods of Determining College Outcomes*. San Francisco: Jossey-Bass, 1991.

Ewell, P. T. *Information on Student Outcomes: How to Get It and How to Use It*. Boulder, Colo.: National Center for Higher Education Management Systems, 1983.

Ewell, P. T. *Assessment, Accountability and Improvement*. Washington, D.C.: American Association for Higher Education, 1987.

Ewell, P. T. *Examining a Brave New World: How Accreditation Might Be Different*. Boulder, Colo.: National Center for Higher Education Management Systems, 1998.

Frazer, M. "Quality Assurance in Higher Education." In Craft, A. (ed.), *Quality Assurance in Higher Education: Proceedings of an International Conference Hong Kong*. Washington, D.C.: The Falmer Press, 1991.

Gaither, G. H. (ed.) *Assessing Performance in an Age of Accountability: Case Studies*. New Directions for Higher Education, no. 91. San Francisco: Jossey-Bass, 1995.

George, M. D. "Assessing Program Quality." In Wilson, R. F. (ed.), *Designing Academic Program Reviews*. New Directions for Higher Education, no. 37. San Francisco: Jossey-Bass, 1982.

Halpern, D. F. "Student Outcomes Assessment: Introduction and Overview." In D. F. Halpern (ed.), *Student Outcomes Assessment: What Institutions Stand to Gain*. New Directions for Higher Education, no. 59. San Francisco: Jossey-Bass, 1987.

Healy, P. "Education Department Proposes Rules to Increase Flexibility In Accreditation." *Chronicle of Higher Education*, July 9, 1999.

Kells, H. R. *Self-Regulation in Higher Education: A Multi-National Perspective on Collaborative Systems of Quality Assurance and Control*. Higher Education Policy Series, no. 15. London: Jessica Kingsley Publishers, 1992.

Marchese, T. "Third Down, Ten Years to Go." *AAHE Bulletin*, 1987, *40*, 3–8.

McGuinness, A. C. "The States and Higher Education." In P. G. Altbach, R. O. Berdahl, and P. J. Gumport (eds.), *American Higher Education in the Twenty-First Century: Social, Political, and Economic Challenges*. Baltimore, Md.: Johns Hopkins University Press, 1999.

Middle States Association of Colleges and Schools, Commission on Higher Education. *Directory: Accredited Membership and Candidates for Accreditation, 1997–98*. Philadelphia: Commission on Higher Education, 1997.

National Center for Education Statistics. *The National Assessment of College Student Learning: State-Level Assessment Activities, a Report of the Proceedings of the Third Study Design Workshop*. Washington, D.C.: National Center for Education Statistics, 1996.

National Governors' Association. *Time for Results: The Governor's 1991 Report on Education*. Washington, D.C.: National Governors' Association Center for Policy Research and Analysis, 1986.

Palomba, C. A., and Banta, T. W. *Assessment Essentials: Planning, Implementing, and Improving Assessment in Higher Education*. San Francisco: Jossey-Bass, 1999.

Paulson, C. P. *State Initiatives in Assessment and Outcome Measurement: Tools for Teaching and Learning in the 1990s: Individual State Profiles*. Denver: Education Commission of the States, 1990.

Ratcliff, J. L. "Assessment, Accreditation, and Evaluation of Higher Education in the US." *Quality in Higher Education*, 1996, *2*(1).

Ratcliff, J. L. "Institutional Self-Evaluation and Quality Assurance: A Global View." In A. Strydom and L. Lategan (eds.), *Enhancing Institutional Self-Evaluation in South African Higher Education: National and International Perspectives*. Blomfontein, RSA: Unit for Research in Higher Education, University of the Orange Free State, 1998.

Rossman, J. E., and El-Khawas, E. *Thinking About Assessment: Perspectives for Presidents and Chief Academic Officers*. Washington, D.C.: American Council on Education and American Association for Higher Education, 1987.

Rowntree, D. *Assessing Students: How Shall We Know Them?* New York: Nichols Publishing Company, 1987.

Study Group on the Conditions of Excellence in American Higher Education, National Institute of Education. *Involvement in Learning: Realizing the Potential of American Higher Education*. Washington, D.C.: U.S. Government Printing Office, 1984.

Uehling, B. S. "Serving Too Many Masters: Changing the Accreditation Process." *Educational Record*, 1987, *68*(3), 38–41.

U.S. Department of Education. "Secretary's Procedures and Criteria for Recognition of Accrediting Agencies." *Federal Register*, 1988, 53(127), 25088–25099.

van Vught, F. A. "Intrinsic and Extrinsic Aspects of Quality Assessment in Higher Education." In D. F. Westerheijden, J. Brennan, and P. A. M. Massen (eds.), *Changing Contexts of Quality Assessment*. Utrecht: Lemma, 1994.

van Vught, F. A., and Westerheijden, D. F. *Quality Management and Quality Assurance in European Higher Education: Methods and Mechanisms*. Luxembourg: Office for Office Publications, European Community, 1993.

Vroeijenstijn, A. I. *Improvement and Accountability: Navigating Between Scylla and Charybdis: Guide for External Quality Assessment in Higher Education*. Higher Education Policy Series, no. 30. Bristol, Pa.: Jessica Kingsley Publishers, 1995.

Wolff, R. A., and Astin, A. W. "Assessment 1990: Accreditation and Renewal." Paper presented at the Fifth American Association of Higher Education Conference on Assessment in Higher Education, Washington, D. C., 1990.

Young, K. E., and others. *Understanding Accreditation*. San Francisco: Jossey-Bass, 1983.

RECOMMENDED READINGS

Banta, Trudy W., Lund, Jon P., Black, Karen E. and Oblander, Frances W. (eds) (1996). *Assessment in Practice: Putting Principles to Work on College Campuses.* Jossey Bass: San Francisco.

Delaney, Anne Marie (1997). The role of institutional research in higher education. *Research in Higher Education* v38, n1 p1-16.

Ewell, Peter (1999). Linking performance measures to resource allocation: exploring unmapped terrain. *Quality in Higher Education.* v5, n3, p. 191-209.

Ewell, Peter T. (1999). Assessment of higher education quality: promise and politics. In Messick, Samuel J. (ed. 1999). *Assessment in Higher Education: Issues of Access, Quality, Student Development and Public Policy.* Lawrence Erlbaum: Nahwah, New Jersey.

Fetterman, David M. (1990). Ethnographic auditing: a new approach to evaluating management. *New Directions for Institutional Research.* V17, n4, p. 19-34.

Gray, Peter J. (1997). Viewing assessment as an innovation: leadership and the change process. *New Directions for Higher Education.* v25 n4 p5-15.

Hoey, J. Joseph, and Gardner, Denise C. (1999). Using surveys of alumni and their employers to improve an institution. *New Directions for Institutional Research.* v26. n1 p43-59.

Hubelbank, Jeanne H. (2001). Evaluation as a catalyst for change. ED458264.

Ingram, R. T. and Weary, W. A. (200). Presidential and Board assessment in higher education: purposes, policies and strategies. ED441364.

Layzell, D. T. (1999). Linking performance to funding outcomes at the state level for public institutions of higher education: past, present, and future. *Research in Higher Education,* v40, n2 pp233-46.

Linn, Robert L. (2001). Assessments and accountability (condensed version). *Practical Assessment, Research & Evaluation.* 7(11). Available online: http://ericae.net/pare/getvn.asp?v=7&n=11.

Meade, P., Morgan, M.,& Heath, C. (1999). Equipping leaders to capitalize on the outcomes of quality assessment in higher education. *Assessment & Evaluation in Higher Education,* v24 n2 pp.147-56.

Peterson, Marvin W., and Augustine, Catherine H. (2000). External and internal influences on institutional approaches to student assessment: accountability or improvement? *Research in Higher Education.* V41 n4 p443-79.

Schmidtlein, Frank A. (1999). Emerging perspectives on organizational behavior: implications for institutional researchers. *New Directions for Institutional Research.* v 26, n4 p61-71.

Shenkle, Cynthia W., Snyder, Robert S., and Bauer, Karen W. (1998). Measures of campus climate. *New Directions for Institutional Research.* V25 n2 p.81-99.

Stufflebeam, Daniel L. (1998). Lessons in contracting for evaluations. *American Journal of Evaluation.* v21 n3 p287-296.

DISCUSSION & REFLECTION

Why is the involvement of faculty important in the institutional assessment process?

In what ways do accreditation and assessment work at cross purposes? Why does or does it not matter?

What is the appropriate role of institutional research in the program review process?

What are the pros and cons for recruiting wide involvement in institutional assessment?

SECTION III

TEACHING & LEARNING

TEACHING & LEARNING

Introduction

Teaching and learning continues to be the primary mission of postsecondary institutions in the 21st century. The literature on measuring and valuing the teaching and learning processes is prolific and grows at the speed of light. In addition to the quantity of information, the related topics are numerous; narrowing the scope was a Herculean task. Therefore this section is more expansive than some of the other sections. This section addresses the process of curriculum development, classroom assessment, factors that affect faculty performance, and technology in the delivery of course content (e.g. distance education). In addition to assessment and evaluation strategies that focus on instructional techniques, the literature in this section, included or identified, addresses culturally-relevant pedagogy and its influence on learning among diverse groups.

CLASSIC READINGS

COGNITIVE MEASURES IN ASSESSING LEARNING

JONATHAN WARREN

Cognitive measures play a limited but crucial role in educational assessment. They are defined here as procedures for observing and recording students' intellectual accomplishments. The information they provide should inform students about what they have and have not learned, faculty members about the successes and failures of their instruction, and department heads and deans about the suitability of the curriculum in bringing students to the desired academic capabilities. The first of these functions requires information about individual students; the other two, information about collective learning.

The Cognitive Complexity of Learning

In the past several decades, cognitive science has grown dramatically as a discipline and as a context in which to examine and perhaps restructure education. One point on which cognitive scientists agree is that knowledge and cognitive skills, or methods of using and manipulating knowledge, are both necessary components of successful intellectual activity (Gardiner, 1985; Simon, 1980). A second point of agreement is that cognitive or intellectual activities are numerous and diverse: "Even if the processes by which individuals reason or classify may be similar the world over, the actual products and *the ways they are thought about* may be so different as to make illuminating generalizations elusive" (Gardiner, 1985, p. 357; emphasis added). The failure of educators to settle on common goals for the teaching of thinking is understandable (Nickerson, Perkins, and Smith, 1985).

Although there can be only slippery generalizations about the most useful cognitive processes or domains of learning in the undergraduate years, attempts to grasp such generalizations are frequent. A common response to recent criticism of higher education's fragmented curricula has been to construct new "core" curricula that incorporate general intellectual goals—problem solving, historical consciousness, global awareness, analytical reasoning, and other broad rubrics that have not often served as explicit goals of instruction. As those goals are introduced into existing courses and curricula, methods for evaluating their impacts on student learning are needed; yet their variety, in both content and processes, creates problems in assessing how well students reach them.

The Gap in Information About Learning

The assessment of students' learning has remained strangely out of step with the growing complexity of that learning. Only the rare institution, such as Alverno College, has any record of the substance of what its students have learned (Alverno College Faculty, 1985). Typically, the only record related

Reprinted from *Implementing Outcomes Assessment: Promise and Perils-New Directions for Institutional Research,* no. 59 (1988), Jossey-Bass Publishers, Inc.

to learning is the list of courses students took and the grades they received. Grades indicate students comparative levels of accomplishment of unspecified kinds of learning, relative to the unknown achievement of anonymous groups of other students. No adequate evaluation can be made, nor record kept, of the success of an educational enterprise without information about the substantive learning of its students—their knowledge of content and their facility with advanced cognitive processes.

The simple convenience of grades and test scores gives them great appeal; their cost, in terms of loss of meaning when widely diverse kinds of performance are forced onto a single scale, tends to be ignored. Grades represent a mix of different kinds of knowledge, cognitive skills, personal qualities or work habits, and faculty emphases. Nevertheless, these components are all presumed equivalent when a student's performance is placed on a one-dimensional scale of achievement. Standardized tests have the same one-dimensional quality, purposely built into them for high reliability. However widely an achievement test's items sample the domain of a field, the resulting score is based on the assumption that the items contribute to a single, uniform dimension of knowledge or ability. For some purposes, such as for indicating which applicants are best prepared for admission to an educational program, that assumption is acceptable; a general picture of academic preparation can be conveyed without providing details. In contrast, when the information's purpose is to provide a record of what students have accomplished in a program, and when that record is used by faculty, administrators, and external constituencies, the details of the learning and their variations become important. Grades may be acceptable as general indicators of relative academic success, but for evaluating the specific success of a particular educational program, more informative indicators are needed. We take pride in students who achieve academic honors, but we can seldom say in any detail what these students accomplished that other students did not. If a group of foreign professors visiting an American university were to ask about the accomplishments of, say, its history graduates, the only information they could be given would be impressionistic. The local faculty members could describe what they hoped their students would accomplish and the usual degree of student success, but they would have nothing to document or demonstrate those accomplishments. If pressed, or if embarrassed by their inability to show any evidence of what their students had learned, the faculty might bring out syllabi, textbooks, or sample examinations, but these would only indicate expectations for learning; nothing would describe what typical students in those courses had actually learned or what the more capable students had learned beyond what was typical. Some of the host faculty members might then describe their grade distributions, pointing out that almost 50 percent of the history majors got B's or better in their history courses, 50 percent C's, and only 1 or 2 percent D's and F's. Yet some of the host history faculty might find those figures embarrassing, thinking that more than half the history majors should have history grade point averages above C. Others might take pride in the same information, seeing as evidence of the department's rigor that not even half the students averaged better than C. In fact, however, grade distributions have no known reference points and no one substantive interpretation; they say nothing about the quality of learning, in terms of either content or cognitive skills.

The seriousness of the gap in information about what students learn is illustrated in a recent article on engineering education (Kerr and Pipes, 1987). The authors argue that undergraduate engineering education has declined over the past thirty years because engineering curricula have shifted their emphases from the poorly defined problems typical of engineering practice (which often require intuitive rather than analytical approaches) to the analytical methods of theoretical science. Graduating engineers, they claim, are less able to handle typical engineering problems than former graduates were. Their evidence comes from comparisons of college catalogues and textbooks, from which only limited inferences can be drawn about what engineering students learn. Whether current engineering graduates are actually less able to solve poorly defined problems than former graduates were can be known only from the percentages of engineering students today and in previous years who have worked successfully with various kinds of problems. To be complete, that information should describe variations in student achievement in terms of cognitive processes required to solve the problems, as well as in terms of content; neither kind of information appears in catalogues or textbooks.

Monitoring trends in the content, strengths, and weaknesses of the educational product is part of using assessment to demonstrate accountability to external constituencies, but information on the substance of what students have learned also has other uses. The special strengths of similar programs, or of courses that differ in their emphases, can be identified. Several courses' combined effects on student learning can be disentangled from their individual effects. The effects of different kinds of educational preparation for a program can be separated from the effects of the program itself. Differences between what ordinary students learn and what the best students learn can suggest modifications of instruction to accommodate students who have distinct purposes or abilities. Indicators that lack information on what was learned cannot adequately serve purposes such as these.

Sources of Information on Learning

In the following discussion, the phrase *indicators of learning* refers to the collective learning of groups of students, which is assumed to be reportable beyond the boundaries of those groups. A professor who observes that a student's oral or written report shows particularly keen understanding of a complex issue, and who reports that to thestudent, is engaging in the gathering and reporting ofinformation about student learning. Similar observations of other students, if cumulated into a summary statement of the students' collective performance, would contribute to an indicator of learning, as the term is used here.

Course Examinations. The periodic examinations faculty members give their classes—quizzes, midterms, and finals—overwhelm all other sources of information on learning, in terms of time and effort given them. Those examinations have strengths most other indicators lack. First, they are directly related to the material studied. Even when wide agreement exists about the content of an undergraduate field, as in chemistry, every department has its own strengths and areas of emphasis, which are often not adequately represented in exams prepared outside the courses in which the material is taught. Second, the frequency of exams in each course makes them more comprehensive of the material covered than any so-called comprehensive exam given only at the end of an academic year. Third, they permit timely feedback about where students have succeeded and where further effort is needed. Fourth, they perform the same function for the faculty, providing information on students' difficulties soon enough for instructors to help. Fifth, they avoid the pressures of comprehensive exams, which some students find intimidating. Sixth, exams in a course usually elicit students best efforts, but that is not always true with end-of-year exams given for the benefit of the institution. Finally, course exams require no additional time outside regular course activities from either faculty or students.

Course exams do have weaknesses, particularly if the information is to be used outside a particular course. First, as noted above, course exams rarely leave any record of what students have learned. Second, they provide no reference group against which collective learning (whether substantive or not) in a particular course or program can be compared. Much of the meaning of test results is lost in the absence of suitable reference groups. If a large proportion of students in a course get every question on an exam right, no one can be sure whether the test was too easy and the course undemanding, or whether the students were particularly capable and had learned the material unusually well. Faculty members can and do compare performances of current and past classes, but they rarely know what similar students in similar courses at other institutions have accomplished. Their expectations may be unnecessarily low or unrealistically high. Moreover, even the information that does let faculty make sense of their students' test results is often left unrecorded. Finally, course exams are often justifiably criticized for testing only what is tested easily, but often not well. The higher cognitive skills essential to academic success are sometimes difficult to observe. This is a universal problem in the assessment of learning, however, and whether it applies more severely to course exams than to other forms of assessment is questionable. If the exercise of higher cognitive skills depends on their substantive content, then faculty members are in a better position than external testing agencies to assess them. Many faculty members make good tests. Improving their test-making skills, when necessary, is not difficult.

Informal, Course-Based Observations. Apart from the formal assignments and examinations that faculty members give students, and the papers, reports, and test results that students give to their professors, there is a variety of less formal kinds of communication between faculty and students. The approach that faculty members take to a topic, the questions they raise and pursue, the kinds of assignments they give, and the attitudes they convey—through these and more subtle cues—tell perceptive students not only which issues are important but also the reasons for their importance. The questions students ask, the comments they make, and even their body language are all cues to learning that faculty members pick up (Rice, 1987). These observations are usually unsystematic, intuitive, and unrecorded, yet their results often influence grades; and grades, with all their limitations, are the most important record of learning now used.

Except in large classes, faculty members rarely have difficulty knowing which students are understanding the material, picking up the fine points, and incorporating them into an integrated understanding of a course. Faculty also know which students do the assignments, study the material regularly but mechanically, miss subtle connections among a course's concepts and issues, and leave with an acceptable grade but with only a superficial grasp of what a course was about.

The informal, intuitive sources of information that faculty members in small classes use for evaluating their students can be made more systematic and used in large as well as small classes. Faculty members can often translate the informal indicators of learning that they use intuitively into one- to five-minute written exercises, given to students at the beginning or the end of class. The results can be examined quickly for indications of where the class collectively lags in understanding or completely misses the point. At the end of the term, those collective results, briefly recorded, can constitute a detailed and virtually continual documentation of the development of understanding among the students in the course and of the variations in their collective accomplishment.

Locally Developed Comprehensive Examinations. Comprehensive exams developed by an institution for its own use are one alternative to course exams for documenting what students have learned. They may be given at the end of each academic year, at the end of the sophomore and senior years, or on completion of a program. They may be written or oral; composed of multiple choice questions, essay questions, quantitative problems, or mixes of these; or focused on learning in the students' major fields or on general education. They may be observed and graded by local faculty, or by experts from other institutions or from outside higher education (Fong, 1987; O'Neill, 1983).

Whether comprehensive exams are developed within or outside an institution, persons other than those who taught the students usually assess them. This procedure can remove the "conflict of interest" held to exist when the instructor sets the standards, instructs the students, and evaluates their performance. It may also improve learning by allowing students and faculty to be collaborators rather than adversaries in learning. Yet the adversarial relationship is fostered more by the assignment of grades than by the examination process itself. When exams are used only as sources of information, for students and for faculty, about the substance and level of learning that has occurred, then the adversarial nature of the relationship is diminished.

Comprehensives may introduce students to perspectives on course material that differ from those of their instructors. That result, although it is unfair to students if it is used to evaluate them individually, can be valuable to the institution if it indicates portions of the curricula that have been unintentionally slighted. Developed at the students' own institution, comprehensives can be kept relevant to local curriculum and simultaneously separate assessment from teaching.

Removing assessment from individual courses has another potential advantage: Comprehensive exams may be designed to indicate how well students have integrated the learning from several courses or incorporated experiences from outside courses. Comprehensive exams provide an opportunity for documenting the synergistic effects courses are hoped to have.

Whether local or external, comprehensives have inherent weaknesses. They cannot realistically cover the entire scope of student learning, even when given each academic year. Coming at the end of a year, their results cannot be used as guides to study or instruction. They are costly in terms of student and faculty time. Finally, if they have any effect on students' academic standing, the resulting pressure on students is liable to bias the results, but if they do not affect grades, some students will not take them seriously.

One of the strengths claimed for comprehensives is that they indicate what students have really learned, rather than what they have learned just long enough to pass an exam, but that may be another weakness. Some of what students have learned a few months before the comprehensive will have been forgotten by the time the exam is given but could quickly be relearned should the need arise. Thus, comprehensives may not showsome prior learning, but that does not mean the learning has been lost.

Other weaknesses, although not inherent, require careful circumvention. The material covered in comprehensives, in addition to being "uncomprehensive," may be uneven and haphazard, largely because so much material must be covered in so little time. Further, the learning that students demonstrate is rarely recorded, whether the exams are oral or written. Particularly if exams are oral, their scope, relevance, and validity may all be questionable.

An irony in the use of comprehensive exams is that their results typically take the form of a single grade. Assessment results that leave no record of the substance of learning, putting the record they do leave in a form suitable only for one-dimensional learning, are hardly comprehensive.

Externally Developed Comprehensive Examinations. Comprehensive exams developed outside an institution differ from locally developed comprehensives. The most important differences are the external exams' systematic coverage of the most common areas of a field and their provision of an independent reference group for interpreting results. Externally developed exams are usually multiple-choice tests devised by commercial testing agencies or state agencies. Comprehensive oral exams are occasionally conducted by persons from outside an institution, but they are more similar to locally developed than to external comprehensives, since they follow locally developed guidelines.

Multiple-choice exams tend to be technically well constructed, with high reliability in the form of internal consistency—that is, high interitem agreement but that reliability makes these tests less valid as indicators of accomplishment across complex areas of learning. Even in well-specified fields like organic chemistry or mechanical engineering, competence does not consist of any uniform body of knowledge, understanding, and intellectual capabilities, which every competent person in the field can be assumed to possess. Nevertheless, such assumptions underlie tests that have high internal consistency. The variety and the complexity of learning in any field, even among graduates in highly structured fields, are too great to be accommodated by a test that assumes a single dimension of competence.

The provision of a reference group, which gives institutions a yardstick against which the performance of their own students can be measured, is also an illusory benefit. The characteristics of the students and institutions that constitute the reference group are seldom even known, and this lack of information makes comparisons questionable.

Commercially developed tests of such general academic skills as critical thinking and problem solving have become more popular with growing attention to general education. They are similar to commercial tests of achievement in subject-matter fields. Faculty members, however, are less sure of what constitutes something like critical thinking or problem solving than of what makes up the content of their own fields, and they look for expert help; but lack of agreement among the experts, as well as the interdependence between knowledge and cognitive processes, raise doubts about the superiority of external-tests of general skills over locally developed tests.

Promising Prospects

Several related trends are apparent. The most obvious is the growing expectation of legislatures, governing boards, and academic administrators for information on students' academic accomplishments to be made available. At present, few constraints are placed on the forms that such information should take. The virtual absence, however, of any information on the substance of student learning (except at the occasional institution like Alverno College) is unlikely to be ignored for long.

Several years ago, colleges and universities responded to the pressure for assessment of students' learning by looking to external test developers. The trend among institutions now seems to favor relying more on their own ability to assess the learning they want their own students to demonstrate. Greater interest in short-essay tests and free-response problems, rather than in multiple-choice tests, is accompanying that shift to local resources. As faculty members shift their purposes in examining students' perfomrance from assigning grades to investigating the substantive and cognitive effects of instruction, they will begin to engage in the kind of instructional research Cross (1986) has urged them to adopt.

Retreat from external test development accompanies a tendency among neighboring institutions to pool assessment efforts. Collaboration can lead to better specification of instructional objectives and more accurate assessment. Faculty members teaching courses with overlapping goals can include a few common questions on their retrospective exams, and have accessible, identifiable reference groups to compare performance among students.

Institutions concerned with students' collective learning need not test every student on the same material. A department can organize the core of its program—the key kinds of understanding, capabilities, and appreciations required into 120 ten-minute exercises (a daunting 20-hour test). To make such time requirements more manageable, three of the exercises can be incorporated into the final exams of each of 40 upper-division courses in several fields. If some redundancy is built into the exercises and if the upper-division courses are chosen carefully, the results can indicate students' accomplishments accurately and comprehensively (including variations within the same field of study and across different fields). Collaboration of several neighboring institutions can extend the usefulness of results while distributing the costs of test development.

There should be continual interplay among the processes of clarifying instructional purposes, devising assessment exercises to reflect them, observing results, improving instruction to meet revised purposes, sharpening purposes and assessment exercises, and so on. Alverno College's elaborate but decentralized assessment program clearly demonstrates that interplay (Alverno College Faculty, 1985). With such a process, neither teaching nor learning remains stagnant, and changes and accomplishments are documented.

Potential Perils

Separating assessment from instruction has advantages as well as risks. Students may see an assessment program that is not directly related to their courses as an unnecessary burden, and faculty members may find little value in the program's results. If so, the program will be abandoned as a sterile process, and more promising attempts to assess what students have learned will have trouble getting accepted.

Few major changes in curricula or academic procedures occur without the involvement of faculty committees, yet that form of faculty involvement is often not enough; the committee perspective is too general. Committees tend to draft new statements of educational goals and then work from them toward the selection or construction of assessment devices. These goal statements, with their related assessment procedures, tend to be so broad that they have little direct bearing on courses that are currently taught. Such a procedure implies that what has already been taught and assessed is not in itself an appropriate guide to what should be done, and faculty members are reluctant to embrace the results of assessments conducted in this way.

A more productive approach is to examine what faculty members already assess, how they do it, and how closely the results reflect their expectations for student learning. That process will probably suggest clarification and restatement of purposes. It may also indicate purposes that are inadequately assessed or suggest improved or expanded assessment procedures, but the recommendations will have grown from and respected faculty members' previous efforts.

The introduction of a wholly new, externally devised assessment process is rarely necessary and is often self-defeating. An assessment program that builds on what already exists not only can provide better information than a new one on the quality of education but also can be linked more readily to the improvement of teaching and learning.

References

Alverno College Faculty. *Assessment at Alverno College.* (Rev. ed.) Milwaukee, Wisc.: Alverno Productions, 1985.

Cross, K. P. "A Proposal to Improve Teaching." *AAHE Bulletin,* 1986, 39 (1), 9–14.

Fong, B. "The External Examiner Approach to Assessment." Paper commissioned by the American Association for Higher Education at the second National Conference on

Assessment in Higher Education, Denver, June 14–17, 1987.

Gardner, H. *The Mind's New Science: A History of the Cognitive Revolution.* New York: Basic Books, 1985

Kerr, A. D., and Pipes, R. B. "Why We Need Hands-On Engineering Education." *Technology Review,* 1987, 90 (7), 34–42.

Nickerson, R. S., Perkins, D. N., and Smith, E. E. *The Teaching of Thinking.* Hillsdale, N.J.: Erlbaum, 1985.

O'Neill, J.P. "Examinations and Quality Control." In J. R. Warren (ed.), *Meeting the New Demand for Standards.* New Directions for Higher Education, no. 43. San Francisco: Jossey-Bass, 1983.

What We Can Learn from Coursework Patterns About Improving the Undergraduate Curriculum

James L. Ratcliff

Most faculty and administrators are committed to improving the quality of undergraduate education. To make improvements, it is necessary to know what students learn in order to decide what ideally they should learn. Assessment plans and programs can monitor institutional performance relative to student learning. Over the past decade, colleges and universities have made substantial efforts to establish student outcomes assessment programs and to revise and reform the undergraduate curriculum. Unfortunately, these two endeavors have not concretely and substantively informed one another.

The 1980s were a decade of examination of the state and quality of education programs. National reports urged faculty and academic leaders to improve baccalaureate programs. The Study Group on the Conditions of Excellence in American Higher Education (1984), formed under the U.S. Department of Education, urged colleges to provide students clear academic direction, standards, and values. It urged researchers to use college student assessment information and to explore the use of student transcripts as resources in understanding more about which subjects students study in college and what they learn. The practical applications, procedures, and techniques of student and curriculum assessment described in the present volume are a direct outcome of those recommendations. Beginning in 1985, we developed specific procedures to determine the gains in student learning that were directly associated with enrollment in different patterns of undergraduate coursework.

In February 1985, the Association of American Colleges (AAC) issued the report *Integrity in the College Curriculum: A Report to the Academic Community* (Committee on Redefining the Meaning and Purpose of Baccalaureate Degrees, 1985), which concluded that undergraduate education was in a state of crisis and disarray. The report attacked the "marketplace"-oriented curriculum based solely on student choice, asking "Is the curriculum an invitation to philosophic and intellectual growth or a quick exposure to the skills of a particular vocation?" (p. 2). The report called on colleges and universities to live up to their stated goals for general education and liberal learning by providing a coherent curriculum. For AAC, a coherent curriculum at least entails inquiry, literacy, understanding of numerical data, historical consciousness, science, values, art, international and multicultural experiences, and study of some discipline in depth (Eaton, 1991). AAC reasserted the belief that an undergraduate education should produce learning outcomes common to all students irrespective of their major or minor fields of specialization.

At least three studies have tried to determine what improvements in the college curriculum have been accomplished since 1985. Zemsky (1989) examined thirty-five thousand student transcripts from

---

Reprinted from *Assessment and Curriculum Reform - New Directions for Higher Education*, no. 80 (1992), by permission of Jossey-Bass Publishers, Inc.

thirty colleges and universities to determine the shape and substance of the undergraduate curriculum that the students had encountered. Zemsky found that the curriculum continued to lack structure and coherence, that students' enrollment in science and mathematics was quite limited, and that the humanities lacked sequential, developmental patterns of learning. Lynne V. Cheney (1989) analyzed humanities enrollments in colleges and universities to determine if there had been a fundamental change in baccalaureate programs between 1983 and 1989. She found little, if any, change in undergraduate degree requirements. She lamented,

> It is possible to graduate now, as it was five years ago, from *more* than 80 percent of our institutions of higher education without taking a course in American history. In 1988–89, it is possible to earn a bachelor's degree from:
>
> - 37 percent of the nation's colleges and universities without taking any course in history;
> - 45 percent without taking a course in American or English literature;
> - 62 percent without taking a course in philosophy;
> - 77 percent without studying a foreign language [Cheney, 1989, p. 5].

Not only was their little evidence of increased structure and rigor to the curriculum during this time period, there was also evidence that the curriculum was not having much impact on student learning. Astin (1991), in a national study of student transcripts, general education requirements, and student test scores and self-reports found no relationship between any general education curriculum structure and improvement in student learning.

There were strident calls in these national reports and studies to improve undergraduate education, and colleges and universities did not remain idle. During the past decade, more than 90 percent of colleges and universities have engaged in some kind of revision or reform of their undergraduate curriculum (Gaff, 1989). The American Council on Education repeatedly reported in *Campus Trends* (El-Khawas, 1988, 1990) that most colleges and universities were engaged in curriculum reform. These efforts led Eaton (1991, pp. 61, 63) to raise some rather uncomfortable questions about this flurry of activity:

> From a negative point of view, one can point to little in the way of completed curricular modifications or, more important, changes in student performance that . . . emerged . . . as the 1980's ended. Worse, one might view the decade . . . as an essentially unimportant ten-year saga during which the higher-education community continued an apparently endless and unproductive dialogue with itself on academic issues as opposed to engaging in construction action. . . .
>
> . . . Did institutional descriptions of academic reform fail to focus on those intended to benefit but, instead, confused expectations of student performance with descriptions of faculty involvement?

There has not been a meaningful and substantive connection between undergraduate curriculum content and improved student learning. The increased national attention given to improved student performance and stronger academic direction, standards, and values demands that we make more substantive links between what students study in college and gains in their learning. This volume offers a model for linking general education curriculum and student outcomes assessment. Before I describe this unique model, and before the contributors to this volume show how it can be used to answer tough questions of academic policy and curriculum reform, we first must examine why faculty and administrators are focusing more attention on the assessment of student outcomes.

Impetus for Assessment

A variety of both external and internal factors are compelling institutions not only to consider assessment but also to formalize plans and take specific actions to measure the educational impact of an institution on its students. One group of external factors involves state initiatives. Dissatisfaction with student learning has led an increasing number of states to expect colleges and universities to implement student assessment programs. Earlier state policies toward assessment took a decentralized approach, allowing institutions to develop their own systems of assessment. However, state policy makers are becoming increasingly dissatisfied with assessment programs that do not improve student learning. The result has been new state proposals for common student outcomes testing (Ewell,

1991). Some states have already adopted formal assessment requirements and many other states are moving in this direction. Every student in Florida who is preparing to receive an associate's degree from a two-year institution or who plans to become a junior in a four-year institution is required by the state to take the College Level Academic Skills Test. Since 1979 Tennessee has based part of its public college and university funding on student assessment results. Colleges and universities in Tennessee test seniors in general education and in their chosen majors, survey alumni, and use the results of assessment activities to guide improvements at the institutions (Banta and others, 1990).

Another set of external factors is composed of accreditation organizations. Most of the six regional accreditation associations have begun to incorporate outcomes assessment as a criterion for institutional approval. The North Central Association of Colleges and Universities has conducted regional seminars on assessment and prepared a workbook to aid in the evaluation of institutional effectiveness and student achievement. In addition, accreditation bodies that approve programs in the disciplines are beginning to include outcomes assessment in their criteria for approval.

Due to these external factors, institutions often have developed and implemented assessment programs to provide accountability. However, there are also internal factors that have encouraged institutions to undertake assessment activities for the sake of academic improvement. The information gathered from assessments can help reform the curriculum, strengthen academic programs and student services, and, consequently increase student satisfaction and enhance student recruitment and longterm retention. Using the information from assessment activities, faculty can give specific attention to the need for self-improvement in teaching and evaluating students in their own individual courses. The model described in this volume is focused on assessment for the purpose of academic improvement.

Development of the Coursework Cluster Analysis Model

Assessments describe and document the nature and extent of learning that has occurred. They cannot tell us, however, which courses most consistently produce gains in learning for specific groups of students over time at particular institutions. Such information would be extremely useful. Knowledge about the degree to which different courses contribute to different learning outcomes would provide a college or university with an empirical basis for curriculum review. Knowledge of such links between coursework and learning would complement faculty wisdom, student evaluation, and other means of appraising the extent to which particular sets and sequences of courses have their intended effects. Such information could also be used to improve the academic advising and guidance that students receive in making course selections (Ratcliff and others, 1990a, 1990b, 1990c, 1990d).

Over the past four years, my colleagues and I have developed a model for linking assessments of the general learning of undergraduates with their coursework (Ratcliff, 1987, 1988, 1989; Ratcliff and others, 1990a, 1990b, 1990c, 1990d, Ratcliff and Jones, 1990, 1991; Jones and Ratcliff, 1990a, 1990b, 1991). This research has proceeded under the rubric of the Differential Coursework Patterns Project, and the model for linking coursework to student assessment has been referred to as the Coursework Cluster Analysis Model (CCAM). Its development and testing was supported, first, by the Office of Educational Research and Improvement of the U.S. Department of Education. Subsequent qualitative validity studies of the Graduate Record Examination (GRE) item types, trend analyses of coursework patterns, and studies of the applicability of the model to curriculum reform, assessment program development, and academic advising have been supported by the Exxon Education Foundation. The CCAM has been tested at six institutions: Stanford and Georgia State universities, and Clayton State, Evergreen State, Mills, and Ithaca colleges. In addition, the CCAM has been applied to student reports of enrollment patterns and American College Test-Comprehensive (ACT-COMP) scores at the University of Tennessee, Knoxville (Pike and Phillippi, 1989). Research on the uses and limitations of the CCAM is continuing as part of the National Longitudinal Study of Student Learning at the National Center on Postsecondary Teaching, Learning, and Assessment.

In the most typical applications, assessment instruments are administered to graduating seniors. Since 1986, we have examined over seventy-two thousand courses appearing on the transcripts of approximately sixteen hundred graduating seniors. Each group of seniors came from a cross section of majors. They also reflected the full range of academic ability, as indicated by their Scholastic Aptitude Test (SAT) scores, for the general population of students at each institution. The results of posttests were compared with the results of corresponding pretests of the same students. Well-known standardized instruments were used: the SAT, GRE, ACT, and ACT-COMP, as well as the Kolb Learning Styles Inventory. Locally constructed measures of student-perceived course difficulty also were used. A great strength of the CCAM and an asset that seems to enhance its acceptability to faculty are that the model is not dependent on instruments supplied by external vendors. It can use a variety of locally developed instruments, tailored to particular needs and extensively employing local judgment. A college, for instance, might administer its own essay examinations to freshmen and seniors, and its own faculty might grade them holistically; so long as the final evaluation, or its subparts, can be translated into a numerical scale, this instrument would be entirely adequate for the purpose of the CCAM.

A common stumbling block in the development of an assessment program is that of determining what form of test or assessment information to use. Curriculum reviewers, reformers, and researches quickly acknowledge that there is no clear conception of what constitutes general learning. Such recognition emerges regardless of whether it is the college curriculum or the various tests and assessment devices that are being examined. A college that attempts to reach consensus among its constituents either on general education goals or on the "best" measure of general learned abilities will foster heated discussion. The quest for consensus on what should be the common intellectual experience of undergraduates may end in irresolution or, worse, abandonment of the assessment initiative. Instead of searching for the ideal measure of general learning in a college, those charged with assessment can better direct their energies toward the selection of a constellation of assessment means and measures that appear to be appropriate criteria for describing one or more dimensions of the general learning goals of the college.

The CCAM provides a basis for determining the relative extent to which each measure explains general student learning within a given college environment. If we have nine different assessment measures, for example, we can determine what proportion of the variation in student scores is explained by each measure. This information leads to a decision point for the academic leader or faculty committee charged with the development and oversight of the assessment program. If a measure of general learning does not explain much of the variation in student scores, one option is to conclude that the measure is inappropriate to the students and the education program or that particular college or university. In short, the CCAM can assist in the discard of that particular form of evaluation as superfluous and unnecessary. An alternative conclusion is that the institution is not devoting sufficient attention to the type of learning measured. Here, an examination of the assessment instrument relative to the curriculum is called for. Again, the CCAM can point to those courses and classes that were associated with gains in student learning on the measure in question.

Steps in the Coursework Cluster Analysis Model

The CCAM is grounded conceptually to the finding that student learning varies more greatly within institutions than between them. The selection, testing, and adoption of a specific methodology for the analysis of coursework patterns were based also on repeated empirical investigation of the relationship between different patterns of coursework and variation in student learning. In this chapter, I describe the general methodology of the CCAM. The rationale and procedures of cluster analysis are described with reference to its application to the investigation of coursework patterns. Since cluster analysis currently is not widely employed in educational research, I begin this section by contrasting cluster analysis with other statistical methods of potential value in the assessment of student learning.

Previous assessment and transcript analysis studies have used the general linear model and regression analysis (Astin, 1970a, 1970b; Benbow and Stanley, 1983; Pallas and Alexander, 1983; Prather and Smith, 1976a, 1976b). The rationale for the use of regression is based on practical and theoretical justifications. Regression analysis allows maximum design flexibility and is statistically robust. Transcript analyses involve large amounts of data. For example, Prather and Smith (1976b) examined 8,735 student transcripts that collectively contained 189,013 individual course grades. Regression analysis provides an effective technique for presenting the diverse nature of the data while maintaining a consistent analysis rationale. However, the general linear model does not provide a direct means of assessing the additive and temporary aspects of course patterns, that is, course combinations and sequences. Moreover, use of linear regression alone would conceptualize the problem as that of finding the one best fit between students and learning experiences. It would not account for the appropriateness and benefits of different learning experiences for different groups of students.

The term *coursework* is used here to refer to the categorization of the courses in which students enrolled according to the multiple assessment criteria of their general education and liberal learning. It is the systematic and unique way in which a college or university labels and arranges its courses (for example, Honors 101, French 340); that scheme or arrangement of classes is already known in a disaggregate form on student transcripts. Identification is the allocation of individual courses to be established in categories on the basis of specific criteria (for example, Biology 205 is classified by many universities as a sophomore-level class in the Department of Biology).

Discriminant analysis is used in the CCAM to test the validity of the groupings and to identifythose assessment criteria that tell us most about collegiate learning experiences. Discriminant analysis is a process used to differentiate between groups formed on an a priori basis (see Biglan, 1973, for an example). Discriminant analysis does not discover groups; rather, it identifies a set of characteristics that can significantly differentiate between the groups. The process allows the analyst to allocate new cases to one of the a priori groups with the least amount of error. In contrast, *cluster analysis* recovers groups representing particular patterns from diverse populations (Lorr, 1983; Romesburg, 1984). In the CCAM, cluster analysis is used to classify courses according to student achievement criteria, while discriminant analysis is used to test and provide secondary validation of the cluster groupings and to identify those criteria that significantly differentiate one cluster of coursework from another.

Cluster analysis is sometimes confused with factor analysis. Factor analysis is different from cluster analysis in that the analyst's attention is on the similarity of the variables (attributes). The aim is to identify a small number of dimensions (factors) that can account for individual differences on the various measures or attributes. Thus, the aim of factor analysis is to reduce or consolidate the number of attributes of a variable set, whereas the purpose of a cluster analysis is simply to classify or taxonomize data into groups on the basis of a set of attributes. Cluster analysis refers to a wide variety of techniques used to classify entities into homogeneous subgroups on the basis of their similarities.

The end products of cluster analysis are clusters or pattern sets. Since the exact number and nature of the course patterns is not known in advance, the clustering process is actually technically preclassificatory. In other words, cluster analysis techniques are used to construct a classification scheme for unclassified data sets. In this way, cluster analysis empirically arranges the courses of a college curriculum using student decision-making behavior (as represented on transcripts) as the primary source of information. The courses are classified in a hierarchical dendrogram or tree. The relationship between courses is determined by their similarity on the criteria used in the classification. In this way, the similarity between courses is determined empirically, rather than by arbitrary concepts (for example, life sciences) or levels (for example, freshmen-level survey). This conceptual-empirical approach was selected due to the lack of agreement in the higher education literature on a common research paradigm, model, or philosophy for the organization of coursework (Bergquist, Gould, and Greenberg, 1981; Biglan, 1973; Fuhrman and Grasha, 1983; Gaff, 1983; Rudolph, 1977; Sloan, 1971; Veysey, 1973).

Cluster analysis conforms to the conceptual restrictions placed on the CCAM to assess the effect of coursework patterns on student learning. Cluster analysis provides a statistical procedure for examining coursework using multiple criteria. It can classify different sets of coursework according to different net effects of learning associated with them. It can accommodate both quantitative and qualitative attributes of varying dimensions. Thus, the criterion selected need not be test scores; nominal ordinal interval, and ratio data have been successfully used as attributes in cluster analysis (Romesburg, 1984). Cluster analysis uses these attributes to arrive at patterns of coursework independently of any institutionally prescribed a priori distinctions. Therefore, it can test the combinations, sequences, and progressions of courses within the undergraduate curriculum. It leads to the discovery of clusters (or patterns) of coursework in student transcripts, based on the multiple measures of student assessment employed. Since the purpose of the CCAM is to group coursework homogeneously relative to student learning criteria (Lorr, 1983; Romesburg, 1984), cluster analysis serves as the primary methodology for the analytical model.

Overview of the CCAM Steps. There are several steps to using the CCAM. First, student residual scores are derived. A residual score is the difference between the student's actual score on the outcomes assessment measure and the score predicted by the entrance measure used. Next, student transcripts are examined. Courses reported on them are clustered into patterns based on the residual scores of the students who enrolled in them. The resulting coursework patterns are then grouped or classified according to any of a wide variety of student or institutional factors. Patterns can be classified according to factors such as the entering ability level of the student, the type of coursework selected (general education, prerequisites), the campus at which the student enrolled, or the residence facilities housing the students. Adult versus traditional college-age students, commuter versus residential students, and part-time versus full-time students' coursework can be compared. Within systems of higher education with course comparability, transfer schemes, and articulation agreements, the model can be used to determine if coursework associated with students from branch campuses or with transfer students is associated with the same types of improvement in learning as found for students native to the campus.

A Closer Look at the CCAM Steps. The CCAM research design uses official student transcripts and assessment instrument scores as data sources for a sample of graduating senior students. To describe the model and to illustrate how CCAM is executed, I here use the nine item-type categories of the General Test of the GRE as examples of multiple measures of general learned abilities of college seniors. Standardized and nonstandardized, locally developed and commercially available assessment instruments and measures can be used with CCAM. In the following example, SAT scores are used as controls for the academic abilities of these students when they first entered college. The student transcripts are used as the unobtrusive record of the sequence of courses in which these seniors enrolled.

The first objective of the CCAM is to determine the extent of student improvement in general learned abilities over the time of their baccalaureate program. To achieve this objective, the residual score of each GRE item type for each student is calculated first; the residual score is the difference between the student's actual score and the score predicted by the student's corresponding SAT score. It is derived by regressing the outcomes measure (in this case, GRE item types) on the entrance measures (in this case, SAT scores). Thus, for each student outcomes measure there is a student residual score for each person in the sample group.

The second objective is to determine patterns of coursework on the student transcripts that are associated with the student score residuals. Cluster analysis gives us these patterns, using student residual scores (GRE item-type residuals) as attributes of the courses in which students enrolled. To achieve this second objective, we create a data matrix where all of the courses to be analyzed are in the columns and all of the assessment measures or criteria are in the rows. Each cell in this matrix is then filled with the appropriate mean course residual score. For example, let us assume that we have student assessment data on writing ability and understanding of scientific knowledge, and a writing sample that has been holistically scored. For the course Introduction to Political Systems, we calculate the mean of residual scores for all students enrolling in it for each of these measures. We do this for Introduction to Political Science and every other course on the students' transcripts that we select to analyze.

Now, with several rows of assessment data, a column for each course analyzed, and a course mean residual score in every cell of the data matrix, we are ready to determine how similarly students who enrolled in different courses performed. The course mean residual score is the metric value that we are going to use to make the comparisons of coursework. To determine how courses are similar to one another in this way, we use the correlation coefficient (Pearson's r) as the indicator of similarity.

Our task is to see how the performance of students in the course Introduction to Political Systems is similar to the performance of students in other courses, However, students take more than one course, so courses taken by a particular group of students will cluster together. That is because the course mean residuals for each assessment measure should look about the same for all of the courses taken by this group of students.

So, if we correlate the writing sample score of Introduction to Political Systems with the sociology course Mass Behavior, then the correlation will be high if students for both courses showed comparable improvement on that measure. What we are doing, then, is creating a second matrix to record our correlation coefficient. In this matrix, all of the rows are the courses analyzed, and all of the columns are a duplicate listing of all of the courses. Each cell contains the coefficient representing the extent to which each course is related to all other courses on all the assessment criteria. Obviously, the greater the assessment criteria, the more precision in establishing the relationship. Construction of these two data matrices, the raw data matrix and the course resemblance matrix, may seem like a lot of work. Fortunately, use of a computer with popular statistical programs, such as SPSS and SAS, makes the task easy. We do not even see these matrices as they are calculated at lightning speed as we move along performing the CCAM cluster analysis.

Once the resemblance matrix indicating the proportional relationship of courses is established, a clustering method is selected and executed to arrange a tree or dendrogram of courses related by the student score gains. Next, we conduct a discriminant analysis on the resulting clusters of coursework. The discriminant analysis tells us the extent to which the courses have been correctly classified according to the assessment criteria, which of the assessment criteria were correlated with particular discriminant functions, and which coursework clusters were associated with the improvement of student learning according to which assessment criteria. From the discriminant analysis, an association can be inferred between coursework patterns (clusters) and the assessment criteria (student score residuals on the multiple measures of learning). The cluster analysis procedure groups courses frequently chosen by students according to the strength of their associated effect on the student score gains.

The CCAM classifies the most frequently enrolled courses according to their associated effect on student improvement in learning. The procedure classifies courses according to a ratio index of similarity to other courses. This procedure is designed to examine those courses in which most students enroll. Thus, the analysis is limited to only a fraction of all of the courses in a college curriculum. For example, in the historical data base used in model building and testing, a 5 percent sample of student transcripts enabled an examination of only 5 percent of the courses appearing on those transcripts (the percentage of courses enrolling five or more students from the sample group). However, the courses examined in that 5 percent corresponded closely to those courses identified as meeting the college's distributional degree requirements in general education. The quantitative procedures and techniques are described in greater detail in Ratcliff, Jones, and Hoffman (1992).

The linking of coursework to assessment results is critical given the diversity of the undergraduate curriculum today. Most colleges and universities have an expansive curriculum representing the explosion of explosion of knowledge, diversity of students, and modes of inquiry that characterize higher education in the twentieth century. Given this observation about the undergraduate curriculum, we find that up to 20 percent of the courses are not to be found on the transcripts of the preceding or following year's graduating seniors. The reason for this is that annual course schedules do not represent all of the courses found in the college catalogue. Certain courses are given on a one-time experimental basis, and some are canceled due to lack of enrollment. Typically, the undergraduate student chooses thirty-five to forty-five courses to fulfill the baccalaureate degree requirements from a list of twenty-five hundred to five thousand courses at a large research university or from eight hundred to fifteen hundred courses at a liberal arts college. Therefore, what students learn and how much they learn at a given institution varies from year to year based on variations in course offerings and student course selections. This variation in student learning within a single institution often is greater than the variation in student learning across institutions.

Findings from Research Based on the Coursework Cluster Analysis Model

Students who take different coursework learn different content, cognitive skills, values, and attitudes. Student learning varies greatly in complex institutions of higher education because of their broad arrays of curriculum offerings. Critical to the success of general and liberal education for students in these institutions is some means for recognizing curriculum diversity and its effects. Thus, the more complex the curriculum offerings the greater is the challenge to determine the relationship between coursework taken and learning achieved.

Based on measures of general learning and the transcripts of graduating seniors, the coursework taken by students who showed large gains in these measures can be identified. In our research, we found that different patterns and sequences of coursework produced different types of gains in learning. For example, course sequences in a wide range of disciplines such as business, biology, and philosophy were associated with gains in student learning in analytical reasoning. Student improvement in mathematics was associated with coursework in economics, business, music, physical therapy, mathematics, and quantitative methods in management. Student gains in reading comprehension were associated with coursework in marketing, accounting, management, music, and history. These findings and relationships are described and illustrated more fully in Jones (this volume (Chapter Three), where the CCAM is used to test the viability of a core curriculum to engender improvement in students' learned abilities.

Consistently, we have found that students who take different coursework learn different things and develop different abilities. There are two lessons from this research. First, the courses that students take in college have a bearing on what they learn. Second, the structure of general education in the institutions that we examined did not produce a profound effect on the types of learning that we examined. While the current general requirements of American colleges and universities may show little effect on the development of general learned abilities of students (Astin, 1991) the specific coursework taken by those students does have an effect (Ratcliff and Jones, 1990, 1991). We believe that improvements in student learned abilities can be achieved by revising undergraduate curriculum experiences to emulate the coursework clusters, patterns, and sequences taken by those students who show large gains in student learning. Here lies the potential power of assessment to guide and monitor the reform of undergraduate education.

What the Coursework Cluster Analysis Model Can Do

The CCAM provides a way for faculty and administrators to make more substantive links between what students study in college and what they learn. It suggests that an ideal coursework pattern is one in which what is to be learned is well matched to the background, preparation, and interests of the learners. The more diverse the student population, the greater is the need for alternative coursework patterns to fulfill the general education requirements.

The model and method of analysis defined in this volume permit a college or university to achieve several tasks of curriculum reform: determine which assessment measures best describe the kinds of learning that take place among students at the institution, determine which parts of the curriculum are currently not monitored or described by the present assessment methods and measures, determine which patterns of coursework are associated with which kinds of learning and with which groups of students, determine the extent to which transfer students benefit from the same or different general education coursework as that taken by students who began their baccalaureate program at the same institution, determine the extent to which a core curriculum or a distributional requirement produces the greatest gains in learning among different groups of undergraduates at the same institution, and determine which course sequences contribute to general education and liberal learning and which do not. The

CCAM has limitations as well. It is designed for assessment of general education and liberal learning, not learning within the major; those institutions that have a distribution plan of general education in which students have a fairly wide range of curriculum choices to fulfill the requirements for their baccalaureate; the identification of coursework *associated* with improvement in student learning in general education and liberal learning. It does not tell us that coursework *caused* the learning. Subsequent research and analysis are required to determine which factors contributed to that learning.

Advantages to Assessing Coursework Pattern

The CCAM provides a number of advantages and benefits in the assessment of general education. First, the model can use multiple measures of assessment, thereby allowing for a broader picture of student learning than any one measure can paint. It provides institutions with information regarding the extent of variation in student assessment results that is explained by any one of the measures used. This information can be helpful in a number of ways. Faculty and administrators need not decide on an ideal set of assessment measures. The extent to which such measures may overlap in describing student learning can be identified. The mix of assessment measures appropriate to the goals of the institution and the characteristics of the student population can be continuously monitored. When students show small amounts of growth on an indicator of student learning, the college or university can either develop strategies for improving student learning in the area identified or else discard the measure as inappropriate to the institution and its students.

Efforts to assess general education and liberal learning can become quickly bogged down in discussions over which measures, indicators, or examinations to use. Faculty feel pressured to commit to a set of measures that may not accurately reflect their visions of the goals of general education. By using multiple measures and by leaving the process of choosing measures open to continuous revision and updating, the college or university can proceed to develop a rational, cogent, and informative assessment plan. Eaton (1991, p. 66) has written about tensions that emerge over the discussion of the desired outcomes of general education and the desirability of such a contingency approach: "These tensions emerge when we are either unwilling or unable to commit some defensible approach to general education for fear that our commitment will be found lacking in some way. Waiting around for the ideal general education scenario, however, serves little purpose and harms students even more than a general education effort that possesses some flaws."

If a general education innovation holds promise to enhance student learning in some way, then there should be a means to ascertain whether or not that improvement has occurred. Linked analysis of assessment and enrollment data holds the promise of identifying when and, more important, under what circumstances the general education curriculum has been improved. The CCAM provides useful information to the college or university about the mix of assessment measures that reflects what the students learn and what the institution intends to teach them.

The model can provide concrete useful information about the curriculum to guide reform efforts. It is a tool ideally suited to institutions of higher education with distributional general education requirement and a wide array of programs, electives, and majors. From a catalogue of hundreds or thousands of courses, the CCAM can identify the courses taken by students who showed the greatest improvement in learning. For example, if one of the assessment measures that a college selects is a test of analytical reasoning, then the CCAM can identify those groups of courses taken by students who showed significant improvement in that area of general learning.

The finding that different courses engender different types of learning is actually a corollary to a larger, more important research finding affirmed in our research but best described by Pascarella and Terenzini (1991). They describe and analyze twenty years of research indicating that *differences in student learning are far greater within institutions than between them.* Given this finding, it stands to reason that students taking different coursework and having different extracurricular experiences should show differences in subject matter learned, in the type and extent of their general cognitive development, and in their values and attitudes toward learning.

The finding that variation in student learning is greater within institutions than between them also means that one intellectual shoe does not fit all freshmen feet. The efficacy of a single set of courses, a core, in fostering the intellectual development of college students can be easily examined using assessment results. Likewise, the efficacy of specific combinations and sequences of coursework can be scrutinized relative to the long-term learning gains of students. The specific learning preparation, interests, and outcomes of different groups of students can be examined, whether they are low ability, high ability, transfer students, or students from specific curricula or majors.

The student population can be subdivided by ability, by gender, race, or ethnicity, or by major. Then the CCAM can identify if the coursework associated with gains in learning among the total group is the same as that for the subgroups. Curriculum planners and curriculum committees can readily use this information. Courses in the general education sequence that are not associated with gains in student learning can be revised, enhanced, or dropped. CoursesCourses outside the general education requirements that contribute to gains in student learning can be included in the general education curriculum.

The model can also produce information that leads to better academic advising, since it links the coursework that students take with their improvement in learning. Students can choose from lists of courses taken by others with similar backgrounds and abilities—others who showed gains in performance and learning. This procedure takes advising beyond the mere listing of formal degree requirements. As more data are amassed, increasingly greater precision is generated in the linking of coursework and student learning. The CCAM may even be amenable to the development of a microcomputer-based advising system utilizing a relational data base of prior students' course-taking patterns and assessment results. Such a computer-based advising system would yield an array of effective coursework tailored to the abilities and interests of individual students and within the parameters of institutional degree requirements. In subsequent chapters, we explore and exemplify how the linking of curriculum information (transcripts, catalogue studies, course syllabi, and examinations) with student outcomes assessment data can guide undergraduate curriculum reform.

References

Astin, A. W. "The Methodology of Research on College Impact, Part 2." *Sociology of Education*, 1970a, *43*, 223–254.

Astin, A. W. "The Methodology of Research on College Impact, Part 2." *Sociology of Education*, 1970b, *43*, 437–450.

Astin, A. W. *Assessment for Excellence: The Philosophy and Practice of Assessment and Evaluation in Higher Education.* New York: Macmillan, 1991.

Banta, T., and others, *Bibliography of Assessment Instruments*. Knoxville, Tenn.: Center for Assessment Research and Development, University of Tennessee, 1990.

Benbow, C. P., and Stanley, J. C. "Differential Course-Taking Hypothesis Revisited." *American Educational Research Journal,* 1983, 20(4), 469–573.

Bergquist, W. H. Gould, R. A., and Greenberg, E. M. *Designing Undergraduate Education*: A Systematic Guide. San Francisco: Jossey-Bass, 1981.

Biglan, A. "The Characteristics of Subject Matter in Different Academic Areas." *Journal of Applied Psychology, 1973, 57* (3),195–203.

Cheney, L. V. *50 Hours: A Core Curriculum for College Students*. Washington, D.C.: National Endowment for the Humanities, 1989.

Committee on Redefining the Meaning and Purpose of Baccalaureate Degrees Association of American Colleges. *Integrity in the College Curriculum: A Report to the Academic Community.* Washington, D.C.: Association of American Colleges, 1985.

Eaton, J. S. *The Unfinished Agenda: Higher Education and the 1980s*. New York: Macmillan 1991.

El-Khawas, E. *Campus Trends, 1988*. Higher Education Panel Reports, No. 77. Washington, D.C.: American Council on Education, 1988.

El-Khawas, E. *Campus Trends, 1990*. Higher Education Panel Reports, No. 80. Washington, D.C.: American Council on Education, 1990.

Ewell, P. "Assessment and Public Accountability: Back to the Future." *Change,* 1991, 23, 12–17.

Fuhrman, B., and Grasha, A. *A Practical Handbook for College Teachers*. Boston: Little, Brown, 1983.

Gaff, J. G. *General Education Today: A Critical Analysis of Controversies, Practices, and Reforms*. San Francisco: Jossey-Bass, 1983.

Gaff, J. G. "General Education at the Decade's End: The Need for a Second Wave of Reform. *Change*, 1989, 21, 11–19.

Jones, E. A., and Ratcliff, J. L. "Effective Coursework Patterns and Faculty Perceptions of the Development of General Learned Abilities." Paper presented at the annual meeting of the Association for the Study of Higher Education, Portland, Oregon, November 1990a.

Jones, E. A., and Ratcliff, J. L. "Is a Core Curriculum Best for Everybody? The Effect of Different Patterns of Coursework on the General Education of High and Low Ability Students." Paper presented at the annual meeting of the American Educational Research Association, Boston, April 1990b.

Jones, E. A., and Ratcliff, J. L. "Which General Education Curriculum Is Better: Core Curriculum or the Distributional Requirement?" *Journal of General Education*, 1991, *40*, 69–101.

Lorr, M. *Cluster Analysis for Social Scientists: Techniques for Analyzing and Simplifying Complex Blocks of Data*. San Francisco: Jossey-Bass, 1983

Pallas, A. M., and Alexander, K. L. "Sex Differences in Quantitative SAT Performance: New Evidence on the Differential Coursework Hypothesis." *American Educational Research Journal*, 1983, 20 (2), 165–182.

Pascarella, E. T., and Terenzini, P. T. *How College Affects Students: Findings and Insights from Twenty Years of Research*. San Francisco: Jossey-Bass, 1991.

Pike, G. R., and Phillippi, R. H. "Generalizability of the Differential Coursework Methodology: Relationships Between Self-Reported Coursework and Performance on the ACT-COMP Exam." *Research in Higher Education*, 1989, *30* (3), 245–260.

Prather, J. E., and Smith, G. *Faculty Grading Patterns*. Atlanta: Office of Institutional Planning, Georgia State University, 1976a.

Prather, J. E., and Smith, G. *Undergraduate Grades by Course in Relation to Student Ability Levels, Programs of Study, and Longitudinal Trends*. Atlanta: Office of Institutional Planning Georgia State University, 1976b.

Ratcliff, J. L. *The Effect of Differential Coursework Patterns on General Learned Abilities of College Students: Application of the Model to a Historical Database of Student Transcripts*. Report on Task No. 3 for the U.S. Department of Education, Office of Educational Research and Improvement, Contract No. OERI-R-86-0016. Ames: Iowa State University, 1987.

Ratcliff, J. L. "The Development of a Cluster Analytic Model for Determining the Associated Effects of Coursework Patterns on Student Learning." Paper presented at the annual meeting of the American Educational Research Association, New Orleans, April 1988.

Ratcliff, J. L. "Determining the Effects of Different Coursework Patterns on the General Student Learning at Four Colleges and Universities." Paper presented at the annual meeting of the American Educational Research Association, San Francisco, March 1989.

Ratcliff, J. L., and Jones, E. A. "General Learning at a Women's College." Paper presented at the annual meeting of the Association for the Study of Higher Education, Portland, Oregon, November 1990.

Ratcliff, J. L., and Jones, E. A. "Are Common Course Numbering and a Core Curriculum Valid Indicators in the Articulation of General Education Credits Among Transfer Students?" Paper presented at the annual meeting of the American Educational Research Association, Chicago, April 1991.

Ratcliff, J. L., Jones, E. A., and Hoffman, S. *Handbook on Linking Assessment and General Education*. University Park: National Center for Postsecondary Teaching, Learning, and Assessment, Pennsylvania State University, 1992.

Ratcliff, J. L., and others. *Development and Testing of a Cluster-Analytic Model for Identifying Coursework Patterns Associated with General Learned Abilities of College Students: Final Report on Stanford University Samples Nos. 1–2*. Prepared for the U.S. Department of Education, Office of Educational Research and Improvement, Contract No. OERI-R-86 0016. Ames: Iowa State University, 1990a.

Ratcliff, J. L., and others. *Development and Testing of a Cluster-Analytic Model for Identifying Coursework Patterns Associated with General Learned Abilities of College Students: Final Report on Ithaca College Samples Nos. 1–2*. Prepared for the U.S. Department of Education, Office of Educational Research and Improvement, Contract No. OERI-R-86 0016. Ames: Iowa State University, 1990b.

Ratcliff, J. L., and others. *Development and Testing of a Cluster-Analytic Model for Identifying Coursework Patterns Associated with General Learned Abilities of college students: Final Report on Ithaca College Sample No. 3.* Prepared for the Exxon Education Foundation. University Park: Center for the Study of Higher Education, Pennsylvania State University, 1990c.

Ratcliff, J. L., and others. *Development and Testing of a Cluster-Analytic Model for Identifying Coursework Patterns Associated with General Learned Abilities of college students: Final Report on Ithaca College Sample Nos. 1-2.* Prepared for the U.S. Department of Education, Office of Educational Research and Improvement, Contract No. OERI-R-86-0016. University Park: Center for the Study of Higher Education, Pennsylvania State University, 1990d.

Romesburg, H. C. *Cluster Analysis for Researchers.* Belmont, Calif.: Lifelong Learning, 1984.

Rudolph, F. *Curriculum: A History of the American Undergraduate Course of Study Since 1636.* San Francisco: Jossey-Bass, 1977.

Sloan, D. "Harmony, Chaos, and Consensus: The American College Curriculum." *Teachers College Record* 1971, *73*, 221–251.

Study Group on the Conditions of Excellence in American Higher Education. National Institute of Education. *Involvement in Learning: Realizing the Potential of American Higher Education.* Washington, D.C.: Government Printing Office, 1984.

Veysey, L. "Stability and Experiment in the American Undergraduate Curriculum." In C. Kaysen (ed.), *Content and Context: Essays on College Education.* New York: McGraw-Hill, 1973.

Zemsky, R. *Structure and Coherence: Measuring the Undergraduate Curriculum.* Washington, D.C.: Association of American Colleges, 1989.

Learning Outcomes and Their Effects

Robert M. Gagné

Abstract: The outcomes of learning are persistent states that make possible a variety of human performances. While learning results are specific to the task undertaken, learning investigators have sought to identify broader categories of learning outcomes in order to foresee to what extent their findings can be generalized. Five varieties of learning outcomes have been distinguished and appear to be widely accepted. The categories are (a) intellectual skills (procedural knowledge), (b) verbal information (declarative knowledge), (c) cognitive strategies (executive control process), (d) motor skills, and (e) attitudes. Each of these categories may be seen to encompass a broad variety of human activities. It is held that results indicating the effects on learning of most principal independent variables can be generalized within these categories but not between them. This article identifies additional effects of each type of learning outcome and discusses the current state of knowledge about them.

The question of understanding how human beings learn has been a central theme of psychological research since the time of the English associationist philosophers Hobbes, Locke, and Mill, and experimental work of Ebbinghaus (1913) in 1885. From that time until the present day, learning has been understood as a change of state of the human being that is remembered and that makes possible a corresponding change in the individual's behavior in a given type of situation. This change of state must, of course, be distinguished from others that may be effected by innate forces, by maturation, or by other physiological influences. Instead, learning is brought about by one or more experiences that are either the same as or that somehow present the situation in which the newly acquired behavior is exhibited.

Psychologists who have studied the phenomenon of learning have sometimes confined their observations to human learning. Such learning was studied by the followers of the Ebbinghaus tradition and was usually referred to as *verbal learning*. Verbal learning was studied by such investigators as Robinson (1932), McGeoch (1932), Melton (1963), Postman (1961), and Underwood (1957), among others. Many students of learning, however, did not hesitate to study the behavior of animals as well as humans nor to relatethe phenomena observed across the species gap. Pioneers in this tradition include Thorndike (1898), Guthrie (1935), Tolman (1932), and Hull (1943). Other differences in fundamental approaches to the study of human learning arose from points of view noted by Bower and Hilgard (1981) as empiricism versus rationalism, contiguity versus reinforcement, and gradual increments versus all-or-none spurts. These issues persist down to the present day and cannot be said to have been resolved in the sense of having attained a consensus of scientists.

Perhaps, though, the most distinctive differences among studies of learning, as reported to us by various investigators, are differences in the *behavior-in-situation* that identifies the new learning. This is often referred to as the *learning task*, a phrase that implies that its specification includes both the external situation and the behavior that interacts with it. This tendency to identify learning with the situation is reflected in texts having learning as a subject, such as Hulse, Deese, and Egeth (1975), or Hill (1981). When Melton (1964) assembled chapters in *Categories of Human Learning*, they dealt with

Reprinted by permission from *American Psychologist*, (1984)

such familiar situations as the classically conditioned eye blink, operant conditioning of pigeons, rote learning of verbal associates, incidental learning of word pairs, and perceptual-motor skills learning. Even when theories of learning are addressed directly, as by Bower and Hilgard (1981), we find the theoretical ideas tied to situations such as dogs salivating to the sight of food, pigeons pecking at circular spots, rats running to food boxes, or people learning paired associates.

The advent of the cognitive psychology of learning, as represented in books done by Klatzky (1980), Bransford (1979), and Anderson (1980), among others, has broadened the situations employed for the study of learning. Thus, we now have insightful studies of the learning of elementary arithmetic (Resnick & Ford, 1981), of constructing geometric proofs (Greeno, 1978b), of story comprehension (Stein & Trabasso, 1982), and of the prediction of rainfall (Stevens & Collins, 1982). Most surely, it is a welcome change to find investigators of human learning choosing schoolroom situations for learning or at least situations that have what might be called "face validity" with tasks encountered by students. The greater diversity of such situations, as contrasted with the narrowly defined learning of paired associates on a memory drum, is a welcome change. If there are cautions to be noted, they may be expressed in the hope that these new school-learning tasks will not themselves become frozen into narrow channels of study, so that we end up with the "psychology of arithmetic learning," the "psychology of reading learning," the "psychology of geometry learning," and the like. I do not think this will necessarily happen. Nevertheless, in our enthusiasm for a newly found freedom from a set of traditional learning tasks, we should, I think, keep firmly in mind that a psychology of learning seeks generalizations that are not tied to particular learning situations. The history of paired-associate learning should help us remember this lesson. For many years, studies of paired associates sought to discover *general* principles about the learning of associations. As understanding increased, however, such studies came to be seen as dealing with a very particular kind of learning task called "paired-associate learning." Many, perhaps most, of the results obtained apply only to that specific learning task.

Should the study of learning continue to be situation bound? Of course, the conceptions of Skinner (1969) offer a way out. Those who view learning as a matter of arranging contingencies of reinforcement can demonstrate how that principle applies to virtually every situation. The case for application of reinforcement techniques as a way of arranging situations for learning is entirely convincing; it is indeed difficult to find contrary evidence. Yet the tendency of learning investigators to seek more detailed specifications for learning situations, from mazes to geometry, implies that reinforcement contingencies are not enough. Greater specificity continues to be sought in the description of the interaction between learner and environment—in the *task,* in other words. Students of learning phenomena continue to find dimensions of the learning situation that do not contradict the operation of reinforcement but that must be described in greater detail.

How can we achieve a psychology of learning that is not tied to specific situations or tasks and that at the same time has the potential for generalization that we value as a scientific goal? My suggestion is that now is a good time to look closely and intensively at the question, what do people learn? This question must be examined as broadly as possible. By this I mean, we need to gain an idea of what all kinds of people learn—not only school children or laboratory subjects but masons, carpenters, astronauts, politicians, housewives, and word-processing operators. Most of the overt behavior people engage in during each day, of course, is what they have learned to do. As observers of behavior, we know what has been learned by perceiving what people can do. In other words, we know that learning has occurred when we observe its outcomes or effects.

How can we find principles of learning that can be generalized and that are not tied to specific subject matter? Actually, it seems to me that learning psychologists, particularly those in the information-processing tradition, are coming close to a satisfactory answer to this question. I trust they will continue to keep the appropriate goal in mind and will not be too seriously distracted by trendy issues suggested by neighboring disciplines. The question continues to be, how do people learn what they learn? That is not the same question, obviously, as how does a person become an expert? Certainly, expertness is learned, but many people learn many things without ever becoming experts.

Categories of Learning Outcomes

A number of years ago (Gagné, 1972), I proposed a set of categories of learning outcomes that seemed to me to possess certain desirable distinctive properties. While I do not intend here simply to cover the same ground, it is worthwhile to state what the characteristics of such categories should be:

1. Each category of learning outcomes should be distinguishable in terms of a formal definition of the class of human performance made possible by the learning.
2. Each category should include a broad variety of human activities that are independent (excluding the extremes) of intelligence, age, race, economic status, and so on. The possibility of special categories (e.g., music virtuosity, expert wine tasting) is acknowledged but is not relevant to the main point. In order not to be narrow, each category must apply to widely diverse set of human activities.
3. Each category should be seen to differ in the nature of information-processing demands for its learning. Specifically, each kind of outcome should require different (a) substantive type of relevant prior learning, (b) manner of encoding for long-term storage, and (c) requirements for retrieval and transfer to new situations.
4. It should be possible to generalize the principles concerning factors affecting the learning of each category to a variety of specific tasks *within* the category but not to learning tasks in other categories. Excluded here is the factor of reinforcement, assumed to apply to all categories.

With such characteristics in mind for the principles of learning that can be generalized, I identified five categories of learning outcomes: (a) intellectual skills, (b) verbal information, (c) cognitive strategies, (d) attitudes, and (e) motor skills. I will discuss each of these categories again from the viewpoint of contemporary learning psychology and from the standpoint of learning effects. Where possible, I will mention a few of the things I think we still need to discover about the effects of learning.

Intellectual Skills

As a category of learning outcome, intellectual skills have in recent times appeared to find their proper place in the scheme of things. Intellectual skills include concepts, rules, and procedures. Perhaps the best known synonym is *procedural knowledge* (Anderson, 1976, 1980). Some investigators prefer the computer-derived language of Newell and Simon (1972), who call this category *production systems.* Some would prefer to distinguish procedures, conceived as having a number of sequential steps, from rules, which may have only two or three. Since I view them as the same category, I have used the phrase "procedural rules" (Gagné, 1977) for the former.

Does procedural knowledge show itself as a learning outcome in a great diversity of human activity? Of course it does. Consider all the rules that govern the use of language both in speaking and writing. This complex set of rules applies to reading in the sense of the phonological and semantic processing of printed discourse. Intellectual skills are easiest to exemplify in the field of mathematics, where there are rules for computation, for interpretation of word problems, and for verifying mathematical solutions (Resnick & Ford, 1981). Procedural rules are involved in the application of scientific principles to real-world problems (Larkin, 1980). But beyond the various subjects of school learning, procedural rules govern a great many common activities of our daily lives—driving an automobile, using a lawnmower, making a telephone call, or shopping in a supermarket. Think of what kinds of knowledge are possessed by a technician in an nuclear power plant or by an aircraft mechanic. Obviously the knowledge most highly relevant to jobs like these, or to a whole host of other jobs, involves items of procedural knowledge, ranging from the simple to the highly complex. There should be little doubt, then, that intellectual skills of this sort occur in an enormous variety of essential human activities.

As described by Anderson (1980), the representation in memory of procedural knowledge is production systems. Each production has a *condition* and an *action.* For example, "IF the goal is to generate a plural of a noun and the noun ends in a hard consonant THEN generate the noun + s" (Anderson, 1980, p. 239). What is apparent about this representation is that it includes a number of concepts that have previously been learned, such as *noun, plural, end* (of word), *hard consonant, add* (a letter to a word), and *s* . Intellectual skills, then, must typically be composed of concepts. An individual who possesses such a rule is able to apply it to *any* noun ending in a hard consonant, even one that may be have been previously encountered (such a *nib*). The other characteristic of procedural knowledge is also made apparent by this example. A procedure involves a *sequence*—first an individual takes one action, then another, followed by another. In the case of this example, the steps might be described as follows: (a) identify the word as a noun; (b) identify an ending consonant; (c) identify the ending consonant as a hard sound; (d) recall *s*; (e) add *s* to the word; and (f) give the plural.

In summary, the possession of an intellectual skill (an item of procedural knowledge) is shown when a person is able to apply a sequence of concepts representing condition and action to a general class of situations.

What do we know, or need to know, about the learning effects of this kind of learning outcome? First, it would seem likely that very simple rules, involving only a small number of steps, are acquired abruptly. For instance, determining the sign of a product of two positive and negative numbers involves two fairly simple rules that would seem to be learned in an all-or-none fashion. What could possibly be gradual about such learning? It would appear, then, that there must be a phase of learning that ought to be identifiable as *initial acquisition*. If learning has occurred, the rule or procedure can be applied to any instance; if the application cannot be made, learning in this initial sense has not yet happened. But in a sense I am using it here, learning *cannot* have occurred partially. The evidence for these ideas is currently weak; yet they appear to be of some importance for the understanding of this kind of learning outcome.

There is more to this story, however, particularly when we consider procedures that are complicated and have many steps. Learning must somehow be devoted to acquiring the sequence of the procedure in such a way that it can be retrieved readily. Neves and Anderson (1981) discuss a possible way of processing for what they call *proceduralization*. Going beyond that stage, they point out that continued practice may lead to composition, which involves combining production systems, to speeding up the action of the procedure, and ultimately to *automatization*. These, then, are some of the additional possibilities for learning effects when we are dealing with this type of outcome called procedural knowledge. It is notable that these effects of practice do not involve a change in the nature of the outcome itself; being able to add two-digit numbers is still the same outcome. But the procedure may be accomplished by somewhat different process and more rapidly. It may come to demand a smaller amount of the attentional resource, as Shiffrin and Schneider (1977) suggest. Yet the essential outcome remains the same. The effects of learning, beyond the stage of initial acquisition, must be looked for in processing changes, not in changes in the nature of the outcome itself.

Verbal Information

A second category of learning outcome is what I have called *verbal information*. *Declarative knowledge* is probably a better name, implying that its presence is shown by the ability of a person to "declare" or "state" something. Yet I do not necessarily retreat from the supposition that such knowledge, when it is displayed, typically takes the form of verbal statements.

As a learning outcome, is declarative knowledge a widespread and diverse occurrence? It is curious that when attempting to address this question, it is necessary to take account of the fact that there are different kinds of packages for this information. There are "facts" that may be more or less isolated from other knowledge, such as the names of particular persons, the names of the months of the year, or the names of metric measures of length. Another kind of "package," however, is meaningfully connected prose or poetry that is learned and recalled in verbatim form. We recall the "Salute the Flag" and the words of the "Star Spangled Banner." Some of us may recall Hamlet's soliloquy and the "seven ages of man" and the words to Cole Porter's song "You're the Top," in both the square and profane versions.

Still another kind of package for declarative knowledge is composed of organized, meaningful domains to be identified and recalled in a great variety of ways. We realize that the name for a common class of objectives, an era of history, or one of the nations of the world can call up for us a complex of interconnected knowledge. A number of different suggestions have been made by various theorists regarding the nature of organization attained by such knowledge in its stored form. One suggestion is that knowledge is organized as networks of units connected to properties (Collins & Loftus, 1975). Another is that concepts form a semantic space and are related to each other in terms of their attributes (Smith, Shoben, & Rips, 1974).

But of greater immediate relevance is the idea that knowledge is stored in networks of propositions. Each proposition is complete with its syntactic structure—at least a subject and predicate and probably a good deal more than that. Many investigators hold the view that the organization of each such network forms a *schema.* A schema is a representation of a situation or event. It may be viewed as a prototype that indicates the usual sequence of events to be expected. Events (such as those of a story) may be stored as a *script,* according to Schank and Abelson (1977), who also describe other forms of organized knowledge called *goals, plans,* and *themes,* from which scripts can be constructed. While it is not yet clear that the concept of schema has been well defined in a general sense, it surely represents a widely accepted way of describing organized knowledge.

What, then, is the nature of the learning outcome for this category of declarative knowledge? This question must be answered differently for the different "packages" in which such knowledge comes. On the one hand, the investigator seeks the exact reinstatement of a word, phrase, or sequence of words in sentence form. If an individual has learned the names of persons, objects, or foreign-language words, exact reproduction of these entities is expected. If someone has committed Lincoln's Gettysburg address to memory, that person is expected to be able to repeat the address word for word without paraphrase or omission. On the other hand, what will convince someone that a student "comprehends" or "understands" a chapter in a textbook such as that dealing with the history of disarmament in the 1920s? Obviously, no one expects such knowledge to be displayed by a verbatim recitation of the chapter's text, word by word. A recognition of the "main ideas" may be expected or perhaps a description of the learner's schema.

It should be possible now for me to propose a definition that runs as follows: the learning of verbal information (declarative knowledge) may be confirmed when the learner is able either to: (a) reinstate in speech or writing the word or sequence of words in the same order as presented; or (b) reconstruct an organized representation of a verbal passage, containing identifiable main and subordinate ideas arranged in a meaningful schema.

One of the most interesting facts about such knowledge, which we do not yet fully understand, is the following. Despite the fact that both of these packages are varieties of declarative knowledge, they are intuitively very different. Most teachers would strongly aver, for example, that being able to recite Lincoln's Gettysburg address is very different from displaying "understanding" of President Lincoln's message. It is conceivable that a learner might be able to recite the speech without being able to recount any of its meaning. Nevertheless, knowing the address in verbatim form may well contribute to a performance that intends to produce only a paraphrase of its main ideas. There are puzzles here about memory that have not yet been explained. It is clear that knowing the sequence of main ideas in a long passage of prose or poetry is helpful in remembering that passage in a verbatim sense. Is the reverse true? Is the retention of a passage in the sense of a schema influenced by certain partial features, words, or phrases that are remembered the their precise form? It may be helpful to think about this question in terms of "levels of processing" (Craik & Lockhart, 1972).

As for the question of learning effects, this also must deal with the distinction between verbatim reinstatement and the recounting of main ideas or themes. As we know from the work of Gates (1917) and other studies of more recent vintage, added practice in the form of recitation increases the quality of verbatim recall. Errors and hesitations are reduced, and the performance becomes more sure. But additional learning experience with passages of meaningful prose has quite a different effect. As learning proceeds, additional links with other concepts and other networks of concepts are formed. What is learned is elaborated (Anderson, 1980) or processed more deeply (Craik & Tulving, 1975). The schema as originally acquired becomes more elaborate as the empty slots in its outline are filled in. It seems clear, then, that the effects of continued learning of this second kind of package are very different from such effects on verbatim learning. In this case, there is a definite qualitative change in the performance of the learner. New elements, additional ideas, are added to the main themes with which the learning began.

Notable, too, are the differences in learning effects for declarative knowledge from those I previously described as applicable to procedural knowledge. For verbatim reinstatement, it is not at all evident that the learner goes through any phases comparable to what Neves and Anderson (1981) called composition, speed-up, or automaticity. While a familiar word may be more rapidly responded to than an unfamiliar one, it is not evident that the other criteria of automatism, such as the allocation of attentional resources, are applicable to verbatim recall of verbal material in quite the same manner as to an intellectual skill. Of course, when we consider the other package, the reconstruction of meaningful discourse, the effects are very different indeed. Rather than a condensation of procedural steps, as in what is called *composition,* we see the effect of greater and greater elaboration. These are some of the reasons for believing that procedural knowledge and declarative knowledge are highly distinctive kinds of learning outcomes.

Cognitive Strategies

Most cognitive learning theorists distinguish another type of cognitive skills besides the procedural knowledge previously mentioned. Most speak of these learned entities as *executive control processes* (Atkinson & Shiffrin, 1968) or more generally as *strategic knowledge* (Greeno, 1978a). In many studies of learning and of human problem solving, it has been repeatedly shown that learners bring to new tasks not only previously learned declarative knowledge and procedural knowledge but also some skills of when and how to use this knowledge. Cognitive strategies for recalling word pairs may consist of constructing images and sentences, and such techniques have been taught to both children and adults (Rohwer, 1970). Strategies for encoding and for cueing retrieval are suggested by research from many sources (Anderson, 1980; Brown, 1978). Strategies of problem solving have been the subject of a good deal of research (Wickelgren, 1974). Greeno (1978b) has written an excellent article on geometric problem solving.

Cognitive strategies vary considerably in the degree of specificity or generality they process. Some appear to be highly specific to the task being undertaken or to the problem being solved. A strategy of checking subtraction by converting numbers to multiples of ten is surely a useful strategy of limited generality. Strategies such as constructive search, limiting the problem space (Greeno, 1978a), and dividing the problem into parts have been suggested as having general applicability. The strategy called *means-end analysis* is very general in its applicability, according to Newell and Simon (1972). Correlated with the specificity of cognitive strategies may be their ease of learning and recall. Some strategies seem very easy to communicate to learners faced with a particular learning or problem-solving situation ("put the two words into a sentence" is an example). Usually, though, these are the strategies that are very specific to the task. More general strategies, such as "break the problem into its parts," although clear to the learner in relation to one task, may not be readily transferable to other novel problem-solving situations.

The definition I suggest for this kind of learning outcome is as follows. A cognitive strategy enables a learner to exercise some degree of control over the process involved in attending, perceiving, encoding, remembering, and thinking. Strategies enable learners to choose at appropriate times the intellectual skills and declarative knowledge they will bring to bear on learning, remembering, and problem solving, Differences in strategies are usually inferred from differences in efficient processing (as it occurs in learning, thinking, etc.). Evidence of strategies and their use comes from learner's reports, or protocols, of their own processing methods.

Despite the inferential nature of the evidence for one cognitive strategy or another, it is difficult to deny their existence or their role as executive processes that influence other forms of information processing. If we admit that cognitive strategies apply not just to problem solving but to all of the kinds of processing involved in cognition—perceiving, learning, remembering, thinking—then there must be many kinds of strategies for almost any conceivable kind of task. Greeno (1978a) has written about the ways strategies enter into problem solving, as has Newell (1980). Learning-to-learn strategies have recently been critically discussed by Langley and Simon (1981).

The effects of continued learning, or continued practice, on cognitive strategies are not well known. Presumably, though, they behave somewhat like intellectual skills. For one thing, cognitive strategies are often learned abruptly. When children are told to remember a set of pictures by putting them in categories, they do it right away and are not particularly better at it after five trials than after one. If a learner discovers a "working backwards" strategy for solving a Tower of Hanoi problem, he or she puts it into effect abruptly and continues to use it thereafter. Whether or not strategies exhibit practice changes, such as composition and automatization, has not been shown. It seems reasonable to suppose, though, that these executive skills may behave similarly to their more pedestrian cousins, the procedural skills, which have external rather than internal targets for their effects. The problem of how to make cognitive strategies generalizable to new learning and problem-solving situations is also a feature shared with procedural knowledge. The question of transfer of training for both these categories of intellectual skills continues to be a problem not yet well understood.

Motor Skills

We're all familiar with the motor skills we use in writing, using tools, skating, riding bicycles, and performing various athletic activities. These performances are based on the possession of learned skills. Should we bother to distinguish them from intellectual skills, or should we simply call them all *skills* and let it go at that? I think the distinction is an important one. Of course, all performances are in some sense "motor," or we would be unable to observe them at all. Stating something, pointing at something, or pushing a button are all motor responses. In fact, they are motor skills that we have learned in the early years of life and have practiced ever since. But if we are attempting to identify a category of learning outcome that reflects new learning, we must have in mind activities such as fly casting, top spinning, lariat twirling, or others that have not previously been done. A skill is identified as a *motor skill* when gradual improvements in the quality of its movement (smoothness, timing) can be attained only by repetition of that movement. That is to say, learning consists of practice of the movement itself, under conditions in which reinforcement occurs, resulting in gradual improvement in the skill (Singer, 1980).

Surely it is evident that procedural knowledge (intellectual skill) does not have these characteristics. Intellectual skills frequently seem to be acquired abruptly, and this is never the case with motor skills. Practice of intellectual skills means applying a general rule to varied examples. It is not apparent that the practice of motor skills can be described in such terms since it requires repetition of the particular muscular movements involved. Finally, there seems nothing comparable in the area of intellectual skills to the increase in smoothness and timing of movement that is observed in motor skills. I would emphasize, then, that although both deserve to be called skills, the intellectual type and the motor type should not on that account be considered a single category.

Fitts and Posner (1967) provided a description of three phases in learning of a motor skill. The earliest they called a *cognitive phase*, and this was devoted primarily to the learning of the procedure that underlies the skill, the *executive subroutine*. For example, in making a tennis serve, the movements required involve shifting body weight to one foot, tossing the ball in the air bringing the racquet up, and striking the ball with the racquet while aiming in a particular direction. All of these movements must be learned as a procedure during the early phase of skill learning, even though at that time the motor skill itself may be of minimal quality. A next phase, according to Fitts and Posner, is an *associative* phase, during which all the parts of the skill come to be fitted together. This phase, of course, establishes the smoothness and timing we recognize as characteristic of motor skill. A third phase they called *autonomous*, in which skill can be exercised without the need for much attention. Presumably, this is the same as what is meant by automatization.

Fitts and Posner, then, have provided us with a basic account of learning effects, so far as this category of learning outcome is concerned. Motor skills begin with the learning of the sequence of muscular movements, the executive subroutine. Continued practice, (successive repetitions of this same set of movements) brings about increased quality of skilled performance, observable as improved timing and smoothness. Continued practice, sometimes over long periods of time, results in automatization of the skill, evidenced by the ability to carry on the skill in the presence of potentially interfering activities.

If the effects of continued practice of motor skills are similar to those of intellectual skills, this similarity may be structurally true, or it may be a kind of coincidence. Is the improvement in smoothness and timing of a motor skill comparable to what is meant by composition and speed-up of procedural knowledge? As a general description, these terms sound right. Yet it is not easy to accept the idea that a well-practiced intellectual skill (such as mentally adding positive and negative numbers) exhibits a phase that can be characterized as smooth or well-timed. One other learning effect that should be mentioned for this category of motor skill is the fact that improvement in performance continues for very long periods of time (Fitts & Posner, 1967). Any particular level of performance at which the skill is treated as fully learned is presumably an arbitrary limit. However, this does not seem a proper way to describe the effects of long-continued practice of a intellectual skill. Whatever comparison is made, motor skills are different.

Attitudes

The fifth kind of learning outcome to be considered is an attitude. There can be little doubt about pervasiveness of efforts to establish and modify our attitudes. The medium that is most heavily devoted to such aims is television. The commercial messages of television are textbook examples of how attitudes are affected. Not only that, it seems likely that the remaining television fare, including soap operas, continues to produce and reinforce attitudes toward the various problems of everyday living. Whether these attitudes are beneficial in the long run is a matter of opinion,but their existence is surely apparent. Of course, there are other sources that attempt to modify our attitudes, and these include all other communication media with which we are surrounded. Even schools do a great deal to establish attitudes. Schools are fairly successful in establishing socially beneficial attitudes (such as fairness or thoughtfulness of others) in the primary grades but are apparently much less successful in getting across attitudes such as avoidance of smoking or harmful drugs in later years. At any rate, we can readily realize that many forces are at work in our society to determine our attitudes.

Attitudes are inferred internal states. We cannot observe them directly, but must make inferences from one or another kind of observable behavior. Furthermore, as many investigators have pointed out. (Rokeach, 1969; Triandis, 1971), the relation between reported attitudes and overt behavior is seldom found to be a close one. Attitudes are sometimes described as having both cognitive and emotional components. These ideas surely have an intuitive appeal, but they do little to provide a scientific explanation of attitudes. All we are able to say is that attitudes *influence* behavior. They do not determine human performance in the sense that both procedural and declarative knowledge do; they appear instead to modulate behavior. Thus, when performance itself is considered, the distinctive qualities of attitudes can readily be seen.

I find my definition of attitude to be remarkably similar to Allport's (1935), or at least it seems to be highly compatible with it. An attitude is an internal state that influences the choice of personal action. As an example, a positive attitude toward listening to classical music influences the behavior of an individual to choose such listening when a choice is provided. An attitude of rejection toward using a harmful drug influences the behavior of rejection when the individual is confronted with choices of this nature.

What about learning effects of this category of learning outcome? The contrast with other kinds of outcome is marked. Whereas we expect declarative knowledge, procedural knowledge, and cognitive strategies to be acquired in some circumstances when learners are told what we want them to learn, it appears extremely unlikely that attitudes are ever acquired this way. Communications that attempt to establish attitudes directly, whether by persuasive logic, emotional appeal, or otherwise, have consistently been found to be ineffective (McGuire, 1969). Whatever conditions must be arranged for the learning of attitudes, they must apparently be different from directly telling learners what we want them to learn.

Are there, then, distinctive conditions for attitude learning? This world appear to be the case, although it can't be said that the precise nature of these conditions is well understood. Some investigators see conflicts in beliefs or between beliefs and other information as origins of attitudes; others give emphasis to contingencies of reinforcement. I am impressed with the evidence found by Bandura (1969) and his associates, which assigns a critical function to the *human model*. It seems to me that at least one highly common way in which attitudes are acquired or changed is through the mediation of a human model. Bandura has described the typical procedure by which such learning occurs; it involves a statement or demonstration of the choice of personal action by the model, followed by learner observation of reinforcement to the model, which is called *vicarious reinforcement.* My view is that this is more than simply observational learning, although I have no doubt of the reality of such learning. However, I tend to think that for attitude learning, the human model is an essential component. What is encoded, I suggested, is a representation of the human model making the choice of action, which is compared with the planned behavior of the learner himself or herself.

Other differences in learning effects serve to distinguish attitudes from other learning outcomes. It is a common observation that particular attitudes may persist for many years and be highly resistant to change. Such persistence may take place regardless of the frequency with which the action choice takes place. Reinforcement of action choices seems to have its expected effect. However, we do not appear to know with any degree of assurance what happens to an attitude when it is "practiced," or when it is displayed in many different circumstances over a period of time. The way attitudes are represented in memory may turn out to be a matter of considerable complexity.

Why Five Kinds of Learning Outcomes?

Now I have described five kinds of learning outcomes, stated why they appear to be different from each other, and suggested some areas in which the effects of learning are still not well understood.

It seems to me that the recognition of distinctive characteristics for these five learning outcomes has gained increasingly wide acceptance among learning psychologists in recent years. The distinction of motor skills from verbal learning has a long history in psychology. Attitudes have usually been assumed to occupy a special place as learned entities. Developments in the psychology of information processing have lead to an emphasis on the distinction between verbal information and intellectual skills (or declarative and procedural knowledge). Investigation of artificial intelligence and human problem solving has given renewed evidence of the need to infer executive control processes, or cognitive strategies, in human thinking. Accordingly, it seems that students of learning and its processes have come to accept and to depend upon these five distinctions.

No particular reason exists to think of these five different learning outcomes as constituting a taxonomy or as having been derived for that reason. As I have tried to show, the five learning outcomes exist because they differ, first, as human performances; second, because the requirements for their learning are different despite the pervasiveness of such general conditions as contiguity and reinforcement; and third, because the effects of learning, and of continued learning, appear also to differ from each other.

There are good reasons why we should not be content with the idea that learning is learning is learning. Of course, learning has some common conditions for its occurrence that are quite general. Those of us who have tried to apply principles of learning in practical situations, whether in connection with school learning, military training, or adult professional development, have become keenly aware that greater detail in specification of learning conditions is required than is provided by general "laws of learning" (cf. Gagné, 1962, 1977). The contrasting viewpoint about types of learning is equally unacceptable. This is the view that we must discover and formulate principles of mathematics learning, science learning, automobile repair learning, and so on. We overlook truly important generalities, for example, when we refuse to look at the resemblances in learning outcomes between, say, arithmetic and reading, geometry and composition, or between the procedures of office management and the procedures of aircraft maintenance.

These five outcomes of learning represents a middle ground but not because a compromise has been sought. Instead, they are categories within which generalizations can legitimately be drawn, according to both reason and empirical evidence. They are also categories between which generalizations about learning are either impossible or very risky. Within these categories of declarative knowledge, procedural knowledge, cognitive strategies, motor skills, and attitudes, we have a continually increasing store of knowledge of when and how learning occurs. The effects of learning on these outcomes are better known for some than for others. For each of these categories, there are questions to be explored about the effects of continued or repeated learning experiences.

It appears to me that psychological research has been well served by these five categories. I believe they are widely accepted as distinctions and that the results of research are made more readily interpretable when the learning effects of these outcomes are made clear. To understand the learning differences and the memory-storage differences among these five outcomes is an intriguing challenge for cognitive theory.

References

Allport, G. W. (1935). Attitudes. In C. Murchison (Ed.), *Handbook of social psychology* (pp. 798–844). Worcester, MA: Clark University Press.

Anderson, J. R. (1976). *Language, memory, and thought.* Hillsdale, NJ: Erlbaum.

Anderson, J. R. (1980). *Cognitive psychology and its implications.* San Francisco: Freeman.

Atkinson, R. C., and Shiffrin, R. M. (1968). Human memory: A proposed system and its control processes. In K. W. Spense & J. T. Spense (Eds.), *The psychology of learning and motivation* (Vol. 2). New York: Academic Press.

Bandura, A. (1969). *Principles of behavior modification.* New York: Holt, Rinehart & Winston.

Bower, G. M., and Hilgard, E. J. (1981). *Theories of learning* (5th ed.). Englewood Cliffs, NJ: Prentice-Hall.

Bransford, J. D. (1979). *Human cognition.* Belmont, CA: Wadsworth.

Brown, A. L. (1978). Knowing when, where, and how to remember: A problem of metacognition. In R. Glaser (Ed.), *Advances in instructional psychology* (Vol. 1, pp. 77–157). Hillsdale, NJ: Erlbaum.

Collins, A. M., and Loftus, E. F. (1975). A spreading-activation theory of semantic memory. *Psychological Review, 82,* 407–428.

Craik, F. I. M., and Lockhart, R. S. (1972). Levels of processing: A framework for memory research. *Journal of Verbal Learning and Verbal Behavior, 11,* 671–684.

Craik, F. I. M. and Tulving, E. (1975. Depth of processing and the retention of words in episodic memory. *Journal of Experimental Psychology: General, 104,* 268–294.

Ebbinghaus, H. (1913). *Memory.* (H. A. Ruger & C. E. Bussenius, Trans.). New York: Teachers College.

Fitts, P. M., and Posner, M. I. (1967). *Human performance.* Belmont, CA: Brooks/Cole.

Gagné, R. M. (1962). Military training and principles of learning. *American Psychologist, 17,* 83–91.

Gagné, R. M. (1972). Domains of learning. *Interchange, 3,* 1–8.

Gagné R. M. (1977). *The conditions of learning* (3rd ed.). New York: Holt, Rinehart & Winston.

Gates, A. I. (1917). Recitation as a factor in memorizing. *Archives of Psychology, 40,* 1–104.

Greeno, J. G. (1978a). Natures of problem-solving abilities. In W. K. Estes (Ed.), *Handbook of learning and cognitive processes:* Vol. 5. *Human information processing* (pp. 239–270). Hillsdale, NJ: Erlbaum.

Greeno, J. G. (1978b). A study of problem solving. In R. Glaser (Ed.), *Advances in instructional psychology* (Vol. 1, pp. 13–75). Hillsdale, NJ: Erlbaum.

Guthrie, E. R. (1935). *The psychology of learning.* New York: Harper & Row.

Hill, W. F. (1981). *Principles of learning: A handbook of applications.* Palo Alto, CA: Mayfield.

Hull, C. L. (1943). *Principles of behavior.* New York: Appleton-Century-Crofts.

Hulse, S. H. Dees, J. and Egeth, H. (1975). *The psychology of learning* (5th ed.). New York: McGraw-Hill.

Klatzky, R. L. (1980) *Human memory: Structures and processes* (2nd ed.). San Francisco: Freeman.

Langley, P., and Simon, H. A. (1981). The central role of learning in cognition. In J. R. Anderson (Ed.), *Cognitive skills and their acquisition* (pp. 361–380). Hillsdale, NJ: Erlbaum.

Larkin, J. H. (1980). Teaching problem solving in physics: The psychological laboratory and the practical classroom. In D.T. Tuma & F. Reif (Eds.), *Problem solving and education: Issues in teaching and research* (pp. 111–125). Hillsdale, NJ: Erlbaum.

McGeoch, J. A. (1932). Forgetting the law of disuse. *Psychological Review. 39,* 352–370.

McGuire, W. J. (1969). The nature of attitudes and attitude change. In G. Lindzey & E. Aronson (Eds.), *Handbook of social psychology* (2nd ed., Vol. 3, pp. 136–314). Reading, MA: Addison-Wesley.

Melton, A. W. (1963). Implications of short-term memory for a general theory of memory. *Journal of Verbal Learning and Verbal Behavior. 2,* 1–21.

Melton, A. W. (Ed.). (1964). *Categories of human learning.* New York: Academic Press.

Neves, D. M., and Anderson, J. R. (1981). Knowledge compilation: mechanisms for the automatization of cognitive skills. In J. R. Anderson (Ed.), *Cognitive skills and their acquisition* (pp. 57–84). Hillsdale, NJ: Erlbaum.

Newell, A. (1980). One final word. In D.T. Tuma & F. Reif (Eds.), *Problem solving and education* (pp. 175–189). Hillsdale, NJ: Erlbaum.

Newell, A., and Simon, H. A. (1972). *Human problem solving.* Englewood Cliffs, NJ: Prentice-Hall.

Postman, L. (1961). The present status of interference theory. In C. N. Cofer (Ed.), *Verbal learning and verbal behavior* (pp. 152–179). New York: McGraw-Hill.

Resnick, L. B., & Ford, W. W. (1981). *The psychology of mathematics for instruction.* Hillsdale, NJ: Erlbaum.

Robinson, E. S. (1932). *Association theory today.* New York: Appleton-Century.

Rohwer, W. D., Jr. (1970). Images and pictures in children's learning. *Psychological Bulletin, 73,* 393–403.

Rokeach, M. (1969). *Beliefs, attitudes and values.* San Francisco: Jossey-Bass.

Schank, R., and Abelson, R. (1977). *Scripts, plans goals and understanding.* Hillsdale, NJ: Erlbaum.

Shiffrin, R. M. & Schneider, W. (1977). Controlled and automatic human information processing: II. Perceptual learning, automatic attending, and general theory. *Psychological Review. 84,* 127–190.

Singer, R. N. (1980). *Motor learning and human performance* (3rd ed.). New York: Macmillan.

Skinner, B. F. (1969). *Contingencies of reinforcement: A theoretical analysis.* New York: Appleton-Century-Crofts.

Smith, E.E., Shoben, E.J., and Rips. L.J. (1974). Structure and process in semantic memory: A featural model for semantic decision. *Psychological Review, 81,* 214–241.

Stein, N. L., and Trabasso, T. (1982). What's in a story: An approach to comprehension and instruction. In R. Glaser (Ed.), *Advances in instructional psychology* (Vol. 2, pp. 213–267). Hillsdale, NJ: Erlbaum.

Stevens, A. L., and Collins, A. (1982). Multiple conceptual models of a complex system. In R. E. Snow, P. A. Federico, and W. E. Montague (Eds.), *Aptitude, learning, and instruction: Vol. 2 Cognitive process analyses of learning and problem solving* (pp. 177–197). Hillsdale, NJ: Erlbaum.

Thorndike, E. L. (1898). Animal intelligence: An experimental study of the associative processes in animals. *Psychological Review, Monograph Supplement, 2,* 8.

Tolman, E. C. (1932). *Purposive behavior in animals and men.* New York: Appleton-Century.

Triandis, H. C. (1971). *Attitude and attitude change.* New York: Wiley.

Underwood, B. J. (1957). Interference and forgetting. *Psychological Review. 64,* 49–60.

Wickelgren, W. A. (1974). *How to solve problems.* San Francisco: Freeman.

CURRENT READINGS

HOW ARE WE DOING? TRACKING THE QUALITY OF THE UNDERGRADUATE EXPERIENCE, 1960S TO THE PRESENT

GEORGE D. KUH

Over the past 15 years, the national reports about undergraduate education have two things in common. First, they presume that the quality of undergraduate education is not what it once was (Association of American Colleges, 1985, 1991; Boyer, 1987; Cheney, 1989; Education Commission of the States, 1995a; Study Group, 1984; Wingspread Group, 1993). Second, the presumption of declining quality is based primarily on the perceptions of various groups of stakeholders, not systematic studies of student performance. Except for transcript analyses (Adelman, 1995; Zemsky, 1989), there are precious few studies comparing the experiences of different cohorts of undergraduates and what happens to them as a result of participating in higher education. Without benchmarks spanning several decades, we cannot determine whether the quality of undergraduate education has gone up or down, or if recent efforts to reform undergraduate education are having the desired effects. Perhaps students today are benefitting as much or more as their counterparts of two and three decades ago. This would be an impressive accomplishment, inasmuch as the number of undergraduates has increased by more than a third since 1970, and the college-going experience for many students looks different—at least on the surface—than the typical experience of the 1960s and 1970s (Astin, 1997; Pascarella & Terenzini, 1997).

> In reality, many students now come to college . . . less prepared to undertake academic inquiry and have less leisure for scholarly pursuits. Their interest in education is likely to be far more practical than that of the student of 30 years ago. . . . Students these days may need to work on basic skills [and] regard college as vocational preparation in a much less abstract sense than students once did. (Menand, 1997, pp. 48–49)

Menand's description confirms what in the faculty psyche is a fundamental difference between the character of the current cohort of undergraduates and that of earlier generations. Faculty wistfully recall that students in the 1960s and 1970s were more intellectually engaged and wanted more from college than simply tickets for a comfortable life. Such recollections are not necessarily accurate, however. Consider Norman Cousins's depiction of undergraduates in 1960:

> The distance [has seldom been greater] between the interested and the disinterested, between the intellectually curious and the routine, between the concerned and the detached. . . . [Some] follow national and world affairs with genuine concern; they seem to be able to distinguish between good and poor sources of information; they know how and what to read. . . . They seem alert, alive, responsible. But the melancholy fact is that they tend to be few in number, very few, and the drop to the others is almost precipitous. . . . Most . . . have a mechanistic view of college. The purpose seems to be to get out of

Reprinted by permission from *Review of Higher Education* 22, no. 2.

> school as uneventfully and expeditiously as possible, rather than to get out of it the most that is possible. . . . Grades are . . . purely utilitarian. . . . They lead to . . . good jobs. (Cousins, 1960, p. 22)

Taken at face value, these descriptions of the typical undergraduate by Louis Menand in the mid-1990s and Norman Cousins almost four decades earlier suggest that what college students today do and get from higher education may not be all that different from previous cohorts.

Purpose

In this paper I examine the quality of the undergraduate experience in the 1990s using data from students spanning four decades: the 1960s, 1970s, 1980s, and 1990s. I address two questions: First, did college students in the 1960s and 1970s gain more from their undergraduate experience than subsequent cohorts? If so, the calls for reforming undergraduate education in the 1980s and since would be justified. Second, are reforms having the desired effects? That is, is the quality of the undergraduate experience improving?

Methods

Instrument

The data reported in this paper reflect the responses of undergraduates to similarly worded items used in survey research from the late 1960s through 1997. The first instrument was a questionnaire developed by C. Robert Pace (1974) for a comparative study of students at different types of institutions. The rest of the data were collected at subsequent points in time using the College Student Experiences Questionnaire (CSEQ) (Pace, 1984). The CSEQ (1990b) assesses what matters to student learning in college by collecting information about students' background (e.g., age, race, gender, place of residence, enrollment status, and parent education) and their experiences in three areas. The first area is the amount of time and energy (quality of effort) students devoted to various activities during the current school year. All items on the CSEQ's 14 activities scales and the four additional reading and writing items correlate positively with many desired outcomes of college (Pace, 1987, 1990b). The second major section of the CSEQ is made up of 23 gain scales which represent a broad array of outcomes that experts agree are among the most important goals of higher education. Students' responses to the CSEQ gains items can be considered value-added judgments in that the results are consistent with other evidence collected over decades. The third section collects information about students' perceptions of eight key dimensions of their institution's environment. Because changes were made in the wording of several items from the second (1983–1989) to the third (1990–1998) editions of the CSEQ, I used only those items common to both editions in the analysis, unless specified otherwise.

Data Sources

This study draws on two sets of data from multiple sources collected at four different time periods. The first two periods, 1969 and 1979–81, predate the national calls for educational reform in the mid-1980s; the latter two periods (1990–1991 and 1996–1997) are coterminous with the dissemination of various statements of good practices in undergraduate education (e.g., American Association for Higher Education, 1992; Chickering & Gamson, 1987). Thus, comparing student responses at different points in time between 1969 and 1997 can provide an indication of whether institutional efforts at improving undergraduate education are having the desired effects.

The first data set is composed of students' responses to gains items on a questionnaire administered in 1969 (Pace, 1974) and responses to comparable items from 1979–1981 (Pace, 1984), 1990–1991, and 1996–1997 taken from the CSEQ national data base at Indiana University. The 1969 data represent 7,369 end-of-year juniors at 79 colleges and universities (Pace, 1974); the 1979–1981 data are from 2,135 seniors at 30 colleges and universities (Pace, 1984); the 1990–1991 data are from 7,376 seniors at 54 institutions; and the 1996–1997 data are from 8,647 seniors at 49 institutions.

The second data set represents students' responses to items on the CSEQ activities scales. The mid-1980s data were collected between 1983 through 1986 from 25,606 students at 74 colleges and universities (Pace, 1987); the mid-1990s data are from 50,188 students at 66 institutions collected between 1992 through 1996 (Kuh, Vesper, Connolly, & Pace, 1997). Taken together, the colleges and universities from which the data are drawn represent reasonable, though not perfect, cross-sections of institutions from different parts of the country and include doctoral-granting universities, comprehensive colleges and universities, and liberal arts colleges.

Results: Were the Calls for Reforms Justified?

Table 1 shows the proportions of upper-division students saying they made substantial progress in important areas. That is, they gained "quite a bit" or "very much" in intellectual and communication skills, personal and social development, knowledge breadth and depth, science, literature, and the arts, and vocational preparation. The gains of the four cohorts are comparable in four areas, as about three-quarters of the students from all the time periods for which data are available for the respective item reported substantial progress in critical thinking, self-directed learning, and social development; and more than two-thirds reported increases in breadth and depth of general education and background for further study.

In four areas (writing, vocational preparation, functioning as a team member, and familiarity with computers) the proportions of students reporting substantial gains increased markedly. In the case of writing and functioning as a team member, the increases were steady over time, from less than half in 1969 to two-thirds in 1997 for the former and from 57% in 1981 to 71% in 1996–1997 for the latter. In the case of vocational preparation, a jump of almost 20% occurred between 1969 and 1981 (Table 1). While these upward trends were consistent for all types of institutions, the proportions varied by institutional type. For example, there was a difference of 15 points on writing gains between students at selective liberal arts colleges (SLAs) and students at doctoral universities (DUs) (Kuh, Vesper, Connolly, Pace, 1997) in 1997 and a difference of 18 points on vocational preparation gains between students at comprehensive colleges and universities (CCUs) and general liberal arts colleges (GLAs) in 1981 (Pace, 1984).

At the same time, declining proportions of students reported substantial progress across time in five areas: (a) personal development, (b) awareness of different philosophies and cultures, (c) understanding of science and experimentation, (d) broadening acquaintance and an enjoyment of literature, and (e) understanding and enjoyment of art, music, and theater. Figure 1 shows that sharp drops of about 20% in literature and the arts occurred prior to the 1980s, leveling off in 1996–1997 with only about 36% reporting substantial gains in literature, and 30% in the arts.

Figure 2 shows that the 7% drop in students reporting substantial gains in self-understanding has been gradual over time (from 84% in 1969 to 77% in 1996–1997). A modest decline also occurred after 1981 in the proportion of students who made substantial progress in developing their values (73% to 69%); this question was not included on the 1969 survey. The decrease in proportions of students reporting substantial progress in values development was uniform across all types of institutions, though it was most pronounced at general liberal arts colleges (GLAs) where a 6% drop occurred on developing values (69% to 63%) and self-understanding (78% to 72%), with a 9% drop in understanding and getting along with others (81% to 72%). These data are not shown in a table but are reported in Kuh, Vesper, Connolly, and Pace (1997). A portion of the declines may be attributed to shifts in curricular emphases as there now appear to be two distinct clusters of GLAs which are distinguishable by the proportions of students majoring in traditional liberal arts area and applied areas (Pace, 1997). One subset is the traditional GLA, colleges where substantial proportions of students major in the liberal arts fields. Pace (1997) contends that a second form has evolved, the vocational liberal arts college (VLA), which is more of a baccalaureate vocational training institute in which the majority of students major in applied areas. (See also Delucchi, 1997.) At the traditional GLAs, more than 70% of students report substantial progress in developing their values compared with only 59% at the VLAs (Pace, 1997).

Another perspective on the quality of undergraduate education can be seen in the fractions of students who gain very little in certain areas. The areas where the largest proportions of students in the mid-1990s gained very little include the performing arts (33%), science (30%), literature (29%), and knowledge of other parts of the world (26%). In the mid-1980s, similar proportions of students at DUs and CCUs reported very little progress in these areas with the proportions of students at SLAs and GLAs being only slightly smaller in the mid-1980s.

TABLE 1
Upperclass Students Reporting "Substantial Progress"[1] in Selected Outcome Areas (in percentages)

Goal Statement	*1969*[2]	*1979 –81*[3]	*1990 –91*[4]	*1996 –97*	Goal Statement
Intellectual and Communication Skills					
Critical thinking: logic, inference, nature, and limitations of knowledge	72	70	70	73	Ability to think analytically and logically
		80	75	75	Ability to see relationships, similarities, differences between ideas
		85	82	81	Ability to learn on one's own
			54	65	Familiarity with computers
Writing and speaking: clear, correct, effective communication	49	54	64	67	Writing clearly and effectively
Personal and Social Development					
Social development: experience and skill in relating to other people	75	79	79	75	Understanding other people; ability to get along with different people
Personal development: understanding one's abilities and limitations, interests, and standards of behavior	84	82	79	77	Understanding oneself: one's abilities, interests, and personality
		73	71	69	Developing one's own values and ethical standards
		57	68	71	Ability to function as a team member
Breadth and Depth					
Vocabulary, terminology, and facts in various fields of knowledge	69	71	70	68	Gaining a broad general education about different fields of knowledge
Awareness of different philosophies, cultures, and ways of life	69	63	56	58	Becoming aware of different philosophies, cultures, and ways of life
Background and specialization for further education in some professional, scientific, or scholarly field	71	74	69	71	Acquiring background and specialization for further education in some professional, scientific, or scholarly field
Science, Literature, and Arts					
Science and technology: understanding and appreciation	43	39	34	38	Understanding the nature of science and experimentation
		40	31	34	Understanding scientific and technical developments
Broadened literary acquaintance and appreciation	57	37	36	36	Broadening one's acquaintance with and enjoyment of literature
Aesthetic sensitivity: appreciation and enjoyment of art, music, drama	53	34	34	30	Developing an understanding/enjoyment of art, music, drama
Vocational training	40	59	60	57	Acquiring knowledge and skills applicable to a specific job or type of work (vocational preparation)

[1] "Very much" or "quite a bit"
[2] C. R. Pace. (1974). *The demise of diversity? A comparative profile of eight types of institutions.* Berkeley: Carnegie Commission on Higher Education.
[3] C. R. Pace. (1984). *Measuring the quality of student experiences.* Los Angeles: Center for the Study of Education, UCLA Graduate School of Education.
[4] Figures for this column and the next (1996–1997) are from the College Student Experiences Questionnaire Research and Distribution Program, Indiana University.

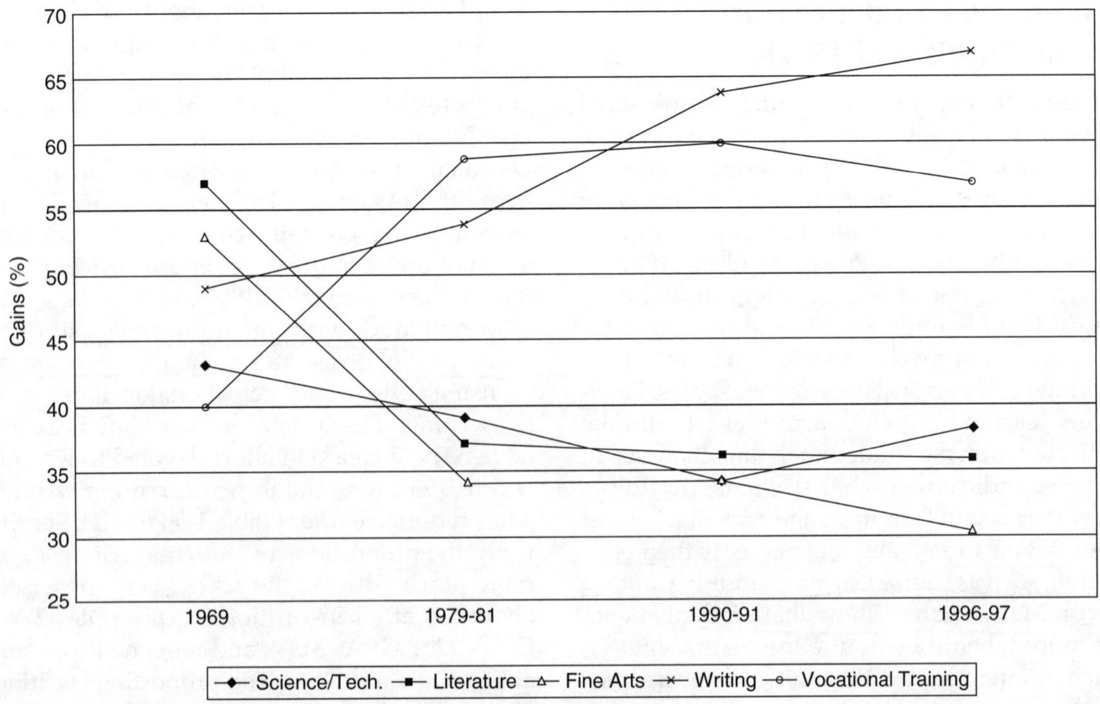

Figure 1 Liberal Arts, Writing, and Vocational Preparation Gains

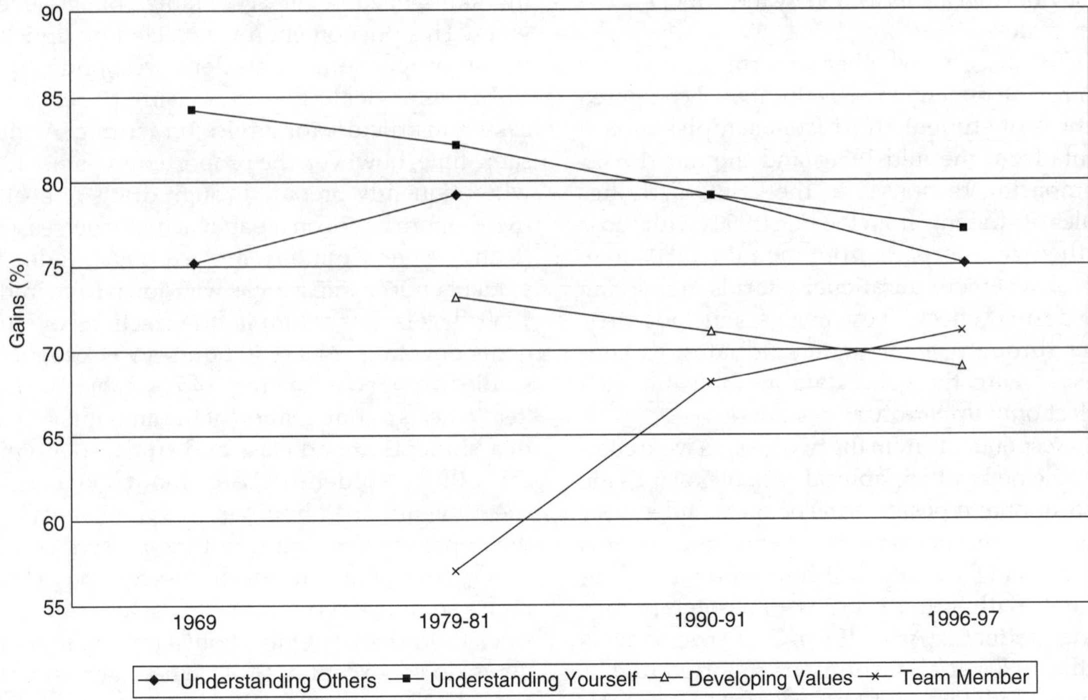

Figure 2 Personal and Social Development Gains

Comparing Student Effort in the 1980s and 1990s

Assessments of student learning and personal development gains are necessary but incomplete evidence of the quality of undergraduate education. Indeed, relying exclusively on outcomes indicators may underestimate the quality of the undergraduate experience in the 1990s. After all,

if a teaching-to-learning paradigm shift (Barr & Tagg, 1995) is underway, it will take time for these new approaches to show their effects in learning and personal development gains. However, learning-centered activities should be reflected almost immediately in changes in process indicators—what students are doing, how they spend their time, and how much effort they devote to activities that matter to their education, such as course learning, studying, and so forth. Many sources show that students benefit more when they do the things that matter, such as interacting with faculty and peers, participating in active and cooperative learning activities, and using the library and other information resources (Astin, 1984, 1993; Pace, 1990a; Pascarella & Terenzini, 1991). Thus, we can anticipate what will happen to outcomes by looking at what students are doing with their time—behaviors that are measured by the CSEQ's activities scales.

To discern whether reform efforts are improving undergraduate education, I compared indices of student effort from samples of students from the mid-1980s and the mid-1990s. Comparing responses to the CSEQ activities scales of students from the mid-1990s with those of their counterparts from the mid-1980s may reveal whether educational reforms are having the desired effect. These analyses include first-year through senior undergraduates, as contrasted with the gains data in Table 1 which reflect only upper-division students.

Respondents from the two groups were comparable on key biographical variables across the institutional types in terms of age, gender, year in school, marital status, and enrollment status (more than 90% were full-time students). Consistent with other studies of contemporary undergraduates (Astin, 1997), CSEQ respondents in the 1990s at all institutions reported higher grades, with the largest increases at CCUs, a 9% jump, from 31% with B+ or better grades in the 1980s to 40% in the 1990s (Table 2); DUs and SLAs had smaller increases, about 5%. The mid-1990s respondents were somewhat more diverse in terms of race and ethnicity (Table 2), especially at DUs (explained in part by the presence of several California universities and the University of Hawaii in the mid-1990s sample); also, more students at SLAs and CCUs were working. This is not surprising, given the changes in the composition of undergraduates over the past 25 years (Pascarella & Terenzini, 1997).

Compared with the mid-1980s, student effort in the 1990s was greater in two areas: (a) using athletic and recreational facilities, and (b) writing. These data are not shown in the tables. The increase in effort devoted to writing is consistent with the upward trend in writing gains reported earlier (Table 1, Figure 1). Specifically, the proportions of students writing 10 or more papers during the school year increased about 5% at all institutional types (DUs 27%; CCUs 22%; GLAs 31%), and remained constant at SLAs at about 45%. The proportions writing 10 or more essays were about the same at all institutions. According to Adelman (1995, 1996), students in the 1980s took more writing courses than their counterparts in the 1970s, though many of these courses were "developmental" in nature, designed to help students acquire writing skills needed for acceptable college-level work. This phenomenon is reflected by upticks in the proportions of students responding to CSEQ items dealing with revising papers and asking instructors for advice on writing. At the same time; however, the proportions of students who frequently prepared rough drafts or spent five or more hours on a paper actually decreased (Kuh, Vesper, Connolly, & Pace, 1997). Indeed, student effort in most areas was down from mid-1980s levels. For example, the fractions of students devoting at least 40 hours a week to their studies dropped an average of 7% (Table 2). This item reflects a combination of the amount of time that students attend class and study, so a typical fulltime student (90% of the respondents) spending about 15 hours in class and studying the appropriate amount of time prescribed by faculty (two hours outside of class for every class hour) should devote more than 40 hours per week to academics. Only about a third of the students do so, except at SLAs where almost half exceed 40 hours per week.

Several items from the course learning scale corroborated the diminished effort pattern in

TABLE 2
Selected Respondent Characteristics

Characteristics	*DUs*		*CCUs*		*SLAs*		*GLAs*		*URBs*	
	80s	*90s*	*80s*	*90s*	*80s*	*90s*	*80s*	*90s*	*80s*	*90s*
College Grades										
A	11	13	8	12	7	12	12	11	NA	8
A−, B+	25	28	22	28	39	40	26	28	NA	27
B	29	29	27	28	34	31	29	28	NA	28
B−, C+	28	23	32	26	17	14	25	26	NA	25
C, C−, or lower	7	7	11	6	3	3	8	7	NA	12
Plan Advanced Degree										
Yes	64	73	62	72	82	80	67	69	NA	78
No	36	27	38	28	18	20	33	31	NA	22
Hours/Week on School Work										
Less than 20 hours/week	7	9	8	12	4	4	8	10	NA	16
About 20 hours/week	15	19	19	23	11	14	17	21	NA	23
About 30 hours/week	37	39	39	38	31	36	37	37	NA	32
About 40 hours/week	27	23	23	19	33	31	26	22	NA	19
About 50 hours/week	14	10	11	8	21	15	12	10	NA	10
Hours/Week Spent on Job										
None, not employed	43	47	45	39	34	26	34	33	NA	26
About 10 hours	17	16	14	16	43	50	28	28	NA	9
About 15 hours	14	13	11	13	14	13	13	12	NA	13
About 20 hours	15	14	16	16	7	6	12	13	NA	24
About 30 hours	5	5	6	8	2	3	5	7	NA	12
More than 30 hours	6	5	8	8	0	2	8	7	NA	16
Race/Ethnicity										
American Indian	1	1	1	2	1	1	1	1	NA	1
Asian or Pacific Islander	6	15	1	1	5	4	2	2	NA	16
Black, African American	5	5	14	8	3	2	3	8	NA	11
Hispanic, Latino	3	4	1	3	1	2	3	2	NA	11
White	85	73	83	83	90	88	90	85	NA	59
Other	0	2	0	2	0	3	0	2	NA	2

that, at all types of institutions, declines of about 10% occurred in the percentages of students indicating they frequently ("often" or "very often") tried to see how facts and ideas fit together and thought about practical applications of their studies. (This information does not appear in the tables.) On the latter item (practical applications), the greatest drops were at DUs and GLAs, with DUs down 10% (76% to 66%) and GLAs down 15% (77% to 62%). In addition, the proportion of students who frequently draw on information from their readings when talking with peers was down on average about 10%, and a similar though less pronounced trend was apparent in the proportion of students who frequently referred to something their professor said when talking with friends. Finally, the proportion of students reading 10 or more assigned books also decreased about 12% at SLAs, 10% at DUs and CCUs, and 5% at GLAs.

The diminished-effort trend also extended to the formal extracurriculum including participation in campus organizations, student union activities, and so forth. One reason may be that more students are working more hours and, therefore, have less discretionary time to devote to such activities. But employment does not explain the decline in out-of-class involvements at predominantly residential SLAs and GLAs where two-thirds to three-quarters of the students work only 10 or fewer hours per week.

Limitations

This study is limited in several ways. First, it is possible that the CSEQ underestimates the amount of time students devote to learning activities. For example, students increasingly are using technology or participating in class-based cooperative learning activities that are not directly measured. In addition, because different colleges and universities are represented in the various time periods, institutional sampling may affect the results in unknown ways. Also, the trends may not hold for any given institution, or groups of students at a particular college or university, such as honors students. And finally, these findings apply primarily to full-time, traditional-age students, as is the case with most longitudinal studies of undergraduates (Astin, 1997; Pascarella & Terenzini, 1991, 1997). That is, although respondent characteristics such as age, enrollment status, and residential experience were comparable across the cohorts, the demographic characteristics of undergraduates have changed markedly since the 1960s.

Another concern is whether the responses of students across decades have the same meaning. Writing is a case in point. Perhaps the increase in proportions of students reporting substantial gains is artificially inflated due to floor effects. That is, compared with previous cohorts, more students in the 1990s start college with less well developed writing skills and, therefore, a larger fraction say they have substantially gained in this area because they had considerable improvement to make in order to become minimally competent. In other words, "substantial progress" in the minds of today's students may be comparable to what students of a decade or two ago might have considered little progress.

Conclusions and Implications

The results point to four major conclusions. First, substantial fractions of students (more than half to as many as four-fifths) make substantial progress in many areas considered vital to living a self-sufficient, civically responsible, and economically productive life after college. These areas include intellectual and communication skills (synthesis, analysis, writing, self-directed learning), personal and social development skills (understanding self and others, being able to function as a team member), and vocational training. Second, the proportions of students reporting substantial progress in several areas traditionally considered the domain of general education (e.g., appreciation and understanding of literature, the arts, science, values development) have decreased since 1969. Third, compared with their counterparts of a decade ago, students in the 1990s devote less effort to activities related to learning and personal development. Finally, despite lower levels of effort, students are getting higher grades as the fraction of college students reporting B+ or better grades is now at an all-time high. The direction of these trends is consistent for all institutional types, though in some instances the magnitudes differ slightly.

Taken together, these results provide a mixed review for the quality of undergraduate education in the 1990s. On the one hand, comparable proportions of students make substantial progress in certain areas as in the 1960s: critical thinking, preparation for advanced study, general knowledge of a variety of fields, and understanding and getting along with others. And in some other important areas, such as writing, vocational preparation, and ability to function as a team member, greater proportions of students in the 1990s say they have gained substantially. However, in the case of writing, this does not necessarily mean that the quality of writing in the 1990s is superior to that produced by earlier cohorts. While the fraction of students reporting substantial progress in vocational preparation is higher than in 1969, the increase occurred during the 1970s and has since leveled off, even though record numbers of students say they are attending college primarily to obtain a good job.

In other important areas, students in the 1990s are benefitting less from college than previous cohorts. General education may not be the cultural wasteland some believe it to be (Bloom, 1987; Cheney, 1989), but there is ample cause for concern as the fractions of students who report gaining very little in their familiarity with literature, arts, and science are almost a third—an alarmingly high number. Process indicators from other studies such as the National Longitudinal Study of the Class of 1972 and the High School and Beyond offer a partial explanation in that students in the 1980s took fewer courses in these areas compared with students in the 1970s (Adelman, 1995). That is, students are not gaining as much in science and literature because they are not studying these subjects to the same extent as earlier cohorts.

Also disconcerting are the gradual declines since the 1980s in such areas as awareness of different cultures, personal development, and values development. Understanding and getting along with others are competencies that have never been more important, yet the proportions of students in the mid-1990s reporting substantial progress in these areas are down from the high levels established in the early 1980s. Even though these declines are modest in magnitude, they are nonetheless troubling because they have occurred during a period when universities have made concerted efforts to help students understand and appreciate diversity in the human experience.

In short, the calls for reforming undergraduate education in the 1980s and beyond seem to have been justified. Although the quality of undergraduate education has not declined as much as some critics contend, both gains measures and process indicators such as the quality of effort (activities) scales indicate that reform efforts may have had some modest, positive effects. For example, in areas considered important for success after college—communication skills (writing), working in teams, learning on one's own, and vocational preparation—the proportions of students reporting substantial gains are at or close to the high-water marks since 1969.

Shapiro's (1997) trenchant insights into the present condition of undergraduate education are instructive. Fueling the current perception of low quality in undergraduate education is that this aspect of the university has not improved as quickly or responded as successfully to the needs of society as faculty efforts in research. While agreeing that improvement is needed, Shapiro asserts that undergraduate education has never been better than at present, all things considered. Moreover, he contends that quality is most appropriately judged by the extent to which undergraduate programs are responding adequately to civic needs, which is the rubric used in the past to evaluate the quality of undergraduate education. That is,

> the transformation of the undergraduate curriculum from one era to another was seldom a case of good triumphing over evil or of a more powerful educational ideology replacing a less forceful one. More often . . . the most important changes were inspired by new societal needs. (p. 71)

At the same time, contemporary undergraduates are shortchanging themselves by not devoting as much effort to the activities that matter to their education as did their counterparts of a decade ago. Equally troubling, they are being shortchanged by their teachers. That is, it appears that faculty are contributing to the diminished-effort phenomenon by asking less from students in return for higher grades. Since 1990 the percentage of college freshmen reporting A-grades the previous year (for the vast majority this means the senior year of high school) increased by nearly 50% (Astin, 1997). This entitlement expectation carries over to college as record numbers of freshmen say they will make at least a "B" average and graduate with honors (Astin, 1997). Student culture is surely a mediating factor in the amount of effort students put forth, as always (Horowitz, 1987); that is, returning students "teach" new students how much academic effort is required to get by. That students are getting higher grades for lower levels of effort suggests that a tacit agreement has been struck between faculty and students in the form of a disengagement compact: "You leave me alone, and I'll leave you alone" (Kuh et al., 1991). The faculty side is not requiring too much from students in terms of reading and written work in exchange for a decent grade—at least a B—provided that students don't make a fuss about the class or ask for too many meetings outside of class or too many comments from faculty on students' written work or exams. Many students are willing to uphold their end of the deal.

Corroboration for this interpretation comes from many quarters (Kennedy, 1997; Sacks, 1996; Shapiro, 1997). Even such selective, affluent residential liberal arts colleges as Kenyon are affected, as Kluge (1993) laments:

> Faculty have been encouraged to remove themselves, to disengage somewhat from a full, complete, intense commitment to students. . . . We're teaching less, there's less

> emphasis on faculty keeping office hours and attending meetings, more celebration of publication and other accomplishments. Students are aware of that, aware of it when you go from asking for four papers to asking for one, aware of it when you go from ten office hours a week to two. That suggests disengagement. (p. 38)

More evidence comes from our (Kuh & Vesper, 1997) study of student exposure to three best practices in undergraduate education: faculty-student interaction, peer cooperation, and active learning (Chickering & Gamson, 1987). After controlling for student background characteristics, perceptions of the institutional environment, and general education gains, student engagement between 1990 and 1994 increased only in student-faculty interaction and only at small colleges (SLAs, GLAs). At doctoral-granting universities the trends were in the opposite direction, toward less student-faculty interaction and less active learning.

The disengagement trend is mirrored in downward trends in personal development and values gains, suggesting a diminishing influence of higher education on personal development. Understanding self and others and being knowledgeable about different cultures and ways of life are essential to functioning effectively in a diverse society. Several years ago the Wingspread Group (1993) challenged higher education to give more attention to values. But between 1989 and 1995, faculty became less interested in the development of their students' values (Sax, Astin, Arredondo, & Korn, 1996). Are faculty members unwitting players in a silent tragedy, the erosion of higher education's commitment to students' personal development?

One explanation of the disengagement trend is the system of graduate school socialization and institutional rewards that compels faculty members to devote considerable time to research, even though they may prefer teaching (Sax et al., 1996). Time is finite; the more time devoted to scholarly activities the less that can be allocated to undergraduate instruction, broadly defined. Another equally pernicious but infrequently discussed trend that may contribute to disengagement is the increasing reliance on part-time faculty in undergraduate programs. Given the importance of faculty-student interaction to many desired outcomes of college, it stands to reason that student effort will decline if faculty effort also declines. Part-time faculty understandably have less time to devote to various class-related activities, such as holding office hours, meeting with students outside of class, or advising student groups. Perhaps full-time and part-time faculty induce differential levels of student effort, resulting in differential gains by students. Thus, the greater the fraction of part-time faculty, the lower the amount of student effort across the range of activities that matter.

Implications

Students learn what they study. Thus, the most obvious and immediate implication of these findings is that institutional improvement efforts must be redoubled, especially those focusing on areas considered foundational to general and liberal education, such as science, literature, and the arts. By softening requirements in these areas, higher education has reaped what it sowed: students who acquire less knowledge in these areas than earlier cohorts. Simply instituting a longer list of required courses is not a promising solution, however, even if it could be orchestrated. Whatever strategies may be used to reverse the downward trend in proportions of students reporting progress in these areas, an intermediate step is needed: rethinking what constitutes liberal education in the present context. Shapiro's (1997) view merits consideration:

> While the concept of a liberal education continues to reign as an article of faith . . . it often masks many important differences in educational philosophies and objectives. Perhaps our chief folly . . . has been to shape our rhetoric as if there were no history of change and controversy on these issues and only one proper curriculum for everyone. There has never been a "right" curriculum. . . . A liberal education needs to prepare all thoughtful citizens for an independent and responsible life of choice that appreciates the connectedness of things and peoples. This involves the capacity to make moral and/or political choices that will give our individual and joint lives greater and more complete meaning, an understanding of how the world works, the capacity to distinguish between logical and illogical arguments, and an understanding of the inevitability of diversity. . . . It would also be helpful if a liberal education encouraged and enabled students to distinguish between self interest and community interest,

> between sentimentality and careful thought, between learning and imagination, and between the power and limitations of knowledge. (pp. 88–90)

The accelerating rate of change and increasing complexity of postmodern life demands that higher education focus on cultivating deep (as contrasted with) surface learning. The familiar surface learning approach is characterized by information recall. In contrast, learners who use a deep approach "seek meaning in study, reflect on what they read and hear, and undertake to create (or re-create) their personal understanding of things" (Marchese, 1997, p. 88). If deep learning and associated intellectual skills (analysis, synthesis, self-directed learning) are more a function of instructional approach than learner disposition (Marchese, 1997), one inescapable conclusion is that faculty are key actors in helping students cultivate such competencies. This means that faculty will have to devote more effort than at present to such activities, at least in the short term.

Finer-grain analyses are needed to determine if the diminution of effort and gains is universal or whether it is specific to certain groups of students, major fields, and institutions. It would be especially instructive if we could integrate effort and outcomes data with course-taking patterns in those areas typically considered general education. In addition, studies are needed to discover the effects of participation in remedial courses and distance education on effort and gains. At some colleges and universities, students perform at levels (both effort and gains) that exceed the predictions of traditional input measures. Among these high-performing colleges are certain HBCUs and Involving Colleges (Fleming, 1984; Kuh et al., 1991). If this is still the case, what can be learned from them with regard to intentional efforts to induce higher levels of student effort and improve learning?

In part, student effort is down, especially in educationally purposeful out-of-class activities, because smaller proportions of undergraduates today experience what was in the past called "college life"—full-time study in residence which, according to Menand, provides "leisure for scholarly pursuits" (p. 49). This kind of educational environment is replete with learning opportunities such as accessible faculty, playing fields, libraries, concert halls, and peers from different backgrounds who are difficult to avoid and whose presence in dorms, dining halls, and classes challenge one's values and world view. In relative terms, opportunities for serendipitous campus-based learning beyond the classroom is substantially attenuated for the majority of undergraduates today.

This does not necessarily mean that student development must be unavoidably blunted, as there are plenty of similar challenges to be faced off-campus in jobs, community agencies, families, churches, and so forth. What it does mean is that the curriculum becomes an even more important organizing framework for learning and personal development—at least the chunk for which colleges and universities can assume responsibility. Faculty typically ignore a powerful lever for learning: whether students use ideas introduced in their classes in their lives outside the classroom. It is now clear that students are more likely to learn at deeper levels when they apply what they are studying in different venues in the company of peers who share a similar intellectual experience. Creating educational environments that induce such behavior requires focused, collaborative efforts by faculty, instructional designers, student affairs professionals, and others.

A Final Word

Pundits are fond of using the familiar A through F grading scheme to evaluate the performance of the American educational system. Based on the results of this study, what grade accurately represents the quality of the undergraduate experience in the United States? Given that less than 75% of seniors in the 1990s reported substantial gains in most areas, a C grade for higher education seems warranted. If we assign a series of grades to account for different aspects of the complicated, multifaceted nature of the undergraduate experience in such domains as vocational preparation, critical thinking, and self-directed learning, then higher education deserves at least a B, inasmuch as the performance of colleges and universities as reflected by student reports of their gains is comparable to that of the 1960s. But in science, literature, and the arts, it's hard to justify anything higher than a D. With regard to effort, neither students nor institutions have earned anything better than a C. This level of effort falls well short of the collective commitment to excellence our students and nation need and deserve.

References

Adelman, C. (1995). *The new college course map and transcript files: Changes in course-taking and achievement, 1972–1993.* Washington, DC: Office of Educational Research and Improvement, U.S. Department of Education.

Adelman, C. (1996, October 4). The truth about remedial work: It's more complex than windy rhetoric and simple solutions suggest. *Chronicle of Higher Education*, p. A56.

American Association for Higher Education (1992). *Principles of good practice for assessing student learning*. Washington, DC: American Association for Higher Education.

Association of American Colleges (1985). *Integrity in the college curriculum: A report to the academic community*. Washington, DC: Association of American Colleges.

Association of American Colleges and Universities (1991). *Reports from the field: Project on liberal learning, study-in-depth, and the arts and sciences major*. Washington, DC: Association of American Colleges and Universities.

Astin, A. W. (1984). Student involvement: A developmental theory for higher education, *Journal of College Student Personnel, 25,* 297–308.

Astin, A. W. (1993). *What matters in college: Four critical years revisited.* San Francisco: Jossey-Bass.

Astin, A. W. (1997). The changing American college student: Thirty year trends, 1966–1996. *The Review of Higher Education, 21*(2), 115–135.

Barr, R. B., & Tagg, J. (1995, November/December). From teaching to learning: A new paradigm for undergraduate education. *Change*, 13–25.

Bloom, A. (1987). *The Closing of the American mind.* New York: Simon & Schuster.

Boyer, E. (1987). College: The undergraduate experience in America. New York: Harper & Row.

Cheney, L. V. (1989). *50 hours: A core curriculum for college students*. Washington, DC: National Endowment for the Humanities.

Chickering, A. W., & Gamson, Z. F. (1987). Seven principles for good practice in undergraduate education. *AAHE Bulletin, 39*(7), 3–7.

Cousins, N. (1960, April 30). Stroll on the American campus. *Saturday Review*, 43(18), 22.

Delucchi, M. (1997). "Liberal arts" colleges and the myth of uniqueness. *Journal of Higher Education, 68,* 414–426.

Education Commission of the States (1995a). *Making quality count in undergraduate education*. Denver, CO: Education Commission of the States.

Education Commission of the States (1995b). *Toward common ground: Defining and assuring quality in undergraduate education*. Denver, CO: Education Commission of the States.

Ewell, P. T., & Jones, D. P. (1993). Actions matter: The case for indirect measures in assessing higher education's progress on the National Education Goals. *Journal of General Education*, 42, 123–48.

Ewell, P. T., & Jones, D. P. (1996). *Indicators of "good practice" in undergraduate education: A handbook for the development and implementation*. Boulder, CO: National Center for Higher Education Management Systems.

Fleming, J. (1984). *Blacks in college: A comparative study of students' success in black and in white institutions.* San Francisco: Jossey-Bass.

Holland, D. C., & Eisenhart, M. A. (1990). *Educated in romance: Women, achievement, and college culture.* Chicago: University of Chicago Press.

Horowitz, H. L. (1987). *Campus life: Undergraduate cultures from the end of the eighteenth century to the present.* New York: Knopf.

Kennedy, D. (1997). *Academic duty*. Cambridge, MA: Harvard University Press.

Kluge, P. F. (1993). *Alma mater: A college homecoming.* Reading, MA: Addison-Wesley.

Kuh, G. D., Schuh, J. H., Whitt, E. J., & Associates (1991). *Involving colleges: Successful approaches to fostering student learning and personal development outside the classroom.* San Francisco: Jossey-Bass.

Kuh, G. D., & Vesper, N. (1997). A comparison of student experiences with good practices in undergraduate education between 1990 and 1994. *The Review of Higher Education, 21*(1), 43–61.

Kuh, G. D., Vesper, N., Connolly, M. R., Pace, C. R. (1997). *College Student Experiences Questionnaire: Revised norms for the third edition*. Bloomington, IN: Center for Postsecondary Research and Planning, School of Education, Indiana University.

Marchese, T. J. (1997). The new conversations about learning. In B. Cambridge (Ed.), *Assessing impact: Evidence and action* (pp. 79–95). Washington, DC: American Association for Higher Education.

Menand, L. (1997, April 20). Everybody else's college education. *New York Times Magazine*, 48–49.

Pace, C. R. (1974). *The demise of diversity? A comparative profile of eight types of institutions*. Berkeley: Carnegie Commission on Higher Education.

Pace, C. R. (1984). *Measuring the quality of college student experiences.* Los Angeles: University of California, The Center for the Study of Evaluation, Graduate School of Education.

Pace, C. R. (1987). *CSEQ: Test Manual and Norms: College Student Experiences Questionnaire.* Los Angeles: University of California, Los Angeles, Center for the Study of Evaluation.

Pace, C. R. (1990a). *The undergraduates: A report of their activities and progress in college in the 1980s.* Los Angeles: Center for the Study of Evaluation, UCLA Graduate School of Education.

Pace, C. R. (1990b*). College Student Experiences Questionnaire, Third Edition.* Los Angeles: University of California, The Center for the Study of Evaluation, Graduate School of Education. (The CSEQ is now distributed by the Center for Postsecondary Research and Planning, Indiana University.)

Pace, C. R. (1997, November). *Connecting institutional types to student outcomes.* Paper presented at the annual meeting of the Association for the Study of Higher Education, Albuquerque, NM.

Pascarella, E. T., & Terenzini, P. T. (1991). *How college affects students: Findings and insights from twenty years of research.* San Francisco: Jossey-Bass.

Pascarella, E. T., & Terenzini, P. T. (1997). Studying college students in the 21st century: Meeting new challenges. *The Review of Higher Education, 21*(2), 151–165.

Sacks, P. (1996). *Generation X goes to college: An eye-opening account of teaching in postmodern America.* Chicago: Open Court.

Sax, L. J., Astin, A. W., Arredondo, M., Korn, W. S. (1996). *The American college teacher: National norms for the 1995–96 HERI faculty survey.* Los Angeles: University of California, Los Angeles, Higher Education Research Institute.

Shapiro, H. T. (1997). *Cognition, character, and culture in undergraduate education: Rhetoric and reality.* In R. G. Ehrenberg (Ed.), The American university: National treasure or endangered species? (pp. 58–99). Ithaca, NY: Cornell University Press.

The Study Group on the Conditions of Excellence in American Higher Education (1984). *Involvement in learning.* Washington, DC: U.S. Department of Education.

Wingspread Group on Higher Education (1993). *An American imperative: Higher expectations for higher education.* Racine, WI: Johnson Foundation.

Zemsky, R. (1989). *Structure and coherence: Measuring the undergraduate curriculum.* Washington, DC: Association of American Colleges and Universities.

Evaluating the Results of Multicultural Education: Taking the Long Way Home

Jeffrey S. Beaudry, Ph.D.

Assistant Professor, Department of Professional Education, University of Southern Maine

James Earl Davis, Ph.D.

Assistant Professor, Department of Educational Studies, University of Delaware

Editor's Notes:

Jeffrey Beaudry and James Davis remind us that, as faculty members, we have a responsibility to evaluate our courses for the purpose of continual improvement. When we make the commitment to modify our courses to incorporate multicultural content, instructional strategies, assessment processes, and/or interactions, we have an additional responsibility to determine the impact of those changes. Evaluation of multicultural course or program change can inspire further transformations and support continued institutional progress. The authors offer fourteen guidelines for engaging in course and program evaluation that also encourage activism in supporting systemic improvement. They argue that without institutional commitment, even dramatic evidence of the efficacy of incorporating multicultural content and processes will have limited impact.

The guidelines extend generic recommendations for course evaluation by including emphases on faculty self-assessment of cultural understanding, integrating evaluation with content, use of evaluation teams that include multicultural expertise, reporting data by all diversity categories, being sensitive to labeling, and developing a systemic view. In presenting their guidelines, the authors review the literature, including available instrumentation for assessing attitude change. They also critique one of Beaudry's own experiences in evaluating a diversity program. They conclude with the idea that evaluating our efforts to incorporate multicultural education in our courses can result in changes to ourselves and our students.

In recent years, stories about the nature and impact of multicultural education have appeared with some regularity in higher education media. Competing voices demand more concerted efforts in support of multicultural content and a more diverse faculty on the one hand, and decry these same efforts as infringements upon academic freedom, on the other. As Morey emphasizes in the final chapter,

Reprinted from *Multicultural Course Transformation in Higher Education*, (1997), Allyn & Bacon.

achieving sustained commitment to the value of multicultural education requires building institutional capacity to plan, implement, and evaluate changes that support diversity. In fact, evaluation of outcomes produced by multicultural transformation can lend some objectivity to the passionate debate. In this era of educational reform, the key values of *education for all* and a *commitment to equity* inspire us to understand the meaning, as well as the impact of multicultural education through evaluation. Despite prevailing constraints of limited resources, emerging standards of accountability for multicultural education are expanding the roles expected of faculty and administrators to include evaluation and assessment.

Multicultural evaluation studies are just beginning to be reported in the literature. One reason may be the relative recency of multicultural change efforts; another stems from the complexities involved. As defined in Chapter 1, multicultural education encompasses gender equity; the complex, lifelong development of cultural, ethnic, national, and personal identity; issues of disability; and the effects of social class. Moreover, multicultural education is conceptualized "as a field that consists of 1) content integration, 2) the knowledge construction process, 3) prejudice reduction, 4) an equity pedagogy, and 5) an empowering school culture and social structure" (Banks, 1994b, p. 4). Goals vary from increased achievement of ethnic students and acquisition of new scholarship (content) to valuing of diversity (affect) to working effecting social change (behavior). The unit of evaluation might be a single transformed course (e.g., Chapter 11, introductory economics), an entire program (e.g., Chapter 12, teacher preparation), or an institution (Chapter 16) and involve any number of subject matter disciplines.

Nevertheless, recognition of the moral imperative has encouraged faculty and administrators in higher education to shift the question from "if" to "when and how" multicultural transformation will occur in each course and on each campus. The reforms in higher education now focus on *education for all*, not for the few. However, this is a time for risk-taking and passion mixed with rigorous evaluation and caution. To be culturally competent means at times to proceed carefully, anticipate and learn from controversy, and respectfully allow for the inclusion of multiple perspectives (Yen, 1992).

The purpose of this chapter is to suggest guidelines for evaluating multicultural course change. We begin with a brief review of research in multicultural education to highlight themes and recommendations for evaluation. We then examine specific applications of course evaluation in higher education, concentrating on the conditions, process, and impact of multicultural education on teaching and learning. A sample case in evaluating organizational change illustrates one experience in practice. We conclude with a consideration of multicultural course evaluation within the broader institutional context. Fourteen guidelines for evaluating multicultural change emerge from and are interspersed with these discussions (see Table 1).

TABLE 1
Guidelines and Suggestions for Evaluating Cultural Infusion

Course Evaluation

- Review the research literature in multicultural education to identify evaluation strategies and useful outcomes.
- Increase the effectiveness of the program by using diverse strategies, lengthening course sequences, and including experiential and field-based learning.
- Understand the connections among beliefs, needs, and goals through self-assessment and then through needs assessment.
- Multiple data sources and data collection methods strengthen inferences and empower stakeholders.
- Comparisons strengthen evaluation findings.
- Integrate evaluation with course content whenever possible.
- Reciprocal benefits occur for students, faculty and administrators engaging in multicultural team-building activities.

Institutional Culture and Context—Systemic Evaluation

- Establish and monitor a positive campus climate, include a focus on explicit support for cultural diversity.
- Evaluate benefits and costs.
- Identify diverse audiences and customize variations on evaluation reports.
- Support diverse, ethnic scholars.
- Be sensitive to the side effects of labeling students by racial categories.
- Publish enrollment data with breakdowns by cultural/ethnic and gender breakdowns.
- Develop a systemic evaluation perspective to multicultural education.

Reviewing the Research on Multicultural Education

Persistent inquiry is vital to critically probe the assumptions of multicultural education and to expand definitions, strategies, and questions for future research. The knowledge base for multicultural education is developing rapidly. Two recent exemplars of research-based publications are Carl Grant's book *Research and Multicultural Education* (1992), and the *Handbook of Research on Multicultural Education* (Banks & Banks, 1995). With its coherence, strength, and discipline, multicultural education research validates basic concepts, offers definition and critical review, provides concrete examples of promising practices, and assists in raising performance standards for students and faculty.

Guideline #1: Review the Research Literature in Multicultural Education to Identify Useful Outcomes and Evaluation Strategies

Faculty members frequently raise the question of how multicultural education can improve the quality of teaching and learning in a given course. The integration of multicultural education with teaching, learning, and assessment has been discussed in previous chapters. This chapter seeks to extend and deepen the understanding of evaluation of courses and programs. One way to assess the strength of multicultural education is to sample the reviews of literature on this topic (Beaudry, 1992; Banks, 1994b). Two reviews merit particular consideration because they clarify the types of outcomes examined in the literature on multicultural education and employed empirical criteria for their selection of studies. Sleeter and Grant (1987) used a vote-count procedure to rate the outcomes of ten empirically based research articles. They found that

> 90 percent of the studies measured changes in attitudes, particularly negative prejudice toward minority racial and ethnic groups. Measures of multicultural knowledge were examined in 30 percent of the studies, while teachers' behaviors were examined in 20 percent of the studies. Of the measured outcomes, 50 percent showed improvement and 50 percent showed mixed results immediately after coursework. In follow-up measures, changes in knowledge and changes in attitudes were reversed and showed a decline to original, pre-program levels. (Beaudry, 1992, p. 77)

The second review, by Grant and Secada (1989), focused strictly on examining the effects of multicultural education on pre-service and in-service teacher education programs. Their selection criteria specified that the research had to have a design that included a comparison group and that the field be limited to preservice and inservice education. The types of outcomes studied were changes in participants' attitudes and knowledge and their adoption of appropriate teaching and learning behaviors. Analyses indicated that 52 percent of the studies on preservice teacher education reported positive outcomes; approximately 42 percent for inservice. "Some of the findings are that length and intensity of the program were positively correlated with increasing multicultural knowledge and changing attitudes, that courses were more effective than workshops, and that two or more courses (especially combined with field experiences) were more effective than just one" Beaudry, 1992, p. 77).

Beaudry's (1992) review of research questioned the value of quantitative synthesis of the multicultural education research literature. The meta-analysis technique initially considered was abandoned for the reason that it blends results without adequate reflection on the cultural validity of the methods and results. In a symposium on multicultural validity, House (1992) argued that even to think of using meta-analysis was an assimilationist strategy, one that was antithetical to liberationist ideology and critical theory and therefore unsuited to understanding multicultural validity. Certainly measurement has been abused by eugenic theorists to the detriment of women, people of color, the disabled, and low socioeconomic class (Gould, 1981).

Meta-analysis may represent the extreme in reductionist research methods by creating a single index or metric at the expense of richer, contextual understanding and combining disparate findings. Meta-analysis may mask a study's ill-defined research topic, for example, or may not be feasible due to insufficient numbers of research studies or poor statistical reporting (Beaudry, 1992). However, research reviews are a powerful, though taken-for-granted evaluation tool.

Evaluation of multicultural education cannot be restricted to descriptive and qualitative methods as the sole means of constructing and validating our new models and new meanings. Ongoing research reveals continuing disciplined efforts to build a knowledge base in multicultural education. Is meta-analysis a standard for judging the maturity of the multicultural education literature (Walberg, 1985)? The whole issue over meta-analysis remains a highly charged, unanswered question. A relevant example is the fierce debate prompted by Willig's favorable conclusions on the effectiveness of bilingual education (1985) and the critical response by Baker (1987). It is not simply a matter of the preferred and defensible method of inquiry. Rather, evaluation is linked with the politics of deciding what is worthwhile. It is in dialogue and argument that we challenge our knowledge, values and commitment to evaluating multicultural education research literature. In conclusion, knowing the paradigms of multicultural education can contribute directly to course and program design, evaluation, and subsequent theorizing.

Guideline #2: Increase the Effectiveness of Teaching Multicultural Education by Lengthening Courses and Including Experiential and Field-based Learning

There are elements in the design of courses and programs for multicultural education that increase effectiveness (Banks, 1994a; Grant & Secada, 1989). For example, courses taught in conjunction with fieldwork and hands-on experiences have demonstrated greater effectiveness than stand-alone courses (Grant, 1981; Ladson-Billings, 1991). Having multicultural field-based experiences in teacher education is currently a standard supported by the National Council for Accreditation of Teacher Education (NCATE, 1990). Undergraduate courses designed as long-term immersion in Native American tribal cultures revealed tremendous effects (Mahan, 1982; Noordhoff & Kleinfeld, 1991). Even a single course of sufficient length (4 or more credits) and depth is likely to make a difference on teachers' classroom behaviors as indicated by Sleeter's analysis of teachers' behaviors and the credits received in human relations (1985). Based on the evaluation of multicultural education courses, offering options to students in courses may be advantageous. For example, Noordhoff and Kleinfeld (1991) and Ahlquist (1992) indicated that dialogue and reflective writing were not sufficiently motivating, even when mixed with field experiences. Noordhoff and Kleinfeld added videotaping to the experience and reflection and seemed to achieve better results (1991).

These learnings can be transferred to professional programs in health care, law, and engineering. Still, faculty members' skepticism and often their personal biases represent a continuing challenge to integrating equity and ethnic and cultural identity issues into their courses. It is a continuous challenge to sustain the developmental interaction between attitude and action.

Excitement over positive short-term results should be tempered by recent research findings. Again, studies have indicated that short-term workshops and mini-courses (Adeeb, 1994) have limited success. This caution also applied to a series of inservice workshops to support implementation of school-wide programs (Sleeter, 1992) aimed at reduction of prejudice in teachers and students. As McGee Banks noted, "To a great extent, we know what to do. What we seem to lack is the ability to act" (1993, p. 43). How can the strenuous and risk-filled task of evaluating results assist in efforts to change attitudes and actions? If we are thinking about how to incorporate multicultural themes in our courses, how do we strengthen the design of teaching and learning and evaluation?

Applications of Evaluation Principles to Multicultural Infusion in Courses and Programs

In this section specific guidelines for evaluating multicultural education will be discussed. These critical concepts focus on: 1) self-assessment of sensitivity and understanding of cultural diversity by faculty and students, 2) triangulation of data sources and methods, 3) applications of evaluation models that incorporate comparison groups and multiple measures (i.e., use of baseline and follow-up data collection), 4) integrating course content with evaluation, and 5) inclusion of multiple stakeholders on evaluation teams.

Guideline #3: Understand the Connections Among Beliefs, Needs, and Goals Through Self-assessment, Then Through Needs Assessment

Efforts to infuse cultural diversity into higher education focus on two key stakeholders—students and teachers. Faculty members must reflect on their own cultural and cross-cultural beliefs and assumptions before trying to influence their students' beliefs (Banks, 1994b). Faculty can seek out professional development opportunities, consult the literature, and begin to conduct classroom-based inquiry into multicultural education.

As an essential first step to design or to infuse multicultural education in a course, faculty members must first think about and clarify their own personal, ethnic, cultural, and national identity. The critical, implicit need is for faculty members to develop cross-cultural competencies (Banks, 1994b; Larke & McJamerson, 1990). How to get started is a matter of resolve, since resources are readily available through literature, videos, and professional associations like the National Association of Multicultural Education.

It is also necessary to assess student needs, as this information will provide the rationale for creating reasonable goals. (See Stecher & Davis, 1987). Some questions can be answered through needs assessment. What is it that multicultural education approaches can provide that will change and benefit students? Is your location one of rural isolation or urban center? What are the implications for the course? For the university? Is the university community (i.e., students and parents, faculty, administrators, and staff) predominantly White, of mixed cultural and ethnic background, gender, and social class? Specifically for the course, what are the purposes and goals to be attained? Is the focus to be some combination of attitudes and awareness, behaviors, and knowledge? What types of classroom experiences will be used to demonstrate and model the desired goals? What are the acceptable standards for judging multicultural education outcomes (See Stufflebeam, McCormick, Brinkerhoff, & Nelson, 1985)?

In some colleges and universities, the need for multicultural education may already be established, and faculty can rely on this work to justify changes in courses. For example, there may already be strategies for dealing with language-different students, for faculty with English as a native language and as a second language (see Chapter 7). A college may have developed a cadre of students, faculty, and administrators who would serve as a resource for translation of documents and interviews. If a needs assessment has not been completed, the research literature can provide the initial rationale for making research-based changes.

Guideline #4: Multiple Data Sources and Data Collection Methods Strengthen Inferences and Empower Stakeholders

Use of diverse evaluation strategies strengthens any recommendations and inferences. Triangulation of multiple data sources and data collection methods is a major goal for multicultural evaluation. Stratified sampling is important and in some cases, over-sampling the groups of interest. (See Henry, 1990, *Practical Sampling*). Key factors in survey research are the sample size and sampling strategy. As mentioned above, evaluation can add a significant component to students' understanding of quality if it is integrated with teaching and learning activities. Again, faculty should evaluate change in manageable steps and through well-researched field tests before implementing complex designs with lengthy, comprehensive surveys (Scriven, 1975).

Faculty may choose to measure general attitudes, knowledge, and behaviors solely with quantitative instruments. Survey instruments like the *Cultural Diversity Awareness Inventory;* the *Cross-cultural Adaptability Inventory* (Kelley & Meyers, 1992); the *Bogardus Social Distance Scale;* the *Diversity Awareness Profile* (Grote, 1994), and socio-demographic profiles of participants have been the most frequent choices. Contreras (1988) and Wayson (1988) used another set of instruments including the *Multi-Factor Attitude Inventory;* the *Multicultural Education Survey;* the *Ethnic History and Cultural Awareness Survey;* and the *Multicultural Teaching Scale*. While valuable for evaluation, many of these instruments are new, and little is known about their validity and reliability. That is, few of these instruments have been used and replicated in other studies, leaving big gaps in knowledge about their psychometric properties (e.g., latent factors and expected results or norms). For this reason, it becomes even more critical to obtain information about the surveys directly from authors and from the literature.

Surveys can be modified to suit the specific interests of faculty. For example, a faculty member may wish to use only the items pertaining to the culturally diverse family from the twenty-six items on the *Cultural Diversity Awareness Inventory*. Consisting of twenty-six items, the instrument contains five sections: 1) cultural awareness and acceptance of people who are culturally different, 2) the relationship with culturally different parents and families, 3) perceptions of difficulties in cross-cultural communications, 4) issues related to assessment, and 5) creating a multicultural environment using multicultural methods and materials (Larke & McJamerson, 1990). To increase the usefulness and meaning of these items, the user should provide space after each item for comments and explanation and ask students to write their reflections about each item. The instructor should take the time to assist students in responding to the surveys in order to maximize thoroughness and minimize missing data, and to decrease the threat of not knowing how this information will be used.

A very promising approach provides more linkage of surveys with interviews by using the same or modified items for interview protocols (Morgan, 1993). Frequently evaluators adapt existing instruments or are compelled to create new instruments. As yet there are few well-accepted measures for multicultural education use. The specific development of questions for surveys is one of fascination and inspiration, initially linked to issues of content, construct, and face validity. A search of ERIC produced a growing cache of multicultural evaluation instrumentation. What may be useful now would be further rigorous reviewing of these instruments from a multicultural education perspective to strengthen construct validity. Another useful activity would be to focus on the process of translating instruments from English into other languages. Attending to this process involves forward translation (from English into the second language), as well as back translation (second language to English). From a multicultural education perspective, the two-way procedure addresses face validity and content validity issues.

Surveys, while efficient, represent a limited choice of data collection methods. Especially in a sensitive area like multicultural education, a need exists to verify results of surveys with observations or by review of documents. It would be useful to determine the "amount of over-reporting and under-reporting of behavior by checking respondents' reports with external records" (Bradburn & Sudman, 1979, p. 164). The existence of cultural differences in perspectives suggests that it would be useful to have respondents rate the topics to understand their perceptions of the topics' importance and how comfortable they feel talking about or responding to various issues. For example, in many models of multicultural education the family and parental involvement in education are central themes. Parents assume very different roles in various cultures, and responses to direct questions may create discomfort in students (Campbell, 1994). One way to arrange an interview or a survey on perceived threatening topics is to create a scenario depicting a problematic situation and ask students to respond to the situation as a member of their cultural or ethnic group. Padilla (1993) gives an excellent example of using the narrative vignette, "Josefina Goes To College," as a stimulus to guide discussions in focus groups of Hispanic undergraduate students. Based on the dialogue prompted by the vignette, researchers identified two themes: the struggle to achieve an education and overcome internal and external barriers and the difficulty of maintaining an ethnic identity (Padilla, 1993).

A significant reason for evaluating courses for multicultural education is to search for and understand the influences of culture, ethnicity, gender, and social class on achievement and success in school. One of the most persistent themes in the research in multicultural education is the preference for anthropological inquiry methods (i.e., interviews, participant-observation) in evaluating cultural diversity in courses (Arvizu & Saravia-Shore, 1990). This trend does not signify a call advocating cultural relativism. Rather the value of anthropological approaches is that field methods like ethnography have provided face-to-face, in-depth understanding of complex issues while preserving the language, values, and customs of ethnic groups, cultures and societies (Fetterman, 1989). Investigating the complex question of whether ethnic or cultural groups define cultural and language differences as barriers to overcome, or as "markers for collective identity that must be maintained" (Ogbu, 1990, p. 428) will necessitate some combination of qualitative and quantitative methods.

The process of asking key stakeholders for their perceptions about cultural diversity then facilitates the crossing of cultural, ethnic, gender, language, and social class boundaries "without feeling threatened" (Ogbu, 1990, p. 429). The issue of being threatened is a real one which must be protected first by procedures in human subjects research, especially confidentiality and participants' informed consent. For example, the use of *race* as a category for discrimination and categorical breakdowns of data today are extremely sensitive issues which result in students receiving mixed messages (Davis, 1992). While requesting racial self-identification has provided a categorical scheme for ensuring equal opportunity, the practice has serious psychological side effects on bicultural students (Belgarde, 1994) and confounds the vision of multicultural education which seeks to deal directly with attitudes and behaviors exhibiting negative prejudice of one group over another. Belgarde indicated that Native American students were particularly vulnerable to the dual loss of identity and the ceremony and appropriate community events (1994). Evaluation must relate to the academic and social activities of students (Padilla, 1993).

In addition to one-to-one interviews and observations, focus group interviewing of five to eight students represents an alternative, group strategy for inquiring into students' thinking before, during, and/or after a course (Krueger, 1988; Morgan, 1993). Morgan and Krueger (1993) suggest that focus groups be used for evaluation and research and not for building consensus, resolving conflict, or making decisions. Faculty can have another trained interviewer moderate the focus group to allow for dialogue by students whose culture and background may foster reluctance to criticize their teacher. As mentioned above, the prompts for focus groups can be questions or narrative vignettes (Padilla, 1993). The focus group approach may lead to the development and improvement of written survey items and to individual interviews (Morgan & Kreuger, 1993).

The payoff from in-depth data collection strategies may reside in the power of communications and language to convey the complex and sensitive issues relating to cultural diversity. The challenge is to honor the process and participants by devoting the time and resources for thorough data analysis and interpretation. In higher education there may be resources available in graduate students who are interested in multicultural education. In addition to moderating and observing, students can be invaluable as translators. Cummins (1986) argues forcefully that teachers and students should learn in, and in this case be evaluated in their native language and English. Using interviews and face-to-face data collection strategies encourages students to form significant contacts and relationships with faculty (Padilla, 1993). In this way, the data collection becomes a part of the program intervention.

Guideline #5: Comparisons Strengthen Evaluation Findings

The strength of evaluation findings for a group of students in a course can be enhanced significantly by establishing a comparison with other groups or by comparing changes over time, as in a pre- and post-test evaluation design. Or, data from interviews and surveys can be compared with data from other groups, resulting in a quasi-experimental design (Cook & Campbell, 1979). Employing a comparison group constitutes one of the most worthwhile techniques for strengthening the evaluation design. Analysis of the composition of the groups by gender, ethnicity (particularly language use), and level of education is vital for comparison. For example, attitudes of business managers were compared with business-major students after they were given a short diversity education course. No significant improvement "in attitudes towards diversity on the basis of age, gender, race/ethnicity was found for business managers, while gender accounted for the only significant difference in business-major students, with females improving their attitudes" (Samiian, p. viii, 1994).

An even stronger evaluation model takes advantage of multiple measures and repeated data collection. The repeated measures design for small groups and the longitudinal or time series design are extensions of pre-test and post-test, with additional measures at selected intervals (Cook & Campbell, 1979). As earlier mentioned, interviews conducted at the beginning and end of courses can be an important starting point for course evaluation, as repeated interviews contribute to in-depth understanding and a validating of students' perceptions. Follow-up measures and observations that take place six months or a year or two years after the educational experiences add even more weight to arguments for supporting multicultural education. Follow-up measures of students, or impact evaluation, may consist of surveys or observations of classroom behaviors, assessment of workplace climate, and attitudes. Universities can employ institutional research departments to facilitate the identification of comparison groups, sampling strategies for evaluation, survey design, and even data collection and analysis.

Guideline #6: Integrate Evaluation with Course Content Whenever Possible

In addition to developing multiple assessment measures, evaluation strategies can be extremely beneficial if they are integrated with teaching activities. A suggestion for integrating teaching and evaluation is to involve students in developing and understanding the criteria for assessing quality. That is, plan the time to seek out student perceptions of activities by debriefing after midterm tests, simulations, and selected lectures. After a test, instructors might allow students to see their test, talk through the answers and questions, and promote a dialogue in which instructors justify their beliefs and assumptions with the students as they construct their understanding of the subject matter. The potential threat to instructors' authority can be outweighed by the critical awareness of the connection between evaluation and pedagogy, especially the pervasive image that tests contain secret, privileged information. It is vital for faculty to take the risk as an evaluator to be forced to justify their beliefs to various audiences (students first!) concerning the connections between subject matter and evaluation. This step toward equalizing power relations supports faculty efforts to transform the instructional component of a course (see Chapter 2).

Use of cooperative learning strategies for inclusive instruction can also support evaluation (Chapter 5). Cooperative groups provide a venue for applying open-ended assessment strategies advocated by cognitive-based instruction (Mercer, 1989). For example, in mathematics the evaluative questions could focus on four dimensions of classroom activities: 1) content or conceptual understanding, 2) procedural knowledge, 3) strategies to solve problems, and 4) communications. For each of these criteria a set of scales would be constructed representing substantive requirements indicating varying degrees of success (Stenmark, 1989, p. 17).

Another principle of multicultural education is to use simulations and experiential learning for instruction, assessment, and course evaluation. For example, in-class theater can bring experience directly into the classroom. Students can direct, act in, and re-write dialogue. If students read Sartre's *No Exit* or Ntozake Shange's *For Colored Girls Who Have Considered Suicide When the Rainbow Is Enuf*, they can dramatize different parts, re-write dialogue individually or problem-solve as group, and reflect on their experience. Evaluating these activities can occur through an observation instrument developed over the time span of two or three courses through focus group debriefing interviews.

Guideline #7: Students, Faculty, and Administrators May Benefit from Team-building

Depending on the characteristic of the students, instructor, and course content, a team of individuals with relevant expertise might provide a more valid and comprehensive evaluation than any single individual can offer. For example, evaluating the impact of multicultural change intended by a course on second language development taken by students with diverse cultural backgrounds may benefit from someone with expertise in the student' language and cultural as well as persons with expertise in the course content and in evaluation. The team approach to evaluating multicultural education has been used by researchers like Slaughter (1991) who involved "language different stakeholders in cross-cultural evaluation teams." (Beaudry, 1992, p. 82). It is also suggested that a support team of faculty be available for translation of instructional materials, interview transcripts, examinations, and surveys. The team members might be the instructor/evaluator and representative students or colleagues.

A Vignette: Languages, Communications, and Cultural/Ethnic Identification in a Multicultural Education Course

As a professor at a university in New York City, the first author had the opportunity to teach and evaluate a course offered to participants in the Teacher Opportunity Corps, a program to recruit minorities into teaching. I was challenged by the issues of language competencies and cultural definitions of key concepts. The program provided academic as well as social support through campus-based activities. The academic program consisted of two courses, one entitled *Multicultural Education* and the second *Teaching the At-risk Child*. The implied relationship of these concepts led me to question the assumptions and beliefs of these courses as they were taught by the instructors and interpreted by the participants. The course instructor for *Teaching the At-risk Child* was an African American woman. I am a White, Euro-American male and taught the course on multicultural education. I am multilingual, speaking German and Arabic and have lived in Latin America, Europe, and in Egypt where I worked three years as an instructional technology consultant.

I outlined a two-year study for evaluating this effort. The first step to evaluating the course was to develop a database of demographic background information on all students. The evaluation design focused on three questions: 1) As a result of the course, what was the students' understanding of the terms *multicultural education* and *at-risk* student? 2) Did improvements occur in students' self-esteem and perception of education? 3) Did improvements occur in students' attitudes about cultural diversity, as measured by the *Cultural Diversity Awareness Inventory*? The primary data sources were the students and the faculty.

The first part of the evaluation was to be based on individual student interviews at the end of the course. All 21 students were interviewed by experienced graduate research assistants during the final three weeks of the semester. The interviews were taped, transcribed, and analyzed with The *Ethnograph*, a computer-based text-analysis program. Questions on the interview protocol focused on their definitions of the key terms—multicultural education and at-risk students. How had their field experiences assisted them in understanding these terms? If the students spoke another language, was there a clear translation of these terms? Most of the bilingual students were Spanish-speaking. Did they have a term like at-risk in their vocabulary? What was their experience in school; did they have teachers of the same cultural or ethnic background as role models? Did they think that matching students based on cultural or ethnic background made a difference? The analysis of the interviews occurred after the course was completed. Participation in the interviews was mandatory and accounted for 10 percent of their final grade. Interviews were conducted with each cohort of students in the course.

While the content of the students' interviews was not part of their course grade, the process of interviewing produced some very significant findings and side effects. Students were curious as to why their opinion mattered, as though it was part of their grade. This concern prompted discussion about the need for evaluating participants' perceptions. Even though most students had grown up in New York City, they had very few, if any role model teachers of the same ethnic or cultural background. They expressed highly divergent opinions about intentionally matching students and teachers based on ethnicity and culture. Some students felt threatened by the questions dealing with matching students based on ethnicity and culture. Finally, when asked to translate the term "at-risk," bilingual Spanish-speaking students seemed to be unfamiliar with a Spanish term that would have a similar meaning. The students' overwhelming response was that the term did not have any straightforward translation. Checking with Spanish-speaking colleagues confirmed that there was difficulty in defining and translating this term.

Administering and evaluating the surveys was more efficient but also incurred difficulties. As part of the evaluation of the Teacher Opportunity Corps program, all students were asked to complete the Coopersmith Self-esteem Inventory and Schutz's Val-Ed (FIRO) and FIRO-B. The results of these surveys indicated no changes in students' self-esteem or perceptions of education based on pre- and post-course measures. In some cases, students became resentful of the continuous barrage of surveys and forms to complete. Students suggested that more time be spent discussing the purposes, the language of the surveys, and assumptions in order to increase the usefulness of the results. In essence, the survey method as an evaluation tool was a topic of intense interest, and the discussion revolved ground the measurement issues of face validity and construct validity. An indicator of students' uncertainty and ambivalence to the surveys was the inconsistency of some respondents as shown by inflated lie scale scores on the self-esteem inventory.

Results from the *Cultural Diversity Awareness Inventory* were designed to be a part of the course, and concepts were directly related to course-teaching activities. Pre- and post-course surveys of each group indicated little change. However, comparing different cohorts showed significant differences in areas of parents and families and in the effects of cross-cultural communications. Even more compelling was the tremendous difference in survey results when comparisons were made between the predominantly White, female sample reported by Larke and McJamerson (1990) and our very culturally and ethnically mixed urban samples. This finding was especially significant because it suggested that we pursue further study of the linkage between students' background and experience and type of community—urban, suburban, rural—with variables related to changes in attitudes.

As a whole, the results clearly attest to the need for the faculty/evaluator and students to interact as partners in the evaluation from the course's inception. What could I have done differently? As junior faculty we could have worked more closely together, but the constraints of teaching, research, and raising families seemed to conspire against our collaboration. I could have used focus group interviews to accommodate cultural learning patterns related to the benefits of group learning for African Americans (Shade, 1982) and Latinos (Rakow & Bermudez, 1993). The qualitative evaluation design could have been improved by sampling. By the same token, students could have interviewed each other, and we could have used these analyses for reflection and improvement. Empowering students to think reflectively was an evaluation objective.

A persistent question in multicultural education concerns the effects of matching teachers and students by ethnicity and culture. On the one hand we should seek to integrate classrooms and experience. Yet, matching students and teachers is perceived as beneficial for social as well as academic integration (Beaudry, 1990). This is an issue for teachers as well as evaluators (Delgado-Gaitan, 1993). While it is not necessary to have multilingual competency, knowledge of cultural diversity can provide the foundation for trust and understanding that is necessary for evaluation and research.

Evaluating Multicultural Change within the Institutional Context

What are some of the persistent themes in this literature? Evaluating multicultural education should be a developmental process, based on the construction of knowledge between and among faculty, students, and administrators. In designing the evaluation of multicultural education, it is suggested that faculty begin with the breadth-first approach to gain understanding of multicultural literature and clarify personal cultural and cross-cultural values. After this step, faculty should take on in-depth evaluation of courses to explore the value of integrative, interdisciplinary, and experiential teaching and learning experiences.

But previous research findings indicate that if positive changes in teacher attitudes and practices are not accompanied by organizational learning, the innovations dissipate (Chapter 16; Beaudry, 1992; Sleeter; 1992). A few faculty can achieve astonishing results and not be accepted or supported by their college or university. Even where multicultural scholarship is well established there can be negative reactions to campus changes supportive of diversity. A similar, disturbing trend was also observed by Warshaw, Olson, and Beaudry (1991). In their study of bilingual programs in elementary schools, the more complete and pervasive the program, the more polarized the participants, especially the monolingual teachers. Administrators often were the limiting factor in the implementation of programs supporting cultural diversity. With faculty members committed to revising courses, what can colleges and universities do to facilitate the improvement of multicultural education through evaluation? The following discussion outlines issues and evaluation strategies for administrators and faculty at the college and institution level. Integrated guidelines focus on obtaining central administrative support and commitment to resources; considering the audiences for evaluation reporting; supporting ethnic scholars; considering the impact of labeling; reporting enrollment data by all categories of diversity; and developing a systemic view.

Guideline #8: Establish a Positive Campus Climate by Getting the University Administration to Be Explicit About Their Support of Multicultural Education

First, the values of multicultural education must be accepted by department heads, deans, and presidents. A great deal of pressure is removed from individual faculty if multicultural education is justified through needs assessment and strategic planning by the university administrators.

In this manner, the institution acknowledges that multicultural values are important and relevant, and university-wide needs assessment and planning can produce standards to evaluate desired outcomes.

Accomplishing a thorough needs assessment at the institutional level will facilitate other actions taken by encouraging more faculty to change courses. (Needs assessment data also provide excellent background for grant-writing.) Those interested in evaluation will be able to more clearly assess whether their course goals are unrealistically high or unnecessarily low. As a result, faculty, administrators, and evaluators can risk raising the standards of judgment regarding multicultural education results.

A promising example of bringing needs assessment together with cultural diversity can be found in the collection of possible strategies for change in the *Resource Guide for Assessing Campus Climate* (California Postsecondary Education Commission, 1992). The measurement strategies and instruments are presented, and strengths and weaknesses for evaluation are considered. The California Postsecondary Education Commission completed a three-year study "on the feasibility of developing an educational equity assessment system designed to obtain information on the perceptions of institutional participants about their campus climate" (1992, p. I). Needs assessment is a very essential and powerful evaluation tool that can have important effects on multicultural education.

Related to institutional leadership is the more specific concern of encouraging faculty research and evaluation on multicultural course and program change. One strategy involves the targeting of funding opportunities and special recognition for such endeavors. An additional consideration is university requirements governing human subjects. It is critical to ensure that evaluation of courses, also a research endeavor, is allowed and facilitated by university and faculty regulations. Evaluating courses could be considered action research, so that rules and restrictions may apply.

Guideline #9: Encourage Institutional Commitment to Benefits and Costs of Multicultural Education

Changes to incorporate multicultural education require long-term support in terms of both time and money as well as a formidable political will. While there are few data about resource support of multicultural education, a leading institution for innovation and sound education, Alverno College, "spends about 3 percent of its operating budget to research and improve its programs, a relatively large amount for an institution of higher education" (Ann Bradley in the May 11, 1994 issue of *Education Week*). What level of resources and funding are required to support research and implementation of multicultural education? Infusion means resource support, a very clear, measurable indicator of institutional commitment.

Guideline #10: Clarify the Audiences for Evaluation Reports

The purpose for evaluation and the audience that will receive the report are highly connected. Typically, faculty members choose to evaluate the impact of their efforts to integrate multicultural content and strategies in a course in order to satisfy their professional curiosity about the effects of multicultural change in general and to derive information for self-improvement. In such cases, the audience should be the faculty member or the faculty member and students.

However, additional audiences can benefit from course evaluation. An accumulation of evaluations can further the knowledge base for professionals in higher education and the specific content fields who are seeking to engage in multicultural course change (see Morris, Fitz-Gibbon & Freeman, 1987). In addition, evaluations of course and program modifications to support diversity can enhance the institution's self-study for accreditation agencies in the various disciplines. Finally, university administrators might find the reports useful for data-driven decisions and risk-taking.

Guideline #11: Support Ethnic Scholars

We suggested earlier that evaluation teams might benefit from the expertise of ethnic scholars. However, the recruitment of minority scholars must occur as a process of building evaluation capacity, and not as coercing available minority faculty who may have other interests and little time to spare (Padilla, 1994). Padilla argues that unless the minority scholar has teaching or research interests in the evaluation project, the extra work in the capacity of translator or emergency counselor may be likened to the imposition of a tax due to cultural background. Administrators who are not sensitive to this issue "fail to understand that ethnic issues cannot be turned on and off like a faucet" (Padilla, 1994, p. 26). The lesson is twofold: we must understand that faculty have their own interests, and we must request faculty consent and be ready to accept "no" as an answer.

Guideline #12: Be Sensitive to the Side Effects of Labeling and Affirmative Action

How have labels been incorporated in multicultural research and evaluation? This question has relevance in terms of the accuracy of our interpretations of data and consequent policy decisions. More specific requests for students to self-identify by selecting census categories can communicate a disregard for complex issues of cultural and ethnic identification (including assimilation, biculturalism, and bi- or multiracialism).

Affirmative Action is a program which is iconoclastic and controversial. Disaggregation of data according to census categories is a process with sociological as well as psychological consequences for individuals depending on their ethnic or cultural identity. What are the implications of disaggregating data and the act of labeling (Davis, 1992; Belgarde, 1994)? In one case, careful scrutiny of the admissions records for Asian Americans shifted the discourse from the stereotyped view of Asian Americans being overrepresented in graduate school to an informed evaluation based on records. In fact, Asian Americans were underrepresented in graduate schools. Through litigation the participants redefined the problem (Takaki, 1992, p. 9). Technical issues may drive continuing quantifying and categorizing of groups for the sake of program support, but there may be a price to pay.

Guideline #13: Publish Enrollment Data with Breakdowns by Gender, Culture, Ethnicity, and Social Class in All Reports

At the risk of belaboring the point, it is important to include gender and social class as well as culture and ethnicity in multicultural evaluation. In an evaluation of activities by the Holmes consortium of universities, Fuller (1992) realized too late that all of the institutional evaluation emphasis was on ethnicity and culture and not on gender or social class.

What is the composition of the classroom by gender, by cultural or ethnic background, by age and experience? It may be that teacher preparation courses have a predominance of White female students. However, upper division organic chemistry, physics, and calculus courses may reflect a predominance of White male students. It is useful to have breakdowns of course enrollments by culture and ethnicity as well. What is the match between students and teachers based on culture, ethnicity, language, gender, and social class? How can this knowledge be respectfully acknowledged and become a part of the classroom or part of change efforts?

Guideline #14: Develop a Systemic Perspective of Multicultural Education

The idea of systemic improvement, not systematic change, has been documented (e.g., Fullan, 1991). Hagans, Crohn, Walkush, and Nelson (1992) developed five analytic dimensions and questions useful for evaluating systemic improvement related to multicultural change: 1) infusion—is the improvement accepted within components of the existing system? 2) pervasive—does the improvement spread throughout the entire system? 3) potent—does the improvement have the power and robustness to make visible desired processes and outcomes? 4) coherence—is there increased close coupling and stronger, more diverse relationships between and among components? and 5) sustainable—do the components become a part of and improve the culture and climate of the system?

Adding the following two dimensions and questions to the evaluation of institutional progress with respect to other goals will help ensure changes that are also responsive to diversity: 6) multicultural—does the proposed improvement focus on the social agenda addressing gender, culture, ethnicity, and social class; is it explicit in accepting inclusion and respectful of diversity? 7) reflective and transformative—how can we evaluate and hold the system accountable? A systemic perspective is important for evaluating results of multicultural infusion because long-term change can be expected only to the extent that the values are solidly imbedded in the complex, varied components that comprise a higher education organization.

Concluding Comments

Banks proposes that individuals should analyze their own cross-cultural behavior (1994b). Applying this dictum to evaluating courses for multicultural change, we suggest that instructors consult the resources mentioned in previous discussions, consider questions that connect with their own interests, and seek to integrate teaching and learning, cultural knowledge and content, and evaluation.

There is the suspicion that interest and commitment to multicultural education is not sufficient to overcome other competing needs (Sleeter, 1992). Apparently, the need has been broadly accepted but not manifested in action. This discrepancy between talk and action may be the most recurring theme of evaluation applied to multicultural change. Why is this the case? As part of implementing and evaluating multicultural course change, all faculty must seek to understand their own cultural, gender, and social class biases. Further, we must directly examine our own constructions of these terms as evidenced in both our ideas and actions. If we collectively force consistency between our constructs and behaviors in favor of multicultural change, then our courses and their evaluations may increasingly reflect actual implementation of multicultural values.

It is critical to understand that multicultural evaluation integrates the content of the course being evaluated with the people (faculty, students, evaluator) and processes of evaluation. The list of guidelines and recommendations presented in this chapter thus constitute a mixture of methodology and substantive ideas. Banks (1994b) pulls together multicultural teaching, learning, and evaluation by noting that faculty must seek to 1) diversify their teaching strategies to include cooperative learning and individual learning, 2) implement gender equity in their teaching, 3) provide students with opportunities to develop and understand their own evaluation capacity, and 4) integrate evaluation with teaching. As for Banks' tenants regarding multicultural education, our guidelines for evaluating multicultural course change apply across disciplines.

It is critical for faculty in all disciplines, but especially mathematics and science, to be challenged to implement multicultural education since these areas reflect the most serious underrepresentation of ethnic and cultural minorities and women. Faculty in these disciplines may have to ascertain how their courses can positively influence and attract students rather than acting as a filter. How can their courses become more involved in language-based learning activities? Faculty need to reflect on the connection between their own pedagogical and evaluation assumptions and their cross-cultural experiences. The goal is for students to be included in the teaching and learning process. The goal of evaluating courses is for faculty to facilitate students' understanding of quality.

Implemented as described, evaluating our courses for multicultural change can result in changes to ourselves and our students. In our role as course evaluators, faculty may become participants in the process of change and choose to conduct liberating inquiry (Grant & Sleeter, 1986), research as praxis (Delgado-Gaitan, 1993; Lather, 1986), and as emergent alternative discourse (King, 1994). The meaning of multicultural education is defined and negotiated with the participation of key stakeholders who must strive to develop their own multicultural evaluation competence. Evaluating and critiquing the goals, activities, and outcomes of a course for multicultural change is a significant step toward transformative education.

Measuring the Outcomes of Non-Cognitive Educational Objectives

Allen H. Miller, W. Imrie Bradford, and Kevin Cox

The worth of a book is to be measured by what you can carry away from it.

James Bryce

In the previous chapter we referred to Bloom's (1956) *Taxonomy of Educational Objectives* in which three domains were identified: cognitive, affective and psychomotor. Much of the emphasis in higher education is on the attainment of cognitive objectives and, because these objectives influence and are influenced by the types of assessment used, there is more discussion of cognitive objectives than non-cognitive. Nevertheless, with changes in traditional curricula and the incorporation of schools of art, music and drama into a greater number of universities, we must not overlook the importance of non-cognitive objectives, even in traditional university disciplines.

Affective Objectives

Affective objectives are defined by Krathwohl *et al.* (1964) as those "which emphasize a feeling tone, an emotion, or a degree of acceptance or rejection". "Affective objectives", they add, "vary from simple attention to selected phenomena to complex but internally consistent qualities of character and conscience." The authors identify five major levels at which students respond to educational objectives in the affective domain. The names of the levels and the subdivisions within each level are those used by Krathwohl *et al.* (1964); the descriptions which follow them are the present authors' interpretation of a summary by Bloom *et al.* (1971). It may be used as a guide for tertiary teachers who wish to compare the levels reached by students at different stages in a course, or indeed within a single lecture or tutorial. The difficulty for a college or university teacher is not so much in recognizing the importance of affective objectives as in deciding whether to include them as part of the formal scheme of assessment and, if they are to be assessed, in what way and with what degree of weighting.

1. Receiving

a sign is present that the student is prepared to learn

This may be indicated by the student's presence at classes. Krathwohl's group note that this basic level of "receiving" may itself become manifest at three sub-levels, namely:

Reprinted from *Student Assessment in Higher Education,* (1998), Kogan Page Publishers.

a) *Awareness* of visual or oral stimuli from the lecturer, without necessarily being able to recall the nature of the stimuli.

Most of us can recognize that this is the *highest* level managed by at least some of our students in the less exciting parts of our lectures and therefore we seek ways of varying the stimuli in order to raise the level of our students' responses.

b) *Willingness* to receive stimuli from the teacher with no attempt being made by the student to avoid the stimuli.

Attempts to avoid the stimuli from the lecturer would include occasions when a student masks out the sound of a lecture by engaging in conversation with another student or listening to music through headphones.

c) *Controlled or selected attention* occurs when a student shows signs of attending to some stimuli in an environment where there are many.

Students may, for example, only pay attention in a lecture when the lecturer displays new material by means of an overhead projector (or unexpectedly leaves the room!).

2. Responding

the student displays a minimum level of commitment to the material being taught yet may appear to be gaining some satisfaction from the subject.

As with "awareness", "responding" may be demonstrated at three sublevels:

a) *Acquiescence in responding*—a passive obedience by the student to any instructions from the teacher.

Examples of acquiescence would be writing down definitions or examining a specimen in a laboratory.

b) *Willingness to respond*—the student voluntarily obeys instructions, not because the student fears any kind of penalty or reproof.

c) *Satisfaction in response*—a student appears to derive some satisfaction from his or her voluntary response to the teacher or the instructional materials.

It is sometimes difficult for a teacher to distinguish between Stages 2 b) and 2 c), at least over a short period. Over a longer period evidence of students' satisfaction or enjoyment is shown by their willingness to undertake further work on a particular topic.

3. Valuing

an appreciation by the student of the worth of pursuing particular educational objectives

As with other major levels, this level may be further subdivided into:

a) *Acceptance of a value*—indicated when a student is prepared to be identified with certain beliefs or points of view

b) *Preference for a value*—intermediate stage between acceptance and commitment, and

c) *Commitment*—belief is expressed in action on the part of the student.

4. Organization

an attempt by the student to arrange a set of values into a hierarchical system so that relationships between different beliefs held by the student become clear

Where there are apparent conflicts, the student identifies which belief is the more important. Two subdivisions of this level have been identified:

a) *Conceptualization of a value*—the student can see how one set of values relates to another or how a new attitude or belief fits into the student's previously held set of beliefs

b) *Organization of a value system*—the student is beginning to develop a philosophy of life which incorporates a "complex of possibly disparate values" which the student attempts to bring into an ordered relationship with one another.

5. Characterization by a Value or Value Complex

the highest level of the affective objectives which is reached when the student consistently behaves in accordance with the set of values which he or she has adopted

There are two sub-levels, namely:

a) *Generalized set*—an unconscious cluster of attitudes which guides a student's actions without conscious forethought on the part of the student

b) *Characterization*—the value system has become the student's philosophy of life.

It should be clear from the above descriptions that each level of Krathwohl's affective domain is likely to be evident in almost any course in higher education. Their importance in fields such as theology, counselling, medicine, social work and law is obvious. An essential part of the day-to-day work of a graduate in each of the above professions is with individual clients, where ethics, beliefs and value systems of consultant and client may be in conflict, or at least need to be recognized. One would therefore expect that at some stage during their professional training undergraduates will be required to demonstrate their acceptance of certain values in other people, and their preference for and commitment to a value system which is not inconsistent with the values of the relevant branch of their chosen profession. For example, it was recognized by Krathwohl *et al.* (1964) that commitment to a particular attitude or belief is shown in a student's attitudes.

> There should be actions on behalf of the value, belief, or sentiment—actions which by their very nature imply a commitment. For example, as a consequence of the social studies objective "Identification with a current social problem", one student volunteers to assist a juvenile-delinquent group worker in a neighbourhood community center and devotes every Saturday during the school year to his work, while another student becomes interested in capital punishment and reads widely on the subject, attends lectures and public meetings, and talks with public officials and criminologists. (p. 150)

The researchers state that there may be occasions when a student has no opportunities for demonstrating directly the type of commitment being sought, in which case the teacher must devise ways of testing students' beliefs and attitudes through such activities as role plays or sociodrama. Testing the higher levels of affective objectives by means of formal examination questions, or even by reports on projects similar to those described in the above quotation, would be a less valid method of assessing these objectives than would direct observation of a student's actions over time. The difficulty for the teacher is in awarding a mark or grade as it is virtually impossible to compare students who are engaged in very different types of activities. The most logical solution would appear to be for the lecturer to draw up a set of guidelines which state the minimum acceptable standards for community involvement (or whatever the activity is) and use these guidelines to determine whether each student has satisfied course requirements or not with regard to "commitment".

Psychomotor Objectives

Although originally recognized and defined by Bloom's team in 1956, a limited taxonomy for this domain was not produced until ten years later (Simpson, 1966) and the more detailed version six years after that (Harrow, 1972). Krathwohl *et al.* (1964) define psychomotor objectives as those "which emphasize some muscular or motor skill, some manipulation of material and objects, or some act which requires neuromuscular coordination". As is to be expected, more attention has been given to the psychomotor domain by teachers of very young children, by those responsible for training apprentices and armed service personnel and by sports coaches than by other university teachers. In some traditional university courses it has long been recognized that certain manipulative skills were essential, particularly in subjects such as dentistry and surgery, but the existence of a hierarchy of skills may not always have been acknowledged.

A comparison of the taxonomies developed by Simpson (1966) and Harrow (1972) with other classifications which are less well known reveals quite different approaches (Harrow, 1972). The taxonomy described by Harrow is more detailed and, while designed to cover the maturation and development of neuromuscular coordination in children, it is readily applicable to higher education.

The terms she uses to describe the six main levels and their subcategories are virtually self-explanatory. Consequently we will reproduce them here with only the briefest of explanations when there is any likelihood of confusion. The examples are selected from those given by Harrow (1972). The levels and their sub-categories are as follows.

Reflex Movements

As Harrow rightly points out, reflex movements are not normally the concern of course designers, although in those rare cases when a student is lacking a particular reflex due to a birth defect, faulty maturation, disease or an accident, their absence could seriously inhibit the development of higher-order manipulative skills.

Basic-fundamental Movements

These include changes in locomotory patterns, bending and twisting the body, and manual dexterity, all of which are normally developed within the first few years of life, and are therefore of much greater interest to parents of young children and to pre-school teachers than they are to teachers in higher education. Nevertheless, teachers at the secondary and tertiary levels are becoming more aware of the importance of these skills as more students are encountered with physical handicaps. A certain level of manual dexterity is required for typing, when using the keyboard for entering data on a computer or for manipulating apparatus in science laboratories, and very high levels of manual dexterity are required when playing a musical instrument or dissecting specimens in a biological laboratory.

Perceptual Abilities

Harrow describes four types of discrimination—kinaesthetic, visual, auditory and tactile—and adds a fifth sub-category which she describes as coordinated activities (eg eye-hand or eye-foot coordination). It is not difficult to imagine how these abilities need to be developed to high levels of sensitivity in sports psychology, the training of air pilots, musical performance, and craft work, to give a few examples from some of the newer disciplines in higher education.

Physical Abilities

The types of physical abilities described by Harrow—namely, endurance, strength, flexibility and agility—are all important for athletes, ballet dancers and players of musical instruments, and normally the level of performance improves during secondary and tertiary education as students in more traditional fields of study engage in extra-curricular sporting or musical activities. Some, if not all, of these physical skills are also essential in medicine, dentistry, physiotherapy, veterinary science, forestry and mechanical engineering.

Skilled Movements

At this level reasonably complex movements or "adaptive skills" have to be learned. Harrow differentiates between "simple" skills (eg typing, skating, sawing, piano playing), "compound" (eg tennis, violin playing) and "complex" (eg aerial gymnastics, high diving).

Non-discursive Communication

There are two sub-categories at this level, namely "expressive movement" (including posture and carriage, gestures and facial expressions) and "interpretive movement" (including aesthetic and creative activities). These range from non-verbal communication skills which are so important in the training of teachers, counsellors, lawyers and medical practitioners to the more difficult expressive and interpretive movements required of actors and dancers.

Relationships between the Domains of Objectives

In describing the various domains and levels of objectives we have chosen to give a greater emphasis to the cognitive domain as this is an essential ingredient of all university study. The examples of test questions and learning experiences illustrate a continuing need for university teachers, course designers and constructors of test questions to ensure that the level of understanding expected of students is being achieved and that students are not forced into superficial learning strategies by the nature of the assessment tasks. The authors believe that the cognitive domain considerations in this book are much wider than those addressed by many practitioners. Consequently we include recommendations and examples of a full range of taxonomies which specify, for example, "understanding", "know-how" and "problem solving". The experiential taxonomy, which was described in the previous chapter, combines both cognitive and affective student experiences as does the taxonomy for professional education, which is described below.

As was hinted earlier, objections have been raised to the apparently rigid separation into three domains as proposed by Bloom and those who followed. The areas of higher education where alternative approaches have been advocated include medicine (eg Engel and Clarke, 1979), engineering (Carter, 1985) and training for the armed services (Hartley, 1984). In each case these authors demonstrate the futility of trying to separate objectives into the three domains, claiming that successful graduates in their respective fields are required to demonstrate, often in the one operation, their possession of appropriate and adequate knowledge and skills coupled with desirable attitudes. Their position is well summarized by Hartley (1984) who writes:

> Breaking learning into domains is an artificial classification . . . (which) does not always truly describe real situations. The performance of physical skills involves knowledge, attitudes, motivation and motor skills. (p. 41)

A good example of the above dictum may be seen in the modern approach to the training of athletes in higher education institutions. In preparing potential record-breakers attention is given to increasing an athlete's knowledge of how the body responds to stress. Each athlete's previous performance is analysed and attitudes which will enhance success are encouraged while attitudes likely to interfere with physical performance are discouraged. At appropriate stages in the training program, and particularly just before peak performance is required, a series of closely supervised training sessions is used to develop the highest levels of coordination and endurance in appropriate sets of muscles and nerves.

A Taxonomy of Objectives for Professional Education

Carter (1985, p. 137) criticizes the Bloom *Taxonomy* for failing to distinguish between knowledge and skills. Although Carter himself uses the term "taxonomy", his pattern of the various types of objectives commonly found in professional education (in his case, engineering) could better be described as a matrix (see Table 1).

As may be seen from Carter's matrix, most of the higher levels in Bloom's cognitive domain are classified by Carter as "mental skills". The type of psychomotor objectives originally identified by Bloom and later described by Harrow are termed "manual skills" and are included with certain cognitive skills under the heading "action skills". Carter's "manual skills" probably do not encompass the higher psychomotor skills described by Harrow nor does he give reasons for including manual skills with organizing, decision making and problem solving when he describes action skills. The only one of his examples of a manual skill where the close links between Bloom's three domains can be readily demonstrated is surgery which, to be effective, demands high levels of

TABLE 1
Summary of a Taxonomy of Objectives for Professional Education (Carter, 1985)

	Mental Characteristics	*Attitudes and Values*	*Personality Characteristics*	*Spiritual Qualities*	
Personal Qualities	Openness Agility Imagination Creativity	Things Self People Groups Ideas	Integrity Initiative Industry Emotional resilience	Appreciation Response	**Being**
	Mental Skills	*Information Skills*	*Action Skills*	*Social Skills*	
Skill	Organization Analysis Evaluation Synthesis	Acquisition Recording Remembering Communication	Manual Organizing Decision making Problem solving	Co-operation Leadership Negotiation & persuasion Interviewing	**Doing**
	Factual Knowledge		*Experimental Knowledge*		
Knowledge	Facts Structures Procedures Concepts Principles		Experience Internalization Generalization Abstraction		**Knowing**
	Cognitive		**Affective**		

cognitive skills and an attitude of care for the patient, as well as delicate neuro-muscular control.

Despite the fact that Carter makes no reference to Harrow's higher psychomotor objectives (or to Harrow's work at all), Carter's matrix is a most valuable contribution to educational thought and, in our opinion, of more direct use to teachers in higher education than any of the earlier books on educational objectives. Its great strength is in the importance this matrix gives to what Carter calls "personal qualities" or "being", which includes the personality characteristics of integrity, initiative, industry and emotional resilience, and the fact that he links this section of his matrix so closely with the group of objectives he calls "social skills" (cooperation, leadership, negotiation and persuasion, interviewing). In fact the highest point in his matrix of objectives would be seen in this group of skills because successful development of these is dependent on acquiring a suitable body of knowledge and the necessary attitudes.

In an explanation of his category, "spiritual qualities", Carter states:

> the category includes qualities other than those of a religious character. It is concerned with the capacity for awe and wonder, with the ability to appreciate, value and respond to both the world of nature and the highest levels of human achievement. Some would wish to add that most important of all is the ability to respond to the One who is the Author of all these things. The importance of spiritual qualities may not lie so much in their utility as in their importance in the development of a mature and balanced person. (p. 145)

It would be generally accepted that it is unfortunate when skilled or semi-skilled workers have an aversion to their jobs. Interest in the job will mean that a person is more likely to take pride in each task, will seek opportunities for further learning and, if the job involves contact with other people, will be cooperative with other members of the team and sympathetic in dealing with members of the public.

Relating Objectives to Assessment Procedures

These two chapters will not be complete until the reader spends some time looking through the descriptions of the various taxonomies, checking against a course outline and asking which of the objectives are important in the course being planned or taught.

Beard and Hartley (1984) give a number of examples of relationships between objectives, learning activities and assessment in higher education quoting from courses in history, medical science, French language, design and art. They also list a set of more general objectives specifying aspects of knowledge, skills and attitudes which students should develop during their years at university. A selection from these objectives will illustrate how Beard and Hartley relate objectives to methods of teaching, students' learning activities and the type of assessment to be used or feedback given to the student. For the more comprehensive list the reader should consult both the original work and an earlier publication by Beard *et al.* (1974).

As examples of higher order mental skills (not to be confused with the psychomotor domain described earlier) Beard and Hartley state that "university teaching in general should enable the student to be verbally articulate and to make his [*sic*] own independent judgements". These skills, they claim, may be developed through "giving papers, effective argument in discussion groups and tutorials, meeting contradictions, and contrasting points of view". Students' acquisition of skills may be assessed through "criticism by other students and tutors, by 'compare and contrast' questions in examinations and by the evaluation of arguments". Under the heading of attitudes the authors state that "an aim in university teaching is to foster in the student enthusiasm for learning". Student activities which are likely to develop this attitude are non-assigned reading, extra-curricular meetings (eg science clubs) and their acquisition of this attitude will be judged by the "extent of extra-curricular activity" or "posing new problems for (the student's) own investigation".

The types of assessment which Beard and Hartley list as the most appropriate for testing the above objectives are informal and rarely contribute to a student's final grade. In fact some objectives are really only achieved, and therefore measurable, after a person has completed a course and entered the workforce. For this reason many professions such as teaching, law, theology, engineering and medicine insist on a transition year of postgraduate training, satisfactory field experience, a period of probation when first entering the profession, or some combination of these before a person is deemed to be qualified to practice.

The Concern for Information Literacy: A Major Challenge for Accreditation

Howard L. Simmons

Why should accreditors have a concern for information literacy? One might just as well ask why accreditors should have a concern for student learning. If an accrediting body concludes—as the Middle States Commission has concluded already—that it is important for institutions to produce more information-literate graduates, then information literacy becomes a critical factor in the improvement, evaluation, and assessment of the quality of undergraduate education. But agreement about the importance and value of information literacy to the improvement of undergraduate education is easy when compared with the accreditor's challenge of promoting the development of effective bibliographic instruction and information literacy programs on college and university campuses.

Besides addressing the benefits of information literacy rather broadly, this chapter identifies the various campus constituencies that must be involved in effecting appropriate programs designed to make students more information literate and independent learners. Some observations also are made relative to what information professionals and other educators might do collaboratively to address the concern for information literacy, all within the context of the accreditation process.

Though there are still those who would dismiss the concept of information literacy as yet another educational fad, the concept is slowly gaining acceptance in the academy as one strategy for improving precollegiate and undergraduate education. I would be the first to admit that information literacy is still not well understood by many in higher education, particularly since some confuse the concept with "computer literacy" or assume that *information literacy* is somehow synonymous with *technical applications*. Nevertheless, it has the potential to be more effective in enhancing the teaching and learning process than any other educational strategy in current use.

And just why am I so confident of this? Precisely because I am convinced that until a person *learns how to learn* or until undergraduate students really learn how to find, select from, analyze, interpret, and use information effectively, they will continually have difficulty improving their abilities to think critically and analytically, to use their powers of reason, or to solve problems. I am equally convinced that information literacy programs (or any resource-based learning programs) must be integral components of undergraduate curricula if they are to be effective or taken seriously by faculty and academic administrators.

In her most recent article, Patricia Breivik (1993) comments about the wise use of information technology by suggesting that when "a goal is information literacy among all students, then those students must have access to computers for self-directed use, and training opportunities and software

Reprinted from *The Challenge and Practice of Academic Accreditation*, edited by Edward D. Garten, (1994), Greenwood Publishing Group.

must be available to facilitate their use of computers and networks" (50). She goes on to note "Students also must have continual practice—both as part of the curriculum and as part of their extracurricular activities—in accessing and using information successfully in all its formats" (50).

Early Emphasis Needed for Best Results

It terms of their undergraduate experience, it is encouraging to learn that some educational leaders (Montgomery 1992) are promoting "the integration of library information skills into curriculum areas" and "suggesting ways in which information skills can be taught naturally within given subject areas" (529). And in a similar fashion, actions now being taken by states (Pennsylvania State Board of Education 1993) and postsecondary institutions (State University of New York 1992) call for the development and improvement of the information literacy skills of students at the K–12 level. Even a portion of the 1994 annual meeting of the American Association of Colleges for Teacher Education will be devoted to the topic "Bringing the information Age into the Curriculum." This is a significant development, given the influence of this group in the preparation of teachers. As one example of the resolve of teacher preparation institutions to strengthen the information skills of their students, a special committee of the American Library Association (Association of College and Research Libraries 1992) developed a fairly detailed set of recommendations to be followed by prospective and in-service teachers, making it clear that the "document [was] intended to reflect the important role of school library media specialists as partners with teachers in curriculum development and information skills instruction" (586).

Finally, that Patricia Senn Breivik as one of education's leading and well respected proponents of information literacy is given a proper forum (Breivik and Jones 1993) to open up discourse with other academic colleagues is further evidence of the increasing value being placed on information literacy. In that "discourse," the collaborators not only discuss the new demands of our information age, but they also conclude that "[w]hen a liberal education . . . is defined by and supports the goal of graduating information-literate students, it will have renewed power in the Information Age" (27).

Information Literacy Cannot Stand Alone

From an accrediting perspective, information literacy must be seen as a concept inextricably connected to the improvement of the undergraduate curriculum—and not just a "hobbyhorse" of librarians and eccentric accrediting officials like me. In my judgment, information literacy—when it is narrowly conceived—will continue to be viewed by some as a peripheral activity unless it is an integral component of the teaching and learning process. Broadly construed, information literacy should be seen as a strategy for improving a student's ability to learn how to learn. With an expanded emphasis in regional accrediting bodies on the assessment of student learning outcomes, information literacy is increasing in importance in the Middle States region and elsewhere.

I believe it is in this connection that librarians, chief academic officers, and others will find the basis for extending the concept of information literacy far beyond the confines of the traditional library. Effective use of information resources—within the library and beyond—assumes that students have mastered the skills to exploit these resources fully, that they have learned how to learn. Students who simply look for facts to support their preconceived ideas and conclusions still have not learned how to learn.

While I am encouraged that the winds of change are already beginning to have positive effects on the campuses of our schools, colleges, and universities, there is still much to be done to ensure that information literacy becomes firmly established in self-study, evaluation, assessment, and accrediting processes for the purpose of improving the teaching and learning process in general and student learning outcomes in particular. Therefore, this chapter not only devotes attention to why the development of more information-literate students is necessary, but it also offers some suggestions as to how librarians, other information specialists, chief academic officers, department heads, and faculty might more aggressively promote the value of information literacy. At the same time, identify some of the challenges—including some "sacred cows" and cynicism—that will have to be confronted and overcome before there is full realization of the benefits of information literacy, especially the difficult challenge of improving undergraduate education.

As I concluded in a recent essay on information literacy and accreditation (Simmons 1992): "Accrediting bodies such as the Middle States CHE need to go a step further in encouraging the colleges and universities that they accredit to view information literacy and other resource-based learning programs as essential elements in assessing quality, student learning outcomes, and institutional effectiveness" (22).

Taking the Challenge Seriously

What will constitute that further step? What will be the nature of our efforts to encourage a stronger emphasis on information literacy in the undergraduate curriculum? How might we suggest that information literacy be integrated most effectively into the teaching and learning process at the undergraduate level. And who must be involved in assuring that the goal of producing more information-literate graduates will be achieved?

Though I am aware that there are actually an undetermined number of steps—not just one step—that can be taken, my purpose here is to provide the perspective of one who has personally benefited from information literacy skills through years of schooling and career advancement.

Given the enormous opportunity to reinvigorate the undergraduate curriculum through the strategic use of information, it seems particularly advantageous for accrediting bodies to include information literacy in the assessment of institutional effectiveness and student learning outcomes.

As a consequence, for the Middle States Commission on Higher Education (Middle States Association of Colleges and Schools 1990), the following an especially relevant.

> Of paramount importance in assessing the effectiveness of library utilization is the ability in the self-study process to describe and document the strategies and activities used to provide an effective program of bibliographic instruction and information literacy. Library instruction can range from the preparation and use of special discipline focused bibliographic instruction to credit courses in bibliography to sophisticated data retrieval systems. Which areas are drawn upon heavily, which slightly? What does analysis of library usage suggest about teaching methods and their effectiveness? These and similar questions, as well as general circulation and acquisition figures, yield valuable insight into library usage. . . . Equally important is the examination of faculty requests for special bibliographies for their courses and the extent to which faculty require students to use learning resources other than the textbook. (8)

It should be clear that the actual development and implementation of effective information literacy programs must be the responsibility of each accredited institution, which should be encouraged by accreditors to view information literacy as important to the improvement of the quality of the undergraduate experience. That will mean that parties participating in evaluation and assessment protocols—including campus constituent groups and others involved in developing and reviewing self-study and assessment results—will need to collaborate with accrediting bodies if the challenge to address the concern for information literacy is to be successful.

Collaboration of All Constituencies Needed

Who are these campus constituent groups? Why is their cooperation and collaboration indispensable to accrediting bodies' efforts to ensure that information literacy is a critical factor in assessing institutional effectiveness and student learning outcomes? And what about those external to the campus? What will be the nature of their efforts to help accrediting bodies address the concern for information literacy? Since campus constituencies and accrediting review groups bring unique perspectives to this challenge, what might be the specific contribution(s) of each? Perhaps the more critical question should be: How will all of these entities, hopefully working toward the same goal of quality improvement at the undergraduate level, collaborate to ensure that undergraduates leave college with more information skills than when they entered?

Every constituent group on campus needs to be involved in any program to improve institutional quality. Therefore, effective information literacy programs must have the collaboration of librarians and other information associates, faculty, students, administrators, and trustees. Each should have a particular role in the process of developing strategies and programs that ultimately should result in more self-directed, independent, information-literate students and graduates. And just as campus constituencies have definite roles to play, so do many outside of the campus who interact with students, professors, and administrators. These might include other universities and colleges, employers, vendors, and a panoply of other information providers and access points. In fact, the very central role played by technology in facilitating information literacy makes it crucial to include these sources.

Now to the special contributions and involvement of the campus constituencies.

Student Involvement?

Since the raison d'être of any college or university is the education of its students, no program of information literacy—however well intentioned—can succeed without the active participation of students. It is simply axiomatic to note that students must take primary responsibility for their own learning, and more "*how*" than "*what.*" While availing themselves of every opportunity to pursue truth, students must discern early the importance of enhancing what Adam Robinson (1993) terms "cyberlearning" skills. These skills naturally involve critical thinking abilities that focus on intellectual skills of a higher education order than rote memory. In the process of becoming more independent learners, students must also begin viewing faculty as facilitators of learning rather than as purveyors of specific pieces of information. In searching for information for the resolution of issues related to life and work, students must subject the information to probing questions. Evidence to suggest that students are becoming more conscious of the need to become more information literate might include: the use of course bibliographies prepared for them by faculty; the greater use of reference services; enrollment in courses on library research; and greater utilization of on-line search and computer data banks.

Information-literate students must never be satisfied with an instructional program that is centered almost entirely on that which can be learned from textbooks and lecture notes. In the final analysis, students must become self-directed learners who have mastered the research tools in the search for knowledge and truth.

Faculty Involvement?

Naturally, the faculty, including librarians, should utilize every means available, as the American Library Association admonishes, "to teach users how to take full advantage of the resources available to them." I do not have much worry about what most librarians as teachers will do to implement a sod program of information literacy, but I do have concern that many other teaching faculty have little direct involvement in either helping to develop the collections or in ensuring that they themselves and their students make full use of existing learning resources. It is sad to note that some institutions still rely solely on library instruction programs consisting only of printed brochures on the introduction to the library, or brief orientation sessions at the beginning of each term for students enrolled in English classes.

On the other hand, there are those institutions that provide specially prepared course and program bibliographies on faculty request; credit and noncredit courses in bibliographic instruction and information literacy; various forms of computer access to data (e.g., compact disk read-only memory [CD-ROMs]) and on-line searches; group and individualized instruction; telecourses; special reference services; and videotapes.

At those institutions where faculty build into their instructional programs strong requirements for library research, we find the greatest effectiveness in getting students to take full advantage of the collections and in promoting the use of resources as a means of improving learning outcomes. Requirements as reflected in course syllabi and student learning contracts and in the nature and extent of student and faculty use of library materials give us some indication of faculty commitment to increased effectiveness. Obviously, when faculty members rely almost exclusively on textbooks and make limited or no demands on students to complete library research on topics within a course or program, it is understandable when students also rely heavily on their textbooks, poorly written lecture notes, and limited or no understanding of how to exploit the full range of information available in a number of formats and locations.

Administration Involvement?

Academic and student development administrators in particular, through appropriate and timely planning, must ensure that there are provisions for easy access by faculty and students to needed information resources and instruction in locating and using them. Administrators must be constantly alert to the need for adequate library and other information to support current and proposed academic programs. It will be critical for academic administrators to do everything possible to ensure that the institutional mission statement and the required general education core include expectations for information literacy.

As part of any overall program for institutional assessment of outcomes, chief academic officers, working closely with professional librarians and other faculty must ensure that the institution's investment in library/learning resources is utilized effectively. Academic deans must ensure that course outlines reflect a requirement for the use of learning resources other than the textbook and should monitor the quality of research papers completed as a partial requirement for course and degree credit.

Self-Study Steering Committee Involvement?

Besides being able to benefit from the cooperation and collaboration of students and faculty, accreditors will likely find their concern for information literacy best addressed through the medium of self-study steering committees especially since self-study processes stress the evaluation of the institution's mission, goals, and objectives, as well as emphasize institutional assessment goals and the standards of the accrediting body. Moreover, it would be an unusual self-study steering committee that did not focus on information processing skills or that did not include a relevant focus on the quality of the undergraduate experience. But it is incumbent on library and information specialists to ensure that self-study designs and work plans provide for the review of programs designed to produce more self-directed, information-literate students.

Trustee Involvement?

For example, members of governing boards, according to Middle States Association standards, are "responsible for the institution's integrity and quality" and must view the library as one of the central foci in maintaining and improving quality. Thus, it is the responsibility of the trustees to provide adequate financial resources to allow the library to develop fully in support of the institution's mission.

Accreditor Involvement?

What should be the response of the accrediting body? In addition to ensuring that its standards and policies include appropriate attention to role of information literacy in improving undergraduate quality, accrediting commissions should develop and implement orientation materials designed to give team evaluators and chairs useful guidance in evaluating and assessing information literacy vis-à-vis institutional effectiveness and student learning outcomes. The accrediting commissions should also expect team members to examine course outlines; syllabi; student research papers, theses, and dissertations; the institution's information literacy program; the annual budget devoted to the support of learning resources; the quality and extent of the institution's collections and means of access to other information sources; and evidence that institutional resources are used by students and faculty.

As for accredited institutions, accreditors not only should expect self-studies to reflect an analysis of library collections in relation to the institution's mission and program offerings; in addition, they should expect those documents to show a demonstrable relationship between its program of bibliographic instruction, actual utilization of learning resources by faculty and students, and learning outcomes. And there should be an expectation that course outlines and syllabi reflect a strong component of student research and recommended readings. Therefore, it is important for each accredited and candidate institution to develop and utilize the library or learning resource center, or information resources more broadly, as a central focus of its teaching/learning process.

How Can Library and Information Specialists Help?

In the first place, the library profession should take a number of important steps to ensure that the concept of information literacy is fully understood and that measures are put in place to facilitate the implementation of effective information literacy programs. In this regard, the library profession should (1) collaborate with other colleagues in higher education to connect information literacy more closely with the assessment of the undergraduate experience; (2) in consultation with higher education associations (including accrediting bodies) and learned societies, design and implement workshops for target groups of educators, such as chief academic officers, department heads, and faculty; (3) enlist the aid of academic administrators to identify faculty members who can serve as role models in the innovative ways in which they encourage library research and information literacy among their students; (4) collaborate with schools and colleges of education to ensure that teacher training curricula emphasize the role of information literacy in improving students' learning skills; (5) be more assertive in getting accrediting bodies to revise their standards and evaluative criteria to reflect stronger requirements for bibliographic instruction, information literacy, and the essential relationship between information literacy and the assessment of effective teaching and learning processes; and (6) continue efforts already under way to redefine the roles and staffing patterns for academic libraries so that the professional librarian as teacher can devote considerable more time to assisting students and other faculty in improving their information management skills.

I conclude, as I began, with the notion that the effectiveness of the undergraduate curriculum in part is predicated on students' having learned how to learn, the primary thesis of a recently published guide (Robinson 1993) to help students master the learning process. Information literacy is the sine quo non of this process, inasmuch as it signifies the essential skills on how to locate, evaluate, interpret, and use information effectively for the entire range of learning needs.

Whether students are concerned about improving their basic academic skills, about enhancing their general intellectual skills, or about sharpening their technical/professional quotient, information management skills are absolutely essential. And when it comes to assessing whether or not students have achieved their learning objectives, information literacy can become the focal point for the assessment. In each case, there must be critical attention to the degree to which students have developed the ability to formulate analytical questions rather than merely giving descriptive responses to questions. When institutions are able to document in self-study processes and evaluation teams are able to document in their reports that students have improved their information literacy skills significantly, accreditors and institutions alike will probably be able to celebrate real success in improving undergraduate quality and outcomes.

References

Association of College and Research Libraries. 1992. "Information Retrieval and Evaluation Skills for Education Students." *College and Research Libraries News* 53(9): 583–88.

Breivik, Patricia Senn. 1993. "Investing Wisely in Information Technology. Asking the Right Questions." *Educational Record* 74(3): 47–52.

Breivik, Patricia Senn, and Dan L. Jones. 1993. "Information Literacy: Liberal Education for the Information Age." *Liberal Education* 79(1): 24–29.

Middle States Association of Colleges and Schools. 1990. *Designs for Excellence Handbook for Institutional Self-Study*. Philadelphia: Middle States Association of Colleges and Schools.

Montgomery, Paul K. 1992. "Integrating Library, Media, Research, and Information Skills." *Phi Delta Kappan* 73(7): 529–32.

Pennsylvania State Board of Education. 1993. "Rules and Regulations: Title 22—Education (Curriculum)." *Pennsylvania Bulletin Part II* 23(30): 3552–61.

Robinson, Adam. 1993. *What Smart Students Know*. New York: Crown.

Simmons, Howard L. 1992. "Information Literacy and Accreditation: A Middle States Association Perspective." In *Information Literacy: Developing Students as Independent Learners*, edited by D. W. Farmer and T. F. Mech. New Directions in Higher Education Series, no. 78. San Francisco: Jossey-Bass.

State University of New York. 1992. *SUNY 2000 College Expectations*. Report of the SUNY Task Force on College Entry-Level Knowledge and Skills. Albany State University of New York.

It Takes a Community to Educate Students

Ursula Wagener and Michael T. Nettles

Since their inception, Historically Black Colleges and Universities (HBCUs) have targeted academic achievement. Before student retention became "hot"—before the new technologies and slogans of enrollment management, faculty responsibility for teaching, and learning communities—the HBCUs concentrated on creating environments in which many students, even ones who are under-prepared by conventional measures, could succeed academically.

Over the last decade, the fiscal pressures on higher education, combined with new kinds of students—older, part-time, transient, less well prepared academically—have thrust student retention until graduation to the forefront of higher education's national agenda. Given their experiences, and their own need to refocus on retention, we believe HBCUs have a lot to say to colleges and universities across the nation.

Founded with the purpose of educating disadvantaged blacks after the Civil War, HBCUs retain a missionary zeal to foster the intellectual and social development of their students. As institutions whose primary purpose is to teach undergraduates, these colleges and universities do not treat academic support for students as an "add on." They do not regularly appoint special retention committees. Rather, they cultivate an ethos to enable faculty to view classroom learning and curricular activities outside of class as a continuum and student development as the responsibility of administrators *and* faculty.

Constituting only 3 percent of the more than 3,800 U.S. institutions of higher education, HBCUs enroll about 16 percent of the black student in college. HBCUs produce approximately 27 percent of all BAs and of all bachelor's degrees in science and engineering awarded to African Americans annually. Of the African Americans who earn doctorates, approximately 35 percent have their baccalaureate origins in HBCUs.

What accounts for this success? At the private HBCUs, the entire academic community unites to educate a student. Administrative leaders understand the importance of graduating students, not just to enhance the image of the college or to generate additional tuition revenues, but to fulfill the institutional mission. HBCU faculty foster a critical variable in improving academic achievement and graduation rates: strong student/faculty relationships, within and outside the classroom. Many HBCU students take responsibility for their peer playing the roles of tutor, counselor, and peer dean. All three groups, administrators, faculty, and students, play an important role in "the careful cultivation of history"—the generation of a historically centered belief that they are special people in a special place—reasserting the alumni achievements.

The HBCUs accomplish these ends in difficult circumstances. On an absolute scale, their rates of graduation in six years and under—ranging from 30 to 70 percent—are hardly the highest in the country. But their students are among the most disadvantaged in the nation. More than one-third of The College Fund/UNCF students—UNCF is a national organization of 39 private HBCUs—come

Reprinted from *Change,* March–April 1998.

Hampton University

Students	
Total Number of Students:	5,177
Total Number of Undergraduates:	4,477
% Male:	41
% Female:	59
% African American:	87
% Full-time:	89
% Part-time:	11
Average Combined SAT:	1003 (Fall 1997)
Graduation Rate/6 Yrs.:	58-60% (1987 Cohort)
Geographic Distribution/All Students:	
Northeast (Predominantly Regional):	32%
International:	3%
Faculty	
Total Number of Faculty:	278
% African American:	52
% Female:	47
% PhDs:	71
Faculty/Student Ratio:	1:16
Institutional Data	
Endowment:	$133.9 million (July 1997)
Tuition:	$8,948
% Students on Financial Aid:	79
Ave. Size of Financial Aid Package:	65% of Tuition Costs

**Data on students and faculty, with the exception of graduation rates and SAT data, are for fall 1996; institutional data are for fall 1997.*

from families with a total income of less than $25,000, in contrast to approximately 20 percent of families of students attending four-year private no sectarian colleges nationally. African-American freshmen tend to come from less well educated families, often with a single parent, thus with fewer home resources to rely on than the average white student. All of this makes retention tough.

This article focuses on three successful HBCUs—Hampton University, Xavier University, and Spelman College, all part of a five-year project funded by The Pew Charitable Trusts to help improve academic achievement and graduation rates at 10 private black colleges and universities. (Other colleges and universities in the program include Dillard University, Fisk University, Howard University, Morehouse College, Johnson C. Smith University, Rust College, and Tougaloo College.)

We chose these three institutions because of the progress each has made in improving academic achievement and retention and because the institutions' leaders—William R. Harvey at Hampton University, Norman Francis of Xavier University, and Johnnetta Cole, past president of Spelman College—brought stability, financial resources, innovation, and standards of excellence to their institutions. Each school draws upon an institutional ethos of academic achievement that is simultaneously spiritual, cultural, and historical. These characteristics suggest that leadership and a culture of community responsibility for academic achievement are key to graduation rates at all institutions of higher education.

Hampton University

Hampton University's campus on a scenic 204 acres along Virginia's Hampton River manifests the traditions of the American college: physically beautiful, bucolic, it gives a sense of a world that once was and always will be. The Emancipation Oak, 98 feet in diameter and designated as one of the world's 10 great trees by the National Geographic Society, stands as testimony that the Emancipation Proclamation was read to Hampton area residents there in 1863. The campus' buildings

Hampton University

Kathryn Kisabeth, professor of physical education, sees students on an intensive basis during the first two weeks of the second semester and then helps them to become as independent as possible. One strategy she uses to help students prepare for tests is a "memory dump," in which everything one knows is put on a piece of paper, then checked against class notes, with weak parts redone afterward. "Note blending" involves combining notes from the text with notes from class. A student then highlights the overlaps and uses this as a basis for studying for tests.

Freddye Davy, professor of education and director of the honors college, uses a different approach: "I try to work with their heads. A student who is admitted to Hampton University obviously has the basic skills to graduate. I work through an assignment with each student, finding out what was difficult. Then I make the student teach that to someone else. In my group sessions, I ask students to bring in different types of questions and discuss them. They practice making presentations."

tie past and present together: the Memorial Church contains pews that were built in 1886; the William R. and Norma B. Harvey Library was built in 1992. They also point to the enormous diversity of programs, including nursing, mass media, aviation, marine biology, and architecture. The university today combines its historic commitment to technical and professional occupations with the liberal arts.

Hampton's image of itself is inseparable from its past. In the 19th century, an elaborate code of conduct existed, transformed in the 20th century into an emphasis on character development, leadership, and service to society. Out of standards of behavior and values comes academic achievement.

Governance and Accountability

Hampton President William R. Harvey has asserted institutional responsibility for students' intellectual, personal, and moral development for 20 years. When asked about his priorities, he invariably includes "building character and values in our students" high on the list. One symbol of this is Hampton's Code of Conduct, featured prominently on the first page of the university's catalogue. A contractual obligation agreed to by all students, the code is comprehensive:

- To respect himself or herself;
- To respect the dignity, feelings, worth, and values of others;
- To respect the rights and property of others;
- To prohibit discrimination, while striving to learn from differences in people, ideas, and opinions;
- To practice personal, professional, and academic integrity, and to discourage all forms of dishonesty, plagiarism, deceit, and disloyalty to the Code of Conduct;
- To foster a personal professional work ethic;
- To foster an open, fair, and caring environment;
- To be fully responsible for upholding the Hampton University Code.

To connect values and conduct to academic achievement, Hampton has built an extensive network of student support systems, or in Harvey's words, "We have high expectations, but don't just throw our students out there. [Hampton] also puts out a helping hand." This has meant organizing the management system so that it impels administrator involvement in student performance. Hampton's vice president for student affairs, Rodney Smith, and his colleagues are responsible for knowing the status of every student—particularly those who are in trouble by mid-semester. But they understand that the data are only useful if they prompt early intervention. Smith himself gets personally involved in keeping students from dropping out, often playing "bad cop" with students in academic difficulty. To those students who are not showing up for tutoring and counseling sessions with faculty, his discourse goes as follows:

> You're not showing up for your sessions. I take that as an indicator that you don't want to be here at Hampton University. [The student denies that this is the case.] When you leave my office, call your faculty mentor and apologize. I expect you to show up for every session from now on. Is that clear? If I see you again in my office, I'll take that as grounds for recommending your dismissal from the university.

Faculty Beyond the Classroom

When interviewed for faculty positions at Hampton, candidates are asked whether they can adhere to Hampton's Code of Conduct. The hiring process emphasizes the university's concern about shaping student values and the faculty role in that process. Each faculty member is asked to complete a yearly performance contract with objectives relating to teaching, research, and service. Department chairs conduct evaluations of teaching, and students evaluate faculty on their teaching. This emphasis on accountability has raised standards and reinforced the faculty role in teaching and student development.

A highly structured example of faculty engagement in student achievement is the faculty development advisor (FDA) program, begun in 1994 with support from The Pew Charitable Trusts. FDAs (the initial 10 grew to 21 in 1996–97) are carefully selected and trained through workshops on student characteristics and problems; information on courses, majors, academic programs, and administrative regulations; and discussions of learning styles and time management. Faculty meet once a month to share what works and what doesn't.

During the fall semester, the FDAs, sometimes referred to by students as "Fantastically Dedicated Angels," assist with student advisement and registration and serve as volunteer instructors in "University 101: The Individual and Life," a required semester-long freshman orientation course. In the spring, each FDA is actively engaged on a weekly or biweekly basis with five to 15 freshmen on academic probation, trying to unravel the problems that keep the students from achieving academically, monitoring and helping students to organize their study habits, leading small discussion groups, and sharing food and friendship through social activities.

The indicators suggest that the FDA program has been successful. The percentage of freshmen on academic probation has decreased, from 20 percent of the freshmen in 1994–95 to 15 percent in 1996–97. Faculty have shown increased willingness to participate, although certain departments like education and physical education are much more active than others.

The growth in faculty numbers combined with the decline in the number of freshmen on academic probation has cut the average number of students per FDA from 15 to 5. The $200 per semester each FDA receives is hardly the motivation. Rather, as Kathryn Kisabeth notes, "The FDA program allows me to help others achieve. It is my way of contributing to other people."

It is easy on many college campuses around the country to find a special program that engages faculty commitment to student academic success. What is important about the FDA program at Hampton, however, is that it is part of a larger culture that is supportive of student development. The faculty are part of a community that takes responsibility for monitoring and intervening on behalf of a student's educational achievement. Going beyond the classroom, many teachers personally engage students, instill in them pride in their future alma mater, and teach them the behaviors and skills required for success.

The Responsibility of Peers

Because Hampton's mission to prepare leaders is built upon an ethos of community responsibility, students play a large role in their peers' development. One example is the new counseling center, a second activity initially supported by The Pew Charitable Trusts. Located in the middle of campus for easy access, the center combines psychological, social, personal, and academic counseling.

Fifty peer counselors help to carry out the work of the center. As Vice President Rodney Smith puts it, "Dr. Linda Malone-Colon [the center director] clones herself." Malone-Colon is a superb professional with missionary zeal, a highly developed and acute intuitive sense about students, and a knack for organization and working with others. She is especially committed to her group of voluntary peer tutors. Applicants are interviewed and selected on the basis of dependability, enthusiasm, empathy, communication skills, and faculty recommendations.

All new peer counselors participate in an intensive three-day training workshop on how to conduct workshops and counsel peers. Malone-Colon has cloned herself so well that peer counselors have taken ownership of interviewing and selecting applicants. As one peer counselor put it, "Working at the center has sharpened both my organizational and interpersonal skills. Dr. Malone-Colon is a terrific role model."

Like other American colleges and universities, Hampton knows that graduation rates are part of its image. They help define perceptions of quality, shape student applications and enrollments, and influence fiscal resources. But at Hampton, the commitment to helping students succeed is not imposed from the outside. It draws upon an ethos of commitment to students' moral and personal development.

History and tradition permeate the present. President William Harvey provides leadership for student development; his deputies take responsibility for making it happen; faculty shape student values and behaviors inside and outside the classroom; and students care about each other. While not all faculty and students are as committed as our portraits illustrate, the goals of academic achievement and retention are central to institutional mission at Hampton.

Xavier University of Louisiana

If we had to choose one word to characterize Xavier University of New Orleans, it would be "struggle." The only black Catholic college in the Unites States, Xavier was founded in 1915 by

Katharine Drexel of the Sisters of the Blessed Sacrament, an order dedicated to serving the educational needs of Native and African Americans. Since 1966, Xavier has been governed by a combined lay/religious board of trustees, but the Catholic legacy remains the basis of the prevailing belief that all students can learn. As one Sister put it: "The values, standards, and high expectations we bring to our work help to establish an environment at Xavier where teaching and learning can flourish."

Xavier today remains very much a Catholic university, although fewer than 50 percent of the students are Catholic and the faculty are overwhelmingly lay. The Sisters of the Blessed Sacrament maintain a strong influence, retaining one-third of the board of trustees' seats. Mass is celebrated daily. Students are required to take two courses in theology and two in philosophy. The environment stresses spiritual and moral values—honesty, integrity, discipline, and service.

Paralleling and intersecting with its Catholic heritage is Xavier's black culture, one that also holds high expectations for students and understands the importance of education and discipline to individual betterment. At Xavier, monitoring students' behavior—class attendance, meetings with faculty advisors, tutoring sessions—plays an important role.

Xavier's physical environment reflects its struggle, and its success. Crammed between Interstate 10 and the Palmetto Canal, the campus combines massive buildings of Gothic design with ultramodern, imposing high-rises. Its tree-shaded walks almost belie the surrounding urban environment and poverty-stricken neighborhood. The university's more than 3,500 students are predominantly African American, female, and full-time with standardized test scores that show increases in recent years. Average combined SAT scores are over 1000. Xavier graduates 45 percent of its student body, considerably higher than the national average of 34 percent for African Americans.

Nonetheless, Xavier's students struggle, many against intractable problems. Academic preparation is often poor, given inferior public schooling. Many students are first-generation college students, making adjustment to college difficult. Three-quarters of the student body is on financial aid; many students work full-time while attending school full-time, or stop out periodically. Financial pressures are always severe, and the university's financial aid budget is limited.

Continuities of Leadership

President Norman Francis is both African American and Catholic. He has been at Xavier almost continuously since 1948 when he enrolled as an undergraduate. In 1968, Francis became Xavier's first African-American lay president. Over the subsequent 30 years, the university increased its endowment tenfold, expanded its enrollment by almost 3,000, established excellence in science, and extended its campus to include an $8 million science complex and a $10 million engineering building.

For his accomplishments, Francis became nationally recognized, serving as president of the American Association for Higher Education, president of the United Negro College Fund, and chairman of the Educational Testing Service and

Xavier University of Louisiana

Students	
Total Number of Students:	3,526
Total Number of Undergraduates:	2,624
% Male:	30.3
% Female:	69.7
% African American:	96
% Full-time:	97.9
% Part-time:	2.1
Average Combined SAT:	1019
Graduation Rate/6 Yrs.:	45% (1987 Cohort)
Geographic Distribution/ All Students:	
Louisiana:	57%
Southern Region:	77%
Faculty	
Total Number of Faculty:	215
% African American:	35.8
% Female:	33.5
% PhDs:	Approx. 70
Faculty/Student Ratio:	1:14.3
Institutional Data	
Endowment:	$ 23.9 million
Tuition:	$8,100
% Students on Financial Aid:	85
Ave. Size of Financial Aid Package:	$5,947 (Need-based)

**Data on students and faculty, with the exception of graduation rates, are for fall 1996; institutional data are for fall 1997.*

the College Board. For all his visibility, however, Francis' heart has remained at home; he exudes a determination to provide others with the educational opportunities he was fortunate enough to attain.

In 1982, Francis hired Antoine Garibaldi as chairman and professor of education. He named Garibaldi dean of the college of education in 1989 and vice president of academic affairs in 1991, before Garibaldi left to become Howard University's provost and chief academic officer in 1996. A nationally recognized scholar on issues of assessment and academic achievement and retention, Garibaldi concentrated on strengthening student academic support services. He introduced a structured orientation program in which upperclass-men serve as peer deans, as well as a year-long, non-credit freshman orientation course; a writing center and reading laboratory; tutoring services; a program in which students who have not selected a major are helped to choose one; and a procedure wherein the academic standing committees of the university regularly review students who are experiencing academic difficulty.

The duo of Francis and Garibaldi defined leadership and management in terms of their impact on student learning, drawing upon and renewing Xavier's ethos of commitment to and concern for individual betterment.

The Faculty

Xavier's academic support structures are dependent upon faculty involvement. The science faculty, for example, have provided a model of superior teaching, advising, and monitoring. Building on Xavier's historical strength in the natural sciences—beginning with the establishment of a Pharmacy College in 1927 (the only pharmacy school in southern Louisiana today)—faculty fashioned a science program that has achieved national recognition.

It took a 20-year commitment, reaching down to junior and senior high schools, and the leadership of a unique individual to cooperatively build summer science programs for students. Chemistry Professor J.W. Carmichael, the recent recipient of the Harold McGraw Education Leadership Award, led the faculty in totally revamping the way in which science students are educated. The result is a science program that customizes instruction, scrapping traditional textbooks in favor of teacher-made workbooks that include detailed learning goals, sample problems, and daily homework assignments.

Faculty encourage cooperative studying by moving all sections of mathematics and science courses through a syllabus at approximately the same pace and by organizing student study groups. In class, faculty question, probe, and challenge, rather than lecture. Each faculty member counsels 35 students and monitors them closely, which requires a weekly meeting to report grades. The goal is to catch academic difficulties early and to intervene quickly.

The successes represent students who often have combined SAT scores of below 1000, who come from economically disadvantaged families, and who attended inferior public schools. Many would likely have dropped out, or certainly would not have become science majors, if not for the faculty's willingness to intervene. The intensity of the intervention is even more surprising when one remembers that Xavier faculty teach a regular load of four courses or 12 credit hours per semester.

Faculty intervention has spread to mathematics. As one focus of The Pew Charitable Trusts' funded initiative, directed by extremely competent Jarlene Hall DeCay, Xavier targeted and carefully planned a Mathematics Laboratory. Faculty, peer tutors, and 12 computers with math software are available to students in need of assistance. All mathematics faculty volunteer one to two hours a week in the Math Lab. As Vaidyanath Vinod, assistant professor of mathematics, told us, the lab "is becoming popular. It's . . . assumed as one of the faculty's natural activities, equal with teaching. [I] absolutely feel responsible for student success."

The Students

The ethos of helping others has spread to students. About one-third of all undergraduates are involved in some kind of community service; about one-tenth serve their peers as tutors and deans. Keandra Johnson, a mathematics tutor, comments on how students model themselves after faculty: "[This willingness to help others] comes from the teachers and their willingness to help you." As Lamont Jones, an Xavier senior and premed student, put it: "If you have knowledge, you should share it. That's my responsibility, to bring others up to my level."

Both the Math Lab and the Academic Support Program, which intervenes to provide special support for students on academic probation and those at risk mid-semester, utilize student tutors. A number of students come to the Math Lab ostensibly to do their homework; once they enter, tutors initiate conversations, asking whether a person wants help, thus breaking the ice. As one tutor explains: "You have to get students out of the mind-set that getting help means you are stupid. You have to figure out what they know and build on that."

So what are the results? Increasing proportions of mathematics students are passing the sophomore mathematics competency exam (the Collegiate Assessment of Academic Proficiency), from 65 percent in the fall of 1994 to 76 percent in the spring of 1997. Xavier's Academic Support Program has helped to increase GPAs. Those students who spent more than 20 hours in the Academic Support Program during the spring 1996 semester increased their GPAs by .71, on average, over the previous semester. Freshman to sophomore retention rates have improved slightly. In 1995, 76 percent of the entering freshman class returned for a sophomore year, in 1996, 78.2 percent returned; in 1997, 76.2 percent returned. Finally, Xavier's six-year graduation rate of 45 percent, as already noted, is significantly above the national average of 34 percent for African Americans.

Retention at Xavier is everyone's business. That is not to suggest that all serve or that everyone is served. The science faculty are a unique group, and they began their work some 20 years ago before considerations of scholarship were taken into account in promotion and tenure reviews. With increasing numbers of lay people as faculty, it becomes more difficult today to maintain the historic ethos of responsibility. Because commuter students spend less time on campus, this group, which is almost two-thirds of the student population, tends to be less well served than resident students. Nonetheless, President Francis and members of the Xavier community work hard to continuously renew a communitywide culture of service. For Xavier, this struggle is essential to its identity.

Xavier's Success in the Sciences

- Xavier trained 25 percent of the 6,000 African-American pharmacists in the United States today.
- Xavier's premed graduates have an 80 percent acceptance rate at medical and dental schools, better than twice the national average.
- In 1992, 1994, and 1996, Xavier placed 34, 54, and 77 African Americans in medical school, respectively—more than any other college in the United States.

Spelman College

Spelman is an outstanding Historically Black College for women run predominantly by women. From Spelman's origins, two themes have dominated: academic excellence and women's educational and professional advancement.

The history of Spelman's remarkable women began in 1881 when Sophia Packard and Harriet Giles, sent by the American Baptist Home Mission Society of New England, opened a school in the basement of Atlanta's Friendship Baptist church with $100 and 11 pupils. Packard and Giles met John D. Rockefeller at a church meeting in Cleveland, Ohio, a year later. In 1884, the Rockefeller family completed the purchase of nine acres and five frame barracks (used by Federal troops after the Civil War), and the name of the school was changed to Spelman Seminary, in honor of Mrs. Rockefeller's mother.

Strong women presidents were to lead Spelman for the next 65 years, including Packard and Giles as the first two presidents. In 1929, Spelman affiliated with Atlanta University and Morehouse College in the Atlanta University Center, allowing Spelman students access to the resources of a major university center. The center later was enlarged to include Clark College, Morris Brown College, the Interdenominational Theological Center, and the Morehouse Medical School.

Albert E. Manley (1953–76), the first male and first black to become president, broke the tradition of women leaders but continued the tradition of excellence, encouraging Spelman women to enter medicine, law, international affairs, engineering, business, and industry. His successor, Donald Stewart (1976–86), currently president of the College Board, initiated Spelman's first full-fledged chemistry department, beginning the college's competitiveness in the sciences. In 1987, leadership reverted to a woman, with Johnnetta Cole (1987–97) assuming a presidency that would propel Spelman into the national media. Most recently, Audrey Forbes Manley, a 1955 graduate of Spelman, wife of former president Manley, and former Acting U.S. Surgeon General, has taken the helm.

With an enrollment of over 1,900, Spelman today receives more than 10 times the number of applications needed to fill each year's entering class. The average combined SAT score is 1073. Spelman offers majors in 22 fields, with special prelaw and premedical sequences available. Forty percent of the current students major in sciences, significantly higher than the percentage of women science majors nationally. Spelman awards the second-highest number of baccalaureate degrees granted to African Americans in mathematics. The college is ranked second among the top 26 institutions that send African Americans on to science and engineering doctorate programs (Howard University is first). Seventy-two percent of Spelman women graduate in six years, almost double the national average of 37 percent for African-American women.

Spelman College

Students	
Total Number of Students:	1,899
Total No. of Undergraduate Students:	1,899
% Male:	0
% Female:	100
% African American:	96
% Full-time:	98
% Part-time:	2
Average Combined SAT:	1073
Graduation Rate/6 Yrs.:	72% (1987 Cohort)
Geographic Distribution/ All Students:	
Out of State:	78%; 45 States & 29 Foreign Countries
Faculty	
Total Number of Faculty:	138
% African American:	64.5
% Female:	62.3
% PhDs:	83
Faculty/Student Ratio:	1:11
Institutional Data	
Endowment:	$156.4 million (July 1, 1997)
Tuition:	$8,560
Financial Aid Budget, 1996–97:	Spelman Allocation = $321,712
% Students on Financial Aid:	85

**Data on students and faculty, with the exception of graduation rates, are for fall 1996; institutional data, except where specified differently, are for fall 1997.*

A Remarkable Leader

During Johnnetta Cole's presidency (1987–97), Spelman became a media sensation for its academic excellence, outstanding women students, and enormous success in fund-raising. Cole's success in fund-raising was remarkable, increasing Spelman's endowment from $40 million (1987) to more than $143 million (1997) and attracting donors like Bill and Camille Cosby and Oprah Winfrey. A recently completed campaign raised $113.8 million, the largest sum ever raised by an HBCU. These and other accomplishments—such as her chairing the board of directors of the United Way Metropolitan Atlanta as well as the board of the Department of Education's Fund for the Improvement of Post Secondary Education—made Cole a national figure in higher education.

In the midst of these successes, Cole never lost sight of Spelman's mission. As she told a reporter: "It's about education, it's not about money. It's about raising the intellectual inquiry. How could I be the head of Spelman and not remain an intellectual and a teacher?" Out of this commitment grew her determination to redefine faculty roles at Spelman, fashioning them to fit an HBCU, but also an increasingly competitive national higher education market. Salaries were made more competitive. The faculty teaching load was reduced from four to three courses per semester, allowing faculty more time to engage in scholarship, while at the same time continuing a tradition of commitment to students.

The Faculty

Like all selective women's liberal arts colleges, Spelman benefits from strong faculty role models, small classes, and rich faculty/student interaction. With a student/teacher ratio of 11 to

1 and over 84 percent of the faculty holding doctorates or other terminal degrees, the Spelman faculty was ranked 21st among the nation's liberal arts colleges in *U.S. News & World Report*'s 1996 listing.

Teaching and advising constitute central roles for Spelman faculty, even as research publications have come to play a larger role in promotions. Faculty teach three courses per semester and advise 40 to 60 students, depending on departmental needs. Faculty development programs have tried to connect research and teaching. A research associates program, for example, brings faculty and students together on research projects.

Sheila McClure, director of Spelman's research infrastructure program and associate professor of biology, suggests another aspect of this integration. McClure teaches an introductory biology course, where she delivers "scholarly attitude lectures" when she senses students feel overwhelmed by course material or are discontented with grades. The lectures cover time management and the necessity of making choices. McClure also uses the "please see me" strategy, expecting to meet with each student once during the course of the semester to talk about academic performance and adjustment to college.

Multiple roles as researcher, teacher, and advisor are time-consuming. Given Spelman's aspirations to national recognition, maintaining them as equally integral to the institution's culture is not easy. But it would be difficult to imagine Spelman without its taking on the challenge.

The Administrators and the Students

Spelman's philosophy mandates early intervention before problems snowball. Data systems allow administrators to track students' academic progress and to intervene at the middle or end of semester for those students who are in trouble. Student testimony indicates that Spelman's academic support network is vast: a Big Sister program connects upperclass women to incoming students; a freshman orientation course helps incoming students to adjust to campus; the Learning Resources Center, the focal point of The Pew Charitable Trusts' initiative, offers academic advisement, peer tutoring, and instruction in study techniques; the counseling center helps reorient students who have lost sight of why they are in college; the Writing Center helps students improve their writing skills; faculty notify the academic dean when students are in trouble and need follow-up from that office. As student Sheronda Sheppard put it, "I like the system of 'checks and balances' [that makes] sure students don't slip through the cracks."

As is the case at many other selective liberal arts colleges, key administrators at Spelman are often faculty; Christine Farris, an associate professor of education, for example, staffs the Learning Resources Center. Interviews with individual students confirm that faculty, administrators, and other students constitute an academic safety net that the college provides. For one, students confirm that faculty hold high expectations for them—such as a certain level of discipline and maturity—and that this helps students to achieve higher levels academically. They rate faculty/student relationships very positively, noting at the same time that student initiative is important. Arnita Welch, a Spelman senior, rates faculty a "95 out of 100" for their interaction with students.

Students also help each other. The Peer Tutoring Program recruits and trains qualified students skilled in a variety of academic disciplines. Many departments, like the sciences, sponsor their own tutors. Tutoring is widespread at Spelman because it is seen as a means of improvement and not as remediation. During new student orientation, students are indoctrinated with the idea that tutoring is not for dumb students but for those who want to improve academically.

It Takes a Community

We have told an enormously positive story of academic achievement and retention at Hampton, Xavier, and Spelman. The successes do not come easily. Many students have overwhelming financial needs, work full-time, and are poorly prepared academically. The schools are constrained in what they can afford. As long as they recruit and enroll disadvantaged students, they will never achieve the 90-percent-plus graduation rates of the very selective private institutions. And yet Hampton, Xavier, and Spelman have clearly been doing something special to graduate students.

Retention is an integral part of mission. Hampton, Xavier, and Spelman maintain and renew the mission of their post-Civil War founders.

Hampton remains committed to students' personal and moral development. Xavier's Catholic heritage still dictates the importance of service to others. The Spelman tradition empowers women students to achieve educationally and professionally. The use of institutional resources to aid student intellectual and social development comes naturally. Retention is not a special initiative on the periphery; it flourishes at the core of each institution. Teaching and helping students to learn constitute central tasks, and institutional incentives and rewards reinforce these behaviors.

Intervention is based on early identification. Through a variety of mechanisms, Hampton, Xavier, and Spelman identify students in trouble before it's too late. Early warning systems identify students in academic difficulty at mid-term or before and get them channeled to counseling and tutoring resources. Cynthia Spence, Spelman's associate academic dean, articulates the organizational culture: "My institution is firmly convinced that retention must be proactive. When a student receives the first below-average grade in a course. . . , she must be targeted. When intervention is early, it is very effective."

The role of the president is crucial. Presidents power the infrastructure in a way that allows innovation to flower and members of the community to act with generosity toward each other. As Hampton's president, William Harvey acts on the belief that building character, values, and manners is central to education. As an Xavier graduate and a first-generation college student, Norman Francis understands the power of high expectations, of monitoring academic work, and of student responsibility for peers. Johnnetta Cole embodied the essence of Spelman College, its focus on excellence and women's leadership. Presidential leadership shapes community wide empowerment around learning.

These snapshots of three HBCUs provide a telling message. These are institutions with cultures where faculty, administrators, and students share a commitment to academic achievement no matter how well or poorly prepared their students are. They have presidents who make student development central to their mandates and shape their organizational structures toward that end. They have faculty who engage student learning inside and outside the classroom. And they encourage students to care about each other's academic successes. The lesson of our work at Hampton, Xavier, and Spelman is that retention is everyone's business.

Assessment to Improve College Instruction

K. Patricia Cross

University of California, Berkeley

Once upon a time when both Warren and I were young, I was asked to review Warren's book on *Success in College* (Willingham, 1985), along with three other books speaking to the general theme of "Making College Students Successful" (Cross, 1985). I commented at the time that Warren's book stood out as the most scholarly of the four. By characterizing his work as "scholarly," I meant that he proceeded in an orderly and analytic way to build new knowledge on the foundations of what was already known about the success of students in college. Many researchers today do a pretty good job of writing about their own little corner of the research domain, but then they leave their pieces of new information scattered about the landscape, hoping perhaps that someday someone may be able to stack them to build a significant piece of knowledge. Warren is typically generous and scholarly as he contributes his work to the building of knowledge.

Using Warren's characteristic approach to scholarship as my model, I want to begin this chapter by recognizing some of the past work that has gone into research on college teaching. Effective teaching is one of the most important handles we have on helping students to become successful learners. And it becomes even more important as increasing numbers of students enter college without adequate habits or skills for learning.

Some of the work on college teaching attempts to describe the characteristics of good college teachers. The descriptions range from global essays, to extensive lists of behavioral characteristics, to a reduction to the parsimonious, basic dimensions of good teaching. The global images are perhaps best captured by essayists. Joseph Epstein's (1981) book, *Masters: Portraits of Great Teachers,* for example, is a collection of essays written by former students of some exceptional teachers. While I am struck by the rich variety in both authors and teachers, Epstein points to some commonalties among these memorable teachers. "What all the great teachers have in common is love of their subject, an obvious satisfaction in arousing this love in their students, and an ability to convince them that what they are being taught is deadly serious." (p. xii).

Joseph Lowman (1984), after reviewing the research on great teachers, comes to a similar conclusion. He contends that excellence in teaching can be described by two major dimensions of expertise—intellectual skills and interpersonal skills. Excellent teachers, he says, are outstanding on one of these dimensions and at least competent on the other. That's something to think about. Could one become a great teacher by possessing *either* a great love of subject matter or a great love of students, heeding Lowman's caution, of course, that one could not be a complete klutz in the other domain? That seems to capture what teaching is all about; it is interacting with students to engage them in the intellectual work of learning. Memorable learning experiences for most of us have probably come either

Reprinted from *Assessment in Higher Education: Issues of Access, Quality, Student Development and Public Policy*, edited by Samuel J. Messick, (1999), by permission of Lawrence Erlbaum Associates, Inc.

from the intellectual excitement of an idea or from the emotional rapport with a teacher who cared a lot and motivated us to do our very best—or in the best of all possible worlds, from teachers who excelled in both intellectual excitement and interpersonal rapport.

But these broad, somewhat idealized, portraits of exceptional and inspirational teachers are not always helpful to more average teachers trying to improve their teaching. For them there is the work of researchers who develop comprehensive lists of the behavioral characteristics of good teachers—in the hope, perhaps, that if we know more concretely what good teachers do, we can emulate those behaviors. Data on the characteristics of good teachers are collected in several ways, usually by asking people to describe an "ideal" or "best" teacher, or by the use of student rating scales to differentiate "good" from "poor" teachers.

An impressive synthesis of this work was done by Kenneth Feldman (1988), who located 31 studies in which students and faculty from the same institutions had been asked to rate the various components of effective teaching. In a meta-analysis across all 31 studies, he was able to rank the characteristics of good teachers with pretty good agreement among the raters. The top ten characteristics are these: The teacher: 1) communicates at a level appropriate to the level of the group, 2) is well prepared for class, 3) is knowledgeable about the subject matter, 4) stimulates interest, 5) is enthusiastic, 6) explains things clearly, 7) is available and helpful, 8) respects students, 9) is concerned about students' learning, and 10) is fair. The only characteristic that faculty put in the top ten that students did not was the ability of the teacher to challenge students intellectually, which was rated 6th by faculty and 17th by students. There is nothing very surprising about this list of virtues. Any teacher who has all of those characteristics—or even most of them—is quite likely to be a good, maybe even excellent, teacher.

Other investigators have tried to synthesize the voluminous research on teacher characteristics by reducing it to the most basic dimensions. Factor analyses of the items typically found in rating scales show that four generic characteristics can pretty well cover the characteristics of good teachers across the disciplines. Those four traits, under which all other traits can be clustered are: 1) Skill, which represents all those characteristics having to do with the ability to communicate in an interesting way, 2) Rapport, which involves empathy, interaction with and concern for students, 3) Structure, which concerns class organization and presentation of course materials, and 4) Load, which refers to workload and instructor demands (Kulik & McKeachie, 1975).

By this time, a great deal of research has been done on the characteristics of good college teachers, in part because of growing pressures to evaluate teaching. Most of the characteristics that distinguish "good" teachers from "poor" have found their way into student rating scales, and researchers have continued to study the validity of student rating scales. At latest count, there were more than 1,300 studies of the validity of student evaluations of teachers (Cashin, 1990). And the conclusions from that research are consistent enough, and the pressures from society strong enough, that the great majority of colleges in the United States now use some form of student evaluations of instruction. The question now is, how useful are the ratings in improving instruction?

The research to date suggests that teachers, especially poor teachers whose self-perception of their teaching is better than their ratings, do change as a result of feedback (Centra, 1973; Murray, 1985) Much remains to be done, however, in improving feedback procedures. One observer of the administrative uses of student ratings writes:

> Evaluation results (if faculty get them back) are returned via some . . . impersonal, albeit efficient method. Generally, results come back to faculty via the mail. . . . They come with varying amounts of statistical cybernetics to decipher and varying degrees of helpful instructions. . . . One we know lists all sixty faculty members by the last four digits of their social security numbers and then rank orders them from top to bottom by their overall rating of effectiveness. To be last on such a list is devastating. Being tenth from the bottom is hardly encouraging. And to what end? . . . If the data do not help them identify specific areas in need of alteration, and if no opportunities to discuss the results are provided, faculty may be motivated to become defensive, not better teachers. (Gleason-Weimer, 1987, p. 9).

There is some evidence to suggest that feedback deserves more attention than we in higher education have been giving it. Peter Cohen (1980) located 22 research studies comparing student ratings of instruction under conditions of feedback to teachers and no feedback. In a meta-analysis, synthesizing the results of these studies, he found that the feedback group received higher end-of-term global ratings in 20 of the 22 comparisons. If the feedback was augmented by consultation with a consultant on teaching improvement, however, the average instructor raised his or her ratings from the 50th to the 74th percentile by the end of the semester. Thus relatively small changes made by individual instructors add up to very substantial improvement, we should think, for the institution. It would be hard to think of a grand policy decision that would bring about that amount of change in so brief a period of time.

Granted, the improvement was in students' perceptions of instruction, but students "do a pretty good job of distinguishing teachers on the basis of how much they have learned" according to one researcher who found a correlation of .43 in a meta-analysis of 41 studies looking at the relationship between student ratings and student achievement (Cohen, 1981, p. 305). While not everyone is so positive about the validity of student ratings (Dowell & Neal, 1982), most of those advising caution in their use do so, not on grounds that teachers cannot get useful feedback from students, but that administrators should be cautious about depending on student evaluation in promotion and tenure decisions. As the pressures for teaching effectiveness increase, folks are inventing a number of interesting and useful ways to evaluate and reward good teaching (See, for example, Edgerton, 1994).

Despite this generally favorable report on the use of student ratings to improve instruction, much remains to be done in involving college and university faculty in the improvement of instruction. My colleague Tom Angelo and I have been working for the past decade on methods that will engage college teachers in self-assessment of the effectiveness of teaching and learning in their own classrooms. We call this Classroom Assessment. The advantages of the active involvement of teachers in assessing their own effectiveness are several:

First, the focus of Classroom Assessment is on student learning rather than on faculty performance. Rather than students judging the performance of their teachers—which has a ring of audacity about it to many college faculty—teacher and students together are assessing what students are learning in that classroom. Classroom Assessment serves a pedagogical as well as an assessment function. Through Classroom Assessment, students are monitoring their own learning as well as providing information to the instructor about the impact of the teaching on their learning.

A second advantage of Classroom Assessment lies in the shift of emphasis from studying the characteristics of teach***ers*** to looking at the process of teach***ing***. This enables us to consider context. Teaching is highly context-specific. What works in some classrooms won't work in others. Thus, studying the dynamic process of teacher-student interaction in a particular context will tell us more than studying the static, and sometimes unalterable, characteristics of teachers (Bloom, 1980).

Finally, college teachers need better feedback on their teaching, and Classroom Assessment can provide immediate information while the lesson is still fresh in the minds of both teacher and students and while there is still time to take corrective action.

As a group, today's college teachers are not very well prepared for their profession of teaching. Fresh from graduate school and armed with voluminous and intricate knowledge of their specialty, they stand before a freshman class with little understanding of how students learn. The ultimate purpose of research on teaching is to help teachers understand how teaching causes learning. Nevertheless, we speak of teaching *and* learning as though they were on parallel tracks. But it is the intersection of teaching and learning that should interest us. We should be talking about teaching *for* learning or what teachers can do to *cause* learning. That kind of language, however, makes a lot of college teachers very nervous.

"Causing" learning is not a comfortable concept for many of us in higher education. Throughout much of the history of higher education, we have devoted a lot of effort and money to discover how to *select* students who will be successful in the learning environments that we offer. Now, the question for the great majority of colleges is not how to select students who will be successful, but rather how to make successful those who come. And it is an agonizing and urgent question for many teachers, especially those in open-admissions colleges. A major purpose of Classroom Assessment is to help teachers make the connection between their teaching and student learning.

With those needs in mind, Tom Angelo and I set out to develop some practical Classroom Assessment Techniques (CATS) that could be used by college faculty members without training in assessment or the research methods of the social sciences. Our purpose was not to use assessment to provide information for use by others in evaluating performance, but rather to provide information to teachers and students about the effectiveness of teaching and learning in a given classroom. We hypothesized that if the purpose of assessment is to improve the quality of undergraduate learning, then the following premises should prevail:

1. The assessment must involve directly those who are actually engaged in teaching and learning, namely teachers and students.
2. If assessment is to make a difference, it must address the questions that are of interest to teachers. Specifically, teachers must formulate their own assessment questions and designs to provide the type of information that will inform their teaching.
3. Feedback from assessment to the people who can do something about it—namely teachers and students—must be timely and accurate.

Collecting what we could find from the literature and from our experience in talking with teachers, we compiled a book of 50 CATS that range in difficulty from extremely simple to complex. The 50 CATs are grouped into three large clusters—one on assessing "Course-Related Knowledge and Skills," one on assessing "Learner Attitudes, Values and Self-Awareness," and one on assessing "Learner Reactions to Instruction" (Angelo & Cross, 1993).

Fortunately, there exists a succinct synthesis of the research on effective student learning over the past several decades. Shortly after *A Nation at Risk* (National Commission on Excellence in Education, 1983) appeared in the mid-80s, calling for major educational reform, a group of distinguished researchers in higher education responded by writing a reform report for higher education entitled, *Involvement in Learning* (Study Group on the Conditions of Excellence in American Higher Education, 1984). Building heavily on the work of Alexander Astin, they concluded that there are three "critical conditions for excellence" in undergraduate education. They identified those conditions as (1) holding high expectations for student performance, (2) encouraging active student involvement in learning, and (3) providing useful assessment and feedback.

Since the primary purpose of Classroom Assessment is to provide useful feedback to both teacher and students, let us start with those "critical conditions for excellence." It is fairly obvious that learners need assessment and feedback. Good teachers spend a lot of time grading papers, making comments and corrections to let students know how they are doing and how they can do better. But teachers themselves get very little assessment and feedback on their teaching. Student evaluations at the end of the semester can be helpful, but they give very little information about the contextual nature of any particular lesson. By the time the evaluations are due, teachers as well as students have forgotten the particulars of any lesson. Both teacher and students need to be able to monitor the effectiveness of their teaching or learning immediately, while it is in process.

For those of you who are not familiar with Classroom Assessment, let me give a concrete example of Classroom Assessment's most famous CAT—the Minute Paper, invented by a physics professor at Berkeley. The Minute Paper is a very simple device, that provides immediate feedback to the instructor on what students are learning and, equally important, it incorporates pedagogical principles that are important to students' learning. It works like this: Shortly before the end of a class period, the instructor asks students to write brief answers to two questions: (1) What is the most important thing that you learned in class today? and (2) What is the main, unanswered question you leave class with today?

In his first report on the Harvard Assessment Seminars, Light (1990) states that early on in the Seminars, he asked faculty members what single change would most improve their current teaching.

> Two ideas swamped all others. One is the importance of enhancing students' awareness of "the big picture," the "big point of it all," and not just the details of a particular topic. The second is the importance of helpful and regular feedback *from students* so a professor can make mid course corrections. (p. 35)

The Minute Paper seems to address both of these desires. It asks students to reflect on the "big picture"—the most important idea—of a specific class session, and it provides feedback to the instructor on how students are experiencing the class.

Pedagogically, we know that little is learned without the students' active involvement in making ideas and information their own. Some students just never stop to reflect, to put it all together, and draw some synthesis about what they have learned from a given class session. Class ends; they close their notebooks, assuming that whatever they have written will be useful for the exam when they get around to thinking about it, and are off to the next class. Other students just can't seem to distinguish between central and peripheral ideas. Their Minute Papers consist of a trivial sentence or two about whatever was said just prior to the request for the Minute Paper.

The Minute Paper asks all students in the class to reflect on what they have learned, to synthesize and articulate it in a few brief sentences, to commit that learning to writing, and to think actively about what they did not understand. Thus, even if the instructor failed to learn something important about students' responses to the teaching of that class session, the Minute Paper would still be worthwhile as a pedagogical technique.

But teachers do learn a great deal from the Minute Papers. Light (1990) comments in his report that "This extraordinarily simple idea [of Minute Papers] is catching on throughout Harvard. Some experienced professors comment that it is the best example of high payoff for a tiny investment they have ever seen" (p. 36).

I use the Minute Paper in my own graduate classes, and I never cease to be amazed at how revealing answers to these simple questions are. In the worst of all possible cases, I find that I'm not quite sure what the major message is myself, and students have discovered that. More often, I find an interpretation that surprises me or some confusion about an issue that can be rather easily cleared up in the next class period.

The second critically important condition for excellence in undergraduate education is active involvement in learning. We hear a lot today about the necessity for active involvement on the part of learners. But active involvement is not a new idea. Charles Gragg, the inspired teacher at the Harvard Business School 50 years ago, put it eloquently when he wrote these words:

> No one can learn in any basic sense from another except by subjecting what that other has to offer to a process of creative thinking; that is unless the learner is actively and imaginatively receptive, he will emerge from the experience with nothing more than a catalog of facts and other people's notions." (Gragg, 1940)

Classroom Assessment involves both teachers and students in learning. One of the reasons for the popularity of Classroom Assessment with college teachers, I think, is that it is a creative activity, directed and applied by teachers to satisfy their own intellectual curiosity about their work. Classroom Assessment Techniques, as they have grown and evolved over the years, offer an opportunity for various levels of teacher involvement.

This is illustrated by the experience of a writing teacher who modified the Minute Paper to get some idea of what students were learning from the small-group work sessions that she used to engage students in critiquing one another's papers. She asked students to answer these two questions when they had finished their small-group work session: 1) What specific suggestions did members of your group offer to you that are likely to help you improve your draft essay? and 2) What suggestions did you offer to others that are likely to help them improve their draft essays?

The good news is that she found that most students mentioned things they had learned from others that they thought would improve their papers. The bad news is that only 3 out of 24 students could think of something they had offered that might have been helpful to the other students in their group!

At this point, the teacher had several different options about the level of her involvement in teaching students how to make the small-group sessions more productive. She might let the CAT do the pedagogical work of reminding students that they are expected to contribute as well as to benefit from the work of the group sessions. For students, just having to respond to the question about benefits and contributions is a gentle reminder of the two-sided obligation of collaborative learning. At a somewhat higher level of involvement, the teacher might spend a little time in class discussion, eliciting suggestions from students about how the group work might be made more productive. Or she might decide to get more heavily involved yet by devising some learning exercises that teach students to critique each other's papers helpfully.

In any case, this illustrates an important use of CATs beyond assessment and feedback. CATs can be used to involve students in monitoring their own learning. One of the major conclusions from the research on cognition over the past 20 years is that students who monitor their own learning are more effective learners than those who do not. Good learners are aware of themselves as learners; they are able to watch themselves in the process of learning, and therefore able to direct and control their use of learning strategies.

Classroom teachers can help students become self-regulated learners through a variety of rather simple Classroom Assessment Techniques. For example, a CAT labeled "Punctuated Lectures" calls for stopping the class occasionally to ask students to reflect on what they were doing during the lecture and how their behavior, while listening, helped or hindered their understanding. They are then asked to write down any insights about their own learning that they have gained and give feedback to the teacher in brief anonymous notes. This form of pedagogical assessment not only teaches students to become more aware of how they are using their learning time; it also informs the teacher about distractions in the environment. A similar assessment technique called "Productive Study-Time Logs" assesses the effective use of study time. It asks students to keep brief records of how much time they spend studying for a particular class, when they study, and how productively they study.

The third condition for excellence identified by the authors of *Involvement in Learning* is "holding high expectations for student performance." What teachers expect of students often determines what students expect of themselves. Holding high expectations for students, by its very nature, has to be geared to the performance of individuals. It is not a normative or competitive matter. A teacher cannot constructively hold high expectations for a student by hoping that the student will do better than someone else. Rather the expectation must be based on the premise that individuals will improve their own performance. Classroom Assessments are, by definition, noncompetitive, non-graded, and usually anonymous. Students are engaged in trying to become more aware of their own learning, and CATs help students to assess themselves.

It is also true, of course, that in using Classroom Assessment Techniques, teachers are setting an example of holding high expectations for their own performance as teachers. As a matter of fact, one of the advantages of Classroom Assessment that is mentioned most frequently by teachers, is the bonding that is formed between students and teacher when teachers are demonstrating their own interest in using assessment for self-improvement. While I have been both gratified, and frankly surprised, by the enthusiasm of college teachers for Classroom Assessment, CAT is not without its critics.

Some ask, can't teachers fool themselves, evaluating their teaching by making and using CATs that tell them what they want to hear? Yes, of course. But our experience is that teachers who use CATs are too hard on themselves rather than too easy. They tend to want to find out what is *wrong* with their teaching rather than what is *right* about it. We have also found that while we thought that one of the big advantages of Classroom Assessment was that teachers could do it in the privacy of their own classrooms, teachers tell us that a major advantage is that Classroom Assessment promotes discussion about teaching. Most teachers seem to want to share their data and its interpretation with their peers. Anything that encourages faculty to develop a campus culture "where faculty talk together about teaching, inquire into its effects, and take collective responsibility for its quality" (Hutchings, 1993, p. v) may be a step in the right direction.

Other critics ask, isn't Classroom Assessment a bit simplistic? Doesn't the improvement of learning involve far more than an individual classroom and individual lessons? Yes, of course. But classrooms are the building blocks that we have chosen for education, and if we cannot find out what goes on in the classroom, and how it can be improved, then it isn't very likely that we can improve the quality of education.

Doesn't Classroom Assessment take time away from teaching? Ah, that is the most common complaint of teachers. How can we cover the material, they ask, if we take time away from teaching it? Actually, it makes no difference how much material the teacher is covering if students aren't getting it. The point of Classroom Assessment is to find out how much of the material covered students are learning. Moreover, Classroom Assessment, used well, *is* using class time to engage students in learning.

Since Classroom Assessment is, in many respects, a child of the larger institutional assessment movement, it shares the family problem of the tension between assessment for accountability imposed from without and self-assessment undertaken for purposes of improvement. Peter Ewell warns that, ". . . once started, assessment in some form *is going to happen*." (Ewell, 1991, p. 17, emphasis in original). I believe that the appropriate form of assessment in a healthy profession is self-assessment, and both students and teachers should be doing it.

References

Angelo, T. A., & Cross, K. P. (1993). *Classroom assessment' techniques: a handbook for college teachers*, Second Edition. San Francisco: Jossey-Bass.

Bloom, B. (1980). The new direction in educational research: alterable variables. *Phi Delta Kappan* (Feb.), 382–385.

Cashin, W. E. (1990). Assessing teaching effectiveness. In P. Seldin (Eds.), *How Administrators Can Improve Teaching*. San Francisco: Jossey Bass.

Centra, J. A. (1973). Effectiveness of student feedback in modifying college instruction. *Journal of Educational Psychology, 65*, 395–401.

Cohen, P. A. (1980). Effectiveness of student rating feedback for improving college instruction: A meta-analysis of findings. *Research in Higher Education*, 13(4), 321–342.

Cohen, P. A. (1981). Student ratings of instruction and student achievement: A meta-analysis of multisection validity studies. *Review of Educational Research, 51*, 281–309.

Cross, K. P. (1985). Making students successful: The search for solutions continues. *Change*, November/December, 48–51.

Dowell, D. A., & Neal, J. A. (1982). A selective review of the validity of student ratings of teaching. *Journal of Higher Education, 53*, 51–62.

Edgerton, R. (1994). A national market for excellence in teaching. *Change*, September/October, *26*(5), 4–5.

Epstein, J. (Ed.). (1981). *Masters: Portraits of great teachers*. New-York: Basic.

Ewell, P. (1991). Assessment and public accountability: Back to the future. *Change*, 23(6), 12–17.

Feldman, K. A. (1988). Effective college teaching from the students' and faculty's views: matched or mismatched priorities? *Research in Higher Education, 28*, 291–344.

Gleason-Weimer, M. (1987). Translating evaluation reports into teaching improvement. *AAHE Bulletin* (April), 8–11.

Gragg, C. I. (1940). Teachers also must learn. *Harvard Educational Review, 10*, 30–47.

Hutchings, P. (1993). *Using cases to improve college teaching*. Washington, D.C.: American Association for Higher Education.

Kulik, J. A., & McKeachie, W. J. (1975). The evaluation of teachers in higher education. In F. N. Karlinger (Ed.), *Review of research in education*. Itasca, Illinois: F.E. Peacock.

Light, R. J. (1990). *The Harvard assessment seminars*. Cambridge, MA: Harvard University.

Lowman, J. (1984). *Mastering the techniques of teaching*. San Francisco: Jossey-Bass.

Murray, H. G. (1985). Classroom teaching behaviors related to college teaching effectiveness. In J. G. Donald & A. M. Sullivan (Eds.), *Using research to improve teaching. New Directions for Teaching and Teaming*, No. 23. San Francisco: Jossey-Bass.

National Commission on Excellence in Education (1983). *A nation at risk*. Washington, D.C.: U.S. Department of Education.

Study Group on the Conditions of Excellence in American Higher Education. (1984). *Involvement in Learning*. Washington, D.C.: Department of Education, National Institute of Education.

Willingham, W. (1985). *Success in college*. New York: The College Board.

The Undergraduate Classroom Experience: Factors Associated with Its Vitality

J. Fredericks Volkwein

Director of Institutional Research
and Associate Professor of Educational Administration and Policy Studies

Alberto F. Cabrera

Associate Professor
Pennsylvania State University

Abstract

Since the classroom experience is central to the purpose of educational institutions, we need to examine those factors that exert positive and negative influences upon it. The data in our study contain measures that reflect an array of concepts from the student-institution fit literature, including academic and social integration, student effort and involvement, encouragement of family and friends, financial need and ability to pay, race and campus climate, and goal clarity. The most beneficial classroom experiences are reported by upper division students who perceive a campus climate of racial harmony and tolerance, and who report the highest levels of academic integration in the form of faculty concern for students and the student's own academic effort and involvement.

The Research and Policy Problem

The undergraduate classroom represents the formal structure in collegiate organizations where learning officially takes place. Nevertheless, the literature on outcomes assessment rarely focuses on the vitality of this experience explicitly. The Pascarella and Terenzini "Moby Book" (1991) presents and discusses the existing array of theories and models of student change, and while several models note the importance of faculty and student interaction, explicit attention to the classroom is either absent or not at all prominent in the discussion. Indeed, most of the empirical studies that provide support for the models by Tinto, by Bean, and by Cabrera and their associates, focus as much on advising and study habits and faculty-student interaction *outside* the classroom, as they do on the dynamics *within* the classroom.

Paper presented at the Annual Meeting of the Association for the Study of Higher Education.

In using these models to examine a variety of desirable student outcomes, Volkwein and his research colleagues in several studies have found that the classroom experience is the single most important influence explaining student growth and satisfaction (Volkwein et al., 1986; Volkwein, 1991; Volkwein & Carbone 1994; Volkwein & Lorang, 1996). Terenzini's NCTLA model (1995) is the first to explicitly identify classroom experiences as having a prominent role in producing learning outcomes. In their recent studies at the NCTLA, Pascarella and Terenzini and their research colleagues have now begun to incorporate measures of course learning, instructor effectiveness, and other academic experiences into their examination of learning outcomes (Terenzini et al., 1995, 1996; Pascarella et al. 1996). At least two of these studies (Terenzini et al., 1995; Pascarella et al. 1996) have found that the CSEQ measures of instructor organization, skill, clarity, and support have exerted heavily significant influences on student outcomes.

Given the importance of the classroom experience, both conceptually and empirically, the purpose of this study is to examine the factors in the undergraduate experience that appear to be the most strongly associated with vitality in the classroom, as reported by students.

Conceptual Theoretical Framework

There are at least three major assertions regarding the nature of adjustment to college. The most traditional view is that academic preparedness for college and clear goals are the main factors accounting for differences in persistence behavior, academic performance, and other educational outcomes (Feldman & Newcomb, 1969). A second group of alternative yet complementary perspectives fall under the general description of student-institution fit models (Pascarella & Terenzini, 1991). Perhaps the most widely researched of these models claims that student persistence and growth depends on the degree of successful integration into the academic and social structures of the institution (Spady 1970, 1971). Tinto has advanced this model and elaborated on it with the additional claim that successful adjustment to college involves severing ties with family and past communities in order to successfully integrate the student into the new academic community (1987, 1994). Another complementary perspective to the student-institution fit model focuses on the importance of student involvement and effort (Astin 1984, Pace 1984). Others argue that support from friends and family are important enhancements to college adjustment (Bean 1980: Bean and Metzner 1985; Nora 1987; Nora et al. 1990). Yet another branch of this literature emphasizes the importance of financial variables and the student's ability to pay (Cabrera et al. 1990: St. John, 1994).

A third set of assertions rest on the role that perceptions of prejudice and discrimination play in student adjustment. Exposure to a campus climate of prejudice and discrimination has gained increased attention as the main factor accounting for the differences in persistence rates between minorities and non-minorities (e.g. Fleming, 1984; Hurtado, 1992, 1994; Hurtado, Carter & Spuler, 1996; Smedley, Myers & Harrel, 1993). Many authors argue that intolerance towards minority students establishes a climate of racial prejudice and discrimination that permeates both academic and social interactions, and thus figures prominently in explaining their maladjustment with the institution (Hurtado, 1992, 1994; Hurtado, Carter & Spuler, 1996; Loo & Rolison, 1986; Murguía, Padilla, & Pavel, 1991). The resulting low involvement with the different campus communities impinges on the minority student's cognitive and affective development as well as persistence (Fleming, 1984; Loo & Rolison, 1986; Smith, 1989, 1992; Tracey and Sedlacek 1984, 1985, 1987; Suen, 1983; Loo and Rolison 1986). Not all studies have supported these claims (Arbona and Novy 1991; Nettles, Thoeny and Gosman 1986; Cabrera and Nora 1994), and there is at least preliminary evidence that perceptions of prejudice and racial disharmony affect White and minority students alike (Nora & Cabrera, 1996).

Since the classroom experience is central to the purpose of educational institutions, we need to examine those factors that exert positive and negative influences upon it. The data in our study contain measures that reflect an array of concepts from the student-institution fit literature, including academic and social integration, student effort and involvement, encouragement of family and friends, financial need and ability to pay, race and campus climate, and goal clarity.

Methodology

The study is conducted at a research university with a matriculated undergraduate population of about 10,000 students. The study uses multivariate regression analysis to examine responses to the Spring 1994 undergraduate outcomes survey. This survey is part of the University's ongoing assessment program and is administered every three years. It contains over 180 items of information in four categories:

1. Background information about age, class year, sex, ethnicity, employment, admissions status, type of enrollment, major, financial aid, and residence.
2. Student plans, goals, and reasons for attendance.
3. Levels of Student satisfaction with an array of campus services and facilities, as well as with various aspects of the institution's academic, administrative, and social environments or climates.
4. A variety of cognitive and non-cognitive experiences and outcomes, including classroom experiences, faculty contact, course taking patterns, graduation plans, anticipated loan indebtedness, Grade Point Average (GPA), and self-reported growth.

The regression analysis for this study is conducted on 496 representative undergraduates who responded to the 1994 outcomes survey by completing at least 90% of the survey questions. The 496 are representative with respect to age, gender, and admissions status. Seniors and ethnic minorities were over-sampled to ensure their generous representation in the database since these are the populations of greatest interest. While not every undergraduate field of study is present in the sample, the 15 largest majors are represented in approximate proportion to their numbers in the undergraduate student body. Table 1 lists the variables that are assembled for the regression model.

TABLE 1
Descriptive Statistics and Marginal Distributions (N = 496)

Variables & Multi-item Scales	*Count*	*Cell %*	*Mean*	*S.D.*	*Alpha*
Demographics (dummy vars.)					
Ethnic Minority (non-White)	137	27.6			
Male	298	60.1			
Class Year (dummy vars.)					
Upper Division	345	69.6			
Lower Division	151	30.4			
Academic Integration:					
Faculty Contact (1 item)			3.01	1.30	
Faculty Concern (2 items)			3.38	.88	.74
Involvement/Effort (2 items)			3.68	.98	.76
Social Integration					
Peer Relations (2 items)			4.01	1.01	.87
Goal Commitment					
Goal Clarity (3 items)			3.93	.93	.72
Campus Climate					
Harmony/Tolerance (5 items)			2.81	.66	.67
Perceptions of Prejudice (2 items)			2.72	.97	.89
Encouragement					
Friends (1 item)			3.70	1.23	
Family (1 item)			4.13	1.08	
Economic Factors					
Financial Difficulty (1 item)			2.90	1.32	
Financial Need (3 items)			2.46	1.68	.81
Work Study (dummy var.)	200	40.3			
Classroom Experiences (7 items)			3.69	.70	.86

Dependent Variable

This research focuses on the classroom experiences reported by respondents to the university's outcomes survey. The dependent variable is a scale of classroom experiences developed by Terenzini and his colleagues (1980, 1982, 1984, 1987) [alpha = .73], and enhanced by Volkwein and his colleagues (1991, 1994, 1996) [alpha = .89]. This is a seven-item scale on which students report the extent to which they have classes in which they are intellectually challenged, learn something new, are given stimulating assignments, etc. [Students respond on a five-point scale: 1 = rarely/never, 2 = less than half the time, 3 = about half the time, 4 = more than half the time, 5 = almost always.]

Independent Variables

The constructs and variables used in the analysis are shown in Table 1 and are drawn directly from the student-institution fit literature in general, and from the Cabrera and Tinto Models in particular. The specific measures listed in the table for academic integration, social integration, campus climate, encouragement, finances, and goal commitment are borrowed not only from Cabrera's work (1992, 1993), but also from studies by Pascarella and Terenzini, 1982; Terenzini, et al., 1982, 1984; Nora 1987; Nora, et al. 1990; Volkwein, et al., 1986; Volkwein 1991; Volkwein & Carbone, 1994; and Volkwein & Lorang, 1996. The alpha reliabilities for the various multi-item scales used in these studies are recalculated for this population; and as shown in Table 1, many exceed .80 and all but one are above .70.

Results

The results of our analysis are shown in Table 2. The significant beta weights are attached to the variables reflecting faculty concern (.33), racial harmony (. 15), student effort (.14), upper division status (.13), goal clarity (.08), and encouragement from friends (.07). The adjusted R-square exceeds .42 which is quite strong for a study measuring a student self-reported behavior. Thus, the most beneficial classroom experiences

TABLE 2

Regression Analysis Results (Dependent Variable = Classroom Experiences)

Variables & Scales	*Beta*	*S.E.*
Demographics:		
Ethnic Minority (non-White)	−.058	.0587
Male	.028	.0553
Class year:		
Upper Division	.130**	.0629
Academic Integration:		
Faculty Contact (outside class)	.018	.0218
Faculty Concern	.333**	.0308
Involvement/Effort	.139**	.0287
Social Integration		
Peer Relations	−.032	.0263
Goal Commitment:		
Goal Clarity	.079**	.0302
Campus Climate:		
Racial Harmony/Tolerance	.149**	.0424
Perception of Prejudice	−.018	.0281
Encouragement:		
Friends	.067**	.0234
Family	−.001	.0270
Economic Factors:		
Financial Difficulty	.020	.0280
Financial Need	−.009	.0235
Work Study	.010	.0553

*$p < .05$
**$p < .01$
$F^{**}_{(15,6.0446)} = 22.28$; $R^2 = .4437$; $R^2_{adjusted} = .4238$

are reported by upper division students who perceive a campus climate of racial harmony and tolerance, and who report the highest levels of academic integration in the form of faculty concern for students and the student's own academic effort and involvement. Of significant, but secondary importance as influences on the classroom experience are the 3-item scale of goal clarity and the single item reflecting personal support from friends.

The prominent roles of faculty concern and student effort in the classroom experience are consistent with several branches of the student-institution fit literature. Indeed, a favorable classroom experience and faculty respect for students and student effort may all mutually reinforce each other. If so, this situation occurs more frequently in classes attended by juniors and seniors than by freshmen and sophomores.

Given the discussions in the literature, we expected to observe significant influences by the variables reflecting gender, financial need and ability to pay, and race and perceptions of prejudice. However, these variables are not influential with this population. We are not surprised by the non-significance of gender because other studies at this particular university have found few male-female differences. We are surprised, however, that the economic variables do not intrude into the classroom and influence the quality of that experience. Apparently, these students do not take their financial problems into the classroom. The non-significance of race/ethnicity challenges some of the statements in the literature about the permeability of discrimination throughout all aspects of the undergraduate experience. We did not find it. Additionally, racial harmony in our study exerts greater *positive* influences on the classroom environment than perceptions of prejudice exert *negative* ones. This invites closer examination.

Thus, in this study we have explored a number of student variables that the literature suggests might influence the classroom experience. The most beneficial classroom experiences are reported by upper division students who perceive a campus climate of racial harmony, and who report the highest levels of academic integration in the form of faculty concern for students and the student's own academic effort and goal clarity. Such findings are entirely consistent with the mainstream of the student-institution fit literature.

This line of research is important because of the current national interest in the undergraduate experience and the instructional contributions that faculty make. Our dependent variable—which we believe reflects classroom vitality—is a scale of items that reflect the presence in the classroom of well-prepared, caring, and interesting instructors who give meaningful assignments, according to the students. Thus, our classroom scale emphasizes faculty *behaviors,* rather than faculty *characteristics*. Apparently these faculty behaviors not only stimulate student learning, but also overcome student differences in race, sex, financial need, and family background—differences that under conditions of good teaching are left at the classroom door.

Future research on this topic should incorporate measures that reflect other aspects of the students and their classroom experiences, including test scores, transfer status, prior achievement, and academic major. In the meantime, additional analyses are planned with this dataset. The possibility of interaction effects cannot be ignored, and we plan to undertake other regressions holding some of our key variables in and out of the analysis. Also, structural equation modeling may reveal additional dynamics among these variables. We also plan to conduct a similar analysis using a multi-campus dataset.

This preliminary research suggests, however, that a wholistic assessment of the undergraduate classroom experience is significantly influenced by student perceptions about campus climate, especially those aspects of campus climate reflecting faculty concern for students, racial harmony, and student involvement. This is entirely consistent with a campus agenda that encourages faculty attentiveness, student conscientiousness, and tolerance among all members of the campus community.

References

Arbona, C. & Novy, D. M. (1990). Noncognitive dimensions as predictors of college success among Black, Mexican-American and White students. *Journal of College Student Development,* 31: 415–421.

Astin, A. (1984). Student involvement: A developmental theory for higher education. *Journal for Higher Education Bulletin,* 38: 11–12.

Bean, J. P. (1980). Dropouts and turnover: The synthesis and test of a casual model of student attrition. *Research in Higher Education,* 12: 155–187.

Bean, J. P. and Metzner, B. S. (1985). A conceptual model of nontraditional undergraduate student attrition. *Review of Higher Educational Research,* 55(4): 485–540.

Cabrera, A. F. & Nora, A. (1994). College students' perceptions of prejudice and discrimination and their feelings of alienation. *Review of Education, Pedagogy, and Cultural Studies,* 16, 387–409.

Cabrera, A. F., Stampen, J. L. and Hansen, W. L. (1990). Exploring the effects if ability-to-pay on persistence in college. *Review of Higher Education,* 13(3): 303–336.

Feldman, K. and Newcomb, T. (1969). *The impact of college on students.* San Francisco: Jossey-Bass.

Fleming, J. (1984). Blacks in college: A comparative study of students' success in Black and in White institutions. San Francisco: CA.: Jossey-Bass.

Hurtado, S. (1992). The campus racial climate: Contexts of conflict. *Journal of Higher Education,* 63: 539–569.

Hurtado, S. (1994). The institutional climate for talented Latino students. *Research in Higher Education,* 35: 21–41.

Hurtado, S., Carter, D. F. & Spuler, A. (1996). Latino student transition to college: Assessing difficulties and factors in successful college adjustment. *Research of Higher Education,* 37(2): 135–158.

Loo, C. M. & Rolison, G. (1986). Alienation of ethnic minority students at a predominantly white university. *Journal of Higher Education,* 57: 58–77.

Murguia, E., Padilla, R. V., and Pavel, M. (1991). Ethnicity and the concept of social integration in Tinto's Model of Student Departure. *Journal of College Student Development,* 32: 433–446.

Nora, A. (1987). Determinants of retention among Chicano student: A structural model. *Research in Higher Education,* 26(1): 31–59.

Nora, A., Attinasi, L. C. and Matonack, A. (1990). Testing qualitative indicators of college factors in Tinto's attrition model: A community college student population. *Review of Higher Education,* 13(3): 337–356.

Nora, A. & Cabrera, A. F. (1996). The role of perceptions of prejudice and discrimination on the adjustment of minority students to college. *The Journal of Higher Education,* 67(2): 119–148.

Nettles, M. T., Thoeny, A. R., and Gosman, E. J. (1986). Comparative and Predictive Analyses of Black and White Students' College Achievement and Experiences. *Journal of Higher Education,* 57(3): 289–318.

Pace, C. (1984). *Measuring the quality of college student experiences.* Los Angeles: University of California, Higher Education Research Institute.

Pascarella, E. T., Edison, M., Hagedorn, L. S., Nora. A., and Terenzini, P. T. (1996). Influences on students' internal locus of attribution for academic success in the first year of college. *Research in Higher Education* 37: 731–756.

Pascarella, E. T. and Terenzini, P. T. (1982). Contextual Analysis as A Method for Assessing Residence Group Effects. *Journal of College Student Personnel,* 23: 108–114.

Pascarella, E. T. and Terenzini, P. T. (1991). *How College Affects Students.* San Francisco, CA: Jossey-Bass Inc.

St. John, E. P. (1992). Workable Models for Institutional Research on the Impact of Student Financial Aid. *Journal of Student Financial Aid,* 22(3): 13-26.

Smedley, B. D., Myers, H. F. and Harrell, S. P. (1993). Minority-status stresses and the college adjustment of ethnic minority freshmen. *Journal of Higher Education,* 64: 434–452.

Smith, D. G. (1989). *The challenge of diversity: involvement or alienation in the Academy?* In J. D. Fife (ed.), ASHE-ERIC Higher Education Reports (Report # 5). Washington, DC.: The George Washington University Press.

Smith, D. G. (1992). Diversity. In M. A. Whiteley, J. D. Porter and R. H. Fenske (eds.), The premier for institutional research. Tallahassee, Florida: Association for Institutional Research Press.

Spady, W. (1970). Dropouts from higher education: An interdisciplinary review and synthesis. *Interchange,* 1: 64–85.

Spady, W. (1971). Dropouts from higher education: Toward an empirical model. *Interchange,* 2: 38–62.

Suen, H. (1983). Alienation and attrition of Black college students on a predominately White campus. *Journal of College Student Personnel,* 24: 117–121.

Terenzini, P. T., Pascarella, E. T., Theophilides, C., and Lorang, W. (1985). A replication of a path analytic validation of Tinto's theory of college student attrition. *Review of Higher Education,* 8: 319–340.

Terenzini, P. T., Springer, L., Pascarella, E. T., and Nora, A. (1995). Influences affecting the development of students' critical thinking skills. *Research in Higher Education,* 36: 23–39.

Terenzini, P. T., Springer, L., Yaeger, P., Pascarella, E. T., and Nora, A. (1996). First-generation college students: Characteristics, experiences, and cognitive development. *Research in Higher Education* 37: 731–756.

Terenzini, P. T., Theophilides, C. & Lorang, W. (1984a). Influences on students' perceptions of their academic skill development during college. *Journal of Higher Education,* 55: 621–636.

Terenzini, P. T., Theophilides, C., & Lorang, W. (1984b). Influences on students' perception of their personal development during the first three years of college. *Research in Higher Education* 21: 178–194.

Terenzini, P. T. and Wright, T. (1987a). Influences on students' academic growth during four years of college. *Research in Higher Education* 26: 161–179.

Terenzini, P. T. and Wright, T. (1987b). Students' personal growth during the first two years of college. *Review of 'Higher Education,* 10: 259–271.

Tinto, V. (1987). *Leaving College: Rethinking the Causes and Cures of Student Attrition.* Chicago: University of Chicago Press.

Tracey, T. J. & Sedlacek, W. E. (1987). Prediction of college graduation using noncognitive variables by race. *Measurement and Evaluation in Guidance,* 19: 177–184.

Tracey, T. J. & Sedlacek, W. E. (1985). The relationship of noncognitive variables to academic success. A longitudinal comparison by race. *Journal of College Student Personnel,* 26: 405–410.

Tracey, T. J. & Sedlacek, W. E. (1984). Noncognitive variables in predicting academic success by race. *Measurement and Evaluation in Guidance,* 16: 171–178.

Volkwein, J. F., King, M., & Terenzini, P. (1986). Student-faculty relationships and intellectual growth among transfer students. *Journal of Higher Education* 57: 413–430.

Volkwein, J. F. (1991). Improved Measures of Academic and Social Integration And Their Association with Measures of Student Growth—Paper presented at Annual Meeting of the Association for the Study of Higher Education, Boston, MA.

Volkwein, J. F., & Carbone, D. A. (1994). The impact of departmental research and teaching climates on undergraduate growth and satisfaction. *Journal of Higher Education,* 65(2): 149–167.

Volkwein, J. F. and Lorang, W. G. (1996). Characteristics of extenders: Full-time students who take light credits loads and graduate in more than four years. *Research in Higher Education,* 37(1): 43–68.

Culturally Responsive Pedagogy and the Assessment of Accomplished Teaching

Lloyd Bond

Abstract

This article addresses the complexities and psychometric challenges facing efforts to devise a standards-based performance assessment of teaching that is appropriate for teachers in a wide variety of contexts and that also satisfies psychometric considerations of reliability and validity. In particular, the question of whether a general assessment of teaching practice can be sufficiently comprehensive to honor and recognize accomplished, culturally relevant pedagogy is considered. Drawing upon the experience of the National Board for Professional Teaching Standards, it is argued that such an assessment, although presenting enormous technical challenges, is both possible and practically attainable.

The task of developing a comprehensive, performance-based assessment of teaching that is appropriate and valid for the wide variety of teachers and teaching contexts found in the United States presents an enormous technical challenge. Review of the history of performance-based assessments of teaching is certainly not encouraging. Such attempts have been characterized by direct classroom observation of teachers, typically by principals and instructional and curriculum specialists, using standardized observational instruments with specified rating categories such as waiting time, clarity, student engagement, use of visual aids, and so on. Detailed behavioral checklists have also been used. These methods require the observer to take sample observations at specified time intervals.

To be sure, observing teachers during their instruction and interaction with students in actual classroom settings is a vital part of any valid assessment, but such brief observations fall far short of a comprehensive evaluation. Moreover, they provide only a limited view of teachers' subject-matter knowledge and give no indication of how teachers organize a coherent unit of instruction over time, or how they analyze, assess, or provide feedback on students' work. Nor do such observational procedures capture how teachers interact with their colleagues as members of learning communities, or how they reflect upon and alter their practice with experience. A comprehensive assessment of teaching would cover all of these aspects and more. It also would appraise:

(1) the extent to which teachers set attainable and worthwhile learning goals for their students;

(2) how teachers select, adapt, and create curricular resources that support active student exploration and learning;

Reprinted by permission from *The Journal of Negro Education* 67, no. 3 (summer 1998).

(3) how teachers' instruction over time integrates reading, writing, speaking, and listening opportunities for students; and

(4) how teachers work with parents, families, and community resources in the service of student growth and learning.

Beyond the above disciplinary considerations, a valid system of teacher assessment must also be sufficiently flexible and comprehensive to recognize and honor excellence in teaching wherever it occurs, be it in an overcrowded school serving largely at-risk students or a poorly funded school in an economically depressed rural community. In essence, such an assessment should be insensitive to context. That is, it should not depend upon the ethnicity of the teacher or the facilities available to her, nor should it depend upon the ethnicity, prior preparation, or abilities of the students taught.

The publication in 1983 of the Nation at Risk report was a landmark event in the history of public education in the United States (National Commission on Excellence in Education, 1983). This publication was a wake-up call to the American people that our schools, and therefore our society, were in trouble. The follow-up report, A Nation Prepared, called for the formation of a National Board for Professional Teaching Standards (NBPTS, or "the National Board") (Carnegie Forum on Education and the Economy, 1986). The NBPTS, which was duly formed in 1987, has a threefold purpose: (a) to establish high and rigorous standards for what accomplished teachers should know and be able to do, (b) to develop and operate a national voluntary system to assess and certify teachers who meet those standards, and (c) to advance educational reforms responsive to this mission for the purpose of improving student learning. Consistent with the organization's philosophy that teachers be centrally involved in all its operations, including majority membership on its 63-member national board of directors, the majority of members on NBPTS standards committees are practicing teachers in the relevant disciplines.

The philosophical foundation for NBPTS's teaching certification system are its five core propositions:

(1) Accomplished teachers are committed to students and to their learning.

(2) Accomplished teachers know the subjects they teach and how to each those subjects to students.

(3) Accomplished teachers are responsible for managing and monitoring student learning.

(4) Accomplished teachers think systematically about their practice and learn from experience.

(5) Accomplished teachers are members of learning communities. These five propositions form the foundation of the National Board's approach to delineating content standards for each of the more than 20 certification areas that it covers. Selected through an extended and open process of nomination and review, the standards committees for each of these areas are charged with the responsibility of defining what accomplished practice means in each area. The resulting standards documents become the content domain for development of relevant assessments.

The NBPTS assessment system is completely performance-based, incorporating two major components: (a) a candidate-prepared portfolio component consisting of six exercises, and (b) a one-day assessment center component that directs examinees to generate four essay responses to content and content-pedagogical prompts. The NBPTS portfolio component is an enormously rich and complex assessment that alone requires up to two hundred hours to complete during the course of the school year. Teachers must present evidence, in the form of videotapes and reflective commentaries, of their actual classroom instruction in both small group and whole class settings. They must also present student work samples and other artifacts of their teaching, along with explanatory commentary, as well as demonstrate their ability to monitor and assess student progress. Additionally, they must show how they plan and carry out a unit of instruction, how they alter their practice as a function of feedback and experience, how they involve families and community resources in their practice, and how they continue their development as members of a professional community.

In 1991, shortly after the contract for developmental work on the first two NBPTS certificate assessments was assigned, a Technical Analysis Group (TAG), composed of some of the nation's leading measurement experts, was formed to ensure the technical measurement quality of the assessments. Since then, this group has completed over 100 psychometric investigations of NBPTS assessments. This article reviews the research undertaken by members of this group with respect to the differential certification rates obtained by various demographic groups of teachers and teacher candidates (adverse impact), and to the possible presence of bias in various components of the assessment system. Before considering these studies in detail, it is useful to distinguish between adverse impact and bias.

Adverse Impact and Bias in Teacher Assessment

An assessment is said to have an adverse impact with respect to a specified population subgroup if the rate at which examinees in that subgroup are certified is substantially below the certification rate of a normative reference group (Equal Employment Opportunity Commission, 1978). For example, if the certification rate for African American examinees is substantially below that of European American candidates, then the assessment is said to exhibit adverse impact with respect to African Americans. The important point to note is that a differential certification rate alone is sufficient evidence of adverse impact, but the reasons for this differential are not relevant to the determination of such an impact. Differential certification rates may result from assessor bias, from biases in the conceptualization of the domain to be assessed, from characteristics of the scoring scheme that disadvantage some examinees, or from differential access to professional or collegial help in preparing portfolio materials, to name a few. The exercises in an assessment and the methods of scoring, however, may be totally free of these deficiencies. In other words, differential certification rates ray not be traceable to any flaws in the assessment system itself. Rather, they may represent genuine group differences in the knowledge, skills, and abilities being assessed. The mere presence of adverse impact gives no clue as to which reason or set of reasons is operative. These reasons must be investigated as a separate matter.

By contrast, an assessment is said to exhibit bias if significant, systematic differences in performance among subgroups of the examinee population can be ascribed to actual flaws or deficiencies in one or more aspects of the assessment system itself that have the affect of disadvantaging members of a specific group (Shepard, 1982). Such deficiencies may be due to construct-irrelevant factors in the assessment. For example, in an assessment of mathematical proficiency, it is desirable to assess this construct as "purely" as possible, without confounding the measurement with linguistic ability. It thus becomes important to keep the demands of competence in the language in which the test is written to a minimum. If the examination includes word problems, then the vocabulary and linguistic demands of the problems must be as simple as possible. Otherwise, persons less proficient in the language of the test, such as those for whom the test's language is a second language, may be disadvantaged because of purely linguistic, as distinct from mathematical, considerations.

Alternately, bias may enter into an assessment even when the assessment does not contain construct-irrelevant factors. For example, an assessment may properly demand only the knowledge, skills, and abilities specified in the content domain, but these may be sampled in a nonrepresentative way, such that some abilities and skills (e.g., writing) are overemphasized and others (e.g., classroom management) are underemphasized. To the extent that subgroups of the population differ in these abilities, the assessment disadvantages some examinees.

External Sources of Bias and Adverse Impact

Performance on a complex assessment like the National Board's can be affected by a variety of factors, some of which are external to the assessment and some of which are internal. To investigate possible external factors, NBPTS asks candidates to provide selected demographic information, including postbaccalaureate degrees, years of teaching experience, a description of the students in their class, and a classification of their school location (rural, urban, or suburban). Examinees' scores on each assessment exercise are systematically compared by school location, gender, and ethnicity. The following sections present the results of TAG investigations into these factors.

School Location Findings. TAG research has found that the location of the school in which a teacher teaches appears to be unrelated to the probability that he or she will achieve Board certification. As of the 1996–97 test administration cycle, approximately 33% of teachers who described their schools as "rural" achieved NBPTS certification compared to 34% who described their schools as "urban" and 42% who described their schools as "suburban." Although the differences tend to favor suburban teachers slightly, school location per se does not appear to be a powerful factor in whether or not a teacher attains certification.

Gender Findings. Female candidates have been certified by NBPTS at a somewhat higher rate than male candidates to date. Approximately 40% of female candidates have achieved Board certification compared to approximately 25% of male candidates (Bond, 1998). One must keep in mind, however, that the majority of NBPTS certificate fields developed thus far have been for teachers of primary and middle school grades, in which females outnumber males by a considerable margin. Whether the above pattern will continue once the full complement of assessments for secondary school teachers are brought on line is unknown.

Ethnicity Findings. The legally recognized criterion for adverse impact is that it exists whenever a given focal group's certification rate is less than 80% of the certification rate of the reference or normative group. If one takes White teacher candidates, whose rate of certification is slightly over 40%, as the reference group, then adverse impact exists for a focal group if its rate is less than 32%. Though the rates of certification for all the major U.S. ethnic minority groups are below this 32% figure, only the certification rate for African American teacher candidates, approximately 11%, is substantially so (Bond, 1998). Although NBPTS is understandably more concerned about identifying and removing any internal components of its assessments that may unfairly disadvantage African American teachers, TAG researchers have also examined the influence of external factors that may affect Black teachers' rates of certification such as educational background, years of teaching experience, number of advanced degrees received, and level of support received during portfolio preparation.

Years of Teaching Experience. As of the 1996–97 administration cycle, 62% of all European American candidates and 54% of all African American candidates submitting to NBPTS certification testing have held degrees beyond the baccalaureate. Further, 58% of all White candidates and 62% of all Black candidates up to that cycle had 10 or more years of teaching experience (Bond, 1998). Taken together, these figures do not present a compelling case for years of experience or advanced degrees as fruitful sources of adverse impact.

It should also be noted that the putative quality of the school from which examinees received their highest degree does not seem to be related in any direct way with the probability of their being certified. For example, the mean scaled score of African American candidates for NBPTS certification who obtained their highest degree from an historically Black college or university (HBCU) is virtually identical with that of African American candidates who obtained their highest degree from predominantly White, Research[1] universities (Bond, 1998).

In traditional assessments, obtaining help and advice from others is considered unethical. Not so with the NBPTS certification system. Examinees may not only obtain advice and support from others, they are encouraged to do so. They are also advised to have colleagues critique and offer editorial suggestions on their written responses and reflective essays, to observe and offer suggestions on the videotapes of their classroom practice, and to get technical help in videotaping. However, these aspects of the assessment come at a price: they introduce additional potential sources of unfairness. For example, some candidates teach in school districts that offer outstanding facilities, knowledgeable colleagues, and highly capable support staff to assist teachers in preparing for certification or portfolio preparation. Other schools and districts have excellent relationships with nearby universities, from which educational researchers can be enlisted to offer additional support.

Support in Portfolio Preparation. To investigate the possibility that adverse impact may result in part from differing levels of collegial, administrative, and technical support available to examinees, TAG researchers conducted in-depth phone interviews of selected candidates for the 1993–94 Early Adolescence/Generalist and Early Adolescence/English Language Arts certificates. The interviews lasted approximately one hour each. Thirty-seven of the 40 African American examinees who submitted complete scorable portfolios and 60 European American candidates, whose profiles matched the African

American candidates as closely as possible on available information such as school location and years of teaching experience, were interviewed. Of course, subjective evaluations of the support one receives depend in part upon the level of support one is accustomed to. Therefore, to determine the absolute rather than the relative level of support received, candidates were asked to describe in detail the exact nature of the support they received. Specifically, they were asked which and how many colleagues or other school personnel viewed, commented on, and/or helped them in the preparation of their classroom videos; and who, if anyone, helped with editing of the various reflective essays required in the portfolio. Candidates were also asked to describe in detail what was discussed during any portfolio preparation meetings, organized by the National Board's network of field test coordinators, that they may have attended.

TAG analysis of the results of the survey suggest that the level and quality of support, per se, were not major factors in the adverse impact observed in these two certificate fields. In virtually all categories of collegial, administrative, and technical support, White and Black candidates received comparable support. However, these results are admittedly tentative, and further research on the relationship between quality and amount of support and certification rate is necessary.

Internal Sources of Adverse Impact

The NBPTS assessment and certification system is a complex one, and sources of bias and unfairness may burrow their way into the system in any number of ways. To date, three potential sources of adverse impact that are internal to the system itself have been investigated by TAG researchers: assessor training factors, interactions of candidate ethnicity and exercise type, and interactions of assessor and candidate ethnicity.

Assessor Training Factors. The qualifications for NBPTS assessors are the same as those for Board certification candidates. Assessors must be practicing teachers in the certificate area for which they will assess, and they must have three years of teaching experience. They must also undergo a rigorous training and calibration regimen and attain an acceptable level of proficiency before they can engage in operational scoring. However, teachers who successfully complete this training are assigned candidate cases without regard to their own teaching backgrounds or the backgrounds of candidates whom they assess. The Board does not attempt to match assessors with candidates. Thus, teachers who have taught only in poorly funded rural schools can be assigned to assess teachers in advantaged suburban settings, teachers in advantaged suburban schools can assess teachers in overcrowded urban settings, and vice-versa.

How can the training and calibration NBPTS assessors receive assure fairness under these circumstances? The Board has adopted several safeguards in this respect. For instance, an important part of assessor training involves the use of training and benchmark cases. Training cases are candidate submissions that have been prescored by experienced assessors and are used to train and calibrate assessors. Benchmark cases are candidate submissions that have been prescored and annotated by experienced assessors. The annotations cite and highlight the specific evidence, along with the connection to the standards of performance, that the assessors used in making their evaluation. Benchmarks provide a mechanism whereby assessors develop a common understanding of qualitative words used in scoring rubrics such as "insightful," "vague," "coherent," and "consistent." These annotated submissions are a permanent component of the assessor manual and are referred to often in the course of assessing candidate work. The manual is the assessor's constant companion during scoring, his or her "bible," as it were.

It should be easy to see why the choices related to which candidate submissions become training cases and which ones become benchmark cases are important: these cases serve as exemplars of the scoring "families." Several criteria are used in this selection process. First and foremost, the selected training and benchmark cases must present compelingly clear examples of one of the four scoring families. Second, cases are selected to represent a wide variety of teaching styles as exemplars of the various score families. Benchmark cases are chosen to help assessors see that while the surface features of two teachers' approaches to instruction may differ markedly, the deep structure of their practice is similar. The variety criterion for benchmark selection stems from the Board's conviction that there is no "one best way" to teach.

Some situations, for example, call for a decidedly student-centered approach to instruction, while others require teachers to be more didactic. The Board's standards of accomplished practice honor both forms of instruction. Third, it is important that training and benchmark cases not reinforce stereotypical notions about who is and who is not an excellent teacher. Submissions from European American suburban teachers with innumerable advantages can be found among the training and benchmark exemplars of the lowest scoring family, and African American teachers in the most challenging of inner-city schools can be found among the exemplars of the highest scoring family. This is as it should be. No group of teachers has a corner on excellence, nor are there any teaching contexts that render excellence impossible.

An important component of NBPTS assessor training is a module devoted exclusively to the issue of assessor biases. The objective of this component is to identify and minimize factors that might cause bias in scoring decisions. Having biases is inevitably a part of being a thinking person—indeed, everyone has conscious and unconscious biases. Yet, biases can be both positive and negative, and some may lead assessors to make judgments during assessment that reflect their own personal preferences rather than the candidates' performances. For this reason, the Board's bias training is designed to help assessors honestly identify their personal biases about social groups as well as their preferences for teaching practices. Each assessor creates a personal "hit list" of his or her strongly held opinions and preferences. Assessors are subsequently instructed to be especially careful about these biases during the assessment process. (A partial indication of the effectiveness of these procedures is described in the section on assessor race by candidate race interactions.)

Interactions of Candidate Ethnicity and Exercise Type. A fundamental requirement of any assessment is that observed differences in performance between individuals or groups reflect only the construct or constructs presumed to be measured and not other irrelevant constructs. Moreover, the relative emphasis of the knowledge, skills, and abilities measured in the assessment exercises should accurately reflect their relative importance in the conceptualization of the content domain. These requirements are essential if the interpretations made on the basis of assessment scores are to be valid for all examinees.

In the present context, any analysis of differential performance by ethnicity must take into account the fact that African American candidates have scored significantly below their European American counterparts on all of the NBPTS assessments. If the sources of differential performance are traceable to some construct-irrelevant property or to properties of the exercises themselves, or if it is traceable to an inappropriate privileging of some components over others, then it is unlikely that each exercise contains a different deficiency or flaw that disadvantages some group of examinees. A more likely circumstance is that all of the exercises contain some common characteristic or set of characteristics. One plausible characteristic is writing ability. As a practical matter, NBPTS assessments rely heavily upon examinees' ability to write about what they know and how they teach. All of the assessment exercises require examinees to produce written material, with some exercises requiring much more writing than others. Do exercises that require more writing result in larger mean differences by ethnicity? The analysis of the results from the Early Adolescence/Generalist certificate is typical. In this assessment, the exercise demanding the most writing by far is the "Interpreting Content" (IC) exercise, which requires examinees to produce three extensive essays in five different content-knowledge areas. By contrast, the "Analyzing Your Lesson" (AYL) exercise requires only a minimal amount of writing.

To investigate the extent to which the differing writing demands of these exercises are related to differential performance by ethnicity, two separate, unequal N, factorial analyses of variance were performed (Bond, 1998). In the first analysis, two levels of ethnicity (African American/European American) were crossed with two levels of writing demand (IC/AYL scores). In the second analysis, race was crossed with IC scores and the average scores on all other exercises in the assessment. The central comparisons in both analyses were the ethnicity by writing demand interactions. In both comparisons, the interaction effect was found to be nonsignificant. A comparison of cell means, however, revealed that the trend, though nonsignificant, was in the direction of relatively higher scores by European American candidates on the writing-intense IC exercise.

The mean scores for White and Black candidates on this exercise were 2.65 and 1.90, respectively, on a scale from 0.75 to 4.25. This compares with White and Black examinee scores of 2.26 and 1.76, respectively, on the AYL exercise.

Similar analyses have been conducted on the interaction of candidate ethnicity with exercises that entail edited writing as opposed to those that require extemporaneous writing. Comparative analyses have also been performed on exercises for which the examinees' ethnicities are known and those for which ethnicities are unknown (Bond, 1998). In these analyzes as well, no significant interaction effects were found.

Interactions of Assessor and Candidate Ethnicity. In NBPTS assessor training programs, efforts are made to train assessors to evaluate candidate performances through a common set of criteria that are firmly grounded in the Board's certification standards. Potential assessors must internalize those standards and apply them in an even-handed way. The very small number of teachers who do not meet the standards attests to the success of this training. However, it is important to note that agreement among qualified assessors is not perfect. Indeed, one would be suspicious if such agreement was the case, for then the scoring system could be reduced to an almost clerical, formulaic process with no room for assessors to draw upon their own experience as filters through which to view the scoring rubrics and performance criteria.

An issue of fundamental concern is the possible existence of assessor ethnicity by candidate ethnicity interactions. Do African American assessors, when evaluating the performance of African American examinees, discern positive aspects of the performance that European American assessors either overlook, misconstrue, or even disparage? More generally, does a candidate's evaluation depend upon a possible interaction between his or her ethnicity and that of the assessor? To achieve adequate statistical power to answer these questions, analysis of assessor ethnicity by candidate ethnicity interactions was performed on data collapsed across all NBPTS certificate areas (Bond, 1998).

In this analysis, a total of 72 cases in which African American candidates were assessed by both a White and a Black assessor were identified. Additionally, 527 cases were identified in which a White candidate was assessed by both an Black and a White assessor. In the latter case, it was possible to perform some analyses within certificate areas. The results of these analyses were unambiguous. In every unequal N analysis of variance test performed (i.e., both those collapsed across certificate areas and those performed within certificate areas), no evidence of assessor-by-candidate ethnicity interaction was found to exist. African American examinees did not appear to be disadvantaged by having their performances evaluated by European American assessors, and vice-versa. The lens through which assessors evaluated candidate performances did not appear to be affected by either their own ethnicity or the ethnicity of the certificate candidate.

Though these results are encouraging, they are not the final word. Candidates and assessors change each year, and new exercises are continually being introduced into the assessments. It is therefore essential that studies of assessor-by-candidate interactions continue to be conducted.

Additional Investigations of Bias and Adverse Impact: The Spencer Studies

In 1996, NBPTS was awarded a major grant from the Spencer Foundation to subject its assessment system to a thorough adverse-impact analysis. The certificate area chosen for the study was Early Adolescence/English Language Arts (EA/ELA), which corresponds roughly to middle school. In particular, the investigations were to focus on elements within the assessment itself, as distinct from possible external sources of adverse impact such as differences in years of experience, differences in quality of professional education, and so on. A summary of the findings of these investigations follow.

Instructional Styles and NBPTS's Vision of Accomplished Practice

A pervasive perception among observers of the Board's work is that its assessment and certification system privileges and honors constructivist, "student-centered," and permissive approaches to instruction over didactic, "teacher-centered," and more authoritarian instructional styles. Educational researchers have argued that the latter of these two teaching styles is often more effective for the very children that the majority of African American teachers teach (Irvine & Fraser, 1998). Do these two circumstances combine to put many African American teachers at a disadvantage in the Board's assessment program? A panel of EA/ELA teachers and educational researchers examined in detail the NBPTS EA/ELA standards and scoring scheme as well as the Board's application of the scoring scheme to candidate cases with a view toward answering this question. Beyond determining whether the EA/ELA assessment contains elements that may disadvantage African American examinees, this review team also sought to understand, as a matter of sound measurement practice, teaching practices and methods that have evolved in response to different teaching contexts. Their investigation focused on the following question: Do patterns of performance exist for African American teachers that are different than those for European American teachers who receive the same evaluation on the EA/ELA assessments exercises in general and on the video-exercises in particular?

In conducting their analyses, rather than follow the evaluation procedure used by the Board (in which assessors are trained to score only a single exercise), subpanels of the review team "read across" the entire portfolio and assessment center exercises submitted by candidates in the study sample. In preparation for this activity, the panelists engaged in a far-ranging, no-holds-barred discussion of any biasing elements that might have burrowed into the assessment. They considered several elements, such as the potentially wide variation in the background of assessors and examinees, and the extent to which assessors were sensitized to the sometimes extraordinarily difficult circumstances under which many urban teachers must work. The panel also discussed at length the effect that candidate dress, demeanor, speech and dialect, teaching style, and subtle cultural aspects of teacher-student interaction might have on assessor evaluations. The intent of these preliminary investigations was not to reach consensus but to alert all panelists to the variety of issues they would have to consider in their review.

The 15-member read-across panel was divided into five groups, each consisting of a university-based teacher educator/researcher, a practicing ELA classroom teacher, and an ELA curriculum specialist. The performance materials of all 37 African American candidates who took the 1993–94 and 1994–95 EA/ELA assessments were distributed among the five groups. In the first round of analysis, the panelists in each group independently reviewed[2] every African American candidate's entire performance packet to determine (a) if they contained any "culturally related" markers that might adversely affect their evaluation by assessors[3]; and (b) whether the candidate was accomplished or not accomplished according to the panelists' interpretations of the EA/ELA standards. The results of this process are summarized in Table 1.

Twelve of the 37 African American candidates were deemed accomplished by at least one panel member. Of the 5 who received certification, 4 supplied materials that contained no cultural markers. Six candidates failed to obtain certification, but at least one panel member deemed those candidates accomplished and at least one felt that cultural markers present in their performance packets might have adversely affected the evaluations they received. A contingent analysis revealed a pattern related to these 6 candidates that requires further study: for all 6 cases, the panel characterized their instructional styles as a combination of student-centered and teacher-centered approaches. However, examination of the written notes of the NBPTS assessors who originally rated these 6 candidates revealed that they uniformly characterized the

TABLE 1
Round-One Summary Results of "Read-Across" Panel

		Number of Candidates Rated "Accomplished"			
		Yes	**Uncertain**	**No**	**Total**
	Yes	6	11	5	22
Presence of Cultural Markers	**No**	6	2	5	13
	Total	12	13	10	35*

**Two candidates used for orientation purposes were not reviewed by the panel.*

TABLE 2
Agreement/Disagreement Between Review Panel Ratings and NBPTS Certification Decisions

African American Candidates	
Accomplished (Panel)/Certified (NBPTS)	5
Accomplished (Panel)/Not Certified (NBPTS)	5
Not Accomplished (Panel)/Certified (NBPTS)	0
Not Accomplished (Panel)/Not Certified (NBPTS)	22
European American Candidates	
Accomplished (Panel)/Certified (NBPTS)	1
Accomplished (Panel)/Not Certified (NBPTS)	2
Not Accomplished (Panel)/Certified (NBPTS)	0
Not Accomplished (Panel)/Not Certified (NBPTS)	14

candidates' instructional styles as exclusively teacher-centered.

The second round of review consisted of a much more thorough examination by the read-across panelists of the performance packets of all the African American candidates and 20 European American candidates, the latter of whom who were matched as closely as possible to the former on total score and teaching context. Each candidate's materials were reviewed by five panelists. Unfortunately, the amount of time required for this process was seriously underestimated; consequently, only about half the candidates were reviewed by five panelists while the remainder were reviewed by only three panelists. Each panelist supplied detailed comments on various aspects of the candidates' practice (e.g., writing ability, teaching style, adequacy and relevance of evidence provided, etc.). The panel produced eight large volumes of detailed commentary of candidate performance packets, along with ratings of various aspects of those performances. Additionally, the panelists provided an overall summative judgment on whether the candidates were or were not accomplished, according to their understanding of the NBPTS's vision of accomplished practice as embodied in the EA/ELA certification standards. These summative judgments are presented In Table 2.

The read-across panelists agreed with 86% of the NBPTS assessors' certification decisions. Decision consistency indices for Board assessments (including EA/ELA) have been estimated by its Technical Analysis Group to be around 85%. In other words, for any randomly chosen set of candidates, if a different set of assessors had evaluated their performances, the certification decisions would have been the same in 85% of the cases. Thus, the panelists' evaluations are consistent with the judged reliability of the EA/ELA assessment. This suggests that the panelists did not perceive any pervasive pattern of erroneous certification decisions with respect to African American candidates.

Beyond determining whether its EA/ELA assessment contains elements that may disadvantage African American candidates, the National Board also sought to understand, as a matter of sound assessment practice, the teaching styles and methods that may have evolved in response to different teaching contexts. In that regard, it was important to ask whether different patterns of performance could be found for African American teachers than for European American teachers who receive the same evaluation, both on the exercises in general and on the video-exercises in particular? The panel could find no convincing evidence of differential teaching styles between comparably scored Black and White teachers.

Varying Views of Accomplished Practice

What elements and aspects of teaching practice do African American teachers consider important for outstanding teaching? Are these perceptions consistent with the NBPTS's vision of accomplished practice? In an attempt to address these questions, four members of the read-across panel identified 25 African American teachers and former teachers in urban settings (Detroit, Atlanta, Boston, and San Diego) who agreed to participate in four focus group discussions. The charge presented to these groups was fourfold. First, they were asked to discuss the scope and content of the NBPTS certification standards and to note how, if at all, the standards differed from their own views about what constitutes accomplished practice. Second, the teachers were asked to discuss the portfolio instructions provided with the 1997–98 version of the EA/ELA certification assessment, with a view toward possible sources of adverse impact that these instructions might contain. Third, in response to concerns that African American teachers may differ from the National Board in their views about the importance of the 10 exercises in the 1997–98 EA/ELA assessment, the focus groups were asked to apply their own weights to the exercises. Fourth, they were asked to evaluate the small-group-discussion exercise components of the portfolios of two EA/ELA candidates from the 1996–97 administration cycle, using their own admittedly limited understanding of NBPTS's vision of accomplished practice.

Intense, in-depth discussion over eight days by individuals who feel passionately about their work and profession obviously produces an enormous amount of data, albeit much of it anecdotal and personal. The focus groups found it difficult to attain genuine consensus on any particular issue. With this caveat in mind, the results may be summarized as follows: In general, all four groups viewed the NBPTS's EA/ELA certification standards, portfolio instructions, and scoring scheme favorably. Moreover, none of the focus groups was able to identify any single problem in the overall assessment system that, if fixed, would materially improve the lower rates of certification of African American candidates. Rather, they tended to view this disparity as systemic and largely external to the assessment program itself. Among the focus groups' major conclusions were the following:

Absent powerful incentives, accomplished African American teachers would generally not seek NBPTS certification for fear of risking their excellent reputations on a process that offered 50-50 odds of failure.

District-imposed curricular constraints as well as constraints imposed by students may militate against the certification of African American teachers, given that many African American teachers teach in districts that require rather rigid adherence to content and procedures that are in conflict with the Nation Board's vision of accomplished practice.

Given that academically advanced students tend to make their teachers look good, those who teach students who are seriously behind, as many African American teachers do, are forced to teach lessons that may appear trivial to assessors who may not be sufficiently sensitive to this issue. (In this vein, several members of the focus groups noted that African American teachers rarely got the chance to teach Advanced Placement or accelerated classes.)

The practice by some principals of keeping African American teachers "out of the loop" regarding professional activities such as conferences and developmental workshops presents a serious obstacle for these teachers.

The focus groups' view of the relative importance of the various exercises in the overall assessment was quite similar to that of NBPTS. They tended to weight the portfolio exercises as slightly more important and the assessment center exercises as slightly less important than the current NBPTS weights. These differences, however, were small. Moreover, the teachers' evaluations of the two selected small-group-discussion performances were remarkably similar to those of NBPTS assessors. The two candidates were deliberately chosen to reflect "outstanding" examples of classroom practice (a score of 4.13 on the 0.75-to-4.25 scale) and "average" performances (a score of 2.00). The mean scores attributed to the candidates by the focus groups were 3.87 and 1.50, respectively. These evaluations were somewhat below those of the NBPTS assessors but well within the range of scores that might reasonably be expected.

Peer/Principal Nominations for EA/ELA Assessment

Ladson-Billings (1994) and several other researchers have obtained moderate agreement among teachers and principals in schools serving predominantly African American student populations with regard to the identification of these schools' outstanding teachers. One question arises, however: How do teachers viewed as outstanding by their peers and by others who are knowledgeable of their ability perform on the National Board's assessments? The study designed to answer this question was by far the most problematic of all of the Spencer-sponsored studies. Nominations of outstanding EA/ELA African American teachers were solicited from peers, principals, and other knowledgeable professionals. The nominated teachers were then contacted and invited to take the assessment. If they did not already have external support to cover certification costs, the Spencer grant assumed this cost.

Thirty-two such nominations were obtained. All 32 nominated teachers were contacted by mail and invited to apply for certification. Of the 32 teachers contacted, 16 eventually indicated a desire to sit for certification. Of these 16, six later had a change of heart and declined to formally apply, leaving a pool of 10 teachers. Given that approximately 60% to 65% of those who apply for NBPTS certification do not complete the portfolio component of the assessment during the operational year, TAG researchers frequently contacted all 10 teachers to monitor their progress and encourage them to complete the process. Notwithstanding, 3 candidates never returned their portfolios, and 1 candidate completed a portfolio but did not complete the assessment center component.

Despite the high attrition levels noted, the study ended on a hopeful note. Of the 6 candidates who completed the entire assessment process (portfolio and assessment center exercises), 3 easily achieved certification, obtaining total assessment scores well above the minimum score required for certification. Of the 3 who did not achieve certification, 2 obtained scores within 30 points of the 275-point minimum required to achieve that goal, and 1 obtained a score within 50 points of the minimum. The Board has since instituted a policy whereby the exercise scores of candidates who fail to achieve NBPTS certification in one attempt are automatically retained or "banked" for three years. The 3 participants in this study who were not certified have been strongly encouraged to retake those exercises on which they scored below 275.

To be sure, a sample of 6 candidates is small, and it is not known how the 6 who completed the assessment compared with the 26 teachers who were initially nominated. Nevertheless, given the 11% certification rate of all African American candidates thus far, these limited results are extremely encouraging. They suggest that the criteria employed by the African American teachers, principals, and others who nominated the teachers in this study were in large part consonant with the National Board's vision of accomplished practice.

Conclusion

An assessment of teaching ability that is appropriate and valid for the wide variety of teachers and teaching contexts found in the United States presents enormous technical challenges. The continued existence of substantially lower certification rates for African American teachers on NBPTS assessments is one such challenge. The evidence so far, incomplete as it is, suggests that this lower rate is not the result of any discernible biases in the assessment system itself. Rather, adverse impact may well be traceable to more systemic factors in U.S. society at large. Through its major contractor, the Educational Testing Service, as well as its independently contracted researchers, the National Board for Professional Teaching Standards continues a vigorous program of research and development on potential threats to the validity of its teacher assessments. Though they are by no means the last word on the matter, these assessments come closer to the ideal of comprehensiveness, validity, reliability, and fairness than any other system yet devised.

Notes

1. The National Board's 12-point scoring scale is divided into four families. Scores of 1−, 1, and 1+ constitute the score-1 family; scores of 2−, 2, and 2+ constitute the score-2 family; and so on.
2. Although the panelists were instructed to review these performances individually without discussing them with other panelists, this instruction was not always followed.
3. Culturally related markers were not, nor could they be, precisely defined; rather, panelists used a written summary of the previous discussion.

References

Bond, L. (1998). Validity and equity in the assessment of accomplished teaching: Studies of adverse impact and the National Board for Professional Teaching Standards. Paper presented as an invited address (Division D) at the annual meeting of the American Educational Research Association, San Diego, CA.

Carnegie Forum on Education and the Economy. (1986). A nation prepared: Teachers for the 21st century: The report of the Task Force on Teaching as a Profession. Washington, DC: The Forum. Equal Employment Opportunity Commission. (1978). Uniform guidelines on employee selection procedures. *Federal Register,* 43, 38296–38309.

Irvine, J. J., & Fraser, J. W. (1998, May 13). Warm demanders: Do national certification standards leave room for the culturally responsive pedagogy of African-American teachers? *Education Week,* pp. 41-.

Ladson-Billings, G. (1994). The dreamkeepers: Successful teachers of African-American children. San Francisco: Jossey-Bass. National Commission on Excellence in Education. (1983). *A nation at risk: The imperative of educational reform.* Washington, DC: U.S. Government Printing Office.

Shepard, L. A. (1982). Definitions of bias. In R. A. Berk (Ed.), *Handbook of methods for detecting test bias.* Baltimore, MD: The Johns Hopkins University Press.

Teaching in Dangerous Times: Culturally Relevant Approaches to Teacher Assessment

Gloria Ladson–Billings

University of Wisconsin–Madison

New teacher assessment tools claim to provide more authentic evaluation of teacher competency. However, some aspects of these new assessment tools may actually serve to reinscribe a narrow set of teaching practices that fail to serve all children well—particularly children of color and children living in poverty. This article looks at some of the debate surrounding teacher assessment and raises questions about what is missing in so-called "authentic" assessments of teachers.

Introduction

In the popular book, *Dangerous Minds* (initially released as *My Posse Don't Do Homework* in 1992) former-Marine-turned-teacher LouAnne Johnson is credited with turning around the "class from hell"—a group of urban African American and Latino students on the road to failure in school and in life. This book (and subsequent motion picture) was just one more of what Strop (1996) identifies as among the "teacher-as-savior" genre of films—movies that construct an image of teachers, particularly White teachers, as "rescuing" urban students of color from themselves, their families, and their communities (Baker, 1996). Closer examination of these celluloid pedagogies reveals characters who, with missionary-like zeal, struggle to give their otherwise hopeless students hope, raise these students' abysmally low levels of self-esteem, and steer them away from the path of wanton self-destruction.

Unfortunately, most of the teachers in this film genre pay little or no attention to the academic achievement of their students. Thus, while many audiences applaud the Hollywood teacher-images' amazing social work, interpersonal, and cross-cultural communication skills, few real-life educators and/or educational researchers would point to any of these histrionic teachers as exemplary classroom instructors. Nonetheless, what the actors teaching on the silver screen do with students Delpit (1995) dubs "other people's children" is seen as just fine—as long as no one in the real world tries to do the same things with the children whom most of the nation's educators view as "their own."

Given the changing demographics of the student body in the United States and the bifurcation of public school student populations into groups of haves and have-nots, it is important to understand that, rather than confronting dangerous minds, teachers of urban students of color are teaching in dangerous *times*. One of the most urgent issues facing this perilous era and the cadre of teachers who serve in it is that of being able to more accurately measure what students know and are able to do. Much attention has been paid to new forms of student assessment that purportedly do just that

Reprinted by permission from *The Journal of Negro Education* 67, no. 3 (summer 1998).

(Newmann & Associates, 1996). However, communities of color, which historically have raised questions about the potential biases built into traditional test measures, have challenged the purpose and design of many of the new assessments (The College Board, 1985; Educational Testing Service, 1991).

The scrutiny of student assessment has been accompanied by a focus in the educational community at large on teacher assessment (Darling–Hammond, 1988; Wise, Darling–Hammond, & Berry, 1987). Within three years after the publication of the U.S. Commission on Excellence in Education's (1983) *A Nation at Risk* report, two national studies focusing on the need to improve the nation's teaching force emerged: the Holmes Group's (1986) *Teachers for Tomorrow's Schools* and the Carnegie Task Force on Teaching as a Profession's (1986) *A Nation Prepared: Teachers for the 21st Century*. Among the suggestions offered by these bodies in the mid-1980s were: (a) higher standards for admission into the teaching profession, (b) elimination of the undergraduate degree in education, and (c) improved assessment measures for both preservice and inservice teachers. This era also saw the creation of the National Board for Professional Teaching Standards (NBPTS) and the Interstate New Teacher Assessment and Support Consortium (INTASC). These organizations function in the teaching field much like medical boards and bar associations function in medicine and law, respectively. Yet, rather than rely on the old "input" model, in which teacher-worthiness is judged by the kinds of courses teachers have completed, NBPTS and INTASC sought to create more authentic forms of assessment for teachers (Newmann & Associates, 1996). These new assessments target "outputs"—that is, what teachers know and are able to do. However, as Shulman (1989) notes, they also present a dilemma:

> . . . in teaching we face a fundamental paradox, a confusion between what is real and what is proxy. We have turned assessment upside-down in thinking about the relationships between tests and the accomplishments they claim to represent. (p. 13)

This article examines contemporary processes of teacher assessment in the real rather than the celluloid world of make-believe. It also suggests ways that assessment might do a better job of identifying strengths of teachers that can be translated into real classroom practices that meet the needs of real urban students of color, who historically have been underserved by public schooling. It is these students who are increasingly being misrepresented as having "dangerous minds" rather than as living and learning in dangerous times.

Authentic Assessment and the Teacher-Testing Phenomenon

In the mid-1980s the nation seemed fixated with testing its teachers. Whereas California and Oregon began a basic competency testing program for each new teaching credential, some southern states began testing teachers who were already in the classroom. Predictably, these testing measures had an adverse impact on the already shrinking pool of African American teachers (Whitaker, 1989). They also focused attention on a critical question: How is it that teachers who have been awarded college degrees are unable to pass basic competency tests in reading, writing, and mathematics? An even larger question emerged as well: Rather than penalize preservice teachers after graduation, why not penalize teacher education institutions for graduating teacher candidates who are ill-prepared to pass certification tests? Though none would argue that school districts school certify incompetent teachers, those states calling for teachers to be tested, either at the end of their baccalaureate education or after years of teaching experience, typically failed to engage a cyclical or recursive process that held schools and colleges of teacher education responsible for ensuring that their graduates meet minimum standards as a consequence of matriculation.[1]

The problem of teachers not passing competency tests seems inconsequential when compared to the larger issue of what these tests reveal about teachers' ability to teach. For example, given that all California teachers who have received regular (not provisional or emergency) teaching certificates within the past 10 years have passed that state's teacher competency test, could one not argue that all of California's teachers are good teachers? Probably not. What, then, is the purpose of such tests? The most compelling argument is to be found in the tests' political symbolism. Creating tests as screens or barriers to admission seems to appease the public outcry for higher standards, even when those standards have no relationship to performance. The more relevant question thus becomes: How can teachers' ability to teach be tested? More specifically, how equitable and reliable are teacher assessment measures for ensuring that teachers will be effective in classrooms of urban children of color?

Fear of the "Next Best Thing"

Almost 10 years ago, I was among a group of scholars of color who were assembled to consult on a well-funded teacher assessment project. The project—with its use of portfolios, on-site observations, videotapes, and assessment center exercises—was to serve as a prototype for assessing exemplary teachers in a variety of subject areas. Early in our efforts, we raised questions about the invisibility of teachers of color among the pool of teachers rated as exemplary using this new form of assessment. One of our major concerns was that the innovative assessment would be seen as *the* answer to the profession's prayers, and, as a consequence, be more "dangerous" for teachers and students of color than the conventional pencil-and-paper teachers' examinations.

Lest readers think that scholars (and teachers) of color stand at the ready to discount any form of teacher assessment, it is important to relate the potential dangers inherent in reifying new forms of assessment without placing them under a critical gaze. As part of that critical gaze, three aspects of these assessments will be examined to discern the ways in which taken-for-granted notions of authenticity may reproduce inequity. Those aspects are (a) teaching contexts, (b) use of videotaping, and (c) portfolio assessments.

Teaching Contexts

Many of the new teacher assessments presently being used or considered fail to take into consideration the very different contexts in which teachers find themselves. More pointedly, teachers of color are more likely to find themselves in poor, urban school communities than are White teachers. When these teachers walk into their district's, state's, or professional organization's assessment centers for certification testing, the context in which they carry out their teaching may not be given any weight The example of one assessment center activity that I personally critiqued as part of my involvement in the consulting project described above provides a case in point.

In this instance, the videotape prepared and presented to the assessors by an African American teacher who taught in an overcrowded, underfunded urban public school yielded only assessor discussion about how stark and bare her classroom seemed compared to those of other examinees. This teacher did not have an intricate, handmade "spider's web" draped across her classroom as a visible reminder of a reading unit's insect theme, as did the teacher from a suburban district who submitted a video. Nor did the African American teacher have a big comfortable sofa, beanbag chairs, pillows, and a carpeted floor on which her students could gather for reading and informal discussion, as depicted in the videotape of a teacher from a school in a college-town district. Thus, by comparison, the assessors seemed summarily unimpressed with the environment that the Black teacher created for her inner-city students.

In my later conversation with this teacher, I learned that because of overcrowding at her school she did not have a real room for her classes and instead taught out of a makeshift closet. Additionally, the school was on a year-round schedule, which meant that students attended school in nine-week shifts and then were off for two weeks before the next shift began. This meant that every nine weeks she was required to take down everything in her "room" and reassemble it after the break. Nothing in the teacher assessment process was designed to take into consideration teaching under these circumstances. Furthermore, if new assessments continue to discount the inequities already built into schools by virtue of unequal funding and other material resources, they will continue to discount the creative ways some teachers deal with scarcity and push students to higher intellectual heights.

Use of Videotaping

Recent examinations of teaching have made extensive use of videotaping to document teaching performances (Berliner, 1988). Because videotaping gives us the luxury of "seeing" teaching, it has gained increased credibility as a purportedly objective "eye" on the classroom. However, videotaping a classroom also reveals how cameras do, indeed, lie.

At best, a classroom videotape is an artificial representation of teaching. Even unedited videotape of classroom activity reveals but a partial view of the classroom setting and what transpires there. The videocamera can capture only selected slices of classroom life. When the camera lens is focused on the teacher, viewers cannot see how students are reacting and responding to the teaching or interacting with and responding to each other. Conversely, focus on the students cuts viewers off from the teacher's pedagogical moves.

Yet, is this the very teaching really is? Can teachers yell, "Cut!" and re-teach a "scene" each time a student is confused or behaving inappropriately? No. Teaching is more episodic, random, and unpredictable than movies. The dynamic of the classroom creates ups and downs, zigs and zags, that may come across as confused and unfocused through the flat, unforgiving lens of a videocamera.

The use of videotaping in research generally is for the purposes of analysis, interpretation, and/or professional development. Researchers employing this technique often are more concerned with the quality of the teaching and classroom activity segments captured than with the technical quality of the videotape (Ladson–Billings, 1994). However, when the purpose of a classroom videotape is assessment and evaluation, teachers, as vested participants, often choose to "create" a tape that features the best of their teaching. Like feature films, their tapes often bear the marks of careful editing to present the subjects in their best light. Schools and districts with resources and personnel equipped to produce high-quality videotapes can make mediocre teaching appear much better than it really is. Conversely, excellent teachers with limited access to good equipment and videographic skills may be left with poor-quality tapes that fail to illuminate any of the magic that transpires in their classrooms.

Portfolio Assessment

The use of teaching portfolios has been hailed as one of the best ways to assess teaching performance (Bird, 1990). By assembling examples of students' work, teaching plans and units, pedagogical journals, letters, commendations, and other artifacts of teaching, teachers have an opportunity to showcase the best of their teaching practice. Modeled after the professorate practice, in which faculty assemble required and relevant materials for tenure and promotion committee review, portfolio assessment is designed to provide examinees with maximum control over what examiners see. Teachers can select and arrange the specific artifacts they wish to present.

On the surface, this seems a fair and equitable way to assess teaching: allow teachers to show what they believe is their best work and/or the products of that work and judge it. However, the seemingly fair portfolio assessment process also has equity pitfalls. Imagine, for example, a teacher who was prepared at one of the nation's Research 1 institutions. Somewhere during her preparation program, she probably heard about teaching portfolios. Perhaps she was both taught and required to construct a portfolio during her student teaching semester. Because of the careful coaching and mentoring she received during her preservice years, she is capable of constructing a first-rate portfolio by the time she starts teaching. By contrast, her colleague who was prepared at a small, historically Black college did not have the same access to portfolio preparation training. Both are good teachers, but one is more capable of using a portfolio to document her abilities and skills than is the other and subsequently receives a better score on this aspect of the assessment.

Imagine another teacher who did not attend a Research I university teacher preparation program but who landed a teaching position in an affluent well-financed school district. As is true in many such districts, teacher turnover is quite low. Teachers spend their entire careers in this district's schools. With just a few new teachers to be mentored, this district can bring more of its considerable resources to bear on helping those teachers who want (or need) to construct portfolios. Contrast this teacher with another new teacher laboring in an underfunded, poorly staffed district who also wants to participate in portfolio assessment. This latter teacher's district is stretched to its fiscal limits and struggling to keep up with constant personnel changes. It has neither enough resources nor personnel to help one teacher construct a portfolio. Thus, while portfolio assessment seems a theoretically fair way to judge teaching' practice, closer examination reveals potential inequities in its use and availability.

A Culturally Relevant Approach to Teacher Assessment

Educational researchers and scholars of color have long suspected that traditional teacher assessment techniques systematically screen out teachers of color from the teaching field (Grant, 1989; Haberman, 1989). If the proposed new teacher assessment techniques continue in this vein,[2] do alternative assessments need to be formulated? If so, what proficiency or skill areas must these assessments address? My own previous work with teachers who are successful with African American students suggests that considerations of teachers' abilities to engender academic achievement, cultural competence, and sociopolitical consciousness among their students may be a way to rethink teacher performance (Ladson–Billings, 1994, 1995a, 1995b). Additionally, assessments that consider aspects of teachers' culture might prove more equitable for teachers of color.

Student Academic Achievement as a Teacher Assessment Measure

Teaching is hard work. Managing a classroom can be made to seem effortless, but even casual observers come to admire the work entailed in keeping more than 20 students quiet and under control. But is merely managing bodies enough? For what purpose are students in the classroom, anyway? Regardless of the elegance of one's teaching performances, the bottom line in teaching is always how much learning takes place. Do students demonstrate competence in academic areas? Are they able to formulate questions? propose solutions? apply knowledge to new and different situations?

Most portfolio assessments require teachers to supply examples of individual students' work; rarely do they set performance criteria for a teacher's entire class. However, a central focus on helping as many children as possible achieve academically is one of the hallmarks of culturally relevant teaching. Subsequently, assessment of culturally relevant teaching practice would require teachers to show evidence of academic achievement for all their students or to provide educationally defensible explanations for why any students do not meet this criteria (e.g., consistently poor attendance records, high transience rates, identified special needs, nonprovision of special educational services).

One way to determine teachers' ability to enhance students' academic achievement is to collect baseline data on students' knowledge and skills at the beginning of the school year and compare those findings to end-of-year data. Often, students from upper-income, dominant-culture communities come into a classroom knowing much of what teachers purport to teach them. Thus, their typically superior performance on standardized measures is actually an indication of what they already know. By contrast, a teacher who moves a low-income student of color who is two or more levels below grade levels at the beginning of the school year to grade-level performance by year's end is fostering more academic achievement than is a teacher of incoming students who perform above grade level and maintain that same level of performance.

In an earlier study of successful teachers of African American students (Ladson–Billings, 1994), I related the case of a sixth-grade teacher I called Margaret Rossi. According to Ms. Rossi's logic, every student in her class was entitled to the very best she had to offer as a teacher. Because she recognized the gatekeeping function that algebra performs in the school curriculum, Ms. Rossi decided that nothing would prevent her from making sure that her students had access to higher mathematics. She subsequently insisted that her students study algebra. Regardless of their previous mathematics achievement, she pushed, prodded, cajoled, and coached all her students to learn the basic principles of algebra. Students with poor computational skills were allowed to use calculators. Those who had reading difficulties were paired with peer tutors. No student in her class was exempt from studying algebra—not even James, the student whom Ms. Rossi identified as an "allegedly special education" candidate.

I also related the examples of two other teachers I called Ms. Lewis and Ms. Deveraux, who pushed their low-income students of color to excel in literacy. Ms. Lewis used the more "progressive" and modern whole-language approach, which is based on a philosophy of immersing students in good literature as they learn to read for meaning. Ms. Deveraux used the more "traditional" phonetics or skills-based approach because she believed that her students needed to learn the sounds that are associated with letters in order to form and decode words. The debate over which is better—phonetics or whole-language—has become heated in the public and professional discourse on literacy. However, for these two teachers, the only important issue was whether or not their students were actually learning to read. Interestingly, the research lens through which these two teachers' practice was examined revealed that students in both classes became proficient readers. Yet, how might an assessor regard to more traditional, skills-based approach of Ms. Deveraux? Would the fact that she did not employ modern techniques indicate that she was not an exemplary teacher?

Unless a teacher's students are demonstrating academic progress, one cannot contend, with good conscience, that the teacher is exemplary. Indeed, it is not the teaching method or strategy that should be the criteria for good teaching, but rather the academic accomplishments of students. Do students who were previously unable to read demonstrate an ability to read after spending a year in a teacher's classroom? Can students who were not able to compute and solve problems at the beginning of the school term provide evidence that they can do so by the end of it? These students' performances should be the benchmarks upon which we put our confidence in teacher effectiveness, and they do not have to be demonstrated solely on standardized tests. However, effective teachers must be prepared to provide powerful examples of what their students know and can do.

Cultural Competence as a Teacher Assessment Measure

This second area does not lend itself to conventional forms of measurement. Its goal is to ensure that teachers support the home and community cultures of students while helping students become proficient in the cultures of schooling and education. What makes this ability to foster cultural competence among students difficult is the finding that far too many teachers in U.S. schools possess only a surface understanding of culture—their own or anyone else's. As noted in another of my earlier studies (Ladson–Billings, 1996), many middle-class White American teachers fail to associate the notion of culture with themselves. Instead, they believe that they are "just regular Americans" while people of color are the ones "with culture." This notion of regularity serves a normalizing function that positions those who are "not regular" as "others." Not recognizing that they too are cultural beings prevents these teachers from ever questioning taken-for-granted assumptions about the nature of human thought, activity, and existence.

Culturally relevant teachers know when to introduce relevant examples from their students' backgrounds and experiences to make learning more meaningful. For example, when the African American students in Ms. Deveraux's class indicated that the only females who could be princesses were White, blond-haired, and blue-eyed, she quickly brought out a copy of John Steptoe's (1987) *Mufaro's Beautiful Daughters* for them to read. This lavishly illustrated children's book, with its richly detailed story of African royalty and traditions, provided her students with the necessary counter-knowledge to challenge their misguided notions about nobility and people of African descent.

The goal of fostering cultural competence requires teachers to help raise students' awareness of prejudice and discrimination as well as their ability to react to and constructively cope with these negative social realities. For example, before Ms. Lewis took her inner-city African American students on a camping trip, she talked candidly with them about the fact that they would be coming in contact with White students and counselors. She encouraged them to think proactively about what they might do if any White person exhibited insensitive or racist attitudes toward them. Fostering cultural competence also requires teachers to support students' home language/dialect while simultaneously teaching them Standard English. That is, rather than chastise students for using the language/dialect they use when speaking with family and friends and in their communities, effective teachers help students understand when and where code-switching, or alternating the use of Standard English and home language/dialect in formal and informal settings, is preferable or necessary.

Unfortunately, nothing in the current teacher assessment battery addresses how well teachers' foster cultural competence within their students. Perhaps this is because few test constructors have ever considered the importance of cultural competence for students, nor would they even recognize it when it is being demonstrated by teachers.

One assessment of cultural competence that came to my personal attention involved in art teacher who taught in a predominantly African American high school.[3] The classroom video submitted by this teacher depicted a demonstration lecture by a cosmetologist whom the teacher had invited to her class to discuss the intricate hair braiding done by Black African women as an art form. The assessors rated this teacher's submission poorly, claiming that cosmetology belonged in vocational education, not art. Their lack of understanding about the relationship between hair and art in African societies kept them from accepting a broader notion of the relevance of this demonstration.

Sociopolitical Consciousness as a Teacher Assessment Measure

In addition to ensuring that students achieve academically and are culturally competent, culturally relevant teachers develop a sociopolitical consciousness in their students. The use of this term, "sociopolitical consciousness," is important, lest readers come to equate it with the more simplistic, almost vacuous term, "critical thinking." Whereas there certainly is nothing wrong with critical thinking per se, what often masquerades as critical thinking in most classrooms is a set of prescriptive steps and practices that may reflect important processes but that are attached to relatively inane content. For instance, students might be asked to imagine that they are legislators who must decide whether or not to provide aid to a country that is deforesting its rainforest. Although this is a serious ecological issue, how can students come to think critically about it given only vicarious knowledge?

A different kind of critical thinking—what I term sociopolitical consciousness or an activist civic and social awareness—is demonstrated by Tate (1995) in his focus on a teacher he calls Sandra Mason. According to Tate, Ms. Mason's middle school mathematics students came to class upset each morning because their route to school was impeded by indigent panhandlers who aggressively approached them for money to purchase cheap liquor from one of the many liquor stores near the school. Instead of ignoring the students' concerns, Ms. Mason decided to incorporate the problem of negotiating around these alcohol-dependent throngs into a classroom lesson. Her students examined city zoning ordinances and learned that their city was divided into "wet" and "dry" zones that determined where alcoholic beverages could be sold. The schools that served poor communities of color were located in wet zones. The students calculated the amount of money that was being generated by the liquor stores in the school neighborhood (and lost to the community since most of the store owners lived elsewhere), and they developed an action plan for rethinking zoning in the city. This involvement with real problems raised the students' sociopolitical consciousness and made mathematics a more meaningful activity for the students. It also made teaching more challenging for Ms. Mason, but it enabled her to help her students understand that what happened in school had relevance for their everyday lives.

How should teachers' abilities to develop students' sociopolitical consciousness be assessed? Certainly, this is a more complex skill than can be exhibited on a pencil-and-paper test. Yet, if we say that students must exhibit this trait; then teachers have to demonstrate their ability to teach in ways that support that kind of learning.

Who Can Handle *Whose* Business?

If assessment practices both powerful and subtle enough to evaluate the aspects mentioned above—academic achievement, cultural competence, and sociopolitical consciousness—could somehow be devised, who would carry them out? This is not a trivial question, nor is it a trivial matter. The complexities of the new types of assessments required will demand assessors who are capable of cultural translations of pedagogical expertise. These assessors will have to be able to answer several questions such as the following:

- When is direct instruction the right methodology to use?
- How does one determine the difference between a teacher who is unduly harsh or one who is, as Kleinfeld (1975) maintains, warmly demanding?
- What difference does it make if teachers slip in and out of students' home language to make a point to their students?
- Can all assessors determine the pedagogical significance of teachers' culturally specific behaviors?

Current practices for assessing exemplary teachers rely on scoring rubrics. Assessors are trained in the use of these rubrics by reviewing single examples of exemplary, good, average, and sub-par teaching practices. This method of assessment has proved devastating for teachers of color. The assessors themselves often are not necessarily exemplary teachers; typically, they are merely teachers who have been trained in the use of the scoring rubrics. Thus, their abilities to make accurate judgments and more complex interpretations of teaching practice are not confirmed.

For the sake of example, consider three high-profile teachers of students of color. Marva Collins, Jaime Escalante, and Kay Tolliver. Both Collins and Escalante have had their pedagogical excellence profiled in feature-length films (Dave Bell Associates, 1981; Levin, 1981; Musca & Menendez, 1988). Tolliver has been the subject of a series of educational films aired on Public Broadcast System stations (Heard & Mikuriya, 1993, 1995–98; Hendry & Mikuriya, 1995–98, 1996). Neither Collins nor Escalante demonstrate the innovative and student-centered approaches embedded in the new standards initiatives such as those developed by NBPTS or INTASC, yet both are exemplary teachers. Collins, for example, early performed her teaching miracles in the attic of her home, where she started the Westside Preparatory School (Collins & Tamarkin, 1982). Although her emphasis on the traditional European literary canon as the center of the curriculum is somewhat questionable, she clearly exemplifies the tenets of culturally relevant teaching—that is, an emphasis on academic achievement, cultural competence, and sociopolitical consciousness. Whether or not one agrees or disagrees with her teaching style, it is difficult to quarrel with her results. The same can be said of Escalante. Thus, assessors must set aside any preferences they or the standards might indicate for teachers' use of diverse curriculum content in order to recognize, not as limitations but as strengths, the ways that these teachers propel students to achieve academically, enhance students' awareness of their cultural heritage and their ability to challenge prejudice and discrimination, and empower students to address societal inequities.[4]

On the other hand, Kay Tolliver's teaching style is very much in line with innovative teaching standards. Her mathematics classes involve lots of student investigation, cooperative and collaborative learning, and close tie-ins between home knowledge and school knowledge. Nonetheless, an assessor would have to guard against the seductions of style and ask questions about the impact of Tolliver's teaching on her students' academic achievement, cultural competence, and sociopolitical consciousness. In Tolliver's case, she does attend to these issues. However, Delpit (1995) has documented instances in which teachers have done exactly what the "experts" suggest and still failed to be effective with students of color. Some teachers have engaged their students of color in process writing and invented spelling techniques, reading with trade books, open classrooms, and student-initiated projects—all of which have had impressive track records with White middle-class students—yet these methods, sometimes improperly understood and implemented, have failed to raise student achievement.

And what happens to those teachers of color who lack the flair and panache of Collins, Escalante, or Tolliver? What assessment method recognizes the effectiveness of a teacher of color who labors long and hard, without recognition or support, to produce academic excellence, cultural competence, and sociopolitical consciousness in students of color? What are the chances that these "garden-variety" teachers of color can walk into an assessment center and have their practice accurately judged? How should their practice be assessed? What do culturally relevant assessments for teachers look like?

Assessment measures that value and reward culturally relevant teaching have not yet been constructed. The most sophisticated teaching tasks, documentation, and scoring rubrics developed to date have not even begun to capture the complexities of such teaching. There are, however, a few promising practices that may allow for a fundamental rethinking of what it means to assess culturally relevant teaching. These include considerations and demonstrations of situated pedagogies, teaching cases, and reflective practice. A brief description of each follows.

Rethinking Teacher Assessment

Situated Pedagogies

What form must teacher assessment take to consider the situated nature of teaching? This is one question that must be addressed in the development of culturally relevant teacher assessments. Ellsworth and Lather (1996) have argued the importance of understanding the situatedness of pedagogy as something that does not occur in a vacuum. They maintain that the situations in which teachers (and students) find themselves define the pedagogical possibilities. For example, teaching the fiction of Mark Twain to 8th graders is not the same as teaching it to 11th graders or college sophomores or graduate students. Alternately, what counts as excellence in an urban setting may be markedly different from what is regarded as excellence in a suburban setting. That is, the teacher who exhibits exemplary practices in an affluent suburban community may be a miserable failure in a poor urban community. Even what is thought of as the "same" setting can vary from year to year and class to class; for example, a teacher's first-period class can be quite different from her sixth-period class. Moreover, policies that promote tracking and ability grouping can make one teacher seem to be teaching in two (or more) different schools.

Teaching Cases

Shulman (1991) has explored the use of teaching cases for professional development. She suggests that teachers can develop more powerful ways to analyze and improve their practice when they are asked to detail the dilemmas they face in the classroom and to think critically about those dilemmas. Her work has been used to guide the practice of intern teachers, mentor teachers, and teachers working in diverse classroom settings. Shulman further asserts that case methodology provides a way to codify the knowledge base of teaching.

As an assessment tool, developing and analyzing teaching cases might serve to unpack some of the nested and complex aspects of teaching. For example, consider an assessment task in which teachers are presented with teaching cases that address particular subject areas, student characteristics, or teaching strategies. As part of such an assessment, teachers might be asked to make judgments about the quality of the decisions made by the teacher in each case and to offer suggestions for improvement. How teachers understand and describe aspects of a case may provide some insights into how they think about their own practice. The critical aspect of developing such assessment tasks rests in the ability to create well-written, complex cases that lend themselves to multiple interpretations. Here again, the scoring rubrics will have to be sufficiently rich and flexible to handle the variety of way examinees might interpret the cases.

Reflective Practice

Liston and Zeichner (1987) began focusing on reflective teaching because their research on elementary teacher education candidates indicated that their student–teachers were technically proficient but demonstrated little concern for or understanding about why they were doing what they were doing or to what end. Liston and Zeichner's work distinguishes itself from the more instrumental approaches to teacher reflection, in which teachers merely think about how to do what they already know how to do and want to do. It also differs from practical approaches to reflection, wherein teachers deliberate about the means and purposes of their practices. Instead, their work focuses on critical reflection that engages the ethical and moral dimensions of teaching.

Another example of reflective practice is exemplified in the work of Gomez and Tabachnick (1992), who believe that through "telling teaching stories" (p. 129), preservice teachers can be prompted to reflect in the critical ways outlined by Liston and Zeichner. Their work involved asking preservice teachers to bring stories of their experiences with diverse types of learners to class or examination and re-examination from multiple vantage points. Their technique required these teachers-to-be to probe deeply into teaching situations in an attempt to make sense of classroom problems and predicaments. Rather than neatly wrapping up the problem situation at the end of their class, Gomez and Tabachnick encourage the prospective teachers to "live with" their stories and revisit them throughout the school term (p. 132). Often, these teacher–candidates would arrive at the end of the semester with powerful new insights on a teaching story or incident that was presented earlier. Similarly, a culturally relevant teacher assessment could engage teachers in reflection about the ethical and sociocultural nature of their work. Accordingly, teachers should be able to articulate their dilemmas, successes, and failures to support their professional development in working with students of color.

Concluding Thoughts

What do we know about teacher assessment? How is it that African American teachers so regularly and predictably fail current assessments, yet the presence of White teachers is no assurance that African American or other students of color will achieve? What is the nature of the technical problems related to designing culturally relevant teacher assessments? Can teacher assessment be considered without a concomitant look at student assessment? In other words, can failing students have successful teachers? These questions are important because more states and local school districts are looking at new ways to assess both preservice and inservice teachers. What these assessments will look like, what opportunities teachers will have for demonstrating teaching competence, and how these assessments will include or exclude potential teacher candidates need careful and critical examination.

The work of teaching is both complicated and complex. How we educators come to understand it has implications for how we assess it. If we construct teaching as a set of technical tasks, then we will devise assessments designed to score these tasks. However, if we understand teaching as a highly complex endeavor undertaken by professionals, then we are compelled to develop assessments that are highly sophisticated and nuanced. Regardless of how we construct teaching as a profession, the challenge of ensuring high-quality performances from teachers and students remains. Without improvement in both, we will continue to live in dangerous times.

Notes

1. It should be noted that some historically Black colleges and universities (HBCUs) have initiated programs that provide additional training for graduates from their education schools and departments who fail to pass state or national teacher assessments (Eleanor Jenkins, faculty member at Florida A&M University, personal communication, June 1992).
2. For example, during a recent round of NBPTS testing, *no* candidates of color passed the Early Adolescence/English Language Arts Assessment (Ladson–Billings, personal communication with NBPTS staff, June 1997).
3. The author is not at liberty to disclose the exact source of this information; however, she has firsthand knowledge that the report of this incident is accurate.
4. I would be less than honest if I did not confess having some reservations about the teaching styles of both Collins and Escalante. However, I have no doubt that almost every student who is taught by either of them benefits greatly.

References

Baker, B. (1996). *A history of the present: Teacher as rescuer and the child study movement*. Unpublished doctoral dissertation, University of Wisconsin–Madison.

Berliner, D. (1988). Implications of studies of expertise in pedagogy for teacher education and evaluation. In Educational Testing Service (Ed.), *New directions for teacher assessment* (Invitational Conference Proceedings; pp. 39–67). Princeton, NJ: Educational Testing Service.

Bird, T. (1990). The schoolteacher's portfolio. In L. Darling–Hammond & J. Millman (Eds.), *Handbook on the evaluation of elementary and secondary school teachers* (pp. 241–256). Newbury Park, CA: Sage.

Carnegie Task Force on Teaching as a Profession. (1986). *A nation prepared: Teachers for the 21st century*. New York: Author.

The College Board. (1985). *Equality and excellence: The educational status of Black Americans*. New York: College Entrance Examination Board.

Collins, M., & Tamarkin, C. (1982). *Marva Collins' way*. Los Angeles: J. P. Tarcher.

Darling–Hammond, L. (1982). Teacher quality and educational equality. *The College Board Review, 148*, 16–23, 39–41.

Dave Bell Associates (Producers). (1981). *Success! The Marva Collins approach* [Film]. Hollywood, CA: Media Five.

Delpit, L. (1995). *Other people's children*. New York: The Free Press.

Educational Testing Service. (1991). *The state of inequality*. Princeton, NJ: Author.

Ellsworth, E., & Lather, P. (Eds.). (1996). Special Issue on "Situated Pedagogies." *Theory Into Practice, 35*.

Gomez, M. L., & Tabachnick, B. R. (1992). Telling teaching stories. *Teaching Education, 4*, 129–138.

Grant, C. A. (1989). Urban teachers: Their new colleagues and curricula. *Phi Delta Kappan, 70*, 764–770.

Haberman, M. (1989). More minority teachers. *Phi Delta Kappan, 70*, 771–776.

Heard, S. R. (Producer), & Mikuriya, R. (Director). (1993). *Good morning, Ms. Tolliver* [Video-documentary]. Los Angeles: FASE Productions.

Heard, S. R. (Producer), & Mikuriya, R. (Director). (1995–1998). *The Eddie files* (Videodocumentary series]. Los Angeles: FASE Productions.

Hendry, D. (Producer), & Mikuriya, R. (Director). (1995–1998). *The Kay Tolliver files* [Videodocumentary series]. Los Angeles: FASE Productions.

Hendry, D. (Producer), & Mikuriya, R. (Director). (1996). *Teacher talk* [Videodocumentary series]. Los Angeles: FASE Productions.

The Holmes Group. (1986). *Teachers for tomorrow's schools*. East Lansing, MI: Author.

Johnson, L. (1992). *Dangerous minds*. New York: St Martin's Press.

Kleinfeld, J. (1975). Effective teachers of Eskimo and Indian students. *School Review, 83*, 301–344.

Ladson–Billings, G. (1994). *The dreamkeepers: Successful teachers of African American children*. San Francisco: Jossey–Bass.

Ladson–Billings, G. (1995a). Toward a theory of culturally relevant pedagogy. *American Educational Research Journal, 35*, 465–491.

Ladson–Billings, G. (1995b). But that's just good teaching! The case for culturally relevant pedagogy. *Theory Into Practice, 34*, 159–165.

Ladson–Billings, G. (1996). Your blues ain't like mine: Keeping issues of race and racism on the multicultural agenda. *Theory Into Practice, 34*, 248–255.

Levin, P. (1981). *The Marva Collins' story* [Film]. Los Angeles: Warner Brothers.

Liston, D., & Zeichner, K. (1987). Reflective teacher education and moral deliberation. *Journal of Teacher Education, 38*, 2–8.

Musca, T. (Producer), & Menendez, R. (Director). (1988). *Stand and deliver* [Film]. Los Angeles: Warner Brothers.

Newmann, F., & Associates. (Eds.). (1996). *Authentic achievement: Restructuring schools for intellectual quality*. San Francisco: Jossey–Bass.

Shulman, L. (1989). The paradox of teacher assessment. In Educational Testing Service (Ed.), *New directions for teacher assessment* (Invitational Conference Proceedings; pp. 13–27). Princeton, NJ: Educational Testing Service.

Shulman, L. (1991). Revealing the mysteries of teacher-written cases: Opening the black box. *Journal of Teacher Education, 42*, 250–262.

Simpson, D., & Bruckhiemer, J. (Producers), & Smith, J. N. (Director). (1997). *Dangerous minds* [Film]. Los Angeles: Hollywood Pictures.

Steptoe, J. (1987). *Mufaro's beautiful daughters: An African tale*. New York: Lothrop, Lee & Shepard.

Strop, J. (1996). *Teacher as savior. Film representations of teachers*. Unpublished manuscript, University of Wisconsin–Madison.

Tate, W. F. (1995). Returning to the root: A culturally relevant approach to mathematics pedagogy. *Theory Into Practice, 34*, 166–173.

Whitaker, L. (1989, January). The disappearing Black teacher. *Ebony*, pp. 122, 126.

Wise, A. E., Darling–Hammond, L., & Berry, B. (1987). *Effective teacher selection: From recruitment to retention*. Santa Monica, CA: The Rand Corporation.

Pushed to the Margins

Sources of Stress for African American College and University Faculty

Carolyn J. Thompson and Eric L. Dey

Introduction

> Learning early on that good grades were rewarded while independent thinking was regarded with suspicion, I knew that it was important to be "smart" but not "too smart." . . . to ask too many questions, to talk about ideas that differed from the prevailing community world view, to say things grown Black folks relegated to the realm of the unspeakable was to invite punishment and even abuse. (bell hooks, 1996, p. 361)

The role of faculty as scholar is one of asking questions, investigating issues, and discussing and challenging world views. That role is intensified for African American faculty, because the prevailing community world views of the academy itself are frequently challenged by African Americans' presence in it. Cornel West (1993) contends that what is required for African American faculty to secure their career in academia is that they imitate dominant paradigms using African American subject matter. Depending on their degree of incongruence with the dominant paradigm, African American faculty experiences are frequently demoralizing as well as stifling to their intellectual creativity.

West (1993) further asserts that to become a Black intellectual is a choice that results in self-imposed marginality, disconnecting the individual from the larger African American community while not providing full membership in the larger academic community. Heightening this marginality for many scholars is the workplace, where the cultures of predominantly white colleges and universities are both white-normed and white-dominated, challenging the experiences of faculty from underrepresented groups to be qualitatively different and disconnected from those of the dominant culture (Harvey, 1996). Marginality is often experienced by African American faculty in their disciplines based on their scholarly agenda; in their departments based on their teaching agenda; in the larger college community based on an institution-preferred agenda; and in the African American community based on an agenda that is misunderstood and frequently benefits few. Moreover, seldom are African American faculty able to avoid what Finkelstein (1984) refers to as the stress of being a token. Former Harvard law professor, Derrick Bell (1994) refers to the role of successful African Americans as a "tightrope act," where the role of race in both successes or failures cannot be denied. Bell elaborates that with success often comes the dilemma of maintaining ethical bearings, sometimes seen as "employment and self-hatred [on one side], on the other, the equally dubious honor of unemployment with integrity" (Bell, 1994, p. 159).[1] Thus, balancing the demands of academic life and the multi-marginality of being underrepresented by race, scholarly agenda, and the larger academic and social communities becomes a common experience of African American faculty. The stress related to performing and succeeding in academe, given this multi-marginality, is not always anticipated or understood by the individual, especially in view of the purported desired diversity of colleges and universities today. Marginality is often neither observable nor acknowledged by others within the academy. This article examines issues of stress among African American faculty at predominantly white colleges and universities and further explores the role of stress among male and female faculty.

There is a good deal of research on occupational stress. Much of it uses a definition similar in orientation to one proposed by McGrath, which describes the conditions under which stress is likely to occur, conditions where an individual perceives that her or his capabilities and resources for adequately responding to a demand are threatened and where there is uncertainty about the outcomes from meeting these demands (McGrath, 1976). The competing workload agendas of most college and university faculty often intensify these stress-producing conditions.

Researchers have given attention to stress among college and university faculty, but with limited attention to the dimensions of stress. Dey's (1994) research expands on previous faculty stress research (Finkelstein, 1984; Gmelch, Lovrich, & Wilke, 1984) by including "off-campus" sources of stress (e.g., family obligations) which can be substantial for faculty but have previously not been given much attention. Even less attention has been devoted to understanding stress among faculty from underrepresented populations—African Americans, Asian Americans, Latinos, and Native Americans. In earlier work on faculty stress, differences have been noted between women and men faculty (Dey, 1994; Smith, 1995), underrepresented and white male faculty (Dey, 1994), and more specifically, white and African American faculty (Smith & Witt, 1996). The results of this research suggest a need for further investigation and greater understanding of stress among populations that since their recent inclusion in the academy have been marginal. Because of the marginality experienced by all underrepresented groups (Harvey, 1996), including women, research needs to focus on each individual population as a way of understanding the relationship of their work condition to their marginality. The present study builds and expands on previous research by focusing on one underrepresented population—African American faculty. It is not a comparative study, because evidence of-similarities will not increase our understanding of the marginality of the population. There are presently no models to guide the examination of stress, or other conditions, in relation to marginality; however, the intent here is to begin to understand the experiences and conditions of African American faculty in predominantly white institutions as a way of understanding how to promote their retention within the profession as well as the attractiveness of faculty careers to African Americans.

African Americans, Asian Americans, Latinos, and Native Americans constitute between 20 and 25% of the U.S. population, yet fewer than 10% of the academic positions are held by members of these groups. A survey of the professoriate by Astin, Korn, and Dey (1991) suggests a decline in the number of faculty from these populations during the decade of the 1980s. Whereas surveys of faculty conducted between 1973 and 1980 evidenced an increase from 6.2% to 9.1% (Bowen & Schuster, 1986), in 1990, only 8.9% of faculty in universities and four-year and two-year colleges were from underrepresented groups. Thus, recent recruitment efforts have not been able to substantially address the retention or degree of underrepresentation these populations experience in their roles as faculty in U.S. colleges and universities.

Among the critical points in the educational structure, recruitment and hiring and promotion and tenure have been identified as targets for increasing the availability of underrepresented faculty, including women (Blackwell, 1988). Studying occupational stress among African American faculty in predominantly white institutions is a way to begin to understand the work conditions that affect their decisions to stay in or leave academe. Until we are able to understand better the specific experiences of African American and other underrepresented faculty and develop corresponding programs and policies to increase the attractiveness of these careers, it seems likely that colleges and universities will continue to have limited success achieving and sustaining diversity among their faculties.

This research seeks to help fill this void. Specifically, it attempts to address directly several limitations in the existing faculty stress research by first providing a clearer picture of the experiences of one underrepresented population—African American faculty. Secondly, institutional differences will be considered so that sources of stress for African American faculty win be examined at universities, four-year, and two-year colleges. Each of these institutional contexts provides a different faculty experience, and we will delineate these differences. Finally, this study will consider the possibility of gender differences in the faculty experience. Previous research has shown gender to have strong implications for faculty stress (Dey, 1994; Smith, 1995), and we hope to provide a better understanding of the multi-marginality of African American women in the academy.

Data Set

Data used in this study are from a national survey of college faculty and administrators conducted by the Higher Education Research Institute (HERI) at UCLA in the fall and winter of 1992 (Dey, Ramirez, Korn, & Astin, 1993). The questionnaire is based largely on the instrument used in the 1989 faculty survey (see Astin, Korn, & Dey, 1991), which was designed in conjunction with a national study of the outcomes of general education programs funded by the Exxon Education Foundation. The revised 1992 instrument is based on results of the 1989 survey, suggestions from faculty respondents, as well as suggestions from the HERI advisory board and researchers who are actively involved in studying faculty issues. In addition to demographic and biographic information, the revised questionnaire content focuses heavily on issues such as how faculty members spend their time, how they interact with students, which methods of teaching and examining students they prefer, how they perceive the institutional climate, and what their primary sources of stress and satisfaction are. The instrument also allows participating institutions to focus on faculty issues specific to their institution.

Institutional sampling. Letters of invitation to participate in the survey were sent to the chief academic and institutional research officers at nearly 2,600 institutions nationwide. Of the total population of invited institutions, 344 institutions agreed to administer the survey. Of these 344 institutions, 55 were dropped from the national data base because of low response rates, leaving 289 institutions. A careful examination of the characteristics of the participating institutions reveals that every major type of institution is well represented (Dey, Ramirez, Korn, & Astin, 1993).

Survey response. The rate of response to the survey was high, exceeding the response rate in the 1989 survey. Of the 72,417 questionnaires mailed out, 43,940 usable returns were eventually received, constituting a 61% response, which compares favorably to the 55% response rate achieved in the 1989 faculty survey (see Astin, Korn, & Dey, 1991). Factors contributing to the higher response rate were (1) the questionnaire format—it contained nearly 200 questions, yet was limited to four pages and required a minimal reading coupled with a maximum amount of responding; (2) its appeal to faculty—questions addressed a wide range of issues of concern to faculty and their institution, and respondents were told that their institution would receive a profile of faculty responses to each item; and (3) follow-up—a second wave of questionnaires was sent to nonrespondents approximately four weeks after the first wave had been sent.

Sample

The sample available for these analyses are all African American respondents, for whom the sample selection was based on two additional criteria: They must have indicated on the survey that their primary responsibility was teaching (rather than administration), and they had to be presently employed in predominantly white institutions. We were left with responses from 796 faculty. Although this number is small in comparison to the overall sample, it should prove adequate for the goals of this study.

Limitations of the Study

Several limitations are evident in this study. First, the questionnaire was not specifically designed to study occupational stress or marginality. As such, some conditions that have been linked to stress, such as psychological hardiness (Rush, 1995), career burnout (Dillon & Tanner, 1995), and work politics (Dua, 1994); as well as to marginality and stress, such as social class—based on class while growing up (Zweigenhaft & Dumhoff, 1991)—are not among the constructs available to include in our study. Second, although the data are generally representative of the national population of faculty, the African American sample available for and once refined for this study is quite small. In addition, because the specific response rate for African Americans is not known, we may not be dealing with a representative sample of African American faculty. Consequently, caution must be taken when generalizing the findings. However, we think that the strength of understanding stress among this population far outweighs the weaknesses when we consider how little attention African American faculty issues have been given in the literature.

Method

Analysis

Faculty stress was assessed using the responses to 18 items developed by the researchers at HERI that were designed to capture a variety of potential sources of stress, plus a single item designed to capture a faculty member's level of stress overall. Although empirical data are not available to test the degree to which these self-reported sources of stress relate to those captured by other instruments, many items are similar in content, and all are similar in design to those used in previous survey-based studies of faculty stress (such as the Faculty Stress Index used in Gmelch, Lovrich, & Wilke, 1984). Self-report measures of stress can be criticized on the grounds that they may be subject to distortions related to social desirability, denial, or rationalization. In response to this critique, Derogatis (1982) conducted a thorough review of the subject and concluded that the strengths of self-report stress assessments typically outweigh their weaknesses. Moreover, relatively objective measures of stress based on medical measurements or clinical evaluations are well beyond the scope of these analyses and would appear impossible to implement in the large-scale, multi-institutional sample used as the basis of this study.

In order to understand more clearly specific areas of stress represented in the 18 stress items, we performed a series of factor analyses. Our first objective was to determine whether there were different dimensions of stress for male and female faculty (and to a lesser extent for faculty in different types of institutions). A series of preliminary, confirmatory factor analyses based on previous work in this area (Dey, 1994) evidenced only minor differences across these groups, and the need to conduct separate confirmatory analyses was unnecessary. The results suggest that, as a group, African American male and female faculty are more alike than different in terms of the dimensions of stress they experience.

Similar procedures were employed and results obtained as in Dey's (1994) earlier work. A series of factor analyses were performed on the 18 stress items that were included on the questionnaire. These items asked faculty to rate the extent to which the areas had been a source of stress within the past two years. The items were rated on a 3-point scale: not at all, somewhat, or extensive. After computing a number of different factor solutions, we determined that several items had extremely low factor commonalities ($h^2 < 0.10$) and should be dropped. A second series of Exploratory Factor Analyses (using the maximum likelihood method for extraction with oblique rotations, because we assumed the underlying stress constructs to be correlated) were conducted using the 14 remaining variables. As in Dey's previous work, it was apparent that the solution that yielded the most interpretable results had four factors. The items loading upon each of these factors could be logically supported and were consistent in their direction of loading. Because of the similarity of the stress factors previously identified among college faculty in general, we labeled these factors time constraints, home responsibilities, governance activities, and promotion concerns.

Variables identified and used in the four stress factors are as follow: (1) *time constraints* includes lack of personal time, time pressures, and teaching load; (2) *home responsibilities* includes household responsibilities, child care, children's problems, and marital friction; (3) *governance activities* includes faculty meetings, committee work, and consulting with colleagues; and (4) *promotion concerns* includes the review and promotion process, research and publishing demands, and subtle discrimination (which includes sensing prejudice, racism, and sexism).

Finally, we regressed each of the 5 dependent variables upon a set of 41 independent variables that were chosen to represent activities and experiences within the institution as well as institutional type—universities, four-year colleges, and private institutions (a dichotomous variable indicating employment at a two-year college was omitted from the regression analyses as the referent category).

Results

To understand the differences in African American male and female faculty in different institutional types, bivariate relationships between the stress constructs and the faculty groups were explored. We examined the data looking at female and male faculty in three types of institutions—universities, four-year colleges, and two-year colleges—resulting in six groups. The data in Table 1 present results of extensive sources of stress for faculty experienced within the past two years. The most common sources of stress are experienced in the areas of time constraints, promotion concerns, and overall stress; less stress is reported by all faculty in the areas of governance activities and home responsibilities. Women faculty in universities as well as four-year colleges experience greater levels of stress than men in all areas, but significantly more in the two most common areas, time constraints and promotion concerns. Moreover, regardless of the type of institution, women experience significantly more overall stress than their male counterparts. This gender difference is consistent with previous research reported by Smith (1995).

A one-way analysis of variance comparing the 6 groups of African American faculty showed significant differences across the groups for overall stress level, time constraints, and promotion concerns. A post-hoc Scheffe test was computed for these three variables to determine which of the subgroups were significantly different from the others ($p < 0.05$). For the overall stress item, men at two-year colleges were significantly different than both men and women faculty at universities and women at four-year colleges. In addition, men at four-year colleges differed significantly from women at four-year colleges and women at universities. For the time constraints factor, men at two-year and four-year colleges differed significantly from women at both four-year colleges and universities. Women at universities and two-year colleges differed significantly in their responses to this item. In terms of promotion concerns, women at two-year colleges were the least likely to report stress in this area, their stress level was significantly lower than that of their women counterparts at four-year colleges and universities.

We further explored institutional differences by looking at the combined male and female faculty samples in each of the three types of institutions. The results, presented in Table 2, show that for the three most common sources of stress—time constraints, promotion concerns, and overall stress—university faculty experience the greatest amount, whereas those in two-year colleges experience the least. A one-way analysis of variance revealed significant institutional differences in these three critical areas; overall stress ($F = 10.79$, $df\ 2/766$, $p < 0.01$), promotion concerns ($F = 10.66$, $df\ 2/793$, $p < 0.01$), and time constraints ($F = 4.62$, $df\ 2/793$, $p < 0.05$). If, as

TABLE 1
Differences Across Stress Measures by Institutional Type and Gender

		Institutional Type					
	African American	*University*		*Four-Year College*		*Two-Year College*	
Stress Measure	*Faculty*	*Men*	*Women*	*Men*	*Women*	*Men*	*Women*
Time constraints	5.13	5.01	6.21	4.49	5.88	4.43	4.72
Home responsibilities	2.57	2.26	2.56	2.62	2.82	2.37	2.43
Governance activities	3.09	2.79	2.98	2.97	3.28	3.49	3.34
Promotion concerns	4.47	4.52	5.03	4.29	4.89	3.95	3.52
Overall stress level	2.31	2.28	2.52	2.23	2.48	1.93	2.19
N	796	126	87	251	200	63	69

Note: Time constraints, home responsibilities, governance activities, and promotion concerns are factorially derived scales that were first standardized and then rescaled to range from 0 to 10. Reliabilities for these four constructs are time constraints = 0.71, home responsibilities = 0.68, governance activities = 0.64, and promotion concerns = 0.54. Overall stress level in past two years is measured using a 3-point self-report scale, where 1 = little or none and 3 = extreme.

TABLE 2
Analysis of Variance: Stress by Institutional Type

	Institutional Type									
	All		*University*		*Four-Year College*		*Two-Year College*			
Stress Measure	*Mean*	*SD*	*Mean*	*SD*	*Mean*	*SD*	*Mean*	*SD*	*F*	*sig.*
Time constraints	5.12	(2.74)	5.50	(2.66)	5.10	(2.79)	4.58	(2.61)	4.62*	0.0101
Home responsibilities	2.57	(2.23)	2.38	(2.13)	2.70	(2.28)	2.40	(2.17)	1.96	0.1412
Governance activities	3.09	(2.20)	2.86	(2.15)	3.10	(2.18)	3.41	(2.31)	2.57	0.0768
Promotion concerns	4.46	(2.09)	4.72	(2.10)	4.55	(2.08)	3.72	(1.95)	10.66**	0.0000
Overall stress level	2.30	(0.65)	2.37	(0.63)	2.34	(0.64)	2.06	(0.66)	10.79**	0.0000
N	796		213		451		132			

Notes: Time constraints, home responsibilities, governance activities, and promotion concerns are factorially derived scales that were first standardized and then rescaled to range from 0 to 10. Reliabilities for these four constructs are time constraints = 0.71, home responsibilities = 0.68, governance activities = 0.64, and promotion concerns = 0.54. Overall stress level in past two years is measured using a three-point self-report scale, where 1 = little or none and 3 = extreme.
*$p < 0.05$. **$p < 0.01$.

Blackwell (1988) points out, the promotion and tenure process should be a target area for increasing underrepresented faculty (including women), then greater attention needs to be given to mentoring African Americans for faculty roles in four-year college and university settings. This is especially critical for African American women, given the observed inadequacy of graduate level mentoring for them (Turner & Thompson, 1993), and given that the institutional differences in these analyses appear to be driven by the more apparent gender differences.

Researchers have argued that some stress is positive and is related to areas of job satisfaction (Olsen, Maple, & Stage, 1995). An examination was made to determine whether any relationship exists between the 5 stress constructs and each of the 14 satisfaction variables. We also tested an additional indicator of job satisfaction, which asks faculty if they would still choose to be professors if they could do it all over again. The results, presented in Table 3, indicate that in most cases there is a significant negative relationship (as indicated by one or more asterisks), suggesting that the more of the particular type of stress experienced, the less satisfied faculty are. Although not all the stress measures are universally related in a negative direction to the satisfaction items (see for example the results related to home responsibilities), this is the predominant trend. There were no significant positive relationships found. This suggests that although there may be some motivational outcomes of stress (e.g., feeling challenged by one's work), among the African American faculty studied here stress consistently is associated with lower levels of satisfaction.

Further support for our interpretation of stress as negative is evidenced in the relationships between areas of satisfaction and promotion concerns. The more stress African American faculty experience related to promotion, the less likely they are to be satisfied in their relationships with other campus professionals: professional relationships with faculty ($r = -0.36$), social relationships with faculty ($r = -0.31$), and relationships with campus administrators ($r = -0.36$). Moreover, the strongest negative relationship is evident between promotion concerns and overall job satisfaction ($r = -0.38$). The significant negative relationships in these areas should come as no surprise, given that promotion concerns is a construct that includes discrimination based on prejudice, racism, and sexism, along with research and publishing demands and the promotion process. If the scholarship areas of African American faculty are marginalized by other professionals who, in turn, determine the worth of that scholarship and their worth as colleagues, then less satisfying relationships would contribute to substantial stress in this area. Therefore, for all stress constructs we conclude that our interpretation is accurate. For this sample of African American faculty all stress items are associated with negative rather than positive states of being.

Because of the significant gender differences in stress apparent in our examination of institutional differences, we also wanted to examine whatever differences might be apparent among

TABLE 3
Zero-Order Correlations of Stress and Satisfaction Items

Predictor Variables	*Overall Stress*	*Time Constraints*	*Home Responsibilities*	*Governance Activities*	*Promotion Concerns*
Would you still be a professor if you could do it all over again?	−0.15**	−0.09**	−0.02	−0.03	−0.17**
Level of satisfaction with					
Salary and fringe benefits	−0.06*	−0.06*	−0.09**	−0.02	−0.12**
Opportunities for scholarly pursuits	−0.13**	−0.20**	0.00	−0.12**	−0.20**
Teaching load	−0.12**	−0.24**	−0.01	−0.12**	−0.15**
Quality of students	0.00	−0.06*	0.01	−0.08**	−0.07*
Working conditions	−0.13**	−0.20**	0.01	−0.12**	−0.16**
Autonomy and independence	−0.11**	−0.09**	0.05	−0.14**	−0.22**
Professional relationships with other faculty members	−0.17**	−0.12**	0.02	−0.14**	−0.36**
Social relationships with other faculty members	−0.21**	−0.15**	−0.02	−0.13**	−0.31**
Competency of colleagues	−0.08**	−0.01	0.07*	−0.17**	−0.25**
Visibility for jobs at other institutions	−0.10**	−0.09**	−0.04	−0.04	−0.17**
Job security	−0.18**	−0.13**	−0.09**	−0.02	−0.30**
Undergraduate course assignments	−0.14**	−0.16**	−0.11**	−0.06*	−0.19**
Relationships with campus administrators	−0.19**	−0.11**	0.00	−0.11**	−0.36**
Overall job satisfaction	−0.26**	−0.21**	−0.06*	−0.12**	−0.38**

*$p < 0.05$. **$p < 0.01$.

the predictor variables. Table 4 presents the results and reveals that approximately half of the predictor variables are significantly related to gender. The variables can be classified into three basic categories—professional status, home supports, and work experiences. The first four significant variables in the table—academic rank,[2] having a doctorate, base salary, and having tenure—indicate that the professional status of men is higher than that of women. Men are more likely to be full professors than assistant professors or lecturers, have doctoral degrees, have higher salaries, and be tenured. The lower professional status of African American women faculty may suggest their greater vulnerability to certain areas of stress, such as promotion concerns and overall stress, as well as their vulnerability to the effects of marginality.

The second set of variables significantly related to gender indicate that men are more likely to have supportive home networks than do women. Men are more likely to be married or living with a partner, to have a family, and to spend less time on household chores. Family supports allow faculty greater opportunities to become part of the larger community social network, possibly through interactions with the families of their children's friends or with friends of a spouse or partner. This is especially meaningful when considering that many faculty must relocate to acquire their jobs. Those with families (who are more likely to be men) are therefore less likely to experience community isolation. The fact that men spend less time on household chores than women suggests that men can have more supports outside of the workplace; the fact that women spend more time on household chores may explain why women experience greater stress related to time constraints at work.

Among the work experience variables that are significantly related to gender, Table 4 reveals that men spend more time on scholarly endeavors, the kind that are likely to be rewarded in the

TABLE 4
Gender Differences Across the Predictor Variables

	Correlation with Faculty Gender	*Mean Value for*		*Variable Range*	
		Men	*Women*	*Min.*	*Max.*
Academic rank	0.16**	2.46	2.78	1	4
Has doctorate	−0.13**	1.62	1.49	1	2
Base institutional salary	−0.21**	4.05	3.48	1	7
Tenured	−0.12**	1.43	1.31	1	2
Years at present institution	−0.05	10.86	9.04	0	47
No. of children 0–4 years of age	−0.20**	1.39	1.16	1	4
No. of children 5–12 years of age	−0.20**	1.74	1.38	1	5
No. of children 13–17 years of age	−0.10*	1.48	1.34	1	5
No. of children 18+ years of age	−0.10*	2.20	1.93	1	5
Single	0.14**	1.13	1.25	1	2
Married (or with partner)	−0.20**	1.71	1.51	1	2
Hours/week: Administration	0.00	4.99	4.99	2	18
Hours/week: Teaching	0.05	10.48	10.80	3	27
Hours/week: Research/writing	−0.12**	2.94	2.51	1	9
Hours/week: Creative products	0.00	1.69	1.71	1	9
Hours/week: Client consultation	0.05	1.47	1.60	1	9
Hours/week: Community service	0.04	2.15	2.24	1	9
Hours/week: Outside consulting	−0.03	1.64	1.57	1	9
Hours/week: Household duties	0.15**	3.45	4.10	I	9
Held administrative post	−0.11**	1.44	1.32	1	2
Received award for teaching	−0.06	1.30	1.25	1	2
Spouse/Partner is an academic	−0.14**	1.36	1.22	1	2
Commute a long distance to work	0.00	1.24	1.24	1	2
Spouse/Partner works in same city	−0.12**	1.49	1.36	1	2
Was sexually harassed here	0.11**	1.03	1.09	1	2
Developed new course	0.00	1.59	1.59	1	2
Held faculty senate office	−0.04	1.21	1.17	1	2
Primarily interested in research	−0.08*	2.14	2.00	1	4
No. of articles	−0.23**	2.69	2.00	1	6
No. of chapters	−0.09**	1.54	1.38	1	5
No. of books	−0.07*	1.61	1.47	1	6
No. of exhibitions, performances	0.01	1.52	1.56	1	7
No. published in past two years	−0.04	2.16	2.05	1	7
Research work done with others	−0.01	1.52	1.50	1	3
Worked with students on research	−0.11**	1.68	1.57	1	2
Had funded research	−0.08*	1.44	1.36	1	2
Served as a paid consultant	0.00	1.48	1.47	1	2
University	−0.04	1.29	1.24	1	2
Four-year college	0.00	1.57	1.56	1	2
Private institution	0.04	1.25	1.28	1	2

Note: Negative correlations indicate that women scored lower on the predictor than men. Academic rank coded on a 4-point scale, where 1 = professor and 4 = assistant professor.
*$p < 0.05$. **$p < 0.01$.

promotion process. Conducting research and writing, having research funds, research interests, and students to aid in their research productivity may be indicative of men's higher professional status, resulting in the greater likelihood of their having supports and resources in place to pursue and complete scholarly endeavors. This would also explain why male faculty have more publications of all types—articles, chapters, and books—than their female peers. The only work-related experience that women encounter significantly more often than men is being sexually harassed. Thus the lower scholarly productivity of African American female faculty, compared to their male counterparts, along with their lower professional status may help explain the higher levels of stress experienced by African American female faculty.

Explaining Stress

Table 5 presents the results of the regressions explaining stress as defined by the five

TABLE 5
Standardized Regression Results

	β_s *Predicting*				
Independent Variables	*Overall Stress*	*Time Constraints*	*Home Responsibilities*	*Governance Activities*	*Promotion Concerns*
Academic rank	−0.047	−0.041	0.040	−0.155**	0.009
Has doctorate	−0.001	0.023	−0.043	−0.087	0.035
Base institutional salary	−0.003	−0.093*	−0.090*	−0.055	−0.055
Tenured	−0.027	−0.043	0.002	−0.007	−0.073
Years at present institution	−0.019	−0.035	−0.046	0.010	−0.043
No. of children 0–4 years of age	0.026	0.011	0.190**	−0.071	−0.046
No. of children 5–12 years of age	−0.041	−0.060	0.149**	−0.107**	−0.070
No. of children 13–17 years of age	−0.047	0.006	0.086*	0.122**	−0.004
No. of children 18+ years of age	0.002	−0.057	0.014	−0.050	−0.029
Single	−0.054	0.002	−0.135**	0.122*	−0.064
Married (or with partner)	−0.076	0.035	−0.085*	0.032	−0.116*
Hours/week: Administration	0.070	0.004	−0.048	0.049	−0.049
Hours/week: Teaching	0.019	0.009	−0.074*	0.027	0.058
Hours/week: Research/writing	−0.049	−0.020	0.020	−0.080	−0.003
Hours/week: Creative products	0.000	−0.001	0.001	0.002	−0.049
Hours/week: Client consultation	0.014	−0.026	−0.049	−0.041	0.032
Hours/week: Community service	0.002	0.059	−0.030	0.058	0.022
Hours/week: Outside consulting	−0.019	−0.058	0.016	−0.025	0.015
Hours/week: Household duties	0.062	0.074	0.301**	0.064	0.069
Held administrative post	0.009	−0.026	0.008	0.016	−0.024
Received award for teaching	−0.002	−0.023	−0.037	0.089*	−0.030
Spouse/Partner is an academic	0.061	0.007	0.025	−0.006	0.053
Commute a long distance to work	0.019	0.023	0.018	−0.004	−0.020
Spouse/Partner works in same city	−0.036	−0.024	−0.009	0.003	−0.019
Was sexually harassed here	0.086*	0.116**	0.029	0.069	0.093**
Developed new course	0.065	0.078*	−0.050	0.116**	0.065
Held faculty senate office	−0.059	0.020	−0.001	0.066	−0.033
Primarily interested in research	0.194**	0.087*	0.015	0.039	0.085*
No. of articles	−0.084	0.023	−0.023	−0.015	−0.030
No. of chapters	0.004	0.002	0.003	−0.015	−0.020
No. of books	−0.026	−0.021	0.065	−0.005	0.031
No. of exhibitions, performances	0.059	−0.042	0.010	0.040	0.064
No. published in past two years	0.051	0.091*	−0.011	0.053	0.078
Research work done with others	0.003	−0.016	0.000	0.040	−0.008
Worked with students on research	0.060	0.026	−0.046	−0.042	0.093*
Had funded research	0.007	0.039	0.065	0.021	0.020
Served as a paid consultant	−0.018	0.077*	0.076*	0.052	−0.063
University	0.121*	0.019	0.033	−0.101	0.136*
Four-year college	0.138*	−0.022	0.111*	−0.078	0.134*
Private institution	−0.005	0.080*	−0.006	0.007	−0.040
Female	0.152**	0.166**	0.049	−0.005	0.029
Multiple *R*	0.379	0.396	0.566	0.358	0.385
R-square	0.144	0.157	0.321	0.128	0.148
Adjusted *R*-square	0.097	0.111	0.284	0.080	0.102

Note: Academic rank coded on a 4-point scale, where 1 = professor and 4 = assistant professor.
*$p < 0.05$. **$p < 0.01$.

constructs—time constraints, home responsibilities, governance activities, promotion concerns, and overall stress. Based on our earlier examination of institutional differences across stress measures (see Table 1), the areas where faculty experience the least amount of stress are those of home responsibilities and governance activities. Looking at the variables that explain stress related to home responsibilities, more than half are home- (rather than work-) related sources. Number of children and hours spent on household duties are positively related to stress in this area, whereas marital status has a negative relationship. The results show that married faculty experience less stress, perhaps in part because they have a partner with whom to share responsibility for household chores. Married faculty are more likely to be men, and traditional societal views have seen the attention of men to household chores as added contributions rather than expectations or responsibilities. Married women faculty may not perceive their household duties as adding stress, with whatever support they receive from their spouse helping to reduce stress in this area. On the other hand, single faculty (unless they are also parents) may be better able to balance attention of their household chores with the demands of their professional work, thereby reducing stress from household responsibilities. Of the professional status variables, faculty who have higher salaries (who are also likely to be men) experience less stress related to home responsibilities. Roughly 30% of stress related to home responsibilities is accounted for in this model.

Although stress related to governance activities is an area where relatively low levels are reported among African American faculty in general, women tend to experience higher levels than their male counterparts in each type of institution (see Table 1). This is further evidenced by the presence of being single as a positive predictor and academic rank as a negative predictor of stress in this area, because African American women faculty are more likely to be single and of lower academic rank (see Table 5). Having adolescent children positively contributes to greater stress in this area, whereas those who have preadolescent children experience less stress. This may suggests that professional demands in this area are competing with faculty's needs to devote time to the demands or needs of adolescent children. Also contributing to stress in this area are teaching activities—being rewarded for teaching and developing new courses. This suggests that governance activities compete for time desired to devote to quality student learning experiences. Governance activities are usually centered around scheduled meetings and often demand much more time than planned. Moreover, devoting more time to governance activities would restrict the flexibility faculty usually have in deciding how they work best, causing problems in their time management.

Common stressors. Areas where African American faculty tend to experience greater amounts of stress are promotion concerns, time constraints, and overall stress. Most of the variables that explain stress in these areas are associated with the work experience as well as being a woman. Sources of stress common to these three areas will be discussed together. The two common predictors of all three stress areas are having research interests and being sexually harassed. The presence of having research interests as a common predictor of the three most common stressors may be indicative of the role of internal motivation in sustaining African Americans in a profession that marginalizes many while offering few external rewards. Their research may serve the void-filling function of correcting historical omissions, while offsetting some of the negative aspects of the workplace that contribute to stress in these areas. At first look, one might consider this a positive experience, because earlier research (Olsen, Maple, & Stage, 1995) evidences a positive relationship between research interests and job satisfaction. However, for those who concentrate their research on African Americans, this focus is often a vehicle through which others reinforce the marginality of African American faculty. Sustaining the integrity of their work while finding sources for publication and validation presents problems for many African American scholars when promotion decisions are being made. This has historically been the response to African American scholarship and is not unlike the initial response to feminist scholarship.

Sexual harassment as a predictor of these three stress areas—time constraints, promotion concerns, and overall stress—suggests that being victimized in this way poses concerns for both male and female African American faculty. Because the perpetration of harassment is associated with the exertion of power, and because being African American, either female or male, is associated with low status both in the academy and in the larger society (much like being a female of any race), African Americans appear to be likely targets when power is exercised over their desire to advance or remain in this profession. This predictor suggests that African American male and female faculty, along with being targets, share a concern as to how their responses to these incidents will affect their ability to advance professionally.

Results found in research by Dey, Korn, and Sax (1996) showed that African American women (and women of color, generally) are not more likely to be harassed because they are African American, but because they are in low status jobs. However, African American women experience "constant cultural assaults on their identity" (Dugger, 1996, p. 36), stemming from historical stereotypes. Thus even when negative labels are not publicly used, others may be exercising their historical, cultural privilege to victimize those whom they have been socialized to view as of lower status. One African American woman's response to why she had remained silent about the long-term harassment she had received in the workplace was "When the president of the United States gets on national television and discounts the credibility of an educated professional . . . like Anita Hill, what chance do I have that someone is going to believe me?" (Boyd, 1993, p. 11). These concerns and others may be exacerbated by colleges' and universities' responses to harassment and victimization of any kind. Many institutions have just begun to acknowledge the seriousness of these incidents, and many have yet to provide adequate resources for the resolution of these issues. To the extent that they do not also recognize the emotional costs to victims and the resulting loss of time, energy, and motivation due to demoralization, the adequacy of the supports already in place must be questioned. Thus marginalization in the workplace may result from being alienated by victimization as well as from inadequate resources for addressing these concerns, thereby contributing to greater stress in these areas.

Other variables explaining these stressors are "being married" or "living with a partner" as a negative predictor and "mentoring students in research" as a positive predictor of promotion concerns. The former indicates that married faculty are less likely to experience stress related to promotion concerns, possibly suggesting that some of the effects of marginalization are reduced by not being isolated both in and out of the workplace. The latter predictor suggests a possible concern that the commitment to mentor students in research may negatively impact faculty productivity, creating additional concerns related to faculty promotion. Working in environments that value and expect more research—universities and four-year colleges—also contributes to stress related to both promotion concerns and overall stress.

Contributing to time constraint-related stress along with research interests are having lower salaries, developing new courses, producing research, working as a paid consultant, and working in private institutions. When we consider other variables significantly correlated with time constraints (see Table 6), we find that faculty who are tenured and have been at their present institution longer experience less stress in this area, whereas faculty who spend more time writing, publishing, and developing courses experience more stress. These are time-consuming faculty responsibilities for which junior faculty (those with lower salaries) are more likely to be devoting time. Moreover, faculty who spend time consulting, regardless of rank, may be attempting to offset the hardship incurred by their lower institutional base salary.

One of the greatest contributors of stress in two areas where greater stress is experienced—time constraints and overall stress—is being an African American woman. This may be partially explained by their fairly recent entry into a white, male-dominated profession and the responses of others to them in these roles. African American women are not new to juggling home and family responsibilities with work force participation. They have constructed definitions of womanhood that include both (Davis, 1981). Whereas white feminists portray the home as a major source of women's oppression, many African American women find home and family affirming of their humanity and a refuge from the hostility of the larger society (Dugger, 1996). However, because many African American women in faculty roles are single and in a profession that usually requires relocation to secure a job, the affirmation of home and family are not always readily available to them. Thus marginality among

TABLE 6
Zero-Order Correlations of Predictor and Dependent Variables Used in the Regressions

Predictor Variables	*Overall Stress*	*Time Constraints*	*Home Responsibilities*	*Governance Activities*	*Promotion Concerns*
Academic rank	−0.01	0.00	0.10**	−0.11**	0.03
Has doctorate	0.08*	0.12**	−0.01	−0.05	0.10**
Base institutional salary	0.00	−0.07	−0.18**	−0.00	−0.08
Tenured	−0.05	−0.07*	−0.09*	0.09**	−0.12**
Years at present institution	−0.06	−0.09**	−0.08*	0.04	−0.10**
No. of children 0–4 years of age	−0.00	0.01	0.43**	−0.14**	−0.06
No. of children 5–12 years of age	−0.07	−0.06	0.37**	−0.12**	−0.11**
No. of children 13–17 years of age	−0.05	−0.02	0.26**	0.10*	−0.04
No. of children 18+ years of age	−0.07	−0.12**	0.04	−0.02	−0.11**
Single	0.02	0.01	−0.25**	0.07*	0.04
Married (or with partner)	−0.08*	−0.02	0.13**	−0.05	−0.13**
Hours/week: Administration	0.06	−0.01	−0.03	0.08*	−0.07
Hours/week: Teaching	0.01	0.02	−0.01	0.07	0.08*
Hours/week: Research/writing	0.07	0.08*	0.03	−0.07	0.12**
Hours/week: Creative products	0.07	0.00	0.00	0.08*	0.05
Hours/week: Client consultation	0.00	−0.05	−0.05	−0.00	0.00
Hours/week: Community service	0.01	0.02	−0.02	0.09*	0.01
Hours/week: Outside consulting	0.01	−0.03	0.00	0.02	0.03
Hours/week: Household duties	0.07	0.11**	0.43**	0.03	0.05
Held administrative post	−0.01	−0.05	−0.05	0.06	−0.07*
Received award for teaching	−0.02	−0.04	−0.07*	0.11**	−0.05
Spouse/Partner is an academic	0.03	−0.01	0.05	0.00	0.01
Commute a long distance to work	0.02	0.03	0.05	−0.01	0.00
Spouse/Partner works in same city	−0.05	−0.05	0.06	0.00	−0.05
Was sexually harassed here	0.13**	0.14**	0.01	0.08*	0.12**
Developed new course	0.11**	0.16**	0.01	0.12**	0.12**
Held faculty senate office	−0.04	0.03	0.02	0.09*	−0.03
Primarily interested in research	0.20**	0.15**	0.03	−0.02	0.16**
No. of articles	0.00	0.07*	−0.04	0.01	0.02
No. of chapters	0.02	0.06	−0.02	0.01	0.01
No. of books	0.01	0.00	0.00	0.04	0.03
No. of exhibitions, performances	0.11**	0.01	0.04	0.09*	0.11**
No. published in past two years	0.13**	0.16**	0.00	0.06	0.16**
Research work done with others	−0.04	−0.07	0.01	0.02	−0.06
Worked with students on research	0.12**	0.10**	−0.06	0.00	0.16**
Had funded research	0.09*	0.13**	0.04	0.00	0.12**
Served as a paid consultant	0.03	0.11**	0.03	0.07	0.00
University	0.06	0.08*	−0.05	−0.06	0.07*
Four-year college	0.06	0.00	0.07*	0.00	0.05
Private institution	0.04	0.11**	0.01	−0.02	0.00
Female	0.17**	0.20**	0.04	0.05	0.08*

Note: Academic rank coded on a 4-point scale, where 1 = professor and 4 = assistant professor.
*$p < 0.05$. **$p < 0.01$.

many African American women faculty is frequently heightened by their distance from loved ones and their participation in often unwelcoming environments. The stress related to meeting regular faculty productivity demands while also juggling role expectation as outsiders in a white, male-dominated profession are usually not anticipated or acknowledged by others.

Conclusions

McGrath (1976) has suggested that stress exists where the element of threat is related to the availability of resources for successfully meeting the demands of one's job. From this perspective the types of experiences that explain heightened levels of stress along with the marginality of African

Americans in academe are likely to contribute to the undesirability of faculty positions as well as the retention of faculty within them. Added to this is the amount of time between the completion of tasks and their outcomes (e.g., acceptance of publications, evaluation, and promotion). Being a member of a population that is regarded as having low status in the larger U.S. society and culture as well as in the academy coupled with the lower-ranking faculty status of most African Americans in predominantly white colleges and universities compounds the decision-making process related to remaining in a profession where the rewards are both long-range and few. Because their role in the academy further distances African American faculty from their own community, the decision to remain in a work environment that is devoid of rewards and laden with demands comes into question. The historical, inequitable treatment of women in the workplace compounds the issues of low status due to both race and gender for African American women faculty even further. Stress as a condition of work has the potential to impact negatively the overall well-being and the employment decisions of African American faculty in general and that of African American women in particular.

One area of grave concern has to do with the sexual harassment of both African American male and female faculty, because it further reinforces their race-related social status. Harassment is a power vehicle used to demoralize and marginalize victims. Through these data we are unable to determine the likelihood of African Americans for reporting incidents of harassment or their means of coping with these experiences. This is an area clearly in need of further examination, not only because of the threat to the professional advancement of African American faculty but because of the potential danger to individual health. Research on racial discrimination and health (Krieger & Sidney, 1996) evidenced blood pressure to be highest among African Americans who experience discrimination in multiple areas of their life but perceive limited or no resources for overcoming the adversities. Conversely, those who experienced adversity but had resources or outlets to address unfair treatment had lower blood pressure. How African American faculty perceive the adequacy of college and university services and potential responses to their charges and emotional needs should be addressed. These experiences threaten the individual's perceived potential to advance professionally, even when the victim's work is valued.

If issues of power, status, and victimization are evident through the examination of sexual harassment, it is possible that they would be even more evident through examination of issues of racial discrimination. However, these issues are beyond the scope of this study, given the unavailability of specific questions in this area. Moving beyond the boundaries of culture-imposed stereotypes and their resulting discrimination is an ongoing process and challenge even for the most well-intentioned. Rabbi Stephen Fuchs (1996, p. 60) captures this difficulty in an article on race relations when he quotes the work of an anonymous poet:

> It's easy to sit in the sunshine
> And talk to the man in the shade
> It's easy to sit in a well-made boat
> And tell others just where to wade
> It's easy to tell the toiler
> How best to carry his pack
> But you'll never know the weight of the load
> Until the pack is on your back.

Given the importance and salience of these issues today, our social perceptions of both gender and racial groups must be challenged as we attempt to tackle discrimination and harassment issues of all types. It is an area that, even without further examination, can be directly addressed by colleges and universities through policies and practices. As colleges and universities struggle to diversify their faculties, the need to recognize the challenges that African Americans and other marginalized groups face is critical. The need for each member of the academic community to recognize his or her contribution to the marginalization of others is even more critical. Balancing the demands of a scholarly career with the multi-marginality often experienced in academic careers is a difficult challenge and one that often goes unobserved by the academy. Understanding the cost in emotional well-being and physical health to marginalized groups in these situations is a first step, but only a first step, in helping to resolve these concerns. Much more research and progress are needed to support institutional efforts to increase faculty racial and gender diversity.

Notes

1. Derrick Bell quotes writer Jill Nelson.
2. Academic rank is coded so that 4 = lowest rank (assistant professor or lecturer).

References

Astin, A. W., Korn, W. S., & Dey, E. L. (1991). *The American college teacher: National norms for the 1989–90 HERI faculty survey.* Los Angeles: Higher Education Research Institute, UCLA.

Bell, D. (1994). *Confronting authority: Reflections of an ardent protester.* Boston, MA: Beacon Press.

Blackwell, J. (1988). Faculty issues: The impact on minorities. *Review of Higher Education, 11,* 417–434.

Bowen, H., & Schuster, J. (1986). *American professors: A national resource imperiled.* New York: Oxford University Press.

Boyd, J. A. (1993). *In the company of my sisters: Black women and self-esteem.* New York: Dutton Books.

Davis, A. (1981). *Women, race, and class.* New York: Random House.

Derogatis, L. R. (1982). Self-report measures of stress. In L. Goldberger &. S. Breznitz (Eds.), *Handbook of stress: Theoretical and clinical aspects.* New York: Free Press.

Dey, E. L. (1994). Dimensions of stress: A recent survey. *Review of Higher Education, 17,* 305–322.

Dey, E., Korn, J., & Sax, L. (1996, March/April). Betrayed by the academy: The sexual harassment of women college faculty. *Journal of Higher Education, 67,* 149–173.

Dey, E. L., Ramirez, C., Korn, W. S., & Astin, A. W. (1993). *The American college teacher: National norms for the 1992–93 HERI faculty survey.* Los Angeles: Higher Education Research Institute, UCLA.

Dillon, J. F., & Tanner, G. (1995). Dimensions of career burnout among educators. *Journal of Mass Communication Educator, 50*(2), 4–13.

Dua, J. K. (1994). Job stressors and their effects on physical health, emotional health, and job satisfaction in a university. *Journal of Education Administration, 32,* 59–78.

Dugger, K. (1996). Social location and gender-role attitudes: A comparison of Black and White women. In E. Ngan-Ling Chow, D. Wilkinson, & M. Baca Zinn (Eds.), *Race, class & gender: Common bonds, different voices.* Thousand Oaks, CA: Sage Publications.

Finkelstein, M. J. (1984). *The American academic profession.* Columbus, OH: Ohio State University Press.

Fuchs, R. S. (1996, April). Farrakhan: Can Jews meet him half way? *Emerge Magazine,* 58–60.

Gmelch. W. H., Lovrich, N. P., & Wilke, P. K. (1984). Sources of stress in academe: A national perspective. *Research in Higher Education, 20,* 477–490.

Harvey, W. B. (1996). Faculty responsibility and tolerance. In C. Turner, M. Garcia, A. Nora, & L. Rendon (Eds.), *Racial and ethnic diversity in higher education,* ASHE Reader Series. Needham Heights, MA: Simon & Schuster Custom Publishing.

hooks, b. (1996). Black women intellectuals. In C. Turner, M. Garcia, A. Nora, & L. Rendon (Eds.), *Racial and ethnic diversity in higher education,* ASHE Reader Series. Needham Heights, MA: Simon & Schuster Custom Publishing.

Krieger, N., & Sidney, S. (1996). Racial discrimination and blood pressure: The CARDIA study of young Black and White adults. *American Journal of Public Health, 86,* 1370–1378.

McGrath, J. E. (1976). Stress and behavioral organizations. In M. Dunnette (Ed.), *Handbook of industrial and organizational psychology* (pp. 1351–1395). Chicago: Rand McNally.

Olsen, D., Maple, S., & Stage, F. (1995, May/June). Women and minority faculty job satisfaction: Professional role interests, professional satisfaction, and institutional fit. *Journal of Higher Education, 66,* 267–293.

Rush, M. C. (1995). Psychological resiliency in the public sector. "Hardiness" and pressure for change. *Journal of Vocational Behavior, 46,* 17–39.

Smith, E. (1995). The multiple sources of workplace stress among land-grant university faculty. *Research in Higher Education, 36,* 261–282.

Smith, E., & Witt, S. (1996). A comparative study of occupational stress among African American and White university faculty: A research note. In C. Turner, M. Garcia, A. Nora, & L. Rendon (Eds.), *Racial and ethnic diversity in higher education,* ASHE Reader Series. Needham Heights, MA: Simon & Schuster Custom Publishing.

Turner, C. S. V., & Thompson, I. R. (1993). Socializing women doctoral students: Minority and majority experiences. *Review of Higher Education, 16,* 355–370.

West, C. (1993). *Race matters.* New York: Vintage Books.

Zweigenhaft, R., & Dumhoff, G. W. (1991). *Blacks in the white establishment? A study of race and class in America.* New Haven, CT: Yale University Press.

Investigating the Evaluation Procedures for a Distance Learning Undergraduate Degree in LIS

Susan D. Lithgow, Clare Thomas and Marianne Taylor

Abstract

This article is based on a process evaluation carried out at the Department of Information and Library Studies (DILS) at the University of Wales Aberystwyth (UWA). The research investigated the effectiveness of the existing evaluation procedures for the BSc Econ in Information and Library Studies by distance learning. After briefly discussing the research process, the article then describes the findings in relation to the perceived gaps in the evaluation procedures, including the importance of disseminating the evaluation results. It was found that changes to the course occurred in response to feedback from various sources and that evaluation data was used in ways that differ from their perceived purposes. Finally, the article relates these findings to the different concepts of quality found to be appropriate to a BSc ILS Distance Learning programme taught both on and off-campus.

The Evaluation Context

The Department of Information and Library Studies (DILS) at the University of Wales Aberystwyth (UWA) has substantial experience in providing distance learning courses. Initially this was at postgraduate level, but since 1993 it has also run an undergraduate programme (BSc Econ ILS) by distance learning, for students working within the profession who do not have a qualification at the professional level. For these students the usual full-time paths to gaining such a qualification present geographical, financial and other barriers. The student profile is predominately female with students working in a wide range of information organisations such as public, academic and school libraries as well as business and media organisations.

The Open Learning Unit (OLU) at DILS UWA was established in conjunction with the BSc Econ ILS programme, but is now responsible for the administration of all the DILS distance learning programmes and for supporting staff and students involved in them. Staff are employed in the

Reprinted by permission from *Education Libraries* 24, no. 2/3, (2000).

development of programmes both by working with academic staff within DILS to produce materials in a format suitable for distance learning, and by commissioning outside experts in the field to produce specialist modules. The unit also develops other media to support learning both on and off campus, such as a computer conferencing system. Finally staff are responsible for training throughout the University and beyond and actively involved in research within the field of distance learning. Currently the OLU has ten full and part-time staff members and supports 414 distance learners, 249 of whom are BSc Econ students.

The Evaluation Rationale and Objectives

The rationale for the evaluation discussed in this article arose from several factors, both internal and external, including the innovative nature of the BSc Econ ILS by distance learning and the desire to expand the research base of the OLU in conjunction with DILS. Externally there have also been recent developments that justified research in this area. The Quality Assurance Agency (QAA) is responsible for the assessment of teaching quality in the higher education sector in the UK. It has recently proposed a shift from a series of single event inspections (quality assessment) to a focus on universities' own review processes (quality audit) (QAA, 1998). The Dearing Report in the UK on Lifelong Learning has drawn attention to issues concerning widening participation to higher education for adults including those in the workplace (Dearing, 1997). Finally, there is a global interest in developing distance learning programmes, and within the LIS community it has also been posited as an alternative means of delivering education to information professionals at all levels (Fasick, 1995).

The remit of this research was to try and identify those aspects of evaluation which were of concern to the users of the existing evaluation procedures in order to create a more cohesive system, relevant to the needs of those users and future users. The research team began by identifying the users of the current evaluation procedures and proceeded to investigate:

- users' perceptions of the existing evaluation procedures
- the effectiveness of the existing evaluation procedures
- the identification of gaps in coverage in existing evaluation procedures.

Methodology

As a process evaluation (Patton, 1980) the research demanded a mainly qualitative approach since the evaluation process, as opposed to the outcomes of the course, was being examined. Moreover, it was hoped that findings from the research project would allow the unit to understand some of the perceptions of the users of the evaluation procedures and the effectiveness of the present quality assurance system. It would also provide qualitative information about any gaps identified and contribute to the specific content of any future evaluation tools. In this respect, it was also essentially a self-evaluation as defined by Calder (1995) and Harris and Bell (1986) in which a department or unit reflects on its present practices with a view to (if necessary) developing them in a way that is more appropriate to meeting the expressed needs of both its internal and external users.

Although the research noted the difficulties about validity when using mixed approaches to evaluation at a theoretical level (Jakupec and Kirkpatrick, 1998) nevertheless the literature revealed that it was legitimate in the context of an internal evaluation to use both quantitative and qualitative methods (Morgan 1984; Dillon and Gunawardena, 1992). The fact that much distance education research and evaluation is bounded by context was seen as pertinent to research in an innovative area of ILS education and in the particular circumstances of a programme taught at a distance from within a traditional university department. The research therefore relied upon a series of complementary methods of data collection to find out the views of students and staff including:

- Literature Search: This was carried out in various areas, for instance, quality in higher and distance education, the concept of dual-mode universities, and student feedback.
- Focus Groups and Interviews: These provided an illuminative dimension to the research and the results also influenced the production of the questionnaires.

- Student and staff questionnaires: These covered the respondents' perception of evaluation and their experiences of the evaluation procedures including the identification of perceived gaps.
- 'Brown papering' of procedures and observation of evaluation sessions.

In relation to identifying gaps in the evaluation procedures, the research was interested in ascertaining how quality was perceived in distance higher education and in locating any performance indicators that could be applicable to a programme which is taught to distance learners from within a conventional campus-based department. Rumble terms universities which teach in this way as 'dual mode' and in many ways DILS UWA operates as a dual mode department (Rumble, 1992).

The research team was aware of the debates about the difficulty of defining quality in higher and distance education. As many commentators have pointed out, quality in education is a contested concept (Green, 1994). This is related to the difficulty of transferring from industrial and managerial domains, terminology such as quality assessment, quality control, and quality assurance which are thought inappropriate to measure the complexity of a process such as higher education (Barnett, 1992; Tait, 1993).

In terms of the performance indicators for distance education the literature search revealed some key publications, such as the European based project, the SATURN Quality Guide for Open and Distance Learning (SATURN, 1992) and within the UK, the Manpower Services Commission's handbook, Ensuring Quality in Open Learning (Manpower Services Commission, 1987). However whilst these were useful, they were found to be very wide in scope and concerned with providers of distance education in a variety of situations such as work-place training as well as education at different levels. Other works by Calder (1994a), Thorpe (1993), and Rowntree (1992) were useful in identifying the key areas of evaluation for distance education in the university sector. The recent UK Quality Assurance Agency Guidelines on the Quality Assurance of Distance Education were published towards the end of this research.

For the BSc Econ at UWA, the academic and professional evaluation of the programme lies with the quality procedures for all courses validated by the university and also by the professional accreditation bodies concerned, which are the UK Library Association and Institute of Information Scientists. The official UWA quality document contains references to support for distance learners and a distance learning quality checklist is distributed to Heads of Department, to remind departments involved of the quality indicators required at UWA.

From within these broad contextual issues of quality in distance higher education the research team devised the focus-group schedules and in the light of those findings, the student and staff questionnaires. Five focus groups were held at the annual residential school, representing a sample of all the BSc student intakes present. The subsequent student questionnaires were sent out to all 222 BSc Econ distance learning students and 82 were completed and returned—a response rate of 37%. The staff questionnaire was sent out to all 30 staff in DILS and 20 were completed and returned—a response rate of 67%. The subsequent results from these, together with the results from the other methods described above, led to the emergence of a number of themes. Given the mainly qualitative nature of this research, the team depended on the focus groups and the open questions to give an indication of the intensity and priority of particular issues of concern to users.

The remainder of this article will focus on the perceived gaps in the existing evaluation procedures as demonstrated by the research and consider how they might relate to issues of quality and evaluation in distance education. It will then go on to look at the relationship between the perceived purposes of the evaluation procedures and their actual use. Finally some of the issues this raises for staff and students concerned will be addressed.

Findings: Perceived Gaps in the Existing Procedures

Before looking in more depth at the gaps identified by the research, it should be noted that key evaluation procedures were found to be in place. For example, the evaluation of the module materials and of the residential schools was well established. These occur firstly through the Module Evaluation Form (MEF) which is placed at the end of each module and which students can return with their assignments to the Open Learning Unit. The evaluation of residential schools takes place at the end of the week in a face to face evaluation session between staff and students. It starts with a set agenda, covering study school administration, on-campus IT and Library Services, counselling and teaching, but the format also encourages students to raise any aspect of the course that they wish. It should be noted that the majority of users considered that these, together with other informal opportunities, provided adequate means of evaluation—especially from a student viewpoint.

In spite of the above, about a third of users, both staff and students, identified gaps in the existing evaluation procedures in response to direct survey questions or as a result of focus-group discussions and interviews. The gaps identified in the evaluation procedures were broadly categorised as:

1. Organisation-Related—those concerned with the evaluation of student support at a distance.
2. Course-Related—those concerned with the gaps in the evaluation of the wider teaching process.
3. Student-Related—those concerned with the student learning experience and environment.
4. Process-related—those concerned with the dissemination of the evaluation data.

Inevitably these categories are not mutually exclusive and indeed the findings supported the view that in the context of distance education, educational, administrative and supportive processes are necessarily interwoven.

In looking at the perceived gaps in this way, it is evident that they are principally concerned with the needs of students when studying away from the campus and with students and staff involved in educational and administrative processes which are characteristic of distance education. Moreover, the research showed that the gaps identified were often related to processes that are 'intangible' and difficult to measure. In this respect they reflect the concerns with quality issues that were identified in the literature search as particularly important to distance education. The issues related to each of the four main categories will now be discussed in turn.

(1) Organisation-Related Issues

These were seen as quality issues that related to the support provided by the orgnisation for students when studying at a distance and comprised the evaluation of:

- OLU support and information provision
- the personal tutorial system
- access to academic tutors
- resources such as Library Services.

It has been shown that support for distance learners will be interpreted in different ways by different institutions. This can include both academic and personal counselling, and administrative services or may be focused on particular aspects of the overall provision. (Robinson, 1995). In the case of DILS UWA, the Open Learning Unit undertakes all of the administrative work for delivering materials, dealing with finance, responding to enquiries, and circulating information. Students are also assigned a personal tutor from Open Learning Unit staff with whom they meet at every study school and are encouraged to contact whenever they are experiencing difficulties or for general guidance when away from the campus. The unit informs students of their progress through the course at six-monthly intervals and there is a lunchtime help-line every week. While many students identified the various ways of contacting the Open Learning Unit (e-mail, computer conferencing, telephone, letter) as opportunities for informal ad-hoc evaluation of the course itself, they did not identify any formal means of evaluating these services unless they arose for some reason at the evaluation at the end of the residential school. Students are also encouraged to contact their academic tutors either directly or through the OLU but again this service is not formally evaluated. The identification of these particular gaps can be related to issues of support for students from the organisation when they are away from the campus.

The evaluation of supporting distance learners in these ways is obviously not easily measured. Apart from efficiency indicators concerning speed of response, they can also be related to more intangible human processes, which are often complicated by the distance involved. Students and staff are both employed in other duties. While a phone call will often provide the most satisfactory and speedy response, it was suggested by some focus group discussions that it can also be difficult to judge the convenient moment and that this will effect the quality of the interaction. Students also gave examples of kinds of difficulties inherent in measuring consistency of response, which will naturally occur when staff attempts to provide adequate support at a distance. Two contrasting student comments were:

> I have phoned on occasions when I was seeking clarification of something and sometimes it's useful and sometimes it isn't, depends on who you get on the other end of the phone to be honest.
>
> I was unsure about the Information and Society module, so I e-mailed, but he rang me up and spoke to me and sorted me out.

The identification of these gaps in the evaluation procedures suggests that users were concerned with quality not only in terms of the kind of information they receive but also in terms of timeliness and consistency of response.

This would equate with the ways in which some distance learning experts link the provision of support for distance learners to the quality criteria used by service management theory (Sewart, 1993; Ljosa, 1993). Ljosa for instance, links the intangible interactions of service delivery with the processes of education and with the focus in distance education on students and delivery systems. Such interactions are compared to what such theories refer to as 'the moment of truth' when a customer experiences the value of what is delivered. These moments are often intangible and ephemeral but are also crucially part of how students value the institution.

The provision of library services is another area that has been increasingly recognised as important in the support of distance learners (Unwin, 1998). In fact the provision of a postal service from the campus library to distance learners is another innovative dimension to this course. Just before the research began, the library had carried out a user survey of its services to distance learners, and the provision of on-campus facilities is evaluated at the end of each study school. However, some users did identify the lack of an on-going formal evaluation of these services as a gap in the evaluation procedures.

The importance of finding ways of providing and evaluating the support provided for students at a distance has been one that Sewart (1993) has demonstrated as being critical to the success of educational programmes. Moreover, these gaps would seem to accord with Sewart's contention that student support acts as an adjunct to the teaching materials in allowing students to experience the discrete elements of the process as a whole.

(2) Course-Related Issues

These were quality issues which lay outside the evaluation of teaching materials but which were part of the wider teaching-learning process. These comprised:

- assignment turnaround times
- assignment feedback in terms of consistency and quality of feedback comments
- clarity of instruction around assessed tasks
- modules in terms of their relevance and up-to-dateness.

The BSc Econ distance learning programme provides a large amount of flexibility with regard to setting assignment deadlines. Students can decide their own pace within the minimum target of completed modules per annum. In distance education, the provision of flexibility with regard to course structure can provide more choice to students and may in itself be an indication of the quality of a course in terms of 'openness'. However in a dual-mode situation, this can add to administrative complexity and put pressure on staffs who are working to two different schedules. In order to create a more coherent pattern for both students and staff, the OLU and DILS have set a number of marking dates that span the academic year. Student assignments are held until these dates and handed over to staff as assignment batches. The nominal assignment return period is one month, including administrative procedures. The OLU monitors this process and provides on-going information to students in cases where there is likely to be any delay in the return of marked assignments.

The research revealed that students wished to have the opportunity to evaluate assignment turnaround time. Staff also felt that assignment turnaround was important and identified it as a quality issue particularly in terms of focusing on the student as stakeholder but did not cite it directly as a gap. In contrast to other perceived gaps in the evaluation procedures, student respondents often commented more extensively on the reasons for their dependence on timely feedback from assignments and this gave the researchers an insight into why this was an important quality issue for student respondents. They did so in terms familiar to the evaluators of distance education. In distance education, assignment feedback is part of the important process of creating a "learning dialogue". The speed and quality of feedback also contributes to student motivation and reassurance, particularly at the start of the course when there is a concern about 'being on the right track' and towards the end when students are anticipating their final result. The speed of assignment turnaround is often cited as a crucial performance indicator for higher education in general and because of its nature for distance education in particular. However, it has also been asserted that the speedy return of assignments does not in itself guarantee the quality or consistency of the feedback in terms of teaching. Again this has been shown to be particularly important in correspondence teaching (Thorpe, 1993). As Helen Lentell (1995) states, 'To return student assignments quickly is important, but is it the same as giving students the kind of feedback they need in order for them to learn and progress' (p. 122). Once again this moves the focus of evaluation from the easily measured to the more complex interactions of the process of learning and the results of the research confirmed that students were also interested in evaluating the quality and consistency of assignment feedback. In relation to this, a comment made in one of the focus groups could also be connected to the issue of timeliness of evaluation and how some students perceive the purpose of evaluating the learning materials as part of the process of learning which is not complete until assessment feedback has been received. The student seems to move evaluation from the product or learning materials to the process of the teaching-learning transaction. It may also be related to the evaluation of the clarity around assessment tasks. This is in itself an area in which the OLU provides on-going support that extends the work in the modules to an on-going activity—again, a process rather than product. As a student commented:

> But you don't always realise that you misunderstood it until it's too late—we evaluate the module after we've just done it and it says "was the question clear" and you say "yes" because you think you've understood it—then you send it off, get the feedback and you're told that you've misunderstood it so then you could do with evaluating it at that point, and also you'd be able to evaluate the marking because one assignment came back with very useful comments and I appreciated them but there was no point to say this.

The measurement of assignment turnaround in a dual mode context is a question of balancing the different aims of the course in relation to providing flexibility for distance learners and enabling staff to provide a coherent response across a cohort when marking. For a significant minority of student respondents, the flexibility of the course in relation to submission of assignments and the ability to work with a large measure of autonomy were more important indicators than that of assignment turnaround. As one student respondent said:

> To be honest I do not pay particular attention to the marking or return dates. I feel that this is just an added pressure, and would rather see my work completed to my satisfaction, than rush to get it in by a marking date.

As already discussed, at the end of each module the OLU has provided a module evaluation form (MEF) and this covers many aspects of the learning process particularly in relation to the module materials. This was identified as the main format for the summative evaluation of the module that a student has just completed and which can be sent in with the assignment. The majority of users felt that the MEF was a satisfactory format for evaluating the course materials. However, in spite of its comprehensive nature, a number of staff and student respondents agreed that the MEF did not cover some aspects of the course materials that they thought important to evaluate, such as the relevance and currency of materials used in the modules and module revision schedules.

The problems of relevance and up-to-dateness are referred to by Cresswell and Hobson, (1996) as one of the areas in which (particularly for distance education) misunderstandings of the purpose of the materials included in a course may occur between students and authors. They point out that this often occurs in professional education. The fact that this was perceived as a gap in the evaluation of the BSc by a number of students and staff would seem to confirm this view. However, while Cresswell and Hobson show that authors and students can have opposing points of view in relation to the relevance and up-to-dateness of teaching materials, this research found that it was an issue that both staff and students would regard as important to evaluate. Perhaps this is due to the nature of the profession, which is one where academic staff and those working in the field cannot ignore the rapid changes taking place.

(3) Student-Related Issues

These gaps relate to quality issues that were concerned with the environment in which distance learners study. This is sometimes referred to as the 'student learning milieu' and may be of particular interest to providers of a professional LIS course undertaken by those simultaneously working in the field. These were:

- employer support
- student experience in a learning environment
- longitudinal evaluation.

For some students and staff the ways in which the course interacts with the workplace was seen as an area that might be subject to evaluation. For instance, a small number of users identified the attitude of employers and the different levels of support that students receive in the workplace as a gap in the evaluation procedures. It also arose in focus group discussions and was clearly of interest to students, who related it specifically to financial support, colleagues' support and their different status within different institutions.

In the focus groups there was much discussion around the kind of environment in which the students studied and worked. This was in terms both of the various levels of support that students experienced and on their status as learners currently working at the level of both theory and practice. Students also referred to their working life when reflecting on how they measured their progress, citing the ways in which they could apply the course directly, or how their learning enabled them to view their organisations from a new theoretical perspective. The evaluation of these aspects of the learning process must fulfill the call by some distance learning experts that evaluation and research in distance education should extend beyond the materials, or support systems to the experience of the students themselves (Evans, 1994).

In terms of LIS education by distance learning, the impact of studying for a degree and qualification by this method may be of interest in terms of the kinds of skills students are given in the programme and their implementation not only in the future when they move into the professional side of work, but the impact on their present employment and employers. In relation to this, students assumed very often that student destinations formed part of the evaluation procedures. Some staff cited longitudinal data as a perceived gap in the evaluation. The focus group discussions revealed this was not as simple a measure as it might be for full-time students moving into a new career. For adult learners the reasons for taking a degree may be more varied and cannot always be measured by simple destination routes. This was evidenced here in the wide range of different responses that students gave in terms of motivation for undertaking the programme and ambitions for the future. These ranged from intrinsic motivations such as 'I'm doing it for myself' to a fourth year student whose extrinsic motivation was such that he was able to project his firm plans to progress from his present position to that of 'County Librarian'. The results also showed that many students would agree that they gained more confidence in their professional and personal lives and that what they valued in studying for the BSc Econ was also an expansion of their opportunities. As one put it:

> I just think at the end of it, I've just got a choice, that's how I feel about the degree, it gives me a choice and I don't know what that'll be until I get to that time. It's a nice thought.

Moreover, the data from the focus groups also revealed that some students were already in professional posts while others had obtained higher level posts during their studies. For instance, one small group consisted of six students who were returning for their dissertation study school, which students can choose to attend either during their third study school or separately towards the end of their studies. It emerged that four of these students had moved into higher level posts while doing the course and the pressure of coping with demanding new positions had resulted in them taking longer than anticipated to complete the degree.

Again this would indicate that in terms of performance measurement and evaluation, the criteria used by students and staff in discussing the value of this course is more complex than the straightforward recording of student destinations. It involves a range of relevant variables including present employment, and employer and student expectation.

(4) Process-Related Issues

Arguably the most significant gap that emerged from this evaluation was in regard to the process itself, particularly in terms of 'closing the feedback loop'. These were identified as:

- access to evaluation data
- feedback on evaluation data
- dissemination of the results of evaluation.

The identification of these gaps emerged in the comments that respondents made in the student and staff surveys and in relation to the findings about the effectiveness of evaluation procedures in terms of the link between evaluation and follow up action.

Distance education has been described as 'two-way communication', and it would seem that for these students, evaluation was also an important means of maintaining a dialogue with the course providers and enhancing their sense of belonging to the institution. For instance, the comments of student and staff respondents demonstrated that they valued the opportunity for contact and immediate interchange of views which the face to face evaluation sessions at the end of study school allowed them. However, when students are evaluating modules at a distance, they are doing so in isolation and many identified the dissemination of the overall results as a gap in the feedback process. Here too, course evaluation was seen to have a role in creating a sense of belonging to the institution and this was evident in the kinds of reasons that students gave for returning completed module evaluation forms (MEF) apart from those of providing feedback. Evaluation was seen as a chance to express their thoughts and feelings about the course and was evidenced by the occurrences in the questionnaire data of the words 'contact' or 'communication'. It may explain why 80% of student respondents stated they always returned the module evaluation form but only 25% believed that it led to changes in the modules.

A significant number of staff also identified a gap in the circulation of feedback data. They were aware of the difficulties of analysing and disseminating evaluation data that was seen as time-consuming and logistically complicated. In traditional courses, it is often up to staff to devise course evaluations. Evaluation results are seen as a means of private reflection on how successfully the curriculum is delivered. Distance education is much more reliant on formats that can be used across the board and can therefore make useful comparisons. Also the evaluation centres on the extent to which the learning materials facilitate student learning and may be less concerned with content. It was striking that student comments in the survey with regard to the evaluation of modules through the MEFs were directed more to the Open Learning Unit than to academic staff.

Staff wished to have a more comprehensive, holistic evaluation of the course, perhaps by an overall quantitative evaluation. This related to questions of ownership, access to data, and the realistic use of time and resources. In terms of module evaluation, staff often required more detailed, qualitative information and more effective means of making the results available.

Action as a result of evaluation feedback is recognised as an important but sometimes neglected phase of the evaluation process. Harvey (1999) states:

'Despite the "customer rhetoric", students are not repeat purchasers of products but participants in a learning process designed to improve their life chances. Feedback will only play a significant role in empowering students if it leads to action'.

In relation to the desire to know what action was taken in relation to the evaluation of this course, many students expressed a desire to have 'feedback on feedback', including information on how evaluation data was used by course providers. About a quarter were able to cite instances of change occurring as a result of evaluation or sometimes in ways that seemingly contradicted evaluation. In particular, the feedback given at the end of study school sessions and concerned with those issues having to do with residential schools was seen as formative and led directly to changes which benefited those participating in future years. Examples of this were given in the survey and included improvements to accommodation and to pre-course provision, timetable changes, the pace of study school and improvements to library access, the marking system, and IT provision.

With regard to changes occurring as a result of feedback through the MEFs, and in common with much student course evaluation, students are not able to directly identify any changes made, since they do not re-take the module. Some students were able to cite examples of changes to modules as a result of informal communication at study school. The majority of students felt that feedback through the MEFs should lead to improvements in the modules and assumed that this was the primary role of the module evaluation form.

From a staff perspective, it was evident that although the module evaluation data was used, it was more likely to be in ways that went beyond its stated or perceived purposes. For instance, it was found that the module evaluation forms were used when staff wished to check the reception of the course in a general way. They were used formatively by staff developing new courses. They were also used by the OLU in its role as the interface between academic concerns and support issues for students in providing study guides, clarifying assessment tasks, or organising the sessions at study school. However, on the evidence of this research, the use of MEF data to make on-going changes to current modules was found to be somewhat limited.

It also seemed that academic staff often used other means of evaluation when judging the effectiveness of current modules. For instance, a small number of academic staff respondents indicated that they made changes to modules as a result of their assessment of how students had coped with the modules after they had marked a batch of essays. This is indicative of the kind of tacit evaluation that is used in on-campus situations where tutors can modify any changes made as a result of evaluation gained through other contacts with students and may be an example of professional reflective practice. In relation to this, some academic staff also reported that changes were more often made to modules as a result of informal feedback from students by e-mail or telephone. It would seem that they were using these means almost in replication of the kind of instantaneous feedback that they would receive from on-campus students.

This might indicate that more change would occur in relation to the MEFs if they were analysed and disseminated rather than being made available for individual consultation as at present. It also suggests that staff is responding in traditional ways to adhoc informal feedback, or, as indicated elsewhere in the research, that in order to facilitate change to modules as result of feedback through the module evaluation form, staff would prefer more qualitative information. These results confirmed the views of some commentators who maintain that change as a result of feedback in organisations is not a simple causal relationship between input and output (Morgan, 1993).

Moreover, in their comments on the evaluation of the course in terms of action, staff often cited the pressures of time and resources as limitations on the kind of practice they saw as ideal. The relationship between feedback and subsequent improvements to courses is very much an issue where political, resource, and management issues will exert as much influence as feedback from students.

Conclusions: Evaluation of an LIS Course in a Dual-Mode Department

The evaluation of programmes delivered in two modes has been linked with the debate about how far distance education remains a distinct mode of delivery and how far it can be said to be converging with traditional education within universities. Lippiatt (1997) feels that the convergence of both modes can be reflected in the convergence of evaluation criteria in a way that is mostly unproblematic and formulates a range of performance indicators that are relevant to both modes. Others feel that distance education is a more complex process with more to evaluate and more complex criteria (Thorpe, 1993). The findings of this research in relation to gaps in the existing evaluation procedures would confirm this latter view. While the central evaluation of the learning materials and on-campus teaching were found to be adequately evaluated, it emerged that there existed a perception of gaps in the evaluation procedures. These dealt with the evaluation of the student experience when studying at a distance, their on-going support, learning environment, and the teaching received through assignment feedback.

Users were also interested in evaluating the intangible aspects such as the kind of service they received in terms of administrative and academic support. These have less to do with the learning materials and more with the process of learning accompanied by support, administration, and the wider teaching-learning transaction. Robinson (1994) has referred to these as the 'conditions for learning' in which 'quality lies in the totality of products, delivery, services and general ethos' (p. 186). Moreover these can be said to be of greater importance to distance education and therefore to be of particular significance in a dual-mode situation.

In distance education generally, evaluation itself has become more process-oriented, both in terms of the administrative and support services that are necessary for a successful distance education programme and a related 'customer-oriented' approach. Morgan (1997) asserts that the impetus for easily measured outcomes and the production of performance indicators for higher education now comes mainly from governmental agencies and that the evaluation of distance education can be said to have moved 'beyond the packages.' Nevertheless the evaluation of the learning materials remains crucial and takes on a new significance in a dual mode situation where outside assessors need to be aware of what the material is trying to achieve in terms of facilitating learning (Rowntree, 1998). However, this research further demonstrates that students also wish to evaluate the whole learning transaction after feedback.

In relation to performance indicators, some gaps could be directly correlated to the criteria applied across both on and off-campus modes such as assignment turnaround times and student destinations. However, when explored in detail these were shown to require more complex indicators than those applied to traditional on-campus graduates in terms of more diverse motivations for studying. For instance, monitoring and evaluating the destinations of this group of students is not only a matter of quantitative analysis which can be compared across the board with various sectors but may also be of interest to see what happens to the 'products' of an innovative ILS course. In relation to this, the users of this evaluation system were also interested in the evaluation of their student learning environment and the social contexts of their learning. The evaluation of the level of support that they are given from employers and colleagues in terms of finance, mentoring, resources, and available study time may be valuable as evidence of the ways in which other groups of learners within and without the LIS community are supported in developing their professional expertise through continuing education at different levels throughout their careers. In relation to this, it has been suggested that distance education needs to extend evaluation to adult learning styles (Calder, 1994b). For this particular group of distance learners, their learning environment is directly related to their course and as such, could be an area of research into constructivist ideas of learning as students identify and evaluate their experience of distance learning in relation to their working lives.

Finally, the gaps identified could be seen to demonstrate how, for providers of distance education, 'the complexities of the administrative, supportive, and educational processes of distance education are interwoven in every part of the system' (Ljosa, 1993, p. 187). This interdependence was revealed in relation to the identification of gaps in the evaluation procedures such as the support of students at a distance, assignment turnaround, and the dissemination and utilisation of feedback, which were shown to be the responsibility of both academic and administrative staff.

Calder (1995) feels that it is important for 'learning organisations' to identify their predominate evaluation in order to achieve a balanced system and advocates the multiple use of collected data as one way of achieving this economically. It was clear that much of the data the Open Learning Unit holds about students and systems at a monitoring level could form the basis of a more informative evaluation system. The identified gaps in the evaluation procedures suggest that at present, the evaluation of the course centres on the learning materials and on the campus experience of distance learners. By considering how to extend this to the experience of students at a distance through the evaluation of administrative, supportive, and educational processes, the course-providers can create a more balanced, holistic, internal evaluation system that was in itself, the primary goal of this self-evaluation.

Added Material

Susan D. Lithgow is a Development Officer responsible for producing course material for library and information studies distance learning students and developing a research profile for the Open Learning Unit at the University of Wales, Aberystwyth. E-mail: sd1994@aber.ac.uk

Clare Thomas is Director of the Open Learning Unit at the University of Wales, Aberystwyth. She leads a staff team of 10 who work to develop and support open and distance learning development, primarily for the 500+ library and information staff who are studying for undergraduate and postgraduate qualifications with DILS, and also across the University. E-mail: cmt@aber.ac.uk

Marianne Taylor is a Development Officer in the Open Learning Unit at the University of Wales, Aberystwyth, where her main responsibilities include administration, organising study schools, student support, and study skills development. E-mail: mmt@aber.ac.uk

The contact address for all three authors is: Open Learning Unit, Department of Information and Library Studies, University of Wales Aberystwyth, Llanbadarn Fawr, Ceredigion, SY23 3AS, Wales, UK.

Phone: +44 (0) 1970-622159; Fax: +44 (0) 1970-662190.

References

Barnett, R. (1992). *Improving Higher Education: Total Quality Care.* Buckingham: Society for Research into Higher Education and Open University Press.

Calder, J. (1994a). *Programme Evaluation and Quality.* London: Kogan Page.

Calder, J. (1994b). "Course Feedback: its Costs and Benefits; its Limitations and Potential." In Dhanarajan et al., eds. *Economics of Distance Education.* Hong Kong: Open Learning Institute of Hong Kong, 241–255.

Calder, J. (1995). "Evaluation and Self-improving Systems." In Lockwood, F., ed., *Open and Distance Learning Today.* London: Routledge, 361–369.

Cresswell, R. and Hobson, P. (1996). "Fallacies and Assumptions in the Use of Student Evaluation of Distance Education Teaching Materials." *Distance Education,* 17 (1), 132–144.

Dearing, R. (1997). *Higher Education in the Learning Society.* National Committee of Inquiry into Higher Education, 1997. (Led by Sir Ron Dearing). UK: HMSO.

Dillon, C. and Gunawardena, C. (1992). "Evaluation Research in Distance Education." *British Journal of Educational Technology,* 23 (3), 181–194.

Evans, T. (1994). *Understanding Learners in Open and Distance Education.* London: Kogan Page.

Fasick, A. (1995). "The Future of Education for the Information Professions." *Education Libraries,* 19 (2), 15–19.

Green, D., ed., (1994). *What is Quality in Higher Education?* Buckingham: Society for Research into Higher Education, Open University Press.

Harris, D. and Bell, C. (1986). *Evaluating and Assessing for Learning.* London: Kogan Page.

Harvey, L. (1999). "The Sense in Satisfaction." *The Times Higher Education Supplement,* London, UK, January 15, 29.

Jakupec, V. and Kirkpatrick, D. (1997). "Problems of Generalisation in Higher Degree Research in Distance Education" in Evans, T. et al, eds., *Research in Distance Education.* Geelong, Australia: Deakin University Press, 4, 197–210.

Lentell, H. (1995). "Quality: Is It Always a Move to Better Things?" in D. Sewart, ed. *One World Many Voices: Quality in Open and Distance Learning.* Selected Papers from the 17th World Conference of the International Council for Distance Education, Birmingham, United Kingdom, 26–30 June, International Council for Distance Education, Gjerdrums vei 12, N-0486 Oslo 4, Norway, The Open University, Walton Hall, Milton Keynes, MK7 6AA, UK, (2), 121–24.

Lippiatt, D. (1997). "The Continuity of Quality Assurance in DOL and Traditional Education" in C. P. Chooi et al., eds. *Quality Assurance in Distance and Open Learning.* Papers prepared for the 11th Annual Conference of the Asian Association of Open Universities (AAOU), Kuala Lumpur, Malaysia, November 11–14, Institut Teknologi MARA, 40450 Shah Alam, Selangor, Malaysia (1), 157–62.

Ljosa, E. (1993). "Understanding Distance Education." In Keegan, D., ed., *Theoretical Principles of Distance Education.* London: Routledge, 175–187.

Manpower Services Commission. (1987). *Ensuring Quality in Open Learning: a Handbook for Action.* Manpower Services Commission, Sheffield, UK. Available from MSC, Room W1111, Moorfoot, Sheffield, S1 4PQ, UK.

Morgan, A. (1984. "Report on Qualitative Methodologies in Research in Distance Education." *Distance Education,* 5 (2), 258–266.

Morgan, A. (1993). "Theorising Quality and Quality Assurance in Open and Distance Learning." In Tait, A., ed. *Conference on Issues of Quality for New Models of Education,* 28–30 September 1993,

Downing College, Cambridge, UK, The Open University UK, East Anglian Region, 175–183.

Morgan, A. (1997). In Evans, T. et al., eds. *Research in Distance Education,* 4, Geelong, Australia: University Press.

Patton Quinn, M. (1980, 1990). *Qualitative Evaluation and Research Methods.* London: Sage Pubs.

Quality Assurance Agency for Higher Education, UK (QAA), (1998). Higher Quality, The Bulletin for the QAA, 4, (4). *Quality Assurance Agency for Higher Education,* Southgate Street, Gloucester, GLI 1UB, UK, http://www.qaa.ac.uk

Quality Assurance Agency for Higher Education, UK (QAA), (1999). *Guidelines on the Quality Assurance of Distance Learning, Quality Assurance Agency for Higher Education,* Southgate Street, Gloucester, GLI 1UB, UK.

Robinson, B. (1994). "Assuring Quality in Open and Distance Learning." In Lockwood, F., ed. *Materials Production in Open and Distance Learning.* London: Paul Chapman Pubs.

Robinson, B. (1995). "Research and Pragmatism in Learner Support." In Lockwood, F., ed. *Open and Distance Learning Today.* London: Routledge, 221–231.

Rowntree, D. (1992). *Exploring Open and Distance Learning.* London: Kogan Page.

Rowntree, D. (1998). "Assessing the Quality of Materials-Based Teaching and Learning." *Open Learning,* 13 (2), 12–22.

Rumble, G. (1992). "The Competitive Vulnerability of Distance Teaching Universities." *Open Learning,* 7 (2), 31–45.

SATURN. (1992). *Quality Guide for Open and Distance Learning: Pilot.* SATURN, Keizersgracht 756, 1017 EZ Amsterdam, The Netherlands.

Sewart, D. (1993). "Student Support Systems in Distance Education." *Open Learning,* 8 (3), 3–11.

Tait, A. (1993). "Systems, Values and Dissent: Quality Assurance for Open and Distance Learning." *Distance Education,* 14 (2), 303–314.

Thorpe, M. (1993). *Evaluating Open & Distance Learning.* UK: Longman.

Unwin, L., K. Stephens et al. (1998). *The Role of the Library in Distance Learning: a Study of Postgraduate Students, Course Providers and Librarians in the UK.* London; New Providence, NJ: Bowker-Saur.

What's the Difference?

Outcomes of Distance vs. Traditional Classroom-Based Learning

Jamie P. Merisotis and Ronald A. Phipps

What's the difference between distance learning and traditional classroom-based instruction? This question has become increasingly prominent as technology has made distance learning much more common. In fact, there is now at least one major Web site, maintained by North Carolina State University's Thomas Russell, dedicated to this question. The Russell Web site (and a recently published companion book) is called *The No Significant Difference Phenomenon*, and compiles various articles, papers, and research studies on distance learning.

With few exceptions, the bulk of these writings suggest that the learning outcomes of students using technology at a distance are similar to those of students who participate in conventional classroom instruction. The "no significant difference" finding has become accepted as fact in the policy community in particular, where at least some public officials have pronounced that the last college campus has been built.

We decided to examine the issue of distance learning's effectiveness by reviewing the available evidence on the subject. This was accomplished simply through a thorough review of the literature, including everything from original research to how-to articles to policy papers. We were determined to find out the answers to several key questions: What are the findings of the research on the effectiveness of distance education? Are they valid? Are there gaps in the research that require further investigation and information? What does the literature suggest for the future?

Because so much has been written about distance learning in higher education—there are now at least half a dozen journals that deal with college-level distance education as their main theme—we limited the scope of our review to material published during the 1990s. This still left us with the task of reviewing several hundred articles, papers, and dissertations.

It turns out that the vast majority of what is written about distance learning is opinion pieces, how-to articles, and second-hand reports that don't include original research with subjects (students or faculty) who are being studied. We focused our inquiry on the original research, including experimental, descriptive, correlational, and case studies, since this is the only appropriate way to assess the differences between distance and classroom-based learning. We certainly don't think we reviewed every study published since 1990, but our analysis clearly captured the most important and salient of these works.

Reprinted from *Change* 31, no. 3, (May–June 1999).

What Does the Research Say?

One of our most important conclusions from this review is that there is a relative paucity of original research dedicated to explaining or predicting phenomena related to distance learning. Despite the large volume of written material concentrating on distance learning, the amount of original research is quite limited. Our analysis encompassed about 40 of these original works of research—a number far smaller than is often cited as "evidence" that there is no significant difference.

From this more limited group of original research, three broad measures of the effectiveness of distance education are usually examined. These include

- Student outcomes, such as grades and test scores;
- Student attitudes about learning through distance education; and
- Overall student satisfaction toward distance learning.

Most of these studies conclude that, regardless of the technology used, distance-learning courses compare favorably with classroom-based instruction and enjoy high student satisfaction. For example, many experimental studies suggest that the distance-learning students have similar grades or test scores, or have the same attitudes toward the course. The descriptive analyses and case studies focus on student and faculty attitudes and perceptions of distance learning. These studies typically conclude that students and faculty have a positive view toward distance learning.

A closer look at the research, however, suggests that it may not be prudent to accept these findings at face value. Several problems with the conclusions reached through this research are apparent. The most significant problem is that the overall quality of the original research is questionable and thereby renders many of the findings inconclusive.

The findings of the original research must be read with some caution. Assessing the quality of the original research requires a determination that the studies adhered to commonly accepted principles of good research. This kind of analysis is much more than an academic exercise. These principles are essential if the results of the studies are to be considered valid and generalizable. If a study does not abide by these principles, the results can be erroneous or misleading, and thereby lead to conclusions that result in poor public policy.

Key Shortcomings of the Research

Below are four shortcomings of the original research:

1. Much of the research does not control for extraneous variables and therefore cannot show cause and effect. Most experimental studies of distance learning are designed to measure how a specific technology (the "cause") impacts upon some type of learning outcome or influences student attitudes toward a course (the "effect"). For this relationship to be assessed accurately, other potential "causes" must not influence the measured outcomes. But in almost all of the experimental research, there was inadequate control of extraneous variables. As a result, it was often difficult to rule out differences other than the technology as the "causal agents."

2. Most of the studies do not use randomly selected subjects. The single best way of controlling for extraneous variables is to assign students randomly to both the experimental and control groups. However, many of the published studies reviewed used intact groups for comparison purposes. As a result, these studies run the risk of having a number of variables—such as pedagogy, student characteristics, and time-on-task—affect academic achievement or student satisfaction, not just the technology used to provide the education at a distance. Of course, random selection doesn't guarantee that the control and experimental groups are similar in all attributes, but it is accepted practice in good research.

3. The validity and reliability of the instruments used to measure student outcomes and attitudes are questionable. An important component of good educational research relates to proper measurement of learning outcomes and/or student attitudes. In short, do the measurement instruments—the final examinations, quizzes, questionnaires, or attitude scales developed by the teacher—measure what they are supposed to measure? A well-conducted study would include evidence of the validity and reliability of the measurement instruments so that the reader could have confidence in the results. But in almost all of the studies reviewed, this information was lacking.

4. Many studies do not adequately control for the feelings and attitudes of the students and faculty—what the educational research refers to as "reactive effects." Reactive effects are a number of factors associated with the way in which a study is conducted and the feelings and attitudes of the students involved. One reactive effect, the "Novelty Effect," refers to increased interest, motivation, or participation on the part of students simply because they are doing something different, not necessarily better. Another, called the "John Henry Effect," refers to control groups or their teachers who feel threatened or challenged by being in competition with a new program or approach and, as a result, outdo themselves and perform well beyond what would normally be expected. In many studies, precautions were not taken in the research to guard against these effects.

Gaps in the Research

Notwithstanding the fact that the overall quality of the research needs improvement, there are several important issues regarding the effectiveness of distance learning that require further investigation and information. These gaps must be filled so that public policy discussions can be based on accurate and adequate information. Specific issues include the following.

1. The research has tended to emphasize student outcomes for individual courses rather than for total academic programs. A major gap in the research is the lack of studies dedicated to measuring the effectiveness of total academic programs taught using distance learning. Virtually all of the comparative or descriptive studies focus upon individual courses. This raises serious questions about whether a total academic program delivered by technology compares favorably with a program provided on campus. In addition to cognitive skills and verbal, quantitative, and subject-matter competence, outcomes with regard to critical-thinking skills, attitudes and values, moral development, and so on need to be addressed. This is especially important since public policy is typically aimed at providing access to degrees or programs of study, not just single courses.

2. The research does not take into account differences among students. A substantial portion of research on distance learning has been conducted to demonstrate no significant difference in achievement levels between groups of distance and traditional learners. However, there is wide variance of achievement and attitudes within the groups, which indicates that learners have a variety of different characteristics. The factors influencing these differences could include gender, age, educational experience, motivation, and others. Gathering samples of students and amalgamating them into averages produces an illusory "typical learner," which masks the enormous variability of the student population. Further research needs to focus on how individuals learn, rather than on how groups learn.

3. The research does not adequately explain why the course dropout rates of distance learners are higher. A number of studies showed that higher percentages of students who participated in distance-learning courses dropped out before the courses were completed compared to students in conventional classrooms. The issue of student persistence is troubling both because of the negative consequences associated with dropping out and because the research could be excluding these dropouts—thereby tilting the student outcome findings toward those who are "successful."

4. The research does not take into consideration how the different learning styles of students relate to the use of particular technologies. Our understanding of how the learner, the learning task, and a particular technology interact is limited. Learner characteristics are a major factor in the achievement and satisfaction levels of students participating in distance education. Information regarding a student's preferred learning style will influence how the course is designed and what type of technology is used. Additional research could result in more information regarding why different technologies might be better suited for specific learning tasks.

5. The research focuses mostly on the impact of individual technologies rather than on the interaction of multiple technologies. Much of the literature on distance learning focuses on one technology and either describes its effectiveness or compares it to the conventional classroom experience (or does both). Most technologies, however, are multifunctional and can be adapted to address a wide range of learning outcomes. Unfortunately, there are few studies that examine more than one technology—or the synergistic effects of certain technologies—in addressing specific educational outcomes and student groups. The few studies that are available do not provide ample grounds for generalization because of a range of limitations, including small sample sizes and lack of sufficient explanation of the instructional treatment.

6. The research does not include a theoretical or conceptual framework. There is a vital need to develop a more integrated, coherent, and sophisticated program of research on distance learning that is based on theory. Theory allows researchers to build on the work of others and, thereby, to increase the probability of addressing the more significant questions regarding distance learning. Using theory as a guiding framework also allows the research to be replicated and enhances its generalizability, thereby making individual studies more meaningful.

7. The research does not adequately address the effectiveness of digital "libraries." Students participating in distance learning, particularly those in remote locations, are often introduced to a digital "library" that provides access to bibliographies, as well as to the full text of a variety of resources. The library is at the core of the higher education experience and, particularly at the graduate level, is an integral part of the teaching/learning process. Some digital libraries boast an enormous array of resources, with the implicit notion that they can provide the same service as the traditional library. But do digital libraries provide adequate services for the academic pro-grams they are established to support? Anecdotal evidence seems to suggest that the curricular objectives of some distance-learning courses have been altered because of a limited variety of books, journals, and other resources available online.

Implications

Research on distance learning has been driven by what many are calling the "information revolution." Advancements in technology offer both the general public, and faculty in particular, a dizzying array of unprecedented challenges. Technology is having, and will continue to have, a profound impact on colleges and universities in America and around the globe.

Distance learning, which was once a poor and often unwelcome stepchild within the academic community, is becoming increasingly more visible as a part of the higher education family. But the research and literature reviewed for this paper indicate that the higher education community has a lot to learn about how, and in what ways, technology can enhance the teaching/learning process, particularly at a distance.

As with other educational innovations that have come before it, there is some danger that the innovations made possible through distance education are advancing more rapidly than our understanding of its practical uses. Princeton historian Robert Darnton makes this point in "The New Age of the Book," an essay in the March 18, 1999 *New York Review of Books* about a similar realm: electronic publishing. Darnton observes that, since its inception, electronic publishing has passed through three stages: "an initial phase of utopian enthusiasm, a period of disillusionment, and a new tendency toward pragmatism."

In the context of the research on distance learning and its effectiveness, more emphasis has been placed on the "utopian" possibilities of the technology and its potential to do as well as classroom-based instruction. But not enough "pragmatism" has been applied to allow for a discussion of distance learning's practical implications as a supplement to enhance teaching and learning.

There are at least three broad implications that can be derived from our review of the original research and the other literature. The first is that the notion of "access to college" in the distance-learning context is unclear. Many of the advocates of distance learning tout access to college-level education as a *raison d'être* for the proliferation of distance education. Indeed, in some states public policy leaders are recommending using distance education in lieu of "bricks and mortar" learning.

Of particular concern is access as it relates to the efficacy of computer-mediated learning. Unlike two-way interactive video, where students and the instructor can see and talk to each other in a conventional classroom, computer-mediated learning requires special skills of students and more sophisticated technical support if students are to interact fully. Questions that need to be asked include: What is the "quality" of the access? Does the student have the necessary skills to use the technology? What are the best ways to participate in asynchronous communication? Is there adequate technical support? And perhaps most important: Will the cost of purchasing a computer and maintaining software be prohibitive for a substantial number of students?

Second, it seems clear that technology cannot replace the human factor in higher education. Faculty involved in distance education find themselves acting as a combination of content experts, learning process design experts, process implementation managers, motivators, mentors, and interpreters. In short, technology "can leverage faculty time, but it cannot replace most human contact without significant quality losses," as William Massy has stated.

Third, although the ostensible purpose of much of the research is to ascertain how technology affects student learning and student satisfaction, many of the results seem to indicate that technology is not nearly as important as other factors, such as learning tasks, learner characteristics, student motivation, and the instructor. The irony is that most of the research on technology ends up addressing an activity that is fundamental to the academy, namely pedagogy—the art of teaching. To that extent, the research has had a salutary effect in that a rising tide lifts all boats. Any discussion about enhancing the teaching/learning process through technology also has the beneficial effect of improving how students are taught on campus.

Consider this example. In 1987, the American Association for Higher Education published "Seven Principles for Good Practice in Undergraduate Education," which distilled findings from the research on the undergraduate experience. The principles were revived in 1996 by Arthur Chickering and Stephen Ehrmann to enable those using new communication and information technologies to enhance the teaching/learning process. In one form or another, the principles have been incorporated in a variety of publications on good practice, and were evident in many of the studies.

AAHE's principles of good practice include those methods that

- encourage contacts between students and faculty;
- develop reciprocity and cooperation among students;
- use active learning techniques;
- give prompt feedback;
- emphasize time-on-task;
- communicate high expectations; and
- respect diverse talents and ways of learning.

In a sense, the discussion has come full circle. The research on distance learning has a long way to go, and much of it is inconclusive. On the other hand, technology has helped the academy to continue its focus on the essential goals of teaching and learning. As a result, either implicitly or explicitly, the key question that needs to be asked is: What is the best way to teach students?

Evaluating for Distance Learning: Feedback from Students and Faculty

JOAN S. THOMSON

Associate Professor, Rural Sociology, Agricultural and Extension Education
The Pennsylvania State University

SHARON B. STRINGER, PH.D. CANDIDATE

Agricultural and Extension Education, The Pennsylvania State University

Abstract

This paper describes the development and evaluation of a World Wide Web-based component for a required freshman seminar at the Pennsylvania State University College of Agricultural Sciences. Students (n = 170) were given a pre-test to assess their access to, knowledge of, and proficiency with computers. The pre-test was designed to address four broad categories: computer use, ability, and perceptions; Internet perceptions and use; communication preferences; and demographic information. This formative evaluation assessed student needs and helped the project team to continue to develop course content for the semester. A summative evaluation was given at the end of the semester to ascertain students' perceptions of web-based assignments and needed changes for future courses. In addition, one faculty member from each section participated in a phone survey, answering questions about their experiences with the course. It was concluded that using a computer-based asynchronous teaching model is quite different from the more traditional model and requires special considerations; practitioners should incorporate formative and summative evaluations to enhance learner satisfaction, to ensure goal attainment, and to demonstrate accountability. (DLS)

Distance learning methodologies support a wide variety of academic programs for residential and off-campus students. These delivery technologies, including audio and video teleconferencing, computer conferencing, and web-based instruction are changing the way students interact with subject matter and faculty. In addition to enhancing traditional learning practices, distance learning technologies affect how students engage the global community through on-line resources. Internet site design and user compatibility provide a starting point to integrate computers into instruction.

Web-based instruction, for example, is growing faster that any other instructional technology (Crossman, 1997). With a computer connection, students and faculty use the web to exchange information and access resources from around the world. The popularity of web-based instruction is attributed to its convenience and flexibility of access (Daugherty and Funke, 1998).

The innovative nature of distance education methodologies demands close examination regarding the issues and practices relevant to educational quality and integrity. Reeves and Reeves (1997) concluded that there are many issues relevant to the web that have to be fully investigated for their

Proceeds of the 14th Annual Conference on Distance Teaching and Learning, August 5–7, 1998.

pedagogical soundness. Web resources are viewed as a means by which to keep courses current, however, accuracy and timeliness plague sites that are not regularly updated.

While some faculty embrace the challenge to incorporate new technologies into the learning environment, others are overwhelmed by them (Collis, 1993). Dillon and Walsh (1992) found that faculty involved in distance education acquire more positive attitudes as their experience with distance education increase. Herther (1997) suggests that the quality of learning through distance education be evaluated before web-based instruction is subsumed and adopted into university practices.

Evaluation is an integral part of course delivery and development. Cost-benefit, learner satisfaction, goal attainment, and accountability require faculty to gather and submit feedback on the effectiveness of course process and content. Evaluation studies provide timely feedback and constructive criticism to the developers and designers using information technology while the curriculum is still evolving (Collis, 1993). Positive evaluations encourage administrative support of policies, practices, and infrastructure relevant to distance education. Furthermore, insights gained broaden faculty understanding of the commitments necessary to develop quality programs that enhance the traditional learning environment.

Collis (1993) suggests that distance education projects are marginally evaluated. Furthermore, when they are evaluated, the evaluations focus on either client satisfaction or factors correlated with learner persistence or attrition. This paper focuses on participants' feedback about the content and relevance of web-based instruction. Students and faculty were queried about product and process. The importance of faculty and learner feedback in furthering the distance education mission is stressed. Formative evaluations were used to provide information about improving the course. Summative evaluation were carried out to make judgments about the basic worth of incorporating web-based technology into the freshmen seminar.

Integrating Distance Education Technologies

Beginning fall 1999, the Pennsylvania State University will require all entering students to take a freshmen seminar. The purpose of the seminars is to support the transition of students to the University environment. Penn State's College of Agricultural Sciences offers *Be a Master Student!* (AG 150) as a two-credit course to entering freshmen. The course focuses on 1) facilitating the student's transition to the university community, and 2) increasing each student's understanding of the issues and opportunities in the agricultural sciences.

To address an identified need, a web-based component was added to the AG 150 curriculum in fall 1997. The intent was to use communications technology to enhance the agricultural sciences component of the curriculum, making the course available to Penn State students and non-students throughout the Commonwealth. The goal was 1) to develop web-based resources that would facilitate the exploration of current issues in the agricultural sciences and their associated resources at Penn State, and 2) to develop a series of activities or lesson plans for students and faculty teaching AG 150 to integrate into the curriculum.

Before this project, computer-based instruction was not available to faculty teaching AG 150. The website supplements the classroom experience by providing a solid core of common resources across sections and campuses as well as the opportunity for students and instructors to interact electronically outside of class. In addition, faculty could draw course assignments from a plethora of web-based resources.

Project Development

Technology-based instruction requires much planning and collaboration. Integration of technology resources for AG 150 was a complex task. It required the synergy and patience of faculty, support staff, and students. The website developed to supplement instruction in the College's freshmen seminar was not created by faculty currently teaching the course. Two faculty members from the College of Agricultural Sciences team taught each of the nine sections. Faculty, often independent and accustomed to teaching autonomously, were required to work in teams to collaboratively develop course materials. Thus, it was imperative that tools and other opportunities be developed to demonstrate to the teaching faculty how the site could support their instructional objectives.

Web-based instruction is a relatively new methodology in higher education, and many issues still need to be addressed. Lack of faculty incentives, limited access to technology, and insignificant support can hinder successful delivery (Bowen and Thomson, 1994). Lessons learned through formative and summative evaluations of the instructional technology portion of the AG 150 seminar provide a road map for faculty pursuing web-based instruction.

Because the University has made the freshmen seminar a requirement, AG 150 has become a model for other colleges to follow. This prototype includes among other things—World Wide Web-based instruction with virtual tours, career path designs, faculty interviews, and links to many relevant resources on the Internet. The site http://www.cas.psu.edu/docs/CASOVER/AG150.index.htm is relevant to anyone interested in agricultural issues.

Evaluation Process

To test the goals for the project and to learn even more about this new learning approach, it was agreed from the outset to collect as much data as reasonable. The population for the study was all of the students in AG 150 *Be a Master Student!* during fall semester, 1997. Because the number of students in AG 150 was small ($N = 170$), a census was used. Students were given a pre-test at the beginning of the semester to assess their access to, knowledge of, and proficiency with computers. The pre-test instrument used was designed to address four broad categories: 1) computer use, ability, and perceptions; 2) Internet perceptions and use; 3) communication preferences; and 4) demographic information. The formative evaluation assessed student needs and helped the project team continue to develop course content for the semester.

During the semester, faculty used the website to supplement in-class lectures and provide resources for assignments. Three of the nine sections specifically used the AG 150 web site. One instructor maximized the AG 150 site by using it in another course. Instructors indicated that helping students determine how to evaluate the credibility of web-based resources now needed to be incorporated into their instruction.

A summative evaluation was given at the end of the semester to ascertain students' perceptions of web-based assignments and needed changes for future courses. Students were queried on using the Web for AG 150 and other courses. Among the 170 students registered, 142 usable, completed post-test questionnaires were collected, an 84% response rate. One of the faculty members from each section participated in a phone survey, answering questions about their experiences with the course.

Findings

The formative evaluation queried students about course content, expectations, and use of the World Wide Web. The survey findings indicated that generally, freshmen access to and knowledge of computers is increasingly. Of the 142 students who were surveyed during fall 1996, 57% owned computers. Among those who owned their computers, 46% ($n = 66$) indicated that their computers were connected to the Internet. Among the two-thirds ($n = 108$) who owned their computers in fall 1997, 72% indicated that their computers were connected to the Internet. Also fall 1997, three-quarters of the students (74.6%) responded that they were already using computers at least once a day. Almost half of the students (45%) stated that they used the Web for class assignments. Forty-four percent indicated that a course that required a web-based supplement appealed to them. The students also indicated interest in learning about job opportunities, internships, and University resources. In response to student surveys, faculty integrated additional content on career opportunities into the course before the semester's end.

The summative evaluation addressed learner satisfaction with the technology. When asked what they liked most about using the Web, two-thirds ($n = 93$) of the students expressed that they liked its convenience and wealth of information. Typical reasons students gave for using the Web:

- "It's easy to get a lot of information without leaving home."
- "It's a hands-on approach to learning."
- "I think it is important to be able to use the Web, because it is such a prevalent means of communication."

In addition, students expressed a concern regarding the reliability of web-based information. When prompted about the accuracy of web-based information, 57% of the 142 students indicated that they considered the source to determine if information is credible.

This freshmen seminar is one of many projects to integrate distance education technologies into University curricula. In every section, students were expected to submit at least some, if not all, assignments via e-mail. The results indicated that students who do not own personal computers must be considered when designing technology-based instruction. Instructors consistently commented on the increasing computer literacy among students during the past two years. Specifically noted was that students with the fewest computer skills were non-University Park (main) campus based. Faculty involved in recruitment for the College in addition to the freshmen seminar recognized the Web's potential as a recruitment tool among secondary students as well as among those in higher education who are outside the agricultural sciences. For the site to be used in this way, faculty noted that placement on the College's homepage becomes crucial.

Conclusion

The project revealed that using a computer-based, asynchronous teaching model is quite different from the more traditional model and requires special considerations. Although entering freshmen are expected to be increasingly computer literate, students enter the university with varying levels of expertise. To optimize the students' educational experiences, faculty will need to be aware of the competencies students bring in order to maximize their learning opportunities.

Furthermore, it is important to note that access to technology is not a significant incentive for faculty to embrace new teaching methodologies. Relevance to subject matter, timeliness of information, and facilitation of instructional objectives are required for successful integration of web-based resources.

While many students enter the university with Internet experience, some faculty are still learning how to incorporate instructional technologies into learning opportunities. Faculty need administrative support and opportunities to develop effective technology-based courses. Faculty must openly communicate with students and each other throughout the learning experience to develop curricula that effectively use distance education technologies. Web-based information is easily accessible and convenient, however, its reliability and accuracy can be questionable. Faculty that incorporate web-based instruction into the curriculum should develop ways for students to test the accuracy of information found on the web.

The evaluation process is key in the communications process. Identifying relevant issues and problems during the course provides opportunities to develop solutions for quality educational programs. Student feedback during the learning process helps to shape the course and improve the learning experience. Practitioners that seek to integrate distance education methodologies into existing curriculum should incorporate formative and summative evaluations to enhance learner satisfaction, to ensure goal attainment, and to demonstrate accountability.

References

Bowen, B. E. and Thomson, J. S. (1994). *The Influence of Institutional Policies Procedures, and Structures in Strengthening Access to Higher Education through Distance Education.* Project report prepared by the Department of Agricultural and Extension Education, Penn State University, University Park, PA.

Collis, B. A. (1993, August). Evaluating Instructional Applications of Telecommunications in Distance Education. *Educational and Training Technology International*, 30(3), 266–274.

Crossman, D. M. (1997). The evolution of the World Wide Web as an emenology tool. In B. K. Kahn (Eds.) *Web-Based Instruction.* Englewood Cliffs: NJ. Technology Publications.

Daugherty, M. and Funke, B. (1998, March). *University and Student Perceptions of Web-Based Instruction.* A paper presented at the International Conference on Technology and Education. Santa Fe, NM.

Dillon, C. L. and Walsh, S. M. (1992). Faculty: The neglected resource in distance education. *The American Journal of Distance Education*, 6(3), 5–21.

Herther, N. K. (1997, September). Education over the Web: Distance Learning and the Information Professional. *Online*, 21(5), 63–72.

Newman, D. R., Johnson, C., Webb, B., & Cochrane, C. (June 1997). Evaluating the Quality of Learning and Computer-Supported Co-Operative Learning. *Journal of the American Society for Information Science*, 48(6), 484–495.

Reeves, T. C. and Reeves, P. M. (1997). Effective dimensions of interactive learning on the World Wide Web. In B. H. Kahn 9 eds. *Web-Based Instruction* (pp. 59–67). Englewood Cliffs: NJ. Educational Technology Publications.

Assessing the Classroom Environment of the Virtual Classroom

Susan M. Powers, Michaeleen Davis, and Eileen Torrence

Indiana State University

Abstract

This pilot study was conducted in order to determine whether a virtual classroom can be assessed, and whether it can be done using already proven techniques for classroom environment assessment. Study participants were 20 graduate students in education enrolled in three different courses offered at a distance via the World Wide Web. Each of the courses was offered by the same instructor and was designed following the same principles. Data were gathered by mailing each student a copy of the College and University Classroom Environment Inventory (CUCEI), which is composed of 49 questions that rate the following seven different factors of the college classroom environment; student cohesiveness; individualization; innovation; involvement; personalization; satisfaction; and task orientation. Thirteen surveys were returned for a 65% return rate. Researchers also collected qualitative information including papers and presentations; discussion questions; online lectures; peer discussion and feedback; and student reflective journals and time logs. Findings indicated that the survey results backed up the qualitative data, and that the CUCEI was promising in its ability to assess the virtual classroom environment and provide instructors with valuable information about student perceptions of the environment. (DLS)

Introduction

Distance Learning is by no means a new phenomenon. However, the new technologies provide a twist to distance learning that is making it grow and expand at overwhelming numbers. The National Center for Educational Statistics reports that in 1995, a third of US post-secondary schools offered distance education courses with another quarter of the population planning to do so in the next three years. When you then consider the rapid proliferation of internet-based courses as a distance learning option and then consider that the World Wide Web (WWW) has only been "popular" for the past 5 years, it is indeed overwhelming.

While the numbers alone are enough to amaze and dazzle, what is more interesting are the instructional design and pedagogical issues that form the basis of these courses (Ritchie & Hoffman, 1997). The technical skills to build a course-web site and all the accompanying technologies are merely psychomotor skills ranging from the simple to the highly complex, and many courseware packages now

Paper presented at the Annual Meeting of Mid-Western Education Research Association, October 14–17, 1998.

remedy the need for instructors to worry about developing those skills (Hansen & Frick, 1997). Hill (1997) lists some of these key issues, which include the pedagogical, technological, organizational, institutional, and ethical. What is missing from these areas of research focus is the psychosocial environment of the classroom. Research has demonstrated that the classroom environment, in terms of psychosocial factors, accounts for appreciable amounts of variance in the cognitive and affective outcomes for students (Fraser, 1981).

However, can a classroom environment which is in fact not physically tangible, and it exists on the "virtual space" be assessed? And, if there really is such a thing as a virtual classroom environment, can it be assessed using already proven techniques for classroom environment assessment. That query is the focus of this preliminary examination of the virtual classroom environment.

Background

Individuals do not act outside the context of their environment. The bond of this physical and social environment interaction with the individual has troubled philosophers since the time of Aristotle (Huebner, 1980). The question therefore consistently posed is how can the environment serve to enhance the development and learning of the student?

The study of the classroom environment accesses and assesses the shared perceptions of the instructors and students situated in that environment (Fraser, 1989). The advantage of this type of assessment over outsider observational data collection is that both students and instructors have the long-term viewpoint of the class and are not basing their perceptions on small sample observations. The instructors and students also place their assessment in context with other educational experiences.

Moos (1974) provides a scheme where there are three classifications to describe human environments. The first is the relationship dimension which describes the nature and intensity of personal relationship and the extent to which there is mutual support and assistance. The second dimension is called the personal development dimension and concerns the degree to which personal growth and self-enhancement occur within an environment. The third dimension is systems maintenance which measures how orderly and responsive the environment is to change.

A number of instruments have been developed to assess a variety of human environments, including K-12 classrooms, psychiatric hospitals, prisons, and residence halls. One instrument developed by Moos and Trickett (1974) is called the Classroom Environment Scale (CES) and has been used in many of these environments even though it's initial development was for the secondary classroom. DeYoung (1977) piloted a short-form of the CES at the university level.

Another instrument developed specifically for higher education is called the College and University Classroom Environment Inventory (CUCEI). This instrument has seven scales which cover the areas of Personalization, Involvement, Student Cohesiveness, Satisfaction, Task Orientation, Innovation, and Individualization (Fraser, 1986). The scales determine the fit between a student's perception of the actual classroom environment and their preferred environment. The CUCEI was developed expressly for the purpose of assessing environments of higher education classrooms and was developed for classes of 30 students or less and not intended for large lecture classes or lab settings.

In possible conflict with the assessment of a classroom environment (the traditional physical space) is the concept of the virtual classroom, such as courses offered over the World Wide Web. Through Internet classrooms, students and faculty can communicate asynchronously and synchronously. Learning on the Internet can take the form of (a) electronic mail (e-mail) and electronic discussion groups (listservs or chat rooms); (b) bulletin boards or newsgroups; (c) downloadable course materials or tutorials; (d) interactive tutorials on the Web; (e) real-time, interactive conferencing; and (f) infomatics, the use of on-line databases (Kerka, 1996). These methods provide usage, response and impact considerations different from the traditional classroom setting (Kuehn, 1994).

The study of classroom environment is critical if teachers want to be able to exercise control over the environment to the betterment of learning. However, with the growth of distance learning, it is also important to determine what instructor and student perceptions are of the virtual environment. Verduin and Clark (1991) state that the separation of teacher and learner does not allow for a truly shared learning experience, but Moore (1973, 1994) concludes that distance learners must be emotionally independent, self-motivated, and more autonomous in order to compensate for the transactional distance in the distance classroom. Initial examinations are being made of student perceptions of this learning environment (Powers & Mitchell, 1997). This study showed that students do perceive that at least two of Moos' dimensions are present (personal development and relationship). The question does remain unanswered as to whether an effective person-environment fit is taking place and the extent to which the instructor might be able to control those factors. This paper describes a pilot study which makes an initial examination of the virtual classroom environment in terms of traditional measures.

Methodology

This study details the results of a pilot study which examined the classroom climate or environment of a virtual course. Study participants were graduate students enrolled in three different courses offered at a distance over the World Wide Web (WWW). Each of the three courses was offered by the same instructor and was designed following the same design principles. One course dealt with the history and theories of Instructional Technology. The second course focused on information technology and media literacy. The topic of the third course was on the technologies of distance learning. Twenty students were enrolled in these three different courses.

The courses consisted of lecture notes placed by the instructor on the WWW, readings of seminal works on the topics, classroom discussion completed through web conferencing and email discussion groups, synchronous chat sessions and presentations made by the students and posted to the WWW. Course requirements included consistent, regular weekly participation in class discussion on the web and response to peers' presentations and ideas.

As an exploratory study into the evaluation and assessment of the virtual classroom environment, data was gathered from a variety of sources. First, a traditional classroom environmental assessment tool was used. Each student (20) was mailed a copy of the College and University Classroom Environment Inventory (CUCEI) (Fraser, Treagust & Dennis, 1986). See Table 1 for sample questions from the CUCEI. The CUCEI is composed of 49 questions which rate seven different factors of the college classroom environment: Student cohesiveness; individualization; innovation; involvement; personalization; satisfaction; and task orientation. Comprehensive validation research has been completed on this instrument to confirm the internal consistency reliability and discriminant validity of the instrument (Fraser et al., 1986). Students rate each question on a four-point scale

TABLE 1
Sample Items from CUCEI

Student Cohesiveness 5. Students know exactly what has to be done in our class. 7. All students in the class are expected to do the same work, in the same way, and in the same time. (scores reversed)	*Individualization* 8. The instructor talks individually with students. 14. Students are generally allowed to work at their own pace.
Innovation 15. The instructor goes out of his/her way to help students. 19. The group often gets sidetracked instead of sticking to the point. (score reversed)	*Involvement* 23. Students in this class pay attention to what others are saying. 25. Classes are a waste of time. (scores reversed)
Personalization 32. Classes are boring. (scores reversed). 33. Class assignments are clear so that everyone knows what to do.	*Satisfaction* 37. There are opportunities for students to express their opinions in this class. 39. Students enjoy going to this class.
Task Orientation 44. The instructor dominates class discussion. (scores reversed) 46. Classes are interesting.	

of Strongly Agree (SA), Agree (A), Disagree (D), and Strongly Disagree (SD).

This instrument can be delivered in two different formats, preferred and actual. The questions as worded in Table 1 represent the actual format, i.e. how students perceive a classroom environment to actually be. In the preferred form, the questions would be the same, but the word "would" is inserted. For example, "Students *would* know exactly what has to be done in our class. For the purposes of this study, only the actual form was used because the research team wanted to determine if this instrument could play a role in the evaluation of virtual classroom environments.

Twenty students were mailed a copy of the CUCEI, along with an explanation letter and a postage-paid, addressed return envelope. Thirteen surveys (.65%) were returned in sufficient time to be included in this discussion. The data from the surveys was entered into SPSS for analysis. Sums were generated for each environmental scale and then means and standard deviations were found for each of these sums (the CUCEI is scored on a 1–5 scale with 1 being Strongly Agree, 5 being Strongly Disagree and 3 given to no answer). Additionally, for investigating the usefulness of the instrument for virtual classrooms, means were generated for each survey item, as well as frequency data for each item to determine the degree to which students considered the questions to be answerable from the perspective of a virtual classroom.

In addition to the data collected with the CUCEI, qualitative information from the course was also collected in order to assist with interpretation of CUCEI results. The data included papers and presentations, discussion questions, on-line lectures, peer discussion and feedback, and student reflective journals and time logs. All qualitative data was content analyzed in terms of the factors of the CUCEI. This process was completed to examine what factors the students and the instructor perceived as important virtual classroom climate issues.

Results and Discussion

The information received from administration of the CUCEI provided valuable information about the classroom environment of a web-based class. The results of the survey provided quantifiable data to support the qualitative information gathered and the instructor's impressions. First, the results which lead to the viability of the use of the CUCEI in this context will be examined, followed by a discussion on the student assessment of their virtual classroom environment.

Use of CUCEI for Virtual Classes. Of the forty-nine questions asked in the CUCEI, one or more students did not answer 15 of the questions. At first glance that seems to be a large percentage of the total number of questions. However, it is important to see how many students didn't answer these questions in order to make determinations on the viability of the instrument (See Table 2).

The researchers predetermined that one or two blank responses was not a critical issue. There could be numerous reasons why a student does not answer a certain item. When three or more students do not answer that same item, than the time must be taken to examine the possible reasons behind the lack of response. Of the original 15 items which received at least one non-answer, only 6 remained when this qualifier is used. These six items appear to fall into two different categories: lack of a tangible, physical classroom to assess and the nature of an asynchronous web-based environment.

When students participate in a web-based course, their "classroom" could be one of dozens of places. For example, a student might consider the computer lab where s/he works to be his/her classroom. A student who works mostly or entirely at home might consider that particular space to be where s/he attends class. Other students might be able to think in the more abstract and consider the website itself to be the classroom in which they will function. Finally, other students may not be able to conceptualize a classroom that does not exist within four walls, has desks, tables and chairs, chalkboard, and needs a good cleaning.

Therefore it is not surprising that those questions that appear to concern a physical classroom space were unanswerable to students. In particular, those questions that deal with the arrangement of the room and the degree to which the instructor moves around the room. The mean score for Item 29 (instructor moves around classroom) was 2.69, indicating that those students who answered the item tended to agree with the question. The mean score for Item 34 (seating arrangement) was 2.38, once again indicated that those who responded agreed with the statement. One example, and a typical example, of how some students might struggle with the concept

TABLE 2
Frequency Data on Unanswered CUCEI Items

Item	*Scale*	*Frequency*
4. The students look forward to coming to class.	Cohesiveness	3
13. New and different ways of teaching are seldom used in the class.	Individualization	1
16. Student "clock watch" in this class.	Innovation	2
19. The group often gets sidetracked instead of sticking to the point.	Innovation	2
21. Students have a say in how class time is spent.	Innovation	2
25. Classes are a waste of time.	Involvement	2
38. The instructor seldom moves around the classroom to talk with students.	Personalization	5
31. It takes a long time to get to know everybody by his/her first name in this class.	Personalization	1
32. Classes are boring.	Personalization	1
34. The seating in this class is arranged in the same way each week.	Personalization	7
39. Students enjoy going to this class.	Satisfaction	3
40. This class seldom starts on time.	Satisfaction	3
41. The instructor often thinks of unusual class activities.	Satisfaction	3
45. Students in this class are not very interested in getting to know other students.	Task Orientation	1
46. Classes are interesting.	Task Orientation	1

of a virtual classroom that doesn't have the characteristics of a traditional classroom is represented in this quote from a student who is trying to figure out where all the discussion points fall together:

> I noticed that [another student] sent the responses to her questions [the listserv]. This is not our chat line, do we use this address only for our assignments? Thanks again for your help. I am working on getting a picture, but have not been successful up to this date.

The student has had no problems with the assignments: rather her frustration lies in figuring out where in the virtual classroom she needs to go to tell the class as a whole something. This type of struggle would not be typical in the traditional seminar classroom.

The remaining troublesome items fall under the category of the asynchronous nature of the classes (i.e., students access course materials at any time). These items concern student going to a class (which might be construed as physically going) and class starting time. The mean for Item 4 (students look forward coming to class) was 2.23 and shows that the students who did answer the item agreed with the question, and the same with Item 39 (students enjoy going to class) with a mean of 2.15. In terms of the issue of class starting time (Item 40), even though 3 students didn't feel as though they could answer the question, the mean of 1.92 indicates strong agreement with the statement. The final item under this category, involving unusual class activities (Item 41), had a mean of 2.69, and again demonstrates agreement with the statement. Under this category, each of these items were left unanswered by 3 students, and the same students each time.

E-mail and listservs are examples of asynchronous communication. The message can be read, studied, and a response sent at staggered times and at the participant's convenience. E-mail provides students direct contact with each other and the instructor without the time restraints of office hours and class time, or space restraints of distance (Kerka, 1996; Partee, 1996). The flexibility of asynchronous class structures superimposed on the responsibility necessary to function in an asynchronous environment may cause problems for some students and generate uncertainty as to when and where they should be doing class work, as demonstrated in the following journal entry by a student:

> I am sorry. I read your message about not posting until Tuesday afternoon, but I posted my 15th question today. I am trying to get ahead because I am going to be gone next week. So sorry. Let me know if I need to send again. Thanks for your patience. When do we need to be available to chat tomorrow?

Although none of what the student worried about was a serious problem, the ability to do class work at times other than regular classroom hours was providing some dissonance for her.

Overall, the CUCEI items appeared to fair well in the virtual classroom. The two items that were most difficult for students to answer were not impossible for everyone to answer. Furthermore, the difficulty which might arise from conceptualization of the virtual classroom environment might be alleviated as the prevalence of web-based courses grows and student experience and understanding of the environment also grows.

Assessment of the Virtual Classroom Environment. The CUCEI assesses seven different factors of the classroom environment. On each of these factors, an individual's total score of 7 would indicate high satisfaction (Strongly Agree) with the environment, and a score of 35 would indicate high dissatisfaction (Strongly Disagree). Table 3 provides the minimum, maximum, mean and standard deviation score for each scale.

For the most part, the scores from each scale are similar to the others scales. The mean scores for the seven items indicate high agreement with the statements in the survey depicting the classroom environment. The strongest degree of agreement appears to be on the Involvement scale. Students felt that the instructor was involved with the students and that the students were able to be involved and participate with each other. This information from the instrument provides invaluable feedback because it addresses one of the biggest fears both students and faculty have about internet-based courses, and distance education courses in general. However, the ability of students to adapt to this environment and to take the initiative for making those connections among participations is exemplified in this message that a student sent as a welcome message (unsolicited) to all other students in the class:

> I'm looking forward to working with you all, those who were in class today and those who I'll meet in cyberspace. Good luck.

For those students who desire and need the involvement with others, the virtual environment may require and force them to be more active about developing relationships as opposed to passively awaiting others to do so for them.

It is also interesting to note that the other scale that stands out is the Personalization scale. This scale not only had higher minimum, maximum, and mean scores, but also four of the seven items on the scale were not answered by at least one individual. Two of these four items were the items that had large numbers of students not responding (Items 29 and 34). This scale concerns how students assess the environment in terms of responsiveness to them as a person, and to what degree they are able to assert their personality. Again, the difficulty some students felt about answering questions dealing with the make-up of the classroom might have affected the overall results of the scale. Students in these three web-based courses spend a great deal of time presenting their work to all students in the class and receiving constructive feedback. Students consistently comment about how much they appreciate hearing from the peers about their work and the recognition it places upon their efforts, as well as the way this sharing forced them to reflect back on their own work:

Scale	*Minimum Sum*	*Maximum Sum*	*Mean*	*Std. Dev.*
Student Cohesiveness	9	23	14.23	3.98
Individualization	10	25	14.07	4.09
Innovation	9	23	14.46	4.33
Involvement	9	19	14.54	2.84
Personalization	12	26	16.23	3.66
Satisfaction	7	24	13.15	4.45
Task Orientation	9	22	14.84	3.46

> Very impressive and detailed paper. Your insight on aspects on privacy and the Internet was very good. You raised many questions and forced me to rethink many simple ideas such as the privacy US mail has and the lack of privacy Internet communication has. I look forward to learning from your perspective.

Overall, the CUCEI provided valuable feedback about the classroom environment. It placed the comments collected by students in another framework that was more quantifiable. As an assessment tool of the virtual environment, it generally appeared to provide good information.

Conclusion

The CUCEI appears to be promising in its ability to assess the virtual classroom environment and provide instructors with valuable information about student perceptions of the environment. One thing this pilot study did not do was to complete a pre-test of the instrument that would provide students' preferred environment. As a follow-up study, it would be interesting to assess students' preferred classroom environment and contrast that with the actual environment. However, to understand the virtual classroom environment better and because a virtual classroom environment can be in many ways substantially different than the traditional classroom, it might be important to assess two different preferred classroom environments. The first administration would examine the preferred classroom environment in general terms. The next administration would examine the students' preferred distance classroom environment, followed by assessing the actual perceptions of the virtual classroom.

Fraser (1981) describes how classroom environmental research can provide a practical basis for aligning the environment to make a better person-environment fit. For example, even though an instructor may not choose for pedagogical reasons to make all adjustments to bring profiles in line, the assessments allow the instructor to know how much weight is placed upon certain scales, i.e., greater emphasis on student cohesiveness than individualization. Finally, the use of the assessment instrument also serves as tool to encourage all those involved to develop greater understanding of the virtual classroom.

References

DeYoung, A. J. (1977). Classroom climate and class success: A case study at the university level. *Journal of Educational Research, 70,* 252–257.

Fraser, B. J. (1981). Using environmental assessments to make better classrooms. *Journal of Curriculum Studies, 13*(2), 131–144.

Fraser. B. J. (1986). *Classroom Environment.* Croom Helm: London.

Fraser, B. J. (1989). Twenty years of classroom climate work: Progress and report. *Journal of Curriculum Studies, 21*(4), 307–327.

Fraser, B. J., Treagust, D. F. & Dennis, N. C. (1986). Development of an Instrument for Assessing Classroom Psychosocial Environment at Universities and Colleges. *Studies in Higher Education, 11*(1), 43–54.

Hansen, L. & Frick, T. W. (1997). Evaluation guidelines for web-based course authoring systems. In Badrul Khan (Ed.) *Web Based-Instruction.* Englewood Cliffs. New Jersey: Educational Technology Publications.

Hill, J. (1997). Distance learning environments via the world wide web. In Badrul Khan (Ed.) *Web Based-Instruction.* Englewood Cliffs, New Jersey: Educational Technology Publications.

Huebner, L. A. (1980). Interaction of student and campus. In U. Delworth, G. R. Hanson (Eds.). *Student Services: A Handbook for the Profession.* San Francisco: Jossey-Bass.

Kerka, S. (1996). Distance learning, the Internet and the world wide web, ERIC Digest No. 168, (ERIC ED 395 214).

Kuehn, S. (1994). Computer-mediated communication in instructional settings: A research agenda. *Communication Education, 43,* 171–182.

Moore, M. G. (1973). Toward a theory of independent learning & teaching. *Journal of Higher Education, 44*(9), 661–679.

Moore, M. G. (1994). Autonomy and interdependence. *American Journal of Distance Education, 8*(2), 1–4.

Moos, R. H. (1976). *The Human Context: Environmental Determinants of Behavior.* New York: Wiley-Interscience.

Moos, R. H. & Trickett, E. J. (1974). Manual: *Classroom Environment Scale.* Palo Alto, CA: Consulting Psychologists Press.

Moos, R. H. (1974). *The Social Climate Scales: An Overview.* Palo Alto, CA: Consulting Psychologists Press.

Partee, M. (1996). Using email, web sites & newsgroups to enhance traditional classroom instruction. *T.H.E. Journal, 23*(8), 79–82.

Powers, S. M. & Mitchell, J. (1997). Student perceptions and performance in a virtual classroom environment. Paper presented at the Annual Meeting of the American Educational Research Association (AERA), Chicago, Illinois, March 1997. ERIC Document: ED 409 005.

Ritchie, D. C. & Hoffman, B. (1997). Incorporating instructional design principles with the world wide web. In Badrul Khan (Ed.) *Web-Based Instruction*. Englewood Cliffs, New Jersey: Educational Technology Publications.

Verduin, J. R., & Clark, T. A. (1991) *Distance Education*. San Francisco, CA: Jossey-Bass, Inc., Publishers.

Customized Internet Assessments
Evaluating Another Dimension of Web Technology

EUGENE P. WAGNER

Online assessments, one area of Internet technology that educators are still trying to develop, can involve complicated programming beyond the reach of many instructors. This article describes a program that enables instructors to create their own online assessments with complete control over content and choices for the types of questions asked.

The Internet has proven to be a force to be reckoned with, having grown into a sizeable information resource unimaginable just 10 years ago (Rose 1996). Already distance-education courses, one product of the recent technology boom, have increased dramatically in their numbers and offerings because they are now conveniently available through the Internet (Kennepohl and Last 1997; Holmes and Warden 1996). Student interaction in traditional courses has also dramatically changed with the use of e-mail, chat rooms, live online discussions, online bulletin boards, and streaming audio and video (Mounts 1996; Sherritt and Basom 1997; Forsyth 1996; Aviv and Golan 1998). Instructors at high schools, colleges, and large research universities are adding web dimensions to their classes through course homepages that offer lecture notes, syllabi, interactive materials, exercises, and links to other Internet sites pertinent to the course (Byers 1997; Spain and Allen 1990; Nadelson 1997; Tissue 1996; Waldow, Fryhle, and Bock 1997; Lustick 1996; Bergland 1996; Dodge 1995). Clearly, educators have tapped the Internet to create an extended classroom resource for students.

One area of Internet technology that educators are striving to develop is online assessments. The difficulty with interactive online assessments is that the programming can be very complicated (Natal 1998). For example, to create a multiple-choice assessment in which the users can enter answers, submit the assignment, and receive immediate feedback on their performance requires computer programming knowledge of databases, common gateway interfacing (CGI), hypertext mark-up language (HTML), and program languages such as perl, javascript, C, and visual basic.

To design and post the assessments, many instructors rely on the Internet materials provided by the publisher of the textbook adopted for the course or use the publisher's web site connected to the text that may offer online assessments and quizzes as well as other learning materials. While these sites are simple enough to use, they have one major flaw: the publisher or programmer develops the questions and the format for the assessment, not the instructor. The result is a resource that does not properly examine students on the content and conceptual understanding that instructors intended for their courses.

Reprinted from *Journal of College Science Teaching* 20, no. 7 (2001), National Science Teachers Association.

A program that enables instructors to create their own online assessments with complete control over the content and choices for the types of questions used, such as multiple-choice, fill-in-the-blank, fill-in calculations, and essays, has many benefits. First, class time can be used to interact with the students and discuss the material rather than administering quizzes. Time outside of class can also be used in a more beneficial manner. Instead of grading vast amounts of quizzes, which can be overwhelming with a large lecture class, instructors can spend more time working on presentations for the course. The advantage of automatic grading and recording of results is that it enables the instructor to give more graded assignments during a semester without a significant time commitment. Students can take quizzes at any time of the day and in any place that has Internet access.

The benefit of online assessment has led me to develop a program that allows instructors to create their own assessments and manage student grades with only a basic knowledge of HTML programming and the Internet. The program has been tested over the past two years and can be used with any course in which online assignments are advantageous. (To learn more about this program, go to *http://chemweb.chem.pitt.edu/demo*; to view examples of program screen displays, log on to *www.nsta.org/pubs/jcst.*)

Program Requirements

Most instructors take a great deal of care in developing assessments that follow the specific content of their courses. Therefore, the ideal online assessment program must allow instructors to create customized assignments and have complete control over the content and format of the assessment. Second, the program must be able to grade the assessments automatically and post the grades to a sheet accessible to students online. The program thus creates more opportunities for assessment without increasing the paper and grading load of the instructor.

The third requirement addresses the issue of possible student dishonesty. Any time students are completing an assignment without supervision, the instructor must rely on student integrity, but if the assessment has a time limit and each student receives a unique assessment, the likelihood of dishonesty will decrease. If a student completes other supervised assignments and there is a large disparity between supervised and unsupervised assignment scores, it will indicate a potential concern for academic integrity.

Another requirement of the program is that it must be useful for constructing online assessments in any discipline. Chemistry is arguably one of the most difficult subject areas in which to create an assessment because of the many different symbols, mathematical and chemical equations, and pictures required to convey the material. Therefore, if the online assessment program is designed to work for chemistry, it should be applicable to other disciplines. The web pages that appear should be simple in design, aesthetically pleasing, and easy to use. Finally, both instructors and students should only be expected to be knowledgeable Internet users, not experienced computer programmers.

Program Description

Two interfaces exist for this program: the faculty interface for the creation and maintenance of the online assessments and grade sheet (fig. 1) and the user interface for students to access their assessments and grades. After the instructor logs on to the faculty interface, a menu with options for constructing and maintaining both the grade sheet and assessments is displayed. An assignment is first created by adding it to the online grade sheet through the faculty interface. This is similar in manner to adding a new column to a spreadsheet program.

After creating an online assignment in the grade sheet, it must be designed through the quiz construction interface either by manually selecting specific questions in the database or by automatic question selection based on criteria specified by the instructor. All questions in the database can be edited and deleted, and the instructor can also create new questions for the database. To create a quiz through manual selection of questions, the instructor first selects the assignment and the number of questions for the assignment on the faculty interface. Upon entering this information, the next screen displays a textbox next to each question group where the question identification numbers (QIDs) are entered. When a student accesses a quiz, it is created by randomly selecting one question from each question group. The frequency in which each question is randomly selected for a quiz decreases as the number of questions in a question group increases. For example, if a 10-question quiz is created from 10 question groups with each group consisting

Figure 1. ***Screen display of the faculty interface. Each cell in the table consists of text and selection boxes to input the necessary information for linking to the option described on the gray hyperlink button.***

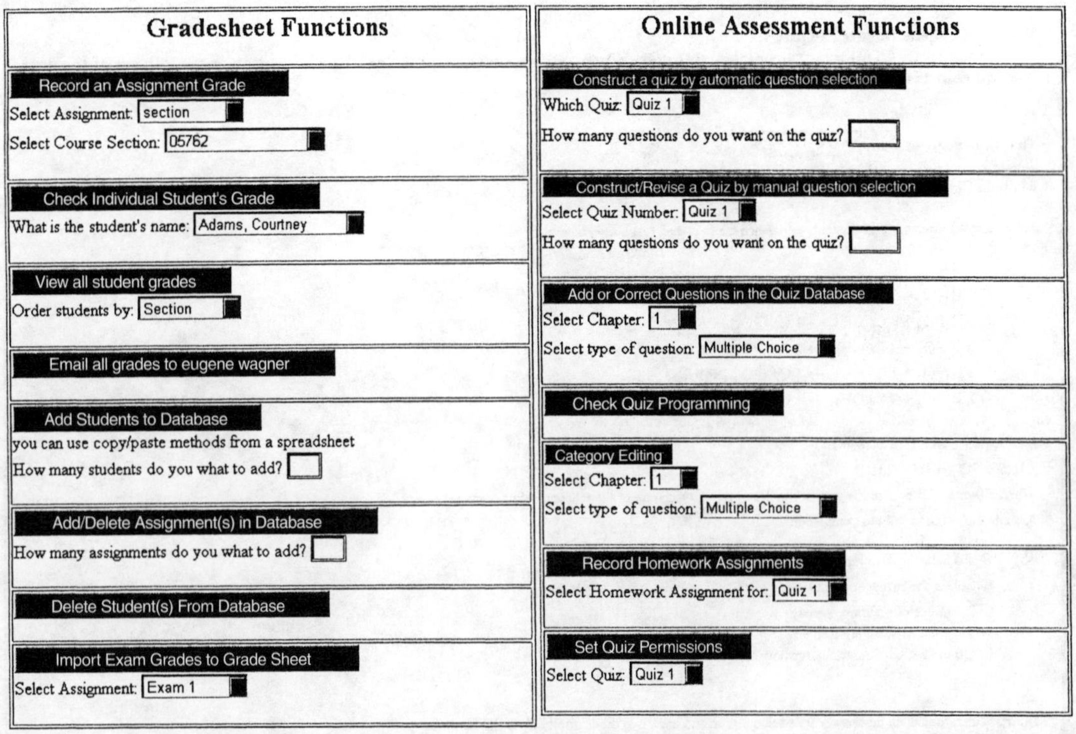

Gradesheet Functions	Online Assessment Functions
Record an Assignment Grade Select Assignment: section Select Course Section: 05762	Construct a quiz by automatic question selection Which Quiz: Quiz 1 How many questions do you want on the quiz?
Check Individual Student's Grade What is the student's name: Adams, Courtney	Construct/Revise a Quiz by manual question selection Select Quiz Number: Quiz 1 How many questions do you want on the quiz?
View all student grades Order students by: Section	Add or Correct Questions in the Quiz Database Select Chapter: 1 Select type of question: Multiple Choice
Email all grades to eugene wagner	Check Quiz Programming
Add Students to Database you can use copy/paste methods from a spreadsheet How many students do you what to add?	Category Editing Select Chapter: 1 Select type of question: Multiple Choice
Add/Delete Assignment(s) in Database How many assignments do you what to add?	Record Homework Assignments Select Homework Assignment for: Quiz 1
Delete Student(s) From Database	Set Quiz Permissions Select Quiz: Quiz 1
Import Exam Grades to Grade Sheet Select Assignment: Exam 1	

of four possible choices, there is the possibility of creating over one million different versions of the quiz. While only four of these quiz versions will be completely unique, four questions per question group typically provides an adequate number of assessment versions for a class of 100 students to significantly discourage academic dishonesty.

After the QID information is entered, the instructor enters the time limit and the dates the assessment will be available to the students. This faculty interface webpage also shows the question and correct answer for each QID selected for the quiz. Instructors are encouraged to print this page and keep a hard copy of the parameters selected for the quiz.

The questions selected for an assessment may also be completed through an automatic process. The instructor starts in the same manner as before by selecting the number of questions for the assignment. Upon submitting this information, the instructor specifies the following criteria for the selection of each question: 1) book chapter covering the material, e.g., stoichiometry, 2) category of the question, e.g., balancing equations or mole problems, and 3) type of question, e.g., multiple-choice, fill-in-the-blank, fill-in calculation, or essay. The program will then display the results as before with a textbox containing the selected QIDs next to the question groups that can be edited as necessary. The final step, as

TABLE 1

Correlation of the online quizzes, PEP, and CES usage and score to the common exam average for the spring 1999 semester. In all cases the p value for significance was <0.001. There was a total of 249 students enrolled in four course sections.

Assignment	*Usage of Resources Correlated to Exam Average*	*Score on Resources Correlated to Exam Average*
Quizzes	0.57	0.70
PEP	0.33	0.33
CES	0.27	0.28

Figure 2. ***Screen display of an online assessment. Four different question formats are displayed: multiple-choice, calculation, fill-in-the-blank and essay.***

Welcome eugene wagner to Quiz 3.
You have exactly 25 minutes to complete this quiz! When you are finished, push the SUBMIT button at the bottom of the page to have your results graded.

Time remaining for Quiz: 24:29

Multiple Choice Instructions: Select the best answer by clicking in the circle next to your choice.

1. Choose whole number coefficients to balance the following reaction equation.

$$H_3PO_4 + Ca(OH)_2 \rightarrow Ca_3(PO_4)_2 + H_2O$$

- ○ $1\ H_3PO_4 + 3\ Ca(OH)_2 \rightarrow 1\ Ca_3(PO_4)_2 + 6\ H_2O$
- ○ $3\ H_3PO_4 + 3\ Ca(OH)_2 \rightarrow 1\ Ca_3(PO_4)_2 + 6\ H_2$
- ○ $2\ H_3PO_4 + 3\ Ca(OH)_2 \rightarrow 1\ Ca_3(PO_4)_2 + 6\ H_2O$
- ○ $1\ H_3PO_4 + 1\ Ca(OH)_2 \rightarrow 1\ Ca_3(PO_4)_2 + 1\ H_2O$
- ○ $2\ H_3PO_4 + 3\ Ca(OH)_2 \rightarrow 1\ Ca_3(PO_4)_2 + 5\ H_2O$

2. SO_2 reacts with H_2S as follows:
$2\ H_2S + SO_2 \rightarrow 3\ S + 2\ H_2O$
When 6.0 moles of H_2S reacts with 5.0 moles of SO_2, which one of the following statements is correct? Assume the reaction goes to completion.

- ○ 3.0 moles of H_2S remain unreacted
- ○ SO_2 is the limiting reagent
- ○ 9.0 moles of sulfur are formed.
- ○ 15 moles of sulfur are formed.
- ○ 1.0 mole of H_2S remain unreacted

Instructions: Calculate the answer for each question and enter it in the textbox below the question.
If you need to use exponential notation, input your answer like this: 7.06E-10 (7.06×10^{-10}).

3. How many atoms of hydrogen are there in 10.0 g of NH_3?

[   ] atoms

Fill in the blank instructions: Enter your answer for each question in the textbox below the question. Make sure you spell the word(s) correctly.

4. Combustion of a hydrocarbon requires __________ , which is found in air.

[   ]

Short answer instructions: Enter your answer for each question in the textbox below the question. These questions will be graded by the instructor and added to your quiz score.

5. Discuss the process that occurs when an alkali metal reacts with water. How does its reactivity compare with an alkaline earth metal? Is the resultant solution acidic or basic? Explain your answer and propose a experimental method to test and measure the pH of the solution.

before, prompts the instructor to enter the time limit and dates available for the assessment. At this point the construction of the online assessment is complete and ready for the students.

Students access the online assessments and grades by first logging on to the web site and selecting the grade report option. All column titles generated in each table are based on the grade sheet constructed by the instructor through the faculty interface. When a student chooses an online assessment, the program first determines whether the specific assignment has

Figure 3. ***Screen display for entering a calculation-type question into the database. HTML formatting tags can be seen in both the question text area and the units text box.***

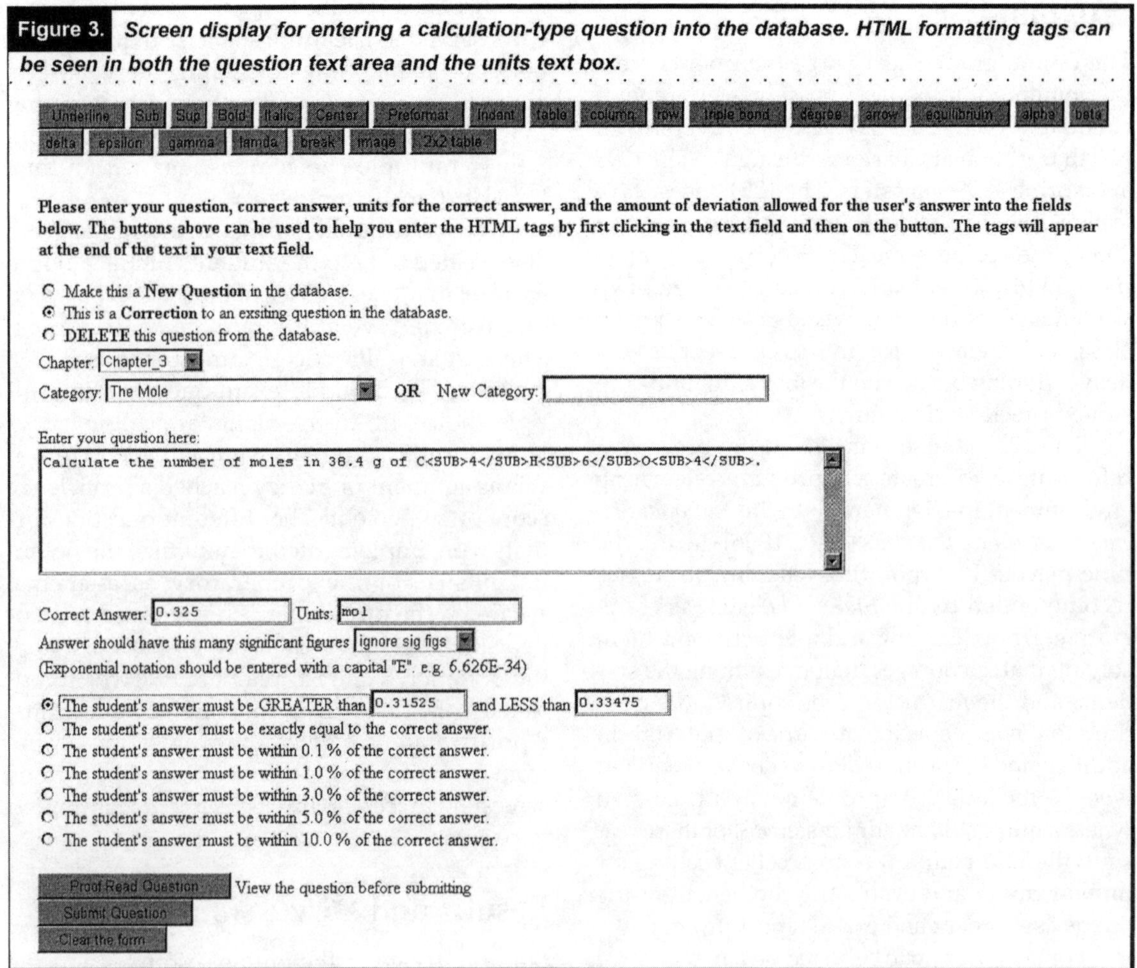
Underline | Sub | Sup | Bold | Italic | Center | Preformat | Indent | table | column | row | triple bond | degree | arrow | equilibrium | alpha | beta | delta | epsilon | gamma | lamda | break | image | 2x2 table

Please enter your question, correct answer, units for the correct answer, and the amount of deviation allowed for the user's answer into the fields below. The buttons above can be used to help you enter the HTML tags by first clicking in the text field and then on the button. The tags will appear at the end of the text in your text field.

- Make this a **New Question** in the database.
- This is a **Correction** to an exsiting question in the database.
- **DELETE** this question from the database.

Chapter: Chapter_3

Category: The Mole **OR** New Category:

Enter your question here:

Calculate the number of moles in 38.4 g of C₄H₆O₄.

Correct Answer: 0.325 Units: mol

Answer should have this many significant figures ignore sig figs

(Exponential notation should be entered with a capital "E". e.g. 6.626E-34)

- The student's answer must be GREATER than 0.31525 and LESS than 0.33475
- The student's answer must be exactly equal to the correct answer.
- The student's answer must be within 0.1 % of the correct answer.
- The student's answer must be within 1.0 % of the correct answer.
- The student's answer must be within 3.0 % of the correct answer.
- The student's answer must be within 5.0 % of the correct answer.
- The student's answer must be within 10.0 % of the correct answer.

Proof Read Question — View the question before submitting

Submit Question

Clear the form

already been completed, and then, if applicable, the status of the student's required preliminary assignment. If these conditions are met, the quiz is generated by random selection of one question from each question group (fig. 2). The timer that loads with the quiz page counts down from the time limit to zero, and it will automatically submit the quiz if the student does not do so before time expires. Instructions for each type of question are also given with the quiz.

After the quiz is submitted, it is automatically graded and entered into the grade sheet, and the itemized question scores and the overall score on the assignment are reported back to the student on the webpage as well as to the instructor via e-mail. Answers to the essay questions are also reported in the e-mail to the instructor and must be graded by the instructor. For other assignments, grades can be manually entered into the online grade sheet.

Since the questions are to be viewed on the Internet, HTML tags must be incorporated for formatting subscripts, superscripts, symbols, and so forth. The buttons that appear at the top of the editing form (fig. 3) will input the appropriate HTML tags for some of the more common formatting situations, but it is helpful if the user has a basic knowledge of HTML language when using the editing form. A button at the bottom of the form allows the user to view the format of the question as it will appear on a quiz before submitting the question into the database. Open-ended calculation problems require setting the additional parameters of percent deviation from the correct answer and significant figures allowed for an answer to be graded as correct. For example, if the parameters of an open-ended calculation problem were set with three percent deviation and the appropriate number of significant figures equal to three, then the correct response for a question asking for the results of 12.507/4.01 ranges from 3.22 to 3.03. The significant figures parameter can be set to "ignore" if desired.

Program Use

The online grade sheet and assessments were implemented into the first-semester general chemistry course (1251) at the University of North Carolina at Charlotte during the fall 1998 and spring 1999 semesters. The 1251 course typically enrolls 650 students in the fall semester and 250 in the spring semester. Section sizes range from 30 to 130 with an average class size of 78 students. Administering weekly quizzes during class, which was typical in this course, placed a heavy grading burden on the instructor and consumed precious class time.

The 1251 course was also in the process of reformation to create a more active-learning environment in alignment with the *National Science Education Standards* (NRC 1996) during the time period. Incorporating teaching strategies recommended by the *Standards*, such as cooperative-group learning and interactive problem solving that encourages dialogue among the students and the instructor, can require more class time to cover a specific amount of material. In addition, the 1251 course does not have a required weekly recitation or problem-solving session where a quiz could be administered. For these reasons, the 1251 course was an excellent setting for implementing and evaluating the benefit of the online assessment and grade report program.

For the program to be tested on a manageable population, the program was restricted to one out of seven 1251 sections offered in the fall 1998 semester. In the spring semester, all four 1251 course sections incorporated the online assessments and grade report, and instructors managed their own database of assessment questions, quizzes, and student grades. The 1251 curriculum operated under a common exam plan in which all students enrolled were administered the same exams regardless of their section or instructor. The common exams accounted for 90 percent of the course grade and the remaining 10 percent was specific to each instructor's course section.

For the web-enhanced course sections, 10 online chapter quizzes accounted for the remaining 10 percent of the course grade. Access to each quiz required completion of a corresponding chapter homework assignment consisting of questions from the end of each chapter in the textbook. Each quiz was worth one percent of the total course grade. Although the homework assignment was checked for completion, it was not calculated into the student's score. The homework served as a learning exercise requiring students to spend time reviewing the chapter's material in a directed effort before progressing to the online quizzes. The quizzes ranged from 8 to 14 multiple-choice questions with a time limit of 20 to 40 minutes.

Two additional online assessments were also created to help the students prepare before each exam. These assessments were optional and were not weighted into the course grade. The first step, Practice Exam Problems (PEP), consisted of 25–30 old exam questions in multiple-choice, fill-in-the-blank, and fill-in calculation formats. Students were allowed to repeat this assignment until they reached a proficiency score of 60 percent. The different question formats were implemented to minimize the potential misuse of the preparatory assessments. Attaining the proficiency score allowed the students to access the final exam preparatory step, the Common Exam Simulator (CES), which consisted of 25-30 multiple-choice questions. Approximately half of these questions came from common exams administered in previous semesters. Access to this assessment was limited to one use.

Results and Discussion

Both the usage of the online resources and the scores recorded for the online assignment were correlated to each student's common exam average (n=249) using Pearson's correlation coefficients (Table 1). These results show a very good direct correlation between using the online resources and exam average as well as the scores reported for the online resources and the exam average. Table 2 shows the average percent use for the online quizzes, PEPs, and CESs as they relate to the letter grade achieved for the course. The differences between mean usage of the online resources and semester grades was conducted through ANOVA.

Over the past year, there has never been a case where a student has completed all quizzes, PEPs, and CESs and earned a semester grade lower than C. Students who completed all quizzes, the PEP, and the CES leading up to an exam averaged 16 percent higher on the exam than those who failed to complete every assignment for the common exam. The differences seen through these analyses are significant and prove

TABLE 2
Average usage of the online quizzes, PEPs, and CESs corresponding to overall grades for the spring 1999 semester. The last column shows the average number of times the grade sheet was accessed by a student during the semester.

Semester Grade	*Percent of Quizzes Taken*	*Percent of PEPs Taken*	*Percent of CESs Taken*	*Grade Sheet Access per Semester*
A	96.7	44.2	24.2	26.4
B	96.7	25.0	8.3	19.7
C	84.6	21.8	8.1	20.8
D	68.8	13.7	3.0	14.6
F	43.0	9.5	1.6	8.9

the usefulness of this Internet-based program for student learning.

While the correlation of scores recorded for each online assessment to the exam score seems obvious, it is important to verify this positive effect and to show that these types of assignments incorporate appropriate questions and concepts that prepare students for the exams. It is interesting to note that the usage of the online resources can also be used as a predictor of success on the exams. This same process can be achieved without the use of the computer by using in-class quizzes, distributing old exams, and returning graded assignments to students. The time commitment, however, in and out of class to provide these learning experiences is enormous. Furthermore, monitoring and reporting student progress on exam preparation using assignments such as old exam questions is only possible if the the assignment is collected, graded, and returned to the students in a timely manner. This is not an issue with the online program. The three other 1251 instructors in the spring semester independently stated that they finished covering the material for the exams more quickly than before using these resources, and they spent the "extra" time in class presenting more in-depth discussions of the material and more extensive reviews for the exams.

Comments from the student course evaluations indicated a positive effect of online assessments. An interesting observation was that the online grade report appeared to put the students a little more at ease in the general chemistry course where anxiety usually runs high. Even though students can calculate their percent grade for the class, the ability to view the instructor's online grade sheet empowers students to verify their grades on the assignments and to calculate their averages for the course. In fact, the online grade sheet was clearly the most popular page on the general chemistry web site, with one student accessing the grade sheet over 200 times in one semester. No negative comments concerning the online assessments were written on the course evaluations, but there was one verbal report during the semester of students helping each other on the quizzes. This issue is always a concern with any unsupervised assignment completed for a grade in class. However, if students are discussing chemistry and solving problems in a collaborative manner outside of class, there will most likely be an increase in their knowledge of the subject and performance in the class. If there is a disparity between supervised and unsupervised assignment grades, then a true academic integrity issue exists. This disparity was not observed in any of the 1251 course sections.

Observations by the faculty suggest that there is a small number of students who do not wish to use the Internet as part of the course. Others have reported some student and faculty anxiety toward the use of computers in education in the past (Bollentin 1998; Corwin and Marcinkiewicz 1998; Perry, Perry, and Hosack-Curlin 1998; Skinner 1988; Reed and Judkins 1986; Cavin, Cavin, and Lagowski 1981). As computer literacy and use increases, this population will most likely decrease. We have found that the large majority of the students enjoy, and to some degree expect, their courses to utilize resources on the Internet.

Future Goals

The online assessments and grade reporting program have been a tremendous success in the first semester general chemistry program, and use of these resources continued in the following academic year. Four out of the six instructors teaching 1251 in the fall 1999 semester used the online assessments, and five of the six instructors use the online grade report. In the spring 2000 semester, the common exam incorporated open-ended calculation problems. The online assessments were still used for chapter quizzes, but they also incorporated fill-in-the-blank and calculation-question formats similar to the PEP to prepare students properly for the exams. There are approximately 750 questions in the database covering the material typically discussed in a first-semester general chemistry course, and questions for the second-semester general chemistry course are currently being added to the database. The program continues to be developed and utilized in the general chemistry curriculum at the University of Pittsburgh.

Although the interface for adding questions has been used with few problems, future programming changes will make it easier to use by eliminating the need to enter or see any HTML tags. Other interfaces will be altered and formatted into a more user-friendly style. The program will also be able to collect statistical data on assignments and questions in the database. In doing so, the instructor will be able to investigate objectively the specific questions and concepts that are difficult for the individual student and the entire class.

Both industrial and grant support are being sought to provide these resources to schools at all levels. The programs are easily distributed since there is no software for instructors or students to download or install, and access to the resources only requires a user ID and password. The program's function is independent of the subject matter and can be used for any type of course or discipline in which online assessment would be advantageous.

Note

Funding for this work was supported in part by a grant from the University of North Carolina at Charlotte.

References

Aviv, R., and G. Golan. 1998. Pedagogical communication patterns in collaborative telelearning. *Journal of Educational Technology Systems* 26(3): 201–208.

Bergland, B. 1996. Using the internet in the introductory composition classroom. Paper presented at the Annual Meeting of the Conference on College Composition and Communication, Milwaukee, WI, March 27–30.

Bollentin, W. R. 1998. Can information technology improve education? Measuring voices, attitudes and perceptions. *Educom Review* 33(1): 50–52, 54.

Byers, D. N. 1997. The effect of computer-assisted instruction on the attitudes of college students toward computers and chemistry. Paper presented at the Technology in Education Conference, San Jose, CA, April 21–22.

Cavin, C. S., E. D. Cavin, and J. J. Lagowski. 1981. The effect of computer-assisted instruction on the attitudes of college students toward computers and chemistry. *Journal of Research in Science Teaching* 18(4): 329–333.

Corwin, T., and H. Marcinkiewicz. 1998. Prediction of and differences in computer use when universally available. Paper presented at the National Convention of the Association for Educational Communications and Technology, St. Louis, MO, February 18–22.

Dodge, B. 1995. WebQuests: A technique for Internet-based learning. *Distance Educator* 1(2): 10–13.

Forsyth, I. 1996. *Teaching and Learning Materials and the Internet*. London: Kogan Page Limited.

Holmes, C. O., and J. T. Warden. 1996. CIStudio: A worldwide Web-based, interactive chemical information course. *Journal of Chemical Education* 73(4): 325–331.

Kennepohl, D. and A. M. Last. 1997. Science at a distance. *Journal of College Science Teaching* 27(1): 35–38.

Lustick, D. 1996. The elements of cyberspace. *The Science Teacher* 63(8): 32–35.

Mounts, R. D. 1996. Chemistry on the web. *Journal of Chemical Education* 73(1): 68–71.

Nadelson, L. 1997. Online assignments: Student web pages report results to the world. *The Science Teacher* 64(3): 23–25.

Natal, D. 1998. Online assessment: What, why, how. Paper presented at the Technology Education Conference, Santa Clara, CA, May 6.

National Research Council (NRC). 1996. *National Science Education Standards*. Washington DC: National Academy Press.

Perry, T. T., L. A. Perry, and K. Hosack-Curlin. 1998. Internet use by university students: An interdisciplinary study on three campuses. *Internet Research* 8(2): 136–41.

Reed, J. H., and J. Judkins. 1986. Evaluation of a holistic CAI system in introductory chemistry. *Journal of Computers in Mathematics and Science Teaching* 6(1): 21–27.

Rose, T. G. 1996. The Future of Online Education and Training. In: Online Information 96. Proceedings of the International Online Information Meeting, London, December 3–5.

Sherritt, C., and M. Basom. 1997. Using the Internet for higher education. *Opinion Papers:* 16 pages.

Skinner, M. E. 1988. Attitudes of college students toward computer assisted instruction: An essential variable for successful implementation. *Educational Technology* 28(2): 7–14.

Spain, D. J., and J. Allen. 1990. Instructional computing as replacement for recitation in freshman chemistry. *Journal of Chemical Education* 67(9): 766–769.

Tissue, B. M. 1996. Applying hypermedia to chemical education. *Journal of Chemical Education* 73(1): 65–71.

Waldow, D. A., C. B. Fryhle, and J. Chris Bock. 1997. CIRRUS: A chemistry Internet resource for research by undergraduate students. *Journal of Chemical Education* 74(4): 441–442.

Learning and Technology: Implications for Culturally Responsive Instructional Activity and Models of Achievement

Richard P. Durán

University of California, Santa Barbara

New forms of learning achievement are being made possible by the introduction of computers and multimedia into classroom activities. With proper planning, it is possible to improve the cultural responsiveness of instruction while addressing students' attainment of critical subject matter and curriculum standards. This article describes several instructional activities that allow students to express their own cultural heritage through the development of World Wide Web pages and video dramatizations of important historical events and personages. These activities raise the possibility of innovative performance assessments that are suited to new forms of achievement.

Introduction

We in the United States are in the midst of a fundamental transformation of classroom learning and schooling that is being made possible by the widespread availability of computers and other electronic technologies in the schools and elsewhere. The promised revolution in schooling through use of computers did not materialize as expected 20 years ago, yet now the rapid diffusion of powerful microcomputers and other multimedia devices in schools has begun to affect large numbers of students (Viadero, 1997). This diffusion has dramatic implications for efforts to improve the schooling outcomes of students from culturally and linguistically diverse backgrounds. However, we educators have only just begun to understand how this diffusion can be harnessed in the service of improving outcomes for these students.

One of the reasons for this lack of vision is that the new forms of learning being made possible through technology are creating altogether new forms of student achievement that defy the simple application of popular notions of achievement. Achievement as shown through evidence of memory for facts and concepts tied to subject-matter learning and focused solving of specific problem tasks in a subject area remain important forms of school achievement. Whereas those notions of achievement are not outmoded, there have evolved new forms of learning, facilitated through technology, that suggest expanded definitions of what might count as learning. This article explores some of the latter possibilities by describing the computer and other electronic media learning experiences of culturally and linguistically diverse elementary school students. As it demonstrates, the emergence of the World Wide Web (WWW) and other forms of electronic media in the everyday life of schools is having a transformative effect on the education of children. Though many think of the electronic revolution in school learning as based primarily on computers, other multimedia electronic technologies are beginning to have a dramatic effects on classroom learning and strategies that can be used to realize the learning standards adopted by state and local education agencies. These and other new technologies have fundamental importance for multiculturalism in educational practice.

Isla Vista's "Web Workers"

Isla Vista Elementary School is located just north of Santa Barbara, California, in the urban nonincorporated community of Goleta, home to more than 75,000 residents. The school serves over 700 children representing more than 15 language backgrounds. More than 60% of its students are Latino; however, there is a growing awareness among the children, teachers, and families of Isla Vista of their membership in the global community. Evidence of this is found on the school's WWW home pages where, beneath a graphic showing children's hands linked around planet Earth, the moniker of the Isla Vista School reads: "Home to the Children of Isla Vista and the World." There is a similar awareness on their part of the centrality of their own racial/ethnic group identity and of the linkage of this identity to everyday presentations of the self as a member of a diverse community.

Freddy[1] exemplifies this awareness. He is a sixth-grade African American student at Isla Vista in a Spanish–English bilingual classroom taught by Mr. Victor Reyes. Mr. Reyes is an active participant in a learning community of teachers sponsored by CRESPAR, the Center for the Education of Students Placed At Risk, a federally funded national educational research center based at Johns Hopkins University and Howard University. The teacher learning community is implementing innovative instruction emphasizing students' active learning of subject-matter knowledge. This instruction includes offering students ample opportunity to draw connections between their learning of traditional subject matter and their personal and social identities.

Freddy has much going for him. He speaks English as his first language, yet he is comfortable in a class where Spanish is also spoken as a language of instruction. He is also a classroom leader and a member of a prestigious group of Isla Vista students who have volunteered to be "Web Workers." These students put in extra time in the school computer laboratory learning how to develop personal web pages that are posted on the school's web site. In the classroom, Web Workers have developed an additional identity: they actively help other children develop their own web pages. Indeed, the World Wide Web provides students like Freddy with new forms of electronic literacy and an opportunity to project their identity and voices outward onto and throughout the Internet. "Freddy's PHAT Page," as he has dubbed his personal web site, is a window into his life understandings and the ways in which both his in-school and out-of-school worlds link to those understandings. Most importantly, this window was constructed by Freddy working in collaboration with other students and his classroom teacher, Mr. Reyes.

Mr. Reyes asked his students to include reading reports on fictional pieces and essays of their choosing on their home pages so that others accessing those pages could understand what students have learned through their reading. He also encouraged them to include summaries of what they had learned in science, history, and the social sciences as well as additional material expressing issues and perspectives of personal value to be shared with others. All of this work was reviewed and graded by Mr. Reyes prior to being electronically "published" on the students' web sites.

Freddy's web site is illustrative of but one embodiment of technology's new effects on schooling. His "PHAT Page" is a good example of this new form of publishing about learning and personal values. Through it, one encounters four reading reports on fictional pieces that Freddy read during the year. The site also includes a quiz Freddy developed to test viewers on the countries of origin of his favorite imported automobiles. Additionally, it presents video/sound clips of his favorite rap and soul musical pieces, and animations and graphics depicting the good and mellow side of "street life." On another of his pages, Freddy proudly describes his family and their strong interests in education and multiculturalism. His site also includes links to other pages spanning a diverse universe of interests. Freddy's spinning "home" logo—in blue-and-white, three-dimensional letters at the bottom of each page—keeps viewers from getting lost by reminding them that they can always easily return to the directory page of Freddie's web site by simply clicking the cursor on the icon. It is also a constant reminder that Freddy is a Web Worker, a virtuoso in the multimedia land of the World Wide Web, because only "advanced" web page developers know how to construct three-dimensional, spinning, multicolor icons.

Media Literacy and Content Learning at La Patera School: The "History on the Silver Screen" Project

Welcome to the fifth- and sixth-grade classrooms of teachers Loret Peterson and Chris Carrera of La Patera Elementary School. La Patera resembles Isla Vista school in many ways. Though the school is located in a more affluent section of Goleta, it busses in a large number of students from less affluent parts of town. La Patera serves children from almost as many language backgrounds as Isla Vista, is largely Latino, and, until fall 1998, it offered a Spanish–English bilingual program.

Like Mr. Reyes, Ms. Peterson and Mr. Carrera are also CRESPAR learning community project teachers. Both have a strong interest in helping students develop new forms of learning through collaborative learning techniques and use of technology. Yet, rather than emphasizing students' development of WWW pages as in Mr. Reyes's classroom, Ms. Peterson and Mr. Carrera have created a different emphasis. They utilize student collaborative learning, along with videorecording and broadcast technology, to effectuate their history and social science curricula.

With help from studio staff of the local cable television provider, students in Ms. Peterson's and Mr. Carrera's class received hands-on training in developing a variety of television programs integrated with the core curriculum. Working in small groups with the television staffers, the students have designed and recorded television news and interview programs that have been broadcast on the local cable educational channel. Every group investigation follows a certain pattern that is repeated three to four times during the school year. The goal of these efforts is to produce videotaped student dramatizations that convey the meaning and outcomes of important historical events. More recently, the students began attempting a more ambitious agenda, expanding beyond news broadcasting. With guidance from their teachers, they undertook the development of a year-long "History on the Silver Screen" television series. "Silver Screen" activities involve groups of three to four students in investigating a history/social studies topic tied to the selected content and learning standards mandated by the local school district and the state.

The "Silver Screen" curriculum is itself a cycle of learning activities. It is also a good example of the careful planning needed to integrate collaborative learning, concerns for multiculturalism, technology, and classroom learning objectives. Ms. Peterson and Mr. Carrera must pick and choose content areas and units within topic areas that can be covered through these activities, and decide how other topic units will be covered by other means. For example, at the fifth grade level in Ms. Peterson's class, students traced the history of the United States from pre-Columbian times to the eras of European colonization, the American Revolution, and the westward expansion. Based on her past experience with the "Silver Screen" curriculum, Ms. Peterson chose to implement only three (or possibly four) "Silver Screen" units with her class in the coming school year. In the fall and winter, she planned to ask her students to enact dramas about important historical events related to the Native American settlers of the Americas and the European colonization. Her spring plans called for students to depict the rise and abolition of slavery and explore its connections to the Civil Rights movement. Given sufficient time after these activities, the students could enact dramas related to the westward expansion.

While "Silver Screen" units are intended to advance student knowledge of important historical and social science content, this objective is tied to other objectives such as helping students acquire skills in conducting cross-disciplinary research investigations, collaborating with other students, and using technology. The curriculum provides a balance between structured, guided instruction and students' exercise of freedom and responsibility for their own learning. Through it, students learn how to be "junior" historians and researchers.

The foundational phase of the "Silver Screen" curriculum is part of a more general plan for instruction that involves teaching students how to do cross-disciplinary research in the classroom. This phase introduces students to the use of diagrams for concept mapping and shows them how to make comparative interpretations of human experiences. It also introduces the "KWLQ" technique, a learning scheme for the conduct of group investigations organized around four critical questions:

1. *K*: What topic do we want to investigate, and what do we already know about it?
2. *W*: What more do we want to learn about the targeted topic?
3. *L*: After conducting an investigation, what have we learned?
4. *Q*: What questions remaining to be answered about the topic?

Concept mapping is introduced in this phase as a tool for developing explicit outlines to guide enactment of KWLQ components and as a guide for the associated reports that students must generate in connection with this activity.

Another part of the foundational curriculum focuses on the interpretive reading of narrative texts, such as fairy tales, from the perspective of the world views that might be held by the characters in those stories. The goals of these activities are to have students actively explore the possibility of multiple interpretations of human experience, and learn how to communicate those perspectives to others as well as begin to investigate how perspectives might influence historical accounts of experiences.

Following these foundational learning activities, students are introduced to the "Silver Screen" unit activities. Each features four subactivities:

1. group and individual identification of an historical topic for research, followed by research on the topic;
2. group authorship of a drama script;
3. enactment of the drama script and the conducting of rehearsals prior to videotaping; and
4. video production and taping (with assistance from cable television staff), followed by class viewing and discussion of the video products.

Each subactivity requires students to exercise a variety of literacy and thinking skills as well as skills in using technology. In the first subactivity, students in small groups must generate and evaluate possible topics for research and script development based on criteria set by the teacher. Each student in a group is given the opportunity to nominate a topic and to offer opinions on the relevance and importance of topics suggested by other students. In exploring possible topics and carrying out research on the chosen topic, students must engage a variety of information resources including but not restricted to CD-ROMs and WWW sites with relevant content. In the second subactivity, students must negotiate the development of a drama script that can communicate to others what they have learned from their research. They must delegate responsibilities for various parts of their scripts among the members of their groups, then they must edit the final product. In carrying out these two subactivities, students make ample use of the computer and related wordprocessing software to develop and store their thoughts and other products. The third subactivity involves student groups in the production of their dramas including creating and building props, making costumes, and conducting rehearsals. In the final phase, student groups record and edit the videos of their dramas. This last phase also includes previewing the videos before the entire class and entertaining whole-class discussion and critique.

In its entirety, the "Silver Screen" process intimately acquaints students with video production and recording equipment. It also helps them acquire critical skills in reasoning about the knowledge communicated by video media. Its instructional activities exemplify the rich range of content and problem-solving skills that can be enhanced by thoughtfully incorporating technology into instruction. Most importantly, it positions technology not as a sole route to learning but rather as an enhancing methodology. It deepens students' awareness of the multiple ways in which subject-matter information can be accessed, organized, and presented in the development of learning products in a complex learning sequence. At each step in the process, students are guided to understand how they are consumers of knowledge and now knowledge can be synthesized and communicated to other audiences—with and without electronic technology.

Assessment Issues Related to Innovative Approaches to Teaching and Learning

The "Silver Screen" curriculum represents an active form of learning in which learning is demonstrated through the effective social communication of students' understandings as complex bodies of interconnected ideas. This social demonstration of learning is very different from the types of evidence of learning demonstrated by students' performance on standardized achievement tests administered in isolated "test events." It is also very different from performance-based assessments such as written essays developed as stand-alone measures. Notwithstanding, it is important to affirm that existing standardized tests of subject-matter learning should not be entirely shelved. These tests are very useful and reliable tools for assessing certain kinds of skills in an on-demand manner. They are excellent tools for assessing numerous specific skills and specific pieces of knowledge that students should be expected to master. However, new tools are needed for assessing the outcomes of the new forms of achievement that are being made possible by the increasing use of technology in learning. This is especially the case in those learning contexts in which social collaboration among learners is an essential component. Traditional assessment methods focus on the capabilities of individuals working in isolation. New constructs representing learning made possible through technology must be devised, and new strategies for gathering evidence and evaluating the qualities of student performances in new kinds of learning must be shaped.

At first glance, checklist-type assessment strategies that could determine whether students have attained learning standards in a "yes" or "no" manner appear useful. For example, the recently adopted State of California Language Arts Standards specify that by the 12th grade, in response to the listening and speaking standards, students are expected to be able to deliver multimedia presentations that:

1. combine text, images, and sound—synthesizing information from a wide range of materials including television, videos, films, newspapers, magazines, CD-ROMs, Internet resources, and computer media-generated images;
2. select an appropriate medium for each element of presentation;
3. use the selected media skillfully, including editing and monitoring for quality;
4. test audience responses and revise the presentation accordingly (California Academic Standards Commission, 1997).

It seems clear that the fifth- and sixth-graders in Ms. Peterson's and Mr. Carrera's classes should be able to meet these standards by the time they graduate from high school, if their subsequent instruction continues to emphasize technology as a tool for learning and the communication of learning.

Yet, just being able to answer "yes" to an item asking whether students have acquired skills such as those listed above is not enough. Effective and informative assessments can profitably include such checklist assessment procedures, but more is needed. To begin, classrooms must be reconceptualized as learning cultures and learning communities in order to understand how learning activities facilitate students' development of agency as learners. Bruner (1996) suggests that educators have been slow to question their own assumptions of what teaching and learning are about. He further maintains that this view is detrimental to improving educational outcomes for students who are low performers. However, students' motivation and interest in learning, and their demonstrations of learning proficiency, are seldom "up for negotiation" between teachers and students.

Durán, Escobar, and Wakin (1997) propose that learning is fundamentally a process of predication. They assert that because it is the basic propensity of the human mind to create meaningful interpretations and associations of experience that guide moment-to-moment activity, students need to become invested in their learning. That is, they need to view themselves as active learners whose self-identity incorporates an enthusiasm for new learning and a connection to learning as an ongoing process connected to self-development and social development.

Consider, for example, the statements of one of Ms. Peterson's students, reflecting on his group's completion of a "Silver Screen" drama project based on their investigation of slavery and the emergence of the civil rights movement:

> I like doing the movie assignment. We are learning about history and drama by acting out history! My favorite part is reading and acting out Dr. Martin Luther King, Jr.'s speech, because I think I understand what he meant. I am also learning how to be a good actor and how not to be nervous when I'm on stage. I like it. I learn how to write scripts, and it can help me to get a great career.

Though the overall degree and depth of this student's learning cannot be gauged by one anecdotal comment, this comment is a powerful conveyance of the student's sense of empowerment as a learner. Classrooms so often fail to connect with students because they do not engage them as living personalities in the manner stated above. Rarely do we teachers fully recognize that students are ready to learn when learning is about "sense making," or that which is valued and that can be appropriated by learners to demonstrate competence and the potential for further personal development.

Wolf (1993) suggests an interesting and worthwhile reconceptualization of assessment of particular value to the foregoing points. She proposes that entire episodes of learning (e.g., a "Silver Screen" project cycle) might be viewed as involving many imbedded assessments and learning reactions to assessments. Therefore, under ideal circumstances, as students proceed through complex learning activities in collaboration with other students, they will have the opportunity to reflect collectively and individually on the quality of learning and how to improve it. Most importantly, if instruction is framed appropriately, students will have the opportunity to respond to feedback and demonstrate improved learning proficiency throughout the course of a learning episode. Black and William (1998) lend support to this perspective in their review of major instructional intervention studies focusing on alternative assessment methods to evaluate learning outcomes. They report evidence that instructional interventions emphasizing regular student assessment (including self-assessment) throughout the course of instruction lead to the greatest achievement gains when these formative assessments include indicators of efficacy including but extending beyond standardized achievement test scores.

Concluding Comments, with Additional Implications for Assessments Made Possible Through Technology

It is fair to state that new assessment techniques aimed at capturing the breadth and depth of students' learning through collaboration with the assistance of technology are in their early stages. One obvious direction to consider is the refinement of portfolio assessment methods (Johnson & Rose, 1997). Consistent with Wolf's (1993) suggestions and the findings of Black and William (1998), portfolios might include individual student products produced during learning episodes as well as students' self-evaluations of their work. Subsequent to their formation, individual products in a portfolio (including students' self-evaluations) might be scored using specially designed rubrics to assess particular aspects of students' learning accomplishments.

A more ambitious and innovative way to proceed would be to use the technology itself to present student portfolios prior to evaluation. One possibility that I have been exploring recently involves constructing a relational database representation of instructional activities and products created by students. The three facets of the database (activities, products, and the student himself or herself) could provide historical documentation of (a) the major activities conducted by the student in carrying out a learning episode (such as a "Silver Screen" cycle), (b) the products generated by students in particular activities (i.e., those associated with each episode), and (c) the identification of individual students or groups of students who participated in the activities and generated products. This database could conceivably include electronic documents and selective multimedia digitization of students' work; it could even be extended to link this sort of information across different learning episodes.

Such complex collections of information could be treated as "texts" in themselves. Database information could be sorted, aggregated, and clustered to foreground alternative interpretation of students' achievement within and across learning episodes over time. For example, it would be possible to explore the La Patera students' self-evaluations of their "Silver Screen" products, determine how these self-evaluations were connected to collaborations with other students, and learn how the evaluations changed over the course of the year. The study of students' self-evaluations could be coupled with direct access to their digitized products for subsequent scoring and interpretation against learning rubrics.

As fantastic as such possibilities seem, the future is already upon us and, as teachers, we must be prepared to offer the necessary vision to realize the full impact of technology on teaching, learning, and assessment. As this article suggests, this vision should build upon carefully constructed and implemented curriculum models. These models should focus on what we want students to learn while giving students a chance to personalize their learning. They should also focus on the implementation of interesting sense-making activities that make such learning possible, and on how student performances in classroom activities show evidence of intended learning achievement in a manner enhancing the assessment of achievement. This article also serves as an reminder that increased use of electronic technology in instruction should be viewed as a tool to serve these goals, not as an end in itself. As teachers, we must be careful to avoid introducing technology into instruction just because it is available. By doing so, we run the risk of not attending to students' learning needs as the fundamental reason for schooling and instruction.

Note

1. A pseudonym.

References

Black, P., & William, D. (1998). Assessment and classroom learning. *Assessment in Education*, 5(l), 7–74.

Bruner, J. (1996). *The culture of education*. Cambridge, MA: Harvard University Press.

California Academic Standards Commission. (1997, October 1). *Language arts: Reading, writing, listening and speaking standards*. Sacramento: California State Department of Education.

Durán, R. P., Escobar, F., & Wakin, M. (1997). Improving instruction for Latino elementary school students: Aiming for college. In M. Yepes–Baraya (Ed.), *Proceedings from the 1998 ETS invitational conference on Latino education issues* (pp. 39–51). Princeton, NJ: Educational Testing Service.

Johnson, N. J., & Rose, L. M. (1997). *Portfolios: Clarifying, constructing, and enhancing*. Lancaster, PA: Technomic.

Viadero, D. N. (1997, November 10). A tool for learning. *Education Week* (Special Issue entitled "Technology Counts: Schools and Reform in the Information Age"), pp. 12–18.

Wolf, D. P. (1993). Assessment as an episode of learning. In R. Bennett & W. Ward (Eds.), *Construction versus choice in cognitive measurement* (pp. 213–240). Hillsdale, NJ: Erlbaum.

RECOMMENDED READINGS

Brookhart, S. M. (1999). The art and science of classroom assessment. The missing part of pedagogy. *ASHE-ERIC Higher Education Report*, v27 n1.

Dasher-Alston, Robin M. and Patton, Gerald W. (1998). Evaluation criteria for distance learning. *Planning for Higher Education*, v27 n.1 pp. 11-17. Fall.

Day, Michael (2000). Teachers at the crossroads: evaluating teaching in electronic environments. Computers and Composition v17 n1 p31-40.

Diamond, Robert M. (1998). *Designing and Assessing Courses and Curricula: A Practical Guide.* Jossey-Bass: San Francisco.

Ducheneaux, Teton, McDonald, J. D. (1999). Biculturalism and Native American college students' performance on the WAIS-III. ED453463.

Foster, Lenoar (1997). A collaborative distance graduate degree program: A case study for building the 'Professional Community.' *Resources in Education.* ED 406358.

Gardiner, Lion F., Anderson, Caitlin and Cambridge, Barbara L. (eds.) (1997). Learning through assessment: a Resource Guide for Higher Education. AAHE Assessment Forum. Washington, DC.

Kasworm, Carol E., and Marienau, Catherine A. (1997). Principles for assessment of adult learning. In Rose, A,D, and Leahy, M. A. (eds.)(1997) Assessing Adult Learning in Diverse Settings: Current Issues and Approaches. *New Directions for Adult and Continuing Education*, n75, pp. 5-16. Fall 1997.

Lesser, Diana and Ferrand, Judy (2000). Effect of class size, grades given and academic field on student opinion of instruction. *Community College Journal of Research and Practice* v24 n4 pp. 269-277.

Lindner, Parker (1998). Assessment tools for distance learning: a review of the Literature. Washington State Board for Community and Technical Colleges. Olympia, WA. ED426725.

Mayes, Larry D. (1998). Assessing faculty workload: a review of the University of Kentucky Community College System process and outcomes. *Community College Journal of Research and Practice* v 22, n2 pp. 145-150.

Sanchis, Gariela R. (2001). Using web forms for online assessment. *Mathematics and Computer Education*, v.35. n.2 pp.105-113.

Ting, Siu-Man Raymond (2000). Predicting Asian Americans' academic performance in the first year of college: an approach combining SAT scores and noncognitive variables. *Journal of College Student Development*, v41, n4, p442-449.

Discussion & Reflection

How credible are student evaluations for assessing quality instruction?

How can culturally relevant pedagogy be assessed with confidence of validity and reliability?

Why is the link between teaching and learning important in assessment/evaluation?

What challenges are there to measuring learning and cognitive growth? How can these challenges be resolved?

How does technology enhance and deter learning in higher education?

What should be considered when assessing faculty productivity? Why?

Section IV

Student Performance & Outcomes

Student Performance & Outcomes

Introduction

Students are the most important stakeholders in higher education and the "value added" of the college experience is a strong indicator of institutional performance. Despite the development of academic and social programs, attention to institutional climate and efforts to incorporate faculty-student relationships in the institutional reward structure, student attrition continues to be a concern. Calls for accountability address the question of whether college makes a difference. Thus, the impact of college on students is often the focus of assessment and evaluation efforts, and rightly so since students are expected to leave college prepared to be contributors to rather than dependents on society. Literature in this section addresses student retention, issues of access and college choice. Diversity continues to be an important objective in higher education and considerable research documents the benefits of diverse populations in higher education. Literature in this section, identified or included, presents a discussion on diversity (e.g. ethnicity, gender and race), college impact on learning, retention and student outcomes.

Classic Readings

Focusing on Student Academic Outcomes

Joanne M. Alexander and Joan S. Stark

Approaches to Outcomes and Outcome Assessment

A number of researchers have attempted to classify outcomes and specify approaches for assessing outcomes. In this section, approaches by Ewell, Astin, Lenning et al., and Bowen are discussed.

Ewell (1983) discusses three approaches that have been used to measure student outcomes: academic investigation perspective, student-personnel perspective, and management perspective. Actually these approaches are based on the purpose of the investigators and thus use different perspectives on outcomes, have different goals for using outcomes, and involve different data requirements.

Academic investigation (research) is the oldest and most commonly used reason for measuring student outcomes. The college experience is investigated in a typical research fashion: theories about student growth are developed, tested, and refined as a result of data collection. From this perspective, most of the research on student outcomes has been done by psychologists and sociologists. Frequently psychologists have focused on the impact of college on personal and cognitive development and sociologists have concentrated on such issues as the impact of college on social mobility and socialization of students into the professional fields. In this perspective the goal to explain (and ultimately to predict) human behavior and the data collected must have high empirical quality and be objective. While some of the relationships discovered in this research have been used by institutional policy makers, it should be noted that divisional utility is not the goal; the purpose is to successfully account for a given outcome.

The student personnel approach uses student outcomes as a means for evaluating students for admission to programs and placement on completion of the program. The data are also used for counselling students in career selection and for evaluating the effectiveness of programs for meeting student needs. In this perspective the goal of outcome measurement is to gain assessment information about individual students. Data is considered useful if it provides information for student placement or if it is diagnostic of student problems. The theoretical constraints of data collection are not crucial when using this approach.

The management perspective for measuring outcomes is a still different approach to outcome assessment. From this perspective the focus is on the use of outcome assessment as a method to improve administrative decisions, particularly those involving program planning and budgeting. The goal of outcome assessment in this perspective is to improve the quality of resource-allocation decisions. To meet this goal, data must be empirically valid, reliable, and perceived by the decision makers as relevant to the decision.

Reprinted from *Focusing on Student Academic Outcomes: A Working Paper,* (1986).

Ewell's classification of approaches to student outcomes is useful because it calls attention to varied uses of outcomes and the ways in which different goals influence the collection of student outcome information.

In addition to classifying approaches to outcome assessment based on proposed uses, researchers have attempted to classify types of educational outcomes. Astin (1974) developed a taxonomy of student outcomes involving three dimensions: type of outcome, type of data, and time. The types of outcome are split into two domains: cognitive and affective. The cognitive domain includes outcomes such as basic skills, general intelligence, and higher-order cognitive processes. The affective domain includes outcomes often described as attitudes, values, and self-concept.

The data dimension is also split into two domains: behavioral and psychological. This dimension distinguishes between outcome data that are covert and those that are observable. The behavioral domain refers to observable activities of the individual. The psychological domain refers to the internal states or traits of the individual. While the actual outcomes may be the same, the ways in which the information is gathered to represent them are different.

The primary two dimensions of Astin's approach are shown in Table 1. This typology has been widely accepted as method for classifying outcomes. In Astin's typology the third dimension, time, stresses the importance of including both the long- and short-term outcomes of college. Some examples of applying the time dimension to the outcome cells are provided in Table 2.

In addition to the typology, Astin (1974) provided some insights into the assessment of educational outcomes. To him the fundamental purpose of assessment is to produce information that is useful for decision making. Thus measurement should begin with a value statement—an idea about what future state would be desirable or important.

Lenning and Associates (1983) at the National Center for Higher Education Management Systems (NCHEMS) developed an extensive framework for identifying the universe of major "outputs" and outcomes of postsecondary institutions. In developing this taxonomy, the authors sought to develop an exhaustive list of outcomes to assist in the assessment of managerial effectiveness. As a result of the management perspective, Lenning et al. did not focus exclusively on student outcomes but rather included them in two of the several categories: human characteristics outcomes and knowledge, technology, and art forms outcomes. Viewed in Astin's terms, the human characteristics outcomes include primarily affective and personality characteristics, as well as skill outcomes. The knowledge, technology, and art form category includes the typically cognitive outcomes:

Table 1
A Typology of Student Outcomes

Data	Outcome	
	Affective	Cognitive
Psychological	Self-concept Values Attitudes Beliefs Drive for Achievement Satisfaction with College	Knowledge Critical Thinking Ability Basic Skills Special Aptitudes Academic Achievement
Behavioral	Personal Habits Avocations Mental Health Citizenship Interpersonal Relations	Career Development Level of Educational Attainment Vocational Achievements Level of Responsibility Income Awards or Special Recognition

Source: Alexander W. Astin, R. J. Panos, and J. A. Creager, *National Norms for Entering College Freshmen-Fall 1966* (Washington, D.C.: American Council on Education, 1967): p. 16.

Table 2
Outcomes Over Time

Outcome	Data Indicator	Short-Term Indicator	Long-Term
Affective	Behavioral	Choice of major field of study	Current Occupation
Affective	Psychological	Satisfaction with college	Job Satisfaction
Cognitive	Behavioral	Persistence	Job Stability
Cognitive	Psychological	LSAT score	Score on law boards

Source: Astin, 1974, p. 33

both specialized and general knowledge and scholarship. Additional outcome categories in this framework include (1) economic (e.g. economic security, standard of living), (2) resource and service provision (e.g., teaching, facility provisions) and (3) other maintenance and change (e. g., traditions, organizational operation). A listing of the complete NCHEMS taxonomy is included in Appendix A. Clearly this framework includes both long- and short-range student outcomes as well as outcomes at the program and institutional level.

Bowen (1974) took a slightly different approach from the two previous researchers when discussing outcomes. Instruction is related to the outcome of learning and changes in human traits. Research and scholarship relates to the outcomes of preservation, discovery, and interpretation of knowledge, artistic and social criticism, philosophical reflection, and advancement of the fine arts. Public service results in societal outcomes such as improved health, solutions to social problems and agricultural productivity (p. 2–3).

Of these three services, Bowen believes that instruction is the primary goal of higher education and bringing about desired changes in students is central to this mission. Bowen's approach could be viewed, therefore, as primarily academic in nature. He focused on investigating the changes that occur among students without emphasizing the use of these measures in either placement or decision making.

In a later work, Bowen (1977) broadened his view of student learning and offered a more elaborate catalogue of accepted goals. This catalogue of goals serves also as a typology of student outcomes derived from three widely accepted goals of instruction. These three general goals are: educating the whole person, addressing the individuality of students, and maintaining accessibility. The first goal, educating the whole person, refers to the idea that education should cultivate both the intellectual and affective dispositions of persons, thereby enhancing intellectual, moral, and emotional growth. The second goal, addressing individuality, requires that the uniqueness of individuals be taken into account in the educational process. Accessibility refers to the notion that education should be readily available to a broad range of persons.

According to Bowen, the catalogue of goals derived from these general goals constitutes both a model for the educational system and the criteria by which the system can be judged. While Bowen recognized that his goal typology has utopian qualities, he posits that it provides a useful model that can be used to shape and guide institutional functioning.

In Bowen's scheme specific educational goals are divided into two groups: goals for individual students and goals for society. The five categories of goals for individual students include: cognitive learning, emotional and moral development, practical competence, direct satisfactions from college education, and avoidance of negative outcomes. In a further subdivision, cognitive learning includes ten specific areas of learning. They are:

1. Verbal skills: Ability to read, speak, and write clearly and correctly.
2. Quantitative skills: Understanding of mathematical and statistical concepts.
3. Substantive knowledge: Acquaintance with Western culture and traditions and

familiarity with other cultures. Knowledge of contemporary philosophy, art, literature, natural science, and social issues. Understanding of facts, principles and vocabulary within at least one selected field.

4. Rationality: Ability to think logically, and analytically, and to see facts clearly and objectively.
5. Intellectual tolerance: Openness to new ideas, curiosity, and ability to deal with ambiguity and complexity.
6. Esthetic sensibility: Knowledge of and interest in literature, the arts and natural beauty.
7. Creativeness: Ability to think imaginatively and originally.
8. Intellectual integrity: Respect for and understanding of the contingent nature of truth.
9. Wisdom: Ability to balance perspective, judgment and prudence.
10. Lifelong learning: Sustained interest in learning. (Bowen, 1977, pp. 35–36)

Bowen's remaining four categories of student goals are focused primarily on affective and long term student outcomes.

Bowen also suggested seven principles that should be used in the identification of outcomes and thus in outcome assessment at particular colleges. The first principle is that inputs should not be confused with outputs. Bowen claims that high institutional expenditures (an input) do not guarantee equivalently high outcomes; the differences between inputs and outputs has too often been ignored. The only valid outcome measurement is of the development and changes that occur in students as a result of their college experience.

The second principle suggests that assessment should be linked to all educational goals, not just to those developments easily measured or related to economic success. Bowen offers his catalogue of goals as a starting point on which to build an assessment plan.

The third principle states simply that educational outcomes should relate to the person as a whole; and the fourth principle posits that outcome assessment should include the study of alumni as well as current students. The fifth principle suggests that outcome assessment should measure changes that occur as a result of the college experience.

The sixth principle states that an evaluation scheme must be practical: not too time-consuming or expensive. The assessment should focus on major goals of the institution and need not be based on the entire population of students. However, results must be reported in a form that the general public can read and understand.

The final principle asserts that assessment should be controlled from within the institution rather than being imposed by external agencies. Assessment programs should be designed for each institution, keeping the special missions and philosophies of the institutions in mind.

Ewell (1983) mentions additional outcome dimensions that should be considered. These include whether (1) the effects are short- or long-term, (2) the student is aware or unaware of the outcome, (3) the effect is direct or indirect (i.e., how closely the outcome is connected to the educational program), and (4) the outcome is intended or unintended. These dimensions represent important differences between outcomes that should be considered in outcome research and assessment.

In more recent work than that reviewed earlier, Astin (1979) identifies three core measures of student outcomes that should be included in a student outcome data base. First, students' successful completion of a program of study should be included. More specifically, information is needed to determine whether students' accomplishments are consistent with their original goals. Second, a measure of cognitive development must be included and more than grade point average and class standing are needed. Preferably, repeated measurement will be used so that change can be assessed by comparing performance at two points in time. Third, measures of student satisfaction should include satisfaction with the quality of the curriculum, teaching, student services, facilities, and other aspects of the college.

Beyond these essential measures, the student data should include information gathered on entry, during the educational process, and at exit or another designated point of time. Student characteristics should be recorded when they first enroll, information on what happens to the student while enrolled at the college must be available, and measures of the degree of attainment of desired or behavioral objective at exit must also be assessable. This approach, developed by Astin, is known as the "value-added" approach. It asserts that outcome measures alone tell us very little about institutional effectiveness or impact. By controlling for entry characteristics, however, a more accurate picture of outcomes will emerge. In the absence of such data, outcome measures may be grossly misinterpreted when used for assessing institutional effectiveness because most outcomes are highly dependent on the characteristics of students at entry.

NCRIPTAL's Delimited Outcome Framework

As discussed earlier, NCRIPTAL's mission includes both conducting basic research on the effects of various aspects of the teaching and learning environment on student outcomes and providing leadership and assistance to institutions in their own assessment and evaluation efforts. Thus, in the terms of Ewell's "perspectives," we must engage in a dual approach, combining the academic-investigative spirit of basic research and a management perspective that can help institutions construct their own assessment processes and uses of the information.

Fulfilling this dual mission with available resources requires delimination of the arena in which our work will be conducted and a selection of outcome measures and assessment principles that seem most closely related to practical concerns in improving teaching and learning. Existing typologies, such as that proposed by Astin (see Tables 1 and 2), the list of principles by Bowen, and the important distinctions mentioned by Ewell, as well as the work of many other scholars, have been helpful in formulating our plans. In Table 3 we have summarized some of these propositions, attempting to group them as accurately as possible under the "technical parameter" headings discussed earlier, namely, "type of outcome to be measured," "level of measurement," and "form of measurement." This grouping forms the basis for our discussion of outcome measures to be used in NCRIPTAL's work. It bears repeating that only these three parameters of type, level, and form are discussed because we have already focused our work on a specific purpose (improvement of teaching and learning) and assume that results will be used for decisions consonant with that purpose. Furthermore, our efforts are based on the assumption that the administrative locus of assessment activities and evaluative decisions about this information all rest within the college or university.

Type of Outcome Measures

However desirable it might be for researchers and institutions to follow Bowen's suggestion to assess all possible outcomes and relate outcomes to the development of the whole person, such a global program would readily encounter problems of feasibility and lack of consensus. Nonetheless, our discussion of outcome measures begins with the whole-person approach in an effort to determine which subsets of this universe are of greatest importance.

During such discussions we found many benefits, but some pitfalls, in Astin's encompassing four-fold typology of student outcomes (see Table 1). Specifically, although Astin acknowledged interactions between affective and cognitive outcomes, his typology used these concepts as two different primary dimensions. Consequently, the typology made little provision for attention to cognitive-personal outcomes or affective-academic outcomes. Yet, many cognitive psychologists and personality theorists believe that, particularly for students who enter college with undeveloped motivation or low self-efficacy, affective outcomes may be related to academic as well as to personal and social growth. As a result of these and related discussions, we drew a slightly different type of typology framework which notes three "arenas" of student growth in college and three forms through which changes in these arenas may be observed. The resulting nine-cell framework, which we stress was derived a priori from our accumulated experience, is shown in Table 4.

The *arena* dimension refers to the various aspects of life in which the outcome is important. The three arenas are personal, social, and academic. The personal domain includes outcomes like personal worth, feelings about oneself, satisfaction with personal accomplishments, ability to make decisions, and using one's skills appropriately. The social arena outcomes include ability to function in interpersonal relationships, citizenship, social responsibility, social awareness, and contributions to society. The academic

Table 3
Propositions and Caveats about Type, Level, and Form of Outcome Measurement

	Bowen	Ewell	Astin
Type of Outcome Measures	Assess all outcomes, even those difficult to measure.	Distinguish intended and unintended outcomes.	
	Relate outcomes to whole person.	Distinguish outcomes of which student is aware and unaware.	
	Focus on changes attributable to college.	Distinguish outcomes closely linked to educational program.	
	Focus on major institutional goals.		
Level of Outcome Measures	Study alumni as well as current students.	Distinguish short- and long-term outcome measures.	Record whether students completed program and whether accomplishments were consistent with their goals.
Form of Outcome Measures	Separate inputs and outputs.		Measure at various points in time; include information at entry, during program, and on exit.
	Use practical and feasible means.		Use measures of cognitive development beyond grade point average.
			Include measures of student satisfaction.

arena includes academic achievement, self-efficacy, motivation, critical-thinking abilities, problem-solving skills, and goal exploration behaviors.

The form dimension also has three categories: cognitive, motivational, and behavioral. This dimension specifies the form in which the outcome is demonstrated. Cognitive outcomes are internal outcomes. Typically they occur within individuals' mental processes and their existence is inferred, usually through testing. Motivational outcomes consist largely of the feelings that individuals have about themselves, their capabilities, and the world around them. These outcomes are generally self-reported, though some social-psychological methods exist that tap these attitudes more discretely. Behavioral outcomes may be reported by the individual or directly observed.

As mentioned earlier, NCRIPTAL's research program will focus on the academic arena shown in Table 4. In selecting this subset of the universe of college outcome measures for attention, we risk posing for others the same difficulty that Astin's typology posed for us. We acknowledge that the personal and social arenas cannot be separated from the academic arena; one's personal and social development affects one's academic development and the reverse is also true. Nonetheless, by constructing a framework that includes three cells, academic-cognitive, academic-motivational, and academic-behavioral, we are able to encompass a broad set of outcomes of primary concern to colleges and the public as well as to incorporate recent theories of cognitive development. Table 5 shows a more detailed view of the academic arena and the types of outcomes that seem to fit into each of the three major cells.

Table 4
A Whole-Person Approach to College Student Outcomes

Form of Demonstrated Change	Arenas of Growth and Development		
	Social	Personal	Academic
Cognitive			
Motivational			
Behavioral			

At first glance, some observers will believe we have violated Bowen's principle of separating inputs and outputs by classifying as outcomes some of those items listed in the academic-motivational cell. Traditionally, motivation, self-efficacy, involvement, and effort have been viewed as fixed attributes students bring to the educational process. Our view that these characteristics are subject to change (in an intended or unintended direction) as a result of the educational process is, in part, what caused us to modify previously existing outcome typologies. Although little attention has been given to these ideas, most colleges would agree, for example, that improved motivation is an outcome to be sought. While the original motivation a student brings to college is an input, a new motivational level based on educational experiences becomes an outcome the student takes to the next stage of learning.

An additional previously neglected aspect of the iterative outcomes conception relates to Ewell's distinction between student awareness or lack of awareness of changes. Although we have not included it in the list at this time, if students are to take increased responsibility for their learning, awareness itself may be an outcome to be sought.

Level of Outcome Measures

As already mentioned, both practicality and technical difficulties have caused us to set aside Bowen's suggestion that alumni be studied in addition to current students. Instead, NCRIPTAL's agenda will focus on outcome measures that can be related directly to classroom and program educational experiences. In general, our unit of analysis will be the individual student and groups of students sharing a common educational experience in a course or program. Whenever possible, outcome measures for special populations of students (e.g., minorities, women, adult students) will be examined in relation to similar data for traditional students.

Astin's point about whether students' eventual accomplishments are constant with their goals will be a special focus of one of our research programs. In fact, goals of students at

Table 5
NCRIPTAL's Outcome Framework

Forms of Measurement	Academic Arena
Cognitive	Achievement (facts, principles, ideas, skills) Critical-thinking skills Problem-solving skills
Motivational	Satisfaction with college Involvement/effort Motivation Self-efficacy
Behavioral	Career and life goal exploration Exploration of diversity Persistence Relationships with faculty

college entry are subject to change in both intended and unintended directions. Since there would likely be disagreement about what constitutes positive change, we have included an academic-behavioral outcome called "career and life goal development." The implication is that the student should gain in ability to explore, consider, and make decisions about eventual goals.

Form of Outcome Measures

For many institutions, there may be an inherent conflict between observing Bowen's caveat about feasibility of measurement and adopting Astin's value-added approach, which statistically controls for student entry characteristics when observing changes in student outcomes over time. This is particularly true if measures of cognitive development, such as reasoning skills and critical thinking, are used to supplement more traditional measures of academic achievement. In developing new measures and in assisting institutions with the use of already developed measures, NCRIPTAL will attempt to help simplify the appropriate use of outcome measures. The next section of this paper describes some of the academic measures already in use by colleges and alerts the reader to some new measures that NCRIPTAL staff hope to make available for future use.

Contemporary Approaches to Assessing Student Achievement of General Education Outcomes

Trudy W. Banta

"With Great Difficulty"

"Specific Disciplines Are the New Focus of Movement to Assess Colleges' Effectiveness" was the title chosen for the *Chronicle of Higher Education* article describing the fourth national conference on assessment held in Atlanta in June 1989. Denise Magner, the author of the article, stated: "As the move toward greater assessment of the educational accomplishments of colleges and universities enters its fifth year, educators say it is drifting from its initial focus on general course requirements to a wider interest in evaluating individual majors."[1]

I remember trying to resist Magner's thesis when she asked about my perceptions of what was happening at the conference. I believed that while the number of faculty interested in talking about assessment within their own disciplines certainly was growing, this did not necessarily mean that fewer colleges and universities were interested in assessing their general education programs. My experience in the last eighteen months in visiting campuses and talking with colleagues at national meetings has served to confirm that belief. Moreover, an inspection of the list of projects currently supported by the Fund for the Improvement of Postsecondary Education (FIPSE) reveals no less than a dozen ongoing studies of ways to improve the assessment of general education. Only one-third as many FIPSE projects are concerned with assessment in major fields.[2] On many campuses where a comprehensive approach to assessment is being considered, concern about measuring student achievement in general education is actually promoted by faculty discussion of methods for assessing student achievement in the major. As groups of faculty begin to talk about measuring student learning in the major, they find that they share with colleagues in other disciplines a concern about students' basic skills and knowledge as developed in a program of liberal studies. Then faculty in various disciplines will ask that some central action be taken to assess student achievement in general education as a means of freeing them to focus specifically on the knowledge and skills developed within the curriculum in the major.

Despite the relative ease with which faculty can agree that there are some domains of knowledge and basic skills in which all graduates should develop competence, specifying exactly what knowledge and which skills is much more difficult. According to Jerry Gaff, "Developing an education philosophy shared by all segments of the college community and finding the means to carry

Reprinted from *Journal of General Education* 40, (1991), by permission of Pennsylvania State University Press.

that philosophy out in practice is an aspiration realized only infrequently, with great difficulty, and after long struggle."[3]

In thinking about ways to assess the core of liberal studies, which provides the foundation for upper-division work at a four-year institution and the basis for a transfer program at a community college, faculty must think first about goals and the methods for implementing those goals, and only then about assessment. Many institutions have no written statements of goals. Among those that do, few have in place a formal audit process that provides for continuous faculty review of course syllabi and classroom tests to guarantee that the goals are being put into practice. And only in the last five years have substantial numbers of institutions begun to work on the assessment of student achievement of general education goals.

By 1989, however, more than 60 percent of the chief academic officers responding to the annual American Council on Education survey of 456 public and private colleges and universities reported that faculty on their campuses were assessing the outcomes of general education or making plans to do so.[4] If these faculties are simply looking at goals and measuring student outcomes without at the same time studying how the goals are being implemented, the long-term results may be disappointing. If, for example, it is determined through assessment procedures that students are not attaining a particular goal, in the absence of an audit process it may be impossible to determine why students are not achieving according to faculty expectations. Are the students failing to grasp certain concepts as they are being presented? Or does the explanation lie in the fact that the course intended to promote the mastery of the concepts no longer includes any reference to them? Only if faculty can obtain accurate, specific information about what needs to be changed can they effect improvements that will enhance student learning.

Beginning with Standardized Measures

In the wave of higher education assessment that began in the early 1980s, there was a rush to tap the inventory of extant standardized instruments to assess student achievement in general education. For instance, by that time both the College Level Examination Program (CLEP) tests in English composition, humanities, math, natural science, and social science/history and the Sequential Tests of Educational Progress (STEP) in English expression, reading, math, science, and social studies were established measures for assessing student attainment. Northeast Missouri State University (NEMU) secured its reputation as a "self-regarding institution"[5] on the basis of administering the ACT assessment test of academic aptitude to entering freshmen and again at the end of the sophomore year in an attempt to assess "value added" by the general education curriculum. NEMU also became one of the first institutions to use ACT's College Outcome Measures Program (COMP) exam, which was designed specifically to assess growth in general education outcome areas during the college years. By the end of the decade, the Academic Profile from ETS, ACT's Collegiate Assessment of Academic Proficiency (CAAP), and the College Basic Academic Subjects Exam (CBASE) published by Riverside had joined the COMP exam in this arena.

Initially, faculty were motivated by the knowledge that these standardized exams were readily available, presumably reliable and valid, and accompanied by norms that would permit comparison of the performance of their students with that of students at similar institutions across the country. However, thoughtful objections to the use of standardized exams were soon raised. First, these instruments may not test what a particular faculty is teaching—virtually no group of individuals at a single institution can cover the entire range of specialties in a given discipline. Since the format is usually multiple-choice, standardized exams also have been criticized because they assess primarily lower-order intellectual skills. These tests may be standardized on unrepresentative norm groups: most of the new generation of exams developed specifically to assess general education outcomes provide user norms, and the users may not be at all typical of a given institution or its approach to general education. Moreover, little is known about the nature of the student samples these "user" institutions employ, or about the timing of the tests or the level of motivation with which students approach the testing experience. Standardized exams usually yield only a few subscores, thus making it difficult to decide exactly what piece of the curriculum or method of instruction ought to be investigated for flaws when scores are lower than expected. Finally, no standardized test score comes with an explanation of *why* it may be lower than anticipated. And the level of mystery about what should be done to improve low scores is intensified by the lack of detailed knowledge about the method faculty are using to deliver the knowledge and skills associated with an institution's goals for general education.

If there ever was a bloom on the rose called standardized testing, it faded rather quickly as the method of choice for assessing program effectiveness in higher education. As early as 1986, Russ Edgerton, president of the American Association for Higher Education (AAHE), warned that many of the standardized tests faculty were trying to use in assessing program outcomes had actually been designed to measure individual attainment; that is, how one student performs relative to others taking the test rather than what groups of students learn in college.[6]

Even the president of the Educational Testing Service, Greg Anrig, in "A Message for Governors and State Legislators" in 1986, noted that "testing alone cannot evaluate institutions."[7] Anrig emphasized that higher education is concerned with far more than the minimum competencies that national exams might measure with a fair degree of accuracy. He urged faculty at each institution to identify the types of knowledge and skills they hoped to develop in graduates and to use this information to shape an assessment program encompassing "a wide range of data and measures."

In one of the largest studies to date of the use of standardized exams in general education assessment, Robert Thorndike found that the COMP exam and pilot versions of the Academic Profile and the CAAP were not appropriate measures of general education, as defined by faculty in the state of Washington. According to Thorndike, "None of the tests measured the separate academic skills (communication, computation, and critical thinking); rather, these tests primarily measured verbal and quantitative aptitude."[8] Further, test scores were not sensitive to specific aspects of the college experience, such as estimated time spent studying and credits earned.

These results have been confirmed by Gary Pike at the University of Tennessee, Knoxville, who compared the ACT-COMP exam with pilot versions of the Academic Profile and the CAAP in a series of controlled studies begun in 1987.[9] Each of these studies used the following sources of data: (1) A group of seven faculty members representing five colleges conducted content analyses of the three exams, matching the content of each with the university's formal statement of goals for general education; (2) all seniors (participation in general education testing is a graduation requirement, and seniors were randomly assigned to take one or the other of the tests being studied) were asked to rate the exam they took on the basis of its usefulness in measuring general education knowledge and skills and its appeal to their interest; (3) students volunteering to take *both* tests under investigation were interviewed individually to determine their reactions and preferences; and (4) several technical analyses of students' scores were conducted, including a study of scale intercorrelations and reliabilities, a principal components analysis, and an investigation of the sensitivity of each exam to the effects of education. Faculty concluded that neither the COMP nor the Academic Profile nor the CAAP measured student mastery of more than 30 percent of the knowledge and skills specified in the goals for general education at UTK. Fewer than half of the students tested considered any of the three exams a "good test" of what they had learned in their general education program. Significant correlations among the subscales on each test, coupled with the principal components analyses, provide strong evidence that the instruments are simply measures of intellectual ability. They appear to be insensitive to the effects of education and thus offer little or no additional information beyond that derived from tests of entering ability such as the ACT or SAT.

Results of a similar study at UTK comparing the COMP and the College BASE[10] provided only slightly more encouragement for the use of a standardized test in assessing general education outcomes. According to the judgment of the faculty evaluators, the College BASE covered 36 percent of the university's goals for general education. Factor analysis confirmed the existence of a factor structure corresponding to the subject scores offered by the CBASE developers. CBASE scores were not significantly correlated with student demographic characteristics, such as age, gender, and race, as was the case with the COMP, Academic Profile, and CAAP. Moreover, the CBASE was found to be slightly more sensitive to the effects of coursework than were the other tests. However, the CBASE does not cover adequately the attitudes and values dimensions of general education; it too is highly sensitive to entering ability. And since the CBASE is just beginning to be used broadly for general education assessment, the generalizability of its user norms is quite limited.

The process of brining faculty together to discuss the goals for general education, the supporting curriculum and methods of instruction, the quality of student learning, and means of improving all of the foregoing constitutes the single greatest benefit to be derived from assessing outcomes. Since faculty may in fact come together for these discussions before selecting and again after administering a standardized exam, this kind of test could provide a useful starting point for assessment at any institution. Ohio University, Austin Peay State University in Tennessee, and Northeast Missouri State University, among others, still use the COMP exam to stimulate faculty discussion about their programs of general education.

However, faculty at many institutions are now moving ahead to develop their own measures of student achievement in general education. An indication of the national trend in this direction comes from the 1990 American Council on Education survey of chief academic officers: 66 percent reported that they are developing their own assessment instruments, an increase from just 45 percent in 1988.[11] Moreover, in 1989 Alexander Astin and associates at UCLA, following some disappointing personal experiences in trying to use standardized measures of cognitive skills, obtained an Exxon grant to initiate a multiyear study of alternative forms of assessment. The starting point for this research is faculty and student opinion about issues that might be considered within a collegiate general education program. A second component is a look at student change over four years in certain attitudes and behaviors after four years in college. Data are being collected from faculty and students at 50 colleges and universities with "distinctive approaches" to general education chosen from the 546 institutions that administered Astin's national survey of college freshmen in Fall 1985.[12]

The remainder of this article addresses the components of the planning-implementing-assessing model discussed above. Examples are drawn from contemporary practice to illustrate goal-setting, auditing to ensure implementation, and finally, assessment.

Beginning with Goals

The faculty at Alverno College in Milwaukee are recognized as pioneers in basing a program of liberal education on a set of specific objectives for learners. In the late 1960s the faculty began to question what knowledge and skills were needed for competent adult functioning and developed descriptions of eight abilities that characterized the kind of person Alverno faculty as educators seek to develop.[13] Since 1973, a student earning a degree at Alverno must have demonstrated satisfactory levels of competence in all the following broad abilities: communications, analysis, problem-solving, valuing, social interaction, responsibility toward the global environment, citizenship, and aesthetic responsiveness.[14]

In the early 1980s, the faculty at King's College in Pennsylvania began an intensive study of their approach to liberal learning and developed a list of eight "transferable skills of liberal learning," which they hoped to strengthen in each King's graduate: critical thinking, creative thinking and problem-solving strategies, writing, oral communication, quantitative analysis, computer literacy, library and information technologies, and values awareness.[15]

In the mid-1980s, the state higher education coordinating agencies in Virginia and New Jersey promulgated mandates for assessment that included explicit references to the need for goal-setting. At James Madison University in Virginia, faculty adopted a comprehensive approach to student development during college that included goals for cognitive, moral and psychosocial growth.[16] In New Jersey, all public institutions were required to submit to the State Board of Higher Education by June 1989 faculty-developed statements of goals for general education that would serve as the basis for assessment plans. These documents were reviewed by external consultants, and each institution subsequently received a detailed written assessment of the perceived strengths and weaknesses of its goals statement.

The recognition of differential institutional missions and programs implicit in the Virginia and New Jersey requirements that institutions prepare for assessment by developing their own goals statements stands in stark contrast to the assessment mandates in a few other states. In Tennessee and South Dakota, for example, the policies issued in 1979 and 1985, respectively, simply specified that standardized exams be used in assessment. In Tennessee, the issue of institutional goals for general education is ignored in the directive that every two- and four-year institution in the state must administer the COMP Objective Test to its graduates in order to assess general education outcomes.[17]

Recognizing that faculty might need assistance in constructing goals statements, the College Outcomes Evaluation Program (COEP) staff of the New Jersey Board of Higher Education commissioned a reference work on the topic. Lion Gardiner's *Planning for Assessment: Mission Statements, Goals, and Objectives* subsequently has been made available at no charge to all New Jersey institutions.[18] And at King's College, recognition that faculty need preparation for the task of redefining curricula led the chief academic officer to offer five years of faculty development experiences prior to the first discussions of new goals for general education.

Monitoring Implementation

In 1982, in his study of general education competence and persistence, Aubrey Forrest emphasized the need for the "curriculum audit," or a careful ongoing monitoring by faculty of the courses designed to promote student achievement of the institution's goals for general education.[19] In his reference work, *Good Practices in General Education*,[20] Forrest included materials collected from a variety of institutions that illustrate how faculty can construct course syllabi and exam questions to ensure that the general education program as presented by faculty actually develops stated outcomes in students.

The Alverno faculty has established comprehensive mechanisms for guaranteeing that its eight abilities are developed with the curriculum. Every faculty member is conscious of the various levels of each of the eight abilities that students must develop, and every course is designed to ensure learning of one or more of the abilities. In every course, as well as at key points outside courses, students participate in faculty-designed performance-based assessments, the outcomes of which become part of their permanent records. In addition, students learn to assess themselves.[21]

At King's College, faculty are expected "to be able to explain clearly to students the specific way the intended educational outcomes of the curriculum related to the College's definition of an educated person."[22] Moreover, continuous efforts are made to prepare faculty to implement changes in their own teaching related to the eight liberal learning goals of the college. Faculty have been trained for their roles in teaching writing across the curriculum, critical thinking, computer literacy, valuing, quantitative analysis, library and information technologies, oral communication, and problem-solving.

At James Madison University, a review process has been established to ensure that student activities outside the classroom play specified roles in promoting the cognitive, moral, and psychosocial goals of the institution. At another Virginia institution, Longwood College, a transcript has been developed to furnish a record of student involvement in college activities that contribute to the accomplishment of 14 goals for knowledge and skills. Students also complete an "Involvement Survey," which helps them note their progress toward the 14 goals and detect areas of development that they may be neglecting.[23]

Contemporary Assessment Strategies

Recognizing that use of standardized instruments to measure student achievement in general education will, at best, provide evaluative data bearing on only a portion of the curriculum, faculty at many institutions have taken assessment into their own hands. Since the beginning of the last decade, several institutional consortia, all supported by grants from the Fund for the Improvement of Postsecondary Education, have been formed for the purpose of inventing new assessment strategies.

Consortium Approaches

In 1986 the Association of American Colleges brought together representatives of 18 diverse institutions for the purpose of conducting an experiment with alternative approaches to assessing learning in liberal arts majors. The set of guiding principles adopted by this consortium are applicable to assessment in general education as well. Bobby Fong has summarized these principles as follows: (1) Assessment should use instruments that provide evaluative feedback that can be used to improve instruction and learning and to strengthen academic programs. (2) Assessment instruments should be sufficiently supple to take into account the diversity of educational missions across institutions. (3) Assessment should provide opportunities for students to demonstrate what they know, not merely where gaps exist in their knowledge. In addition to testing for common learning, assessment should give students ways to show that they have developed unique competence and knowledge. (4) Assessment instruments should allow students to work through a problem or issue so that they can receive credit for the process they use as well as the solution they reach.[24] The AAC consortium also acted on the belief that assessment should include participation by qualified outside parties to avoid the risk of being skewed toward local concerns and standards. Thus faculty from triads of similar institutions served as external examiners for each other's students.

In the early 1980s, the American Association of State Colleges and Universities developed a consortium of ten colleges for the purpose of evaluating the general education component of baccalaureate programs in those institutions. The Academic Program Evaluation Project (APEP) was based on the assumption that generic intellectual skills are measurable and can be used to evaluate student learning. The APEP took place on each campus according to a series of five stages that would soon become a familiar sequence in similar projects: defining generic skills; identifying performance indicators, criteria, and testing procedures; assessing student performance and program effectiveness; judging student and program performance; then making decisions and developing policies.[25]

In 1986 the University of Kentucky began a similar sequence of steps with a consortium of 14 private liberal arts colleges in central Appalachia. These institutions worked cooperatively to develop a plan for assessing the outcomes of their general education programs that eventually included four components: a freshman essay repeated in the senior year, the Academic Profile, the College Student Experiences Questionnaire, and senior interviews. The interviews, which were considered the most valuable of the four components, took place in groups composed of three students with a faculty member guiding a two-hour discussion. In the discussion, students were given a chance to demonstrate generic skills through responses to such questions as, What is an educated person? What is an effective citizen? What is the role of the artist in a culture? What is work? What were two or three of your most important college experiences? Interviewees on the 14 campuses were taped, then transcribed centrally and analyzed using a phenomenological/ethnographic approach.[26]

Building upon their own assumptions about assessment as learning, the Alverno College faculty in 1987 developed a consortium of 23 institutions for the purpose of demonstrating in a wide variety of institutional settings that faculty could design and implement assessment procedures to facilitate and measure student achievement of general education outcomes. The 68 college and university educators who met at Alverno for three annual summer workshops were asked to work on one of the expected general education outcomes that their institution had identified. In an extended process, they worked out specific components of that outcome within a course of program and identified indicators of student performance that would facilitate making judgments about student success in attaining the outcome. Finally, they designed methods of assessment. The educators then developed criteria for judging student performance, providing feedback to the learner, and evaluating the assessment procedure itself. Monographs describing more than 30 field-tested instruments for assessing liberal arts outcomes, as well as processes for validating such instruments, will be published by Alverno College in 1991.[27]

Institutional Approaches

The paradigm of assessment-as-learning pioneered by the faculty at Alverno College almost twenty years ago stands as a primary example of the way in which an assessment program can transform an institution. Alverno is known throughout the world for its ability-based curriculum. More recently, other institutions have effected fundamental changes in their approaches to general education via innovative approaches to assessment. Projects at King's College, Kean College, Lehman College, and the University of Connecticut provide examples.

Since the mid-1980s, faculty at King's College have been experimenting with course-embedded assessment, which is intended to be "diagnostic and supportive of student learning." The purpose of assessment at King's is to "provide systematic feedback to students on their academic progress toward meeting the expectations of faculty throughout all four years of undergraduate studies."[28] All core curriculum courses use pre- and postassessments that are common to all sections of the course and designed by faculty teams. Postassessments are administered to students two weeks before the end of each course so that instructors will have ample time to provide feedback to students. The postassessment is an integral part of the final grade for each course, and thus student motivation to do their best work is ensured. Courses are designated for delivery of one or more of the eight transferable skills of liberal learning that guide the King's approach to general education. Each student has a Competence Growth Plan that provides a record of his or her progress toward achieving the eight skills. As students complete their assessment experiences in the designated courses, progress is noted in their individual plans. The activities associated with implementing this course-embedded assessment model serve to evaluate the outcome-oriented curriculum designed by the King's faculty.

At Kean College, faculty have developed essay items to evaluate knowledge of content and critical thinking skills in five areas: composition, emergence of the modern world, intellectual and cultural traditions, inquiry and research, and landmarks of world literature.[29] These items are incorporated in course exams, and students' responses are read twice—once by the course instructor for purposes of assigning a grade, then again by a faculty committee looking at response patterns across students and across courses for purposes of evaluating the effectiveness of the general curriculum. The Kean faculty also gather evaluative data from faculty and student surveys designed to elicit perceptions about the curriculum.

At Lehman College of the City University of New York, faculty undertook an evaluation of the general education curriculum in 1986. As at Kean, questionnaires were developed for faculty and for students to gauge their perceptions of the effectiveness of the curriculum. Other measures were obtained from student records, including persistence in college since the inauguration of a new general education curriculum, grade point averages, length of time needed to meet central college requirements, and the mix of courses taken. The Lehman faculty then developed procedures for testing student's abilities to read verbal tests, interpret quantitative data and present it graphically, evaluate data and arguments, and argue for points of view on complex issues. A significant part of this project was the training of faculty to score these assessments of cognitive abilities.[30]

In 1986 the University of Connecticut faculty adopted a plan scheduled to begin in September 1988 that would require all entering students to complete a structured menu of courses in six cognitive areas: foreign language, literature and the arts, Western/non-Western civilization, philosophy and ethics, social science, and science and technology. The program was also intended to develop students' skills in writing, quantifying, and computing. In 1988 some 50 faculty organized into six teams, corresponding to the categories of the curriculum, for the purpose of reviewing course syllabi, examinations, and available assessments. Multidisciplinary groups, each of which was chaired by an individual from a discipline other than the dominant one in the given area, developed a series of tasks for assessing student achievement that was pilot-tested during 1988–89. A wide variety of measures was constructed, including multiple-choice items as well as tasks such as identifying the rationale behind philosophical positions, and responding aesthetically to a painting, a poem, or a piece of music.[31] The University of Connecticut faculty also measured student response to the general education program in two ways: Students were asked to record their perceptions of their abilities in the six goal areas, and a series of focus groups was conducted to obtain qualitative information about the program.[32]

The development of tasks as prompts for constructed responses by students is an approach that has guided one state's approach to assessing the generic skills of sophomores in all of its public colleges and universities. The College Outcomes Evaluation Project (COEP) of the State Board of Higher Education in New Jersey engaged a representative group of faculty in constructing free-response tasks to measure students' skills in gathering, analyzing, and presenting academic information in the domains of social science, natural science, and humanities/fine arts. By subdividing the three major skills, a taxonomy of 48 skills was devised. The skill of analyzing, for instance, is composed in part of forming hypotheses and drawing conclusions. The tasks, which were pilot-tested as the General Intellectual Skills (GIS) Assessment during 1989–90, consists of series of problems or questions that proceed from less to more demanding as they draw a student toward a solution or answer. Core scoring is used to evaluate responses, with each task reading by four evaluators—two scoring skills and two scoring writing competence.[33]

Specific Techniques

Faculty are experimenting with a number of specific assessment techniques as they attempt to identify strengths and weaknesses of their general education programs. For instance, faculty at the State University of New York at Fredonia concluded that historical, scientific, cultural, and ethical understanding could be assessed using paper-and-pencil tasks. In the first task students were asked to list ten of the most important events in human history, then describe three consequences of one event's not having taken place. Responses were scored for chronological ordering, selection of important events, understanding of cross-cultural cause-and-effect relationships, and the presence of ethnocentrism and presentism. The second task asked students to consider an imaginary European exchange student's criticisms of American practices or problems. Responses were scored according to the same set of constructs, with the exception that sense of history was eliminated and the criteria of understanding of mainstream American values and questioning of stereotypes were added.[34]

Portfolios are growing in popularity as assessment tools that can be used in a wide variety of settings. Examples of materials that might be collected in a portfolio include course assignments, research papers, materials from group projects, artistic production, self-reflective essays, correspondence, and taped presentations. Student performances can be recorded using audio- or videotapes. Potential materials for the cassette-recorded portfolio are speeches, musical performances, visual arts productions, foreign-language pronunciation, group interaction skills, and demonstrations of laboratory techniques or psychomotor skills.

Pioneering work in portfolio assessment was conducted at Alverno College in the 1970s. Today, faculty who have participated in one of Alverno's periodic workshops are undertaking their own experiments. For instance, at Millsaps College in Mississippi faculty are developing with FIPSE support a curriculum-embedded assessment procedure that will "measure and promote students' development as thinkers and writers by using writing done in course and assembled in individual portfolios."[35] Faculty assessors are developing criteria for assessing student writing that use analysis of content and the process of revision for clues that may signal cognitive growth.

While the concept of using portfolios is immediately appealing to many faculty, portfolio assessment is not easily implemented, as the FIPSE project director, David Lutzer, at Virginia's College of William and Mary, discovered. In the first year of their general education assessment project, the William and Mary faculty collected portfolios from instructors rather than students. They simply asked for some samples of what seniors were writing. The resulting portfolios were so lacking in uniformity that they proved nearly impossible to evaluate.[36] With a little more experience in this arena, Lehman College faculty devised specific criteria for portfolios, including number, length, and type of manuscripts to be submitted. Scoring of portfolios is also problematic, but Millsaps, Lehman, and others have reported that teaching instructors to use holistic scoring has constituted a valuable faculty development experience that proved to be somewhat unanticipated benefit of engaging in assessment activities.

Technology is also being employed to advance the state of the art of assessment. At Texas College of Osteopathic Medicine, Frank Papa and Jay Shores are using expert systems to assess the problem-solving skills of medical students and then to provide individualized instruction designed to improve these skills.[37] And at the University of Denver, Karen Kitchener and her colleagues are developing an interactive, computerized test of reflective judgment and teaching faculty how to use the resulting assessment information to adapt their instruction to the developmental characteristics of their students.[38] Both of these projects are supported by grants from FIPSE.

What Have We Learned from Assessment?

What have we learned from the extensive activity that has taken place over the last decade in attempting to assess general education? According to Jim Watt of the University of Connecticut, "during the first year, committees involving over 50 faculty members evaluated course content, and translated the goal statements into evaluation instruments. A very encouraging outcome of this process was the level of discussion of general education which the project generated within the faculty."[39] It is this focused discussion among faculty who are interested in improving student learning that has been one of the most salient positive features of assessment. And this benefit becomes evident immediately. It usually happens before faculty even begin to collect evidence from students. Then after the data begin to come in, faculty who are really invested in the process will see ways to improve the environment for learning, which is by far the most important outcome of assessment.

Faculty have learned that they must be more systematic in stating their goals for general education, in auditing the means of implementing the goals, and then in assessing outcomes in ways that provide evidence that can be used to confirm or to modify the original goals. This iterative process is not well understood, and certainly not widely practiced, in higher education; engagement in assessment may serve to increase understanding and thus improve practice. Faculty have also learned that assessment cannot be episodic—rather, it must be ongoing in an effort to provide for continuous improvement of the environment for student learning.

With regard to specific techniques, faculty have not found standardized tests to provide substantial assistance in suggesting modifications in courses or curricula that would improve general education. However, standardized exams may provide a starting point for the focused discussion that has been identified as a principal benefit of faculty involvement in assessment activities.

Recognizing the weaknesses inherent in standardized exams, faculty in consortia of institutions as well as individual colleges and universities have begun to experiment with a variety of homegrown assessment methodologies. Most of these could be characterized as qualitative in nature. Students are asking to construct their own responses orally and/or in writing, thus revealing much more about the extent of their knowledge and unique abilities than could ever be captured in responses to multiple-choice items. Extended interviews and collections of work in the form of portfolios are giving faculty opportunities to assess student learning comprehensively. Assessment activities that are embedded in courses are most likely to elicit students' best efforts. Finally, interactive computer technology is being developed that not only assesses current status but also can assist students to improve their skills and grasp of content.

While most of the recent development activities have produced measures of students' cognitive abilities and knowledge, faculty seeking ways to assess the effectiveness of general education programs have also sought some information about faculty and student perceptions of quality. Questionnaires and interviews have been employed for this purpose on a number of compuses. Student investment in activities, such as use of the library, that are assumed to promote learning has been noted through the use of instruments like the College Student Experiences Questionnaire. Student records have yielded information on persistence rates, college grades, and course-taking patterns that can also play a valuable role in assessing the effectiveness of the general education program.

Jerry Gaff has observed that assessment of general education outcomes has had a positive impact on the sense of identity and community within institutions that have approached assessment with seriousness of purpose. Involvement in assessment activities has also produced direction for faculty development and sparked faculty renewal. These changes have subsequently been associated with improved student satisfaction and retention.[40] These observations are borne out in the comments of some of the most committed practitioners.

In describing portfolio assessment at Lehman college, Dick Larson has said, "Our scoring constructs an *affirmative* statement about students' achievements, not a list of deficits. We also learn useful information about what faculty ask students to write, how they make assignments, and how they respond to students' writings."[41] According to Minda Rae Amiran, "[Students'] answers are immensely rich and educators at SUNY Fredonia are learning much about their students' socioethical understanding. The detailed descriptions of the eight constructs are also helping them refocus assignments and teaching methods in general education courses."[42] In summing up the impact of the changes in general education stimulated by the outcomes-oriented approach at King's College, Peter Ewell has written, "As evidenced by rising enrollments, and improved academic profile of entering students, and growing regional reputation. King's exemplifies an ancient piece of wisdom. The heart of academic institution is its curriculum. If the integrity of the curriculum is maintained and its effectiveness demonstrated, external benefits will naturally follow."[43]

Notes

1. Denise K. Magner. "Specific Disciplines Are the New Focus of Movement to Assess Colleges' Effectiveness," *Chronicle of Higher Education*, 5 July 1989, A26.
2. *Fund for the Improvement of Postsecondary Education Program Book* (Washington, D. C.: FIPSE, 1990).
3. Jerry G. Gaff. *General Education Today: A Critical Analysis of Controversies, Practices, and Reforms* (San Francisco: Jossey-Bass, 1983), xi.
4. Elaine El-Khawas. *Campus Trends, 1989*. Higher Education Panel Report No. 78 (Washington, D.C.: American Council on Education, July 1989), vii.
5. Peter T. Ewell, *The Self-Regarding Institution: Information for Excellence* (Boulder, Colo.: National Center for Higher Education Management Systems, 1984).
6. Russell Edgerton, "An Assessment of Assessment." Closing Plenary Session of the Educational Testing Service Annual Invitational Conference, New York, 25 October 1986.
7. Gregory R. Anrig "A Message for Governors and State Legislators: The Minimum Competency Approach Can Be Bad for the Health of Higher Education." (Princeton, N.J.: Educational Testing Service, 1986).
8. Robert M. Thorndike, "Assessment Measures," *Assessment Update* 1(3) (1989):8.
9. Gary R.Pike and Trudy W. Banta, *Using Construct Validity to Evaluate Assessment Instruments: A Comparison of the ACT-COMP Exam and the ETS Academic Profile.* American Educational Research Association, San Francisco, 28 March 1989; and Gary R. Pike, "A Comparison of the College Outcome Measures Program (COMP) and the collegiate Assessment of Academic Proficiency Exams," in *Performance Funding Report for the University of Tennessee, Knorville 1988-1989* (Knoxville, Center for Assessment Research and Development, University of Tennessee, 1989), II-1–27.
10. Gary R. Pike, "Comparison of ACT COMP and College BASE," in *1989–90 Performance Funding Report for the University of Tennessee, Knoxville* (Knoxville: Center for Assessment Research and Development, University of Tennessee, 1990), 47–57.
11. Elaine El-Khawas, *Campus Trends, 1990,* Higher Education Panel Report Number 80 (Washington, D. C.: American Council on Education, July 1990), vii.
12. Alexander Astin et al., *A National Study of General Education Outcomes* (Los Angeles: Higher Education Research Institute, University of California, Los Angeles, 1989).
13. Alverno College Faculty, *Assessment at Alverno College* (Milwaukee: Alverno College, 1979).
14. Alverno College Faculty, *Liberal Learning at Alverno College* (Milwaukee: Alverno College, 1989).
15. D. W. Farmer, *Enhancing Student Learning: Emphasizing Essential Competencies in Academic Programs* (Wilkes-Barre, Pa.: King's College, 1988), 57.
16. T. Dary Erwin, "Virginia Assessment Requirements," paper presented at the Strategies for Assessing Outcomes Workshop, Knoxville. Tennessee. 5 November 1990.
17. *Performance Funding Standards for Public Colleges and Universities* (Nashville: Tennessee Higher Education Commission. 9 February 1990).
18. Lion F. Gardiner. *Planning for Assessment: Mission Statements, Goals, and Objectives*. (Trenton: New Jersey Department of Higher Education. 1989.)
19. Aubrey Forrest, *Increasing Student Competence and Persistence: The Best Case for General Education* (Iowa City: ACT National Center for the Advancement of Educational Practice, 1982).
20. Aubrey Forrest, *Good Practices in General Education* (Iowa City: American College Testing Program, 1986).
21. Georgine Loacker, Lucy Cromwell, and Kathleen O'Brien, "Assessment in Higher Education: To Serve the Learner." In *Assessment in Higher Education,* ed. C. Adelman (Washington, D.C.: Office of Educational Research and Improvement. 1986).
22. Farmer. *Enhancing Student Learning,* 12
23. Longwood College, *Longwood College Involvement Project* (Farmville, Va.: Longwood College, 1986).

24. Bobby Fong, "Old Wineskins: The AAC External Examiner Project." *Liberal Education 74(3)* (1988):12–16.
25. "Defining and Assessing Baccalaureate Skills: Ten Case Studies. A Report on the Academic Program Evaluation Project." American Association of State Colleges and Universities, Washington, D.C.: 1986.
26. Karen W. Carey and Charles F. Elton, *The Appalachian College Assessment Consortium* (Lexington: University of Kentucky, 1990).
27. Judeen Shulte, *Refocusing General Education Outcomes Through Assessment-as-Learning,* paper presented at the FIPSE Project Directors' Meeting, Washington, D.C., 27 October 1990.
28. Farmer. *Enhancing Student Learning,* 157.
29. Peter J. Gray, "Campus Profiles," *Assessment Update* 2(3) (1990):4–5.
30. Personal communication from Richard Larson, 15 October 1989.
31. Barbara D. Wright. "But How Do We Know It'll Work?" *AAHE Bulletin* 42(8) (1990):14–17.
32. James Watt, "Assessing General Education Outcomes: An Institution-Specific Approach," in *Fund for the Improvement of Postsecondary Education Program* Book (Washington D.C.: FIPSE, 1990), 60.
33. Personal communication from Robert J. Kloss, 23 April 1990.
34. Fredonia Designs Socioethical Assessment Measures," *Assessment Update* 1(4) (1989):4.
35. Austin Wilson, "Assessing Student Intellectual Growth Through Writing," in *Fund for the Improvement of Postsecondary Education Program Book* (Washington, D.C.: FIPSE, 1990), 103.
36. David Lutzer, "Assessing General Education," panel presentation at the FIPSE Project Directors' Meeting, Washington, D.C., 27 October 1990.
37. Frank Papa and Jay Shores, "Expert Systems-Based Clinical Tutorial Project," in *Fund for the Improvement of Postsecondary Education Program Book* (Washington D.C.: FIPSE, 1990), 160.
38. Karen Strohm Kitchener, "Assessing Reflective Thinking Within Curricular Contexts," in *Fund for the Improvement of Postsecondary Education Program Book* (Washington, D.C.: FIPSE, 1990), 67.
39. Watt, "Assessing General Education Outcomes," 60.
40. Jerry Gaff, "Assessing General Education," panel presentation at the FIPSE Project Directors' Meeting, Washington, D.C., 27 October 1990.
41. Larson, 15 October 1989.
42. Fredonia Designs Socioethical Assessment Measures," 4.
43. Peter T. Ewell, Foreword, in *Enhancing Student Learning: Emphasizing Essential Competencies in Academic Programs,* ed. D. W. Farmer (Wilkes-Barre, Pa.: King's College, 1988), viii.

In Their Own Words: What Students Learn Outside the Classroom

George D. Kuh

I've learned a lot about a lot of things . . . I care more about how I interact with other people. That is, I care about helping people learn and sharing my ideas with others. I definitely feel more confident in conveying what I have to say. I can express myself better . . . . An important part of what I've done [is] the classes and seeing how things connect and seeing how things work in an in-depth way. (Earlham College senior).

Assessments of student learning in college usually focus on academic aspects of the undergraduate experience—the classroom, laboratory, studio, and library. Transcripts and test scores, however, reflect only a fraction of how students change (Light, 1992). Wilson (1966), for example, estimated that more than 70% of what students learn during college results from out-of-class experiences. According to Moffatt (1989):

> For about 40% of students, the do-it-yourself side of college [what took place outside the classroom] was the most significant educational experience. And for all but 10%, extracurricular learning had been at least half of what had contributed to their maturation so far in college (p. 58).

Other scholars also have linked many of the benefits of attending college to out-of-class activities and experiences (Astin, 1977; Bowen, 1977; Boyer, 1987; Chickering, 1969; Feldman & Newcomb, 1969; Pace, 1979, 1990; Pascarella & Terenizini, 1991; Thomas & Chickering, 1984). These benefits include, among other things, gains in confidence, self-esteem, and altruistic values (Astin & Kent, 1983; Pascarella, Ethington, & Smart, 1988). Out-of-class experiences that contribute to these and other aspects of student learning and personal development include conversations with faculty after class and collaboration in research and teaching projects, living in a residence hall, working on or off campus, participating in institutional governance, involvement in clubs and organizations, and voluntarism.

For the most part, the research methods used to assess the impact of college have been quantitative and positivistic (Pascarella & Terenzini, 1991). Such methods require that researchers determine both the questions to be asked and the response categories. Attinasi (1992) argued that "progress in understanding college student outcomes . . . has been retarded by our failure to adequately take into consideration the meanings that the phenomenon of going to college holds for students" (p. 68). This view holds that it is impossible to understand the human experience *without* taking into account the complicated, mutually shaping events, actions, and motivations of the individual or group under study. According to Bogdan and Biklen (1982), "people act, not on the basis of

Reprinted from *American Educational Research Journal* 30, no. 2, American Educational Research Association.

predetermined responses to predefined objects, but rather as interpreting, defining, symbolic animals whose behavior can only be understood by having the researcher enter into the defining process" (p. 38). Attinasi (1992) recommended use of "phenomenological interviews" whereby the inquirer gains access to the meanings individuals attach to their own experience using a semi-structured interview guide.

There is a tradition of using qualitative research methods (e.g., phenomenological interviews) to discover what happens to students during college (Freedman, 1967; Madison, 1969; White, 1966). Several such inquiries culminated in popular, wide-used theories of college student development (i.e., Chickering, 1969; Kohlberg, 1984; Perry, 1970). However, the bulk of qualitative research about college students was conducted 25 years ago with traditional-age (18–22) students enrolled full time who lived on campus. Today, only about one sixth of undergraduate students fit that description (Levine, 1989). As Pascarella and Terenzini (1991) concluded, "specifying the effects of college for the vast numbers of non-traditional students . . . may be the single most important area of research on college impacts in the next decade" (p. 632). Through the use of interviews, we may be able to discover those aspects of college considered important by students whose frames of reference were not taken into account when many of the current research instruments and models of college impact were developed.

Purpose

The purpose of this study was to discover, by asking undergraduates to reflect on their college years, the impact of out-of-class experiences on their learning and personal development. Three research questions guided the study: (a) What did students learn from their experiences outside the classroom? (b) In what ways have they changed since starting college? and (c) Do the outcomes considered by students to be important differ by typeof institution attended and student background characteristics?

Although seniors from multiple institutions participated, this study did not seek to obtain generalizable results. Rather, the purpose was to generate an accurate and trustworthy picture of the perceptions and experiences of learning and personal development of undergraduates as told by the students themselves. As we shall see, most students found it difficult to bifurcate their college experience into two separate categories of learning; that is, one linked to experiences outside the classroom and the other a function of the formal curriculum.

Conceptual Framework

According to Pascarella and Terenzini (1991), studies of what happens to students during college follow one of two general approaches: developmental and college impact.

Developmental Approaches

The vast majority of theory-driven research on change during the college years is developmental (Kuh & Stage, 1992). Inquiries grounded in this perspective emphasize discrete periods or stages of development that are presumed to emerge in an orderly and hierarchical manner. Developmental models are heavily influenced by psychological theory; therefore, intrapersonal dynamics are considered to be more important to development than the environment. Some developmental theories focus on the *content* of the changes in cognitive, affective, and behavioral domains (e.g., psychosocial, typological) that occur during college while others describe the *processes* (cognitive-structural, person-environment interaction) by which these changes take place (Kuh & Stage, 1992; Pascarella & Terenzini, 1991; Rodgers, 1989).

An example of the latter is Baxter Magolda's (1992) study of cocurricular influences on intellectual development. Using the Epistemological Reflection model, Baxter Magolda found that students' ways of knowing, or epistemologies, influenced their interpretations of the importance of out-of-class experiences. For example, when asked to talk about important aspects of the collegiate experience, absolute knowers (i.e., students who assume knowledge is certain) tended to talk about how they had to "adjust" to college life (e.g., take more responsibility for their own affairs); transitional knowers described the importance of peers to learning how to function effectively in the college environment; and independent knowers talked of how they "discovered their own voices" (Baxter Magolda, 1992, p. 211) through dealing with people different from themselves.

College Impact Approaches

The study reported in this paper uses the college impact approach to discover outcomes that college students associated with out-of-class experiences. To account for learning and personal development, college impact models emphasize interactions between students and the institution's environments (broadly conceived). For example, in Pascarella's (1985) model, outcomes (learning and cognitive development) are a function of reciprocal influences among the structural and organizational characteristics of the institution (e.g., enrollment, control, selectivity, affluence), student background characteristics (e.g., sex, aspirations, aptitude, ethnicity), the perceptual and behavioral environments created by interactions with peers and institutional agents (e.g., faculty seem friendly and helpful, peers are competitive), and the "quality" of effort (i.e., time and energy) students invest in educationally purposeful activities.

Various outcome taxonomies have been developed to account for changes that occur during college (Astin, 1973; Bowen, 1977; Lenning, 1976; Micek, Service, & Lee, 1975). These taxonomies typically encompass two types of outcomes, affective and cognitive, which can be assessed using either psychological instruments or observations and reports of behavior, or both. (Astin, 1977; Kuh, Krehbiel, & MacKay, 1988; Pascarella & Terenzini, 1991). An example of an affective outcome is enhanced aesthetic awareness, which could be assessed psychometrically, such as with the estheticism scale of the *Omnibus Personality Inventory* (Heist & Yonge, 1968). A behavioral measure of aesthetic awareness could be observations or self-report information about frequency of participation in cultural events.

The most comprehensive synthesis of college outcomes is Pascarella and Terenzini's (1991) review of 2,600 studies. They divided affective and cognitive outcomes into nine domains: knowledge and subject matter competence, cognitive skills and intellectual growth, psychosocial changes, attitudes and values, moral development, educational attainment, career choice and development, economic benefits, and quality of life after college. Pascarella and Terenzini found that, in general, college attendance typically was associated with "net" and "long-term effects" for each of the domains. Net effects are changes due to attending college, as contrasted with changes resulting from maturation or experiences other than college. Long-term effects refer to whether the changes that occur during college persist after college.

Research conducted using the college impact approach reflects aggregated group effects. Although not every student changes on every domain, on average, college attendance is associated with modest gains in verbal and quantitative skills, substantial gains in knowledge (particularly in the major), and increased cognitive complexity; greater social maturation, personal competence, and freedom from irrational prejudice; increases in appreciation for the aesthetic qualities of life; clarification of religious views; substantial gains in personal autonomy and nonauthoritarianism; and modest decreases in political naivete and dogmatism. Also, college students become more introspective and more aware of their own interests, values, and aspirations. The crystallization of these diverse aspects of personality functioning into a sense of identity is one of the most important outcomes of college (Bowen, 1977; Chickering, 1969; Feldman & Newcomb, 1969; Pascarella & Terenzini, 1991). Equally important, the college experience leaves a "residue" (Bowen, 1977) manifested as an openness to new information and ideas, a facility for meeting and dealing with a wide variety of persons, and a practical sense of competence and confidence that enables a college-educated person to successfully cope with novel situations and problems.

Methods

To determine the impact of out-of-class experiences on student learning and personal development, seniors were interviewed from 12 institutions in different regions of the continental United States.

Participants

Participants were students classified as seniors at the following institutions: Berea College, Earlham College, Grinnell College, Iowa State University, Miami University of Ohio, Mount Holyoke College, Stanford University, The Evergreen State College, University of California, Davis, University of Louisville, Wichita State University, and Xavier University of Louisiana. These institutions were selected because they were known to provide rich out-of-class learning and personal development opportunities for their students (Kuh et al., 1991). Each institution was visited twice by a team of two to four investigators; the interviews with students on which this study is based were conducted during the second visits to these colleges.[1]

The institutional contact (typically someone designated by the chief student affairs officer) was asked to identify 10 to 12 seniors who, as a group, reflected a range of involvement in various aspects of the undergraduate experience. For example, we asked that no more than half the students selected for interviews be a highly visible student leader (e.g., editor of the student newspaper, varsity athlete, president of a social organization); the remainder, then, would likely be more typical of undergraduates at that institution in their level of campus involvement. We also requested that several students from historically underrepresented racial and ethnic groups be invited to participate. For the two metropolitan colleges, Louisville and Wichita State, a proportionate number of older, part-time, and commuting students were represented.

Problems related to scheduling and other vagaries (e.g., some students did not show up at the appointed hour) resulted in fewer than 10 students being interviewed at some institutions (i.e., Iowa State = 7; Xavier = 7; UC Davis = 9). Because members of the research team were employed at two of the institutions, they were able to conduct some interviews beyond the target number of 10. As a result, 28 students from Stanford University and 18 students from Wichita State University are included among the respondents.

In all, 149 seniors were interviewed: 69 men, 80 women; 101 whites, 30 African Americans, 6 Hispanics, 6 Asian Americans, and 6 international students; 129 students of traditional age (18–23) and 20 older than 23 years of age. Even though the numbers of students from most of the institutions are relatively small, as a group the participants reflect the diversity that characterizes undergraduate students enrolled in institutions of higher education in the United States.

Data Collection

A semistructured interview protocol was developed for this study and was field-tested during the first campus visit during the fall of 1988. The protocol subsequently was reduced to four general probes designed to elicit the most important things that the respondent learned during college—about oneself, others, interpersonal relations, cultural differences, academics, and so on—rather than the interviewer suggesting specific categories of outcomes. The four probes were: (a) Why did you choose to attend this college and in what ways has it been what you expected? (b) What are the most significant experiences you had here? (c) What are the major highlights of your time here? Low points? High points? Surprises? Disappointments? and (d) How are you different now than when you started college?

Interviews were conducted between January and June of 1989. Prior to the interviews, students received a letter from the investigators outlining the purpose of the study. By informing them in advance about the topics to be covered, some students were able to give the topics considerable thought before the interview.

Interviews were conducted by eight people. Seven of the interviewers were members of the College Experiences Study (CES) research team; by the time these interviews were conducted (during the second visit to the institutions), all the CES project staff had acquired extensive interviewing experience. The eighth interviewer, a graduate student in higher education, concluded 16 of the 28 interviews with Stanford students as part of an internship.[2]

No systematic effort was made to match interviewers and respondents on gender, race, and ethnicity. The interviews occurred in private rooms in campus buildings (e.g., administration buildings, libraries, student unions) that were reserved for this purpose. Interviews ranged in time from 35 minutes to 1 and one-half hours; the modal length was about 1 hour. All interviews were tape-recorded and transcribed verbatim.

Data Analysis

Transcribing interviews required 16 months (April, 1990 through July, 1991). Four people participated in the analysis of interview transcripts. Three were doctoral students in higher education with some training in qualitative research methods. They did not conduct any of the interviews. The fourth person (the author) conducted 21 of the interviews.[3]

To accomplish the purpose of the study, a two-stage, multimethod data analysis procedure was used. The first stage was inductive and the second deductive. As Reichardt and Cook (1979) argued:

> There is no need to choose a research method on the basis of a traditional paradigmatic stance. Nor is there any reason to pick between the two polar opposite paradigms. . . . There is every reason (at least in logic) to use them together to satisfy the demands of . . . research in the most efficacious manner possible. (p. 27)

The inductive stage began by examining what respondents said were—for them—important benefits of attending college that they associated with out-of-class experiences. The interview transcripts were analyzed using a five-phase iterative procedure. First, each transcript was reviewed by one of the doctoral students who assigned an identification number to the transcript including the institution, a student identification number, and the student's age, sex, and ethnicity. This initial reading of the transcripts yielded a set of eight categories reflecting outcomes mentioned by the participants (Miles & Huberman, 1984). Second, another reader analyzed several dozen transcripts and, based on her suggestions, the initial set of outcome themes was revised and expanded to 10 categories. Third, a transcript was selected which was read by all four readers to determine how well these themes accommodated the student-reported outcomes contained in this transcript. This revised set of themes was then discussed at some length by the four readers. The product of these discussions was a taxonomy comprised of 13 outcome categories. Fourth, four additional transcripts were selected; each reader read a copy of all four. The experience of coding these transcripts was discussed, and several minor revisions were made to the taxonomy including the addition of the miscellaneous "other" category. Finally, all 149 transcripts were read and coded by the author, which included assigning outcome category numbers in the margin of the transcript next to relevant passages. Thus, a single "human instrument" was responsible for analyzing and interpreting all the data, thereby avoiding potential interrater reliability problems.

The second stage of data analysis was deductive. As Miles and Huberman (1984) suggested, one can more quickly analyze massive amounts of data in the form of words by transforming categories of information into numbers; in addition, numbers can protect against investigator bias, thus ensuring intellectual honesty. Following Miles and Huberman, after the transcripts were coded, quantitative data analysis procedures were used to identify patterns in the data that had empirical and conceptual integrity, not to test hypotheses about out-of-class experiences and student learning.

Measures of central tendency were computed for each outcome category. A factor analysis was performed to determine whether the outcome categories (excluding the miscellaneous "other" category) could be reduced to a more wieldy number of outcome domains. Using the factor solution, *t*-tests and analysis of variance (ANOVA) were used to determine if the outcomes mentioned by students differed by certain student background characteristics (age, sex, ethnicity) and institutional size (large = 5,000 or more undergraduates, which included Iowa State, Louisville, Miami, Stanford, UC Davis, and Wichita State; small = fewer than 5,000 undergraduates, which included Berea, Earlham, Evergreen State, Grinnell, Mount Holyoke, and Xavier); control (public = Evergreen State, Iowa State, Louisville, Miami, UC Davis, Wichita State; private = Berea, Earlham, Grinnell, Mount Holyoke, Stanford, Xavier), and mission (liberal arts = Berea, Earlham, Evergreen State, Grinnell, Mount Holyoke, Xavier; metropolitan = Louisville, Wichita State; comprehensive = Iowa State, Miami, Stanford, UC Davis). . . .

Discussion

This section is divided into four parts: (a) the contribution of the study to the literature, (b) reflections on using interview data to assess college outcomes, (c) limitations of the study, and (d) thoughts on using quantitative data analysis procedures with qualitative data.

Contribution of the Study

The outcome categories that emerged from the inductive analysis of senior interview transcripts were, for the most part, similar to those developed by others to define and categorize college outcomes (e.g., Bowen, 1977; Ewell, 1984; Feldman & Newcomb, 1969; Lenning, 1976; Micek, Service, & Lee, 1975). For example, compared with the categories used by Pascarella and

Terenzini (1991), the only outcomes *not* mentioned by seniors were those that cannot be determined until after graduation—educational attainment, economic benefits, and quality of life after college.

Given the focus of the study—learning and personal development associated with out-of-class experiences—it was not surprising that some outcomes, such as academic skills, were mentioned less frequently than other outcomes, such as autonomy and confidence. At the same time, it is disappointing that knowledge application was not mentioned by more than a quarter of the respondents. Collegiate environments offer innumerable opportunities to use information obtained from many courses of study (e.g., political science, psychology, sociology) in dealing with the problems and challenges of daily life. To encourage more knowledge application, faculty could structure assignments that require students to illustrate how they are using class material in other areas of their lives. Institutional agents whose primary work is with students outside the classroom (e.g., student affairs staff, academic advisors) could promote more knowledge application by asking students on a regular basis to apply what they are learning in class to life outside the classroom. Simple illustrations of how this might work are the residence hall director who routinely invites students during casual conversation to share the three or four most important things they learned that week, or the student government advisor who challenges student leaders to apply material from their political science, psychology, and communications classes to their student government role.

One outcome frequently mentioned by participants as important was learning about and gaining experience with people from different racial, ethnic, and cultural backgrounds (Altruism and Estheticism). Earlier studies of attitudinal changes during college usually found increased tolerance for racial and ethnic differences (e.g., Clark, Heist, McConnell, Trow, & Yonge, 1972; Hyman & Wright, 1979; Winter, McClelland, & Stewart, 1981), an affective psychological outcome (Astin, 1973). This study suggests that experiences outside the classroom are an important venue where students not only develop an appreciation for people from backgrounds different from their own (the affective psychological outcome), but also cultivate skills that enable them to relate personally to such students (an affective behavioral outcome).

College impact models emphasize the influence of institutional and student characteristics on learning and personal development (Pascarella, 1985; Pascarella & Terenzini, 1991; Tinto, 1987; Weidman, 1989). Institutional control, size, and mission were associated with differences in Cognitive Complexity, Knowledge and Academic Skills, and Altruism and Estheticism. However, in this study sex was the only student characteristic associated with a difference in reported outcomes (Cognitive Complexity). That other student background characteristics were not systematically associated with differences in outcomes may be explained by the nature of the institutions. These institutions shared a number of properties, including cultural assumptions that every student can succeed and that every student is expected to participate fully in the life of the institution (Kuh et al., 1991). These colleges and universities have created something akin to a level playing field, an institutional context wherein student characteristics become neutral factors in terms of their learning and personal development (Kuh & Vesper, 1992).

Pascarella and Terenzini (1991) found that within-college differences (i.e., what a student does in college) were greater than between-college differences (i.e., type of institution attended). Few studies compared the effects of attending *specific* institutions on college impact, such as assessments of gains of students attending Indiana University, Ball State University, and Hanover College. Therefore, whether *individual* institutions have distinctive impacts on their students is not known because any differences in student outcomes that may be associated with salience and character of institutional mission become obfuscated by aggregating data from a number of institutions. For example, do students at colleges such as Berea, Earlham, and Grinnell, where the institutional mission emphasizes service to others, report patterns of outcomes that differ from those of their counterparts at other college and universities that do not emphasize service in their missions? Of course, institutions with salient service-oriented missions attract many students with humanitarian interests. Therefore, efforts to examine the relationship between institutional mission and student outcomes must attempt to estimate the relative contributions of the institutional environment and students' pre-college predilections to changes compatible with those valued by the institution's missions and philosophy. The contextual properties of these 12 colleges and universities differed in myriad, subtle ways that may influence student learning (Kuh et al., 1991), a point to which we shall return in the "Limitations" section.

Using Interviews to Assess Outcomes

The words of seniors describing the role of out-of-class experiences to their learning and development during college are compelling evidence of the value of using interviews to assess the impact of college on students. At the same time, using unstructured interviews to better understand what happens to students is not without potential pitfalls.

The quality of the information obtained from interviews is a function of the respondent's capacity to reflect on and discuss the topics under investigation and the interviewer's skill in creating the conditions which encourage the respondent to talk freely. Many seniors interviewed for this study spoke with clarity and precision about how they benefited from out-of-class experiences. Others, when asked to reflect on changes associated with experiences outside the classroom, invariably used illustrations from both in-class and out-of-class experiences. In other instances, students described a seamlessness between learning in and out of the classroom, suggesting that the boundaries between academics and student life beyond the classroom—often perceived by faculty and administrators to be real—were blurred so as to be indistinguishable to students. Still others were not very articulate in talking about how or whether they had changed during college. The best example is a Rhodes Scholar who, during the course of a 75-minute interview, was asked three times to describe how he had changed. Each time, however, he took the conversation in other directions. In all likelihood, this student—who had achieved national honors and a spate of institutional recognitions—benefited more from the undergraduate experience than his interview transcript revealed.

Finally, another plausible explanation for variation in the richness of interviews is the nature of a student's experiences in college. Some respondents may not have learned or changed very much as a result of experiences outside the classroom. Recall that seniors at small colleges with liberal arts missions were more likely to report changes in Cognitive Complexity, Knowledge and Academic Skills, and Altruism and Estheticism. Small classes and dorms place a greater obligation on students to actively participate; therefore, students at small colleges may have more opportunities to engage in activities—both in and out of the classroom—that require reflection and application of knowledge and skills (Barker, 1968; Chickering, 1969); thus, they have more practice in expressing themselves orally. At the same time, it may be that students who choose to attend small colleges are predisposed to such behavior and that these apparent differences in outcomes are a function of college recruitment, and not college impact (Pascarella & Terenzini, 1991).

Limitations

This study has several limitations. The first, and perhaps most important, is the nature of the institutions from which participants were selected. These colleges and universities were known to provide high quality out-of-class learning opportunities. Thus, it is possible that the range and degree of changes reported by students in this study may be richer than those of students at other institutions. Indeed, comparative analyses of *College Student Experience Questionnaire* (Pace, 1987) data indicated that students from these 12 institutions were more involved in their education (i.e., expended greater effort in their studies and educationally purposeful out-of-class activities) and benefitted more thantheir counterparts at other institutions (Kuh et al., 1991; Kuh & Vesper, 1992). Thus, the special qualities of these colleges and universities should be considered when determining the transferability of these findings.

Although these institutions are similar in that they provide rich out-of-class learning environments, they differed—as mentioned earlier—in other ways that influence student learning. More information about the contextual conditions of these colleges would provide a framework within which to interpret students' experiences and explain, perhaps, why what appear to be similar experiences and outcomes differ qualitatively. One example must suffice.

All of the quotations from students at The Evergreen State University mention their program of study. This may seem out of place in a paper focused on out-of-class experiences, unless one is familiar with the Evergreen ethos. At this college, many students have difficulty distinguishing between in-class and out-of-class learning. During our first visit to this campus, before we began interviewing for this study, we discovered that students viewed the terms, "in class" and "out of class" as irrelevant. At Evergreen, learning and personal development is a 24-hour-a-day activity, an expectation reinforced by an academic program that is markedly different from the traditional curriculum in which students select majors and take four or five courses a semester. Evergreen students ("junior learners" in the vernacular of that campus) match up with faculty ("senior learners") and form groups of 20 to 40 or so to study some topic in depth from an interdisciplinary perspective for a few months to, on occasion, a year. For many students, these groups, called "Programs," constitute one's primary academic *and* affinity groups. That is, the Program *is* the college experience, and to ask students to compartmentalize their learning experiences contradicts the mission of the institution and makes no sense to students. Hence, an understanding of the contextual conditions of these institutions would allow additional interpretations of these data.

Another limitation is the nature of the data—student reports of what happened to them since coming to college. Self-report data have been found to be moderately correlated ($r = .25$ to $r = .65$) with objective measures of knowledge acquisition (Pascarella & Terenzini, 1991). Nonetheless, memories are selective, and it is possible that students failed to mention certain changes. Recall could have been prompted by the use of a structured protocol based on an existing taxonomy of outcomes, such as Lenning (1976) or Micek, Service, and Lee (1975): This approach was rejected because it was incompatible with the phenomenological interview method. However, if respondents could have reviewed a verbatim transcript, or summary of their comments, they might have added other changes (Kvale, 1983). Therefore, the data reported in this paper almost certainly underestimate the benefits students derive from attending college in general and from out-of-class experiences in particular.

Finally, multiple investigators were needed to interview students at a dozen institutions in different regions of the country. Although all research team members were skilled in interviewing techniques, some were more successful than others in getting students to talk about the impact of out-of-class experiences on their learning and personal development.

A Note on Using Quantitative Data Analysis Procedures with Qualitative Data

The appropriateness of mixing quantitative and qualitative methods is the subject of continuing debate (Howe, 1988; Jick, 1979; Smith & Heshusius, 1986). The issues are complicated and cannot be resolved here; rather, the purpose here is to illustrate an important tradeoff associated with being "shamelessly eclectic" (Rossman & Wilson, 1991) in mixing methods: efficiency versus investigator influence. As mentioned earlier, employing quantitative procedures allows the researcher to more quickly identify patterns in large amounts of information (Miles & Huberman, 1984). However, using quantitative data analysis procedures limits the investigator's capacity to understand the nature, meaning, and impact of the information, the natural by-product of joining personal interpretations as one analyzes the data inductively (Peshkin, 1988).

This study took a middle road in that many weeks were devoted to the inductive analysis of more than 12 dozen interviews prior to employing quantitative techniques to distill patterns in the data. These procedures (e.g., factor analysis, ANOVA) allowed the researcher to classify the information in ways (e.g., by institutional type) that would have required substantially more time using the inductive approach exclusively.

Conclusions

This study provides a contemporary view of the changes students attributed to out-of-class experiences. Based on their "voices," four conclusions about student learning and personal development associated with out-of-class experiences are warranted.

First, consistent with earlier studies (e.g., Wilson, 1966), experiences beyond the classroom made substantial contributions to student learning and personal development. All students reported personally meaningful changes in one or more areas considered to be important outcomes of college (e.g., interpersonal and practical competence, critical thinking). The relationships among these outcomes were complex, suggesting cumulative and mutually shaping effects of knowledge, and enhanced capacity for critical thinking, personal reflection, competence, and self-direction. With all the attention given to outcomes assessment (Ewell, 1991), it is disappointing that the contributions of out-of-class experiences to learning and personal development have received so little attention, particularly given that students attach so much importance to such experiences.

Second, knowledge acquisition and academic skills were more frequently associated with classroom, laboratory, and studio activities than with out-of-class experiences. When talking about how they had changed during college many students mentioned skill areas such as writing and knowledge about specific subjects. The quotations illustrating this outcome domain suggest that students view the classroom as the primary source of these changes. At the same time, although students attributed gains in knowledge to classroom assignments and experiences, life outside the classroom provided ample opportunities to test the value and worth of these ideas and skills.

Third, student background characteristics were, for the most part, unrelated to the learning and personal development outcomes they considered important. The kinds and degree of changes reported by seniors in this study were similar, regardless of age and ethnicity. It is reassuring to know that the benefits associated with attending college reported by "new majority students" (i.e., students of color and those who are over the age of 23, attend college part time, live off campus, have families, or work more than 20 hours a week; Ehrlich, 1991) did not differ from those of traditional age and white students. The lone difference associated with sex regarding application of knowledge is a reminder that collegiate climates for learning often are less empowering for women than for men. If women are taken seriously in and out of the classroom by faculty and administrators, perhaps they will be encouraged to the same extent as their male counterparts to apply what they are learning.

Finally, the type of institution attended was related to differences in the frequency with which certain outcomes were mentioned. For example, students at the smaller colleges with a liberal arts mission more frequently reported changes in intellectual and aesthetic areas. To what degree pre-college characteristics of students contribute to these differences cannot be determined from this study. However, others have argued that a salient, consistently articulated mission focuses student effort (Chickering, 1969; Keeton, 1971). To the extent that this is the case of these colleges, the results of this study affirm Bowen's (1977) conclusion that large size does not necessarily offer educational advantages.

There is more to discover about the contributions of out-of-class experiences to student learning and personal development. For example, studies that attempt to link various out-of-class experiences (e.g., voluntarism, student government, on-campus job) with specific outcomes would be useful to institutional decision-makers responsible for weighing the merits of allocating resources to such activities. Because many of the benefits of college attendance seem to persist well beyond graduation, it would be instructive to examine the relationships between involvement in out-of-class activities and the long-term effects of college. The words of a senior from The Evergreen State College convey a thought consistent with this last point:

> My educational experience here, it's been more like preparing for my journey. [College] has been a journey within itself, but it's more a preparation for my real journey.

Notes

1. The research reported in this paper was funded in part by grants from The Lilly Endowment, Inc., the National Association of Student Personnel Administrators, and the Education Division of the Marriott Corporation. However, any endorsement by these agencies of the findings presented here should not be inferred.
2. I gratefully acknowledge the splendid work of collaborators on the College Experiences Study. Without them, the information on which this paper is based could not have been gathered: Rosalind Andreas, Herman Blake, James Lyons, Lee Krehbiel, Kathleen MacKay, John Schuh, Carney Strange, and Elizabeth Whitt. Also Jeff McCollough, while he was a graduate student at Indiana University, did an internship at Stanford (his alma mater), part of which included interviewing Stanford students.

3. The contributions of Caitlin Anderson, James Arnold, and John Downey, all doctoral students in higher education at Indiana University, were essential to completing this project. They played key roles in developing the outcomes taxonomy distilled from the interview transcripts and made many helpful comments on an earlier draft of this paper. Special thanks also are due to Nick Vesper of Indiana University who cheerfully, skillfully, and in a most timely fashion, performed the computer analysis of outcomes data. Finally, I wish to acknowledge the helpful comments of John Centra and Elizabeth Whitt on an earlier version of this paper and the suggestions of the anonymous reviewers and John Rury.

References

Astin, A. W. (1973). Measurement and determinants of the outputs of higher education. In L. Solmon and P. Taubman (Eds.), *Does college matter? Some evidence on the impacts of higher education.* New York: Academic Press.

Astin, A. W. (1977). *Four critical years: Effects of college on beliefs, attitudes, and knowledge.* San Francisco: Jossey-Bass.

Astin, H. S., & Kent, L. (1983). Gender roles in transition: Research and policy implications for higher education. *Journal of Higher Education, 54, 309–324.*

Attinasi, L. C., Jr. (1992). Rethinking the study of college outcomes. *Journal of College Student development, 33,* 61–70.

Barker, R. (1968). *Ecological Psychology: Concepts for studying the environment of human behavior.* Stanford, CA: Stanford University Press.

Baxter Magolda, M. B. (1992). Cocurricular influences on college students' intellectual development. *Journal of College Student Development, 33,* 203–213.

Bogdan, R. C., & Biklen, S. K. (1982). *Qualitative research for education: An introduction to theory and methods.* Boston: Allyn and Bacon.

Bowen, H. R. (1977). *Investment in learning.* San Francisco: Jossey-Bass.

Boyer, E. (1987). *College: The undergraduate experience in America.* New York: Harper & Row.

Chickering, A. W. (1969). *Education and identity.* San Francisco: Jossey-Bass.

Clark, B. R., Heist, P., McConnell, T. R., Trow, M. A., & Yonge, G. (1972). *Students and colleges: Interaction and change.* Berkeley: University of California, Center for Research and Development in Higher Education.

Ehrlich, T. (1991). *Our university in the state: Educating the new majority.* Bloomington: Indiana University.

Ewell, P. T. (1984). *The self-regarding institution: Information for excellence.* Boulder, CO: National Center for Higher Education Management Systems.

Ewell, P. T. (1991). Assessment and public accountability: Back to the future. *Change, 23*(6), 12–17.

Feldman, K. A., & Newcomb, T. M. (1969). *The impact of college on students.* San Francisco: Jossey-Bass.

Freedman, M. B. (1967). *The college experience.* San Francisco: Jossey-Bass.

Heist, P., & Yonge, G. (1968). *Omnibus Personality Inventory manual (Form F).* New York: Psychological Corporation.

Hyman, H., & Wright, C. (1979). *Education's lasting influence on values.* Chicago: University of Chicago Press.

Howe, K. R. (1988). Against the quantitative-qualitative incompatibility thesis or dogmas die hard. *Educational Researcher, 17*(8), 10–16.

Jick, T. D. (1979). Mixing qualitative and quantitative methods: Triangulation in action. *Administrative Science Quarterly, 24,* 602–611.

Keeton, M. (1971). *Models and mavericks.* New York: McGraw-Hill.

Kohlberg, L. (1984). *Essays on moral development: Vol. 2. The psychology of moral development: The nature and validity of moral stages.* New York: Harper & Row.

Kuh, G. D., Krehbiel, L., & MacKay, K. A. (1988). *Personal development and the college student experience: A review of the literature.* Trenton, NJ: New Jersey Department of Higher Education, College Outcomes Evaluation Program.

Kuh, G. D., Schuh, J. S., Whitt, E. J., Andreas, R. E., Lyons, J. W., Strange, C. C., Krehbiel, L. E., & MacKay, K. A. (1991). *Involving colleges: Successful approaches to fostering student learning and personal development outside the classroom.* San Francisco: Jossey-Bass.

Kuh, G. D., & Stage, F. K. (1992). Student development theory and research. In B. R. Clark & G. Neave (Eds.), *Encyclopedia of higher education* (pp. 1719–1730). Oxford and New York: Praeger.

Kuh, G. D., & Vesper, N. (1992, April). *A comparison of student learning at "involving" and "other" metropolitan universities.* Paper presented at the Annual Meeting of the American Educational Research Association, San Francisco.

Kvale, S. (1983). The qualitative research interview: A phenomenological and hermeneutical mode of understanding. *Journal of Phenomenological Psychology, 14,* 171–196.

Lenning, O. T. (Ed.). (1976). *Improving educational outcomes.* San Francisco: Jossey-Bass.

Levine, A. & Associates. (1989). *Shaping higher education's future: Demographic realities and opportunities, 1990–2000.* San Francisco: Jossey-Bass.

Light, R. J. (1992). *The Harvard assessment seminars: Explorations with students and faculty about teaching, learning, and student life* (Second report). Cambridge, MA: Harvard University Graduate School of Education and Kennedy School of Government.

Madison, P. (1969). *Personality development in college.* Reading, MA: Addison-Wesley.

Micek, S. S., Service, A. L., & Lee, Y. S. (1975). *Outcome measures and procedures manual. Boulder,* CO: National Center for Higher Education Management Systems, Western Interstate Commission on Higher Education.

Miles, M. B., & Huberman, A. M. (1984). *Qualitative data analysis: A sourcebook of new methods.* Beverly Hills, CA: Sage.

Moffatt, M. (1988). *Coming of age in New Jersey: College and American culture.* New Brunswick, NJ: Rutgers University Press.

Pace, C. R. (1979). *Measuring outcomes of college: Fifty years of findings and recommendations for the future.* San Francisco: Jossey-Bass.

Pace, C. R. (1987). *CSEQ: Test manual and norms: College Student Experiences Questionnaire.* Los Angeles: The Center for the Study of Evaluation, Graduate School of Education, University of California, Los Angeles.

Pace, C. R. (1990). *The undergraduates: A report of their activities and progress in college in the 1980s.* Los Angeles: University of California at Los Angeles, Center for the Study of Evaluation.

Pascarella, E. T. (1985). College environmental influences on learning and cognitive development: A critical review and synthesis. In J. Smart (Ed.), *Higher education: Handbook of theory and research (Vol. 1).* New York: Agathon.

Pascarella, E. T., Ethington, C. A., & Smart, J.C. (1988). The influence of college on humanitarian/civic involvement values. *Journal of Higher Education, 59,* 412–437.

Pascarella, E. T., & Terenzini, P. T. (1991). *How college affects students: Findings and insights from twenty years of research.* San Francisco: Jossey-Bass.

Perry, W. G., Jr. (1970). *Forms of intellectual and ethical development in the college years. A scheme.* New York: Holt, Rinehart, & Winston.

Peshkin, A. (1988). In search of subjectivity—one's own. *Educational Record, 17*(7), 17–22.

Reichardt, C. S., & Cook, T. D. (1979). Beyond qualitative versus quantitative methods. In C. Reichardt & T. Cook (Eds.), *Qualitative and Quantitative methods in evaluation* (pp. 7–32). Beverly Hills: Sage.

Rodgers, R. F. (1989). Student development. In U. Delworth & G. Hanson (Eds.), *Student services: A handbook for the profession* (pp. 117–164). San Francisco: Jossey-Bass.

Rossman, G. B., & Wilson, B. L. (April, 1991). *Numbers and words revisited: Being "shamelessly eclectic."* Paper presented at the Annual Meeting of the American Educational Research Association, Chicago.

Saufley, R. W., Cowan, K. O., & Blake, J. H. (1983). The struggles of minority students at predominantly white institutions. In J. Cones III, J. Noonan, & D. Janha (Eds.), *Teaching minority students: New directions for teaching and learning, No. 16* (pp. 3–15). San Francisco: Jossey-Bass.

Shrader, W. (1969). *College ruined our daughter: Letters to parents concerning the baffling world of the college student.* New York: Harper & Row.

Smith, J. K., & Heshusius, L. (1986). Closing down the conversation: The end of the quantitative-qualitative debates among educational inquirers. *Educational Researcher, 15*(1), 4–12.

Thomas, R., & Chickering, A. W. (1984). *Education and Identity* revisited. *Journal of College Student Personnel, 25,* 392–399.

Tinto, V. (1987). *Leaving college: Rethinking the causes and cures of student attrition.* Chicago: University of Chicago Press.

Weidman, J. (1989). Undergraduate socialization: A conceptual approach. In J. Smart (Ed.), *Higher education: Handbook of theory and research (Vol. 5).* New York: Agathon.

White, R. W. (1966). *Lives in progress* (2nd ed.). New York: Holt, Rinehart, & Winston.

Wilson, E. K. (1966). The entering student: Attributes and agents of change. In T. Newcomb & E. Wilson (Eds.), *College peer groups* (pp. 71–106). Chicago, Aldine.

Winter, D., McClelland, D., & Stewart, A. (1981). *A new case for the liberal arts: Assessing institutional goals and student development.* San Francisco: Jossey-Bass.

CURRENT READINGS

COLLEGE IMPACT ON STUDENT LEARNING: COMPARING THE USE OF SELF-REPORTED GAINS, STANDARDIZED TEST SCORES, AND COLLEGE GRADES

GUADALUPE ANAYA

To examine the impact of college researchers have used a variety of measures of learning and fairly comparable results have been obtained. This study undertakes a direct comparison of three learning indicators: college grade-point average, student-reported growth (Verbal and Quantitative), and GRE scores (Verbal, Quantitative, and Composite). The same set of independent variables was regressed onto each dependent measure using a national sample of 2,289 students. Substantive interpretation are presented and comparisons are made for paired regressions using alternate indicators. This paper provides evidence suggesting that (1) student-reported cognitive growth survey items have a modest relative validity; (2) the attenuation associated with the use of residual gain scores does not invalidate their use; and (3) comparable results are obtained when using the college GPA and standardized test scores. It is concluded that the alternate measures can be used as proxies for more direct measures of learning.

A case for the use of short-term measures of progress has been presented by a technical resource group to the National Education Goals Panel (Ewell and Jones, 1993). The literature was reviewed to explore the validity of alternate indicators, such as self-reports of educational outcomes, as proxies for more direct measures. In fact, student self-reports of cognitive growth along with standardized test results and college grades have been the more commonly used outcome measures in college impact studies (Pascarella and Terenzini, 1991). Each type of indicator appears to be associated with different types of studies. Pascarella and Terenzini (1991) reported that studies using college grades or student-reported learning have primarily examined within-college factors; on the other hand, the studies using standardized measures generally focused on between-college factors. Reviews of the literature suggest that fairly similar results have been obtained, thus providing support for the use of alternate measures of learning (Anaya, 1992; Ewell and Jones, 1993). Because studies have examined the impact of different elements of the college experience, the existing research precludes a direct examination of the substantive results obtained with each type of measure (Pascarella and Terenzini, 1991). This study uses self-reports of learning, college grade-point average (GPA), and performance on a standardized test (GRE) as indicators of learning. A direct comparison of the results

Reprinted by permission from *Research in Higher Education* 40, no. 5 (1999).

can provide evidence about the relative validity of alternate learning indicators for college impact studies.

Alternate Measures of Student Learning

The GPA has been the measure of choice by researchers interested in examining the influence that college programs and experiences may have on the cognitive development of students. There are two problems associated with college GPA as a measure of cognitive skill development: validity and generalizability. In the first case, the grade assigned to a student in a course typically does not take into account the student's performance level at the beginning of the course; there is no "pretest" available for the final grade in the course. In essence, college grades are normative rather than criterion-based indicators of cognitive performance. A second major limitation of using college GPA is that it is a nonstandardized measure. This limits the generalizability of research results unless we assume (1) that a GPA of 3.8 at one college or in one subenvironment (major) is equivalent to a 3.8 GPA at another college or in another subenvironment; and (2) that the differences in GPA reflect differential learning for students in a given environment (e.g., major or course). Using college GPA makes generalizations about the impact of college problematic (Duran, 1983), since it does not provide a basis for comparing college effects either between or within institutions. Nonetheless, it is generally assumed that grades reflect learning.

Student-reported measures of learning or cognitive change are regularly used in college impact studies. The College Student Experiences Questionnaire (Pace, 1979), the College Student Survey (Higher Education Research Institute, 1989), and the Follow-Up Survey (Higher Education Research Institute, 1989) are widely used survey instruments that include student self-reports of growth. Students are asked to estimate and report the degree of cognitive change since they entered college. Essentially students are asked to estimate the degree of cognitive change over a stated period of time in each of several areas of knowledge and competence. The results of research using items from the aforementioned questionnaires are consistent with research using other measures of academic achievement (Anaya, 1992; Astin, 1993; Pace, 1984) even though measurement characteristics may have affected the research results. However, Pike (1995, 1996) has suggested that student-reported measures possess a certain degree of "convergent" validity vis-à-vis standardized instruments. Pike (1995, 1996) examined the convergent validity of survey items reflecting the four domains of the College BASE. These studies yielded stronger associations between these two types of measures for the mathematics domain than for the English domain. The student-reported method of studying college impact is attractive from a methodological perspective in that it can cover a wide range of learning and developmental outcomes. It is attractive from a practical perspective since it is fairly inexpensive to survey students and to ask them to report how much they have learned or changed since entering college.

Research using standardized tests, such as the SAT and GRE, has generally examined between-institution or academic domain effects (Angoff and Johnson, 1990; Hartnett and Centra, 1985; Pike and Phillippi, 1989). Standardized measures can provide a basis for examining between- and within-institutional influences, but there are a few limitations associated with the characteristics of standardized instruments, with variations in the performance of different groups and methodological issues. First, standardized tests generally measure limited domains of human cognitive development or learning: verbal, quantitative, and analytical. (Although ACT's College Outcomes Measures Project, ETS's Academic Profile, the General Examinations of the College Level Examination Program, and academic subject area instruments measure a broader set of domains, they are in limited use.) Second, limitations may also arise given that the performance of women and minorities on these standardized tests has been lower than that of men and whites, respectively (Angoff and Johnson, 1990). Third, college impact studies that use multiple regression or residual gains have elicited criticism because performance on a standardized test is most strongly associated with prior achievement. The variation in posttest performance that remains after controlling for the effects of the pretest is relatively small (Baird, 1985). Thus, the proportion of variance accounted for by collegiate factors has been said to be minuscule compared to that accounted for by prior academic performance. Astin (1991) and Pascarella and Terenzini

(1991) have argued that standardized instruments can still provide useful information even though the effects of educational programs or treatments are comparatively small.

In summary, the three types of measures discussed here are part of the functioning of colleges and universities (e.g., screening students, assessing programs), and institutional researchers and practitioners generally take into account the limitations of each. The cumulative evidence suggests that the results obtained with the alternate measures are consistent (Anaya, 1992; Ewell and Jones, 1993) and recent research suggests that self-reports of learning may possess a certain degree of convergent validity with standardized tests (Pike, 1995, 1996).

The Study

The research question addressed in this study is essentially a methodological one. Nevertheless a conceptual framework is used in selecting variables that might be associated with student learning. Active learning (Bjork, 1979; Shuell, 1986), cooperative learning theory (Deutsch, 1949; Johnson et al., 1981), and involvement theory (Astin, 1984) provide the conceptual basis.

The concept of active learning emanates from human learning research (Shuell, 1986). Learning has been found to be positively associated with variable encoding (Craik, 1981; Mandler, 1978) and levels of processing (Craik and Lockhart, 1972). This research suggests that learning material can be processed to a greater or lesser degree, and that the learner's involvement in the learning process varies from, more or less, passive to active. This conclusion has also been indicated by the research on the mediating effects of cooperative techniques on human learning processes (Anaya, 1990). Cooperative learning techniques optimize learning outcomes because they facilitate a student's active involvement in the learning process (Anaya, 1990). Cooperative learning activities provide students with opportunities to take part in the selection of learning goals and materials, discuss how they will achieve their learning goals, plan their activities, share their learning experiences, and work together toward a common learning goal. Thus, when students tutor each other, discuss course content, or work on class projects together it is likely that they will process the learning material more actively (Lambiotte et al., 1987).

Along a similar vein, involvement theory states that a student's progress toward any developmental goal is hypothetically a direct function of the amount of time and energy that the student invests in activities related to the achievement of that goal (Astin, 1984). One would expect that environments and activities directly related to quantitative skill development would be positively associated with verbal learning. For example, students majoring in the physical sciences (or those taking a large number of courses that emphasize numerical understanding) find themselves in educational environments conducive to quantitative skill development. Astin (1984) indicates that, since a student's time and energy are finite, the student is engaged in a zero sum game when it comes to competition among different forms of involvement. One form or level of involvement may facilitate verbal skill development while another form or level of involvement may hinder it (e.g., high levels of involvement in extracurricular activities). Survey items indicating quantitative and qualitative distinctions in the activities engaged in by students were selected. Survey items indicating student-student learning interactions were selected as the closest approximations to cooperative and active learning activities (Anaya, 1992). Each of the alternate measures was regressed onto the same set of independent variables and evaluated using the enter method.

Sample and Instruments

This study uses a subset of a nationally representative sample of 1985 first-time freshmen. The subset consists of 2,289 students who took the GRE in 1989, completed the Follow-Up Survey (FUS) in 1989, and completed the Student Information Form (SIF) in 1985. The mean and standard deviations for the GRE Verbal scores are 547 and 107, and for the Quantitative scores they are 609 and 124. The variability of the GRE scores for this sample is comparable to that reported by the Educational Testing Service (1987): 118 and 132, respectively. The surveys include items on student demographics, achievement, expectations, values, goals, self-ratings, academic and co-curricular activities, and teaching or learning activities. Data for this study also include student SAT and GRE scores.

Variables in the Study

Three types of measures of learning are used: average college grades, standardized test scores, and student-reported gains. The undergraduate GPA is measured on a 6-point scale: (1) C− or less; (2) C; (3) C+, B−; (4) B; (5) B+, A−; and (6) A. The GRE Verbal, Quantitative, and Composite scores make up the second type of measure. The GRE test range is 200–800 and the Composite score is the sum of the two test scores. The third type of learning measure consists of the students' responses to cognitive change survey items. These items asked students to indicate how much they had changed since entering college. Students responded to a set of items regarding their development. They responded to the following question: "Compared to when you entered college as a freshman, how would you now describe your" on a variety of developmental items. The items included: (a) in analytic and problem-solving skills (expected in this study to be related to the GRE quantitative measure); (b) in writing skills (expected in this study to be related to the GRE verbal measure); and (c) in foreign-language skills. The response options are on a 5-point scale: (1) much weaker, (2) weaker, (3) no change, (4) stronger, and (5) much stronger.

Two types of independent variables are included in this study. First, student characteristics that might be associated with student learning are statistically controlled, including demographic characteristics, high school achievement, and precollege motivations and expectations. The second group of independent variables includes both between-college variables and within-college or subenvironment variables. The within-college variables include structural variables and student involvement in academic activities, courses, classroom learning activities, and nonacademic activities (Appendix A). Prior achievement as indicated by high school grade-point average and SAT scores is used as the pretest. Because of the large sample size (N = 2,289), a PIN of .005 is used in the regression. The regression blocks and variables are:

Precollege factors: race—dummy coded for African-American, Asian-American, Mexican-American, and white; gender—1 = male, 2 = female; mother's and father's level of education, 1–8; number of years of high school English, math, and foreign languages, 1–7; the student's level of commitment to career/financial goals 1–18; and degree aspirations, 1–6.

Institutional characteristics: institutional type dummy coded for public university, private university, public 4-year, and private 4-year; and selectivity, sum of SAT Verbal and SAT Math.

Within-college factors—academic environments and nonacademic activities: academic major, years lived on campus, 0–4; participation in clubs and sports 0–15; participation in college clubs and organizations, 1–27; hours per week (hpw) socializing with friends, and speaking with faculty outside of class, 1–8.

Learning activities: number of courses emphasizing writing skills, math or numerical understanding, scientific understanding, historical perspectives, and foreign-language courses, 1–5; interacting (discussions) with classmates, 0–9; tutored a student, received tutoring, worked on an independent research project, had a class paper critiqued by a professor, guest in a professor's home, took an essay exam, and worked on a group project for a class, 1–3; and hours per week (hpw) reading for pleasure, hpw attending classes/labs, and hpw studying/doing homework, hpw talking with faculty outside of class, 1–8.

Results and Discussion

This study is conducted in two phases. In the first phase the task of identifying student-reported change items that correspond to the GRE Verbal and Quantitative subscores is undertaken. In the second phase a comparison is made of the results of three pairs of analyses. Learning in two domains is examined using the GRE Verbal and Quantitative scores as well as student-reported measures corresponding to these two domains. The Verbal and Quantitative test score regression results are compared with self-reported gains regression results. The undergraduate GPA and the GRE Composite score (GRE Verbal plus GRE Quantitative) are used as general measures of student learning. The cumulative test score regression results are compared with the college grade-point average regression results.

Phase 1

The task here is to ascertain which survey item (or combination of items) corresponds most closely with each GRE scale. Using the student's

TABLE 1
The GRE Quantitative and Analytical Residual Gains Scores Regressed on the Student Reported Gains

Survey Item	β	R^2	*Constant*	*F*	σF
GRE quantitative equivalent		0.20	−21.40	15.067	.000
Analytical and problem-solving skills	16.27				
Foreign-language skills	−4.90				
Writing skills	−6.9				
GRE verbal equivalent		0.12	−50.81	8.731	.000
Writing skills	6.85				
Analytical and problem-solving skills	5.87				

self-reported change to replicate the analysis presents several problems. First, the selected "pretests" for the analyses are the student's SAT scores. These pretests provide a statistical control for the student's precollege achievement, producing a measure of "change" that is basically a residual gain score. However, when a student reports cognitive change, precollege achievement is presumably already "controlled" because the survey asks the student to report change since entering college. Second, in using student-reported change, one cannot be sure if the student-reported cognitive skill is the same as what the GRE is measuring. How, then, for comparison purposes does one decide which self-reported skills are the closest "equivalents" to the GRE scores? There are two ways to deal with this problem: a priori and empirical. The a priori method is to factor analyze all self-reported change measures that relate to cognitive development, to examine the factor structure, and to select those factors whose content most resembles that of the GRE Verbal and Quantitative scales. The empirical approach would be to correlate self-reported change with actual SAT-GRE residual gains and to choose those self-reported change items that yield the highest correlation. For example, the residual gain scores on the Verbal test can be computed by regressing the GRE Verbal score on the SAT Verbal score. The residual would be calculated for each subject as follows: $GRE_{Verbal} - (a + bSAT_{Verbal})$. The latter method is used to determine which, if any, of the student-reported change items best correspond to the GRE scores.

The empirical method of treating student-reported change involves a three-stage "cross-validation" process. Using a random 50% sample, residual gain scores are computed by regressing the GRE scores on the SAT scores: $GRE = a + b(SAT_{Verbal}) + b(SAT_{Math})$. Thus, best-fit coefficients for computing residual gain scores on the actual GRE in the independent sample can be obtained. In the second stage, residuals are calculated using the formulas obtained in the first stage as follows: $GRE - GRE_{predicted}$. The residual gain scores, in turn, are regressed onto the self-reported gain items: in analytic and problem-solving skills, in writing skills, and in foreign-language skills.

The GRE Verbal and Quantitative residual gain scores were regressed on the student-reported cognitive change items (Table 1). The self-assessment of analytic and problem-solving skills entered both Verbal and Quantitative (residual gains) regressions. The magnitude of the betas and the constants in these formulas indicates, as might be expected, that this item is more closely associated with Quantitative scores. The data point to a stronger association between the survey items and the Quantitative scores, and are consistent with the data reported by Pike (1995, 1996). These results indicate that there is some validity, albeit modest, to student-reported cognitive growth, assuming that residual scores are valid indicators of student learning. Alternately, it could be surmised that the apparent convergence of these measures indicates that the attenuation inherent in residual scores is not so serious as to invalidate residual scores. The cross-validation portion of this work constitutes the third and final stage, where the regression weights obtained in stage two are applied to the second random half of the sample. The self-reported verbal gains measure contains two survey items and the quantitative measure consists of three survey items (Table 1). The combined self-reported items are weighted (Table 1) and used as a set of alternate measures. The independent samples are used to minimize the possibility of capitalizing on error in the final test of the validity of the empirically derived student-reported estimates of cognitive growth.

Each of the learning measures in the study is paired with a second one deemed to most closely correspond with it. The first pair includes student performance on the GRE Verbal test and student-reported verbal gains survey items. The second pair includes student performance on the GRE Quantitative test and student-reported quantitative gains survey items. The third pair of learning measures are indicators of general learning: the GRE Composite score (the sum of the Verbal and Quantitative scores) and the college grade-point average. The results of the pairs of regressions are compared in the following section to determine the nature of the substantive conclusions that might be reached with each type of measure and to examine the relative validity of each.

Phase 2

The analysis for each dependent variable employed a least-squares regression solution. The independent variables were blocked and entered hierarchically using the Statistical Package for the Social Science (SPSS) multiple regression program. Standardized betas from two stages in the regression analysis are reported and the correlations are used to examine the differences in effects coefficients. The first two blocks constitute the input variables and include precollege achievement measures and student characteristics. The beta in the first step of the block following the input blocks is extracted from the computer output for each of the variables in the study and recorded as the "after input" betas. The next three blocks of variables include the between- and within-college variables. The (final) beta in the regression solution and the beta for the variable after the input blocks (after inputs) are reported because a simple comparison of the variables that are statistically significant in the final step of the regressions for the alternate measures is not, in every case, very informative. The fact that a variable is statistically significant in one regression and not the other does not always mean that different effects are operating.

First, due to chance sampling variations, two "different" but highly correlated variables that enter the two different regressions could be serving as proxies for each other because of multicollinearity. Second, a variable can enter one regression and not the second simply because a coefficient did not quite reach significance in the second regression. This may not necessarily be due to a significant difference between the two coefficients. That is, the fact that a coefficient is significantly different from zero in the first regression and not in the second regression does not mean that the two coefficients are significantly different from one another. Therefore, it would be inappropriate to merely compare the final equations. A sounder basis for determining whether similar results have been obtained is to compare the simple correlations (Appendix C), as well as the coefficients for the variables, following control of inputs across different regressions. The multiple regression procedures described here provide a robust method for analyzing the environment-outcomes relationships of interest in college impact studies (Astin, 1991).

Precollege Factors

The student inputs comprise the first two blocks in the regression analysis (Tables 2, 3, and 4). Prior academic achievement was controlled in all of the regressions by entering high school grade-point average and SAT Verbal and Math scores in the first block. The SAT scores and high school grades bear a direct correspondence with the GRE scores and college GPA measures of learning, respectively. In the student-reported gains regression, the coefficients for the precollege achievement variables are smaller, nevertheless they are significant predictors.

The second block of student inputs includes demographic data, courses taken in high school, and freshman-year educational and career goal measures. Tables 2, 3, and 4 show a negative association between being female and learning as measured by performance on the GRE tests. What might account for these results? First, the zero-order correlations between being female and the GRE Verbal, Quantitative, and Composite scores are negative: –.20, –.40, and –.35 respectively. Second, the after inputs regression coefficient for gender (female) remains negative: –.05, –08, and –.11. Thus, after controlling

TABLE 2
College Environments and Learning Activities Regressed on Student GRE Verbal Scores and Student-Reported Verbal Gains

	GRE Verbal		*Student-Reported Verbal Gains*	
Variables in the Equation	*Standardized* β	β *After Inputs*	*Standardized* β	β *After Inputs*
Academic achievement				
Average high school grades	0.3762**	0.0473**	0.0104**	0.0444*
SAT Verbal score	0.819**	0.7315**	−0.0084**	0.0082
SAT Math score	0.1242**	0.1086**	−0.0679	−0.0427
Student characteristics & precollege factors				
Female	−0.0401**	−0.0454**	(−0.0153)	0.0013
Asian-American	(−.0080)	−0.0037	−0.0611**	−0.0168**
Goal: Career & financial achievement	−0.0537**	−0.0575**	(0.0262)	0.037*
Institutional characteristics				
Public 4-year	−0.0787**	−0.0787**	(−.0238)	−0.0196
Private 4-year	(−.0313)**	−0.0251	0.1066**	0.1066**
Institutional selectivity (SATV + SATM)	0.0508**	0.0508**	0.0739**	0.0739**
Within college factors, nonacademic activities & learning environments				
College athletics	−0.0515**	−0.0410**	(−.0227)	−0.0081
Major 89: Professions	−0.0331**	−0.0399**	(−.0215)	−0.0501*
College clubs & organizations	−0.0355**	−0.0406**	(−.0064)	0.0518*
Learning activities				
Hours per week reading for pleasure	0.0701**	0.0615**	(.0291)	0.0616*
Guest in professor's home	(.0026)	0.0039	0.1025**	0.1567**
Received tutoring	−0.0481**	−0.0553**	(−.0206)	0.0104
Discussions (interactions) with student	(.0230)*	0.0347*	0.1903**	0.2443**
Hours per week in class/labs	−0.0409**	−0.056**	(.0128)	0.0149
Hours per week—study/homework	(.0262)*	0.018	0.0718**	0.1256**
# of foreign-language courses	0.0429**	0.0462**	(−.0061)	0.0759**
# of courses emphasizing writing skills	(.0202)*	0.0351*	0.2801**	0.2824**
# of courses emphasizing numerical skills	−.0402**	−.0544**	(.0385)	−.0030
Independent research project	0.0323**	0.0353*	(.0482)*	0.1237**
Paper critiqued by professor	(.0208)*	0.0359*	0.0929**	.2203**
Multiple R	0.8707		0.3848	
Adjusted R^2	0.7563		0.1439	

Note: Coefficients are enclosed in parentheses for variables not statistically significant in the final equation. A PIN of .005 was used.
*$p < .01$.
**$p < .005$.

for demographic characteristics and prior achievement, being female is still negatively associated with learning gains. That is, the negative association remains once student inputs have been statistically controlled. Third, the final coefficient for the variable remains negative in the GRE test score regression: –.04, –.14, and –10. The final regression coefficients take into account environmental characteristics, within-college factors, and student involvement in learning activities. The "gender gap" present when students enter college apparently persists over the course of time. The GRE regression results suggest that different conditions are associated with learning for different groups of students, specifically men and women. The negative association with being female holds to some degree in all of the pairs across alternate measures. In the case of quantitative learning, the coefficient is statistically significant in the final equation for both measures (Table 3). While this is not true for the verbal learning equations, the betas are relatively similar in size: –0.04 for the GRE score and –0.02 for self-reported

TABLE 3
College Environments and Learning Activities Regressed on Student GRE Quantitative Scores and Student-Reported Quantitative Gains

	GRE Quantitative		*Student-reported quantitative gains*	
Variables in the equation	*Standardized β*	*β After Inputs*	*Standardized β*	*β After Inputs*
Academic achievement				
Average high school grades	0.4608**	0.0779**	0.0854**	0.0393
SAT Verbal score	0.4258**	0.0173	−0.0572**	−0.1241**
SAT Math score	0.8349**	0.7505**	0.2782**	0.2259**
Student characteristics & precollege factors				
Female	−0.1372**	.0779**	−0.0781**	−0.0172
Years of high school math	0.0607**	0.0655**	(.0061)	0.0399*
Years of high school English	−0.0295**	−0.0292**	(.0088)	−0.0037
Institutional characteristics				
Private 4-year	−0.0355*	−0.0355**	(.0406)*	0.0023
Within college factors, nonacademic activities & learning environments				
Major 89: Physical sciences	0.0541**	0.0759**	(.0441)*	0.0952**
Major 89: Engineering	0.0353**	0.0754**	0.068**	0.1408**
Major 89: Life sciences	0.0306**	0.0185	(.0248)	0.0278
Learning activities				
# of courses emphasizing numerical stills	0.1305**	0.1305**	0.2648**	0.2648**
# of courses emphasizing writing skills	−0.0591**	−0.0640**	−0.0878**	−0.0959**
# of foreign-language courses	(−.0086)	−0.0414**	−0.3897**	−0.3897**
Worked on a group project for a class	−0.0341**	−0.0099	(.0061)	0.0637**
Tutored	0.0309**	0.0472**	(.0342)	0.0827**
Discussions (interactions) with student	(.0039)	−0.0229	0.0555**	0.0188
Hours per week in class/labs	(−.0144)	0.0090	0.0704	0.1085**
Multiples *R*	0.893		0.523	
Adjusted R^2	0.79672		0.2702	

Note: Coefficients are enclosed in parentheses for variables not statistically significant in the final equation. A PIN of .005 was used.
* $p < .01$.
** $p < .005$.

verbal gains (Table 2). A conclusion that could be drawn from these results is that conditional effects are operating in the cases of verbal and quantitative cognitive development. At this point, we have evidence suggesting that similar substantive conclusions about conditional effects might be reached using alternate learning indicators.

Institutional Factors

Tables 2, 3, and 4 indicate that the use of alternate measures might yield mixed results. Attending a selective institution is positively associated with learning as measured by the GRE Verbal scores, student-reported verbal learning, and GRE Quantitative scores. On the other hand, attending a selective institution, it is negatively associated with student-reported quantitative learning. These data might reflect the differential impact of highly selective institutions on different learning domains. However, attending a four-year private institution is negatively associated with learning as measured by the GRE Composite score, college GPA, and GRE Verbal scores. This institutional characteristic is positively associated with student-reported verbal learning. It could be argued that in the case of between-college factors the data may lead to contradictory conclusions when different types of learning indicators are used.

Within-College Factors

The results for the within-college factors are consistent within the pairs of regressions for verbal and quantitative learning. One could reach similar conclusions with the GRE and student-

TABLE 4
College Environments and Learning Activities Regressed on Student GRE Composite Scores and Student-Reported College GPA

	GRE Composite		College Grade Point Average	
Variables in the Equation	*Standardized β*	*β After Inputs*	*Standardized β*	*β After Inputs*
Academic achievement				
Average high school grades	0.4736**	0.0780**	0.3793**	0.3081**
SAT Verbal score	0.6833**	0.3804**	0.2033**	0.2576**
SAT Math score	0.5674**	0.5247**	−0.0254**	0.068**
Student characteristics & precollege factors				
Female	−0.0998**	−0.1070**	(−.0239)	0.0144
Black	(.0028)	−0.0024	−0.0571**	−0.1051**
Goal: Career & financial achievement	−0.0351**	−0.0346**	−0.066**	−0.0636**
Years of high school foreign language	(.0120)	0.0157	(.0437)	0.0778**
Institutional characteristics				
Public 4-year	−0.0443**	−0.0443**	−0.1520**	−0.152**
Private 4-year	−0.04**	−0.04**	(−.0474)	0.0391
Institutional selectivity (SATV + SATM)	0.0414**	0.0402**	−0.2830**	−0.2830**
Within college factors, nonacademic activities & learning environments				
Major 89: Physical sciences	0.0394**	0.0439**	(−.0219)	−0.0158
Major 89: Engineering	(.0308)*	0.0354**	(0.0300)	−0.0016
Major 89: Life sciences	(.0212)*	0.0161	−0.0925**	−0.09**
College clubs & organizations	−0.0337**	−0.0435**	(−.0083)	0.0389
College athletics	(−.0168)	−0.0134	−0.0682**	−0.1073**
Member of fraternity/sorority	(−.0168)	−0.0268**	−0.0682**	−0.0558**
Learning activities				
Worked on a group project for a class	−0.0338**	−0.0333**	(−.0080)	−0.0365
Tutored	0.0356**	0.0259*	0.1273**	0.0972**
Received tutoring	−0.0368**	−0.0268*	−0.1108**	−0.1462**
Worked on professor's research project	(.0073)	0.0279**	0.0864**	0.0764**
Time talking with faculty outside of class	(.0018)	−0.0135	0.0638**	0.0927**
Hours per week in class/labs	−0.0468*	−0.0192	(.0081)	−0.0722**
Independent research project	0.0287**	0.0188	(.0283)	0.0953**
# courses emphasizing numerical skills	0.0591**	0.059**	−0.1055**	−0.1156**
Took essay exams	−.0298*	−.0448**	(−.0490)*	(−.0232)
Hours per week—study/homework	(.0167)*	0.0199	0.1040**	0.1101**
Multiple R	0.9108		0.577	
Adjusted R^2	0.8283		0.32834	

Note: Coefficients are enclosed in parentheses for variables not statistically significant in the final equation. A PIN of .005 was used.
*$p < .01$.
**$p < .005$.

reported measures regarding within-college effects. The data in Tables 3 and 4 suggest two general conclusions. First, within-college environments (activities) that are directly associated with the learning outcome are positively associated with the learning indicator. Table 3 shows that having a major in physical science or engineering is positively associate with quantitative learning as measured by both performance on the GRE Quantitative exam and student-reported quantitative learning gains. As suggested earlier, in some instances it is necessary to go beyond a simple comparison of the variables that enter the regressions for the alternate measures to determine if different effects are operating. For example, in Table 3 we can see that majoring in the physical sciences is statistically significant in the regression equation for the GRE measure. In the student-reported equation, the final coefficient, .04, is not statistically significant (Table 3). We can take a closer look at the relationships between this independent variable and the alternate indicators of learning by comparing the simple correlations (Appendix B) and the after-input coefficients (Table 3, the point at which inputs are statistically controlled in each of the regressions). The simple correlations, after input coefficient and final coefficient, are .27, .08, .05 for the GRE Quantitative measure and .16, .10, .04 for the student-reported Quantitative gains measure. The after-input coefficient, .10, in this case is statistically significant (PIN = .005). The final coefficient is significantly different from zero in the first regression and not in the second regression, but the two coefficients are not significantly different from each other. Therefore, we cannot conclude that the alternate measures provide evidence that different effects are operating. A similar comparison of the final regression coefficient with the after-input coefficient for other variables in the study (Tables 2, 3, and 4) indicates that this is so for several variables. The recommendation made by the National Education Goals Panel (Ewell and Jones, 1993) in favor of the use of proxies (e.g., grades, self-reports) until more direct measures are available is supported by the data.

Second, the converse of the first general conclusion is somewhat supported: Within-college environments (activities) that are not directly associated with the learning outcome are negatively associated with the learning indicator. Participation in college sports and in student organizations is negatively associated with verbal learning as indicated by performance on the GRE Verbal test (Table 2). However, this relationship does not hold for the student-reported learning indicator. Table 4 also yielded mixed results; in some cases, the results of the regression for both indicators of general learning (GRE Composite and College GPA) support these general conclusions, and in others only one of the indicators does so. This may be due in part to the lack of a one-to-one correspondence between the pairs of learning measures. The conclusions reached using alternate measures are not always consistent. But, as with the precollege factors, they are not contradictory.

Learning Activities

Fairly comparable results regarding the impact of learning activities are obtained with the alternate measures. The GRE Verbal score and the student-reported verbal gains are positively associated with several learning activities: the amount of time spent reading for pleasure, student-student interactions, the amount of time spent studying or doing homework, the number of courses that emphasize writing, working on an independent research project, and having a paper critiqued by a professor. Similarly, both quantitative learning measures are positively associated with the number of courses taken that emphasize numerical skills and tutoring another student. Consistency within the pairs of regression is also evident with the variables negatively associated with learning. Furthermore, all of the learning measures, except college GPA, are positively associated with the number of courses taken in an academic domain directly related to the measure. This study and earlier studies conducted by Gray and Taylor (1989) and by Jones and Ratcliff (1990) imply that the depth or level of exposure to college courses enhances student learning. The data also support previous research that academic departments are differentially associated with academic performance (Angoff and Johnson, 1990; Hartnett and Centra, 1985; Pike and Phillippi, 1989). In sum, all three pairs of learning measures manifest a substantial degree of consistency in this block of the regression. The data in this block (across the three pairs of regressions) support two general conclusions similar to those reached regarding the within-college factors: (1) learning activities that are directly associated with the learning outcome are positively associated with the learning indicator, (2) learning activities that are not directly associated with the learning outcome are negatively associated with the learning indicator.

Additional substantive conclusions can be made about the impact of learning activities. First, the analyses conducted in this study yielded some mixed results regarding the influence of group learning activities. In the case of the GRE Composite and college GPA (Table 4), tutoring is positively associated with learning, but receiving tutoring appears to hinder learning. This may be due to the nature of these activities as they are experienced by students on college campuses. Both activities can be classified as group learning activities with the potential to actively involve students in the learning process. However, these two learning activities may be qualitatively different. It may be that the tutor is more actively involved in the learning process. The student who is the recipient of tutoring may, in contrast, be a passive or even a reluctant participant (e.g., if required to obtain tutoring). The tutor is relearning the material in the process of teaching it to another student. The tutee, on the other hand, may be investing time and energy in counterproductive attitudes and behaviors. If this is the case, the tutee is expending time and energy, both finite resources, which are not available for productive learning activities. Second, as with prior research, the results of this study indicate that student-student and faculty-student interactions facilitate learning (Anaya, 1992, 1996; Astin, 1993). Third, the data provide additional and more consistent support for the two general conclusions reached regarding within-college factors. Learning activities that are most directly linked with the learning outcome are positively associated with the learning indicator.

The self-reported learning measures were derived on the basis of their correlations with residual GRE scores. However, in the case of the number of courses taken that emphasize writing skills, the coefficient is .02 in the GRE Verbal regression and .28 in the student-reported verbal gains regression. What can possibly account for the difference in the size of the coefficient? There may be several explanations for this result. First, the student-reported learning measure had only a weak relationship with residual GRE Verbal scores, in spite of the fact that it was empirically derived from those scores. Second, the student-reported verbal gains indicator appears to be measuring a broader set of "verbal" skills than the GRE Verbal score. That is, (a) the self-reported measure reflects writing skills more than the GRE Verbal does; and (b) the common factor variance between the two measures is not accounted for by writing skills.

Limitations of the Study

Before entertaining observations about the relative validity of the alternate indicators of learning, it is important to remember that these measures differed from each other in several ways. There is a lack of a one-to-one correspondence between the standardized measures and the student-reported gains and college GPA measures. Efforts to minimize the problem with the student-reported measures have been included in the study design (e.g., the use of empirically derived student-reported indicators), but there remains the possibility that we could obtain a better "fit" by using student-reported change measures that more directly correspond to the GRE scores. Additionally, the standardized test scores are on a continuous scale; the college GPA is on a 6-point ordinal scale; and the self-reported verbal and quantitative gains measure are comprised of 5-point ordinal scale survey items (two and three survey items, respectively). Finally, the study used a sample of students who took the GRE, a subsample of students who are perhaps more academically inclined than their peers.

Summary

The measures used in this study have been utilized as performance indicators in college impact studies. Although the research employing the college GPA and self-reports of learning has focused on within-college factors, and the research using standardized test scores has focused on between-college factors (Pascarella and Terenzini, 1991), fairly comparable results have been reported (Anaya, 1992; Ewell and Jones, 1993). The emphasis in college impact studies on different college factors precludes a direct comparison of the relative validity of these measures; consequently, this study set out to conduct a direct examination. The comparison of the data using the college grade-point average, standardized test scores, and self-reports of learning suggests that the each measures some aspect of student learning and each appears to be a valid measure of learning. The results (1) allow for similar substantive conclusions to be drawn using each of the alternate measures; (2) suggest that activities directed at eliciting domain-related outcomes yield more comparable data across types of learning indicators; and (3) different, though not contradictory, results are obtained in a few cases. First, a direct examination of the substantive results across types of measures indicates that both between- and within-college factors are associated with learning. The data are generally consistent across types of measures (e.g., test scores and student-reported gains). Second, the weight of the evidence suggests that domain-specific learning environments and activities promote specific learning outcomes. For example, majoring in the sciences and the number of courses taken that emphasize mathematical skills are positively associated with learning as measured by self-reported quantitative gains survey items and by performance on the GRE Quantitative test. On the other hand, environments and activities not associated with the learning outcome are in some cases not associated with measures of the outcome, and in other cases they are negatively associated with measures of the outcome. For instance, being a guest in a professor's home is positively associated with verbal learning but is not associated with qualitative learning; and the number of foreign-language courses taken is negatively related to quantitative learning. Independent variables less directly related to the learning domain yield comparable results but with less consistency across the three types of measures. Nonetheless, despite the lack of one-to-one correspondence and the use of ordinal measures, the data are fairly comparable across pairs of alternate measures. Third, the few inconsistencies observed in the data (within the pair of verbal learning results) are possibly due to the relatively more limited degree of correspondence between the verbal measures (GRE Verbal score and self-reported verbal gains). The direct comparisons provide additional evidence that these indicators can lead to comparable conclusions regarding the impact of college on student learning and that they can serve as proxies for more direct measures of learning.

Future research on the use of alternate measures should concentrate on using student-reported change, standardized tests, and grades in domains that more closely correspond to one another. If indeed the GRE Verbal is a composite of reading speed, reading comprehension, vocabulary, and knowledge of grammar, then a corresponding composite based on self-reports of growth in these specific areas should produce data more comparable to standardized test data. The results reported here suggest that self-reported gains are valid measures and therefore future research using self-reported growth measures should branch out to other cognitive areas.

APPENDIX A
Descriptive Statistics for Variables in the Study

Variables in the Study	*Mean*	*Standard Deviation*
College GPA	4.67	.87
GRE Composite score	1156.70	206.14
GRE Verbal score	547.89	107.51
Reported Verbal gains	608.81	124.08
GRE Quantitative score	3.82	12.23
Reported Quantitative gains	2.45	7.07
SAT Verbal score (SATV)	551.44	99.85
SAT Math score (SATM)	589.77	106.45
Average high school grades	6.78	1.23
Female 89	1.64	.48
White	1.90	.30
Black/African-American	1.05	.21
Asian-American	1.04	.20
Mexican-American	1.01	.09
Mother's education	5.449	1.802
Father's education	6.15	1.92
Years of HS English	6.03	.35
Years of HS math	5.93	.62
Years of HS foreign language	4.98	1.26
Goal: Career & financial achievement	13.85	3.12

APPENDIX A (*Continued*)
Descriptive Statistics for Variables in the Study

Variables in the Study	*Mean*	*Standard Deviation*
High degree planned anywhere eighty-five	5.30	.73
Institutional selectivity (SATV + SATM)	6.18	1.86
Public university	1.15	.36
Public 4-year	1.14	.35
Private university	1.25	.43
Private 4-year	1.45	.50
Major 89: Humanities	1.21	.41
Major 89: Life sciences	1.10	.30
Major 89: Engineering	1.11	.31
Major 89: Physical sciences	1.12	.32
Major 89: Social sciences	1.27	.44
Major 89: Professional	1.20	.40
Years lived on campus	2.98	1.28
Involvement in college clubs & organizations	12.44	3.23
Involvement in college athletics	7.70	2.18
Member of fraternity/sorority	1.22	.41
Worked on professor's research project	1.36	.48
# of courses emphasizing writing skills	3.37	1.22
# of courses emphasizing math/numerical skills	3.07	1.16
# of foreign-language courses	2.32	1.20
Student-student interactions	7.14	1.21
Time talking with faculty outside of class	2.95	.96
Guest in professor's home	1.56	.58
Time in class/labs	6.33	1.18
Time study/homework	6.21	1.38
Time reading for pleasure	2.51	1.20
Independent research project	2.10	.83
Discuss course content with students	2.65	.49
Worked on a group project for a class	2.05	.67
Tutored	1.76	.68
Essay exams	2.55	.58
Received tutoring	1.19	.42
Papers critiqued by professor	2.42	.63

APPENDIX B
Correlations Between Alternate Measures of Student Learning and Independent Variables in the Study

	College GPA	*GRE Composite*	*GRE Verbal*	*Self-Reported Verb Gains*	*GRE Quantitative*	*Self-Reported Quantitative Gain*
SAT Verbal score	.3156**	.7654**	.8468**	−.0057	.5374**	−.0189
SAT Math score	.2547**	.8386**	.6089**	−.0377	.8656**	.1653**
HS GPA	.3830**	.4719**	.3751**	.0052	.4590**	.0855**
Female	−.0292	−.3493**	−.2016**	.0216	−.4057**	−.1343**
White	.1199**	.1602**	.1660**	.0540**	.1224**	.0190
Black/African-American	−.1710**	−.2843**	−.2403**	.0036	−.2641**	−.0234
Asian-American	.0067	.0677**	.0094	−.0643**	.1043**	.0168
Mexican-American	−.0399	−.0374	−.0244	−.0232	−.0411*	−.0189
Mother's education	.0387	.1880**	.1860**	0.0109	.1427**	−.0562*
Father's education	.0643**	.2575**	.2595**	−.0071	.2031**	.0088
Years of HS English	−.0130	.0644**	.1031**	.0089	.0178	−.0076
Years of HS math	.0504*	.2712**	.1205**	−.0541**	.3461**	.1270**
Years of HS foreign language	.1071**	.2035**	.2348**	−.0015	.1346**	−.0185
Goal: Career & financial success	−.1309**	−.1735**	−.2337**	.0224	−.0857**	.0618**
High degree planned 1985	.0411*	.1715**	.1796**	.0197	.1293**	.0287
Institutional selectivity	.0141	.5547**	.4943**	.0351	.4932**	.0296
Public university	.0505*	−.0244	−.0616**	−.0681**	.0128	.0516*
Public 4-yr. college	−.1541**	−.1236**	−.1786**	−.0460*	−.0505*	.0268
Private university	.1008**	.2634**	.2357**	−.0318	.2333**	.0091
Private 4-yr. college	−.0213	−.1176**	−.0320	.1081**	−.1677**	−.0613**
Major 89: Humanities	.0851**	.0360	.1857**	.0942**	−.1011**	−.2574**
Major 89: Life sciences	−.0681**	.0234	.0060	−.0741**	.0338	.0688**
Major 89: Engineering	.0386	.2489**	.0784**	−.0465*	.3456**	.2726**
Major 89: Physical sciences	.0426*	.2053**	.0781**	−.0041	.2734**	.1610**
Major 89: Social sciences	−.0488*	−.1278**	−.0504*	.0440*	−.1686**	−.1070**
Major 89: Professional	−.0456*	−.2744**	−.2634**	−.0491*	−.2278**	−.0155
Years lived on campus	−.0017	.1637**	.1487**	.0489*	.1431**	.0145

APPENDIX B (*Continued*)
Correlations Between Alternate Measures of Student Learning and Independent Variables in the Study

	College GPA	*GRE Composite*	*GRE Verbal*	*Self-Reported Verb Gains*	*GRE Quantitative*	*Self-Reported Quantitative Gain*
College clubs & organizations	.0366	−.1607**	−.1371**	.0659**	−.1483**	−.0267
Sports and athletics	−.1231**	.0541**	−.0437*	.0034	.1277**	.0904**
Member of fraternity/sorority	−.0852**	−.1218**	−.1357**	−.0246	−.0847**	.0376
Professor's research project	.0847**	.0767**	.0329	.0039	.0989**	.1156**
# of courses emphasizing writing	.0231	−.0415*	.0922**	.2857**	−.1487**	−.1996**
# of courses emphasizing math	−.0349	.2762**	.0198	−.0277	.4417**	.3728**
# of foreign-language courses	.0928**	.0464*	.1449**	.0829**	−.0484*	−.4062**
Discussions with students	.0518*	.0758**	.1612**	.2471**	−.0137	−.0670**
Time talking with professor out of class	.0455*	−.1542**	−.1240**	.1239**	−.1488**	−.0002
Guest in professor's home	.0788**	.0350	.0807**	.1759**	−.0117	−.0162
Time in class/labs	−.0256	−.0059	−.0721**	.0043	.0527*	.1436**
Time study/homework	.1504**	.1982**	.1581**	.1229**	.1923**	.0375
Time reading for pleasure	.0008	.0374	.1123**	.0593**	−.0351	−.0768**
Independent research project	.1126**	.1080**	.1542**	.1369**	.0459*	−.0046
Discuss course with students	.0414*	.0531*	.0572**	.1802**	.0387	.0547**
Group project	−.0742**	−.1747**	−.2132**	.0735**	−.1056**	.1050**
Tutored	.1458**	.0962**	.0213	.1074**	.1414**	.0965**
Essay exams	−.0455*	−.1517**	−.0253	.1414**	−.2301**	−.2045**
Received tutoring	−.2144**	−.1425**	−.1902**	.0040	−.0719**	.0731**
Papers critiqued by professor	.0057	−.0722**	.0439*	.2309**	−.1580**	−.1446**

*$p < .05$.
**$p < .01$.

APPENDIX C
Correlation Matrix for Learning Environments and Experiences Variables in the Study

Variable	*Selectivity*	*Public University*	*Public 4-yr.*	*Private University*	*Private 4-yr.*	*Humanities*	*Life Sciences*	*Engineering*
College selectivity	1	−.1700**	−.1139**	.2826**	−0.0199	.0839**	−0.0258	.1707**
Public university		1	−.1704**	−.2420**	−.3814**	−.0722**	0.0225	.0803**
Public 4-yr.			1	−.2324**	−.3663**	−.1028**	−0.0127	.0483*
Private university				1	−.5201**	0.0109	−.0410*	.1761**
Private 4-yr.					1	.1203**	0.0294	−.2373**
Humanities major						1	−.1738**	−.1795**
Life sciences major							1	−.1182**
Engineering major								1
Physical sciences major								
Social sciences major								
Prof. major								
Yrs. lived on campus								
College clubs/officer								
College sports								
Fraternity/Sorority								
Prof's research								
# writing courses								
# numerical courses								
# foreign-language courses								
Discussions with students								
Time talking with professor								
Guest in prof's home								
Time in class/lab								
Time doing homework								
Time spent pleasure reading								
Independent research								
Discuss course content with students								
Group project								
Tutored								
Essay exam								
Received tutoring								
Paper critiqued by prof								

APPENDIX C (*Continued*)
Correlation Matrix for Learning Environments and Experiences Variables in the Study

Variable	*Physical Sciences*	*Social Sciences*	*Professional*	*On Campus*	*College Clubs*	*College Sports*	*Fraternity Sorority*	*Prof's Research*
College selectivity	0.0406	−0.0025	−.2300**	.2802**	−.1649**	.1870**	−.1035**	0.0291
Public university	−.0594**	−0.0124	.0558**	−.2879**	−.0768**	−.0544**	0.0153	.0827**
Public 4-yr.	0.0234	−.0637**	.1287**	0.0147	−0.0183	.1411**	−.0441*	−.0697**
Private university	−.0470*	0.0009	−.0806**	0.0324	−0.005	−0.003	.0534*	.0577**
Private 4-yr.	.0637**	.0469*	−.0634**	.1791**	.0765**	−.0470*	−0.0271	−.0628**
Humanities major	−.1879**	−.3086**	−.2541**	0.0209	0.0043	−.0993**	−.0452*	−.2197**
Life sciences major	−.1237**	−.2032**	−.1673**	−0.0327	−0.0114	0.0125	0.0125	.1740**
Engineering major	−.1278**	−.2099**	−.1728**	.0516*	−.0760**	.1023**	0.0197	.0875**
Physical Science major	1	−.2197**	−.1809**	.0483*	−.0744**	.0599**	−.0490*	.1080**
Social Science major		1	−.2972**	−0.0153**	0.0268	−0.0322	−0.0117	0.0209
Prof's major			1	−.0590**	.0944**	−0.001	.0741**	−.0876**
Yrs. lived on campus				1	.0659**	.1327**	−0.0193	−.0552**
College clubs/officer					1	0.0362	.2437**	0.0344
College sports						1	0.0107	0.0072
Fraternity/Sorority							1	0.0225
Prof's research								1
# writing courses								
# numerical courses								
# foreign-language courses								
Discussions with students								
Time talking with professor								
Guest in prof's home								
Time in class/lab								
Time doing homework								
Time spent pleasure reading								
Independent research								
Discuss course content with students								
Group project								
Tutored								
Essay exam								
Received tutoring								
Paper critiqued by prof								

APPENDIX C (*Continued*)
Correlation Matrix for Learning Environments and Experiences Variables In the Study

Variable	*Writing Classes*	*Numbers Classes*	*Foreign Language*	*Student Discuss*	*Talk with Prof*	*Prof's Guest*	*Class Time*	*Homework*
College selectivity	0.0299	.1105**	.0852**	.1132**	−.1424**	.0635**	−.0699**	.2385**
Public university	−.1054**	0.0368	−.0476*	−.0986**	−.0852**	−.1473**	0.029	−.0562**
Public 4-yr.	−0.0286	.1401**	−.0821**	−.1404**	0.0123	−0.02	.1738**	−.0578**
Private university	−.0472*	.0497*	0.0308	−0.0069	−.1387**	−.1212**	−0.0273	.0453*
Private 4-yr.	.1325**	−.1664**	.0723**	.1761**	.1767**	.2302**	−.1169**	.0413*
Humanities major	.3296**	−.3479**	.2873**	.1661**	0.0367	.1578**	−.1131**	.0433*
Life sciences major	−.1309**	0.019	−.0938**	−.0737**	0.0154	−0.0344	.1518**	−0.0026
Engineering major	−.1941**	.4172**	−.2321**	−.1033**	−.0811**	−.0890**	.0978**	.1275**
Physical sciences major	−.1487**	.3953**	−.0539**	−.0739**	0.0112	0.0371	.0507*	0.0115
Social sciences major	.0678*	−.1847**	.0845**	.1232**	−0.014	−0.0339	−.1066**	−0.0344
Prof. major	−0.0396	−.1012**	−.0904**	−.1096**	0.0206	−.0578**	0.0003	−.1133**
Yrs. lived on campus	.0590**	.0523*	.0446*	.0914**	0.0408	.1472**	−0.0116	.1069**
College clubs/officer	.0899**	−.0735**	.0562**	.1274**	.4774**	.1498**	0.0283	0.0284
College sports	−0.0059	.2285**	−.0552**	0.0292	.0939**	.0477*	.0666**	.0861**
Fraternity/Sorority	−0.0007	−0.0214	−.0660**	−.1009**	0.0022	−0.0176	0.0188	−.0944**
Prof's research	−.1064**	.1510**	−.0960**	0.0097	.1399**	.0444*	.1181**	0.0227
# writing courses	1	−.1337**	.1967**	.2461**	.1071**	.1487**	−.0486*	.0776**
# numerical courses		1	−.2196**	−.1263**	−0.011	−.0497*	.1753**	.1001**
# foreign-language courses			1	.1815**	0.0241	.1191**	−.0584**	.0788**
Discussions with students				1	.1740**	.2025**	−.0438*	.1402**
Time talking with professor					1	.3004**	.0516*	.0895**
Guest in prof's home						1	0.0084	.0957**
Time in class/lab							1	.1229**
Time doing homework								1
Time spent pleasure reading								
Independent research								
Discuss course content with students								
Group project								
Tutored								
Essay exam								
Received tutoring								
Paper critiqued by professor								

APPENDIX C (*Continued*)

Correlation Matrix for Learning Environments and Experiences Variables In the Study

Variable	*Reading Time*	*Independent Research*	*Discuss Course*	*Group Project*	*Tutored*	*Essay Exam*	*Received Tutoring*	*Paper Critiqued*
College selectivity	−.0686**	.0931**	.0495*	−.1167**	−.0692**	−0.0323	−0.0267	.0476*
Public university	0.0181	−.0804**	−0.0315	−0.0221	−0.0329	−.1098**	−0.0293	−.0996**
Public 4-yr.	0.0141	−.1302**	−0.0099	.1883**	.0814**	−.0657**	.2275**	−0.0231
Private university	−0.0038	−0.0222	−0.0405	−.1031**	−.0935**	−0.0343	−.0818**	−.0523*
Private 4-yr.	−0.0237	.1744**	.0715**	−0.0245	.0425*	.1554**	−.0645**	.1314**
Humanities major	.0878**	.0879**	.0509*	−.1560**	−.0664**	.1705**	−.0969**	.2172**
Life sciences major	−.0467*	0.0369	−0.0166	−.0651**	−0.0139	0.0299	0.0122	−.0751**
Engineering major	−.0538*	−.0503*	.0544**	.2127**	.0496*	−.3083**	.0749**	−.1896**
Physical sciences major	−0.001	−0.0038	0.0019	−.0685**	.1976**	−.1649**	0.0194	−.1604**
Social sciences major	−0.0111	.0482*	−.0479*	−0.0331	−.1148**	.1799**	−0.0228	.1342**
Prof. major	0.0011	−.1291**	−0.0303	.1350**	0.0068	−0.0216	0.0408	−0.0351
Yrs. lived on campus	−0.0103	.0674**	.0522*	0.0133	.0632**	.0583**	0.015	.0490*
College clubs/officer	.0636**	.0949**	.0749**	.1063**	.1597**	.1150**	.0445*	.1155**
College sports	.0411*	−0.0138	.0415*	.1327**	.0994**	0.0243	.1732**	0.0213
Fraternity/Sorority	−.0801**	−0.0065	−0.0296	0.0126	−0.005	0.0335	0.0103	−0.0179
Prof's research	−0.0122	.2505**	.0423*	0.0026	.0819**	−.0814**	−0.0054	0.0067
# writing courses	.0946**	.1366**	.0988**	0.0199	0.0316	.3109**	0.0125	.3283**
# numerical courses	−0.0058	−.0535*	.0434*	.1529**	.2344**	−.2567**	.1788**	−.2159**
# foreign-language courses	.0677**	.0574**	0.0101	−.1266**	0.0233	.1907**	0.0053	.1472**
Discussions with students	.1354**	.1892**	.6017**	.1138**	.1207**	.2266**	0.0372	.3432**
Time talking with professor	.1452**	.2470**	.1493**	.0945**	.1970**	.0829**	.0826**	.1353**
Guest on prof's home	0.0176	.1767**	.1449**	0.0355	.1679**	.1071**	0.0159	.1843**
Time in class/lab	−0.03	0.0289	.0960**	.1089**	.0883**	−0.0196	.0926**	−0.0228
Time doing homework	−.0854**	.1455**	.1744**	0.0132	.0994**	0.024	.0542**	.0507*
Time spent pleasure reading	1	.0587**	0.0374	−0.0065	.0456*	0.0272	0.003	.0687**
Independent research		1	.0982**	−0.0316	0.0363	.0979**	−.0511*	.2010**
Discuss course content with students			1	.2352**	.1751**	.0844**	.0811**	.1712**
Group project				1	.1356**	0.0134	.1764**	.1054**
Tutored					1	0.0018	.1439**	0.0349
Essay exam						1	−0.0051	.3790**
Received tutoring							1	0.0225
Paper critiqued by prof								1

References

Anaya, G. (1990). Toward the enhancement of learning outcomes: Methods and learning principles revisited. *UCLA Journal of Education* 3: 13–25.

Anaya, G. (1992). *Cognitive development among college undergraduates*. Unpublished doctoral dissertation, University of California, Los Angeles.

Anaya, G. (1996). College experiences and student learning: The impact of academic and nonacademic activities. *Journal of College Student Development* 37(6): 1–12.

Angoff, W. H., and Johnson, E. G. (1990). The differential impact of curriculum on aptitude test scores. *Journal of Educational Measurement* 27: 291–305.

Astin, A. W. (1984). Student involvement: A developmental theory for higher education. *Journal of College Student Personnel* 22: 297–308.

Astin, A. W. (1991). *Assessment for Excellence: The Philosophy and Practice of Assessment and Evaluation in Higher Education*. New York: Macmillan.

Astin, A. W. (1993). *What Matters in College: Four Critical Years Revisited*. San Francisco: Jossey-Bass.

Baird, L. L. (1982). Value added: Using student gains as yardsticks of learning. In C. Adelman et al. (eds.), *Performance and Judgment: Essays on Principles and Practice in the Assessment of College Student Learning*. Washington, DC: Office of Educational Research and Improvement.

Bjork, R. A. (1979). Information-processing: Analysis of college teaching. Unpublished manuscript. University of California, Los Angeles.

Craik, F. I. M. (1981). Encoding and retrieval effects in human memory: A partial review. In A. D. Baddeley and J. Long (eds.), *Attention and Performance IX*. Hillsdale, NJ: Erlbaum.

Craik, F. I. M. and Lockhart, R. S. (1972). Levels of processing: A framework for memory research. *Journal of Verbal Learning and Verbal Behavior* 11: 671–684.

Deutsch, M. (1949). A theory of co-operation and competition. *Human Relations* 2: 129–152.

Duran, R. P. (1983). Prediction of Hispanics' college achievement. In M. A. Olivas (ed.), *Latino College Students* (pp. 221–245). New York: Teachers College Press.

Educational Testing Service (1987). *Guide to the Use of the Graduate Record Examinations Program, 1987–88*. Princeton, NJ: Educational Testing Service.

Ewell, P. T., and Jones, D. P. (1993). Actions matter: The case for indirect measures in assessing higher education's progress on the national education goals. *Journal of General Education* 42: 123–148.

Gray, M. W., and Taylor, A. (1989). Study factors influencing student performance in mathematics on the Florida college-level academic skills test (CLAST). *Journal of Negro Education* 58: 531–543.

Harris, J. (1970). Gain scores on the CLEP General Examination and an overview of research. Paper presented at the annual meeting of the American Educational Research Association, Minneapolis.

Hartnett, R., and Centra, J. (1985). The effects of academic departments on student learning. *Journal of Higher Education* 48: 491–507.

Higher Education Research Institute (1989). *Follow-Up Survey*. University of California, Los Angeles.

Johnson, D. W., Maruyama, G., Johnson, R., Nelson, D., and Skon, L. (1981). Effects of cooperative, competitive, and individualistic goal structures on achievement: A meta-analysis. *Psychological Bulletin* 89: 47–62.

Jones, E. A., and Ratcliff, J. R. (1990). Is a core curriculum best for everybody? The effect of different patterns of coursework on the general education of high and low ability students. Paper presented at the annual meeting of the American Educational Research Association, Boston, Massachusetts.

Lambiotte, J. G., Dansereau, D. F., O'Donnell, A. M., Young, M. D., Skaggs, L. P., Hall, R. H., and Rocklin, T. R. (1987). Manipulating cooperative scripts for teaching and learning. *Journal of Educational Psychology* 79: 424–430.

Mandler, J. M. (1978). A code in the node: The use of story schema in retrieval. *Discourse Processes* 1: 14–35.

Pace, C. R. (1979). *Measuring the Outcomes of College*. San Francisco: Jossey-Bass.

Pace, C. R. (1984). *Measuring the Quality of College Student Experiences*. Higher Education Research Institute, Graduate School of Education, University of California, Los Angeles.

Pascarella, E. T. and Terenzini, P. T. (1991). *How College Affects Students*. San Francisco: Jossey-Bass.

Pike, G. R. (1995). The relationship between self reports of college experiences and achievement test scores. *Research in Higher Education* 36(1): 1–21.

Pike, G. R. (1996). Limitations of using students' self-reports of academic development as proxies for traditional achievement measures. *Research in Higher Education* 37(1): 89–114.

Pike, G. R., and Phillippi, R. H. (1989). Generalizability of the differential coursework methodology: Relationships between self-reported coursework and performance on the ACT-COMP. *Research in Higher Education* 30: 245–260.

Shuell, T. J. (1986). Cognitive conceptions of learning. *Review of Educational Research* 56: 411–436.

WHO WILL SUCCEED IN COLLEGE? WHEN THE SAT PREDICTS BLACK STUDENTS' PERFORMANCE

JACQUELINE FLEMING

African American students feel greater than usual concern over whether the Student Aptitude Test (SAT) gives a true reading of academic aptitude but have little understanding of when the SAT does and does not predict the grades they will achieve in college. Clearer insights about predictive validity issues for them may come from several nontraditional studies based on academic and psychosocial data. While educational underachievement prior to test-taking (Bracey, 1993; Horn & Carroll, 1997; Smith & Choy, 1995a, 1995b; Young & Smith, 1997) and issues activated during test taking are important (Jencks & Phillips, 1998; Steele & Aronson, 1995; Watson, 1972), this discussion focuses on the consequences of a given test score for future success in college. Data from several sources provide analyses of predictive validity by dominant race of the college and by gender. Analyzing SAT correlates sheds new light on the problem of predictive validity in minority populations.

Predictive Validity for White and Black Students

Within certain important limits, the SAT tells us which *White* students will succeed in college, despite charges that test scores do not reflect ability and do not help colleges make better selection decisions (Crouse & Trusheim, 1988; Neill & Medina, 1989). Nonetheless, the SAT-College GPA correlations among majority students are consistent. While prediction from SAT scores to grades usually includes high school grades and may lead to complex prediction equations, the SAT-College GPA correlation is the essential predictive validity statistic. Fleming and Garcia's (1998) review of 12 studies of predictive validity among White students, which included studies conducted for up to thirteen years with up to eleven different samples, found that the average correlation was 0.342. The square of the correlation indicates the amount of variance accounted for by the SAT in college GPA; in this case the variance accounted for was 11.7%. (See Fig. 1.) With the exception of a study by Pennock-Roman (1990) which produced generally low correlations, the remaining eleven studies were distinguished by the consistency with which test scores showed either moderate or strong ability to predict college grades. In short, few measures rival test scores in consistency of prediction. Virtually the only other measure able to indicate how a student will fare in college is the high school grade point average.

SAT scores may not give the same reading of future success for African American students because the predictive validity is lower than for White students. However, the evidence for lower Black

Reprinted by permission from *Review of Higher Education*, spring 2002.

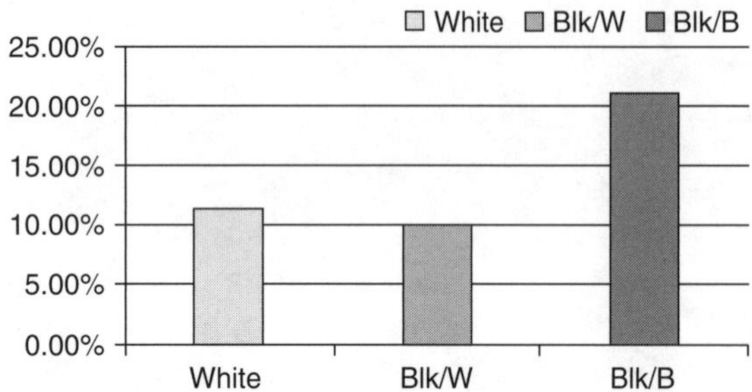

Figure 1 Percentages of Variance in Grades Accounted for by SAT for White Students, Black Students in White Colleges, and Black Students in Black Colleges. Adapted from Fleming (1990).

predictive validity is actually inconsistent and does not fall neatly into a single category. Some researchers have found strong positive SAT-GPA correlations for Black students (e.g., Breland, 1978; Morgan, 1990), while other authors have reported that the SAT score bore no relationship to grades (e.g., Boyd, 1977; Miller & O'Connor, 1969), that students performed *better* than their test scores would indicate (Houston, 1983), and that students performed *worse* than their test scores would indicate (Breland, 1978; Crouse & Trusheim, 1988; Nettles, Thoeny, & Gosman, 1986; Kane, 1998; Temp, 1971; Vars & Bowen, 1998). Indeed, contrary to popular opinion, overprediction (performing worse) is the most consistent occurrence in Black predictive validity studies, and few cogent explanations have been offered.

Fleming and Garcia (1998) examined eight validity studies reporting correlations for Black students (Fig. 1). The average correlation was 0.315, accounting for an average of 9.9% of the variance in college grades. While this figure is lower than that for majority students, it is a difference of only 1.8%—not as low as opinion would suggest. This difference does not support an argument for differential predictive validity. Jencks (1998) comes to a similar conclusion: that test scores have a moderate correlation with grades and that test scores predict a little better for Whites than for Blacks. Fleming and Garcia (1998) also found that the variability in correlations was substantially greater for Black student samples, where correlations ranged from −.01 to 0.48 (from 1% to 23% of the variance). It may be that the greater variability, which has yet to be adequately explained, creates the impression of inconsistency and therefore unreliability of prediction. Also, the Black students in these eight studies were all attending predominantly White colleges.

Predictive Validity and Race of College Environment

Are there certain subgroups of Black students whose success the SAT can foretell with better accuracy? That is, are there minority students for whom the SAT does predict as well as for White students? The answer is yes. The SAT predicts success better for Black students attending historically Black colleges and universities.

Fleming (1990) reported the first indication of such a trend. Five predominantly Black colleges participated in that study. Each submitted test scores (either SAT or ACT), high school grade averages, and college grade point averages for freshmen and seniors for whom all three indices were available. A total of 1,551 students were included in the analysis. The five colleges chosen were different in key respects. The first was a single-sex (male) institution. The second was a nonselective institution with an open admissions policy. The third was a Catholic college. The fourth was a large urban university. The fifth was a small private school in the rural south. These institutional differences represent much of the variety of college types found among historically Black institutions. The results indicated that in all five colleges, standardized test scores predicted college grade point average exceptionally well. The correlations ranged from .340 to .570, with an average correlation of .456. Thus, the average variance accounted for was a high 20.1%. Test scores, then, appear to be more than adequate predictors of college grades in Black colleges.

In addition, Fleming (1990) reported data from three institutional studies. An unpublished study from Morehouse College (1984) found that test scores correlated from .41 to .48 with college grades. Another unpublished report from Xavier University (1984) found that test scores strongly predicted grades with a correlation of .61. Finally Ramist, Lewis, and McCamley-Jenkins (1994), in a then-unpublished study, found that the SAT score predicted college grades moderately well at 11 predominantly

Black colleges. The average correlation was .38. The average correlation from these three studies was 0.478, accounting for an average of 22.9% of the variance. As shown in Figure 1, when correlations from all four studies were considered, the average correlation was 0.462, accounting for an average of 21.4% of the variance. The fact that such strong results occurred in eight different samples, one of which included eleven colleges, demonstrates a consistency of effect that is unusual in studies of Black students. This degree of consistency has been typical only in studies of White students. The difference in predictive validity (i.e., variance accounted for) between White and Black students in White colleges was only 1.8% in favor of White students, but the difference between White students and Black students in Black colleges was 9.7% in favor of Blacks in Black colleges. Furthermore, the difference between Blacks in White colleges and Blacks in Black colleges was 11.5% in favor of Blacks in Black colleges. These effects occurred despite lower average test scores among Blacks in Black colleges and a more constricted range of scores.

There has been no suggestion in the psychometric literature that the predominant race of the college or the quality of student adjustment could influence predictive validity. These findings, however, suggest that college environment makes a considerable difference: Being at a Black colleges facilitates the SAT-GPA correlation among Black students. The findings also imply that differential adjustment to the college environment has an influence on SAT predictive validity.

Predictive Validity, College Environment, and Gender

Are there any finer distinctions that would shed light on those for whom the SAT works best? To answer this question, Fleming and Garcia (1998) reanalyzed freshmen in 15 college samples from Fleming's (1984) *Blacks in College* study. The data bank allowed an unusual opportunity to examine predictive validity by race of college environment. The resulting analysis provided some confirmation of the previous findings and showed that when the freshmen samples were split by sex, the predictive validity of the SAT was best for Black males in Black colleges.

Subjects for the study included 1,069 Black freshmen in 15 different colleges for whom test scores and transcripts were available. There were 543 freshmen in seven predominantly Black colleges (229 males and 314 females), and 526 Black students in eight predominantly White colleges (200 males and 326 females). In addition, there were 204 White freshmen in three White colleges (124 males and 80 females). Average sample size was 78 for students in Black colleges and 66 for Blacks in White colleges. The 15 colleges were located in four states: Georgia, Texas, Mississippi, and Ohio.

Approximately 29% of the test scores in Texas and Mississippi were ACT scores, which we converted to SAT scores using the Marco and Abdel-Fattah (1991) formula. We examined correlations for test scores with semester as well as cumulative grade averages. This analysis reports correlations using semester GPA. Ramist, Lewis, and McCamley-Jenkins (1994) have cautioned against pooling course grades into a composite GPA with no control for comparability of courses, but they also found that pooling was not an important problem for African American student scores. Further, there was no correction for restriction of range of test scores, which may underestimate the size of the predictive validity coefficients (Ramist, Angoff, Broudy, Burton, Donlon, Stern, & Thorne, 1984).

When we examined composite freshmen samples, the differences in predictive validity were not as dramatic as those Fleming (1990) found. (See Fig. 2.) This time, SAT predictive validity was better for Black freshmen in White colleges (0.304 or 9.2% of the variance) than for White freshmen in White colleges (0.298 or 8.9% of the variance), but the difference was only 0.3%. Predictive validity was better for Black freshmen in Black colleges (0.397 or 15.8%) compared to Black freshmen in White colleges (0.298 or 9.2%), with a difference of 6.6%. The constricted differences in predictive validity estimates in this analysis (Fleming & Garcia, 1998) compared to Fleming (1990), may stem from the fact that the latter study's results had been obtained from one researcher using similar methods, instead of from a review which drew estimates from many different studies using different procedures. On the other hand, Fleming and Garcia (1998) included only 15 colleges, while the estimates in Fleming (1990) included a much larger number of samples.

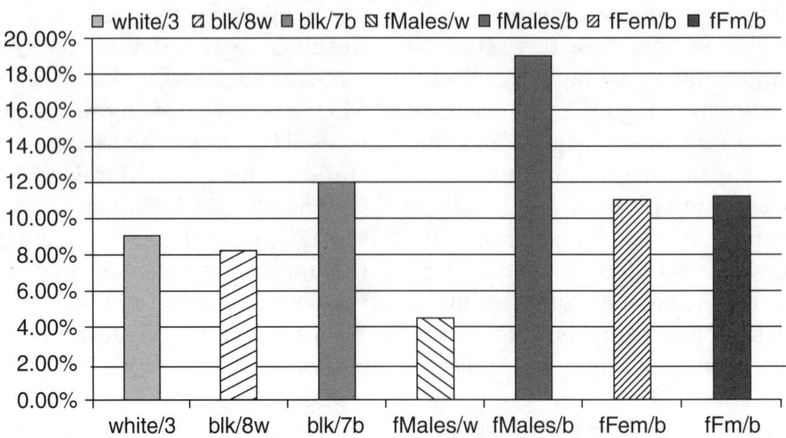

Figure 2 Percentage of Variance in Grades Accounted for by SAT by Race, Predominant Race of College, and Sex, Interacting with Race of College. Adapted from Fleming Garcia (1998).

When the samples were split by sex, the differences were startling. (See Fig. 2). Among Black freshmen males, the average correlation in Black colleges was 0.436 (accounting for 19.0% of the variance) versus 0.219 (accounting for 4.8%) in White colleges. Again, the variability of predictive validity coefficients for males was significantly greater in White colleges and included strong positive correlations, zero-order correlations (the SAT was unrelated to performance), and even negative correlations (the better the SAT scores, the worse the academic performance). Among Black freshmen females, there was virtually no difference in predictive validity: 0.334 (11.2% of the variance accounted for) in Black colleges versus 0.338 (11.4%) in White colleges.

In short, predictive validity is best for Black males in Black colleges, poor for Black males in White colleges, with no differences for Black females. Clearly, the consequences of the college environment for SAT predictive validity are vastly different for Black males and females. These differences support literature findings that Black males develop best in Black, not White, colleges (Fleming, 1984; Gibbs, 1988) and parallel society's differential treatment of Black males and females. Better predictive validity coefficients may well reflect adjustment advantages in general or a relative lack of prejudice and racism in particular.

Correlates of the SAT

These differences are illuminating but, except for differences in average variance, not statistically significant in a sample of 15 colleges. Predictive validity was not significantly different by sex or race of college environment, even though the disparities in estimates were dramatic for the predictive validity literature. This finding raises the question of whether there is some statistically significant way of foretelling the success of Black students. Therefore, Fleming (in press) analyzed whether SAT correlates would shed light on adjustment issues. The findings indicate that the SAT in White colleges is associated with a significantly larger number of psychosocial correlates that appear to undermine academic adjustment.

Previous research makes it clear that Black students adjust better to Black colleges than to predominantly White colleges. Black students who attend predominantly Black schools tend to have higher average grades, a richer learning environment, better relationships with faculty members, exhibit better cognitive development and display greater effort and engage in more academic activities than Black students who attend White schools (Berry & Asamen, 1989; Bohr, Pascarella, Nora, & Terenzini, 1995; DeSousa & Kuh, 1996; Ford, 1996; Kraft, 1991). In Black schools, Black students show better social adjustment, have more extensive social support networks, show greater social involvement, and engage in more organizational activities (Allen, 1985; Cheatham, Slaney, & Coleman, 1990; Jay & D'Augelli, 1991; Nottingham, Rosen, & Parks, 1992; D'Augelli & Herschberger, 1993; Schwitzer, Griffin, Ancis, & Thomas, 1999).

However, there is virtually no research on the relative adjustment of Black high achievers in both Black and White colleges, if high achievement is defined by higher SAT scores. Systematic studies of a wide range of correlates of standardized tests that might inform the nature of adjustment of high achievers to college are rarely conducted. Miller and O'Connor (1969) described an achiever personality, while recent research has identified math and foreign language proficiency (Pelavin & Kane, 1990), and a proactive orientation to college life—particularly help-seeking behavior (Fleming, Garcia, & Embaye, 1997). Unfortunately, higher SAT scores among minority students are also associated with low or lack of teacher support (Fleming & Morning, 1998).

I wanted to fill a void in the literature about African American students by going beyond the question of the SAT's predictive validity. To do so, I examined the wide-ranging consequences of SAT scores for academic adjustment and psycho-social functioning. I analyzed correlates of the SAT in the 15 colleges (seven samples from historically Black colleges and eight from predominantly White colleges) in which students responded to the same instruments. Subjects for the study were freshmen and seniors in Fleming's (1984) study of *Blacks in College* for whom test scores were available. The sample consisted of 1,485 students, including 746 Black students in seven Black schools (543 freshmen and 203 seniors); and 739 Black students in eight White schools (526 freshmen and 213 seniors). I grouped freshmen and seniors, not differentiating by gender. I examined consequences of the SAT for college adjustment using ten measures of academic performance, seven measures of math and verbal performance, two categories of academic adjustment measures, seven categories of measures of psychosocial adjustment, and two categories of measures of background information including SES. (For details, see Fleming, in press).

Previous analyses have looked at SAT correlations with social class and other background variables *across* institutions, concluding that SAT scores increase with social advantages (Chambers, 1988). This study, however, examined correlates *within* colleges where SAT scores were more similar than different and where the range of socioeconomic status scores was more restricted than in the general population of test takers. I controlled SES through partial correlations, i.e., by eliminating any correlate that was reduced to nonsignificance after conducting a correlation that partialed out the effects of SES. However, a measure of SES was never significantly correlated with the SAT in any of the 15 samples.

This investigation determined the frequency with which variables or categories of variables were correlated with the SAT and concerns only important correlates of the SAT—that is, those contributing unique variance in a regression equation. For each of the 15 samples, the SAT (or its ACT equivalent) was correlated with each variable or measure in the study. Correlates that were statistically significant at or beyond the .05 level of significance, and which produced correlation coefficients of .30 or higher (i.e., a moderate effect size, visible to the naked eye), were selected for further analysis (Cohen, 1988). I entered correlates that survived the partial correlations at significant levels into a multiple regression equation. This discussion is limited to correlates that contributed unique variance in regression equations for the 15 colleges and to correlates loading first in regression equations for each college. (For an analysis of all first-order correlates, see Fleming, in press). Thus, the analysis describes trends in important correlates of standardized tests. Correlations rarely emerged for the same variable in more than a few colleges, even when a substantial number of correlations appeared in the same category of variables. To fully utilize all 15 samples or cases, I converted significant regressed variables to present-absent categorical variables for later groupings.

The results showed that higher test scores were most strongly associated with a preponderance of psychosocial correlates as opposed to academic correlates. Furthermore, high SAT scorers in Black colleges did indeed exhibit evidence of better academic adjustment. (See Fig. 3.) The profile of the African American high-SAT scorer gleaned from regressed correlates showed that test scores were associated with:

- Psycho-social attributes, averaging 2.93 correlates per school in 100% of the colleges. The largest category was Black ideology correlates, 75% of which indicated low Black ideology, including 100% of the correlates in Black colleges and 67% of the correlates in White colleges. The second major category was self-concept, the vast majority of which were positive intellectual self-concepts. (See Fig. 4.)

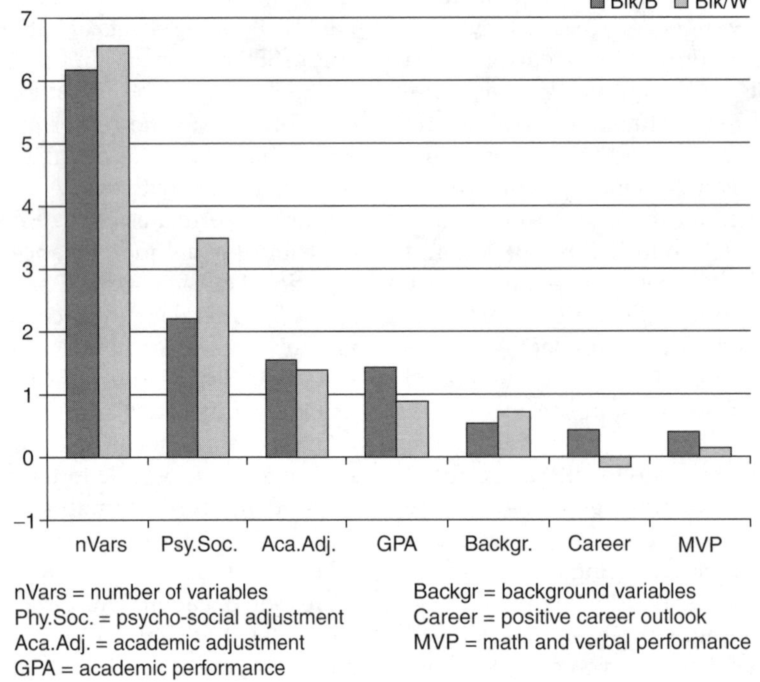

Figure 3 Summary of Regressed SAT Correlated: Mean Number of Correlates per School in Selected Categories for Black Students in Seven Black and Eight White Colleges. Adapted from Fleming (in press).

- Academic adjustment correlates, averaging 1.47 per college in 87% of the colleges. They were largely career related but included both positive and negative career issues (e.g., aspires to medical career, frustrated by teacher attitudes).
- Academic performance correlates, averaging 1.13 per college in 80% of the colleges.
- Education-related background correlates averaging 0.67 per college in 53% of the colleges.

High scorers could thus be described as (a) having an intellectual identity, if not a strong Black identity, (b) being focused on both positive and negative academic adjustment issues, (c) being better academic performers, and (d) having backgrounds richer in educational advantages.

Consideration of the variables that loaded first in each regression equation confirms the importance of psychosocial variables for African American students. In order of frequency, 40% of the strongest correlates were psycho-social, 33% were academic performance correlates, 23% were academic adjustment correlates, and 7% were math and verbal performance.

It appears that the pattern of correlates may be related to the pattern of predictive validity estimates. Considering regressed correlates, students in White colleges exhibited fewer father-related background advantages and a less positive career outlook, but fewer indications of psychosomatic symptoms. The strongest correlates of the SAT showed no statistically significant differences as a function of predominant race at the college. However, in White colleges psychosocial correlates were most likely to load first (in 63% of the colleges), while in Black colleges GPA correlates were most likely to load first (in 43% of the colleges). Thus, for Black students in White colleges, higher SAT scores were less likely to be associated with career optimism or the advantages associated with educated fathers. Their relatively low SAT predictive validity appears consistent with the findings. These results suggest that the greater occurrence of psychosocial correlates of the SAT in predominantly White colleges somehow interferes with academic performance.

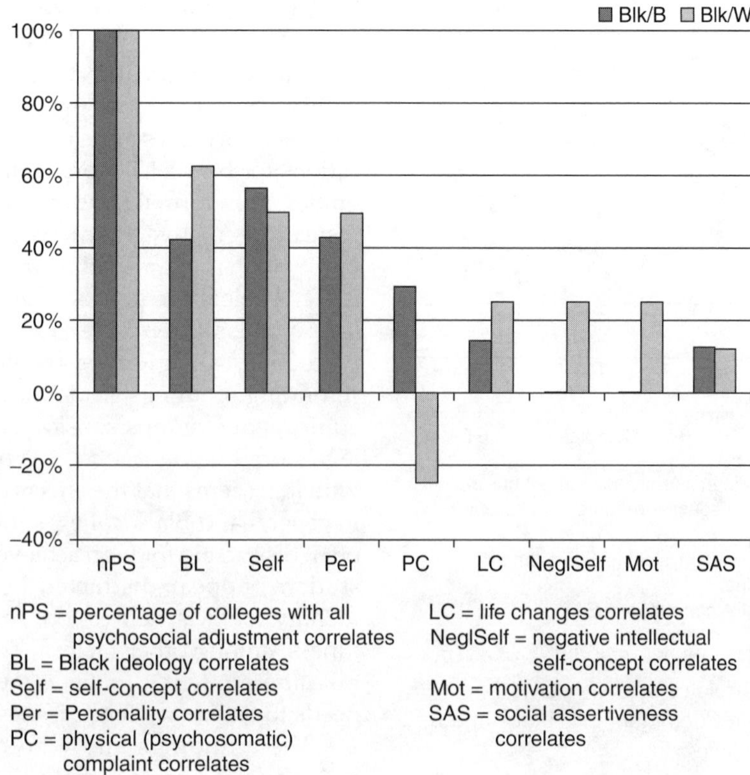

Figure 4 Percentage of Colleges with Psychosocial Adjustment Correlates in Selected Categories for Black Students in Seven Black Colleges and Eight White Colleges. Adapted from Fleming (in press)

Predicting Predictive Validity of the SAT

Do any of the correlates of the SAT portend success better than the interaction of the student's sex and the predominant race at a given college? With these correlates, the next analysis attempted to predict predictive validity. That is, I correlated the presence (or frequency) of categories of correlates with the Fleming and Garcia (1998) SAT-GPA correlations. My objective was to identify the types of correlates that were associated with higher predictive validity. I entered significant correlates of the SAT into a regression equation with predictive validity as the dependent variable. (See Fig. 5.)

Using the SAT-GPA correlation with semester GPA as the dependent variable, I found four significant regressed correlates. The variable loading first in the regression equation was "colleges with academic adjustment correlates of the SAT" (b = .764)—that is, not the number of academic adjustment correlates per college, but the presence or absence of academic, adjustment correlates in a given college. The category of academic adjustment correlates was 60% negative. Attempts to separate the components of this variable into positive and negative adjustment issues did not improve prediction. Thus, this finding suggests that in schools where high scoring students are concerned with academic adjustment issues in general, the SAT-GPA correlation is higher.

The second factor was "colleges with the presence of education-related background correlates of the SAT" (b = .511). Again, this variable assessed not the number of such correlations but their presence. In short, a global measure of social class provided insignificant correlations with the SAT, while specific advantages related to education—such as good high school preparation—were far more significant. The third factor was "colleges with the absence of psychosomatic complaints" (b = .419). Psychosomatic complaints were SAT correlates in 20% of the predominantly Black colleges but were counter-indicated (by negative SAT correlations) in 25% of the predominantly White colleges. This finding suggests that both psychological health and physical health are critical to optimal functioning.

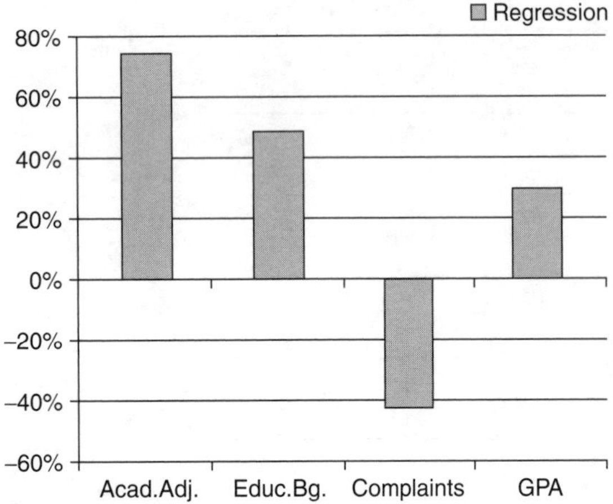

Acad.Adj. = schools with academic adjustment correlates
Educ.Bg. = schools with education-related background correlates
Complaints = schools with physical (psychosomatic) complaints
GPA = schools with GPA correlates of SAT

Figure 5 Predicting Predictive Validity: Regression of SAT Correlates on SAT = GPA Correlation Coefficient in 7 Black and 8 White Colleges

The fourth factor was "colleges with GPA correlates" (b = .310). Again, it is the presence of any such correlations with the SAT, rather than the number, that is significant. These four variables accounted for 93% of the variance in SAT-Semester GPA predictive validity ($F = 31.33$, $p < .001$).

Taken together, the results suggest that high-scoring African American students will perform better academically: (a) if they are more focused than other students on academic adjustment issues, including satisfactions and frustrations alike; (b) if they bring educational background advantages with them to college; and (c) if they are physically and psychologically healthy. Stated another way, if high SAT scorers are in colleges where they (the students) are able to focus on academics, their background advantages can make a positive difference in performance.

Who Will Succeed in College?

This research has shown that the predictive validity of the SAT in a series of samples is better for Black students in Black colleges, particularly for Black males. While psychosocial issues were more characteristic of high SAT scorers in White colleges, they were not directly linked to predictive validity. Similarly, the preponderance of psychosocial correlates appear at first to have implications for how SAT scores translate into better grades, but a formal test reveals that they do not. Instead, predictive validity was associated primarily with academic adjustment issues. Hence, it is not solely the predominant race of the college or the student's sex per se that has such predictive value. Rather, the key factor is concentrating on things academic. While academic adjustment overlaps considerably with the college's predominant race, it is not synonymous with it. It seems that the effects of White colleges in general and Black colleges for women are too often distracting for high achievers. High-scoring students appear distracted by issues of race, identity conflicts, depression, and psychosomatic illness, among other factors. These distractions take the student's focus away from where it needs to be: on academic issues.

These findings imply both good and bad news. The bad news is that colleges differ in the extent to which they facilitate Black student achievement; and most students, unaware of what they are up against, fall victim to the prevailing winds in their college setting. The good news is that individual students can perform up to and beyond their ability by choosing to focus their energies on academics. The SAT score may indicate some, perhaps wide, limits to academic potential, but the student also has wide latitude to make ability count.

References

Allen, W. R. (1985). Black student, White campus: Structural, interpersonal and psychological correlates of success. *Journal of Negro Education, 54,* 135–147.

Berry, G. L., & Asamen, J. L. (1989). *Black students.* Newbury Park, CA: Sage.

Bohr, L., Pascarella, E. T., Nora, A., & Terenzini, P. T. (1995). Do Black students learn more at historically Black or predominantly White colleges? *Journal of College Student Development, 36,* 75–85.

Boyd, W. M. (1977). SAT's minorities: The dangers of under-prediction. *Change, 9,* 48–64.

Bracey, G. W. (1993). The third Bracey Report: The condition of public education. *Phi Delta Kappan, 2,* 105–117.

Breland, H. M. (1978). Population validity and college entrance measures. *Research Bulletin* (RB 78–6) Princeton, NJ: Educational Testing Service.

Chambers, G. A. (1988, March 7). *All of America's children: Variants in ACT test scores—what principals need to know.* Paper presented at the NASSP Annual Convention, Anaheim, CA. Available from author, Division of Educational Administration, University of Iowa, Iowa City, IA 52242.

Cheatham, H. E., Slaney, R. B., & Coleman, N. C. (1990). Institutional effects on the psycho-social development of African American college students. *Journal of Counseling Psychology, 37,* 453–458.

Cohen, J. (1988). *Statistical power analysis in the behavioral sciences.* New York: Academic Press.

Crouse, J., & Trusheim, D. (1988). *The case against the SAT.* Chicago: University of Chicago Press.

D'Augelli, A. R., & Herschberger, S. L. (1993). African American undergraduates on a predominantly White campus: Academic factors, social networks, and campus climate. *Journal of Negro Education, 62,* 67–81.

DeSousa, D. J., & Kuh, G. D. (1996). Does institutional racial composition make a difference in what Black students gain from college? *Journal of College Student Development, 37,* 257–267.

Fleming, J. (1984). *Blacks in college: A comparative study of students' success in Black and in White institutions.* San Francisco: Jossey-Bass.

Fleming, J. (1990). Standardized test scores and the Black college environment. In K. Lomotey (Ed.), *Going to school: The African American experience* (pp. 145–154). Albany: State University of New York Press.

Fleming, J. (in press). The significance of historically Black colleges for high achievers: Correlates of standardized test scores in African American students. In K. Freeman & M. C. Brown (Eds.), *Historically Black colleges at the millennium: Perspectives, policy and practice.* Stamford CT: Ablex Press.

Fleming, J., and Garcia, N. (1998). Are standardized tests fair to African Americans? Predictive validity of the SAT in Black and White colleges. *Journal of Higher Education, 69,* 471–495.

Fleming, J., Garcia, N., & Embaye, F. (1997). The approach to college of the high SAT scorer: An analysis of correlates in minority students. *Texas Southern University Research Journal, 5,* 54–75.

Fleming, J., & Morning, C. (1998). Correlates of the SAT in minority engineering students: An exploratory study. *Journal of Higher Education, 69,* 89–108.

Ford, C. A. (1996). *Student retention: Success models in higher education.* Tallahassee FL: CNJ Associates.

Gibbs, J. T. (Ed.) (1988). *Young, Black and male in America: An endangered species.* Dover MA: Auburn House.

Horn, L. J., & Carroll, C. D. (1997). *Confronting the odds: Students at risk and the pipeline to higher education.* Statistical Analysis Report. OERI Publication No. NCES 98–094. Washington, DC: U.S. Department of Education, National Center for Education Statistics.

Houston, L. N. (1983). The comparative predictive validities of high school rank, the Ammons Quick Test, and two Scholastic Aptitude Test measures for a sample of Black female college students. *Educational and Psychological Measurement, 43,* 1123–1126.

Jay, G. M., & D'Augelli, A. R. (1991). Social support and adjustment to university life: A comparison of African American and White freshmen. *Journal of Community Psychology, 19,* 95–108.

Jencks, C. (1998). Racial bias in testing. In C. Jencks & M. Phillips (Eds.), *The Black-White test score gap.* Washington DC: Brookings Institution Press.

Jencks, C., & Phillips, M. (1998). The Black-White test score gap: An introduction. In C. Jencks & M. Phillips (Eds.), *The Black-White test score gap* (pp. 1–51). Washington DC: Brookings Institution Press.

Kane,T. J. (1998). Racial and ethnic preferences in college admissions. In C. Jencks & M. Phillips (Eds.), *The Black-White test score gap* (pp. 431–456). Washington DC: Brookings Institution Press.

Kraft, C. L. (1991). What makes a successful Black student on a predominantly White campus? *American Research Journal, 28,* 423–443.

Marco, G. L., & Abdel-Fattah, A. A. (1991). Developing concordance tables for scores on the enhanced ACT assessment and the SAT. *College & University, 66,* 187–194.

Miller, D. M., & O'Connor, P. (1969). Achiever personality and academic success among disadvantaged college students. *Journal of Social Issues, 25,* 193–116.

Morehouse College (1984). *Computational Chart: Freshman predicted index.* Atlanta, GA: Author.

Morgan, R. (1990). Predictive validity within categorizations of college students: 1978, 1981, and 1985. ETS Research Report 90–14. Princeton, NJ: Educational Testing Service.

Neill, D. M., & Medina, N. J. (1989, May). Standardized testing: Harmful to educational health. *Phi Delta Kappan,* 688–697.

Nettles, M. T., Thoeny, A. R., & Gosman, E. J. (1986). Comparative and predictive analyses of Black and White students' college achievement and experience. *Journal of Higher Education, 57,* 289–318.

Nottingham, C. R., Rosen, D. H., & Parks, C. (1992). Psychological well-being among African American university students. *Journal of College Student Development, 33,* 356–362.

Pelavin, S. H., & Kane, M. (1990). *Changing the odds: Factors increasing access to college.* New York: College Examination Board.

Pennock-Roman, M. (1990). *Test validity and language background: A study of Hispanic American students at six universities.* New York: College Entrance Examination Board.

Ramist, L., Angoff, W. H., Broudy, I. L., Burton, N. W., Donlon, T. E., Stern, J., & Thorne, P. A. (1984). The predictive validity of the ATP tests. In T. F. Donlon (Ed.), *The College Board technical handbook for the scholastic aptitude and achievement tests.* New York: College Entrance Examination Board.

Ramist, L., Lewis, C., and McCamley-Jenkins, L. (1994). *Student group differences in predicting college grade: Sex, language, and ethnic groups.* College Board Report No. 93–1, ETS RR No. 94–27. New York: College Entrance Examination Board.

Schwitzer, A. M., Griffin, O. T., Ancis, J. R., & Thomas, C. R. (1999). Social adjustment experiences of African American college students. *Journal of Counseling and Development, 77,* 189–197.

Smith, T. M., & Choy, S. P. (1995a). *High school students ten years after "A nation at risk." Findings from: "The condition of education 1994."* OERI Publication No. NCES 95–764. Washington DC: U.S. Department of Education, National Center for Education Statistics.

Smith, T. M, & Choy, S. P. (1995b). *The educational progress of Black students: Findings from: "The condition of education 1994."* OERI Publication No. NCES 95–765. Washington DC: U.S. Department of Education, National Center for Education Statistics.

Steele, C. M., & Aronson, J. (1995). Stereotype threat and the intellectual test performance of African Americans. *Journal of Personality and Social Psychology, 69,* 797–811.

Temp, G. (1971). Validity of the SAT for Blacks and Whites in thirteen integrated institutions. *Journal of Educational Measurement, 8,* 245–251.

Vars, F. E., & Bowen, W. G. (1998). Scholastic aptitude test scores, race, and academic performance in selective colleges and universities. In C. Jencks & M. Phillips (Eds.). *The Black-White test score gap.* Washington DC: Brookings Institution Press.

Watson, P. (1972, September). IQ: The racial gap. *Psychology Today,* 48.

Young, B. A., & Smith, T. M. (1997). *The social context of education. Findings from: "The condition of education 1997."* OERI Publication No. NCES 97–091. Washington, DC: U.S. Department of Education, National Center for Education Statistics.

Xavier University of Louisiana (1984, March). *Student success at Xavier.* Institutional Research, Xavier University.

Making School to College Programs Work

Academics, Goals, and Aspirations

Linda Serra Hagedorn and Shereen Fogel

Introduction

As many of the other chapters have indicated, despite the existence of special programs designed to assist urban, rural, and minority youth from low-income areas to attain college degrees and subsequent occupational success, the stark reality remains—only a small number will earn a bachelor's degree or beyond (U.S. Department of Education, 2000; Levine & Nidiffer, 1997; Bureau of the Census, 1997). As Swail and Perna have indicated, the government, private foundations, and others have instituted many programs to counteract obstacles preventing these students from going to college. But despite the proliferation of programs, there remains a lack of research to assess effectiveness. As Patricia Gándara noted, most of the literature regarding special programs does not include empirical data to test for efficacy. Moreover, the existing evaluations tend to be short-term and do not follow students to college graduation and beyond. But most important, the extant literature is not counterfactual; in other words it does not disclose what would have happened to the subjects sans intervention.

The present chapter is divided into three sections. In the first section we present the literature on various key components that have been shown to be significant predictors of college attendance and subsequent college retention. In section two, we fashion a model of evaluation designed to assist policy makers to evaluate school-to-college programs subsequently testing it through the evaluation of three college preparation programs. To conclude the chapter, we present the voices of students included in our analyses. Like the other two chapters in this section of the book, we provide policy suggestions based on our empirical findings.

The three programs of interest were located in California. Chapter 7 (Yonezawa, Jones, and Mehan) aptly described the unique conditions and politics of the state. Although one may argue that California is unique in many ways, the directions that the state has recently taken are also in practice in other states (i.e., bans on affirmative action in admissions and elimination of remedial courses in public universities) and still other states are following California's example. Within this increasingly hostile environment we examine the efficacy of programs through the following specific questions:

- Do students enrolled in school-to-college preparation programs enroll in college in greater proportion than their non-program counter-parts?
- Do school-to-college programs affect student cognitions, such as academic self-efficacy, goal orientation, and ego anxiety?
- What are the ingredients for college preparation programmatic success?

Reprinted by permission from *Increasing Access to College: Extending Possibilites for All Students,* edited by W.G. Tierney and L.S. Hagedorn, (2002), State University of New York Press.

The Literature

College admission and subsequent retention are highly related to academics (Gladieux & Swain, 1998; Maeroff, 1999). In chapter 2, Cliff Adelman reminds us that one of the most consistent and dominant variables capable of predicting degree completion is "Academic Resources, a composite index of pre-collegiate preparation that is dominated by the *academic intensity and quality of one's high school curriculum.*" But it is important to link academic achievement with important and key factors such as family characteristics, student self-efficacy, goal orientation, academic support, college information, and the development of study skills.

Based on its strong link with academic performance (U.S. Department of Education, 2000), family involvement has become a salient issue in the popular and academic literature and a focal point of many federally funded programs. However, much of the literature linking families and achievement is correlational rather than causal and focuses on demographic traits such as parent income, education, or occupation (Leslie & Oaxaca 1998; also see Jun and Colyar, chapter 9). While the evidence may indicate a relationship, the demographic conditions of parents may be only a proxy for another construct more directly responsible for student achievement—family social and cultural capital (Clark, 1983; Delgado-Gaitan, 1991; Delpit, 1988; Funkhouser & Gonzales, 1998; Lam, 1997; Lareau, 1987).

As Jun and Colyar will elaborate in the following chapter, the essence of Cultural Capital Theory is that families of each social class transmit the cultural values, knowledge, skills, abilities, manners, style of interaction, pronunciation, and language facility consistent with their social standing. Pierre Bourdieu (1977; 1986) provides a framework of cultural capital, asserting that cultural capital of middle and upper class students provides privilege in terms of educational mobility, economic security, organizational contexts, and personal support systems integral to predicting educational achievement. Many college preparation programs supplement student cultural capital by exposing students to activities and role models that most middle and upper class students would find commonplace but that would be less likely to occur without intervention.

While the range of cultural capital can be quite extensive, equally extensive is the range of academic capital—the level and intensity of experienced academic rigor (Bourdieu & Passeron, 1977; Clark, 1991; Coleman, 1990; Kozol, 1991; McDonough, 1994; Mehan et al., 1996). As Gándara has noted, academic capital is typically higher in wealthy communities. For example, while 86 percent of high school graduates from high-income families are academically qualified for admission to higher education institutions, less than 53 percent of low-income graduates are similarly qualified (U.S. Department of Education, 1998). The situation is compounded by deficits of background knowledge and experiences related to college. In other words, students from lower socioeconomic neighborhoods and family situations may not have taken the appropriate courses or established proper scholastic habits, resulting in grades and test scores that do not meet the admission standards of colleges and universities. Further, the situation is exacerbated when students have language deficits and attend schools with insufficient resources. In addition, college attendance can also be threatened by a lack of familiarity regarding the process and availability of college financial aid (Carger, 1996; Levine & Nidiffer, 1996). The relationship between family socioeconomic status and academic achievement is neither perfect nor linear. Simply stated, parents who are familiar with and understand the importance of higher education are more likely to convey and support the social and academic characteristics leading to college attendance. Overall, many low-income students are not "college familiar"—they are unlikely to have participated in campus visits, spoken with college representatives, leafed through college catalogs, or participated in other activities that create "college readiness" (see Attinasi, 1989). In response to the deficits and conditions aforementioned, school-to-college programs typically seek to expand students' cultural and academic capital and to provide them with the experiences and knowledge consistent with that of their more affluent and privileged peers.

Student Cognitions

Self-Efficacy

Involvement in a college preparation program may positively influence students' cognitive beliefs about themselves and their abilities. Bandura (1977) defines self-efficacy as beliefs regarding one's self-capabilities to organize and execute the courses of action required to accomplish specific tasks. Self-efficacy is related to academic performance by affecting the tasks people choose, the amount of effort they expend, and how long they persevere in the face of obstacles (Bandura, 1993; Bandura, 1997; Dweck, 1986; Middleton & Midgley, 1997; Pajares, 1996). A meta-analysis by Zimmerman, Bandura, and Martinez-Pons (1992) indicated that academic self-efficacy has an impact on academic achievement directly as well as indirectly by influencing self-regulatory practices and goals.

Within a socio-cognitive framework, self-efficacy encompasses the cognitive beliefs of one's ability and the expectations of the environment's support of success. While many studies focus on self-efficacy in terms of beliefs about ability (Anderman & Young, 1994; Schunk, 1996; Skaalvik, 1997), less attention has been given to the impact of these beliefs on the student's ability to navigate the environment. For high self-efficacy, it is important that students believe both that they are able to accomplish a given task, and if successful, fair and appropriate gains will be achieved. Without a high sense of self-efficacy, task engagement is unlikely (Clark, 1998), as people do not choose to engage in tasks in which they are likely to fail or not be appropriately recognized or rewarded. College preparation programs frequently work with students to increase their feelings of self-worth and to encourage them to adopt an "I can do it" attitude.

Goal Orientation

Goal theory is a prominent perspective in explaining aspects of motivation (Wiener, 1990; Dweck & Leggett, 1988; Skaalvik, 1997). In addition to goals, orientation is also important when explaining why people engage in specific tasks. There are two main types of goal orientation, mastery and performance (Dweck & Leggett, 1988; Nicholls, 1984).

Individuals with a mastery orientation engage in learning tasks primarily for the enjoyment derived from learning new information, and/or to increase competency in a given area. In comparison, individuals with a performance orientation engage in learning tasks primarily to gain or maintain favorable judgments of their ability (Pintrich & Schunk, 1996). Simply put, a person with a mastery orientation learns for the love of learning, while one with a performance orientation learns in order to be perceived in a positive way.

Adopting either a mastery or performance orientation is associated with subsequent patterns of behavior, cognition, affect, and performance (Ames, 1992; Dweck, 1986; Dweck & Leggett, 1988). Mastery goals are generally associated with more positive patterns of educational behavior, affect, and cognition (Ames & Archer, 1988). For example, mastery-oriented students are believed to be more persistent when faced with challenging tasks, to choose appropriate level tasks, and to partake in active task engagement (Dweck & Leggett, 1988).

Performance goals are generally associated with less adaptive patterns of behavior, affect, and cognition (Ames & Archer, 1988). Performance-oriented students often attribute their performance to fixed, uncontrollable causes such as unfair grading practices or bad luck; while mastery-oriented students more often attribute their performance to changeable, controllable causes such as the amount of effort expended when attempting to accomplish a task (Roedel, Schraw, & Plake, 1994). In addition, performance-oriented students are more likely to assess their ability through feedback from past performances. After failing a task such as a test, performance-oriented students are inclined to believe that their performance reflects low ability (Reisetter & Schraw, 1998; Dweck & Leggett, 1988). Because performance-oriented students are more likely to believe their ability is a fixed entity, they may be less likely to expend significant effort to try to improve their performance in the future. As a result, performance-oriented students often prefer less challenging tasks that maximize success and minimize failure.

Mastery-oriented students are more likely to use feedback effectively after poor performance to determine how they may improve in the future. Since mastery-oriented students often view intelligence as incremental and alterable, they may expend more effort even after a poor performance (Reisetter & Schraw, 1998). Furthermore, mastery-oriented students frequently prefer challenging tasks that offer the greatest opportunity for growth (Ames & Archer, 1988; Nicholls et al., 1989). Mastery-oriented students generally use more self-regulatory strategies, persist longer on tasks, expend more overall effort, and achieve more than performance-oriented students (Bandura, 1996; Pintrich & Schrauben, 1992; Pajares, 1996). Within this framework, the type of goal orientation with which a student approaches school has impact on their successive academic performance, which in turn affects their choice to enroll in college. Thus many college preparation programs take steps to instill within the students the "love of learning."

Goal Orientation and Achievement Behavior

Historically, mastery and performance goal orientations were believed to be two ends of the same spectrum. Current research, however, indicates that goal orientation is actually multidimensional. That is, individuals hold varying amounts of performance and mastery goal orientations simultaneously. Accordingly, having a high level of one orientation does not necessarily mean a low level of the other. Rather, one can be high mastery- and high performance-oriented simultaneously. It is the various combinations of mastery and performance goal orientations (goal configurations) that are associated with cognition and behavior in a variety of areas. Table 1 illustrates four goal configurations and related cognition and behavior.

While performance orientation is generally cast as producing less advantageous patterns of achievement behavior, recent research has indicated that performance-orientation does not necessarily lead to negative behavior patterns. Rather, it is those performance-oriented students who also can be classified as "high ego anxiety" that are more likely to exhibit the negative achievement behavior patterns often associated with performance orientation. The combination of high performance orientation and high ego anxiety is termed performance-avoid approach.

TABLE 1
Cognition and Behavior by Goal Orientation Configuration

	High Mastery/Low Performance	*High Mastery/High Performance*	*Low Mastery/High Performance*	*Low Mastery/Low Performance*
Value of learning	Self fulfillment and social affiliation	Self fulfillment, social affiliation, and status	Status, social affiliation, and self-protection	Utility, status
Ability and effort	Emphasis on effort	Innate ability enhanced by effort	Ability, with effort in areas of innate ability	Ability with selective effort
Locus of Control	Internal emphasis	Internal and external	External	External with selective internal
Social responsibility	To self	To self, family, and others	To family and others	To self
Role of interest in learning	Important but controllable	Important but controllable with outside help	Critical, controlled by ability perceptions	Critical, controlled relevance perceptions
Role of the teacher in the learning process	Not critical	Important as an ally and support	Critical as gatekeeper of success or failure	Important as pertains to interest and relevance, otherwise, not
Influences of goal orientation	Parents, supportive family, and culture	Parents, family culture with high performance	Performance-oriented family, sibling competition	Detachment, neutrality, utility
Affective dimension	Enthusiasm, hopeful, high expectations for success in all areas	Enthusiastic, hopeful, high expectations, but more anxious	Hurt, hostile, fearful, anxious, resigned endurance, sense of betrayal	Resignation indifference, detachment, passivity, independent choices

In contrast, students who are performance oriented but do not have high-ego anxiety exhibit advantageous behavior patterns similar to mastery-oriented students. This orientation is known as performance-approach. Therefore, it is not whether one is performance oriented, but rather if one has high ego anxiety along with a performance orientation that determines achievement behavior patterns.

Since student cognitions substantially affect achievement behavior, the relationship between college preparation program and student cognition may be an important evaluation consideration.

The Evaluation Model

The School to College Programs Included in the Analyses

This study focused on three programs that served low socioeconomic urban areas, emphasized college preparation, targeted low-achieving to marginal achieving students, and were longitudinal—spanning multiple grades including twelfth.

Program 1. Grand Outreach[1]

The Grand Outreach program targets historically underrepresented minority students with demonstrated potential but marginal grades. Grand Outreach operates throughout California in more than 100 school districts and public higher education sectors. Its mission is to ensure that all students, especially the disadvantaged and underachieving with academic potential, will: succeed in a rigorous curriculum, participate in mainstream school activities, enroll in baccalaureate-granting institutions, and subsequently become responsible citizens and leaders. Direct student services include preparation for college admissions and placement testing, academic support for rigorous curriculums, advisement and career preparation, parent education, and instruction on writing. Most Grand Outreach programs provide an informational class, often meeting before school or during a regularly scheduled class period.

Program 2. Partial Support

The Partial Support Program assists promising students from disadvantaged backgrounds to graduate from high school, pursue postsecondary education, and become contributing members of the community. Accordingly, the Partial Support Program aims to expose at-risk students to college preparatory curriculum, and to provide appropriate mentors for student support. Students who complete high school and are accepted to a post-secondary institution receive a partial college scholarship, renewable for up to five years.

Program 3. Total Immersion

The Total Immersion program operates on a college campus providing multiple levels of academic and nonacademic services. Total Immersion targets middle-achieving (C average), low-income students from underrepresented minority groups. Program students meet daily at the college in before-school sessions that target reading, writing, and mathematics, as well as mandatory sessions on skill development encompassing note taking, extent of time spent on various activities, problem solving, and critical thinking. The program also provides mandatory parent sessions as well as individual, group, and family counseling to assist students in dealing with emotional and psychological issues.

Students Included in the Analyses

The analyses presented in this chapter involve 203 students (112 girls, 95 boys) from low socioeconomic, urban areas in Southern California that were seniors in high school during the 1998–1999 school year. While 144 of the students were enrolled in one of the three college-preparation programs previously described, 63 were not enrolled in a special program but were enrolled in the college prep track of the same high schools attended by the program participants and fit the ethnic and socioeconomic demographics profile. Students enrolled in college preparation programs will hereafter be called the treatment group while those not enrolled in special programs served as an effective control group.

Data Collection and Instrumentation

Initial data collection occurred between September and December 1998. Control group students and those enrolled in Programs 1 and 2 completed survey forms at their high school. Program 3 students were surveyed at the location of their program. All students heard the same introductory comments and were assured of the confidentiality of their responses. All students completed a seven-page survey of questions targeting demographic information, family background and expectations, friends, courses, achievement and college enrollment tests, academic plans, goal orientation, academic self-efficacy, ego anxiety, extent of time spent on various activities, college preparation program participation, grades, and assessment of college preparation program support. Students' cognitive beliefs, such as academic self-efficacy, goal orientation, and ego anxiety, were measured by three separate inventories included within the survey. These inventories were adapted from the Self-efficacy scale of the Expectancy Component of the Motivated Strategies for Learning Questionnaire Manual (NCRIPTAL, 1991); the Roedel, Schraw, & Plake Goal Orientation Inventory (1994); and the Shorkey, Whiteman Ego Anxiety Scale (1977). In addition, two items measuring agency component of self-efficacy were also included on the survey.

Follow-up surveys were sent to both treatment and control students at two points following the initial contact. The first follow-up was mailed approximately six months after students completed the initial survey and was intended to coincide with participant's receipt of college admission notification. The second follow-up was sent one year after the initial contact and was intended to verify that students were actually enrolled and had matriculated at their chosen college.

Analysis

The preliminary analysis consisted of (1) coding variables; (2) developing valid and reliable scales; (3) exploring demographics such as age, ethnicity, and course-taking patterns, and (4), performing preliminary comparisons between the treatment and no-treatment groups. College attendance was coded in two ways. First, we created a dichotomous variable to indicate if students were attending college (1) or not (0). Second, we created a separate variable in which college attendance was coded by the type of institution attended (0 = no college, 1 = community college, 2 = four-year college or university). We performed two analyses of variance tests to see if in general, students enrolled in college preparation programs (treatment) were more likely to attend college and/or were more likely to attend a four-year institution (rather than a two-year) as compared to those not enrolled in a special program (no treatment).

Conceptual Framework of Model

The hypothesized model begins with measures of the type and degree of participation in college preparation programs that are hypothesized to influence students' cognitions, achievement behavior, actual achievement, and subsequent enrollment in higher education. The model was analyzed with EQS structural equations program for Windows v5.7b. The analyses were conducted in two stages: the measurement model followed by the structural model. The model was derived from the two-stage Commitment and Necessary Effort (CANE) model of motivation (Bandura, 1997; Ford, 1992; Pintrich & Schunk, 1996). The first stage, "goal commitment," was defined as the active pursuit of a goal over time (Clark, 1999). The model hypothesized that commitment results from the self-assessment of three key factors: personal agency (self-efficacy), value (goal orientation), and affect (mood). According to the CANE model, goal commitment increases with increases in value, mood, and personal agency.

The hypothesized model consists of four domains of variables operationalized using four measured variables and five latent variables described in Table 2. A fifth domain, family characteristics, was originally proposed but due to lack of variance, was excluded from the final model.

Test of the Model

Once the measurement model was determined to measure all latent constructs adequately, the structural model was tested. The structural model tested the factors to determine the extent of causation as related to college attendance. The final model (presented in Figure 3) proposes that greater involvement in a college preparation programs (as determined by academic, informational, study skills building, and enrichment activities) affects student cognitions by increasing student's academic self-efficacy, decreasing ego anxiety, which in turn increases mastery goal orientation, and performance goal-approach orientation while minimizing performance goal-avoid orientation. Student cognitive beliefs are then manifested in an increase in enrollment in

TABLE 2
Structural Model Constructs

College Enrollment	*From Follow-up, Coded As "1" for Yes and "0" for No.*
GPA	1 low (mostly Cs and Ds and mostly Ds or below) 2 middle (mostly Bs, mostly Bs and Cs, and mostly Cs), 3 high (mostly As and mostly As and Bs),
Courses	Summation of basic math, algebra, geometry, general science, biology, chemistry, physics, foreign language, advance placement, and honors courses. Weighted according to importance in college admissions.
Time spent studying	Self-reported number of daily hours spent studying or doing homework as reported on the initial survey.
Mastery goal orientation	Based on Roedel, Schraw, & Plake's (1994) Learning and Performance Orientation scale
Ego Anxiety	Based on Shorkey-Whiteman (1977) Ego-Anxiety Scale
Academic Self-efficacy	Based on the Motivated Strategies Learning Questionnaire (MSLQ) (NCRIPTAL, 1991)
College preparation program involvement	Measures of involvement and participation regarding academic support, information sessions, enrichment activities, and study skills development

college readiness courses and time spent in study, which in turn increases GPA. Finally, the model proposes that the increase in college readiness courses and higher grades lead to an increase in college enrollment.

Findings

Overall, the families of the students in all four groups (three college preparation programs and the control group) were quite similar. An analysis of variance revealed no statistically significant differences among program and control group students regarding parent/s educational attainment or expectations regarding their child's academic success.

According to student responses, approximately 66 percent of mothers and 55 percent of fathers did *not* finish high school, yet *all* students reported that their parents would be disappointed if *they* did not finish high school. In addition, no significant differences were found in the number of parents in the treatment as compared to the control group who expected that their child would attend college.

Courses

Although there were no significant differences between treatment and control group student enrollment in basic courses such as basic math, analysis of variance equations indicated distinct differences between treatment and control group with respect to advanced courses. Students in the treatment group were significantly more likely to have taken or be enrolled in algebra, geometry, biology, chemistry, foreign language, advanced placement (AP) courses, and honors courses than control group students. Table 3 provides the statistical significance of the course-taking tests.

College Enrollment

Figures 1a and 1b provide graphic representations of student aspirations with respect to the type of college they attend. In the year following high school graduation, only 9 percent of the treatment group students were not enrolled in college as compared to 24 percent of the control group students. Although 6 percent of the treatment students were attending one of the campuses of the University of California,[2] none of the control group students were similarly enrolled. Further, of the 23 percent of the treatment students who reported attending a four-year college other than one in the public California system, many were at prestigious private institutions such as the University of Southern California. One student was at Stanford University. Significantly more students in the control group were attending community college than students enrolled in any of the three treatment groups ($F = 31.52, p < .05$).

TABLE 3
ANOVA Results by Course Type

		Treatment Group (School-to-College Program)		*Control (No-Treatment) No Special Program*	
Course	*F Statistic*	*Mean (E)*	*SD (E)*	*Mean (C)*	*SD (C)*
Algebra	5.94*	.99	.08	.93	.25
Geometry	5.69*	.95	.22	.85	.36
Science	23.73†	.97	.16	.74	.44
Chemistry	33.05†	.89	.31	.53	.50
Physics	0.17ns	.42	.50	.46	.50
AP Courses	13.45†	.80	.40	.52	.50
Honors	57.32†	.83	.38	.29	.46

*$p < .05$;
†$p < .01$.

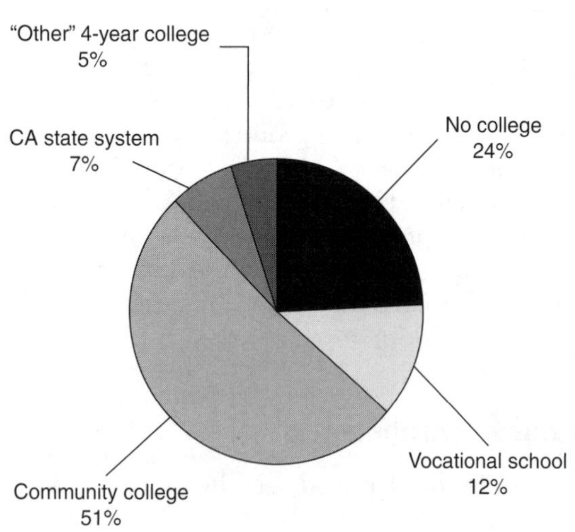

Figure 1a College Choice (Control)

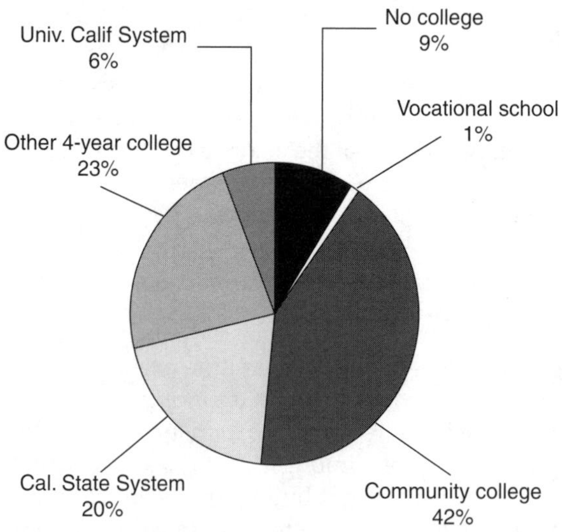

Figure 1b College Choice (Treatment)

Testing the Model

We proposed and tested the measurement model via confirmatory factory analysis (CFA) to determine if measured variables appropriately loaded on latent factors (see Kline, 1998). We further checked to be sure that no indicators were associated with more than one latent variable (crossloading). Both the Lagrange Multiplier modification index, and the Wald (W) statistic were consulted to assure a good fit (Bentler, 1980; Bentler & Bonnet, 1980; Newcomb, 1990). In addition, the fit of the measurement model was examined by the chi-square to degrees of freedom ratio ($\chi^2/df = 155.94/94 = 1.66$), (Carmines, & McIver, 1981), the Comparative Fit Index (CFI = .96), and the Non-Normed Fit Index (NNFI = .95).

The standardized measurement model including factor loadings and residual variances is provided as Figure 2. Factor loadings may be interpreted as regression coefficients (i.e., factor loadings estimate the direct effects of the factors), while residuals are squared to indicate the variance unexplained.

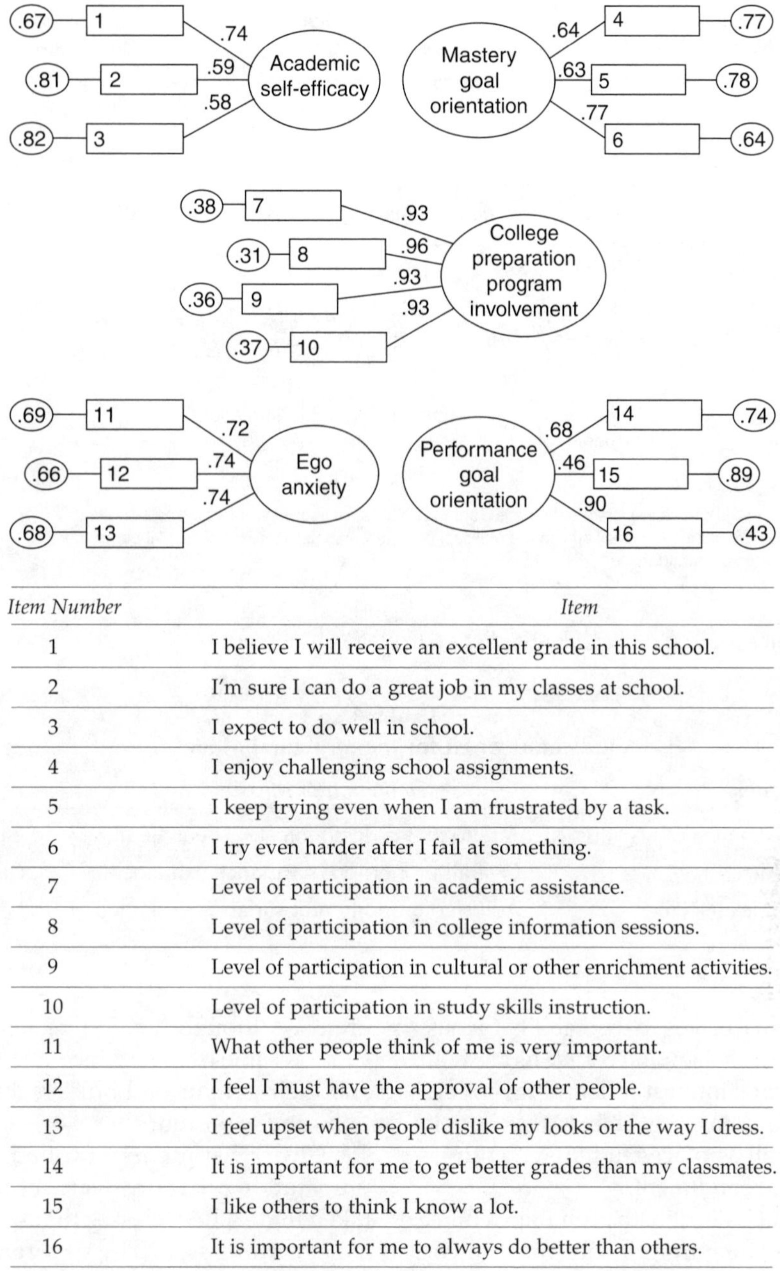

Item Number	*Item*
1	I believe I will receive an excellent grade in this school.
2	I'm sure I can do a great job in my classes at school.
3	I expect to do well in school.
4	I enjoy challenging school assignments.
5	I keep trying even when I am frustrated by a task.
6	I try even harder after I fail at something.
7	Level of participation in academic assistance.
8	Level of participation in college information sessions.
9	Level of participation in cultural or other enrichment activities.
10	Level of participation in study skills instruction.
11	What other people think of me is very important.
12	I feel I must have the approval of other people.
13	I feel upset when people dislike my looks or the way I dress.
14	It is important for me to get better grades than my classmates.
15	I like others to think I know a lot.
16	It is important for me to always do better than others.

Note: Rectangles are measured variables, large circles are latent constructs, and small circles are residual variances. Factor loadings are standardized and *all* are significant ($p < .05$).

Figure 2 Confirmatory Factor Analysis (CFA) Model

Structural Model

The hypothesized model, presented in Figure 3, and the data for this study fit well. As seen in Table 4, the examined indicators of fit all supported adequate model fit.

While the model confirms a significant and direct connection between college preparation program involvement and course enrollment, several other indirect paths were also found to influence course enrollment. Our model shows that involvement in a college preparation program influences students' academic self-efficacy, or beliefs regarding ability to succeed academically. Increases in academic self-efficacy then significantly increase students' mastery goal orientation, which in turn leads to significant increases in enrollment in college readiness courses. By

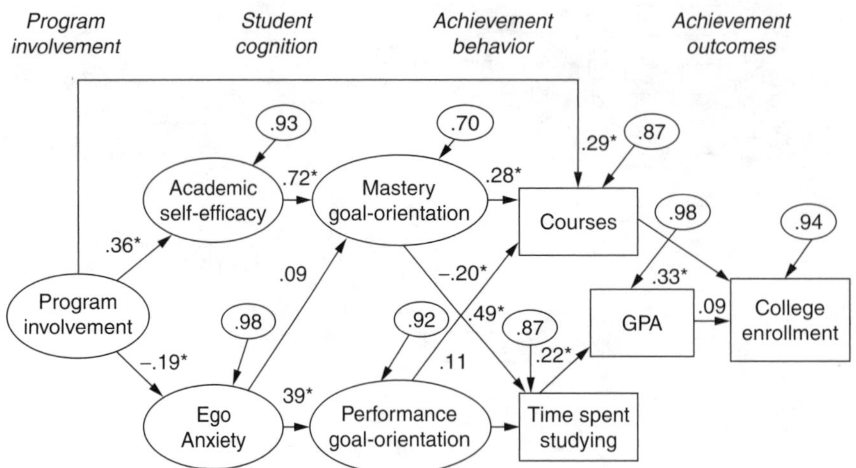

Note: Large circles are latent constructs, rectangles area measured variables, single-headed arrows are paths, and small circles are residual or disturbance terms (variances). All parameter estimates are standardized.
$^*p < .05$.

Figure 3 Structural Model Predicting College Enrollment

TABLE 4
Indicators of Fit for the Structural Model

Fit Index	*Definition or Measure*	*Statistic*
Chi-square/degrees of freedom (χ^2/df)	A ratio of 3 or less indicates adequate fit.	243.13/161 = 1.51
Comparative Fit Index (CFI)	Overall proportion of variance explained.	CFI = .92
Non-Normed Fit Index (NNFI)	Adjusted proportion of variance explained.	NNFI = .9I

increasing students' beliefs in their ability to master the content in a challenging course along with igniting a student's interest in learning, college preparation programs are able to effectively encourage as well as place students in courses leading to college enrollment.

An additional indirect path promoting course enrollment originating from involvement in college preparation program begins with ego anxiety (i.e., student's concern about negative judgments from others.). Lower ego anxiety, operationalized as a decrease in the concern of negative judgments by others, directly leads to decreases in performance orientation or the drive to engage in tasks for an external reward or confirmation.

Conclusions from the Model

The students enrolled in school-to-college programs were not demographically different from their peers who were not enrolled in special programs. Although it could be said that all of the subjects came from low-income homes, both they and their parents had universally high expectations and aspirations.

Clearly, students enrolled in the college preparation programs were more likely to have taken high-school classes that ultimately lead to college admission. The differences were most marked for chemistry, advanced placement, and honors course. Because the direct path from college-level courses to college enrollment in the tested model was highly significant, the policy implications for college preparation programs are evident. Courses likely work in several ways to produce college enrollment. First, the appropriate coursework prepares students to score in the acceptable ranges in college admission tests. Further, college admission committees examine high school transcripts for the enrollment of courses that will allow the student to enroll in true college-level courses.

College Enrollment

Figures 1a and 1b clearly displayed the different college enrollment patterns of the treatment and no-treatment groups. Specifically, students enrolled in southern California school-to-college programs do enroll in college in greater numbers than their no-treatment counterparts. In addition, treatment group students are less likely to enroll in a community college. Although in some circumstances the choice to attend a community college may be wise, attendance at a four-year institution is more likely to yield a bachelor's degree in a timely fashion (Cohen & Brawer, 1996).

One of the most important contributions of this model is the redefinition of the role of high school courses and grades in college enrollment. While both popular knowledge and college admissions policies often emphasize the importance of high school grades, the model indicates that courses taken in high school may actually be a better predictor of college enrollment than grade point average.

This finding supports the recent emphasis on the role of appropriate courses in college preparation. Current research studies such as Cliff Adelman's "Answers in the Tool Box" study emphasize that despite the concern for high school GPA, grades are not the best predictors of college success (Adelman, 1999). Adelman again emphasized the role of taking the "right" courses *before* college to increase the chances of graduating from college in chapter 2 of this book. Although this connection may almost seem intuitive, many high school students are not taking the most rigorous courses because (a) they fear that harder courses may yield lower grades and lower grades may affect their college admission eligibility; (b) the rigorous courses are not offered at their school; or (c) they are hesitant to take courses requiring high levels of study if they are unaware or unadvised of the significant advantages.

While courses appear to be the best predictor of college enrollment, our model indicates higher levels of mastery performance orientation were not only associated with increased enrollment in college readiness courses, but also increased the amount of time students spent studying. Further, increased study time led to better grades. While this model does not suggest that higher grades increase one's chances of attending college, there may be other benefits of high grades such as scholarship opportunities, awards, and admission to more prestigious institutions.

Cognitions

School-to-college programs may positively affect student cognitions such as academic self-efficacy, goal orientation, and ego anxiety. Involvement in a college preparation program both increases academic self-efficacy and decreases ego anxiety. Thus, students may come to believe in their abilities to obtain a postsecondary education. As academic self-efficacy increases, so does mastery goal orientation. Thus, students may be transformed into life-long learners who appreciate education for its own sake. The combination of these student cognitions may naturally lead to less fear in enrolling in courses in the hard sciences or those designated as "AP" or "honors." As the model clearly indicated, the importance of taking the right high school courses cannot be over-emphasized.

Finally, in answer to our third query, the ingredients for southern California college preparation programmatic success appear to be actions that promote enrollment and success in pre-college courses. Students can be motivated to enroll in courses expected to be challenging by assisting them academically and providing "out of class" enrichment. Practice and exposure to academic content may show students they can do and thus increase academic self-efficacy. Further, programs should strive to enhance students' mastery goal orientation to develop a love and hunger for learning.

Student Voices

In this final section of the chapter, we present the voices of four students whose views were especially poignant, compelling, and useful in understanding how college preparation programs work. Two of the students, Juan and Sandra, were enrolled in a special enrichment program, while the other two, Alma and Trevor, were control group students. Together, they weave a story of the interplay of public education, private enrichment programs, and life's circumstances.

Juan (Partial Support Program—Not Enrolled in College)

Juan started the Partial Support enrichment program in the tenth grade and attended sponsored functions sporadically throughout high school. Juan confessed that he wanted to go to college and still does, but "things just didn't work out right now." While in his senior year in high school, Juan applied to three institutions, The University of California at Los Angeles, California State at Dominguez Hills, and Loyola Marymount.

> Even when I was filling out the applications I like knew it wasn't going to happen. . . . not yet. I was like doing it because it was what I was supposed to do but I knew it wasn't going to happen.

Juan was accepted at Dominguez Hills and told everyone that he was planning to attend there in the fall. But as the time came closer, he began to feel differently. By summer, Juan was working with his uncle in a family-owned business and knew that the time wasn't right for him to leave home.

> I was working, making money, and being my own self and just didn't feel like going back to school again. A lot of people, especially my parents, told me I should go to college, but I just didn't want to go back to homework and studying and all of that stuff. I needed a change.

In answer to "is there something that the program could have done that would have resulted in his enrollment in college?" he thought a minute and said, "maybe give me more money for college and living. It is hard to see that it makes sense to go to school and spend all kinds of money and take out loans when I can work and make money."

Will Juan ever go to college? He insists he will but he needs to do it in his own time frame and not at the urging of school counselors or program officers.

Sandra (Total Immersion Program—Enrolled in a Private Research University)

Sandra's story boasts of success. She represents the student that a college preparation program could use as their spokesperson. Although Sandra was raised in a very rough part of Los Angeles and attended schools in high crime areas, both Sandra and her parents always had high aspirations for her. When coming into the Total Immersion program in the seventh grade, Sandra and her family knew that she would be attending a private university someday and that her life would be transformed through the experience. Sandra participated in everything the program offered. Her parents[3] attended meetings every week.

Sandra is now enrolled at an elite private university and lives near the campus. She is happy to be at the institution but confesses that the work is a lot harder than what she expected.

> I took all of the hard college-bound courses in high school. I took physics, chemistry, geometry, and foreign language. The work here is really hard, but I know that I am doing ok only because I took all of the hard courses in high school and I had extra help in the program. I had to work hard in high school and that was good because now I know how to work hard and I have to keep on doing that. Being a scholar in the "Total Immersion" program, I couldn't hang out like a lot of kids do. I am glad about that now because I go out with friends and all, but I also know how to work hard and say no to some parties.

In answer to the question would she be in college today if it were not for the Total Immersion Program, Sandra said she doubted it. Her high school friends who were not in the program were not in college and she guessed she wouldn't be either. Sandra is an example of success and will likely continue to be a great spokesperson for the Total Immersion Program.

Alma (Control—Not Enrolled in College)

Initially, Alma was very hesitant to speak to us. She even accused us of "looking down on her" because she wasn't in college. Early in the interview she said "just because you guys are in a college you think everyone should go; but I know lots of people who never went to college and they are doing good and are even rich and stuff, so not everyone needs to go to college." As our conversation progressed, however, we fell into a more relaxed conversation in which Alma seemed to be more comfortable.

Alma was in the college track in high school. She thought she would go to college but never really knew what she wanted to become. She is interested in the entertainment field and expressed a desire to be an actress, a model, or even work behind the scenes such as a hairdresser or costumer. Part of the reason Alma didn't go to college was because she just didn't know the type of courses to take to work in the entertainment field. While in her senior year in high school Alma's counselor helped her to request applications from several colleges and universities including UCLA, California State University at Northridge and the University of Texas at Austin. But, Alma confessed that she never completed any of them because she just didn't have the time or the inclination.

Today, Alma's time is filled with her part-time job and her fiancé. She has no immediate plans for college but has not totally dismissed the idea of "someday." We finally asked Alma if she had more support such as assistance in filling out applications or had been taken on campus visits if she might be attending college today. Her response after a long pause was "who knows, I'm happy now and that's all that's important."

Trevor (Control Group, Presently Attending a Community College)

Trevor told us that he never considered college an option—he always planned on attending. He maintained good grades in high school and managed to stay out of trouble despite enrollment in a high school with a large gang population. He reported that he considered four-year universities and even thought about going away from home and joining a fraternity, but deep in his heart he knew that the Ivy League wasn't for him. Trevor reported that his decision was influenced by most of his friends who were going to college and were planning on attending the community college. He also confessed to low SAT scores that would likely have been a problem at prestigious universities. Today, Trevor is enrolled in three courses (10 units) at the community college and holds down a part-time job. He is taking U.S. history plus a mathematics and English course that are both below college level.

We asked about "getting ready experiences" such as campus visits and financial aid forms. Trevor said that he had been on the UCLA campus once, but had not visited any other four-year schools. He had filled out the federal financial aid forms with the help of the high school counselor. With the full support of his family, Trevor had not applied to any four-year colleges because his mind was made up that he would attend the community college.

Trevor aspires to be a lawyer. At this time he does not know where he would like to transfer—"I have time to worry about that. . . . maybe I will go to New York or someplace."

We asked Trevor why he never considered a four-year university and his response was typical of many of the community college students we interviewed. Simply put, nobody ever looked beyond the community college as a postsecondary possibility.

> Four year university? You mean UCLA or something? Whenever I talked about college it was always community college. My counselor, my teachers, and everyone only talked about community college. Maybe it's because UCLA is for rich kids.

During the interview we tried to give Trevor advice about courses and credits, and he seemed to be hearing the information for the first time.

Conclusion

As other authors of the chapters in this book have attested, college preparation programs hold important keys to increasing the college-enrollment levels of low-income and other students. Thus, it appears appropriate to continue to focus efforts on enabling students to believe in themselves, to learn how to learn, and to face academic challenge without fears. We emphasize the importance of offering and encouraging students to enroll in those high school courses that will produce college enrollment. An important way that preparation programs can promote college success is to counsel students to enroll in those courses that will assist them to stay on the college track. However, enrolling the students may not be enough. The programs can further assist students to succeed in rigorous courses through academic assistance, tutoring, and instruction in note taking and study skills. Academics are important!

While the model provided the skeletal structure of how programs can assist students, the voices added the flesh. Through Juan we see that enrollment in a special program may not be enough. Students like Juan needed more guidance to become mastery oriented and immersed in learning. From Alma we learned that without special assistance, students may not realize the lifetime implications of education. Trevor demonstrated that good grades and ambition may not be enough. Finally we see Sandra who enrolled in the "right" courses, partook of the "getting ready" activities, and believed in her abilities—she appears to be the picture of success.

Our evaluation covered only one year's time. To revisit the sample in five years, ten years, or even twenty years may change the picture and the conclusions. For now, however, we close with the positive tone that college preparation programs appear to assist some students to go to college. The United States is frequently called "the land of opportunity"—a country where it is presumed that the trio of ability, determination, and hard work can overcome deficits in wealth or family standing. College preparation programs may be one appropriate medium to develop the ability, encourage determination, and promote hard work among students lacking great wealth or influential family standing.

Notes

1. All program names are pseudonyms.
2. The public postsecondary system is composed of three tiers of institutions. The top tier is the University of California system that admits only the top 12.5 percent of the state's high school graduates. The California State system, middle tier, has less stringent admission policies (generally admits the students in the top 50 percent of their graduating class). The California Community Colleges have an open door policy and hence are considered the third tier.
3. Sandra's mother always attended. Her father attended when his work and/or other schedules allowed. Sandra indicated that her mother rearranged her schedule so that she could be present for everything.

References

Adelman, C. (1999). *Answers in the Tool Box: Academic Intensity, Attendance Patterns, and Bachelor's Degree Attainment.* Washington DC: Office of Educational Research and Improvement.

Ames, C. (1992). Achievement goals and the classroom motivational climate. In D. H. Schunk, & J. L. Meece (Eds.), *Student Perceptions in the Classroom* (pp. 327–343). Hillsdale, NJ: Erlbaum.

Ames, C., & Archer, J. (1988). Achievement goals in the classroom: Student's learning strategies and motivation processes. *Journal of Educational Psychology, 80* (3), 260–267.

Anderman, E. M., & Young, A. J. (1994). Motivation and strategy use in science: Individual differences and classroom effects. *Journal of Research in Science Teaching, 31* (8), 811–831.

Attinasi, L. F. (1989). Getting in: Mexican Americans' perceptions of university attendance and the implications for freshman year persistence. *Journal of Higher Education, 60,* (3), 247–277.

Bandura, A. (1977). Self-efficacy: Toward a unifying theory of behavioral change. *Psychological Review, 84* (2), 191–215.

Bandura, A. (1993). Perceived self-efficacy in cognitive development and functioning. *Educational Psychologist, 28* (2), 117–148.

Bandura, A. (1996). Multifaceted impact of self-efficacy beliefs on academic functioning. *Child Development, 67,* (3), 1206–1222.

Bandura, A. (1997). *Self-Efficacy: The Exercise of Control.* New York: W. H. Freeman and Company.

Bentler, P. M. (1980). Multivariate analysis with latent variables: Causal modeling. *Annual Review of Psychology, 31,* 419–456.

Bentler, P. M., & Bonnet, D. G. (1980). Significance tests and goodness of fit in the analysis of covariance structures. *Psychological Bulletin, 88,* 588–606.

Bourdieu, P. (1977). Cultural Reproduction and Social Reproduction. In J. Karabel & A. H. Halsey (Eds.), *Power and Ideology in Education.* New York: Oxford University Press.

Bourdieu, P. (1986). The Forms of Capital. In J. G. Richardson (Ed.), *Handbook of theory and research for the sociology of education* (pp. 241–258). New York: Greenwood Press.

Bourdieu, P., & Passeron, J. (1977). Reproduction in education, society, and culture. *SAGE studies in social and educational change, 5.* Beverly Hills: CA.

Carger, C. L. (1996). *Of Boarders and Dreams: A Mexican-American Experience of Urban Education.* New York: Teachers College Press.

Carmines, E., & McIver, J. (1981). Analysis models with unobserved variables: Analysis of covariance structures. In G. Bohrnsedt & E. F. Borgatta (Eds.), *Social measurement: Current issues* (pp. 65–115). Beverly Hills, CA: Sage.

Clark, M. L. (1991). Social identity, peer relations, and academic competence of black adolescents. *Education and Urban Society 24,* 41–52.

Clark, R. (1983). *Family Life and School Achievement: Why Poor Black Children Succeed or Fail.* Chicago: University of Chicago Press.

Clark, R. E. (1998). The CANE model of motivation to learn and to work: A two-stage process of goal commitment and effort. In J. Lowyck (Ed.), *Trends in Corporate Training.* Leuven, Belgium: University of Belgium Press.

Cohen, A. M., & Brawer, F. B. (1996). *The American Community College.* San Francisco: Jossey-Bass.

Coleman, J. S. (1990). *Foundations of social theory.* Cambridge: Harvard University Press.

U.S. Department of Education, National Center for Education Statistics (1998). *The Condition of Education 1998,* NCES 98-103. Washington, DC, U.S. Government Printing Office.

Delgado-Gaitan, C. (1991). Involving parents in schools: A process of empowerment. *American Journal of Education, 100* (1), 20–46.

Delpit, L. D. (1988). The silenced dialogue: Power and pedagogy in educating other people's children. *Harvard Educational Review, 58* (3), 280–298.

Dweck, C. S. (1986). Motivational processes affecting learning. *American Psychologist, 41,* 1040–1048.

Dweck, C. S., & Leggett, E. L. (1988). A social-cognitive approach to motivation and personality. *Psychological Review, 95* (2), 256–273.

Funkhouser, J. E., & Gonzales, M. R. (1998). *Family Involvement Children's Education: Successful Local Approaches.* Washington DC: U.S. Department of Education, Office of Research and Education.

Gladieux, L. E., & Swain, W. S. (1998). Financial aid is not enough. *The College Board Review* (185).

Kline, R. B. (1998). *Principles and practice of structural equation modeling.* New York: The Guilford Press.

Kozol, J. (1991). Seasons of darkness. *Teacher Magazine, 3,* (2), 35–45.

Lam, S. F. (1997). *How the family influences children's academic achievement.* (ERIC Document Reproduction Service No. ED 411 095).

Lareau, A. (1987). Social class differences in family-school relationships: The importance of cultural capital. *Sociology in Education, 60* (2), 73–85.

Leslie, L. L., & Oaxaca, R. L. (1998). Women and minorities in higher education. In J. C. Smart (Ed.), *Higher education: Handbook of Theory and Research Vol. 8,* (pp. 304–352). New York: Agathon Press.

Levine, A., & Nidiffer, J. (1996). *Beating the Odds: How the Poor Get to College.* San Francisco: Jossey-Bass.

McDonough, P. (1994). Buying and selling higher education: The social construction of the college applicant. *Journal of Higher Education 4,* 383–402.

Maeroff, G. I. (1999). *Altered destinies: Making Life Better for Schoolchildren in Need.* New York: St. Martin's Press-Griffin.

Mehan, H., Hubbard, L., Lintz, A., & Villanueva, I. (1996). *Constructing School Success: The Consequences of Untracking Low-Achieving Students.* New York: Cambridge University Press.

Middleton, M. J., & Midgley, C. (1997). Avoiding the demonstration of lack of ability: An underexplored aspect of goal theory. *Journal of Educational Psychology, 89* (4), 710–718.

National Center for Research to Improve Postsecondary Teaching and Learning (NCRIPTAL). (1991). *A manual for the use of motivated strategies for learning questionnaire (MSLQ)* (Technical Report 91-B-004). Ann Arbor, MI: The Regents of the University of Michigan.

Newcomb, M. D. (1990). What structural modeling techniques can tell us about social support. In I. G. Sarason, B. R. Sarason & G. R. Pierce (Eds.), *Social Support: An Interactional View* (pp. 26–63). New York: Wiley and Sons.

Nicholls, J. (1984). Achievement motivation: Conceptions of ability, subjective experience, task choice, and performance. *Psychological Review, 91,* 328–346.

Nicholls, J., Cheung, P., Lauer, J., & Pataschnick, M. (1989). Individual differences in academic motivation: Perceived ability, goals, beliefs, and values. *Learning and Individual Differences, 1,* 63–84.

Pajares, F. (1996). Self-efficacy beliefs in academic settings. *Review of Educational Research, 66* (4), 543–578.

Phipps, R. (1998). College remediation: What it is, what it costs, what's at stake. Washington, DC; The Institute for Higher Education Policy.

Pintrich, P. R., & Schrauben, B. (1992). A social cognitive model of student motivation. In D. H. Schunk & J. L. Meece (Eds.), *Students' Perceptions in the Classroom* (pp. 149–159). Hillsdale, NJ: Erlbaum.

Pintrich, P. R., & Schunk, D. H. (1996). *Motivation in Education: Theory, Research, and Applications.* Englewood Cliffs, NJ: Prentice-Hall.

Reisetter, M., & Schraw, G. (1998). *The Multi-Dimensionality of Goal Orientations: A Qualitative Study.* Paper presented at AERA annual conference, San Diego, CA.

Roedel, T. D., Schraw, G., & Plake, B. S. (1994). Validation of a measure of learning and performance goal orientations. *Educational and Psychological Measurement, 54* (4), 1013–1021.

Schunk, D. H. (1996). *Self-evaluation and self-regulated learning.* Paper presented at the Graduate School and University Center, CUNY, New York.

Shorkey, C. T., & Saski, J. (1983). A low reading-level version of the Rational Behavior Inventory. *Measurement and Evaluation in Guidance, 46,* 95–98.

Shorkey, C. T., & Whiteman, V. L. (1977). Development of the rational behavior inventory: Initial validity and reliability. *Educational and Psychological Measurement, 37,* 527–533.

Skaalvik, E. M. (1997). Self-enhancing and self-defeating ego orientation: Relations with task and avoidance orientation, achievement, self-perceptions, and anxiety. *Journal of Educational Psychology, 89* (1), 71–81.

U.S. Bureau of the Census (1997). *Educational attainment, by race, and Hispanic origin.* [http:/ www. census.gov/population/www/socdemo/ education.html].

U.S. Department of Education, National Center for Education Statistics (2000), *The Condition of Education 2000,* (NCES 2000–062), Washington, DC: U.S. Government Printing Office.

Weiner, B. (1990). History of motivational research in education. *Journal of Educational Psychology, 82* (4), 616–622.

Zimmerman, B. J., & Martinez-Pons, M. (1990). Student differences in self-regulated learning: Relating grade, sex, and giftedness to self-efficacy and strategy use. *Journal of Educational Psychology, 82,* 51–59.

Zimmerman, B. J., Bandura, A., & Martinez-Pons, M. (1992). Self-motivation for academic attainment: The role of self-efficacy beliefs and personal goal setting. *American Educational Research Journal, 29* (3), 663–676.

INCREASING AFRICAN AMERICANS' PARTICIPATION IN HIGHER EDUCATION

AFRICAN AMERICAN HIGH-SCHOOL STUDENTS' PERSPECTIVES

KASSIE FREEMAN

Researchers and policymakers rarely include the individuals who are the focus of their studies in the development of solutions to their own problems. Although individuals or groups are often asked their opinions about their plight, they are seldom asked to participate in the development of programs or models that will improve their lives. The very individuals who would be most affected and who should be the first to be consulted are not given a voice in the dialogue, as if they had no stake in these important decisions that determine the course of the policies that will affect their lives. The process of deciding how to increase African Americans' participation in higher education, one of the most important commodities for upward mobility in our society, provides a prime example. African American high-school students are rarely, if ever, asked for their perceptions of the problems or, more important, for their ideas about possible solutions.

My intent in this study was to explore African American high-school students' perceptions of barriers to African Americans' participation in higher education and to explore their perceptions of effective programs for addressing the problems. In particular, this study asked two primary questions: What are the barriers African Americans face in their decision to participate in higher education? What are the solutions that African American students recommend to increase African Americans' participation in higher education? Of particular interest was how these students' responses could add to college choice and economics of education literature and to policy making.

This study is a qualitative inquiry across a range of cities, schools, and family circumstances, and it was intentionally designed to give African American students an opportunity to express their perceptions in their own voices. The study concludes that such voices provide valuable insights for researchers and policymakers.

Research in Context

There is still reason for great concern about African Americans' participation in higher education. The most recent (1994) *Status on Minorities in Higher Education* report indicates that African Americans continue to trail Whites in their rate of college participation by 9% (42% to 32.9%). The editors, Carter

Reprinted by permission from *Journal of Higher Education* 68, no. 5 (September–October 1997).

and Wilson (1994) in this thirteenth annual status report indicate that, in fact, "overall, the 1993 college participation rate for African American high-school graduates showed little change from 1992" and that African Americans had "experienced little improvement in college participation since 1990, when they posted a rate of 33 percent" (p. 2). The 1992 *Status on Minorities in Higher Education* report indicated that "unlike enrollment figures, which provide a snapshot of college attendance for a particular period, participation rates track both the current enrollment and the recent postsecondary attendance patterns of a given age group, particularly youth ages 18 to 24" (Wilson, 1992, p. 6). According to that report, the participation rate of African Americans in higher education in 1991 showed a 1.8% decline from 1990.

Findings on African Americans' participation in higher education from the 1994 *Status on Minorities in Higher Education* report are particularly troubling, because educators and economists are in agreement on the importance of increasing African Americans' participation in higher education. Reports such as that of the Hudson Institute Workforce 2000 have indicated that by the twenty-first century, one of three jobs will require schooling beyond the secondary level. In his book *Faded Dreams,* Carnoy (1995) discussed the importance of African Americans increasing their educational opportunities. More specifically, Simms (1994) discussed the direct relationship between higher education and African Americans' participation in the economy.

Other economics of education theorists (i.e., Becker, 1975; Cohen 1979; Freeman, R., 1976; Schultz, 1961; Thurow, 1972) have documented that although White Americans, over time, receive a higher return on their investment in higher education than African Americans, those African Americans who do attend higher education institutions fare better than those who do not. Previous research findings (Freeman, K., 1989) on the difference between White Americans' and African Americans' return on investment in graduate business training (using seven of the MBA programs that comprise the Consortium schools) revealed that African American MBA graduates in those programs received higher starting salaries, on average, than did White Americans. African Americans who receive a higher education also benefit themselves and society non-monetarily. For instance, those African Americans who are educated are more likely to educate their children.

Even though these findings suggest that African Americans are better off attending higher education institutions, the 1994 *Status on Minorities in Higher Education* report indicated that the African American college participation rate in the 1990s has fluctuated between stagnation and decline and that although the 1990s have shown a slight increase in African American enrollment in higher education, there is still a sizeable gap between White American and African American participation.

Much of the research on the cause of stagnation or decline in African American college participation has focused on the increasing investment students need to make to obtain a higher education, brought about, for example, by rising tuition costs and a decline in financial aid. (Nettles, 1988; Wilson, 1989). Little research has been conducted on African Americans' perception of the value of a college degree (the return on investment). Is it worth the cost? The recent cutback in funding for higher education specific to minorities makes it even more imperative to derive new ways of motivating African Americans to attend college.

Researchers have tended to focus on increasing the motivation and aspiration of African American students to attend higher education while excluding cultural considerations; the prescription for attracting and retaining students has been based on models that have paid little, if any, attention to the heritage and culture of African Americans. Moreover, through their policies and practices, policymakers and educators alike have tended to focus on remedies for increasing African American students' participation in higher education with little or no input from the students themselves.

Few studies have given voice to African American students, who are the ones that are in the best place to assess the problems and judge the programs that have most benefited them or their peers. By all accounts, the college choice process for African American high-school students is a complicated process, which necessarily has to take into consideration the context of their culture; otherwise, the solutions could be based on models that may not fit the circumstances of these students. It has been my intent with this research to review previous background information on the choice process and at the same time allow these students to voice their own personal accounts. In order to increase African American students' participation in higher education—and it is obvious that current models are not working—it is critical that educators and policymakers better understand how these students, based on their experiences, perceive what has worked for them and will work for others like them.

College Choice: To Participate or Not to Participate in Higher Education

Although there is much that researchers know about the process of choosing a college education, there is still much to learn about the decision-making process of underrepresented groups. Many questions are still unanswered: Are the influences that determine the choice to go to college the same for different cultural groups? At what age does the process to choose higher education begin? What role does econometrics really play in the process for groups such as African Americans? What role does secondary school play in the college choice process of underrepresented groups? Although these and other questions remain unanswered, this research explores what has been written about the majority culture to determine similarities and differences as they relate to African American students' perceptions.

Most of the recent college choice research focuses on college destination (Hearn, 1991; McDonough, Antonio, & Trent, 1995), better understanding of college matriculation decisions (Hossler & Vesper, 1993), or the marketing of colleges (Litten, Sullivan, & Brodigan, 1983; McDonough, 1994). However, much of this research—and even the multitude of earlier research that focused on how students choose to participate in postsecondary schooling—overlooked or did not include factors that were culture specific (Alexander et al., 1978; Alwin & Otto, 1977; Anderson & Hearn, 1992; Boyle, 1966; Hossler & Gallagher, 1987; Mortenson, 1991; Stage & Hossler, 1989). For example, although research certainly focused on social and cultural capital, it usually assessed these issues across all groups, not specifically the cultures of groups individually. Bourdieu and Passeron (1977), for example, tend to be the most widely cited on the topic of cultural capital; yet, it is not clear what their specific experiences have been with different cultures within the United States. The intent of the research presented here is to point out that although many theories on how students choose to participate in a college education are applicable to students of all socioeconomic groups, researchers recognize the need to better understand the choice process for minority students (Hossler, Braxton, & Coopersmith, 1989; McDonough, Antonio, & Trent, 1995).

Discussions of aspiration and decision making about attending higher education generally focus on cultural and social capital, economics and financial capital, or some combination of the two (Hossler, Braxton, & Coopersmith, 1989). However, Orfield et al. (1984) conducted a comprehensive study of access and choice in higher education in Chicago, which concluded that minorities are channeled into college based on defined geographic locations—where they live. Although most choice theorists would include the concept of channeling—a concept that is greatly underexamined—under the cultural and social models of decision making, it was considered separately in the framework for this study.

Cultural and Social Capital

In simplest terms, the concepts of cultural and social capital mean assets, in the form of behaviors, on which individuals and/or families can draw to meet a certain set of established values in a society. These societal values are generally established by majority groups in society and encompass such behaviors as the way individuals speak and the way they dress. The more individuals are able to meet these established standards, the more they are accepted by different institutions (e.g., schools) in society. Researchers such as DiMaggio and Mohr (1985) have suggested that cultural capital is typically a set of specialized social behaviors that makes one accepted at different levels of society. Other theorists (e.g., Coleman, 1990) have indicated that although social capital is related to cultural capital, it is more related to relations among persons. For example, Coleman (1988) explains social capital as the networks that provide information, social norms, and achievement support.

There is no doubt, however, that the cultural and social capital that students bring to the primary school classroom has tremendous implications for how they will be accepted, treated, and given the necessary information on which to make choices that will lead to postsecondary schooling. According to Cicourel and Mehan (1985), students are provided different educational opportunities because they arrive in school with different types of culture capital. It is generally accepted that African Americans do not bring the same kind of social and cultural capital to the classroom as Whites bring. It may have been this very underexplored phenomenon that led Orfield et al. (1984) to indicate that some researchers had posited a theory that Blacks and Whites form aspirations in different ways and to say, "There has been little exploration of the social consequences of the huge gap between Black hopes and the reality of higher education for Blacks" (p. 16).

The sociological model of student choice (which is the umbrella model for cultural and social capital), at least as described by Hossler, Braxton, and Coopersmith (1989), focuses on the factors that influence aspiration. This model describes family socioeconomic level and student academic ability as predictors of students' aspiration for college. It is important to note that in a study with socioeconomic status held constant, African Americans were more likely than Whites to begin college (Olivas, cited in Orfield et al., 1984, p. 34).

Hossler, Braxton, and Coopersmith further indicate that expectations from others, such as parents, teachers, and friends, also influence student aspiration. According to Orfield et al. (1984), next to socioeconomic status, the secondary school a student attends is the primary structure that provides access to college. It is the school curriculum (academic vs. technical-vocational), counseling (regarding college availability and preparation), and grading that have tremendous impact on students' choice to participate or not to participate in higher education.

However, if it is the case, as some theorists (Bourdieu & Passeron, 1977; Coleman, 1988, 1990; Collins, 1979) have suggested, that postsecondary aspiration and high-school academic decision making grow out of the cultural and social capital of families, it seems logical that aspiration and choice are based on culture and not necessarily on societal (elite) values. It is ironic that models to increase aspiration have generally been based on society at large, completely ignoring the culture, in this case, of African Americans.

Econometric Model and Financial Capital

In addition to cultural and social capital as one of the major rationales for how students choose college participation, the econometric model and financial capital have also been postulated as rationales in the decision-making process (Anderson & Hearn, 1992; Hossler, Braxton, & Coopersmith, 1989; Orfield et al., 1984). In the econometric model, as these college choice theorists and economics of education theorists (i.e., Becker, 1975; Cohn, 1979; Johns, Morphet, & Alexander, 1983) have suggested, expected costs and future earnings expected from attending college are the primary considerations that impact students' perception of the value of higher education, although economic status, race, and education of parents may also have bearing on future earning potential.

The notion of future earning potential as it relates to African American students' participation in higher education has been a very much underexplored topic. For example, Barnes (1992) completed a study on African American twelfth-grade male stayins (those who were persisting through high school), and in their responses found the following about those students' economic goals: "It is interesting that 43.7 percent indicated they wanted to become wealthy or comfortable rather than identify an occupation" (p. 96).

Socioeconomic factors, such as parental income level, occupation, educational level, and number of siblings, are also posited as indicators of students' choices regarding college participation (Alwin & Otto, 1977; Anderson & Hearn, 1992; Boyle, 1966; Hossler & Gallagher, 1987). Parental income and educational level have both a direct and an indirect effect on college choice. Indirectly, the lower the parental income and education levels, the less information they will have available to assist their children with financial decision making. Directly, as stated by Orfield et al. (1984), "Family income is viewed as causing inequalities in educational access" (p. 30). As an example, "Because family income is much lower for minority students than for

White students, the former are three to four times more dependent on federal financial aid than the latter" (Morris, cited in Orfield et al., 1984, p. 25).

Although research is replete with information about the impact that the lack of financial aid has on participation in higher education (Cross & Astin, 1981; Nettles, 1988), what is increasingly clear is that there is a void in understanding how, in their decision-making process on college participation, different cultural groups interpret or perceive the expectations of future earnings.

Channeling

The term channeling can be defined as the environmental forces (whether individuals, institutions, or circumstances) that influence the direction of students' choice. Channeling, as it relates to college choice, cuts across social and cultural capital and economic and financial capital. That is, the more capital an individual has, whether cultural or economic, the more likely it is that he or she will be influenced by forces internal to the home. Aside from the influences inside the home, students are also channeled by influences outside the home in directions that impact their decision-making process to participate in higher education.

Outside the home, high-school teachers and counselors have tremendous influence on channeling students to choose or not to choose college participation (Barnes, 1992; Morrison, 1989; Orfield et al., 1984). According to Barnes (1992), 47.5% of the African American twelfth-grade male stay-ins in her study reported that "assignment to excellent teachers helped keep them in school" (p. 106). She further stated, "It seems clear that one way to hold African-American males' attention and keep them interested in their school work is to assign them the best teachers in school. These teachers will hold their interest, educate them, and help them graduate" (p. 106).

Counselors play an equally important function. Morrison (1989) wrote, "An opportunity for minority students and their parents to engage in programs that provide current institutional information, a visual campus overview, interaction with faculty and alumni, and questions and answers can be of considerable benefit" (pp. 13–14). It typically is the school counselors who help facilitate this process for high-school students.

As further support of the importance of environmental influences on students' decision making, one of the most recent studies that specifically investigated the choice process of underrepresented groups was a study by Levine and Nidiffer (1996). In their book *Beating the Odds: How the Poor Get to College,* they analyzed interviews of 24 students from impoverished conditions, including African American students. They found a common theme among their subjects in their comments on "how they came to attend college" (p. 65). This common element, "was an individual who touched or changed the students' lives" (p. 65). Similarly, this was found to be a frequent comment of the students who were interviewed for this study.

The quality of high school understandably also has implications for whether students will choose college participation (Alexander et al., 1978; Anderson & Hearn, 1992; Boyle, 1966). For example, students at the top of their class in an inner-city school are less likely than their counterparts in a suburban school to have had access to college recruiters, are less likely to have visited a college campus, and are less likely to have had access even to the basic information necessary for college choice. Students who attend private/independent schools and suburban schools would more likely be influenced and channeled to attend higher education institutions than students who attend inner-city high schools. More than the location of the school itself, it is the services these schools provide—the assistance of teachers and counselors. "Schools in affluent suburbs encourage college attendance and channel their students into college preparatory curricula; schools in poor or working class neighborhoods tend to prepare students for jobs not requiring college training" (Jencks, cited in Orfield et al., 1984, p. 28).

Channeling, when used effectively, can mediate social and cultural differences, can impact the financial aid process and the economic outlook of students, and can influence the type of postsecondary school that is selected and the subsequent college experiences. As Orfield et al. (1984) explained, in discussing the concept of channeling, "Changes in the school situation can change outcomes" (p. 28).

In summary, research from student choice theorists has provided information for understanding the factors that motivate majority students to participate in higher education. New research has been helpful in finding some common influences on the underrepresented poor (Levine & Nidiffer, 1996); however, additional research on the specific factors that influence African American students' motivation and aspiration to attend postsecondary schooling is sorely lacking. Hossler, Braxton, and Coopersmith (1989) and Orfield et al. (1984) have suggested that further research is necessary to examine minority motivation and aspiration to attend or not to attend a college or university. The research presented in this article contends that the best way to understand the motivating factors impacting the choice of African Americans to participate in higher education is to ask African American students, for they are in the best position to assess the problems and to offer possible solutions.

Design of the Study

To investigate the questions raised in this study, a qualitative inquiry method using groups was utilized. Why the qualitative approach? The voices of students are rarely heard in the debates regarding their lives, and the voices of disempowered students are even more silent, as stated by Nieto (1992). The purpose of this approach—using group interviews—was to allow a greater and more diverse number of African American students a voice and thus to provide a deeper understanding of their consideration of the value of higher education. According to Nieto (1992), qualitative studies can enable us to examine "particular situations so that solutions can be hypothesized and developed" (p. 5).

Data Collection Procedures

The data for this research were gathered through structured group interviews. A protocol was developed for the interviews based on pilot testing of a survey that was administered to a sampling of students in an inner-city school and in a private school in Atlanta, Georgia. (Atlanta was selected as a test site because of convenience of location.) After reviewing the responses on the survey, the researcher was left with many unanswered questions. The students' write-in responses indicated a desire to explain more about their answers, and therefore group interviews, as outlined by Nieto (1992), were determined to be an effective means of hearing students' voices.

Although there was a formal protocol, the interviews and guiding questions were generally flexible and informal in order to allow students to express their issues and concerns more freely. For better control of reliability in the questioning process, the researcher personally conducted all of the focus group interviews. The interviews were audiotaped, and the tapes were transcribed by a professional transcriber. The data were reread several times to confirm coding.

Primary patterns and themes in the interview transcripts were evaluated based on procedures outlined in Miles and Huberman (1984), who explain that "pattern codes are explanatory or inferential codes, ones that identify an emergent theme, pattern, or explanation" (p. 67), and further, that "the bedrock of inquiry is the researcher's quest for repeatable regularities" (p. 67). The data were analyzed using what Miles and Huberman (1984) refer to as a "start list," a deductive approach and cross-group analysis. A master list of codes was developed around the conceptual framework, the pilot test, and the research questions, using general categories with descriptive marginal remarks. Based on the master codes, cross-group analysis was used to determine commonality in themes and patterns among the responses of the different groups.

Student and Site Selection

Focus group sessions were conducted in each of five cities that have large African American populations (Atlanta, Chicago, Los Angeles, New York, and Washington, DC). These cities were selected based on the previous work of Neimi (1974) and Simms (1995). Both indicated that these cities have the largest cross-section of African American populations, and Simms further noted that they are among the metropolitan cities where African Americans have the highest median income and lowest poverty rates.

Group interviews included African American students (male and female) in tenth, eleventh, and twelfth grades. These grades were the focus of this study because it is typically in these grades that students already have formed their perceptions about the worth of the investment in postsecondary education. In order to include a cross-section of school types, students in inner-city, suburban, magnet, and private schools (private and independent are used interchangeably throughout this article) in these cities were included.

As a first step, school board administrators in each city were asked to recommend schools based on the researcher's request for the stated school types. In each school, the principal or headmaster selected the group participants based on criteria the researcher outlined: all African Americans, equal number by gender, grade, and socioeconomic background (particularly in private schools). It is often difficult to gain access to private schools to conduct research; therefore, when this study was given the support of the National Association of Independent Schools, it was decided to oversample private/independent schools to obtain as much research data as possible from this school type. In addition, the researcher wanted to assess the differences in responses to the research questions by students from different socioeconomic levels within the African American race. Such a cross-section of schools, particularly private schools with African American students, would be inclusive of a broader range of socioeconomic levels.

A total of 70 students participated in 16 group interviews. The breakdown by school, gender, and grade is as noted in Table 1. In the inner-city school in New York and in one of the inner-city schools in Washington, DC, interviews were conducted with two small classes. In each case, one class was college preparatory and one class was not college bound. Because these classes were much larger in size than the groups, the numbers are not included in the total participant numbers in Table 1; however, the responses

TABLE 1
Profile of School Participants in African American High School Focus Groups

				Gender		Grade Level		
School Type	*School Location*	*No. of Schools*	*Participants*	*Male*	*Female*	*12th*	*11th*	*10th*
Inner-City								
	Chicago	2						
	School A		2	1	1	1	1	0
	School B		4	2	2	3	1	0
	New York*	1						
	Washington, DC	2						
	School A		3	0	3	1	0	2
	School B*							
Magnet								
	Chicago	1	6	3	3	3	3	0
	Los Angeles	1	4	1	3	1	3	0
	Washington, DC	1	5	2	3	3	0	2
Private								
	Atlanta	1	5	3	2	5	0	0
	Chicago	2						
	School A		6	3	3	5	1	0
	School B		7	3	4	3	2	2
	Los Angeles	2						
	School A		5	2	3	2	2	1
	School B		5	2	3	1	2	2
	New York	2						
	School A		6	1	5	3	2	1
	School B		5	2	3	0	0	5
Suburban								
	Atlanta	1	7	6	1	7	0	0
Totals		16	70	31	39	38	17	15

*At the request of school officials, intact classes were interviewed as groups; therefore, the number of individual participants is not relevant to this table.

of students from these classes were coded and are included in the analysis. In group analysis it is acceptable to include these responses, because the study was designed to find patterns and themes based on the theoretical framework and the research questions. Though it is recognized that there is an uneven distribution of school types across cities, the diversity and the number of schools and students participating in the study allowed a representative sampling.

The background of the students varied, but there were some commonalities. In most cases, across school types, the students were first generation college-goers—most were from homes where the parents were not formally (college/university) educated. Though students were not asked any questions about income, because the researcher's interest was in the students' responses in the aggregate, the school distribution provided a basis for assumptions about income level. That is, it would not be expected that the income of parents of students who attended inner-city schools is as high as that of parents of students who attend private schools. It is important to note, however, that several African American students in private/independent schools were on scholarships.

Data Analysis

As a result of the pilot test it was decided that the best way to examine students' perceptions of the value of higher education was to ask questions in a way that was not specific to their own college plans. One of the high-school principals said that American society places so much emphasis on higher education that for students to answer that they do not plan to attend a higher education institution following graduation or that they do not perceive higher education to be worth the cost automatically makes them feel as if they were a failure. Martin Carnoy of Stanford University (personal communication, 1991) indicated that if the question is made specific to the student, the student's response might imply that higher education is worth the investment, but "for other people not me."

Thus, to encourage students to express their perceptions of the barriers (costs) to African Americans' participation in higher education, my question to them was, "Will you help me to better understand why there seems to be a lack of interest among African American high-school graduates regarding participation in higher education." In this way, students could more freely describe the barriers they perceived. This guiding question also served the two-fold purpose of eliciting not only statements of barriers to participation but also expressions of student-perceived "solutions" to these barriers. Themes were developed from the most frequently stated responses by the students. As Levine and Nidiffer (1996) noted about the findings from the interviews of their subjects: "When asked how they came to attend college, each of them told almost the same story" (p. 65). Although the students in this sampling attended different school types and lived in different geographic regions, their responses varied little. It was like listening to the same song—different school, different city.

Students Discuss the Issues

Across school types and cities, four themes emerged from students' responses about their perceptions of barriers to African Americans' participation in higher education. These responses can basically be grouped into two broad categories: (1) economic barriers and (2) psychological barriers (see Figure 1). The responses relating to economic barriers can be described as a fear of (a) not having enough money to attend college or (b) not getting a job that pays appropriate to the level of education after completing higher education. In regard to psychological barriers, which appear to pose even greater challenges to educators and policymakers, the students' responses stressed three issues: (a) college never being an option, (b) the loss of hope, and (c) the intimidation factor. The students' responses to these issues were surprisingly similar across school types.

Economic Barriers

Money and Jobs

The students' answers were either related to fear of not getting a job that pays adequately or of not having enough money to attend college. For example, a student attending a suburban school in Atlanta stated the following:

> A lot of people lose hope in college. They pass, and they are still not making a lot of money. They are still struggling.

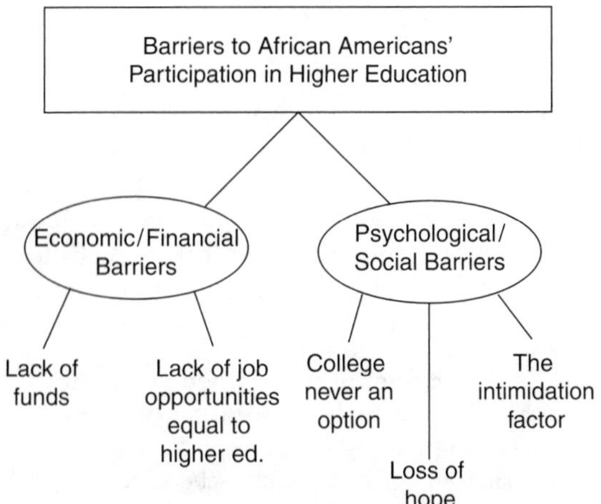

Figure 1 African American High-School Students' Perceptions of Barriers to African Americans' Participation in Higher Education

A student attending an independent school in Atlanta responded:

> It does not guarantee a job. [They] may not see the point.

That statement was echoed in many different ways by students across the country. In one independent school in Chicago, a student responded:

> People are unaware that there are opportunities out there after college. People just kind of see it as: you get out of college and then what do you do?

At an independent school in New York, a student said this:

> Well, maybe, because a lot of times when you are growing up, you might get the feeling and the outlook that, you know, it makes no sense because the jobs are not out there. A lot of people feel that way, like, "Why am I going through all this when I am not going to get a job, a job equivalent to what I would get if I didn't go? So what's the point." I know a lot of people feel that way.

The responses of students in inner-city schools more often focused on making money. They spoke of the need to have an income during and immediately after high school instead of postponing earning wages for four more years. For example, at an inner-city school in Chicago, a student responded in this way:

> They [high-school students] start making so much money.

The issue of lack of money to attend college was also a concern expressed by students across cities and school types. One student at a suburban school in Atlanta responded with a statement that was frequently repeated by the students:

> They don't have money to go.

Another student attending an inner-city school in Washington, DC, simply stated:

> Money.

Psychological Barriers

College Never an Option

Another rationale that students often expressed as to why there was a decline in African Americans' participation in higher education was that college had never been presented as an option. The responses here centered on several factors, such as not being pushed by parents or by school personnel or, generally, as not receiving encouragement from anyone. A student at an independent school in Los Angeles passionately stated this:

> Well, from personal experience, friends of mine are just not interested in college at all. They are into sports or something like that. It just seems that there is just not a want to go to college. People just don't want to do it. When I ask them, "Well, what are you going to do when you graduate from high school?" they don't know, but college has never been given to them as an option. It's never given. I don't know if that starts in the home with parents.

At an inner-city school in New York, a student had this to say:

> Parents. Some parents say like, "You are not going to go to school."

A student attending a magnet high school in Chicago responded in this way:

> Well, I think part of the problem is like you don't have anybody to help you, to want you to excel, to inspire you that you need to get a higher education, to help you understand that "we are here for you, and we are going to help you get through this."

A magnet school student in Los Angeles responded in a similar manner:

> There seems to be a decline, I think, because there is motivation but it is coming from the wrong people. A lot of people are not as strong as myself, for instance, and you might need to hear you need to go to college from somebody else. I am not the one you want to tell you. You might need your parent or your best friend to tell you. They are not the ones telling you.

Loss of Hope

The third theme that emerged out of this question was that students lose hope, which in some ways is similar to the previous theme—college never given as an option. It differs in that students seemed to be saying here that African Americans are missing a passion for pursuing higher education or that the benefits of college are not recognized. For example, a student at an independent school in Los Angeles said,

> One of the things that I was really upset about in the school systems [public], how they took a lot of the fine arts, and that upset me, because kids—I mean I know that I did—need a passion, and they need something to look for, a goal. They need to say, "Well, I can go there, I will achieve my goal," and I think a lot of people don't have the drive, unfortunately.

A student attending another private school in Los Angeles echoed that response:

> There is a negative influence, and people don't have hope any more for the future. I know a lot of people like that. They don't care anymore. They just don't care about their future, and they don't have any hope.

At a suburban school in Atlanta, a student had this response:

> You watch TV, and you watch, like, movies, and you see kids stressed out and struggling in college and stuff. They don't want to go through all that.

In Chicago, a student attending an inner-city school perceived it in this way:

> Most [students] just want to live a ghetto life. Because they belong to a gang at a young age, they don't come to school; the whole school is a gang bang. They don't come to school.

The Intimidation Factor

The final and most prevalent theme that emerged in response to the interviewer's question was what students referred to as the "intimidation factor." Interestingly, students attending independent schools generally held this perception about students attending inner-city schools. A student attending a private school in Chicago stated the following:

> I think that a lot of times when you go to public school, higher education can be a really intimidating factor, especially if you go to like an inner-city public school, because you are used to seeing, you know, nothing but Black people going to school. If you see a White person at your school, hey, they are rare. But when you go to higher education, it seems as though that's really all you see, and you are sort of intimidated by these people who may not have necessarily gone to an independent school but who have had the benefit of a White education.

Students attending public schools who had visited a college/university campus were more likely to agree with that assessment than those who had not visited a campus. For example, a student attending a suburban school in Atlanta, said the following after an overnight stay at a university:

> I went and stayed overnight at a university in Georgia, and I got to see how things are after classes and stuff, how they act. To tell you the truth, before I visited it, I was more excited about going there. After I visited it and saw a lot of the people there, it seems like they are not used to being around [Blacks]. That visit kind of turned me more off than on.

By way of explanation, he offered the following:

> I visited such and such college, and I go there and everybody, well most of the people there are White, there is not a lot of Black people. To me I have always been around all Blacks. I just don't see myself being comfortable around [them], having a White person for a roommate. I just know that I am going to have to adjust when I go.

These students were asked whether they believed that the American society overemphasizes higher education participation. The intent of the question was to further understand if they perceived the worth of an investment in higher education for African Americans in general. Across school types, these students believed that not enough emphasis is placed on higher education participation. For example, a student in an inner-city school in Chicago said,

> I don't. I mean, because I feel that there is not enough emphasis put on it, you know, pressuring a child to go to college. You have to. You can't even get a job at McDonald's without a high-school diploma. So just imagine what, say four more years, five more years for me, 1999, I couldn't even probably get a job, period. Nowhere. So I don't think there is enough emphasis put on it—about going to college.

At another inner-city school in Chicago, a student stated something similar:

> It is a big deal. You want to become something better.

In New York at an inner-city school, a student responded,

> The world is changing; you have to get more than a college education now. You have got to have more than a college education.

A student in a private school in Chicago remarked,

> I mean people whose families haven't gone to college or haven't gotten asked if they should go to college. I think those families don't think about going to college, and I think that's bad. I think that people should figure out a way to make everyone understand that college is really an important part of what you do.

In sum, in spite of these students' perceived costs to African Americans' participation in higher education, they still perceived that the benefits far outweigh the costs. That is, they perceived that this country does not emphasize the benefits of participation in higher education enough.

Students Offer Solutions

The students did not hesitate to voice their opinions about what models were needed to increase African Americans' participation in higher education—it was as though they were waiting to be asked. As evidence of the seriousness of their thoughts about ways to increase African American students' participation in higher education, it is important to note how their suggestions for solutions are closely aligned to their perceptions of the barriers. Notable also, is the similarity of the students' responses across geographic regions, school types, socioeconomic levels, and gender.

The sense of being accepted for who they are and having someone who encourages them to maximize their potential were the themes that were stressed most often. It is not surprising, then, that many students expressed "teaching other people about their culture" as one possible solution. Another response that was frequently voiced was having "more Black teachers—who want to be there." In fact, according to these students, what happens inside the walls of schools holds great importance for motivating African American students to participate in higher education. Therefore, the themes that emerged from these students' suggestions for solutions mostly centered on the conditions of the place where students are being taught—how schools are equipped, who is teaching, how they are teaching, and what they are teaching as it relates to who they are. Their responses can be classified into the following categories: (a) improve school conditions, (b) provide interested teachers and active counselors, (c) instill possibilities early, and (d) expand cultural awareness. (See Figure 2 for students' suggestions for programs/models.)

A student attending an independent school in Los Angeles captured the essence of the students' responses across cities when he stated the following:

> I think that if we were to start a program, it would start in the elementary school and junior high school; in my opinion the kids would be more interested in learning then, [and] they would want to go to college and learn more. I think that the schools themselves in the Black neighborhoods [would], if more money was put into them, if [they had] better teachers. My hat is off to teachers, but I think that teachers need to be paid more to make them want to teach more. I think that if we do that and then still if African Americans are not excited about going to college, then we need a program; then I think we really need to just upgrade and improve the schools in our neighborhoods.

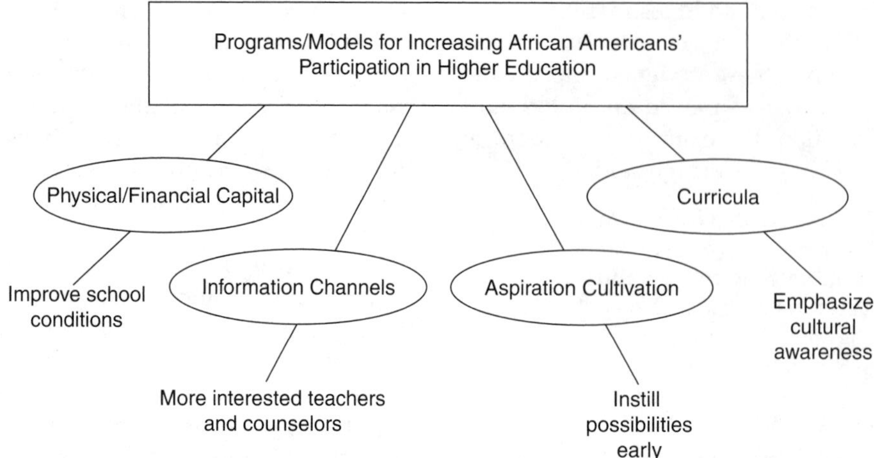

Figure 2 African American High-School Students' Suggestions for Programs/Models to Increase African Americans' Participation in Higher Education

Improve School Conditions

The suggestion of the need to improve the conditions of the schools was stated frequently—the need to improve the physical condition of the building as well as the contents of the building, such as having more computers available for students. The following statements were heard from students across school types and across cities:

> My cousin, she still lives in DC and she is still in elementary school, but for like the first three years up to the third grade she went to the same elementary school that I went to, and from the time I had been there until then it had just been in a steady decline, so finally my aunt just took her out and put her in a White school. [To transfer her child to another public school] she had to either lie or pay a fine or something. But [at] all costs she said, "My kid can't go to this school." At this White school, it is like four stories, huge and sprawling with lockers and science rooms, but in the other school, it was dingy, with cockroaches, rats. She used to hate to read; she used to scream and cry when she used to have to read. Now she comes home and starts her homework. She reads for pleasure now. That's the reason why I know that if the schools were improved, they would have a chance. (Independent school student, Los Angeles)

> I know the reason why we don't have the things we need; it's because we are a minority school. Because my cousin goes to another high school, and they have a computer at every desk. We have a computer lab. You have to make an appointment to go the computer lab because it is always full. (Magnet school student, Los Angeles)

> The school must know what it wants to do. (Independent school student, New York)

More Interested Teachers and Actively Involved Counselors

Even more frequently stated than the need to improve schools, interested teachers and active counselors were repeatedly suggested as ways to motivate students to participate in higher education. The students placed greater emphasis on their perceived value of having teachers who instill a passion in students, who believe in African American students' ability to learn, and who push students to maximize their potential. Students voiced their opinions about the role of the teachers in motivating students in this way:

> I have been fortunate enough to have a teacher who made me work for everything. Mr. Sweeney [name changed] is a real mathematics teacher. Some other mathematics teacher might not be as good, but what I learned was college math analysis, and that is because Mr. Sweeney got out his paycheck and went and bought these college prep books. (Magnet school student, Los Angeles)

> . . . then also have a lot of Black teachers. (Independent school student, New York)

> A program, like a different type of teaching program. Like [now] most students are in the chairs, and teachers are at the board. I think

more discussions should be involved in the classrooms and not so much reading the books. (Inner-city school student, New York)

Enthusiastic teachers come across interesting. Teachers are everything. (Independent school student, New York)

There are not that many Black teachers here at all. I mean, this school is an excellent school for an education, but it would probably even be better. (Independent school student, Chicago)

I think it's school. I don't have many friends outside of school, but the couple that I do have, the way they [describe it], it's like the teachers don't even care if they come to school everyday and stuff like that, and I don't know if it's exaggerated, but it is completely different from here. (Independent school student, Chicago)

Teachers and friends, or something, encourage them to go on with their education. (Inner-city school student, Washington, DC)

You know, I had teachers who, like, were strong. They motivated you to do your work and helped you a lot. I think some schools in the Black community, they don't have enough money to buy books that will teach the kids; so, you know, the teachers don't want to teach it, then it is not good material and the students don't want to learn. So I think it is like you got to get your money together, put it in the schools where it counts, you know, and help these kids. (Independent school student, Los Angeles)

In addition to some students' stated responses about the importance of having counselors actively involved in the process to increase African American students' participation in higher education, observations and conversations with school officials confirmed students' statements. It was personally noted by the researcher that in those schools that had structured counseling programs, there tended to be a greater number of students interested in higher education participation. As would be expected, the private schools had active college-related events, and in those public schools that did have active counseling programs, the success in stimulating and preparing students to participate in higher education seemed equal to that of private schools. The following statements demonstrate how strongly students felt about active counselor involvement in assisting students in the college process:

Because we are pushed. We are pushed to go on to higher education and then get a job. That's Ms. Getter's [name changed] whole basis [for] being here basically. (Magnet school student, Los Angeles)

Maybe get some college programs in high school. To prepare them for college so they won't go and be scared what it is going to be. (Inner-city school student, New York)

Counselors generally have the information as far as scholarships. Certain counselors have information about internships, different opportunities for us so that you can get to work, specific jobs where you get to go into that field of your interest to see if that's what you really want to do. If you keep in contact with these individuals [counselors] then, I mean, these who haven't really had, have the opportunity. (Magnet school student, Washington, DC)

Counselors do not help. They discourage you, especially in public schools. They tell you such things as, "You are not qualified." They do not care. (Independent school student, New York)

I have got career beginnings. It's a program to help me decide what college I want to go to and where. And [it] helps you with your financial aid. (Inner-city school student, Chicago)

They let us know about upcoming scholarships from this point on. They have something like a senior letter, and every time a new scholarship comes up, they put it on that list. (Suburban school student, Atlanta)

Junior year you start having classes about college courses. You have to have required meetings with the counselor. (Independent school student, Chicago)

Counseling. (Inner-city school student, Washington, DC)

Instill Possibilities Early

The idea of instilling at an early age an awareness of the possibilities of attending college, as voiced by these students, affirmed the need for providing students with information on possibilities, requirements, and outcomes earlier than in high school. In addition, these students discussed the need to develop excitement about higher education and prospects for jobs after completing higher education. A group of students attending the same private school in New York summarized it best:

> I think what you should do [is] like early, start really early in third, fourth, fifth grade. Get them involved in stuff that you know you have to [learn] to go to college to get a degree like in communications. Give them a lot of opportunities, and in turn take them places and get them excited about, you know, get them out in the world to get an education.
>
> Show more Black people with jobs that pay, who have been to college.
>
> Oh yeah, just to show people who have been to college, Black people preferably, who have jobs that pay a lot of money, like maybe engineers and architects. More higher paying jobs for people who are Black.
>
> We have to learn how to make college seem like the best four years of your life. (Independent school student, New York)
>
> I would tell someone in the younger age bracket to always look for a challenge, and school is always going to be a challenge. (Magnet school student, Washington, DC)
>
> If you can show them what they can be or who is successful and how far they could really go, you know, if they do this and do that, you are already showing them like a light they could try to get to. (Independent school student, Los Angeles)
>
> Invest more in younger age. (Independent school student, New York)
>
> They [students] just have to realize, and they are not realizing it soon enough, because by the time they get in here they have got to pay for those classes that they didn't pass. (Suburban school student, Atlanta)
>
> I think people can be helped more when they are younger. It's like hard to convince tenth or eleventh graders that never cared about college or anything. (Independent school student, Los Angeles)

Emphasize Cultural Awareness

Out of very passionate discussions about their culture, students, particularly those students who attended independent schools, voiced the need to increase cultural awareness as a way to motivate more African Americans to participate in higher education. Also included in this category was the need for more male role models.

> We need more Black male role models. (Independent school student, Los Angeles)
>
> More role models that don't play sports all the time. I mean, I love them. I love basketball, but we need to get kids at a young age to love education and to feel the need that they have to do this to survive in the world, because without it you are just going to be like lost. (Independent school student, New York)
>
> I think when they are young you need to teach them backgrounds of other cultures, not only European. European history, and then are you saying [it's] the ideal school or something like that? (Independent school student, New York)
>
> I have had a hard time in African American history because I don't know about Black history, because I was never taught. I was always taught other things. It's so backwards. I think it's crazy. How do you skip the years which were some of the most important times, which helped in the creation of America. How do you skip that—from early to modern? (Independent school student, Chicago)
>
> There should be Black history. (Independent school student, New York)
>
> I know early world history, and they do not incorporate African Americans in their history. (Independent school student, Chicago)
>
> They don't really teach you about Black history. Like this is Black history month; we will focus on Black people. But it is not worked into the curriculum as a whole like, you know, as a whole thing. (Independent school student, New York)

Within their communities across cities, students, particularly students attending private schools, indicated tremendous pressure to be accepted, describing the feeling of "living in two different worlds." Several students described their experiences of having their friends in their communities accuse them of "acting White," because they attended private schools, and at the same time feeling the pressure to make themselves accepted in their school environment.

Interpretations and Implications of Students' Thoughts

This study clearly points out how important it is that researchers not only include individuals as subjects in their studies but also include their voices in the development of solutions to their problems. This would particularly appear to be appropriate when studies cut across cultures. Student choice and economics of education theorists have long documented the factors that influence the decision-making process of students (see the college choice section for a listing of theorists), but one rationale why these models and programs have failed to increase African Americans' participation in higher education might be a lack of understanding of how these models and programs would work within the context of the African American culture.

For example, these research findings do not disagree with those of the student choice theorists, which note the importance of parental education and income. However, when these students describe barriers and possible solutions to African Americans' participation in higher education, they stress the importance of the elementary and secondary school environments. The school system plays an even greater role when neither parent has participated in higher education, for many of the students in this sample came from such homes. Understanding this in the context of the African American culture has merit.

However, this finding should not be interpreted as meaning that students who do not live in the traditional two-parent family, particularly in the inner city, are not aware of the value of higher education. The research presented in this article suggests that although these students are aware of the barriers to African Americans' access to higher education, they still perceive that it is worth the costs. In fact, researchers such as Anderson and Hearn (1992) and Orfield et al. (1984) have indicated that when socioeconomic background is held constant, African Americans have a higher aspiration to participate in higher education than Whites. Therefore, researchers should use caution in interpreting lack of information as lack of interest. In fact, these students offered viable options as ways of increasing the information channels.

As indicated by these students, it has become increasingly clear that the information pipeline to students, particularly to those students who do not benefit from having the information on the value of higher education passed down to them through their families, must begin much earlier, and it must be incorporated in some structured format within the schools. It is in this way, as Orfield et al. (1984) have suggested, that channeling can improve the choice process for students. In response to those who say that public schools cannot be all things to all people or that schools are already doing enough, this process of channeling does not imply that the information process has to be a specific course imposed on teachers. However, it is noteworthy that among the schools participating in this study, the public schools with structured counseling programs (all independent schools had them) had a larger number of students participating in higher education.

When the students who were interviewed in this study discussed instilling an awareness of possibilities early, they appeared to be saying that the problem is more than a lack of information. Their responses could be interpreted as meaning that if schools are not going to provide information through teachers and counselors, then, at a minimum, educators should not take away students' passion for achieving higher education by instilling in them the idea that because of their social and cultural background, they cannot aspire to attain it. This interpretation would support these students' voiced perceptions that the psychological barriers of "loss of hope" and "college never an option" are strong factors impacting African Americans' participation in higher education. It is here, in the further study of social and cultural capital, that researchers can shed more light for educators on why these students voiced the perception that they are not instilled with a passion to participate in higher education but are actually being discouraged. The negative side of the cultural capital concept, as defined by Bourdieu and Passeron (1977), is that educators come to their classrooms with established views of acceptable actions and values expressed in behavior patterns that are typically based on the majority culture. In school settings where students do not meet those "established views," these educators early on begin the process of stripping away the students' personal cultural values, which can lower their perception of their worth and leave them without hope of ever becoming high achievers and ultimately robbing them of their passion for pursuing preparation for a college education.

Given these realities, it is understandable that these students would echo the importance of emphasizing cultural awareness. This aspect of their model (see Figure 2) is one that student choice and economics of education theorists have not explored and one that could bear more extensive review. What exactly is the role that increasing cultural awareness in the curriculum plays in increasing students' participation in higher education? According to these students, it would at least improve their sense of self and instill a passion for learning. Ogbu (1988) wrote about the burden of "acting White," and these students appeared to be saying that "acting White" is just the reality of being Black in America. That is, instead of feeling as though their interpretation of "acting White" were a negative about their culture, I interpret it to mean that if their culture were more included in the curriculum and in other aspects of the American society, African American students could be themselves across settings and not have to leave their culture behind in their homes. This research also demonstrates that the views of students, at least in this sample, cut across class lines, a finding that provides impetus for the growing notion that cultural views (that is, behaviors, values, and frames of reference) outweigh class differences.

It seems logical, then, that African Americans, and in this case African American high-school students, are in the best position to assist educators and policymakers in the development of solutions for increasing African Americans' participation in higher education. This research poses some challenging questions for policymakers: In the absence of parental encouragement to attend college after high school, what are ways of including African American students in decision making regarding their lives? What different roles can K-12 and postsecondary schools play in addressing students' concerns related to cultural considerations? How should educators address these students' concerns of the psychological barriers that they perceive Africans Americans face in making college choices? How can educators and policymakers address these students' fear of future earnings not being appropriate to the level of education after completing higher education?

Commentary

These findings demonstrate that the students who participated in this research tended to voice concerns and solutions that could impact the process of choosing a college education for African Americans in general. Workable solutions have to come from the sources most familiar with the circumstances. There is good reason for optimism. Based on the extensive research student choice and economics of education theorists have developed on understanding the college choice process, the development of models and programs to increase African American students' motivation and aspiration to participate in higher education is within reach. The research presented in this article points out that the missing link to previous research has been the voices of the students. The next step is for educators and policymakers to work with African American students, to empower them, to investigate their thoughts more formally, and to develop sites to test their models.

It is clear that current models are not working and that these students' ideas are solid ones. It would be difficult to find anyone who would disagree that physical and financial resources are necessary for inner-city schools, that better teachers and interested counselors are needed, that instilling possibilities earlier is indicated, and that having, across all school types, a curriculum that is inclusive of all cultures (not just for one event or one month) is desperately lacking.

However, all too often, researchers unfamiliar with the historical and structural differences of cultures continue to define the problems and develop the solutions based on models that are applicable to the majority population. In order to develop workable programs and models, educators and policymakers must begin the process of hearing the voices that are all too often regulated to the margins, for, logically and intuitively, those are the only voices that can possibly hold the solutions.

References

Alexander, K., D'Amico, R., Fennessey, J., & McDill, E. (1978). *Status composition and educational goals: An attempt at clarification.* Report 244. Baltimore: Johns Hopkins University Center for Social Organizations of Schools.

Alwin, D. F., & Otto, L. B. (1977, October). High school context effects on aspiration. *Sociology of Education, 50,* 259–273.

Anderson, M., & Hearn, J. (1992). Equity issues in higher education outcomes. In W. E. Becker & D. R. Lewis (Eds.), *The economics of American higher education* (pp. 301–334). Norwell, MA: Kluwer Academic Publishers.

Barnes, A. S. (1992). *Retention of African American males in high school.* New York: University Press of America.

Becker, G. S. (1975). *Human capital* (2nd ed.). New York: Columbia University Press.

Bourdieu, P., & Passeron, P. (1977). *Reproduction in education, society and culture.* London: Sage Publications.

Boyle, R. (1966). The effect of the high school on students' aspirations. *The American Journal of Sociology, 6,* 628–639.

Carnoy, M. (1995). *Faded dreams: The politics and economics of race in America.* New York: University of Cambridge Press.

Carter, D., & Wilson (Eds.). (1994). *Status on minorities in higher education.* Washington, DC: American Council on Education.

Cicourel, A. V., & Mehan, H. (1985). Universal development, stratifying practices, and status attainment. *Research in Social Stratification and Mobility, 4*(5), 728–734.

Cohn, E. (1979). *The economics of education.* Cambridge, MA: Harper & Row.

Coleman, J. S. (1988). Social capital in the creation of human capital. *American Journal of Sociology, 94,* 95–120.

Coleman, J. S. (1990). *Foundations of social theory.* Cambridge, MA: Belknap Press of Harvard University.

Collins, R. (1979). *The credential society: An historical sociology of education and stratification.* San Diego, CA: Academic Press.

Cross, P., & Astin, H. (1981). Factors affecting Black students' persistence in college. In G. Thomas (Ed.), *Black students in higher education* (pp. 76–90). Westport, CT: Greenwood Press.

DiMaggio, P., & Mohr, J. (1985). Cultural capital, educational attainment, and marital selection. *American Journal of Sociology, 90*(6), 1231–1261.

Freeman, K. (1989). *The returns to schooling: The impact of career counseling on Black-White MBA starting salaries.* Unpublished doctoral dissertation, Emory University, Atlanta, GA.

Freeman, R. B. (1976). *The overeducated American.* New York: Academic Press.

Hearn, J. C. (1991). Academic and nonacademic influences on the college destinations of 1980 high school graduates. *Sociology of Education, 64,* 158–171.

Hossler, D., Braxton, J., & Coopersmith, G. (1989). Understanding student college choice. In J. C. Smart (Ed.), *Higher education: Handbook of theory and research: Vol. 5* (pp. 231–288). New York: Agathon Press.

Hossler, D., & Gallagher, K. (1987). Studying student college choice: A three-phase model and the implications for policymakers. *College & University, 62*(3), 207–221.

Hossler, D., & Vesper, N. (1993). *Consistency and change in college matriculation decisions: An analysis of the factors which influence the college selection decisions of students.* Paper presented at the annual meeting of the American Educational Research Association, Atlanta, GA.

Johns, R. L., Morphet, E. L., & Alexander, K. (1983). *The economics and financing of education* (4th ed.). Englewood Cliffs, NJ: Prentice-Hall.

Levine, A., & Nidiffer, J. (1996). *Beating the odds: How the poor get to college.* San Francisco: Jossey-Bass.

Litten, L., Sullivan, D., & Brodigan, D. (1983). *Applying market research in college admissions.* New York: The College Board.

McDonough, P. (1994, July/August). Buying and selling higher education: The social construction of the college applicant. *Journal of Higher Education, 65*(4), 427–446.

McDonough, P., Antonio, A., & Trent, J. (1995). *Black students, Black colleges: An African American college choice model.* Paper presented at the meeting of the American Educational Research Association, San Francisco, CA.

Miles, M. B., & Huberman, A. M. (1984). *Qualitative data analysis.* Newbury Park, CA: Sage Publications.

Morrison, L. (1989). The Lubin House experience: A model for the recruitment and retention of urban minority students. In J. C. Elam (Ed.), *Blacks in higher education: Overcoming the odds* (pp. 11–27). New York: University Press of America.

Mortenson, T. (1991). *Equity of higher educational opportunity for women, Black, Hispanic, and low income students.* American College Testing Program.

Nettles, M. (1988). *Financial aid and minority participation in graduate education.* Princeton, NJ: Minority Graduate Education Project for Educational Testing Service.

Niemi, A. W. (1975, January). Racial differences in returns to educational investment in the South. *American Journal of Economics and Sociology, 34,* 87–94.

Nieto, S. (1992). *Affirming diversity: The sociopolitical contest of multicultural education.* White Plains, NY: Longman Publishing Group.

Ogbu, J. U. (1988, Winter). Cultural diversity and human development. In D. T. Slaughter (Vol. Ed.), *Black children and poverty: A developmental perspective: Vol. 42. New directions for child development* (pp. 11–28). San Francisco: Jossey-Bass.

Orfield, G., Mitzel, H., Austin, T., Bentley, R., Bice, D., Dwyer, M., Gidlow, L., Herschensohn, J., Hibino,

B., Kelly, T., Kuhns, A., Lee, M., Rabinowitz, C., Spoerl, J., Vosnos, A., & Wolf, J. (1984). *The Chicago study of access and choice in higher education* (Report prepared for the Illinois Senate Committee on Higher Education). Chicago: Illinois Senate Committee.

Schultz, T. W. (1961). Investment in human capital. *American Economic Review, 51,* 1–17.

Simms, M. (1995, July). The place to be: Washington. *Black Enterprise,* 24.

Stage, F., & Hossler, D. (1989). Differences in family influences on college attendance plans for male and female ninth graders. *Research in Higher Education, 30*(3), 301–315.

Thurow, L. C. (1972). Education and economic equality. *Public Interest, 28,* 66–81.

Wilson, R. (Ed.). (1989). *Status on minorities in higher education.* Washington, DC: American Council on Education.

Wilson, R. (Ed.). (1990). *Status on minorities in higher education.* Washington, DC: American Council on Education.

Wilson, R. (Ed.). (1992). *Status on minorities in higher education.* Washington, DC: American Council on Education.

Comparing Retention Factors for Anglo, Black, and Hispanic Students

Dr. Margaret M. Johnson, OP

Vice President for Planning, Research, and Evaluation

Dr. David Molnar

Director of Institutional Research

Abstract

This study examined differences and similarities in first-year college retention among Anglo, Black, and Hispanic students. Data were gathered on nearly 3,000 new undergraduate students who entered Barry University in Miami Shores, Florida, between 1991 and 1995, including full-time, part-time, and transfer students. Data included demographic information, standardized test scores, academic performance at previous institutions, and academic performance at Barry University. The students also completed two surveys during their first year on their subjective experiences at the university. The study found that first-year grade point average (GPA) had a far greater impact on the odds of retention than any other factor, contributing 81 percent to a predictive model of retention. Taken together, variables interacting with ethnicity or citizenship contributed less than seven percent to the retention model. It was also found that Black students had 50 percent greater odds of persistence assuming all other factors being equal. Only Black and Hispanic students' GPAs were affected by satisfaction with opportunities for academic help outside of class, while concerns about financial difficulties affected persistence only for resident aliens, regardless of ethnicity. (Contains 45 references.) (MDM)

Purpose

As our student populations become more diverse—by ethnicity, age, academic preparation, etc.—we must no longer blindly treat the student body as if all students were cut from a single cookie cutter mold. Different groups may take different paths to successful completion of college, and they may be impacted differently by the factors that influence student retention and academic achievement. By understanding the extent to which factors impact different groups, an institution can tailor retention strategies to address each group's special circumstances. In this way we can preserve the ethnic diversity we initially invited in recruiting students.

This paper compares and contrasts the factors correlated with first-year retention for Anglo, Black, and Hispanic students, by citizenship category, at a private, urban university. It is a well established

Paper presented at the Annual Meeting for the Association for Institutional Research, May 1996.

concern that Black and Hispanic students have higher dropout rates nationally. Do all groups face the same "risk" factors, and which risks are more prevalent among students from these minorities? Or do different groups face different risk factors? Because Barry University is so ethnically diverse, it allows us to explore how these groups respond to essentially the same environment. In contrast, the literature has focused more on the retention of minorities in traditionally Black or Hispanic institutions or alternatively in institutions in which they are a tiny fraction of the student body. These studies have not allowed us to separate the impact on retention of differences among institutions from the differential impact of ethnicity.

Review of the Literature

This portion of the paper offers a brief review of the literature on retention and attrition in higher education. The discussion starts with an overview of the problem, i.e., the need for theoretical models predictive of retention and attrition among college students; it continues with a description of the work of Tinto and Bean, pioneers in this field of research. The final section reviews modifications of the models proposed by Tinto and Bean.

Need for Theoretical Models

In 1972 the National Longitudinal Survey of the High School Class of 1972 indicated that nearly 60% of every 100 first-time entrants to the four year college would leave their first institution of registration without completing their degree program (Eckland and Henderson, 1981). Of this number approximately 29 would leave higher education permanently. The remaining 31 would transfer to other institutions of higher education immediately or "stop-out" and re-enter after some interval. In other words, out of every 100 entrants, nearly 65 would eventually earn a degree and approximately 44 would do so from the institution of initial entry.

Tinto (1985) notes that some students leave college involuntarily; i.e., because of grades or some other problem with the institution. However, he notes that approximately 85% of withdrawals are voluntary. The failure to distinguish between voluntary and involuntary withdrawal, permanent from temporary has, according to Tinto (1975), led to inaccurate estimates of withdrawals in higher education. It is Tinto's contention that this lack of precision leads to inappropriate policy decisions. He also contends that the lack of a theoretical, longitudinal model disallows researchers from isolating the significant factors that lead to the decision to withdraw. Knowing that students leave is insufficient. Policy makers need to know why students leave.

Bean (1980) quotes Summerskill, who reviewed 35 different studies of student attrition between 1913 and 1962 and found that the median loss of students was 50%. From his review of studies conducted in the 70's Bean concludes that attrition statistics remain fairly consistent. Bean concurs with Tinto on the need for a conceptual model that investigates the determinants of student attrition.

Institutions of higher education do need to know why students leave their campuses; if not to provide a more congenial climate for student learning and success, then certainly for institutional survival.

Proposed Models

Tinto's theoretical model premises student dropout as a longitudinal process of interactions between the individual and the academic and social systems of the institution of higher learning. In other words, it is the student's experiences in these two systems that continually modify his goal commitment and institutional commitment which, in turn, affect the decision to persist or leave (Tinto, 1975).

Tinto draws from Durkheim's theory of suicide in developing his model; he posits a similarity in the factors that lead to suicide with those that lead to withdrawal from college, i.e., insufficient moral and social integration. The former is a result of holding highly divergent values from those of society; Tinto, following the insight of Spady, likens this to the inability to integrate into the moral and academic climate of the institution. The latter corresponds to failure to integrate into the social systems of the college (Tinto, 1975).

Tinto's model also draws upon the cost benefit theory of economics. A student is constantly analyzing the benefits of investing time and monies into education against alternative forms of personal investment. This analysis processes the cost of staying against the benefit in the light of future employment, social status, personal satisfaction, etc. The cost and benefits analysis is impacted by the student's social and academic integration into the institution; both affect his personal goal commitment and institutional commitment.

Essentially Tinto's model called the Student Integration Model by researchers, hypothesizes the decision to persist or to leave as complex series of interactions between goal commitment (intention to persist), and institutional commitment (identification with moral and academic climate of the institution), which respectively influence academic and social integration, the significant factors in the decision. The model accepts the research findings that family background, e.g., social and economic status, parent support and expectations, as well as previous schooling as measured by GPA, are factors impacting goal commitment and institutional commitment. The measures of academic integration are grade performance and intellectual development as perceived by the student; social integration is measured by peer-group and faculty interactions.

In summary the Student Integration Model emphasizes students interactions within the college environment, both social and academic, as the factors influencing attrition. The theory hypothesizes that persistence is a function of the match between an individual's motivation and academic ability and the institution's academic and social characteristics. The coincidence of this match shapes the individual's commitment to complete college (goal commitment) and his commitment to the respective institution (institutional fit). The stronger these commitments the more likely is the decision to persist (Cabrera, Castaneda, Nora & Hengsler, 1992).

Tinto did not test his model; however, in their test of the model, Terenzini and Pascarella (1978) confirmed that precollege traits were not significantly related to attrition and that integration into the academic systems of the institution may be more important than involvement in social systems. They observed that, after all other variables have been controlled, stayers reported more frequent contact with faculty, found the academic program more exciting and enjoyable as well as enlightening and provocative.

Terenzini and Pascarella did observe differences in responses between white students and black students. For example, the amount of self-perceived progress in intellectual development appeared virtually unrelated to attrition among minority students, but was strong among non-minority students. Also affective appeal was more contributive to stayers among minorities than among non-minorities. In their conclusion these researchers suggested that attrition reduction efforts needed to focus on what happens to students in academic areas after they arrive on campus.

Bean (1980) noted the inadequacy of the Tinto model in that it did not distinguish between the determinants of student attrition (analytic variables) and correlates of student attrition (demographic variables). This failure to distinguish rendered the model unsuitable for path analysis to test causal links. Bean proposed a causal model of student attrition, adapted from Price's theory of employee turnover in work organizations. The basic assumption is that students leave institutions of higher learning for reasons analogous to those that cause employees to leave work organizations. The model contains the dependent variable, dropping out; the intervening variables are: satisfaction and institutional commitment, organizational determinants and background variables.

Bean found that the background variables, socioeconomic status and GPA, positively affected goal commitment and university GPA. These organizational determinants, along with intellectual development, practical value, institutional quality, institutional integration and communication, staff/faculty relations, campus work, major area and major certainty, and campus organizations positively influenced satisfaction. Satisfaction was positively related to institutional commitment which showed an inverse relationship to dropping out.

As tested, Bean's 1980 model accounted for 21 percent of the variance for females and 12 percent of males. Institutional commitment was the most important variable for both men and women. The opportunity variables (opportunity to transfer, to get a job, remain as a dependent at home) were significant in determining institutional commitment and opportunity to transfer had the highest path coefficient for those variables significantly related to institutional commitment for women.

In 1982 Bean proposed a revised model, containing ten rather than twenty-three (23) independent variables. Background variables were excluded. Based on the effects coefficients, the overall ranking of the independent variables in influencing dropout were, in descending order: intent to leave, grades, opportunity to transfer, practical value, certainty of choice regarding institutional fit, loyalty to institution, family approval, courses, student goals, certainty of major and job certainty.

Intent to leave, measured by the student's response to the question of returning the next semester or the next year, showed a negative relationship to the three attitudinal variables: loyalty, certainty of choice of institution, and practical value. In this study Bean divided his sample into four groups: high-low confidence women and high-low confidence men. While intent to leave and the three attitudinal variables were significant for each group, the effects of the remaining variables on attrition differed among groups, thus illustrating the complexity of establishing causal relationships to explain attrition (Bean, 1982).

In his 1985 explanatory model Bean posited "drop syndrome" as the dependent variable, which is defined as "a conscious, openly discussed intention to leave coupled with actual attrition." By thereby controlling the variable "intent to leave," he was better able to isolate the independent variables influencing attrition. In this model academic, social-psychological and environmental factors (exogenous variables) are expected to influence the socialization/selection process; the socialization/selection process influences the endogenous variables: college grades, institutional fit, and institutional commitment. The endogenous variables are expected to influence the dropout syndrome (Bean, 1985).

The results of the study supported previous research in demonstrating that socialization is a dominant force in affecting dropout decisions. The study found that social life has large significant effects on institutional fit and that the attitudes of peers have a much greater effect than those of faculty. Bean concludes that peer support is an important element in the retention of students (Bean, 1985).

Cabrera, Castaneda, Nora, and Hengstler (1992) note that the models of Tinto and Bean have many common elements: both claim that persistence is the result of a complex set of interactions over time; both argue that precollege characteristics affect how well students adjust to their institutions, and both agree that persistence is an effect of the successful match between student and institution, i.e., what Tinto labels institutional commitment corresponds to institutional fit in Bean's Student Attrition Model (SAM). One difference lies in the emphasis that the Student Attrition Model places upon the role external factors: family approval, encouragement of friends, finances, perceptions about opportunity to transfer, play in shaping attitudes and decisions. In addition, Tinto's Student Integration Model regards academic performance as an indicator of academic integration while Bean's Student Attrition Model considers it an outcome variable resulting from social-psychological processes.

Cabrera, *et al.*, tested the two models for their predictive quality and validated the finding that college persistence is the product of a complex set of interactions among personal and institutional factors. The hypothesis that intent to persist is the outcome of a successful match between student and institution was likewise supported. Tinto's Student Integration Model appeared the more robust of the two models when judged in terms of the number of hypothesis validated; however, Bean's Student Attrition Model accounted for more variance in both Intent to Persist and Persistence. This finding is attributed to Bean's proposition that the role external factors play is far more complex and comprehensive than the Student Integration Model purports (Cabrera, Castaneda, Nora & Hengstler, 1992). The role of external factors, especially Encouragement from Significant Others, was validated by Nora. (Nora, 1991)

Building upon their previous research on both models (SIM & SAM) on the Student Integration Model and Student Attrition Model, Cabrera, Castaneda, and Nora (1993) constructed a baseline model that incorporated both theoretical frameworks. The variables included were those validated by testing the two models. The exogenous or environmental variables were: encouragement from family and friends, and finance attitudes (I am satisfied with the amount of financial support, e.g., grants, loans, family, job, I have received.). The endogenous variables were: academic integration as revealed by student satisfaction with courses, evaluation of personal performance and academic experiences; academic performance, social integration, institutional commitment, and goal commitment.

When tested the integrated model supported the structional relationships hypothesized by Tinto and Bean between academic and social integration factors as well as those among commitment factors. Support was also found for the role of external factors in facilitating the integration of the student into the academic scene and in maintaining institutional commitment (Cabrera, Castaneda & Nora, 1993).

Retention/Attrition Research with Non-Traditional and Ethnic Students

Both the Student Integration Model and Student Attrition Model have been hypothesized and tested in four-year institutions of higher education with traditional students: 18–24, residing on campus, attending full time. Yet research indicates that enrollment of non-traditional students, i.e., those who commute, are 25 or older, do not attend full time, has greatly increased and in some institutions constitutes the majority (Bean & Metzner, 1985). The differences between the traditional and non-traditional student are significant in studying the causes of attrition. Typically the non-traditional student is older, more mature, self-directed, and pragmatic. For this student the social environment of the institution is less significant and academic concerns are paramount; there is less interaction with faculty and students and much greater interaction with the non-collegiate, external environment. (Bean & Metzner, 1985)

Bean and Metzner present a conceptual model for explaining attrition among nontraditional students. Based on the stereotype of the non-traditional student, the model presumes that socialization in the college environment is not important and that socialization in the external environment is. The model proposes that dropout decisions are primarily based on four sets of variables: (1) poor academic performance; (2) intent to leave, influenced by psychological outcomes (utility, satisfaction, goal commitment and stress) as well as by academic variables; (3) background variables: primarily high school performance and educational goals; and defining variables, i.e., age, enrollment status, sex, ethnicity and residence; (4) environmental variables: finances, hours of employment, outside encouragement, family responsibility, and opportunity to transfer. Intent to leave is used in this model in place of institutional commitment, because research suggests redundancy when both are included; also, intent to leave is more accurate for short term students and is a very strong predictor of attrition even when institutional commitment is controlled. (Bean & Metzner, 1985)

The model hypothesizes that when environmental and academic variables are both good, i.e., favorable for persistence, students should remain in college; when both are poor, the student should leave; when academic variables are good but environmental variables are poor, the student should leave; conversely, when academic variables are poor but environmental variables are good, the student is expected to stay. Bean and Metzner admit the tentative nature of this model and propose it primarily as a framework for further study with non-traditional students (Bean & Metzner, 1985).

In his study Nora (1987) tested a modified version of Tinto's Student Integration Model on a Chicano student population in two-year colleges. Exogenous variables included were: high school grades, parents' education and encouragement by significant others; endogenous variables were academic integration, social integration, institutional/goal commitment and the dependent variable, retention. The results of the test indicated that academic and social integration did not have significant direct effects on retention as was reported by other researchers testing Tinto's model. Furthermore, Tinto emphasized the importance of initial institutional and goal commitment on retention but only when they were mediated through academic and social integration. However, in Nora's study, institutional and goal commitment not only had a direct effect on retention, but were also considerably more important in determining retention (Nora, 1987).

In testing the fit of this model, Nora established that the precollege variables, grades and encouragement explained 20% of the variance in institutional commitment; that the endogenous variable, institutional commitment, explained 42% of the variance in academic integration, and finally, that the two exogenous variables and the one endogenous variable accounted for 24% of the variance in social integration. Essentially Nora's research reflected the overall strength of his hypothesized model; it was not entirely supportive of Tinto's model (Nora, 1987).

In her work analyzing factors affecting Hispanic student transfer behavior, Kraemer (1995) noted that nationwide, one-fourth of all community college students are minorities; furthermore, these students have the lowest retention rates and the highest transfer losses. Nora and Rendon (1990) indicated that although 80 percent of Hispanic community college students express the desire to transfer to a four-year institution, national transfer rates for Hispanics and for most minorities, remain between 5 and 20 percent. Significant variables explaining transfer behavior in Kraemer's study were: mathematic ability, academic achievement, and intent to transfer. Since transfer is a form of persistence the significance of these variables can perhaps be extrapolated to the analysis of retention in Hispanic students.

The Nora and Rendon study (1990) of Hispanic community college students examined their "predisposition to transfer." The model supported the fact that a high degree of congruence between student and environment led to a predisposition to transfer. All five factors in the model: parents' education, encouragement, initial goal and institutional commitments, social integration and academic integration were significant and together explained 65 percent of the variance.

Grossman, Dandridge, Nettles and Thoeny (1983) cite attrition studies that show that more blacks than whites drop out of college, particularly after the first and second years. Blacks are also more likely to engage in part-time employment and interrupted schooling, resulting in significantly lower four-year completion rates. In their study of student retention Grossman, Dandridge, Nettles and Thoeny (1983), focused on the relationship between race and student progression. They tracked students' progress from entry to degree completion by comparing those who left school with those who remained, thereby looking at both attrition and retention behaviors. They also compared different groups of students in terms of persistence and dropping out behaviors.

This study isolated the following variables as significant in predicting attrition and progression in college: mean SAT score, mean family income, type of institution, financial aid, and race. The study concluded that low attrition for blacks could be attributed to high SAT scores, high family income, attendance at a predominantly black institution. The study also revealed that racial differences in performance disappeared when other student and institutional characteristics were accounted for through multiple regression techniques. Differences were explained by variables other than race (Grossman, Dandridge, Nettles and Thoeny, 1983).

In another study of student attrition, Mallinckrodt (1988) found that student perceptions of social support and the intent to leave were significant predictors of persistence for both black and white students. However, white students looked to family for support whereas black students sought support from the campus community. The limitations of this study were noted: small sample of traditional undergraduate students.

The results of Nelson's study (1994) are reminiscent of the Mallinckrodt finding that persistence is causally related to support from the campus community. While Mallinckrodt does not define campus support in terms of students, faculty, and services. Nelson explicitly relates campus support to academic assistance, personal counseling, social enrichment and career counseling. Reporting from previous studies, Nelson describes the freshman dropout as one who: did not receive intrusive academic counseling, did not attend tutorial sessions, did not tend to participate in social activities, did not use academic facilities, and did not participate in student union activities. Nelson notes that African-American students who persist generally utilized campus support services.

Bennett and Okinaka (1990) adapted Bean's 1982 student attrition model to construct a conceptual model of black student attrition. This conceptual model was tested in 1982 and revised in 1985. Independent variables included in this model seem to reflect research findings supporting a positive correlation between social integration and retention. These variables are: pre-college positive inter-racial contact, positive collegiate inter-racial contact, amount of pre-college and college inter-racial contact, membership in ethnic organizations, friends on campus, opportunities on campus to help, openness to human diversity, and college adjustment. The latter variable replaced feelings of trauma or alienation used in the 1982 study. Analysis of the college adjustment items (25) yielded four factors: (1) PREPAREDNESS, degree to which a student feels prepared, (2) INSTRUCTORS, perceptions of instructors, (3) RELATE, the way students perceive their social relationships on campus, and (4) ACCOMPLISH, student's sense of accomplishment. The criterion variable in the 1985 study was persistence, whereas the 1982 study used intent to leave. The sample for the 1985 study was the same group used in 1982, i.e., the persisters and non-persisters of the 1982 freshman class.

Data revealed persistence rates of 73% for Asian students, 79% for whites, 35% for Blacks, and 48% for Hispanics. Regression analysis of model variables indicated that college grade point averages were not significant predictors of retention for Asian and white freshmen but were significant predictors for Black freshmen. The negative relationship between the factor RELATE (how students perceive their social relationships on campus) and persistence of Black freshmen was unexpected. In other words, those freshmen who felt the most alienated or negative about their social relationships were most likely to be persisters. Among Black freshmen those who felt most prepared for college also felt the least satisfied with the social environment on campus but attained the highest GPA. These findings suggest that Black students who feel the least alienated in terms of the factor PREPARE will persist even though they feel the most alienated in terms of RELATE (Bennett and Okinaka, 1990).

Consistent with this finding is the indication that Black students who belong to a predominantly Black organization felt most dissatisfied with campus social environment, yet those students who valued this membership most highly felt most prepared for college. A comparison of the degree of satisfaction expressed by Black freshman and that expressed by Black seniors or persisters seems to suggest that experiences on campus increased the sense of alienation. Black seniors expressed greater alienation than Black freshmen. Black students who experienced the most positive interracial contacts on campus felt most positive about their social relationships and instructors. Positive pre-college interracial contacts predict positive collegiate interracial contacts as well as openness to human diversity, i.e., attitudes about interracial dating and marriage, and attitudes about equity policies (Bennett and Okinaka, 1990).

The model tested by Bennett and Okinaka shows that satisfaction, openness and college adjustment are important predictors of persistence among Asian, Black and White freshmen. For Hispanics none of the model's variables appear related to persister status.

A preponderance of the research has shown that Blacks have a higher rate of attrition than Whites (Bennet and Bean, 1984, MacKinney and Allen, 1982, Pascarella, Smart, and Ethington, 1986). Lenning, Beal and Sauer (1986) reported that Blacks have a higher rate of attrition even when high school academic ability is controlled. The study conducted by Lichtman, Bass and Ager (1989) at an urban commuter university supports the research that Blacks have a higher rate of attrition than whites. In the Lichtman study 57% of the Blacks dropped out; by contrast, 38% of the whites left during the same time studied. In support of Lenning, *et al.*, the study found that for each high school GPA category, i.e., below 3.25 and above 3.25, the dropout rate for blacks is significantly higher. In considering college grade point average, the study found that Blacks and whites performing below 3.0 dropped out at about the same rate: however, above 3.0 Blacks dropped out 2.37 to 3.47 for every white who left. At every level of the ACT Blacks dropped out at a higher rate than whites (Lichtman, Bass & Ager, 1989).

Bean and Metzner (1985) hypothesized that students who commute are less affected by the social integration variables in Tinto's Student Integration Model and more affected by academic integration variables and academic outcomes, namely college GPA. The findings of the Lichtman, Bass and Ager study appear inconsistent with this hypothesis. Blacks with higher GPAs (3.0 and above) dropped out at a greater rate than whites with the similar GPA, whereas Black students and white students with GPAs less than 3.0 dropped out at the same rate. This finding has not been reported in previous research (Lichtman, Bass and Ager, 1990).

Consistent with the research of Bennett and Okinaka (1990) and Lichtman, Bass and Ager (1989), are the findings of Smedley, Myers, and Harrell (1993). These researchers hypothesized that minority status stress conferred an additional risk for poor college adjustment for minority students. Given that all college freshman experience the stress of financial problems, pressures from home, conflicts with faculty and peers, Smedley, *et al.*, propose that these pressures are compounded for Black students on white campuses because of their sense of alienation in the collegiate environment. This burden of added stress would contribute to negative outcomes for Black students.

The results of the study confirmed the hypothesis. The results indicated that chronic student role strains and life event stresses are important correlates of psychological distress for minority freshmen and that minority status stresses contributed substantially to this correlation. The study supported previous research on minority freshmen that showed psychological distress, regardless of sources, was not as important as academic aptitude, i.e., prior academic preparation and performance in explaining current academic achievement. However, the significant association of minority status-related achievement stresses with lower GPA suggests that conflicts between academic expectations and questions about readiness to compete academically are important additional sources of academic vulnerability for minority students. The students in this study evidenced considerable psychological sensitivity and vulnerability to the campus climate, to interpersonal tensions between themselves and white students and faculty, and to experiences of actual and perceived racist attitudes (Smedley, Myers, & Harrell, 1993).

The study also confirmed the intuition that minority-status stress heightened freshman anxiety over academic preparedness, sense of legitimacy as an university student, and perceptions of white students and faculty. This heightened concern reflected a sensitivity to the stigmatized "special status" of a student admitted under an affirmative action program and interfered with the student's ability to bond with the university (Smedley, Myers, & Harrell, 1993).

Theoretical Framework

The theoretical framework which motivated the choice of predictors investigated in this study is described by the flow chart in Figure 1. The persistence decision is an outcome of a complex sociological and psychological process of academic and affective socialization interacting with institutional characteristics as well as with personal background and individual characteristics. The persistence decision is determined by four conceptual variables: academic outcomes, social/psychological outcomes, institutional effectiveness, and background variables external to the institution and preceding student's initial enrollment. Refer to the original text *Comparing Retention Factors for Anglo, Black, and Hispanic Students,* by Margaret M. Johnson and David Molnar for the entire discussion.

Methodology

Introduction to Logit Regression

Ordinary least squares (OLS) regression is not appropriate for analyzing the determinants of a dichotomous dependent variable (Y) like retention. Two problems stand out. First, the required assumption that the error terms have constant variance is untenable. If the expected value of Y is close to 1, then the error terms will all be large (if observed $Y = 0$) or small (if observed $Y = 1$). All the error terms will be approximately 0.5 if the expected value of Y is close to 0.5. Consequently, while the estimated OLS coefficients would be unbiased, the standard errors would be incorrectly estimated. Second, any linear model eventually predicts values of Y greater than 1 or less than 0, impossible predictions since the dependent variable is interpreted as the probability of retention. The function estimated should approach the {0, 1} boundaries asymptotically.

Logit regression[1] overcomes these problems by transforming the dependent variable. Let P be the probability that the student is retained. The odds favoring retention are: $P/(1 - P)$. For the sample of students analyzed in this paper $P = 0.74$ so the odds or retention are 2.8 or nearly 3 to 1. By taking the natural logarithm of the odds, we obtain a logit: $L = \log_a\{P/(1 - P)\}$. Logit regression refers to models with a logit as the dependent variable:

$$L_i = 6_0 + 6_1 X_{i1} + 6_2 X_{i2} + \ldots + 6_{K-1} X_{i,K-1}$$

Since the logit is a linear function of the predictors (X variables), the probability of retention is a nonlinear S-shaped function like that in Figure 2. Since the logit function is flattest near the extremes, it reflects the intuitive notion that marginal changes in predictors will have the least impact when the probability of persistence is near 0 or 1. Consequently, the impact of any single retention factor is dependent upon the values of the other factors which jointly determine the position on the S-shaped curve.

Logit models are estimated by maximum likelihood rather than by least squares. Maximum likelihood methods ask, "What parameter values make this sample most likely?" Logit regression techniques assume that (1) the model is correctly specified as a linear function of the X variables, which are measured without error, (2) the observations are independent, and (3) none of the X variables are linear functions of the others. If these conditions are met, the maximum likelihood estimates of the parameters are unbiased, minimum variance, and normally distributed in large samples.

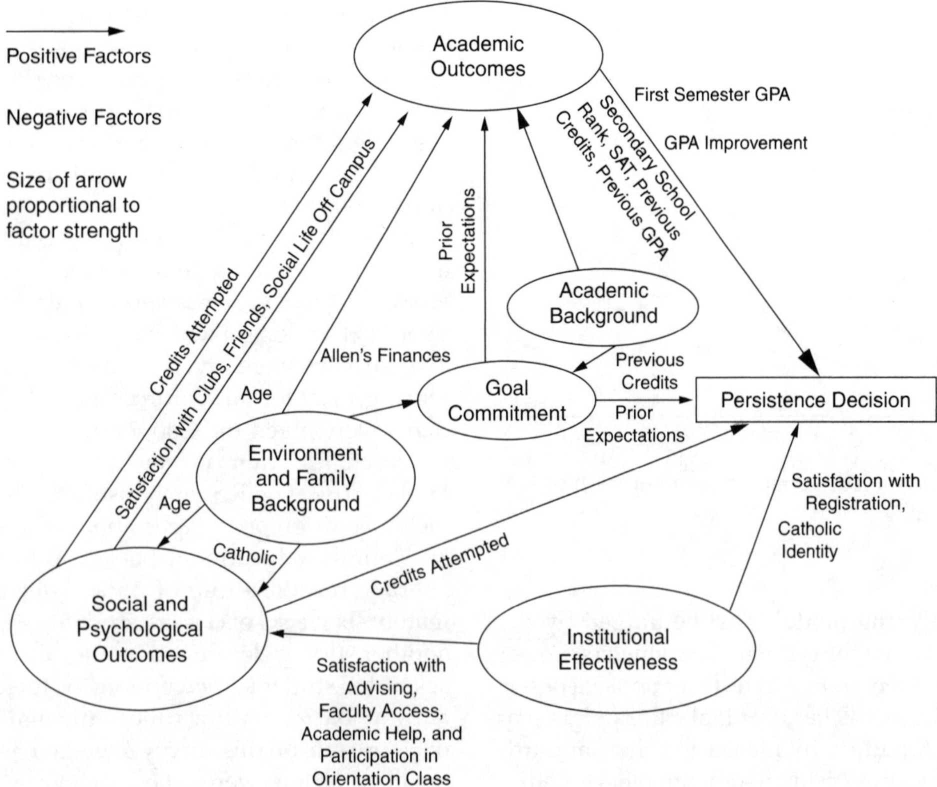

Figure 1 Theoretical Model of First-Year Student Persistence

The coefficient, 6_j, tells us how much the logit increases for a unit increase in X_j. However, the probability of retention is a nonlinear function of the logit, making it difficult to interpret the coefficients in terms of the impact of the predictors on the probability of retention. One interpretation of the coefficient, 6_j, is that each unit increase in X_j multiplies the odds favoring retention by e^{6j} if all the other X's stay the same. e^{6j} is called the odds ratio and is often used comparatively to describe the strength of an effect. The stronger the relation between X and retention, the farther the odds ratio will be from 1—greater than 1 if increases in X encourage retention and less than 1 if increases in X discourage retention.

Alternatively, we can describe the effect of X in terms of probabilities rather than odds. The effect of X_j on the probability of retention depends on the values of the other X's and has the least effect when the predicted probability is near 1 or 0. The effect of a unit change in X_j on the predicted probability of retention, under the assumption that the other X's are at their mean values, is reported in this paper as the delta-p statistic (see Peterson, 1984). The delta-p statistic measures the strength of the effect of X_j on the predicted probability of retention.

Goodness-of-fit measures are less easy to interpret than with OLS regression. **McFadden's Rho-squared** is a transformation of the likelihood ratio statistic which tests the hypothesis that all coefficients except the constant are zero. It is intended to mimic an R-squared in that it is always between 0 and 1, and a higher Rho-squared corresponds to a better fit. However, it tends to be much lower than R-squared with values between 0.2 and 0.4 considered very satisfactory.

The success of the model in classifying students can be judged by the proportion of the sample for which the retention decision is correctly predicted. The **success index** is the gain the model shows over a purely random model which assigns the same probability of retention (the sample mean) to every student in the sample. The smaller the success index, the poorer the performance of the model.

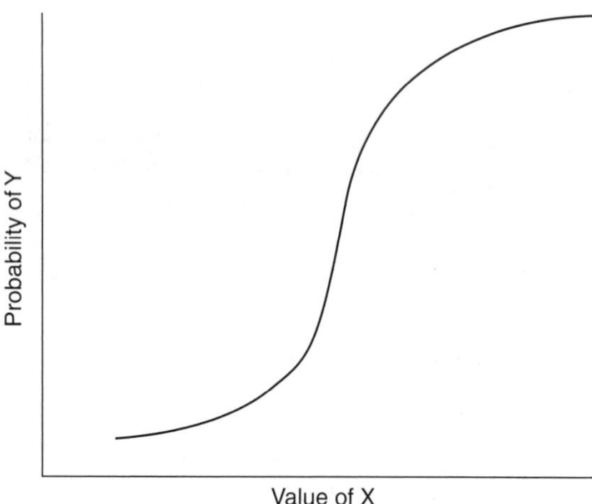

Figure 2 Predicted Probability as a Function of X

Finally, the model must be judged by the extent to which the estimated parameters are not unduly influenced by a handful of unusual observations. Cook's D helps us make this judgement for each X pattern by measuring the standardized change in *all* estimated parameters together that results from deleting all cases with that X pattern. The parameter estimates in this study were improved by deleting 12 "high influence" observations out of a sample of 2850.

Data Sources

Data were gathered for nearly 3,000 new undergraduate students who entered the university between the Fall term 1991 and the Spring term 1995. The sample includes full-time (83% of sample) and part-time students, transfer (60%) and first-time in college students, commuter (70%) and residential students, but it excludes students enrolled exclusively in the adult degree program or the weekend programs in physical or occupational therapy. The average age was 24 and the sample contained 67% Florida residents, 65% women, 53% minority students and 28% resident aliens or international students. Seventy one percent of the students received financial aid from some source in the first year. The analysis focuses on student persistence into the second year at Barry, which is not necessarily the student's sophomore year[2] or second year in college. Students are defined as a persisters if they are enrolled three terms after the initial enrollment or have graduated from Barry. A very small number of students who "stop-out" but returned during the time frame of this study were coded as persisters.

Data used to predict persistence come from three sources. The students' admissions records yield demographic information, standardized test scores, and data on academic performance at previous institutions. The students' academic record at Barry yields grades, credits attempted, and credits transferred from previous college level work. The final source is survey data on the students' perceptions of their subjective experiences. Two surveys were given to first-year students. During orientation, before classes begin, students were given the Cooperative Institutional Research Program survey developed by the Higher Education Research Institute. This survey yielded data on prior expectations of graduation and family educational background with an average response rate of 36%. After approximately six weeks of classes, students were given another survey, developed by the author, which asked for students' perceptions of their experience at Barry. With a follow-up mailing, the response rate on this survey averaged 39%. Since not all questions were asked each year, the sample size may vary for different questions as shown by the descriptive statistics in Table 2. All the variables defined in Table 1 are statistically significant.

Model Specification

Missing observations for some of the variables was a problem in specifying the model. Table 2 shows that some of the variables, especially survey results, were available for only part of the sample. In order to get the best estimates for coefficients, the first round of estimation included only variables that were available for essentially the whole sample. For a second round of estimation, the coefficients for the first round were "locked in" by creating an artificial variable which was a linear combination of the statistically significant variables from the first round. A limitation of this strategy is that variables introduced in a subsequent round could not fully "compete" with variables from an earlier round for explanatory power, but this limitation is outweighed by the value of estimating coefficients from the largest available sample.

For two variables missing values were replaced by estimated values from a linear

TABLE 1
Definition of Variables

Variable	*Definition*
ACADhlp	Five point scale indicating the extent to which "opportunities outside of class to receive help with academic problems" meets expectations
ACCESS	Five point scale indicating the extent to which the student agrees "faculty are accessible to students, not only through office hours, but elsewhere on campus"
ADVISING	Five point scale indicating the extent to which "the quality of advice and information I received about course selection and course requirements" meets expectations
AGE	Student's age at matriculation
ALIEN	1 if resident alien, 0 if not
ANGLO	1 if white non-Hispanic, 0 if not
ATTEMPT	Number of credits attempted in first semester
BLACK	1 if Black or Black Hispanic, 0 if not
CATHOLIC	1 if self-identified Catholic, 0 if not
CLUBS	Five point scale indicating the extent to which "opportunities to participate in clubs and organizations on campus" meets expectations
EXPECT	Five point scale indicating the extent to which the student agrees "I expect to receive my degree from Barry University"
FINCDIF	Five point scale indicating the extent to which the student agrees "I am concerned that financial difficulties may affect my ability to stay at Barry"
FRNDS	Five point scale indicating the extent to which the student agrees "I am finding some of my best friends here at Barry"
FULLTIME	1 if student enrolled for 12 or more credits in first semester, 0 if not
GPA1	Student's GPA after first semester
GPA21	Student's cum GPA after second semester minus student's GPA after first semester
INTRNL	1 if international student, 0 if not
NOprevCRD	1 if student received no transfer credits from any source, 0 if not
ORI100	1 if student enrolled in Orientation Course, 0 if not
prevCRD	1 if no transfer credits, 2 if 60 or fewer transfer credits, 3 if more than 60 transfer credits
prevGPA	Student's GPA from high school or previous college(s)
READING	Average placement test score for English language reading
REGISTRA	Five point scale indicating the extent to which "the registration process" meets expectations
SAT	Student's SAT score
SOCoff	Five point scale indicating the extent to which "social opportunities off campus" meets expectations
ssRANK	Student's rank in secondary school
TRANSFER	1 if 15 or more transfer credits or grades reported from previous college, 0 if not
US	1 if United States citizen, 0 if not

regression. The variable GPA21 shows academic achievement "momentum" by taking the difference between the cumulative GPA after the second semester and the first semester GPA. This variable was estimated for 71 students (2.5% of sample) who left after only one semester. EXPECT was estimated for 1813 students (64% of sample!) because prior expectations of graduation is a retention factor that theoretically precedes in time factors reflecting the students' experience of this institution. Consequently, it was vital that this variable be entered in the first

TABLE 2
Descriptive Statistics for Variables

Variable	*Sample Size*	*Mean*	*Standard Deviation*
ACADhlp	1001	2.297	0.921
ACCESS	923	2.275	0.997
ADVISING	1028	2.622	1.034
AGE	3494	23.774	7.259
ATTEMPT	3513	13.425	3.805
CLUBS	975	2.625	0.866
EXPECT	1029	1.895	1.079
FINCDIF	841	2.710	1.323
FRNDS	425	2.214	1.032
GPA1	3330	2.840	0.920
GPA21	2481	−0.029	0.372
prevCRD	3285	32.555	30.083
prevGPA	2741	2.830	0.585
READING	1496	12.988	2.745
REGISTRA	1030	3.081	1.061
SAT	2405	868.598	156.915
SOCoff	956	2.748	0.993
ssRANK	880	0.351	0.256

round of analysis to give it the fullest chance for explanatory power. Estimated values of the variable were used so that the sample size would not be dramatically reduced in the first round of analysis. This decision may be criticized because there is self-selection bias in the subsample of students who reported prior expectations. One indication is their attrition rate was 6% lower.

Results

Table 3 shows the results of the logit regressions that were used to estimate the direct impact of retention factors on persistence. The odd's ratio shows that first-semester GPA has a far greater impact on the odds of retention than any other factor. As one measure of the goodness-of-fit this logit regression classified 78% of the students correctly in contrast to a purely random model that would have classified 65% of the students correctly. Note that Black students have 50% greater odds of persistence, assuming all other factors being equal. Table 4 shows that this assumption is not viable for Black transfer students whose GPA is 0.3 lower after controlling for other determinants. For international students, their English reading ability is a modest retention factor. Note that this factor operates directly on the odds of retention rather than indirectly through an impact on GPA, as might be expected. Perhaps international students can compensate for weak reading skills in terms of their first semester grades, but the extra effort and stress reduces the odds of persistence. Financial concerns reduce the odds of retention only for resident aliens. In our environment these are mostly Cuban and Haitian immigrants. Since aliens receive financial aid in nearly the same proportion as U.S. citizens (72% vs. 75%) and on average receive larger awards after controlling for income, this may be a cultural phenomenon more than an objectively financial one.

For statistically significant predictors of GPA1, indirect impacts were estimated from ordinary least squares coefficients given in Table 4. The size of the standardized coefficients give the best estimate of the relative impact of each variable on GPA. The significant negative GPA differential for transfer students between Blacks and other ethnicities is disturbing and unexplained by this analysis. One speculation is that this effect is a function of the "quality" of the schools from which Black students are likely to transfer. Satisfaction with opportunities to receive academic help outside of class has a modest impact on grades only for minority students. Only for U.S. citizens does the accessibility of the faculty outside of class and office hours have an impact on grades. This may suggest that the mentor relationship with faculty members is an expectation unique to American citizens. Since the distribution of responses was similar for citizens and non-citizens, this evidence is suggesting that citizens are not more satisfied with faculty mentoring—they are just more affected. An interesting result is the negative impact on grades (equal for all ethnic groups) of some of the factors that lead to social and psychological integration—CLUBS, FRNDS, and SOCoff.

Table 5 provides the best summary of the relative impact of individual retention factors. The logit model improves our ability to correctly classify students (persistence vs. attrition) to 78% from the 65% correct for a purely random model. The first column shows how much of this "improvement" is attributable to each variable.

TABLE 3
Logit Regression Results for First-Year Retention

Independent Variable	*Coefficient*	*Odd's Ratio*
First round of variable entry N = 2838		
Square root of GPA1	3.0046***	16.35†
GPA21	1.3924***	1.65†
ATTEMPT	0.1207***	1.44
NOprevCRD	−0.6327***	0.53
CATHOLIC	0.3958**	1.49
BLACK	0.3899**	1.48
EXPECT	0.4442***	1.39†
ORI100	0.5306***	1.70
AGE	−0.0230**	0.89
Second round of variable entry N = 1484		
READING*INTRNL	0.0613***	1.21†
Third round of variable entry N = 588		
REGISTRA	0.2251*	1.28†
FINCDIF*ALIEN	−0.2817*	0.68†

*$p \leq .05$;
**$p \leq .01$;
***$p \leq .001$ one-tail test.
†Odd's ratio adjusted for unit change of one standard deviation.

TABLE 4
OLS Regression Results on First Semester GPA

Independent Variable	*Coefficient*	*Standardized Coefficient*
First round of variable entry: N = 1875, R^2 = 0.29, Standard error of estimate = 0.77		
prevGPA	0.4258***	.28
prevCRD	0.1994***	.16
SAT	0.0010***	.16
EXPECT	0.1876***	.16
FULLTIME	0.4162***	.13
TRANSFER*BLACK	−0.2900***	−.09
TRANSFER*nonBLACK	0.1308**	.07
AGE	0.0177***	.09
Second round of variable entry N = 717, R^2 = 0.29, Standard error of estimate = 0.74		
ssRANK	0.2975*	.09
Another second round N = 632, R^2 = 0.32, Standard error of estimate = 0.67		
CLUBS	−0.1126***	−.12
ACADhlp*nonANGLO	0.0626**	.09
FRNDS	−0.0968**	−.09
ADVISING	0.0631*	.08
SOCoff	−0.0586*	−.07
Third round of variable entry N = 511, R^2 = 0.33, Standard error of estimate = 0.65		
ACCESS*US	0.0388*	.06

*$p \leq .05$;
**$p \leq .01$;
***$p \leq .001$ one-tail test.

TABLE 5
Factors Increasing First Year Retention

Retention Factor	Contribution to Model's Predictive Success	*Impact on Probability of Retention* Direct Impact	Thru 1st Semester GPA	Total Impact	Unit of Change
Higher first semester GPA	53.9%	0.41***		0.41	.92†
GPA improves 1st to 2nd semester	13.6%	0.07***		0.07	0.35†
More credits attempted in 1st semester	9.9%	0.05***	0.04***	0.09	3 credits
Prior expectation of graduation	7.3%	0.05***	0.06***	0.11	0.74†®
Aliens with less financial concerns	5.7%	0.05*		0.05	1.34†®
Intrnl students' English reading skill	5.1%	0.03***		0.03	3.14†Ř
No previous college credits	4.0%	−0.09***	−0.08***	−0.18	
Higher GPA at previous institution(s)	3.8%		0.11***	0.11	0.58†
Participant in orientation course	2.5%	0.08***		0.08	
non-Black transfer students	1.8%	−0.06**	0.10**	0.04	
Black transfer students	1.6%	0.06**	−0.10**	−0.04	
Satisfaction with registration process	1.6%	0.03*		0.03	1.06†®
Age	1.5%	−0.02**	0.04***	0.02	5 years
Black freshman	1.4%	0.06**		0.06	
Catholic students	1.3%	0.06**		0.06	
Satisfaction with opportunities to participate in clubs & organizations	0.6%		−0.04***	−0.04	0.87†®
Higher SAT	0.6%		0.07***	0.07	157†
Minority students satisfaction with opportunities for academic help	0.5%		0.03**	0.03	0.92†®
Agrees with "finding some best friends at Barry"	0.4%		−0.04**	−0.04	1.03†®
Satisfaction with academic advising	0.3%		0.03*	0.03	1.03†®
Satisfaction with social opportunities off campus	0.2%		−0.03*	−0.03	0.99†®
US citizen's experience that faculty are accessible elsewhere on campus	0.2%		0.02**	0.02	1.00†®
Secondary school class rank	0.2%		0.01*	0.01	1 decile

*$p \leq 0.5$;
**$p \leq .01$;
***$p \leq .001$ one-tail test.
†Represents one standard deviation.
®Survey response on a 5 point scale.
ŘOn a reading grade level scale.

For instance, more than half the model's ability to improve prediction or classification of students' persistence/attrition status comes from the contribution of GPA1.

The next three columns estimate the impact of a unit change in the predictor on the probability of retention, i.e., the delta-p statistic. Direct, indirect, and total impacts are shown. Since predictors are not measured in comparable units, these estimated impacts cannot be directly compared without adjustments. The last column shows the unit of change for each variable. In many cases they are made roughly comparable by using one standard deviation while in other cases a "natural" unit was used, like 3 credits constituting a single course. When the retention

TABLE 6
Factors Improving First-Year Retention by Ethnic and Citizenship Groups

Citizenship/Ethnic	*All Citizenship Groups*	*U.S. Citizens*	*Resident Aliens*	*International Students*
All ethnic groups	▶higher GPA ▶some previous college credits ▶prior expectation of graduation ▶more credits attempted in 1st semester ▶participation in orientation course ▶2nd semester improvement in GPA ▶self-identified Catholic ▶satisfaction with registration process * higher GPA at previous institution * higher SAT * dissatisfaction with opportunities to participate in clubs & organizations *▶older at time of matriculation * satisfaction with academic advising * disagrees with "finding some of my best friends at Barry" * dissatisfaction with social opportunities off-campus	*satisfaction with access to faculty in addition to class and office hours 73% retention 72% of sample	▶no concerns about financial difficulties 76% retention 13% of sample	▶higher English language reading achievement score 77% retention 15% of sample
Anglos	* transfer student 47% of sample	73% retention 41% of sample	1% of sample	80% retention 5% of sample
Hispanics	* transfer student * satisfaction with opportunities for academic help outside of class 27% of sample	74% retention 20% of sample	79% retention 5% sample	72% retention 4% sample
Blacks	* first-time in college * satisfaction with opportunities for academic help outside of class 20% of sample	71% retention 9% of sample	75% retention 6% of sample	81% retention 5% of sample

▶ Factors marked with this bullet have a direct impact on the probability of first year retention.

* Factors marked with this bullet have only an indirect impact on retention through their impact on first semester GPA.

factor is dichotomous, the column is left blank. In general both a variables impact on the probability of retention and its contribution of the model's predictive power give a similar impression of the factor's "strength." Occasionally a factor appears to be out of line. For instance, because resident aliens' financial concerns have a relatively high variability, the variable makes a relatively large contribution to the model's predictive power even though its impact on the probability of retention is more modest.

Conclusions and Implications

Taken together variables interacting with ethnicity or citizenship contribute less than 7% of the model's total predictive power. For comparison, academic background variables together contribute 12% and academic outcomes account for 81%. Clearly differences of ethnicity and citizenship play only a modest role in our efforts to understand the forces that determine persistence and attrition. Table 6 displays all the statistically significant retention factors by the ethnic and citizenship groups to which they apply. It is perhaps reassuring that students from different ethnic groups respond more similarly than differently to the collegiate environment. This suggests that, for the most part, uniform retention strategies are likely to be equally effective across ethnic and citizenship groups.

One exception is that the availability of opportunities for academic help outside of class is especially important for minority students. Perhaps the staffing of learning and writing centers on campus should make those services especially friendly and attractive to minorities without stigmatizing them. Finally, additional research is called for to understand the apparent disadvantage of black transfer students at our university.

Ethnic and citizenship groups are not uniformly defined across the country. Here Hispanics are Cubans not Mexican–Americans and Black aliens are probably Haitians while Black international students are more likely to be from Jamaica or the Bahamas. These "micro" differences in ethnicity point out the limited utility of ethnic categories in the first place, and they suggest that each campus may need to replicate this type of research for its own environment and its own ethnic and citizenship mix. At the very least, this research will help us improve access to education and equal treatment for all cultures.

Notes

1. The Systat Logit module was used for this analysis.
2. Students transferred an average of 33 credits from previous college level work.

References

Aldrich, J. H. and Nelson, F. H. (1984). *Linear Probability, Logit and Probit Models.* Beverly Hills: Sage.

Beal, P. E. and Noel, L. (1980). *What Works in Student Retention.* Iowa City, Iowa: The American College Testing Program and the National Center for Higher Education Management Systems.

Bean, J. P. (1980). Dropouts and turnover: the synthesis and test of a causal model of student attrition. *Research in Higher Education,* 12(2), pp. 155–187.

Bean, J. P. (1982). Student attrition, intentions, and confidence: interaction effects in a path model. *Research in Higher Education,* 17(4), pp. 291–318.

Bean, J. P. (1985). Interaction effects based on class level in an explanatory model of college student dropout syndrome. *American Educational Research Journal,* 22(1), pp. 35–64.

Bean, J. P. and Metzner, B. S. (1985). A conceptual model of nontraditional student attrition. *Review of Educational Research,* 55(4), pp. 485–540.

Bennet, C. and Bean, J. P. (1984). A conceptual model of black student attrition of a predominantly white university. *Journal of Educational Equity and Leadership,* 4, pp. 173–188.

Bennett, C. and Okinaka. (1999): Factors related to persistence among asian, black, hispanic, and white undergraduate at predominantly white university: comparison between first and fourth year cohorts. *The Urban Review,* 22(1), pp. 33–40.

Cabrera, A. F., Catañeda, M. B., Nora, A., and Hengetler, D. (1992). The convergence between two theories of college persistence. *Journal of Higher Education,* 63(2), pp. 143–164.

Cabrera, A. F., Nora, A., and Catañeda, M. B. (1993). College persistence: structural equations modeling test of an integrated model of student retention. *Journal of Higher Education,* 64(2), pp. 125–139.

Eaton, S. B. and Bean, J. P. (1995). An Approach/Avoidance Behavioral Model of College Student Attrition. *Research in Higher Education,* 36(6), pp. 617–646.

Eckland, B. and Henderson, L. (1981). *College Attainment Four Years After High School.* Washington, D.C.: National Center for Educational Statistics.

Farabaugh-Dorkins, C. (1991). Beginning to understand why older students drop out of college. *The Association for Institutional Research,* 39, pp. 1–10.

Greenfeig, B. R. and Goldberg, B. J. (1984). Orienting returning adult students. *New Directions for Student Services,* 25, pp. 79–91.

Grosman, E. J., Dandridge, B. A., Nettles, M. T., and Thoeny, A. R. (1993). *Research in Higher Education,* 18(2), pp. 209–236.

Hahn, R. W. (1974). In defense of dropping out. *Community College Review,* Winter, pp. 35–40.

Holahan, C. K., Green, J. L., and Kelley, H. P. (1983). A 6-year longitudinal analysis of transfer student performances and retention. *Journal of College Student Personnel,* July, 1983, pp. 305–310.

Kraemer, B. A. (1995). Factors affecting hispanic student transfer behavior. *Research in Higher Education,* 36(3), pp. 303–322.

Lechtman, C. M., Bass, A. R., and Ager, J., W., Jr. (1989). Differences between black and white students in attrition patterns from an urban commuter university. *Journal of College Student Personnel,* January, 1989 (3), pp. 4–10.

Lenning, O. T., Beal, P. E., and Souer, K. (1980). *Retention and Attrition: Evidence for Action and Research.* Boulder, CO: National Center for Higher Education Management Systems.

Levitz, R. and Noel, L. (1986). Keeping students sold. *Career Training,* September, pp. 18–21.

Lovacchini, E. V., Hall, L. M., and Hengstler, D. (1985). Going back to college: some differences between adult students and traditional students. *College and University,* 61(1), pp. 43–53.

Mallinekrodt, B. (1988). Student retention, social support, and dropout retention: Comparison of black and white students. *Journal of College Student Development.* January, 1988, pp. 60–64.

Metzner, B. S. and Bean, J. P. (1987). The estimation of a conceptual model of nontraditional undergraduate student attrition. *Research in Higher Education,* 27(1), pp. 15–38.

Murdock, T. A. (1987). It isn't just money: the effects of financial aid on student persistence. *The Review of Higher Education,* 11(1), pp. 75–101.

Nelson, W. L. (1994). Receptivity to institutional assistance: an important variable for African-American and Mexican American student achievement. *Journal of College Student Development,* 35, pp. 378–383.

Noel, L. *Steps for Mobilizing a Campus-wide Retention Effort.* (pamphlet) Iowa: Noel/Levitz Centers for Institutional Effectiveness and Innovation.

Noel, L. (1976). College student retention—a campus-wide responsibility. *The National ACAC Journal,* 21(1), pp. 33–36.

Noel, L., Levitz, R., Saluri, D., and Associates (1985). *Increasing Student Retention.* California: Jossey-Bass, Inc.

Nora, A. (1987). Determinants of retention among Chicago college students: a structural model. *Research in Higher Education,* 26(1), pp. 31–59.

Nora, A. and Wedham, E. (1991). "Off-campus experiences: the pull factors affecting freshman year attrition on a commuter campus." Paper presented at the annual meeting of the American Educational Research Association. Chicago.

Nora, A. and Rendon, L. I. (1990). Determinants of predisposition to transfer among community college students: a structural model. Research in Higher Education, 31(3), pp. 235–255.

Norl, L., Levitz, R., Salieri, D., and Associates. (Ed.) 1985. *Increasing Student Retention.* San Francisco: Jossey-Bass.

Pascarella, E. T., Smart, J. C., and Ethington, C. A. (1986). Long-term persistence of two year college students. *Research in Higher Education,* 24, pp. 47–71.

Pedrini, Bonnie, C., and Pedrini, D. T. (1988). Grade point average: stepwise multiple predictors for disadvantaged and control freshmen. *Psychology,* 25(1), pp. 54–57.

Petersen, T. (1984). A comment on presenting results from logit and probit models. *American Sociological Review,* 50(1), pp. 13–131.

Ramist, L. (1981). College student attrition and retention. *Findings,* VI(2), pp. 1–4.

Rowser, J. F. (1990). A retention model for African American students. *The Western Journal of Black Studies,* 14(3), pp. 166–170.

Sewall, T. J. (1984). A study of adult undergraduates: What causes them to seek a degree? *Journal of College Student Personnel,* 25(4), pp. 309–314.

Smedley, B. D., Myers, H. F., and Harrell, S. P. (1993). Minority-status stresses and college adjustment of ethnic minority freshmen. *Journal of Higher Education,* 64(4), pp. 434–452.

Southern Association of Colleges and Schools. *Criteria for Accreditation: Commission on Colleges* (1992–1993 Edition). Decatur, GA.

Terenzini, P. T. and Pascarella, E. T. (1978). The relation of students precollege characteristics and freshman year experience to voluntary attrition. *Research in Higher Education,* 9, pp. 347–366.

Tinto, V. (1975). Dropout from higher education: a theoretical synthesis of recent research. *Review of Education Research,* 45(1), pp. 89–125.

———(1987). *Leaving College.* Chicago: The University of Chicago Press.

Wilson, R. C., Gaff, J. G., Dienst, E. R., Wood, L., and Bavry, J. L. (1975). *College Professors and Their Impact on Students.* New York: John Wiley and Sons.

Improving Minority Students' Performance on College Admission Tests

Michael T. Nettles, Catherine M. Millett, and Marne K. Einarson

Why do underrepresented minorities test relatively low on admission tests? How can these tests be improved to predict student success? The authors argue that we need to address differences in backgrounds, learning styles, and study habits; and they outline a research agenda to come up with a solution.

Soon after high school graduates learn whether they have been admitted by their chosen college or university or will have to select an alternate, and their euphoria or disappointment subsides, they face the challenge of performing in freshman classes. Their memories of test anxiety have faded, but their test scores, which were used as a criterion in the admission process, may now be used by their chosen colleges to assess both their past academic achievement and to predict their performance in their first year.

Beyond admission decisions, the extent to which college and university faculty rely on admission test scores to gauge expected student achievement or to forecast student performance in individual courses is uncertain. What is certain is that faculty employ a variety of assessment techniques in an effort to evaluate the knowledge and skills that students have accumulated, and to assess the new knowledge and skills that they expect students to gain in their freshman year. The modes of assessment vary and include dialogues with professors, essays, oral and written reports and papers, and examinations taken in class or at home. These often represent a different approach to assessment from the one students experienced in admission examinations or in prior school curricula. Student performance on admission tests and on freshman-year assessments, and the congruence between the two, as well as the validity of admission tests in general, are vital centennial issues for the College Board.

In addition to initial impressions gained from freshman-year assessments, colleges and universities predict first-year performance on the basis of past academic performance and achievement. Evidence of past performance typically includes admission test scores, high school grade-point average (GPA), recommendations from high school teachers and guidance counselors, and other factors such as the type of high school curriculum, the quality of the high school, and students' special talents.

Predicted college GPA is typically a precise measure based on observing the match between the students' entering test scores and their first-year grades over time; therefore, the vast majority of students can be counted on to achieve their projected GPA. Some, however, do not and are therefore viewed as underperformers. In particular, African-American and Hispanic students more often than their white and Asian counterparts fall short both on admission tests scores and in achieving predicted freshman-year performance. This phenomenon is commonly referred to as either overprediction or underperformance, and indeed it could be both. In addition to improving the admission test and freshman-year academic performance of underrepresented minorities, one of the challenges for the College Board is to gain a clearer understanding of the relationship between these two measures and of what leads to overprediction or underperformance. Given the College Board's preeminent role in admission testing and its commitment to eliminating performance gaps between population groups, correcting the ethnic and social-class differences in performance and improving predictive validity should be at the top of the Board's equity agenda.

The Racial/Ethnic Conundrum in College Admission Testing

More students overall and more minority students aspire to attend college. Yet performance on admission tests and the use of admission criteria for predicting college performance remains a challenge for educators. The number of students expressing an interest in attending college by taking admission tests grew from about 1.5 million in 1991 to over 2 million in 1999. Roughly 70 percent of the more than 2.6 million high school graduates in recent years have taken admission tests. All of the major racial/ethnic groups have contributed to the increase, and with the exception of the decline in the number of Native Americans taking the ACT, each minority group represented a larger share of the test-taking population in 1999 than in 1991 and 1995.

Table 1 illustrates both the increasing number of students from minority racial/ethnic groups and their increasing representation among SAT I and ACT test-takers. The increase in African Americans taking the SAT between 1991 and 1999 was 16.9 percent, going from 97,008 to 113,377. African Americans represented 10.1 percent of all SAT test-takers in 1991 and 10.3 percent in 1999. The increase in African Americans taking the ACT between 1991 and

TABLE 1
SAT I and ACT Test-Takers by Race/Ethnicity and Year

	1991 *N*	*%*	*1995* *N*	*%*	*1999* *N*	*%*	*% Change in Participation 1991–99*	*% Change in Representation 1991–99*
SAT I								
African American	97,008	10.1	99,252	10.0	113,377	10.3	16.9	0.2
Asian American	42,607	4.4	48,523	4.9	60,878	5.6	42.9	1.2
Hispanic/Latino	55,211	5.7	67,050	6.8	81,632	7.5	47.9	1.8
Native American	7,828	0.8	8,955	0.9	8,225	0.8	5.1	0.0
White	676,404	70.2	665,750	67.4	707,851	64.6	4.6	(5.6)
Other Citizen	11,422	1.2	19,344	2.0	30,756	2.8	169.3	1.8
Noncitizen	73,150	7.6	80,258	8.1	92,989	8.5	27.1	0.9
Missing	80,206		107,524		159,876			
Total	1,043,836		1,096,656		1,255,584		13.7	
ACT								
African American	71,722	9.5	87,462	10.1	100,282	10.5	39.8	1.0
Asian American	14,306	1.9	19,622	2.3	24,357	2.6	70.3	0.7
Hispanic/Latino	30,661	4.1	42,193	4.9	46,361	4.9	51.2	0.8
Native American	9,285	1.2	11,220	1.3	10,612	1.1	14.3	(0.1)
White	584,986	77.9	645,915	74.4	718,498	75.5	22.8	(2.4)
Other Citizen	21,982	2.9	35,542	4.1	22,870	2.4	4.0	(0.5)
Noncitizen	18,129	2.4	25,772	3.0	28,527	3.0	57.4	0.6
Missing	45,912		77,562		67,506			
Total	796,983		945,288		1,019,013		26.7	

Note: Figures are based on test-takers in each senior cohort year with data on race, sex, and admission test score.
Sources: ACT, Inc. (1999) and College Board and Educational Testing Service (1999) unpublished tabulations.

1999 was even greater—39.8 percent, going from 71,722 to 100,282. African Americans represented 9.5 percent of ACT test-takers in 1991 and 10.5 percent in 1999. Table 1 also shows that the increase in Hispanics taking the SAT was 47.9 percent between 1991 and 1999. Similarly, the increase in Hispanics taking the ACT was 51.2 percent between 1991 and 1999.

The greater the number of minorities and the larger the proportion of college admission test-takers they represent, the more important it is to ensure that they share in the benefits of college access and achievement that accrue from the tests. It is important that those minority students who are admitted achieve the expected performance standards and graduate to prepare for graduate and professional schools and to achieve upward mobility in the workforce.

Performance of Racial/Ethnic Groups on College Admission Tests and in College

Although the number of underrepresented students among test-takers has increased, African-American, Hispanic, and Native American students do not perform as well as their Asian and white peers. Consequently, they are not benefiting equally from the tests. Although the increasing number of Asian-American and Hispanic test-takers has not resulted in large declines in their mean group performance, the increasing number of African Americans has been accompanied by a growing gap between their scores and those of other population groups. In fact, African Americans are the lowest performing group: their scores are the farthest below white and Asian students.

Table 2 shows the distribution within four selected SAT score ranges by racial/ethnic group and comparable ACT score ranges for the 1999 cohort of SAT I and ACT test-takers. The performance gaps between racial/ethnic groups are perhaps most apparent in the proportion of each group in the lowest and highest score ranges. For example, approximately 80 percent of African-American, 70 percent of Hispanic, and from 57.1 to 72.8 percent of Native American students scored in the lowest range on both tests compared with from 36.8 percent to 50.4 percent of Asian and white students. Fewer than 4 percent of African-American, 9 percent of Hispanic, and 13 percent of Native American students achieved scores in the highest SAT I score range compared with 31 percent of Asian and 23 percent of white students. On the ACT, fewer than 2 percent of African-American, 6 percent of Hispanic, and 7 percent of Native American students achieved scores in the highest range compared with 22 percent of Asian and 16 percent of white students.

Problems in Recruiting African-American and Hispanic Students

College admission tests, such as the SAT and ACT, are vitally important for colleges and universities as they seek to identify prospective students and make admission decisions based at least partially on predicted achievement. Among the important challenges facing the most selective and highly selective institutions[1] is the very small number of African-American, Hispanic, and Native American students who earn competitive scores on the SAT and ACT. The low supply of eligible underrepresented minority students places severe constraints on the efforts of these institutions to diversify their student bodies.

Even within the various score ranges, the mean performance of African Americans, Hispanics, and Native Americans falls below that of whites and Asians. Table 3 presents the mean scores of SAT and ACT test-takers at the various score ranges, African Americans have the lowest overall average and the lowest averages within each score range. Overall, the average score on the SAT was 852 for African Americans, 921 for Hispanics, 964 for Native Americans, 1077 for Asian Americans, and 1054 for whites. Similarly, the average score on the ACT was 17.1 for African Americans, 19.1 for Hispanics, and 19.0 for Native Americans, 22.4 for Asian Americans, and 21.8 for whites. Asian and white test-takers had the highest mean scores overall and at each range, and the largest gap in mean test scores at each range was between African Americans and Asians and whites. In the highest SAT score range of 1200 and above, the average score for African Americans was 1279 compared with 1336 for Asians and 1307 for whites. In the highest ACT score range of 27 and above, the average score for African Americans was 28.3 compared with 29.3 for Asians and 28.9 for whites.

Although admission test scores are usually not the sole criterion by which students are

TABLE 2
Frequency and Percentage of SAT I and ACT Test-Takers by Score Range and Race/Ethnicity, 1999

	SAT V + M Score Range Less than 1000		*1000 to 1090*		*1100 to 1190*		*1200 and Above*		
SAT	*N*	*%*	*N*	*%*	*N*	*%*	*N*	*%*	*Total N*
African American	89,560	79.0	12,644	11.2	6,773	6.0	4,400	3.8	113,377
Asian American	22,395	36.8	10,126	16.6	9,511	15.6	18,846	31.0	60,878
Hispanic/Latino	53,915	66.0	12,770	15.6	7,977	9.8	6,970	8.6	81,632
Native American	4,695	57.1	1,477	18.0	1,037	12.6	1,016	12.3	8,225
White	273,018	38.6	145,925	20.6	124,931	17.6	163,977	23.2	707,851
Other Citizen	13,198	42.9	5,451	17.7	4,641	15.1	7,466	24.3	30,756
Noncitizen	49,693	53.4	14,168	15.2	11,587	12.5	17,541	18.9	92,989
	ACT Score Range Less than 22		*22 to 23*		*24 to 26*		*27 and Above*		
ACT	*N*	*%*	*N*	*%*	*N*	*%*	*N*	*%*	*Total N*
African American	87,880	87.6	6,196	6.2	4,467	4.5	1,739	1.7	100,282
Asian American	10,994	45.1	3,522	14.5	4,529	18.6	5,312	21.8	24,357
Hispanic/Latino	33,759	72.8	5,032	10.9	4,830	10.4	2,740	5.9	46,361
Native American	7,727	72.8	1,162	10.9	1,041	9.8	682	6.4	10,612
White	361,860	50.4	111,564	15.5	131,704	18.3	113,370	15.8	718,498
Other Citizen	13,699	59.9	3,053	13.3	3,386	14.8	2,732	11.9	22,870
Noncitizen	19,983	70.0	3,033	10.6	3,142	11.0	2,369	8.3	28,527

Note: Figures are based on test-takers in the 1999 senior cohort with data on race, sex and admission test score.
Sources: ACT, Inc. (1999) and College Board and Education Testing Service (1999) unpublished tabulations.

admitted to colleges and universities, they often serve as the initial screen through which applicants must pass to be considered. Thus even when admission test scores are a small factor, they have consequences for the type of college to which students are admitted. And because students are usually attuned to where they are likely to be admitted, they most often only apply to institutions that are likely to admit them. The more selective the institution, the higher the test score students need to compete for admission.

Table 4 presents the distribution of first-time, full-time freshman enrollment by students' race or ethnicity for colleges and universities of various levels of selectivity in 1997. Categories of institutional admission selectivity are based on Barren's classifications of postsecondary institutions. (*see* Appendix, page 327). Only 3 percent of African-American freshmen enrolled in the nation's most competitive and only 5 percent enrolled in highly competitive colleges and universities. The representation of African Americans and Native Americans in the top two admission selectivity tiers of colleges and universities is the lowest among the various racial or ethnic groups. The representation of Hispanic students in the top two tiers was slightly higher than that of African-American and Native American students (3 percent in the most competitive and 7 percent in the highly competitive institutions) but below that of white and Asian students. Four percent of white freshmen were enrolled in the most competitive institutions while 10 percent were enrolled in highly competitive institutions. Asian students had the highest representation of all racial or ethnic groups in the most competitive and highly competitive institutions (10 percent and 19 percent, respectively).

Overprediction or Underperformance?

After addressing issues regarding the use of admission tests for deciding which students to admit, the next step is to ensure that the teaching and learning process provides the maximum opportunity for all students to succeed. Although

TABLE 3
SAT I and ACT Mean Test Scores by Race/Ethnicity, 1999

	Mean Score within Score Range				
SAT I	*Overall Mean*	*Less than 1000*	*1000 to 1090*	*1100 to 1190*	*1200 and Above*
African American	851.94	782.67	1040.47	1138.66	1278.70
Asian American	1076.68	844.27	1044.84	1143.98	1336.01
Hispanic/Latino	921.05	812.51	1040.93	1139.86	1290.60
Native American	963.64	828.68	1043.53	1138.58	1292.62
White	1053.79	866.14	1044.24	1142.58	1307.07
Other Citizen	1035.88	835.19	1044.96	1143.32	1317.22
Noncitizen	981.63	807.62	1043.48	1142.79	1318.20
All SAT I Test-Takers	1016.98	837.81	1043.78	1142.38	1309.62
ACT	*Overall Mean*	*Less than 22*	*22 to 23*	*24 to 26*	*27 and Above*
African American	17.07	16.08	22.43	24.77	28.28
Asian American	22.38	17.93	22.49	24.97	29.32
Hispanic/Latino	19.12	17.04	22.45	24.85	28.61
Native American	18.98	16.81	22.45	24.88	28.65
White	21.75	18.13	22.48	24.91	28.91
Other Citizen	20.64	17.54	22.46	24.89	28.89
Noncitizen	19.29	16.79	22.46	24.90	28.92
All ACT Test-Takers	21.01	17.64	22.48	24.90	28.91

Note: Figures are based on test-takers in the 1999 senior cohort with data on race, sex, and admission test score.
Sources: ACT, Inc, (1999) and College Board and Educational Testing Service (1999) unpublished tabulations.

educators question the predictive validity of standardized admission tests for African-American, Hispanic, and Native American students, these tests have typically been found to be stable and valid predictors of freshman-year academic performance. This simply means that the higher a student's admission test score, the higher his or her college grades are likely to be. But because of the variation in types of colleges and universities, curriculum requirements, course workloads, and faculty grading practices, there is also most likely to be variability in the relationship between admission criteria and freshman grades. Even when minority students achieve similarly high test scores and gain the same level of access, even at the nation's most prestigious colleges and universities, African-American, Hispanic, and Native American student achievement in college typically does not rise to the predicted level of performance. As a group, African Americans are the lowest performers among all the racial/ethnic groups on admission tests and in college courses. On average, Hispanic and Native American student performance is nearly half-way between African Americans and whites. Among the negative consequences for African-American, Hispanic, and Native American students of having lower average test scores in the upper range are the following:

- When admitted by the most selective and highly selective colleges and universities, students with relatively lower average scores are at a disadvantage in their freshman courses and that leads to relatively low grades.[2]
- Low grades often result in disappointment, restrictions on participation in sports, academic probation, parental disapproval, lower employment prospects, and competitive disadvantages in getting scholarships for graduate school.[3]
- Students with low freshman grades are more likely to migrate to leniently graded major fields (nonquantitative),[4] to continue to receive relatively low grades in courses beyond freshman year, and to be more likely to drop out of college.[5]

TABLE 4
First-Time Full-Time Freshmen Enrolled in Fall 1997 by Institutional Selectivity and Race/Ethnicity

		Number and Percent Freshmen Enrolled						
Selectivity	*# Institutions*	*Total*	*Black*	*Hispanic*	*Native Am*	*International*	*White*	*Asian*
Total	1,892	1,153,923	126,404	95,584	9,008	24,278	830,759	67,890
Column %	100%	100%	100%	100%	100%	100%	100%	100%
Row %		100%	11%	8%	1%	2%	72%	6%
Most competitive	52*	50,932	3,196	2,780	272	2,328	35,542	6,814
Column %	3%	4%	3%	3%	3%	10%	4%	10%
Row %		100%	6%	5%	1%	5%	70%	13%
Highly competitive	89	114,986	5,777	6,690	475	2,918	86,140	12,986
Column %	5%	10%	5%	7%	5%	12%	10%	19%
Row %		100%	5%	6%	0%	3%	75%	11%
Very competitive	250	241,047	14,404	14,175	1,756	4,591	188,645	17,476
Column %	13%	21%	11%	15%	19%	19%	23%	26%
Row %		100%	6%	6%	1%	2%	78%	7%
Competitive	588	411,940	52,344	22,638	3,172	8,073	305,553	20,160
Column %	31%	36%	41%	24%	35%	33%	37%	30%
Row %		100%	13%	5%	1%	2%	74%	5%
Less competitive	297	158,958	30,435	11,539	1,375	2,490	107,089	6,030
Column %	16%	14%	24%	12%	15%	10%	13%	9%
Row %		100%	19%	7%	1%	2%	67%	4%
Noncompetitive	125	87,234	13,370	5,566	1,235	1,491	63,627	1,945
Column %	7%	8%	11%	6%	14%	6%	8%	3%
Row %		100%	15%	6%	1%	2%	73%	2%
Other	491	88,826	6,878	32,196	723	2,387	44,163	2,479
Column %	26%	8%	5%	34%	8%	10%	5%	4%
Row %		100%	8%	36%	1%	3%	50%	3%

Note: Institutional selectivity is based on categories of admission selectivity published in Barron's Profile of American Colleges. Barron's criteria for determining admission selectivity include median admission test scores, high school rank, and grade averages of prior freshman classes. These categories are associated with the following median freshman admission test scores: "most competitive" = 655 to 800 SAT I, and 29 and above ACT; "highly competitive" = 620 to 654 SAT I, and 27 or 28 ACT; "very competitive" = 573 to 619 SAT I, and 24 to 26 ACT; "competitive" = 500 to 572 SAT I, and 21 to 23 ACT; "less competitive" = below 500 SAT I, and below 21 ACT; "noncompetitive" institutions require evidence of high school graduation; "other" includes specialized institutions (e.g., art, business, etc.) and institutions not rated by Barron's.

*One "most competitive" institution was not included in the IPEDS 1997 Fall Enrollment data file and could not be included here.

Sources: Barron's *Profile of American College's 1999* and *Integrated Postsecondary Education Data System 1997 Fall Enrollment.*

APPENDIX
Most Competitive and Highly Competitive Colleges and Universities in 1999

Most Competitive Colleges and Universities (N = 53)
*Rank 10: Median Freshman SAT I Score of 655 to 800: A to B+; Top 10% to 20% of High School Class**

Amherst College, MA	Duke University, NC	United States Air Force Academy, CO
Barnard College, NY	Georgetown University, DC	U.S. Coast Guard Academy, CT
Bates College, ME	Georgia Institute of Technology, GA	U.S. Military Academy, NY
Boston College, MA	Grove City College, PA	U.S. Naval Academy, MD
Bowdoin College, ME	Harvard University, MA	University of Chicago, IL
Brown University, RI	Harvey Mudd College, CA	University of Notre Dame, IN
CA Institute of Technology, CA	Haverford College, PA	University of Pennsylvania, PA
Carnegie Melton University, PA	Johns Hopkins University, MD	University of Virginia, VA
Claremont McKenna College, CA	Massachusetts Institute of Tech, MA	Vassar College, NY
Colby College, ME	Middlebury College, VT	Wake Forest University, NC
Colgate University, NY	New College of Univ of S. Florida, FL	Washington and Lee University, VA
College of the Holy Cross, MA	Northwestern University, IL	Washington University, MO
College of William and Mary, VA	Pomona College, CA	Webb Institute, NY
Columbia University, NY	Princeton University, NJ	Wellesley College, MA
Cornell University, NY	Standard University, CA	Williams College, MA
Dartmouth College, NH	Swarthmore College, PA	Yale University, CT
Davidson College, NC	Tufts University, MA	

Highly Competitive Colleges and Universities (N = 89)
*Rank 9: Median Freshman SAT I Score of 645 or More; GPA B+ to B; Top 20–35% of High School Class (N = 16)**

Brandeis University, MA	Illinois Inst of Technology, IL	Rose-Hulman Inst of Technology, IN
Bryn Mawr College, PA	Illinois Wesleyan University, IL	Smith College, MA
Case Western Reserve University, OH	Kenyon College, OH	Stevens Institute of Technology, NJ
Colorado College, CO	Oberlin College, OH	University of the South, TN
Emory University, GA	Reed College, OR	Vanderbilt University, TN
Grinnell College, IA	Cooper Union for Science & Art, NY	Rice University, TX
Wesleyan University, CT		

*Rank 8: Median Freshman SAT I Score of 620 to 654; GPA B+ to B; Top 20–35% of High School Class (N = 73)**

Austin College, TX	Lyon College, AR	Trinity University, TX
Babson College, MA	Macalester College, MN	Tulane University, TX
Beloit College, WI	Mary Washington College, VA	Union College, NY
Boston University, MA	Miami University, OH	U.S. Merchant Marine Academy, NY
Brigham Young University, UT	Mount Holyoke College, MA	Univ of California at Berkeley, CA
Bucknell University, PA	New York University, NY	Univ of California at Davis, CA
Carleton College, MN	Penn State University, PA	Univ of California at Los Angeles, CA
College of New Jersey, NJ	Pepperdine University, CA	Univ of California at Santa Barbara
College of the Atlantic, ME	Pitzer College, CA	University of Florida, FL
Colorado School of Mines, CO	Providence College, RI	University of Georgia, GA
Connecticut College, CT	Rhodes College, TN	Univ of Illinois at Urbana-Champaign
Drew University, NJ	Saint Louis University, MO	University of Miami, FL
Franklin and Marshall College, PA	Saint Mary's College of Maryland	University of Michigan/Ann Arbor

APPENDIX (*Continued*)
Most Competitive and Highly Competitive Colleges and Universities in 1999

Furman University, SC	Saint Olaf College, MN	Univ of North Carolina at Chapel Hill
George Washington University, DC	Santa Clara University, CA	University of Puget Sound, WA
Gettysburg College, PA	Sarah Lawrence College, NY	University of Richmond, VA
Hamilton College, NY	Scripps College, CA	University of Rochester, NY
Hampshire College, MA	Skidmore College, NY	Univ of Southern California, CA
Jewish Theological Seminary, NY	Southwestern University, TX	Univ of Wisconsin/Madison, WI
Kettering University, MI	SUNY College at Binghamton, NY	Ursinus College, PA
Knox College, IL	SUNY College Environ Science, NY	Villanova University, PA
Lafayette College, PA	SUNY College at Geneseo, NY	Wheaton College, IL
Lawrence University, WI	Syracuse University, NY	Whitman College, WA
Lenroh University, PA	Trinity College, CT	Worcester Polytechnic Institute, MA
Loyola College in Maryland, MD		

*Barron's uses an average of SAT I: Verbal and SAT I: Math scores for this table.
Source: Barron's *Profiles of American Colleges, 1999 Edition.*

Factors Related to Performance on Admission Tests and in College

Admission test scores can only be understood in the context of a variety of personal and academic characteristics and experiences. In addition, many noncognitive psychosocial student and faculty behaviors, experiences, and interactions, as well as institutional characteristics, should also be examined as possible influences on performance in college. These considerations may yield insights for developing strategies to improve minority student admission test performance and the predictive validity of admission tests.

The research literature examining factors that influence college admission test performance is rather sparse. Students' academic performance as reflected in patterns of high school course work and grades, particularly in math, have been identified as important predictors of admission test scores.[6] Differences in high school preparation and grades alone, however, do not explain the gap in admission test performance observed between underrepresented minority and other racial/ethnic groups. Other factors contributing to variations in test scores across groups include psychosocial or noncognitive factors,[7] and home, school,[8] and neighborhood environments.[9]

Research on the prediction of African-American and other underrepresented minority student performance has succeeded in identifying the overprediction/underperformance phenomenon but has fallen short of providing explanations of the type needed for designing efforts to improve performance in college. Because of the general absence of data and information about what happens in the college teaching and learning process, statistical analyses and research leave much room for speculation about how African-American, Hispanic, and Native American students learn compared with their majority counterparts.

Some of the student and faculty interactions, behaviors, and experiences that should be addressed include students' study habits; the level of student effort; interactions between students and faculty; the effectiveness of faculty; the quality of student work; faculty criteria for judging student work; the congruence between performance on admission tests, their content, and the content of college courses; and the congruence between the content and rigor of high school and college courses. An important initial step toward improving performance in college and, in turn, the predictive validity of college admission tests would be to develop standards of performance and communicate them to students.

Limitations in Current Methods of Predicting College Grades

The value of admission tests as instruments for selecting students and predicting their college performance, and the likelihood of degree completion and success after graduation is often debated. The debate is particularly delicate when it centers on underrepresented minority students whose test scores tend to be lower and hence to have more tenuous predictive validity. Yet the vast majority of four-year colleges and universities require students to take a test as part of the application and admission process, and the most selective colleges and universities use the test scores for making decisions about which students to consider for admission based largely on their projections of success at the institution.

Although mathematical models reveal with a degree of precision what a college student's GPA is likely to be, they often fail to shed light on the art and science of teaching and learning as it plays out in the college experience, or to provide a complete image of a student's previous learning experiences and capabilities. Colleges and universities need to learn much more about the backgrounds and experiences of their admitted students and their approaches to learning to know whether the students are a good match and whether they are likely to achieve their academic potential in a particular academic setting. The academic community should take a closer look at the skills that freshmen have on arriving at college, and whether those skills are the ones needed to succeed. Once required skills are articulated, then the question becomes how to best represent them in admission criteria.

College admission test scores may provide just the lip of the iceberg of information needed by colleges and universities in their efforts to ensure that underrepresented minority students succeed. New research and development on existing measurement instruments might lead to richer criteria for selecting minority students and forecasting their success and for improving their academic performance in college. Perhaps the instruments used for predicting performance can be improved with better information about performance expectations in college. Simply stated, by understanding the content and style of the best student performance in college, institutions and test developers alike can learn how to improve both measurement instruments and minority student performance. This, in turn, may lead to greater progress toward eliminating overprediction of college performance.

A Centennial Research Agenda

Research aimed toward improving African-American, Hispanic, and Native American students' admission test performance should focus on the factors that contribute to relatively high test scores among these groups to design strategies that might be useful for the broader population of underrepresented minority test-takers. Research on the predictive validity of admission test scores for college performance would help explain why African Americans, Hispanics, and Native Americans receive lower college grades than their majority counterparts even when they are predicted to attain the same grades. Without knowing the quality of student work, the faculty criteria for judging student work, the content and type of work required in college courses, the expectations of faculty, and the character of faculty/student interactions, researchers can only speculate about the possible sources of the differentials in predictions and grades that suggest underperformance.

Research questions related to relatively low admission test performance include:

- How do groups of underrepresented minority (African American, Hispanic, and Native American) admission test-takers compare with each other and with their white and Asian counterparts in terms of socioeconomic backgrounds and high school experiences and achievements?
- What are the differences in the socioeconomic backgrounds and high school experiences and achievements of underrepresented minority male and female test-takers? How do they contrast with their white and Asian counterparts?
- What are the differences in the socioeconomic backgrounds and high school experiences and achievements of underrepresented minority test-takers in various regions of the United States? How do they compare with regional differences among white and Asian test-takers?
- How are the composition and characteristics of underrepresented minority test-taking groups changing over time? How do they contrast with the composition and characteristics of white and Asian test-taking groups?

- What factors contribute to the admission test performance of underrepresented minority test-takers? How do these factors differ for white and Asian test-takers?

Research questions related to the predictive validity of admission tests include:

- Is the content and rigor of the academic work that African-American, Hispanic, and Native American students do in high school qualitatively different from that to which their white and Asian counterparts are exposed?
- Is the quality of work produced by underrepresented minority students the same as that of their white and Asian counterparts when they have similar college admission test scores?
- Do the performance gaps observed between majority and minority freshman students result in higher rates of attrition and lower cumulative grade-point averages through graduation?
- What information can college and university faculty provide about the quality of student work that will improve underrepresented minority student performance in college?
- How do faculty articulate the differences in the quality of work produced by African-American, Hispanic, Native American, Asian, and white students?
- Are the academic aspirations of underrepresented minorities the same as their white and Asian counterparts?
- Have underrepresented minority students learned the study habits and strategies required for high academic performance?
- Is the quality of work produced by underrepresented minorities in freshman college courses as high as their white and Asian counterparts?
- What is the congruence between the type of learning required for achievement on college admission tests and that required in first-year college curricula and how is this reflected in the grades of underrepresented minorities compared with their white and Asian counterparts?

Are judgments about performance made by college and university faculty fair to all students?

One Approach

One approach toward understanding the predictive validity of admission criteria, particularly test scores, with respect to grades in individual college courses, cumulative grade-point average and, ultimately, graduation with a bachelor's degree is to learn more about what happens in freshman courses. We propose that faculty who teach first-year courses learn more about the predictive validity of the tests that are used to forecast student success. Only then would we be able to identify the factors that contribute to differences in student performance and subsequent grades earned. Some of the areas we should focus on are: writing ability, prior subject knowledge, research skills, writing mechanics, and student performance on different types of classroom assignments. Strategies could then be developed to help students and faculty address differences in backgrounds, learning styles, and study habits with the goal of developing programs to help both students and faculty.

References

1. The Appendix lists the 53 most competitive and 89 highly competitive colleges and universities in the United States in 1999.
2. L. Ramist, C. Lewis, and L. McCamley-Jenkins, *Student Group Differences in Predicting College Grades: Sex, Language, and Ethnic Groups,* ETS RR No. 94-27, (New York: College Entrance Examination Board, 1994): J. P. Noble and R. Sawyer, *Predicting Grades in Specific College Freshman Courses from ACT Test Scores and Self-Reported High School Grades* (Iowa City, Iowa: American College Testing Program, 1987).
3. R. Sabot and J. Wakeman-Linn. "Grade Inflation and Course Choice." *Journal of Economic Perspective* 5 (1991): 159–70.
4. W. W. Willingham, J. W. Young, and M. M. Morris, *Success in College: The Role of Personal Qualities and Academic Ability* (New York: College Entrance Examination Board, 1985).
5. T. K. Schurr, E. S. Arthur, and R. E. Virgil. "Actual Course Difficulty as a Factor in Accounting for the Achievement and Attrition of College Students." *Educational and Psychological Measurement* 47 (1987): 1049–54.

6. D. Chaplin, J. Hannaway, S. Bell-Rose, and S. Creaturo, *African-American High Scorers Project: Student Activities, Course Taking, School Performance, and SAT Performance,* Technical Report Three (New York: Andrew W. Mellon Foundation and Urban Institute, 1998).
7. J. E. King, *Improving the Odds: Factors that Increase the Likelihood of Four-Year College Attendance Among High School Seniors.* College Board Report No. 96–2 (New York: College Entrance Examination Board, 1996); C. M. Steele and J. Aronson, "Stereotype Threat and the Test Performance of Academically Successful African Americans," in C. Jencks and P. Meredith, eds., *The Black-White Test Score Gap* (Washington, D.C.: Brookings Institution Press, 1998), 401–27.
8. C. Jencks and M. Phillips, eds., *The Black-White Test Score Gap* (Washington, D.C.: Brookings Institution Press, 1998).
9. Chaplin et al., 1998.

What Are Colleges Doing About Student Assessment?

Does It Make a Difference?

Marvin W. Peterson and Marne K. Einarson

Introduction

An increasing number of colleges and universities have engaged in some form of student assessment activity over the past decade (El-Khawas, 1988, 1990, 1995). Administrators and faculty have invested considerable time and effort in promoting, supporting, and implementing these assessment efforts. Yet concerns have been raised that assessment activities are difficult to mount successfully (Ewell, 1988a; Gray & Banta, 1997) and seldom produce discernible impacts on students' or institutions' performance (Astin, 1991; Ratcliff & Associates, 1995).

Student assessment, particularly scholarship taking an institutional perspective, is an emerging arena of study in higher education. A rich prescriptive literature exists. Scholars and practitioners have produced many books and monographs that offer guidelines for how institutions might best approach and support their student assessment efforts (cf. Banta & Associates, 1993; Banta, Lund, Black, & Oblander, 1996; Rossman & El-Khawas, 1987; Sims, 1992). Less available is nationally representative empirical evidence concerning how institutions have conducted student assessment and to what effect. Studies have collected descriptive data regarding the content and methods of institutions' assessment approaches (Cowart, 1990; Ory & Parker, 1989; Steele & Lutz, 1995). But there has been little systematic examination of organizational and administrative patterns at the institutional level developed to support student assessment efforts (Ewell, 1997; Johnson, Prus, Andersen, & El-Khawas, 1991) or how institutions have used and been affected by assessment information (Banta et al., 1996; Ewell, 1988b; Gray & Banta, 1997).

The purpose of our study was to extend current understanding of how postsecondary institutions have approached, supported, and promoted undergraduate student assessment, and the institutional uses and impacts that have been realized from these assessment efforts. In addition, we were interested in examining the congruence between institutional approaches to student assessment found in the prescriptive literature and actual institutional practices.

Reprinted by permission from *The Journal of Higher Education* 72, no. 6 (November–December 2001).

Review of the Related Literature

We began our research by conducting an extensive review of the literature on student assessment in postsecondary institutions. Details of this literature review and its results are available elsewhere (see Peterson & Einarson, 2000; Peterson, Einarson, Trice, & Nichols, 1997). For this study, we focused on the following conceptual domains: (1) the relationship of institutional context to student assessment; (2) institutional approaches to student assessment; (3) organizational and administrative support for student assessment; (4) assessment management policies and practices; and (5) institutional uses and impacts of student assessment information. Our review considered prescriptive literature offering recommendations for institutions embarking on student assessment and empirical literature providing evidence of institutional practices and consequences with respect to student assessment. Findings from the literature review are summarized below.

Institutional Context

The literature suggests that variations in the student assessment practices observed across postsecondary institutions are related to differences in broad characteristics of institutional context. Differences by institutional type have been observed in the content and methods of student assessment approaches (Johnson, Dasher-Alston, Ratteray, & Kait, 1991; Steele & Lutz, 1995; Steele, Malone & Lutz, 1997). Fewer studies have found differences in forms of organizational and administrative support for student assessment by institutional type (Patton, Dasher-Alston, Ratteray, & Kait, 1996), control (Johnson et al., 1991) and size (Woodard, Hyman, von Destinon, & Jamison, 1991). These findings suggest that patterns of assessment management policies and practices and institutional uses and impacts from assessment may also differ by institutional type, control, and size. No such comparative research was found.

Institutional Approaches to Student Assessment

Institutional approach to student assessment refers to the content and technical aspects of student assessment. Three dimensions of institutions' approaches to student assessment were relevant to this study: the content or type of student data collected, methods employed to collect assessment data, and the analyses conducted with assessment data.

Institutions may collect data concerning students' cognitive (e.g., higher-order cognitive processes, subject-matter knowledge), affective (e.g., values, attitudes) and behavioral (e.g., course completion, hours spent studying) performance or development (cf. Alexander & Stark, 1986; Astin, 1991; Bowen, 1977; Ewell, 1984; Lenning, Lee, Micek, & Service, 1977). Second, institutions may employ various methods to collect assessment data. Choices include comprehensive examinations or inventories; integrative or performance-based methods such as capstone projects, demonstrations, or portfolios; surveys or interviews; or the collection of institutional data such as enrollment or transcript data (Ewell, 1987c; Fong, 1988; Johnson, McCormick, Prus, & Rogers, 1993). Third, assessment approaches vary in the nature of analyses conducted with collected data. Institutions may analyze data at various levels of aggregation such as individual students or student subgroups, courses, academic programs or departments, schools or colleges, or the institution as a whole (Alexander & Stark, 1986; Astin, 1991; Ewell, 1984, 1988b). Approaches also vary in the complexity of analyses conducted. Analysis options range from producing descriptive summaries of student data to conducting relational studies of students' performance to aspects of their educational experiences such as course-taking patterns, exposure to different teaching methods, and interactions with faculty (Astin, 1991; Ewell, 1988b).

Scholars assert that a positive relationship exists between institutional uses and impacts of assessment and the comprehensiveness of an institution's assessment approach—that is, the extent to which an institution collects data on various domains of student functioning (Astin, 1991; Ewell, 1988b; Johnson et al., 1993), uses a variety of assessment methods (Ewell, 1984, 1988b; Halpern, 1987; Jacobi, Astin, & Ayala, 1987; Terenzini, 1989), analyzes data at several levels of aggregation (Astin, 1991; Ewell, 1988b), and studies the relationship between student performance and institutional experiences (Ewell, 1988b, 1991; Johnson et al., 1993).

Extant research shows institutions have adopted circumscribed approaches to student assessment. Although variance in content emphasis has been observed among types of institutions, most have focused on assessing cognitive rather than behavioral or affective domains of student development (Cowart, 1990; Gill, 1993; Johnson et al., 1991; Patton et al., 1996; Steele & Lutz, 1995; Steele et al., 1997). There is conflicting evidence regarding the assessment methods used by institutions. Some studies observed an increase in the tendency of institutions to use complex measures such as portfolio assessment (El-Khawas, 1992, 1995), whereas others found that institutions were most likely to rely on easily collected and quantifiable measures such as course completion and grade data (Cowart, 1990; Gill, 1993; Patton et al., 1996; Steele & Lutz, 1995). No research was located that examined institutional choices regarding the level of aggregation of data analysis. There is limited evidence of institutions conducting relational studies of student performance and institutional experiences (Gill, 1993; Patton et al., 1996; Steele et al., 1997).

Organizational and Administrative Support for Assessment

Three dimensions of organizational and administrative support have been discussed in the literature as important influences on the effectiveness of institutions' student assessment efforts: institutional support strategy, leadership and governance patterns, and evaluation of student assessment processes.

Institutional support strategy refers to an institution's choices about the overall purpose or functions of its assessment efforts. Scholars pro-pose that assessment strategies that emphasize internal purposes such as institutional improvement rather than external purposes such as meeting state-level or accreditation requirements will foster internal support for assessment and enhance the likelihood of garnering positive impacts from assessment (Aper, Cuver, & Hinkle, 1990; Braskamp, 1991; Ewell, 1987a). An institution's academic mission reflects strategic choices regarding educational goals and activities to be pursued. Whether or not an institution's academic mission prioritizes undergraduate teaching and learning (Banta & Associates, 1993; Hutchings & Marchese, 1990) and student assessment (Duvall, 1994) as valued institutional activities or specifies intended educational outcomes (Braskamp, 1991) may be predictive of assessment support and impacts.

Supportive leadership on the part of senior administrators (Banta et al., 1996; Ewell, 1988a; Rossman & El-Khawas, 1987) and faculty (Banta & Associates, 1993; Sell, 1989; Young & Knight, 1993) is thought to play a critical role in promoting an institution's student assessment efforts. The nature of governance processes for student assessment is also expected to influence internal support for assessment and the likelihood of achieving assessment impacts. On the one hand, a centralized approach as reflected in the existence of a formal policy for student assessment or creation of a central coordinating office may do much to symbolize an institution's commitment to assessment (Ewell, 1984; Thomas, 1991). More often, scholars have advocated a decentralized governance approach involving a broad range of internal participants, particularly faculty, as a means of enhancing the acceptance and use of assessment results (Astin, 1991; Banta et al., 1996; Eisenman, 1991; Ewell, 1984; Terenzini, 1989).

Finally, student assessment is expected to contribute most to the improvement of student and institutional performance when it is approached as a constantly evolving process rather than an episodic activity (Wolff, 1992). Accordingly, scholars have characterized evaluation of the assessment process as an important means by which institutions can enhance the institutional impact of their student assessment efforts (Dennison & Bunda, 1989; Ewell, 1988b; Sims, 1992).

Institutions have reported engaging in student assessment activities for a variety of internal and external purposes (El-Khawas, 1995). Descriptive data suggest that assessment support strategies that give equal or greater weight to internal improvement purposes than to external accountability purposes have developed more comprehensive student assessment approaches (Hyman, Beeler & Benedict, 1994; Johnson et al., 1991; Muffo, 1992). There is limited evidence that an increasing number of institutions have developed institution-wide student assessment plans (Gill, 1993; Patton et al., 1996) and that the centralization of decision making varies across the phases of planning, implementing, and using information from student assessment (Johnson et al., 1991; Patton et al., 1996). Results from one study suggest that few institutions have evaluated their student assessment approach (Patton et al., 1996).

Assessment Management Policies and Practices

Scholars contend the extent to which institutions devise specific policies and practices to support their student assessment activities and integrate them with other institutional processes is a powerful means of promoting internal support for and institutional impacts from assessment (Ewell, 1988a; Sell, 1989). Institutions have been encouraged to link internal resource allocation processes to their assessment efforts (Ewell, 1984, 1987a, 1987b, 1987c, 1988a; Thomas, 1991); to develop comprehensive computerized student assessment information systems to manage collected data (Astin, 1987; Ewell, 1984, 1988a; Terenzini, 1989); to regularly communicate student assessment purposes, activities, and results to internal and external constituencies (Ewell, 1984; Mentkowski, 1991; Thomas, 1991); to devise policies encouraging student participation in assessment activities (Duvall, 1994; Erwin, 1991; Loacker & Mentkowski, 1993); to provide professional development on assessment-related topics (Ewell, 1988b; Gentemann, Fletcher, & Potter, 1994; Young & Knight, 1993); and to integrate student assessment with processes for academic planning and review (Barak & Sweeney, 1995; Chaffe-Stengel, 1992; Ewell, 1984, 1988a, 1997). Conflicting opinions have been offered as to whether institutions should link policies concerning faculty evaluation and rewards to student assessment involvement or results (Ewell, 1984; Halpern, 1987; Ryan, 1993).

A few studies have provided descriptive data on the extent to which institutions have implemented policies and practices regarding communication of assessment information (Patton et al., 1996), student assessment information systems (Astin, 1987; Gill, 1993), faculty development (Steele & Lutz, 1995), and program review (Barak & Sweeney, 1995) to support their assessment efforts. In one relational study, the breadth of the intended audience for assessment reports was predictive of achieving positive outcomes from institutions' student assessment projects but resource allocation practices were not (California State University Institute for Teaching and Learning [CSUITL], 1993). Despite the reputed importance of this dimension of student assessment support, it has received limited attention in empirical studies.

Uses and Impacts of Student Assessment Information

Scholars suggest that student assessment information can be used in many areas of institutional planning and decision making, including institutional mission and goals (Banta et al., 1996; Ewell, 1984; Jacobi et al., 1987); academic programs (Ewell, 1987a, 1987b, 1988a, 1997; Gentemann et al., 1994); student support services (Banta, 1985; Williford & Moden, 1993; Young & Knight, 1993); academic resource allocation (Ewell, 1984, 1987a, 1987b, 1987c, 1988b; Thomas, 1991); and faculty evaluation and rewards (Ewell, 1984, 1988b; Jones & Ewell, 1993).

The ultimate measure of the effectiveness of an institution's student assessment efforts is the extent to which these efforts contribute to improvements in student and institutional performance (American Association for Higher Education [AAHE], 1992; Banta & Associates, 1993; Ewell, 1987b, 1988b, 1997). Clearly, enhancing students' academic performance is an important potential institutional benefit of engaging in student assessment. In addition, assessment may have positive impacts on faculty behavior and attitudes and on institutions' relationships with the external environment (Banta & Associates, 1993; Banta et al., 1996; Ewell, 1997).

The bulk of evidence concerning institutional uses of assessment information comes from descriptions of single institutions' assessment efforts (cf. Banta et al., 1996; Banta & Associates, 1993). Limited evidence from multi-institutional research reveals that institutions have most often used assessment information in decisions about program review (Barak & Sweeney, 1995) and least often in decisions regarding faculty rewards (Cowart, 1990; Steele & Lutz, 1995).

A few institutions have noted increases in student achievement on standardized examinations (Bowyer, 1996; Krueger & Heisserer, 1987; Magruder & Young, 1993), grade point averages (RiCharde, Olny, & Erwin, 1993), retention (RiCharde et al., 1993; Walleri & Seybert, 1993), and satisfaction with educational experiences (Katz, 1993; Krueger & Heisserer, 1987; Williford & Moden, 1993). However, two multi-institutional studies produced conflicting evidence regarding the impact of student assessment on student grade achievement (CSUITL, 1993; Johnson et al., 1991).

Descriptions of assessment practices undertaken at various institutions suggest that student assessment efforts may stimulate changes in the teaching methods used by faculty, including greater use of teaching approaches that promote student involvement in learning (Banta & Moffett, 1987; Friedlander, Murrell, & MacDougall, 1993; Walleri & Seybert, 1993; Young & Knight, 1993). Reports of individual institutions' assessment experiences also suggest that these efforts may have a positive effect on faculty satisfaction (Katz, 1993; Young & Knight, 1993) and interest in teaching (Friedlander et al., 1993; Hutchings & Marchese, 1990), and may stimulate campus discussions about undergraduate education (Hutchings & Marchese, 1990). Multi-institutional studies found little evidence that student assessment had led to changes in faculty teaching methods (CSUITL, 1993; Cowart, 1990) but have documented more positive faculty attitudes toward assessment activities (CSUITL, 1993), increases in faculty interaction and cooperation (Johnson et al., 1991), and increased sensitivity to the student experience (Hyman et al., 1994) as benefits derived from assessment.

There has been less consideration of the association between institutions' student assessment efforts and relationships with their external environment. The most frequently reported external use of assessment information is responding to state and accreditation reporting requirements (Cowart, 1990; El-Khawas, 1989, 1995; Ory & Parker, 1989). A few institutions have documented a positive relationship between their assessment efforts and allocations of state funding, number and quality of student applicants, and reputation of their institution (Young & Knight, 1993; Williford & Moden, 1993; McClain et al., 1986).

Overall, descriptive data about institutions' assessment approaches are relatively plentiful in the assessment literature. There is comparatively less information available concerning patterns of organizational and administrative support, management policies and practices, uses and impacts of assessment information, and the way these patterns differ by institutional type. The bulk of existing knowledge concerning postsecondary student assessment comes from descriptions of assessment efforts on individual campuses.

Research Questions

The purpose of this study was to provide a current and comprehensive portrait of institutions' approaches to student assessment, specific dimensions of organizational and administrative support for student assessment, assessment management policies and practices, and institutional uses and impacts stemming from assessment. We were interested in examining whether patterns of assessment approaches, organizational and administrative support, management policies and practices, and uses and impacts differed by institutional type. The research questions addressed in this study were:

1. What approaches to student assessment have institutions adopted? How do assessment approaches vary by institutional type?
2. What organizational and administrative support patterns for student assessment have institutions adopted? How do assessment support patterns vary by institutional type?
3. What assessment management policies and practices have institutions adopted? How do assessment management policies and practices vary by institutional type?
4. What uses and impacts from student assessment have institutions reported? How do assessment uses and impacts differ by institutional type?

Conceptual Framework

Based on our literature review, we developed a conceptual framework of institutional support for student assessment comprised of five domains: institutional context student assessment approaches, organizational and administrative support, assessment management policies and practices, and uses and impacts of student assessment. This framework is displayed in Figure 1.

Variables

Variables included in each domain of this framework are listed below. The variable names used in our analyses and tables are italicized. Operational definitions for all variables in the model and reliability estimates where appropriate are provided in Appendix A.

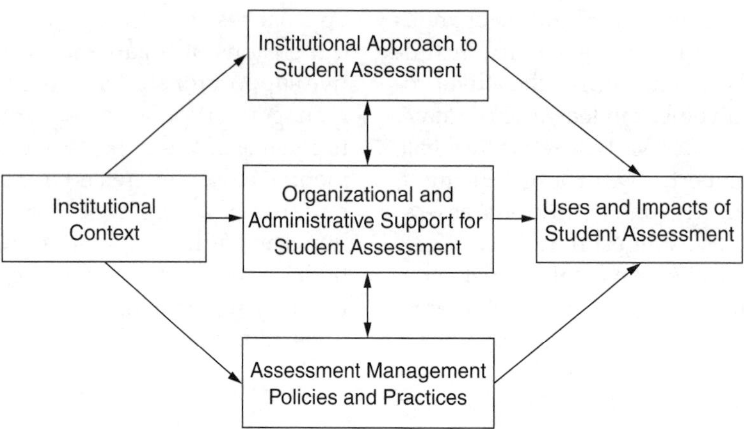

Figure 1 Conceptual Framework of Institutional Support for Student Assessment

Institutional Context

This domain was measured by *institutional type* (associate of arts, baccalaureate, master's, doctoral and research).

Institutional Approach to Assessment

The content of institutions' assessment approaches was measured by the extent to which they collect data on students' *cognitive, affective,* and *postcollege* development or performance. Three variables measured assessment methods—the number of comprehensive tests or inventories used (*number of instruments*), use of integrative or performance-based assessment methods (*student-centered methods*), and use of methods involving external constituencies (*external methods*). Analysis approach was measured by the *number of studies* conducted of student performance and institutional experiences, and the number of levels at which assessment data are aggregated and reported (*number of reports*).

Organizational and Administrative Support for Assessment

Four variables represented institutional strategy for assessment—*mission emphasis* on undergraduate education and assessment, and the importance of internal reasons (*internal purposes*), accreditation requirements (*accreditation purposes*), and state requirements (*state purposes*) as purposes for engaging in student assessment. Leadership and governance patterns for assessment were measured by the number of *administrative and governance activities* used to promote assessment, *administrative and faculty support* for assessment, whether the institution has a *formal centralized policy* and uses an *institution-wide planning group* for assessment. Evaluation was measured by whether an institution has formally or informally evaluated its assessment process (*conducted evaluation*).

Assessment Management Policies and Practices

Measures were developed for nine dimensions of assessment policies and practices: whether assessment data are incorporated in *academic planning and review* processes; use of assessment data for *budget decisions*; information system support for assessment (*computer support*), breadth of internal access to assessment information on individual students (*access to information*); breadth of distribution of assessment reports (*distribution of reports*); policies promoting *student involvement* in assessment; *professional development* policies on assessment for faculty and academic administrators; professional development policies on assessment for *student affairs* personnel; and policies linking *faculty evaluation* and rewards to student assessment involvement or results.

Uses and Impacts of Assessment

Academic decisions measured institutional use of student assessment information in academic decisions such as academic program planning, curriculum, academic support services, and academic resource allocation. *Faculty decisions* measured the extent to which assessment information has influenced institutions' decisions regarding faculty promotion and tenure and salary increases or rewards. Four measures of the impact of student assessment on students were used: *student satisfaction, retention and graduation* rates, *grade performance,* and achievement on external examinations (*external achievement*). Four items served as measures of the impact of student assessment on faculty: *campus discussions* of undergraduate education, *faculty satisfaction, interest in teaching,* and changes in *teaching methods.* Finally, four items measured the impact of student assessment information on external indicators of institutional performance: *student applications* or acceptance rates, allocation of *state funding,* regional *accreditation evaluation,* and *institutional reputation.*

Method

Sample

The present study is part of a national research effort on student learning and assessment in postsecondary institutions undertaken by Project Five of the National Center for Postsecondary Improvement. Based on our literature review and pilot testing with chief academic officers in four types of institutions (associate of arts, baccalaureate, doctoral, and research), we developed and refined a survey of "Institutional Support for Student Assessment." The survey is a comprehensive inventory of external influences on student assessment, institutional approaches to student assessment, organizational and administrative policies and practices supporting student assessment, and institutional uses and impacts of student assessment. In January 1998, the survey was mailed to chief academic officers at all postsecondary institutions recognized by the United States Office of Education that offer undergraduate programs at the associate or baccalaureate degree level, excluding specialized and proprietary institutions (n = 2,524). These administrators were instructed to direct the survey to the individual or individuals most familiar with the patterns of undergraduate student assessment within the institution. Completed surveys were received from 1,393 institutions for an overall response rate of 55%. Response rates by institutional type varied from a low of 53% for baccalaureate colleges to a high of 65% for research institutions.

Analyses

We supplemented data collected via our survey with variables for institutional type, control, and enrollment from the 1995 Integrated Post-secondary Education Data System (IPEDS). We used two data reduction approaches to identify patterns of variables in each conceptual domain and to condense the number of variables used in bivariate analyses. Survey items with an interval response scale were factored using an oblique rotation method. Several sections of the survey inventory consisted of dichotomous or categorical variables that did not lend themselves to factor analysis. In most instances, we reduced data by summing scores within sections to create an additive index of practices or policies in existence at institutions.

Descriptive mean scores of the variable indices were used to examine student assessment approaches, organizational and administrative support practices, assessment policies and practices, and uses of student assessment information in all respondent institutions. One-way analysis of variance was used to examine differences in these measures across five types of institutions: associate of arts, baccalaureate, master's, doctoral, and research. For each measure, post hoc multiple comparisons were conducted using the Tukey method to identify significant differences among specific institutional types. The eta-squared statistic was used to measure the proportion of the variability in each measure accounted for by institution type. Impacts of student assessment information were categorical variables. The Pearson chi-square statistic was used to test for significant differences in reported impacts by institutional type. Although not presented in the tables, adjusted residuals were used to identify which cross-tabulation cells departed most from the hypothesis of independence, and standardized residuals were used to determine the contribution of each cell to the chi-square statistic.

Results

Institutional Approaches to Student Assessment

Our first research question concerned the approaches to student assessment adopted by institutions. Eight variables were used to examine institutions' student assessment approaches. Table 1 displays means and standard deviations of assessment approach variables for all respondent institutions and by institutional type.

TABLE 1
Institutional Approaches to Student Assessment

	Institutional Type							
	All N = 1298	*Assoc. of Arts* N = 539	*Baccalaureate* N = 309	*Master's* N = 311	*Doctoral* N = 64	*Research* N = 78	*F*	*Eta Squared*
Content								
Cognitive assessment[1]	1.67	1.57^{b}	1.81^{a}	1.75^{a}	1.69^{ab}	1.50^{b}	10.881^{***}	0.201
	(0.58)	(0.58)	(0.58)	(0.55)	(0.55)	(0.53)		
Affective assessment[2]	1.87	1.70^{d}	2.06^{ab}	1.94^{c}	1.86^{abcd}	2.01^{abc}	26.901^{***}	0.113
	(0.54)	(0.49)	(0.58)	(0.51)	(0.64)	(0.53)		
Post-college assessment[2]	2.29	2.29^{a}	2.32^{a}	2.34^{a}	2.21^{ab}	2.09^{b}	3.302^{*}	0.072
	(0.60)	(0.59)	(0.60)	(0.59)	(0.64)	(0.60)		
Methods								
Number of instruments[3]	9.41	8.63^{b}	9.67^{a}	10.41^{a}	10.52^{a}	9.17^{ab}	14.211^{***}	0.045
	(3.49)	(3.33)	(3.40)	(3.45)	(3.49)	(3.51)		
Student-centered methods[4]	1.37	1.24^{b}	1.51^{a}	1.46^{a}	1.50^{a}	1.33^{b}	56.501^{***}	0.200
	(0.30)	(0.27)	(0.31)	(0.27)	(0.28)	(0.22)		
External methods[5]	2.04	2.03	1.98	2.10	2.05	2.05	1.713	0.045
	(0.57)	(0.60)	(0.54)	(0.53)	(0.54)	(0.58)		
Analyses								
Number of studies[6]	2.22	1.80^{c}	2.32^{b}	2.44^{b}	2.92^{ab}	3.33^{a}	11.284^{***}	0.048
	(2.32)	(2.12)	(2.36)	(2.39)	(2.59)	(2.36)		
Number of reports[7]	2.48	2.31^{b}	2.18^{b}	2.82^{a}	2.94^{a}	3.13^{a}	15.255^{***}	0.045
	(1.46)	(1.48)	(1.31)	(1.42)	(1.47)	(1.57)		

Note: Standard deviations are in parentheses. Post hoc pairwise multiple comparisons were tested using the Tukey method. For each variable, means whose superscripts contain a common letter (e.g., [a]) are *not* significantly different ($p > 0.001$); means whose superscripts do not contain a common letter *are* significantly different ($p < 0.001$). Response categories for all additive indices: 1 = yes; 0 = no. Factor scale A: 1 = not collected; 2 = collected for some students; 3 = collected for many students; 4 = collected for all students. Factor scale B: 1 = not used; 2 = used in some units; 3 = used in most units; 4 = used in all units.

[1] Four-item factor: scale A.
[2] Three-item factor: scale A.
[3] Thirty-item additive index.
[4] Four-item factor: scale B.
[5] Two-item factor: scale B.
[6] Nine-item additive index.
[7] Five-item additive index.
$^{*}p < 0.05$.
$^{***}p < 0.001$.

All Institutions

In general, the extent of data collection among all institutions was limited. Institutions collected postcollege assessment data (students' vocational outcomes, further education, and postenrollment satisfaction with institution) more extensively than data concerning current students' cognitive performance or affective development. Institutions reported substantial use of comprehensive tests or instruments as means of collecting assessment data. Despite considerable interest in the literature concerning alternative methods of assessing student performance, student-centered methods such as portfolios and capstone projects were either not used or were used in only some departments. Use of external assessment methods (those involving external constituencies such as employers and alumni) was comparatively greater. Institutions produced and provided reports of student assessment results at several levels of aggregation. It appears these reports were primarily descriptive in nature as institutions reported conducting few studies of the relationship between aspects of students' institutional experiences and student performance.

By Institutional Type

Statistically significant differences by institutional type were evident on all assessment approach variables except the use of external assessment methods. However absolute differences among institutional types in the means and standard deviations for each assessment approach measure were generally very small. The eta-squared statistic shows that institutional type accounted for a substantive proportion (greater than 5%) of the variance in only four approach measures—the collection of cognitive, affective and postcollege assessment data and the use of student-centered assessment methods.

Like all types of institutions except research universities, associate of arts colleges collected postcollege data from some to many of their former students. However, they collected significantly fewer affective and cognitive data than baccalaureate and master's institutions and used significantly fewer standardized instruments and student-centered assessment methods than all but research institutions. Associate of arts colleges conducted significantly fewer assessment studies than other institutional types and produced fewer assessment reports than all but baccalaureate colleges.

Baccalaureate and master's institutions shared similar assessment approach profiles. While baccalaureate colleges collected significantly more affective data than master's institutions, both collected significantly more cognitive data than associate of arts and research institutions and significantly more postcollege data than research institutions. They used significantly more standardized instruments than associate of arts colleges and made greater use of student-centered methods than associate of arts and research institutions. Both fell in the mid-range of number of assessment studies conducted. Along with associate of arts institutions, baccalaureate colleges produced significantly fewer reports of assessment data than did other types of institutions.

Doctoral institutions were neither significantly higher nor lower than other institutional types in their collection of cognitive, affective, and postcollege data. Like baccalaureate and master's institutions, they used significantly more standardized instruments than associate of arts colleges and more student-centered assessment methods than associate of arts and research institutions. They conducted significantly more relational studies of assessment data than associate of arts colleges and produced more assessment reports than associate of arts and baccalaureate colleges.

In terms of content and methods, research universities reported the least extensive assessment approaches. They collected significantly fewer postcollege data than all other types of institutions and fewer cognitive data than baccalaureate and master's institutions. They made significantly less use of student-centered assessment methods than all but associate of arts colleges. However, they conducted significantly more studies of relationships between students' institutional experiences and performance than all other institutional types and provided assessment reports at significantly more levels of aggregation than associate of arts and baccalaureate colleges.

Organizational and Administrative Support for Student Assessment

Our second research question addressed the organizational and administrative support patterns that institutions have developed to promote student assessment on campus. Nine variables were used to measure institutional support strategy, leadership and governance for assessment, and evaluation. Table 2 displays means and standard deviations for these variables for all respondent institutions and by institutional type.

All Institutions

Institutions reported a moderate degree of mission emphasis on undergraduate education and its assessment. Preparing for accreditation self-study emerged as the most important purpose for engaging in student assessment activities, followed by meeting state reporting requirements and internal improvement. Institutions had introduced two to three administrative and governance activities to promote student assessment. Administrators and faculty were perceived as being somewhat to very supportive of student assessment. Half of respondent institutions had a formal centralized policy stipulating specified student assessment activities of all academic units, almost three-quarters had an institution-wide group responsible for assessment planning and policy development, and half had either formally or informally evaluated their student assessment process.

By Institutional Type

There were statistically significant differences by institutional type on all dimensions of organizational and administrative support but evaluating the assessment process. With the exception of conducting assessment for state purposes, these differences were small in absolute magnitude and most often reflected differences between research universities and associate of arts, baccalaureate and master's institutions. As shown by the eta-squared statistic, institutional type accounted for more than 5% of the variance in only two organizational and administrative support measures—conducting student assessment for internal purposes and for state purposes.

There were several similarities in the profiles of organizational and administrative support for assessment reported by associate of arts, baccalaureate, and master's institutions. Compared to research institutions, they gave significantly higher importance ratings to internal improvement and preparing for an accreditation self-study as purposes for conducting assessment, reported significantly higher administrative and faculty support for assessment, were more likely to have a formal centralized assessment policy and more likely to use an institution-wide planning group for student assessment.

Differences were also observed among these three institution types. Associate of arts colleges were significantly less likely to have an explicit mission emphasis on undergraduate education and assessment than were baccalaureate and master's institutions. Associate of arts colleges gave significantly greater importance to meeting state requirements as an assessment purpose—rating this as moderately to very important—than all other types of institutions. They used significantly fewer administrative and governance activities to support assessment than master's institutions.

There were few significant differences between doctoral and other types of institutions on measures of organizational and administrative support for assessment. Doctoral institutions gave a significantly higher importance rating to preparing for an accreditation self-study as a purpose for conducting assessment than did research institutions and attributed significantly less importance than associate of arts institutions to conducting assessment for state purposes.

Research institutions presented the weakest profile of organizational and administrative support for assessment. As discussed above, they scored significantly lower than all but doctoral institutions on most measures considered within this domain.

Assessment Management Policies and Practices

Our third research question addressed the use of assessment management policies and practices to support student assessment. Table 3 displays means and standard deviations of nine dimensions of assessment management policies and practices for all institutions and by institutional type.

All Institutions

On the whole, institutions rarely used student performance indicators to reward academic units in the budget process or competitively allocate resources among academic units. Information

TABLE 2
Organizational and Administrative Support for Student Assessment

	Institutional Type							
	All *N = 1312*	*Assoc. of Arts* *N = 544*	*Baccalaureate* *N = 315*	*Master's* *N = 313*	*Doctoral* *N = 65*	*Research* *N = 79*	*F*	*Eta Squared*
Institutional Support Strategy								
Mission emphasis[1]	1.54	1.46[b]	1.64[a]	1.64[a]	1.50[ab]	1.27[b]	5.320***	0.005
	(0.85)	(0.90)	(0.77)	(0.84)	(0.87)	(0.73)		
Internal purposes[2]	2.49	2.53[a]	2.51[a]	2.48[a]	2.37[ab]	2.28[b]	5.185***	0.138
	(0.50)	(0.51)	(0.50)	(0.45)	(0.51)	(0.51)		
Accreditation purposes[3]	3.60	3.61[a]	3.63[a]	3.67[a]	3.69[a]	3.14[b]	11.300***	0.007
	(0.65)	(0.66)	(0.63)	(0.55)	(0.58)	(0.92)		
State purposes[3]	2.88	3.37[a]	2.30[c]	2.76[b]	2.60[bc]	2.41[bc]	54.650***	0.064
	(1.18)	(.90)	(1.21)	(1.17)	(1.26)	(1.27)		
Leadership and Governance								
Administrative and governance activities[4]	2.34	2.20[b]	2.33[ab]	2.62[a]	2.42[ab]	2.16[ab]	5.212***	0.013
	(1.22)	(1.18)	(1.29)	(1.21)	(1.25)	(1.12)		
Administrative and faculty support[5]	17.04	17.20[a]	17.09[a]	17.06[a]	16.51[ab]	16.05[ab]	3.606***	0.033
	(2.74)	(2.86)	(2.91)	(2.37)	(2.88)	(2.27)		
Formal centralized policy[6]	0.50	0.54[a]	0.55[a]	0.47[a]	0.37[ab]	0.28[b]	6.951***	0.017
	(0.50)	(0.50)	(0.50)	(0.50)	(0.49)	(0.45)		
Institution-wide planning group[6]	0.71	0.73[a]	0.73[a]	0.73[a]	0.62[ab]	0.45[b]	6.950***	0.011
	(0.46)	(0.44)	(0.45)	(0.45)	(0.49)	(0.50)		
Evaluation								
Conducted evaluation[6]	0.49	0.52	0.47	0.49	0.50	0.36	2.039	0.010
	(0.50)	(0.50)	(0.50)	(0.50)	(0.50)	(0.48)		

Note: Standard deviations are in parentheses. Post hoc pairwise multiple comparisons were tested using the Tukey method. For each variable, means whose superscripts contain a common letter (e.g., [a]) are *not* significantly different ($p > 0.001$); means whose superscripts do not contain a common letter *are* significantly different ($p < 0.001$). Response categories for all additive indices: 1 = yes; 0 = no. Factor scale A: 1 = no importance; 2 = minor importance; 3 = moderate importance; 4 = very important.

[1] Three-item additive index.
[2] Four-item factor: scale A.
[3] Single item: scale A.
[4] Seven-item additive index.
[5] Four-item additive index: 1 = very unsupportive; 2 = somewhat unsupportive; 3 = neutral or unknown; 4 = somewhat supportive; 5 = very supportive.
[6] Single item: 1 = yes; 0 = no.
** $p < 0.01$.
*** $p < 0.001$.

TABLE 3
Assessment Management Policies and Practices

	Institutional Type							
	All N = 1293	*Assoc. of Arts* N = 538	*Baccalaureate* N = 304	*Master's* N = 313	*Doctoral* N = 308	*Research* N = 78	*F*	*Eta Squared*
Budget decisions[1]	0.08 (0.32)	0.07 (0.29)	0.07 (0.32)	0.10 (0.33)	0.05 (0.22)	0.18 (0.51)	1.440	0.003
Computer support[2]	0.80 (0.90)	0.89^{a} (0.94)	0.66^{b} (0.87)	0.75^{ab} (0.86)	0.69^{ab} (0.79)	0.92^{ab} (0.91)	4.018^{**}	0.003
Access to information[3]	3.48 (1.65)	3.80^{a} (1.53)	3.35^{b} (1.66)	3.34^{b} (1.62)	2.77^{b} (1.85)	2.94^{b} (1.88)	11.776^{***}	0.034
Distribution of reports[4]	2.44 (1.38)	2.54 (1.42)	2.42 (1.24)	2.34 (1.32)	2.31 (1.48)	2.26 (1.66)	1.663	0.016
Academic planning and review[5]	2.78 (0.97)	2.87^{a} (0.99)	2.82^{ab} (0.99)	2.72^{abc} (0.89)	2.48^{bc} (0.95)	2.43^{c} (0.85)	5.089^{***}	0.302
Student involvement[6]	2.64 (0.85)	2.71^{ab} (0.88)	2.80^{a} (0.80)	2.56^{b} (0.83)	2.41^{bc} (0.77)	2.14^{c} (0.79)	11.040^{**}	0.156
Professional development[5]	1.88 (0.79)	2.04^{a} (0.82)	1.79^{b} (0.77)	1.81^{b} (0.76)	1.83^{ab} (0.73)	1.45^{c} (0.60)	11.975^{***}	0.292
Student affairs[7]	1.93 (1.17)	2.21^{a} (1.27)	1.66^{b} (1.07)	1.78^{b} (1.07)	1.80^{ab} (1.08)	1.68^{b} (0.95)	13.505^{***}	0.042
Faculty evaluation[8]	1.25 (0.66)	1.14^{b} (0.62)	1.37^{a} (0.74)	1.31^{a} (0.63)	1.26^{ab} (0.63)	1.22^{ab} (0.59)	6.866^{***}	0.352

Note: Standard deviations are in parentheses. Post hoc pairwise multiple comparisons were tested using the Tukey method. For each variable, means whose superscripts contain a common letter (e.g., ^{a}) are *not* significantly different ($p > 0.001$); means whose superscripts do not contain a common letter *are* significantly different ($p < 0.001$). Response categories for all additive indices: 1 = yes; 0 = no. Scale for all factors: 1 = not done at all; 2 = done in a few depts; 3 = done in some depts; 4 = done in many depts; 5 = done in most depts.

[1]Two-item additive index.
[2]Three-item additive index.
[3]Five-item additive index.
[4]Six-item additive index.
[5]Four-item factor scale.
[6]Three-item factor scale.
[7]Two-item factor scale.
[8]Five-item factor scale.
$^{**}p < 0.01$.
$^{***}p < 0.001$.

system capabilities for student assessment, indicated by the computer support index, were limited. Institutions provided fairly broad internal access to student assessment information but somewhat less access through the distribution of assessment reports. Institutions used student performance data in academic planning and review processes and had policies encouraging student involvement in assessment activities in some departments. They made comparatively less use of policies providing professional development on student assessment for faculty, academic administrators, and student affairs personnel and seldom linked faculty evaluation and reward policies to student assessment involvement or results.

By Institutional Type

With the exception of budget decisions and the distribution of assessment reports, there were statistically significant differences in the extent to which different types of institutions used assessment management policies and practices. Absolute differences among institutional types were slightly larger in this assessment domain than in the approach and support domains. Institutional type differences were also reflected in the large eta-squared statistics associated with the use of four areas of assessment management policies: academic planning and review, student involvement, professional development for faculty and academic administrators, and faculty evaluation.

Overall, associate of arts institutions made the most extensive use of assessment management policies and practices. They used more sophisticated information systems to manage student assessment data and provided significantly greater internal access to these data than other types of institutions. They made significantly greater use of assessment information in academic planning and review and had significantly more extensive policies encouraging student involvement in assessment than research universities. They had significantly more extensive professional development policies for faculty, academic administrators and student affairs personnel than all types of institutions but doctoral universities. Although it was rare for any type of institution to link student assessment to faculty evaluation and rewards, associate of arts colleges did so least of all institutional types.

There were several similarities in the extent to which baccalaureate, master's, doctoral, and research institutions used these assessment management policies and practices. They did not differ significantly from each other in their computer support for assessment, provision of internal access to assessment information, and the extent of their policies providing professional development on assessment for student affairs personnel or linking student assessment to faculty evaluation. In particular, master's and doctoral institutions fell in the mid-range of responses relative to other types of institutions, often reporting neither significantly more nor less extensive use of assessment policies and practices to support student assessment.

However, a few distinctions among these institutional types were also observed. Baccalaureate colleges reported significantly less computer support for assessment than associate of arts colleges and made greater use of policies promoting student involvement in assessment than master's, doctoral, and research universities. Research universities were significantly less likely to use assessment data in academic planning and review processes than associate of arts and baccalaureate colleges; made significantly less use of policies encouraging student involvement in assessment than all but doctoral institutions; and provided significantly less professional development on student assessment for faculty and academic administrators than all other types of institutions.

Institutional Uses and Impacts of Student Assessment

Assessment Information Uses

Our fourth research question considered institutional uses and impacts of student assessment information. Two indices were used as measures of the influence of student assessment information on institutional decision making. Academic decisions was a ten-item factor reflecting the influence of student assessment information on decisions such as academic program planning, academic support services, teaching methods, and academic resource allocation. Faculty decisions was a two-item factor measuring the influence of student assessment information on institutions' decisions regarding faculty promotion and tenure and salary increases or other

TABLE 4
Uses of Student Assessment Information

		Institutional Type						
	All *N = 1302*	*Assoc. of Arts* *N = 519*	*Bacca-laureate* *N = 295*	*Master's* *N = 296*	*Doctoral* *N = 63*	*Research* *N = 69*	*F*	*Eta Squared*
Academic decisions[1]	1.40 (0.41)	1.40[ab] (0.42)	1.40[ab] (0.41)	1.44[a] (0.38)	1.32[ab] (0.42)	1.29[b] (0.34)	2.549*	0.866
Faculty decisions[2]	1.28 (0.62)	1.20[b] (0.57)	1.44[a] (0.71)	1.30[ab] (0.60)	1.22[ab] (0.59)	1.19[b] (0.50)	8.042***	0.014

Note: Standard deviations are in parentheses. Post hoc pairwise multiple comparisons were tested using the Tukey method. For each variable, means whose superscripts contain a common letter (e.g., [a]) are *not* significantly different ($p > 0.001$); means whose superscripts do not contain a common letter *are* significantly different ($p < 0.001$). Scale for both factors: 1 = no action taken or influence unknown; 2 = action taken, data not influential; 3 = action taken, data somewhat influential; 4 = action taken, data very influential.

[1] Ten-item factor scale.

[2] Two-item factor scale.

* $p < 0.05$.

*** $p > 0.001$.

rewards. Specific items and alpha coefficients for each factor appear in Appendix A. Table 4 displays means and standard deviations for these assessment uses for all institutions and by institutional type.

All Institutions

As Table 4 shows, student assessment information has had limited influence on institutions' academic decisions and even less on faculty-related decisions. These low scores for assessment information uses reflect the fact that many institutions reported they had not monitored the items comprising these indices (for full results of individual items comprising these indices, see Peterson, Einarson, Augustine, & Vaughan, 1999c). The percentage of institutions reporting they did not know the nature or extent of assessment information influences ranged from 22% for modifications to student academic support services to 70% for faculty salary increases or rewards. When institutions had monitored assessment uses on specific items, they were most likely to report that assessment information had been somewhat influential with respect to decision making.

By Institutional Type

There were statistically significant differences by institutional type in reported use of assessment information in academic and faculty decisions. For example, post hoc comparisons reveal that master's institutions made significantly greater use of assessment information in academic decisions than research institutions. Baccalaureate colleges reported significantly more influence of assessment data in faculty-related decisions than either associate of arts or research institutions. Further, the eta-squared statistic shows that institutional type accounted for a large proportion of the variance in using assessment information in academic decisions. But statistical significance notwithstanding, absolute differences in the use of assessment information by types of institutions were negligible. All types reported that assessment information had either none or no known influence on academic and faculty decisions.

Assessment Information Impacts

Four measures of the impact of student assessment on students were used: student satisfaction, retention or graduation rates, grade performance, and achievement on external examinations. Four items served as measures of the impact of student assessment on faculty: campus discussions of undergraduate education, faculty satisfaction, interest in teaching and changes in teaching methods. Four items measured the impact of student assessment information on external indicators of institutional performance: student applications or acceptance rates, allocation of state funding, regional accreditation evaluation, and institutional reputation. For each item, respondents indicated whether they had not monitored the impact of assessment information, had monitored and observed a negative impact, had monitored and observed no impact, or had monitored and observed a positive impact. Table 5 presents the distribution of responses for all institutions and by institutional type. Chi-square was used to test the significance of differences in responses across institutional types.

All Institutions

Table 5 clearly shows that the majority of institutions had not monitored assessment-related impacts. Institutions were more likely to have monitored assessment impacts on students and faculty than on external performance indicators. When monitoring had taken place, negative impacts were almost never reported.

Approximately one-fifth of institutions reported positive impacts of assessment information on three indirect indicators of student performance—student satisfaction, retention or graduation rates, and achievement on external examinations. A smaller proportion had documented positive impacts of assessment information on student grade achievement. More than one-third of institutions reported that assessment information had stimulated campus discussions of undergraduate education and encouraged faculty to change their teaching methods, while one-fifth attributed increased faculty interest in teaching to their student assessment efforts. There was a mixed profile of assessment impacts on faculty satisfaction. Whereas one-tenth of institutions reported a positive impact from student assessment information on this impact measure, five percent reported a negative impact; although a small proportion, this was the largest negative response associated with any impact measure.

Conversely, institutions were most likely to report a positive impact from student assessment information on their regional accreditation evaluation—with more than two-fifths of institutions doing so. One-fifth of respondents credited their student assessment efforts with an improvement in institutional reputation. Fully 90% of institutions had either not monitored or did not know the impact of assessment information on student applications or state funding allocations.

By Institutional Type

There were no statistically significant differences by institution type in the monitoring and nature of assessment impacts on any of the four measures of student performance, faculty interest in teaching, accreditation evaluation and institutional reputation. Standardized and adjusted residuals were examined to identify cells making the greatest contribution to significant institutional type differences for the remaining faculty and external impact measures.

Institution types differed significantly on three of the four faculty impact items: campus discussions of undergraduate education, faculty satisfaction, and changes in teaching methods. The significant chi-square statistics associated with these three items were chiefly the product of the greater tendency of baccalaureate institutions, relative to other types of institutions, to have monitored and documented positive assessment impacts. Associate of arts, master's, and doctoral institutions were in the mid-range of responses, while research institutions reported monitoring and documenting positive impacts on these faculty-related measures less often than would be expected if monitoring of these impacts were independent of institution type.

Institution types differed significantly on two measures of external impacts from student assessment information: student application or acceptance rates and state funding allocations. Significant chi-square statistics were primarily due to the difference in the responses of associate of arts and baccalaureate colleges on these impact measures. Baccalaureate institutions were more likely than associate of arts institutions to have monitored the impact of assessment information on student application rates, and to have documented no associated impact. However, associate of arts institutions were more likely than baccalaureate institutions to have monitored the impact of assessment on their state funding allocations and to have documented a related positive impact. The other three types of institutions generally fell between these two extremes of responses.

Discussion

Several limitations of the study must be noted. Like much survey research, our data consists of institutions' self-reports of assessment practices, policies, uses and impacts. Our survey was initially directed to the chief academic officer within each institution. Particularly in larger institutions, it would be difficult for any one individual to be knowledgeable about the wide range of institutional policies and practices

TABLE 5
Impacts of Student Assessment Information

	Institutional Type						
	All N = 1302	*Assoc. of Arts N = 519*	*Baccalaureate N = 295*	*Master's N = 296*	*Doctoral N = 63*	*Research N = 69*	*Chi Square*
Student Impacts							
Student satisfaction							12.537
Not monitored	58.1	59.6	53.7	58.3	60.9	62.9	
Monitored/negative impact	1.0	1.1	0.7	1.7	0.0	0.0	
Monitored/no known impact	21.2	20.1	26.5	17.7	21.9	21.4	
Monitored/positive impact	19.6	19.2	19.1	22.3	17.2	15.7	
Retention/graduation rates							8.127
Not monitored	49.9	49.0	46.8	51.8	57.1	55.1	
Monitored/negative impact	0.8	0.9	1.0	0.7	0.0	0.0	
Monitored/no known impact	28.6	27.1	31.6	28.6	28.6	27.5	
Monitored/positive impact	20.7	23.0	20.5	18.9	14.3	17.4	
Grade performance							17.992
Not monitored	58.9	54.0	59.1	64.6	65.6	64.3	
Monitored/negative impact	0.6	0.8	1.0	0.3	0.0	0.0	
Monitored/no known impact	27.6	28.6	29.2	25.2	25.0	25.7	
Monitored/positive impact	12.8	16.6	10.6	9.9	9.4	10.0	
External achievement							9.783
Not monitored	60.8	59.7	59.1	62.5	61.5	68.1	
Monitored/negative impact	0.3	0.2	0.7	0.3	0.0	0.0	
Monitored/no known impact	19.8	19.3	22.1	18.3	16.9	23.2	
Monitored/positive impact	19.1	20.8	18.2	18.9	21.5	8.7	
Faculty Impacts							
Campus discussions							29.833**
Not monitored	51.5	57.5	42.1	48.0	54.7	59.2	
Monitored/negative impact	1.0	1.1	1.0	1.3	0.0	0.0	
Monitored/no known impact	13.9	13.6	14.6	12.6	18.8	14.1	
Monitored/positive impact	33.6	27.8	42.4	38.1	26.6	26.8	
Faculty satisfaction							31.330**
Not monitored	67.9	68.2	58.9	70.7	75.0	85.5	
Monitored/negative impact	5.3	4.2	7.7	6.1	1.6	4.3	
Monitored/no known impact	16.7	16.0	20.4	16.2	15.6	8.7	
Monitored/positive impact	10.1	11.6	13.0	7.1	7.8	1.4	

TABLE 5 (Continued)
Impacts of Student Assessment Information

	Institutional Type						
	All N = 1302	*Assoc. of Arts* N = 519	*Baccalaureate* N = 295	*Master's* N = 296	*Doctoral* N = 63	*Research* N = 69	*Chi Square*
Interest in teaching							20.520
Not monitored	65.3	65.0	60.7	66.4	71.4	77.1	
Monitored/negative impact	1.3	1.9	1.0	1.0	0.0	1.4	
Monitored/no known impact	13.8	15.3	17.7	9.6	11.1	5.7	
Monitored/positive impact	19.6	17.8	20.7	22.9	17.5	15.7	
Teaching methods							22.206*
Not monitored	46.2	47.4	39.8	47.5	43.8	61.4	
Monitored/negative impact	0.2	0.4	0.0	0.0	0.0	0.0	
Monitored/no known impact	15.7	15.8	21.1	11.9	15.6	8.6	
Monitored/positive impact	37.9	36.4	39.1	40.6	40.6	30.0	
External Impacts							
Student applications							21.674*
Not monitored	78.8	82.6	72.2	78.6	81.3	76.4	
Monitored/negative impact	0.8	1.0	0.3	1.0	0.0	1.4	
Monitored/no known impact	13.4	9.9	20.1	12.0	12.5	16.7	
Monitored/positive impact	7.1	6.5	7.4	8.4	6.3	5.6	
State funding							30.188**
Not monitored	80.5	77.3	89.5	80.8	75.4	72.1	
Monitored/negative impact	1.1	1.3	0.4	1.4	1.6	0.0	
Monitored/no known impact	10.6	10.6	6.9	11.8	13.1	17.6	
Monitored/positive impact	7.8	10.8	3.2	5.9	9.8	10.3	
Accreditation evaluation							13.091
Not monitored	42.5	45.1	41.4	38.9	37.1	48.5	
Monitored/negative impact	2.8	2.5	2.4	3.4	3.2	4.4	
Monitored/no known impact	12.5	12.5	14.6	10.2	9.7	16.2	
Monitored/positive impact	42.1	39.9	41.7	47.4	50.0	30.9	
Institutional reputation							14.109
Not monitored	63.7	65.6	59.5	62.0	71.0	69.0	
Monitored/negative impact	0.6	0.4	0.7	1.0	0.0	1.4	
Monitored/no known impact	13.7	11.7	16.4	13.3	16.1	16.9	
Monitored/positive impact	21.9	22.4	23.4	23.7	12.9	12.7	

Note: Due to rounding column percentages for each impact item may not total 100%. Differences by institutional type were estimated using chi-square test of independence.
* $p < 0.05$.
** $p < 0.01$.

tapped by survey questions. However, these administrators were instructed to redirect the survey for completion by other individuals within the institution as appropriate. In our request for the names of individuals to serve as future points of contact for survey results, we most often received the names of individuals other than the chief academic officer—usually an institutional research or student assessment officer. This suggests that chief academic officers did indeed redirect the survey for completion as needed and enhances the credibility of the responses we received. An additional limitation of our research was its focus on an institution-wide perspective. This did not permit the examination of variations in assessment practices and policies within individual programs or departments or at the classroom level.

Despite these limitations, this study contributes a current and comprehensive national portrait of the nature and extent of undergraduate student assessment activities, institutional support practices, and uses and impacts within and across specific types of postsecondary institutions and allows a comparison of recommended to actual practices for student assessment among postsecondary institutions. Finally, these findings suggest future research directions.

Institutional Approaches to Student Assessment

Our first research question addressed the nature of student assessment approaches institutions have adopted. Scholars contend that the comprehensiveness of an institution's assessment approach may be positively related to the degree of internal support for assessment and the uses and impacts of assessment information achieved.

Institutions have adopted assessment approaches that are less extensive than those recommended by assessment scholars. Our findings confirm prior research regarding the moderate scope of assessment approaches undertaken by institutions. On the whole, institutions emphasize the collection of easily quantifiable postcollege measures, such as employment outcomes and further education, over more complex measures, such as higher-order cognitive skills and affective development. They make greater use of traditional assessment methods, such as standardized instruments, than less traditional methods, such as portfolios or capstone courses. Although they provide descriptive profiles of student assessment results, they seldom study the relationship between students' institutional experiences and student performance.

We found statistically significant differences in assessment approach measures by institutional type, although absolute differences were of little practical significance for several measures. Institution-type differences in student assessment approaches appear to be reflective of related variations in institutional mission (Austin, 1994; Clark, 1987). Despite their institutional focus on undergraduate education, associate of arts institutions have undertaken the least comprehensive assessment approaches. The highly diverse and mobile student population served by these open admission institutions may render the assessment and analysis of student performance more difficult than in other types of institutions. In contrast, baccalaureate institutions have the most comprehensive data collection efforts. This may be related to the student-development focus of these institutions. Their comparatively low emphasis on data analysis and reporting may be indicative of lower institutional research capacity relative to graduate institutions. It also suggests that student assessment may occur more often at the classroom or department level than as an institution-wide activity. Master's and doctoral institutions both scored in the middle range for most assessment approach variables. This may be due to these institutions' competing responsibilities toward undergraduate and graduate education. Finally, research institutions' low scores for data collection and assessment methods are likely associated with their greater emphasis on graduate rather than undergraduate education. Their high scores for assessment studies and reports reflect a well-developed capacity for educational research.

Organizational and Administrative Support for Student Assessment

Our second research question examined the organizational and administrative support patterns used by institutions to promote student assessment. Scholars and practitioners of student assessment assert that conducting assessment for internal purposes, strong leadership support, a combination of centralized and decentralized governance structures, and ongoing evaluation of assessment efforts are important means by which institutions can effectively support and benefit from student assessment.

A mixed profile of support practices was observed across all institutions. As has been noted in previous studies (El-Khawas, 1992, 1995), regional accreditation requirements appear to be responsible for stimulating many institutions' assessment efforts; whereas meeting state requirements and informing internal improvement are comparatively less important purposes underlying institutions' decisions to engage in assessment. There is limited evidence of explicit leadership support for assessment through mission emphasis or administrative/governance activities. Many institutions have established formal centralized policies concerning student assessment, and most utilize some degree of internal participation in assessment planning. Only half of institutions have evaluated their assessment process.

Significant differences by institutional type were evident in patterns of organizational and administrative support practices for student assessment. These were largest for the importance accorded to state-related purposes for conducting assessment. Differences reflect the governance styles associated with specific types of institutions (Austin & Gamson, 1983; Birnbaum, 1988, Clark, 1987). For associate of arts and baccalaureate colleges, institutional control also plays a role in shaping support patterns.[1] Associate of arts institutions have a comparatively strong profile of organizational and administrative support practices—an emphasis that is congruent with their more bureaucratic or administratively driven governance style relative to other types of institutions (Cohen & Brawer, 1996). These institutions view assessment as serving both internal and external purposes. The high importance attributed to meeting state requirements is attributable to the large proportion of these institutions under public control. Baccalaureate institutions are more often privately controlled institutions and thus place the least emphasis on fulfilling state-related purposes for assessment. Together with master's institutions, they fall in the middle range of administrative control and faculty autonomy. In contrast, research universities and, to a lesser extent, doctoral universities operate as professional bureaucracies—institutions in which management functions and external accountability are the responsibility of administrators, while teaching and scholarship are the responsibility of an autonomous faculty. The governance style and emphasis on graduate education characteristic of these institutions likely contributes to their comparatively low scores on organizational and administrative support practices for undergraduate student assessment.

Assessment Management Policies and Practices

Our third research question considered the extent to which institutions have intentionally used specific policies and practices to support student assessment. Scholars have depicted assessment management policies and practices as powerful levers for integrating student assessment with other institutional functions and processes, thereby fostering internal support for and institutional impacts from assessment.

Institutions have provided moderate internal access to and distribution of student assessment information. There appear to be some efforts to integrate student assessment processes with academic planning and review processes. Many institutions have also adopted policies to encourage student involvement in assessment activities. However, there is less evidence of providing professional development on student assessment to faculty, academic administrators, and student affairs personnel, and almost no efforts to link student assessment with faculty evaluation and reward policies.

Observed differences in the use of assessment management policies and practices among institutional types are consistent with institutional missions and governance styles. Of all types of institutions, associate of arts institutions are most likely to link student assessment to academic planning processes and to provide professional development on assessment to faculty and administrators. This administrative focus on assessment support is congruent with the comparatively strong administrative control associated with these institutions. Baccalaureate institutions, on the other hand, are more likely to have policies encouraging faculty and student involvement in assessment. This profile is reflective of their strong student orientation and suggests that student assessment in these institutions is more often a faculty than an administrative or student affairs responsibility. The relatively moderate use of these policies and practices by master's and doctoral institutions seems characteristic of their dual focus on graduate and undergraduate education. Finally, in keeping with their emphasis on graduate education and high degree of faculty autonomy, research institutions present the least extensive profile of assessment management policies and practices in support of undergraduate student assessment.

Uses and Impacts of Student Assessment

Our fourth research question examined the institutional uses and impacts of student assessment. Assessment scholars clearly contend that the assessment of student performance should not be an end in itself but a means to educational and institutional improvement (AAHE, 1992; Banta & Associates, 1993; Ewell, 1988b).

As has been reported elsewhere in the literature (cf. Banta et al., 1993; Banta & Associates, 1996), most colleges and universities have not monitored the influence of student assessment information on institutional decision making or its impact on student performance, faculty behavior, and external performance indicators. In comparative terms, baccalaureate institutions are most likely of all institutional types to monitor assessment uses and impacts, but in absolute terms, even their rate of reported monitoring of impacts is low. To date, the majority of postsecondary institutions have little documented evidence of whether and to what degree their assessment efforts have influenced decision making or produced discernible impacts on students, faculty, or external constituencies.

Institutions may be doing little monitoring of assessment uses and impacts for a variety of reasons—among them the brief amount of time in which some institutions have been engaged in assessment efforts, the difficulty of disentangling assessment influences and impacts from those of other sources, and the dearth of external requirements to provide evidence of having used assessment information or improved as a consequence of assessment efforts. Given the extensive claims made for the value of student assessment and the substantial human and financial resources invested in assessment activities, institutions need to give greater priority to examining and evaluating the uses and impacts of student assessment.

Future Research

This study provides a systematic comparative examination of institutional approaches to, support practices for, and uses and impacts of undergraduate student assessment. Despite more than a decade of assessment scholarship and activity, results show that most institutions have adopted limited student assessment approaches, developed selected institutional mechanisms to support and promote assessment, and have not monitored the uses and impacts of their assessment efforts. Results also show that patterns of assessment approaches, support practices, and uses and impacts vary among types of postsecondary institutions.

The present study has not examined the relationship of assessment approaches, organizational and administrative support practices, and assessment management policies and practices to institutional uses and impacts of assessment information. Certainly, this is an important research goal. Quantitative multivariate analyses of our survey data have been used to test the relationships among these domains in the conceptual framework. Results of these analyses are available elsewhere (see Peterson & Augustine, 2000a, 2000b).

The present study also supports the importance of conducting analyses within specific types of institutions. Such examinations of institutional assessment approaches, organizational and administrative support patterns, assessment management policies and practices, uses and impacts of student assessment, and relationships among these domains have been conducted. Reports for associate of arts (Peterson, Augustine, Einarson & Vaughan, 1999a), baccalaureate (Peterson, Augustine, Einarson & Vaughan, 1999b), master's (Peterson, Einarson, Augustine, & Vaughan, 1999a) and research and doctoral (Peterson, Einarson, Augustine, & Vaughan, 1999b) institutions are available from the National Center for Postsecondary Improvement.

A qualitative research approach would illuminate institutional processes involved in promoting and supporting student assessment. Conducting case studies of institutions with comprehensive student assessment processes that have produced institutional impacts may help identify institutional best practices in student assessment. A final phase of our research takes this approach and will provide further guidance to institutions in selecting assessment approaches, organizational and administrative practices, and assessment management policies that can promote the use of student assessment information and contribute to enhanced performance.

Finally, the literature on student assessment has highlighted the critical role of institutional culture and climate for student assessment in promoting its use to improve institutional performance (Banta & Associates, 1993; Banta et al., 1996; Jones & Ewell, 1993). Research on this domain of institutional dynamics is extremely important. Although not addressed as part of this national survey, developing an instrument for assessing culture and climate is an important facet of our case studies in the final phase of this project.

APPENDIX A
Variable Definitions

Variable	*Definition*
Institutional Characteristics	
Institutional type	Five-item nominal variable: associate of arts, baccalaureate, master's, doctoral, and research institutions.
Institutional Approach to Student Assessment	
Cognitive assessment	Four-item factor scale reflecting the extent to which an institution collects data on current students' cognitive performance: competence in major field; general education competencies; higher-order cognitive skills; vocational or professional skills (1 = not collected; 2 = collected for some students; 3 = collected for many students; 4 = collected for all students); Cronbach alpha = 0.71.
Affective assessment	Three-item factor scale reflecting the extent to which an institution collects data on current students' affective development and satisfaction: experiences and involvement with institution; satisfaction with institution; personal growth and affective development (1 = not collected; 2 = collected for some students; 3 = collected for many students; 4 = collected for all students); Cronbach alpha = 0.68.
Postcollege assessment	Three-item factor scale reflecting the extent to which an institution collects data from former students: vocational or professional outcomes; further education; satisfaction and experiences with institution (1 = not collected; 2 = collected for some students; 3 = collected for many students; 4 = collected for all students); Cronbach alpha = 0.83.
Number of instruments	Thirty-item additive index of comprehensive examinations, inventories or standardized instruments (institutionally developed, state provided, and commercially available) used by institution to collect ten types of assessment information: student plans or expectations; basic college-readiness skills; higher-order cognitive skills; general education competencies; competence in major; vocational or professional skills; personal growth and affective development; experiences or involvement with institution; satisfaction with institution (1 = instrument used; 0 = instrument not used).
Student-centered methods	Four-item factor scale reflecting the extent to which an institution uses integrative or nontraditional assessment methods: performance in capstone courses; portfolios or comprehensive projects; observations of student performance; individual interviews or focus groups (1 = not used; 2 = used in some units; 3 = used in most units; 4 = used in all units); Cronbach alpha = 0.61.
External methods	Two-item factor scale reflecting the extent to which an institution uses assessment methods that collect data from external constituencies: employer interviews or focus groups; alumni interviews or focus groups (1 = not used; 2 = used in some units; 3 = used in most units; 4 = used in all units); Cronbach alpha = 0.63.
Number of studies	Nine-item additive index of the number of studies an institution conducts on the relationship between student performance and institutional experiences: course-taking patterns; exposure to different teaching methods; student-faculty interaction; extra-curricular activities; residence arrangements; financial aid

(*Continued*)

APPENDIX A (*Continued*)
Variable Definitions

Variable	*Definition*
Number of studies	and/or employment; admission standards or policies; academic advising patterns; classroom, library and/or computing resources (1= conduct study; 0 = do not conduct study).
Number of reports	Five-item additive index of the levels of aggregation at which student assessment data are provided as reports: institution-wide; schools or colleges; academic programs or departments; special populations or subgroups of students; by course or groups of courses (1 = report provided; 0 = report not provided).
Organizational and Administrative Support	
Mission emphasis	Three-item additive index reflecting an institution's mission statement emphasis on undergraduate education and its assessment: emphasizes excellence in undergraduate education; identifies educational outcomes intended for students; refers to student assessment as important activity (1 = yes; 0 = no).
Internal purposes	Four-item factor scale reflecting the importance of internal institutional purposes for undertaking student assessment: guiding undergraduate academic program improvement; improving achievement of undergraduate students; improving faculty instructional performance; guiding resource allocation decisions (1 = no importance; 2 = minor importance; 3 = moderate importance; 4 = very important); Cronbach alpha = 0.79.
Accreditation purposes	Single item: importance of preparing for institutional accreditation self-study as a purpose for undertaking student assessment (1 = no importance; 2 = minor importance; 3 = moderate importance; 4 = very important).
State purposes	Single item: importance of meeting state reporting requirements as a purpose for undertaking student assessment (1 = no importance; 2 = minor importance; 3 = moderate importance; 4 = very important).
Administrative and governance activities	Seven-item additive index reflecting the number of administrative or governance activities used by an institution to promote student assessment: annual institution-wide assessment forums or seminars; rewards or incentives for administrators promoting use of assessment in unit; incentives for academic units to use assessment information; assessment workshops for administrators; board of trustees committee addresses assessment; faculty governance committee addresses assessment; student representation on assessment committees (1 = yes; 0 = no).
Administrative and faculty support	Four-item additive index reflecting the degree to which chief executive officer, academic and student affairs administrators, and faculty support student assessment (1 = very unsupportive; 2 = somewhat unsupportive; 3 = neutral or unknown; 4 = somewhat supportive; 5 = very supportive).
Formal centralized policy	Single item: institution has formal institutional plan or policy requiring specified student assessment activities of all academic units or programs (1 = yes; 0 = no).
Institution-wide planning group	Single item: institution has institution-wide group for student assessment planning and policy setting (1 = yes; 0 = no).
Conducted evaluation	Single item: institution has formally or informally evaluated its student assessment process (1 = yes; 0 = no).
Assessment Management Policies and Practices	
Budget decisions	Two-item additive index reflecting formal use of assessment information in the budget process: to competitively allocate resources among academic units; to reward academic units for improvement (1 = yes; 0 = no).
Computer support	Three-item additive index reflecting institutional capacity to collect and manage student assessment information: computerized student information system includes student performance indicators; student information system tracks individual students; student assessment database integrated with other institutional databases (1 = yes; 0 = no).

Variable	*Definition*
Access to information	Five-item additive index reflecting internal accessibility of assessment information on individual students by: institutional research or assessment professionals; senior academic administrators; department chairs or academic program administrators; student affairs professionals; faculty advisors (1 = yes; 0 = no).
Distribution of reports	Six-item additive index reflecting the number of constituent groups to whom student assessment reports are regularly distributed: students; faculty; academic administrators; student affairs professionals; employers; general public (1 = yes; 0 = no).
Academic planning and review	Four-item factor scale reflecting the incorporation of student assessment data into academic planning and review processes for: academic departments or undergraduate programs; general education or core curriculum; courses; student academic support services (1 = not done at all; 2 = done in a few departments; 3 = done in some departments; 4 = done in many departments; 5 = done in most departments); Cronbach alpha = 0.84.
Student involvement	Three-item factor scale reflecting the extent to which an institution has policies or practices to promote student involvement in assessment activities: inform students about assessment purposes and uses; require students to participate in assessment activities; provide students with individual feedback on assessment results (1 = not done at all; 2 = done in a few departments; 3 = done in some departments; 4 = done in many departments; 5 = done in most departments); Cronbach alpha = 0.69.
Professional development	Four-item factor scale reflecting existence of professional development policies or practices on student assessment for faculty and academic administrators: provide funds for faculty to attend or present at assessment conferences; offer student assessment workshops or consultation for faculty; provide assistance (e.g., paid leaves, stipends, course reduction) to improve faculty use of student assessment; provide student assessment workshops for academic administrators (1 = not done at all; 2 = done in a few departments; 3 = done in some departments; 4 = done in many departments; 5 = done in most departments); Cronbach alpha = 0.77.
Student affairs	Two-item factor scale reflecting existence of professional development policies or practices on student assessment for student affairs personnel: require assessment training for student affairs staff; provide student assessment workshops for student affairs administrators (1 = not done at all; 2 = done in a few departments; 3 = done in some departments; 4 = done in many departments; 5 = done in most departments); Cronbach alpha = 0.84.
Faculty evaluation	Five-item factor scale reflecting existence of faculty evaluation and reward policies and practices related to student assessment: promotion evaluation considers evidence of student performance; salary evaluation considers evidence of student performance; promotion, tenure or salary reviews consider faculty participation in student assessment; promotion, tenure or salary reviews consider scholarship on assessment; public recognition or awards for faculty use of student assessment (1 = not done at all; 2 = done in a few departments; 3 = done in some departments; 4 = done in many departments; 5 = done in most departments); Cronbach alpha = 0.77.
Institutional Uses and Impacts of Student Assessment	
Academic decisions	Ten-item factor scale reflecting the use of student assessment information in academic decisions: modifying instructional or teaching methods; designing or reorganizing academic programs or majors; revising or modifying general education curriculum; creating or modifying out-of-class learning experiences; revising undergraduate academic mission; modifying student academic support services; modifying student assessment plans or processes; designing or reorganizing student affairs units; allocating resources to academic units; creating or modifying distance learning initiatives (1 = no action or influence unknown; 2 = action taken, data not influential; 3 = action taken, data somewhat influential; 4 = action taken, data very influential); Cronbach alpha = 0.83.

(Continued)

APPENDIX A (*Continued*)
Variable Definitions

Variable	*Definition*
Faculty decisions	Two-item factor scale reflecting the use of student assessment information in faculty decisions: deciding faculty promotion and tenure; deciding faculty salary increases or rewards (1 = no action or influence unknown; 2 = action taken, data not influential; 3 = action taken, data somewhat influential; 4 = action taken, data very influential); Cronbach alpha = 0.79.
Faculty impacts	Four single items reflecting student assessment impacts on faculty: affected campus discussions of undergraduate education; contributed to faculty satisfaction; contributed to faculty interest in teaching; led to changes in teaching methods used (1 = not monitored, do not know; 2 = monitored, negative impact; 3 = monitored, no known impact; 4 = monitored, positive impact).
Student impacts	Four single items reflecting student assessment impacts on students: contributed to student satisfaction; affected student retention or graduation rates; affected student grade performance; affected student achievement on external examinations (1 = not monitored, do not know; 2 = monitored, negative impact; 3 = monitored, no known impact; 4 = monitored, positive impact).
External impacts	Four single items reflecting student assessment impacts on external indicators of institutional performance: student applications or acceptance rates; allocation of state funding; regional accreditation evaluations; and institutional reputation or image; (1 = not monitored, do not know; 2 = monitored, negative impact; 3 = monitored, no known impact; 4 = monitored, positive impact).

Note

1. Separate analyses, not reported here, revealed differences by institutional control within institutional type on study measures. Control-related differences were most salient to associate of arts colleges (93% in our study were public) and baccalaureate colleges (88% in our study were private).

References

Alexander, J. M., & Stark, J. S. (1986). *Focusing on student academic outcomes: A working paper* (Technical Report No. 86-A-002.1). Ann Arbor: University of Michigan, National Center for Research to Improve Postsecondary Teaching and Learning.

American Association for Higher Education. (1992). *Principles of good practice for assessing student learning*. Washington, DC: American Association for Higher Education.

Aper, J. P., Cuver, S. M., & Hinkle, D. E. (1990). Coming to terms with the accountability versus improvement debate in assessment. *Higher Education, 20,* 471–483.

Astin, A. W. (1987). Assessment, value-added, and educational excellence. In D. F. Halpern (Ed.), *Student outcomes assessment: What institutions stand to gain* (New Directions for Institutional Research No. 84, pp. 47–63). San Francisco: Jossey-Bass.

Astin, A. W. (1991). *Assessment for excellence: The philosophy and practice of assessment and evaluation in higher education*. New York: American Council on Education/Macmillan.

Austin, A. E. (1994). Understanding and assessing faculty cultures and climates. In M. K. Kinnick (Ed.), *Providing useful information for deans and department chairs* (New Directions for Institutional Research No. 84, pp. 47–63). San Francisco: Jossey-Bass.

Austin, A. E., & Gamson, Z. F. (1983). *Academic workplace: New demands, heightened tensions* (ASHE-ERIC Higher Education Report No. 10). Washington, DC: Association for the Study of Higher Education.

Banta, T. W. (1985). Using outcomes information at the University of Tennessee, Knoxville. In P. T. Ewell (Ed.), *Assessing educational outcomes* (New Directions for Institutional Research, No. 47, pp. 19–32). San Francisco: Jossey-Bass.

Banta, T. W., & Associates. (1993). *Making a difference: Outcomes of a decade of assessment in higher education*. San Francisco: Jossey-Bass.

Banta, T. W., Lund, J. P., Black, K. E., & Oblander, F. W. (1996). *Assessment in practice: Putting principles to work on college campuses*. San Francisco: Jossey-Bass.

Banta, T. W., & Moffett, M. S. (1987). Performance funding in Tennessee: Stimulus for program improvement. In D. F. Halpern (Ed.), *Student outcomes assessment: What institutions stand to gain* (New Directions for Higher Education No. 59, pp. 35–43). San Francisco: Jossey-Bass.

Barak, R. J., & Sweeney, J. D. (1995). Academic program review in planning, budgeting, and assessment. In R. J. Barak & L. A. Mets (Eds.), *Using academic program review* (New Directions for Institutional Research No. 86, pp. 3–17). San Francisco: Jossey-Bass.

Birnbaum, R. (1988). *How colleges work: The cybernetics of academic organization and leadership*. San Francisco: Jossey-Bass.

Bowen, H. R. (1977). *Investment in learning*. San Francisco: Jossey-Bass.

Bowyer, K. A. (1996). Efforts to continually improve a nursing program. In T. W. Banta, J. P. Lund, K. E. Black, & F. W. Oblander (Eds.), *Assessment in practice: Putting principles to work on college campuses* (pp. 128–129). San Francisco: Jossey-Bass.

Braskamp, L. A. (1991). Purposes, issues, and principles of assessment. *NCA Quarterly, 66,* 417–429.

California State University Institute for Teaching and Learning. (1993). *Academic challenges: Student outcomes assessment*. Long Beach: California State University, Institute for Teaching and Learning.

Chaffe-Stengel, P. (1992). Integrated program review: Lessons from assessment research at California State University, Fresno, *Student outcomes assessment: What makes it work? Assessment practices and experiences in the California State University*. Long Beach: California State University Institute for Teaching and Learning.

Clark, B. (1987). *The academic life: Small worlds, different worlds*. Princeton, NJ: Carnegie Endowment for the Advancement of Teaching.

Cohen, A. M., & Brawer, F. B. (1996). *The American community college* (3rd ed.). San Francisco: Jossey-Bass.

Cowart, S. C. (1990). *A survey on using student outcomes measures to assess institutional effectiveness*. Iowa City, IA: American College Testing Program.

Dennison, G. M., & Bunda, M. A. (1989). Assessment and academic judgments in higher education. In P. J. Gray (Ed.), *Achieving assessment goals using evaluation techniques* (New Directions for Higher Education No. 67, pp. 51–70). San Francisco: Jossey-Bass.

Duvall, B. (1994). Obtaining student cooperation. In T. H. Bers & M. L. Mittler (Eds.), *Assessment and testing: Myths and realities* (New Directions for Community Colleges No. 88, pp. 47–52). San Francisco: Jossey-Bass.

Eisenman, C. D. (1991). Faculty participation in assessment programs. *NCA Quarterly, 66,* 458–464.

El-Khawas, E. (1988). *Campus trends 1988*. Higher Education Panel Report No. 77. Washington, DC: American Council on Education.

El-Khawas, E. (1989). How are assessment results being used? *Assessment Update, 1* (4), 1–2.

El-Khawas, E. (1990). *Campus trends 1990*. Higher Education Panel Report No. 80. Washington, DC: American Council on Education.

El-Khawas, E. (1992). *Campus trends 1992*. Higher Education Panel Report No. 82. Washington, DC: American Council on Education.

El-Khawas, E. (1995). *Campus trends 1995*. Higher Education Panel Report No. 85. Washington, DC: American Council on Education.

Erwin, T. D. (1991). New opportunities: How student affairs can contribute to outcomes assessment. In U. Delworth, G. R. Hanson, & Associates (Eds.), *Student services: A handbook for the profession* (2nd ed., pp. 584–603). San Francisco: Jossey-Bass.

Ewell, P. T. (1984). *The self-regarding institution: Information for excellence*. Boulder, CO: National Center for Higher Education Management Systems.

Ewell, P. T. (1987a). *Assessment, accountability, and improvement: Managing the contradiction*. Boulder, CO: National Center for Higher Education Management Systems.

Ewell, P. T. (1987b). Assessment: Where are we? The implications of new state mandates. *Change, 19*(1), 23–28.

Ewell, P. T. (1987c). Establishing a campus-based assessment program. In D. F. Halpern (Ed.), *Student outcomes assessment: What institutions stand to gain* (New Directions for Higher Education No. 59, pp. 9–24). San Francisco: Jossey-Bass.

Ewell, P. T. (1988a). Implementing assessment: Some organizational issues. In T. W. Banta (Ed.), *Implementing outcomes assessment: Promise and perils* (New Directions for Institutional Research No. 59, pp. 15–28). San Francisco: Jossey-Bass.

Ewell, P. T. (1988b). Outcomes, assessment, and academic improvement: In search of usable knowledge. In J. C. Smart (Ed.), *Higher education: Handbook of theory and research* (Vol. 4, pp. 53–108). New York: Agathon Press.

Ewell, P. T. (1991). Assessment and public accountability: Back to the future. *Change, 23*(6), 12–17.

Ewell, P. T. (1997). Strengthening assessment for academic quality improvement. In M. W. Peterson, D. D. Dill, L. A. Mets, & Associates (Eds.), *Planning and management for a changing environment: A handbook on redesigning postsecondary institutions* (pp. 360–381). San Francisco: Jossey-Bass.

Fong, B. (1988). Assessing the departmental major. In J. H. McMillan (Ed.), *Assessing students' learning* (New Directions for Teaching and Learning No. 34, pp. 71–83). San Francisco: Jossey-Bass.

Friedlander, J., Murrell, P. H., & MacDougall, P. R. (1993). The community college student experiences questionnaire. In T. W. Banta & Associates (Eds.), *Making a difference: Outcomes of a decade of assessment in higher education* (pp. 196–210). San Francisco: Jossey-Bass.

Gill, W. E. (1993, June 12, 1993). *Conversations about accreditation: Middle States Association of Colleges and Schools focusing on outcomes assessment in the accreditation process*. Paper presented at the Double Feature Conference on Assessment and Continuous Quality Improvement of the American Association for Higher Education, Chicago, IL.

Gentemann, K. M., Fletcher, J. J., & Potter, D. L. (1994). Refocusing the academic program review on student learning. In M. K. Kinnick (Ed.), *Providing useful information for deans and department chairs* (New Directions for Institutional Research No. 84, pp. 31–46). San Francisco: Jossey-Bass.

Gray, P. J., & Banta, T. W. (Eds.). (1997). *The campus-level impact of assessment: Progress, problems and possibilities* (New Directions for Higher Education No. 100). San Francisco: Jossey-Bass.

Halpern, D. F. (Ed.). (1987). *Student outcomes assessment: What institutions stand to gain* (New Directions for Higher Education No. 59). San Francisco: Jossey-Bass.

Hutchings, P., & Marchese, T. (1990). Watching assessment: Questions, stories, prospects. *Change, 22*(5), 12–38.

Hyman, R. E., Beeler, K. J., & Benedict, L. G. (1994). Outcomes assessment and student affairs: New roles and expectations. *NASPA Journal, 32*(1), 20–30.

Jacobi, M., Astin, A., & Ayala, F. (1987). *College student outcomes assessment: A talent development perspective* (ASHE-ERIC Higher Education Report No. 7). Washington, DC: Association for the Study of Higher Education.

Johnson, R., McCormick, R. D., Prus, J. S., & Rogers, J. S. (1993). Assessment options for the college major. In T. W. Banta & Associates (Eds.), *Making a difference: Outcomes of a decade of assessment in higher education* (pp. 151–167). San Francisco: Jossey-Bass.

Johnson, R., Prus, J., Andersen, C. J., & El-Khawas, E. (1991). *Assessing assessment: An in-depth status report on the higher education assessment movement in 1990*. Higher Education Panel Report No. 79. Washington, DC: American Council on Education.

Jones, D. P., & Ewell, P. (1993). *The effect of state policy on undergraduate education: State policy and college learning*. Boulder, CO: Education Commission of the States.

Katz, A. M. (1993). Helping a campus in transition. In T. W. Banta & Associates (Eds.), *Making a difference: Outcomes of a decade of assessment in higher education* (pp. 54–65). San Francisco: Jossey-Bass.

Krueger, D. W., & Heisserer, M. L. (1987). Assessment and involvement: Investments to enhance learning. In D. F. Halpern (Ed.), *Student outcomes assessment: What institutions stand to gain* (New Directions for Higher Education No. 59, pp. 45– 56). San Francisco: Jossey-Bass.

Lenning, O. T., Lee, Y. S., Micek, S. S., & Service, A. L. (1977). *A structure for the outcomes of postsecondary education*. Boulder, CO: National Center for Higher Education Management Systems.

Loacker, G., & Mentkowski, M. (1993). Creating a culture where assessment improves learning. In T. W. Banta & Associates (Eds.), *Making a difference: Outcomes of a decade of assessment in higher education* (pp. 5–24). San Francisco: Jossey-Bass.

Magruder, W. J., & Young, C. C. (1993). Value-added talent development in general education. In T. W. Banta, J. P. Lund, K. E. Black, & F. W. Oblander (Eds.), *Assessment in practice: Putting principles to work on college campuses* (pp. 169–171). San Francisco: Jossey-Bass.

McClain, C. J., Krueger, D. W., & Taylor, T. (1986). Northeast Missouri State University value-added assessment program: A model for educational accountability. *International Journal of Institutional Management in Higher Education, 10*(3), 252–261.

Mentkowski, M. (1991). Creating a context where institutional assessment yields educational improvement. *Journal of General Education, 40,* 255–283.

Muffo, J. A. (1992). The status of student outcomes assessment at NASULGC member institutions. *Research in Higher Education, 33,* 765–774.

Ory, J. C., & Parker, S. A. (1989). Assessment activities at large, research universities. *Research in Higher Education, 30,* 375–385.

Patton, G. W., Dasher-Alston, R., Ratteray, O. M. T., & Kait, M. B. (1996). *Outcomes assessment in the Middle States Region: A report on the 1995 outcomes assessment survey*. Philadelphia, PA: Commission on Higher Education of the Middle States Association of Colleges and Schools.

Peterson, M. W., & Augustine, C. H. (2000a). External and internal influences on institutional approaches to student assessment: Accountability or improvement? *Research in Higher Education, 41,* 443–479.

Peterson, M. W., & Augustine, C. H. (2000b). Organizational practices enhancing the influence of student assessment information in academic decisions. *Research in Higher Education, 41,* 21–52.

Peterson, M. W., Augustine, C. H., Einarson, M. K., & Vaughan, D. S. (1999a). *Designing student assessment to strengthen institutional performance in associate of arts institutions*. Stanford, CA: Stanford University, National Center for Postsecondary Improvement.

Peterson, M. W., Augustine, C. H., Einarson, M. K., & Vaughan, D. S. (1999b). *Designing student assessment to strengthen institutional performance in baccalaureate institutions*. Stanford, CA: Stanford University, National Center for Postsecondary Improvement.

Peterson, M. W., & Einarson, M. K. (2000). An analytic framework of institutional support for student assessment. In J. C. Smart (Ed.), *Higher education: Handbook of theory and research* (Vol. 15). New York: Agathon Press.

Peterson, M. W., Einarson, M. K., Augustine, C. H., & Vaughan, D. S. (1999a). *Designing student assessment to strengthen institutional performance in comprehensive institutions*. Stanford, CA: Stanford University, National Center for Postsecondary Improvement.

Peterson, M. W., Einarson, M. K., Augustine, C. H., & Vaughan, D. S. (1999b). *Designing student assessment to strengthen institutional performance in doctoral and research institutions*. Stanford, CA: Stanford University, National Center for Postsecondary Improvement.

Peterson, M. W., Einarson, M. K., Augustine, C. H., & Vaughan, D. S. (1999c). *Institutional support for student assessment: Methodology and results of a national survey*. Stanford, CA: Stanford University, National Center for Postsecondary Improvement.

Peterson, M. W., Einarson, M. K., Trice, A. G., & Nichols, A. R. (1997). *Improving organizational and administrative support for student assessment: A review of the research literature*. Stanford, CA: Stanford University, National Center for Postsecondary Improvement.

Ratcliff, J. L., & Associates. (1995). *Realizing the potential: Improving postsecondary teaching, learning, and assessment*. University Park: The Pennsylvania State University, National Center on Postsecondary Teaching, Learning, and Assessment.

RiCharde, R. S., Olny, C. A., & Erwin, T. D. (1993). Cognitive and affective measures of student development. In T. W. Banta & Associates (Eds.), *Making a difference: Outcomes of a decade of assessment in higher education* (pp. 179–195). San Francisco: Jossey-Bass.

Rossman, J. E., & El-Khawas, E. (1987). *Thinking about assessment: Perspectives for presidents and chief academic officers*. Washington, DC: American Council on Education and the American Association for Higher Education.

Ryan, G. J. (1993). After accreditation: How to institutionalize outcomes-based assessment. In C. Praeger (Ed.), *Accreditation of the two-year college* (New Directions for Community Colleges No. 83, pp. 75–81). San Francisco: Jossey-Bass.

Sell, G. R. (1989). An organizational perspective for the effective practice of assessment. In P. J. Gray (Ed.), *Achieving assessment goals using evaluation techniques* (New Directions for Higher Education No. 67, pp. 21–41). San Francisco: Jossey-Bass.

Sims, S. J. (1992). *Student outcomes assessment: A historical review and guide to program development*. Westport, CT: Greenwood Press.

Steele, J. M., & Lutz, D. A. (1995). *Report of ACT's research on postsecondary assessment needs*. Iowa City, IA: American College Testing Program.

Steele, J. M., Malone, F. E., & Lutz, D. A. (1997). *Second report of ACT's research on postsecondary assessment needs*. Iowa City, IA: American College Testing Program.

Terenzini, P. T. (1989). Assessment with open eyes: Pitfalls in studying student outcomes. *Journal of Higher Education, 60*, 644–664.

Thomas, A. M. (1991). Consideration of the resources needed in an assessment program. *NCA Quarterly, 66*, 430–443.

Walleri, R. D., & Seybert, J. A. (1993). Demonstrating and enhancing community college effectiveness. In T. W. Banta & Associates (Eds.), *Making a difference: Outcomes of a decade of assessment in higher education* (pp. 87–102). San Francisco: Jossey-Bass.

Williford, A. M., & Moden, G. O. (1993). Using assessment to enhance quality. In T. W. Banta & Associates (Eds.), *Making a difference: Outcomes of a decade of assessment in higher education* (pp. 40–53). San Francisco: Jossey-Bass.

Wolff, R. A. (1992). CSU and assessment—second down and eight yards to go: A view from the scrimmage line, *Student outcomes assessment: What makes it work?* (pp. 73–80). Long Beach: California State University, Institute for Teaching and Learning.

Woodard, D. B. Jr., Hyman, R., von Destinon, M., & Jamison, A. (1991). Student affairs and outcomes assessment: A national survey. *NASPA Journal, 29*(1), 17–23.

Young, C. C., & Knight, M. E. (1993). Providing leadership for organizational change. In T. W. Banta & Associates (Eds.), *Making a difference: Outcomes of a decade of assessment in higher education* (pp. 25–39). San Francisco: Jossey-Bass.

Do Institutional Characteristics Affect Student Gains from College?

Robert K. Toutkoushian and John C. Smart

Academics have long striven to better understand how colleges affect students and whether student gains during their undergraduate careers are influenced by specific characteristics of students and their respective institutions. As Pascarella (1991) noted, "The impact of college on students forms, perhaps, the single largest base of empirical investigations in higher education" (p. 455).[1] The interest of campus administrators in the topic has certainly been heightened in recent years by increased calls from stakeholders for accountability and cost efficiency in higher education. While some institutional characteristics are beyond an administrator's control, such as public vs. private status, they can influence other institutional characteristics such as the size, selectivity, mission, and level of expenditures.

Academics argue that an institution's characteristics should have an influence on different aspects of student gains. Tinto (1975) asserts that institutional characteristics contribute to student retention since an institution's resources place limits on student development and integration. Economists likewise predict that an institution's characteristics affect student gains in much the same way that a firm's characteristics (e.g., size, quantity of inputs used in production) influence the quality of its products/services. Obviously, institutions with more financial resources can hire better faculty, expand their libraries, and purchase more and better computer equipment for students and faculty. Others argue that priorities of allocation can affect student gains, since some of the ways institutions use financial resources (e.g., instruction) may be more closely related to student learning than others (e.g., administration).[2]

Unfortunately, the empirical evidence to date offers little guidance for administrators. While Solmon and Wachtel (1975), Wachtel (1976), and Bowen (1977) found that institutional characteristics do matter, the majority of studies that have considered the topic conclude that institutional effects contribute little, if anything, to student growth after controlling for student background and acquired characteristics.[3] Studies by Hanushek (1972), Rock, Centra, and Linn (1970), Rock, Baird, and Linn (1972), James, Alsalam, Conaty, and To (1989), and James and Alsalam (1993) do not support the concept that "money matters." Rather, their specific findings are consistent with Pascarella and Terenzini's (1991) overall conclusion that institutional characteristics such as size, type of control, curricular emphasis, and selectivity "are simply not linked with major differences in *net* impacts on students" (p. 589; emphasis theirs).

Determining whether institutional characteristics influence student gains is not only important in its own right for finding ways to help students, but also for critiquing the usefulness of "performance

Reprinted by permission from *Review of Higher Education* 25, no. 1 (fall 2001).

indicators" of higher education institutions. Recent years have seen rising interest among many legislatures, college administrators, and other education stakeholders in using quantitative measures of institutional characteristics to monitor and evaluate colleges and universities (e.g., Taylor & Massy, 1996). The choice of indicators is rarely based on any evidence that they actually do affect educational outcomes; thus, such studies may not offer clear policy prescriptions for administrators.[4] Some agencies have gone further and use these indicators to rate institutions (McDonough et al., 1998). Most notably, *U.S. News and World Report* bases its measure of "academic excellence" on such institutional characteristics as selectivity, retention, student-faculty ratio, and expenditures per student. In this study, we use data about a national sample of students to investigate whether expenditures per student affect students' self-perceived gains. The data, compiled by the Higher Education Research Institute (HERI) at UCLA, began with a cohort of first-year students in 1986 and a follow-up survey in 1990; the information includes students' background characteristics, their activities and accomplishments during college, and their self-assessments of gains in a variety of areas. We focus specifically on gains in five areas that correspond to objectives common to students and their respective institutions: interpersonal skills, learning/knowledge, tolerance/awareness, graduate/professional school preparation, and communication skills.

The unique aspect of this study is its combination of student-level data with institution-level data for each school, making it possible to identify whether institutional characteristics such as expenditures contribute to self-reported student growth after taking student characteristics and their experiences as undergraduates into account. Our findings suggest that several institutional characteristics, such as the level and targets of institutional spending, can affect students' self-reported gains. The results also highlight the importance of recognizing the many ways in which students can benefit from college and that particular characteristics (and subsequent policies) may have differential effects on outcomes.

While studies of student gains have used different factors in their analyses, most can be grouped into three categories: student background characteristics, student characteristics acquired during college, and institutional characteristics. The consensus in the literature is that student background characteristics, such as ability/high school performance, gender, race/ethnicity, and socioeconomic status, can contribute to student gains during their postsecondary education (e.g., Astin, 1968; Pascarella & Terenzini, 1978; Dumont & Troelstrup, 1980). Tinto's (1975) theory suggests that a student's background characteristics would influence gains because of the effects these characteristics have on his or her commitment to succeed in academia. In addition, other studies have shown that what students do while attending college ("acquired characteristics") contribute to their gains.[5]

Questions about how to identify and measure student gains from college have contributed to the considerable size of this literature. Students can potentially benefit in many different ways from attending college, not all of them mutually reinforcing. Certainly some students are interested in attending college to pursue intellectual growth, while others may focus on more pragmatic benefits from college such as acquiring job-specific training and increasing their employment and earnings prospects. Students may also desire less tangible gains such as personal/social growth during college. Leaning, Vanderwell, and Brue (1975), for example, describe seven categories of student outcomes: academic learning, intellectual and creative development, personality development, motivation/vocational development, social development, aesthetic/cultural development, and moral/philosophical development.[6] Multiple measures also exist for each concept, each with its advantages and limitations. A handful of studies have used the future earnings of graduates to measure student gains, while more studies rely on student performance measures like scores on standardized tests or college grades. Other researchers argue in favor of self-reported gains since it is difficult to quantify student gains in certain dimensions such as "social awareness."[7] The value of self-reports on gains has been examined by scholars like Dumont and Troelstrup (1980), who conclude that self-reported gains are highly correlated with quantifiable measures of student progress. Pike (1995) and others, however, caution researchers about the use of self-reported gain scores; since this study relies on self-reported student gains, the reader should refer to this literature for more information.

Research Procedures

Sample

We took the data for this study from a random sample of first-year students in 1986 who subsequently took a follow-up survey in 1990. Both surveys were by the Cooperative Institutional Research Program (CIRP) sponsored by the Higher Education Research Institute (HERI) at the University of California at Los Angeles. We included only students who returned the 1990 survey, have been enrolled for four years of college, and have stayed at their first institution. After eliminating remaining observations with missing values on all independent variables of interest, our final sample size was 2,269 students attending 315 different institutions. The 1990 survey focused on students' actual college experiences and perceived growth during college. HERI used a variety of sources to construct the data set that we use here. For example, its data on financial and enrollment characteristics of institutions came through HEGIS/IPEDS.

Variables

From the survey data, we constructed a number of independent variables relating to student and institutional characteristics. (For specific variables, see the Appendix.) The first block of variables represent student background characteristics. We created four categories to represent a student's race/ethnicity (Asian, Black, White, other); we also constructed variables for family income, gender, whether the individual was a first-generation college student, and his or her self-reported high school grade point average.[8] We also constructed three control variables to represent the different reasons that students reported going to college. These variables were based on responses to 11 survey questions asking students to rate each reason for their decision to attend college on a three-point scale (1 = "not important," 2 = "somewhat important," 3 = "very important"). To help group common reasons for attending college and reduce the number of variables needed to represent these motivations; we applied factor analysis to the responses for these 11 questions and derived three reasons for attending college with the CIRP choices that yielded these answers:

1. Intellectual/personal growth. CIRP choices: "to gain a general education and appreciation of ideas," "to make me a more cultured person," "to improve my reading and study skills," "to learn more about things that interest me," and "to prepare myself for graduate or professional school."
2. Career preparation. CIRP choices: "to be able to make more money," and "to be able to get a better job."
3. Miscellaneous. CIRP choices: "there was nothing better to do," "my parents wanted me to go," "wanted to get away from home," and "I could not find a job."

We saved these three factor scores as independent variables and included them in the list of controls for a student's background.[9]

The second block of variables correspond to measures representing student-acquired characteristics. We derived four variables from their responses to questions about how they allocated their time during college: the percentage of hours/week spent on school activities (includes time in classes/labs, plus hours spent studying and doing homework), percentage of hours per week working for pay, percentage of hours per week talking with faculty outside of class, and the total hours/week spent on any of these three activities or socializing. We also created a variable to represent the percentage of years that a student reported living on campus to determine if a student's proximity to campus had an effect on his or her perceived gains.

In this study, however, we primarily focused on the third block of independent variables representing institutional characteristics. These measures are based on data for each institution as of 1985–1986. For each institution, we created two dummy variables for whether the institution's admissions had "high" or "low" selectivity based on average SAT scores of first-year students. Other institutional variables that we created from the data include the level of enrollments, the level of tuition and fees, the student-faculty ratio, the institution's Carnegie classification, the percentage of graduate students, the percentage of minority students, and the average faculty salary at each college/university.[10]

In this study, we pay particular attention to the effects of institutional expenditures on

student gains. The institutional variables that we use include the level of spending per student, and the percentages of expenditures devoted to instruction, academic support, or institutional support. The category of instruction would typically include expenditures for faculty salaries and teaching supplies. Academic support encompasses student advising/counseling. Finally, institutional support commonly consists of administrative expenditures. We posit that if money matters, then expenditures per student might have a positive effect on student gains—in other words, that higher expenditures could lead to more/better inputs for helping students. Likewise, if the way in which institutions spend money matters, then we would expect student gains to rise as the percentage of expenditures used for instruction and/or academic support rise, or as the percentage of expenditures for institutional support fall.

We derived the dependent variables of interest through student responses to 20 different questions of self-reported gains from college. In the 1990 survey, students were asked to identify the gains that they feel they have made since their first year in 20 different areas, such as "general knowledge" and "writing skills." Their choices for responses were: 5 = "much stronger," 4 = "stronger," 3 = "no change," 2 = "weaker," 1 = "much weaker." We conducted a factor analysis to help group the responses from the 20 questions into common aspects of student gains, resulting in six factors:[11]

1. Work/interpersonal skills. CIRP choices: "leadership abilities," "ability to work independently," "interpersonal skills," "confidence in academic abilities," "public speaking ability," "competitiveness," and "ability to work cooperatively."
2. Learning/knowledge. CIRP choices: "general knowledge," "analytical and problem-solving skills," "knowledge of a particular field or discipline," "ability to think critically," and "job-related skills."
3. Tolerance/awareness. CIRP choices: "cultural awareness and appreciation," "tolerance of persons with different beliefs," and "acceptance of people from different races/cultures."
4. Preparation for graduate school. CIRP choices: "interest in pursuing a graduate/professional degree" and "preparation for graduate or professional school."
5. Communication skills. CIRP choices: "foreign language ability," "job-related skills," and "writing skills."
6. Miscellaneous. CIRP choices: "job-related skills" and "religious beliefs and convictions."

In the following analysis, we focus on the first five of these factors for student gains and create variables for each of them based on the factor scores.

Analyses

We used multiple regression analysis to examine how the selected student and institutional characteristics affect student gains. As described above, we consider five different measures of student gains (work/interpersonal skills, learning/knowledge, tolerance/awareness, preparation for graduate school, and communication skills) and estimate two regression models for each of these five dependent variables. The first model (1) controls for student background characteristics (Asian, White, Black, female, family income, first-generation status, high school GPA, reason for attending college) and selected institutional characteristics (expenditures per student, percentage of expenditures for instruction, percentage of expenditures for academic support, institutional selectivity, percentage of graduate students, percentage of minority students, student-faculty ratio, and Carnegie classification).

The second model (2) adds controls for student-acquired characteristics (percentage of hours/week on school work, percentage of hours/week working for pay, percentage of hours/week talking with professors outside of class, total hours spent per week on selected activities, percentage of years living on campus) and other institutional characteristics (enrollments, tuition and fees, average faculty salary, percentage of expenditures for institutional support) to the list of regressors. The use of two models allows us to examine whether the primary institutional characteristics of interest here influence student gains and also whether any observed relationships between institutional characteristics and student gains during college are due to the effects of student-acquired characteristics or other institutional characteristics that are correlated with the expenditure variables.[12] To control for the effects of stratified sampling and nonresponse bias, we weighted all observations based on the supplied weights from HERI.[13]

Results

Table 1 displays descriptive statistics for the variables used in this study.

Beginning with institutional expenditure characteristics, we note that the institutions examined here spent on average over $10,000 per student, with considerable variation within the sample. We found similar differences when we looked at the distribution of expenditures across schools. On average, these institutions spent 39% on instruction, 13% on institutional support, and 9% on academic support; however, these percentages vary widely across the sample as evidenced by the minimum and maximum for each expenditure category. Among the other institutional characteristics in Table 1, it can be seen that 58% of the students in the sample attend either

TABLE 1
Descriptive Statistics

Variable	*Mean*	*Standard Deviation*	*Min.*	*Max.*
Expenditures per student	$10,137	$6,254	$2,504	$46,393
% expenditures for instruction	39%	7%	15%	58%
% expenditures for academic support	9%	3%	2%	31%
% expenditures for institutional support	13%	5%	3%	33%
High selectivity for admission	0.28	0.41	0	1
Low selectivity for admission	0.31	0.43	0	1
Enrollments	12,182	11,670	169	50,372
% graduate students at institution	12%	10%	0%	57%
% minority students at institution	15%	15%	1%	100%
Tuition	$3,455	$2,606	$0	$11,154
Student/faculty ratio	20.2	4.8	8	35
Research I or II institution	0.28	0.41	0	1
Doctoral I or II institution	0.14	0.32	0	1
Comprehensive I or II institution	0.36	0.44	0	1
Average faculty salary	$37,320	$7,064	$14,757	$76,573
Asian	0.03	0.16	0	1
Black	0.07	0.24	0	1
White	0.79	0.37	0	1
Female	0.53	0.46	0	1
Family income	$49,386	$31,751	$3,000	$150,000
First-generation student	0.27	0.41	0	1
High school GPA	3.26	0.59	1.00	4.00
Total hours/week at selected activities	57.7	14.5	10.5	124.0
% hours/week on school	46%	14%	2%	98%
% hours/week on work	16%	13%	0%	78%
% hours/week outside contact w/faculty	3%	3%	0%	36%
% years living on campus	60%	34%	0%	100%

Notes: Number of observations = 2,269. Data were obtained from a random sample of freshmen in 1986 who were subsequently followed up in a 1990 survey by the Cooperative Institutional Research Program (CIRP) sponsored by the Higher Education Research Institute (HERI) at the University of California at Los Angeles. All observations in this table are weighted, based on stratified sampling weights and nonresponse weights.

a comprehensive or liberal arts institution. Likewise, 28% of the students in the sample attended an institution with highly selective admissions as measured by average SAT scores of incoming first-year students.

With regard to student characteristics, the data show that while the majority of students were White (79%), there was good representation of students from other race/ethnicity categories. About one out of every four students was a first-generation college student, and the average family income was nearly $50,000 per year. Students on average allocated 46% of their time to school-related activities, 16% to working for pay, and about 3% to talking with faculty outside of class. On average, students spent fifty-eight hours per week on these activities and on socializing.

Table 2 provides the estimated coefficients from the alternative multiple regression models for the five separate measures of student gains that we examine in this study. We organized the findings according to the three sets of independent variables defined earlier.

Institutional Characteristics

The results in Table 2 show that institutional expenditures do contribute to self-reported gains for students. After controlling for student background and acquired characteristics, higher per-student expenditures are positively related to student gains in interpersonal skills and learning/knowledge acquisition. There is also limited evidence that the way in which expenditures are allocated among major categories has an influence on student gains along these five different dimensions. Students enrolled at institutions with a higher proportion of expenditures devoted to academic support, for example, report having lower gains in learning/knowledge and communication skills. At the same time, it is interesting that the proportion of expenditures on institutional support also has a positive effect on gains in learning/knowledge, and that the proportion of expenditures allocated to instruction has no consistent impact on self-reprted student gains.

In addition to expenditures, other institutional characteristics also influenced various dimensions of student gains. Beginning with institutional selectivity, students in more highly selective institutions (as represented by entrance exam scores) are more likely to report higher gains in communication skills but lower gains in interpersonal skills, while students in low selectivity institutions experienced higher gains in tolerance/awareness (similar results were reported by Hagedorn et al., 1999). Students enrolled in larger institutions report lower gains than other students in interpersonal skills, tolerance/awareness, and preparation for graduate school. Interestingly, students enrolled at institutions with higher concentrations of graduate students report lower self-perceived gains in learning/knowledge. This finding could reflect the fact that many research institutions use graduate students, rather than full-time faculty, to teach a significant number of undergraduate courses.

The percentage of minority students at an institution has a small positive effect on student gains in tolerance and communication skills but negative effects on learning. We also tested for whether student gains were affected by the racial/ethnic diversity of the institution by including an additional variable for the squared percentage of minority students. If student gains were higher at more diverse institutions, then the coefficient on this variable would be negative and statistically significant. Of the five measures of student gains considered here, however, we found only evidence of such gains for graduate school preparation. Overall, the results do not support the notion that student-perceived gains are affected by the racial/ethnic diversity of the institution.

Holding all other factors constant, attending a higher-priced college or university may contribute to lower gains in interpersonal skills, and there is marginal evidence of positive gains in knowledge/learning. Contrary to conventional wisdom, higher student-faculty ratios lead to reductions in student gains in only one area (communication skills) out of the five gain measures considered here. This finding in particular should raise questions about overreliance on student-faculty ratios as a measure of institutional quality or performance. The Carnegie classification of an institution tends to have an important influence on student gains in learning/knowledge, with learning/knowledge gains being highest in research or doctoral institutions. At the same time, however, gains in interpersonal skills were lower at research institutions than at liberal arts colleges. Finally, there is no clear evidence that, after controlling for the other

TABLE 2
Multiple Regression Models Explaining Student Gains in Five Factor Scores

	Dependent Variable Equals Factor Score for Student Self-Perceived Gains in:									
	Interpersonal Skills		*Learning/Knowledge*		*Tolerance/Awareness*		*Graduate School Preparation*		*Communication Skills*	
Variable	*(1)*	*(2)*	*(1)*	*(2)*	*(1)*	*(2)*	*(1)*	*(2)*	*(1)*	*(2)*
Expenditures per Student ($1,000)	0.010* (2.35)	0.009* (1.97)	0.012** (2.83)	0.009† (1.95)	−0.005 (1.18)	−0.009* (2.09)	−0.006 (1.46)	−0.008† (1.76)	−0.005 (1.17)	−0.006 (1.38)
% Expenditures for Instruction	0.002 (0.83)	0.008* (2.17)	−0.004 (1.24)	−0.005 (1.37)	−0.001 (0.46)	0.002 (0.59)	−0.006† (1.91)	0.006 (1.58)	0.002 (0.57)	−0.004 (0.92)
% Expenditures for Academic Support	0.0002 (0.03)	−0.001 (0.22)	−0.012* (1.96)	−0.018** (2.66)	0.0008 (0.12)	0.011† (1.70)	0.004 (0.66)	0.016* (2.39)	−0.015** (2.58)	−0.020** (2.96)
% Expenditures for Inst. Support	—	0.012† (1.87)	—	0.019** (2.87)	—	−0.002 (0.30)	—	0.007 (1.01)	—	−0.007 (1.11)
High Selectivity for Admissions	−0.155** (2.60)	−0.215** (3.49)	0.0008 (0.01)	0.026 (0.41)	0.198** (3.27)	0.073 (1.17)	0.107† (1.76)	0.061 (0.97)	0.134* (2.33)	0.163** (2.65)
Low Selectivity for Admissions	0.013 (0.26)	0.011 (0.22)	−0.003 (0.05)	0.035 (0.69)	0.162** (3.07)	0.196** (3.89)	0.075 (1.43)	0.083 (1.61)	−0.004 (0.08)	0.056 (1.12)
Enrollments (1000s)	—	−0.009** (2.73)	—	0.002 (0.76)	—	−0.012** (3.74)	—	−0.011** (3.30)	—	−0.0008 (0.24)
% Graduate Students	0.0006 (0.19)	0.002 (0.68)	−0.012** (3.98)	−0.011** (3.26)	0.001 (0.44)	−0.006† (1.70)	0.006† (1.76)	0.004 (1.18)	−0.001 (0.44)	−0.002 (0.70)
% Minority Students	−0.002 (1.32)	−0.0004 (0.25)	−0.004* (2.50)	−0.005** (2.79)	0.003† (1.84)	0.004* (2.12)	0.001 (0.72)	−0.0004 (0.24)	0.004* (2.45)	0.005** (2.91)
Tuition ($1,000)	—	−0.039** (3.91)	—	0.020* (1.98)	—	0.010 (1.02)	—	0.007 (0.64)	—	0.005 (0.53)
Student/Faculty Ratio	0.007 (1.17)	0.022** (3.41)	0.018** (3.14)	−0.001 (0.16)	−0.007 (1.33)	0.003 (0.42)	0.001 (0.24)	0.012† (1.75)	−0.017** (3.15)	−0.020** (3.12)

(Continued)

TABLE 2 (*Continued*)

	Dependent Variable Equals Factor Score for Student Self-Perceived Gains in:									
	Interpersonal Skills		*Learning/Knowledge*		*Tolerance/Awareness*		*Graduate School Preparation*		*Communication Skills*	
Variable	*(1)*	*(2)*	*(1)*	*(2)*	*(1)*	*(2)*	*(1)*	*(2)*	*(1)*	*(2)*
Research I/II Institution	−0.257** (2.97)	−0.311* (2.35)	0.268** (3.04)	0.651** (4.88)	0.086 (0.98)	0.175 (1.31)	−0.142 (1.62)	0.005 (0.04)	0.129 (1.55)	0.316* (2.40)
Doctoral I/II Institution	−0.065 (0.78)	−0.199** (1.98)	0.247** (2.92)	0.528** (5.21)	0.094 (1.12)	0.056 (0.55)	−0.198* (2.37)	−0.256* (2.48)	0.116 (1.46)	0.323 (3.23)
Comprehensive I/II Institution	0.038 (0.65)	−0.187* (2.55)	0.014 (0.24)	0.251** (3.40)	−0.003 (0.05)	−0.057 (0.77)	−0.029 (0.48)	−0.150* (1.99)	0.014 (0.25)	0.190** (2.60)
Average Faculty Salary ($1000s)	—	0.004 (0.83)	—	−0.002 (0.33)	—	0.014** (2.69)	—	0.0006 (0.12)	—	−0.003 (0.60)
Asian	0.100 (0.76)	0.194 (1.51)	−0.603** (4.47)	−0.390** (3.00)	−0.155 (1.16)	−0.087 (0.67)	0.044 (0.33)	0.082 (0.62)	0.122 (0.96)	0.111 (0.86)
White	−0.013 (0.18)	0.023 (0.35)	−0.052 (0.74)	−0.048 (0.74)	−0.054 (0.78)	−0.073 (1.12)	−0.024 (0.35)	0.017 (0.26)	−0.003 (0.05)	−0.034 (0.53)
Black	0.446** (3.79)	0.436** (3.85)	0.098 (0.82)	0.163 (1.43)	0.069 (0.58)	0.028 (0.24)	0.202† (1.70)	0.462** (3.97)	−0.038 (0.33)	−0.079 (0.70)
Female	−0.120** (2.88)	−0.048 (1.13)	−0.039 (0.92)	−0.039 (0.90)	0.339** (8.01)	0.250** (5.81)	0.138** (3.27)	0.051 (1.16)	0.129** (3.21)	0.123** (2.90)
Family Income ($1,000)	0.0004 (0.57)	0.001* (1.97)	0.001* (2.20)	0.001* (2.14)	−0.002** (3.30)	−0.002** (2.85)	−0.0006 (0.85)	−0.0003 (0.49)	0.002** (3.20)	0.003** (3.98)
First Generation Student	0.078† (1.71)	0.156** (3.23)	−0.008 (0.18)	0.051 (1.04)	−0.007 (0.15)	0.133** (2.73)	−0.051 (1.11)	−0.031 (0.62)	0.023 (0.53)	−0.014 (0.29)
High School GPA	−0.082* (2.42)	−0.078* (2.24)	0.061† (1.75)	0.026 (0.73)	−0.095** (2.75)	−0.036 (1.02)	−0.005 (0.16)	−0.017 (0.48)	−0.0009 (0.03)	0.031 (0.90)

TABLE 2 (*Continued*)

	Dependent Variable Equals Factor Score for Student Self-Perceived Gains in:									
	Interpersonal Skills		*Learning/Knowledge*		*Tolerance/Awareness*		*Graduate School Preparation*		*Communication Skills*	
Variable	*(1)*	*(2)*	*(1)*	*(2)*	*(1)*	*(2)*	*(1)*	*(2)*	*(1)*	*(2)*
Attend College for Intellectual/Personal Growth (factor 1)	0.146** (7.15)	0.120** (5.85)	0.090** (4.33)	0.106** (5.10)	0.063** (3.02)	0.088** (4.23)	0.127** (6.17)	0.107** (5.07)	0.073** (3.71)	0.070** (3.41)
Attend College for Career Preparation (factor 2)	0.077** (3.53)	0.076** (3.56)	−0.013 (0.56)	0.027 (1.28)	−0.033 (1.47)	−0.048* (2.26)	−0.008 (0.36)	0.012 (0.53)	−0.031 (1.48)	−0.044* (2.10)
Attend College for Other Reasons (factor 3)	0.021 (1.02)	0.002 (0.09)	−0.050* (2.38)	−0.046* (2.18)	0.070** (3.36)	0.063** (2.97)	0.012 (0.57)	−0.004 (0.17)	−0.031 (1.59)	−0.018 (0.85)
% Hours/Week School	—	−0.004** (2.53)	—	0.008** (4.80)	—	−0.004* (2.47)	—	0.009** (5.15)	—	−0.0002 (0.11)
% Hours/Week Work	—	−0.004* (2.10)	—	−0.005** (2.79)	—	−0.0006 (0.32)	—	−0.0004 (0.21)	—	0.0009 (0.51)
% Hours/Week Faculty Contact	—	0.017** (2.66)	—	−0.005 (0.77)	—	0.005 (0.83)	—	0.006 (1.00)	—	0.016** (2.57)
Total Hours/Week at Selected Activities	—	0.006** (4.26)	—	0.008** (5.96)	—	0.003* (2.16)	—	0.006** (3.98)	—	−0.002 (1.15)
% Years Living on Campus	—	0.001†	— (1.67)	−0.002**	— (3.64)	0.002**	— (2.79)	−0.001†	— (1.84)	0.002**
Intercept	0.107 (0.50)	−0.737* (2.16)	−0.309 (1.42)	−0.847* (2.46)	0.359† (1.66)	−0.602 (1.75)	+0.139 (0.65)	−1.174** (3.34)	0.130 (0.63)	0.297 (0.87)
R-squared	0.06	0.11	0.05	0.09	0.07	0.08	0.05	0.06	0.04	0.06
F-test for overall model fit	7.81**	9.06**	5.44**	7.72**	8.83**	6.45**	5.59**	5.01**	4.62**	4.79**
Sample size	2,433	2,269	2,433	2,269	2,433	2,269	2,433	2,269	2,433	2,269

Notes: T-statistics (absolute value) are shown in parentheses below each coefficient.
$^{**}p < .01$.
$^{*}p < .05$.
$^{\dagger}p < .10$ (two-tailed test). Dependent variables are factor scores based on 20 questions relating to student gains. All observations are weighted, based on the stratified sampling design and nonresponse bias.

factors in the model, the level of faculty compensation contributes to student gains in any of these areas but tolerance/awareness.

Student Background Characteristics

With regard to a student's race/ethnicity, we found that Asian students reported lower gains than students in other race/ethnicity categories in their learning/knowledge, while Black students experienced higher gains in interpersonal skills and graduate school preparation. Women students experienced significantly higher gains than men students in tolerance/awareness and communication skills. Students from higher-income families described themselves as having higher gains than students from lower-income families in their interpersonal skills, learning/knowledge, and communication skills but smaller gains in tolerance/awareness. Also of interest, first-generation college students experienced higher gains than students with college-educated parents in interpersonal skills. Higher-ability students, as represented by their high school GPA, did not report greater gains than students with lower high school GPAs in any of these five measures and, in fact, had lower gains in interpersonal skills.

The data show that students' motivation for attending college can have a large impact on their realized gains after four years. Students who attended college for intellectual or personal growth had significantly higher gains than other students in all five measures of student gains. Similarly, students who indicated that they were attending college for career preparation had higher gains in interpersonal skills, and students who said that they attended college for miscellaneous reasons reported lower gains than other students in learning/knowledge but higher gains in tolerance and awareness.

Students-Acquired Characteristics

Students who invested a greater proportion of their time in school work experienced greater gains in learning/knowledge and graduate/professional school preparation but lower gains in interpersonal skills and tolerance/awareness. A very encouraging finding is that hours spent talking with faculty outside of class had a positive contribution to student gains in two of the five dimensions of student gains examined here. This finding is consistent with a large body of literature that has focused on the benefits of student-faculty interactions in postsecondary education.

Time spent working for pay during college did not contribute positively to student gains in any of these areas and, in fact, lowered self-reported student gains in interpersonal skills and learning/knowledge. This finding is particularly important given the concern expressed within academe that students often spend an excessive amount of time during college working for pay. The total hours spent by students on these main activities have a positive effect on gains in four of the five measures of student gains and perhaps reflect student motivation.[14] Finally, students who spent more of their college career living on campus reported higher gains in tolerance/awareness and communication skills but lower gains in learning/knowledge, suggesting that the main benefits of campus living are social rather than academic.

Summary and Discussion

Two important points can be made from this study. The first is that students anticipate gaining more benefits than knowledge alone from their postsecondary education; therefore, any discussion or analysis of "student gains" should recognize these various dimensions and not simply focus on gains in learning. Factors such as having a more racially diverse institution may not lead to greater student gains in learning but may nonetheless contribute to students' development through raising their tolerance and awareness of social issues. While gains in these areas are even more difficult to quantify than in learning, they are important benefits that should be taken into account when administrators are designing policies (such as changing admissions standards) in an effort to achieve other institutional goals and objectives.

The second important finding is that there are a number of ways in which institutional and student characteristics can potentially contribute to greater student benefits from postsecondary education. Beginning with the institutional characteristics, the level of spending can have a direct impact on student gains in interpersonal skills and learning. This correlation presents a challenge for institutions facing pressure from legislators, parents, and other constituencies to contain the growth of education costs. Likewise, allocating more money to academic support apparently has an adverse effect on student gains in knowledge and communication skills. Becoming more selective in the admissions process may raise the quality of entering first-year students but, in and of itself, does not seem to contribute to student gains in learning. In fact, students in more selective institutions reported lower gains in interpersonal skills.

Smaller appears to be better in higher education, which also raises some interesting challenges as the demand for higher education rises, due in part to the progression of baby boomers' children through the K-12 system. The racial/ethnic diversity of an institution has positive benefits for student growth in tolerance/awareness and communication skills, and there is some evidence that student gains in learning are higher in more expensive institutions. Finally, despite the rhetoric about the effects of class size on learning, there is no convincing evidence that students gain more from college along these dimensions when the student-faculty ratio is lower.

Turning to student characteristics, Asian students report experiencing lower gains than other students in learning, while Black students report the greatest gains in interpersonal skills and graduate school preparation. Similarly, men and women appear to differ considerably along the dimensions in which they derive the greatest gains. Women report higher gains than men in tolerance/awareness, communication skills, and possibly graduate school preparation, yet achieve lower gains in interpersonal skills. Given the dramatic gains in higher education participation among women during the past 20 years, these gender differences in what students report deriving from college have implications for institutions as they consider the changing needs of students over time. First-generation students fare as well as students with college-educated parents in terms of the self-perceived benefits from college; in fact, they reported having higher gains in interpersonal skills and tolerance/awareness. This finding, together with the observation that students with lower high school grade point averages school report similar gains from college as those with higher GPAs, is certainly encouraging for policy makers who have been promoting the benefits of a college education and advocating greater access to higher education for all types of students.

Students also play a major role in influencing their own destiny; investing more time in their education can contribute to higher gains in different aspects while combining work and college may detract from general knowledge acquisition. With the growing number of students working part-time during the school year (70% of the students in this sample worked at least one hour for pay during the school year), this is a major policy concern for institutions. Likewise, we found that a student's motivation for attending college has a large impact on the gains that he or she ultimately receives from college.

In part, these factors reflect other personal traits of students, such as interest in learning or acquiring job skills and general attitude towards education. They do emphasize, however, that institutions are limited in the control they have over the gains their students realize from postsecondary education, since students also influence what they gain from college.

These findings should certainly be useful in evaluating the extent to which institutional characteristics such as expenditures per student, selectivity, and cost can be used as precise measures of institutional quality. Some of the commonly used indicators of institutional prestige/quality (e.g., more selective admissions, higher average faculty salaries, and/or lower student-faculty ratios), do not contribute to greater gains in student acquisition of knowledge, interpersonal skills, or graduate school preparation. In evaluating alternative postsecondary destinations, students should be interested in identifying the type of environment in which to realize the greatest value added from their education.

Many college-bound students look to such popular institutional rankings as that produced by *U.S. News and World Report* to guide their selection. The rankings, however, are typically defined as a weighted average of institutional and student characteristics, many of which have not been shown to contribute to student gains in the ways assumed for forming the rankings. As noted by Gaither, Nedwek, and Neal (1994), "A leap of faith exists between concerns over input or contextual characteristics and outcomes. This leap of faith represents the untested assumption that the educational system and its institutions, programs, or culture explain variations in outcomes" (p. 90).

The findings we present here suggest placing more emphasis on student outcomes/gains in assessing institutional performance; furthermore, if rankings are intended to capture the value added that students might expect to realize at different institutions, then the measures used to derive such rankings should not be based on factors that capture the quality of students.

APPENDIX

Variables	*Definitions*
Student Background Characteristics	
Family income	The midpoint of the self-reported family income category for respondents. Fourteen different income categories in the survey. Family incomes in the highest category ($150,000 or more) were set equal to $150,000.
First-generation student	Dummy variable equal to one if the student indicated that neither parent had completed at least some college education, zero otherwise.
Student-Acquired Characteristics	
Total hours/week	Average number of hours spent per week on the following activities: school work, talking with faculty outside class, working for pay, socializing with friends, partying, doing volunteer work, or involvement with student clubs/groups. The midpoints of each class are used to derive hours spent in each activity.
Percentage hours/week on school	Percentage of total hours per week in classes/labs, studying, or doing homework.
Percentage hours/week with faculty	Percentage of total hours per week spent talking with faculty outside class.
Percentage years on campus	Percentage of a student's four years in college living on campus. Includes living in a dormitory, fraternity/sorority house, or other campus student house.
Institutional Characteristics	
Expenditures per student	Total expenditures per FTE student, in thousands of dollars. Includes expenditures for instruction, research, public service, academic support, library, student services, institutional support, physical plant, unrestricted and restricted awards, and mandatory transfers.
Percentage of expenditures for instruction	Percentage of total expenditures for the general instructional activities within academic divisions of the institution.
Percentage of expenditures for academic support	Percentage of total expenditures for activities that support the teaching, research, and service functions of the institution.
Percentage of expenditures for institutional support	Percentage of total expenditures on items that facilitate the operational functioning of the institution on a daily basis.
High selectivity for admissions	Dummy variable equal to one if the institution's admission criteria is described as being high or very high, zero otherwise (average SAT scores > 1,100 for public universities, 1,175 for private universities and nonsectarian colleges, 1,025 for public colleges and Roman Catholic institutions, and 1,050 for Protestant colleges). Definitions are based on stratification cell variable provided by HERI.
Low selectivity for admissions	Dummy variable equal to one if the institution's admission criteria are described as being low or very low, zero otherwise (average SAT scores are below 1,000 for public universities, 1,050 for private universities, 950 for private nonsectarian and Roman Catholic colleges, 935 for public colleges, and 875 for Protestant colleges). Definitions are based on stratification cell variable provided by HERI.
Tuition	The level of tuition and fees for the institution in 1985. For students with the same home state as the institution's state, the in-state tuition and fees were used. Likewise, when a student's home state differed from the institution's state, the out-of-state tuition and fees were used.

Notes

1. Feldman and Newcomb (1969) cited over 1,500 studies that have investigated the relationship between college and student outcomes, and Pascarella and Terenzini's book *How College Affects Students* (1991) contains over 154 pages of references to studies.
2. Rock, Centra, and Linn note that their variable for expenditures per student included expenditures for items and services that may not be "directly related to improving the quality of the educational process" (1970, pp. 117–118). Likewise, Solmon and Wachtel (1975) assert that Hanushek's (1972) finding that expenditures do not affect student gains implies that "monies are being spent on the wrong things" (p. 76).
3. See, for example, Astin and Panos (1969) and Pascarella and Terenzini (1991). Kuh, Pace, and Vesper (1997) found that student perceptions of their institutional environment contributed little to self-reported gains, and Pascarella (1991) concludes "the net effects of traditional college 'quality' measures on an individual's socioeconomic attainments are very small" (p. 459).
4. As Taylor and Massy note: "There is no 'right' or 'wrong' value for any indicator" (1996, p. xv). For a more extensive critique of the use of performance indicators, see Gaither, Nedwek, and Neal (1994).
5. Kuh, Pace, and Vesper (1997) recently showed that active learning and cooperation among students were the best predictors of student gains. Banta et al. (1987), Ratcliff (1988), and Pike (1992) have investigated the effects of coursework on student gains. The literature particularly emphasizes student-faculty interactions. See Lamport (1993) for a review. Chickering (1969) and Spady (1970), among others, posited that the frequency of student interactions with faculty would contribute positively to student gains during college. For supporting evidence, see Feldman and Newcomb (1969), Wilson, Wood, and Gaff (1974), Pascarella, Terenzini, and Hibel (1978), Pascarella and Terenzini (1978), and Terenzini, Theophilides, and Lorang (1984). Also see Bean & Metzner (1985), Cabrera, Nora, and Castaneda (1993), and Pascarella (1985).
6. Likewise, Kuh, Pace, and Vesper (1997) group student gains into five categories: general education, personal/social development, intellectual skills, science and technology, and vocational preparation. For similar categorizations, see Wilson et al. (1974), Terenzini, Theophilides, and Lorang (1984), and Pace (1990).
7. Studies that use graduates' earnings as a measure of gains include Solmon and Wachtel (1975), Wachtel (1976), and James et al. (1989). Similarly, Astin (1968), Rock, Centra, and Linn (1970), Rock, Baird, and Linn (1972), Pascarella and Terenzini (1978), Pascarella, Terenzini, and Hibel (1978), and Pike (1992), among others, advocate the use of student test scores and grades for assessing student gains. For a sampling of research in favor of self-reported gains, see Nichols (1967), Terenzini, Theophilides, and Lorang (1984), DeSousa and Kuh (1996), and Kuh, Pace, and Vesper (1997).
8. We computed family income as the midpoint of the income class reported by students on the 1986 survey. For the purpose of this study, a student is defined as a first-generation student when neither parent attended any college.
9. The authors will provide complete results from the factor analysis upon request.
10. The enrollment totals represent the total headcount for undergraduate and graduate students in 1985 (source: HEGIS). The level of tuition and fees is set equal to the reported resident rate when the student attended an institution in his or her home state and is likewise set equal to the nonresident rate for those students attending an institution that is not the same as their home state (source: 1985 College Board Survey). We collapsed the Carnegie classifications into four categories: research, doctoral, comprehensive, and liberal arts. We took the student-faculty ratios from the 1986 HEGIS Faculty Salary and Tenure Survey. HERI provided all of these data.
11. We based the factor analysis on responses to question #16 from the 1990 CIRP survey: "Compared with when you entered college as a freshman, how would you now describe your . . ." The complete results from the factor analysis are available from the authors upon request.
12. Due to missing observations on several independent variables, the number of valid observations in the second model for each dependent variable was 2,269 contrasted to 2,433 in the first model. To determine if these observations affected the results presented here, we reestimated each of the first regression models after excluding these observations with missing data and found that the results were very similar to those presented here. We also estimated similar models by adding controls for college major and again found no significant differences in

the signs or significance patterns of the institutional characteristics of interest to this study.

13. The weights for each observation were computed as the stratified sampling weight times the nonresponse weight, divided by the average total weight in the sample.
14. The intraclass correlation coefficients for the student gain measures were very low (ranging from 0.03 and 0.10), suggesting that a hierarchical linear modeling approach would yield results similar to those reported in this study.

References

Astin, A. (1968, August). Undergraduate achievement and institutional "excellence." *Science, 161*, 661–668.

Astin, A., & Panos, R. (1969). *The educational and vocational development of college students*. Washington, DC: American Council on Education.

Banta, T., Lambert, E., Pike, G., Schmidhammer, J., & Schneider, J. (1987). Estimated student score gain on the ACT COMP exam: Valid tool for institutional assessment? *Research in Higher Education, 27*(3), 195–217.

Bean, J., & Metzner, B. (1985). A conceptual model of nontraditional undergraduate student attrition. *Review of Educational Research, 55*, 485–540.

Bowen, H. (1977). *Investment in learning*. San Francisco: Jossey-Bass.

Chickering, A. (1969). *Education and identity*. San Francisco: Jossey-Bass.

Cabrera, A., Nora, A., & Castaneda, M. (1993). College persistence: Structural equations modeling test of an integrated model of student retention. *Journal of Higher Education, 64*, 123–136.

DeSousa, D. J., & Kuh, G. (1996). Does institutional racial composition make a difference in what Black students gain from college? *Journal of College Student Development, 37*(3), 257–267.

Dumont, R., & Troelstrup, R. (1980). Exploring relationships between objective and subjective measures of instructional outcomes. *Research in Higher Education, 12*(1), 37–51.

Feldman, K., & Newcomb, T. (1969). *The impact of college on students*. San Francisco: Jossey-Bass.

Gaither, G., Nedwek, B., & Neal, J. (1994). *Measuring up: The promises and pitfalls of performance indicators in higher education*. ASHE-ERIC Higher Education Report, No. 5. Washington, DC: George Washington University, Graduate School of Education and Human Development.

Hagedorn, L., Pascarella, E., Edison, M., Braxton, J., Nora, A., & Terenzini, P. (1999). Institutional context and the development of critical thinking: A research note. *Review of Higher Education, 22*(3), 265–285.

Hanushek, E. (1972). *Education and race*. Lexington, MA: Heath.

James, E., & Alsalam, N. (1993). College choice, academic achievement and future earnings. In E. P. Hoffman (Ed.), *Essays on the Economics of Education* (pp. 111–138). Kalamazoo, MI: W. E. Upjohn Institute for Employment Research.

James, E., Alsalam, N., Conaty, J., & To, D. (1989). College quality and future earnings: Where should you send your child to college? *American Economic Review, 79*(2), 247–252.

Kuh, G., Pace, C. R., & Vesper, N. (1997). The development of process indicators to estimate student gains associated with good practices in undergraduate education. *Research in Higher Education, 38*(4), 435–454.

Lamport, M. (1993). Student-faculty informal interaction and the effect on college student outcomes: A review of the literature. *Adolescence, 28*(112), 971–990.

Lenning, M., Vanderwell, J., & Brue, E. (1975). *The many faces of college success and their nonintellective correlates*. Iowa City, IA: American College Testing Program.

McDonough, P. M., Antonio, A. L., Walpole, M., & Perez, L. X. (1998). College rankings: Democratized college knowledge for whom? *Research in Higher Education, 39*, 513–537.

Nichols, R. (1967). Personality change and the college. *American Educational Research Journal, 4*, 173–190.

Pace, C. R. (1990). *College student experiences questionnaire* (3rd ed.). Los Angeles: University of California, Center for the Study of Evaluation, Graduate School of Education.

Pascarella, E. (1985). College environmental influences on learning and cognitive development: A critical review and synthesis. In J. C. Smart (Ed.), *Higher education: Handbook of theory and research* (Vol. 1, pp. 1–61). New York: Agathon Press.

Pascarella, E. (1991). The impact of college on students: The nature of the evidence. *Review of Higher Education, 14*(4), 453–466.

Pascarella, E., & Terenzini, P. (1978). Student-faculty informal relationships and freshman year educational outcomes. *Journal of Educational Research, 71*, 183–189.

Pascarella, E., & Terenzini, P. (1991). *How college affects students*. San Francisco: Jossey-Bass.

Pascarella, E., Terenzini, P., & Hibel, J. (1978). Student-faculty interactional settings and their relationship to predicted academic performance. *Journal of Higher Education, 49*, 450–463.

Pike, G. (1992). Using mixed-effect structural equation models to study student academic development. *Review of Higher Education, 15*(2), 151–177.

Pike, G. (1995). The relationship between self reports of college experiences and achievement test scores. *Research in Higher Education, 36*(1), 1–21.

Ratcliff, J. (1988, April). *Developing a cluster-analytic model for identifying coursework patterns associated with general learned abilities of college students.* Paper presented at the annual meetings of the American Educational Research Association, New Orleans.

Rock, D., Baird, L., & Linn, R. (1972). Interaction between college effects and students' aptitudes. *American Educational Research Journal, 9,* 149–161.

Rock, D., Centra, J., & Linn, R. (1970). Relationships between college characteristics and student achievement. *American Educational Research Journal, 7,* 109–121.

Solmon, L., & Wachtel, P. (1975). The effect on income of type of college attended. *Sociology of Education, 48*(1), 75–90.

Spady, W. (1970). Dropouts from higher education: An interdisciplinary review and synthesis. *Interchange, 2,* 38–62.

Taylor, B., & Massy, W. (1996). *Strategic indicators for higher education.* Princeton, NJ: Peterson's.

Terenzini, P., Theophilides, C., & Lorang, W. (1984). Influences on students' perceptions of their academic skill development during college. *Journal of Higher Education, 55*(5), 621–636.

Tinto, V. (1975). Dropout from higher education: A theoretical synthesis of recent research. *Review of Educational Research, 45*(1), 89–125.

Wachtel, P. (1976). The effect on earnings of school and college investment expenditures. *Review of Economics and Statistics, 58*(3), 326–331.

Wilson, R., Wood, I., & Gaff, J. (1974). Social-psychological accessibility and faculty-student interactions beyond the classroom. *Sociology of Education, 47,* 74–92.

Community College Transfer Students: A Case Study of Survival

Barbara K. Townsend

The transfer process between community colleges and four-year colleges and universities has long been under heavy scrutiny, partly because many minority students use two-year schools as their entry point into higher education. Transfer rates between the two-year and four-year sectors as well as the degree attainment of community college transfer students have been examined at the national level (Cohen, Brawer, and Bensimon 1985; Grubb 1991; Pascarella, Smart, and Ethington 1986; Richardson and Bender 1985; Trent and Medsker 1968), with some scholars focusing specifically on the transfer of minority students (Astin 1982; Olivas 1979; Pincus and DeCamp 1989). Others examine transfer rates between specific two-year and four-year institutions (e.g., Illinois Community College Board 1986; Kissler, Lara, and Cardinal 1981), while still other scholars try to identify student characteristics that indicate a predisposition to transfer (e.g., Nora and Rendon 1991) and what characteristics predict success at the senior institution (e.g., Townsend, McNerney, and Arnold 1993). Practitioner-oriented works often focus on what community colleges can do to improve the process or mechanics of transferring (Kintzer and Wattenbarger 1985; Pincus and Archer 1989) and occasionally on how four-year institutions can facilitate transfer (Donovan, Schaier-Peleg, and Forer 1987; Wechsler 1989). Only recently has the question been raised, "What should faculty and administrators at four-year colleges and universities do to ensure the retention and graduation of community college students once they are at the senior institution?"

Normed to the mores and educational expectations of the community college, community college transfer students often suffer "transfer shock" (Hills 1965) at senior institutions. Usually manifested by a dip in grade point average, this shock may be so severe that individual students drop out. Sometimes they go to another school whose environment is more compatible with their academic abilities and psychological needs; sometimes they abandon a four-year degree as a goal.

Influenced by Vincent Tinto's (1975, 1987) theory of why students may withdraw from a particular institution, student retention studies frequently concentrate on how students integrate themselves into a school's social and academic systems. However, since many community college transfers are commuter students, they may have fewer opportunities or be less willing to integrate themselves into a college or university's social system (Tierney 1992). If administrators and faculty at senior-level institutions wish not only to attract but also to retain community college transfer students, they must pay attention to the academic system and provide a teaching-learning environment conducive to community college transfer students' success.

Reprinted by permission from *Review of Higher Education* 19, no. 2 (winter 1995).

Although several in-depth studies have examined the teaching-learning environment in individual community colleges (Kempner 1990; London 1978; Richardson, Fisk, and Okun 1983; Weis 1985), little attention has been paid to the academic environment at the four-year college or university level from the perspective of the community college transfer student. Researchers have been more inclined to examine minority students' perceptions of their experience at four-year institutions and factors affecting their persistence or withdrawal. For example, Louis Attinasi (1989) conducted a qualitative study of freshmen Mexican American students at a Southwestern university to see what influenced their "getting in" and staying in the institution.

Focus of the Study

To aid in understanding possible obstacles to the transfer and retention of community college students who have moved to the university, I conducted a case study that focused on the perceptions of a group of community college transfer students about two significant situations: the transfer process itself and the academic environment into which they transferred. A fundamental premise of this study is that understanding how community college transfer students view the transfer process and their academic experiences at the community college and the university is crucial to improving the enrollment and retention of community college transfer students in the four-year sector.

This descriptive, exploratory study had two objectives. The first was to learn how students viewed the transfer process, including if and how both the community college and the university facilitated the process, and what each institution could have done to have made the process easier. The second objective was to learn how students perceived certain aspects of each institution's academic environment, defined in this study as a composite of (1) academic standards, (2) classroom atmosphere, including interactions between students and teachers and among students, (3) tests and assignments, (4) attendance policies, (5) faculty attitudes and behaviors, and (6) student attitudes and behaviors.

My assumptions or "guiding hypotheses" (Marshall and Rossman 1991) about transfer process, were: (1) students would perceive community college representatives as aiding them in the transfer process, (2) students would view community college representatives as more helpful than university representatives, and (3) students would report difficulties in the transfer process, perhaps to a degree that they questioned their decision to transfer. My assumptions about the academic environment of the two institutions were: (1) students would perceive the university's academic standards as higher than those of the community college, (2) students would consider their community college academic experience as helpful but sometimes insufficient preparation for university-level academics, and (3) students would perceive community college faculty as more caring and helpful but less rigorous than university faculty members.

The population for this study consisted of full-time students at an urban university who had transferred from a particular urban community college between fall 1987 and spring 1992. These students might have attended other community colleges prior to attending the community college in the study, but none had attended a four-year college or university. I limited the population to students from a particular community college so that all students in the study could make the same institution-specific comparisons.

The population for this study consisted of forty-four students. Seven (16 percent) had graduated from the university when data collection began, 16 (36 percent) were no longer attending the university, and 21 (48 percent) were still enrolled.

The community college in the study is large and public with an open admissions policy. In fall 1992 it enrolled over 5,000 students in credit courses and over 10,000 students in noncredit courses. I chose this particular community college because of its racial and ethnic diversity, including a large number of international students.[1] Of the students taking credit courses at this institution in fall 1992, 24 percent were Asian, 22 percent black, 13 percent Hispanic, 1 percent Native American, 39 percent white, and 1 percent other. Given the diversity of the school's student body, I assumed that, as a group, transfer students from this college would be more racially and ethnically diverse than transfer students from the area's suburban community colleges. Racial and ethnic diversity would be an advantage in this study since I assumed that such students would provide perspectives not bounded or dominated by one racial or ethnic group.

The university is a private, religiously affiliated, moderately selective university in the Carnegie Doctorate-Granting I classification. It is located in the same metropolitan area as the community college. Its fall 1992 enrollment was over 5,700 full-time and 3,800 part-time undergraduate students[2] and almost 6,000 full and part-time graduate and professional students. Transfer students average 8 percent of the university's undergraduate student body. In fall 1992, 53 percent of the 493 undergraduate transfer students came from community colleges, including 9 percent from the community colleges within the city in which the university is located.

I chose this particular university for the study for two reasons: (1) It is officially committed to diversifying its student body and thus supports efforts to enroll community college transfers. At the time of this study, it was participating in a grant-funded program with the community college to improve transfer between the two institutions. (2) While university faculty are stereotypically portrayed, especially in the community college literature, as absorbed in their subject matter and not particularly interested in their undergraduate students (e.g., Seidman 1985), many members of the university in this study pride themselves on the institution's teaching- and student-centered approach. Given this faculty orientation and the university's espoused commitment to teaching and student-centered approach, I assumed its academic environment might be more compatible with that of the community college than might a large public university's. Since I was interested in learning what assisted and what deterred community college transfer students' academic success in the university, I decided to select a best-possible environment for the students. On the other hand, if the transfer students found that the academic environment of this particular university inhibited their academic success, I assumed the situation would be far worse in a university and with a faculty less committed to teaching and a student orientation.

Methodology

I chose the method of interviewing students to gain a sense of how they understood their transfer and academic experiences and to uncover dynamics in the transfer process and in their classroom experiences that could not be elicited through responses on a survey instrument.

I contacted the twenty-one students enrolled at the university in spring 1992, first by letter and then by phone, to ascertain their willingness to be interviewed about the transfer process and their academic experiences at both schools. During the summer and fall of 1992, ten students agreed to be interviewed on campus for a period lasting from one to two hours. One declined to be interviewed after coming to the interview session and learning more about the study. To accommodate students' schedules, four of the nine students were interviewed in pairs. The interviews were conducted by a white, female, graduate student close in age to the students. Working on a master's degree in college student personnel, she had never attended a community college but had a strong interest in working with international students and was then doing so part-time at the university. I felt that these factors would facilitate greater candor from the interviewees.

With the nine students who consented to be part of the study, in-depth focused interviews were used to elicit answers to questions about how the students viewed the transfer process and how the academic environment of the two schools compared. (See Appendix.) All students were asked the same base questions, with additional follow-up questions as the interviewer deemed necessary. For example, if the interviewee, when asked about the university faculty, chose to discuss their accessibility to students, the interviewer then followed up by asking the student to compare the availability of the community college faculty. If students gave responses whose meaning was unclear to the interviewer, she asked them to clarify their meaning or give her an example.

The interviews were taped and transcribed. Paraphrasing was occasionally used when the respondent digressed into some personal matter beyond the study. Such paraphrases are clearly noted in the transcriptions. I coded responses to each question by themes and categories developed after several readings of the interview data (Strauss and Corbin 1990). To strengthen the reliability of the analysis, I had a colleague code responses to three of the questions.

As another way of ascertaining what might inhibit the academic success of community college transfer students, I also contacted sixteen community college transfer students who were no longer attending the university. Due to time and funding constraints, I did not attempt interviews but rather sent these individuals a researcher-designed, one-page survey incorporating both close-ended and open-ended questions. It asked respondents to: (1) evaluate the teaching at both the community college and the university, (2) compare the teaching-learning process at both institutions, (3) assess how well the community college prepared them academically for the university, (4) state their reason(s) for leaving the university, and (5) state what the university could have done to help them stay. After two mailings of the survey, five students had responded to the survey (31 percent response rate). However, five of the surveys were undeliverable because of address changes. Thus the adjusted response rate was 45 percent.

Findings

The findings will be presented in two parts: (1) the perceptions of community college transfer students who were still enrolled at the university, and (2) the survey responses of students who had withdrawn from the university.

Perceptions of the Transfer Process

The students still enrolled in the university reported that they neither sought nor received help from the community college in the transfer process. Rather almost all of them chose to rely upon themselves or occasionally on friends or relatives. The following comments were typical:

> Hispanic male: I knew about the Transfer Center but I decided not to use it. I didn't consult anyone at the community college.[3] I did it myself.

> White international female: The only office I contacted was admissions at the community college because I needed my transcript sent to the university.

> White international female: I didn't receive any assistance from the community college but rather from a friend at the university.

> Asian female: My brothers and sisters also transferred from the community college to the university, and since I had their help, I didn't seek help from anyone at the community college. I never went to any counselors. I never really talked to anybody.

One student seemed forced to rely on herself since the community college failed to meet her request for help:

> Hispanic female: I tried to get help from the community college, but no one could help me. . . . Everyone I asked, they told me they didn't know. So I said, 'Forget it, I'll just come to the university, I found out after I left the community college I was supposed to see a guidance counselor there. I didn't know that. It was too late. . . . So I just came over here and they gave me the name of my dean and I made an appointment.

Only one student used the community college's center established to aid potential transfer students.[4] This student made it clear she could not have attended the university without the transfer center's help since it was there she learned about the state financial aid that was available.

Although almost every student claimed she or he had transferred "on my own," three of the nine students also indicated they had received help from a university admissions representative who visited the community college campus and provided applications, information about transferability of courses, and financial aid information. In other words, the students perceived they did it by themselves, but the community college actually assisted in the process by inviting university representatives to recruit on campus. Similarly the university assisted by sending representatives to the community college for recruitment purposes.

In general, the students who came to the university on their own initiative to find out how to transfer praised university staff for their helpfulness. Only one student complained that "as a transfer student, they wouldn't help me." She added that part of the problem was that "everyone was on vacation at that time" because she decided to start in a summer session.

None of the students chose to participate in the university's sole official effort to socialize transfer students to the university, an orientation for transfer students from both two-year and four-year schools. In some instances, the students' self-reliance was again apparent in their reasons for not attending the orientation:

> Asian international female: I was aware of the orientation but decided not to go. I was only interested in knowing which building

> housed the nursing program. However, my first day I was lost and it might have been a good idea if I'd gone to the orientation.
>
> White female: There was one offered but I didn't go. I work a lot. I just found my way around.
>
> Black male: I'm from [the city] so I pretty much know where everything is.
>
> Hispanic male: I knew there was one but I decided not to go. I think I had to work that day.

Sometimes the students developed self-reliance because the institution failed to communicate with them. Three of the students received no information or incomplete orientation information, so they could not have attended the orientation even if they had wanted to do so. While it is possible that students had failed to inform the university of their correct mailing address, from the students' perspective, the university was responsible for the poor communication.

Although most students declared they had "done it on my own" and sometimes complained about both institutions' poor communications with students during the process, almost uniformly they assessed the transfer process as "easy." Typical comments were, "I was very satisfied with the whole procedure and the university advisor;" "It was too easy. It was great;" "Everything ran smoothly;" and "No criticisms. No suggestions. I thought it was just perfect".

Thus my findings in the study did not support my guiding hypotheses about the transfer process. Students did not perceive that they had received transfer help from the community college and actually found university representatives more helpful than community college representatives in the transfer process. Further, students saw the transfer process as "easy," not difficult.

Perceptions of Each Institution's Academic Environment

Most students perceived the university's academic standards as higher or "more difficult" than those of the community college. Only two thought the standards were "almost the same thing," and none found the standards easier at the university. Typical comments of students who thought the university's standards were higher were:

> Hispanic male: There's definitely a higher standard at the university than for the community college. The university courses are definitely harder. The introductory courses are less introductory . . . not as basic . . . courses are academically more demanding.
>
> Asian international female: At the university you really have to study to get very good grades . . . At the community college I just didn't feel challenged. I really didn't study as much and I was on the dean's list. And like here, I would study and still I'm not on the dean's list.
>
> Hispanic male: The university grading was more what I expected in college than at the community college where they were amazed if you knew how to use a semicolon.

Also as I had expected, when asked how well the community college had prepared them for the university, most of the students either said it had not prepared them sufficiently or said it been inadequate in only a few areas. The harshest comment was: "Honestly, I think high school prepared me more for what the university was going to be than the community college did." Three students felt unprepared in math, one in writing and public speaking, one in general knowledge (defined as "not knowing a lot of the readings others in the university classes did"), and one in the sciences. Suggestions for improving the preparation included the following:

> Hispanic male: The community college students should be aware of the academic rigors of the university before they enroll. Someone should state clearly to them what will be expected of them academically.
>
> Asian international female: The community college could provide a more rigid classroom atmosphere. [She then added, rather paradoxically:] I just felt like at the community college you didn't have to be so formal, which is nice.

Assignment and Tests

As is typical of community college students nationally (e.g., Doughterty 1987; Kissler, Lara, and Cardinal 1981), the students in this sample had limited experience with writing assignments or essay tests at the community college. Eight of the nine students indicated that university faculty required more writing, both for assignments and for tests, than did community college faculty. As one student said, "I have found the key to doing well at the university is being able to write."

One international student much preferred the community college's approach to writing, which allowed students to take assignments home rather than dealing with the pressures of in-class writing. A native-born student believed her writing was "not up to par" and "my skills were not as sharp as they could be" because the community college spent so much time on students for whom English was not their native language. She had been an A student in her English class at the community college, but she had also been "the only American in a class of foreign [sic] students."

Most students perceived that university faculty gave few multiple-choice tests. According to one student, even when they did, the tests were very different from the ones at the community college. "I was used to the type of multiple choice test where there was only one right answer and the other ones were off the wall."

Faculty Accessibility and Willingness to Help Students

Most of the students perceived the university faculty as available for questions and consultation outside of class. Two students found them more available than the community college faculty, while two saw university faculty as more distant than the community college faculty. One of these latter students said, "At the university you don't have much of a relationship with professors unless you really go out of your way. At least I haven't had a chance to." She later stated, however, that she had never tried to make an appointment with a teacher at the university and thus couldn't really say if they were available to students.

There were mixed perceptions about the university faculty's willingness to help students. While most students considered university faculty in general helpful, four of the nine students related very negative classroom incidents about specific faculty members.

> Hispanic female: My first computer (teacher) . . . was the worst professor I had ever had. This man should not be teaching. I went to him for help and he told me it was self-explanatory and that if I couldn't understand it I should get out of his class. I was so furious! I never thought a professor could say that to me. I told him that he shouldn't be teaching.

> White female: I had a girlfriend whose physics teacher wouldn't answer any algebra-related questions in class. His response was, "Go learn your algebra and then come back here."

> Black male: I had one teacher who was teaching a very difficult subject and he would just read it straight to us out of the book, and it was way over our heads. And then he would translate it into just as difficult terms . . . Several students approached him about what he was doing, but he didn't change.

> Asian international female: I never had Shakespeare in high school and so I thought, "Oh, I want to try this. . . . So I took this class and it was a big mistake. It seemed like he expected us to understand the book and that was why we were in the class. And for me, I am a student, I want to learn, that is why I am there. . . . I went up to the teacher and told him I really didn't understand a thing, and the teacher just said, 'Oh, there is a counseling center."

It is not difficult to hear the "shock" in students' voices as they encountered these university faculty members' dismissive and unsympathetic responses to their lack of the "appropriate" academic background.

As I had anticipated, community college faculty were sometimes considered more helpful than the university faculty, partly because of how the community college faculty taught. One of the international students who contrasted take-home assignments at the community college with in-class work at the university foresaw increasing problems for the university as it dealt with more international students like her who found it "hard to improve because you don't have time to work things through" with only in-class assignments. Another student preferred the community college faculty's approach of doing in-class work, where "we'd work things out together. At the university it's lecture and you take things home and do it yourself. . . . They throw all this information at you. Then you have ten pages of notes and you sit at home by yourself." Similarly, another student commented, "There are some teachers at the university that make the students understand, 'I'm not willing to answer questions—I'm giving you a lecture—take down notes—study on your own.'"

Classroom Atmosphere

Most students defined classroom atmosphere in terms of students' willingness to help one another and in how comfortable they felt asking questions in class. An unexpected finding was several students' perception that the competitive nature of the university made students reluctant to help one another academically:

> White international female: There is more competition than I expected. At the community college you go to learn, there is no competition. Here I really feel bad for the students because there is so big [sic] pressure. I wish there was a way where they could help each other. . . . At the community college you can learn from everyone's experiences. Students are more encouraged to share in class. . . . At the university students aren't interested in helping one another.

> Asian female: University students are more competitive. In some ways that's good because it makes you work harder, but it's bad because I don't want to get mixed up in that kind of atmosphere where I always have to watch out for myself, you know, watch my back because if I don't keep up to date someone is going to step over me.

> White female: There's peer pressure to be on time at the university. It's not a teacher expectation. It's just that you don't want to miss any information because you're afraid to ask others for the notes.

Similarly, fear that other students, rather than the faculty, would find their questions "dumb" or inappropriate apparently inhibited students from asking questions in the classroom. Students were seemingly more concerned about losing face with one another than with the instructor.

Student Perceptions of Why the Two Schools Differ

An intriguing finding of the study was how the students made sense of the two institutions' differing academic environments. Although not asked why they thought the two institutions differed, several students suggested that community college students collectively were the reason behind any difficulties they, as individuals, might be having in the university. Typical comments included the following:

> Hispanic male: The caliber of students in the community college classes probably had a lot to do with the caliber of teaching. You had to teach to their level . . . Having lots of foreign (sic) students who couldn't speak English well prevented the teachers from going at a faster pace.

> Black male: Many of my teachers at the community college never got all the way through the syllabus by the end of the term. They went so slowly. I don't know whether it was the teacher or the student.

> Asian female: It's the students that make a difference because over there I was always considered a very good student, and I guess that's because everyone else wasn't that good of a student. . . . So I think the junior college needs to get more students who are more competitive or who have better grades. I don't think they have a good mixture of students over there. They are mostly not that well educated (before coming to the community college) . . . I heard from my sister-in-law who goes to school there now that they are letting in people off the street.

> Hispanic male: University students tend to be a lot more serious than the community college students . . . more goal-oriented . . . a lot more responsible. . . . They also tend to be more intelligent for lack of a better word . . . more prepared for a college situation.

In other words, students who articulated a reason for the differing academic standards usually said they stemmed from a difference in the student bodies, with the university having better students than the community college. Several native-born students perceived the great diversity of the community college's student body, and particularly its large number of international students, as an obstacle to high-quality education in the community college. In contrast, they almost unanimously perceived the university's student body as "so white!"

Responses of Students Who Had Left the University without Graduating

Five of the sixteen students who left the university without graduating responded to a one-page survey about their experiences at the university and the community college. Their responses provide another perspective on how community college transfers see the two institutions and what concerns these students may have about their post community college/university education.

A common assumption about students who leave an institution without graduating is that they do so because of academic difficulties. This may have been a reason why some of the sixteen students left the university. Of the nonrespondents, nine had a university GPA of less than 2.0, which is equivalent to a C average. Of these nine, four were dropped for poor scholarship. However, of the five respondents to the survey only one had clearly failed academically and had a 0.0 GPA after one semester. The other four all had passing GPA's, with the average being 2.45. While average GPA was a major difference between respondents and nonrespondents as groups, their characteristics were otherwise similar.

None of the five respondents indicated that differences in academic standards or in the teaching-learning process made them leave the university. Instead, two cited financial reasons and three cited curricular, i.e., a desire for majors  the university did not offer. These three respondents had transferred to other schools. When the two who left for financial reasons were asked what the university could have done to help them stay, one suggested "payment plans for tuition."

When asked if they believed the community college had prepared them adequately for the university, three said yes, one said no, and one wrote that the community college "needs to focus more on written skills and to come up with and express critical thought." When asked which institution's teaching-learning process was more effective for them, four of the five students named the university. Reasons given included the greater "enthusiasm" of the university faculty, the "fast pace at which the university classes moved [that] required more of you to keep up," and the emphasis on critical thinking. Additionally, one respondent preferred the university because "the quality of students is much better which creates a competitive yet educational atmosphere."

Discussion and Implications for Research and Practice

Given the small sample size and the institution-specific nature of the study, the findings of this study can only be considered suggestive, even for the two institutions themselves. By extension, however, the findings are important for community colleges and universities interested in understanding the dynamics of the transfer process and factors affecting the retention of community college transfer students.

What the data suggest is that the community college transfer student who succeeds at this university is a fairly self-reliant student, able to survive with minimal institutional help. These students initially manifested self-reliance during the transfer process and upon initial entry to the university. For example, most of the students relied upon the community college only for mechanical or bureaucratic help such as sending transcripts to the university. Students were far more likely to use the personal resources of friends and family than institutional ones of community college transfer centers and university orientation programs. It may be that the help and encouragement of peers who have made it to the four-year sector are perceived as more accurate and reliable than institutional help.

What this finding suggests for university members is that the more community college transfers they enroll, the more they are likely to enroll. Friends and relatives of recruited and enrolled students are likely applicants because their already enrolled peers can steer them through transfer and entry. The university may also increase the number of transfers from community colleges if its representatives go there, rather than relying completely upon the community college to help students transfer. While at the community college, university representatives can recruit students and facilitate their entrance into the university by providing them with information about applications, transferability of credits, and available financial aid. The community college transfer center can facilitate these encounters between community college students and university representatives.

Once transfer students are enrolled at the university, they apparently continue to rely upon themselves to deal with the university's very different academic environment.[5] Not only are course standards usually higher, with assignments reflecting a premium on writing and critical thinking, but university students' behaviors are also different from those in the community college. Transfer students in this study were surprised at the competitiveness among the university students. Robert Williams (1973), in his discussion of transfer shock, indicated that the community college failed to prepare students for "university-level competition" (1973, 321). The university in this study is not atypical of other universities, so the problem probably affects similar institutions.

Another major difference between the two institutions seems to be faculty attitudes and behavior toward students. Faculty at community colleges generally concentrate on developing students' academic abilities rather than expecting them to demonstrate these abilities and punishing them if they do not (McGrath and Spear 1991). In contrast, if this sample is representative, numerous four-year college and university faculty and administrators reflect an almost Darwinian perspective about academic success: The academically fit will demonstrate their ability and survive, while the less fit will withdraw or flunk out (Boice 1992). From some faculty members' perspective, it is the student's responsibility to correct any deficiencies in academic preparation, not the faculty member's. While all of the students in this study had positive comments to make about university faculty, some of the students described university faculty behavior that suggests a "survival of the fittest" attitude toward students. Even at an institution officially committed to teaching and a student-centered approach, some university faculty seemed reluctant to give students direct assistance if they seemed to lack appropriate academic background.

Thus, community colleges with a student-centered approach designed to raise self-esteem—sometimes at the expense of academic standards (Seidman 1985)—may contribute to the confusion and shock of transfer students facing different standards and expectations at the university. Those who are able to rely upon themselves, not the faculty or fellow students, can survive. Those who expect help from the faculty and students who are not relatives or friends prior to entry to the university may well flounder and go down.

To examine further the likelihood that community college transfer students who succeed academically at the university need to be very self-reliant, future research could include interviews with community college students who dropped out as well as those who graduated from the senior institution to which they transferred. These students' perceptions of what they needed for academic success at the university and how the university could have assisted students would be useful information for those committed to increasing the retention rate of this group of students at the university.

Practical implications of the differing academic environments found in this study are not limited to the two institutions of the study. At the very least, community college faculty who wish to see students well prepared for transfer would be well advised to increase writing assignments and essay tests. The faculty should also talk candidly with prospective transfer students about the probability of more rigorous university grading standards, owing to different institutional missions and faculty attitudes toward the teaching-learning process.

At the university level, faculty should be encouraged to reexamine their attitudes about their responsibility in the teaching process. Also administrators should reexamine the institution's commitment to helping students whose academic backgrounds may be lacking in certain areas. Are students expected to sink or swim? Is this a conscious, deliberately chosen institutional attitude or an unanticipated outcome of failure to reflect about institutional and faculty commitments to students? As faculty and administrators reflect about their responsibilities in teaching, they should consider Alexander Astin's (1985) model of "talent development," which emphasizes faculty and student collaboration in developing students' talents and abilities. His paradigm for the teaching-learning process is suggested in the wistful comments of at least some of the students in this sample on the differences between the community college and the university. If universities are sincere about increasing the enrollment and retention of community college transfer students, an implicit institutional stance of the "survival of the fittest" approach to student success needs to be rethought.

Appendix

Interview Questions

1. Community College Assistance for Transferring

   Did you receive any assistance at the community college when you decided to transfer to the university? Did you ask for any?

2. University Assistance for Transferring

   How about the university? Did you receive any assistance when you decided to transfer in? Did you ask for any?

   How would you evaluate this assistance?

   Is there anything the university should do to better aid students who want to transfer?

3. University Transfer Student Orientation

   Did you attend transfer student orientation at the university? If so, was it helpful?

   Is there anything that was not covered in the orientation session that should have been covered?

4. Student Expectations of the University
   a. General: Is the university what you expected it would be? If not, how is it different?
   b. Academics: Is the university different from the community college as for as academics are concerned? If so, how is it different?
   c. Assignments: Do you have more written assignments at the university that you did at the community college, e.g., book reports, research papers?
   d. Tests: Are the testing procedures used by teachers at the university different from the procedures used by the community college teachers? If so, how are they different?
   e. Teachers: What is your general impression of the teachers at the university? How would you compare them to the community college teachers?
   f. Students: What is your general impression of the students at the university? How would you compare them to the community college students?
   g. Attendance Requirements: How about the university's attendance requirements? Are they different from the community college's?
   h. Classroom Setting and Atmosphere: Are the classroom setting and atmosphere different at the university compared to the community college? If so, how?
   i. Preparation for the University: Do you feel the community college prepared you academically to do well at the university? If not, what might it have done differently?

Notes

1. "International students" means immigrants to the United States, not individuals who are in the country on a temporary study visa.
2. The university differentiates between full-time (12 or more hours each semester) and part-time undergraduate students, admitting them under a different selection process and assigning them to different administrative offices. Consequently, the demographic makeup of the two student bodies is quite different. All of the students in this study were admitted as full-time students.
3. Students naturally used the name of the university or the name of the community college in their responses; I have silently masked these references, here and in the appendix.
4. The community college's transfer center was established in 1989 but was not in full operation until 1991. Six of the students who were interviewed transferred before the center was established.
5. Kevin Doughterty comments on "tougher standards of the four-year colleges" and "poorer academic preparation in the community college" (1987, 99).

References

Astin, Alexander. *Minorities in Higher Education*. San Francisco: Jossey-Bass, 1982.

——. *Achieving Educational Excellence*. San Francisco: Jossey-Bass, 1985.

Attinasi, Louis C. "Getting In: Mexican Americans' Perceptions of University Attendance and the Implications for Freshman Year Persistence." *Journal of Higher Education* 60 (May/June 1989): 247–76.

Boice, Robert. *The New Faculty Member*. San Francisco: Jossey-Bass, 1992.

Cohen, Arthur, Florence Brawer, and Estela Bensimon. *Transfer Education in American Community Colleges*.

Los Angeles: Center for the Study of Community Colleges, 1985.

Donovan, Richard A., Barbara Schaier-Peleg, and Bruce Forer, eds. *Transfer: Making It Work*. Washington, D.C.: American Association of Community and Junior Colleges, 1987.

Dougherty, Kevin. "The Effects of Community Colleges: Aid or Hindrance to Socioeconomic Attainment?" *Sociology of Education* 60 (April 1987): 86–103.

Grubb, William N. "The Decline of Community College Transfer Rates: Evidence from National Longitudinal Studies." *Journal of Higher Education* 62 (March/April 1991): 194–217.

Hills, John R. "Transfer Shock: The Academic Performance of the Junior College Transfer." *Journal of Experimental Education* 33 (Spring 1965): 201–16.

Illinois Community College Board. *Illinois Community College Board Transfer Study: A Five-Year Study of Students Transferring from Illinois Two-Year Colleges to Illinois Senior Colleges in the Fall of 1979*. Springfield: Illinois Community College Board, 1986.

Kempner, Ken. "Faculty Culture in the Community College: Facilitating or Hindering Learning." *Research in Higher Education* 13, no. 2 (1990): 215–35.

Kintzer, Frederick C., and James L. Wattenbarger. *The Articulation/Transfer Phenomenon: Patterns and Directions*. Washington, D.C.: American Association of Community and Junior Colleges, 1985.

Kissler, Gerald, Juan Lara, and Judith Cardinal. "Factors Contributing to the Academic Difficulties Encountered by Students Who Transfer from Community Colleges to Four-Year Institutions." Paper presented at American Educational Research Association, Los Angeles, April 1981.

London, Howard. *The Culture of a Community College*. New York: Praeger Press, 1978.

Marshall, Catherine, and Gretchen B. Rossman. *Designing Qualitative Research*. Newbury Park, California: Sage Publications, 1991.

McGrath, Dennis, and Martin Spear. *The Academic Crisis of the Community College*. Albany, New York: SUNY Press, 1991.

Nora, Amaury, and Laura Rendon. "Determinants of Predisposition to Transfer Among Community College Students: A Structural Model." *Research in Higher Education* 31 (1990): 235–55.

Olivas, Michael. *The Dilemma of Access: Minorities in Two-Year Colleges*. Washington, D.C.: Howard University Press, 1979.

Pascarella, Ernest T., John C. Smart, and Corinna A. Ethington. "Long-term Persistence of Two-Year College Students." *Research in Higher Education* 24 (1986): 47–71.

Pincus, Fred, and Elayne Archer. *Bridges to Opportunity: Are Community Colleges Meeting the Transfer Needs of Minority Students?* New York: College Entrance Examination Board, 1989.

Pincus, Fred L., and Suzanne DeCamp. "Minority Community College Students Who Transfer to Four-Year Colleges: A Study of a Matched Sample of B.A. Recipients and Non-Recipients." *Community/Junior Quarterly of Research and Practice* 13, nos. 3–4 (1989): 191–219.

Richardson, Richard C., Jr., and Louis W. Bender. *Students in Urban Settings: Achieving the Baccalaureate Degree*. ASHE-ERIC Higher Education Report No. 6. Washington, D.C.: Association for the Study of Higher Education, 1985.

Richardson, Richard C., Jr., Elizabeth Fisk, and Morris Okun. *Literacy in the Open-Access College*. San Francisco: Jossey-Bass, 1983.

Seidman, Earl. *In the Words of the Faculty*. San Francisco: Jossey-Bass, 1985.

Strauss, Anselm, and Juliet Corbin. *Basics of Qualitative Research*. Newbury Park, California: Sage Publications, 1990.

Tierney, William. "An Anthropological Analysis of Student Participation in College." *Journal of Higher Education* 63 (November/December 1992): 603–18.

Tinto, Vincent. "Dropouts from Higher Education: A Theoretical Synthesis of Recent Research."*Review of Educational Research* 45 (1975): 89–125.

——. *Leaving College: Rethinking the Causes and Cures of Student Attrition*. Chicago: University of Chicago Press, 1987.

Townsend, Barbara, Nancy McNerney, and Allen Arnold. "Will This Community College Transfer Student Succeed? Factors Affecting Transfer Student Performance." *Community College Journal of Research and Practice* 17 (Fall 1993): 433–44.

Trent, J., and Leland L. Medsker. *Beyond High School*. San Francisco: Jossey-Bass. 1968.

Wechsler, Harold. *The Transfer Challenge: Removing Barriers, Maintaining Commitment*. Washington, D.C. Association of American Colleges, 1989.

Weis, Lois. *Between Two Worlds: Black Students in an Urban Community College*. Boston: Routledge & Kegan Paul, 1985.

Williams, Robert. "Transfer Shock As Seen from a Student's Point of View." *College and University* 48 (Summer 1973): 320–21.

More Than 13 Ways of Looking at Degree Attainment

Dr. Clifford Adelman

Senior Research Analyst, Office of Educational Research and Improvement,
United States Department of Education, Washington, D.C.

The title of this piece, a play on that of Wallace Stevens' poem, "Thirteen Ways of Looking at a Blackbird," reflects the nearly infinite variety of nuances in the basic question about attainment in American higher education.

When newspaper reporters or state legislative aides telephone and ask, "What proportion of college students earn a bachelor's degree?" or "What percentage of community college students earn credentials?" the answers are not clear until the questioner defines who is in the denominator (or what we call the "universe"): all students who graduated from high school? all students who ever said they aspired to a bachelor's degree? all students who entered college? all students who attended a four-year college at any time? all students who entered a four-year college directly from high school?

After the denominator, the numerator is comparatively easy, but still must be specified. For the bachelor's degree, the numerator must include a time "censor": within five years of high school graduation? within five years of entering college? within six years? by age 35? ever?

Of course, we can complicate the numerator with conditions other than those of time, but with each additional degree of complexity, we no longer are asking the basic question.

In July of this year, I was asked the basic question by staff at the Congressional Budget Office. The context for the question was a proposed amendment to the reauthorization of the Higher Education Act, and required a long-term censor—something beyond five or six years.

The purpose of this presentation is not to discuss the proposed amendment, but rather to share with you what I told my colleagues at the Congressional Budget Office.

The source for the data is the postsecondary transcript file of the High School & Beyond Sophomore Cohort longitudinal study. This is the second national longitudinal study conducted by the National Center for Education Statistics. The postsecondary transcripts in those studies enable us to tell very accurate student histories, histories that cross state lines and involve many institutions—for the same student.

At present, this is the only data source in the nation that can answer the basic question about long term degree completion rates in recent years. In these data, we are looking at the history of the scheduled high school graduating class of 1982, from the time of their graduation up to 1993, when most of the cohort was 29 or 30 years old.

Reprinted from *National CrossTalk* 6, no. 4 (fall 1998).

The Four-Year College Story

The basic position I take in Table 1, "Postsecondary Fate to Age 30", is that one is not in the denominator for the calculation of bachelor's degree attainment rates unless one has gone to the trouble of actually enrolling in a bachelor's degree-granting institution. With that simple gesture, one says far more than repeating 100 times "I want to get a bachelor's degree" or "I am working toward a bachelor's degree." It is neither accurate nor fair to judge attainment among those who did not make a minimum attempt by age 30.

If one enters a four-year college directly from high school, and gets by the 60* credit, the odds are about 7 in 8 of completing a bachelor's degree by age 30. That's pretty good! In an age of multi-institutional attendance, such system graduation rates make far more sense than "institutional graduation rates." Institutions may "retain," but it is students who persist. And the last time I looked, federal higher education policy was directed at students, not institutions.

Since all these data came from the college transcript records, I could add the following note: At age 30, and among those who had earned more than 60 credits, a relatively low proportion (9 to 12 percent) of the low proportion (13 to 21 percent) who had not earned a bachelor's degree were still in school.

In other words, the vast majority of non-completers had drifted away from higher education at age 30. While we always are confident that some will return, it is eminently apparent that we are children of time, and that other demands and possibilities of life come to supersede those of formal education after we have passed through our 20s.

The Community College Story

The community college story presented in Table 2 (located on page 391) is both very different and very exciting. For years, we have been beating up on community colleges because of what we perceive to be low degree completion rates.

But students use community colleges for a variety of reasons, not all of which are connected to credentials. Of the entire universe of students who ever enter community colleges, nearly one out of six never earns even a semester's worth of credits. These "incidental" students are excluded from the analysis in "Community College Fate to Age 30" because they are just that—incidental—and it is not fair, or accurate, to include them in a universe with which we judge institutional performance.

Table 2 thus sets a minimum threshold of credits earned by students at community colleges as undergraduates. (It excludes a small number of students who attended community colleges after earning a bachelor's degree as well as those four-year college students who took a course or two at community colleges.)

Table 2 does something else that is very important to judging community college performance in terms of labor market preparation. It takes students who did not complete any credential, looks at their transcript records, and asks whether one can describe a dominant "tone" of study, something analogous to a college major or a balanced general education program.

For example, a student may have accumulated 36 credits (and no credential), of which half are in finite mathematics, electronics, computer programming, computer organization

TABLE 1
Postsecondary Fate to Age 30
1993 Achievement of Students from the High School Class of 1982 Who Attended 4-Year Colleges

	60+ Creds No Degree	*Certificate*	*Assoc.*	*Bachelor's*
Attended 4-Yr College & Earned >60 Creds	12	2	7	79
1st Inst was 4-Yr & No Delay After High School	12	1	4	82
>60 Creds from 4-Yr & No Delay After High School	10	1	2	87

Note: All rows Add to 100%.
Source: National Center for Education Statistics: High School & Beyond Sophomore Cohort (Restricted) Postsecondary Education Transcript File (NCES 98–135).

TABLE 2
Community College Fate to Age 30
1993 Achievement of College-Goers from the High School Class of 1982 Who Attended Community Colleges

	>29 Creds No Degree No Field	*>29 Creds No Degree But Field*	*Certificate*	*Assoc.*
Earned <29 Creds From Comm Col and <11 Credits & No Delay After High School	11	36	15	38
From 4-Yr College	11	36	12	41

Note: All rows add to 100%.
Source: National Center for Education Statistics: High School & Beyond Sophomore Cohort (Restricted) Postsecondary Education Transcript File (NCES 98–l35).

and architecture. There is no doubt of a dominant "tone" to this record. One can say that this student is prepared to enter the labor market in the general area of computer technologies.

This does not mean the student is an automatic JAVA-whiz, nor does it mean that we have witnessed the end of the individual's education and training. What it does mean is the student has derived something from the community college experience that anyone—including employers—can describe. And I don't need to remind readers that a majority of community college students attend in order to establish specific trajectories into the labor market.

At age 30, then, those who have attended community colleges in non-incidental ways have "separated" from the system in a satisfactory manner if they have accomplished one of four ends: 1) transferred to a four-year college and received a bachelor's degree; 2) earned a terminal associate's degree; 3) earned a certificate indicating a coherent course of study that is nonetheless not a full degree program; or 4) taken a sufficient amount of coursework that can be described as a partial major or complete lower-division general education program.

Table 2 shows what I call "community college dominant students"—students who earned 30 or more credits from a community college and fewer than 11 credits from four-year colleges. In this group, the *de facto* "completion rate" (associate's degree + certificate + a classifiable cluster of coursework) is an astounding 89 percent—equivalent to the bachelor's degree completion rate of four-year college students who entered directly from high school and earned more than 60 credits.

For skeptics who say that this "community college dominant" group is small, I beg to differ. We are looking at about 325,000 people from a single high school graduating class.

For the record (and because someone is bound to ask), at the "community college dominant" level, the distribution of classifiable course clusters of those who left without a credential was: complete general education program (23 percent); business and marketing (15 percent); business support occupations (10 percent); arts and applied arts (8 percent); computer science and technology (7 percent); other science and tech (7 percent); trades and crafts (7 percent); and other fields (23 percent). Not all of these are statistically significant percentages, but they give one a decent idea of the distribution.

So What's the Point?

Our system may appear sloppy to some, but our results are better than the popular myths, most of which use the institution, and not the student, as the unit of analysis. We have to be prepared to provide solid answers to those who hold us accountable in terms that the public understands. Our judges have many ways of asking the question, and any appearance of uncertainty on our part in answering will be taken as a sign of vulnerability.

Our focus must be on the student. We have to be clear about the terms of our answers: The terms must be those of common sense, and we must be able to combine them quickly and authoritatively.

The College Experience: A Conceptual Framework to Consider for Enhancing Students' Educational Gains

Lemuel W. Watson

Introduction

Sociologists Pierre Bourdieu and Jean Claude Passeron are known for their work in social, class, and cultural reproduction within the educational systems. Bourdieu (1977) view education as an important social and political force in the process of class reproduction. By appearing to be an impartial and neutral "transmitter" of the benefits of a valued culture, schools are able to promote inequality in the name of fairness and objectivity. Bourdieu refers to this inequality as cultural capital, which is central to his argument Bourdieu's (1977) concept of cultural capital refers to the different sets of linguistics and cultural competencies that individuals inherit by way of the class-location boundaries of their families.

In more specific terms, a child inherits from his or her family sets of meanings, quality of style, modes of thinking, and types of dispositions that are accorded a certain social value and status as a result of what the dominant class or classes label as the most valued cultural capital. Schools play a particularly important role in both legitimating and reproducing the dominant culture, especially at the level of higher education, and embody class interest and ideologies that capitalize on a kind of familiarity and set of skills that only specific students have received by means of their family backgrounds and class relation (Bourdieu, 1977). A four-year college degree has often been referred to as a ticket into the American middle class (Bowles & Gintis, 1976). Upward mobility in American society is defined by changes in occupational status and income and is inextricably aligned to postsecondary education in modern American society (Pascarella & Terenzini, 1991).

How does this cultural capital affect college students and their educational gains? What can be done in institutions of higher education to assist students in their learning and development? More importantly, are there differences between historically Black colleges and universities (HBCUs) and predominantly White institutions (PWIs) and Black and White students' educational outcomes from their undergraduate experiences based on the type of institution? A framework is introduced next in this chapter to address some of the posed questions.

Drawing from the work of Pace (1984) and Astin (1984), Watson's (1994, 1996) conceptual framework for student learning, involvement, and gains was developed to encourage a critical perspective for professionals when planning and addressing students' learning and educational gains. While the model employs familiar theories and concepts, it is unique in proposing a simple and practical

Reprinted from *Examining African American Culture and Heritage in Higher Education Research and Practice,* (1998), Praeger Publishers.

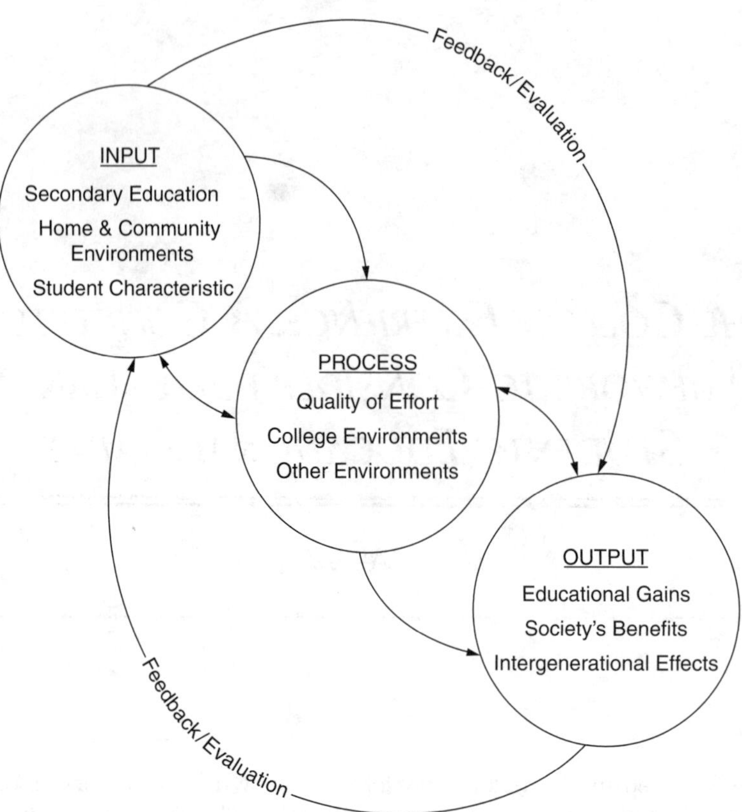

Figure 1 Conceptual Framework for Student Learning, Involvement, and Gains

framework to spark a holistic, creative, systematic, and critical thinking process that may be applied by educators to enhance student learning. The conceptual framework is to be used as a planning tool and is composed of three basic and dynamic components (Figure 1).

1. Input includes characteristics and experiences that students bring with them to college. We seem to do a great job of examining grade point averages (GPAs) and standardized test scores: however, we know little about the students as we move away from these factors. For example, students' experiences in secondary institutions, home, and community environments, as well as, their age, sex, marital status, college class, housing, major, parents' schooling, and race influence their college experience.
2. Process includes behavioral involvement of students on campus; quality of effort (scholarly and intellectual activities, informal personal activities, use of group facilities, organizational activities); and college environment (agents, peers, resources, and places on campus where students expend time and energies). Other environments represent agents, peers, resources, and places off campus where students might spend their time and energies. These places may include off-campus housing, churches, community centers, bars, and sports centers. The process section, the "what" student do, of the framework is an extremely important component of students' lives. It is equally important to understand that both the campus community and general community offer a vast array of activities. More time and energy could be invested, in building partnerships in order to share resources and facilities to enhance learning and the educational gains of students and citizens. This component of the framework encourages us as professionals to expand our notions of designing environments to include other influential factors that may affect learning and educational gains.
3. Output represents educational gains in personal, social, intellectual, vocational,

and cultural preparation while attending an institution of higher education (Pace, 1988), as well as societal benefits and intergenerational effects. The literature on educational outcomes is plentiful. We know that as students proceed through college from their first year to their senior year, they develop along many dimensions (Pascarella & Terenzini, 1991). In fact, central to most development theories is the notion of identity. Hence, part of the definite benefits of college is to develop those values and principles by which students live their lives. Raising the consciousness to a higher level of understanding regarding the value and respect of human existence, collective and individual, is a major contribution to society.

This framework is employed here to demonstrate the importance of considering multiple factors for research, programming, curriculum, and services for students. However, for this chapter a research study is the focus while employing the guidance of the framework. The study that is used in this chapter includes a target sample of 1,600 Black and White undergraduate students enrolled in two HBCUs and two PWIs for the 1993–1994 academic school year. For the PWIs, a random sampling of students was drawn, while the instrument was administered at the HBCUs in compliance with the policies of the United Negro College Fund (UNCF) which prohibits the institutions from revealing students' names and addresses. A total of 862 completed and returned questionnaires were usable. The College Student Experience Questionnaire (CSEQ) was used, which measures the quality of student effort by levels of involvement in the institution, student perceptions of their campus environment, and their belief of how much they have gained across various cognitive and affective skills. The framework helps in identifying the difference between dominant race environments and why various factors in the environment affect the quality of the educational experiences and gains for Black students at PWIs and HBCUs.

Input—Student Characteristics

Therefore, does background affect who goes to college, where one goes to college, and how well one performs in college? (See Figure 2.)

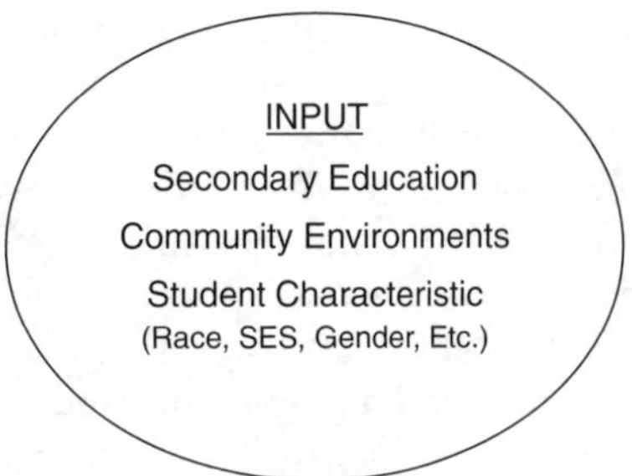

Figure 2 The Effect of Input

To discuss student characteristics, one must consider the student's family background, socioeconomic status or social class, parental education and income, and the student's preparation to enter college. The most commonly observed background characteristics that are related to the gains and experiences of the student in college are social class, parental education, parental income, and academic preparedness (Nettles & Johnson, 1987; Pascarella, Ethington, & Smart, 1988; Tinto, 1975). However, Terenzini and Pascarella (1980) and Bean (1980) have concluded that student background characteristics are insignificant to student performance in college.

The literature on student background characteristics is mixed in regard to student effort, persistence, and gains in college. However, educators cannot ignore the economic conditions of Black students compared to White students and how such conditions impact the college experience. According to a report in 1985 by the College Entrance Examination Board, in 1982, 48% of Black children below the age of 18 lived in households below the poverty line, compared to 17% of White children. In addition, the report found that Black students were more likely to come from a one-parent household compared to White students (Nettles & Johnson, 1987). One out of every five Blacks in the labor market was unemployed in 1982. In addition, statistics show that "70 percent of all Black students who enroll in four year colleges dropout at some point, as compared to 45 percent of white students" (Steele, 1992, p. 70).

The Scholastic Aptitude Test (SAT) is a major determining factor for students' acceptance into college and can be classified as a cultural capital instrument (Hurn, 1985). For example, in 1992, 12 out of nearly 100,000 Black students who took the SAT scored above 750 on the verbal portion of the test, and 520 scored over 700 on the math portion. Yet, only 1% of all Blacks who took the SAT scored over 600 on verbal, and only 2% scored above 600 on the math. White students were 12 times as likely as Blacks to score over 750 on the verbal and 16 times more likely as Blacks to score over 750 on the math portion of the SAT. "Scholastic Aptitude Test scores are profoundly affected by parental incomes and education, books in the home, quality of schooling, ability to purchase SAT coaching aid, cultural differences in the knowledge of words and other nonracial factors" (Goldsby, 1993, pp. 20–21). For these reasons, SAT scores are poor measures of academic ability. Data given in the previous sentence are mention only "because SAT scores are a deciding factor, to a very great degree, on who will be admitted to higher education" (Goldsby, 1993, pp. 20–21; Hurn, 1985).

In this study, the background factors had little effect on students' involvement or educational gains. In a similar study, MacKay and Kuh (1994) found that the level of education for parents was not a significant factor in the educational outcomes of students. The literature on parents' education as a contributing factor to educational gains and success is mixed and indicates different findings for race and sex (Gruca, 1988; Pascarella & Terenzini, 1991).

In summary, one can clearly see how background factors may influence the likelihood of students getting into institutions of higher education. Based on the educational sociologists and reports about the SAT, the argument of cultural capital certainly has merit in a capitalist society like the United States. However, a capitalist society also allows one to rise out of poverty and oppression to achieve a dream. Regardless of background or SAT scores, many students have been accepted into institutions of higher education and perform quite well (Pascarella & Terenzini, 1991). Yet, there are mixed reports on various institutions of higher education and their students' success and gains in regard to student characteristics.

Process—Quality of Effort, College Environments, and Other Environments

Does it really matter where a student attends college? Does it affect his or her educational outcomes? For Black students, is there really a difference between Black and White institutions regarding their educational experience? (See Figure 3.)

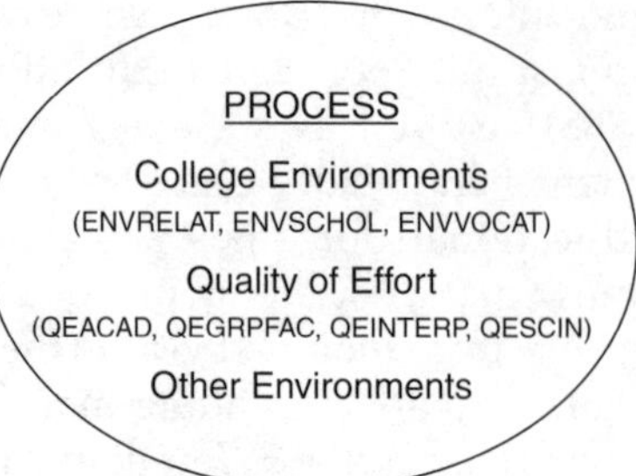

Figure 3 The Effect of Process

Much of the literature of student involvement and persistence mentions the importance of a supportive environment (Astin, 1984, 1993; Bean, 1980; Fleming, 1984; Kuh et al., 1991; Pascarella & Terenzini, 1991; Thompson & Fretz, 1991; Tinto, 1975). Also, various students experience the campus in different ways, which may affect how they invest their time and effort in utilizing institutional resources and agents and, therefore, their educational gains. It is important to find out how the university environment can be made into a place of comfort and warmth for those students who do not feel welcome. Students are often expected to adjust and accommodate themselves to the physical and social environments, and they are rarely given the chance to redesign the environment to meet their desires. Therefore, students, especially Black students, pay a high adaptation cost in terms of dissatisfaction, marginal performance, instability, and avoidance of the environment (Fleming, 1984).

White Institutions (PWIs)

Research on the concerns that Black students face on the campuses at PWIs indicates that some problems are unique to them and other minorities. Because White students are part of the majority and dominant culture, the issue of assimilation does not emerge for them. However, many Black students at PWIs have reported that they have not really felt welcome on campus and have been treated like uninvited guests in a strange land (Livingston & Stewart, 1987). Therefore, before most Black students in PWIs can begin to concentrate on academics, they must first feel comfortable in the residence halls, the classrooms, and social settings. One assumption for the adjustment problem is that the expectations of most Black students are not met at PWIs. Black students go to the institution thinking there will be less racism; yet when they arrive on campus, there is a discrepancy between their ideal environment and reality (Fleming, 1984).

It is important to understand that regardless of ethnicity, most students will encounter problems adjusting to college (Plinar & Brown, 1985; Webster, Sedlacek, & Miyares, 1979). However, since they are the dominant culture at a PWI, most White students do not face racial harassment or individual, cultural, or institutional racism, as do minority groups at PWIs. The struggles that Black students face at PWIs are qualitatively and quantitatively different from those faced by White students (Baum & Lamb, 1983; Fleming, 1984; Ponce, 1988; Sedlacek, 1987).

Black Institutions (HBCUs)

In contrast to the experiences of Black students at PWIs, Allen (1986), Fleming (1984), Watson (1994), and Watson and Kuh (1996) found that at HBCUs Black students experienced more positive psychosocial development and academic achievement. In addition, Black students were supported and encouraged to a greater degree by faculty, and they reported higher satisfaction with the social aspects of the college environment.

Davis (1991) stressed how HBCUs afford the Black students more opportunities to become integrated in the campus life. Fleming (1984) emphasized that the ingredients of social connectedness are present within the HBCU settings because "an individual can achieve feelings of progress, gain a sense of recognition, and know that there are people who will provide an attentive ear" (p. 152).

The positive attributes of HBCUs have a positive impact on the overall development of Black students. Black students show stronger intellectual confidence and a greater feeling of success and satisfaction with academic life than Blacks attending PWIs. The issue of race is less of a concern, and students are able to develop and learn as individuals without having to worry about representing their race (Whiting, 1991). The developmental progress and patterns of Black students at HBCUs are parallel to those of White students in PWIs (Allen, 1992; Fleming, 1984; Watson, 1994; Watson & Kuh, 1996).

In returning to a previous question, does it make a difference where a student, especially a Black student, attends college with regard to that student's involvement and educational gains? According to the findings of the study in this chapter, there is a definite difference for Black students.

Analysis of variance was conducted on the environmental factors for Black majority (Black students at HBCUs), White majority (White students at PWIs), and Black minority (Black students at PWIs) students. (See Figure 4.)

Black majority students showed one significant difference on the three environmental factors compared to White majority and Black minority students. Table 1 shows that the mean for Black majority students ($M = 4.72$) was the lowest of the three groups, which indicates that students at the HBCUs in this study perceived their institutional environment to place less emphasis on ENVSCHOL, the development of academic, scholarly, and intellectual qualities; the development of esthetics, expressive, and creative qualities; and being critical, valuative, and analytical. Figure 5 defines the quality of effort factors.

ENVRELAT	Represents the scholarly and intellectual emphasis of the campus environment
ENVSCHOL	Represents the vocational and practical emphasis of the campus environment
ENVVOC	Represents the supportive personal relationships of the campus environment

Figure 4 College Environmental Factors

Table 1
Group Comparison of Means and Standard Deviations by Racial Status for the Quality of Effort Factors, Environmental Factors, and Gains Factors

	Black Majority n = 502		*White Majority n = 214*		*Black Minority n = 83*		
Factors	*M*	*SD*	*M*	*SD*	*M*	*SD*	*F*
QEACAD	2.51	.47	2.28	.44^	2.44	.46	.000***
QEGRPFAC	2.28	.57	2.13	.47^	2.36	.62	.000***
QEINTERP	2.20	.46	2.05	.42^	2.22	.51	.000***
QESCIN	2.02	.70	1.88	.75	1.97	.80	.059
ENVRELAT	4.88	1.33	5.11	1.05	5.04	1.37	.064
ENVSCHOL	4.72	1.31^	5.35	.90	5.47	1.04	.000***
ENVVOCAT	4.67	1.41	4.85	1.25	4.95	1.25	.118

*$p < .05$.
**$p < .01$.
***$p < .001$.
Note: "^" indicates the group that significantly differs from the others.
Black Majority = Black students at predominantly Black institutions.
White Majority = White students at predominantly White institutions.
Black Minority = Black students at predominantly White institutions.

QEACAD	Represents the scholarly/intellectual activities
QEINTERP	Represents the informal interpersonal activities
QEGRPFAC	Represents the activities in the use of group facilities
QESCIN	Represents the activities related to science

Figure 5 Quality of Effort Factors

The literature on the subject supports this finding and suggests that it may be due to the historical mission of some private Black colleges. In fact, Allen (1987) and Fleming (1984) have stated in their work on Black colleges that Black students exchange psychological well-being, cultural likeness, and supportive academic relations for poor physical facilities and restricted academic programs. In Table 1, no other factors were shown to be significant between the groups, which is a surprise. Given the literature of Black students at PWIs, one would expect that at least one environmental factor would have been significant for Black minority students. The research on the experiences of Black students at PWIs reports that these students often experience feelings of social alienation, intense academic competition, racial stress, lack of campus integration, and isolation (Allen, 1987; Fleming, 1984; Rooney, 1985; Thomas & Hill, 1987).

The results of the analysis of variance show that White majority students differed from Black majority and minority students on three of the four quality of effort factors. (See Table 1.)

White majority students had a lower mean for all three groups, which indicates that they were less involved in QEACAD (academic activities), QEGRPFAC (group and campus facilities), and QEINTERP (informal interpersonal relations) at PWIs. Black majority students had a higher mean for QEACAD than Black minority students, and Black minority students had a higher mean for QEGRPFAC and QEINTERP. What this could signify is that the Black students at HBCUs were more involved in academic activities than Black and White students at

PWIs. However, one could also conclude from the study that Black students at HBCUs would be more involved and more active in an environment where their race is dominant versus their counterparts in PWIs. In addition, one would also expect White students to be more involved with their campus resources and agents than other minority groups at PWIs.

Output—Educational Gains

What makes a difference in students' educational gains at HBCUs and PWIs? (See Figure 6.) The educational outcomes from this study are concerned with the output section of the conceptual framework. (See Figure 7.)

ENVRELAT represents an environment that emphasizes positive relationships with other students, faculty members, and administrative personnel. As was expected from numerous studies on the effects of the environment on student outcomes, Black majority students rank their environmental relationship as contributing to four out of the five gains for educational outcomes.

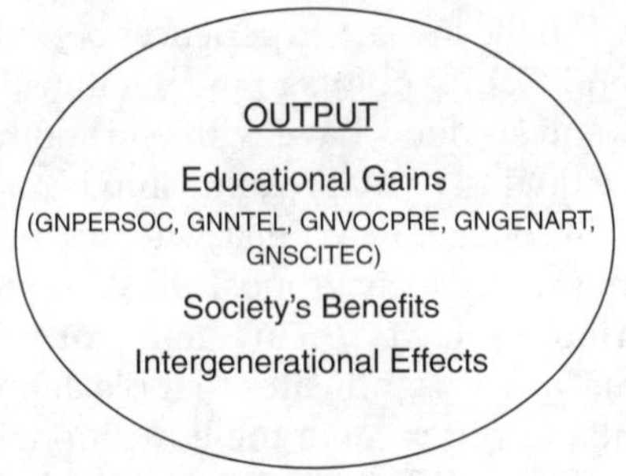

OUTPUT

Educational Gains

(GNPERSOC, GNNTEL, GNVOCPRE, GNGENART, GNSCITEC)

Society's Benefits

Intergenerational Effects

Figure 6 The Effect of Output

(See Table 1.) As expected, in an environment where Black students are the predominant race, their educational gains are impacted positively (Allen, 1992; Fleming, 1984; Gurin & Epps, 1975). ENVRELAT was more significant in gains for Black majority students than for White majority students.

ENVRELAT influenced gains only in personal and social development for Black minority students. Compared to Black and White majority students, one may conclude that being a minority on a campus inhibits other educational gains for students. For example, the two majority groups perceive their environment to value supportive and personal relationships within the campus community, and this factor contributes more to gains for the majority students than for the minority students. (See Table 1.) Allen (1992) reports in his study of Black students on HBCU and PWI campuses that Black students who attend PWIs reported lower academic achievement. Fleming (1984) points out that a supportive community for Black students on HBCUs (1) provides opportunities for friendships of various kinds with various personnel, (2) affords students opportunities to participate in campus life, and (3) allows them to feel a sense of progress and success in their academic pursuits.

ENVSCHOL is an environment that emphasizes the development of academic, scholarly, and intellectual quantities; esthetics, expressive, and creative quantitative; and critical, valuative, and analytical skills. For the majority student groups, ENVSCHOL was the only factor influencing gains in general education, literature, and the arts. However, ENVSCHOL was the greatest contributing factor for gains compared

GAIN PERS/SOC	Represents the personal and social development gains that students believe they have made while attending an institution.
GAIN SCI/TECH	Represents the science and technology gains that students believe they have made while attending an institution.
GAIN GE, LIT, ARTS	Represents the gains one believes he or she has made in their knowledge of general education, literature, and art while attending an institution.
GAIN INTEL SKILL	Represents intellectual and analytical skills gained.
GAIN VOC PREP	Represents vocational preparation gained while attending an institution.

Figure 7 Educational Gain Factor

to all other factors for minority students. ENVSCHOL contributed to gains in personal and social development, gains in intellectual skills, and gains in vocation and career options for Black minority students.

Therefore, it seems that Black students at PWIs obtain greater negative educational outcomes than both Black students at HBCUs and White students at PWIs when they perceive the environment to value academic excellence. This finding could also indicate that Black students at PWIs suffer in both personal and social aspects in order to have better programs and facilities, which may or may not increase their educational outcomes in the end. To the contrary, Astin (1977) states that Black students at HBCUs tend to have higher grades and are less satisfied and less likely to persist to the completion of a baccalaureate than Black students at PWIs.

Quality of effort in academic activities is shown to be significant for Black students at HBCUs for all of the gains factors, GNPERSOC, GNINTEL, GNVOCPRE, GNGENART, and GNSCITEC (see Table 2). Quality of effort in academic activities includes tasks related to library experiences, experiences with faculty, course learning, and writing. It was expected that QEACAD would be significant for all of the gains for Black majority students because of the relationships and support that students have from the faculty at HBCUs (Allen, 1992; Anderson, 1992).

One factor that has an overall influence on the cognitive and affective gains of students in institutions of higher education is student—faculty contact and the quality of that interaction. Talking with faculty outside the classroom, and being a guest in a faculty member's home are associated with the overall satisfaction of the college experiences. Having a class paper criticized by an instructor has a positive partial correlation with gains in general knowledge, knowledge of field or major, analytical and problem-solving skills, writing skills, and preparation for graduate or professional programs (Astin, 1993; Pascarella & Terenzini, 1991).

Also, faculty expectations and attitudes are major issues for the retention and involvement of all students, especially Black students. A study about the college experience of Black undergraduates who attend HBCUs and PWIs found that academic achievement is highest for students who report positive relationships with faculty (Allen, 1992). Likewise, Black students on PWI campuses must rely on White students and professors in making their adjustments to campus life; therefore, the support systems and other coping skills are developed within a White environment with White participants. Black students on HBCUs do not have to deal with the unfamiliar and stressful situation of being a minority (Davis, 1991).

Although the study shows that Black majority students in HBCUs perceived their institutional environment to be less scholarly and intellectual (ENVSCHOL) than that of their White and Black colleagues at PWIs, they were heavily involved with academic activities. This high involvement in academic activities at HBCUs may help explain why HBCUs tend to graduate more Black students than PWIs (Braddock, 1981; Fleming, 1984). This high involvement with academic activities also is associated with every aspect of educational gains for Black students at HBCUs (Fleming, 1984).

Quality of effort in academic activities was one of the two strongest factors for White majority students in regard to gains in GNINTEL, GNVOCPRE, and GNGENART. Most of the research on the in-class experiences between students and faculty points to the relationship that faculty and students have with one another and how the quality of that relationship is related to success in college (Pascarella & Terenzini, 1991). In contrast to majority groups, QEACAD was not a contributing factor to any gains for minority students, and this indicates that Black minority students do not receive the educational gains or payoffs that White students at PWIs receive for their involvement. For example, although Table 1 indicates that Black minority students are more involved than White majority students, Table 1 shows that the quality of effort for White majority students is significant and influences gains. However, for Black minority students, it is not clear why their greater involvement in QEACAD does not influence gains. This is the most disturbing finding and perhaps gives merit to the rationale for using the framework proposed to explore an in-depth examination for an explanation.

Although Fleming (1977) reports that the evaluation of faculty and administration by White students became more positive from the freshman year to senior year, the evaluation made by Black students became more negative

TABLE 2
Regression Analyses for Racial Majority and Minority Students' Quality of Effort Factors, Environmental Factors, and Gains Factors

	Black Majority n = 502			*White Majority n = 214*			*Black Minority n = 83*		
Gains	*B*	*Beta*	*F*	*B*	*Beta*	*F*	*B*	*Beta*	*F*
GNPERSOC									
(Personal & Social)									
QEACAD	.03	.19	.000***	.02	.13	.120	.02	.16	.240
QEGRPFAC	.01	.10	.094	.02	.12	.122	.01	.01	.933
QEINTERP	.01	.10	.118	.02	.01	.138	.02	.16	.410
QESCIN	.01	.05	.261	−.00	−.01	.936	.02	.20	.074
ENVRELAT	.08	.16	.000***	.13	.24	.001***	.17	.35	.002**
ENVSCHOL	.03	.05	.333	−.02	−.03	.694	.22	.31	.003**
ENVVOCAT	.03	.06	.288	.07	.15	.060	−.03	−.05	.629
(Constant)	.23		.289	.50		.146	−.17	.74	
R^2		.31			.33			.52	
Adjusted R^2		.29			.29			.43	
GNINTEL									
(Intellectual Skills)									
QEACAD	.04	.26	.000***	.02	.15	.043*	.01	.07	.647
QEGRPFAC	−.00	−.00	.943	.02	.13	.068	.03	.23	.200
QEINTERP	.02	.12	.049*	.00	.03	.709	.00	.01	.970
QESCIN	.01	.09	.039*	.03	.35	.000***	.02	.20	.022*
ENVRELAT	.10	.17	.000***	.06	.09	.120	.05	.09	.421
ENVSCHOL	.04	.06	.231	.07	.09	.182	.26	.33	.003*
ENVVOCAT	.01	.02	.716	.16	.28	.000***	.05	.08	.438
(Constant)	.07		.766	.76		.034	−.60		.318
R^2		.34			.50		.47		
Adjusted R^2		.33			.47			.38	
GNVOCPRE									
(Vocational Preparation)									
QEACAD	.03	.20	.000***	.03	.15	.033*	−.01	−.04	.798
QEGRPFAC	−.00	−.00	.977	.00	.01	.923	.00	.04	.842
QEINTERP	.01	.07	.274	.01	.05	.495	.04	.29	.202
QESCIN	.02	.14	.002***	.01	.06	.251	.02	.19	.130
ENVRELAT	.05	.09	.061	−.06	−.08	.185	.05	.11	.363
ENVSCHOL	−.00	−.01	.915	−.01	−.01	.905	.17	.25	.034*
ENVVOCAT	.14	.27	.000***	.26	.42	.000***	−.04	−.08	.499
(Constant)	−.00		.995	−.39		.301	.07		.908
R^2		.31			.54			.38	
Adjusted R^2		.29			.51			.27	
GNGENART									
(General Education, Literature, & Arts)									
QEACAD	.03	.22	.000***	.04	.24	.001***	.01	.10	.426
QEGRPFAC	−.01	−.10	.101	−.01	−.08	.238	.01	.10	.514
QEINTERP	.05	.35	.000***	.05	.36	.000***	.06	.50	.009**
QESCIN	.00	.04	.319	−.03	−.31	.000***	−.00	−.05	.633
ENVRELAT	.05	.11	.006***	.14	.23	.000***	.08	.18	.073
ENVSCHOL	.06	.15	.003***	.15	.22	.001***	.05	.09	.370
ENVVOCAT	.03	.06	.259	.01	.03	.623	.04	.09	.334
(Constant)	.04		.805	−.46			.138	−.52	.240
R^2		.42			.52			.58	
Adjusted R^2		.40			.49			.50	

(Continued)

TABLE 2 *(Continued)*
Regression Analyses for Racial Majority and Minority Students' Quality of Effort Factors, Environmental Factors, and Gains Factors

	Black Majority n = 502			*White Majority n = 214*			*Black Minority n = 83*		
Gains	*B*	*Beta*	*F*	*B*	*Beta*	*F*	*B*	*Beta*	*F*
GNSCITEC (Science & Technology)									
QEACAD	.02	.12	.027*	.00	.00	.948	.04	.25	.095
QEGRPFAC	−.01	−.08	.172	−.02	−.09	.147	−.05	−.38	.044*
QEINTERP	.02	.14	.024*	.02	.09	.188	.05	.36	.095
QESCIN	.04	.38	.000***	.09	.75	.000***	.04	.43	.001***
ENVRELAT	.09	.15	.001**	.02	.03	.613	.09	.16	.166
ENVSCHOL	−.01	−.01	.863	−.04	−.04	.487	.15	.18	.111
ENVVOCAT	.06	.10	.062	.12	.16	.014*	−.05	−.08	.428
(Constant)	−.04		.863	.10		.820	.38		.566
R^2		.33			.58			.44	
Adjusted R^2		.31			.55			.33	

*$p < .05$.
**$p < .01$.
***$p < .001$.
Note: Black Majority = Black students at predominantly Black institutions.
White Majority = White students at predominantly White institutions.
Black Minority = Black students at predominantly White institutions.

at PWIs. Yet, MacKay and Kuh's (1994) study shows that the QEACAD of Black students contributed to three of the five gains factors, GNGENART, GNINTEL, and GNVOCPRE, which were the same factors that are presented as contributing factors for White majority students. However, for White majority students, QEACAD was significant only in influencing GNVOCPRE. In summary, when interaction between faculty and students is enhanced and increased in the classroom and out of the classroom, the gains of students are greatly increased.

Activities related to QEINTERP include involvement in art, music, theater, personal experiences, student acquaintances, topics of conversations, and information in conversations. The study shows that QEINTERP was very significant for the Black majority student's GNINTEL (intellectual skills), GNGENART (general education, literature, and the arts), and GNSCITEC (understanding science and new technology). This is not surprising for Black majority students at HBCUs. Fleming (1984) reports that Black students at HBCUs have more positive psychosocial experiences than Black students at PWIs. The literature shows that Black students at HBCUs have higher involvement and gains when studying in their dominant race environment (Allen, 1987, 1992; Fleming, 1984; Watson, 1994; Watson & Kuh, 1996).

However, it was unexpected for QEINTERP not to contribute to gains in GNPERSOC of Black students because of the positive experiences of dating, social, and other interpersonal incidents that are reported at HBCUs. Fleming (1984) also reported that Black students at HBCUs experienced positive psychosocial development due to a critical mass of Black students, staff, administrators, and faculty within a culture more compatible for Black students. The factor QEINTERP also influenced GNGENART (gains in general education, literature, and arts) for both Black and White students at PWIs. MacKay and Kuh (1994) revealed that for Black and White students QEINTERP was the greatest contributing factor across the five gains for both Black and White students.

QESCIN was a contributing factor for gains in all groups in intellectual skills (GNINTEL) and understanding science and new technology (GNSCITEC). For Black majority students, QESCIN was also significant for gains in vocational and career preparation probably because Black students at HBCUs were found to be more focused in the career for science and technology than White majority and Black minority students at PWIs. QESCIN also was a contributing factor for gains in general education for White students in PWIs.

Intergenerational Gains

The evidence to support a connection between the college experiences and long-term gains and "quality of life indexes" is not very strong. While holding economic resources constant, many "quality of life indexes" still exist (Pascarella & Terenzini, 1991). College experiences have a moderate effect on one's health status, family size, consumer behavior, savings and investment, marital satisfaction, and life satisfaction index; they have a weak effect on marital stability, nurturance of children, cultured leisure, and job satisfaction (Pascarella & Terenzini, 1991).

There is some evidence to support that having college-educated parents positively affects the socioeconomic achievement of sons and daughters and the educational attainment of children. It is likely that

> having college-educated parents may enhance the cognitive development of young children through the indirect route of the home environment. Compared to those with less education, college-educated parents, particularly mothers, spend more time with their children in developmental activities such as reading and teaching. The long-term trend of these intergenerational legacies appears to be not only toward greater socioeconomic security and well-being but also toward greater cognitive growth and openness, tolerance, and concern for human rights and liberties. (Pascarella & Terenzini, 1991, p. 586)

Recommendations and Suggestions

Policy decisions at the national, state, and local levels that address the functions and purposes of private HBCUs should focus on matters that are related to students' educational gains. Black students at HBCUs report richer educational experiences than Black students at HBCUs, given their quality of effort, their perceptions of the college environment, and their educational gains. Policymakers and practitioners who work with, and in, HBCUs must understand and recognize that these colleges and universities provide Black students with an avenue that might have been closed for them if it were not for their existence. The findings show that activities related to academic involvement, interpersonal involvement, and relationships with faculty, administrators, and students have a greater influence on educational gains of Black students at HBCUs than at PWIs. Therefore, HBCUs seem to effectively provide Black students with the skills they need to function within the general society.

Exchange programs between private HBCUs and private PWIs should be developed so that minority and majority students and faculty may become aware of practices and relationships that encourage students to succeed. Given that exposure to different people and ways of life influences a number of gains, an exchange program might provide students from HBCUs and PWIs opportunities to experience different cultures and institutions. An exchange program for students at PWIs and HBCUs should allow them to reflect on prejudices and stereotypes and appreciate their educational experiences at both types of institutions.

Because of the quality of effort that Black majority students expend on academic activities at PWIs, faculty and students from PWIs should learn new ways of interacting with Black students who choose to go to HBCUs and use that knowledge to build programs at PWIs for their own students. Faculty from PWIs should also be given the opportunity to participate in an exchange program to observe teaching styles and other interactions of the faculty at HBCUs that allow them to become more involved academically with students. For example, Butler University and Shaw University might consider an exchange program so that students and faculty from a PWI can experience being in a different environment, even as a minority, and increase their awareness and understanding of the differences that exist in an HBCU. This program would help them appreciate and recognize how students of a different race and culture feel in a similar situation and why.

PWIs should find ways of encouraging faculty to become more involved with Black students. In this study, Black and White majority students benefited more from their academic activities than did Black minority students. A key influence in the success of Black students in institutions of higher education is the faculty. Therefore, the mentoring, teaching, and servicing role of faculty in PWIs may need to be encouraged and rewarded for such related activities.

PWIs may need to increase their minority faculty, staff, and student population in order to provide Black students with the support they need to consider themselves a part of the campus community. Fleming (1984) believes that at times of frustration and alienation Black students on PWI campuses need to delve into academic activities instead of allowing those times to divert them from academic pursuits.

A two-way interaction needs to be developed where institutions and students become partners in maximizing educational gains. Perhaps programs need to be developed to teach all students how to take responsibility for their lives. In return, the institution should make sure that support, programming, and appropriate personnel are provided to assist students in utilizing the institution's resources to enhance their educational gains.

References

Allen, W. (1986). *Gender and campus race differences in Black student academic performance, racial attitudes and college satisfaction.* Atlanta, GA: Southern Education Foundation.

Allen, W. (1987). Black colleges vs. White colleges. *Change, 19*(3), 28–34.

Allen, W. (1992). The color of success: African-American college student outcomes at predominantly White and historically Black public colleges and universities. *Harvard Educational Review, 62*(1), 26–44.

Anderson, J. (1988). *The education of Blacks in the south, 1860–1935.* London: University of North Carolina.

Anderson, J., & Adams, M. (1992). Acknowledging the learning styles of diverse student populations: Implications for instructional design. *New directions for teaching and learning.* San Francisco: Jossey-Bass.

Astin, A. (1977). *Four critical years: Effects of college on beliefs, attitudes, and knowledge.* San Francisco: Jossey-Bass.

Astin, A. W. (1982). *Minorities in American higher education.* San Francisco: Jossey-Bass.

Astin, A. W. (1984). Student involvement: A developmental theory for higher education. *Journal of College Student Development, 26,* 297–308.

Astin, A. W. (1993). *What matters in college?* San Francisco: Jossey-Bass.

Baum, M., & Lamb, D. (1983). A comparison of concerns presented by Black and White students to a university counseling center. *Journal of College Student Personnel, 24,* 127–131.

Bean, J. P. (1980). Dropout and turnover: The synthesis and test of a causal model of student attrition. *Research in Higher Education, 12*(2), 155–187.

Bourdieu, P. (1977). The cultural transmission of social inequality. *Harvard Educational Review, 47,* 545–555.

Bowles, S., & Gintis, H. (1976). *Schooling in capitalist America.* New York: Basic Books.

Braddock, J. (1981). Desegregation and Black student attrition. *Urban Education, 15,* 178–186.

Cross, W., Jr. (1971). Discovering the Black referent: The psychology of Black liberation. In J. Dixon & B. Foster (Eds.), *Beyond Black or White* (n.p.). Boston: Little, Brown.

Davis, R. (1991). Social support networks and undergraduate student academic success-related outcomes: A comparison of Black students on Black and White campuses. In W. R. Allen, E. G. Epps, & N. Z. Haniff (Eds.), *College in Black and White* (pp. 143–157). New York: State University of New York Press.

Fleming, J. (1977). The impact of predominately white and predominately Black environments on the functioning of Black students. In *Second annual report to the Carnegie Corporation.* New York: Carnegie Corporation.

Fleming, J. (1984). *Blacks in college.* San Francisco: Jossey-Bass.

Gruca, J. (1988). Intergenerational effects of college graduation on career sex atypicality in women. *Research in Higher Education, 29,* 99–124.

Gurin, P., & Epps, E. (1975). *Black consciousness, identity, and achievement: A study of students in historically Black colleges.* New York: John Wiley & Sons.

Hurn, C. J. (1985). *The limits and possibilities of schooling: An introduction to the sociology of education* (3rd ed.). Boston: Allyn & Bacon.

Kuh, G., Schuh, J., Whitt, E., Andreas, R., Lyons, J., Strange, C., Krehbiel, L., & Mackay, K. (1991). *Involving colleges: Successful approaches to fostering student learning and development outside the classroom.* San Francisco: Jossey-Bass.

Livingston, M. D., & Stewart, M. A. (1987). Minority students on a white campus: Perception is truth. *NASPA Journal, 24,* 39–48.

MacKay, K., & Kuh, G. (1994). A comparison of student effort and educational gains of Caucasian and African-American students in predominantly White colleges and universities. *Journal of College Student Development, 35,* 217–223.

Nettles, M., & Johnson, J. (1987). Race, sex, and other factors as determinant of college students' socialization. *Journal of College Student Personnel, 28*, 512–524.

Nettles, M. T. (1988). *Toward Black undergraduate student equality in American higher education.* New York: Greenwood Press.

Pace, C. R. (1984). *Measuring the quality of college student experiences.* Los Angeles: University of California Higher Education Research Institute.

Pace, C. R. (1988). *CSEQ: Test manual and norms.* Los Angeles: University of California Center for the Study of Evaluation.

Pascarella, E., Ethington, C., & Smart, J. (1988). The influence of college on humanitarian/civic involvement values. *Journal of Higher Education, 59*, 412–437.

Pascarella, E. T., & Terenzini, P. (1991). *How college affects students.* San Francisco: Jossey-Bass.

Plinar, J. E., & Brown, D. (1985). Projections of reactions to stress and preferences for helpers among students from four ethnic groups. *Journal of College Student Personnel, 26*, 147–151.

Ponce, F. Q. (1988). Minority student retention: A moral and legal imperative. In M. C. Terrell & D. J. Wright (Eds.), *From survival to success: Promoting minority student retention* (pp. 25–54). Washington, DC: National Association of Student Personnel Administrators.

Rooney, G. (1985). Minority students' involvement in minority student organizations: An exploratory study. *Journal of College Student Personnel, 26*, 450–455.

Sedlacek, W. (1987). Black students on White campuses: 20 years of research. *Journal of College Student Personnel, 28*, 484–494.

Steele, C. M. (1992). Race and the schooling of Black Americans. *The Atlantic Monthly*, pp. 68–78.

Thomas, G., & Hill, S. (1987). Black institutions in U.S. higher education: Present roles, contributions, future projections. *Journal of College Student Personnel, 28*, 532–545.

Thompson, C. E., & Fretz, B. R. (1991). Predicting the adjustment of Black students at predominantly White institutions. *Journal of Higher Education, 62*(4), 437–450.

Tinto, V. (1975). Dropouts from higher education: A theoretical synthesis of recent research. *Review of Educational Research, 45*, 89–125.

Watson, L. W. (1994). An analysis of Black and White students' perceptions, involvement, and educational gains in private historically Black and White liberal arts institutions. Unpublished doctoral dissertation, Indiana University. Bloomington.

Watson, L. W. (1996). Learning in institutions of higher education. *Planning and Changing: An Educational Leadership and Policy Journal, 27*(3/4).

Watson, L. W., & Kuh, G. D. (1996). The influence of dominant race environments on student involvement, perceptions, and educational gains: A look at historically Black and predominantly White liberal arts institutions. *Journal of College Student Development, 37*, 4.

Watson, L. W., & Stage, F. (under review). A conceptual framework for student learning, involvement, and educational gains. In F. Stage, L. Watson, & M. Terrell (Eds.), Enhancing student learning: Setting the campus context (n.p.). San Francisco: Jossey-Bass.

Webster, D., Sedlacek, W. E., & Miyares, J. (1979). A comparison of problems perceived by minority and White university students. *Journal of College Student Personnel, 20*, 120–165.

Whiting, A. (1991). *Guardians of the flame: Historically Black colleges yesterday, today, and tomorrow.* Washington, DC: American Association of State Colleges and Universities.

"ASSESSMENT, OUTCOMES MEASUREMENT AND ATTRITION" (REFLECTIONS, DEFINITIONS AND DELINEATIONS)

DR. AL JOHNSON

Abstract

This paper addresses issues in assessment of college students, outcome studies, and attrition research in the context of trends toward requiring greater accountability from institutions of higher education. First the paper considers how assessment, student outcomes studies, and attrition research terminology might be more clearly defined. It suggests that these three areas of inquiry, although distinctive, are highly interrelated phenomena. The paper then attempts to operationalize definitions and outline a recursive research model appropriate for research in these areas. Finally, it briefly describes how one small liberal arts university is currently thinking through the process of implementing a longitudinal assessment program including student outcomes studies and student attrition research through a recursive research model and operationalized definitions. Stressed is the need for institutions to plan their research to be consistent with the educational goals of the institution. (Contains 17 references.)

One need not immerse oneself in the literature on college student assessment, outcomes studies and attrition research to any great degree to realize that these areas of inquiry are still very much in the process of being defined as legitimate avenues of educational research. Attrition research began in earnest about a quarter of a century ago, Astin (1975), Cope and Hannah (1975), Tinto (1975), Pascarella and Terenzini (1978), Johnson (1980), while efforts to develop models for assessment and student outcomes studies are more recent, Astin (1991 & 1993), Light (1992), Angelo and Cross (1993), Banta and Associates (1993), Ewell (1985 and 1988), and many others. Despite this volume of literature, there is still a good deal of ambiguity in the way the terms assessment, outcomes measurement, and attrition are defined for research purposes. For example, the National Association of Student Personnel Administrators (1995), recently published a booklet titled "Successful Student Outcomes Assessment." In this short work, NASPA included a partial inventory of available instruments currently in use for assessment and outcomes research. The title of NASPA's publication implies that the terms assessment and outcomes are, if not interchangeable, then at least similar enough so as to require no further delineation regarding the precise meaning of these terms. This notion is further reinforced when one examines carefully the inventory of assessment/outcomes instruments NASPA selected for its partial inventory. That list included more than 27 instruments which addressed topics as diverse as scholastic aptitude, vocational interests, career paths, concepts of work, capacity to realize opportunities, extra-curricular activities, critical thinking, judgement, confidence, sexual identity and a host of other subjects. The diversity of subject matter which these inventories purport to

Reprinted from *College and University 73, no. 2* (fall 1997), by permission from the author. Al Johnson, Ph.D., Associate Executive Director, Northwest Commission on Colleges & Universities, 8060 165th Ave. NE, Suite 100, Redmond, WA 98052.

measure implies that regardless of its emphasis, all student research is, in effect, defacto assessment research. And yet not all researchers would agree. For example, Mentkowski (1994) recently observed that educators must somehow "connect assessment with teaching and learning." She views the assessment process as an altogether different exercise from outcomes research. Her view, which is shared by others, is that outcomes studies strictly speaking should address academic and intellectual growth, an emphasis manifestly different from assessment which is often used to imply data gathering.

Despite the ambiguity in how these research areas are presently defined, there is little doubt that educational administrators recognize the value of the assessment process largely because this research enables them to better understand the students they seek to educate. They also understand that data gathered under the rubric of student assessment and outcomes studies have the potential to mitigate student attrition by anticipating which students a-priori have a demonstrable likelihood of failing to complete an academic program. In a larger context, when institutions establish carefully defined assessment programs, they are in effect demonstrating their interest in learning as much as they possibly can about their students and their students' needs. This in turn reassures legislatures which allocate funds in support of public higher education, governing boards which approve budgets for private institutions, and an increasingly skeptical public that institutions of higher learning are in fact trying to maximize the likelihood of graduation for each student. At a time when an investment *in* higher education is so closely correlated in the public's mind with the value *of* higher education, institutions are seeking to do everything possible to maintain and increase graduation rates thereby justifying the very considerable investment which the cost of a college education represents.

Toward that end, the purpose of this reflection is three-fold. First, observations are offered on how assessment, student outcomes studies and attrition research terminology might be more clearly defined and made more useful to consumers of this research. Second, the suggestion is made that these three areas of inquiry, each distinctive in and of itself, are nonetheless, highly interrelated phenomena. Finally, in operationalyzing definitions and outlining a recursive research model, this paper highlights how one small liberal arts university is currently thinking through the process of implementing a longitudinal assessment program including student outcomes studies and student attrition research.

When administrators plan assessment programs, they must first distill the term assessment into its component parts. Broadly defined, assessment consists of three highly interrelated phenomena each of which has its own distinctive characteristics. The first of these components is assessment itself. According to the (1995) New American Heritage Dictionary of the English Language, the word assessment means to *determine* the *value* of *something* or to *determine* its significance or its extent. In higher education, this implies data gathering; specifically, gathering various kinds of descriptive data on students who comprise the institution's clientele. The term assessment therefore should be carefully defined to mean the collection or assembly of data, demographic, vocational, personal, for example. To employ the term in this way enables researchers to differentiate assessment from other measurement activities. These data can then be used in a variety of ways, perhaps none more important than assisting institutions in learning who their students are as well as what their students' needs are.

The first stage of the assessment exercise is to establish a baseline of data. These data sets should include information on 1) incoming freshmen, 2) sophomores and juniors who can be operationally defined as continuing students, 3) graduating seniors, 4) graduate students, 5) alumni whose graduation date was within 5 years of the date of the survey and finally, 6) alumni whose date of graduation was older than five years. To accomplish this phase of the research, one approach, (there are many others) is to use the National Center of Higher Education Management Systems (NCHEMS) Student Opinion and Information Survey (SOIS) as a survey vehicle. These instruments are specifically designed to collect information, *not to measure academic outcomes*. In addition, these surveys are easy to administer, clearly understood by the students who complete them and easily tabulated for analysis. "NCHEMS" survey instruments enables the researcher to establish comprehensive group profiles which reflect, among other things, students' experiences, expectations, aspirations, specific goals, and their evaluation of the institution and its services. In addition to telling institutions just who their students are, these surveys also summarize additional information having to do with the overall quality of the association between the students and the institution, something all academic and student affairs administrators want to know. In addition, these group profiles can also serve as a valuable foundation upon which strategic planning might be based. In short, the initial phase of the assessment process should be a relatively easy exercise of collecting extensive descriptive data on the institution's audiences. All other things being equal, it seems a perfectly reasonable way to begin the assessment process. In defining assessment in this way, institutions are able to differentiate this activity from student outcomes measurement and attrition research which constitutes separate but obviously related, collateral activities.

To begin the second phase of research, institutions should identify a group of students on whom baseline data reflecting rudimentary academic skills can be established. Those students should be asked to complete a set of examinations which measures verbal and quantitative abilities. The collection of such information is of course commonplace at many institutions. As elsewhere, these baseline data enhance academic advising and program planning. But these data have an additional purpose. Students who participated in this phase of the study can then be tracked to determine whether or not they acquired the skills in English and mathematics that institutions seek to instill in their students. Pre and post designs are particularly appropriate for this purpose. During their first two years, these students then take a variety of typical freshman and sophomore English and mathematics courses. Pre and post test analysis, can determine whether a statistically significant difference could be identified between students' initial scores and their subsequent scores on alternate versions of, for example, the ASSET examination published by the American College Testing Service. If statistically significant differences for these dependent groups are found, institutions may conclude that the intervening course work did, in part, contribute to those differences. Such results however speak only to elementary English and mathematics skills, not to the broader issue of higher order, relational and abstract thinking. As long as the variables used in outcomes measurement are very narrowly defined and easily quantified, it is not a particularly difficult matter to test and retest groups of students to determine whether or not academic objectives are being met. Scores on standardized math and English tests are a case in point. More substantial outcomes measures however, specifically those which test for the acquisition of critical thinking skills and complex problem solving, are much more difficult to identify. In order to determine whether or not certain higher order academic skills have been acquired by students, institutions must first determine exactly what they are attempting to impart to students through the process of education. Most faculty would agree that basic skills in English and math are desirable outcomes of the education process. But beyond this basic agreement, faculty are often quite polarized regarding their opinions on what characterizes an educated person. Variations of the often repeated themes of thinking with clarity, achieving depth and breadth in a field of knowledge, acquiring the capacity to grapple with moral and ethical problems, distilling complex problems into their component parts or learning to appreciate the process whereby knowledge itself is acquired continue to be discussed as desirable traits for educated persons to possess. And herein lies one of the central problems with academic outcomes studies. Not only must each institution decide what it wishes to impart to its students, it must also devise ways to determine whether those objectives have been met. It is a widely accepted truism that the more sophisticated intellectual behavior becomes, the more difficult it is to quantify and measure. It is equally true that the primary reason higher order reasoning skills are often not part of student outcomes research is that university faculties simply cannot agree on what should be taught and how such skills, whatever they are perceived to be, should be measured. In discussions at the University of Great Falls which focused on how one could determine whether or not graduates were reflections of what faculty wanted them to be, it became clear that our perceptions of what constituted an educated person were quite disparate. We also agreed that if left unaltered, our various notions of what an educated person should be would preclude any long term meaningful student outcomes research. If we could not even agree on what belongs in the curriculum, how then could we begin to think through an outcomes process? Responding to this impasse, we began a two-year long dialogue on reconfiguring the core components of our undergraduate curriculum to bring about some common agreement on what comprised a relevant and rigorous course of undergraduate study. Only by establishing common goals were we able to reach some consensus on what our graduates should know. And only then could we undertake a meaningful dialogue on how to begin to structure measurement instruments to tell us if the goals we had set for students were being realized. Student outcomes research therefore has the potential to tell an institution not only a great deal about its students' intellectual achievements but also a great deal about the faculty who educate them. This then, is the real value of student outcomes research and what sets it apart from simple assessment. Outcomes measurement which gauges real intellectual depth and breadth is only possible when faculty share a common vision regarding what intellectual characteristics are desirable and how those skills might be measured appropriately.

The third component of the assessment triptych addresses student attrition research, the goal of which is two-fold. The first task is to develop predictor equations which identify students who fit a "high risk" profile. The second goal is dictated by the results of the first. It entails the design and implementation of programs to decrease the likelihood that a particular student will become an attrition statistic. How is the first goal to be accomplished? Each institution should develop its own set of predictor equations using assessment and outcomes data on students who have graduated compared to those who have not. Multivariate statistics, especially multiple regression and discriminant analysis, are particularly useful in this area of research. Once predictor models have been developed, assessment and outcomes data can then be used to predict into which category, (persisters, voluntary withdrawers, or academic dismissals) any given student's profile suggests he or she is likely to fall. Demographic variables, pre-matriculation academic variables and other measures can be used to isolate the best predictors of subsequent academic standing. Once students are identified as high risk, institutions can intervene with tutorial programs, counseling, remedial work and the like to attempt to mitigate what initially might seem to be an inevitable outcome.

In summary, the three activities commonly referred to as assessment, outcomes measurement and attrition prediction are in reality separate but highly interrelated phenomena. None of the three can be meaningfully understood in isolation or without reference to the other two. As administrators and researchers develop and continue to develop assessment programs, it will be helpful to differentiate these research activities into three specific areas so that each component is clearly defined and its relationship to the other two can be made clear. The assessment process as defined here should be the initial exercise. Periodic outcomes measurement can then be used in conjunction with assessment data to develop and refine predictor equations which can identify at risk students. However, in order for the process to serve the institution and its students, institutions must plan their research so that it is consistent with the overall educational goals as determined by its faculty. Outcomes measurement research methodology must be drawn directly from those goals and aspirations. Models for assessment, for outcomes measurement and for attrition prediction must be developed by individual campuses for localized use. These models must be constructed using clearly defined, operational definitions of assessment and related terms. Failures to provide such definitions almost certainly guarantees continued obfuscation and ambiguity in this area of research which is so important to institutions of higher education.

References

American College Testing Program. (1994). Asset Technical Manual, Iowa City: ACT Publications.

American Heritage Dictionary of the English Language. (1992). Boston: Houghton Mifflin, Co.

Angelo, Thomas, and Cross, K. Patricia. (1993). *Classroom Assessment Techniques: A Handbook for College Teachers.* 2nd Ed. San Francisco: Jossey-Bass.

Astin, Alexander W. (1974). *Measuring the Outcomes of Higher Education*. In H. Brown (ed.), Evaluating Institutions for Accountability. San Francisco: Jossey-Bass.

——— (1991). *Assessment for Excellence: The Philosophy and Practice of Assessment and Evaluation in Higher Education.* New York: MacMillan.

——— (1993). *What Matters In College*? San Francisco: Jossey-Bass.

Banta, T., and Associates. (1993). *Making A Difference.* San Francisco: Jossey-Bass.

Cope, Robert, and Hannah, William. (1975). *Revolving College Doors: The Causes and Consequences of Dropping Out and Transferring*. New York: John Wiley and Sons.

Ewell, Peter T., Ed. (1985). Assessing Educational Outcomes. *New Directions for Educational Research.* No. 47. San Francisco: Jossey-Bass.

——— (1988). Outcomes assessment and academic improvements: In search of usable knowledge. In J. Smart (ed.) *Higher Education: Handbook of Theory and Research.* Vol. 4. New York: Agathon Press.

Johnson, A. E. Jr., and Hutchinson, J. (1980). Identifying persisters, voluntary withdrawers and academic dropouts at a liberal arts college. *Journal of the National Association of Student Personnel Administrators, 18.* 41–45.

Light, R. J. (1992). The Harvard Assessment Seminars. First Report. Cambridge: Harvard University Press.

Light, R. J. (1992). The Harvard Seminars. Second Report. Cambridge: Harvard University Press.

Mentkowski, Marcia. (1994). How assessment practitioners who are educational researchers can contribute to assessment in higher education. *Assessment Update 6* No. 1.

Pascarella, E. T., and Terenzini, P. T. (1978). The relations of students' pre-college characteristics and freshman year experiences to voluntary attrition. *Research in Higher Education. 9.* 347–366.

Successful Student Outcomes Studies. (1995). National Association of Student Personal Administrators. Washington, DC.

Tinto, Vincent. (1995). Dropouts from higher education: a theoretical synthesis of recent research. *Review of Educational Research. 45.* 89–125.

Baccalaureate Degree Attainment and Precollege Academic Preparedness of Underrepresented Minorities

Theresa Y. Smith

Director, Center for Institutional Data Exchange and Analysis
The University of Oklahoma

Abstract

This study analyzed retention and graduation rates of entering minority group freshmen from the 1989–96 cohort at 232 diverse colleges and universities using data from the Consortium for Student Retention Data Exchange (CSRDE), which consistently have indicated that graduation rates are lower for underrepresented minority groups of blacks. Hispanics, and American Indians. Findings are reported for: first-time freshman population, fall 1989 to fall 1996; retention rate by race; graduation rate by race; graduation rates and institutional selectivity: classification of CSRDE institutions by selectivity; enrollment of underrepresented minorities; and graduation rates of underrepresented minorities and institutional selectivity. Major findings indicated that: (1) minority participation in higher education increased at a faster pace than participation by whites; (2) retention and graduation rates were static over time; (3) retention and graduation rates were lower for the underrepresented minority groups of blacks. Hispanics, and American Indians; (4) minority enrollment tended to concentrate disproportionately in the less selective institutions; and (5) graduation rates were higher for the more selective institutions. Results for other studies of educational attainment of underrepresented minorities are reviewed in terms of precollege academic preparedness; high school completion rates; proficiency in reading, mathematics, and science; college admissions test scores; and college enrollment rates. (Contains 23 references.)

Background

One of the major changes in higher education over the last two decades has been the growth of racial diversity in the student population. From 1980 to 1995, college enrollment grew by 18 percent from 12.1 million to 14.3 million. Minority enrollment increased at a much faster rate than whites: the growth rate was 79 percent for minorities compared with only 5 percent for whites. Consequently, the representation of minorities rose from 16 percent of the total higher education enrollment to 25 percent. In terms of head count, minority college students increased from 1.95 million to 3.5 million[1], with more than half of the growth occurring in the last five of the fifteen years (NCES, Table 207, 1997).

Paper presented at the AIR Annual Forum, Seattle.

Recent demographic trends in public elementary and secondary schools suggest that the presence of minorities in higher education will continue to increase. In 1995, minorities constituted 35 percent of the public school enrollment, an increase of five percentage points from 1986 (NCES, Table 45, 1997). As this trend carries forward to the future college population, it is estimated that, by the year 2000, more than 30 percent of the college enrollment will be minorities. Population projections further suggest that the growth of minority population will continue to outpace that of whites. The 1990 census report indicated that minorities made up one-fourth of the national population. The U.S. Census Bureau further projected that, by the year 2050, nearly half of the population will be minorities (Day, 1996).

The dramatic increase of college minority population in the last two decades has generated much attention to the retention and graduation rates of various racial ethnic groups. With the exception of Asian Americans, levels of educational attainment, income and other measures of social well-being are lower for minorities than whites (ACE, 1988). Thus, blacks, Hispanics and American Indians are often referred to as the "underrepresented minorities." As the increases in minority enrollment continue into the next millennium, the success of minorities in educational attainment will take on added importance. The purpose of this paper is to assess minority participation in higher education beginning with the annual report on college retention and graduation rates of 232 colleges and universities in the Consortium for Student Retention Data Exchange (CSRDE).

The 1997–98 CSRDE Report

The 1997–98 CSRDE report is the product of a collaborative effort of the CSRDE members. Data included in this report were provided by 232 colleges and universities. Their characteristics range from public to private, from large to small, from highly selective to liberal in admission requirements and from doctoral to baccalaureate in degree programs. Approximately 34 percent of the 1.15 million 1996 first-time freshmen enrolled in four-year public and private institutions were included in the report. However, the representation was much higher for public than private institutions. The report included 48 percent of the first-time freshmen enrolled in public institutions and only 7 percent in private institutions.

The First-Time Freshman Population, Fall 1989 to Fall 1996

On average, approximately 368,400 new freshmen entered the 232 CSRDE institutions each year. From 1989 to 1996, the overall first-time freshman enrollment decreased by 1 percent, from 388,972 to 384,011, while enrollment of underrepresented minorities increased by 21 percent, from 45,693 to 55,193. Consequently, the representation of underrepresented minorities rose from 11.7 percent of the 1989 new freshman population to 14.4 percent in 1996. Progress in minority participation was made by all racial subgroups.

Retention Rates by Race

Similar to results reported in many other national studies (Cope, 1978; Tinto, 1982; Astin, 1993), retention rates in these 232 institutions have been fairly static over time. In general, there were modest increases in retention rates for all racial subgroups while the overall first-year retention rates for the eight first-time freshman cohorts, from 1989 to 1996, stayed within the range of 77 percent to 79 percent. Second-year retention rates for the seven cohorts, from 1989 to 1995 were in the range of 67 percent to 68 percent.

Complete six-year tracking data for the 1989–91 cohorts indicated that 78 percent of the first-time freshmen continued to the second year and 67 percent progressed to the third year of college. Significant differences existed among the subgroups of students by race. Retention rates were lower for each of the underrepresented minority groups when compared with their white and Asian counterparts. After the first year, the retention rates were 74 percent for blacks, 71 percent for Hispanics and 63 percent for American Indians, compared with 79 percent for whites and 83 percent for Asians. After the second year, the gap in retention rates grew even wider with 60 percent of the blacks, 59 percent of the Hispanics and 49 percent of the American Indians persisted to the third year of college, compared with 68 percent for whites and 74 percent for Asians (Figure 1). When tracking progressed toward the fifth year, 48 percent of the blacks, 50 percent of the Hispanics and 40 percent of the American Indians continued

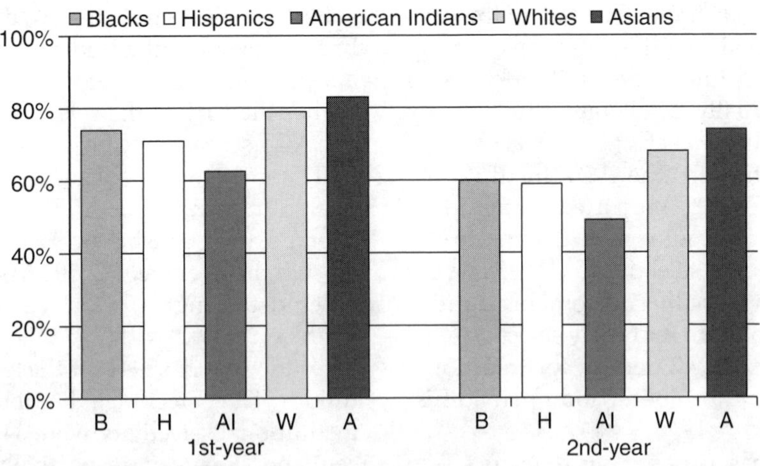

Figure 1 Retention Rates by Race 1989–1991 Freshman Cohorts

or graduated, compared with 61 percent for whites and 65 percent for Asians.

Graduation Rates by Race

As a consequence of higher dropout rates for the underrepresented minorities, smaller percentages of these students completed their baccalaureate degrees. Six-year graduation rates for the 1989–91 cohorts were 37 percent for blacks, 37 percent for Hispanics, 31 percent for American Indians, compared with 55 percent for whites and 54 percent for Asians with an overall graduation rate of 53 percent.

A higher percentage of the minorities continued to the seventh year: the percentages were 8 percent for blacks. 10 percent for Hispanics, 7 percent for American Indians, compared with 5 percent for whites and 8 percent for Asians. Since these students were very likely to graduate, the eventual graduation rates were estimated at 44 percent for blacks, 46 percent for Hispanics, 37 percent for American Indians, compared with 59 percent for whites and 61 percent for Asians and an overall rule of 57 percent for the 1989–91 cohorts (Figure 2).

Graduation Rates and Institutional Selectivity

Institutional selectivity is an important factor in student retention (Cope, 1978; Lenning, 1982; Noel & Levitz, 1983); the more selective institutions tend to have higher student retention rates. Saupe (1988) analyzed data from 27 public research universities and found that admission standards were significant predictors of first-year retention and six-year graduation rates. Astin

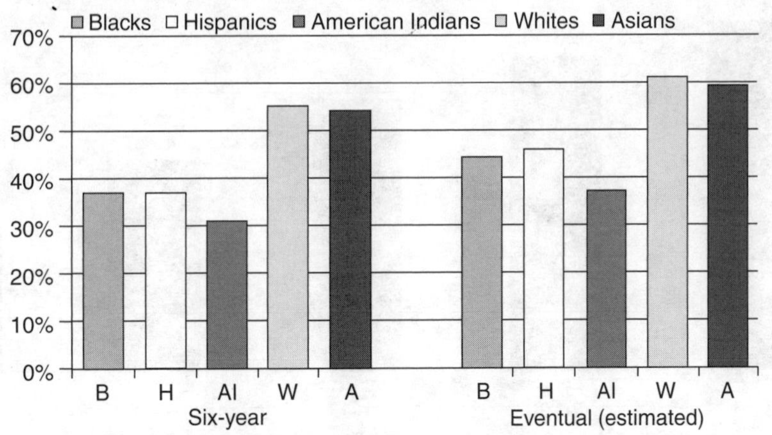

Figure 2 Graduation Rates by Race 1989–1991 Freshman Cohorts

(1993) observed that "more than half of the variance in institutional retention rates can be attributed directly to differences in the kinds of students who initially enroll, rather than to any differential institutional *effect*."

As an illustration, the ACT Institutional Data Profile (ACT, 1994) reported that graduation rates decreased with each decline in the level of institutional selectivity[2]. The five-year graduation rates for public doctoral institutions ranged from 69 percent for highly selective to 53 percent for selective, 42 percent for traditional and 38–40 percent for liberal and open admission institutions.

In a comparison based on data in seven research universities in the "Big Eight," Smith (1992) concluded that students in the higher ACT test score brackets had higher graduation rates. The six-year graduation rates of the 1983–87 first-time freshmen in the study group ranged from 76 percent for the subgroup with an ACT average of 31 or higher to 32 percent for the subgroup with an ACT average below 16. The intermediate six-year graduation rates were 68 percent, 59 percent and 46 percent for the subgroups of ACT 26–30, 21–25 and 16–20 respectively (Figure 3).

Classification of CSRDE Institutions by Selectivity

In order to derive more meaningful comparisons of retention and graduation rates, the 232 institutions were divided into three subgroups: 51 highly selective, 117 selective and 64 less selective institutions. The classification was based on average admission test scores for the 1996 cohorts. Institutions in the highly selective group had an average enhanced ACT composite scores above 24 or an average SAT composite score higher than 1,100; the selective group, an average ACT score between 21 and 24 or an average SAT score between 990 and 1,100; the less selective group, an average ACT score below 21 or an average SAT score below 990.

On the average, 122,507 first-time freshmen entered the highly selective institutions each year, compared with 177,979 for the selective institutions and 67,944 for the less selective institutions. The percentage distributions by type of institutional selectivity were 34 percent, 48 percent and 18 percent respectively.

Enrollment of Underrepresented Minorities

In addition to lower high school graduation rates and lower college participation rates for the underrepresented minorities, Hauptman and Smith (1994, p. 88) noted that

> *"Another concern with current patterns of participation in higher education is that African American and Hispanic students tend to attend certain types of institutions disproportionately. For example, 37 percent of all college student enrollments are in two-year institutions, but 57 percent of all Hispanic students are enrolled in two-year institutions. Similarly, 20 percent of African American college students are enrolled in historically Black colleges and universities."*

Eight years later, these statistics showed little change (NCES, 1997, tables 206 and 220). While 39 percent of the 1995 college students were in

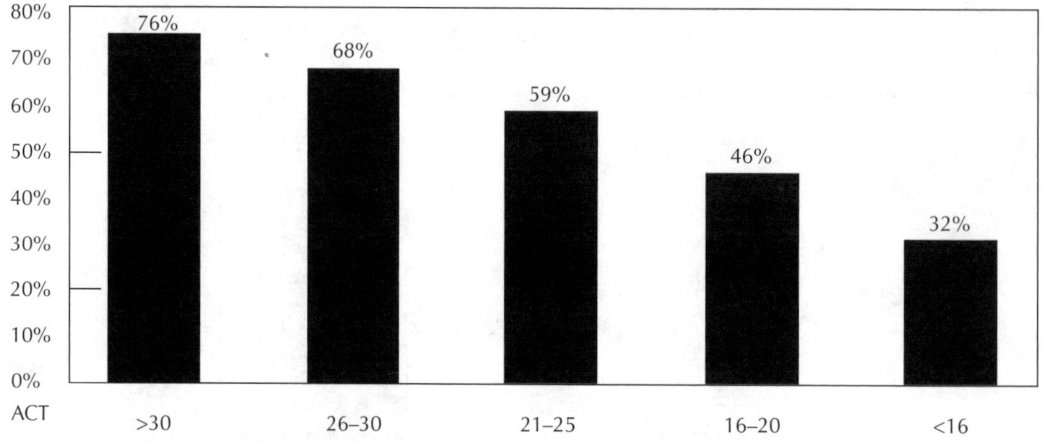

Figure 3 Graduation Rates and ACT Scores in Seven of the "Big Eight" Universities

TABLE 1
Six-Year Graduation Rates by Institutional Selectivity and Race
1989–91 First-time Freshman Cohorts in 232 CSRDE Institutions

Race	*Highly Selective*	*Selective*	*Less Selective*	*Total*
Blacks	52%	36%	25%	37%
Hispanics	55%	38%	25%	37%
American Indians	43%	27%	28%	31%
Whites	69%	51%	42%	55%
Asians	70%	53%	38%	54%
All Races	67%	49%	38%	53%

two-year institutions. 56 percent of the Hispanic students and 43 percent of the black students were enrolled in two-year institutions.

Similar disparity was found in the CSRDE study. The enrollment in less selective institutions consisted of a far higher percentage of the underrepresented minorities. They represented 26 percent of the 1996 first-time freshmen in the less selective institutions but only 11 percent of those in the highly selective and 12 percent in the selective institutions.

Graduation Rates of Underrepresented Minorities and Institutional Selectivity

Consistent with many previous research results, the graduation rates in the CSRDE group were higher for institutions with higher admission test scores. More than 67 percent of the 1989 to 1991 first-time freshmen graduated within six years from the highly selective institutions: the graduation rate decreased to 49 percent for students in the selective and 38 percent for students in the less selective institutions. Similar observations can also be made for almost all of the underrepresented minority groups. The six-year graduation rates for blacks were 52 percent in the highly selective institutions. 36 percent in the selective and 25 percent in the less selective institutions: the respective graduation rates were 55 percent, 38 percent and 25 percent for Hispanics and 43 percent, 27 percent and 28 percent for American Indians (Table 1).

Summary of CSRDE Minority Degree Attainment

Analysis of retention data for the 1989 to 1996 freshman cohorts in 232 CSRDE institutions reaffirmed many of the historical research findings. First, minority participation in higher education increased at a faster pace than whites. Second, retention and graduation rates were static over time. In a period of eight years, the spread of first-year retention rates was 1.5 percentage points from a low of 77.3 percent to a high of 78.8 percent. Moreover, this difference decreased as the study progressed toward the later tracking years. The six-year graduation rates over time showed a difference of less than one percentage point, from a low of 52.4 percent to a high of 53.3 percent. Third, the retention and graduation rates were lower for the underrepresented minority groups of blacks. Hispanics and American Indians. The six-year graduation rates showed a difference of more than 18 percentage points between each underrepresented minority subgroup and whites. Fourth, minority enrollment tended to concentrate disproportionately in the less selective institutions. Finally, graduation rates were higher for the more selective groups of institutions. This observation was applicable to almost all racial subgroups.

Implication: Decreasing Minority Representation from Entry to Graduation

Longitudinal data from 232 institutions in the CSRDE study indicated a decrease in minority representation from entry to graduation. Underrepresented minorities constituted 12.5 percent of the 1989–91 new freshman population, yet they accounted for only 8.8 percent of those who graduated within six years. In terms of head count, 139,240 underrepresented minorities entered the CSRDE institutions from 1989 to 1991 and 51,292

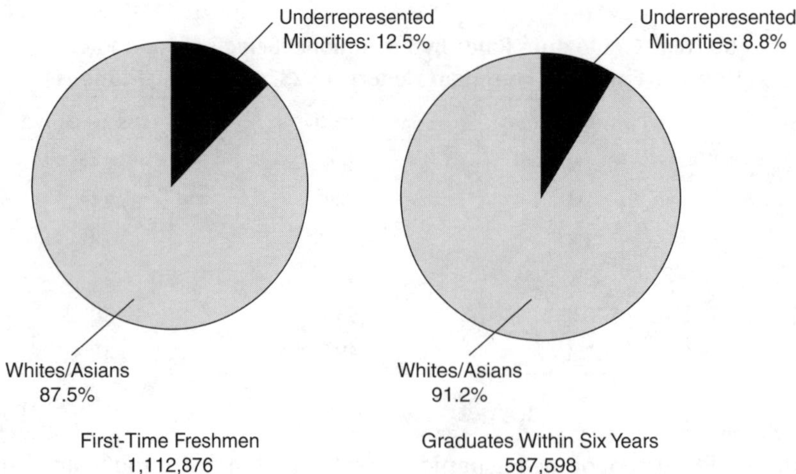

Figure 4 1989–91 Cohorts from Entry to Graduation

graduated within six years (Figure 4). If these underrepresented minorities had graduated at the same rate as whites, the number of graduates would have been 77,139, a difference of 25,847 degrees, or 50 percent, from the 51,292 degrees that were actually awarded to the 1989–91 underrepresented minority freshman cohorts.

In the absence of national longitudinal data, precise analysis cannot be derived as to the number of degrees that would have been necessary for bringing the degree attainment level of underrepresented minorities to that of whites each year. However, results of the CSRDE study and other national studies of graduation rates (NCAA, 1997), suggested that an improvement of 18 percentage points in underrepresented minority graduation rates would be a necessary first step.

Educational Attainment of Underrepresented Minorities

The representation of blacks, Hispanics and American Indians decreased dramatically as they progressed to higher levels of the education ladder. For example, blacks constituted 14 percent of the 18- to 19-year-old population in 1983, but only 12 percent of the high school graduates and 9 percent of the college students for the same year; their representation further reduced to 5 percent of the baccalaureate degree recipients in 1988–89 (Hill, 1992) and only 3 percent of the doctoral degrees in 1990–91 (NCES, 1993).

An NCES survey (NCES, 1997, table 307), *High School and Beyond, Educational Attainment of High School Sophomores by 1992,* reported that significant disparity existed in educational attainment by race. The survey results showed that of the 1980 high school sophomores. 12 percent of blacks, 10 percent of Hispanics and 8 percent of American Indians completed a bachelor's degree or more, compared with 27 percent of the whites and 46 percent of the Asians (Figure 5).

Precollege Academic Preparedness of Underrepresented Minorities

The CSRDE study found that academic preparedness was generally lower for the underrepresented minorities than their white peers. Consequently, a disproportionately larger percentage of the underrepresented minorities attended the less selective institutions with typically lower graduation rates. Even for those who attended the more selective institutions, their average admissions test scores were below the averages for whites.

Astin noted that "Although a number of other entering freshman characteristics add significantly to the prediction of retention, these four variables (a student's high school grades, admissions test scores, sex and race) account for the bulk of the variance in retention. (Astin, 1993, p. 2)." The following analysis of precollege educational statistics of underrepresented minorities offers a necessary context for understanding college retention and graduation rates of minorities.

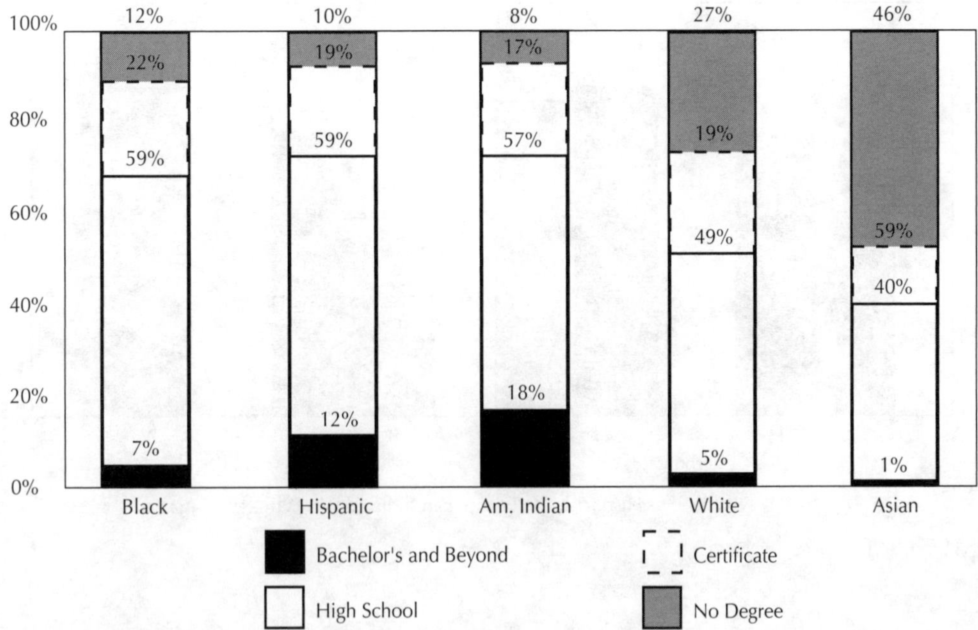

Figure 5 Educational Attainment by Race 1980 High School Sophomores by 1992

High School Completion Rates

According to a report of the U.S. Census Bureau, blacks and Hispanics have narrowed the gap in high school completion in the last few decades. In 1965, only 27 percent of blacks 25 years or older had completed high school, compared with 51 percent for whites. By 1993, the high school completion rates were 70 percent for blacks 25 years or older compared with 82 percent for whites. While data for Hispanics were not available until much later, the report indicated that among Hispanics 25 years or older, 53 percent had completed high school in 1993, compared with 37 percent in 1974 (Adams, 1998).

Despite the substantial improvement in high school completion rates, dropout rates remain to be higher for the underrepresented minorities. The 1996 high school dropout rates of persons 16 to 24 years old were 13 percent for blacks and 29 percent for Hispanics, compared with 7 percent for whites (NCES, 1997, Table 103).

Proficiency in Reading, Mathematics and Science

A series of reports on the test scores from the National Assessment of Educational Progress (NAEP) evaluated the academic performance levels of students in public schools (NCES, 1997). These reports compared the proficiency levels of 9-, 13- and 17-year-olds in reading, mathematics, and science over a period of more than 20 years. In general, the reports showed that blacks and Hispanics had made some improvement over the last 20 years. However, as a group, their academic proficiency continued to be below that of whites. Because of the difficulty in deriving a large enough sample for American Indians, their data were not available in the reports compiled by the U.S. Bureau of the Census, Current Population Survey.

According to the NAEP report, the percentages of students at or above certain levels of proficiency in reading, mathematics and science were consistently lower for underrepresented minorities. For example, the reading test scores indicated that the percentages of 13-year-olds at the level of being "able to search for specific information, interrelate ideas, and make generalization about literature, science, and social studies materials" were 35 percent for blacks and 40 percent for Hispanics, compared with 70 percent for whites. The NAEP mathematics test scores for 17-year-olds placed 31 percent of blacks and 40 percent of Hispanics at the level of "moderately complex procedures and reasoning," compared with 69 percent of whites. Finally, the percentages of 17-year-olds at the level of "analyze scientific procedure" were 17 percent for blacks and 24 percent

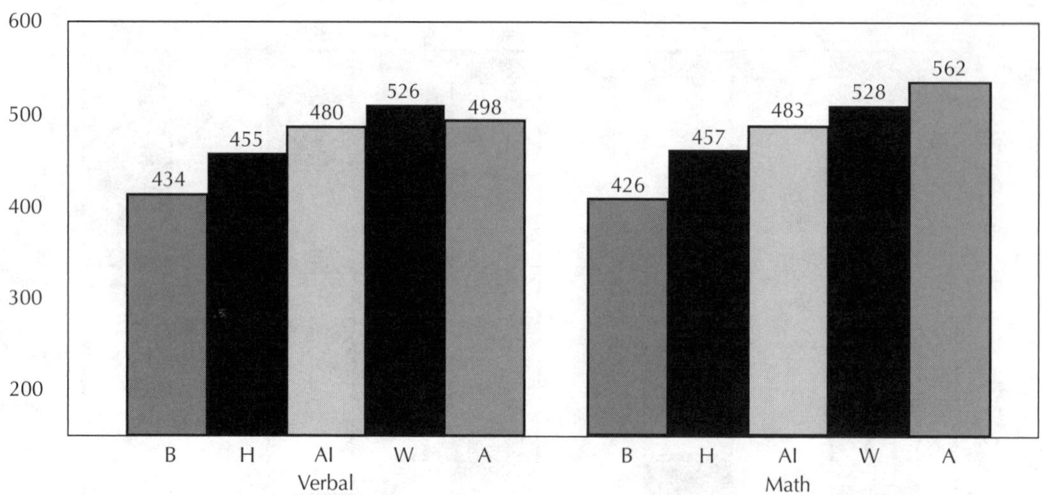

Figure 6 1998 SAT Scores by Race

for Hispanics, compared 59 percent for whites (NCES, 1997, tables 110, 119 and 124).

College Admissions Test Scores

The differences in high school academic proficiency of students by race were echoed in the subsequent national college admissions test results (SAT, 1998, ACT, 1998). The 1998 average SAT verbal test scores were 434 for blacks, 452–461 for Hispanics, 480 for American Indians, compared with 526 for whites and 498 for Asians; the mean mathematics test scores were 426 for blacks, 447–466 for Hispanics, 483 for American Indians, compared with 528 for whites and 562 for Asians (Figure 6). ACT test scores for the 1998 freshman group reflected similar disparity. The 1998 national ACT composite score averages were 17.1 for blacks, 18.5 for Hispanics and 19.0 for American Indians, compared with 21.7 for whites and 21.8 for Asians.

College Enrollment Rates

Although the overall college enrollment trend reflected a more educated population, significant differences by race continue to exist. In 1977, the college enrollment rates as a percent of 18- to 24-year-olds were 21 percent for blacks and 17 percent for Hispanics, compared with 27 percent for whites; in 1996, the percentages were 27 percent for blacks and 20 percent for Hispanics, compared with 40 percent for whites (NCES, 1997, table 186). The differences in high school completion, college enrollment and college graduation rates culminated into a large gap between minorities and whites in baccalaureate degree completion. Among the 25-to-29-year-old group in 1993, 14 percent of the blacks and 11 percent of the Hispanics completed a bachelor's degree or higher, compared with 29 percent of the whites and 51 percent of the Asians (Day and Curry, 1997).

Conclusion

When comparing educational attainment, there may be a tendency to focus solely on the racial differences in today's performance statistics. Much more, however, can be learned from reviewing current data in a historical context. Despite existing disparities, educational statistics in the last 50 years indicated that blacks and Hispanics had made impressive progress in high school enrollment, high school completion and college attendance. "In 1940, only 8 percent of Blacks 25 years old and over had completed high school, compared with 26 percent for Whites. . . . By 1993, 70 percent of Blacks 25 years old and over had completed high school, compared with 82 percent of Whites." Similar progress was made by Hispanics. "Among Hispanics 25 years old and over in 1993, 53 percent had completed high school, up from 37 percent in 1974." (Adams, 1998).

Likewise, minority college enrollment had increased substantially. From 1972 to 1996, the college enrollment rates of 18- to 24-year-olds increased from 18 percent to 27 percent for blacks, from 13 percent to 20 percent for Hispanics, compared with an overall increase from 26 percent to 36 percent. The improvement was even more impressive over a period of 50 years. Before the 1954 Supreme Court decision on "Brown V. Board of Education," most of the public institutions were simply not accessible to blacks. Today, 47 percent of the blacks 25 to 29 years of age had attended colleges and more than 14 percent of these young adults had completed a college education (Day and Curry, 1997).

The progress in high school completion and college attendance of minorities, however, was not matched by an equal gain in their academic preparedness for college. Consequently, minority college graduation rates continued to be low. Without adequate preparation, it is unlikely that individuals can succeed in college. In reviewing the post-secondary remedial work and student success reported in *The Condition of Education, 1996,* Adelman (1997) noted that a larger proportion of minorities were required to take remedial reading in college. Moreover, "Sixty-five percent of those people (who took remedial reading) found themselves in at least three other remedial courses," and "only 24 percent of those who took three or more remedial courses had earned a bachelor's." These facts prompted the assertion that ". . . we cannot continue to let high school graduates believe that they have a good chance of earning a college degree if they leave high school with poor reading skills."

"It takes 10 years to establish a tree; 100 years, a person." This Chinese proverb captures the essence of education. Improving educational attainment takes time; indeed, it takes generations. Among today's college-aged black youth, only 8 percent of their grandparents and 27 percent of their parents had completed a high school education. Twenty years from now, more than 70 percent of the black college-aged students will have parents who are high school graduates and more than 14 percent of them will have parents who are college graduates. Educational statistics in the last five decades provided strong evidences that underrepresented minority children in the next century will be guided by far better-educated parents.

Terenzini et al. (1996) in a study of the first-generation college students concluded that,

> *"In both precollege characteristics and their experiences during their first year in college, first-generation students differ in many educationally important ways from the students higher education has traditionally served. Because of these different characteristics and experiences, they are also a group at-risk. They are a group clearly in need of greater research and administrative attention if they are to survive and succeed in college."*

While past educational statistics suggest a progressively brighter future for minority children, the same statistics also caution that for at least four to five more decades, a large portion of the minorities will most likely continue to be first-generation students. Their precollege academic preparedness, parental education and socioeconomic status will also likely lag behind the majority of their peers. Therefore, it will be an important challenge and responsibility for colleges and universities to help underrepresented minority students bridge these gaps so that they can succeed.

Note

1. From 1980 to 1995, the minority enrollment increases by race were blacks, 1.11 to 1.47 million; Hispanics, 472 thousand to 1.09 million, American Indians, 84 to 134 thousand, and Asian Americans, 286 to 797 thousand.

References

Adams, A. U.S. Census Bureau. *Education attainment.* <http://www.census.gov/prod/1/pop/profile/95/7_ps.pdf>, (accessed: October 3, 1998).

Adelman, C. (1997). *The truth about remedial work: it's more complex than windy rhetoric and simple solutions suggest.* The Chronicle of Higher Education, October 4, 1996.

American College Testing Program. (1994). *National dropout rates.* Iowa City: ACT.

American College Testing Program. (1998). *1998 High School Profile Report–National Data.* Iowa City: ACT.

American Council on Education & Education Commission of the States. (1988). *One-Third of a nation.* A Report of the Commission of Minority Participation in Education and American Life. Washington DC: American Council on Education.

Astin, A. W. (1993a). *What matters in college: Four critical years revisited.* San Francisco: Jossey Bass.

Astin, A. W. (1993b). "How good is your institution's retention rate?" Unpublished Manuscript. University of California, Los Angeles.

Beal, P. & Pascarella, E. T. (1982). Designing retention interventions and verifying their effectiveness. In E. T. Pascarella (Ed.), *Studying Student Attrition.* New Directions for Institutional Research, (pp. 73–88). San Francisco: Jossey-Bass.

Carter, D. J. & Wilson, R. (1993). *Minorities in higher education.* Washington, DC: American Council on Education, Office of Minorities in Higher Education.

College Board. (1998). *1998 profile of SAT and achievement test takers.* Princeton NJ: The College Board.

Cope, R. G. (1978). Why student stay, why they leave. In L. Noel (Ed.), *Reducing the Dropout Rate.* New Directions for Student Services, (pp. 1–12). San Francisco: Jossey-Bass.

Day, J. C. (1996). *Population Projections of the United States by Age, Sex, Race and Hispanic Origin: 1995 to 2050,* U.S. Bureau of the Census Current Population Reports, P25–1130. Washington, DC: U.S. Government Printing Office.

Day, J. & Curry, A. C. (1997). Educational Attainment in the United States: March 1997. U.S. Bureau of the Census, Current Population Reports, P20–505. Washington, DC: U.S. Government Printing Office.

Hauptman, A., & Smith, P. (1994). Financial Aid Strategies for Improving Minority Student Participation in Higher Education. In M. J. Justiz, R. Wilson, & L. G. Bjork (Eds.), *Minorities in higher education,* (pp. 78–106). Phoenix, AZ: Oryx Press and the American Council on Education.

Hill, S. T. (1992). *Blacks in undergraduate science and engineering education* (NSF 92-305). Washington, DC: National Science Foundation Division of Science Resources Studies. Special Report.

Lenning, O. T. (1982). Variable-selection and measurement concerns. In E. T. Pascarella (Ed.), *Studying Student Attrition.* New Directions for Institutional Research, (pp. 35–53). San Francisco: Jossey-Bass.

National Center for Education Statistics. (1993). *Trends in degrees conferred by institutions of higher education: 1984–85 through 1990–91.* Washington, DC: United States Department of Education, Office of Educational Research and Improvement.

National Center for Education Statistics. (1997). *Digest of education statistics.* Washington, DC: United States Department of Education, Office of Educational Research and Improvement.

Saupe, J. L. (1988). *Selectivity in freshman admissions, retention and degree-completion rates: twenty-seven public research universities.* Paper presented at the Mid-AIR Conference, Kansas City, October 19–21, 1988.

Smith, T. Y. (1992). *The Big Eight/Big Ten/SUG Longitudinal Retention Survey: A Report on Findings and Implications,* Paper presented at the Association for Institutional Research (AIR) conference, Atlanta, May, 1992.

Smith, T. Y. (1998), *1997–98 CSRDE Report: The retention and graduation rates of 1989–96 entering freshman cohorts in 232 U.S. colleges and universities.* Norman, Oklahoma: Center for Institutional Data Exchange and Analysis.

Terenzini, P. T., Springer, L., Yaeger, P. M., Pascarella, E. T., & Nora, A. (1996). First-generation college students: characteristics, experiences, and cognitive development, *Research in Higher Education* 37(1): 1–22. San Francisco: Jossey-Bass.

Thomas, G. E. (1991). "Assessing the college major selection process for black students." In W. R. Allen, E. G. Epps & N. Z. Haniff (Eds.), *College in black and white,* (pp. 61–74). Albany, NY: State University of New York Press.

Aptitude vs. Merit: What Matters in Persistence

Edward P. St. John, Shouping Hu,
Ada B. Simmons, and Glenda Droogsma Musoba

The new debate about the use of racial preferences in college admissions has raised questions about the measures of merit used in the admissions process. In Washington and California, the electorate has voted to eliminate racial preferences in admissions. In Texas, the *Hopwood* decision has eliminated the use of racial preferences for admission to public universities, while the University of Michigan is being sued (*Gratz and Hamacher v. Bollinger et al.*) over the use of race as a factor in its admissions process (Schmidt, 1998). These developments have set off a new wave of efforts to find other measures, in addition to standardized tests, that can be used to provide an approach to college admissions that will promote both fairness and diversity. As colleges experiment with different measures of merit that can be used in college admissions, it is also important to consider the potential effects of using these measures on persistence, given that attaining a degree is one of the most important outcomes of higher education (Pascarella & Terenzini, 1991).

The merit-aware index, derived from the differential of individuals' standardized Scholastic Aptitude Test (SAT) and American College Test (ACT) scores and the average score for all college-going students in their high schools, provides an alternative measure of merit that can be used to increase diversity in college admissions (St. John, Simmons, & Musoba, in press). This paper compares the effects of SAT and the merit-aware index on within-year persistence of first-year college students. First, we describe the new policy context that has influenced efforts to find alternative measures that will both identify merit and promote diversity in admissions. Then we describe our research approach and present our analyses of the effects of one alternative measure of merit on persistence and grade point average (GPA). Finally, we consider the implications of the analysis for the new policy debates about affirmative action and diversity.

A Changing Policy Context

Legal challenges to racial preferences in college admissions raise serious questions for the entire higher education community. Historically, standardized admissions tests provided neutral measures of ability, or aptitude, for assessing the quality of applicants (Stewart, 1999). At the very least, the Scholastic Aptitude Test (SAT) and the American College Test (ACT) provide standardized measures of achievement that colleges can use to rate students from different high schools. For decades,

Reprinted by permission from *The Review of Higher Education* 24, no. 2 (2001).

colleges have used these tests as part of the admissions screening process; more recently, these tests have been used as indicators of college selectivity (Hossler & Litten, 1993). However, a new legal context is influencing a rethinking of merit measures in enrollment and raising questions about the long-term effects of alternative measures of merit.

A New Legal Context

The use of racial preferences in addition to standardized tests in undergraduate admissions emerged as a legal issue at the same time that the first round of litigation over college segregation was completed in all states with a history of separate but equal systems of higher education. A brief review of both developments helps set the stage for this analysis.

Although college desegregation began, in West Virginia at least, after the 1954 *Brown v. Board of Education* decision by the U.S. Supreme Court, most states did not take action until after the initial *Adams* decisions in the middle 1970s. In response to these decisions, the Office of Civil Rights in the U.S. Department of Education required the Southern and border states with historically segregated systems to develop plans for systemwide desegregation. Most states developed plans that were eventually approved (Williams, 1977). By 1989, a court decision had been reached in Tennessee; Alabama, Louisiana, and Mississippi were still litigating; and the rest had approved plans.

In 1989, the Mississippi case (*Fordice*) reached the U.S. Supreme Court. Reviewing a Fifth Circuit Court decision that declared Mississippi desegregated because students had a choice about where they attended, the U.S. Supreme Court decided that, although student choice played a role in the desegregation process, the state also needed to eliminate the vestiges of *de jure* segregation. The cases in Mississippi and Alabama were fully litigated, and the Louisiana case was settled under the parameters set by the *Fordice* decision. These cases included mission-related remedies to promote desegregation of historically Black systems, including the use of scholarships to encourage Whites to attend historically Black colleges.

During the same period, the use of race-based scholarships was being litigated in other states. *Podberesky v. Kirwan* in Maryland (Fourth Circuit Court) modified the use of race-based scholarships in Maryland (1994), and the *Hopwood* decision in Texas upheld a Fifth Circuit Court decision to eliminate race-based admissions and scholarships in Texas (1996). In the *Hopwood* decision, the Fifth Circuit panel rejected as a binding precedent Justice Lewis Powell's reasoning in the *Bakke* decision that the use of race to achieve campus diversity is permissible (Olivas, 1997). These decisions began to dismantle the use of student aid, one element of the prior desegregation settlements that had promoted desegregation through student choice. However, knowledge of this litigation did not deter the Fifth Circuit Court judges in Mississippi, Alabama, and Louisiana from including scholarships for Whites as part of the settlements for the Midsouth desegregation cases.

At virtually the same time that the Fifth Circuit Court was beginning to dismantle race-based scholarships and admissions standards in Texas, the citizens of California were questioning the use of racial preferences in college admissions. In 1996, they passed Proposition 209 to eliminate racial preferences in college admissions. In 1998, Washington's citizens passed Initiative 200, a similar measure (Gutiérrez-Jones, 1999). Even more recently, Florida announced that state universities would no longer consider race in admissions decisions, instead granting admission to the top 20% of graduating classes from all high schools in the state (Selingo, 1999).

The courts have also begun to respond to new legal challenges to the use of racial preferences in college admissions. Recently, the University of Michigan has been sued for using racial preferences in its admissions process (Schmidt, 1998; Sugrue et al., 1999). While the case might be settled on a technical issue, it could be difficult for the federal courts to uphold the use of racial preferences. Most recently, Tompkins, a student in Alabama, has challenged the use of race-based scholarships for Whites at Alabama State University (a historically Black institution), a strategy that was implemented as part of the *Knight v. Alabama* decision in 1995 (Center for Individual Rights, 1999).

This new legal context complicates admissions processes in selective public universities. If they use racial preference in admissions, then they either face a need to rethink their admissions practices or are susceptible to legal challenge. While it is possible that the courts will uphold the use of racial preferences in admissions, such decisions would counter both the current direction of federal court decisions and possibly even the will of a majority of voters. There is growing evidence that voters would like to see colleges maintain and improve diversity but to do so without using racial preferences (Ford Foundation, 1999; Newcomb, 1998).

Rethinking Merit Measures

The position that individuals take about the use of racial preferences depends in part on their view of social justice. Many in higher education have argued that there is still reason to use racial preferences (Sugrue et al., 1999). In fact, after reviewing alternative admissions schemes, a Texas Coordinating Board study group suggested that there is no good proxy for race (Olivas, 1997). Some public universities are taking a public position in defense of the use of racial preferences (Bollinger & Cantor, 1998; Schmidt & Healy, 1999). However, given the new legal challenges, many higher education leaders have begun to rethink the use of tests and other measures of merit in college admissions.

States that have already been faced with the elimination of racial preferences have begun to make innovative adaptations. Texas used a deliberate analytic approach to develop a new set of empirical criteria that could be used to redirect student financial aid to a larger percentage of minority students (Hanson & Burt, 1999). The University of Texas has increased diversity back to pre-*Hopwood* levels (Carnevale, 1999; Hanson & Burt, 1999), while the University of California Board of Regents recently decided to use high school class rank rather than test scores in admissions decisions and to admit the top 4% of high school classes to the UC system (Healy, 1999). However, the University of California system still has a lower percentage of minority students than it did before Proposition 209, particularly on the flagship campuses at Berkeley and Los Angeles (Selingo, 2000; Sharlet, 1999).

The use of high school rank offers one way to approach racial parity and the distribution of underrepresented minorities suggests why. American schools (K-12) are now more segregated than they were before the *Brown* decision (Fossey, 1998; Orfield & Easton, 1996). Further, average achievement test scores are consistently lower in rural and urban school districts (Snow, Burns, & Griffin, 1998), a consequence of lower socioeconomic status and poorer quality schools—meaning that they lack the full range of more advanced courses, particularly mathematics, that have been linked to later educational success (Adelman, 1999). Many urban high schools are predominantly Black.[1] Thus, admitting top-ranking students from each high school would produce a more diverse group of students than admitting only top-scorers on nationally normed tests. However, the use of class rank or grades overlooks the original purposes of college admissions testing, which historically were created to help compare students from different high schools fairly (Lemann, 1999; Olivas, 1997). Such comparisons are not possible if admissions decisions are made on the basis of class ranking. Furthermore, the U.S. Civil Rights Commission has taken the position that the use of class-rank "percentage plans will do no better and probably worse" than race-conscious affirmative action (Selingo & Healy, 2000), thus encouraging the consideration of other admissions formulae.

Class-based affirmative action has been offered as a "more principled compromise" to racial preferences, one that can be defended against political and legal attack (Kahlenberg, 1996). Without taking race into consideration, class preferences are designed to benefit the nation's poorest. Yet because of past discrimination which has resulted in economic disadvantage, citizens of color are expected to make disproportionate gains from this policy redirection (Kahlenberg, 1996). Recently, Bernal, Cabrera, and Terenzini (1999) tested this theory, finding only a weak (but statistically significant) correlation between race and socioeconomic status. Furthermore, they found that White students of low socioeconomic status were more likely than Blacks to benefit from such a policy because of sheer numbers and subsequent overrepresentation. Similarly, admissions policies giving first-generation preference to students whose parents did not attend college would favor racial minorities but would also benefit students of uneducated White parents (Olivas, 1997). When the outcomes contradict the aims for which the policies were created, class-based preferences in college admissions and other areas lose some of their appeal.

The testing community has also begun to explore new ways of using standardized tests to measure merit for college. In a *Wall Street Journal* article, Amy Dockser Marcus (1999a) broke the story of the Educational Testing Service's attempts to develop a "Strivers" index. This method would identify students with SAT scores that were at least 200 points higher than would be expected from their background, thus singling out a higher percentage of Black and other minority students than relying on the SAT would produce. In theory, the Strivers formula could identify high-achieving students as part of the admissions process. However, the method has been controversial (Gose, 1999) and has been criticized by the College Board, which sponsors the SAT (Dockser Marcus, 1999b).

William Goggin (1999), a higher education economist, has proposed that colleges use a merit index constructed by subtracting the mean SAT score of the student's high school from the student's own score. This method would produce an index that is sensitive to socioeconomic and racial differences in high schools, similar to high school rank. However, it is consonant with the use of standardized tests in college admissions and K-12 education policy, if not with the historic use of standardized tests in college admissions. Goggin argued that the merit index provides a fair and just approach to admissions:

> Why not create a measure of the extent to which a student's achievement exceeded what could reasonably have been expected given his or her academic background? In particular, why not use a measure of the extent to which the actual test score exceeds the predicted score? Make no mistake, incorporated in the right admissions model, such a merit measure would be as powerful as race and ethnicity in achieving the goals of affirmative action. (p. 9)

The merit-aware index—the differential between individuals' SAT scores and the averages for their high schools—also provides a way of linking college admissions to K-12 education policy. In the past two decades, states have moved toward use of the average scores of high school students or the percentage of students passing standardized tests as measures of high school quality. The merit-aware index is consonant with this logic. It provides a means of evaluating the performance of high school students in relation to their high school peers by adjusting test scores to the quality of high schools.

The merit-aware index was only recently introduced and has not yet been used in college admissions. However, an empirical test of the model has revealed that its use can increase the number and percentage of Black students who are screened into an applicant pool for more complete review (St. John, Simmons, & Musoba, in press). In a simulation of a selective university without large numbers of minority applicants, using the merit-aware index score raised the proportion of African Americans in the screened-applicant pool from roughly 1% who would enter the screened pool using SAT alone to 2.5% using the combination of SAT cutoff and the merit-aware index. Similarly, in another simulation of a selective university with a larger percentage of minority applicants, the proportion of African Americans in the screened-applicant pool rose from 2% to 4.5%, yielding a total minority percentage of 18.2% by using the combination of SAT score and merit-aware index.

In these examples, using SAT alone yielded African American representation in the screened-applicant pool at a rate less than half of parity; using the merit-aware index alone yielded African American representation greater than parity. This means that colleges could adopt the index as a means of selecting meritorious students and increasing diversity. Indeed, it is possible to use the merit index to identify a group of students who merit more complete review as part of a selective admissions process. The process could be used to supplement the use of standardized test scores as a part of the process of selecting a more diverse first-year class without even considering race in the admissions process. However, this method of admissions, like the use of high school rank or high school grades, is potentially subject to criticism for not providing an adequate measure of potential success in college. Therefore, it is important to consider how well the merit-aware index predicts college persistence and grades.

Implications for Persistence

The development of standardized tests has historically been driven by the theory that such tests can identify students who have a high probability of success in college. If an alternative to standardized test scores is used in the admissions process, then a fair test of that alternative's efficacy is whether it predicts persistence as well as standardized tests.[2] If this were the case, then there would be fewer reasons to resist using the merit-aware index to promote diversity in selective public universities. In this study, we compare the predictive value of SAT scores and the merit-aware index on persistence and college grades during the first year of college.

Given that most persistence research focuses on year-to-year persistence rather than within-year persistence, it is appropriate to question the wisdom of examining within-year persistence. However, year-to-year persistence is a measure of how well students integrate into a particular college, rather than a measure of how well they achieve academically. Typically, persistence studies find that academic integration, including college grades, has an impact on persistence (Braxton, Shaw Sullivan, & Johnson, 1997; Pascarella & Terenzini, 1991). Since our concern is with measuring students' ability to complete the first year of college, the year-to-year approach is less appropriate. Indeed, after the freshman year, college grades are better predictors of subsequent persistence than SAT or ACT scores, an issue we address in this paper. Thus, while the focus on within-year persistence may be appropriate for this initial test of the merit-aware approach, future research should examine the ability of the merit-aware index to predict year-to-year persistence.

Research Approach

This study examines the impact of three approaches to measuring student ability in predicting persistence during the first year of college: the SAT test, the merit-aware index, and whether students have a positive score on the merit-aware index (a dichotomous version of merit). Below we describe the method for constructing the merit-aware index, the specifications of the persistence model, the statistical methods, and the study limitations.

The Merit-Aware Index

One of the more difficult issues we faced in the current study was to develop a merit-aware index that we could use in a persistence analysis. Constructing a merit-aware index requires a more complete data set than is available from institutional admissions records. In some states, high school SAT averages are public records. For example, in Indiana where this study was conducted, the Indiana Department of Education disseminates on its web page the average SAT scores for each high school based on the individual scores of all students at that school who took the test. However, we decided to compute a high school average SAT score for this study a little differently.

This study used a random sample of full-time freshmen enrolled in the public system of higher education in Indiana in 1997–1998 drawn from the total population of Indiana students enrolled in state higher education institutions. We drew our sample after computing the merit index for the full data set. For each student, we identified an SAT score for his or her high school, calculated by averaging the SAT scores of all students from that high school who attended a public higher education institution in the state. We matched high school averages with student records by using the high school code. These high school averages then became the base for calculating the merit index. We calculated the merit index for each student by subtracting the average SAT score for his or her high school from the student's SAT score.

We decided to use this locally constructed set of high school averages rather than averages from published sources to reflect the actual range of scores for students who attended institutions within the state system. Had we used the published scores, then the merit-aware index would have included students who attended private colleges or public colleges in other states. Many of these other students would have higher scores than students who remained in public institutions in the state. Since our focus is on state residents who attend the public system of higher education, we decided it was more appropriate to focus on average scores for students enrolled in public colleges and universities. The primary difference between the two measures is that, using the locally constructed mean, a larger percentage of students have positive merit scores. This adjustment was important, since Goggin (1999) suggests that only positive merit scores be considered in the admissions screening process. In this study we used a continuous measure of merit, from the lowest score to the highest score, in one test of the merit-aware index. In a separate analysis we assess the effects of having a positive merit score.

Model Specifications

We defined persistence as the enrollment of first-year students in the spring term following the fall term of their entry—that is, whether students enrolled for the full academic year. Our analyses used a three-step logical model for comparing the effects of the SAT and the merit-aware index on persistence. Below we describe the specification of variables included in each step (see also Table 1), then describe the multiple versions of the analysis included in this paper.

In the first step, we examined the effect of selected social background variables plus the SAT score (in one version) or the merit-aware

TABLE 1
Descriptive Statistics

	First-Year Student Sample	
Variable	*Percentage*	*Mean*
Gender		
Male	49.6	
Female[1]	50.4	
Age (years)		18.6
Ethnicity		
African American	5.0	
Other Ethnicity	4.2	
White	90.8	
Dependency		
Self-supporting	1.3	
Dependent and non-aid applicants	98.7	
Income		
Low Income	4.9	
Lower Middle	11.2	
Upper Middle	21.2	
Upper Income	23.8	
Non-aid applicant	38.9	
SAT range: 350–1,550		986
Merit Index (range:-618–533)		−2.95
Dichotomized Merit Indicator	49.2[2]	
College GPA		
Below C	30.8	
C Average	19.8	
B Average	38.6	
A Average	10.8	
Institution Type[3]		
Two-Year Institution	1.5	
Other Four-Year Institution	60.2	
Research University	38.4	
Degree Program		
Associate	18.0	
Baccalaureate	82.0	
Housing Status		
On-campus	69.3	
Other	30.7	
Persistence	84.7	
N	2,500	

[1] Italics indicate the uncoded comparison variable in the sets of design variables used in the logistic regression models.
[2] Indicates percent of students scoring higher than the mean for their high school.
[3] Some categories may not total 100% due to rounding.

index (in the other versions) on within-year persistence. We rescaled the SAT and merit-aware scores by dividing by 100 in the logistic analyses to make it easier to interpret the delta-p for the SAT and the merit index. We also included gender (males compared to females), age, ethnicity (Blacks and students from other ethnic groups compared to Whites), whether students were self-supporting aid applicants, and income (we divided aid applicants into four quartiles and compared them to students who did not apply for aid). These variables provide an indication of how student background plus test scores (or merit) influence persistence. Further, this set of variables represents the type of precollege information that a university would have when making admissions decisions.

In the second step, we added college grades to the model. Students with below-C grades (below 2.0), mostly-C grades (2.0 to 2.5), and mostly-A grades (above 3.5) were compared to students with mostly B grades (above 2.5 to 3.5). By including college grades in the second step, we were able to estimate the effects of academic achievement in college, beyond the effects of precollege tests and other background variables.[3]

In the third step, we entered a set of variables related to the college setting. These included whether students were enrolled in a research university or two-year college (compared to being enrolled in another type of four-year institution), whether students were enrolled in an associate program, and whether students were living on campus. This analysis provides insight into whether there were any interactions between the direct effects of test scores and student background, and the effects of attending different types of public postsecondary institutions.

This paper includes three versions of the three-step persistence analysis. We analyze the effects of the SAT (Table 2), then the effects of the merit-aware index (Table 3), and finally the effects of a dichotomous variable of having a higher SAT score than an otherwise average cohort member (Table 4).

Statistical Methods

This study uses logistic regression, an appropriate statistical method for dichotomous outcomes (Cabrera, 1994; Hosmer & Lemeshow, 1989). We present three model indicators for each step of the analysis. We use a pseudo R2, the Cox and Snell R2, which provides a proxy for the percentage of variance explained by the model. The Cox and Snell R2 is a more conservative estimate of variance explained than some other possible measures (and thus will be smaller), but it does provide an indication of the improvement of one model over another. The Cox and Snell R2 represents, at most, the proportion of error variance that an alternative model reduces in relation to a null model. Second, we also present a −2 log likelihood (or −2 Log L), which provides an indication of the fit of the model. A lower −2 log L indicates a better fit. We also present the percentage of cases correctly predicted, which provides a direct indicator of the model's predictive quality.

In addition, we present the change in probability measures (delta-p statistics) for the predictor variables in each of the analyses using a method developed by Petersen (1985) and recommended by Cabrera (1994). The delta-p statistic indicates the change in the baseline probability of persistence attributable to a unit change in a given predictor. For the dichotomous variable persistence, the delta-p indicates the change in persistence attributable to having a particular characteristic compared to the comparison group. For example, a positive delta-p of .040 for living on campus means that students who live on campus are four percentage points more likely to persist than first-year students who do not live on campus.

Limitations

This study has a few limitations that readers should consider. First, we use a policy-oriented model of persistence rather than an institutional-fit model. This policy-oriented model is partially consistent with the current discourse within the higher education community about academic integration processes and includes related measures (e.g. college grades). However, it uses no measures of social integration. Nevertheless, we think the model does include the variables needed to assess the persistence effects of shifting from the use of the SAT to the use of a merit-aware index and is consistent with public policy models used to assess the effects of state (St. John, 1999) and federal (St. John, Kirshstein, & Noell, 1991) funding policies. Further, the variables included in the analysis are logically structured and consistent with the types of indicators that public officials routinely assess. It may be

TABLE 2
Logistic Regression Persistence Model: SAT Only

Variable	Step 1 Delta-P	Step 2 Delta-P	Step 3 Delta-P
Gender: male	0.004	0.030*	0.023
Age	−0.107***	−0.111***	−0.094***
Ethnicity			
African American	0.013	0.032	0.025
Other Ethnicity	0.004	0.000	−0.010
Dependency			
Self-supporting	0.008	0.025	0.023
Income			
Low Income	−0.016	−0.021	−0.018
Lower Middle	0.032	0.036	0.041
Upper Middle	0.026	0.015	0.014
High Income	0.026	0.019	0.019
SAT/100	0.018***	−0.001	−0.007
College GPA			
Below C		−0.423***	−0.410***
Mostly C		−0.100**	−0.098**
Mostly A		0.026	0.026
Institution Type			
Two-Year Institution			0.111
Research University			0.062***
Degree Program			
Associate			0.005
Housing			
On-campus			0.043**
Baseline P (%)	84.7%	84.7%	84.7%
Cox & Snell R^2	0.044	0.126	0.137
−2 Log L	2025.114	1800.361	1770.357
% Correctly Pred.	84.7%	85.5%	85.2%
N	2,500	2,500	2,500

* Coefficient significant at .05.
** Coefficient significant at .01.
*** Coefficient significant at .001.

appropriate to conduct studies using the institutional fit model in the future, if the merit-aware index is actually used in admissions in selective public colleges and universities.

Second, we have not included cases with missing variables. In particular, not all of the first-year students in the Indiana public system of higher education had SAT scores reported. However, since our purpose was to compare the effects of two distinct approaches to the use of the SAT, this limitation was not problematic. We conducted a supplemental analysis without test scores (data not shown) which confirms that test scores improve prediction of persistence when grades are not known, but do not add to the prediction of persistence when test scores are known.

Third, our analysis does not include high school grades and other precollege indicators of merit, such as Adelman's (1999) academic resources measure. While the state database includes a few additional precollege measures of student achievement,[4] we thought it was more appropriate to limit this analysis to a comparison of the SAT and the merit index. This limitation was important because of our focus on the alternative uses of tests as predictors of persistence.

TABLE 3
Logistic Regression Persistence Model: Merit-Aware Index Only

Variable	*Step 1 Delta-P*	*Step 2 Delta-P*	*Step 3 Delta-P*
Gender: male	0.005	0.031*	0.024
Age	−0.110***	−0.112***	−0.095***
Ethnicity			
African American	0.000	0.031	0.027
Other Ethnicity	0.001	−0.001	−0.011
Dependency			
Self-supporting	0.012	0.024	0.022
Income			
Low Income	−0.022	−0.021	−0.016
Lower Middle	0.029	0.036	0.043
Upper Middle	0.024	0.015	0.014
High Income	0.025	0.020	0.019
Merit Index/100	0.016***	−0.003	−0.008
College GPA			
Below C		−0.426***	−0.411***
Mostly C		−0.102***	−0.099**
Mostly A		0.028	0.027
Institution Type			
Two-Year Institution			0.111
Research University			0.062***
Degree Program			
Associate			0.004
Housing			
On-campus			0.043**
Baseline P (%)	84.7%	84.7%	84.7%
Cox & Snell R^2	0.042	0.126	0.137
−2 Log L	2029.82	1800.07	1769.69
% Correctly Pred.	84.7%	85.5%	85.4%
N	2,500	2,500	2,500

* Coefficient significant at .05.
** Coefficient significant at .01.
*** Coefficient significant at .001.

It would be appropriate for future studies to undertake analyses comparing the effects of a wider range of measures of merit and achievement on college persistence.

Findings

The analyses below compare the effects of different approaches to using standardized tests on the continuous enrollment of students during their first year of college. First, we provide a brief overview of the population, then describe the three logistic regression analyses.

Population Characteristics

The population of in-state first-year students (Table 1) in Indiana public higher education in 1997–1998 was mostly White (90.8%), but there were substantial percentages of Blacks (5.0%) and other minorities (4.2%). The average age was 18.6. Most students had applied for student aid, as evidenced by the fact that only 38.9% had no income reported. A slight majority of the students (50.4%) were females. Students were spread across the spectrum of income levels with 4.9% being low income, 11.2% lower middle income, 21.2% upper middle income, and 23.8%

TABLE 4
Logistic Regression Persistence Model: Dichotomous Merit Indicator Only

Variable	*Step 1 Delta-P*	*Step 2 Delta-P*	*Step 3 Delta-P*
Gender: male	0.006	0.030*	0.022
Age	−0.113***	−0.111***	−0.093***
Ethnicity			
African American	−0.006	0.033	0.030
Other Ethnicity	−0.002	−0.000	−0.008
Dependency			
Self-supporting	0.010	0.025	0.024
Income			
Low Income	−0.020	−0.021	−0.017
Lower Middle	0.029	0.036	0.042
Upper Middle	0.025	0.015	0.014
High Income	0.026	0.019	0.019
Merit Indicator	0.046***	−0.004	−0.018
College GPA			
Below C		−0.423***	−0.407***
Mostly C		−0.100**	−0.096**
Mostly A		0.026	0.023
Institution Type			
Two-Year Institution			0.112
Research University			0.060***
Degree Program			
Associate			0.007
Housing			
On-campus			0.043**
Baseline P (%)	84.7%	84.7%	84.7%
Cox & Snell R^2	0.042	0.126	0.136
−2 Log L	2030.66	1800.34	1770.84
% Correctly Pred.	84.7%	85.5%	85.2%
N	2,500	2,500	2,500

* Coefficient significant at .05.
** Coefficient significant at .01.
*** Coefficient significant at .001.

upper income; 38.9% did not report their income levels. In their first semester of college, 30.8% of the students had a grade point average (GPA) below C, 19.8% earned a C average, 38.6% had a B average, and 10.8% had earned mostly A's. The majority of students (60.2%) attended four-year institutions that were not research universities. Only 1.5% attended two-year colleges, and 38.4% attended research universities. Eighteen percent were in associate degree programs, and 82% were pursuing a baccalaureate degree. The majority (69.3%) lived on campus.

The Effects of the SAT

Our analysis of the effects of SAT test scores on persistence (Table 2) reveal that SAT scores alone had only a modest direct effect on persistence. In the first step, age was negatively associated with persistence, and SAT scores were positively associated with persistence. Each year of age differential decreased the probability of persistence by first-year students by about 10 percentage points across the three steps of the analysis. In contrast, each 100 points of differential in the SAT test increased the probability of persistence by 1.8 percentage points before grades were considered.

In the second step, first-year college grades predicted persistence substantially better than the SAT. Earning below-C grades during the first semester reduced the probability of persisting in the spring term by more than 40 percentage points, while earning C grades reduced this probability by about 10 percentage points. However, SAT test scores were not significant after grades were considered. Further, when grades were entered, the quality of the model improved: the R2 increased substantially, from .044 to .126, and the −2 log L decreased modestly.

In addition, males were more likely to persist in the second step but not in the third. Since this variable was no longer significant when college setting (institutional type, degree program, and housing) was considered, it is apparent that males have some advantage compared to females because of the type of college attended or the increased probability of living on campus. Clearly, gender differences in persistence is a topic that merits further investigation.

In the third step, we added a set of variables related to the college setting. Attending a research university improved the probability of persistence by 6.2 percentage points, and living on campus improved this probability by 4.3 percentage points. The quality of the model also improved slightly compared to the first model.

It is noteworthy that ethnicity was not statistically significant in any step of the analysis. This finding indicates that in Indiana in 1997–1998, minorities had the same probability of persistence as Whites, all other characteristics being equal. The reasons for this relatively equal probability of persistence merit further investigation.

The Effects of the Merit-Aware Index

The effects of the merit-aware index on persistence (Table 3) were virtually identical to the effects of the SAT (compare to Table 2).[5] The SAT and the merit-aware index had similar delta-p statistics (.018 for a 100 point change in the SAT to .016 for a 100 point change in the merit-aware index). Also, the model indicators were similar for the first step. They were slightly lower for the merit-aware index but not enough to have an obvious impact. Further, the delta-p statistics and model indicators for each of the subsequent steps were virtually identical in the two analyses.

Thus, we conclude that the merit-aware index predicts college persistence *about as well* as the SAT. This means that selective colleges would not lose any quality as measured by the percentage of students persisting or the grades they achieve if the merit-aware index were used in the application screening process. However, they could gain diversity in the student population.

The Effects of Having Merit

The third persistence analysis (Table 4) examined the effect on persistence of a positive score on the merit index (i.e., a dichotomous variable with positive values indicating an SAT score greater than the average score in the student's high school). All statistics, except the delta-p for the alternative merit measure, were virtually identical to those using the merit-aware index, inclusive of positive and negative merit scores (compare to Table 3). Achieving an SAT score higher than the average for the student's individual high school improved the probability of persistence by 4.6 percentage points, indicating that students whose SAT scores exceeded their high school peers were more likely to persist in college their first year. This finding opens a range of alternative uses of the merit-related measures in the admissions process.

Conclusions and Implications

These analyses of the effects of the merit-aware index on college persistence take place within a changing policy context. Clearly there is evidence that the history of racial discrimination in the United States has not been remedied (St. John, 1998; Williams, 1997). Yet because the current practice of using racial preferences is being challenged, alternative ways of measuring merit that might improve diversity are particularly appropriate and timely. Alternative measures of merit can be used to increase diversity in admissions, whether or not racial preferences hold up in federal court.

The merit-aware index (Goggin, 1999) provides a powerful indicator of merit. Previous analyses indicate that this measure can improve ethnic diversity in admissions compared to the use of the SAT alone (St. John, Simmons, & Musoba, in press). This analysis further extends the debate into the domain of college persistence by demonstrating that the merit-aware index is as effective as SAT scores in predicting within-year persistence in college. This finding was true regardless of whether we used a continuous (the merit-aware index derived from the SAT) or dichotomous measure (whether a student achieved a greater-than-average SAT score compared to classmates) of merit. These findings open the door more widely to alternative ways of approaching college admissions decisions.

Essentially, these results could be used to rationalize two different approaches to college admissions. One approach would be to use a merit-aware index as Goggin proposes (1999). This process involves first computing a merit-aware index, then assigning weights to the index that ensure consideration in the screened applicant pool. An alternative approach might be to assign extra points to students with positive scores on the merit-aware index. Both approaches would identify students who, based on their achievement test scores relative to their peers, would have an increased probability of college success.

The primary advantage of shifting to the use of the merit-aware index compared to the use of absolute SAT scores, at least in part of the college admissions process, is that it could change the mixture of diverse students who receive serious considerations in admissions (St. John, Simmons, & Musoba, in press). When the merit-aware index is used, more students from urban and rural high schools would be screened into the initial pool of applicants receiving more complete consideration in admissions. Such a pool would include more diverse students in selective public colleges and universities, more Blacks from the inner city, and more Whites and minorities from rural high schools. Thus, the merit-aware approach could increase opportunity for high-achieving students who attend low-performance high schools. However, it is true that this approach might exclude some minority students in suburban high schools whose SAT scores are higher than the national average but lower than the average for their high schools.

Given its sensitivity toward merit and its success in predicting persistence, the merit-aware index is also relevant in other campus decision-making processes that rely on such criteria—for example, awarding institutional financial aid. While need-based aid is a primary means of equalizing opportunity, many colleges and universities have targeted substantial portions of their institutional aid for attracting abler students. Redirecting some portion of this latter

APPENDIX
Standardized Coefficients of Student Background Characteristics, SAT, and Merit Index on College GPA

Variable	*Background*	*SAT*	*Merit Index*
Male	−.082***	−.128***	−.127***
Age	−.108***	−.024	−.031
Ethnicity			
African American	−.097***	−.026	−.053***
Other ethnicity	.005	.026	.023
Self-supporting	−.002	−.009	−.004
Income			
Low income	−.053*	−.033	−.046*
Lower middle	−.026	−.014	−.029
Upper middle	.024	.027	.016
High income	.049*	.033	.025
SAT/100		.359***	
Merit Index/100			.340***
Adjusted R2	.039***	.152***	.144***
N	2,500	2,500	2,500

* Coefficient significant at .05.
** Coefficient significant at .01
*** Coefficient significant at .001

category of aid and using the merit-aware index in award decisions may enable a campus to accomplish the dual goals of attracting and keeping capable students and creating a diverse campus.

In conclusion, there is sound evidence to support the efforts of selective public universities that are experimenting with alternative measures of merit in college admissions. While the merit index is not a perfect solution to the legal challenges facing admissions offices in public colleges, it may be more workable than many of the alternatives. Indeed, using the merit index in admissions would not only improve diversity but would also maintain persistence rates.

Notes

1. Most rural high schools outside of the South are predominantly White, which means that efforts to expand access for minorities using new merit measures could also expand access for low-income Whites.
2. College grades represent a second measure of collegiate success and are themselves an important factor in persistence to college graduation. A series of multiple regression models estimating the influence of background characteristics, SAT, or the merit-aware index, and campus environmental factors on college grades is presented in the appendix.
3. Adelman (1999) argues for using a composite variable, "academic resources," made up of an SAT-like test score, class rank, grade point average, and intensity of high school curriculum. His model also merits further testing.
4. The state collected information about the type of high school program taken but not information on grades earned in high school.
5. Similarly, the effects of SAT and the merit-aware index on college grades were not dramatically different (i.e., standard deviations for SAT and the merit-aware index were 1.73 and 1.69 respectively; standardized coefficients were .359 and .340 respectively. See the appendix).

References

Adelman, C. (1999). *Answers in the toolbox: Academic intensity, attendance patterns, and bachelor's degree attainment*. Washington, DC: U.S. Department of Education, Office of Educational Research and Improvement.

Bernal, E., Cabrera, A. F., & Terenzini, P. T. (1999, November). *Class-based affirmative action admissions policies: A viable alternative to race-based programs*. Paper presented at the annual meeting of the Association for the Study of Higher Education, San Antonio, TX.

Bollinger, L., & Cantor, N. (1998, April 28). The educational importance of race. *Washington Post*. Online edition: http://www.umich.edu/~urel/admissions/ comments/ washpost.html.

Braxton, J. M., Shaw Sullivan, A. B., & Johnson, R. M., Jr. (1997). Appraising Tinto's theory of college student departure. In J. C. Smart (Ed.). *Higher education: Handbook of theory and research* (Vol. 12, pp. 107–164). Edison, NJ: Agathon Press.

Cabrera, A. F. (1994). Applied logistic regression. In J. C. Smart (Ed.), *Higher education: Handbook of theory and research* (Vol. 10, pp. 225–256). New York: Agathon.

Carnevale, D. (1999, September 3). Enrollment of minority freshmen nears pre-Hopwood levels at U. of Texas at Austin. *Chronicle of Higher Education*, p. A71.

Center for Individual Rights (1999) *Active cases: Tompkins v. Alabama State University*. http://www.cir-usa.org/cs-sum.htm.

Dockser Marcus, A. (1999a, August 31). New weights can alter SAT scores: Family is factor in determining who's a striver. *Wall Street Journal*, pp. B1, B8.

Dockser Marcus, A. (1999b, October 1). President of College Board criticizes controversial "strivers" research project. *Wall Street Journal*, p. B4.

Ford Foundation (1999). *Americans see many benefits to diversity in higher education, finds first-ever national poll on topic*. http://www.fordfound.org.

Fossey, R. (Ed.). (1998). *Readings on equal education*. Vol. 15 of *Race, the courts, and equal education: The limits of the law*. New York: AMS Press.

Goggin, W. J. (1999, May). A "merit-aware" model for college admissions and affirmative action. *Postsecondary Education Opportunity Newsletter*. Mortenson Research Seminar on Public Policy Analysis of Opportunity for Postsecondary Education, pp. 6–12.

Gose, B. (1999, September 17). More points for "strivers": The new affirmative action: Researchers devise ways to reward students who have overcome disadvantages. *Chronicle of Higher Education*, p. A55.

Gutiérrez-Jones, C. (1999). *The affirmative action and diversity project: A web page for research*. Santa Barbara, CA: Department of English, University of California Santa Barbara, http://aad.english.ucsb.edu.

Hanson, G. R., & Burt, L. (1999, May). *Responding to Hopwood: Using policy analysis research to re-design scholarship award criteria*. Paper presented at the meeting of the Association for Institutional Research, Seattle, WA.

Healy, P. (1999, April 2). U. of California to admit top 4% from every high school. *Chronicle of Higher Education*, p. A36.

Hosmer, D. W. Jr., & Lemeshow, S. (1989). *Applied logistic regression*. New York: Wiley.

Hossler, D., & Litten, L. H. (1993). *Mapping the higher education landscape*. New York: College Board.

Kahlenberg, R. D. (1996). *The remedy: Class, race, and affirmative action*. New York: Basic Books.

Lemann, N. (1999). The big test: The secret history of the American meritocracy. New York: Farrar, Straus, and Giroux.

Newcomb, A. (1998, October 13). Weighing in on diversity. *Christian Science Monitor*, p. 7.

Olivas, M. A. (1997). Constitutional criteria: The social science and common law of admissions decisions in higher education. *University of Colorado Law Review, 68*(4), 1065–1121.

Orfield, G., & Easton, S. E. (1996). *Dismantling desegregation: The quiet reversal of Brown v. Board of Education*. Harvard Project on School Desegregation. New York: New Press.

Pascarella, E. T., & Terenzini, P. T. (1991). *How college affects students: Findings and insights from twenty years of research*. San Francisco: Jossey-Bass.

Petersen, T. (1985). A comment on presenting results from logit and probit models. *American Sociological Review, 50*(1), 130–131.

St. John, E. P. (1998). Higher education desegregation in the post-*Fordice* legal environment: An historical perspective. In R. Fossey (Ed.), *Readings on equal education*. Vol. 15 of *Race, the courts, and equal education: The limits of the law*. New York: AMS Press.

St. John, E. P. (1999). Evaluating state grant programs: A study of the Washington state grant programs. *Research in Higher Education, 40*, 149–70.

St. John, E. P., Kirshstein, R., & Noell, J. (1991). The effects of student aid on persistence: A sequential analysis of the high school and beyond senior cohort. *Review of Higher Education, 14*, 383–406.

St. John, E. P., Simmons, A., & Musoba, G. D. (in press). Merit-aware admissions in public universities: Increasing diversity without considering ethnicity. *Thought &Action*.

Schmidt, P., & Healy, P. (1999, October 8). U. of Virginia poised to limit race-based admissions; U. of Georgia keeps its preferences. *Chronicle of Higher Education*, p. A40.

Schmidt, P. (1998, October 30). U. of Michigan prepares to defend admissions policy in court. *Chronicle of Higher Education*, p. A32.

Selingo, J. (1999, November 19). Florida's university system plans to end affirmative action in admissions. *Chronicle of Higher Education*, pp. A36, A38.

Sharlet, J. (1999, April 16). Minority freshman admissions rebound at U of California. *Chronicle of Higher Education*, p. A40.

Snow, C., Burns, M., & Griffin, P. (1998). *Preventing reading difficulties in young children*. Washington, DC: National Academy Press.

Stewart, D. M. (1999). *Affirmative action and the SAT: A message from Donald M. Stewart, President of the College Board*. http://www.collegeboard.org/press/html/971219.html.

Sugrue, T., Foner, E., Camarillo, A., Gurin.P., Bowen, W., Steele, C., Bok, D., Syverud, K., & Webster, R. B. (1999). *The compelling need for diversity in higher education*. University of Michigan. http://www.umich.edu/~urel/admissions/le-gal/expert/toc.html.

Williams, J. B. (1997). *Race discrimination in public higher education: Interpreting federal civil rights enforcement, 1964–1996*. Westport, CT: Praeger.

Table of Cases

Brown v. the Board of Education of Topeka, Kansas, 349 U.S. 294 (1955).

Grantz and Hamacher v. Bollinger et al., No. 97-75231.

Hopwood v. State of Texas, 78 F.3d 932 (5th Cir. 1996) cert. Denied, 116 S. Ct. 2581 (1996).

Podberesky v. Kirwan, 38 F.3d 147 (4th Cir. 1994), cert. Denied, 115 S. Ct. 2001 (1995).

Tompkins v. Alabama State University, No. 97-T-471-N (M.D. Ala. File Mar 31,1997) *United States v. Fordice*, 505 U.S. 717 (1992).

The Positive Educational Effects of Racial Diversity on Campus

Mitchell J. Chang

Abstract

This study examined links between racial diversity on college campuses and positive educational outcomes. Data came from the Cooperative Institutional Research Program database, a longitudinal set of student and faculty surveys and research that assessed the impact of college on students. This study used data from a 1985 freshman survey and the 1989 follow-up of the same students. The survey examined demographics, high school experiences, college expectations, values, attitudes, life goals, self-confidence, and career aspirations. The follow-up survey also asked students to reflect on their experiences and perceptions of college. Information on students' SAT scores, ACT scores, and educational attainment and on African American, Asian American, Hispanic, and White undergraduate student enrollment was collected. Several campus climate measures were merged with the data sets. Faculty data were collected from full-time teachers at the same institutions for which student information was available. Faculty discussed how they spent their time and interacted with students, teaching and evaluation methods, perceptions of institutional climate, and sources of stress and satisfaction. Overall, campus diversity had a small but significant positive impact on students' college experiences. Both socializing across racial lines and discussing issues of race were reported as positive educational experiences. (Contains 36 references.)

Perspective

Does attending a college with a racially diverse population significantly enhance students' educational experiences? Does such diversity on campus create a richer environment for learning? These questions lie at the heart of one of the most contentious issues in higher education today: the use of race-conscious affirmative action in admissions.

Critics of affirmative action argue that diversity by itself has no significant educational benefits and is therefore not a legitimate goal. Moreover, the critics charge, race-conscious policies designed to promote diversity have serious negative effects, including lowering academic standards, "polarizing" campuses, and denying educational opportunities to "more deserving" white students—the "reverse discrimination" argument.

Reprinted from *Diversity Challenged: Evidence on the Impact of Affirmative Action*, edited by Gary Orfield, (2001), Harvard Education Publishing Group.

Some recent important judicial and policy decisions on affirmative action have taken note of this controversy. Both the Fifth Circuit Court of Appeals 1996 ruling in *Hopwood v. Texas* and the 1995 decision of the Regents of the University of California to eliminate race-conscious affirmative action were made in part on the grounds that there are no significant educational benefits to having a racially diverse student body.

The arguments on either side of this critically important issue have often been political, ethical, and ideological. Very little empirical research has asked whether there is indeed a direct link between diversity and positive educational outcomes.

This paper represents one attempt to fill that gap. The data analyzed here, though hardly definitive, point unmistakably to the conclusion that campus diversity does indeed have a small but significant positive effect on students' experience of college. Moreover, they offer no support to the arguments of those who say that the results of efforts to promote diversity have been negative.

Research Objectives and Data Sources

Most educators view a diverse student body as an important educational resource, arguing that diversity creates a richer environment for learning (Rudenstine, 1996; Tien, 1996). Students are said to learn most from those who have very different life experiences from theirs (Sleeter & Grant, 1994). Diversity offers the potential, many educators believe, to challenge students and enrich the intellectual dialogue of the college community (Duster, 1993; Moses, 1994). Further, having a racially diverse campus is seen as a powerful way to teach students the realities of the multiracial world they will eventually be living and working in (Astone & Nuñes-Wormack, 1990; Hall, 1981; Tierney, 1993).

Research by Astin (1993b) and Villalpando (1994) found that emphasizing "multiculturalism" through ethnic studies courses, cultural awareness workshops, cross-racial socialization, and discussion of racial issues—to name just a few campus activities—is associated with widespread beneficial effects on a student's academic and personal development, irrespective of the student's race. Their studies, however, did not directly link the level of diversity on campus with these positive effects. The purpose of the study described here was to ask if such a link exists, by measuring the impact of having a racially mixed student population on students' likelihood of socializing with those of different racial or ethnic groups and of discussing issues of race and ethnicity.

This study draws on several major data sources. The primary source of student data is the Cooperative Institutional Research Program (CIRP) database. CIRP is a longitudinal set of very large student and faculty surveys and research, sponsored by the American Council on Education and the Higher Education Research Institute (HERI) at UCLA. The database is designed to assess the impact of college on students, and is generally considered the most comprehensive collection of information on higher education. The CIRP data used in this study included information from two surveys: the 1985 freshman survey and the 1989 follow-up survey of the same college class in their senior year.[1]

The 1985 survey was administered to new college freshmen during orientation programs and in the first few weeks of fall classes. It included information on students' personal and demographic characteristics, high school experiences, and expectations about college, as well as their values, attitudes, life goals, self-confidence, and career aspirations. The survey was completed by 192,453 first-time full-time freshmen at 365 four-year colleges and universities.[2]

Four years later, in the summer and fall of 1989, the follow-up survey was sent to the home addresses of a sample of the 1985 respondents. The 1989 survey repeated the earlier one's questions on values, attitudes, life goals, self-confidence, and career aspirations. It also asked students to reflect on their experiences and perceptions of college. More than 86,000 students were contacted; approximately 30 percent of them responded. The final sample yielded 18,188 students attending 392 four-year colleges and universities. This sample was statistically adjusted for nonresponse and weighted to approximate the national population of students.[3]

Also included in the data set was information on students' SAT and ACT scores, provided by the Educational Testing Service and the American College Testing Program.[4] The 1989 HERI Registrar's Survey provided additional information on which students had earned bachelor's degrees, which were still enrolled in college, and how many years of college each student had completed. These data were linked with the surveys to form a database designed to assess a wide range of student experiences and undergraduate achievements and to provide longitudinal data for studying how different college environments influence student development. Institutional characteristics (size, type, and so on) and undergraduate ethnic enrollments from 1986, both obtained from the data files of the U.S. Department of Education's Integrated Post-Secondary Data System (IPEDS), were merged with student survey data.

The IPEDS enrollment figures for African American, Asian American, Latino, and white undergraduate students were used to create the measure of campus diversity.

Finally, several campus climate measures were developed from responses to the 1989 HERI Faculty Survey and merged with the data sets. The faculty data were collected from full-time teaching personnel at 212 of the same institutions for which longitudinal student data were available. The survey asked faculty members to describe how they spent their time, how they interacted with students, what teaching practices and evaluation methods they used, their perceptions of the institution's climate, and their sources of stress and satisfaction, as well as demographic and biographical questions.[5]

Defining "Racial Diversity"

Although previous research has examined how college students are affected by "racial diversity" (Allen, 1985, 1992; Astin, 1993a; Hsia & Hirano-Nakanishi, 1989; Hurtado, 1992; Pascarella & Terenzini, 1991), there is little consensus on what constitutes a racially diverse student population. Conventional approaches equate color with diversity; that is, the more nonwhites on campus, the more "diverse" the student body. This approach fails to measure heterogeneity, and thus fails to address the educational rationale for maintaining race-conscious admissions practices—namely, that diversity enriches education because students learn most from those who have very different life experiences from their own.

I therefore designed a measure to assess an institution's ability to provide opportunities for all students to interact with others from different racial groups. Percentages of students from different major racial groups were combined to create an overall measure that equates diversity with heterogeneity. The formula, similar to that used for calculating standard deviation, is

$$\sqrt{\frac{(A - m)^2 + (L - m)^2 + (B - m)^2 + (W - m)^2}{4}}$$

where A is the percentage of Asian American students, L is the percentage of Latinos, B is the percentage of blacks, W is the percentage of whites at each particular institution, and m is the mean, or overall average, of A, L, B, and W across all institutions. This formula yields an inverse measure (the greater the differences from the mean, the less diversity), so the reciprocal of this value was used as the index of diversity.

In effect, this variable measures the variance across all four racial and ethnic groups. For example, if the percentages of the four groups were very similar (e.g., 25%, 25%, 30%, and 20%) at a particular institution, it would have a very low standard deviation, and thus a high index of diversity—in this case, 0.28. If, on the other hand, the percentages were widely disparate (e.g., 80%, 5%, 0%, and 15%) it would have a large standard deviation and a low index of diversity—in this case, 0.03. In this way, I attempted to define racial diversity as an institution's ability to offer opportunities for maximizing cross-racial interaction for all students.

Research Design

This study uses the Input-Environment-Outcome (I-E-O) methodological framework developed by Astin (1991) for assessing the impact of college environmental variables on student outcomes. According to Astin, the impact of the environment, in this case racial diversity, on specific student outcomes is best observed after controlling for student characteristics measured at college entrance.

Four characteristics of entering freshmen reflecting their views and goals regarding racial or ethnic issues were selected as measures of their racial orientation and were controlled when examining the effects of racial diversity on student behavior as measured four years later (see Table 1). Two outcome measures were selected from the 1989 follow-up survey to examine the

TABLE 1
Input and Outcome Measures

Freshman Racial Attitudes (From 1985 Freshman Survey)	*Outcome Measures (From 1989 Follow-Up Survey)*
Views[a]	*Frequency with which students*[b]
"Busing is O.K. to achieve racial balance in the schools."	Socialized with persons from different racial/ethnic groups
"Realistically, an individual can do little to bring about changes in society."	Discussed racial/ethnic issues
Importance of Goals[c]	
Helping to promote racial understanding	
Influencing social values	

[a] Coded as a four-point scale: 4 = "Agree strongly" to 1 = "Disagree strongly."
[b] Coded as a three-point scale: 3 = "Frequently" to 1 = "Not at all."
[c] Coded as a four-point scale: 4 = "Essential" to 1 = "Not important."

effects of racial diversity: the frequency with which students socialized with those of different racial or ethnic backgrounds, and the frequency of their having discussions of racial or ethnic issues. Both of these activities have been shown by earlier research to be associated with students' academic and personal development (Astin, 1993b; Villalpando, 1994).

Researchers have long emphasized the importance of controlling student background characteristics when interpreting the impact of the college environment on outcomes (Astin, 1977; Feldman & Newcomb, 1969; Pascarella & Terenzini, 1991). Because the distribution of students across different college environments is never random, a number of student characteristic, college environment, and student involvement measures were selected as additional controls for this study. Socioeconomic status, race, gender, and measures of student ability have been shown to be consistent predictors of a variety of educational outcomes (Astin, 1982; Featherman & Hauser, 1978; Ortiz, 1986; Pascarella & Terenzini, 1991); this study controls for these differences.

In addition, several college characteristics served as controls to help identify how the effects of racial diversity might vary according to campus environment, following the practice of earlier researchers (Astin, 1977, 1991, 1993a; Pascarella & Terenzini, 1991; Weidman, 1989). These included variables considered important for understanding racial climates on campus: institutional size, location, type, religious affiliation, gender (coed or single-sex), and selectivity. Other measures of peer-group characteristics and faculty environment that have been shown to be important in determining educational outcomes (Astin, 1993a; Astin & Chang, 1995; Hurtado, 1990; Pascarella & Terenzini, 1991) were also included for analysis.

Lastly, a set of variables that measured students' direct involvement and experiences with their institutions was selected from the 1989 follow-up survey. These items were designed to examine variations in students' experiences within individual campuses, and included activities such as enrolling in an ethnic studies course, attending a racial or cultural awareness workshop, being a member of a fraternity or sorority, working full-time while attending college, taking part in intercollegiate or intramural sports, being elected to student government, participating in campus protests or demonstrations, working on a group project for a class, and so on. These particular measures were chosen because they are known to affect some of the outcomes used in this study (Astin, 1977, 1993a; Hurtado, 1990) and are believed to "mediate" the effects of racial diversity (Astin, 1993b).

Analysis and Findings

The various measures of students' initial attitudes and outcomes were combined with all of the control variables in a statistical analysis designed to isolate the effects of racial diversity on the two specified outcomes—the development of interracial friendships and the frequency of discussing racial issues. This analysis was done in relation to 11 student background characteristics, 2) the campus racial diversity measure, 3) other campus characteristics, and 4) intermediate outcomes. Because this model

TABLE 2
Student Socialization and Discussion of Racial Issues as a Function of Campus Diversity

Student Outcomes	*Racial Diversity*			
	Simple r	*B1*	*B2*	*B3*
Socialized with someone of a different race	.16***	.11***	.12**	.12**
Discussed racial issues	.08***	.05***	.04**	.02*

B1 represents the standardized regression coefficient after controlling for student background characteristics.
B2 represents the standardized regression coefficient after controlling for institutional, peer, and faculty characteristics.
B3 represents the final standardized regression coefficient.
*$p < .014$,
**$p < .001$,
***$p < .0005$.

requires a temporal arrangement of variables, college experiences were treated as intermediate outcomes; that is, they occurred after the student's initial exposure to the college environment but while the student was still in college. Variables were entered in the above four-stage sequence to observe changes in regression coefficients. To determine if the effects of racial diversity made a unique contribution, beyond the effects of other variables, Beta coefficients for the racial diversity measure were observed after controlling for student background and college environment, and again after controlling for intermediate outcomes.

The simple statistical correlations for the racial diversity measure and the two outcomes are .16 and .08 (see Table 2). The last three columns in Table 2 show the corresponding correlations after controlling for student background, college environment, and college experiences. The results show that multiracial diversity is a significant, though not strong, positive predictor of students' likelihood of forming interracial friendships and talking about race and ethnicity, even after students' background and campus environment are taken into account.

One could argue that participating in these two outcome activities is in itself a positive experience. More important, however, is that these experiences have been shown to be associated with beneficial effects on students' academic and personal development, regardless of their race (Astin, 1993b; Villalpando, 1994). To verify these effects, additional analyses were conducted on four educational outcomes: retention, satisfaction with college, intellectual self-confidence, and social self-confidence. These outcomes resemble the measures most often used in "racial diversity" studies (Astin, 1993a, 1993b; Hurtado, 1990). Moreover, these outcome measures have corresponding pretest measures that were selected from the 1985 freshman survey (see Table 3).

This further analysis shows that socializing with someone of another racial group is positively related to all four educational outcomes, and that these relationships remained significant even after institutional, peer, and faculty variables were controlled (see Table 4).

But when the effects of other intermediate outcomes were controlled, only the effects on satisfaction with college and social self-confidence remained significant.[6] Thus, socializing with someone of another race appears to have direct effects on two of these educational outcomes, and indirect effects on the other two. Likewise, the experience of talking about racial issues shows significant positive effects on all four outcomes, even after controlling for student background and college environment. When intermediate outcomes were controlled, however, only one of these outcomes, intellectual self-confidence, remained significant.[7]

In sum, these findings strongly suggest that both socializing across racial lines and discussing issues of race are positive educational experiences. Because racial diversity on campus increases the likelihood of students' having these experiences, I conclude that diversity has educational benefits in college.

Implications for Policymakers

Attending college with those of other races and ethnicities increases the likelihood that students will socialize across racial lines and talk about racial matters. The more diverse the student body, the more likely that these activities will take place. In turn, these activities have a positive impact on student retention, overall college satisfaction, and intellectual and social self-confidence among all students. Though racial diversity alone does not appear to directly affect every one of these educational outcomes, it very likely affects all of them indirectly.

The statistical correlations found in this study are relatively small, but they are significant—not

TABLE 3
Educational Outcome Measures

Outcome Measures (1989 Follow-Up Survey)	*Pretests (1985 Freshman Survey)*
Self-Concept	
Academic Self-Concept[a]	Academic Self-Concept
Self-Rating: "intellectual self-confidence"	Identical Self-Rating
Social Self-Concept[a]	Social Self-Concept
Self-Rating: "social self-confidence"	Identical Self-Rating
Retention	
Student Persistence:	Students' best guess as to the chances they will:[c]
Earned a bachelor's degree or above	Drop out temporarily
Student did not withdraw, transfer, or take a leave of absence	Earn a BA
College Satisfaction	
Overall college satisfaction rating[b]	Students' best guess as to the chances they will be satisfied with college[c]

[a]Coded as a 5-point scale: 5 = Highest 10% to 1 = Lowest 10%.
[b]Coded as a 4-point scale: 4 = Very Satisfied to 1 = Dissatisfied.
[c]Coded as a 4-point scale: 4 = Very Good Chance to 1 = No Chance.

TABLE 4
Educational Outcomes as a Function of Students' Experiences

	Socialize				*Discuss*			
Student Outcome	*Simple r*	*B1*	*B2*	*B3*	*Simple r*	*B1*	*B2*	*B3*
Retention	.06*	.04*	.04*	.00	.07*	.04*	.03*	.00
Satisfaction with College	.10*	.09*	.08*	.05*	.11*	.07*	.05*	.00
Intellectual Self-Concept	.08*	.03*	.03*	.01	.10*	.06*	.06*	.05*
Social Self-Concept	.10*	.07*	.06*	.04*	.09*	.05*	.04*	.02

B1 represents the standardized regression coefficient after controlling for student background characteristics.
B2 represents the standardized regression coefficient after controlling for institutional, peer, and faculty characteristics.
B3 represents the final standardized regression coefficient.
*$p < .0005$.

simply in the mathematical sense but also because they exist at all. Critics of affirmative action in college admissions maintain that diversity has no benefit in itself and that efforts to promote it are counterproductive of positive race relations. This study suggests that these critics are wrong, that campuses where diversity has flourished, largely through the impact of affirmative action, confer significant educational benefits on their students.

Given what we know about the racial climate on U.S. campuses and the corrosive forces in society at large that impede dialogue and understanding, even a small positive impact may be extremely important. The modest benefits we see in this study could perhaps be much larger if policymakers choose to move the clock forward instead of turning it back.

Notes

1. The sample used in this study did not include historically black institutions because the controversy over affirmative action in admissions has ignored these institutions (Hacker, 1992). This is not surprising, as their mission, clientele, and history vastly differ from those of predominantly white institutions (Allen, 1987, 1992; Davis, 1991; Fleming, 1984; Jackson & Swan, 1991; Nettles, 1991; Willie, 1981). Because this study sought to inform the use of affirmative action, it was reasonable to limit the sample in this way. Likewise, this study

did not include community colleges because the sample size for that group was too small.

2. See Astin, Green, Korn, and Shalit (1985) for a copy of the survey and a complete description of the sampling procedure.
3. See Higher Education Research Institute (1991) for a copy of the survey and a complete description of the sampling and weighting procedures.
4. ACT scores were converted into equivalent SAT scores by HERI.
5. For detailed information on the Faculty Survey (implementation, sampling, and weighting) see Astin, Korn, and Dey (1990).
6. It is difficult to interpret whether socializing with someone of another racial or ethnic group has a "direct" effect on retention and intellectual self-concept because this particular experience is also an intermediate outcome and a temporal arrangement among intermediate outcomes cannot be established.
7. The same problem described in the preceding footnote applies here.

References

Allen, W. R. (1985). Black student, while campus: Structural, interpersonal, and psychological correlates of success. *Journal of Negro Education, 54,* 134–137.

Allen, W. R. (1987). Black colleges vs. white colleges: The fork in the road for black students. *Change, 19,* 28–34.

Allen, W. R. (1992). The color of success: African American college student outcomes all predominantly white and historically black public colleges and universities. *Harvard Educational Review, 62,* 26–44.

Astin, A. W. (1977). *Four critical years.* San Francisco: Jossey-Bass.

Astin, A. W. (1982). *Minorities in American higher education.* New York: Macmillan.

Astin, A. W. (1991). *Assessment for excellence: The philosophy and practice of assessment and evaluation in higher education.* New York: Macmillan.

Astin, A. W. (1993a). *What matters in college: Four critical years revisited.* San Francisco: Jossey-Bass.

Astin, A. W. (1993b). Diversity and multiculturalism on the campus: How are students affected? *Change, 23,* 44–49.

Astin, A. W., & Chang, M. J. (1995). Colleges that emphasize research and teaching: Can you have your cake and eat it too? *Change, 27*(5), 44–49.

Astin, A. W., Green, K. C., Korn, W. S., & Schalit, M. (1985). *The American freshman: National norms for 1985.* Los Angeles: UCLA, Higher Education Research Institute.

Astin, A. W., Korn, W. S., & Dey, E. L. (1990). *The American college teacher: National means for the 1989–90 HERI Faculty Survey.* Los Angeles: UCLA. Higher Education Research Institute.

Astone, B., & Nuñez-Wormack, E. (1990). *Pursuing diversity: Recruiting college minority students.* Washington, DC: George Washington University, School of Education and Human Development.

Chang, M. J. (1999). Does racial diversity matter? The educational impact of a racially diverse undergraduate population. *Journal of College Student Development, 40,* 377–395.

Davis, R. B. (1991). Social support networks and undergraduate student academic-success-related outcomes: A comparison of black students on black and white campuses. In W. R. Allen, E. G. Epps, & N. Z. Haniff (Eds.), *College in black and white* (pp. 143–157). Albany: State University of New York Press.

Duster, T. (1993). The diversity of California at Berkeley: An emerging reformulation of "competence" in an increasingly multicultural world. In B. W. Thompson & S. Tyagi (Eds.), *Beyond a dream deferred: Multicultural education and the politics of excellence.* Minneapolis: University of Minnesota Press.

Featherman, D., & Hauser, R. (1978). *Opportunity and change.* New York: Academic Press.

Feldman, K. A., & Newcomb, T. M. (1969). *The impact of college on students* (vol. 1). San Francisco: Jossey-Bass.

Fleming, J. (1984). *Blacks in college: A comparative study of students' success in black and in white institutions.* San Francisco: Jossey-Bass.

Hacker, A. (1992). *Two nations: Black and white, separate, hostile, unequal.* New York: Ballantine Books.

Hall, S. (1981). Teaching race. In A. James & R. Jeffcoate (Eds.), *The school in the multicultural society* (pp. 58–69). London: Harper.

Higher Education Research Institute. (1991). *The American college student, 1989: National norms for 1985 and 1987 college freshmen.* Los Angeles: Author.

Hsia, J., & Hirano-Nakanishi, M. (1989). The demographics of diversity: Asian Americans and higher education. *Change, 21,* 20–27.

Hurtado, S. (1990). *Campus racial climates and educational outcomes.* Doctoral dissertation, University of California, Los Angeles. Ann Arbor: University Microfilms International, No. 9111328.

Hurtado, S. (1992). Campus racial climates: Contexts of conflict. *Journal of Higher Education, 63,* 539–569.

Jackson, K. W., & Swan, A. L. (1991). Institutional and individual factors affecting black undergraduate student performance: Campus race and student gender. In W. R. Allen, F. G. Epps, & N. Z. Haniff

(Eds.). *College in black and white* (pp. 127–141). Albany: State University of New York Press.

Moses, Y. T. (1994). Quality, excellence, and diversity. In D. C. Smith, L. L., Woll, & J. Levitan (Eds.), *Studying diversity in higher education.* San Francisco: Jossey-Bass.

Nettles, M. T. (1991). Racial similarities and differences in the predictors of college student achievement. In W. R. Allen, E. G. Epps, & N. Z. Haniff (Eds.), *College in black and white* (pp. 175–191). Albany: State University of New York Press.

Ortiz, V. (1986). Generational status, family background and educational attainment among Hispanic youth and non-Hispanic white youth. In M. A. Olivas (Ed.), *Latino college students.* New York: Teachers College Press.

Pascarella, E. T., & Terenzini, P. T. (1991). *How college affects students.* San Francisco: Jossey-Bass.

Rudenstine, N. L., (1996, March/April). The uses of diversity. *Harvard Magazine,* 48–62.

Sleeter, C. E., & Grant, C. A. (1994). *Making choices for multicultural education: Five approaches to race, class, and gender*. New York: Maxwell Macmillan.

Tien, C. (1996). *Racial preferences? Promoting diversity in higher education: Perspectives on affirmative action and its impact on Asian Pacific Americans.* Los Angeles: LEAP Asian Pacific American Public Policy Institute.

Tierney, W. G. (1993). *Building communities of difference: Higher education in the twenty-first century.* Westport, CT: Bergin & Garvey.

Villalpando, O. (1994). *Comparing the effects of multiculturalism and diversity on minority and white students' satisfaction with college.* Paper presented at the annual meeting of the Association for the Study of Higher Education, Tucson, AZ.

Weidman, J. (1989). Undergraduate socialization: A conceptual approach. In J. Smart (Ed.), *Higher education: Handbook of theory and research.* New York: Agathon Press.

Willie, C. V. (1981). *The ivory and ebony towers.* Lexington, MA: Lexington Books, D. C. Heath.

Human Diversity and Equitable Assessment

Edmund W. Gordon

Yale University and The College Board

The topic of human diversity and its implications for assessment is extremely complex. In this chapter, I will address just four of the major issues arising in this contentious domain. The first issue concerns the relationship between assessment and pedagogy itself. The second issue has to do with the implications of assessment that grow out of an assertion that the problems of diversity are probably not primarily problems for assessment but problems for education. Third, I will discuss the complexities of diversity as distinct from pluralism, both of which have implications for education and assessment. Finally, I explore some notions of how educational assessment can be made more sensitive and more appropriate for persons from diverse cultural backgrounds.

Problems of Assessment or of Pedagogy

With respect to the first issue, I argue that the most fundamental problem concerning human diversity and equity in educational assessment has to do with the effectiveness, sufficiency, and adequacy of teaching and learning. When teaching and learning are sufficient, when they are truly effective, most of the problems posed for equitable assessment as a function of diverse human characteristics become manageable. The problems are not eliminated but they at least become manageable when the educational work on the front end is appropriate. Unfortunately, it often is not. It is when teaching and learning are insufficiently effective for the universe of students served that problems arise in the pursuit of equity for diverse human populations. It can be argued that the problems of equity in educational assessment are largely secondary to the failure to achieve equity through educational treatments. However, the fact that equitable educational assessment is only secondarily a problem of assessment does not mean that those of us in the assessment enterprise have no responsibility for doing something constructive.

It is not by accident that existing approaches to standardized assessment of educational achievement are insufficiently sensitive to the diversity of the student population served as well as to pluralism and the social demands placed upon students—shortly, I will clarify what I mean by pluralism. Prevailing standards by which academic competence is judged are calibrated in large measure against either what most people at a specific level of development are considered able to do or what we agree is necessary in order for students to engage effectively in the demands of the next level of work. The fact that some persons have greater difficulty than others and seem unable to achieve these standards is usually thought to be a problem in the individual or reflective of group differences in abilities. It is not often thought to be a problem of the appropriateness

Reprinted from *Assessment in Higher Education: Issues of Access, Quality, Student Development and Public Policy,* edited by Samuel J. Messick, (1999), by permission of Lawrence Erlbaum Associates, Inc.

of the assessment instruments or of educational practices.

In our efforts to be responsive to diverse learning characteristics and plural social standards, prevailing wisdom suggests that there may be limits to what can be done to design and develop sensitive assessment technology and procedures. We may be able to make the assessment processes more instructive; we may make them more supportive of diverse learning experiences; we may find more varied contexts and vehicles through which students can demonstrate their competencies; the items can be made more process sensitive and could give less emphasis to narrowly defined products. But in the final analysis, any assessment procedure is most likely to reveal the effectiveness of the teaching and learning to which students have been exposed. Thus the facts of diversity and pluralism may have more serious implications for teaching and learning than for equitable educational assessment technology and practice.

Previously, I asserted that this does not mean that those of us in the assessment community are off the hook. What I think it does mean is that both the teaching and learning end and the assessment end need to give greater attention to better understanding of the complexities of human diversity.

Complexities of Diversity and Pluralism

When I speak of diversity of human characteristics, I am generally referring to the different positions people hold in this society, differences in status as well as differences in function. In both education and assessment if we do not distinguish between status characteristics and functional characteristics, we are likely not to make much progress.

Status defines one's position in the social hierarchy and that status, that position, often determines one's access to the resources of the society, to the economic and political power structures. Status influences access to opportunity and access to rewards. It influences how other people treat you, what other people may expect of you, and often what one expects from one's self. Traditionally, differential status has been assigned on the basis of social class or caste, of ethnicity or race, of gender, even of language and national origin. There is a host of so-called social dividers by which we define status.

In contrast, diversity in functional characteristics refers to the *hows* of behavior, to the ways in which behavior is manifested, the ways in which people act. These functional characteristics may be locally associated with certain status groups, but the manner of behavior is not associated with status. We include as functional characteristics such traits as cognitive styles, interests, and identity. With each of these functional characteristics—remembering now that they define the how of behavior, the way people behave—we think more and more that they reflect the way persons engage learning experiences and the way people engage the environments to which they are exposed.

In the past year or so, I have been thinking that this may be too narrow a view of either functional or status characteristics. It may be that the most crucial aspect of the categories into which one falls is its contribution to the way one feels about oneself. Cultural identity may be more important than culture itself. In the modern world there is so much overlap in the manifestations of culture that if we were to focus only on cultural practices, only on the external facts of culture, we would have a hard time explaining how it is that Ed Gordon, who is exposed to so much of what is the mainstream culture of the United States, still acts like an African American, functions like an African American, and most important thinks of himself as an African American. What is important here is Ed Gordon's identification of self with that symbolic culture we call African American. Even when one deconstructs the culture itself, it has elements of many other cultures. Now this point may be made for all of the functional characteristics, that the differences between groups with respect to these functional characteristics are less important than the differences within groups. What may be most important is the contribution that the point of reference—the culture or the group—makes to the way the person identifies the self.

In order to clarify some of their implications for assessment and education, diversity of status and function needs to be distinguished from pluralism. In many of our writings we tend to use pluralism and diversity interchangeably as if they were synonymous. However, pluralism refers to the social demand of demonstrating multiple concurrent competencies in situationally relevant contexts. We recognize pluralistic demands most readily with respect to different cultures and languages. Those of us who are bilingual or multilingual have clear advantages over those of us who are monolingual. Similarly, those of us who can make ourselves at home in more than a single culture have advantages over those who can function in only one culture. I take great pride in being able to go back to North Carolina and be at home with my colleagues there or to come to Princeton or to City College and be at home with my colleagues there. If the context of the settings in which I am called upon to express my competencies qualitatively affects their expression, then this is tantamount to the development of pluralistic competencies. The requirement that all of us are being called upon to develop pluralistic competencies in a diverse world and a diverse society presents problems for us in what to teach and what to assess.

Let us turn next to the questions of equity and equality, which I contend often get confused. Much of our legal approach to democracy has been based upon ensuring that people are treated equally. However, when we come to human services, particularly education and health, equal treatment may actually be dysfunctional for some folks. What one needs is equitable treatment, that is, treatment that is appropriate to the characteristic and sufficient to the need. When we begin to talk about the issues of diversity and of pluralism in the context of equity, I am simply contending that equity in these terms requires considerably more attention, first, so we can better understand it and, second, so that this understanding can inform what we do about inequity.

Because the issues concerning diversity and pluralism are far more complex than is often reflected in public debates, it may be useful to identify some of the possible ways in which a concern for population diversity and pluralistic outcomes impacts upon teaching, learning, and assessment. It is becoming more and more obvious that these sources of variance influence student motivation to engage in academic learning and to master its content. Recent research shows that some African American students are unwilling to engage in appropriate academic activity because they view those activities as identified with another group (Fordham & Ogbu, 1986). Furthermore, it is dysfunctional in their primary social interactions to exhibit behaviors that set them apart from their group rather than place them within the group. In my own work with Thomas and Allen where we are trying to help young citizens improve their cognitive skills and strategies, we found that many of these students actually have relevant strategies (Gordon, Allen, & Armour-Thomas, 1988). The students used them appropriately in a different context but were unwilling to use them in the academic context. Hence, the primary problem is not one of cognitive deficiency but the absence of a disposition to use particular kinds of cognitive skills in particular kinds of situations.

My oldest son, who is an anthropologist, talks about the possibility that much of the behavior we see in young Black males that we call dysfunctional or antisocial is actually resistant behavior. If the society is going to do something productive with these young people, we have to find ways to turn their resistant behavior into socially productive activities rather than try to control or contain the resistant behavior itself.

As a consequence, the ways in which I identify myself, the ways in which I perceive my status and my functional relationships with society, influence the way in which I engage in the learning opportunities of that society. Parenthetically, they probably also influence the ways in which I engage in assessment experiences. Not only do cultural identities influence the ways in which things are acquired but also the ways in which things are played out in day-to-day behavior as well as in assessment functions.

Toward More Equitable Assessment

Many years ago, actually it was in the 1950s, I had the good fortune to work with a German woman who had come to this country just about the time of the rise of Hitler. Her name was Elsa. Elsa was a gentile but she did not want to be part of a society gearing itself up to treat Jews and Gypsies and other so-called undesirable folk the way Germany was treating them at that particular moment. And if I can digress formally at my age, I take advantage of this opportunity to express my politics. It is troubling to me that we see beyond the horizon in this country some of the same mean spirit that one saw in Germany in 1929, 1930, and 1931, namely, efforts to divide people in terms of their group characteristics, some as desirable versus others as undesirable and, more seriously, some as superior versus others as inferior. Worse still, there is a strong tendency to view these group differences as God-given and genetically determined. These beliefs led to the destruction of German society, and many of us have been troubled by Herrnstein and Murray's (1994) treatment of these issues for similar reasons. But, many of us are almost as troubled by the concerted rush to reject these ideas because in the process of doing so we also gave undue prominence to that point of view.

Unfortunately, the nation seems to be ready for this kind of minority-group baiting because we seem to be increasingly fearful of the sufficiency of our material resources to serve all of us adequately, so some of us are to be set apart. Elsa saw this happening in Germany, but she was not politically assertive enough to fight it there. However, she did say that she would not stay in Germany and be a part of it. But Elsa's great contribution was not political but rather her scientific work in trying to assess educational potential in neurologically impaired children. She went to great lengths to construct alternative procedures for doing so. But the piece of her message that I want to stress as we move into a discussion of what can be done to make assessment more responsive to diverse human characteristics is her argument that any serious changes one might wish to make in assessment procedures need to be preceded by a change in our perception of the purpose of assessment.

Elsa saw the traditional purposes of assessment as being focussed primarily, almost exclusively, on classification and prediction. She argued that what we really need in assessment is better description and understanding as a basis for prescribing and intervening. It seems clear that Elsa's message is more appropriate for lower levels of education than for higher education and more appropriate for youngsters with serious disabilities than for those in the normal range. However, there are messages in her work that can be applied to higher education and to a wide range of diverse individuals because, in her view, the assessment experience should result in the examinees having more and better understanding of how they function and of how they can use the assessment information for subsequent learning and development.

What can be done to improve assessment? It must be 20 or 25 years ago now that Sam Messick and I put together a little proposal (that was never funded) to unbundle standardized test data in an effort to identify task demands and associated cognitive processes contributing to the total score. We wanted to isolate clusters of items with common task requirements so that subscores could be constructed at the process level. We hoped to better understand the construct-relevant sources of task difficulty in relation to the ways in which examinees engage or fail to engage relevant cognitive processes, so that we could provide richer score interpretations for informing instruction. Although our study died aborning, recent work by Snow and his colleagues has pursued similar aims in a much more sophisticated fashion, using rich data sets and detailed multivariate analyses (Hamilton, Nussbaum, Kupermintz, Kerkhoven, & Snow, 1995; Kupermintz, Ennis, Hamilton, Talbert, & Snow, 1995).

In the past few years we have seen the emergence of what has been called portfolio assessment, which aims to collect a wide array of qualitative and quantitative information about students in an effort to improve understanding of the person being assessed. Portfolios afford an opportunity for students to present themselves in a variety of ways, even in ways that offer the best picture of the self. Another vehicle is to embed assessment in the curriculum itself or to embed teaching and learning experiences within assessment procedures. However, some of us worry that the assessment tail could wag the instructional dog. We become cautious when assessment is used for instructional as well as for evaluative purposes.

To dispel some of these concerns and to provide some concrete suggestions as to how to make assessment more responsive to human diversity, I next present seven assessment/educational interventions. These seven suggestions are not offered as firm recommendations but rather are in the spirit of needed research and development. The first suggestion is to radically increase the teaching, learning, and assessment experiences, to increase the diversity of the kinds of learning and assessment tasks available as well as diversity in the contexts and demands of learning and assessment. This particular suggestion stems from considerations outlined in earlier sections of this chapter that what we have to build into the assessment experience is a much wider opportunity for choice in ways in which students can demonstrate what they know and do not know.

Incidentally, I recognize that there are problems in systematizing evaluative judgments based on individualized choice of tasks, whether by students or by teachers. This issue of systematization or standardization takes me back to one of Elsa's abiding concerns. Elsa went into retirement and ultimately to her death complaining that she was never able to standardize her assessment procedures. Some of us thought that if her procedures had been standardized, this would have defeated her purpose. It may very well be, as we think about our other research and development suggestions, that if we give too much attention to how we standardize scores now, to how we calibrate them systematically to make comparable judgments across persons and circumstances, it may be counterproductive to the purposes behind assessment responsive to human diversity.

The first of these suggestions was for far greater diversity in the opportunities to learn and to express one's learning in test situations. The second has to do with increased flexibility in the timing of assessments, which was examined by Bennett in Chapter 14.

The third suggestion has to do with recognizing and enhancing the multiplicity of perspectives to which students are exposed in their learning as well as the perspectives from which they are encouraged to express themselves in their assessments. What we see is influenced by the frame of reference or perspective we bring to the stimulus field. When I am exposed to a phenomenon or come to any experience, I see through eyes that have been shaped by a particular background and by particular experiences. If what is being looked for by the person who is assessing or what is being offered by the person who is teaching does not take my perspective into account, my responses and constructions may be misinterpreted. Insensitivity to student perspectives presents problems for us because it is not just that multiple perspectives represent alternative viewpoints, some of them right and some of them wrong. The question of how one selects from a variety of perspectives and makes judgments is one of the research issues that needs to be pursued. I am convinced that at both the instructional level and the assessment level if one is insensitive to student perspectives the interpretation of assessment data will be off-target, distorted, or otherwise invalid. Furthermore, a way of seeing is also a way of not seeing in our assessment and teaching. We have to be much more sensitive to differences in perspective and recognize that these differences are influenced by the cultural backgrounds from which people come.

The fourth suggestion is a proposal to sample from noncanonical as well as canonical voices, knowledge, and techniques. The key question is what is appropriate to the canon in the context of cultural diversity? As we hear new voices in different cultures, their automatic inclusion in the canon is almost as bad as their exclusion. If one is confronted with bad literature from Asian culture or African culture, say, it does not do justice to students from those cultures by accommodating them with the inclusion of bad literature in teaching or assessment. Rather, it is patronizing them. One of the practical problems here is not being sufficiently familiar with these new and diverse voices in literature in general so as to select appropriately a representative teaching or assessment package. Selections from noncanonical sources need to be made with the same care and attention that we give to the more familiar canonical selections.

The fifth suggestion has to do with allowing student self-selected choice as opposed to teacher- or examiner-determined options for demonstrating what is known. The introduction of widespread student choice into assessment presents problems because there is some evidence that students, the people being tested, are not often the best judges of what they ought to be tested on or of the best way of presenting themselves. Hence, we need to do more research not only on the effects of self-selected choice in learning and assessment, but also on how to help students make better decisions about what they need as well as what they want and about how to put their best foot forward. If we go back to my work with Armour-Thomas and Allen (Gordon, Allen, & Armour-Thomas, 1988) on cognitive modifiability, what we began to recognize was that when the target students were able to identify what we were talking about in a context familiar to them, when they were able to use their own experience base, they understood the concepts. But when we presented material in the academic language and academic context, they did not. This finding implies that we should provide choices in learning and assessment that are compatible with the students' own experiences.

As a sixth point, we need to provide opportunities for both individual and cooperative learning as well as cooperative performance opportunities. In Lauren Resnick's (1987) article on learning in and out of school, she reminds us of how in school settings and formal assessment settings, we do not want people to cooperate with each other. Yet on entering the world of work, if you cannot cooperate with others you are lost.

The final suggestion is for student design of tests to cover learner- or examinee-generated knowledge. If you are trying to learn what I know about chemistry, biology, English, or the social sciences, why not give me the opportunity to define the domain of knowledge I think I am an expert in? Some years ago out at the Rand Corporation they were experimenting with approaches to computer-based instruction. One of the lines of investigation being pursued was self-designed tests whereby an examinee constructed his or her own assessment from a pool of items and assessment situations. Letting students define the boundaries of their knowledge and understanding in a subject area may be the best way of assessing their knowledge structures.

Having laid out this program of research-and-development to make assessment more responsive to human diversity, I must remind us of the point at which we began: Unless persons have had adequate educational and social opportunities to learn and develop, whatever we do in assessment is not going to help very much.

References

Fordham, S., & Ogbu, J. U. (1986). Black students' school success: Coping with the "burden of 'acting white'." *Urban Review, 18,* 176–206.

Gordon, E. W., Allen, B. A., & Armour-Thomas, E. (1988). *The development and enhancement of cognitive competence of educationally disadvantaged high school students.* A Report to the Exxon Foundation.

Hamilton, L. S., Nussbaum, E. M., Kupermintz, H., Kerkhoven, J. I. M., & Snow, R. E. (1995). Enhancing the validity and usefulness of large-scale educational assessments: II. NELS:88 science achievement. *American Educational Research Journal, 32,* 555–581.

Herrnstein, R., & Murray, C. (1994). *The Bell Curve: Intelligence and Class Structure in American Life.* New York: Free Press.

Kupermintz, H., Ennis, M. E., Hamilton, L. S., Talbert, J. E., & Snow, R. E. (1995). Enhancing the validity and usefulness of large-scale educational assessments: I. NELS:88 mathematics achievement. *American Educational Research Journal, 32,* 525–554.

Resnick, Lauren B. (1987). Learning in school and out. *Educational Researcher, 16*(9), 13–20.

UNDERSTANDING THE RETENTION OF LATINO COLLEGE STUDENTS

JOHN C. HERNANDEZ

In this qualitative study, the researcher explored the retention of 10 Latino college students, particularly how their experiences and environmental factors contributed to their persistence. The participants ranged in age from 21 to 25 years and included 5 men and 5 women. The findings include 11 major categories or themes. Implications for practice are discussed.

Given the increasing presence of Latinos in the general population and in higher education, the recruitment, retention, and academic performance of Latino college students is a critical issue for research (Mayo, Murguia, & Padilla, 1995). Latinos were one of the nation's fastest-growing populations. According to the latest U.S. Census, Latinos are 8.2% of the total population in the United States (U.S. Department of Commerce, Bureau of the Census, 1991), and demographic projections report that Latinos will become the largest minority group by 2005 ("Facts on Hispanic Higher Education," 2000).

However, in spite of an overall growth in the general population, Latinos continue to be highly underrepresented on the nation's college campuses (Collison, 1999). Data on retention and degree completion rates indicate that most colleges and universities are not succeeding in retaining Latino students (O'Brien, 1993); the author further indicates that "Latino students were the least likely of all racial/ethnic groups to persist in college" (p. 7).

The study of student retention and attrition has become a major concern in higher education, leading to the development of several theories and models that attempt to explain the process of college persistence (Astin, 1984; Bean, 1980; Tinto, 1975, 1987, 1993; Tracey & Sedlacek, 1984, 1987). However, "our understanding of Hispanic college students is not significantly increased by the available student literature" (Olivas, 1986, p. 4).

Research is needed that focuses on the persistence of Latino college students. Only since the mid-1970s have scholars begun to test retention theories and models on various underrepresented groups. Another problematic issue is that previous theories and research studies have treated students as the "problem" to be fixed (Viernes-Turner, 1996); many scholars have considered retention-related issues from the perspective of student failure (Abi-Nader, 1990; Padilla, Trevino, Gonzalez, & Trevino, 1997). Focusing exclusively on failure misses what might be understood were researchers to focus on those students who have overcome barriers and who have sustained their enrollment (Arellano & Padilla, 1996). In more recent years researchers have begun to examine the nature of ethnic minority student experiences from the perspective of the student (Viernes-Turner, 1996).

Reprinted from *Journal of College Student Development 41*, no. 6 (November–December 2000).

Qualitative research methods are remarkably well adapted to explore and understand retention-related issues. Lincoln and Guba (1985) identified qualitative methods as more suitable in dealing with multiple realities because they are keener to the many mutually formed influences that a researcher may encounter. Qualitative research can provide a thick description of the "how?" "why?" and, "in what ways?" type of questions that quantitative studies often cannot address. Additionally, Attinasi and Nora (1992) have suggested that structured survey instruments are unable to adequately capture the complex cultural concepts of our diverse student population.

In this study, the researcher sought to explore and gain a deeper understanding of the retention of Latino college students and the meaning they made of their sustained enrollment. The researcher attempted to capture the experience of students who had graduated or were approaching graduation from college to understand better the factors that facilitated their success. The approach to study this phenomenon from the perspective of successful students is in line with a growing number of researchers who are examining the issue of student retention from the perspective of students who persist (Padilla et al., 1997). A naturalistic or constructivist framework (Lincoln & Cuba, 1985) was selected to capture the multiple voices of Latino students within the context of the college environment. Several research questions guided this study although they did not bind it. The following research questions served to guide and inform this study:

1. What are the factors that influenced the retention and graduation of Latino college students?
2. In what ways, if any, did the environment influence the experience and ultimately the retention of Latino college students?
3. What meaning did students give to these factors? How was this meaning used in their decision to persist in college?

Method

The primary method for data collection was a series of in-depth interviews conducted during the Spring 1998 semester at a large public mid-Atlantic research university. The presence of Latino students at this predominantly White institution is a relatively new development. As recently as 1975, Latinos represented only 0.9% of the undergraduate enrollment. By Fall of 1997, the undergraduate enrollment of Latinos increased to 4.6%.

Participants

Among the 10 students who participated, 5 were men and 5 were women; their ages varied between 21 and 25 years. Six of the participants were born in the United States; the remaining 4 were born in El Salvador, Puerto Rico, Colombia, and Peru. Four of the participants were recent graduates and 6 were seniors scheduled to graduate at the end of the semester in which the study was undertaken. Seven of the participants entered the university as freshmen, and 3 transferred from local community colleges. They were balanced in their choice of majors: 4 in the college of arts and humanities; 3 in the college of business management; 3 in the college of behavioral and social sciences; 2 in the college of engineering; and 1 in the college of life sciences (3 of the participants double majored). Seven of the 10 participants had at one point lived in an on-campus residence facility.

When asked about their father's educational level, 3 participants indicated completion through elementary school, 1 had completed high school, 2 had some college, and 4 had a university degree. The participants' mother's educational level was very similar: 3 indicated completion through elementary school, 3 had completed high school, and 4 had a university degree. Seven participants reported that Spanish was the primary language spoken in their home, 2 reported both English and Spanish as primary languages, and 1 reported English as the primary language spoken at home. Four of the participants described their family's socioeconomic level as "low to medium," and 6 described theirs as "medium to high."

Procedure

Maximum variation sampling was used to select participants who had diverse backgrounds and experiences to "more thoroughly describe the variation in the group and to understand variations in experiences while also investigating core elements and shared outcomes" (Patton, 1990, p. 172).

Prospective participants were identified in several ways. First, the researcher obtained a list of graduating Latino students from the registrar's office; 52 prospective participants were randomly selected from this list and a letter of invitation was mailed to these students. Secondly, the researcher solicited referrals from students by making an announcement and extending an invitation at a meeting of the Latino student union. Finally, faculty and staff were invited to make referrals; this call for referrals was relayed through E-mail to selected university personnel and through the listserv of the Hispanic faculty, staff, and graduate student association. Once initial contact was established with interested respondents, consent to participate in the study was negotiated.

A three-phase interview process (Lincoln & Guba, 1985), which included significant overlaps, was the primary method of data collection. All interviews were tape-recorded; each interview lasted between 60 and 90 minutes. Participants were interviewed in a closed and quiet room on campus to ensure confidentiality and minimal interruptions. Interviews began in January 1998 and continued through April 1998.

Prior to the initial planning stage, a focus group was conducted to pilot the set of questions for Phase 1 of the interviews. The students who participated in the focus group were representative of the sample the researcher proposed to interview. Additionally, the students who participated in the focus group were instrumental in providing input on the clarity of questions, and in assessing the effectiveness of the questions to draw out general information.

Interviews

Phase 1: Orientation and Overview

During the orientation and overview phase (Lincoln & Guba, 1985) the initial approach was to obtain general information that would result in a basic knowledge of what is important for detailed follow-up. A set of open-ended questions were asked during Phase 1 of the interviews (Appendix A). These questions served to obtain general information about the participants while allowing for the establishment of trust and rapport.

Phase 2: Focused Exploration

Phase 2, focused exploration, occurred after the data from Phase 1 was initially analyzed. Each selected participant partook in two activities during this phase. The first activity was an interview, which allowed for detailed follow-up questions from the emerging data from Phase 1, and an interview protocol that focused on the role of the environment (Appendix B).

The second activity during Phase 2 was a guided imagery tour. Participants were invited to take the researcher on a virtual or imaginary tour of the campus to accentuate those aspects of the environment that were most and least supportive to their retention. The idea for the campus tour activity was adopted from a similar activity used in a recent doctoral study (Stevens, 1997). This activity served as a source of rich information and is viewed as a here-and-now activity that allowed the participants to share the meaning they gave to their environment. The responses were analyzed for preliminary units and categories of information. Preliminary categories from the virtual tour were checked and expanded during subsequent interviews.

Phase 3: Member Checks and Closure

Phase 3 is often referred to as the member check phase, and is the result of analyzed data from Phase 2. However, member checking occurred during all of the phases to assure the accuracy of the interview transcripts and to solicit agreement of meanings. Interview transcripts were taken back to the participants to obtain confirmation that the transcripts fully captured the data as constructed by the informants. This procedure allowed each of the participants to correct, amend, or extend the report to establish the credibility of the data.

During Phase 3, participants were invited to a group activity to discuss the emerging themes. The goal of this activity was to bring the participants together and to collectively negotiate the emerging model with the researcher. Two focus groups were convened during June 1998.

Finally, the participants were once more invited to meet as a group to provide feedback on the findings and to negotiate the outcomes. Nine of the 10 participants (1 participant could not be located) were invited to convene as a group in March 1999; 7 of the participants accepted the invitation and participated in this group activity. One of the most important undertakings of this activity was to ask the participants to help explain the relationship among the various categories. The participants were asked the following questions:

1. How do these categories come together to explain your retention?
2. In what ways, if any, do these categories influence each other?
3. Do some categories come before others (are they hierarchical) or are they equal?
4. Are some categories more important than others?
5. Is anything missing?

Data Analysis

The constant comparative method of qualitative data analysis as described by Lincoln and Guba (1985) and Glaser and Strauss (1967) was used to analyze the data in this study. The constant comparative method is a strategy that combines inductive category coding with simultaneous comparison of all observed incidents.

Lincoln and Cuba (1985) described two processes that are used to analyze the data: unitizing and categorizing. Unitizing is the process of coding data. A unit has two characteristics: first, it should be heuristic—aimed at some understanding or some action that the researcher needs to have or take. Second, it must be the smallest piece of information about something that could stand by itself—interpretable in the absence of any additional information. Units of information included phrases, sentences, or paragraphs that met the above stated criteria; a total of 1,154 units were identified. Each unit was recorded on a separate index card, and each index card was noted in a manner that could be understood by someone other than the researcher. Categorizing is the process that organizes the unitized data into broader and provisional categories that "provide descriptive or inferential information about the context or setting from which the units were derived" (Lincoln & Guba, p. 203).

The constant comparative method produced a total of 43 categories; from these, 18 higher order categories were produced. However, of these higher order categories only 11 were relevant to the primary research questions. These 11 categories became the themes that led to the development of a working hypothesis about the retention of Latino college students. The primary research questions were useful in grounding the context of the study and provided a foundation for the emerging data. Only those categories that were deemed relevant to the research questions were used in the development of a working hypothesis. Although the remaining seven higher order categories were interesting in and by themselves, they were not directly related to the focus of the study, and as such were not used.

Establishing Trustworthiness

Lincoln and Cuba (1985) offered the following standards to ensure that the trustworthiness criteria may be operationalized in a naturalistic or constructivist inquiry: credibility (the researcher's interpretations are credible to the respondents), transferability (the study may be useful in another context), dependability (changes over time are taken into account), and confirmability (the data can be confirmed by someone other than the researcher).

Credibility in part was established by using the following techniques or activities: peer debriefing, triangulation, member checks. Peer debriefing is the process of using peers to ensure that the researcher acknowledges the influence of personal perspectives and perceptions on the study and to develop and test next steps and emerging hypotheses (Whitt, 1991). Three female graduate students and a male undergraduate student were invited to participate in the research team and to serve as peer debriefers. The peer debriefers were selected based on their awareness of Latino students, retention issues, qualitative methodologies, or some combination of these areas. Their role allowed the researcher to probe for biases and to clarify the basis for interpretations.

Triangulation typically refers to using multiple sources of data and multiple methods of data collection (Whitt, 1991). Triangulation was achieved in this study by using multiple sources of data (the 10 individual participants and two follow-up focus groups) and multiple methods of data collection (two sets of individual interviews, a sequence of follow-up focus groups, observation, and a guided imagery tour). Additionally, member checks are essential for establishing credibility because they ensure that the researcher's reconstructions are recognizable to participants as adequate representations of their multiple realities. In this study, member checking occurred after each individual interview as well as during the focus groups in the final stage of the study.

A naturalistic or constructivist design makes no attempt to generalize the findings or conclusions to the general population. Transferability was achieved through a thick description of the data. Other researchers must look through these detailed descriptions to make an informed judgment about the appropriateness or transferability to alternate locations.

To meet the criterion of dependability, the researcher provided evidence of the inquiry decisions made throughout the study (Lincoln & Guba, 1985); this was accomplished through the use of an audit, which used an independent analyst, or inquiry auditor, to review all of the materials and analyze the trail of decisions leading to the conclusions. An inquiry auditor was selected based on her understanding of the naturalistic paradigm and of the purpose of this study. The specific role of the auditor was to review all data records, written notes, and other pertinent documents to attest that the findings and interpretations are logical and acceptable.

The final standard to ensure trustworthiness is confirmability, which centers around the question, Can the data be confirmed by someone other than the researcher? According to Lincoln and Guba (1985), the major technique for establishing confirmability is the audit and the use of an auditor. The keeping of a reflexive journal dovetails with the audit process. Lincoln and Guba described the reflexive journal as a diary in which the researcher records a variety of information about self and method. The researcher achieved the intent of journaling by providing a written record for methodological decisions and the rationale for making them; by documenting activities and logistics related to the research study; and by noting personal reflections.

Results

Data analysis produced 11 major categories or themes. The categories depict a variety of interdependent relationships, which when taken together, provide a better understanding of the factors that impacted the retention of 10 Latino college students. As presented below, the themes are arranged in no particular order.

I Want to do it

The belief in and the realization that they possessed the potential to succeed in college was a primary theme expressed by all of the participants. At times this was expressed as a belief in oneself although this concept is more than just having the motivation or the right attitude. This belief blended self-efficacy in that the participants also possessed an "I can" or "I am capable" mentality. Although these two concepts (motivation and efficacy) are different, they were expressed in ways that combined elements of both.

Possessing a positive mental outlook was associated with having the desire to succeed and was demonstrated by overcoming barriers and obstacles that made the participants ever more resilient. For some of the participants this belief was internalized through many years of having to fend for themselves or by observing their parents struggle to overcome a variety of barriers, such as adjusting to life in the United States, socioeconomic hardships, and racial or ethnic discrimination. Additionally, this sense and belief that "anything is possible" seemed to be the driving force behind the participants' belief in themselves. This belief was often reinforced after completing a formidable task or after accomplishing a desired outcome. It ultimately seems to have positively influenced their self-esteem, and a strong belief that "I want to do it."

The Family

Without exception, all of the participants discussed in no uncertain terms the important role that their family had on their retention. However, they gave meaning to this factor by describing the ways in which the family impacted their staying in school. Most of the participants described their family as a source for support and encouragement; however, the family also placed pressure on the participants. For some it was the pressure of knowing that their parents would not support dropping out of college. The notion that they could never drop out of college was reinforced by a fear of disappointing their families. One male participant summed it up by stating, "Oh my God, what an incredible disappointment I'd be for my parents, so I never really saw dropping out as an option."

Friends and Peers

In addition to the family, friends and peers played a role in providing a source of support. One participant discussed the important role that his friends played: they were driven to succeed and "made me want to make sure that I pull, that

I came across the finish line myself." Another participant described one of his friends as an "emissary" because he assisted him in answering questions about what to expect and by introducing him to college life.

Faculty and Staff

All of the participants, in describing individuals who had a positive impact on their staying in school, mentioned individual faculty members, counselors, and advisors. For some it was a personalized, one-on-one relationship; many stated that having professors who were looking out for their well-being was helpful. Similarly, staff also played a vital role in the retention of the participants; each participant discussed the important ways in which these individuals impacted their persistence.

Cocurricular Involvement

All of the participants discussed the impact that being involved had on their retention. Though their level of involvement varied and the type of organizations they chose to interact with were quite diverse, they all discussed the benefits of getting involved, both on and off campus. Some of the participants were actively involved in various student clubs and organizations, whereas others participated as volunteers both on and off campus. Regardless of their level of involvement, most stated in very clear terms the benefit of this involvement.

Finding a Latino Community

Many of the participants indicated that meeting and finding other Latinos on a predominantly White campus had a positive impact on their retention. Some stated that by meeting other Latinos they were better able to cope with the college environment. One of the participants stated that meeting other Latinos "played a part in me being more interested in coming here and staying here." Meeting Latinos of similar backgrounds who were succeeding in college was an important motivating factor; as stated by one participant, "If you see that others like you that have similar backgrounds and similar obstacles that you have had, have made it, and they're still there and they're still working hard, then why can't you?"

Money Matters

Almost all of the participants identified how finances played a role in their retention and how it impacted their education. Some had to struggle to meet the financial demands of a college education; as such, finances was an additional stressor. For others, however, money was not a barrier due to scholarships, financial aid, or parents who had the financial means to support them. The important factor to keep in mind is that the issue of finances was identified as having an impact, either positively or negatively, on their ability to stay in college.

I'm Going to Make It Within the Environment

Many of the participants discussed the personal responsibility that students must take in making the college environment work for them. The participants indicated that the institution provides an array of services and opportunities, but it's up to students to take advantage of these and to select those that will aid them in transitioning through college. In essence, the participants stated that they were responsible for making the environment work for them even when it was not conducive to their educational success.

Environment Equals People

In discussing the role of the environment on their retention, the participants indicated that the people within the environment were what shaped their experiences, whether positive or negative. One participant stated, "I think it had to do more with the people than the actual environment. The people that were in the environment."

Most of the participants were able to identify both positive and negative experiences with people. However, regardless of whether their encounters with these people were positive or negative, their interactions with these individuals gave meaning to how they defined and thought about the college environment.

Personal Experiences Shape the Perceptions of the Physical Environment

Related to the role of people in shaping the environment is the concept of how an individual's personal experiences influence one's perceptions, both positive and negative, of the college environment. One participant explained how the buildings within the physical environment influenced her in both good and bad ways and indicated how these experiences impacted her retention. She provided an example of how she felt about one of the buildings on campus based on an experience that occurred in that building. "If I go to Keys Hall where I had that class I'd be like 'God I hate this building' just because of what happened." Additionally, she described how she would "pick and choose" sections of the physical environment based on her experiences and feelings about specific areas or buildings.

Interestingly, those participants who associated a negative encounter with the college environment did not overgeneralize their sentiments to the entire university; rather they limited this negative association to the specific area of the environment where it had occurred, be it in a building or within a specific department or unit. In fact, many of the participants who experienced negative encounters expressed satisfaction with their overall collegiate experience.

Involvement as a Way to Break Down the Environment

The participants acknowledged the importance of making the environment smaller through involvement in on-campus organizations and activities. Involvement was cited as crucial to breaking down the environment into smaller units—the greater the level of involvement, the greater the likelihood of feeling welcomed. One participant expressed this idea:

> We have about 28,000 undergrads, and 1 of 28,000 is overwhelming and it's scary, but if you get involved in a student group where you know your views correlate, you meet a group of friends, or you get involved with something so that you are 1 of 100 as opposed to 1 of 28,000, so it'll just make it a little smaller and put you in perspective.

Category Relationships

The participants' thorough discussion during Phase 3 resulted in an explanation of how these 11 categories came together for them. A visual depiction of this relationship is shown in Figure 1. This diagram is a conceptual model of the relationships that exist among the 11 categories. It is presented as a conceptual model because it attempts to explain a complex set of relationships; it should not be viewed as an emerging theory because to do so would require additional research.

The conceptual model is made up of 11 circles, one for each of the 11 themes. At the center of the conceptual model is the category "I Want to Do It," which is depicted by a larger circle.

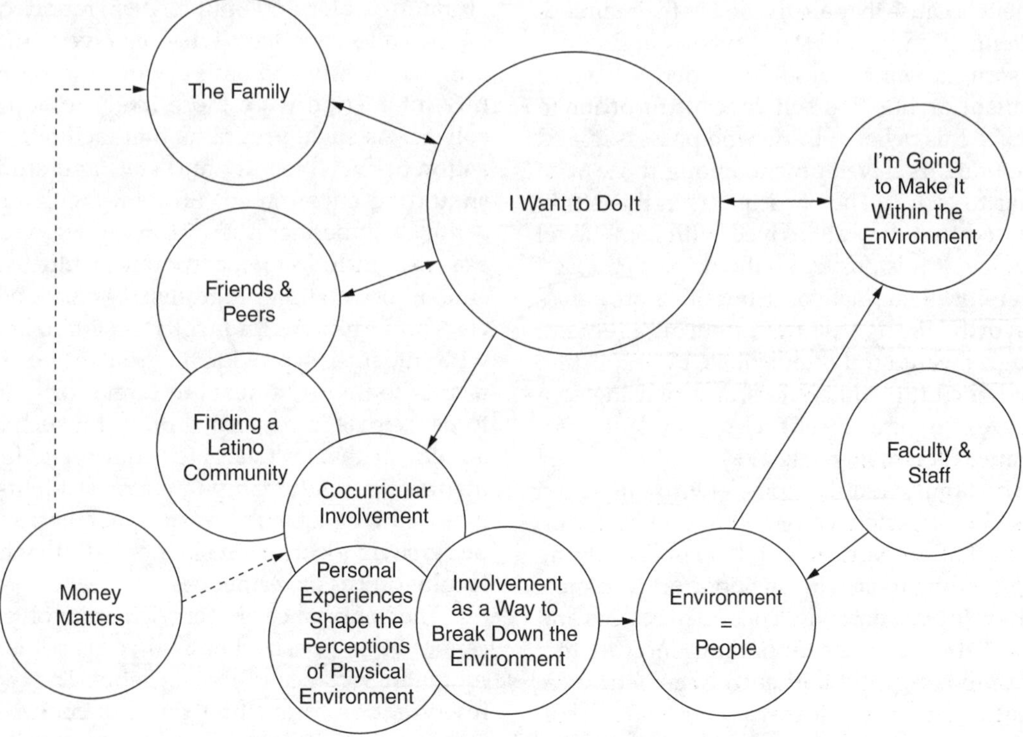

Figure 1 Conceptual Model of the Relationship Among Elements of Latino Student Retention

It is located in the center because it was identified as the core retention element and has greater value than the other categories. All of the remaining retention elements carry similar importance and are depicted by equally shaped circles. Several of the categories overlap each other; this overlapping symbolizes an association between the interconnected circles or categories.

The relationships between these categories are either unidirectional, bidirectional, or indirect. A unidirectional relationship is one where a specific category influences the development of another category. A bidirectional relationship exists when two categories impact and influence each other in a dynamic and interactive way. An indirect relationship, which is depicted in the diagram by a broken line, is a relationship that indirectly shapes the development of another category and whose influence may or may not be as compelling.

Discussion

Validating students' desire to succeed and encouraging their optimistic outlook is a central theme for student retention. Faculty and staff should be made aware of the importance of this type of affirmation, particularly for students who believe they are academically unprepared or students who are unfamiliar with the college environment because they are the first in their families to attend (Rendon, 1994). Advisors and counselors might want to assess a student's level of optimism or positive self-concept in order to reinforce this belief in those who possess it, and to facilitate its development among those who appear to lack it. The participants in this study indicated that they all arrived with some level or degree of this positive outlook. Nonetheless, university personnel contribute to a student's self-worth through words of encouragement, through meaningful interactions, by respecting his or her cultural differences, and by using constructive critique and feedback of a student's performance (Terenzini et al., 1994).

The family and the home environment can be used as an effective retention tool by familiarizing Latino parents with the college setting and providing them with an opportunity to meet and develop rapport with college educators and support staff. The current findings indicate that the family's support and encouragement were crucial to retention. However, more often than not, Latino parents are unfamiliar with the system of higher education in this country (Aguirre & Martinez, 1993). To gain family support, university personnel should engage parents in programs that assist them to become comfortable with and knowledgeable about U.S. higher education. Bilingual and culturally sensitive recruitment materials should be made available. Similarly, parent orientation programs should be designed so parents with limited English proficiency can participate in orientation programs. Parents, spouses, and partners, particularly of first-generation Latino students, should be made aware of the academic rigor and time demands that will be placed on their students.

The challenge to incorporating the family, and parents in particular, as partners in a student's educational attainment is that the system of higher education in the United States treats its students as adults; the family is typically left out of the formula. Euro-Western values of individualism and independence often fail to validate the cultural relevance of collective groups or of the family (Wright, 1987). Perhaps a balance is needed that recognizes an interdependence between the student as an adult, an institution's responsibility to ensure the privacy of its students, and the meaningful interaction of the family.

The importance of having a relationship with faculty or staff was identified as having a positive influence on student retention. Similarly, Hurtado, Carter, and Spuler (1996) reported that Latino college students who perceive a student-centered faculty and have opportunities for faculty interaction were more likely to adjust to college. As such, programs that facilitate interaction between faculty and staff and students should be encouraged. Student-faculty interactions can be increased in many ways. Some examples include: (a) incorporate faculty in new-student orientation programs; (b) create out-of-class opportunities for faculty or staff to interact with students; (c) provide financial incentives for faculty to invite students to dinner or lunch or to participate in a campus program such as an athletic or theater event; (d) coordinate formal mentoring relationships where students are matched with a faculty or staff member; and (e) design living-learning residence halls that house faculty offices or residences.

The importance of cocurricular involvement cannot be emphasized enough; research is clear on the importance of this variable. The current investigation found that through cocurricular involvement students (a) had opportunities to make new friends, particularly peers that came from similar cultural and socioeconomic backgrounds; (b) found a caring and supportive community; and (c) were able to break down the larger environment into meaningful wholes.

Most of the participants found their niche through a Latino student organization. Involvement in a Latino organization was a way to stay culturally grounded and to nurture one's sense of ethnic identity, particularly on a predominantly White campus. Furthermore, Latino students who have representative groups to join at predominantly White institutions may feel less socially isolated and less culturally alienated (Fuertes & Sedlacek, 1989). Students who are active in school will be more likely to develop a sense of belonging on campus, develop potential friendships with support persons, meet role models, and develop leadership skills (Fuertes & Sedlacek, 1989).

When gauging or evaluating a student's level of involvement, faculty and practitioners should acknowledge that many Latino students find meaningful involvement opportunities in off-campus organizations. All too often university personnel fail to recognize the impact of community-based organizations. Because Latinos are family and community oriented, students—particularly commuters—are often engaged in cocurricular activities away from the college setting. Omission of community involvement fails to take into account the cultural importance and value placed on community obligations. Developing linkages with these community-based organizations is important as is recognizing the many community service projects that Latino students support.

Recommendations

Student retention is a complex and multidimensional process; future retention studies should take into account this complexity from the frame of reference of college students. The findings of this investigation raise several questions about future retention research. Additionally the results of this inquiry and the conceptual model in particular provide a framework for future interpretive research.

Further research is needed to explore in greater detail the concept of "I Want to Do It." The desire to succeed was expressed as the single most influential category. This concept may be a combination of previously researched areas, such as positive self-concept (Sedlacek & Brooks, 1976), academic invulnerability and resiliency (Alva & Padilla, 1995; Arellano & Padilla, 1996), and self-efficacy (Bandura, 1977, 1997); or it may be a concept that needs to be uniquely identified and described. Additional questions about this concept that appear unanswered include: Why do some possess this desire to succeed and others do not? Does this variable distinguish persisters from nonpersisters? How is this concept nurtured? Are there precollege influences? Is this belief driven primarily by an internal locus of control or is it influenced by one's environment, or both?

Although the impact of faculty-student interactions has been investigated over time, few researchers have attempted to ascertain the direct influence of nonfaculty staff on student outcomes. Researchers have overlooked the influence of student-staff interactions (Love, 1995). The need to investigate the effect of student-staff interactions is further warranted by the often limited time of faculty to engage in informal interactions with students and because the frequency of student-faculty informal interactions has declined during the past several decades (Pascarella & Terenzini, 1991). Additionally, the culture within higher education rewards informal student contact (Love); thus nonfaculty staff very likely may have a significant impact on student retention.

Further, few researchers have attempted to explain or understand the role of the environment on persistence. The participants in this study experienced the environment not as a whole but rather through its subparts, which included subcommunities. The participants gave meaning to environmental influences and described these influences in unique ways. Additional research is needed to assess the impact of the environment on Latino college students, particularly the role of subcommunities.

Finally, the participants in this inquiry did not generalize negative encounters within the environment to their overall experience. The participants did not internalize these negative perceptions and apply them globally; rather they isolated these incidents and did not allow them to negatively shape their degree of satisfaction with the overall environment and with their university experience. This phenomenon is intriguing and warrants additional research. Is this true of all students or is it unique to ethnic minority students? Is it a survival strategy that ethnic minorities learn from other life experiences? Are these negative encounters processed cognitively and affectively? If so, how do these encounters influence one's behavior?

APPENDIX A
Phase I Interview Questions

1. Tell me a little about yourself.
2. How would you describe your college experience?
   - Probe both academic and social experiences.
3. What were your greatest fears about coming to college?
   - How did you overcome those fears?
4. Was there ever a time when you wanted to drop out or thought about dropping out from college? If yes, could you expand on your response?
5. Do you know anyone who did not persist? How was your experience different?
6. What have been the greatest challenges of your college experience?
   - What was your most negative experience?
7. What have been the greatest triumphs or accomplishments of your college experience?
   - What are you most proud of?
8. To summarize, can you list those things that stand out as the most influential to your staying in school?
9. In what ways did each of these affect or influence your decision to persist and stay in college?
10. As we wrap up are there any additional factors you haven't thought about?
11. Is there anything that you would like to add? Is there anything that you feel I should have asked you?
12. For our next meeting, I would like to ask you to share any essays, writings (your own, i.e., sections of your journal; or the works of others), articles from the press, photographs, awards, anything that you believe depicts your college experience or factors that had an impact on your retention.

APPENDIX B
Phase II Interview Questions

Physical & Social Aspects of the Environment

Hand participant a campus map. Say "I want to talk about the physical spaces on this campus that relate to your staying in college. Examples of physical spaces may include offices, units, buildings, rooms, departments."

1. What areas of this campus are you drawn to the most?
2. Where do you spend most of your time? Is that different from the places you're most drawn to?
3. What areas of the campus have made a difference in your staying in school?
   - Probe BOTH social and academic spaces/locations.
   - Probe BOTH positive and negative areas.
4. What about off-campus environments that have made a difference to your staying in college?
5. Overall, how did the physical environment impact your retention?

Institutional & Climate Issues of the Environment

Say, "I want to talk about the general climate on this campus, how you experienced it, and how the climate influenced your decision to stay in school."

6. How welcomed or valued have you felt on this campus?
7. Did the college environment make you feel that you mattered and that others cared about you? If so, in what ways?
8. Do you feel your concerns and needs have been adequately addressed by the institution? Please explain.
9. Were there climate issues that have been a challenge to your retention and graduation? If so, how did you work them out?
10. Were there people on this campus that had a positive or negative impact on your retention?
11. Overall, how did the climate impact your retention?

References

Abi-Nader, J. (1990). A house for my mother: Motivating Hispanic high school students. *Anthropology and Education Quarterly, 21,* 41–58.

Aguirre, A., Jr., & Martinez, R. O. (1993). *Chicanos in higher education: Issues and dilemmas for the 21st century.* ASHE-ERIC Higher Education Report No. 3. Washington DC: The George Washington University, School of Education and Human Development.

Alva, S. A., & Padilla, A. M. (1995). Academic invulnerability among Mexican Americans: A conceptual framework. *The Journal of Educational Issues of Language Minority Students, 15,* 27–48.

Arellano, A. R., & Padilla, A. M. (1996). Academic invulnerability among a select group of Latino university students. *Hispanic Journal of Behavioral Sciences, 18,* 485–507.

Astin, A. W. (1984). Student involvement: A developmental theory for higher education. *Journal of College Student Personnel, 25,* 297–308.

Attinasi, L. C., Jr., & Nora, A. (1992). Diverse students and complex issues: A case of multiple methods in college student research. In F. K. Stage & Associates (Eds.), *Diverse methods for research and assessment of college students* (pp. 13–27). Alexandria, VA: American Counseling Association.

Bandura, A. (1977). Self-efficacy: Toward a unifying theory of behavior change. *Psychological Review, 84,* 191–215.

Bandura, A. (1997). *Self-efficacy: The exercise of control.* New York: Freeman.

Bean, J. P. (1980). Dropouts and turnover: The synthesis and test of a causal model of student attrition. *Research in Higher Education, 12,* 155–187.

Collison, M. N-K. (1999). For Hispanics, demographic imperative drives educational mandate. *Black Issues in Higher Education, 16,* 56.

Facts on Hispanic higher education. (2000, April). *The Voice, X,* 14.

Fuertes, J. N., & Sedlacek, W. E. (1989). *A needs assessment of Hispanic students at a predominantly White university.* (Research Report #21–89). College Park: University of Maryland, Counseling Center.

Glaser, B. G., & Strauss, A. L. (1967). *The discovery of grounded theory.* Chicago: Aldine.

Hurtado, S., Carter, D. F., & Spuler, A. (1996). Latino student transition to college: Assessing difficulties and factors in successful college adjustment. *Research in Higher Education, 37,* 135–157.

Lincoln, Y. S., & Cuba, E. G. (1985). *Naturalistic inquiry.* Newbury Park, CA: Sage.

Love, P. G. (1995). Exploring the impact of student affairs professionals on student outcomes. *Journal of College Student Development, 36,* 162–170.

Mayo, J. R., Murguia, E., & Padilla, R. V. (1995). Social integration and academic performance among minority university students. *Journal of College Student Development, 36,* 542–552.

O'Brien, E. (1993). *Latinos in higher education* (Research Briefs, Vol. 4, No. 4). Washington, DC: American Council on Education.

Olivas, M. A. (1986). Introduction—Research on Latino college students: A theoretical framework and inquiry. In M. A. Olivas (Ed.), *Latino college students* (pp. 1–25). New York: Teachers College Press.

Padilla, R. V., Trevino, J., Gonzalez, K., & Trevino, J. (1997). Developing local models of minority student success in college. *Journal of College Student Development, 38,* 125–135.

Pascarella, E. T., & Terenzini, P. T. (1991). *How college affects students.* San Francisco: Jossey-Bass.

Patton, M. Q. (1990). *Qualitative evaluation and research methods* (2nd ed.). Newbury Park, CA: Sage.

Rendon, L. I. (1994). Validating culturally diverse students: Toward a new model of learning and student development. *Innovative Higher Education, 19,* 33–51.

Sedlacek, W. E., & Brooks, G. C., Jr. (1976). *Racism in American education: A model for change.* Chicago: Nelson-Hall.

Stevens, A. (1997). *Critical incidents contributing to the development of lesbian identities in college.* Unpublished doctoral dissertation, University of Maryland, College Park.

Terenzini, P. T., Rendon, L. I., Upcraft, M. L., Millar, S. B., Allison, K. W., Gregg, P. L., & Jalomo, R. (1994). The transition to college: Diverse students, diverse stories. *Research in Higher Education, 35,* 57–73.

Tinto, V. (1975). Dropouts from higher education: A theoretical synthesis of recent research. *Review of Educational Research, 45,* 89–125.

Tinto, V. (1987). *Leaving college: Rethinking the causes and cures of student attrition.* Chicago: University of Chicago Press.

Tinto, V. (1993). *Leaving college: Rethinking the causes and cures of student attrition* (2nd ed.). Chicago: University of Chicago Press.

Tracey, T. J., & Sedlacek, W. E. (1984). Noncognitive variables in predicting academic success by race. *Measurement and Evaluation in Counseling and Development, 16,* 171–178.

Tracey, T. J., & Sedlacek, W. E. (1987). Prediction of college graduation using noncognitive variables by race. *Measurement and Evaluation in Counseling and Development, 19,* 177–184.

U.S. Department of Commerce, Bureau of the Census (1991). *The Hispanic population in the United States: March 1991* (Current Population Reports, Series

P-20, No. 455). Washington, DC: U.S. Government Printing Office.

Viernes-Turner, C. S. (with Garcia, M., Nora, A., & Rendon, L.) (1996). Introduction: Higher education's diverse racial/ethnic populations. In C. Turner, M. Garcia, A. Nora, & L. I. Rendon (Eds), *Racial and ethnic diversity in higher education* (pp. xvii–xxiii). Needham Heights, MA: Simon & Schuster.

Whitt, E. J. (1991). Artful science: A primer on qualitative research methods. *Journal of College Student Development, 32*, 406–415.

Wright, D. J. (1987). Minority students: Developmental beginnings. In D. J. Wright (Ed.), *Responding to the needs of today's minority students* (pp. 5–21). San Francisco: Jossey-Bass.

Racial/Ethnic Group Differences in the Realization of Educational Plans

Laura Walter Perna, Ph.D

Visiting Assistant Professor
Department of Educational Policy & Leadership

Abstract

Descriptive and multinomial logistic regression analyses are used to examine racial/ethnic group differences in two-year and four-year college enrollment among bachelor's degree aspirants after controlling for differences in expected costs and benefits, financial resources, academic characteristics, and social and cultural capital. The sample is drawn from the National Educational Longitudinal Study (NELS:90/94).

More students than ever before are aspiring to attain a college degree. Between 1980 and 1990, the percentage of high school sophomores who reported that they expected to earn at least a bachelor's degree rose substantially, from 39% to 69% (Nettles & Perna, 1997). The growth in educational expectations has been particularly dramatic among African Americans. About 70% of 1990 African American high school sophomores expected to finish college, compared with only 35% of 1980 African American high school sophomores. The percentage of African American high school sophomores who expect to finish college is now comparable to the percentage of Whites (Nettles & Perna, 1997).

Despite this increase in the predisposition toward college, however, challenges remain. The percentage of students who actually enroll in a four-year college or university continues to vary by racial/ethnic group, even when only those who reported aspiring to earn at least a bachelor's degree are considered. Analyses of the National Educational Longitudinal Study (NELS:90/94) reveal that, among all those who were high school sophomores in 1990, only 28% of African Americans and 20% of Hispanics were enrolled in a four-year college or university during fall 1992, the fall after their expected high school graduation, compared with 38% of Whites and 43% of Asians. Among 1990 high school sophomores who aspired to complete at least a bachelor's degree, only about 38% of African Americans and of Hispanics were enrolled in a four-year institution during the fall of 1992, compared with about 55% of Whites and Asians. These data suggest that only a fraction of 1990 sophomores are likely to realize their educational goals and that the percentage of students who will realize their goal varies by racial/ethnic group.

Paper presented at the Annual Meeting of the American Educational Research Association. Reprinted by permission of Laura W. Perna, Assistant Professor, Department of Education Policy and Leadership, University of Maryland, College Park.

Certainly not all students have the desire or ability to enroll in college. This research is designed to contribute to our understanding of the barriers that limit college enrollment for students of different racial/ethnic groups by focusing specifically on the enrollment decisions of high school students who report that they expect to complete at least a bachelor's degree.

Pipeline to College

According to Hossler and Gallagher (1987), three stages characterize the college enrollment process: predisposition toward or interest in attending college: search for information about various colleges and universities; and choice of one college or university to attend. This study focuses on the characteristics and enrollment behavior of students who are predisposed toward college, as indicated by their self-reported educational expectations. Other researchers have concluded that a student's educational expectations are among the best predictors of college enrollment (Hossler, Schmit, & Vesper, 1999; McDonough, 1997).

Horn (1997) has suggested that the "pipeline" or path to enrollment in a four-year college or university has five sequential steps: aspiring to complete at least a bachelor's degree; becoming academically prepared to enroll in college; taking college entrance examinations; completing college admissions applications; and matriculating. Horn (1997) found that about two-thirds of all 1992 high school graduates aspired as 10th graders to earn at least a bachelor's degree but that only 40% completed the next four steps including enrolling in a four-year institution. Her analyses focused on differences in the progression through the pipeline between students who were and were not at-risk of dropping out of high school with no attention to racial/ethnic group differences. Other research suggests that a smaller percent of Hispanic than of African American, Asian, and White 1992 high school graduates who are at least minimally academically qualified to attend a four-year college take college entrance exams and apply for admission to a four-year institution (Berkner & Chavez, 1997).

Examinations of differences in college enrollment across racial/ethnic groups have shown contradictory results. St. John and Noell (1989) found college enrollment rates to be comparable for African American, Hispanic, and White high school seniors after controlling for background, ability, and educational aspirations. African American college applicants were less likely than their White peers to enroll, however, after also controlling for financial aid offers. Other researchers have shown that, compared with their White counterparts and after controlling for other differences, African American high school students are less likely to enroll in college (Nolfi, et al., 1978), are less likely to attend highly selective colleges and universities (Hearn, 1984), and are less likely to attend their first-choice institution (Hurtado, Inkelas, Briggs, & Rhee, 1997). Still other research suggests that African Americans are more likely than Whites to enroll in college (Catsiapis, 1987; Kane & Spizman, 1994; Perna, 2000) and tend to enroll in four-year rather than two-year colleges (Rouse, 1994) holding constant other variables.

The variables that predict college enrollment have been shown to vary by race/ethnicity. St. John (1991) found that African American high school seniors were more likely than White seniors to attend college when region, family background, ability, and high school experiences were controlled, but were no more likely than White seniors to attend when educational expectations were also controlled. Hispanic seniors were less likely than other students to attend college when region and family background were controlled, but no less likely than White students when test scores and high school experiences were also taken into account. Jackson (1990) showed that receiving financial aid had a stronger positive effect on the probability of enrolling in college for African American and Hispanic college applicants in 1980 than for their White counterparts, but that the positive effect of financial aid for Hispanics disappeared when background and academic characteristics were also held constant. Using data from the National Educational Longitudinal Study, Perna (2000) concluded that educational expectations were a less important predictor of four-year college enrollment for African American high school graduates than for Hispanic and White high school graduates.

One common approach to examining college enrollment behavior is economic (Hossler, Braxton, & Coopersmith, 1989; Hossler, Schmit, & Vesper, 1999). Econometric models posit that an individual makes a decision about attending college by comparing the benefits with the costs for all possible alternatives and then selecting the alternative with the greatest net benefit, given the individual's personal tastes and preferences (Hossler, Braxton & Coopersmith, 1989; Manski & Wise, 1983). The traditional econometric perspective predicts that the decision to invest in higher education is influenced by expected costs and benefits, financial resources, academic ability, current and expected labor market opportunities, personal preferences and tastes, and uncertainty (Becker, 1962).

Based on her examination of differences in four-year college enrollment among African American, Hispanic, and White high school graduates, Perna (2000) concluded that the explanatory power of traditional econometric approaches to college enrollment decisions is improved when measures of social and cultural capital are used as proxies for differences in expectations, preferences, tastes, and certainty about higher education investment decisions. Qualitative research examining college enrollment behavior has utilized the sociological concepts of social and cultural capital to describe the ways in which knowledge and information about college, as well as the value placed on obtaining a college education, may influence college enrollment decisions (e.g., Freeman, 1997; McDonough, 1997). Like human capital and physical capital, social and cultural capital are resources that may be invested to enhance profitability (Bourdieu & Passeron, 1977) and productivity (Coleman, 1988) and facilitate upward mobility (DiMaggio & Mohr, 1985; Lamont & Lareau, 1988). Social capital may take the form of information-sharing channels and networks, as well as social norms, values, and expected behaviors (Coleman, 1988). Cultural capital is the system of factors derived from one's parents that defines an individual's class status (Bourdieu & Passeron, 1977). Members of the dominant class possess the most economically and symbolically valued kinds of cultural capital (Bourdieu & Passeron, 1977; McDonough, 1997).

Research Method

This study draws upon the expanded econometric framework described by Perna (2000) to explore the facilitators of and barriers to college enrollment among high school sophomores who expected to earn at least a bachelor's degree and examines differences in the predictors of college enrollment among bachelor's degree aspirants of various racial/ethnic groups. Specifically, this study addresses the following research questions:

1. How do the characteristics of bachelor's degree aspirants vary across racial/ethnic group?
2. How do two-year and four-year college enrollment rates vary among bachelor's degree aspirants of different racial/ethnic groups after controlling for other variables related to college enrollment, including expected costs and benefits, financial resources, academic characteristics, and social and cultural capital?
3. How do the predictors of college enrollment vary among bachelor's degree aspirants of different racial/ethnic groups?

Sample

Data from the first (1990), second (1992), and third (1994) follow-ups to the National Educational Longitudinal Study (NELS:90/94) are used to examine the research questions. Sponsored by the U.S. Department of Education's National Center for Education Statistics, the NELS contains data for a cohort of students in the 8th grade (1988), when they are high school sophomores (1990), when they are high school seniors (1992), and when they are two years out of high school (1994). The sample used in this research is limited to individuals who, as members of the spring 1990 high school sophomore cohort, reported that they expected to complete at least a bachelor's degree. As other researchers have concluded, most students have formalized their educational plans by the tenth grade (Horn, 1997; Hossler & Stage, 1992; Hossler, Schmit, & Vesper, 1999) and enter the search stage of the college choice process during the junior year of high school (Hossler, Braxton, & Coopersmith, 1989).

The 1992–94 NCES panel weight (F3F1PNWT) is appropriate for approximating the population of 1990 bachelor's degree aspirants from the sample. To minimize the influence of large sample sizes and the non-simple random sample design on standard errors, each case is weighted by the NCES panel weight divided by the average weight for the sample. The adjusted weighted sample used in these analyses numbers 7,832, representing 1,659,873 students nationwide.

Analyses

Descriptive analyses, including chi-square and one-way ANOVA, are used to identify differences in the characteristics of African American, Asian, Hispanic, and White bachelor's degree aspirants. For the categorical variables, the chi-square value is adjusted for the relatively large sample sizes (even with the adjusted weight) to show the strength of the relationship using the formula: $\phi = \sqrt{(\chi^2/n)}$. For the continuous variables, differences among the four groups are examined further using orthogonal contrasts.

The dependent variable, college enrollment, is measured in October 1992, the fall following the student's scheduled graduation from high school. Three enrollment status categories are considered: 1) enrolled in a four-year college or university; 2) enrolled in a public two-year college; and 3) not enrolled. Students who are enrolled in a for-profit or less than two-year institution are classified as not enrolled.

Because the dependent variable includes three categories, a multinomial logistic regression model, a special case of the general loglinear model, is used to examine the relationship between race/ethnicity and college enrollment after controlling for other variables. Two contrasts are possible with three outcome categories. In this study, enrollment in a four-year institution and enrollment in a two-year institution are simultaneously contrasted to no enrollment.

Multinominal logistic regression models estimate the log-odds of one outcome occurring relative to another outcome. The interpretation of the multinomial logit coefficients is facilitated by the use of odds-ratios. The odds-ratio represents the change in the odds of choosing a particular enrollment status relative to the reference outcome (no enrollment) that is associated with a one-unit change in a particular independent variable. An odds-ratio greater than one represents an increase in the likelihood of four-year or two-year college enrollment relative to no enrollment, whereas an odds-ratio less than one represents a decrease in the likelihood of four-year or two-year college enrollment.

The continuous variables are entered into the model as covariates. The fit of the model is measured by the deviance chi-square, the change in -2 log likelihood when the model is compared to a saturated model. When the model fits well, the observed significance level is large (SPSS, 1999). The Pseudo-R^2 provides an indication of the strength of the relationship between the outcome variable and the independent variables. To examine racial/ethnic group differences in the predictors of college enrollment, the multinomial logit analyses are repeated for each of four groups: African Americans, Asians, Hispanics, and Whites.

Independent Variables

Following the example of Perna (2000), the college enrollment decision is expected to be a function of the following: expected costs and benefits, financial resources, academic characteristics, and social and cultural capital. The specific independent variables included in the analyses are based on the review of prior research and are operationalized based on the variables available in the NELS:90/94 database. Table 1 summarizes the predictor variables.

As in prior research (e.g., Schwartz, 1985; Kane, 1994; Perna, 2000), the expected cost of attendance is measured by the average in-state tuition and fees at public four-year colleges and universities in the student's home state. The average in-district or local tuition and fees at public two-year colleges in the student's home state is also included. Both the average four-year and the average two-year tuition in each state were calculated from analyses of the 1992–93. Institutional Characteristics survey of the Integrated Postsecondary Education Data System and added to the NELS database. Expected benefits are measured by the expected occupation at age 30. Three categories are included: don't know, multiple response, or missing response; professional; or other. Labor market opportunities are expected to influence an individual's calculation of the expected costs and benefits. As in prior research (e.g., Rouse, 1994; Kane, 1994; Perna, 2000), labor market opportunities are measured by the unemployment rate in the state in which the student attended high school. Slate unemployment rates were obtained from the Current Population Survey, March 1992 Supplement and added to the NELS database.

Students are also expected to consider their financial resources when determining the relative costs and benefits of investing in postsecondary education (Becker, 1962). Other researchers (e.g., Hossler, Schmit, & Vesper, 1999) have concluded that parental income is an important predictor of

TABLE 1
Predictors of College Enrollment

Predictor	*Variable*
Sex	Female
Race/ethnicity	African American (l = yes), Hispanic (1 = yes), and Asian (1 = yes). White is the reference group.
Expected costs and benefits	
Four-year college tuition	Average in-state tuition and fees at public four-year colleges and universities in student's home state, divided by 100. Range: 2.19 to 30.46.
Two-year college tuition	Average local tuition and fees at public two-year colleges in student's home state, divided by 100. Range: 4.15 to 42.65.
Expected occupation	Expected occupation at age 30: 1 = Don't know, multiple response, or missing response; 2 = professional: 3 = other.
State unemployment rate	Calculated from the Current Population Survey, March 1992 Supplement.
Financial resources	
Family income	15 category variable representing total family income from all sources in 1991; 0 = none, 15 = more than $200,000. Missing values imputed for 15% of the cases based on the average value for students of the same race and socioeconomic status quartile.
Academic characteristics	
Test score	Composite score on the reading and mathematics tests administered as part of the NELS data collection. Missing values imputed for 22% of the cases based on the average value for students of the same race and SES quartile.
Mathematics coursework	Highest level of mathematics coursework completed: no mathematics coursework data available; Algebra I and geometry, Algebra II, at least one advanced math course. No math or non-academic math coursework is the reference category.
Social and cultural capital	
High school segregation	African Americans and Hispanics comprise 10% to 29% of all students (1 = yes), 30% to 59% of all students (1 = yes), or more than 60% of students (1 = yes). Less than 10% is the omitted/reference category. Missing data are imputed for 17% of the cases based on the average value for students of the same race and high school location (urban, suburban, rural).
High school quality	Percent of 1990–91 high school graduates enrolled in 4-year college. 1 = 0%, 6 = 100%. Missing values imputed for 21% of the cases based on the average for students of the same race and socioeconomic status quartile.
School help with admissions	Student received help at high school with college application, financial aid application, and college essay (1 = yes) and student received no help with application, financial aid, or essay (1 = yes). Receiving help with one or two of these items is the reference category.
Parental expectations	Highest level of education expected for the student by the father and mother: 1 = no more than high school, 2 = some college, 3 = finish college, 4 = advanced degree.
Parental saving	Parent started saving for the student's college education before the student entered the 10th grade (1 = yes) or while the student was in the 10th, 11th, or 12th grades (1 = yes). No savings or no response is the reference category.
Parental involvement	Factor composite comprised of six variables. Alpha reliability coefficient = 0.828.
Peer plans	Share of friends planning to attend a four-year college, 1 = none, 2 = some, 3 = most, 4 = all.
Extracurricular activities	Participated in no, one, or two extracurricular activities. Participating in three or more activities is the reference category.

the realization of educational plans. In this research, financial resources are measured by a 15-category variable representing total family income in 1991. To minimize the amount of missing data, values are imputed for 15% of the cases based on the average value for students of the same race and socioeconomic status quartile.

Prior research consistently shows that individuals with greater ability, generally measured by test scores, are more likely to invest in higher education (Becker, 1962; Sewell, Haller & Ohlendorf, 1970; Alexander & Eckland, 1974; Catsiapis, 1987; Hossler, Braxton, & Coopersmith, 1989; St. John & Noell, 1989; Jackson, 1990; St. John, 1991; Kane & Spizman, 1994; Rouse, 1994; Perna, 2000). In this research, the composite score on the reading and mathematics tests administered as part of the NELS data collection in 1992 is the test score included in the model. Although admissions test scores would have been more reflective of the actual college enrollment process, about one-third of the cases were missing either SAT score or ACT score data. Because the correlations among SAT scores, ACT scores, and NELS composite test scores range from 0.825 to 0.890, the NELS test score is assumed to be an appropriate substitute. To minimize the amount of missing data, NELS test scores are imputed for 22% of the cases based on the average score for students of the same race and socioeconomic status quartile.

A second measure of academic ability and preparation that has been shown to promote college enrollment is participation in an academic or college preparatory curricular track in high school (Alexander & Eckland, 1974; Alwin & Otto, 1977; Thomas, 1980; Borus & Carpenter, 1984; Hossler, Braxton & Coopersmith, 1989; St. John & Noell, 1989; Jackson, 1990; St. John, 1991; Perna, 2000). Nonetheless, Adelman (1999) concluded that "academic track" is an unreliable indicator of the quality and intensity of the high school curriculum. Some research (e.g., Horn, 1997) shows that taking at least one advanced mathematics course is associated with a higher probability of enrolling in a four-year college or university among students who are at-risk of dropping out of high school after controlling for other variables. Therefore, in this research the quality and intensity of the high school curriculum is measured by a series of dichotomous variables that reflect the highest level of mathematics completed: algebra I and geometry; algebra II; and at least one advanced math course. Other or no mathematics coursework is the reference category. To limit the amount of missing data, a dichotomous variable indicating whether mathematics coursework data are available is also included.

Following the example of Perna (2000), the model used in this study expands the traditional econometric approach by considering social and cultural capital to be resources that reflect an individual's expectations, preferences, tastes, and uncertainty about the college investment. One way social and cultural capital may influence expectations, preferences, and uncertainty about college investment decisions is through the provision of knowledge and information about college (DiMaggio & Mohr, 1985; McDonough, 1997). High school segregation and high school quality are included as two measures of the availability of information. High school segregation is measured by the representation of African Americans and Hispanics in the student body. To minimize the amount of missing data, data are imputed for 17% of the cases based on the average value for students of the same race and high school location (urban, rural, or suburban). High school quality is measured by the share of 1990–91 high school graduates enrolled in a four-year college or university. Missing data are imputed for 21% of the cases based on the average value for students of the same race and socioeconomic status quartile.

School personnel may also serve as a source of information about college enrollment procedures and requirements. Some evidence suggests that assistance from school personnel with college admissions applications is associated with a higher probability of enrolling in a four-year college or university among students who are at-risk of dropping out of high school after controlling for other variables (Horn, 1997) and that receiving no help with college admissions requirements reduces the probability of enrolling in a four-year institution among high school graduates (Perna, 2000). In this study, school help with admissions requirements is measured by a series of dichotomous variables, received help at school with college application, financial aid application, and college essay received no help with application aid application, or essay, or received help with one or two of these items (reference category.)

A second manifestation of social and cultural capital refers to the value placed on obtaining a college education (DiMaggio & Mohr, 1985; McDonough, 1997). Although the highest level of education attained by either parent is typically included in analyses of college enrollment behavior as a measure of parental encouragement for the student's educational attainment as well as the availability of information about how to acquire a college education (Hossler, Braxton, & Coopersmith, 1989; Rouse, 1994; Perna, 2000), parents' educational attainment is not included in the analyses for two reasons. First, some analyses suggest substantial discrepancies between the level of education reported by students and the actual level attained by the parents (Adelman, 1999). In addition, parental education is not a variable that is amenable to public policy intervention.

This study includes the following three indicators of parental encouragement and support for higher education, 1) parental expectations measured by the highest level of education that the student perceives to be expected by the father and mother, 2) parental saving for the student's college education, and 3) a factor composite reflecting parental involvement in the student's education. As Hossler, Schmit, and Vesper (1999) noted based on their nine-year longitudinal study of the college going process among Indiana high school students parental saving is likely to be perceived by the student as a "tangible commitment" to higher education. Following the example of others (e.g., Horn, 1997; Perna, 2000), parental involvement is a factor comprised of six variables in the NELS database measuring the frequency of discussions between students and their parents about high school course selections, school activities, topics studied, grades, plans to take the SAT or ACT, and applying to college. The alpha reliability coefficient for this factor is 0.828.

Interactions with peers may also reflect accepted values, norms, and standards for behavior (Steinberg, 1996). One measure of peer encouragement for higher education found to be related to four-year college enrollment in prior research (e.g., Horn, 1997) is the share of peers planning to attend a four-year college or university. A second measure found to be associated with four-year college enrollment (Horn, 1997) reflects involvement in extracurricular activities. A series of dichotomous variables reflecting no, one, two, and three or more extracurricular activities (reference category) are included in the model. Participation in extracurricular activities may also facilitate the transmission of the types of knowledge and information required to succeed in educational settings.

Limitations

As with all secondary data analyses, the specification of the model is limited by the availability of appropriate measures in the NELS database. One potentially important, but unavailable, proxy for information availability is the number of siblings in college, a variable that has been found to be related to college enrollment behavior by other researchers (e.g., Manski & Wise, 1983; McDonough, 1997).

A second limitation is that, in an effort to preserve sample sizes, missing data are imputed for four variables (family income, test score, high school segregation, and high school quality) based on the average value for students of the same racial/ethnic group and socioeconomic status quartile. Imputing missing values in this manner results in an underestimation of the standard errors. As a result, the regression coefficients for these four variables may falsely appear to be statistically significant and, therefore, should be interpreted with caution.

A third limitation pertains to the relatively small numbers of Asians and American Indians in the sample. Asians are included in the analyses although the relatively small number of Asians in the multinomial logistic regression analyses (n = 299) restricts the power to detect statistically significant relationships. An even smaller number of American Indians in the sample (n = 59) prohibits any meaningful examination of college enrollment for this group. Future research should further explore the college enrollment decisions of these two groups.

Findings

Characteristics of Bachelor's Degree Aspirants

The descriptive analyses reveal that 69% of 1990 high school sophomores who aspired to complete at least a bachelor's degree were enrolled in a four-year or public two-year institution in the fall after graduating from high school. This is considerably lower than the finding by Hossler, Schmit, and Vesper (1999) that 82% of 10th graders with college aspirations attended some type of postsecondary educational institution after graduating from high school. Part of the difference is attributable to the definition of the outcome variable. About 5% of those classified as not enrolled in this study were enrolled in a private two-year, private for-profit, or public less than two-year institutions. These students would likely have been classified as enrolled by Hossler and his colleagues. In addition, because of the low response rates to the Hossler, Schmit, and Vesper (1999) nine-year longitudinal study (18% for the 8th and final survey), their sample likely overrepresents "successful" students.

The descriptive analyses also show that only 52% of 1990 high school sophomores who aspired to complete at least a bachelor's degree were enrolled in a four-year college or university in the fall after graduating from high school. The percentage of sophomores who took this step toward realizing their educational goals varies by racial/ethnic group. Table 2 shows that only 39% of African American and 37% of Hispanic bachelor's degree aspirants were enrolled in a four-year institution during the fall of 1992, compared with 56% of Whites and 55% of Asians. More than one-fifth of Hispanics (23%) and Asian (24%) were enrolled in public two-year colleges, compared with 17% of Whites and only 12% of African Americans.

Racial/Ethnic Group Differences in Enrollment Behavior

Table 3 shows the odds-ratios for four-year college enrollment and public two-year college enrollment relative to no enrollment for 1990 bachelor's degree aspirants overall and separately for bachelor's degree aspirants of each of four racial/ethnic groups: African Americans, Asians, Hispanics, and Whites. For all groups, the test of the final model indicating the probability that all of the variables in the model are jointly equal to zero is rejected at the 0.1% level. The difference in the percent of cases correctly classified (89% for four-year college enrollment and 22% for public two-year college enrollment) suggests that the model is substantially better for predicting four-year than public two-year college enrollment decisions.

The multinomial logistic regression analyses reveal that, after controlling for sex, expected costs and benefits, financial resources, academic characteristics, and social and cultural capital, African Americans are more likely than students of other racial/ethnic groups to be enrolled in a four-year college or university in the fall after graduating from high school but less likely than students of other racial/ethnic groups to be enrolled in a public two-year college. The odds of being enrolled in either a four-year or public two-year institution in the fall after graduating from high school appear to be comparable for Asians, Hispanics, and Whites.

Conducting separate multinomial logistic regression analyses for each of the four groups suggests that the predictors of four-year and two-year college enrollment vary among bachelor's degree aspirants of different racial/ethnic groups. For example, among African Americans and Whites, women appear to be more likely than men to be enrolled in a four-year college after controlling for expected costs and benefits, financial resources, academic characteristics, and social and cultural capital. White women also are more likely than their White male counterparts to be enrolled in a public two-year college.

Sensitivity to the costs of attendance also appears to vary by race/ethnicity. An increase in two-year public college tuition and fees is associated with an increased likelihood of four-year college enrollment among Hispanics and a decreased likelihood of two-year college enrollment among Whites. Contrary to expectations based on human capital theory, an increase in the costs of attending a four-year college or university appears to be associated with an increased likelihood of four-year college enrollment among Asians.

The influence of financial resources on the odds of college enrollment also varies by racial/ethnic group. Family income appears to be unrelated to the odds of either four-year or two-year college enrollment among both African Americans and Asians. Among Hispanics, a higher level of family income is associated with a greater likelihood of four-year college enrollment but is unrelated to public two-year college enrollment. Only among Whites does the likelihood of both four-year and public two-year college enrollment increase with family income.

Both test scores and the quality and intensity of the high school curriculum (as measured by mathematics coursework) are important predictors of college enrollment regardless of racial/ethnic group. Nonetheless, test scores appear to be a somewhat more important predictor, and

TABLE 2
Selected Characteristics of 1990 Bachelor's Degree Aspirants by Racial/Ethnic Group

Variable	*Total*	*African American*	*Hispanic*	*Asian*	*White*	*Statistical Significance*
Enrollment status						ϕ = 0.19
Total	100%	100%	100%	100%	100%	
Enrolled in 4-year	51.9	38.6	37.4	55.1	55.7	
Enrolled in public 2-year	16.9	12.3	22.5	23.5	16.7	
Not enrolled or other enrollment	31.2	49.1	40.1	21.3	27.6	
Occupational aspirations for age 30						ϕ = 0.09
Total	100%	100%	100%	100%	100%	
Don't know/missing data	13.8	16.8	15.2	19.0	12.9	
Professional	56.3	58.9	54.9	60.4	55.8	
Other	30.0	24.4	29.9	20.6	31.4	
Family income						W > A > H > AA
Mean	10.7	9.0	9.3	10.7	11.1	
Standard deviation	2.3	2.6	2.4	2.5	2.0	
Test score						(W = A) > H > AA
Mean	54.5	47.5	49.6	56.5	56.1	
Standard deviation	8.1	7.5	8.0	8.0	7.3	
Mathematics coursework						ϕ = 0.24
Total	100%	100%	100%	100%	100%	
Math data missing	16.4	23.6	19.2	16.8	14.7	
No math or non-academic math courses	14.0	27.9	23.0	8.8	10.9	
Algebra I & geometry	11.4	12.8	13.3	8.2	11.1	
Algebra II	29.0	20.0	26.7	23.6	31.2	
At least one advanced math course	29.2	15.7	17.8	42.6	32.1	
% Blacks & Hispanics						ϕ = 0.68
Total	100%	100%	100%	100%	100%	
Less than 10%	48.6	6.0	10.1	32.2	60.8	
10% to 29%	26.2	15.8	15.0	32.5	28.7	
30% to 59%	12.6	24.6	25.7	27.5	8.3	
60% or more	12.6	53.6	49.2	7.7	2.2	
% Graduates in 4-year college						ϕ = 0.15
Total	100%	100%	100%	100%	100%	
10% or less	3.3	3.4	3.9	2.8	3.2	
11–24%	11.3	10.0	14.9	15.0	10.9	
25–49%	48.3	59.9	57.8	41.8	45.5	
50–74%	25.8	19.3	17.1	26.6	28.0	
75–100%	11.3	7.4	6.3	13.9	12.4	
Help with college requirements						ϕ = 0.08
Total	100%	100%	100%	100%	100%	
No help	38.5	37.8	38.4	35.2	38.8	
Help with some requirements	45.1	42.4	38.4	48.9	46.1	
Help with all three	16.4	19.8	23.3	15.9	15.0	
Parents' expectations						ϕ = 0.13
Total	100%	100%	100%	100%	100%	
Less than bachelor's degree	10.7	15.4	14.8	8.4	9.7	
Bachelor's degree	56.7	44.7	52.4	44.8	59.9	
Advanced degree	32.6	39.9	32.8	46.8	30.5	

(Continued)

TABLE 2 *(Continued)*
Selected Characteristics of 1990 Bachelor's Degree Aspirants by Racial/Ethnic Group

Variable	*Total*	*African American*	*Hispanic*	*Asian*	*White*	*Statistical Significance*
Grade parents started college saving						$\phi = 0.17$
Total	100%	100%	100%	100%	100%	
10, 11, or 12th grade	23.6	22.5	21.7	25.0	2.39	
Prior to 10th grade	39.6	29.2	23.8	34.9	43.5	
No saving or no response	36.8	48.3	54.5	40.1	32.6	
						AA > W >H > A
Parental involvement						
Mean	0.00	0.05	−0.10	−0.30	0.02	
Standard deviation	1.00	1.10	1.17	1.05	0.96	
Share of friends planning 4-year						$\phi = 0.13$
Total	100%	100%	100%	100%	100%	
None or a few	13.1	21.8	19.6	10.0	11.4	
Some	17.4	14.1	21.2	14.3	17.5	
Most	52.1	48.4	45.2	49.5	53.6	
All	17.4	15.7	14.0	26.1	17.5	
Number of extracurricular activities						$\phi = 0.07$
Total	100%	100%	100%	100%	100%	
None	13.0	14.6	16.5	15.3	12.2	
One	19.8	20.8	23.6	13.9	19.6	
Two	21.9	19.0	20.6	19.0	22.8	
Three or more	45.2	45.6	39.3	51.7	45.3	

Note: For the categorical variables, the statistical difference column shows the strength of the relationship, calculated using the following formula: $\phi = \sqrt{(\chi^2/n)}$. A ϕ that is below 0.3 represents a "small" effect size; a ϕ that is greater than 0.5 is "large". For the continuous variables, this column shows differences between the four groups found using orthogonal contrasts.
Source: Analyses of NELS:90/94.

advanced mathematics coursework appears to be a somewhat less important predictor, of four-year college enrollment for Asians than for bachelor's degree aspirants of other racial/ethnic groups. Completing at least one advanced mathematics course appears to be a particularly important predictor of four-year college enrollment for African Americans and Hispanics.

Various measures of social and cultural are also related to college enrollment behavior. While parents' educational expectations for the student are unrelated to either four-year or two-year college enrollment among bachelor's degree aspirants, other measures of parental support and encouragement are related. Parental involvement, as measured by the frequency of discussions with parents about school related issues, is positively related to the odds of four-year college enrollment for African Americans, Hispanics, and Whites. The odds of public two-year college enrollment also increase with the level of parental involvement among African Americans and Whites. Contrary to expectations, parental saving beginning in the 10th, 11th, or 12th grade generally appears to be a more important predictor of public two-year college enrollment than of four-year college enrollment for African Americans, Hispanics, and Asians.

The influence of high school segregation also appears to vary across racial/ethnic groups. Contrary to expectations, the likelihood of enrolling in a four-year college or university is greater for African Americans who attend a high school in which African Americans and Hispanics comprised at least 30% of the student body than for African Americans who attended high schools with a smaller concentration of African Americans and Hispanics. For Asians, attending a high school with a higher representation of African Americans and Hispanics appears to be associated with a greater likelihood of public two-year college enrollment.

African American bachelor's degree aspirants who attend a high school in which fewer than one-half of the senior class goes on to a four-year college are less likely than other African Americans to enroll in a four-year college themselves, net of other differences. Whites who attend a high school in which fewer than 25% of the high school graduates enroll in a four-year

TABLE 3
Odds-Ratios for College Enrollment Status in October 1992 Among 1990 Bachelor's Degree Aspirants by Race/Ethnicity

	Total	
Independent Variable	*4-year*	*2-year*
African American	1.40*	0.59**
Hispanic	1.16	1.17
Asian	1.14	1.39
Female	1.30***	1.28**
4-year tuition	1.01	1.00
2-year tuition	1.00	0.96***
No occupational aspirations	1.12	1.08
Professional occupation	1.08	0.97
Unemployment rate	0.97	1.19***
Family income	1.13***	1.10***
Test score	1.06***	0.99
No math coursework data	2.93***	1.13
Algebra I and geometry	2.34***	2.07***
Algebra II	5.73***	2.28***
At least I advanced math	10.41***	2.55***
10–29% Black & Hispanic	0.97	1.07
30–59% Black & Hispanic	1.19	1.31*
60% or more Black & Hispanic	1.22	0.63*
Less than 25% graduates in 4-year	0.70*	2.19***
25–49% graduates in 4-year	0.74*	1.42*
50–74% graduates in 4-year	1.31	1.32
No help with college requirements	0.69***	0.83*
Help with all college requirements	1.13	0.79
Parents' expect less than bachelor's	1.02	1.28
Parents' expect finish college	0.93	1.18
Started saving in 10, 11, or 12th grade	1.53***	1.57***
Started saving prior to 10th grade	1.76***	1.51***
Parental involvement	1.37***	1.17***
No friends planning 4-year college	0.35***	1.17
Some friends planning 4-year college	0.40***	1.40*
Most friends planning 4-year college	0.88	1.50**
No extracurricular activities	0.61***	1.10
One extracurricular activity	0.70***	1.13
Two extracurricular activities	1.08	1.32*
Number of cases in the analyses	6.426	
Improvement in fit—χ^2	2,264.68	
Pseudo R^2 (Cox & Snell)	0.350	
Percent classified correctly	89%	22%

*$p < .05$.
**$p < .01$.
***$p < .001$.
Source: Analyses of NELS: 90/94.

TABLE 3 (*Continued*)
Odds-Ratios for College Enrollment Status in October 1992 Among 1990 Bachelor's Degree Aspirants by Race/Ethnicity

	African American		*Hispanic*	
Independent Variable	*4-year*	*2-year*	*4-year*	*2-year*
Female	1.95**	1.17	0.74	1.10
4-year tuition	1.01	0.97	1.00	1.03
2-year tuition	1.00	0.99	1.11*	0.94
No occupational aspirations	1.14	1.37	0.41	0.59
Professional occupation	0.86	1.05	1.12	0.64
Unemployment rate	0.88	1.17	1.23	1.51
Family income	1.05	1.06	1.20**	1.12
Test score	1.04*	0.98	1.06**	1.02
No math coursework data	3.09**	1.40	3.61*	3.43*
Algebra I and geometry	2.64*	3.45*	2.90	1.30
Algebra II	6.64***	2.14	7.44***	1.47
At least I advanced math	16.79***	2.40	13.53***	1.45
10–29% Black & Hispanic	3.29*	2.64	1.15	1.04
30–59% Black & Hispanic	6.56***	3.41	1.15	0.89
60% or more Black & Hispanic	4.60**	1.69	1.58	0.43
Less than 25% graduates in 4-year	0.18**	7.47	0.99	1.61
25–49% graduates in 4-year	0.21**	2.40	1.03	1.78
50–74% graduates in 4-year	0.40	3.17	1.86	1.22
No help with college requirements	0.96	0.20***	0.89	1.09
Help with all college requirements	1.10	0.27**	1.62	1.18
Parents' expect less than bachelor's	1.95	2.03	1.04	0.53
Parents' expect finish college	1.10	1.33	0.72	0.64
Started saving in 10, 11, or 12th grade	1.79*	3.58**	1.75	3.24**
Started saving prior to 10th grade	1.81*	2.99*	1.06	0.81
Parental involvement	1.41**	1.65**	1.33*	1.24
No friends planning 4-year college	0.51	0.45	0.33*	0.97
Some friends planning 4-year college	0.38*	0.86	0.32*	1.04
Most friends planning 4-year college	1.07	0.91	0.48	0.71
No extracurricular activities	0.59	1.17	0.54	0.60
One extracurricular activity	0.57*	0.44	0.51	1.67
Two extracurricular activities	1.00	0.90	0.73	1.34
Number of cases in the analyses	634		453	
Improvement in fit—χ^2	333.62***		266.62***	
Pseudo R^2 (Cox & Snell)	0.408		0.444	
Percent classified correctly	77%	27%	79%	48%

*$p < .05$.
**$p < .01$.
***$p < .001$.
Source: Analyses of NELS:90/94.

TABLE 3 (*Continued*)
Odds-Ratios for College Enrollment Status in October 1992 Among 1990 Bachelor's Degree Aspirants by Race/Ethnicity

	Asian		White	
Independent Variable	*4-year*	*2-year*	*4-year*	*2-year*
Female	1.53	1.08	1.26**	1.35**
4-year tuition	1.11*	1.11	1.01	1.00
2-year tuition	0.98	0.90	1.00	0.97**
No occupational aspirations	0.54	0.89	1.21	1.11
Professional occupation	0.85	0.78	1.15	1.04
Unemployment rate	0.90	1.30	0.96	1.16***
Family income	0.99	l.08	1.18***	1.11***
Test score	1.14***	1.00	1.07***	0.99
No math coursework data	5.99	3.36	2.53***	0.85
Algebra I and geometry	2.67	2.06	2.22***	2.13***
Algebra II	3.39	1.63	5.80***	2.41***
At least I advanced math	8.61*	0.89	10.27***	2.95***
10–29% Black & Hispanic	1.20	3.87*	0.94	1.04
30–59% Black & Hispanic	2.32	5.10*	0.90	1.05
60% or more Black & Hispanic	1.94	1.31	0.89	0.58
Less than 25% graduates in 4-year	1.35	3.99	0.77	2.21***
25–49% graduates in 4-year	1.26	1.73	0.79	1.40
50–74% graduates in 4-year	2.71	3.11	1.37*	1.31
No help with college requirements	1.49	1.28	0.64***	0.85
Help with all college requirements	7.22**	2.38	1.01	0.80
Parents' expect less than bachelor's	0.37	1.07	0.96	1.27
Parents' expect finish college	0.58	0.96	0.95	1.22
Started saving in 10, 11, or 12th grade	2.38	3.43*	1.46***	1.31*
Started saving prior to 10th grade	1.25	0.87	1.83***	1.55***
Parental involvement	1.07	1.23	1.43***	1.16**
No friends planning 4-year college	0.36	1.12	0.35***	1.37
Some friends planning 4-year college	0.63	3.30	0.43***	1.58*
Most friends planning 4-year college	1.30	2.52	0.94	1.68**
No extracurricular activities	0.90	1.20	0.57***	1.13
One extracurricular activity	1.52	0.94	0.74**	1.18
Two extracurricular activities	2.16	2.72	1.09	1.28
Number of cases in the analyses	299		5,005	
Improvement in fit—χ^2	194.62***		2,128.62***	
Pseudo R^2 (Cox & Snell)	0.428		0.346	
Percent classified correctly	89%	63%	90%	21%

*$p < .05$.
**$p < .01$.
***$p < .001$.
Source: Analyses of NELS:90/94.

college are more likely than other Whites to enroll in a public two-year college. Having no or only some friends who plan to attend a four-year college reduces the odds that a Hispanic bachelor's degree aspirant will attend a four-year college. Receiving help with all college related admissions requirements increases the odds of four-year college enrollment for Asians but is unrelated to four-year college enrollment for African Americans and Hispanics.

Discussion

The analyses presented in this study explored the predictors of college enrollment among high school students who had taken the first step in the process of enrolling in college, namely aspiring to complete at least a bachelor's degree. Several conclusions may be drawn from this research. First, in terms of racial/ethnic group differences in college enrollment behavior, both four-year and public two-year college enrollment rates appear to be comparable for Hispanic, Asian, and White bachelor's degree aspirants after controlling for differences in expected costs and benefits, financial resources, academic characteristics, and social and cultural capital. In contrast, African American bachelor's degree aspirants appear to be more likely to enroll in a four-year college or university and less likely to enroll in a public two-year college than bachelor's degree aspirants of other racial/ethnic groups after taking into account other differences. As noted by Hurtado, Inkelas, Brings, and Rhee (1997), however, only a small number of African Americans are "equal" to Whites in terms of all other characteristics. Specifically, the descriptive statistics (Table 2) show that, compared to White bachelor's degree aspirants, African American bachelor's degree aspirants average lower family incomes and test scores, have had less rigorous mathematics coursework, and attend high schools in which smaller proportions of students go on to college.

The analyses also support the conclusion of Perna (2000) that an econometric framework that has been expanded to include measures of social and cultural capital as proxies for differences in expectations, preferences, tastes, and uncertainty is an appropriate conceptual framework for exploring racial/ethnic group differences in college enrollment behavior. Expanding the traditional econometric model to include measures of social and cultural capital builds on McDonough's (1997) conclusion that the college choice process does not conform to the economist's rational choice model. Moreover, much of the econometric research on college enrollment behavior focuses on family background and academic ability to explain observed differences in enrollment rates. The results of such analyses are often fairly pessimistic since such variables as parental education and test scores have not been amenable to public policy. In contrast, by explicitly examining the influence of social and cultural capital—measures of the ways in which parents' education and class status may influence enrollment decisions—on college enrollment decisions, the results of this research suggest several types of policies and practices that may be more likely to result in increased college enrollment rates.

Specifically, the findings from this study suggest several reasons why African Americans and Hispanics who expect to earn at least a bachelor's degree may be less likely than Whites and Asians to take one of the critical steps toward realizing their goal, namely enrolling in a four-year college or university in the fall after graduating from high school. For example, one important barrier to four-year college enrollment for African Americans and Hispanics appears to be their relative underrepresentation among students enrolled in at least one advanced mathematics course. The descriptive analyses reveal that only 16% of African American and 18% of Hispanic bachelor's degree aspirants have taken at least one advanced mathematics course, compared with 32% of White and 43% of Asian bachelor's degree aspirants. The substantial increase in the odds of enrolling in a four-year college associated with completing at least one advanced mathematics course raises important issues of educational equity since the highest levels of mathematics are not available in all schools. Two lawsuits filed in 1999 in California charge that limited access to advanced placement courses disadvantages African American and Hispanic students in the college admissions process. Among the policies that may begin to address this inequity in the quality and intensity of the curriculum are allowing high school students to take courses at local community colleges with credit awarded to the student from both the high school and the community college, providing additional funds to train teachers and enhance high school course offerings, and offering advanced courses on-line (Adelman, 1999; Hebel, 1999).

Another barrier to four-year college enrollment for Hispanics appears to be related to the level of parental involvement. While the odds of enrolling in a four-year college or university increase for both African American and Hispanic bachelor's degree aspirants with the level of parental involvement, the average level of parental involvement is observed to be lower for Hispanics than for African Americans and Whites (Table 2). Efforts to increase parental involvement should recognize that the decision to become involved in the child's education is likely a function of the parents' role construction or beliefs about appropriate behavior, the parents' sense of efficacy for helping the student succeed in school, and the parents' perception of being invited by the school and the student to participate (Hoover-Dempsey & Sandler, 1997). Parental involvement among Hispanics may be limited by a lack of relevant resources (e.g., their own educational attainment, occupational status, work schedule flexibility) and/or different patterns of family life (e.g., kinship ties, socialization patterns, leisure activities) (Lareau, 1987).

This research also suggests that, for African Americans, the decision to enroll in a four-year college or university is influenced by the values, norms, and other characteristics of the high school attended. Specifically, the multinomial logistic regression analyses show that, after taking into account other differences, four-year college enrollment rates are higher for African Americans who attend segregated high schools and high schools in which the majority of graduates attend a four-year college than for other African Americans. Some caution is necessary in interpreting this finding, however. The descriptive analyses reveal that 54% of African American bachelor's degree aspirants attend a high school in which African Americans and Hispanics comprise at least 60% of the student body. As Orfield (1988) concluded based on his examination of trends in White and minority student experiences in Los Angeles high schools, community colleges, and universities, racial/ethnic group segregation is related to economic segregation and both forms of segregation are related to such measures of educational inequality as high school graduation rates, repeated grades, attendance, and test scores. In other words, only a very small number of African Americans who attend segregated high schools are comparable to African Americans who attend integrated high schools in terms of such important college-enrollment related variables as family income, test scores, and mathematics coursework. Nonetheless, future research should explore the particular characteristics of segregated high schools that may, at the margin, promote four-year college enrollment after controlling for other variables, such as differences in the availability of information about four-year colleges, particularly four-year historically Black colleges and universities, and differences in the ways in which school personnel are communicating to students the value of higher education.

Directions for Future Research

This study also suggests at least three areas for future research. One area for future research pertains to the most appropriate ways to measure social and cultural capital. While the results of this study demonstrate the usefulness of an expanded econometric model for examining racial/ethnic group differences in college enrollment behavior, the results also suggest that additional and/or more appropriate measures of social and cultural capital are needed to further develop our understanding of the barriers that limit college enrollment for students of different racial/ethnic groups. For example, the results of this research suggest that four-year college enrollment rates are higher for African Americans who attend high schools in which at least 50% of high school graduates enter four-year colleges. Particularly for those interested in the implications of such research for policy and practice, better measures are required to understand the specific ways in which high school context influences college enrollment behavior. For example, is this measure of "high school quality" really a proxy for the availability and accessibility of appropriate college guidance counseling?

Second, as evidenced by both the percent of cases correctly classified and the number of statistically significant predictors, the expanded econometric model of college enrollment used in this research is substantially better for predicting four-year college enrollment decisions than for predicting public two-year college enrollment decisions. While students who enroll in two-year institutions likely realize many benefits, only a fraction are likely to complete a bachelor's degree (Lavin & Hyllegard, 1996). Analyses of the Beginning Postsecondary Student Survey show that only about one-fifth of students who enroll in a two-year college transfer to a four-year college or university within five years and that transfer rates are lower for African Americans than for Whites (Nettles, Perna, & Edelin, 1999). In this study, the descriptive analyses show that more than one-fifth of 1990 Asian and Hispanic bachelor's degree aspirants enrolled in a public two-year college in the fall after graduating from high school. Therefore, more needs to be learned about the predictors of public two-year college enrollment. Clearly students are considering different criteria, and applying different weights to these criteria, when considering whether to attend a two-year rather than a four-year institution.

Finally, future research should further explore the sex differences in college enrollment found in this study. The multinomial logistic regression analyses show that, among African American and White bachelor's degree aspirants, women are more likely than men to enroll in a four-year college even after controlling for expected costs and benefits, financial resources, academic characteristics, and social and cultural capital. As evidenced in part by a November 1999 conference entitled. "Fewer Men on Campus: A Puzzle for Liberal Arts Colleges and Universities," college leaders are becoming increasingly concerned about the growing gender imbalance in their undergraduate student bodies (Gose, 1999). Although the number of male undergraduates increased by 11% between 1976 and 1996, the number of female undergraduates increased at a faster rate (51%)(NCES, 1999). Because of the differential growth rates, the representation of men among undergraduates has declined from 52% in 1976, to 48% in 1980, to 44% in 1996. With the exception of nonresident aliens, the number of women undergraduates exceeds the number of men undergraduates regardless of race/ethnicity. But, the magnitude of the gender gap in undergraduate enrollments varies by racial/ethnic group. In fall 1996 women represented 62% of African American undergraduates, compared with 51% of Asians, 55% of Whites, 56% of Hispanics, and 59% of American Indians/Alaskan Natives (NCES, 1999). The analyses presented in this research suggest that, among African Americans and Whites, these observed sex differences are not entirely attributable to differences between women and men in variables that are expected to be related to college enrollment. Therefore, future research should continue to recognize the diversity of student experiences by exploring reasons for differences in college enrollment between women and men of the same racial/ethnic group.

References

Adelman, C. (1999). *Answers in the tool box. Academic intensity, attendance patterns, and bachelor's degree attainment.* Washington, DC. Office of Educational Research and Improvement. U.S. Department of Education.

Alexander, K. L., & Eckland, B. K. (1974). Sex differences in the educational attainment process. *American Sociological Review, 39*(October), 668–682.

Alwin, D. F., & Otto, L. B. (1977). High school context effects on aspirations. *Sociology of Education, 50,* 259–273.

Becker, G. S. (1962). Investment in human capital: A theoretical analysis. *Journal of Political Economy, 70 Supplement* (5), 9–49.

Berkner, L., & Chavez, L. (1997). *Access to postsecondary education for the 1992 high school graduates.* Washington, DC. National Center for Education Statistics. (NCES 98–105).

Borus, M. E., & Carpenter, S. A. (1984). Factors associated with college attendance of high-school seniors. *Economics of Education Review, 3*(3), 169–176.

Bourdieu, P., & Passeron, J. C. (1977). *Reproduction in education, society and culture.* Beverly Hills, CA: Sage Publications.

Catsiapis, G. (1987). A model of educational investment decisions. *Review of Economics and Statistics 69,* 33–41.

Coleman, J. S. (1988). Social capital in the creation of human capital. *American Journal of Sociology, 94*(Supplement), 95–120.

DiMaggio, P., & Mohr, J. (1985). Cultural capital, educational attainment, and marital selection. *American Journal of Sociology, 90*(6), 1231–1261.

Freeman, K. (1997). Increasing African Americans' participation in higher education. African American high school students' perspectives. *Journal of Higher Education, 68*(5), 523–550.

Gose, B. (1999). Colleges look for ways to reverse decline in enrollment of men. *Chronicle of Higher Education,* November 26, p. A73.

Hearn, J. C. (1984). The relative roles of academic, ascribed, and socioeconomic characteristics in college destinations. *Sociology of Education, 57* (January), 22–30.

Hebel, S. (1999). A. P. courses are new target in struggle over access to college in California. *Chronicle of Higher Education,* November 26, p. A32.

Horn, L. J. (1997). *Confronting the odds: Students at risk and the pipeline to higher education* PEDAR. Washington, DC: Office of Educational Research and Improvement. U.S. Department of Education (NCES 98-094).

Hoover-Dempsey, K., & Sandler, H. (1997). Why do parents become involved in their children's education? *Review of Educational Research, 67*(1), pp. 3–42.

Hossler, D., Braxton, J., & Coopersmith, G. (1989). Understanding student college choice. In John C. Smart (Ed.), *Higher Education: Handbook of Theory and Research,* Vol. V. (pp. 231–288). New York: Agathon Press.

Hossler, D., & Gallagher, K. S. (1987). Studying student college choice: A three-phase model and the implications for policy-makers. *College and University, 2*(3), 207–221.

Hossler, D., & Stage, F. (1992). Family and high school experience influences on the postsecondary educational plans of ninth-grade students. *American Educational Research Journal, 29*(2), 425–451.

Hossler, D., Schmit, J., & Vesper, N. (1999). *Going to college: How social, economic, and educational factors influence the decisions students make.* Baltimore Johns Hopkins University Press.

Hurtado, S., Inkelas, K. K., Briggs, C., & Rhee, B. S. (1997). Differences in college access and choice among racial/ethnic groups: Identifying continuing barriers. *Research in Higher Education, 38*(1), 43–75.

Jackson, G. A. (1990). Financial aid, college entry, and affirmative action. *American Journal of Education* (August), 523–550.

Kane, J., & Spizman, L. M. (1994). Race, financial aid awards and college attendance: Parents and geography matter. *American Journal of Economics and Sociology, 53*(1), 73–97.

Kane, T. J. (1994). College entry by blacks since 1970. The role of college costs, family background, and the returns to education. *Journal of Political Economy, 102*(5), 878–911.

Lamont, M., & Lareau, A. (1988). Cultural capital: Allusions, gaps and glissandos in recent theoretical developments. *Sociological Theory, 6*(Fall), 153–168.

Lareau, A. (1987). Social class differences in family-school relationships: The importance of cultural capital. *Sociology of Education, 60*(April), 73–83.

Lavin, D., & Hyllegard, D. (1996). *Changing the Odds: Open Admissions and the Life Chances of the Disadvantaged.* New Haven: Yale University Press.

Manski, C. F., & Wise, D. A. (1983). *College choice in America.* Cambridge: Harvard University Press.

McDonough, P. M. (1997). *Choosing colleges: How social class and schools structure opportunity.* Albany: State University of New York.

National Center for Education Statistics (1999). *Digest of Education Statistics.* Washington, DC, Author.

National Educational Longitudinal Study. Third follow-up (NELS: 90/94). Washington, DC: U.S. Department of Education, National Center for Education Statistics.

Nettles, M. T., & Perna, L. W. (1997). *The African American education data book: Higher and adult education, Volume 1.* Fairfax, VA: Frederick D. Patterson Research Institute.

Nettles, M. T., Perna, L. W., & Freeman, K. E. (1999). Two decades of progress: African Americans moving forward in higher education. Fairfax, VA: Frederick D. Patterson Research Institute.

Nolfi, G. J., Fuller, W. C., Corazani, A. J., Epstein, W. H., Freeman, R. B., Manski, C. F., Nelson, V. I., & Wise, D. A. (1978). *Experiences of recent high school graduates: The transition to work or postsecondary education.* Lexington, Massachusetts: Lexington Books.

Orfield, G. (1988). Exclusion of the majority: Shrinking college access and public policy in metropolitan Los Angeles. *The Urban Review, 20*(3), 147–183.

Perna, L. W. (2000). Differences in college enrollment among African Americans, Hispanics, and Whites. *Journal of Higher Education, 71,* 117–141.

Rouse, C. E. (1994). What to do after high school: The two-year versus four-year college enrollment decision. Chapter 3 in R. G. Ehrenberg (Ed.). *Choices and consequences: Contemporary policy issues in education* (pp. 59–88). New York: IRL Press.

Schwartz, J. B. (1985). Student financial aid and the college enrollment decision. The effects of public and private grants and interest subsidies. *Economics of Education Review, 4*(2), 129–144.

Sewell, W. H., Haller, A. O., & Ohlendorf, G. W. (1970). The educational and early occupational status attainment process: Replication and revision. *American Sociological Review, 35,* 1014–1027.

St. John, E. P. (1991). What really influences minority attendance? Sequential analyses of the High School and Beyond sophomore cohort. *Research in Higher Education, 32*(2), 141–158.

St. John, E. P., & Noell, J. (1989). The effects of student financial aid on access to higher education: An analysis of progress with special consideration of minority enrollments. *Research in Higher Education, 30*(6), 563–581.

Steinberg, L. (1996). *Beyond the Classroom: Why School Reform has Failed and What Parents Need to Do.* New York: Simon & Schuster.

Thomas, G. E. (1980). Race and sex differences and similarities in the process of college entry. *Higher Education, 9,* 179–202.

Recommended Readings

House, J. Daniel (1996). College persistence and grade outcomes: noncognitive variables as predictors for African American, Asian American, Hispanic, Native American, and White students. Paper presented at AIR Annual Forum. Albuquerque, NM, 1996.

Kirano-Nakanishi, M. J. (1994). Methodological issues in the study of diversity in higher education. *New Directions for Institutional Research.* N. 81, pp. 63-85.

Kuh, G. D. (2001). Assessing what really matter to student learning: inside the national survey of student engagement. *Change,* v33, n3 pp. 10-17, 66. May/June.

Maruyama, Geoffrey, Moreno, Jose F., Gudeman, Roxane Harvey, Marin, Patricia (2000). Does diversity make a difference? Three research studies on diversity in college classrooms. ED444409.

Marwick, Judith D. (1998). Academic outcomes assessment: A tool for student learning. ED422991.

Napoli, Anthony R. and Wortman, Paul M. "Psychosocial Factors Related to Retention and Early Departure of Two-Year Community Colleges' Students" Reprinted by permission from *Research in Higher Education 39* no. 4 (August 1998).

Nettles, M. T. & Perna, L. W. (1997). *The African American Education Data Book. Volume I: Higher and Adult Education.* College Fund/UNCF. Fairfax, VA.

Porter, Stephen (1999). Assessing transfer and native student performance at four-year institutions. Paper presented at AIR Annual Forum. ED433790.

Smith, Daryl G. Gerbick, Guy L., Figueroa, Mark A., Watkins, Gayle Harris, Levitan, Thomas, Moore, Leeshawn Cradoc, Merchant, Pamela A. Beliak, Haim Dov, Figueroa, Benjamin (1997) *Diversity Works: The Emerging Picture of How Students Benefit.* Association of American Colleges and Universities: Washington, DC. ED416797

Thompson, G. L. (1999). What the numbers really mean: African American underrepresentation at the doctoral level. *Journal of College Student Retention* v.1, n1, pp. 23-40.

Watson, L. W., and Kuh, G. D. (1996). The influence of dominant race environments on student involvement, perceptions, and educational gains: a look at historically black and predominantly white liberal arts institutions. *Journal of College Student Development,* v37, n4 pp. 415-424. July/August.

DISCUSSION & REFLECTION

How can assessment/evaluation shrink the gap of degree attainment between diverse groups in higher education?

What impact(s) should college have on students? How can college impact(s) be assessed?

Is it possible to distinguish the effects of learning in the classroom from learning that occurs outside the classroom? Why is or is it not important to determine the difference?

In what ways should standardized tests be used (or not used) to determine academic success for students of color? Why?

What new perspectives should drive attrition research in the 21st century?

Section V

Measurement Issues

Measurement Issues

Introduction

This section focuses on the issues of measurement in assessment and evaluation. Issues of validity and reliability are essential to the quality of the assessment and evaluation processes since invalid or unreliable measures render conclusions useless. One factor that contributes to issues of valid and reliable measures is the notion of fairness in measurement. There is a growing body of literature that addresses the importance of fair testing and the influence of culturally relevant assessment. Literature in this section, identified or included, presents the discourse around the issues of fair testing and its role in assessment and evaluation in higher education.

Classic Readings

Code of Fair Testing Practices in Education

Joint Committee on Testing Practices

A. Developing and Selecting Appropriate Tests

Test developers should provide the information that test users need to select appropriate tests.

Test developers should:

1. Define what each test measures and what the test should be used for. Describe the population(s) for which the test is appropriate.
2. Accurately represent the characteristics, usefulness, and limitations of tests for their intended purposes.
3. Explain relevant measurement concepts as necessary for clarity at the level of detail that is appropriate for the intended audience(s).
4. Describe the process of test development. Explain how the content and skills to be tested were selected.
5. Provide evidence that the test meets its intended purpose(s).

Test users should select tests that meet the purpose for which they are to be used and that are appropriate for the intended test-taking populations.

Test users should:

1. First define the purpose for testing and the population to be tested. Then, select a test for that purpose and that population based on a thorough review of the available information.
2. Investigate potentially useful sources of information, in addition to test scores, to corroborate the information provided by tests.
3. Read the materials provided by test developers and avoid using tests for which unclear or incomplete information is provided.
4. Become familiar with how and when the test was developed and tried out.
5. Read independent evaluations of a test and of possible alternative measures. Look for evidence required to support the claims of test developers.

Reprinted from *American Psychologist,* (1989), by permission of American Psychological Association.

6. Provide either representative samples or complete copies of test questions, directions, answer sheets, manuals, and score reports to qualified users.
7. Indicate the nature of the evidence obtained concerning the appropriateness of each test for groups of different racial, ethnic, or linguistic backgrounds who are likely to be tested.
8. Identify and publish any specialized skills needed to administer each test and to interpret scores correctly.

6. Examine specimen sets, disclosed tests or samples of questions, directions, answer sheets, manuals, and score reports before selecting a test
7. Ascertain whether the test content and norm group(s) or comparison group(s) are appropriate for the intended test takers.
8. Select and use only those tests for which the skills needed to administer the test and interpret scores correctly are available.

B. Interpreting Scores

Test developers should help users interpret scores correctly.

Test developers should:

9. Provide timely and easily understood score reports that describe test performance clearly and accurately. Also explain the meaning and limitations of reported scores.
10. Describe the population(s) represented by any norms or comparison group(s), the dates the data were gathered, and the process used to select the samples of test takers.
11. Warn users to avoid specific, reasonably anticipated misuses of test scores.
12. Provide information that will help users follow reasonable procedures for setting passing scores when it is appropriate to use such scores with the test.
13. Provide information that will help users gather evidence to show that the test is meeting its intended purpose.

Test users should interpret scores correctly.

Test users should:

9. Obtain information about the scale used for reporting scores, the characteristics of any norms or comparison group(s), and the limitations of the scores.
10. Interpret scores taking into account any major differences between the norms or comparison groups and the actual test takers. Also take into account any differences in test administration practices or familiarity with the specific questions in the test.
11. Avoid using tests for purposes not specifically recommended by the test developer unless evidence is obtained to support the intended use.
12. Explain how any passing scores were set and gather evidence to support the appropriateness of the scores.
13. Obtain evidence to help show that the test is meeting its intended purpose(s).

C. Striving for Fairness

Test developers should strive to make tests that are as fair as possible for test takers of different races, gender, ethnic backgrounds, or handicapping conditions.

Test developers should:

14. Review and revise test questions and related materials to avoid potentially insensitive content or language.
15. Investigate the performance of test takers of different races, gender, and ethnic backgrounds when samples of sufficient size are available. Enact procedures that help to ensure that differences in performance are related primarily to the skills under assessment rather than to irrelevant factors.
16. When feasible, make appropriately modified forms of tests or administration procedures available for test takers with handicapping conditions. Warn test users of potential problems in using standard norms with modified tests or administration procedures that result in noncomparable scores.

Test users should select tests that have been developed in ways that attempt to make them as fair as possible for test takers of different races, gender, ethnic backgrounds, or handicapping conditions.

Test users should:

14. Evaluate the procedures used by test developers to avoid potentially insensitive content or language.
15. Review the performance of test takers of different races, gender, and ethnic backgrounds when samples of sufficient size are available. Evaluate the extent to which performance differences may have been caused by inappropriate characteristics of the test.
16. When necessary and feasible, use appropriately modified forms of tests or administration procedures for test takers with handicapping conditions. Interpret standard norms with care in the light of the modifications that were made.

D. Informing Test Takers

Under some circumstances, test developers have direct communication with test takers. Under other circumstances, test users communicate directly with test takers. Whichever group communicates directly with test takers should provide the information described below.

Test developers or test users should:

17. When a test is optional, provide test takers or their parents/guardians with information to help them judge whether the test should be taken, or if an available alternative to the test should be used.
18. Provide test takers the information they need to be familiar with the coverage of the test, the types of question formats, the directions, and appropriate test-taking strategies. Strive to make such information equally available to all test takers.

Under some circumstances, test developers have direct control of tests and test scores. Under other circumstances, test users have such control. Whichever group has direct control of tests and test scores should take the steps described below.

Test developers or test users should:

19. Provide test takers or their parents/guardians with information about rights test takers may have to obtain copies of tests and completed answer sheets, retake tests, have tests rescored, and cancel scores.
20. Tell test takers or their parents/guardians how long scores will be kept on file and indicate to whom and under what circumstances test scores will or will not be released.
21. Describe the procedures that test takers or their parents/guardians may use to register complaints and have problems resolved.

Methodological and Analytical Issues in Assessing the Influence of College

Ernest T. Pascarella and Patrick T. Terenzini

The Unit of Analysis

An important question in investigations of the influence of college on student development is the appropriate unit of analysis. This is most apparent when one is analyzing multi-institutional samples where data are collected at the individual level but where it is also possible to obtain average scores at the institutional or other level of aggregation (for example, the Cooperative Institutional Research Program data, the National Longitudinal Study of the High School Class of 1972, High School and Beyond). It is also possible, however, that one needs to consider the appropriate unit of analysis even when the data come from single-institution samples. What, for example, are the effects of classroom climate or residential unit composition on student learning (for example, Pascarella & Terenzini, 1982; D. Smith, 1977; Terenzini & Pascarella, 1984)?

The unit of analysis issue has been a complex and somewhat controversial one in research on the influence of college. It is often the case that scholars interested in essentially the same question have in various studies used institutions, departments, or individuals as the unit of analysis. Consider, for example, studies of the influence of different college characteristics on student learning (for example, Astin, 1968c; Ayres, 1983; Ayres & Bennett, 1983; Centra & Kock, 1971; Hartnett & Centra, 1977). Variation in the unit of analysis has perhaps contributed to the lack of consistent findings in several areas of inquiry (for example, Pascarella, 1985a). As suggested in a sophisticated and cogent discussion by Burstein (1980a), the issue is not so much that one unit of aggregation is more appropriate than another. Rather, the issue needs to be understood in light of the fact that different units of aggregation or analysis are asking different questions of the data. When the institution is the unit of analysis, for example, one is essentially asking what the average influence of certain college characteristics (student body selectivity, average faculty salary, and so on) is on average student development. Thus, one is primarily concerned with average effects among or between institutions. When individuals are the unit of analysis, however, the question is typically whether differences in individual students' collegiate experiences (for instance, academic major, extracurricular involvement, interaction with faculty) lead to differences in specified outcomes. Here the focus is on the effects of different experiences or exposures among or between individual students, even if the data are multi-institutional in form.

By focusing on one question, both institutional and individual levels of aggregation tend to ignore other questions. Aggregating at the level of the institution tends to mask possibly substantial variations between individual students' experiences within the same institution (Cronbach, 1976). Assuming, for example, that an aggregate or global measure of the college environment accurately portrays a homogeneous stimulus experienced by all students in the institution ignores substantial evidence of influential subenvironments in an institution, subenvironments that are more proximal to the

Reprinted from *How College Affects Students: Findings and Insights from Twenty Years of Research,* by permission of Jossey-Bass Publishers, Inc.

student's daily experience (for example, Baird, 1974; Berdie, 1967; Lacy, 1978; Newcomb & Wilson, 1966; Pascarella, 1976; Phelan, 1979; Weidman, 1979). Conversely, using individuals as the unit of analysis tends to ignore the dependencies (or correlations) of individual subject experiences within institutions; that is, the shared educational experience among individual students within the same college leads to the nonindependence of individual behaviors within the college (Burstein, 1980a). Thus, for example, institutional enrollment (size) may facilitate certain types of student-faculty relationships in a small liberal arts college that are quite different from the nature of the student-faculty relationships typically found in large research universities. These types of relationships may differentiate small and large institutions even when individual differences in student characteristics are taken into account. Moreover, as suggested by Burstein (1980a), standard statistical estimation techniques such as ordinary least-squares regression analysis can yield flawed or biased estimates in the presence of within-group dependencies.

Because of the dilemmas inherent in choosing one level of aggregation or unit of analysis over another, a number of scholars have suggested the appropriateness of using multilevels of analysis guided by appropriate theory (for example, Astin, 1970b; Burstein, 1980a, 1980b; Cooley, Bond & Mao, 1981; Cronbach, 1976; Cronbach & Webb, 1975; Terenzini & Pascarella, 1984; Rogosa, 1978). In such analyses, both between-student and between-aggregation effects could be estimated when one has multi-institutional (or even multimajor, multiclassroom, or multiresidential arrangement) data. (The appropriate level of aggregation, of course, depends on the substantive question being asked.) Routine use of a multilevel approach such as this might be one way to permit a more valid and informative comparison of results across studies. It would also permit one to compare differences in the aggregate effects of college (or some other unit of aggregation) with the effects of individual student characteristics and experiences. As suggested by Burstein (1980a), variables can have different meanings at different levels of analysis. Studies that choose colleges as the unit of analysis are asking different questions than studies that use the individual as the unit of analysis; consequently, we should expect different results.

Contextual Analysis

One way of combining aggregate and individual levels of analysis simultaneously is through a procedure known as contextual analysis. Contextual analysis is essentially the study of the influence of group- or aggregate-level variables on individual-level outcomes (Erbring & Young, 1980, Firebaugh, 1978, 1980; Lazarsfeld & Menzel, 1961). In this procedure the individual is the true unit of analysis, but instead of focusing only on the developmental effects of individual college experiences, one also attempts to estimate the effect of being a member of a particular group or aggregation (for example, college academic major, residential unit, classroom).

In its simplest form, contextual analysis can be defined by the following regression equation:

$$Y_{ij} = a + b_1X_{ij} + b_2\overline{X}_j + \text{error},$$

where Y_{ij} might represent the academic achievement (for instance, Graduate Record Examination Scores) of the ith student in college j, X_{ij} might be a measure of academic aptitude for the same student, and X_j would be the average (mean) value of student academic aptitude in college j. In short, X_{ij} might be thought of as a measure of student input or background, while X_j could be considered an estimate of college context or environment. The error or random disturbance term represents errors of measurement plus all causes of Y_{ij} (achievement) unspecified by the equation, such as student motivation and efficiency of study habits (Hanushek, Jackson, & Kain, 1974). The coefficients a (constant) and b_1 and b_2 (regression coefficients) can be estimated by ordinary least-squares regression procedures. A contextual or environmental effect is said to occur in this equation if the aggregate measure of student body aptitude has a significant regression coefficient with individual GRE achievement net of individual aptitude. If the coefficient for the contextual effect is positive, it would suggest that attending a college with a student body composed of "bright" students tends positively to influence a student's standardized academic achievement above and beyond his or her own academic aptitude.

One might posit the causal mechanism underlying the above example as due to the tendency for college faculty to gear the cognitive and conceptual level of instruction to the academic capacities of the students being taught or to the generally "higher" intellectual level of student discourse inside or outside the classroom. Hypothetically, then, students in more selective colleges might benefit from instruction (or an overall environment) geared to higher-level cognitive processes such as analysis, synthesis, and evaluation (Bloom, 1956), the results of which are manifest in higher GRE scores. In positing such a causal mechanism, however, we are again confronted by the disconcerting likelihood that selection (input) and aggregation (environmental) effects are substantially correlated. As such, it is extremely difficult, if not impossible, to accurately estimate and separate the effects of the latter from those of the former (Cronbach, Rogosa, Floden, & Price, 1977; Werts & Linn, 1971). In the above specification of the model, the unique effects of context or environment (as indicated by b_2) are likely to be quite conservative. Thus, a significant regression coefficient for average student body aptitude is reasonably convincing evidence of a unique contextual or environmental influence (Burstein, 1980a).

Frog-Pond Effects

Another approach to the combining of individual and aggregate level data is the "frog-pond" or relative deprivation effect as suggested by the work of Davis (1966), Alexander and Eckland (1975b), and Bassis (1977). This approach suggests that in order to understand individual behavior, one needs to be cognizant not only of individual attributes but also of how individual attributes position one in relationship to an important reference or peer group. In the above example of aptitude and achievement, the regression equation might be specified as follows:

$$Y_{ij} = a + b_1X_{ij} + b_2(X_j + \overline{X}_{ij}) + error$$

In this specification, hypothetical GRE achievement for an individual student (Y_{ij}) is posited as a function of individual academic aptitude (X_{ij}) and the difference between individual aptitude and the average college aptitude. A significant regression coefficient would indicate that a student's academic ability relative to the student average at the college attended has an influence on GRE achievement above and beyond individual aptitude alone. The sign of the regression coefficient would indicate whether the effect is generally beneficial to students below (+) or above (–) the college average.

As demonstrated by Burstein (1980a, 1980b), a regression equation including individual, contextual, and frog-pond effects is not estimable by standard means because the variables representing the three effects have a linear dependency. (The coefficients in an equation with any combination of two of the three effects represented, however, can be estimated.) Burstein (1980a) has suggested a way to deal with this problem. Specifically, he suggests that the investigator obtain more direct measures of the contextual or frog-pond effects. This means giving considerable thought to the specific and underlying causal mechanisms at work. For example, research conducted by Terenzini and Pascarella (1984) found that net of individual levels of institutional commitment, freshman-year persistence was independently and positively influenced by the average level of institutional commitment in the student's residence unit (contextual).

It is also possible that the student's level of institutional commitment relative to that of his or her residential unit peers (frog pond) would add significantly to an understanding of individual persistence or withdrawal behavior (an influence not estimated by Terenzini & Pascarella, 1982). That this effect operates through the influence of social involvement or integration is suggested by the theoretical work of Tinto (1975, 1982, 1987). Thus, instead of entering an unestimable frog-pond term operationalizing the student's standing relative to the average institutional commitment of the residence unit, one could substitute relative standing on level of social involvement. The equation then might be specified as follows:

$$P_{ij} = a + b_1(IC_{ij}) + b_2(\overline{IC}_j) + b_3(\overline{SI}_j - SI_{ij}),$$

where

P_{ij} = an individual student's persistence or withdrawal behavior,

IC_{ij} = an individual student's level of institutional commitment,

$\overline{IC}_j$ = average level of institutional commitment in a particular student's residence unit,

$(SI_j - SI_{ij})$ = an individual student's level of social integration relative to the average in his or her residence unit.

Burstein's (1980a) argument for focusing on direct measures of aggregate and/or frog-pond effects underscores a major conceptual problem in multilevel analysis. This problem, which has been forcefully articulated by analysts such as Hauser (1970, 1974) and Firebaugh (1978), is that contextual or frog-pond effects estimated atheoretically are often mechanistic and distally related to the underlying social-psychological processes they were designed to represent (Burstein, 1980a). For example, contextual or frog-pond effects estimated at the institutional level may have little relevance to and therefore little impact on individual cognitive development during college. Greater understanding may come from estimating contextual and relative standing effects at levels of aggregation that are not only theoretically justifiable but also more proximal and directly related to student learning (for example, classrooms, peer groups, roommates). In short, the most informative multilevel analyses are likely to be those "based on theories in which the source and form of group effects are measured directly" (Burstein, 1980a, p. 207).

It may be, of course, that aggregate effects at almost any level are simply too psychologically remote (or too globally measured) to have important direct effects on student development. Instead, the major aggregate-level influences on student development in college may be indirect, transmitted through their shaping of the individual student's interaction with important agents of socialization on campus, such as peers and faculty.

Change Scores

A substantial amount of the more recent research on the influence of college has a developmental focus and attempts to estimate how exposure to different collegiate experiences or environments leads to differential change on some trait over time. For example, do students who reside on campus tend to change more in critical thinking than students who commute to campus? One way in which this type of question has traditionally been approached is to compare pre- to postdifferences (such as freshman-to-senior scores) on an appropriate measure between groups of interest. If, for example, students residing on campus tend to change more in critical thinking than do those commuting to campus, one might conclude that the residential experience increases the impact of college, at least on critical thinking.

This is an intuitively appealing approach. There are, however, two problems with the use of change scores: reliability and the fact that the magnitude of the change or gain is typically correlated with the initial score (Linn, 1986). Reliability is an issue because change scores incorporate the unreliability of both the pre- and post test measures (Thorndike & Hagen, 1977). This can be a major problem when difference scores are used to make decisions about individuals, but it may not be a major issue when group comparisons are being made (Cronbach, 1970; Linn, 1986). The second problem with change scores, their correlation with the initial score, however, can confound attempts to attribute differential change to exposure to a particular group or educational experience. If one simply compared changes in critical thinking between residents and commuters, it would be extremely difficult, if not impossible, to determine whether the differential changes were due to differences in actual residence status or simply to differences in initial critical thinking status between the two groups.

Comparing simple change or gain scores cannot correct for the lack of random assignment to different groups or collegiate experiences. A better (though not totally adequate) approach would be to employ change or gain in critical thinking as a dependent measure in a regression model that includes both a measure of group membership (for example, 1 = residents, 0 = commuters) and initial level of critical thinking. This would indicate whether or not residence arrangement is significantly associated with critical thinking gains when the influence of initial critical thinking status is partialed out. It is of interest to note, however, that one need not use change scores to obtain essentially the same information. Exactly the same results in terms of the statistical significance of residence status would be obtained if senior-year critical thinking were regressed on a model containing both residence status and initial freshman-year critical thinking (Linn, 1986; Linn & Slinde, 1977). Similarly, in the fictitious example we have been using throughout this appendix, essentially the same *net associations* for *SIZE* and *IWF* would be obtained in either of the following regression equations:

$$IO_2 - IO_1 = IO_1 + SIZE + IWF + \text{error}$$

$$IO_2 = IO_1 + SIZE + IWF + \text{error}$$

In what has come to be regarded as a classic paper, Cronbach and Furby (1970, p. 80) have suggested that "investigators who ask questions regarding gain scores would ordinarily be better advised to frame their questions in other ways." In fact, as suggested above, questions about gain or change can typically be reformulated without sacrificing information. Regression analyses that treat the pretest (precollege) scores no differently from other independent variables in the model and use the posttest (senior-year) scores as the dependent variable provide essentially the same information while avoiding many of the problems associated with change scores (Linn & Slinde, 1977).

This is not to suggest that change should not be studied. Recent work by Bryk and Raudenbush (1987) and Willett (1988), as reviewed by Light, Singer, and Willett (1990), has suggested that the study of change becomes more valid and less ambiguous when it is measured over more than two time points. Light, Singer, and Willett (1990, p. 147) argue that assessing change over three, four, or even more time points permits one to trace the "shape of each student's growth trajectory" rather than just the difference between the beginning and end points. The use of multiple estimates of student status over time is a promising new methodological approach to the assessment of change or growth.

Conditional Versus General Effects

The analytical procedures we have discussed in the preceding sections have all assumed that the net effects of each independent variable on the dependent variable are general. That is, the effect is the same for all students irrespective of their status on other independent variables (Kerlinger & Pedhazur, 1973). Thus, in our fictitious example we are assuming that the net direct effect of *IWF* on IO_2 is the same regardless of the student's level on IO_1 or the size of the institution attended this assumption certainly has the appeal of parsimony (that is, other things being equal, the simplest explanation is often the optimal one). On the other hand, it can be argued that assuming only general effects in one's analytical approach ignores individual differences among students attending the same institution or exposed to the same educational or institutional experience. These individual differences among students may interact with different institutional, instructional, curricular, or other educational experiences to produce "conditional" rather than general effects. In a conditional effect, the magnitude of the influence of certain educational experiences on the dependent measure may vary for students with different individual characteristics. Thus, for example, the magnitude of the direct effect of *IWF* on IO_2 may vary, depending upon the student's precollege level of intellectual orientation (IO_1) or on other individual traits such as gender or race.

It is also possible that there may be patterns of conditional relationships or interactions that involve different levels of aggregation (Bryk & Thum, 1989; Raudenbush & Bryk, 1988). In a contextual analysis, for example, individual aptitude may influence achievement differently depending upon the aggregate level of institutional, departmental, or residence unit aptitude. Similarly, there may be interactions among college experience variables that do not directly involve individual differences among student precollege characteristics. The influence of informal contact with faculty on intellectual orientation, for example, may vary in magnitude in institutions of different size enrollment. Conditional effects of the various types described above may be masked by analyses that consider general effects only. Under certain circumstances this may lead the researcher to conclude that the effects of specific educational experiences are trivial or nonsignificant when, in fact, they may have statistically significant and nontrivial influences for certain subgroups in the sample. Thus, a narrow focus on aggregate means or tendencies as an index of college impact may mask important changes in individuals or student subgroups. (See Clark, Heist, McConnell, Trow, & Yonge [1972] or Feldman & Newcomb [1969, pp. 53–58] for a more extensive discussion of this point.)

The concept of conditional effects determined by the interaction of individual differences among students with different methods of teaching of the presentation of course content has a respected tradition in instructional research. Here it is typically referred to as aptitude (or trait) x treatment interaction (Berliner & Cahell, 1973; Cronbach & Snow, 1977). Underlying its application in instructional research is the more general perspective, stemming from the psychology of individual differences, that not all individuals will benefit equally from the same educational experience. Applications of the investigation of conditional effects with post-secondary samples are provided by Romine, Davis, and Gehman (1970) for college environments and achievement; by Holland (1963) for career choice and academic achievement; by Pfeifer (1976) for race and grades; by Andrews (1981), Born, Gledhill, and Davis (1972), Buenz and Merrill (1968) Domino (1968), Daniels and Stevens (1976), Gay (1986), Horak and Horak (1982), Parent, Forward, Canter, and Mohling (1975), Pascarella (1978), Peterson (1979), Ross and Rakow (1981), and Stinard and Dolphin (1981) for different instructional approaches; by Cosgrove (1986) for the effects of programmatic interventions; by Bean (1985), Pascarella and Terenzini (1979a), and Terenzini, Pascarella, Theophilides, and Lorang (1985) in research on student persistence and withdrawal behavior in college; and by Chapman and Pascarella (1983) on students' levels of social and academic integration in college.

The computational procedure for estimating conditional effects involves the addition of a cross-product term to a general effects equation. Thus, if one is interested in the interaction of IO_1 and *IWF*, the required regression would be the following:

$$IO_2 = IO_1 + SIZE + IWF + (IO_1 \times IWF) + \text{error}$$

Because the cross-product of $IO_1 \times IWF$ is composed of variables already in the equation, its introduction produces a high level of multicolinearity or intercorrelation among the independent variables. Since this can lead to biased and unstable regression coefficients, the estimation of conditional effects is usually conducted via a hierarchical regression approach (Overall & Spiegel, 1969). In this approach, the general effects IO_1, *SIZE* and *IWF* (sometimes called main effects) would be entered in the first step. This would be followed by the addition of the cross-product or interaction term in the second step. If the cross-product of IO_1, $\times$ *IWF* is not associated with a significant increase in R^2, one can then eliminate the cross-product term from the equation and interpret the equation in terms of its general effects results. If, however, the cross-product is associated with a significant increase in R^2, it suggests the presence of a significant conditional effect (that is, the magnitude of the influence of *IWF* on IO_2 varies with the student's precollege status on IO_1).

This being the case, the results yielded by the general effects equation would be misleading. Rather, one would interpret the nature of the $IO_1 \times IWF$ interaction to determine variations in the effects (unstandardized regression coefficient) of *IWF* on IO_2 at different levels of IO_1. Cohen and Cohen (1975) provide a simple computational formula for interpreting the nature of a conditional effect when the two interacting variables are continuous in nature. This formula can also be applied when one variable is categorical (for example, treatment versus control) and one is a continuous covariate (for example, aptitude). In the latter case an additional analysis can be conducted to determine the range of the continuous variable (aptitude) for which significant differences in the dependent variable exist between treatment and control groups (Johnson & Fay, 1950; Serlin & Levin, 1980).

A final point needs to be made about the estimation of conditional effects. The presence of replicable aptitude $\times$ treatment interaction effects has not been particularly common in experimental instructional research. Thus, in correlational data where one needs to rely on less effective statistical controls, the presence of conditional effects can often be artifacts idiosyncratic to the particular sample being analyzed. Considerable caution is therefore recommended in substantively interpreting conditional effects in correlational data. The most trustworthy are those suggested by theory and replicable across independent samples.

Final Note

At about the time this volume went into production, two potentially important books on the methodology of research and assessment in higher education were published. The first, by Light, Singer, and Willett (1990), uses case studies of actual investigations in postsecondary settings to introduce and explicate in greater detail many of the issues in research methodology touched upon in this appendix. The second, by Astin (1990), is a detailed treatment of many of the important conceptual, methodological, and analytical issues involved in assessing the impact of college and the impact of different experiences in college. Of particular relevance to the present discussion is Astin's own technical appendix on the statistical analysis of longitudinal data.

Therein, he deals with many of the statistical and analytical issues we have just discussed, though from a somewhat different perspective. He also demonstrates how elements of regression analysis and causal modeling are combined to assess college effects within his input-environment-output model. Both books provide important conceptual, methodological, and analytical tools for scholars interested in the impact of college on students.

But Is It Rigorous? *Trustworthiness and Authenticity in Naturalistic Evaluation*

Yvonna S. Lincoln and Egon G. Guba

Until very recently, program evaluation has been conducted almost exclusively under the assumptions of the conventional, scientific inquiry paradigm using (ideally) experimentally based methodologies and methods. Under such assumptions, a central concern for evaluation, which has been considered a variant of research and therefore subject to the same rules, has been how to maintain maximum rigor while departing from laboratory control to work in the "real" world.

The real-world conditions of social action programs have led to increasing of the rules of rigor, even to the extent of devising studies looser than quasi-experiments. Threats to rigor thus abound in sections explaining how, when, and under what conditions the evaluation was conducted so that the extent of departure from desired levels of rigor might be judged. Maintaining true experimental or even quasi-experimental designs, meeting the requirements of internal and external validity, devising valid and reliable instrumentation, probabilistically and representatively selecting subjects and assigning them randomly to treatments, and other requirements of sound procedure have often been impossible to meet in the world of schools and social action. Design problems aside, the ethics of treatment given and treatment withheld poses formidable problems in a litigious society (Lincoln and Guba, 1985b).

Given the sheer technical difficulties of trying to maintain rigor and given the proliferation of evaluation reports that conclude with that ubiquitous finding, "no significant differences," it is not surprising that the demand for new evaluation forms has increased. What is surprising—for all the disappointment with experimental designs—is the *continued* demand that new models must demonstrate the ability to meet the same impossible criteria! Evaluators and clients both have placed on new-paradigm evaluation (Guba and Lincoln, 1981; Lincoln and Guba, 1985a) the expectation that naturalistic evaluations must be rigorous in the conventional sense, despite the fact that the basic paradigm undergirding the evaluation approach has shifted.

Under traditional standards for rigor (which have remained largely unmet in past evaluations), clients and program funders ask whether naturalistic evaluations are not so subjective that they cannot be trusted. They ask what roles values and multiple realities can legitimately play in evaluations and whether a different team of evaluators might not arrive at entirely different conclusions and recommendations, operating perhaps from a different set of values. Thus, the rigor question continues to plague evaluators and clients alike, and much space and energy is again consumed in the evaluation report explaining how different and distinct paradigms call forth different evaluative questions, different issues, and entirely separate and distinct criteria for determining the reliability and authenticity—as opposed to the rigor—of findings and recommendations.

Reprinted from *Naturalistic Evaluation–New Directions for Program Evaluation,* edited by D.D. Williams, no. 30 (1986), by permission of Jossey-Bass Publishers, Inc.

Rigor in the Conventional Sense

The criteria used to test rigor in the conventional, scientific paradigm are well know. They include exploring the truth value of the inquiry of evaluation (internal validity), its applicability (external validity or generalizability), its consistency (reliability or replicability), and its neutrality (objectivity). These four criteria, when fulfilled, obviate problems of confounding, atypicality, instability, and bias, respectively, and they do so, also respectively, by the techniques of controlling or randomizing possible sources of confounding, representative sampling, replication, and insulation of the investigator (Guba, 1981; Lincoln and Guba, 1985a). In fact, to use a graceful old English cliché, the criteria are honored more in the breach than in the observance; evaluation is but a special and particularly public instance of the impossibility of fulfilling such methodological requirements.

Rigor in the Naturalistic Sense: Trustworthiness and Authenticity

Ontological, epistemological, and methodological differences between the conventional and naturalistic paradigms have been explicated elsewhere (Guba and Lincoln, 1981; Lincoln and Guba, 1985a; Lincoln and Guba, 1986; Guba and Lincoln, in press). Only a brief reminder about the axioms that undergird naturalistic and responsive evaluations is given here.

The axiom concerned with the nature of reality asserts that there is no single reality on which inquiry may converge, but rather there are multiple realities that are socially constructed, and that, when known more fully, tend to produce diverging inquiry. These multiple and constructed realities cannot be studied in pieces (as variables, for example), but only holistically, since the pieces are interrelated in such a way as to influence all other pieces. Moreover, the pieces are themselves sharply influenced by the nature of the immediate context.

The axiom concerned with the nature of "truth" statements demands that inquirers abandon the assumption that enduring, context-free truth statements—generalizations—can and should be sought. Rather, it asserts that all human behavior is time- and context-bound; this boundedness suggests that inquiry is incapable of producing nomothetic knowledge but instead only idiographic "working hypotheses" that relate to a given and specific context. Applications may be possible in other contexts, but they require a detailed comparison of the receiving contexts with the "thick description" it is the naturalistic inquirer's obligation to provide for the sending context.

The axiom concerned with the explanation of action asserts, contrary to the conventional assumption of causality, that action is explainable only in terms of multiple interacting factors, events, and processes that give shape to it and are part of it. The best an inquirer can do, naturalists assert, is to establish plausible inferences about the patterns and webs of such shaping in any given evaluation. Naturalists utilize the field study in part because it is the only way in which phenomena can be studied holistically and *in situ* in those natural contexts that shape them and are shaped by them.

The axiom concerned with the nature of the inquirer-respondent relationship rejects the notion that an inquirer can maintain an objective distance from the phenomena (including human behavior) being studied, suggesting instead that the relationship is one of mutual and simultaneous influence. The interactive nature of the relationship is prized, since it is only because of this feature that inquirers and respondents may fruitfully learn together. The relationship between researcher and respondent, when properly established, is one of respectful negotiation, joint control, and reciprocal learning.

The axiom concerned with the role of values in inquiry asserts that far from being value-free, inquiry is value-bound in a number of ways. These include the values of the inquirer (especially evident in evaluation, for example, in the description and judgment of the merit or worth of an evaluand), the choice of inquiry paradigm (whether conventional or naturalistic, for example), the choice of a substantive theory to guide an inquiry (for example, different kinds of data will be collected and different interpretations made in an evaluation of new reading series, depending on whether the evaluator follows a skills or psycholinguistic reading theory), and contextual values (the values inhering in the context, and which, in evaluation, make a remarkable difference in how evaluation findings may be accepted and used). In addition, each of these four value sources will interact with all the others to produce value resonance or dissonance. To give one example, it would be equally absurd to evaluate a skills-oriented reading series naturalistically as it would to evaluate a psycholinguistic series conventionally because of the essential mismatch in assumptions underlying the reading theories and the inquiry paradigms.

It is at once clear, as Morgan (1983) has convincingly shown, that the criteria for judging an inquiry themselves stem from the underlying paradigm. Criteria developed from conventional axioms and rationally quite appropriate to conventional studies may be quite inappropriate and even irrelevant to naturalistic studies (and vice versa). When the naturalistic axioms just outlined were proposed, there followed a demand for developing rigorous criteria uniquely suited to the naturalistic approach. Two approaches for dealing with these issues have been followed.

Parallel Criteria of Trustworthiness. The first response (Guba, 1981; Lincoln and Guba, 1985a) was to devise criteria that parallel those of the conventional paradigm: internal validity, external validity, reliability, and objectivity. Given a dearth of knowledge about how to apply rigor in the naturalistic paradigm, using the conventional criteria as analogs or metaphoric counterparts was a possible and useful place to begin. Furthermore, developing such criteria built on the two-hundred-year experience of positivist social science.

These criteria are intended torespond to four basic questions (roughly, those concerned with truth value, applicability, consistency, and neutrality), and they can also be answered within naturalism's bounds, albeit in different terms. Thus, we have suggested credibility as an analog to internal validity, transferability as an analog to external validity, dependability as an analog to reliability, and confirmability as an analog to objectivity. We shall refer to these criteria as criteria of trustworthiness (itself a parallel to the term *rigor*).

Techniques appropriate either to increase the probability that these criteria can be met or to actually test the extent to which they have been met have been reasonably well explicated, most recently in Lincoln and Guba (1985a). They include:

For credibility:

- Prolonged engagement—lengthy and intensive contact with the phenomena (or respondents) in the field to assess possible sources of distortion and especially to identify saliencies in the situation
- Persistent observation—in-depth pursuit of those elements found to be especially salient through prolonged engagement
- Triangulation (cross-checking) of data—by use of different sources, methods, and at times, different investigators
- Peer debriefing—exposing oneself to a disinterested professional peer to "keep the inquirer honest," assist in developing working hypotheses, develop and test the emerging design, and obtain emotional catharsis
- Negative case analysis—the active search for negative instances relating to developing insights and adjusting the latter continuously until no further negative instances are found; assumes an assiduous search
- Member checks—the process of continuous, informal testing of information by soliciting reactions of respondents to the investigator's reconstruction of what he or she has been told or otherwise found out and to the constructions offered by other respondents or sources, and a terminal, formal testing of the final case report with a representative sample of stakeholders.

For transferability:

- Thick descriptive data—narrative developed about the context so that judgments about the degree of fit or similarity may be made by others who may wish to apply all or part of the findings elsewhere (although it is by no means clear how "thick" a thick description needs to be, as Hamilton, personal communication, 1984, has pointed out).

For dependability and confirmability:

- An external audit requiring both the establishment of an audit trail and the carrying out of an audit by a component external, disinterested auditor (the process is described in detail in Lincoln and Guba, 1985a). That part of the audit that examines the process results in a dependability judgment, while that part concerned with the product (data and reconstructions) results in a confirmability judgment.

While much remains to be learned about the feasibility and utility of these parallel criteria, there can be little doubt that they represent a substantial advance in thinking about the rigor issue. Nevertheless, there are some major difficulties with them that call out for their augmentation with new criteria rooted in naturalism rather than simply paralleling those rooted in positivism.

First, the parallel criteria cannot be thought of as a complete set because they deal only with issues that loom important from a positivist construction. The positivist paradigm ignores or fails to take into account precisely those problems that have most plagued evaluation practice since the mid 1960s: multiple value structures, social pluralism, conflict rather than consensus, accountability demands, and the like. Indeed, the conventional criteria refer only to methodology and ignore the influence of context. They are able to do so because by definition conventional inquiry is objective and value-free.

Second, intuitively one suspects that if the positivist paradigm did not exist, other criteria might nevertheless be generated directly from naturalistic assumptions. The philosophical and technical problem might be phrased thus: Given a relativist ontology and an interactive, value-bounded epistemology, what might be the nature of the criteria that ought to characterize a naturalistic inquiry? If we reserve the term *rigor* to refer to positivism's criteria and the term *reliability* to refer to naturalism's parallel criteria, we propose the term *authenticity* to refer to these new, embedded, intrinsic naturalistic criteria.

Unique Criteria of Authenticity. We must at once disclaim having solved this problem. What follows are simply some strong suggestions that appear to be worth following up at this time. One of us (Guba, 1981) referred to the earlier attempt to devise reliability criteria as "primitive"; the present attempt is perhaps even more aboriginal. Neither have we as yet been able to generate distinct techniques to test a given study for adherence to these criteria. The reader should therefore regard our discussion as speculative and, we hope, heuristic. We have been able to develop our idea of the first criterion, fairness, in more detail than the other four; its longer discussion ought not to be understood as meaning, however, that fairness is very much more important than the others.

Fairness. If inquiry is value-bound, and if evaluators confront a situation of value-pluralism, it must be the case that different constructions will emerge from persons and groups with differing value systems. The task of the evaluation team is to expose and explicate these several, possibly conflicting, constructions and value structures (and of course, the evaluators themselves operate from some value framework).

Given all these differing constructions, and the conflicts that will almost certainly be generated from them by virtue of their being rooted in value differences, what can an evaluator do to ensure that they are presented, clarified, and honored in a balanced, even-handed way, a way that the several parties would agree is balanced and even-handed? How do evaluators go about their tasks in such a way that can, while not guaranteeing balance (since nothing can), at least enhance the probability that balance will be well approximated?

If every evaluation or inquiry serves some social agenda (and it invariably does), how can one conduct an evaluation to avoid, at least probabilistically, the possibility that certain values will be diminished (and their holders exploited) while others will be enhanced (and their holders advantaged)? The problem is that of trying to avoid empowering at the expense of impoverishing; all stakeholders should be empowered in some fashion at the conclusion of an evaluation, and all ideologies should have an equal chance of expression in the process of negotiating recommendations.

Fairness may be defined as a balanced view that presents all constructions and the values that undergird them. Achieving fairness may be accomplished by means of a two-part process. The first step in the provision of fairness or justice is the ascertaining and presentation of different value and belief systems represented by conflict over issues. Determination of the actual belief system that undergirds a position on any given issue is not always an easy task, but exploration of values when clear conflict is evident should be part of the data-gathering and data-analysis processes (especially during, for instance, the content analysis of individual interviews).

The second step in achieving the fairness criterion is the negotiation of recommendations and subsequent action, carried out with stakeholding groups or their representatives at the conclusion of the data-gathering, analysis, and interpretation stage of evaluation effort. These three stages are in any event simultaneous and interactive within the naturalistic paradigm. Negotiation has as its basis constant collaboration in the evaluative effort by all stakeholders; this involvement is continuous, fully informed (in the consensual sense), and operates between true peers. The agenda for this negotiation (the logical and inescapable conclusion of a true collaborative evaluation process), having been determined and bounded by all stakeholding groups, must be deliberated and resolved according to rules of fairness. Among the rules that can be specified, the following seem to be absolute minimum.

1. Negotiations must have the following characteristics:
   a. It must be open, that is, carried out in full view of the parties of their representatives with no closed sessions, secret codicils, or the like permitted.
   b. It must be carried out by equally skilled bargainers. In the real world it will almost always be the case that one or another group of bargainers will be the more skillful, but at least each side must have access to bargainers of equal skill, whether they choose to use them or not. In some instances, the evaluator may have to act not only as mediator, but as educator of those less skilled bargaining parties, offering additional advice and counsel that enhances their understanding of broader issues in the process of negotiation. We are aware that this comes close to an advocacy role, but we have already presumed that one task of the evaluator is to empower previously impoverished bargainers; this role should probably not cease at the negotiation stage of the evaluation.
   c. It must be carried out from equal positions of power. The power must be equal not only in principle but also in practice; the power to sue a large corporation in principle is very different from the power to sue it in practice, given the great disparity of resources, risk, and other factors, including, of course, more skillful and resource-heavy bargainers.
   d. It must be carried out under circumstances that allow all sides to possess equally complete information. There is no such animal, of course, as "complete information," but each side should have the same information, together with assistance as needed to be able to come to an equal understanding of it. Low levels of understanding are tantamount to lack of information.
   e. It must focus on all matters known to be relevant.
   f. It must be carried out in accordance with rules that were themselves the product of a negotiation.
2. Fairness requires the availability of appellate mechanisms should one or another party believe that the rules are not being observed by some. These mechanisms are another of the products of the pre-negotiation process.
3. Fairness requires fully informed consent with respect to any evaluation procedures (see Lincoln and Guba, 1985a, and Lincoln and Guba, 1985b). This consent is obtained not only prior to an evaluation effort but is continually renegotiated and reaffirmed (formally with consent forms and informally through the establishment and maintenance of trust and integrity between parties to the evaluation) as the design unfolds, new data are found, new constructions are made, and new contingencies are faced by all parties.
4. Finally, fairness requires the constant use of the member-check process, defined earlier, which includes calls for comments on fairness, and which is utilized both during and after the inquiry process itself (in the data collection-analysis-construction stage and later when case studies are being developed). Vigilant and assiduous use of member-checking should build confidence in individuals and groups and should lead to a pervasive judgment about the extent to which fairness exists.

Fairness as a criterion of adequacy for naturalistic evaluation is less ambiguous than the following four, and more is known about how to achieve it. It is not that this criterion is more easily achieved, merely that it has received more attention from a number of scholars (House, 1976; Lehne, 1978; Strike, 1982, see also Guba and Lincoln, 1985).

Ontological Authentication. If each person's reality is constructed and reconstructed as that person gains experience, interacts with others, and deals with the consequences of various personal actions and beliefs, an appropriate criterion to apply is that of improvement in the individual's (and group's) conscious experiencing of the world. What have sometimes been termed *false consciousness* (a neo-Marxian term) and *divided consciousness* are part and parcel of this concept. The aim of some forms of disciplined inquiry, including evaluation (Lincoln and Guba, 1985b) ought to be to raise consciousness, or to unite divided consciousness, likely via some dialectical process, so that a person or persons (not to exclude the evaluator) can achieve a more sophisticated and enriched construction. In some instances, this aim will entail the realization (the "making real") of contextual shaping that has had the effect of political, cultural, or social impoverishment; in others, it will simply mean the increased appreciation of some set of complexities previously not appreciated at all, or appreciated only poorly.

Educative Authentication. It is not enough that the actors in some contexts achieve, individually, more sophisticated or mature constructions, or those that are more ontologically authentic. It is also essential that they come to appreciate (apprehend, discern, understand)—not necessarily like or agree with—the constructions that are made by others and to understand how those constructions are rooted in the different value systems of those others. In this process, it is not inconceivable that accommodations, whether political, strategic, value-based, or even just pragmatic, can be forged. But whether or not that happens is not at issue here; what the criterion of educative validity implies is increased understanding of (including possibly a sharing, or sympathy with) the whats and whys of various expressed constructions. Each stakeholder in the situation should have the opportunity to become educated about others of different persuasions (values and constructions), and hence to appreciate how different opinions, judgments, and actions are evoked. And among those stakeholders will be the evaluator, not only in the sense that he or she will emerge with "findings," recommendations, and an agenda for negotiation that are professionally interesting and fair but also that he or she will develop a more sophisticated and complex construction (an emic-etic blending) of both personal and professional (disciplinary-substantive) kinds.

How one knows whether or not educative authenticity has been reached by stakeholders is unclear. Indeed, in large-scale, multisite evaluations, it may not be possible for all—or even for more than a few—stakeholders to achieve more sophisticated constructions. But the techniques for ensuring that stakeholders do so even in small-scale evaluations are as yet undeveloped. At a minimum, however, the evaluator's responsibility ought to extend to ensuring that those persons who have been identified during the course of the evaluation as gatekeepers to various constituencies and stakeholding audiences ought to have the opportunity to be "educated" in the variety of perspectives and value systems that exist in a given context.

By virtue of the gatekeeping roles that they already occupy, gatekeepers have influence and access to members of stakeholding audiences. As such, they can act to increase the sophistication of their respective constituencies. The evaluator ought at least to make certain that those from whom he or she originally sought entrance are offered the chance to enhance their own understandings of the groups they represent. Various avenues for reporting (slide shows, filmstrips, oral narratives, and the like) should be explored for their profitability in increasing the consciousness of stakeholders, but at a minimum the stakeholders' representatives and gatekeepers should be involved in the educative process.

Catalytic Authentication. Reaching new constructions, achieving understandings that are enriching, and achieving fairness are still not enough. Inquiry, and evaluations in particular, must also facilitate and stimulate action. This form of authentication is sometimes known as feedback-action validity. It is a criterion that might be applied to conventional inquiries and evaluations as well; although if it is were virtually all positivist social action, inquiries and evaluations would fail on it. The call for getting "theory into action"; the preoccupation in recent decades with "dissemination" at the national level; the creation and maintenance of federal laboratories, centers, and dissemination networks; the non-utilization of evaluations; the notable inaction subsequent to evaluations that is virtually a national scandal—all indicate that catalytic authentication has been singularly lacking. The naturalistic posture that involves all stakeholders from the start, that honors their inputs, that provides them with decision-making power in guiding the evaluation, that attempts to empower the powerless and give voice to the speechless, and that results in a collaborative effort holds more promise for eliminating such hoary distinctions as basic versus applied and theory versus practice.

Tactical Authenticity. Stimulation to action via catalytic authentication is in itself no assurance that the action taken will be effective, that is, will result in a desired change (or any change at all). The evaluation of inquiry requires other attributes to serve this latter goal. Chief among these is the matter of whether the evaluation is empowering or impoverishing, and to whom. The first step toward empowerment is taken by providing all persons at risk or with something at stake in the evaluation with the opportunity to control it as well (to move toward creating collaborative negotiation). It provides practice in the use of that power through the negotiation of construction, which is joint emic-etic elaboration. It goes without saying that if respondents are seen simply as "subjects" who must be "manipulated," channeled through "treatments," or even deceived in the interest of some higher "good" or "objective" truth, an evaluation or inquiry cannot possibly have tactical authenticity. Such a posture could only be justified from the bedrock of a realist ontology and an "objective," value-free epistemology.

Summary

All five of these authenticity criteria clearly require more detailed explication. Strategies or techniques for meeting and ensuring them largely remain to be devised. Nevertheless, they represent an attempt to meet a number of criticisms and problems associated with evaluation in general and naturalistic evaluation in particular. First, they address issues that have pervaded evaluation for two decades. As attempts to meet these enduring problems, they appear to be as useful as anything that has heretofore been suggested (in any formal or public sense).

Second, they are responsive to the demand that naturalistic inquiry or evaluation not rely simply on parallel technical criteria for ensuring reliability. While the set of additional authenticity criteria might not be the complete set, it does represent what might grow from naturalistic inquiry were one to ignore (or pretend not to know about) criteria based on the conventional paradigm. In that sense, authenticity criteria are part of an inductive, grounded, and creative process that springs from immersion with naturalistic ontology, epistemology, and methodology (and the concomitant attempts to put those axioms and procedures into practice).

Third, and finally, the criteria are suggestive of the ways in which new criteria might be developed; that is, they are addressed largely to ethical and ideological problems, problems that increasingly concern those involved in social action and in the schooling process. In that sense, they are confluent with an increasing awareness of the ideology-boundedness of public life and the enculturation processes that serve to empower some social groups and classes and to impoverish others. Thus, while at first appearing to be radical, they are nevertheless becoming mainstream. An invitation to join the fray is most cheerfully extended to all comers.

References

Guba, E. G. "Criteria for Assessing the Trustworthiness of Naturalistic Inquiries." *Educational Communication and Technology Journal,* 1981, 29, 75–91.

Guba, E. G., and Lincoln, Y. S. "Do Inquiry Paradigms Imply Inquiry Methodologies?" In D. L. Fetterman (Ed.), *The Silent Scientific Revolution.* Beverly Hills, Calif.: Sage, in press.

Guba, E. G., and Lincoln, Y. S. *Effective Evaluation: Improving the Usefulness of Evaluation Results Through Responsive and Naturalistic Approaches.* San Francisco: Jossey-Bass, 1981.

Guba, E. G., and Lincoln, Y. S. "The Countenances of Fourth Generation Evaluation: Description, Judgment, and Negotiation." Paper presented at Evaluation Network annual meeting, Toronto, Canada, 1985.

House, E. R. "Justice in Evaluation." In G. V. Glass (Ed.), *Evaluation Studies Review Annual, no. 1.* Beverly Hills, Calif.: Sage, 1976.

Lehne, R. *The Quest for Justice: The Politics of School Finance Reform.* New York: Longman, 1978.

Lincoln, Y. S., and Guba, E. G. *Naturalistic Inquiry.* Beverly Hills, Calif.: Sage, 1985a.

Lincoln, Y. S., and Guba, E. G. "Ethics and Naturalistic Inquiry." Unpublished manuscript, University of Kansas, 1985b.

Morgan, G. *Beyond Method: Strategies for Social Research.* Beverly Hills, Calif.: Sage, 1983.

Strike, K. *Educational Policy and the Just Society.* Champaign: University of Illinois Press, 1982.

Current Readings

Addressing Cultural Context in the Development of Performance-Based Assessments and Computer-Adaptive Testing: Preliminary Validity Considerations

Gwyneth M. Boodoo

Educational Testing Service

Performance-based and computer-adaptive assessments have been proposed for use as instructional assessments and for selection, placement, certification, licensing, and other accountability purposes. As with other assessments, it is important that the development, administration, scoring, and reporting of these assessments, as well as the cultural context in which they are viewed by individuals and subgroups, be considered as much as possible within a construct validity framework. This article examines the research and the steps required to address these concerns. It supports the development of a new conceptual framework and more explicit guidelines for designing culturally responsive assessments.

The introduction of performance-based assessments (PBAs) and computer-adaptive tests (CATs) for large-scale accountability purposes has had a positive and revitalizing impact on the measurement community. These innovations have led to both a reexamination of the bases of test construction and evaluation as well as a rich expansion of the measurement models, theories, and beliefs underlying test development. Though much work will be needed in the coming decades to realize this expansion—for example, fairness issues related to the new assessments have yet to be addressed in systematic fashion (Boodoo, 1992)—the efforts of psychometricians such as Messick (1992), Snow (1993), and others provide firm beginnings (Boodoo, 1994). Additionally, the development, administration, scoring, and reporting of information derived from PBAs and CATs must be carried out such that the cultural context of individuals and subgroups is increasingly taken into account. A new conceptual framework is needed to carry out this complex and important task.

To understand the impact of PBAs and CATs on the assessment of minority students, it is first important to view the development of these instruments in light of current research on and standards for addressing the cultural context of testing as a whole (American Educational Research Association, American Psychological Association, & National Council on Measurement in Education, 1995; Educational Testing Service, 1987). Beyond that, a framework for the development of culturally responsive PBAs and CATs must be created.

Reprinted by permission from *The Journal of Negro Education* 75, (1980).

Standards and Guidelines for Addressing Cultural Context in Testing

In 1985, the American Educational Research Association (AERA), the American Psychological Association (APA), and the National Council on Measurement in Education (NCME) jointly published their *Standards for Educational and Psychological Testing.* This comprehensive document differentiates these standards into three categories: primary, secondary, and conditional. Primary standards are those that should be met by all tests before their operational use and in all test uses unless a sound professional reason is available to show why it is not necessary or technically feasible to do so in a particular case. Secondary standards are desirable as goals but are likely to be beyond reasonable expectations in many situations. Conditional standards are those that may be primary in some situations and secondary in others. The AERA/APA/NCME publication outlines seven technical standards that directly address cultural context in test development relevant to validity, reliability, test design, test content, test format, and norming:

1. Standard 1.20 (Conditional):

   Investigations of criterion-related validity for tests used in selection decisions should include, where feasible, a study of the magnitude of predictive bias due to differential prediction for those groups for which previous research has established a substantial prior probability of differential prediction for the particular kind of test in question. (AERA, APA, & NCME, 1985, p. 17)

2. Standard 1.21 (Primary):

   When studies of differential prediction are conducted, the reports should include regression equations (or an appropriate equivalent) computed separately for each group, job, or treatment under consideration or an analysis in which the group, job, or treatment variables are entered as moderators. (AERA, APA, & NCME, 1985, p. 17)

3. Standard 1.22 (Secondary):

   To the extent that it is feasible, comparisons of regression equations in studies of differential prediction among groups, jobs, or treatments should include all of the explicit variables that are used in making selection or classification decisions. (AERA, APA, & NCME, 1985, pp. 17–18)

4. Standard 2.9 (Conditional):

   When there are generally accepted theoretical or empirical reasons for expecting that reliabilities or standard errors of measurement differ substantially for different populations, estimates should be presented for each major population for which the test is recommended. (AERA, APA, & NCME, 1985, p. 22)

5. Standard 3.5 (Conditional):

   When selecting the type and content of items for tests and inventories, test developers should consider the content and type in relation to cultural backgrounds and prior experiences of the variety of ethnic, cultural, age, and gender groups represented in the intended population of test takers. (AERA, APA, & NCME, 1985, p. 26)

6. Standard 3.10 (Conditional):

   When previous research indicates the need for studies of item or test performance differences for a particular kind of test for members of age, ethnic, cultural, and gender groups in the population of test takers, such studies should be conducted as soon as is feasible. Such research should be designed to detect and eliminate aspects of test design, content, or format that might bias test scores for particular groups. (AERA, APA, & NCME, 1985, p. 27)

7. Standard 4.3 (Conditional):

   Norms that are presented should refer to clearly described groups. These groups should be the ones with whom users of the test will ordinarily wish to compare the people who are tested. Test publishers should also encourage the development of local norms by test users when the published norms are insufficient for particular test takers. (AERA, APA, & NCME, 1985, p. 33)

Presently, the standards are being revised by a joint committee of AERA, APA, and NCME members that has been charged with developing standards for fairness that should provide more direction for including considerations of cultural context in test development.

The Educational Testing Service (ETS) published a revision of its standards for quality and fairness in test development in 1987. The ETS standards reflect and adopt the AERA/APA/NCME standards and tailor them to ETS's particular circumstances and needs. They include 18 procedural guidelines that directly address cultural context in test development and research according to the following policies. The first of these policies states that "ETS will strive to develop tests that will be unbiased with regard to major subpopulations being tested" (p. 7). The second,

> . . . [that] ETS will devote appropriate research efforts to investigating special problems faced by population subgroups in test taking. In addition, ETS will encourage analysis of these groups whenever information about them is pertinent to the research being undertaken. (p. 23)

The procedural guidelines state the following:

> Whenever there are sufficient population subgroup members to permit meaningful analyses, investigate validity for major subgroups if the need for such investigation is indicated by consideration of the intended use(s) of the test scores, the characteristics of the intended test-taking population, or research. (Validity Procedural Guideline 5, p. 9)

> Obtain substantive contributions to the test development process from qualified persons who are not on the ETS staff and who represent relevant perspectives, professional specialties, population subgroups, and institutions. Document their relevant qualifications and characteristics. (Test Development Procedural Guideline 1, p. 10)

> Ascertain basic information for each test to be developed, including the intended population that will take the test, including anticipated major subgroups. (Test Development Procedural Guideline 2b, p. 10)

> Document the rationale for the item type(s) and test format to be used and whether any background or prior experience factors (e.g., age, linguistic or cultural background of intended test takers) affected item-type or test-format selection. (Test Development Procedural Guideline 3a, p. 10)

> For each test, prepare, with appropriate advice and review, test development specifications that cover sensitivity, that is, requirements for the inclusion of material reflecting the cultural background and contributions of major population subgroups. (Test Development Procedural Guideline 4d, p. 11)

> Have subject matter and test development specialists who are familiar with the specifications and purpose of the test and with its intended population review the test items for accuracy, content appropriateness, suitability of language, difficulty, and the adequacy with which the domain is sampled. (Test Development Procedural Guideline 6, p. 11)

> Review individual items, the test as a whole, directions, and descriptive materials to assure that language, symbols, words, phrases, and content that are generally regarded as sexist, racist, negative toward population subgroups, or otherwise potentially offensive are eliminated except when judged to be necessary for adequate representation of the domain. (Test Development Procedural Guideline 7b, p. 11)

> Whenever there are sufficient population subgroup members to permit meaningful analysis, use data on item performance relative to subgroups to enhance the judgments of test developers if the need for such studies is indicated by consideration of the recommended use(s) of the test, the characteristics of the intended test-taking population, or prior research. (Test Development Procedural Guideline 9, p. 11)[1]

> Advise test center staff of the need to minimize distractions and to make examinees comfortable in the testing situation. Instruct staff to be sensitive to the psychological as well as physical needs of examinees. Direct supervisors to consult with or include on the test center staff, when appropriate, subgroup members and persons knowledgeable about handicapping conditions. (Test Administration Procedural Guideline 3, p. 13)

> Whenever there are sufficient population subgroup members to permit meaningful analysis, study the reliability or consistency of reported scores for major subgroups if the need for such studies is indicated by consideration of the intended use(s) of the test, the characteristics of the intended test-taking population, or prior research. (Reliability Procedural Guideline 6, p. 16)

Develop score interpretive information by appropriate method(s) (e.g., norms studies, derivation of program statistics, cut score studies). Describe the method(s) including relevant information about:

- the method of selecting participants on whom the data are based, including information about representation of relevant major subgroups within the defined population. (Score Interpretation Procedural Guideline 6b, p. 20)
- the participation rate of categories of individuals or institutions and their characteristics such as the age, sex, or subgroup composition of the group; weighting systems or other adjustments made to form the norming sample; and whether or not the participants were self-selected. (Score Interpretation Procedural Guideline 6c, p. 20)

Avoid developing interpretive information for population subgroups unless sufficient data are available on each subgroup to make the information meaningful, the information can be accompanied with a carefully described rationale (e.g., guidance purposes) for using it, and the information can be presented in a way that discourages incorrect interpretation and use. (Score Interpretation Procedural Guideline 9, p. 20)

Advise users that when using test scores differently for members of different population subgroups (e.g., using separate sex norms or using racial data in regression equations), such uses should be carefully and rationally supported. (Test Use Procedural Guideline 4, p. 21)

Advise users that whenever individuals are assigned to groups on the basis of test scores, users should undertake periodic examinations of classification rates among major population subgroups. (Test Use Procedural Guideline 5e, p. 21)

Provide for a periodic assessment of research and development priorities to assure an adequate balance of resources directed toward meeting the needs of the educational community and society, including population subgroups. (Research and Development Procedural Guideline 1, p. 24)

Follow review procedures for research proposals and reports that will assure that research is of high quality. Reviews may include sensitivity to language or material that is generally regarded as sexist, racist, or otherwise offensive or inappropriate. (Research and Development Procedural Guideline 4f, p. 24)

Whenever information on sex, ethnic, racial, or other population subgroups is pertinent to the research, studies should be designed to allow analyses of these groups. (Research and Development Procedural Guideline 6, p. 25)

The sensitivity review of items and tests follows the ETS sensitivity review guidelines (ETS, 1992, 1994a, 1994b).

Based on these and other recommendations, the ETS's Graduate Record Examination (GRE), which currently consists of three components (verbal, quantitative, and analytical), is being revised as part of the organization's New Testing Initiative (NTI) to develop a new GRE testing program (ETS, 1996a). The current test is being evaluated or revised. By fall 1999, a GRE writing test will be introduced that measures examinees' general writing ability—specifically, their ability to effectively present and sustain a coherent discussion of their views on a complex issue and/or argument. The new GRE, which is to be delivered to test takers via computer, is being developed to improve the graduate admissions process by providing a broader range of tools for assessing the qualifications of candidates for graduate programs. Specifically, it is a response to calls for more accurate and complete assessment of the skills and abilities important for success in graduate school, a greater emphasis on fair test use, and increased diversity in graduate education (ETS, 1996a).

The emphasis on recognition of increased diversity in the GRE was echoed by the Council of Graduate Schools (1996). Additionally, the NTI's inclusion of multicultural issues in its planning for the new GRE follows the 10 FAME (*F*airness, *A*ccess, *M*ulticultural, *E*quity) principles described by Ramirez (1997). These principles include the following:

1. *Presence*—there are multiple ethnic, racial, and cultural groups involved in the NTI;
2. *Contact and Interaction*—the development of the NTI was characterized by extensive contact and interaction among various ethnic, racial, and cultural groups;
3. *Learning and Understanding*—NTI efforts unfold in such a way that they provide

extensive opportunity for the diverse groups to learn about each other's cultures, values, and customs;

4. *Equal Power Relations*—the different and multiple perspectives that diverse groups bring to the NTI process have the same degree of legitimacy, and power relations between groups are equal and symmetric;
5. *Multicontextual Interracial Interactions*—opportunities are provided for the different cultural groups involved in the NTI to interact across a variety of different settings and contexts;
6. *Cooperation and Collaboration*—the different ethnic, racial, and cultural groups involved in the NTI have common and shared goals, and understand that the best way to achieve these goals is by mutual cooperation and collaboration;
7. *Nonhierarchical Structure Along Ethnic, Racial, and Cultural Lines*—the NTI decision-making process is neither stratified nor distributed along ethnic, racial, or cultural dimensions;
8. *Multiperspectival Analysis of the Human Experience*—the NTI process is one in which the human intellectual/learning experience is analyzed and conceptualized from a variety of ethnic, racial, and cultural perspectives, among them the view that truth is not the exclusive domain of any one cultural group and that human behavior must be viewed from multiple perspectives;
9. *Cultural Diversity*—the NTI process is ethno-diverse, not ethnocentric, and is not based on assimilation, acculturation, or cultural uniformity models; and
10. *Mutually Reinforcement*—the NTI process occurs within an institutional context that supports and sanctions, through its authority figures and leadership structure, the previous 9 FAME principles.

Cultural Context and Testing: Findings from the Literature

Research investigating issues of fairness in computer-based testing is ongoing. Much of this research has centered on the comparison of various gender, ethnic, and racial groups' performance on computer tests vis-à-vis their performance on paper-and-pencil measures with respect to item difficulty, item review, guessing corrections, text reading, writing, timing, and penalties for incompleteness. Generally, the results have shown that the differences remain approximately the same across groups for both forms of test administration (Bridgeman, 1997). Moreover, whereas multiple-choice items presently are more widely used in paper-and-pencil assessment formats, the computerization of tests has opened paths for the introduction and integration of new types of items that require some form of constructed response and restructuring of test content. The potential ease with which these latter types of items can be developed, administered, and scored using computer technology suggests that in the not-too-distant future, computerized assessments offering both constructed and multiple-choice items will be increasingly used to measure performance.

With the development of new and revised assessments and the addition or restructuring of existing test content, research on equity issues has assumed increasing prominence. For example, Gallagher's (1997) research on a proposed GRE mathematical reasoning test sought to determine whether that assessment is fair to women and ethnic minority test takers, or whether it serves as a barrier to members of these groups who seek admission to graduate programs in the mathematics, natural science, and engineering fields. Her research was conducted at 17 institutions of higher learning across the country, including several historically Black colleges and universities (HBCUs) and Hispanic Association of Colleges and Universities (HACU) institutions. The results indicated that the impact for women and minorities was twice the size of that found for the same population of students on the current GRE quantitative measures. Although other measures intended for the same population of students as the proposed mathematical reasoning test show impact in the same range, the decision was made that an impact of this magnitude was unacceptably large. Based on the impact results, factors (e.g., speediness, use of figural material) were identified as potential sources of irrelevant variance for female and minority test takers. These factors and others identified in subsequent research will be taken into consideration in future test redesigns.

In addition to the above standards, several researchers have developed validity criteria that have implications for the development of a framework for addressing cultural context in assessment. Frederickson and Collins (1989), for example, propose directness, scope, reliability, and transparency as suitable criteria. Messick (1992) has identified six aspects of a unified construct validity theory that are applicable to both multiple-choice and performance-based assessments, depending on their purposes:

1. the content aspect, which includes evidence of content relevance, representativeness, and technical quality;
2. the substantive aspect, which refers to theoretical rationales for consistencies in test responses, including process models of task performance;
3. the structural aspect, which refers to appraisals of the fidelity of the scoring structure relative to the structure of the construct domains being examined;
4. the external aspect, which includes convergent and discriminant evidence from multitraite–multimethod comparisons as well as evidence of criterion relevance and applied utility;
5. the generalizability aspect, which entails the extent to which score properties and interpretations generalize to and across population groups, settings, and tasks, including validity generalization of test-criterion relationships;
6. the consequential aspect, which considers the value implications of score interpretation as a basis for action as well as the actual and potential consequences of test use, especially with regard to sources of test invalidity related to issues of bias, fairness, and distributive justice.

Messick also provides guidelines for using these validity criteria in the development of assessments. His guidelines, which are also applicable to both multiple-choice and performance-based assessments, include the following:

- The interpretation and use of performance-based assessments, like that of all assessments, should be validated in terms of all six aspects of construct validity.
- Decisions to include particular student performances or products in an assessment should be rationally tied to the purposes of the testing, the nature of the substantive domain at issue, and the construct theories of pertinent skills and knowledge.
- Given the trade-offs in performance-based assessment between domain coverage and generalizability on the one hand, and time-intensive depth of examination on the other, assessment batteries ought to represent a mix of efficient, structured exercises and less structured, open-ended tasks.
- Where possible, a construct-driven approach should be adopted because the meaning of a construct guides the selection or construction of relevant tasks as well as the rational development of scoring criteria and rubrics.
- The conflict between contextualization and decontextualization of problems or tasks should be resolved by recognizing that both, in separate ways, can serve legitimate instructional and measurement purposes.
- For comprehensive assessment, both complex skills and their component skills, where delineated, should be tested.
- The validity standard implicit in the authenticity of assessment as a measurement concept is the familiar one of construct representation or minimal construct underrepresentation.
- Evidence of intended and unintended consequences of test interpretation and use should be evaluated as an integral part of the validation process.

Linn, Baker, and Dunbar (1991) offer eight additional validation criteria for which evidence should be collected in the development of performance-based assessments. These criteria, which may be considered in one or more of the points noted by Messick, include:

1. the intended and unintended consequences of the assessment,
2. the degree to which performance on specific assessment lead to valid generalizations about achievement more broadly defined,

TABLE 1
Mean GRE Test Scores for Ethnic Groups: 1994–95 (U.S. Citizens Only)

GRE General Test	*American Indian*	*Asian American/ Pacific Islander*	*Black/ African American*	*Mexican American*	*Puerto Rican*	*Other Hispanic*	*White/ European American*
Verbal	465	491	390	439	413	459	499
Quantitative	478	599	407	466	461	490	537
Analytical	512	558	422	481	454	502	564
N	1,861	12,857	24,218	5,710	2,891	5,558	239,273

3. the fairness of the assessment,
4. the cognitive complexity of the processes employed in solving assessment problems,
5. the meaningfulness of the assessment problems for students and teachers,
6. a basis upon which the quality of the assessment content is judged,
7. a basis upon which the comprehensiveness of the assessment content is judged, and
8. the costs of conducting the assessment.

Developing a Framework for Culturally Responsive Assessments

It is quite possible that, without a detailed study of the cultures represented by the subgroups taking a test throughout all stages of the test's design and development, differences found between subgroups on existing assessments may also arise on any new or revised measures. For example, Table 1 presents mean scores for different U.S. ethnic groups, taken from Table A.2 of the GRE technical report, *Sex, Race, Ethnicity, and Performance on the GRE General Test* (ETS, 1996b). The emphasis on differential performance and the use of results of existing tests to revise or develop new tests may in itself cause performance differences to persist, particularly in those areas that require knowledge and skills over and beyond those required to perform successfully on the criteria served by the test. Although it is important to consider differential performance in test development and revision, exclusive use or overemphasis on such results could lead to a post hoc rather than the more preferred, and also more difficult, a priori approach to test development. The latter approach will involve engagement with scholars in disciplines that have not traditionally entered the educational assessment dialogue such as those in the fields of anthropology and sociology.

Many researchers have pointed out the difficulty of comparing concepts of intelligence—or, more generally, measures of cognitive ability—across cultures (Neisser et al., 1996). The implications for assessment if this assertion is correct are enormous. Boykin (1994), for example, argues that the successful education of African American children requires an approach that is less concerned with talent sorting and assessment, and more concerned with talent development. This approach has implications for the ways in which assessments are designed, conducted, scored, and used.

Ogbu (1992) points out that the current emphases on core curricula and multicultural education may not be conducive to testing reform if the relationships between ethnic minority and mainstream European American cultures are not taken into account. As he maintains, two types of ethnic minority cultures can be found in the United States: immigrant or voluntary minorities, who tend to adopt the mainstream culture in order to learn and be successful while retaining their cultural identity; and castelike or involuntary minorities, who ancestors were brought to this continent against their will or usurped of their claims to this land by Europeans, and who remain somewhat ambivalent and oppositional to White culture to this day.

One method for testing Ogbu's theories would be to compare the performance of American and non-American test takers from minority groups on standardized assessments such as the GRE, especially if the differences are examined with respect to the underlying attributes required to perform well on the test. These attributes (content, context, and process variables) have been developed by Tatsuoka and Gallagher (in press) for the first section of the GRE quantitative measures component, and have been scored using Tatsuoka's (1995) rule–space model. Additionally, Tatsuoka and Boodoo's (in press) examination of the performance of various ethnic groups on this assessment has shown that while different groups exhibit similar processing skills, they differ in the basic knowledge (intermediate algebra and geometry) needed to answer test items. Among U.S. citizens, Asian Americans were found to score higher than Whites, who scored higher than Hispanics, who scored higher than Blacks. If indeed differences can be found in the attribute performance of U.S. and non-U.S. test takers from ethnic minority groups, then Ogbu's call for a rethinking of instruction and assessment for these populations would be supported. However, there is no empirical evidence that this is the case.

Conclusion

A large body of work can be drawn upon to develop a conceptual framework for the consideration of cultural context in assessment, with that pertaining to construct definition providing the most important of these resources. Indeed, the research discussed in this article suggests that if a construct is defined to include considerations of both the tasks and the test takers, then it is only natural that cultural context will be a major consideration, to the degree necessary, for the assessment that flows from the defined construct. As such, in the future, there may be no culture-free measures.

Note

1. Item statistics and DIF analyses (Holland & Thayer, 1988) are used for this purpose.

References

American Educational Research Association, American Psychological Association, & National Council on Measurement in Education. (1985). *Standards for educational and psychological testing.* Washington, DC: American Psychological Association.

Boodoo, G. M. (1992). National standards and assessments. *Psychological Science Agenda, 5*(3), 10–11.

Boodoo, G. M. (1994). Performance assessment or multiple choice? *Educational Horizons, 72*(1), 50–56.

Boykin, A. W. (1994). Harvesting talent and culture: African-American children and educational reform. In R. Rossi (Ed.), *Schools and students at risk* (pp. 116–138). New York: Teachers College Press.

Bridgeman, B. (1997, March 5–7). *Fairness in computer-based testing: What we know and what we need to know.* Paper presented at the Graduate Record Examination/Xavier conference on New Directions in Assessment for higher education: fairness, access, multiculturalism, and equity, New Orleans, LA.

Council of Graduate Schools. (1996). *Building an inclusive graduate community: A statement of principles.* San Francisco: Author.

Educational Testing Service. (1987). *ETS standards for quality and fairness.* Princeton, NJ: Author.

Educational Testing Service. (1992). *Sensitivity review guidelines.* Princeton, NJ: Author.

Educational Testing Service. (1994a). *Fairness and the GRE.* Princeton, NJ: Author.

Educational Testing Service. (1994b). *Sensitivity review guidelines for computer-adaptive tests.* Princeton, NJ: Author.

Educational Testing Service. (1995). *Graduate Record Examination F.A.M.E. report (fairness, access, multiculturalism, equity and new testing initiatives).* Princeton, NJ: Author.

Educational Testing Service. (1996a). *Overview of the GRE program in transition.* Princeton, NJ: Author.

Educational Testing Service. (1996b). *Sex, race, ethnicity, and performance on the GRE general test: A technical report.* Princeton, NJ: Author.

Frederickson, J. R., & Collins, A. (1989). A systems approach to educational testing. *Educational Researcher, 18*(9), 27–32.

Gallagher, A. (1977, March). *Equity issues in the development of the GRE mathematical reasoning test.* Paper presented at the Graduate Record Examination/Xavier University conference, "New Directions in Assessment for Higher Education: Fairness, Access, Multiculturalism, and Equity," New Orleans, LA.

Holland, P. W., & Thayer, D. T. (1988). Differential item performance and the Mantel–Haenszel procedure. In H. Wainer & H. I. Braun (Eds.), *Test validity* (pp. 129–145). Hillsdale, NJ: Erlbaum.

Linn, R. L., Baker, E. L., & Dunbar, S. B. (1991). Complex, performance-based assessment: Expectations and validation criteria. *Educational Researcher, 20*(8), 15–21.

Messick, S. (1992). *The interplay of evidence and consequences in the validation of performance assessments* (ETS RR 92-39). Princeton, NJ: Educational Testing Service.

Neisser, U., Boodoo, G., Bouchard, T. J., Jr., Boykin, A. W., Brody, N., Ceci, S. J., Halpern, D. J., Loehlin, J. C., Perloff, R., Sternberg, R. J., & Urbina, S. (1996). Intelligence: Knowns and unknowns. *American Psychologist, 51,* 77–101.

Ogbu, J. U. (1992). Understanding cultural diversity and learning. *Educational Researcher, 21*(8), 5–14.

Ramirez, A. (1997, March 5). *The ten FAME principles.* Paper presented at the Graduate Record Examination/Xavier University conference, "New Directions in Assessment for Higher Education: Fairness, Access, Multiculturalism, and Equity," New Orleans, LA.

Snow, R. E. (1993). Construct validity and constructed-response tests. In R. E. Bennett & W. C. Ward (Eds.), *Construction versus choice in cognitive measurement* (pp. 44–60). Hillsdale, NJ: Erlbaum.

Tatsuoka, K. K. (1995). Architecture of knowledge structures and cognitive diagnosis: A statistical pattern classification approach. In S. Chipman, R. Brennan, & P. Nichols (Eds.), *Alternative diagnostic assessment* (pp. 327–359). Hillsdale, NJ: Erlbaum.

Tatsuoka, K. K., & Boodoo, G. M. (in press). Subgroup differences on the GRE quantitative test based on the underlying cognitive processes and knowledge. In A. E. Kelly & R. Lesh (Eds.), *Methodology for mathematics and science in education.* Hillsdale, NJ: Erlbaum.

Tatsuoka, K. K., & Gallagher, A. (in press). *Variables that are involved in the underlying cognitive processes and knowledge of GRE quantitative tests* (Technical Report). Princeton, NJ: Educational Testing Service.

STAKEHOLDER PARTICIPATION FOR THE PURPOSE OF HELPING ENSURE EVALUATION VALIDITY: BRIDGING THE GAP BETWEEN COLLABORATIVE AND NON-COLLABORATIVE EVALUATIONS

PAUL R. BRANDON

Abstract

Collaborative evaluations, in which program stakeholders participate extensively, typically are conducted for the primary purpose of enhancing the use of evaluation findings, and non-collaborative evaluations, in which stakeholders do not participate extensively, typically are conducted for the primary purpose of generating valid findings. This article shows how the gap can be bridged between these two types of evaluations. The article synthesizes, and elaborates on, a small body of recent research that showed that considerable interaction with stakeholders during the evaluation of small education programs helped achieve the raison d'etre of non-collaborative evaluations—that is, to enhance validity. It is also shown that theories and methods of stakeholder participation for the purpose of enhancing validity, which by and large have been ignored in the collaborative evaluation literature, can improve the quality of collaborative studies.

Introduction

The collaboration of evaluators with program stakeholders for the purpose of improving educational program evaluations began to be studied widely in the 1970s, when citizen participation in educational evaluation was encouraged (Smith, 1983). Since then, researchers have developed several approaches for guiding this collaboration. The two collaborative approaches most commonly applied to the evaluation of education programs in the United States and Canada have been *stakeholder-based evaluation* (SBE) (e.g., Bryk, 1983; Donmoyer, 1990; Henry, Dickey, & Areson, 1991; Tovar, 1989), in which stakeholders are involved somewhat in the beginning and ending phases of evaluations, and *practical participatory evaluation* (PPE) (e.g., Cousins & Earl, 1992, 1995), in which stakeholders are heavily involved as evaluation partners in all evaluation phases.[1]

Reprinted from *The American Journal of Evaluation* 19, no. 3 (1998).

SBE was the first collaborative approach to be widely studied, and PPE is one of the most recent. Evaluators using either of these approaches involve stakeholders for the practical purpose of improving the use of evaluation findings (Bryk, 1983; Cousins, Donohue, & Bloom, 1996, 1997; Cousins & Earl, 1992, 1995; Cousins & Whitmore, 1997). In education settings, both stakeholder-based and participatory evaluators seek to involve administrators, project managers or curriculum coordinators and, in the evaluations of small programs or projects, faculty or operational staff who will help achieve the purpose of enhancing the use of evaluation findings.

The purpose of collaborative evaluations and the extent of stakeholder participation in them typically differs notably from non-collaborative evaluations. Evaluators using non-collaborative approaches focus primarily on the epistemological purpose of generating "valid knowledge concerning program functioning and effects" (Cousins & Whitmore, 1997, p. 8). These researchers also note that extensive stakeholder participation does not occur: "Stakeholders are relegated to the role of data source, though on occasion [they] may be consulted for input" (Cousins & Whitmore, 1997, p. 9).

However, as can be seen in four recent research studies on stakeholder participation in evaluation (Brandon, in press; Brandon & Higa, 1998; Brandon, Lindberg, & Wang, 1993; Brandon, Newton, & Harman, 1993), the distinction between collaborative and non-collaborative evaluations is not always clear. Although the evaluations described in these four studies had characteristics of collaborative approaches, in that program stakeholders in all four participated in significant ways during the beginning or ending phases of evaluations, the evaluations examined in these studies also had characteristics of the non-collaborative approach, in that their primary focus was on collecting and reporting valid findings.

The purposes of this article are to show how these four research studies bridge the gap between collaborative and non-collaborative evaluation and to draw implications of these studies for both approaches. Highlights of the four "bridge studies" are provided to show that evaluator-stakeholder interaction enhanced evaluation validity and that their purposes and methods can help improve the quality of future SBE or PPE evaluations.

Involving Stakeholders to Enhance Validity

In the four recent studies highlighted in this article, stakeholders participated for the purpose of enhancing validity. By validity, it is meant here that adequate and appropriate inferences (Messick, 1989, 1995) are made from data collected and reported in evaluations. This psychometric definition of validity is essentially the same as that given in the standards developed by the Joint Committee on Standards for Educational Evaluation (1994, p. 145), which stipulate that validity is an issue of the "soundness or trustworthiness of the inferences that are made from the results of the information gathering process" (see also Carey & Smith, 1992; Owston, 1986; Rogers, 1995).

Inferences should be *construct valid.* In the psychometric literature, construct validity is a concept that recently has come to subsume all aspects of validity, including (among others) instrument content, the technical quality of instruments or data-collection procedures, and the extent to which inferences from data do not have adverse social consequences (Messick, 1989, 1995; Shepard, 1993).[2]

Avoiding threats to the construct validity of inferences made in program evaluations is an important challenge to evaluators. The key threats to construct validity discussed in the psychometric literature are *construct-irrelevant variance* and *construct underrepresentation* (Messick, 1989). Construct-irrelevant variance occurs when data are collected on constructs that are irrelevant to the stated purpose of the data collection, and construct underrepresentation occurs when data incompletely address the intended construct.

Both threats to validity, which together might be called construct *misrepresentation,*[3] have obvious implications for program evaluators, collaborative and non-collaborative alike. When examining program implementation, for example, invalidity due to construct-irrelevant variance is likely to occur when evaluators examine program aspects that are not intended to be implemented, and invalidity due to construct underrepresentation is likely to occur when evaluators fail to consider key characteristics of implementation such as depth and breadth.

To avoid construct misrepresentation in evaluation, evaluators need to ensure that they have a sufficient level of understanding of the programs they evaluate. It is most important to have this understanding in the beginning phases of evaluations, when studies are formed, and in the ending phases, when findings are summarized and conclusions are drawn. In the beginning phases, evaluators' understanding of programs should be sufficient to ensure that evaluations are based on valid needs and that the questions that evaluations are intended to answer do not misrepresent program implementation, outcomes, or context (i.e., the "program constructs" which evaluations are commissioned to address). In the ending phases of studies, evaluators' understanding of programs must be at a level sufficient for ensuring that their interpretation of findings is well informed. For example, if they know too little about the intricacies of program administration, their recommendations for program revisions might be inappropriate. Similarly, if they do not know how well a program should perform for it to be considered successful, data interpretation might go away.

For evaluators to understand programs sufficiently well to conduct valid studies, they often need the assistance of program experts. Cognitive psychologists (e.g., Glaser & Chi, 1988) and expert-systems researchers (e.g., Hoffman, 1994) have shown that experts not only have factual and practical knowledge unknown by novices but also have knowledge of patterns and themes of which novices are unaware. Furthermore, experts can simplify complex problems, identify which information is relevant to decisions, and effectively communicate their expertise to non-experts (Shanteau, 1988).

Many program stakeholders are program experts. As Huberman and Cox said, "The evaluator is like a novice sailor working with yachtsmen who have sailed these institutional waters for years, and know every island, reef and channel" (1990, p. 165). Stakeholders can help improve evaluators' understanding of programs. By tapping stakeholders' expertise, evaluators are not constrained to using the limited program expertise that they have before beginning an evaluation or that they gain on their own during the course of a study.

The four studies discussed in this article collectively show an approach that can be used to help ensure that evaluators' understanding of programs is sufficient for promoting evaluation validity. Because of the overlap between this purpose and the validity purpose of non-collaborative evaluations, these four studies have clear implications for non-collaborative studies. The four studies also have implications for SBEs and PPEs, because they point out some troublesome oversights in SBE and PPE and suggest methods that collaborative evaluators might wish to consider in future evaluations.

A brief overview of these stakeholder participation studies is given in Table 1. Of the studies, two occurred during the beginning phases of evaluation, when the problems for programs to address are identified (a kind of needs assessment) (Brandon, Newton, & Harman, 1993) or the attributes of programs to address in evaluation questions are stipulated (Brandon, Lindberg, & Wang, 1993). The remaining two studies occurred during the ending phases of evaluation, when recommendations for program improvement are prepared (Brandon, in press) or standards for interpreting the extent to which programs have performed satisfactorily are developed (Brandon & Higa, 1998).[4] All studies described evaluations of small education programs.

Procedures for Guiding Evaluator-Stakeholder Interaction

To tap stakeholders' expertise for the purpose of improving evaluators' understanding of programs (and thereby ultimately enhancing validity), three broad *procedural rules* (Smith, 1997) were followed in the four studies. The procedures (a) provide guidance for non-collaborative evaluators who seek to involve stakeholders for the purpose of enhancing validity, and (b) suggest revisions that SBE and PPE might make in their approaches to involving stakeholders.

Tapping the Expertise of the Appropriate Group

The first procedural rule is that *the participation of stakeholder groups with the appropriate program expertise should be elicited.* These are the groups familiar with the purposes, functions, and operations of the programs; they typically are program personnel such as faculty and staff and program beneficiaries such as students. Together, these groups provide the expertise that evaluators need for fully understanding programs and the evaluation data collected about them.

TABLE 1
Overview of Four Research Studies that Bridge the Gap between Collaborative and Non-collaborative Evaluation

Identifying Homeless Children's Problems (Brandon, Newton, & Harman, 1993)	*Identifying Program Attributes to Address in a Subsequent Evaluation (Brandon, Lindberg, & Wang, 1993)*	*Reviewing Evaluators' Recommendations (Brandon, in press)*	*Developing Standards for Judging Students' Performance (Brandon & Higa, 1998)*
Representatives of homeless parents, teachers serving homeless children, and homeless-shelter providers participated in identifying and prioritizing homeless children's educational problems. The study was a form of needs assessment. Samples of each group participated in interviews and a survey. After the samples were interviewed and surveyed, group representatives were convened in a meeting for reconciling differences among groups. The participation of parents ensured that representatives of program beneficiaries were involved. The scope of the problems identified and prioritized was broader than those reported in previous studies elsewhere, suggesting that parent involvement enhanced the validity of the study's findings.	Faculty and students participated in specifying the program attributes to be addressed in a subsequent evaluation. Samples were interviewed, and a survey was distributed to all members of each group. Representatives of each group participated in a structured meeting to reconcile between-group differences. Faculty retained final decision making authority but students had considerable influence on decisions. The final list of program attributes selected for evaluation included some that would have been ignored had students not participated.	Faculty often have input into accepting or modifying evaluators' recommendations, but students usually do not. In this study, meetings in which students reviewed evaluators' recommendations for program revisions were systematically conducted. Males participated more than females, but post-meeting questionnaire data showed that both sexes agreed with the modifications made to the recommendations. The results of the review were used to modify the recommendations before submitting them in a final evaluation report to faculty and administrators.	Teachers of students who had been administered a program-outcome measure participated in a standard-setting procedure for judging the adequacy of the students' levels of performance on the measure. Teachers were deemed the only appropriate group to set standards because other groups had insufficient knowledge about the students' ability and educational background, the subject taught and assessed, and teaching context. The standards set by the teachers were not so low as to suggest a self-serving bias or so high as to suggest unrealistic expectations.

Program personnel have considerably more knowledge than external evaluators about the program's history, administration, management, and operations. As shown in the summaries of the four studies in Table 1, these stakeholders' expertise can be tapped by involving them in identifying the problems that programs should address (Brandon, Newton, & Harman, 1993) or in stipulating program attributes that should be evaluated (Brandon, Lindberg, & Wang, 1993). Both of these activities help evaluators develop better evaluation questions. The expertise of program personnel can also be tapped by having them review evaluators' recommendations for program revisions (Brandon, in press) or having them specify the standards against which to judge performance on program-outcome measures (Brandon & Higa, 1998).

Program beneficiaries are often familiar with aspects of program implementation or outcomes that neither evaluators nor program personnel know. They should be involved whenever they have this knowledge to contribute, such as in three of the four studies summarized here. In one of these three studies (Brandon, Newton, & Harman, 1993), the evaluators involved homeless parents (who had been excluded from previous similar studies conducted in nearly every state of the nation) when identifying their children's most severe educational problems. In the second study (Brandon, Lindberg, & Wang, 1993), the evaluators involved students in helping to identify program attributes to be addressed in a subsequent evaluation. In the third (Brandon, in press), the evaluators involved students in reviewing the evaluators' recommendations for program improvement before the recommendations were reported to faculty and administrators. The involvement of program beneficiaries was crucial in these studies because they had relevant information to contribute that program personnel did not know.

Stakeholder groups should participate in program evaluations only if they have the appropriate expertise. For example, when setting standards for judging student performance, the evaluators (Brandon & Higa, 1998) elicited the assistance of program teachers. Teachers were the only group asked to participate because others had insufficient knowledge about the students' ability and educational background, the subject taught and assessed, and the teaching context. The school principal did not know enough about the capabilities of the assessed students to set fair standards, and parents knew too little about content-area knowledge or skills or about the teaching context to arrive at fair judgments. Setting standards without fully understanding all aspects of schooling can result in standards unfair to the programs.

Beneficiary participation typically is less important to SBE or PPE evaluators than it was to the evaluators in the studies summarized here. No beneficiaries participated in the PPEs included in the volume edited by Cousins and Earl (1995), for example. (Beneficiaries have been involved more in SBEs; for example, see Donmoyer, 1990 and Greene, 1987.) SBE and PPE evaluators often choose not to involve beneficiaries because the primary purpose of such evaluators is to secure the participation of program administrators, managers, and other primary intended users of evaluation findings. As Cousins and Whitmore (1997, p. 6) said about PPE, "Part of the rationale for limiting participation to stakeholders associated closely with program support and management functions is that the evaluation stands a greater chance of meeting the program and organization decision makers' time lines and needs for information."

Without the contribution of program beneficiaries, the validity of SBEs and PPEs might be threatened, resulting in misguided evaluation questions, ill-informed evaluation recommendations, adverse effects for program beneficiaries, or other consequences of evaluation invalidity. A particularly strong risk to validity is cooption of the evaluation by program staff (Dawson & D'Amico, 1985; see also Perry & Backus, 1995). As Scriven (1997, p. 170) said about empowerment evaluation, a close cousin of PPE, "It is in the interests of staff . . . to make [self-evaluation] results look good, since it is their jobs that are at risk." SBE and PPE evaluators might wish to consider the extent to which they risk these threats to validity and decide if it might be appropriate to include program beneficiaries in their evaluations more frequently.

Tapping Expertise Fully and Carefully

The second procedural rule followed in the four studies is that *stakeholders' program expertise should be fully tapped by applying carefully developed, thorough methods for stakeholder participation.* Although not explicitly discussed, this rule has been addressed in a number of published studies of stakeholder participation (e.g., Deutsch & Malmborg, 1986; Edwards, Guttentag, & Snapper, 1975; Greene, 1987; Henry, Dickey, & Areson, 1991; Lawrence & Cook, 1982; Trochim & Linton, 1986).[5]

Gleaning stakeholder expertise is a form of data collection that is subject, within reason, to validity requirements. One such requirement is that the instruments for gleaning stakeholder expertise be content valid and of sufficient technical quality. In two of the four studies that are the focus of this article (Brandon, Lindberg, & Wang, 1993; Brandon, Newton, & Harman, 1993), a Delphi-like procedure was used in which (a) samples of stakeholders were interviewed, the interview results were content-analyzed, and the content-analysis results used to develop a questionnaire, (b) the questionnaires were administered to stakeholder groups (or samples of the groups), and (c) meetings to reconcile the differences among groups' questionnaire results were held with stakeholder representatives. Interviews and survey administration were tailored to the groups (an issue of ecological generalizability). In both studies, scaling methods (Thurstone pair-comparison scaling or magnitude-estimation scaling) were used to analyze questionnaire results. Also, instruments were pilot tested. In one study, content analysis results were supplemented with information obtained in a review of the literature and a review of program documents (Brandon, Lindberg, & Wang, 1993).

A second validity requirement is that face-to-face decision making among stakeholders should be carefully crafted, organized, and conducted. Efforts to do so were made in all four studies featured here. Brandon, Newton, and Harman (1993) described how evaluators used the Nominal Group Technique to structure stakeholder decision making in a meeting conducted by an experienced facilitator for the purpose of reconciling differences among stakeholder groups. In the second study, Brandon, Lindberg, and Wang (1993) described how evaluators conducted a half-day, tightly-structured meeting (held at a neutral site) of student and faculty representatives, held for the purpose of reconciling differences in their groups' surveyed opinions about the program attributes to address in a subsequent evaluation. In this study, the evaluators (a) prepared and distributed tables showing the students and faculty their respective groups' survey results, (b) contributed factual information when necessary, (c) gave faculty and students equal opportunity to contribute to the discussion, and (d) summarized the stakeholders' comments on flip-charts throughout the meeting, while ascertaining that all participants understood their content. In the third study, Brandon (in press) showed how evaluators involved students in meetings held to review evaluators' recommendations for program revisions. The evaluators began the meetings with a description of prior instances of successful involvement of similar stakeholder groups. (This step is particularly important with students, who might be recalcitrant about participating if their opinions have routinely been ignored in the past.) In a structured format, an evaluator with experience as a facilitator then presented recommendations to the students. The meetings were brief and convenient, and recommendations were jargon-free, carefully edited, and presented as chart essays, an efficient format useful for oral presentation (as suggested by Torres, Preskill, & Piontek, 1996). Students' comments were carefully recorded and used to modify several recommendations. Furthermore, participating students believed their involvement had a noteworthy effect on the recommendations. In the fourth study, when K-12 teachers set standards for judging student performance on a program-outcome measure, the evaluators conducted the standard-setting meeting in three rounds (Brandon & Higa, 1998). In the first round, teachers (who had not yet been given their students' scores) recorded their initial impressions of how well their student groups should have scored. In the second round, teachers reflected on their first-round standards after considering actual distributions of scores for high-scoring schools elsewhere in the district. In the third round, teachers discussed the rationales for the standards they had developed in the first and second rounds; after the discussion, the teachers who saw fit made a final round of revisions to their standards.

The methods for involving stakeholders that are described in the four studies suggest how to glean expertise with care. Regrettably, methods such as these are not emphasized (or at least are not well explicated) in descriptions of SBE or

PPE studies (with the exception of the study by Greene, 1987). Indeed, collaborative evaluators often seem to collect information from stakeholders simply by eliciting their contributions in meetings or semi-structured interviews.

Evaluators conducting SBEs and PPEs might wish to consider adopting methods such as those described in the four studies. These methods help ensure that stakeholder expertise is tapped thoroughly by attending to the details of good information collection, both in formal instruments or data-collection procedures and in structured meetings. The full contribution of stakeholders will help ensure that evaluators can be confident of the validity of the conclusions they draw about programs.

Involving Stakeholders Equitably

The third procedural rule followed in the four studies is that *the equitable participation of stakeholders, both between and within groups, should be ensured.* Stakeholders have differential levels of influence on evaluation decisions because of job position and personal characteristics (Bacharach & Lawler, 1980), particularly when both program staff and program beneficiaries participate in evaluations. Contrary to what we might be led to think by theories of collaborative evaluation, these differences in influence do not go away just because evaluators have declared that they are involving the major stakeholder groups; indeed, unless care is taken to ensure equity, efforts to involve stakeholders in evaluation might actually increase the disparity among groups (Mulder & White, 1970; O'Neill, 1995).

Although this third procedural rule has overtones of transformative participatory evaluation and other approaches that emphasize stakeholder participation for the purpose of social justice (Cousins & Whitmore, 1997), the primary intent of the procedure is simply to ensure that no stakeholder groups' expertise is ignored in evaluation decision making. Much of the effort of the evaluators in two of the four studies discussed here was devoted to helping ensure that no stakeholder group's expertise was tapped less than another's. When representatives of homeless parents, social-service providers, and elementary-school teachers participated in identifying the major educational problems of homeless children (Brandon, Newton, & Harman, 1993), the evaluators included explanations of the purpose of stakeholder participation in the introductions to parent interviews and questionnaires, because parents were inexperienced in need assessments. Interviews of members of all three stakeholder groups took no more than one-half hour each, and questionnaires were brief, thereby helping ensure stakeholders' full participation. Remuneration for completing questionnaires also helped ensure full participation. The evaluators used the Nominal Group Technique, which is designed to ensure equitable group participation, in a meeting to reconcile differences in the survey findings for the three groups. The meeting was small, decreasing the likelihood that any stakeholders would be intimidated. All stakeholder-group representatives attending the meeting had equal access to the evaluation findings. When identifying program attributes to address in a subsequent evaluation (Brandon, Lindberg, & Wang, 1993), faculty and students had similar opportunities to participate in the interviews and survey. The meeting to reconcile group differences was tightly structured, small, and did not include high-level administrators; equal numbers of faculty and students participated. Faculty representatives were chosen because they were likely to cooperate with students in decision making. Between-group differences in position and personalities were minimized so as to ensure full participation. A trained group facilitator gave all participants in the meeting sufficient opportunities to express their opinions. Faculty retained decision-making authority in the meeting, because they had legal responsibility for curriculum decision making, but students were given considerably more influence than usual in curriculum evaluation.

Evaluators in the four studies also took steps to help ensure that individual members of stakeholder groups did not dominate the group's input to the evaluation, again for the purpose of ensuring that all participants' expertise could be tapped. When students participated in meetings to review evaluators' recommendations for curriculum revisions in a medical-school evaluation, for example, the evaluators took steps to ensure that all group members felt they could contribute to the discussions, regardless of gender or personality (Brandon, in press). The meeting facilitator supported equitable discussion by striving to inhibit outspoken participants from dominating the discussions; encouraging clarification, rebuttals, and elaboration by other participants;

asking probing questions; and restating students' comments when necessary. Analyses of observation data and of stakeholder questionnaire data collected during the meetings showed that male students tended to participate somewhat more than females, but that both sexes strongly agreed with the suggested revisions to the evaluator's recommendations. Students also reported that they agreed that their participation affected the evaluators' recommendations. When elementary-school teachers participated in a three-part procedure for developing the standards against which to judge student performance on a measure of program outcomes (Brandon & Higa, 1998), standard setting was conducted in a manner intended to avoid conformity due to social desirability or peer pressure. In the first and second rounds, teachers did not discuss the standards they were setting or the rationales for their standards; in the third round, teachers discussed their rationales without talking about the standards that they had set individually. Training and standard setting were efficient—taking about two hours—thereby helping to ensure teachers' full attention to the standard-setting tasks.

Sometimes program personnel, by virtue of their responsibility for programs, might have more influence than others on the final decisions made in evaluations (Brandon, Lindberg, & Wang, 1993). However, even in these circumstances, evaluators can take steps to ensure that other groups such as beneficiaries contribute their knowledge and perspectives in an equitable manner before final decisions are made.

Inequity resulting from differences in socioeconomic status is clearly an issue for evaluators to address when they develop methods for involving stakeholders, particularly for the purpose of enhancing validity. Differences in participation due to equity differences among stakeholders has been widely discussed in the evaluation and organizational decision-making literatures (e.g., Donmoyer, 1990; Greene, 1987; House, 1990; Mercurio, 1979; Tjosvold, 1987; Wood, 1989). Descriptions of applications of methods for diminishing inequities in evaluations have not been thoroughly discussed in the PPE or SBE literatures, however—a deficit that should be addressed. Evaluators who are learning how to involve stakeholders should be careful to ensure that differential levels of organizational influence do not adversely affect evaluation validity. Practitioners of PPE and SBE might wish to consider the extent to which their current practices do not sufficiently take these differential levels of stakeholder influence into account. In particular, they might want to avoid adverse social consequences to program beneficiaries (an issue of construct invalidity) that might result from inequitable participation.

Conclusion

A clear conclusion of this article is that stakeholder participation can help enhance the likelihood of producing valid evaluation findings. The strength of this conclusion is stronger than it was in any one of the four bridge studies comprising the body of recent research on stakeholder participation, because it is based on a synthesis of these studies. The studies examined stakeholder participation in two tasks in the beginning phase of evaluation and two tasks in the ending phase; together, they support the conclusion that stakeholders can help with a variety of tasks across a breadth of evaluations.

The knowledge that stakeholder participation can enhance validity by increasing evaluators' understanding of programs is important for evaluators who typically have not involved stakeholders extensively in their studies. But the primary original contribution of this article is that this knowledge has implications for collaborative evaluators.

Consider how the purposes of SBE and PPE evaluations have affected methods for stakeholder involvement. The purpose of an evaluation approach tends to determine its procedures (Greene, 1990; Smith, 1995, 1997). The SBE and PPE purpose of enhancing program personnel's use of evaluation findings is likely to incline evaluators toward collecting stakeholder information in unstructured interviews or during informal interactions with stakeholders as fellow members of evaluation teams. These methods are appropriate for gathering information that serves the social role of ensuring the use of evaluative findings.

In contrast, consider how the purpose of enhancing validity affects the selection and development of methods for involving stakeholders. The evaluators in the four studies described in this article applied a repertoire of methods from psychometrics and social-science research when they collected information from stakeholders for the purpose of enhancing validity. Methods were developed or selected to collect information in a thorough and equitable manner from all appropriate stakeholder groups. They were appropriate for the role of helping assure evaluation clients of the soundness of evaluation findings.

If SBE and PPE evaluators were to broaden their purposes to include involving stakeholders for enhancing validity, they would be more likely to adopt methods such as those shown in the four studies. By taking greater care to involve all appropriate stakeholder groups and to apply methods that collect stakeholder information fully and equitably, SBE and PPE evaluators would be informed more fully. Such efforts would improve the credibility of their studies. Collecting stakeholder information equitably and fully would require more evaluation resources, but, as the risk of threats to validity was diminished, evaluation conclusions would be strengthened.

Focusing on validity does not mean that the use of evaluation findings must be ignored. Just as in collaborative evaluations, it is likely that the use of evaluation findings was enhanced in the four studies described in this article, because stakeholders participating in the evaluations were involved during significant steps and in influential ways. Decision makers such as administrators who were not directly involved in the evaluations (because they did not have the type of expertise that the evaluators needed to tap) were more likely to heed evaluation conclusions because they knew that their staff members had been involved in significant phases of the evaluation.

In summary, this article can serve as a guide for structuring interactions with stakeholders during the beginning and ending phases of evaluations. By tapping the expertise of all appropriate stakeholder groups and by using methods to glean this expertise fully and equitably, evaluators can take steps calculated to enhance evaluation validity. Evaluators' confidence in the credibility of their studies should be improved, and, most likely, they will find that their studies will receive greater use.

Author Note

This article is a revised version of a paper presented at the meeting of the American Evaluation Association, San Diego, CA, November 1997. The author is grateful to Nick Smith and Brad Cousins for their reviews of the conference version of this manuscript and to two anonymous reviewers for their helpful comments about the current version. The author also thank-fully acknowledges the contributions of James Harman, Terry Ann Higa, Barbara Newton, Marlene Lindberg, and Jonathan Wang to the development and implementation of the evaluations discussed in the four studies synthesized in this article.

Notes

1. Practical participatory evaluation should be distinguished from *transformative* participatory evaluation (Cousins & Whitmore, 1997), which is not discussed here because its purposes (primarily ideological and political) are different from those of PPE.
2. Most discussions of validity in the program evaluation literature have focused on evaluation designs, addressing issues of external and internal validity (e.g., Cook, 1991). Even when construct validity recently was explicitly discussed in this literature, the focus was on validity within the context of experimental and quasi-experimental design (Conrad & Conrad, 1994).
3. This term was suggested to me by Robert W. Health.
4. This article focuses on four studies which discuss stakeholder participation during the beginning and ending phases of evaluations because stakeholder participation is most important in these phases of evaluations, when purpose is established or conclusions are drawn. It could also legitimately focus on stakeholder participation in the middle phase, when evaluation instruments are developed and data are collected and analyzed, because stakeholders' contributions in this phase can obviously also help enhance validity.
5. However, the methods described in some of these studies are not fiscally feasible for the evaluation of small education programs such as those described in this article.

References

Bacharach, S. B., & Lawler, E. J. (1980). *Power and politics in organizations.* San Francisco: Jossey-Bass.

Brandon, P. R. (in press). Involving program stakeholders in reviews of evaluators' recommendations for program revisions. *Evaluation and Program Planning.*

Brandon, P. R., and Higa, T. A. F. (1998, April). *Setting standards to use when judging program performance in stakeholder-assisted evaluations of small educational programs.* Paper presented at the meeting of the American Educational Research Association, San Diego, CA.

Brandon, P. R., Lindberg, M. A., & Wang, Z. (1993). Involving program beneficiaries in the early stages of evaluation: Issues of consequential validity and influence. *Educational Evaluation and Policy Analysis, 15,* 420–428.

Brandon, P. R., Newton, B. J., & Harman, J. W. (1993). Enhancing validity through beneficiaries' equitable involvement in identifying and prioritizing homeless children's educational problems. *Evaluation and Program Planning, 16,* 287–293.

Bryk, A. (1983). (Ed.), *Stakeholder-based evaluation: New directions for program evaluation 17.* San Francisco: Jossey-Bass.

Carey, M. A., & Smith, M. W. (1992). Enhancement of validity through qualitative approaches: Incorporating the patient's perspectives. *Evaluation and the Health Professions, 15*(4), 107–114.

Conrad, K. J., & Conrad, K. M. (1994). Reassessing validity threats in experiments: Focus on construct validity. In K. J. Conrad (Ed.), *Critically evaluating the role of experiments: New Directions for Program Evaluation 63* (pp. 5–25). San Francisco: Jossey-Bass.

Cook, T. D. (1991). Clarifying the warrant for generalized causal inferences in quasi-experimentation. In M. W. McLaughlin & D. C. Phillips (Eds.), *Evaluation and education: At quarter century. Ninetieth yearbook of the National Society for the Study of Education, Part II* (pp. 115–144). Chicago: National Society for the Study of Education.

Cousins, J. B., Donohue, J. J., & Bloom, G. A. (1996). Collaborative evaluation in North America: Evaluators' self-reported opinions, practices and consequences. *Evaluation Practice, 17,* 207–226.

Cousins, J. B., Donohue, J. J., & Bloom, G. A. (1997, November). *Dimensions of form of collaborative evaluation as predictors of utilization.* Paper presented at the annual meeting of the American Evaluation Association, San Diego, CA.

Cousins, J. B., & Earl, L. M. (1992). The case for participatory evaluation. *Educational Evaluation and Policy Analysis, 14,* 397–418.

Cousins, J. B., & Earl, L. M. (Eds.). (1995). *Participatory evaluation in education: Studies in evaluation use and organizational learning.* Washington, DC: Falmer.

Cousins, J. B., & Whitmore, E. (1997, May). *Framing participatory evaluation.* Paper presented at the annual meeting of the Canadian Evaluation Society, Ottawa.

Dawson, J. A., & D'Amico, J. J. (1985). Involving program staff in evaluation studies: A strategy for increasing information use and enriching the data base. *Evaluation Review, 9,* 173–188.

Deutsch, S. J., & Malmborg, C. J. (1986). A study on the consistency of stakeholder preferences for different types of information in evaluating police services. *Evaluation and Program Planning, 9,* 13–24.

Donmoyer, R. (1990). Curriculum evaluation and the negotiation of meaning. *Language Arts, 67,* 274–286.

Edwards, E. L., Guttentag, M., & Snapper, K. (1975). A decision-theoretic approach to evaluation research. In E. L. Struening & M. Guttentag (Eds.), *Handbook of evaluation research* (pp. 139–181). Beverly Hills, CA: Sage.

Glaser, R., & Chi, M. T. H. (1988). Introduction: What is it to be an expert? In M. T. H. Chi, R. Glaser, & M. J. Farr (Eds.), *The nature of expertise* (pp. xv–xxiix). Hillsdale, NJ: Lawrence Erlbaum.

Greene, J. C. (1987). Stakeholder participation in evaluation design: Is it worth the effort? *Evaluation and Program Planning, 10,* 379–394.

Greene, J. C. (1990). Technical quality versus user responsiveness in evaluation practice. *Evaluation and Program Planning, 13,* 267–274.

Henry, G. T., Dickey, K. A., & Areson, J. C. (1991). Stakeholder participation in educational performance monitoring systems. *Educational Evaluation and Policy Analysis, 13,* 177–188.

Hoffman, R. R. (1994). (Ed.), *The psychology of expertise: Cognitive research and empirical AI.* New York: Springer-Verlag.

House, E. R. (1990). Trends in evaluation. *Educational Researcher, 19*(3), 24–28.

Huberman, M., & Cox, P. (1990). Evaluation utilization: Building links between action and reflection. *Studies in Educational Evaluation, 16,* 157–179.

Joint Committee on Standards for Educational Evaluation. (1994). *The program evaluation standard:* (2nd ed.). Thousand Oaks, CA: Sage.

Lawrence, J. E. S., & Cook, T. J. (1982). Designing useful evaluations: The stakeholder survey. *Evaluation and Program Planning, 5,* 327–336.

Mercurio, J. A. (1979.) Community involvement in cooperative decision making: Some lessons learned. *Educational Evaluation and Policy Analysis, 1*(6), 37–46.

Messick, S. (1989). Validity. In R. L. Linn (Ed.), *Educational measurement* (3rd ed.) (pp. 13–103). New York: American Council on Education/Macmillan.

Messick, S. (1995). Validity of psychological assessment: Validation of inferences from persons' responses and performances as scientific inquiry into score meaning. *American Psychologist, 50,* 741–749.

Mulder, M., & Wilke, H. (1970). Participation and power equalization. *Organizational Behavior and Human Performance, 5,* 430–448.

O'Neill, T. (1995). Implementation frailties of Guba and Lincoln's fourth generation evaluation theory. *Studies in Educational Evaluation, 21,* 5–21.

Owston, R. D. (1986). Establishing validity in evaluation: The Canadian Indian school evaluations. *Evaluation and Program Planning, 9,* 319–323.

Perry, P. D., & Backus, C. A. (1995). A different perspective on empowerment in evaluation: Benefits and risks to the evaluation process. *Evaluation Practice, 16,* 37–46.

Rogers, W. T. (1995). The treatment of measurement issues in the revised *Program Evaluation Standards. Journal of Experimental Education, 61,* 13–28.

Scriven, M. (1997). Empowerment evaluation examined. *Evaluation Practice, 18,* 165–175.

Shanteau, J. (1988). Psychological characteristics and strategies of expert decision makers. *Acta Psychologica, 68,* 203–215.

Shepard, L. A. (1993). Evaluating test validity. In L. Darling-Hammond (Ed.), *Review of research in education* (Vol. 19, pp. 405–450). Washington, DC: American Educational Research Association.

Smith, N. L. (1983). Citizen involvement in evaluation: Empirical studies. *Studies in Educational Evaluation, 9,* 105–117.

Smith, N. L. (1995). The influence of societal games on the methodology of evaluative inquiry. In D. M. Fournier (Ed.), *New Directions for Evaluation 44* (pp. 5–14). San Francisco: Jossey-Bass.

Smith, N. L. (1997, November). An investigative framework for characterizing evaluation practice. In N. L. Smith (Chair), *Examining Evaluation Practice.* Symposium conducted at the meeting of the American Evaluation Association, San Diego, CA.

Tjosvold, D. (1987). Participation: A close look at its dynamics. *Journal of Management, 13,* 739–750.

Torres, R. T., Preskill, H. S., & Piontek, M. E. (1996). *Evaluation strategies for communication and reporting: Enhancing learning in organizations.* Thousand Oaks, CA: Sage.

Tovar, M. (1989). Representing multiple perspectives: Collaborative-democratic evaluation in distance education. *The American Journal of Distance Education,* 3(2), 44–56.

Trochim, W. M. K., & Linton, R. (1986). Conceptualization for planning and evaluation. *Evaluation and Program Planning, 9,* 289–308.

Wood, C. J. (1989). Challenging the assumptions underlying the use of participatory decision-making strategies. *Small Group Behavior, 20,* 428–448.

Predictions of Freshman Grade-Point Average from the Revised and Recentered SAT® I: Reasoning Test

Brent Bridgeman, Laura McCamley-Jenkins, and Nancy Ervin

Abstract

The impact of revisions in the content of the SAT® and changes in the score scale on the predictive validity of the SAT were examined. Predictions of freshman grade-point average (FGPA) for the entering class of 1994 (who had taken the old SAT) were compared with predictions for the class of 1995 (who had taken the new SAT I: Reasoning Test). The 1995 scores were evaluated both on the original SAT Program scale and on the recentered scale introduced that year. The changes in the test content and recentering of the score scale had virtually no impact on predictive validity. Other analyses indicated that the SAT I predicts FGPA about equally well across different ethnic groups. Correlations were slightly higher for higher levels of parental education and family income, and grades were more predictable for students with intended majors in math/science (mathematics, engineering, and biological or physical sciences) than for students with other intended majors. Correlations of the SAT I and the composite of SAT I scores and high school grade-point average (HSGPA) with FGPA were generally higher for women than for men, although this pattern was reversed at colleges with very high mean SAT I scores. When a single prediction equation was used for all students, men tended to get lower grades than predicted and women got higher grades than predicted. African-American and Hispanic/Latino men received lower grades than predicted, but women in these groups performed as predicted by the composite. Both men and women with intended majors in math/science got lower grades than would be predicted by an equation based on scores for all enrolled students.

Introduction

A revised SAT, renamed SAT I: Reasoning Test (SAT I), was first offered in March of 1994. The new test continues to assess verbal and mathematical reasoning and uses the same 200–800 score scale as the test it replaced. There were a number of new features introduced in the revised test. The verbal (SAT I–V) section of the test was lengthened by 15 minutes to accommodate more emphasis on critical reading and to allow time for more students to complete all of the questions. A set of questions based on a pair of related passages was added to allow questions that compare and contrast different styles or points of view. Verbal analogies and sentence completion questions were retained from

Reprinted from *College Board Research Report*, College Entrance Examination Board.

the old test, but antonym questions were dropped. There was an increased emphasis on assessing vocabulary in context. The verbal section now contains 78 questions that are to be answered in 75 minutes; more than half of these questions are based on reading passages. The mathematical (SAT I–M) section was also lengthened by 15 minutes, and a new question type was introduced. The new question type required examinees to enter numerical answers on a special grid. The 60 questions of the revised mathematical section contain 50 multiple-choice questions and 10 of the special grid type. For the new test, examinees are allowed to use their own calculators. Allowing calculators did not result in any major changes in the question specifications, and computations were kept simple so that calculators, while allowed, would not be required.

Over the years, as the population of students taking the SAT changed, average scores were no longer in the middle of the 200–800 score scale. In the 1995 profile of college-bound seniors (College Board/Educational Testing Service, 1995), the mean verbal score was 428 on the original SAT Program scale and the mean mathematical score was 482. Because verbal scores had changed more over time than had mathematical scores, students could easily misinterpret their relative standing in these two academic areas. For example, a student with a 470 on both sections would be well above average on the verbal scale but slightly below average on the mathematical scale. In response to this, a change was made to the SAT I score scale in April of 1995. Scores were realigned so that the middle of both the verbal and mathematical scales would once again be about 500. Recentering affected only the way scores were reported; questions on the recentered test were neither harder nor easier than questions on the test prior to recentering. Scores for the same test could be reported on the original or recentered scales.

The current study was undertaken to determine the effects of the content changes and score recentering on the ability of the SAT I: Reasoning Test to predict freshman grade-point average (FGPA) and to address more generally the factors that may affect correlations of frequently used admission measures with freshman grades. Colleges use SAT I scores as a supplement to other information, notably the high school grade-point average (HSGPA), to make selection decisions. The SAT I and HSGPA were examined both individually and combined as predictors of college grades. The study recognizes that freshman grades are only one indicator of success in college and that much can be gained from considering a broader perspective (Willingham, 1985); nevertheless, the FGPA is an important indicator because it reflects a cumulative judgment of the quality of college-level academic performance made by a number of faculty members in several different disciplines. Although the four-year average might be a preferable criterion, research reviews suggest that there is little or no difference in the size of validity coefficients based on FGPA and those based on the cumulative four-year average (Burton & Ramist, in preparation; Wilson, 1983).

Because students select colleges and colleges select students, the range of SAT scores and HSGPAs found among the enrolled students at a particular college can be much narrower than the range found in the potential applicant population. This restriction in range tends to reduce correlations with FGPA that can be computed only for enrolled students; the real question of interest is how well the scores predict for potential applicants, not for enrolled students. Therefore, correlations were adjusted to estimate what they would have been if the ranges of SAT I scores and HSGPAs were the same for a given college and the full national cohort of college-bound seniors taking the SAT I.

The impact of the change in test content was assessed by comparing data for students from the entering college freshman class of 1994 who had taken the old SAT, with data for students from the entering freshman class of 1995 who had taken the new SAT I. Although cohort effects were necessarily confounded with effects related to changes in the test content, previous research suggests that changes in correlations with FGPA over a single year tend to be quite small, especially when correlations are averaged over several colleges (Willingham, Lewis, Morgan, & Ramist, 1990). A change of .02 or less in the multiple correlation (predicting FGPA from a combination of SAT I–V, SAT I–M, and HSGPA) would be in the range expected for year-to-year fluctuations; a change of more than .02 could reflect a real difference related to changes in test content. For analyses of the effects of recentering, there was no confounding with cohort differences because only the 1995 cohort was used. Raw scores on the same tests were converted to both the original or recentered score scales; thus, the score of each student in the 1995 cohort was available on both the original SAT Program scale and on the recentered scale.

An additional question of interest was whether the changes in test content and test scale had an impact on over/underprediction, that is, the tendency for predictions based on the total group to be either too high or too low for specific subgroups. Overprediction occurs when a subgroup does not perform as well as predicted; its predicted performance is above, or over, its actual performance. A common finding is that college grades of women are underpredicted and grades of ethnic minorities are overpredicted (Breland, 1979; Linn, 1978; Ramist, Lewis, & McCamley-Jenkins, 1994; Sawyer, 1986). The referenced studies all examined gender and ethnic groups separately rather than examining gender effects within ethnic groups. This leaves open the question of whether FGPA for women from minority groups is over- or underpredicted. A study of African-American and Hispanic/Latina women in three colleges suggested that their scores were slightly underpredicted by SAT scores when the predictions were based on males from the same ethnic group (Pennock-Román, 1994). However, Pennock-Román did not evaluate over/underprediction within gender/ethnic groups when the original predictions were based on the regression for all students.

Method

Sample

Data for both the 1994 and 1995 entering classes were provided by 23 colleges. Because the same colleges provided data in both years, we could be more confident that any validity changes were attributable to changes in the test content rather than changes in the mix of colleges providing data. The colleges in the sample represented a combination of public and private institutions (13 public and 10 private), including one junior college. One college had only female students. Each of the six College Board geographical regions was represented, but the sample should not be considered to be a nationally representative sample in a strict sampling sense. In particular, most of the colleges were well above average in selectivity and had relatively high scores in their freshman classes. Seven colleges had average combined SAT I scores above 1250, and only two colleges had average scores below 1000. In the sample, average scores on the recentered SAT Program scale were 566 verbal and 581 mathematical compared to 504 and 506 for all college-bound seniors in 1995 (College Board/Educational Testing Service, 1995). The few students in the 1995 cohort who had scores only from the old SAT were removed from the analyses.

Variables

Colleges were asked to provide the FGPA for all students in the 1994 and 1995 entering classes. In addition, they were asked to provide grades in individual courses, but only seven colleges sent this course-level information. SAT I scores were extracted from SAT Program files at the Educational Testing Service (ETS). If the student had taken the SAT I more than once, the most recent score was used. Demographic information was obtained from the Student Descriptive Questionnaire (SDQ), which about 95 percent of the students voluntarily complete when they register to take tests in the SAT Program. The self-reported HSGPA was also obtained from the SDQ. This HSGPA contains 12 categories from F through A+. This HSGPA was coded such that an F = 0, D− = .7, D = 1.0, D+ = 1.3, . . . A+ = 4.3. FGPA was similarly coded from 0 to 4.3, though 4.0 was the top score for many colleges that did not use A+ grades. Previous research suggests that using the self-reported HSGPA from the SDQ results in multiple correlations (combining SAT scores and HSGPA to predict FGPA) that are about .03 to .04 points smaller than multiple correlations that use the actual school-reported HSGPA (Freeberg, Rock, & Pollack, 1989).

Procedures

With a few exceptions as noted, correlations of predictors with FGPA were corrected for range restriction with the Pearson-Lawley multivariate correction (Gulliksen, 1950, pp. 165–166). This adjustment requires the national standard deviations (SD) for the predictors as well as their intercorrelations. For the original SAT Program scale, these SDs were as follows: SAT I–V, 112; SAT I–M, 124. For the recentered scale the SDs were: SAT I–V, 110; SAT I–M, 111. The SD for HSGPA was 0.66. Correlations were the same for original and recentered scales and were as follows: SAT I–V with SAT I-M, .71; SAT I–V with HSGPA, .48; SAT I–M with HSGPA, .53. Consistent with the approach taken by Ramist, Lewis, and McCamley-Jenkins (1994), we made coefficients more comparable across colleges, gender categories, college major categories, and ethnic groups by applying a single correction, based on the SDs in the full national group taking the SAT, to each subgroup.

All correlations with FGPA were computed within colleges, weighted by the number of students at that college (or in the relevant subgroup in that college), and averaged across colleges. Similarly, multiple correlations that used more than one predictor were computed within college and then the weighted average taken across colleges. If any predictor in the multiple correlations had a negative weight, the multiple correlation was recomputed with that variable removed.

Over/underprediction was analyzed by making predictions based on all students in a college and then, for each gender within an ethnic subgroup, computing the difference between the predicted and actual FGPA (predicted GPA minus actual GPA). The result is in grade-point units, with positive values indicating overprediction and negative values indicating underprediction. Two colleges were excluded from the averages—one had only female students and the other used a 0–15 scale for FGPA rather than the 0–4 (or 0–4.3) scale used at the other colleges. Procedures that are specific to particular analyses are presented with the results and discussion for those analyses.

Results and Discussion

Correlations of FGPA with the old (1994) SAT original scale, new (1995) SAT I original scale, and SAT I recentered scale are presented in Table 1. For the purpose of comparing predictions from old (1994) and new (1995) content and original and revised score scales, there was no need to adjust for range restriction, and the correlations in Table 1 were not adjusted. (The extent to which unadjusted correlations underrepresent the actual relationship of scores to grades may be seen by comparing the unadjusted correlations in Table 1 with the adjusted correlations in the *Total* column of Table 4.) Table 1 presents results separately for males and females and for gender within each of the four major ethnic groups. Note that the number of students in the *Gender Total* category is not simply the sum of the four ethnic categories shown; it also includes students from other ethnic categories and students who did not specify their ethnicity.

A quick glance down the first column of correlations suggests that neither the content changes nor recentering had much impact on predictive validity. This interpretation is reinforced in Table 2, indicating that the change from the old test to the new recentered test resulted in about as many colleges showing increases as decreases. Because no change was made in the way HSGPA was computed, differences noted for HSGPA presumably reflect cohort effects from 1994 to 1995. As noted previously (e.g., Ramist, Lewis, McCamley-Jenkins, 1994), correlations were generally higher for women than for men, but the impact of changes in the test and score scale on predictive validity appears to be equally trivial for men and women.

Predictions within Gender and Ethnic Groups

Because of the somewhat smaller sample sizes, some year-to-year fluctuations in the gender-within-ethnic-group correlations should be expected. Changes from 1994 to 1995 in correlations of HSGPA with FGPA indicate only cohort effects. As indicated in the uncorrected correlations in Table 1, shifts of .05 or greater were found in 3 of the 8 gender/ethnic groups (two down and one up). The only single test score correlation showing a change greater than .05 was SAT–M in the Hispanic/Latino sample, with a decline of .06 for Hispanic/Latino men and an increase of .06 for Hispanic/Latino women. The SAT combined score was relatively stable; the only change greater than .05 was an apparent decline for Hispanic/Latino men of .06, from .30 to .24. Because the SAT combined correlation increased by .03 for Hispanic/Latino women, it would be hard to make an argument that the new content was somehow less predictive for Hispanic/Latino students generally. Adjusting the values in Table 1 for range restriction still showed essentially the same decline for Hispanic/Latino men (from .50 to .43). However, there was not a uniform decline across colleges. In the 8 colleges with at least 50

TABLE 1
Correlations with FGPA for SAT (1994), SAT I (1995) on Original Scale, and Recentered SAT I

			Correlation with Freshman Grade-Point Average									
			Gender Total		*African American*		*Asian American*		*Hispanic/Latino*		*White*	
Score	*Version*	*Total*	*M*	*F*	*M*	*F*	*M*	*F*	*M*	*F*	*M*	*F*
Number of Students	old (1994)	45,100	21,733	23,367	1,074	1,761	3,767	4,047	1,400	1,825	14,545	14,60**
	new (1995)	48,039	23,925	25,114	1,148	1,826	3,778	4,087	1,517	1,934	15,249	15,920
SAT–V	old	.29	.28	.32	.28	.29	.23	.27	.21	.29	.27	.29
	new, OS	.30	.28	.32	.23	.29	.24	.26	.19	.29	.28	.30
	new, R	.30	.28	.32	.23	.29	.24	.26	.19	.29	.28	.30
SAT–M	old	.29	.30	.34	.29	.33	.28	.33	.25	.25	.27	.30
	new, OS	.30	.32	.35	.31	.34	.32	.31	.19	.31	.30	.31
	new, R	.30	.32	.35	.30	.34	.32	.32	.19	.31	.30	.31
HSGPA	old	.36	.37	.35	.29	.34	.32	.28	.32	.34	.37	.35
	new	.36	.37	.34	.34	.29	.28	.26	.30	.29	.38	.34
SAT	old	.34	.34	.39	.35	.38	.32	.38	.30	.34	.32	.34
	new, OS	.35	.35	.39	.35	.37	.36	.37	.24	.37	.33	.35
	new, R	.35	.35	.39	.34	.37	.36	.37	.24	.37	.33	.35
SAT + HSGPA	old	.45	.45	.46	.43	.47	.43	.43	.42	.44	.44	.43
	new, OS	.44	.44	.45	.45	.44	.44	.42	.38	.44	.43	.43
	new, R	.44	.44	.45	.45	.44	.44	.43	.38	.44	.44	.43

Note: OS = original scale; R = recentered scale. For HSGPA, old and new refer only to 1994 and 1995 samples respectively, not to content changes.

TABLE 2
Number of Colleges with Validity Increase or Decrease from SAT (1994)/Original Scale to SAT I (1995)/Recentered Scale

	Verbal	*Math*	*HSGPA*	*SAT + HSGPA*
# Colleges with Validity Increase	11	13	8	9
# Colleges with Validity Decrease	10	10	10	13
# Colleges Validity Unchanged	2	0	5	1

Hispanic/Latino men in both years, the correlation declined in 5 but increased in the other 3. Two colleges in the sample had large Hispanic/Latino populations (more than 200 students in both 1994 and 1995). In one of these colleges, a large state university in the Southwest, the adjusted correlation for Hispanic/Latino men declined from .57 to .50. However, in the other college, a large state university in the West, the adjusted correlation increased from .37 to .46. Thus, there does not appear to be a uniform declining trend or increasing trend in any subgroup, and the observed differences in the mean correlations may simply reflect year-to-year variation.

Correlations for Colleges in Three Score Ranges

Correlations for colleges in three score ranges are shown in Table 3. The score ranges were based on the mean SAT I combined score in the college, using the recentered score scale. The first category included colleges with mean scores of less than 1050, the middle category range was 1050–1250, and the colleges in the highest category had mean SAT combined scores above 1250. The correlations were adjusted for restriction in range. Such adjustments are especially useful when comparisons are being made across categories in which there is more range restriction in one category than another; there is typically greater restriction in the highest score category because colleges in this category tend to be most selective. Within any one score category, the changes in the test and score scale had little or no impact on validity. A previous study of score recentering (Morgan, 1994), suggested that any impact on predictive validity should be quite small, but whatever effects are noted should be positive; Table 3 supports that conclusion.

Consistent with previous findings (Ramist, Lewis, and McCamley-Jenkins, 1994), correlations tended to be higher for the institutions in the highest score category. In addition, the SAT increment, that is, the extent to which SAT scores improve predictions over HSGPA alone, tended to be greatest for colleges in the highest category. For the recentered scores on the new test, the SAT increment was .04 in the lowest category, .06 in the middle category, and .09 in the highest category.

TABLE 3
Adjusted Correlations with Freshman GPA for Colleges in Three Score Ranges

		Version		
Score	*Score Range (V + M)*	*Old (1994)*	*New (1995), OS*	*New, R*
SAT–V	<1050	.47	.46	.46
	1050–1250	.46	.45	.46
	>1250	.57	.54	.55
SAT–M	<1050	.47	.45	.46
	1050–1250	.47	.46	.47
	>1250	.58	.57	.57
HSGPA	<1050	.58	.58	.58
	1050–1250	.55	.52	.53
	>1250	.59	.60	.60
SAT	<1050	.51	.50	.50
	1050–1250	.50	.49	.50
	>1250	.63	.60	.61
SAT + HSGPA	<1050	.62	.62	.62
	1050–1250	.60	.58	.59
	>1250	.69	.69	.69

Note: Five colleges and 4,490 students in <1050 category; 11 colleges and 37,033 students in 1050–1250 category; 7 colleges and 6,516 students in >1250 category. OS = original scale; R = recentered scale.

Table 4 shows the ethnic/gender breakdown for the score categories in Table 3. Because the old test, new test, and recentered scale correlations were all virtually the same, only the correlations for the recentered scores on the new test are included in the table. The pattern of higher correlations in the colleges in the highest score category was not replicated in all groups. Note,

TABLE 4
Adjusted Correlations of Recentered Scores with Freshman Grade-Point Average for Colleges in Three Score Categories

			Correlation with Freshman Grade-Point Average									
			Gender Total		*African American*		*Asian American*		*Hispanic/Latino*		*White*	
Score	*Score Category (V + M)*	*Total*	*M*	*F*	*M*	*F*	*M*	*F*	*M*	*F*	*M*	*F*
Number of Students	<1050	4,490	2,001	2,489	269	320	76	68	170	268	1,398	1,733
	1050–1250	37,033	17,589	19,444	697	1,305	3,560	3,550	1,220	1,556	11,448	12,063
	>1250	6,516	3,335	3,181	182	201	442	469	127	110	2,403	2,174
SAT I–V	<1050	.46	.43	.50	.48	.49	.42	.58	.48	.49	.42	.49
	1050–1250	.46	.44	.49	.32	.48	.50	.50	.39	.48	.42	.47
	>1250	.55	.56	.55	.43	.46	.54	.55	.46	.33	.55	.50
	Total	.47	.46	.50	.37	.48	.50	.50	.39	.46	.44	.48
SAT I–M	<1050	.46	.41	.53	.52	.21	.38	.66	.52	.51	.39	.52
	1050–1250	.47	.47	.51	.40	.52	.57	.54	.40	.50	.44	.48
	>1250	.57	.59	.57	.46	.52	.58	.56	.56	.29	.59	.53
	Total	.48	.49	.52	.44	.52	.57	.55	.40	.48	.46	.49
HSGPA	<1050	.58	.54	.60	.47	.53	.38	.66	.47	.53	.55	.61
	1050–1250	.53	.52	.52	.45	.47	.55	.52	.48	.47	.51	.51
	>1250	.60	.60	.58	.49	.51	.54	.49	.62	.38	.61	.58
	Total	.54	.53	.53	.46	.49	.55	.52	.49	.48	.53	.53
SAT I	<1050	.50	.46	.56	.55	.55	.47	.68	.55	.55	.44	.55
	1050–1250	.50	.50	.55	.42	.55	.59	.57	.43	.55	.47	.51
	>1250	.61	.63	.61	.53	.54	.61	.61	.59	.41	.67	.56
	Total	.52	.51	.56	.47	.55	.59	.58	.44	.53	.49	.53
SAT I + HSGPA	<1050	.62	.58	.66	.59	.62	.55	.77	.59	.62	.58	.66
	1050–1250	.59	.58	.61	.52	.60	.66	.63	.54	.60	.56	.59
	>1250	.69	.70	.68	.61	.61	.67	.67	.72	.66	.70	.66
	Total	.61	.60	.62	.55	.61	.66	.64	.55	.61	.58	.60

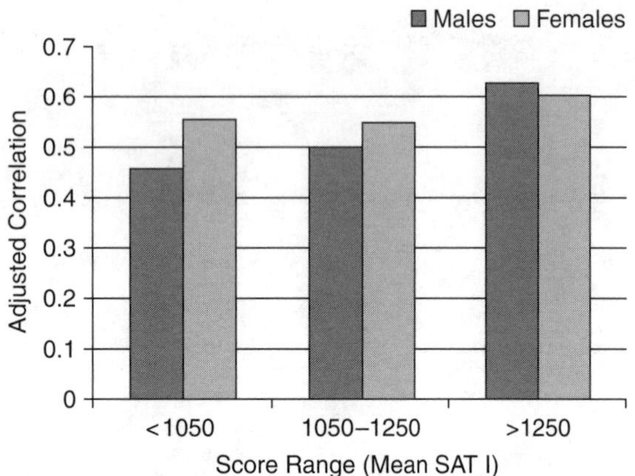

Figure 1 Adjusted Correlations of SAT I Scores with FGPA for Males and Females in Colleges in Three Score Ranges

for example, that the SAT I combined correlation for the highest category colleges was no higher than for the lowest category colleges for African-American, Asian-American, and Hispanic/Latina females and for African-American males as well. In the relatively large white student population sample, the correlations in the colleges in the highest category were much higher for males (.23 and .20 higher compared to the low and middle groups, respectively) but only marginally higher for females (.01 and .05, respectively). As indicated in Figure 1, correlations for the combined ethnic groups suggest that the SAT I combined score is a better predictor for women than for men at the colleges in the lowest score category, but that it predicts FGPA equally well for men and women at the colleges in the highest category. These data are consistent with the argument that behaviors unrelated to the developed abilities measured by the SAT, such as failing to attend class or complete assignments on time, may be more common in males and therefore make male grades more difficult to predict (Stricker, Rock, & Burton, 1993). Because males at most colleges in the highest score category may be as likely as females to attend class and complete assignments, tested abilities should be equally valid for men and women at these institutions.

For the SAT I and HSGPA composite, the same pattern seen for SAT I scores alone was repeated—grades of females were predicted more accurately in the colleges with relatively low mean test scores, but grades of males were predicted more accurately at the colleges with high mean test scores. This pattern was especially evident in the sample of white examinees. In the colleges in the lowest category, the correlation was higher for females by .80, but in the colleges in the highest category, the correlation was .05 higher for males. The previous Ramist et al. (1994) study found a similar pattern with higher correlations for women at the colleges with lower mean test scores, an a very small male advantage at the schools in their higher category; they did not provide information on gender within ethnic groups within mean score categories. The same pattern could also be observed in the uncorrected correlations for the colleges studied by Pennock-Román (1994). The two colleges in her sample that would be classified in the highest category in our sample both showed higher correlations for white males than for white females. In the two colleges with lower mean scores, the pattern was reversed.

Correlations in Individual Colleges

Means and standard deviations of the predictor and criterion scores for each college in the sample are presented in Table 5 along with the adjusted correlations for HSGPA, the SAT I combined, and the SAT I and HSGPA composite. The colleges are arranged in ascending order of the total SAT I combined mean score. The FGPA for the last college listed was on a 0–15 scale; all other colleges were on a 0–4.3 scale. The last column of the table indicates the range in the ability of the SAT I and HSGPA composite to predict freshman grades. The lowest adjusted correlation, and the only correlation in the .40s, was .47; there were four correlations in the .50s, twelve in the .60s, and six in the .70s.

Over- and Underpredictions

Table 6 presents the over- and underpredictions of FGPA. Results for the new content, original scale and new content, recentered scale were virtually identical, so for this analysis only the results for the recentered scale are presented for the new test (SAT I). For the full sample (across ethnic and gender groups), the over/underprediction was exactly the same for the new test as for the old. For the smaller gender within ethnic group breakdowns, differences were what would be expected from sample variations. The

TABLE 5
Means, Standard Deviations, and Adjusted Correlations with FGPA for Recentered SAT I Scores

	SAT I		SAT I–V		SAT I–M		HSGPA		FGPA		Adjusted Correlations		
College Type/Region	*Mean*	*N*	*Mean*	*SD*	*Mean*	*SD*	*Mean*	*SD*	*Mean*	*SD*	*HSGPA*	*V + M*	*V + M + H*
Public/Southwest	850	468	426	85	424	85	3.10	0.58	2.24	0.92	0.53	0.58	0.63
Private Jr. Col./South	962	210	487	78	475	69	3.11	0.53	2.28	0.84	0.68	0.60	0.73
Public/Southwest	1009	1759	506	74	503	71	3.48	0.43	2.45	0.84	0.60	0.49	0.63
Private/Southwest	1010	264	510	81	500	76	3.37	0.53	2.69	0.84	0.49	0.49	0.56
Public/West	1036	1789	515	83	521	87	3.37	0.52	2.77	0.71	0.57	0.47	0.61
Public/Middle States	1063	10862	527	93	536	99	3.38	0.57	2.64	0.83	0.47	0.40	0.50
Public/Middle States	1073	1254	522	85	550	83	3.43	0.41	2.60	0.79	0.50	0.48	0.56
Public/New England	1079	2047	535	87	544	86	3.21	0.47	2.55	0.77	0.49	0.48	0.55
Public/West	1098	2327	524	87	574	84	3.61	0.42	2.75	0.64	0.50	0.54	0.60
Private/South	1106	2186	548	77	558	80	3.47	0.53	2.59	0.87	0.62	0.53	0.66
Public/West	1155	2532	561	92	594	91	3.72	0.40	2.82	0.65	0.54	0.54	0.61
Public/South	1201	2824	601	83	600	80	3.94	0.35	2.84	0.65	0.63	0.65	0.73
Public/West	1204	2602	582	88	622	77	3.82	0.36	2.95	0.54	0.55	0.55	0.63
Public/Southwest	1207	5146	595	83	612	80	3.78	0.43	2.86	0.81	0.57	0.57	0.65
Private/Middle States	1207	2280	606	88	601	83	3.59	0.46	3.10	0.69	0.44	0.37	0.47
Public/West	1209	2973	590	81	618	83	3.84	0.39	3.01	0.58	0.59	0.63	0.70
Private/New England	1264	394	639	65	624	68	3.61	0.38	2.95	0.63	0.62	0.55	0.67
Public/South	1265	1616	611	75	653	69	3.81	0.41	2.78	0.67	0.68	0.67	0.77
Private/South	1277	1193	632	71	645	69	3.79	0.43	2.84	0.73	0.55	0.52	0.61
Private Women/Mid. St.	1280	355	650	70	630	58	3.71	0.34	3.24	0.46	0.52	0.56	0.62
Private/New England	1282	319	643	76	638	69	3.74	0.37	3.06	0.53	0.65	0.59	0.71
Private/Midwest	1325	1516	656	69	669	74	3.95	0.34	3.21	0.49	0.55	0.55	0.62
Private/New England	1456	1123	731	64	726	61	4.09	0.25	12.28	1.73	0.62	0.72	0.77

TABLE 6
Over- (+) and Underprediction (−) of FGPA

Score	Version	*Gender Total*		*African American*		*Asian American*		*Hispanic/Latino*		*White*	
		M	*F*	*M*	*F*	*M*	*F*	*M*	*F*	*M*	*F*
Number of Students	Old (1994)	21,100	22,830	1,024	1,707	3,646	3,923	1,358	1,787	14,199	14,361
Number of Students	New (1995), R	22,327	24,589	1,121	1,770	3,675	3,994	1,480	1,903	14,887	15,713
SAT–V	Old	+.08	−.07	+.23	+.13	+.01	−.09	+.19	+.09	+.07	−.12
	New, R	+.08	3.07	+.26	+.06	+.01	−.07	+.20	+.09	+.07	−.11
SAT-M	Old	+.12	−.12	+.24	+.05	+.13	−.05	+.21	+.04	+.11	−.18
	New, R	+.13	−.12	+.26	−.02	+.14	−.03	+.22	+.02	+.11	−.17
HSGPA	Old	+.04	−.04	+.20	+.18	+.04	−.02	+.20	+.17	+.02	−.10
	New	+.04	−.04	+.22	+.12	+.04	−.01	+.20	+.15	+.01	−.09
SAT	Old	+.11	−.10	+.20	+.04	+.08	−.08	+.17	+.02	+.11	−.15
	New, R	+.11	−.10	+.22	−.03	+.09	−.06	+.19	+.01	+.11	−.14
SAT + HSGPA	Old	+.08	−.07	+.13	+.04	+.07	−.05	+.14	+.04	+.07	−.11
	New, R	+.08	−.07	+.14	−.01	+.07	−.03	+.15	+.02	+.07	−.09

Note: For HSGPA, version refers only to sample (Old = 1994, New = 1995). R = recentered.

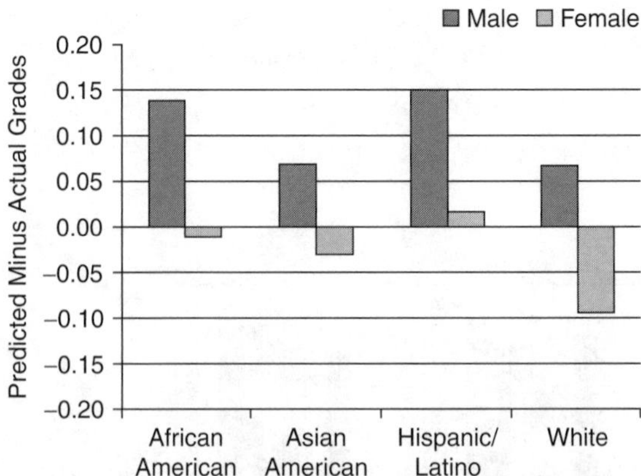

Figure 2 Over- (+) and Underprediction (−) of FGPA from SAT I and HSGPA Composite for Four Ethnic Groups

greatest differences were in the samples of African-American female students, with apparently less overprediction, or a shift from overprediction to underprediction, with the new test. However, because the shift in predictions from HSGPA alone was in the same direction and about as large, the change seems to reflect sample differences and not test content differences.

Consistent with previous findings (e.g., Pennock-Román, 1994; Ramist et al., 1994), there was a modest underprediction of women's grades and the complimentary overprediction of men's grades. As indicated in Figure 2, for the three ethnic minority groups studied, there was virtually no over- or underprediction of women's grades from the combination of SAT I scores and HSGPA. There was moderate to substantial overprediction of men's grades. For all of the three minority groups, but especially for the African-American and Hispanic/Latino groups, there was overprediction of grades for men, i.e., men did not perform as well in college as would be expected from their high school grades and/or SAT I scores. Note that in these groups the overprediction was as great for HSGPA by itself as for the SAT I by itself. In the most highly selective colleges, the underprediction of women's grades from the SAT I and HSGPA composite was slightly less, ranging from −.04 to −.05.

Correlations within Parental Education and Income Categories

Socioeconomic categories, such as the highest educational degree earned by either parent, interact with ethnic categories in a way that makes it difficult to attribute results to ethnic as opposed to socioeconomic categories. In an attempt to disentangle these effects, correlations were run, adjusted for range restriction, for the ethnic/gender groups separately in four parental education categories. The parent education categories were derived from self-reported responses on the Student Descriptive Questionnaire. Students responded for both mother's and father's education level, and the parent with the highest level was used. There are four categories: high school diploma or less (HS), some college but no college degree (HS+), bachelor's degree (B), and graduate degree (G). Students with parents who had some graduate work but no graduate degree were included in the bachelor's degree category. For this and all subsequent analyses, only the recentered scores for the SAT I were used.

As shown in Figure 3 and Table 7, across ethnic groups college grades tend to be more predictable for students whose parents have more education. Within each parental education category, grades were most predictable for Asian-American males, but within-category trends were less clear for the other groups. For example, within the college degree category, SAT I and HSGPA composite correlations were just as high for African-American males as for white males, but correlations for African-American females appeared to be relatively low. In the high school diploma category, SAT I and HSGPA composite correlations were as high for African-American females as for white females. As indicated in Figure 4, analyses run within family income categories revealed the same trends with some within-category variation but a tendency for correlations to be highest in the highest income category.

Comparison of a Standardized HSGPA Report with SDQ HSGPA

One of the problems with using the high school grade-point average to predict FGPA is that high schools use different procedures to compute HSGPA. For example, some schools use all courses while other schools use only academic courses; some schools give extra credit for honors courses and others do not; schools that give extra credit for honors courses may differ in the way in which they define an honors course.

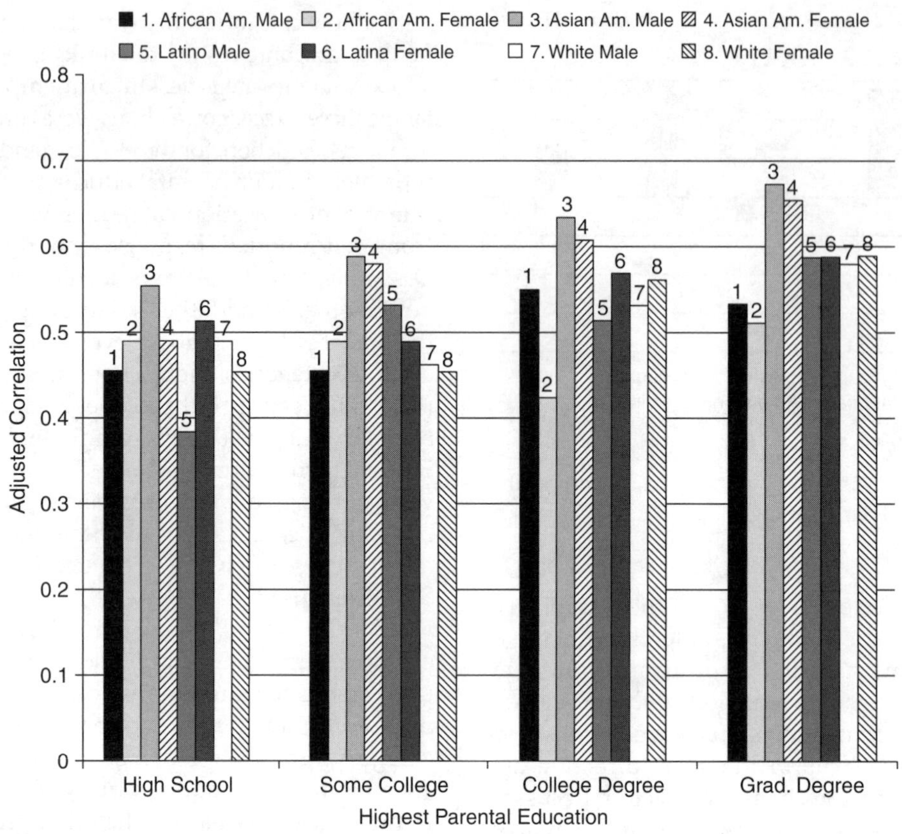

Figure 3 Adjusted Correlations of the SAT I + HSGPA Composite with FGPA by Parental Education Level for Males and Females in Four Ethnic Groups

An attempt to address the problem of the noncomparability of high school grades has been made by the University of California (UC) system. UC applicants from California are required to submit high school grades in a uniform format (University of California, 1999). This special HSGPA includes only academic core courses as defined by the UC system; it explicitly excludes courses such as physical education, typing, and driver education. In addition, a bonus point is assigned for three categories of courses—honors courses that are approved by the UC, Advanced Placement Program® courses, and International Baccalaureate Higher Level courses. Thus, for example, if a student received a B in an approved honors course, this B would be worth 4 grade points rather than the 3 used in nonhonors courses. Applicants to the UC system fill out a special, machine-readable form that contains detailed instructions on how to enter this uniform grade information. Although these grades are self-reports, students know that the colleges receiving these reports frequently confirm them with similar information submitted directly by the high schools.

The uniform California HSGPA (Cal-GPA) is a step in the direction of standardization, but it makes no attempt to make adjustments across high schools in terms of grading standards. There is no assurance that an A in one school represents the same level of accomplishment as an A in the other school.

Data for the current analyses came from freshmen at six UC campuses. Because of the extra credit granted for honors courses, the mean for the uniform California HSGPA (3.86) was higher than the GPA from the Student Descriptive Questionnaire (3.77) obtained from the same students. Standard deviations were comparable (0.37 for Cal-GPA and 0.39 SDQ-GPA). Because the standard deviation of the Cal-GPA in an unselected sample was not available, the range restriction correction used the SDQ-GPA as an explicit selection variable and used the Cal-GPA

TABLE 7
Adjusted Correlations by Highest Parent Education Level between Various Scores and FGPA

Score	Parent Education*	Total	Gender Total		African American		Asian American		Hispanic/Latino		White	
			M	*F*	*M*	*F*	*M*	*F*	*M*	*F*	*M*	*F*
Number of Students	HS	6,211	2,829	3,382	200	329	674	747	425	568	1,439	1,622
	HS+	9,774	4,395	5,379	346	628	578	694	393	565	2,944	3,303
	B	14,940	7,249	7,691	308	470	1,203	1,268	339	373	5,120	5,295
	G	15,986	7,886	8,100	287	364	1,258	1,309	357	422	5,614	5,608
SAT I	HS	.41	.40	.44	.42	.47	.52	.47	.26	.44	.36	.38
	HS+	.40	.40	.43	.36	.47	.54	.52	.41	.46	.35	.39
	B	.46	.46	.49	.51	.38	.55	.57	.40	.53	.44	.47
	G	.49	.49	.52	.42	.43	.61	.57	.51	.53	.48	.51
HSGPA	HS	.45	.45	.42	.34	.39	.44	.38	.37	.46	.48	.41
	HS+	.44	.45	.42	.41	.39	.49	.50	.50	.40	.44	.41
	B	.51	.50	.49	.44	.36	.57	.49	.49	.46	.49	.51
	G	.55	.54	.54	.51	.47	.58	.59	.53	.50	.53	.53
SAT I + HSGPA	HS	.49	.49	.49	.45	.49	.55	.49	.38	.51	.49	.45
	HS+	.48	.48	.48	.45	.49	.59	.58	.53	.49	.46	.45
	B	.55	.55	.56	.55	.42	.64	.61	.51	.57	.53	.56
	G	.60	.59	.60	.53	.51	.68	.66	.59	.59	.58	.59

*HS = High School diploma or less; HS+ = some college; B = Bachelor's Degree; G = Graduate Degree.

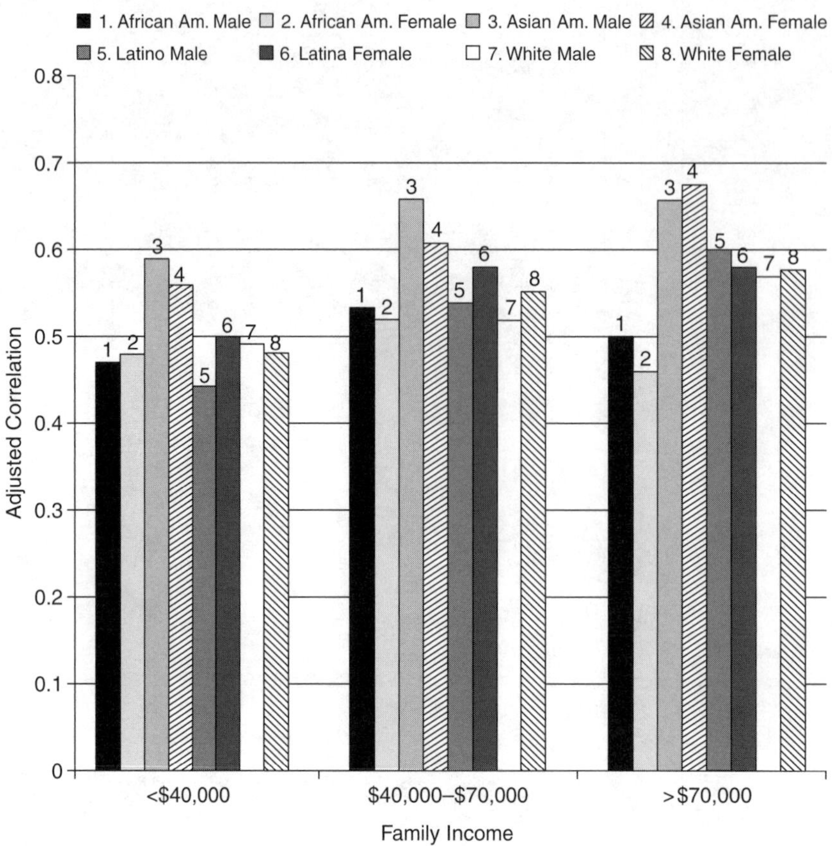

Figure 4 Adjusted Correlations of the SAT I + HSGPA Composite with FGPA by Family Income Level for Males and Females in Four Ethnic Groups

as an implicit selection variable. The Cal-GPA correlated .72 with SDQ-GPA, .26 with SAT I–V, and .30 with SAT I–M. In this sample, SDQ-GPA correlated .17 with SAT I–V and .23 with SAT I–M. Correlations with FGPA, adjusted for range restriction, for both high school grade-point averages are presented in Table 8. Correlations were generally higher for the Cal-GPA than for the HSGPA obtained from the SDQ-GPA. Thus, the uniform procedures for collecting high school GPAs in California did succeed in improving predictions. Both the use of SAT I scores and the use of the uniform California HSGPA are intended to even out some of the inconsistencies in predictions from nonuniform HSGPAs. It then might be expected that adding standardized test scores would show a greater validity boost for the SDQ-GPA than for the Cal-GPA. As can be seen in Figure 5, just such a differential boost was found. For the math/science intended majors, the incremental validity for the SAT over the SDQ-GPA was .08 and over the Cal-GPA it was .05; similarly for the other intended majors the SAT increment was .08 over the SDQ-GPA and

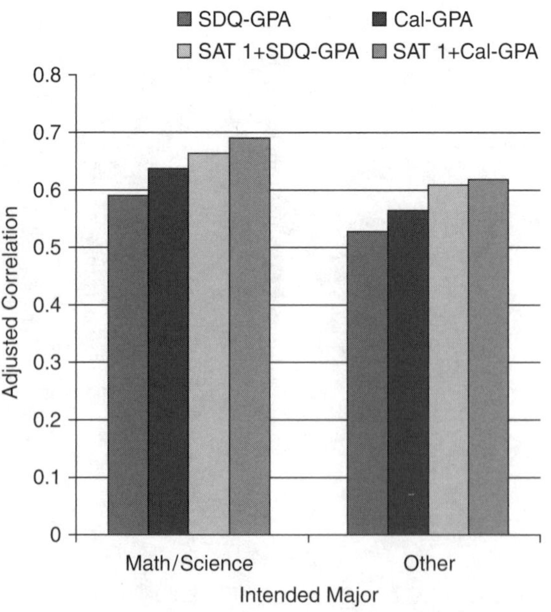

Figure 5 Adjusted Correlations of Admission Measures (SDQ-GPA, Cal-GPA, and Composites Including SAT I) with FGPA for Math/Science and Other Intended Majors

TABLE 8
Adjusted Correlations of Two Measures of HSGPA with FGPA

Score	*Total*	*Gender Total*		*African American*		*Asian American*		*Hispanic/Latino*		*White*	
		M	*F*	*M*	*F*	*M*	*F*	*M*	*F*	*M*	*F*
					Math/Science Intended Major						
Number of Students	6,183	3,274	2,909	61	146	1,563	1,288	363	396	1,001	863
SDQ-GPA	.59	.60	.58	.69	.47	.62	.62	.51	.42	.54	.61
Cal-GPA	.64	.64	.63	.69	.49	.64	.66	.55	.48	.61	.67
SAT I	.59	.58	.63	.58	.54	.58	.64	.57	.51	.57	.68
SAT I + SDQ-GPA	.67	.67	.69	.77	.66	.69	.72	.63	.56	.63	.74
SAT I + Cal-GPA	.69	.69	.70	.79	.69	.70	.73	.64	.57	.66	.74
					Other Intended Major						
Number of Students	7,535	3,068	4,467	.87	192	1,208	1,807	430	?12	1,111	1,427
SDQ-GPA	.53	.53	.52	.38	.52	.50	.49	.45	.48	.53	.49
Cal-GPA	.57	.57	.56	.32	.51	.54	.55	.49	.50	.56	.56
SAT I	.54	.53	.58	.32	.57	.55	.56	.33	.51	.50	.57
SAT I + SDQ-GPA	.61	.61	.64	.50	.64	.60	.61	.47	.57	.59	.62
SAT I + Cal-GPA	.63	.62	.65	.47	.66	.62	.62	.51	.59	.61	.64

.06 over the Cal-GPA. The SAT I significantly improved prediction even when the Cal-GPA was used. When combined with SAT I scores, there was only a .02 point difference between the multiple correlations that used SDQ-GPA and the multiple correlations that used Cal-GPA.

Adjustment for Course Difficulty

Because grading standards differ across courses, students in leniently graded courses may receive higher grades, on average, than students with the same academic background who take strictly graded courses. For some students, the FGPA may consist primarily of leniently graded courses while for other students the FGPA may consist primarily of strictly graded courses. Given that students with the highest scores on admission tests often select the scientific and quantitative courses that are graded most strictly, the correlation between admission test scores and FGPA can be attenuated (Elliott & Strenta, 1988; Goldman & Widawskt, 1976; Ramist, Lewis, & McCamley-Jenkins, 1994).

For the current sample, adjustments were made in the seven colleges that provided grades in individual courses for 1995. A number of different adjustment methods have been proposed and evaluated (Stricker, Rock, Burton, Muraki, & Jirele, 1994). Three adjustment methods were used: a within-course predicted FGPA, a course-grade residual analysis, and an analysis within an intended college major.

The within-course predicted FGPA followed the procedure outlined by Ramist, Lewis, and McCamley-Jenkins (1994). In this adjustment method, admission scores are used to make linear regression grade predictions in each course containing at least seven freshmen. For each student, the predicted grade for each course taken is averaged over all of the courses taken by that student to form a predicted FGPA for that student. The predicted FGPA is then correlated with the actual FGPA. The within-course predictions were performed separately for each predictor (SAT I–V, SAT I–M, and HSGPA) as well as for the combinations of these predictors (SAT I combined; SAT I and HSGPA). If any equation contained negative regression weights, we removed the variable with the negative weight and recomputed the correlation using the remaining predictors. For courses with just a few students, the weight for a single predictor could be negative; in these cases we substituted the mean grade in the course for the regression estimate. Because regression estimates based on optimal weighting of multiple predictors in relatively small samples may inflate correlations by capitalizing on chance, we also computed the SAT I and HSGPA correlation based on uniform weights, that is the simple sum of SAT I–V and SAT I–M and (200 × HSGPA). The same uniform weight equation was used whether the course was predominantly verbal (such as English) or primarily quantitative (such as calculus), thus producing a very conservative estimate.

As shown in Table 9, the correction for course difficulty (with optimal weights) increased the SAT I and HSGPA correlation by about .06 (from .43 to .49) with an additional increase to .65 when also adjusted for range restriction. These corrections for grading differences are somewhat smaller than those found by Ramist, Lewis, and McCamley-Jenkins (1994), but are consistent with those computed by Stricker et al. (1994). The last six rows of Table 9, and Figure 6, show that the conservative uniform weight correlations were nearly as high as those with the optimal regression weights.

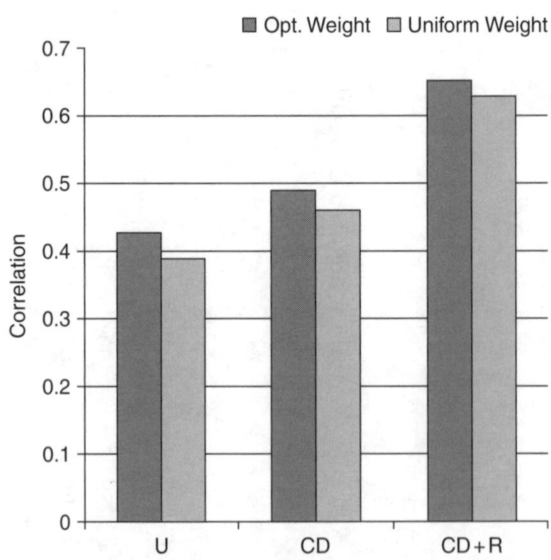

Correction Type—U = uncorrected; CD = corrected for course difficulty; CD + R = corrected for difficulty and range restriction.

Figure 6 Effects of Correction for Course Difficulty and Range Restriction on Correlation of FGPA with SAT I + HSGPA Composite (Optimal Weights and Uniform Weights)

TABLE 9
Correlations with FGPA Adjusted for Course Difficulty and Range Restriction

Score	*Correction Type**	*Total*	*Gender Total*		*African American*		*Asian American*		*Hispanic/Latino*		*White*	
			M	*F*	*M*	*F*	*M*	*F*	*M*	*F*	*M*	*F*
Number of Students		13,344	6,175	7,169	479	713	786	816	599	704	4,002	4,631
SAT I–V	U	.26	.24	.28	.25	.24	.20	.23	.18	.23	.24	.27
	CD	.34	.32	.35	.32	.31	.32	.37	.32	.44	.30	.32
	CD + R	.50	.48	.52	.42	.46	.55	.54	.47	.53	.47	.49
SAT I–M	U	.30	.32	.34	.31	.33	.39	.38	.17	.29	.29	.29
	CD	.37	.37	.39	.38	.38	.42	.40	.31	.47	.34	.34
	CD + R	.52	.52	.55	.48	.52	.62	.56	.46	.56	.51	.52
HSGPA	U	.35	.34	.34	.31	.32	.26	.32	.32	.28	.34	.37
	CD	.42	.41	.42	.41	.40	.37	.39	.42	.47	.41	.40
	CD + R	.59	.56	.60	.51	.54	.58	.59	.56	.58	.56	.59
SAT I	U	.33	.34	.37	.35	.35	.41	.41	.23	.34	.32	.33
	CD	.40	.39	.42	.39	.40	.44	.43	.33	.48	.36	.37
	CD + R	.56	.55	.58	.49	.54	.63	.60	.49	.57	.53	.56
Optimal Weights	U	.43	.43	.45	.43	.44	.46	.47	.41	.42	.41	.42
	CD	.49	.48	.50	.47	.48	.48	.47	.45	.54	.45	.46
SAT I + HSGPA	CD + R	.65	.63	.67	.56	.61	.67	.67	.59	.65	.62	.66
Uniform Weights	U	.39	.39	.41	.37	.38	.39	.41	.29	.35	.37	.39
	CD	.46	.45	.48	.46	.45	.44	.45	.43	.52	.43	.44
SAT I + HSGPA	CD + R	.63	.61	.66	.54	.60	.66	.66	.57	.63	.60	.65

*U is uncorrected correlation, CD is corrected for course difficulty, CD + R is corrected for course difficulty and range restriction.

For the course-grade residual analysis, the overall SAT I and HSGPA prediction equation for a college to predict the average grade for all of the students in a given course was used. The course residual was the difference between the predicted grade of the students in that course and the actual mean grade of the students in that course. Thus, each course had a residual value associated with it, with positive residuals indicating a course with higher grades than would be expected from the admission scores of the students in that course, that is, a course with lenient grading; negative residuals indicated strict grading. For a given student, these residuals were averaged over all of the courses taken by that student. This mean residual was then used as an additional predictor (along with SAT I–V, SAT I–M, and HSGPA) in predicting the FGPA for a student. Results of this procedure were nearly identical to those for the predicted FGPA procedure (mean correlation over colleges of .50 for mean grade-residual analysis compared to .49 for the predicted FGPA procedure).

The third procedure did not directly adjust for differences in course grading; it merely grouped students into more homogeneous categories based on their intended college majors as indicated by their responses to the Student Descriptive Questionnaire. This method has obvious drawbacks in that students frequently change their intended majors before or after enrolling in college, and even students with different majors can have a similar mix of courses during the freshman year. Nevertheless, this approach has the distinct advantage of not requiring colleges to supply any course-level information, so it could be used for all 23 of the colleges in the sample. All majors were grouped into two categories—"math/science" included majors in the physical and biological sciences, engineering, and mathematics; all other majors were put in the "other" category. As indicated in Table 10 and Figure 7, correlations were uniformly higher in the math/science group. Note that because these correlations were adjusted for range restriction the higher correlations in the math/science

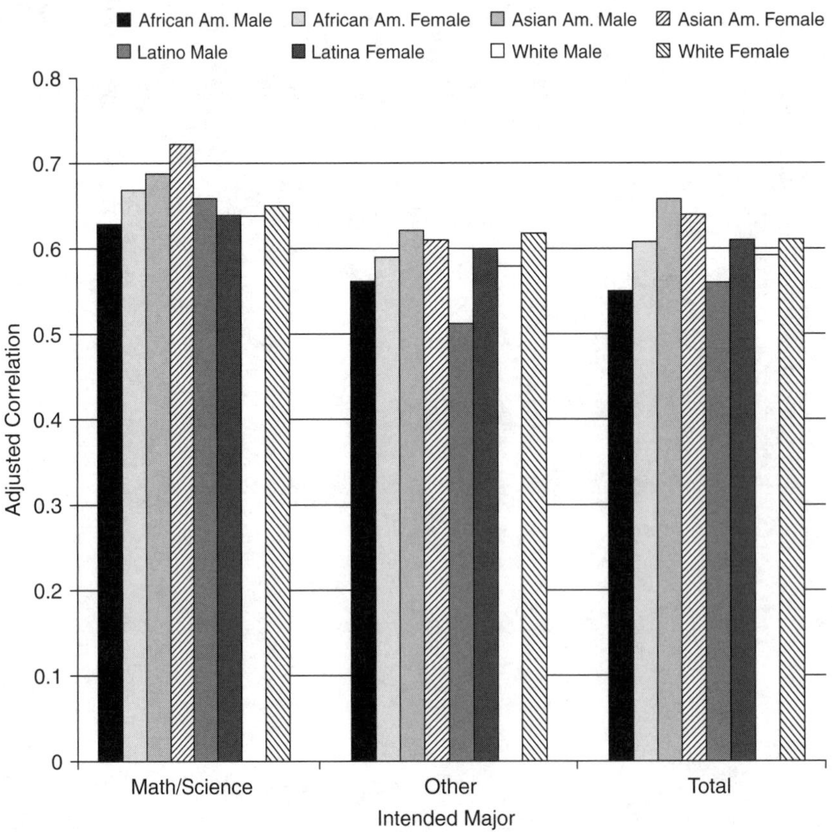

Figure 7 Adjusted Correlations of the SAT I + HSGPA Composite with FGPA by Intended Major for Males and Females in Four Ethnic Groups

TABLE 10
Correlations with FGPA by Intended Major, Adjusted for Range Restriction

Score	Intended Major	Total	Gender Total		African American		Asian American		Hispanic/Latino		White	
			M	*F*	*M*	*F*	*M*	*F*	*M*	*F*	*M*	*F*
Number of Students	M/S	16,742	9,446	7,296	496	631	2,039	1,613	626	624	5,810	4,053
	O	29,553	12,556	16,997	603	1,135	1,627	2,375	826	1,257	8,958	11,498
SAT I–V	M/S	.50	.48	.52	.43	.49	.51	.55	.46	.47	.46	.49
	O	.41	.45	.50	.32	.48	.49	.48	.34	.46	.44	.49
	T	.47	.46	.50	.37	.48	.51	.50	.40	.46	.44	.48
SAT I–M	M/S	.54	.54	.58	.50	.54	.59	.61	.47	.50	.51	.55
	O	.47	.47	.52	.40	.51	.53	.50	.35	.48	.45	.49
	T	.48	.49	.52	.44	.52	.57	.54	.41	.49	.46	.49
HSGPA	M/S	.58	.58	.57	.51	.53	.59	.58	.54	.48	.57	.55
	O	.54	.52	.54	.42	.45	.50	.49	.45	.49	.52	.54
	T	.54	.53	.53	.47	.49	.55	.52	.49	.48	.53	.53
SAT I	M/S	.57	.56	.60	.55	.58	.61	.65	.54	.57	.54	.57
	O	.51	.50	.56	.47	.55	.57	.55	.39	.53	.49	.53
	T	.52	.52	.56	.46	.55	.59	.58	.45	.54	.49	.53
SAT I + HSGPA	M/S	.66	.65	.67	.63	.67	.69	.72	.66	.64	.64	.65
	O	.60	.58	.63	.56	.59	.62	.61	.51	.60	.58	.62
	T	.61	.60	.63	.55	.61	.66	.64	.56	.61	.59	.61

Note: M/S = math/science; O = other; T = total.

TABLE 11
Means and Standard Deviations of Scores and GPAs by Intended Major

	Math/Science		*Other*		
	M	*SD*	*M*	*SD*	*d*
SAT I–V	578	84	560	84	0.21
SAT I–M	628	76	564	83	0.81
HSGPA	3.70	0.43	3.54	0.46	0.36
FGPA	3.01	0.79	2.96	0.74	0.07

Note: The standardized difference between the Math/Science and Other categories, *d*, is the mean difference divided by the square root of the unweighted average of the squared standard deviations.

category cannot be attributed merely to greater variability of scores in that category. The means, standard deviations, and standardized differences (*d*) in Table 11 indicate that the difference in FGPA between the math/science and other groups is considerably smaller than the difference in any of the admission measures, suggesting that grading standards were indeed more rigorous for students whose intended major was in a math/science field.

Over/Underprediction Adjusted for Course Difficulty

Because members of different gender and ethnic sub-groups may differentially sort themselves into courses with relatively strict or lenient grading standards, adjusting for course difficulty can also have an impact on the extent to which grades are over- or underpredicted. For each subgroup, we used the FGPA predicted in the course grade residual analysis (SAT I and HSGPA and Residual) that accounts for course difficulty differences, and then found the differences between the predicted and actual FGPA. These differences are presented in Table 12; as before, positive differences indicate predictions for a group that were higher than the grades actually received (overprediction). The correction reduced the underprediction of women's grades from −0.07 to −0.05; for women in the two colleges in the highly selective category that provided course grades, underprediction was −0.04 before correction and −0.03 after correction.

For the full sample of colleges, not just those that supplied course grades, over/underprediction results by intended major are presented in Table 13. Grade predictions were made without regard to intended major, but differences between predicted and actual grades were computed within major (math/science or other). Results were consistent with the notion that grading standards are more strict in math/science fields. In every gender/ethnic category, grades for students with intended majors in math/science were not as high as predicted from the SAT I and HSGPA equation for the entire college. The generalization that grades of women are underpredicted was not true for these math/science students, though the overprediction for men was notably larger than the overprediction for women.

The results of all of the course-adjustment procedures underscore the importance of taking grading differences into account whenever possible for predictions of FGPA. When adjustments

TABLE 12
Over- (+) and Underprediction (−) of FGPA Adjusted for Course Difficulty

	Gender Total		*African American*		*Asian American*		*Hispanic/Latino*		*White*	
Score	*M*	*F*	*M*	*F*	*M*	*F*	*M*	*F*	*M*	*F*
Number of Students	6,175	7,169	479	713	786	816	599	704	4,002	4,631
SAT I	+.13	−.11	+.23	−.07	+.02	−.12	+.16	−.01	+.13	−.13
SAT I + Residual	+.11	−.09	+.24	−.07	−.03	−.11	+.18	+.02	+.11	−.11
SAT I + HSGPA	+.08	−.07	+.16	−.05	.00	−.07	+.12	+.02	+.09	−.09
SAT I + HSGPA + Residual	+.06	−.05	+.15	−.04	−.05	−.05	+.13	+.05	+.07	−.07

TABLE 13
Over- (+) and Underprediction (−) of FGPA for Students with Math/Science or Other Intended Majors

	Gender Total		*African American*		*Asian American*		*Hispanic/ Latino*		*White*	
Score	*M*	*F*	*M*	*F*	*M*	*F*	*M*	*F*	*M*	*F*
Math/Science Intended Major										
Number of Students	9,519	7,342	513	642	2,072	1,641	653	646	5,846	4,075
SAT I	.13	−.04	.22	−.02	.07	−.01	.20	.08	.13	−.07
SAT I + HSGPA	.12	.02	.17	.03	.08	.03	.20	.11	.13	.01
Other Intended Major										
Number of Students	12,644	17,138	626	1,157	1,653	2,404	847	1,277	9,022	11,597
SAT I	.11	−.13	.23	−.04	.10	−.09	.18	−.03	.09	−.16
SAT I + HSGPA	.04	−.11	.12	−.03	.05	−.08	.13	−.03	.02	−.13

cannot be made, it should at least be acknowledged that the resulting correlations are underestimates of the ability of the admission measures to predict college grades.

Conclusions

The content changes in the SAT and the recentering of the score scale had little or no impact on the overall predictive validity of the test. The SAT I appears to predict about equally well across ethnic groups. At most colleges, grades of females are more predictable than grades of males, but at the most highly selective colleges, the grades of males and females are predicted equally well. Males generally perform slightly worse in their freshman year than predicted from test scores and high school grades; women perform slightly better than predicted. Within African-American and Hispanic/Latino groups, men perform worse than predicted and women perform about as predicted.

Across ethnic groups, grades are more predictable for higher socioeconomic status (SES) students than for lower SES students. This is true for both parent education and income definitions of SES.

Accounting for differences in course grading practices produces a noticeable improvement in predictions of FGPA. Even as simple a procedure as running correlations separately for students who indicate that they would like to be math/science majors has an impact on the size of validity coefficients. Validity coefficients would have been even larger had we adjusted for unreliability in the FGPA criterion as was done by Ramist et al. (1994). However, we had no way of adequately estimating the reliability of the FGPA for all of the schools in our sample. If grade reliability were about the same in our sample as in the Ramist et al. sample (a reasonable but unverifiable assumption), about .05 should be added to the adjusted correlations. Thus, for example, correcting for the unreliability of the FGPA would raise the correlation for the SAT I and HSGPA composite in math/science students from .66 to .71.

Many issues remain to be explored in future analyses of the data base created for this study, notably how SAT II: Subject Tests relate to the other measures in predicting FGPA. In addition, the database can also be used to simulate the effects of different selection models (such as using SAT II scores in the place of SAT I scores) on the quality and ethnic/gender composition of an admitted class. Additional data will be needed to explore longer-term validity issues.

References

Breland, H. (1979). *Population validity and college entrance measures.* Princeton, NJ: College Board Publication Orders.

Burton, N. W., & Ramist, L. (in preparation). *Predicting long term success in undergraduate school: A review of predictive validity studies.* Princeton, NJ: Educational Testing Service.

College Board/Educational Testing Service (1995). *1995 College Bound Seniors.* New York: College Entrance Examination Board.

Elliott, R., & Strenta, A. C. (1988). Effects of improving the reliability of the GPA on prediction generally and on comparative predictions for gender and race particularly. *Journal of Educational Measurement, 25,* 333–347.

Freeberg, N. E., Rock, D. A., & Pollack, J. (1989). *Analysis of the revised Student Descriptive Questionnaire: Phase II, Predictive validity of academic self-report* (College Board Report No. 89-8). New York: College Entrance Examination Board.

Goldman, R. D., & Widawski, M. H. (1976). A within subjects technique for comparing grading standards: Importance in the validity of the evaluation of college achievement. *Educational and Psychological Measurement, 36,* 381–390.

Gulliksen, H. (1950). *Theory of Mental Tests.* New York: John Wiley and Sons.

Linn, R. L. (1978). Single-group validity, differential validity, and differential prediction. *Journal of Applied Psychology, 63,* 507–512.

Morgan, R. (1994). *Effects of score choice on predictive validity.* Princeton, NJ: Educational Testing Service.

Pennock-Román, M. (1994). *College major and gender differences in the prediction of college grades* (College Board Report No. 94-2). New York: College Entrance Examination Board.

Ramist, L., Lewis, C., & McCamley-Jenkins, L. (1994). *Student group differences in predicting college grades: Sex, language, and ethnic groups* (College Board Report No. 93–1). New York: College Entrance Examination Board.

Sawyer, R. (1986). Using demographic subgroup and dummy variable equations to predict college freshman grade average. *Journal of Educational Measurement, 23,* 131–145.

Stricker, L. J., Rock, D. A., & Burton, N. W. (1993). Sex differences in predictions of college grades from Scholastic Aptitude Test scores. *Journal of Educational Psychology, 85,* 710–718.

Stricker, L. J., Rock, D. A., Burton, N. W., Muraki, E., & Jirele, T. J. (1994). Adjusting college grade point average criteria for variations in grading standards: A comparison of methods. *Journal of Applied Psychology, 79,* 178–183.

University of California (1999). *Admissions as a Freshman.* http://www.ucop.edu/pathways/infoctr/introuc/fresh.html

Willingham, W. W. (1985). *Success in college: The role of personal qualities and academic ability.* New York: College Entrance Examination Board.

Willingham, W. W., Lewis, C., Morgan, R., & Ramist, L. (1990). *Predicting college grades: An analysis of institutional trends over two decades.* Princeton, NJ: Educational Testing Service.

Wilson, K. M. (1983). *A review of research on the prediction of academic performance after the freshman year* (College Board Report No. 83-2). New York: College Entrance Examination Board.

FOUR ASSUMPTIONS OF MULTIPLE REGRESSION THAT RESEARCHERS SHOULD ALWAYS TEST

JASON W. OSBORNE AND ELAINE WATERS

North Carolina State University and University of Oklahoma

Most statistical tests rely upon certain assumptions about the variables used in the analysis. When these assumptions are not met the results may not be trustworthy, resulting in a Type I or Type II error, or over- or under-estimation of significance or effect size(s). As Pedhazur (1997, p. 33) notes, "Knowledge and understanding of the situations when violations of assumptions lead to serious biases, and when they are of little consequence, are essential to meaningful data analysis". However, as Osborne, Christensen, and Gunter (2001) observe, few articles report having tested assumptions of the statistical tests they rely on for drawing their conclusions. This creates a situation where we have a rich literature in education and social science, but we are forced to call into question the validity of many of these results, conclusions, and assertions, as we have no idea whether the assumptions of the statistical tests were met. Our goal for this paper is to present a discussion of the assumptions of multiple regression tailored toward the practicing researcher.

Several assumptions of multiple regression are "robust" to violation (e.g., normal distribution of errors), and others are fulfilled in the proper design of a study (e.g., independence of observations). Therefore, we will focus on the assumptions of multiple regression that are not robust to violation, and that researchers can deal with if violated. Specifically, we will discuss the assumptions of linearity, reliability of measurement, homoscedasticity, and normality.

Variables are Normally Distributed

Regression assumes that variables have normal distributions. Non-normally distributed variables (highly skewed or kurtotic variables, or variables with substantial outliers) can distort relationships and significance tests. There are several pieces of information that are useful to the researcher in testing this assumption: visual inspection of data plots, skew, kurtosis, and P-P plots give researchers information about normality, and Kolmogorov-Smirnov tests provide inferential statistics on normality. Outliers can be identified either through visual inspection of histograms or frequency distributions, or by converting data to z-scores.

Bivariate/multivariate data cleaning can also be important (Tabachnick & Fidell, p. 139) in multiple regression. Most regression or multivariate statistics texts (e.g., Pedhazur, 1997; Tabachnick & Fidell, 2000) discuss the examination of standardized or studentized residuals, or indices of leverage. Analyses by Osborne (2001) show that removal of univariate and bivariate outliers can reduce

Reprinted from *Practical Assessment, Research and Evaluation* 8, no. 2.

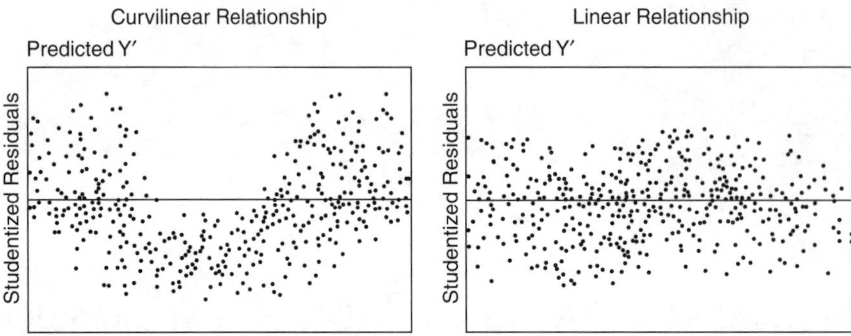

Figure 1 Example of Curvilinear and Linear Relationships with Standardized Residuals by Standardized Predicted Values

the probability of Type I and Type II errors, and improve accuracy of estimates.

Outlier (univariate or bivariate) removal is straightforward in most statistical software. However, it is not always desirable to remove outliers. In this case transformations (e.g., square root, log, or inverse), can improve normality, but complicate the interpretation of the results, and should be used deliberately and in an informed manner. A full treatment of transformations is beyond the scope of this article, but is discussed in many popular statistical textbooks.

Assumption of a Linear Relationship between the Independent and Dependent Variable(s)

Standard multiple regression can only accurately estimate the relationship between dependent and independent variables if the relationships are linear in nature. As there are many instances in the social sciences where non-linear relationships occur (e.g., anxiety), it is essential to examine analyses for non-linearity. If the relationship between independent variables (IV) and the dependent variable (DV) is not linear, the results of the regression analysis will *under-estimate* the true relationship. This under-estimation carries two risks: increased chance of a Type II error for that IV, and in the case of multiple regression, an increased risk of Type I errors (over-estimation) for other IVs that share variance with that IV.

Authors such as Pedhazur (1997), Cohen and Cohen (1983), and Berry and Feldman (1985) suggest three primary ways to detect non-linearity. The first method is the use of theory or previous research to inform current analyses. However, as many prior researchers have probably overlooked the possibility of non-linear relationships, this method is not foolproof. A preferable method of detection is examination of residual plots (plots of the standardized residuals as a function of standardized predicted values, readily available in most statistical software). Figure 1 shows scatterplots of residuals that indicate curvilinear and linear relationships.

The third method of detecting curvilinearity is to routinely run regression analyses that incorporate curvilinear components (squared and cubic terms; see Goldfeld and Quandt, 1976 or most regression texts for details on how to do this) or utilizing the nonlinear regression option available in many statistical packages. It is important that the nonlinear aspects of the relationship be accounted for in order to best assess the relationship between variables.

Variables are Measured without Error (Reliably)

The nature of our educational and social science research means that many variables we are interested in are also difficult to measure, making measurement error a particular concern. In simple correlation and regression, unreliable measurement causes relationships to be *under-estimated* increasing the risk of Type II errors. In the case of multiple regression or partial correlation, effect sizes of other variables can be *over-estimated* if the covariate is not reliably measured, as the full effect of the covariate(s) would not be removed. This is a significant concern if the goal of research is to accurately model the "real" relationships evident in the population. Although most authors assume that reliability estimates (Cronbach alphas) of .7–.8 are acceptable (e.g., Nunnally, 1978) and Osborne, Christensen, and Gunter (2001) reported that the average alpha reported in top Educational Psychology journals was .83, measurement of this quality still contains enough measurement error to make correction worthwhile, as illustrated below.

Correction for low reliability is simple, and widely disseminated in most texts on regression, but rarely seen in the literature. We argue that authors should correct for low reliability to obtain a more accurate picture of the "true" relationship in the population, and, in the case of multiple regression or partial correlation, to avoid over-estimating the effect of another variable.

Reliability and Simple Regression

Since "the presence of measurement errors in behavioral research is the rule rather than the exception" and "reliabilities of many measures used in the behavioral sciences are, at best, moderate" (Pedhazur, 1997, p. 172); it is important that researchers be aware of accepted methods of dealing with this issue. For simple regression, Equation #1 provides an estimate of the "true" relationship between the IV and DV in the population:

$$r_{12}^{*} = \frac{r_{12}}{\sqrt{r_{11}r_{22}}} \qquad (1)$$

In this equation, r_{12} is the observed correlation, and r_{11} and r_{22} are the reliability estimates of the variables. Table 1 and Figure 2 presents examples of the results of such a correction.

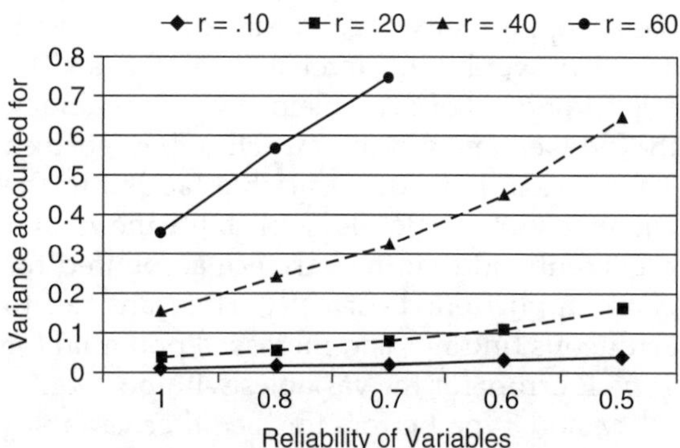

Figure 2 Change in Variance Accounted for as Correlations are Corrected for Low Reliability

As Table 1 illustrates, even in cases where reliability is .80, correction for attenuation substantially changes the effect size (increasing variance accounted for by about 50%). When reliability drops to .70 or below this correction yields a substantially different picture of the "true" nature of the relationship, and potentially avoids a Type II error.

Reliability and Multiple Regression

With each independent variable added to the regression equation, the effects of less than perfect reliability on the strength of the relationship becomes more complex and the results of the analysis more questionable. With the addition of one independent variable with less than perfect reliability each succeeding variable entered

TABLE 1
Values of *r* and r^2 after Correction for Attenuation

Observed	*Perfect Measurement*		*Reliability of DV and IV* .80		.70		.60		.50	
r	*r*	r^2	*r*	r^2	*r*	r^2	*r*	r^2	*r*	r^2
.10	.10	.01	.13	.02	.14	.02	.17	.03	.20	.04
.20	.20	.04	.25	.06	.29	.08	.33	.11	.40	.16
.40	.40	.16	.50	.25	.57	.33	.67	.45	.80	.64
.60	.60	.36	.75	.57	.86	.74	—	—	—	—

Note: For simplicity we show an example where both IV and DV have identical reliability estimates. In some of these hypothetical examples we would produce impossible values, and so do not report these.

has the opportunity to claim part of the error variance left over by the unreliable variable(s). The apportionment of the explained variance among the independent variables will thus be incorrect. The more independent variables added to the equation with low levels of reliability the greater the likelihood that the variance accounted for is not apportioned correctly. This can lead to erroneous findings and increased potential for Type II errors for the variables with poor reliability, and Type I errors for the other variables in the equation. Obviously, this gets increasingly complex as the number of variables in the equation grows.

A simple example, drawing heavily from Pedhazur (1997), is a case where one is attempting to assess the relationship between two variables controlling for a third variable ($r_{12.3}$). When one is correcting for low reliability in all three variables Equation #2 is used:

$$r^*_{12.3} = \frac{r_{33}r_{12} - r_{13}r_{23}}{\sqrt{r_{11}r_{33} - r^2_{13}}\sqrt{r_{22}r_{33} - r^2_{23}}} \qquad (2)$$

Where r_{11}, r_{22}, and r_{33} are reliabilities, and r_{12}, r_{23}, and r_{13} are relationships between variables. If one is only correcting for low reliability in the covariate one could use Equation #3:

$$r^*_{12.3} = \frac{r_{33}r_{12} - r_{13}r_{23}}{\sqrt{r_{33} - r^2_{13}}\sqrt{r_{33} - r^2_{23}}} \qquad (3)$$

Table 2 presents some examples of corrections for low reliability in the covariate (only) and in all three variables.

Table 2 shows some of the many possible combinations of reliabilities, correlations, and the effects of correcting for only the covariate or all variables. Some points of interest: (a) as in Table 1, even small correlations see substantial effect size (r^2) changes when corrected for low reliability, in this case often toward reduced effect sizes, (b) in some cases the corrected correlation is not only substantially different in magnitude, but also in direction of the relationship, and (c) as expected, the most dramatic changes occur when the covariate has a substantial relationship with the other variables.

Assumption of Homoscedasticity

Homoscedasticity means that the variance of errors is the same across all levels of the IV. When the variance of errors differs at different values of the IV, heteroscedasticity is indicated. According to Berry and Feldman (1985) and Tabachnick and Fidell (1996) slight heteroscedasticity has little effect on significance tests; however, when heteroscedasticity is marked it can lead to serious distortion of findings and seriously weaken the analysis thus increasing the possibility of a Type I error.

This assumption can be checked by visual examination of a plot of the standardized residuals (the errors) by the regression standardized predicted value. Most modern statistical packages include this as an option. Figure 3 show examples of plots that might result from homoscedastic and heteroscedastic data.

Ideally, residuals are randomly scattered around 0 (the horizontal line) providing a relatively even distribution. Heteroscedasticity is

TABLE 2

Values of $r_{12.3}$ and $r^2_{12.3}$ after Correction Low Reliability

Examples:				*Reliability of Covariate*			*Reliability of All Variables*		
			Observed	*.80*	*.70*	*.60*	*.80*	*.70*	*.60*
r_{12}	r_{13}	r_{23}	$r_{12.3}$	$r_{12.3}$	$r_{12.3}$	$r_{12.3}$	$r_{12.3}$	$r_{12.3}$	$r_{12.3}$
.3	.3	.3	.23	.21	.20	.18	.27	.30	.33
.5	.5	.5	.33	.27	.22	.14	.38	.42	.45
.7	.7	.7	.41	.23	.00	−.64	.47	.00	—
.7	.3	.3	.67	.66	.65	.64	.85	.99	—
.3	.5	.5	.07	−.02	−.09	−.20	−.03	−.17	−.64
.5	.1	.7	.61	.66	.74	.90	—	—	—

Note: In some examples we would produce impossible values that we do not report.

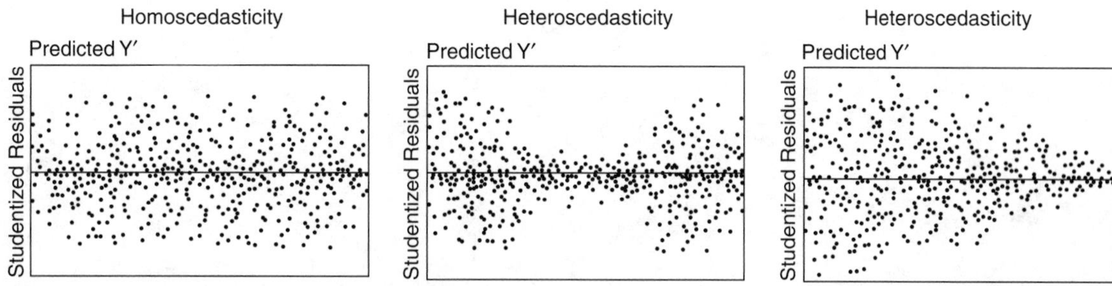

Figure 3 Examples of Homoscedasticity and Heteroscedasticity

indicated when the residuals are not evenly scattered around the line. There are many forms heteroscedasticity can take, such as a bowtie or fan shape. When the plot of residuals appears to deviate substantially from normal, more formal tests for heteroscedasticity should be performed. Possible tests for this are the Goldfeld-Quandt test when the error term either decreases or increases consistently as the value of the DV increases as shown in the fan shaped plot or the Glejser tests for heteroscedasticity when the error term has small variances at central observations and larger variance at the extremes of the observations as in the bowtie shaped plot (Berry & Feldman, 1985). In cases where skew is present in the IVs, transformation of variables can reduce the heteroscedasticity.

Conclusion

The goal of this article was to raise awareness of the importance of checking assumptions in simple and multiple regression. We focused on four assumptions that were not highly robust to violations, or easily dealt with through design of the study, that researchers could easily check and deal with, and that, in our opinion, appear to carry substantial benefits.

We believe that checking these assumptions carry significant benefits for the researcher. Making sure an analysis meets the associated assumptions helps avoid Type I and II errors. Attending to issues such as attenuation due to low reliability, curvilinearity, and non-normality often boosts effect sizes, usually a desirable outcome.

Finally, there are many non-parametric statistical techniques available to researchers when the assumptions of a parametric statistical technique is not met. Although these often are somewhat lower in power than parametric techniques, they provide valuable alternatives, and researchers should be familiar with them.

References

Berry, W. D., & Feldman, S. (1985). *Multiple Regression in Practice.* Sage University Paper Series on Quantitative Applications in the Social Sciences, series no. 07-050). Newbury Park, CA: Sage.

Cohen, J., & Cohen, P. (1983). *Applied multiple regression/correlation analysis for the behavioral sciences.* Hillsdale, NJ: Lawrence Erlbaum Associates, Inc.

Nunnally, J. C. (1978). *Psychometric Theory* (2nd ed.). New York: McGraw Hill.

Osborne, J. W., Christensen, W. R., & Gunter, J. (April, 2001). Educational Psychology from a Statistician's Perspective: A Review of the Power and Goodness of Educational Psychology Research. Paper presented at the national meeting of the American Education Research Association (AERA), Seattle, WA.

Osborne, J. W. (2001). A new look at outliers and fringeliers: Their effects on statistic accuracy and Type I and Type II error rates. Unpublished manuscript, Department of Educational Research and Leadership and Counselor Education, North Carolina State University.

Pedhazur, E. J., (1997). *Multiple Regression in Behavioral Research* (3rd ed.). Orlando, FL: Harcourt Brace.

Tabachnick, B. G., & Fidell, L. S. (1996). *Using Multivariate Statistics* (3rd ed.). New York: Harper Collins College Publishers.

Tabachnick, B. G., & Fidell, L. S. (2001). *Using Multivariate Statistics* (4th ed.). Needham Heights, MA: Allyn and Bacon.

Are Standardized Tests Fair to African Americans?

Predictive Validity of the SAT in Black and White Institutions

Jacqueline Fleming and Nancy Garcia

The controversy over whether standardized tests like the SAT and the ACT are fair to ethnic minorities continues to rage. There is considerable opinion that standardized tests are unfair to African Americans and other minorities. Proponents of standardized tests argue that they offer an objective, common yardstick that helps identify capable students who come from various backgrounds and grading systems. Thus, they prevent discrimination against able minority candidates (College Board, 1983). The National Research Council of the National Academy of Sciences reports that SAT scores predict performance as accurately for blacks as they do for majority applicants. Though the report acknowledges that average scores for whites are higher than those for blacks, just as they are for men compared to women, the averages do not reveal the different abilities of individuals within those groups, which is what the test is intended to identify. Opponents of standardized tests allege that they are inherently unfair to disadvantaged minorities because they are culturally and educationally inappropriate (Hilliard, 1990; Carty-Bennia, 1989), because such tests are frequently wrong in assessing the potential of minorities (Crouse & Trusheim, 1988), and because wide variation in predictive validity suggests unfairness (see Wilson, 1981; Houston, 1983; Temp, 1971).

The evidence for predictive validity of the SAT for white students is consistent (see Table 1). A study by Cameron Fincher (1974) is representative of many large-scale efforts that validate the effectiveness of the SAT. Fincher's work was carried out in 29 institutions of the university system of Georgia over a 13-year period. The average correlation obtained was 0.490 (or 24% of the variance in grades). Ford and Campos (1977) similarly reported a summary of validity data gathered over 10 years from 1964 to 1974, and found the average correlation with freshman grades for the verbal SAT and the math SAT to be 0.370 and 0.320, respectively (13.7% and 10.2% of the variance). This study also found that SAT scores were predicting as well in more recent years as in earlier years, but that the validity of the high-school record and multiple correlations had declined slightly. A study by Ramist, Lewis, and McCamley-Jenkins (1994) reported validity coefficients for students in 11 colleges. The average correlation of the SAT with freshman grades was 0.420 (17.6% of the variance). Willingham and Breland (1982), in a study of 18 independent colleges,

Reprinted by permission from *The Journal of Higher Education* 69, no. 5 (September–October 1998).

TABLE 1A
SAT Validity Coefficients for White Students

Study	*Correlation*	*% Variance*	*Strength of r*
1. Fincher (1984)	0.490	24.0%	moderate
2. Ford & Campos (1977; 783 colleges):			
SATM	0.320	10.2%	moderate
SATV	0.370	13.7%	moderate
3. Wilson (1980; n = 961):			
SATM	0.388	15.1%	moderate
SATV	0.392	15.4%	moderate
4. Wilson (1981; n = 1102):			
SATM	0.301	9.1%	moderate
SATV	0.338	11.4%	moderate
5. Fleming & DuBois (1981; n = 62)	0.410	16.8%	moderate
6. Willingham & Breland (1982; n = 4693)	0.420	17.6%	moderate
7. Goldman & Richards (1974; n = 210)			
SATM	0.370	13.7%	moderate
SATV	0.400	16.0%	moderate
8. Goldman & Hewitt (1976; n = 4259)			
SATM	0.210	4.4%	weak
SATV	0.300	9.0%	moderate
9. Pennock-Roman (1990):			
California 1 (private institution; n = 898):			
SATM	0.240	5.8%	weak
SATV	0.370	13.7%	moderate
California 2 (public institution; n = 1304):			
SATM	0.190	3.6%	weak
SATV	0.290	8.4%	weak
Texas (public institution; n = 4347):			
SATM	0.330	10.9%	moderate
SATV	0.310	9.3%	moderate
Florida (public institution; n = 2565):			
SATM	0.210	4.4%	weak
SATV	0.220	4.8%	weak
Massachusetts (private institution; n = 4473)			
SATM	0.290	8.4%	weak
SATV	0.310	9.3%	moderate
New York (private institution; n = 2033)			
SATM	0.090	0.8%	weak
SATV	0.060	0.4%	weak
10. Dittmar (1977)			
1974 (n = 218):			
SATM	0.439	19.3%	moderate
SATV	0.421	17.7%	moderate
1975 (n = 254):			
SATM	0.410	16.8%	moderate
SATV	0.378	14.3%	moderate
11. Ramist, Lewis, McCamley-Jenkins (1994)	0.420	17.6%	moderate
12. Morgan (1990)			
1978 (n = 89,013):			
SATM	0.500	25%	strong
SATV	0.520	27%	strong
1981 (n = 89,524):			
SATM	0.490	24%	moderate
SATV	0.490	24%	moderate
1985 (n = 74,586):			
SATM	0.310	9.6%	moderate
SATV	0.300	9%	moderate
Average	0.342	11.7%	

TABLE 1B
SAT Validity Coefficients for Black Students

Study	*Correlation*	*% Variance*	*Strength of r*
Black Students in White Colleges:			
1. Miller & O'Connor (1969):			
Females, 1964	0.480	23.0%	moderate
Females, 1965	0.440	19.4%	weak
2. Wilson (1980; *n* = 270):			
SATM	0.410	16.8%	moderate
SATV	0.371	13.8%	moderate
3. Wilson (1981; *n* = 115):			
SATM	0.191	3.6%	weak
SATV	0.236	5.6%	weak
4. Flaming & DuBois (1981); *n* = 96	−0.010	0.01%	weak
5. Ramist, Lewis & McCamley-Jenkins (1994)	0.300	9.0%	moderate
6. Goldman & Hewitt (1976; *n* = 272)			
SATM	0.180	3.2%	weak
SATV	0.280	7.8%	weak
7. Hedges & Majer (1976) (*n* = 161 unidentified minorities)			
SATM	0.315	9.9%	moderate
SATV	0.250	6.3%	weak
8. Morgan (1990):			
1978 (*n* = 5,162):			
SATM	0.430	18.5%	moderate
SATV	0.430	18.5%	moderate
1981 (*n* = 4,086):			
SATM	0.350	12.3%	moderate
SATV	0.330	10.9%	moderate
1985 (*n* = 5,095):			
SATM	0.350	12.3%	moderate
SATV	0.320	10.2%	moderate
Studies Without Coefficients:			
Pfeiffer & Sedlacek (1971)			
Temp (1971)			
Goldman & Hewitt (1976)			
Dalton (1976)			
Boyd (1977)			
Breland (1978)			
Houston (1983)			
Average	0.315	9.9%	
Black Students in Black Colleges:			
1. Morehouse College (1984)			
SATM	0.480	23%	moderate
SATV	0.410	16.8%	moderate
2. Xavier University (1984)	0.610	37.2%	strong
3. Ramist, Lewis, & McCamley-Jenkins (1994)	0.380	14.4%	moderate
4. Fleming (1990):			
Spelman (*N* = 641)	0.341	11.6%	moderate
Morris Brown (*N* = 159)	0.395	15.6%	moderate
Xavier (*N* = 535)	0.565	31.9%	strong
Tougaloo (*N* = 70)	0.555	30.8%	strong
Texas Southern (*N* = 146)	0.424	18%	moderate
Average	0.462	21.3%	
Grand Average	0.362	14.7%	

found correlations averaging 0.420 (17.6% of the variance). Note that validity coefficients are rarely considered alone but in combination with the high-school record, which produces substantially higher multiple correlations.

Several smaller studies rely on data from a single college and also find results similar to the large-scale efforts. For instance, Wilson (1980) found that at a state university the math and verbal SATs correlated 0.388 and 0.392, respectively, with grades (15.5% and 15.1% of the variance). Wilson (1981) also reported data at a highly selective college and found the math and verbal SAT correlations to be somewhat lower, that is, 0.301 and 0.338 (9.1% and 11.4%). At New York University, Fleming & DuBois (1981) found the SAT score to be the best predictor of college grades ($r = 0.410$; 16.8%) in a study that considered several motivational variables. Other studies, both by ETS researchers and by independent researchers, report similar results (Morgan, 1990; Dittmar, 1977; Goldman & Hewitt, 1976; Goldman & Richards, 1974). For all reviewed studies combined, the average correlation for white students was 0.342, accounting for an average of 11.7% of the variance in grades. A study by Pennock-Roman (1990) is the only one reporting relatively low average correlations of 0.243 (5.9% of the variance) for white students in three public and three private institutions.

The evidence for black students in predominantly white schools is more complicated. The few reports available for black students yield variable and contradictory results. Morgan (1990) reported substantial correlations among four to five thousand black students at three different time periods, averaging 0.368 (13.6% of the variance). Breland's (1978) extensive research lead him to conclude that test scores predict similarly for black and white students. Pfeiffer and Sedlacek (1971) concurred. Hedges and Majer (1976) found higher correlations for SATM (0.315) than SATV (0.250), 9.9% and 6.3% of the variance respectively. Goldman and Hewitt (1976) reported relatively low correlations for both SATM and SATV of 0.180 and 0.280, respectively (3.2% and 7.8%). Ramist's comprehensive study of blacks in 11 white colleges showed that although the range of scores for blacks and whites was similar, the level of prediction was substantially less for black students. On the average, black SAT scores correlated 0.300 (9%) with freshman grades; similar scores for white students were 0.420 (17.6%), a differential of 8.6%. Wilson conducted two studies of minority student (half of whom were black) prediction to grades from test scores. In a state university, Wilson (1980) found that the math and verbal SAT correlated 0.410 and 0.371, respectively, with college grades (16.8% and 13.8%), a better level of prediction than found for non-minorities. However, in a second study at an elite university, Wilson (1981) found a much lower level of prediction for minorities, that is, correlations of 0.191 and 0.236 for math and verbal scores, respectively (3.6% and 5.6%). Miller and O'Connor (1969) found that SAT scores did not predict freshman grades at all for their sample of black males at the University of Michigan, although correlation coefficients were not given. For one entering class of black women, the correlation for SAT and grades was 0.440 (19.4%), but for black women in the next entering class, the correlation was 0.100 (1%). Similarly, Fleming and DuBois (1981) reported that SAT scores did not correlate significantly at all with grades among black students at New York University ($r = -0.01$; 0.01%), whereas correlations were in the usual range for white students (i.e., 0.410).

Other studies for which validity coefficients were not available also reported difficulties using test scores to predict college grades. Houston (1983) reported problems in underprediction. A number of authors have found that found that overprediction was a consistent problem (Temp, 1971; Breland, 1978; Crouse & Trusheim, 1988; Nettles, Thoeny & Gosman, 1990). Dalton (1976) viewed the combination of high-school rank and SAT scores to be of limited usefulness in predicting the academic success of black students. Boyd (1977) studied black and Hispanic students at 20 highly selective colleges and concluded that their success in these institutions could not be predicted by the SAT score alone.

From the available studies that do report validity coefficients, the average correlation for black students is 0.315, accounting for an average of 9.9% of the variance (compared to 11.7% for white students, a minor difference of 1.8%). It does, however, appear that the level of prediction from test scores to college grades is highly variable among black students, ranging from −0.01 to 0.48 (from 0.01% to 23% of the variance), variability that has never been adequately explained. Despite the minimal difference in average correlations, variable findings such as these have lead to a widespread belief that standardized test scores are either invalid for black students or fail to measure important abilities. Eight studies of Latino students report relatively low correlations, ranging from −0.080 to 0.370, with an average of 0.232, accounting for 5.4% of the variance (Morgan, 1990; Pennock-Roman, 1990; Duran, 1986; Breland, 1978; Dittmar, 1977; Goldman & Hewitt, 1976; Lowman & Spuck, 1975; Goldman & Richards, 1974).

Note, however, that all of the previous studies of black students were conducted among students attending predominantly white schools. Indeed, when the validity of the SAT for black students in black schools was examined from the few reports available, a more consistent picture of SAT score prediction emerged. Ramist's aforementioned study at the Educational Testing Service included 11 black colleges. Although psychometricians are concerned over the restricted range of test scores at black colleges, the pattern of prediction is nonetheless similar to that of white students in white colleges: SATs correlated 0.38 with freshman grades (14.4% of the variance). An unpublished report by predominantly black Morehouse College (1984) found that math and verbal SATs correlated 0.480 and 0.410 with freshman grades (23% to 16.8%). Xavier University (1984), another predominantly black institution, found that the SAT correlated 0.610 with grades among its freshmen after three semesters (37.2%). Also, for 1982 graduates in arts and sciences, the ACT correlated 0.500 with grades (25%). Fleming (1990), in the only published report available, found that the SAT (or ACT equivalent) provided consistently good prediction to grades, from 0.341 to 0.565 (11.6% to 31.9%), in five black colleges that provided official records for all students who had taken standardized tests, with an average correlation of 0.456 (20.8%). Across studies, the average correlation was 0.462, accounting for an average of 21.3% of the variance (that is, 9.6% better than for white students, and 11.4% better than for blacks in white schools).

Thus, previous research indicates that SAT scores predict grades for black students better if those students attend predominantly black schools than if they attend predominantly white schools. However, previous research has rarely examined predictive validity in both kinds of schools in the same study using the same methods, thus posing problems for comparing validity coefficients. The Ramist et al. (1994) study is the only exception. Therefore, studies using different methods and widely varying numbers of subjects become the only basis for comparison. Although ETS researchers are in the best position to use all available data from a school population, they often do not investigate comparisons of interest to other researchers. Thus, the present study presents correlations for standardized tests and grades for samples of black students in 15 colleges, 7 predominantly black and 8 predominantly white. It also presents correlations for white students in 3 of the predominantly white colleges. It was hypothesized that (a) correlation coefficients would be higher for black students in predominantly black colleges; (b) correlation coefficients would be more variable for black students in predominantly white schools, and (c) correlation coefficients for white students would be higher than for black students in predominantly white schools; (d) there would be no difference in the correlation coefficients for white students in white colleges and for black students in predominantly black colleges.

Method

Subjects

Subjects for the study were students in Fleming's (1984) study of *Blacks in College*, recruited by a series of procedures designed to produce a high volunteer rate. Of the 2,979 students in the original subject pool, standardized test scores were available for 1,843 students (62% of the sample); transcripts were available for 2,711 (91% of the sample); and both were available for 1774 freshmen and seniors, a 40% reduction in sample size that reflects the difficulty of recruiting students who had taken college entrance exams. There were 746 black students in 7 black schools, including 543 freshmen (229 males and 314 females) and 203 seniors (85 males and 118 females); 739 black students in 8 white schools, including 526 freshmen (200 males and 326 females) and 213 seniors (88 males and 125 females). There were also 289 white students in 3 white schools, including 204 freshmen (124 males and 80 females) and 85 seniors (54 males and 31 females). Although the numbers of seniors became quite small in a number of schools, analyses for them are presented for the sake of thoroughness in an area of research where few studies are available.

TABLE 2
Subject Breakdown by School, Class, Sex and Race

School	*Male*		*Female*		
	Freshmen	*Seniors*	*Freshmen*	*Seniors*	*Total N*
Black Students in Black Schools:					
Spelman	0	0	68	40	108
Morehouse	78	31	0	0	109
Clark	20	2	69	12	103
Texas Southern	57	22	68	22	169
Tougaloo	19	6	52	14	91
Wilberforce	33	7	46	7	93
Central State	22	17	11	23	73
Total	229	85	314	118	746
Black Students in White Schools:					
Emory	5	6	13	12	36
University of Georgia	22	11	41	15	89
Georgia Tech	39	11	21	0	71
Georgia College	6	6	36	19	67
University of Houston	37	15	93	30	175
Millsap	10	12	17	7	46
University of Dayton	27	22	42	23	114
Ohio State University	54	5	63	19	141
Total	200	88	326	125	739
White Students in White Schools:					
Georgia Tech	53	28	8	7	96
University of Houston	33	5	28	9	75
University of Dayton	38	21	44	15	118
Total	124	54	80	31	289
Grand total	553	236	720	274	1774

Table 2 presents a breakdown of subjects by school, class, sex, and race.

Procedure

During the initial testing session, students completed a registrar release form allowing the release of their transcripts and standardized test scores. Because both SAT and ACT scores were used by some colleges (primarily in Texas and Mississippi), ACT scores were converted to their SAT equivalents according to a formula made available by the American College Testing Program (Langston & Watkins, 1976), and updated by Marco and Abdel-Fattah (1991). Two measures of academic performance were used for this set of analyses: overall grade point average and cumulative grade point average for the spring semester. For coding purposes, a 4-point system was used uniformly, and differential weighting of letter grades was discarded. Standardized test scores were correlated with semester GPA and cumulative GPA. Correlations were examined for all students, freshman (males and females), and seniors (males and females).

Treatment of Data

Correlations for SAT (or ACT equivalents) and semester GPA and cumulative GPA were computed for all students, freshmen, freshmen males, freshmen females, seniors, senior males, and senior females. These analyses were performed separately for black and white students.

For each set of analyses, the following statistics were also computed: (a) the average correlation coefficient within black schools, white schools, and for white students; (b) the average estimate of variance accounted for; (c) the average standard deviation of the correlation coefficient; (d) independent *t*-test comparisons for mean differences in the correlation coefficients for black schools and white schools ($n = 15$), and comparison of blacks in white schools and with white students ($n = 11$); (e) Levene's test for differences between variances; and (f) the correlation between the SAT/ACT-GPA correlation coefficient and mean SAT (or ACT equivalent) score for each sample, and number of subjects.

Please note that pooling course grades into a composite GPA with no control for comparability of courses can diminish predictive validity (Ramist, Lewis, & McCamley-Jenkins, 1994). However, the problem proved to be minimized with African American students. Also note that there was no correction for restriction of range of test scores, which may underestimate the size of the predictive validity coefficients (see Ramist et al., 1984).

Results

Black Students in Black and White Schools

All Students

For all students combined, with an average sample size of 99 (121 in black schools, and 96 in white schools), validity coefficients were higher for black students in black schools, but the differences in prediction were not great. Table 3 shows that average correlations for semester GPA were 0.347 for students in black schools, compared to 0.288 for students in white schools; the difference in average variance accounted for only 3.7%. Similarly, average correlations for the cumulative GPA were 0.359 and 0.326, respectively; the difference in

TABLE 3
Correlations for SAT with Semester GPA and Cumulative GPA for All Students

Schools	*N*	*Mean SAT*	*r with Semester GPA*	*r with Cumulative GPA*
Black Schools:				
Spelman	108	782	0.323***	0.434***
Morehouse	109	799	0.533***	0.567***
Clark	103	699	0.339***	0.352***
Texas Southern	169	611	0.341***	0.386***
Tougaloo	191	673	0.365***	0.423***
Wilberforce	93	569	0.291**	0.030
Central State	73	602	0.234*	0.321**
Average	121	676	0.347 (12%)	0.359 (12.9%)
White Schools:				
Emory	36	957	0.429**	0.241
University of Georgia	89	830	0.061	0.230*
Georgia Tech	71	1018	0.287*	0.398***
Georgia College	67	634	0.385***	0.333**
University of Houston	199	758	0.399***	0.379***
Millsap	46	900	0.195	0.307*
University of Dayton	116	846	0.166	0.347***
Ohio State	143	679	0.383***	0.374***
Average	96	828	0.288 (8.3%)	0.326 (10.6%)
White Students in White Schools:				
Georgia Tech	97	1192	0.390***	0.486***
University of Houston	76	1025	0.159	0.159
University of Dayton	118	1005	0.357***	0.384***
Average	97	1074	0.302 (9.1%)	0.343 (11.8%)

Note: Variance accounted for in parentheses.
*$p < 0.05$.
**$p < 0.01$.
***$p < 0.001$.

average variance accounted for was only 2.3%. Furthermore, there were no significant differences in variability of the correlations. The mean SAT scores of black students in white schools were significantly higher than those of counterparts in black schools ($t = 2.55, p < 0.05$), indicating that size of the validity coefficient appears not to vary with the mean SAT (ACT) scores of the sample.

Freshmen

Freshmen constituted 72% of the sample and produced an average sample size of 71: 78 for students in black schools and 66 for blacks in white schools. When they were considered alone, students in black schools produced correlations now substantially better than for students in predominantly white colleges. Table 4 shows that the average correlation for semester GPA was 0.397 for students in black schools, compared to 0.304 for students in white schools; the difference in average variance accounted for was a substantial 6.6%. Corresponding figures for the cumulative GPA were 0.371 and 0.310, respectively, with a 4.2% difference in average variance accounted for. However, these differences were not significant in the 15-sample analysis, nor were there significant differences in variability. In terms of both numbers of subjects, averaging 71 students in each school, and consistency of academic experience, this analysis may be the most valid. The validity coefficients, especially for semester GPA, were sufficiently different to suggest that racial composition of the college environment may play some role in the translation of test score potential into academic performance.

TABLE 4
Correlations for SAT and Semester and Cumulative GPA for Freshmen

Schools	*N*	*Mean SAT*	*r with Semester GPA*	*r with Cumulative GPA*
Black Schools:				
Spelman	68	772	0.490***	0.519***
Morehouse	78	800	0.543***	0.543***
Clark	89	699	0.332**	0.351**
Texas Southern	125	611	0.434***	0.422***
Tougaloo	71	659	0.396***	0.410***
Wilberforce	79	566	0.348**	−0.015
Central State	33	611	0.239	0.364*
Average	78	67	0.397 (15.8%)	0.371 (13.8%)
White Schools:				
Emory	18	922	0.420	0.228
University of Georgia	63	845	0.143	0.260*
Georgia Tech	60	1008	0.357**	0.394**
Georgia College	42	618	0.375*	0.261
University of Houston	130	735	0.312***	0.312***
Millsap	27	896	0.269	0.312
University of Dayton	69	841	0.211	0.370**
Ohio State	117	664	0.347***	0.346***
Average	66	816	0.304 (9.2%)	0.310 (9.6%)
White Students in White Schools:				
Georgia Tech	61	1192	0.411***	0.545***
University of Houston	61	1023	0.144	0.166
University of Dayton	82	1101	0.338**	0.330**
Average	68	1105	0.298 (8.9%)	0.347 (12%)

Note: Variance accounted for in parentheses.
*$p < 0.05$.
**$p < 0.01$.
***$p < 0.001$.

Freshmen Males

The greatest differences in test score prediction appeared after splitting the freshmen sample by sex, with males in black schools producing much higher validity coefficients. Males constituted 40.1% of the freshmen sample, with an average sample size of 29: 38 in black schools and 25 in white schools. Table 5 shows that for semester GPA, and average correlation for freshmen males in black schools was 0.436, compared to 0.219 for freshmen males in white schools. The difference in average variance accounted for was quite high, that is, 14.2%. Indeed, the difference in average correlations approaches significance, even in the small sample of 15 cases ($t = 2.05$, $p = 0.065$), and it is the only comparison of means among black students that does approach significance. Furthermore, the correlations for black freshmen males in white schools were significantly more variable than those for black males in black schools, including two negative correlations. Levene's test for unequal variances was significant ($F = 6.63$, $p < 0.05$), the only significant difference in variances among black students found in the study. For the cumulative GPA, the average correlation for black schools was 0.413, compared to 0.175 for white schools, with an average differential of 14%, a substantial but not significant difference. In this case, neither the difference in average correlations nor variances approached statistical significance. Unfortunately, the validity of these coefficients is reduced by the small sample sizes, averaging 31 students, but ranging from 5 to 43 subjects. One of the negative correlations for black males in white schools was a substantial −0.565, but it was based on only 5 subjects. However, the

TABLE 5
Correlations for SAT and Semester and Cumulative GPA for Freshmen Males

Schools	*N*	*Mean SAT*	*r with Semester GPA*	*r with Cumulative GPA*
Black Schools:				
Clark	20	705	0.540**	0.614**
Morehouse	78	800	0.543***	0.543***
Texas Southern	57	592	0.482***	0.493***
Tougaloo	19	722	0.490*	0.500*
Central State	22	622	0.259	0.428***
Wilberforce	33	542	0.299	−0.101
Average	38	664	0.436 (19%)	0.413 (17.1%)
White Schools:				
Emory	5	942	−0.001	−0.565
University of Georgia	22	869	0.068	0.156
Georgia Tech	39	1014	0.470**	0.504***
Georgia College	6	657	0.610	0.686
University of Houston	37	802	0.256	0.230
Millsaps	10	897	0.000	−0.079
Ohio State	54	687	0.431***	0.457***
University of Dayton	27	842	−0.080	0.007
Average	25	839	0.219 (4.8%)	0.175 (3.1%)
White Students in White Schools:				
Georgia Tech	53	1202	0.436***	0.572***
University of Houston	33	1058	0.050	0.044
University of Dayton	38	1016	0.385*	0.386*
Average	41	1092	0.290 (8.4%)	0.334 (11.2%)

Note: Variance accounted for in parentheses.
*$p < 0.05$.
**$p < 0.01$.
***$p < 0.001$.

trends for freshmen, if confirmed, would indicate that the role played by racial composition of the college environment maximizes test score prediction in black schools but is least favorable to test score prediction among black males in white schools.

Freshman Females

Freshman females produced a reversal of the previous trends, producing better correlations in predominantly white schools. Average sample size was 46: 52 in black schools, and 41 in white schools. Table 6 shows that the average correlation for semester GPA for black freshman females in black schools was 0.334, *slightly lower* than the average of 0.338 found for freshman females in white schools. The average differential for semester GPA was only 0.2% of the variance. However, for cumulative GPA, the average correlation for freshman females in black schools was 0.280, *substantially lower* than the average of 0.380 found for black freshmen females in white schools. In this case, the difference in average variance accounted for was a noteworthy 6.6%, indicating better prediction for black women in white schools, although the difference was not statistically significant in the 15-sample study. The mean SAT scores were higher for black freshman females in white schools, compared to those in black schools ($t = 2.49, p < 0.05, n = 14$).

Seniors

By the senior year differences in predictive validity seem to be minimized, and the advantage to students in black schools is less clear-cut. The average sample size was 28: 29 for blacks in black

TABLE 6
Correlations for SAT and Semester and Cumulative GPA for Freshmen Females

Schools	N	Mean SAT	r with Semester GPA	r with Cumulative GPA
Black Schools:				
Spelman	68	772	0.490***	0.519***
Clark	69	697	0.241*	0.234*
Texas Southern	68	627	0.395***	0.376**
Tougaloo	52	636	0.409**	0.439***
Wilberforce	46	581	0.365**	0.015
Central State	11	592	0.104	0.099
Average	52	651	0.334 (11.2%)	0.280 (7.8%)
White Schools:				
Emory	13	913	0.631*	0.623*
University of Georgia	41	832	0.258	0.344*
Georgia Tech	21	997	0.051	0.144
Georgia College	36	610	0.312~*	0.206
University of Houston	93	708	0.357***	0.373***
Millsap	17	895	0.383	0.472~*
University of Dayton	42	840	0.387**	0.568***
Ohio State	63	645	0.328*	0.306*
Average	41	805	0.338 (11.4%)	0.380 (14.4%)
White Students in White Schools:				
Georgia Tech	8	1129	−0.155	−0.139
University of Houston	28	981	0.460**	0.499**
University of Dayton	44	1006	0.298*	0.282
Average	27	1039	0.201 (4%)	0.214 (4.6%)

Note: Variance accounted for in parentheses.
*$p < 0.05$.
**$p < 0.01$.
***$p < 0.001$.

TABLE 7
Correlations for SAT and Semester and Cumulative GPA for Seniors

Schools	*N*	*Mean SAT*	*r with Semester GPA*	*r with Cumulative GPA*
Black Schools:				
Spelman	40	801	−0.036	0.140
Clark	14	696	0.565*	0.438
Morehouse	31	797	0.515**	0.667***
Texas Southern	44	608	0.144	0.358
Tougaloo	20	726	0.255	0.494*
Wilberforce	14	588	−0.058	−0.423
Central State	40	594	0.247	0.273
Average	29	688	0.231 (5.3%)	0.386 (14.9%)
White Schools:				
Emory	18	993	0.389	0.243
University of Georgia	26	793	0.008	0.189
Georgia Tech	11	1053	0.062	0.567
Georgia College	25	665	0.310	0.382
University of Houston	45	802	0.464**	0.395**
Millsap	19	896	0.196	0.394
University of Dayton	45	857	0.079	0.287~*
Ohio State University	24	753	0.472*	0.323
Average	27	852	0.248 (6.2%)	0.348 (12.1%)
White Students in White Schools:				
Georgia Tech	35	1192	0.457**	0.509**
University of Houston	14	1022	0.369	0.498
University of Dayton	36	994	0.402*	0.500**
Average	28	1069	0.409 (16.7%)	0.502 (25.2%)

Note: Variance accounted for in parentheses.
*$p < 0.05$.
**$p < 0.01$.
***$p < 0.001$.

schools and 27 for blacks in white schools. Table 7 shows that the average correlation for semester GPA for black seniors in the black schools was 0.231, now *lower* than the average correlation of 0.248 found for black seniors in white schools. The difference in average variance accounted for was only 0.9%, but the departure from overall trends is striking. Average correlations for cumulative GPA, however, indicated a minimal difference between black seniors in black and white schools in favor of black schools, that is, 0.386 for those in black schools and 0.348 for those in white schools. The average differential was 2.8% of the variance. Also note that the size of the validity coefficients produced in the senior year (i.e., with semester GPA) are relatively low, suggesting that the SAT exerts a smaller influence on academic performance at this stage among black students. Obviously the larger correlations produced by the cumulative GPA are due to a longer history beyond the second semester of the senior year.

Senior Males and Females

To further break down the senior sample stretches the limits of validity, but doing so reveals two trends: a reversal of the findings found for freshmen in both males and females and attenuated SAT score differences among senior males. For senior males, the average number of subjects in each school was 12: 14 for blacks in black schools and 11 for blacks in white schools. Surprisingly, Table 8 shows that better correlations in white schools were accounted for by males rather than females. The average correlation for

TABLE 8
Correlations for SAT and Semester and Cumulative GPA for Senior Males

Schools	N	Mean SAT	r with Semester GPA	r with Cumulative GPA
Black Schools:				
Morehouse	31	797	0.515***	0.667***
Clark	2	870	—	—
Texas Southern	22	608	0.144	0.358
Tougaloo	6	765	−0.049	0.321
Wilberforce	7	566	0.114	−0.322
Central State	17	610	0.353	0.416~*
Average	14	703	0.221 (4.9%)	0.288 (8.3%)
White Schools:				
Emory	6	997	0.190	0.035
University of Georgia	11	853	0.494	0.114
Georgia Tech	11	1053	0.062	0.567~*
Georgia College	6	653	0.448	0.454
University of Houston	15	820	0.535*	0.323
Millsap	12	838	0.481	0.536~*
University of Dayton	22	813	−0.061	0.173
Ohio State	5	718	0.010	0.660
Average	11	843	0.270 (7.3%)	0.358 (12.8%)
White Students in White Schools:				
Georgia Tech	28	1175	0.441*	0.469*
University of Houston	5	995	0.388	0.561
University of Dayton	21	977	0.212	0.213
Average	18	1049	0.347 (12%)	0.414 (17%)

Note: Variance accounted for in parentheses.
*$p < 0.05$.
**$p < 0.01$.
***$p < 0.001$.

semester GPA among senior black males in black schools was 0.221, slightly *lower* than the 0.270 average correlation for senior black males in white schools; the difference in average variance accounted for was 2.4%. However, unlike seniors in general, for cumulative GPA the average correlation of 0.288 was also lower for senior black males in black schools than the 0.358 for those in white schools; the difference in average variance accounted for was 4.5%. Mean SATs were higher for black students in white schools, compared to those in black schools, but the difference only approached significance ($t = 2.02, p = 0.066, n = 13$). (This is the only case in which the means in SAT scores were not significantly different and may account for the similarity in prediction.

For black females, the freshman advantage going to those in white schools was not the case among the seniors. Average sample size was 17: 20 for black females in black schools and 18 for black females in white schools. Table 9 shows that the average correlation for black senior females in black schools was 0.338; for black females in white schools it was a lower 0.322. However, the difference in average variance accounted for was only 1%. For cumulative GPA, the average correlation of 0.339 was higher for black senior females in black schools than the 0.300 for those in white schools. This time, the difference in average variance estimates was still a small 2.5%. The mean SAT was higher for black females in white schools compared to those in black schools ($t = 2.85, p < 0.05, n = 13$). Apparently, the factors influencing black males and females differentially in the freshman year are reversed among seniors. Although the senior differences are very small in terms of variance accounted for, they do indicate the presence of

TABLE 9
Correlations for SAT and Semester and Cumulative GPA for Senior Females

Schools	*N*	*Mean SAT*	*r with Semester GPA*	*r with Cumulative GPA*
Black Schools:				
Spelman	40	801	0.140	−0.036
Clark	12	668	0.592*	0.467
Texas Southern	22	614	0.109	0.135
Tougaloo	14	709	0.690**	0.463~*
Wilberforce	7	619	0.377	0.765*
Central State	23	581	0.120	0.240
Average	20	665	0.338 (11.4%)	0.339 (11.5%)
White Schools:				
Emory	12	991	0.565~*	0.395
University of Georgia	15	749	−0.163	0.427
Georgia Tech	—	—	—	—
Georgia College	19	668	0.274	0.362
University of Houston	30	793	0.455*	0.494**
Millsap	7	994	0.688~*	−0.033
University of Dayton	23	899	−0.068	0.167
Ohio State	19	763	0.500*	0.290
Average	18	837	0.322 (10.4%)	0.300 (9%)
White Students in White Schools:				
Georgia Tech	7	1259	0.739~*	0.683~*
University of Houston	9	1037	0.328	0.463
University of Dayton	15	1018	0.687**	0.791**
Average	10	1105	0.585 (34.2%)	0.648 (50%)

Note: Variance accounted for in parentheses.
*$p < 0.05$.
**$p < 0.01$.
***$p < 0.001$.

different conditions. The smallness of the sample sizes may well compromise the importance of the conclusions, but they may also provide direction for future research.

Comparing White and Black Students in Predominantly White Schools

All Students

Comparisons of white students in 3 of the white schools and black students in 8 white schools generally show better correlations for white students, but only slightly better (see Table 3). Average sample size was 96: 97 for white students and 96 for blacks in white schools. For semester GPA the average correlation of 0.302 was better for white students, compared to 0.288 for black students in white schools, but the differential in average variance accounted for was only 0.8%. For cumulative GPA, the average correlation of 0.343 for white students was also slightly better than the 0.326 for black students, but the differential in average variance accounted for was still only 1.2%. There were no significant differences in average correlations of variances. The mean SAT scores for white students were significantly higher than those of blacks in white schools ($t = 2.87$; $p < 0.05$).

Freshmen

Among freshmen, the differences between black and white students were also slight, but whether white or black students produced higher correlations depended on the measure of GPA used (see Table 4). The average number of subjects was 66 : 68 for white students and 66 for blacks in white schools. For white students the average correlation for semester GPA was 0.298, slightly *lower* than the 0.304 found for blacks in white schools, but the differential in average variance accounted for was only 0.3%. For cumulative GPA, the average correlation for white students was 0.347, *higher* than the 0.310 for black students in white schools, but the average differential was a small 2.4%. The mean SAT scores of white freshmen were higher than those for black freshmen in white schools ($t = 3.44, p < 0.01$).

Freshman Males

Among freshman males, the correlations for white students were higher, but this time the differences were substantial (see Table 5). The numbers of freshman males were relatively small, averaging 29: 41 for white males, and 25 for black males in white schools. For freshman white males the average correlation with semester GPA was 0.290, higher than the 0.219 for black males in white schools. The average difference in variance accounted for was 3.7%. For cumulative GPA, the average correlation for white males was 0.334, considerably higher than the 0.175 for black freshman males in white schools. In this case, the difference in variance accounted for was a substantial 8.1%. The difference did not, however, reach statistical significance in the comparison of 11 cases. The mean SAT scores of white students were significantly higher than those of black students in white schools ($t = 3.21$, $p = 0.01$).

Freshman Females

Among freshman females, a reversal occurred; correlations were substantially higher for black females (see Table 6). The average number of subjects was 37: 27 for white females in white schools and 41 for black freshman females in white schools. For white freshman females the average correlation for semester GPA was 0.201, *lower* than the 0.338 for black females in white schools; the difference in average variance accounted for was 7.4%. The average correlation for white freshman females for cumulative GPA was 0.214, even *lower* than the 0.380 for black females in white schools. This time, the difference in variance accounted for was a noteworthy 9.8%. These trends toward better prediction for black women compared to white women in white schools were not statistically significant in the sample of 11 schools. The mean SAT for white freshman female students was higher than that for black freshman females in white schools ($t = 2.73, p < 0.05, n = 11$).

Seniors

The average differential estimates increase significantly when comparing white seniors and black seniors in white schools (see Table 7). The average sample size was 27: 28 for white students and 27 for blacks in white schools. For semester GPA the average correlation for white seniors was 0.409, much higher than the 0.248 for blacks in white schools. The difference in variance accounted for was 10.5%. Similarly, for cumulative GPA, the average correlation for white seniors was 0.502, whereas the average correlations for black seniors in white schools was only 0.248. In this case the average differential variance estimate was 13.1%. The mean SAT for white students was higher than that for blacks in white schools ($t = 2.62, p < 0.05, n = 11$).

Senior Males

Among seniors, white males produced higher correlations, but the differences were small (see Table 8). Average number of subjects in each sample was 13: 18 for white senior males and 11 for black seniors males in white schools. The average correlation for semester GPA for white senior males was 0.347, higher than the 0.270 for black senior males in white schools; the difference in variance accounted for was 4.7%. In this case, however, the correlations for black males were significantly more variable than those for white males ($F = 7.86, p < 0.05, n = 11$). White senior males also had a higher average correlation of 0.414 for cumulative GPA, compared to 0.358 for black senior males in white schools. The average differential in variance accounted for was not substantial: 4.4%. The mean SAT was higher for white senior males compared to black senior males ($t = 2.40, p < 0.05, n = 11$).

Senior Females

The most dramatic differences were found between the higher correlations of white senior females compared to those of black senior females in white schools (see table 9). The average number of subjects in each sample was 14: 10 for white senior females, and 18 for black senior females in white schools. The average correlation for semester GPA for white females was 0.585, much higher than the 0.322 average correlation found for black senior females in white schools; the difference in average variance accounted for was 25.2%. For cumulative GPA the average correlation for white senior females was 0.648, again much higher than the 0.300 found for black senior females in white schools, producing the highest difference in average variance accounted for in the study, that is, 33%. This difference in mean correlations was also statistically significant ($t = 2.82, p < 0.04, n = 10$). The mean SAT was higher for white females than for black females in white schools ($t = 3.02, p < 0.05, n = 10$).

Discussion

Charges that standardized tests are unfair to African American students persist because of wide variation in predictive validity as well as problems with lack of prediction, underprediction, and overprediction. But several studies suggest that standardized test scores predict academic performance much better for black students who attend predominantly black colleges, with the same consistency and level of prediction usually found for white students (see Fleming, 1990). However, previous research rarely includes data from black students in both kinds of schools in the same study, introducing a source of comparative error. Consequently, the present study examined validity coefficients for black students in 8 predominantly white and 7 predominantly black colleges. Overall, the investigation found that average validity coefficients for cumulative grades were: (1) 0.326 for black students in the white schools, i.e., 10.6% of the variance compared to 9.9% found in eight previous studies; (2) 0.359 for black students in the black schools, i.e., 12.9% of the variance compared to 21.3% in four previous studies; and (3) 0.343 for white students, i.e., 11.8% of the variance compared to 11.7% in twelve previous studies. Although the average validity coefficients for black students in black schools were higher than they were for blacks in white colleges, the average differences of 2.3% and 3.7% of the variance accounted for (in semester and cumulative grades) were small and hardly provided evidence for a case to argue differential predictive validity. The one exception found was for black freshman males. Freshman males in black schools produced significantly higher validity coefficients (i.e., a difference of 14% of the variance). Furthermore, coefficients for black freshman males in white schools were significantly more variable, including positive, negative, and zero-order correlations. An interesting but nonsignificant reversal occurred for black freshman females, who produced higher validity coefficients in predominantly white schools (differences of 0.2% and 6.6% of the variance). Better prediction for black females in consistent with numerous reports that black women have certain achievement advantages in predominantly white settings that are unavailable to black males (Fleming, 1983, 1984; Epstein, 1973; Feagin, 1970; Fichter, 1967; Bernard, 1966). Among seniors, differences were smaller, as were the numbers of subjects, but the coefficients were slightly higher for students in white schools (differences of 0.9% and 2.8%). Splitting the senior sample by sex revealed that black males in white schools accounted for the higher validity coefficients for black students in white schools generally (differences of 2.4% and 4.5%). In short, the overall trends indicate differences that are not great, but the overall trends also mask provocative sex differences in predictive validity.

How seriously should we take these findings, or rather, how valid are they? On one hand, the present data are derived from a 1984 study when black-white SAT scores were more divergent than they are today (e.g., Jones, 1984; Baratz-Snowden, 1987; Wainer, 1988; Ramist, Morgan, & Affleck, 1989). On the other hand, the present data are no older than many studies cited frequently in the standardized testing literature and, furthermore, provide an unusual opportunity to examine validity coefficients for black students in black and white schools. Unlike previous research for black students in black colleges, as well as institutional research that was able to examine validity coefficients for all students in the school or in a given class, the present study was only able to examine coefficients from samples of students who had been recruited. This difference may well be a factor in the difference in average validity coefficients found for students in black schools between the present study and previous studies. When correlation coefficients from all available previous studies reviewed here were examined, the average variance accounted for was 11.4% greater for black students in black schools compared to black students in white schools (and 1.8% greater for white students compared to black students in white schools). It does seem, however, that estimates should not be excluded from consideration if they are based on samples of students rather than the entire population, and in this case the sampling limitation is offset by the advantage of having fifteen samples of approximately 100 students each. It poses a problem that the samples are not equally balanced for academic classification but are composed of 72% freshmen and 28% seniors. Nonetheless, the results were examined separately by class. Finally, it is problematic that some (i.e., 29%) of the scores, in Texas and Mississippi, were ACT scores requiring a conversion to SAT equivalents, so that parties interested in one test or the other may have concerns about the purity of the data. Suffice it to say that the present study is not perfect in possessing data based on entire classes of students, each of whom had taken only one variety of standardized test. Nonetheless, the present study does make a contribution in providing validity coefficients for a wide variety of black students in both black and white schools with good geographic representation and with possibilities for analysis by race, sex, and academic classification.

Previous research has also suggested that standardized tests predict academic performance better for white students than for black students. This study could only consider validity coefficients for white students in three colleges, so that the confidence placed in the findings is not the same as that for comparisons of black students. Nonetheless, the average correlations were generally better for white students, and this was particularly true in the senior year, due largely to the vastly (and significantly) better average correlations of senior white females compared to their black counterparts. There was, however, a substantial reversal among freshmen, in that black female freshmen in white schools produced better correlations than white female freshmen. Also, among freshmen, the correlations of black freshman males were more variable than those of white students. Thus, the overall trends in favor of white students mask sometimes dramatic differences by sex that suggest differential adjustment issues.

There are several issues raised by the findings that relate to the fairness of the SAT for African American students. The first is, does the racial environment of the college make a difference in predictive validity of the SAT? The answer is that it depends on how you look at it. If you look at overall analyses where academic classification and sex are ignored, then racial environment of the college of matriculation appears to make very little difference. If you look at analyses of freshmen where sex is ignored, the differences are worth mentioning but not sufficient to support a serious contention of differential predictive validity. But if you examine freshman separately by sex, the data indicate that racial environment makes a considerable difference for black freshman males in white schools, whose validity coefficients were both lower and wildly variable, ranging from strong positive correlations to zero-order correlations to negative correlations. The variability is consistent with other reports of predictive validity for black males and is suggestive of situational interference in the translation of tested potential into academic outcomes. The problematic situation is not evident in the senior year, but given the high attrition rates for black males, especially in white schools, the present data may be on samples of the relatively few survivors of college. The freshman trends may well be symptomatic of the difficulty in surviving to the senior year.

The second issue is, does the fact that white students produce better correlations suggest that standardized tests are biased against black students? The answer is, again, it depends on how you look at it. Yes, the average overall correlations for white students were better, but these differences were insignificant until the senior year. When sex and year were considered, it does appear that black freshman males were at a disadvantage in terms of highly variable correlations, whereas black freshmen females displayed markedly better correlations than their white counterparts. By the senior year these differences were no longer present, while another equally dramatic scenario in favor of white females appeared. It is possible that the small numbers of subjects create trends that are not stable. It may also be that standardized tests reflect differential influences present in society as well as in college environment. Those trends change, depending on the particular school, sex, year, and race. Because these trends surface in other aspects of psychological investigation, they appear to be products of society rather than products of standardized tests alone.

Do these results shed light on the patterns of correlations found previously among black students, suggesting inconsistency? Indeed, the present study suggests at least three reasons: (1) the number of samples; (2) the composition of the sample; and (3) the number of subjects in the sample. The present study has relied on average correlations across 15 samples to determine trends in SAT prediction. However, looking at any given sample in the study would not necessarily reflect the nature of the average trends. Furthermore, samples composed largely of black males in white schools would give the most inaccurate readings of general trends due to their special variability. Samples of black students in white schools were in general more variable, if not significantly so. Although the numbers of subjects was unrelated to the size of the correlations, small samples should be vulnerable to variable readings.

Does predictive validity vary with the mean SAT score? No. The mean SAT scores of white students were significantly higher than those of black students in white schools; and these were significantly higher than those of black students in black schools. Overall the average correlations were not greatly different between the groups, certainly not significantly so. Furthermore, black students in black schools, who had the lowest SAT scores, produced coefficients midway between black and white students in white schools. It appears that year and sex, but not race of school, are greater determinants of predictive validity than is mean SAT score. This is contrary to concerns expressed by psychometricians that lower means indicate constricted variability that results in lower predictive validity (Ramist et al., 1984).

Future research could examine the adjustment problems in the translation of the SAT into grades by race and sex. Specifically, research could consider correlating test scores with measures of academic, adjustment to determine where interfering adjustment problems may lie.

References

Baratz-Snowden, J. (1987, May/June). Good news, bad news: Black performance on standardized tests. *Change, 19*, 50–54.

Bernard, J. (1966). *Marriage and family among Negroes.* Englewood Cliffs, NJ: Prentice Hall.

Breland, H. M. (1978). Population validity and college entrance measures. *Research Bulletin* (RB 78–6) Princeton, NJ: Educational Testing Service.

Boyd, W. M. (1977). SAT's minorities: The dangers of underprediction. *Change, 9*, 48–49, 64.

Carty-Bennia, D. (1989, March 5). A debate on the SAT focuses on its fairness. *Boston Globe.*

College Entrance Examination Board. (1983a). Facts about the fairness of the Scholastic Aptitude Test. New York: Author.

College Entrance Examination Board. (1983). Facts about the usefulness of the Scholastic Aptitude Test. New York: Author.

Crouse, J., & Trusheim, D. (1988). *The case against the SAT.* Chicago: The University of Chicago Press.

Dalton, S. (1976). A decline in the predictive validity of the SAT and high-school achievement. *Educational and Psychological Measurement, 36*, 445–448.

Dittmar, N. (1977). *A comparative investigation of the predictive validity of admissions criteria for Anglos, Blacks, and Mexican Americans.* Unpublished doctoral dissertation, University of Texas, Austin.

Duran, R. P. (1986). Prediction of Hispanics' college achievement. In M. A. Olivas (Ed.), *Latino college students.* New York: Teachers College Press.

Epstein, C. F. (1973). Positive effects of the double negative: Explaining the success of black professional women. In J. Huber (Ed.), *Changing women in a changing society.* Chicago: The University of Chicago Press.

Feagin, J. R. (1970). Black women in the American labor force. In C. V. Willie (Ed.), *The family life of black people.* Columbus, OH: Merrill.

Fichter, J. H. (1967). Career expectations of Negro graduates. *Monthly Labor Review, 90*, 36–42.

Fincher, C. (1974). Is the SAT worth its salt? An evaluation of the use of the Scholastic Aptitude Test in the university system of Georgia over a thirteen-year period. *Review of Educational Research, 44*(3), 293–305.

Fleming, J. (1983). Black women in black and white college environments: The making of a matriarch. *Journal of Social Issues, 39*(3), 41–54.

Fleming, J. (1984). *Blacks in college.* San Francisco: Jossey-Bass.

Fleming, J. (1990). Standardized test scores and the black college environment. In K. Lomotey (Ed.), *Going to school: The African-American experience.* Albany: State University of New York Press.

Fleming, J., & DuBois, L. (1981). *The role of suppressed and perceived hostility in academic performance: An exploratory study of Black students.* New York: United Negro College Fund, Report to the Spencer Foundation.

Ford, S. F., & Campos, S. (1977). *Summary of validity data from the admissions testing program validity study service.* The College Entrance Examination Board.

Goldman, R. D., & Hewitt, B. W. (1976). Predicting the success of black, chicano, oriental, and white college students. *Journal of Educational Measurement, 13,* 107–117.

Goldman, R. D., & Richards, R. (1974). The SAT prediction of grades for Mexican American versus Anglo American students at the University of California, Riverside. *Journal of Educational Measurement, 11*(2), 129–135.

Hedges, L. V., & Majer, K. (1976). An attempt to improve prediction of college success of minority students by adjusting for high-school characteristics. *Educational and Psychological Measurement, 36,* 953–957.

Hilliard, A. G. (1990). Limitations of current academic achievement measures. In K. Lomotey (Ed.), *Going to school: The African-American experience.* Albany: State University of New York Press.

Houston, L. N. (1983). The comparative predictive validities of high-school rank, the Ammons Quick Test, and two Scholastic Aptitude Test measures for a sample of black female college students. *Educational and Psychological Measurement, 43,* 1123–1126.

Jones, L. V. (1984). White-black achievement differences: The narrowing gap. *American Psychologist, 39*(11), 1207–1213.

Langston, I. W., & Watkins, T. (1976). *SAT-ACT equivalents.* Unpublished manuscript, University of Illinois, University Office of School and College Relations.

Lowman, R., & Spuck, D. (1975). Predictors of college success for disadvantaged Mexican Americans. *Journal of College Student Personnel, 16,* 40–48.

Macro, G. L., & Abdel-Fattah, A. A. (1991). Developing concordance tables for scores on the enhanced ACT Assessment and the SAT. *College & University, 66*(4), 187–194.

Miller, D. M., & O'Connor, P. (1969). Achiever personality and academic success among disadvantaged college students. *Journal of Social Issues, 25*(3), 103–116.

Morehouse College (1984). *Computational chart: Freshmen predicted index.* Atlanta, GA: Office of Admissions.

Morgan, R. (1990). *Predictive validity within categorizations of college students: 1978, 1981, and 1985* (ETS Research Report 90–14). Princeton, NJ: Educational Testing Service.

Nettles, M. T., Thoeny, A. R., & Gosman, E. J. (1986, May/June). Comparative and predictive analyses of black and white students' college achievement and experience. *Journal of Higher Education, 57,* 289–318.

Pennock-Roman, M. (1990). *Test validity and language background: A study of Hispanic American students at six universities.* New York: College Entrance Examination Board.

Pfeiffer, C. M., & Sedlacek, W. F. (1971). The validity of academic predictors for black and white students at a predominantly white university. *Journal of Educational Measurement, 8,* 253–261.

Ramist, L., Angoff, W. H., Broudy, I. L., Burton, N. W., Donlon, T. F., Stern, J., & Thorne, P. A. (1984). The predictive validity of the ATP tests. In T. F. Donlon (Ed.), *The college board technical handbook for the Scholastic Aptitude and Achievement Tests.* New York: College Entrance Examination Board.

Ramist, L., Lewis, C., & McCamley-Jenkins, L. (1994). *Student group differences in predicting college grades: Sex, language and ethnic groups.* College Board Report No. 93–1, ETS RR No. 94–27. New York: College Entrance Examination Board.

Ramist, L., Morgan, R., & Affleck, A. (1989, October 7). *An analysis of score gains for Black SAT takers, 1978 to 1988.* Paper presented at the National Conference of the National Association of College Admission Counselors.

Temp, G. (1971). Validity of the SAT for blacks and whites in thirteen integrated institutions. *Journal of Educational Measurement, 8,* 245–251.

Wainer, H. (1988). How accurately can we assess changes in minority performance on the SAT? *American Psychologist, 43*(10), 774–778.

Willingham, W. W., & Breland, H. M. (1982). *Personal qualities and college admissions.* New York: College Entrance Examination Board.

Wilson, K. M. (1980). The performance of minority students beyond the freshman year: Testing a "late-bloomer" hypothesis in one state university setting. *Research in Higher Education, 13*(1), 23.

Wilson, K. M. (1981). Analyzing the long-term performance of minority and non-minority students: A tale of two studies. *Research in Higher Education, 15*(4), 351–375.

Xavier University of Louisiana. (1984, March). *Student success at Xavier.* New Orleans: Office of Institutional Research.

CULTURALLY RESPONSIVE PERFORMANCE-BASED ASSESSMENT: CONCEPTUAL AND PSYCHOMETRIC CONSIDERATIONS

STAFFORD HOOD

Arizona State University

This article provides a rationale for advocating the development of culturally responsive performance-based assessments as a means of achieving equity for students of color. It first addresses the arguments for and against these types of assessments, noting important psychometric concerns. It then discusses their potential for effectuating culturally responsive instructional approaches. Last, it recommends that existing test development procedures be modified to emphasize the meaningful participation of individuals who are not only experts in the content area being assessed but have deep understandings of the cultural contexts of students of color based on substantial teaching experience in those contexts.

Introduction

The noted educational researcher Edmund Gordon issued a challenge to the assessment community at a conference entitled "Assessment Questions: Equity Answers," sponsored in 1993 by the Center for Research on Evaluation Standards and Student Testing (CRESST). At that conference, Gordon outlined three ways to make assessment more equitable (Rothman, 1994). First, he suggested that we educators and policymakers make better use of available information to allocate resources more equitably. Second, he suggested that we develop new instruments and procedures to tap students' affective traits and not just their cognitive skills. Third, he recommended that we conduct research and development work to build on what is known about cultural pluralism and its impact on teaching and learning.

I agree with Gordon on all three points. Indeed, this article reflects my most recent attempt to elaborate on his second point and to stimulate the generation of ideas that amplify his third point. It begins with a rationale for proposing culturally responsive performance-based assessment as a potential vehicle for achieving equity for students of color. That argument is followed by a discussion of some of the major technical concerns associated with measures of reliability and validity when assessing students of color using performance-based assessments is the central consideration. Finally, the article discusses the probable consequences of employing specific strategies that modify typical test development procedures. It recommends targeting the inclusion of individuals who are not only experts in the content area of the assessment (e.g., mathematics, science, etc.) but also have an in-depth understanding of students' cultural context. This latter focus examines the likely outcomes of involving individuals who are grounded in both the substantial schooling and real-life experiences of the cultural contexts of targeted examinees of color.

At the core of Gordon's second point is the need to develop assessment devices that do not place examinees at a disadvantage simply because their cultural background differs from that of European Americans. In recent years, performance-based assessments have been offered as an alternative to traditional forms of standardized testing because they are believed to be potentially more culturally fair. Certainly, alternatives to the traditional approaches used to assess students of color must be rigorously explored and implemented. We must further consider developing assessments that parallel pedagogical strategies that are grounded in the cultural contexts of examinees of color. If it is true that culturally responsive forms of assessment can quite possibly improve the assessment of what examinees of color know and can do relative to specific learning outcomes, then it is incumbent upon us to begin discussing how these devices can be developed and validated.

In the past few years, the discussions prompted by the Goals 2000: Educate America Act, the proposed National Voluntary Test, and other educational reform efforts have challenged our thinking about curriculum, instruction, and assessment (Howe, 1991; Shepard, 1993). However, when students of color are included in the equation of desirable educational and social outcomes, the complexity of the issues surrounding these reform initiatives increases exponentially. I am fully aware of the embedded complexities that require consideration of existing differences within particular cultural groups (e.g., African, Hispanic, Native, or Asian Americans); however, I am also aware of the formidable challenges as well as the high costs that would likely be associated with developing such assessments. Advocates of performance-based assessment claim that it more accurately measures the higher order thinking skills of students in general and provides a fairer assessment of students of color and those from economically disadvantaged backgrounds (Wiggins, 1989). They further maintain that these assessments require students to display a more comprehensive array of knowledge and skills than do traditional tests, and that they facilitate teachers' opportunities to observe problem-solving behaviors in real-world contexts (Boodoo, 1993; Wiggins, 1989). Performance-based assessments have also been characterized as providing a tight coupling with instruction or grounding in the discipline and as allowing scoring that is more than a quantitative summary of right answers (Garcia & Pearson, 1994). Garcia and Pearson contend that these types of assessments illuminate the reasonableness of the procedures used to complete tasks or solve problems.

The persuasive arguments that traditional testing instruments have failed to assess academic skills and knowledge in the fluid setting of real-life situations have caused many concerned parties—educators, members of the general public, business people, state and federal legislators, and other politicians, among them—to embrace the various forms of performance-based assessments that have emerged. The purported ability of these assessments to provide a more comprehensive view of what students can actually do in the real world appears to give them an edge over traditional tests. Some proponents of performance-based assessments have broadened the range of their claims to suggest that these measures provide a fairer assessment of students of color (Simmons & Resnick, 1993). Messick (1995a), for example, asserts that these measures are "less stigmatizing, more adaptable to individual student needs, less narrow and more faithful to the richness and complexity of real-world problem solving, more instructionally relevant, more useful for public and parental reporting, and more reflective of the actual quality of student understanding" (p. 21).

Although many have claimed that performance-based assessments can do a better job than traditional tests, in truth there is little empirical evidence to support such a claim (Bond, 1995; Gordon & Bowman–Bonilla, 1996; Linn, Baker, & Dunbar, 1991). Upon closer examination, lingering questions remain regarding both the technical adequacy and the responsiveness of performance-based assessments for assessing students of color. Further, as Madaus (1994) attests, regardless of what form of assessment is used, the real issue is whether the inferences and decisions made from test scores are appropriate for different groups.

The claim that performance-based assessments are more likely to provide a fairer assessment of what students of color have learned as a result of schooling implies that these assessments are culturally fair or possibly more responsive to these students' cultural backgrounds (Bracey, 1993). This perspective forces one to seriously consider the merits of developing assessment approaches that incorporate the basic tenets of culturally responsive pedagogical strategies, and that are grounded in the cultural context of diverse groups of examinees. Alternatively, it suggests that the student learning that results from culturally responsive instructional strategies may be more effectively assessed by using approaches that are also culturally responsive.

The Need for Culturally Responsive Performance-based Assessment

Culturally responsive instruction has been generally defined as that which (a) incorporates teachers' adaptations of subject-matter content to reflect the cultures of their students, and (b) helps students become more aware of and knowledgeable about their own cultures and the cultures of others (Hood, 1993). Ladson–Billings (1995a, 1995b), Lee (1990), and other proponents of culturally responsive instruction generally concur with that definition. Through their work, they have shown that teachers who exhibit such qualities have been successful in improving the achievement levels of students of color.

In an evaluation I conducted a few years ago of a training institute for urban and rural teachers (Hood, 1993), I learned that both groups of teachers reported being knowledgeable about culturally responsive instructional strategies. The urban teachers, however, were reportedly more likely than their rural counterparts to use these strategies in their classrooms. In subsequent interviews with selected institute participants, several of the urban teachers, most of whom taught in schools with a majority of students of color, reported experiencing considerable frustration that their use of culturally responsive instructional strategies did not necessarily translate into higher performance on standardized achievement tests. Some were adamant that all too often the results of the standardized achievement tests contradicted their first-hand classroom observations and assessments of students of color. Those assessments, they indicated, revealed higher levels of student performance on targeted learning objectives than reflected by students' scores on standardized tests.

Of course, there could be a number of explanations for this. One explanation comes from Messick (1995a), who suggests that low standardized test scores may be the result of the assessment "missing something relevant to the focal construct (academic achievement) that if present would have permitted the affected students to display their competence" (p. 7). Koelsch, Estrin, and Farr (1995) extend this line of reasoning by suggesting that low test scores for students of color may reflect the failure of test developers to consider these students' cultural experiences in their assessments. As Koelsch et al. state:

> If the student's experiences in a cultural group . . . are not taken into account when assessment tasks are developed and scored, the evaluation process of how well a student has learned with the school's culture will be flawed. A failing performance may indicate the degree of disconnection between the task and the student's frame of reference, rather than the degree of mastery of the knowledge and skills being assessed. (p. 21)

Estrin (1993) concurs, noting that it is not possible to fully understand a student's performance on any assessment without considering her or his language and culture:

> . . . test questions and student responses are understood only in terms of the test taker's background, the testing context, and the cultural lens of the test developer and scorer. What counts as "intelligence," for example, is so culturally variable that a single test of it cannot be valid for all people. (p. 2)

Madaus (1994) extends this position by arguing that differences in the intellectual traditions of U.S. cultural groups may create different conceptions of reality that are not tapped by traditional standardized testing instruments. If one agrees that these contentions are sound, then it is reasonable to suggest that the approaches and devices used to assess students of color must be grounded in the cultural experiences of those students. One must also agree that those experiences must serve as an essential frame of reference for developing assessment instruments.

As Miller–Jones (1989) contends, it might be of value to develop assessment items and tasks that are functionally equivalent or similar to the point of view of the cultural subject. Although he acknowledges the extreme difficulty of accomplishing such a task, he maintains that the positive outcomes could provide convincing evidence of competent performance among individuals from diverse cultural backgrounds.

A Brief Look at Some of the Counterarguments

There are important counterarguments to the above propositions that cannot be easily dismissed. Bracey (1993), for one, maintains that culturally responsive assessment approaches are impractical, given that it may not be technically feasible to implement them, and if it were, the magnitude of the task would make it highly unlikely. Linn (1994a) suggests that while the idea of providing functionally equivalent tasks that are compatible to students' cultural background is appealing, "little is known about the feasibility of constructing such tasks" (p. 572). In his view, even if the extremely difficult responsibility of developing functionally equivalent tasks is undertaken, the task of identifying and selecting culturally specific tasks that are congruent with targeted learning outcomes remains to be addressed. This formidable challenge is compounded by the lingering questions regarding the general technical adequacy of performance-based assessments, most notably, the crucial technical issues of reliability and validity.

Low reliability is indeed a characteristic technical flaw of performance-based assessment (Linn, 1993). One of the central reliability concerns associated with this approach is the higher than average possibility that performance raters may assign different ratings to a task. However, Shavelson, Baxter, and Pine (1992) found interjudge reliability to be less problematic than task variability in affecting scores on performance assessments. An additional complication is the longer amounts of time required to complete performance-based assessments. This limits the number of tasks that can be included and rated, thereby exerting a negative effect on reliability by limiting the sampling of the domain being assessed.

Even proponents of performance-based assessments agree that reliability issues must be addressed in order to ensure the assessments' fairness (Wiggins, 1989). Yet, little guidance has been offered to date regarding how their reliability can be increased. One must also consider how much weight should be attributed to reliability issues because the application of learned skills and knowledge in real-life experiences may result in the inconsistent application of knowledge and skills but the successful completion of performance tasks. Performance-based assessments are more concerned with successful solutions than with how problems are solved. Consequently, inquiries into their validity may initially outweigh concerns about the apparent need to raise their reliability coefficients.

Shepard (1993) notes that Messick's earlier work cemented the consensus on the unified concept of validity while it also extended that consensus "beyond test score meaning to include relevance and utility, value implications, and social consequence" (p. 423). In other words, the validity of an assessment must also be based on whether its consequences are justifiably in the best interests of examinees. As Koelsch et al. (1995) assert, "Consequential validity becomes a huge problem when students' abilities and potential have not been fairly judged because of the inappropriateness of the assessment" (p. 11). Although Messick's consequential basis of validity is controversial and some believe it overburdens the concept of validity (e.g., Woolley, 1996), it has the potential to improve standards for evaluating a test's validity and for making a case for the value of culturally responsive assessments.

Linn et al. (1991) propose eight criteria for evaluating the test validity of performance-based assessments:

1. consequences,
2. fairness,
3. transfer and generalizability,
4. cognitive complexity,
5. content quality,
6. content coverage,
7. meaningfulness, and
8. cost and efficiency.

Importantly, they note that the first criterion involves the collection of evidence regarding the intended and unintended consequences of the assessments on teachers and students, including the ways teachers and students spend their time and think about the goals of education. Thus, they view consideration of the consequential basis of validity as essential if performance-based assessments are to live up to their expectations.

Messick (1994) counters this position by arguing that Linn et al.'s validity criteria should not be exclusively relied upon for the following reasons:

> . . . important validity aspects might be downplayed or left out, particularly those bearing on score interpretation and its value implications. . . . Basic assessment issues as validity, reliability, comparability, and fairness need to be uniformly addressed for all assessments because they are not just measurement principles, they are social values that have meaning and force outside of measurement wherever evaluative judgments and decisions are made. (p. 13)

He elaborates further on the importance of value implications in considering validity by stating:

> The value implications of score interpretation are only part of score meaning, but a socially relevant part that often triggers score-based actions and serves to link the construct measure to questions of applied practice and social policy. (Messick, 1995b, p. 748)

Indeed, Messick is correct in his view that social values have played a major role both in defining high-stakes constructs as well as determining what is acceptable evidence to support their construct validity. However, his work raises several questions: How much have cultural values defined the educational constructs some in U.S. society hold so dearly (e.g., academic achievement, intelligence, etc.)? Whose culture and whose values have defined these constructs? Could it be that these constructs would be defined differently if they were defined by people with different cultural backgrounds? In light of the potential consequences of the projected demographic changes that will occur in the U.S. during the 21st century, the cultural values that have defined the psychometric constructs as well as the agreed-upon evidence that underpins their validity must be reconsidered. It seems quite reasonable to explore new definitions of constructs and validity that are based on a more culturally diverse vision. Therefore, insights on how key constructs are defined and manifested within different cultural contexts are critical. It may be possible to observe these manifestations if assessments are driven by the input of diverse and/or targeted cultural groups. Assessments grounded in the cultural context of examinees may also result in a fairer assessment of different cultural groups on constructs such as academic achievement.

Toward the Development of Culturally Specific Performance-based Assessments: Issues and Considerations

The current movement toward performance-based assessments has the potential to address some of these concerns, but important complications must be addressed. These complications are related to the difficult task of developing performance tasks and scoring criteria that (a) are responsive to cultural differences and (b) adequately assess the content-related skills that are the focus of the assessment. Consequently, it is important for those who define performance criteria to have some understanding of the kinds of tasks that show the greatest promise of being culturally responsive for different or multiple groups. This requires that developers of performance criteria be knowledgeable of the cultural context as well as the specific content area to be assessed. Additionally, developers must be able to appropriately draw upon this knowledge to identify tasks and criteria that bridge context and content.

According to Linn (1994b), the choice of test items and other assessment tasks is a critical component of efforts to address cultural diversity for the purpose of achieving fairness. He asserts that "providing students with some ability to choose content, context, and tasks within specified limits will decrease the likelihood of disadvantaging students from diverse cultural and social backgrounds" (p. 572). In other words, if given the choice, students of color would be more likely to choose test items or performance assessment tasks that are grounded in a culturally familiar context. Baker and O'Neil (1994) agree, noting that no studies to date have provided convincing evidence of the need for culturally specific tasks in performance-based assessment. They recommend, however, that examinees' interest be stimulated through the selection of tasks that are directly related to their particular world and prior knowledge.

Koelsch et al. (1995) have highlighted the importance of developing equitable performance-based assessments in the classroom and designed a workshop to accomplish this purpose. Although their strategies and related workshop activities are targeted toward assisting classroom teachers in the development of equitable performance-based assessments, the advice they offer is also useful in the development of traditionally formatted large-scale assessments. They assert that the criteria for developing authenticity in assessments for students of color should satisfy three conditions: they should "first guide development of performance assessments that connect with students' lives, . . . [second,] allow students to display learning in culturally responsive ways and, . . . [third,] make fundamental connections between school and the world outside of school" (p. 22).

With these conditions in mind, test developers might consider some of the approaches delineated below.

Diversifying Content Committees

The first step in the development of any assessment of student performance is to define the academic domain to be assessed or to establish the content standards. This involves the development of culturally specific tasks and the selection of an appropriate context for performance-based assessment that is firmly grounded in the realm of content validity. As in the development of any standardized academic instrument, the role of content and subject-matter experts is of utmost importance. Thus, the content expertise of the content committee members should be a primary consideration.

However, what if cultural specificity was one of the major priorities in developing performance-based assessments? What if test developers made serious efforts to recruit content experts who had similar cultural experiences and backgrounds or, at a minimum, first-hand experiences in teaching or interacting with the targeted group? It would then be reasonable to expect that members of the content committee would have a genuine appreciation and understanding of the cultural nuances, experiences, and backgrounds that targeted groups of examinees bring to the assessment.

Developing Items/Performance Tasks

Following the initial work on the part of the content committee to identify the assessment objectives, the next step would be to develop performance tasks that are aligned with those objectives. In the case of culturally specific assessments, however, the priority would be to develop tasks that are linked not only to the content objectives but also to the cultural context of the examinees.

But what if test originators also took seriously the recruitment of highly qualified developers of performance tasks who also possess characteristics similar to those mentioned for the above-noted content committee members? What if test developers were also concerned about including those who represented subgroups within the particular targeted cultural group(s)? In that case, for example, it would be desirable for Mexican, Cuban, and Puerto Rican Americans to be represented among those selected to develop culturally specific performance tasks and criteria for examinees who are included under the broad category of "Hispanics" These representatives could be provided with training in developing performance assessment tasks and performance criteria as well as judgmental bias review procedures. This process would necessarily be followed by the systematic and rigorous screening of these tasks for quality and congruence with the targeted learning outcomes.

Rating Performances

Judging students' performance on performance-based assessments is a critical step that can be highly problematic. When the performance criteria are clear and consensually agreed upon as being appropriate for the targeted domain, there should be few problems. Yet even under such optimal conditions, the selection of raters and the reliability of their ratings of student performance are major concerns. Moreover, Bond (1995) indicates that scoring performance-based assessments reliably and validly has major implications for fairness equity. As he notes, raters, like anyone else, can "hold purely prejudicial beliefs that can affect their objective assessments of others" (p. 24). Even if test developers recognize the importance of utilizing raters who are representative of targeted examinees' cultural group and of making representativeness a priority for selection as a performance rater, the potential influences of prejudicial beliefs on ratings of student performance cannot be eliminated. Appropriate steps must therefore be taken to minimize these effects, but once again, what if those who rate examinees' performances on specific tasks both reflected the cultural diversity of the examinees and possessed content expertise in the domain under study? One would expect these raters to have more insight in observing and rating examinees from their particular cultural group. It is also possible that they might have more favorable views of the performance of students from their own cultural group that cannot be attributed to "insider" sensitivity and insight. Such issues can and must be addressed during the training sessions for these observers.

Piloting the Assessments

The next step critical step is to pilot test the promising culturally responsive performance tasks. Major questions to be resolved at this stage relate to the type of statistical information that should be collected and how that information should be analyzed. Issues associated with judging the quality of the tasks and performance criteria as well as the reliability and accuracy of the observations and ratings must also be addressed. Despite the absence of a clear answer to the first set of methodological issues, it is important to collect and present some type of statistical information. Analyses should be conducted to determine the degree of congruence of the assessment tasks with the targeted learning outcomes as well as the identification of patterns of performance that may emerge within groups. During this carefully considered process, the final selection of the performance tasks, criteria, and procedures, along with the protocols for observing and rating performance, must be determined. Then and only then should the major task of conducting extensive research on the merits, appropriateness, and effectiveness of this proposed process begin in earnest.

Concluding Thoughts

Admittedly, I have raised many questions in this article and have not provided answers for all of them. I also confess that some of the ideas proposed herein reflect my own biased perspectives. But who among us is not guilty of this fault? The first priority of efforts to develop culturally responsive assessments is to determine whether the tasks and criteria developed with this goal in mind are congruent with the targeted domain and learning outcomes. It is also critically important to determine early on the extent to which, if given the choice, students of color will select performance tasks that are specific to their particular background when given the opportunity to do so. If these students choose culturally specific performance tasks, then their level of performance relative to the established performance criteria must be determined. Perhaps the students could then be presented with performance tasks from another source that are congruent with the specific domain objective of the culturally specific tasks, possibly the pool of performance tasks from the National Assessment of Educational Progress (NAEP) battery of tests (Berends & Koretz, 1996). If the performance is comparable for high and low scorers, then questions regarding functional equivalence can be addressed. If the discrepancy is such that the high scorers on a culturally responsive assessment also score lower on a traditional assessment such as the NAEP, then it may be possible that the culturally responsive tasks are more stimulating and may more effectively elicit optimal performance. Regardless, one must be certain that both performance tasks match the domain objectives.

It will also be important to determine the extent to which culturally responsive assessments differ across cultural groups. Identifying which types of performance tasks can only be used for one cultural group and not for another may also prove to be an area worth studying. It may be possible that certain culturally responsive assessments are selected by students from cultural backgrounds that differ from those students for whom they were designed. If those students are successful in meeting the performance criteria, it could be an indication that a multiculturally oriented single assessment could have some utility.

If we in the assessment field are successful in developing culturally specific performance items, tasks, criteria, observations, and ratings, then we can and should collect evidence of both the potential positive and negative consequences of culturally responsive assessments. It is very likely that the positive consequences of increased motivation for, optimal performance on, and further insights into the value of these assessments will outweigh the negative consequences. However, using more culturally responsive assessment tools may be a bold step in the right direction for addressing the issue of fairness in educational assessment.

References

Baker, E. L., & O'Neil, H. F. (1994). Performance assessment and equity: A view from the USA. *Assessment in Education, 1*(1), 11–26.

Berends, M., & Koretz, D. M. (1996). Reporting minority students' test scores: How well can the National Assessment of Educational Progress account for differences in social context? *Educational Assessment, 3*(3), 249–285.

Bond, L. (1995). Unintended consequences of performance assessments: Issues of bias and fairness. *Educational Measurement: Issues and Practices, 14*(4), 5–8.

Boodoo, G. M. (1993, Fall). Performance assessments or multiple choice? *Horizons*, pp. 50–56.

Bracey, G. (1993, December). Testing the tests. *School Administrator*, pp. 8–11.

Estrin, E. T. (1993). *Alternative assessment: Issues in language, culture, and equity* (Knowledge Brief No. 11). San Francisco: Far West Laboratory.

Garcia, G. E., & Pearson, P. D. (1994). Assessment and diversity. *Review of Research in Education, 20*, 337–391.

Gordon, E. W., & Bowman–Bonilla, C. (1996). Can performance-based assessments contribute to the achievement of educational equity? In J. B. Baron & D. P. Wolf (Eds.), *Performance-based student assessment: Challenges and possibilities* (95th Yearbook of the National Society for the Study of Education, Part 1; pp. 32–51). Chicago: The University of Chicago Press.

Hood, S. (1993). *An evaluation of the Rural School Action Project/Urban School Action Project Summer Institute.* Oak Brook, IL: North Central Regional Educational Laboratory.

Howe, H. (1991, November). America 2000: A bumpy ride on four trains. *Phi Delta Kappan*, pp. 192–203.

Koelsch, N., Estrin, E., & Farr, B. (1995). *Guide to developing equitable performance assessments.* (ERIC Document Reproduction Service No. ED 397 125)

Ladson–Billings, G. (1995a). But that's just good teaching: The case for culturally relevant pedagogy. *Theory into Practice, 34*(3), 159–165.

Ladson–Billings, G. (1995b). Toward a theory of culturally relevant pedagogy. *American Educational Research Journal, 32*(3), 465–491.

Lee, C. (1990). How shall we sing our sacred song in a strange land? The dilemma of double-consciousness and the complexities of an African-centered pedagogy. *Journal of Education, 172*(2), 45–61.

Linn, R. L. (1993). Educational assessment: Expanded expectations and challenges. *Educational Evaluation and Policy Analysis, 15*, 1–16.

Linn, R. L. (1994a). Evaluating the technical quality of proposed national examination systems. *American Journal of Education, 102*, 565–580.

Linn, R. L. (1994b). Performance assessment: Policy promises and technical measurement standards. *Educational Researcher, 23*(9), 4–14.

Linn, R. L., Baker, E. L., & Dunbar, S. B. (1991). Complex, performance-based assessment: Expectations and validation criteria. *Educational Researcher, 20*, 15–21.

Madaus, G. F. (1994). A technological and historical consideration of equity issues associated with proposals to change the nation's testing policy. *Harvard Educational Review, 64*(1), 76–95.

Messick, S. (1994). The interplay of evidence and consequences in the validation of performance assessments. *Educational Researcher, 23*(2), 13–23.

Messick, S. (1995a). Standards of validity in performance assessments. *Educational Measurement: Issues and Practices, 14*(4), 5–8.

Messick, S. (1995b). Validity of psychological assessment: Validation of inferences from person's responses and performances as scientific inquiry into score meaning. *American Psychologist, 50*, 9.

Miller–Jones, D. (1989). Culture and testing. *American Psychologist, 44*(2), 360–366.

Rothman, R. (1994, Winter). *Assessment questions: Equity answers* (Proceedings of the 1993 CRESST Conference). (ERIC Document Reproduction Services No. ED 367 684)

Shavelson, R., Baxter, G. P., & Pine, J. (1992). Performance assessments: Political rhetoric and measurement reality. *Educational Researcher, 21*(4), 22–27.

Shepard, L. A. (1993). Evaluating test validity. *Review of Research in Education, 19*, 405–450.

Simmons, W., & Resnick, L. (1993, February). Assessment as the catalyst of school reform. *Educational Leadership*, pp. 11–15.

Wiggins, G. (1989). A true test: Toward more authentic and equitable assessment. *Phi Delta Kappan, 70*, 703–713.

Woolley, K. (1996, January 25). *Revised thinking about the nature of validity.* Paper presented at the annual meeting of the Southwestern Educational Research Association, New Orleans, LA.

An Overview of Content Analysis

Steve Stemler

Yale University

Content analysis has been defined as a systematic, replicable technique for compressing many words of text into fewer content categories based on explicit rules of coding (Berelson, 1952; GAO, 1996; Krippendorff, 1980; and Weber, 1990). Holsti (1969) offers a broad definition of content analysis as, "any technique for making inferences by objectively and systematically identifying specified characteristics of messages" (p. 14). Under Holsti's definition, the technique of content analysis is not restricted to the domain of textual analysis, but may be applied to other areas such as coding student drawings (Wheelock, Haney, & Bebell, 2000), or coding of actions observed in videotaped studies (Stigler, Gonzales, Kawanaka, Knoll, & Serrano, 1999). In order to allow for replication, however, the technique can only be applied to data that are durable in nature.

Content analysis enables researchers to sift through large volumes of data with relative ease in a systematic fashion (GAO, 1996). It can be a useful technique for allowing us to discover and describe the focus of individual, group, institutional, or social attention (Weber, 1990). It also allows inferences to be made which can then be corroborated using other methods of data collection. Krippendorff (1980) notes that "[m]uch content analysis research is motivated by the search for techniques to infer from symbolic data what would be either too costly, no longer possible, or too obtrusive by the use of other techniques" (p. 51).

Practical Applications of Content Analysis

Content analysis can be a powerful tool for determining authorship. For instance, one technique for determining authorship is to compile a list of suspected authors, examine their prior writings, and correlate the frequency of nouns or function words to help build a case for the probability of each person's authorship of the data of interest. Mosteller and Wallace (1964) used Bayesian techniques based on word frequency to show that Madison was indeed the author of the Federalist papers; recently, Foster (1996) used a more holistic approach in order to determine the identity of the anonymous author of the 1992 book *Primary Colors.*

Content analysis is also useful for examining trends and patterns in documents. For example, Stemler and Bebell (1998) conducted a content analysis of school mission statements to make some inferences about what schools hold as their primary reasons for existence. One of the major research questions was whether the criteria being used to measure program effectiveness (e.g., academic test scores) were aligned with the overall program objectives or reason for existence.

Reprinted from *Practical Assessment, Research and Evaluation* 7, no. 17 (2001).

Additionally, content analysis provides an empirical basis for monitoring shifts in public opinion. Data collected from the mission statements project in the late 1990s can be objectively compared to data collected at some point in the future to determine if policy changes related to standards-based reform have manifested themselves in school mission statements.

Conducting a Content Analysis

According to Krippendorff (1980), six questions must be addressed in every content analysis:

1. Which data are analyzed?
2. How are they defined?
3. What is the population from which they are drawn?
4. What is the context relative to which the data are analyzed?
5. What are the boundaries of the analysis?
6. What is the target of the inferences?

At least three problems can occur when documents are being assembled for content analysis. First, when a substantial number of documents from the population are missing, the content analysis must be abandoned. Second, inappropriate records (e.g., ones that do not match the definition of the document required for analysis) should be discarded, but a record should be kept of the reasons. Finally, some documents might match the requirements for analysis but just be uncodable because they contain missing passages or ambiguous content (GAO, 1996).

Analyzing the Data

Perhaps the most common notion in qualitative research is that a content analysis simply means doing a word-frequency count. The assumption made is that the words that are mentioned most often are the words that reflect the greatest concerns. While this may be true in some cases, there are several counterpoints to consider when using simple word frequency counts to make inferences about matters of importance.

One thing to consider is that synonyms may be used for stylistic reasons throughout a document and thus may lead the researchers to underestimate the importance of a concept (Weber, 1990). Also bear in mind that each word may not represent a category equally well. Unfortunately, there are no well-developed weighting procedures, so for now, using word counts requires the researcher to be aware of this limitation. Furthermore, Weber reminds us that, "not all issues are equally difficult to raise. In contemporary America it may well be easier for political parties to address economic issues such as trade and deficits than the history and current plight of Native American living precariously on reservations" (1990, p. 73). Finally, in performing word frequency counts, one should bear in mind that some words may have multiple meanings. For instance the word "state" could mean a political body, a situation, or a verb meaning "to speak."

A good rule of thumb to follow in the analysis is to use word frequency counts to identify words of potential interest, and then to use a Key Word In Context (KWIC) search to test for the consistency of usage of words. Most qualitative research software (e.g., NUD*IST, HyperRESEARCH) allows the researcher to pull up the sentence in which that word was used so that he or she can see the word in some context. This procedure will help to strengthen the validity of the inferences that are being made from the data. Certain software packages (e.g., the revised General Inquirer) are able to incorporate artificial intelligence systems that can differentiate between the same word used with two different meanings based on context (Rosenberg, Schnurr, & Oxman, 1990). There are a number of different software packages available that will help to facilitate content analyses (see further information at the end of this paper).

Content analysis extends far beyond simple word counts, however. What makes the technique particularly rich and meaningful is its reliance on coding and categorizing of the data. The basics of categorizing can be summed up in these quotes: "A category is a group of words with similar meaning or connotations" (Weber, 1990, p. 37). "Categories must be mutually exclusive and exhaustive" (GAO, 1996, p. 20). Mutually exclusive categories exist when no unit falls between two data points, and each unit is represented by only one data point. The requirement of exhaustive categories is met when the data language represents all recording units without exception.

Emergent vs. *A Priori* Coding

There are two approaches to coding data that operate with slightly different rules. With *emergent coding*, categories are established following some preliminary examination of the data. The steps to follow are outlined in Haney, Russell, Gulek, & Fierros (1998) and will be summarized here. First, two people independently review the material and come up with a set of features that form a checklist. Second, the researchers compare notes and reconcile any differences that show up on their initial checklists. Third, the researchers use a consolidated checklist to independently apply coding. Fourth, the researchers check the reliability of the coding (a 95% agreement is suggested; .8 for Cohen's kappa). If the level of reliability is not acceptable, then the researchers repeat the previous steps. Once the reliability has been established, the coding is applied on a large-scale basis. The final stage is a periodic quality control check.

When dealing with *a priori* coding, the categories are established prior to the analysis based upon some theory. Professional colleagues agree on the categories, and the coding is applied to the data. Revisions are made as necessary, and the categories are tightened up to the point that maximizes mutual exclusivity and exhaustiveness (Weber, 1990).

Coding Units

There are several different ways of defining coding units. The first way is to define them physically in terms of their natural or intuitive borders. For instance, newspaper articles, letters, or poems all have natural boundaries. The second way to define the recording units syntactically, that is, to use the separations created by the author, such as words, sentences, or paragraphs. A third way to define them is to use referential units. Referential units refer to the way a unit is represented. For example a paper might refer to George W. Bush as "President Bush," "the 43rd president of the United States," or "W." Referential units are useful when we are interested in making inferences about attitudes, values, or preferences. A fourth method of defining coding units is by using propositional units. Propositional units are perhaps the most complex method of defining coding units because they work by breaking down the text in order to examine underlying assumptions. For example, in a sentence that would read, "Investors took another hit as the stock market continued its descent," we would break it down to: The stock market has been performing poorly recently/ Investors have been losing money (Krippendorff, 1980).

Typically, three kinds of units are employed in content analysis: sampling units, context units, and recording units.

- *Sampling units* will vary depending on how the researcher makes meaning; they could be words, sentences, or paragraphs. In the mission statements project, the sampling unit was the mission statement.
- *Context units* neither need be independent or separately describable. They may overlap and contain many recording units. Context units do, however, set physical limits on what kind of data you are trying to record. In the mission statements project, the context units are sentences. This was an arbitrary decision, and the context unit could just as easily have been paragraphs or entire statements of purpose.
- *Recording units*, by contrast, are rarely defined in terms of physical boundaries. In the mission statements project, the recording unit was the idea(s) regarding the purpose of school found in the mission statements (e.g., develop responsible citizens or promote student self-worth). Thus a sentence that reads "The mission of Jason Lee school is to enhance students' social skills, develop responsible citizens, and foster emotional growth" could be coded in three separate recording units, with each idea belonging to only one category (Krippendorff, 1980).

Reliability

Weber (1990) notes: "To make valid inferences from the text, it is important that the classification procedure be reliable in the sense of being consistent: Different people should code the same text in the same way" (p. 12). As Weber further notes, "reliability problems usually grow out of the ambiguity of word meanings, category definitions, or other coding rules" (p. 15). Yet, it is important to recognize that the people who have developed the coding scheme have often been working so closely on the project that they have established shared and hidden meanings of the coding. The obvious result is that the reliability coefficient they report is artificially

TABLE 1
Example Agreement Matrix

		Rater 1			
		Academic	*Emotional*	*Physical*	*Marginal Totals*
	Academic	.42 (.29)*	.10 (.21)	.05 (.07)	**.57**
Rater 2	Emotional	.07 (.18)	.25 (.18)	.03 (.05)	**.35**
	Physical	.01 (.04)	.02 (.03)	.05 (.01)	**.08**
		.50	**.37**	**.13**	**1.00**

*Values in parentheses represent the expected proportions on the basis of chance associations, i.e. the joint probabilities of the marginal proportions.

inflated (Krippendorff, 1980). In order to avoid this, one of the most critical steps in content analysis involves developing a set of explicit recording instructions. These instructions then allow outside coders to be trained until reliability requirements are met.

Reliability may be discussed in the following terms:

- *Stability,* or intra-rater reliability. Can the same coder get the same results try after try?
- *Reproducibility,* or inter-rater reliability. Do coding schemes lead to the same text being coded in the same category by different people?

One way to measure reliability is to measure the percent of agreement between raters. This involves simply adding up the number of cases that were coded the same way by the two raters and dividing by the total number of cases. The problem with a percent agreement approach, however, is that it does not account for the fact that raters are expected to agree with each other a certain percentage of the time simply based on chance (Cohen, 1960). In order to combat this shortfall, reliability may be calculated by using Cohen's Kappa, which approaches 1 as coding is perfectly reliable and goes to 0 when there is no agreement other than what would be expected by chance (Haney et al., 1998). Kappa is computed as:

$$\kappa = \frac{P_A - P_c}{1 - P_c}$$

where:

P_A = proportion of units on which the raters agree

P_c = the proportion of units for which agreement is expected by chance.

Given the data in Table 1, a percent agreement calculation can be derived by summing the values found in the diagonals (i.e., the proportion of times that the two raters agreed):

$$P_A = .42 + .25 + .05 = .72$$

By multiplying the marginal values, we can arrive at an expected proportion for each cell (reported in parentheses in the table). Summing the product of the marginal values in the diagonal we find that on the basis of chance alone, we expect an observed agreement value of:

$$P_c = .29 + .18 + .01 = .48$$

Kappa provides an adjustment for this chance agreement factor. Thus, for the data in Table 1, kappa would be calculated as:

$$\kappa = \frac{.72 - .48}{1 - .48} = .462$$

In practice, this value may be interpreted as the proportion of agreement between raters after accounting for chance (Cohen, 1960). Crocker & Algina (1986) point out that a value of $\kappa = 0$ does not mean that the coding decisions are so inconsistent as to be worthless, rather, $\kappa = 0$ may be interpreted to mean that the decisions are no more consistent than we would expect based on chance, and a negative value of kappa reveals that the observed agreement is worse than expected on the basis of chance alone. "In his methodological note on kappa in *Psychological Reports,* Kvalseth (1989) suggests that a kappa coefficient of 0.61 represents reasonably good overall agreement." (Wheelock et al., 2000). In addition, Landis & Koch (1977, p. 165) have suggested the following benchmarks for interpreting kappa:

Kappa Statistic	*Strength of Agreement*
<0.00	Poor
0.00–0.20	Slight
0.21–0.40	Fair
0.41–0.60	Moderate
0.61–0.80	Substantial
0.81–1.00	Almost Perfect

Cohen (1960) notes that there are three assumptions to attend to in using this measure. First, the units of analysis must be independent. For example, each mission statement that was coded was independent of all others. This assumption would be violated if in attempting to look at school mission statements, the same district level mission statement was coded for two different schools within the same district in the sample.

Second, the categories of the nominal scale must be independent, mutually exclusive, and exhaustive. Suppose the goal of an analysis was to code the kinds of courses offered at a particular school. Now suppose that a coding scheme was devised that had five classification groups: mathematics, science, literature, biology, and calculus. The categories on the scale would no longer be independent or mutually exclusive because whenever a biology course is encountered it also would be coded as a science course. Similarly, a calculus would always be coded into two categories as well, calculus and mathematics. Finally, the five categories listed are not mutually exhaustive of all of the different types of courses that are likely to be offered at a school. For example, a foreign language course could not be adequately described by any of the five categories.

The third assumption when using kappa is that the raters are operating independently. In other words, two raters should not be working together to come to a consensus about what rating they will give.

Validity

It is important to recognize that a methodology is always employed in the service of a research question. As such, validation of the inferences made on the basis of data from one analytic approach demands the use of multiple sources of information. If at all possible, the researcher should try to have some sort of validation study built into the design. In qualitative research, validation takes the form of triangulation. Triangulation lends credibility to the findings by incorporating multiple sources of data, methods, investigators, or theories (Erlandson, Harris, Skipper, & Allen, 1993).

For example, in the mission statements project, the research question was aimed at discovering the purpose of school from the perspective of the institution. In order to cross-validate the findings from a content analysis, schoolmasters and those making hiring decisions could be interviewed about the emphasis placed upon the school's mission statement when hiring prospective teachers to get a sense of the extent to which a school's values are truly reflected by mission statements. Another way to validate the inferences would be to survey students and teachers regarding the mission statement to see the level of awareness of the aims of the school. A third option would be to take a look at the degree to which the ideals mentioned in the mission statement are being implemented in the classrooms.

Shapiro & Markoff (1997) assert that content analysis itself is only valid and meaningful to the extent that the results are related to other measures. From this perspective, an exploration of the relationship between average student achievement on cognitive measures and the emphasis on cognitive outcomes stated across school mission statements would enhance the validity of the findings. For further discussions related to the validity of content analysis see Roberts (1997), Erlandson et al. (1993), and Denzin & Lincoln (1994).

Conclusion

When used properly, content analysis is a powerful data reduction technique. Its major benefit comes from the fact that it is a systematic, replicable technique for compressing many words of text into fewer content categories based on explicit rules of coding. It has the attractive features of being unobtrusive, and being useful in dealing with large volumes of data. The technique of content analysis extends far beyond simple word frequency counts. Many limitations of word counts have been discussed and methods of extending content analysis to enhance the utility of the analysis have been addressed. Two fatal flaws that destroy the utility of a content analysis are faulty definitions of categories and non-mutually exclusive and exhaustive categories.

Further Information

For links, articles, software and resources see

http://writing.colostate.edu/references/research/content/

http://www.gsu.edu/~wwwcom/.

References

Berelson, B. (1952). *Content Analysis in Communication Research.* Glencoe, III: Free Press.

Cohen, J. (1960). A coefficient of agreement for nominal scales. *Educational and Psychological Measurement, 20,* pp. 37–46.

Crocker, L., & Algina, J. (1986). *Introduction to Classical and Modern Test Theory.* Orlando, FL: Harcourt Brace Jovanovich.

Denzin, N. K., & Lincoln, Y. S. (Eds.). (1994). *Handbook of Qualitative Research.* Thousand Oaks, CA: Sage Publications.

Erlandson, D. A., Harris, E. L., Skipper, B. L., & Allen, S. D. (1993). *Doing Naturalistic Inquiry: A Guide to Methods.* Newbury Park, CA: Sage Publications.

Foster, D. (1996, February 26). Primary culprit. *New York,* 50–57.

Haney, W., Russell, M., Gulek, C., and Fierros, E. (Jan-Feb, 1998). Drawing on education: Using student drawings to promote middle school improvement. *Schools in the Middle, 7(3),* 38–43.

Holsti, O. R. (1969). *Content Analysis for the Social Sciences and Humanities.* Reading, MA: Addison-Wesley.

Krippendorff, K. (1980). *Content Analysis: An Introduction to Its Methodology.* Newbury Park, CA: Sage.

Kvalseth, T. O. (1989). Note on Cohen's kappa. *Psychological reports,* 65, 223–26.

Landis, J. R., & Koch, G. G. (1977). The measurement of observer agreement for categorical data. *Biometrics, 33,* pp. 159–174.

Mosteller, F. and Wallace, D. L. (1964). *Inference and Disputed Authorship: The Federalist.* Reading, Massachusetts: Addison-Wesley.

Nitko, A. J. (1983). *Educational Tests and Measurement: An Introduction.* New York, NY: Harcourt Brace Jovanovich.

Roberts, C. W. (Ed.) (1997). *Text Analysis for the Social Sciences: Methods for Drawing Statistical Inferences from Texts and Transcripts.* Mahwah, NJ: Lawrence Erlbaum Associates.

Rosenberg, S. D., Schnurr, P. P., & Oxman, T. E. (1990). Content analysis: A comparison of manual and computerized systems. *Journal of Personality Assessment, 54* (1 & 2), 298–310.

Shapiro, G., & Markoff, J. (1997). 'A Matter of Definition' in C.W. Roberts (Ed.). *Text Analysis for the Social Sciences: Methods for Drawing Statistical Inferences from Texts and Transcripts.* Mahwah, NJ: Lawrence Erlbaum Associates.

Stemler, S., and Bebell, D. (1998). *An Empirical Approach to Understanding and Analyzing the Mission Statements of Selected Educational Institutions.* Paper presented at the annual meeting of the New England Educational Research Organization. Portsmouth, New Hampshire. Available: ERIC Doc No. ED 442 202.

Stigler, J. W., Gonzales, P., Kawanaka, T., Knoll, S. & Serrano, A. (1999). *The TIMSS Videotape Classroom Study: Methods and Findings from an Exploratory Research Project on Eighth-Grade Mathematics Instruction in Germany, Japan, and the United States.* U.S. Department of Education National Center for Educational Statistics: NCES 99-074. Washington, D.C.: Government Printing Office.

U.S. General Accounting Office (1996). *Content Analysis: A Methodology for Structuring and Analyzing Written Material.* GAO/PEMD-10.3.1. Washington, D.C. (This book can be ordered free from the GAO).

Weber, R. P. (1990). *Basic Content Analysis,* 2nd ed. Newbury Park, CA.

Wheelock, A., Haney, W., & Bebell, D. (2000). What can student drawings tell us about high-stakes testing in Massachusetts? *TCRecord.org.* Available: http//www.tcrecord.org/Content.asp?ContentID=10634.

Psychometrics and African-American Reality: A Question of Cultural Antimony

Wade W. Nobles

The problem of psychological assessment has been the historical arena where controversy and criticism has surfaced as the cutting edge issue relative to the African-American community. From the use of the MMPI to evaluate Black men and women in this country's prisons to the use of I.Q. tests to place Black children in EMR classes to the use of various aptitude tests as "gate keepers" to future access and opportunity, psychometry has been an area of fundamental concern. The overarching issue of what is mental functioning and how it is assessed is, in fact, problematic. Grossman[1] has stated in this regard that the factors which determine mental retardation for instance are developmental lags in intellectual functioning, personal independence and social responsibility. As such, mental retardation is defined as "the condition which exists when there is significantly sub-average general intellectual functioning concurrent with deficits in adaptive behavior." Adaptive behavior, in turn, is defined as "the effectiveness, in degree, with which the individual meets the standards of personal independence and social responsibility expected of one's age and cultural group." Retarded mental functioning would, therefore, be a condition where one possesses sub-average intelligence and fails to meet the cultural expectations of one's group. Psychometrically, the determination of mental retardation would be to measure both one's intelligence and attainment of cultural expectations. How does one however measure the attainment of cultural expectations? For that matter, how does one measure intelligence? The failure to do the latter, (fairly or objectively), in fact, is the major point of confrontation between the discipline of Black Psychology and Western Psychology. The essential point of contention (cf: Hilliard[2]; Kamin[3]; BAABP,[4]) in this confrontation was the recognition and/or denial (depending on which group one finds oneself) that intelligence testing was culture bound and cannot in its natural content and form adequately assess the intelligence of African-American people. The problem, of course, is that psychometry itself is culture bound. The field of mental measurement was in part developed and propagated by people committed to a particular social world view and cultural orientation. Psychometry is not the objective and systematic assessment of various mental dispositions and/or attitudes. Psychometry is a "mega-business complex" bringing together the interest of racist science and capitalist commercial interests. The problem with psychometry is actually found in both its historical development and its contemporary practice.

Reprinted from *Testing African American Students. Special Issues of Negro Educational Review,* edited by Asa G. Hilliard, (1991), by permission of Third World Press.

Psychometry and Western Consciousness

The assault on African people by the misuse of tools of psychometry and racist scientific theories is long standing. As early as the turn of the century, white psychologists and educators were amassing their psychometric armaments to justify the continued oppression of African-American people.

The prevailing intellectual atmosphere was and is shaped by racist thinking and assumptions. In 1956, for example, the prestigious literary magazine, "Putnam's Monthly" published the common thinking of the time wherein an anonymous author noted that,

> "the most minute and the most careful researchers have as yet, failed to discover a history or any knowledge of ancient times among the negro races. They have invented no writing; not even the crude picture-writing of the lowest tribes; they have no gods and no heroes; no epic poems and no legend, not even simple traditions. There never existed among them an organized government; they never ruled a hierarchy or an established church."[5]

This unidentified author goes on to conclude in his argument that the few evidences of African splendor or civilization were borrowed from Europe; and that where there is an African religion or creed or knowledge, customs and progress, they too came from outside of Africa. The African in effect has no history and makes no history. Three decades later, Harvard University's William McDougall indicated from his Ivy league citadel that "a policy of segregation of the colored people of the United States is the only sound one."

The establishment of the inferiority of African and African-American peoples via psychometry assessment immediately replaced the shallow pseudo-religious theories of pre-destiny and Divine curse. The most interesting case of this psychometric propaganda occurred shortly after the 1954 Brown vs. Board of Education decision. In 1958, Professor Audrey M. Shuey at Randolph-Macon College in Virginia published *The Testing of Negro Intelligence* (Shuey, 1958) wherein she reviewed over three hundred original investigations of negro intelligence conducted during the previous five decades. Professor Shuey's intention or purpose as noted by Chase (1980) was to interpret the prevailing psychometric wisdom so as to substantiate her belief (offered as a conclusion) that those mental test scores "all taken together, inevitably point to the presences of native differences between Negroes and Whites as determined by intelligence tests" (pp. 521). Parenthetically, the White Citizens Council in addition to distributing (for the cost of $1.00) dozens of so-called scientific pamphlets and bulletins on race and racial problems (particularly Henry E. Carretts', "Race and Psychology"; "Heredity: The Cause of Racial Differences in Intelligence" and "The Relative Intelligence of Whites and Negroes"), the council also distributed Shuey's work. It should also be noted that Dr. Garrett was the chairman of the Department of Psychology at Columbia University and served consecutive terms as the president of **The Psychometric Society**, the Eastern Psychological Association and the American Psychological Association. Garrett waged his psychometric war on African-American people from the halls of the American Psychological Association to the shores of the Patrick Henry Press. Through this latter publication, Garrett's psychometric propaganda was printed in enormous editions (i.e. 200,000 copies of a 26 page pamphlet on classroom desegregation plus 85,000 copies of the second printing) and purposely distributed to newspaper editors and columnists, teachers, preachers, politicians and "influential citizens" in all of the fifty states. A similar example of psychometric warfare was the publication of Carleton Putnam's, "Race and Reason,"[6] which again documented the low I.Q. scores of Blacks as well as our low income and high crime rates.

The Louisiana State Board of Education purchased 5,000 copies of Race and Reason for use in the schools of Louisiana and a self-appointed group of influential "southern gentlemen" organized the Putnam letters committee to pay for the distribution of the writings, teachings and open letters of Carleton Putnam about the race problem.

It should be noted that the Society for the Psychological Study of Social Issues (SPSSI) openly opposed this type of scientific racism and psychometric warfare. In addition to its 1961 resolution attacking such "scholarship," it also sponsored APA member books with a counter perspective on the problems of race, education and society. One of the most important volumes of this effort was the text, *Social Class, Race and*

Psychological Development edited by Martin Deutsch, Irwin Katz and Arthur Jensen,[7] wherein basic scientific data was offered to support the notion that socio-economic and/or environmental causes were the antecedent to differential learning capacity of the poor and non-poor, Black children and White children. Eight years later, however, one of the above mentioned scholars, Arthur Jensen,[8] openly recanted the "error of his ways" and published in the prestigious Harvard Education Review his new found born-again belief or conviction that at least 80% of the intellectual development of human beings is controlled by the genes they inherit from their parents and that as a unitary trait, intelligence can be measured accurately with I.Q. tests. This born-again psychometric warrior further noted that not only is intelligence at least 80% genetic, but that the different races differ in their racial intelligence quotients.

In this regard, he notes in his book, *Educability and Group Differences*[9] that the possibility of a biochemical connection between skin pigmentation and intelligence is not unlikely in view of the biological relation between melanin and some of the neurotransmitter substances in the brain. In effect, Black skin is related to Black brains which have been psychometrically proven to be inferior to white brains. In addition to Jensen, several highly placed "generals," (Harvard University Professor Richard Hornstein; Stanford University Physics Professor William Shockley[10]), of the psychometric wars emerged and gained national prominence and attention.

The evidence for an undeclared psychometric war on African-Americans is rather clearly explained in Allan Chase's[11] *The Legacy of Malthus.* It is not, however, our task to review this record. The psychological war against African-Americans has been fairly well documented (i.e. Hilliard[12]; Nobles[13]; Guthrie[14]). The ultimate question is why?: Why in relation to African people does science become racist and its tools (i.e. psychometry) weapons?

The answer it seems is found in the historical clash of cultures. If one examines, for instance, the historical contact between Africa and the West, the one outstanding sign having special meaning was the invention of "the Negro." It is extremely important to recognize the concept and meaning of "The Negro" is an entirely different and distinct ideological construct from the image and meaning of the African which proceeded its (the concept of the Negro) inclusion into European consciousness. There is no stretching of the point to note that literally from the beginning of human consciousness to the advent of "the Negro," the relationship between the African and the European had been the opposite of what it is now. The contact between cultures began long before the events of the 15th and 16th century which set into motion the ultimate domination and control of Africa. With the exception of a few minor interruptions Black people or the Africans were feared and respected by Whites or European people. The meaning of the Africans in their (the whites) historical consciousness was associated with high culture, superior civilizations and sophisticated human systems of organization (i.e., law, commerce, family, etc).

From the time of the Ionian philosophers, to the Roman Ascension to the Moorish conquest of the Iberian peninsula, evidence abounds that the Europeans viewed the Blacks with awe and respect. The terms Ethiop, Blackamoor, Nubian and African all represented, in the minds of the European, a culture and people who were superior, dominant and their antagon. The psychological requisite for European domination was therefore the destruction of African civilization and the re-definition of the African. These two conditions are, in fact, the necessary and sufficient condition for European world domination. The European, in effect, had to re-define the African so that we differed in mentality, attitude, function (behavior) and belief from that which allowed us to rule the known world and shape the process of human development. Enter here on the stage of human history the necessity for inventing the concept of "Negro" and the permanent installation of a Judeo-Christian Greco-Roman ideological bases of Western civilization. With the establishment of philosophical doctrines of domination and exploitation like the "Imperium Christianum," "Regnum Europe" or "Societas Christianum," Europe emerged from the Dark Ages committed to a new interpretation of history and human consciousness steeped thoroughly and inextricably in Eurocentrism. The requisite condition for the legitimacy of this Eurocentrism was the destruction of the Afrocentric World and the establishment of the human construct known as "The Negro." Having invented "The Negro," European ascension required that it (the Negro) have meaning which proved European superiority. Hence, the adoption of the belief in the inferiority of African people as the guiding perspective of all Western scholarships as pertaining to the African, now re-classified as the Negro. The ultimate proof of European superiority was, of course, not subjective opinion or personal desire but "scientific fact." It is at this point, as mentioned above, that the queen discipline of human understanding, (i.e. psychology) becomes racist and it's tools of mental measurement (i.e. psychometry) as instrument of falsification, domination and exploitation.

Psychometrics, Paradigms and Paradox: The Question of Cultural Antimony

It is indeed unfortunate that the advent of the disciplines devoted to the study of human development (i.e., psychology, anthropology, etc.) paralleled the establishment of Eurocentricism as a world order. As a consequence of this co-terminal development, the question of what is authentic culture and how do we understand and assess the human experience of other people has undergone continuous confusion, debate and criticism.

The way in which a people view the world or universe is critical, if not fundamental, to all the life-space activities they engage in. A people's conceptual universe not only determines their human capacities (e.g. intelligence), it also guides the development of any new human "inventions." How we define and classify both regular and irregular patterns of social interaction, behavior and development is consequently determined and guided by our conceptual universe. In fact, one could go so far as to say that the meaning of human (social) relationships is both defined and determined by one's conceptual universe.

In terms of science the conceptual universe takes the form of a "paradigm." Technically, this paradigm serves as a formalized framework which guides the assessment and evaluation of reality. At the heart of this issue is the fact that the notion of a conceptual universe has implied in it a more central set of ideas. The centricity (i.e., Eurocentrism) of the conceptual universe gives it a particular focus and/or orientation.

Given the necessities of European world domination it is appropriate to re-note that the central set of ideas in the Eurocentric conceptual universe is the "wished for" and "imagined" inferiority of African people. Accordingly, when the Eurocentric conceptual universe takes the form of a scientific paradigm and serves thereby as an instrument for "knowing" there is a fundamental flaw in its allegiance to the requirement of scientific objectivity as pertaining to non-European people. Parenthetically, it should also be noted that as paradigms are replaced, or more accurately, as the centrality of a particular conceptual universe shifts to a different or new set of ideas, how we define and classify patterns of social interaction and human development, including mental measurement, also change.

In the history of the natural sciences one can best find examples of shifts on the central set of ideas which support a particular conceptual universe. For instance, the change from Ptolemaic to Copernican celestial science really represented a paradigmatic shift in conceptualization. Likewise the reconceptualization of mechanical rebounding to electro-static repulsion is a similar shift in the way of "knowing." These changes in paradigm, accordingly, represent a change in the way one conceives/perceives his universe.

What should be apparent, here, is that in the universe of people, our contemporary world has been viewed as Euro-centered. By that, it is simply meant that the core set of ideas viewed as legitimately representing the human condition were (are) based on a European "view" of the universe. This Euro-centrism thus served as the paradigm for knowing. Since the 15th century, the Euro-centric paradigm, accordingly, has been used to define and classify social interaction and human development. Hence, most, if not all, standards of human behavior and understanding are shaped by this Euro-centric paradigm.

The paradigm, indeed influences and shapes all aspects of the scientific enterprise, including its conceptualizations, methodology and techniques. The more general category of cross-cultural research techniques, for example, utilizes various methods and techniques to test hypotheses about human behavior amongst various peoples throughout the world. The application of cross-cultural methods is supposedly to ensure that one's findings relate to human behavior in general and not just to behavior of a single culture. In effect, the intent of cross-cultural research is to "discover" the universality of human behavior.

When one, however, examines the application of racial and comparative research as examples of cross-cultural research an interesting phenomenon occurs. For the most part, racial and comparative research (especially psychometric comparisons) with African-American populations don't explore the "universality" of behavior. Instead, there is the assumption of the innate inferiority of African people. In fact, one can argue that the racial and comparative method in psychometry rather than test the "theory" of Black intellectual inferiority, actually defends and protects the theory from refutation.[15]

The problems associated with cross-cultural research are found in the notion of the "equivalence of culture" which in turn raises questions regarding the "equivalence of meaning," for the variables, subject status, conceptualization, measurements, sampling, analyses and interpretation. If the meaning (and experience) of intelligence, for instance, differs between two cultures then the results of the psychometric assessment of intelligence would in fact be meaningless.

According to Whiting, the acquisition of meaningful information in cross-cultural research depends on the researcher's ability to maximize cultural homogeneity within one's definition of study case. He argues in this regard that to ensure that the local community units are reasonably equivalent with respect to homogeneity, they should ideally have features which serve to reduce the variability of both individual behavior and the cultural beliefs, values and techniques held by the community members. Accordingly, he suggests that comparative units should have the following factors: (1) members have frequent face-to-face contact with one another; (2) they speak the same dialect; (3) they have some degree of sovereignty; and (4) they have a group name.

There are of course two problems with Whiting's criterion for cross-cultural research. The primary and most important flaw is that this strategy is designed so as to minimize cultural differences. The explication of cultural differences for the purpose of establishing universals is really the only valid reason for doing cross-cultural research. Unless of course one is doing mono-cultural research with the intent of demonstrating how deviant one culture is from another (standard) culture. This is not cross-cultural research. The second flaw is that the criteria are really designed to maximize "between" cultural homogeneity. It doesn't, therefore, address the problem of conceptual equivalence between two distinct cultural groups. If one could, nevertheless, identify a culturally homogeneous Black and White group utilizing Whiting's criteria, one would still have remaining, the problem of "stimuli relevance," "comparability of response" and "differential meanings".

Consistent with Whiting's notion, in psychometric assessment the task is, therefore, to maximize cultural homogeneity by minimizing the importance and integrity of race. This occurs most often by classifying race as a "status variable" whose importance in the research process is that status variables need to be controlled, randomized or held constant so that their effects are neutralized, cancelled out or equated for all conditions.[16]

The essential crises of psychometry, of course, is found in the difficulty it has in appropriately defining human intelligence or mental attitudes which are consistent with the cultural meanings of both human communities. It is, therefore, within the realm of culture, that the crises and critical flaw of racial and comparative research, particularly psychometric assessment is found.

In recognition, therefore, that the goal of science is to "understand" and not singularly or only to predict and control phenomena, the task of scientific inquiry is to ultimately establish general laws about human phenomena, which, in turn, serve as instruments for systematic explanation, and provide the basis for dependable prediction. Scientific inquiry and method are, nevertheless, idiosyncratic to a people's cultural deep structure.

In effect, the program in psychometrics is that rather than establish the universality of mental functioning between Black and White people; it, by its very nature, denies the cultural integrity of Black people and thereby fails to explicate the binding cultural laws within each group which is the basis of human mental functioning and which may serve as the key to understanding the universality of human mentalities.

Racial and comparative methods, as currently utilized, are idiosyncratic to the laws and assumptions of primarily Euro-American culture. Hence, if we are to elevate the assessment of Black mental functioning to more than a "tinted reflection" of White mental functioning we must start with a theoretical and empirical framework which is capable of reducing the elements of

Black reality into intellectually manageable properties without compromising the historical truths and cultural principles of African and African-American people.

A Paradox is a statement or tenet which is discordant with what is held to be established belief. Scientific Paradox would, therefore, be those conceptualizations, data and findings which are contrary to established opinion and belief. Even when or especially when the belief or opinion are unstated. Antimony is a contradiction in a law or a contradiction between two binding laws.[17] Culture, as the process which gives a people a general design for living and patterns for interpreting their reality, implies that there are cultural laws (guiding principles) which are consistent with the requirements of the people's cultural deep structure. Accordingly, the "cultural laws" of two different groups can and often are in contradistinction. When the cultural substance or deep structure between two or more cultures stands in contradistinction of each other, it can result in contradiction in their respective meanings of reality. This contradiction of meaning results in a state of "Cultural Antimony."

In effect, the Eurocentric cultural paradigm or the Eurocentric formalized framework which guides the assessment and evaluation of reality stands in contradistinction of the cultural laws which are consistent with the cultural deep structure of African people. The specific cultural Antimony (i.e., contradiction in law or between two laws) is in the assumed white superiority. Keep in mind that up until the 15th century, the cultural law, embedded in the historical consciousness of European people, was the acceptance of African grandeur and superiority. The advent of the construct "Negro" with all its connotations of inferiority, savagery, unholy and uncivilized represents in fact and deed a contradiction in the European historical consciousness.

The Euro-American belief (now presented as objective scientific findings) about African and African-American "inferiority" stands in contradistinction with the belief about African "superiority" which is found in European historical consciousness. The fact that the European community set about to develop scientific theories about Black inferiority and methods (i.e. psychometry) to defend those theories from repetition does not change the state of antimony.

The technical criticism of psychometry has ranged from issues and concerns involving (1) the misuse (or more properly, the political use) of testing; (2) the technical weakness associated with test reliability, objectivity, validity and standardization; (3) the guiding assumption of test construction models (i.e., deficit vs. difference, heterogeneity vs. homogeneity); and (4) the educational, legal and economic implications/applications of test data. Each and every one of these concerns points to serious problems in psychometry. The source of these problems, however, lie in or can be traced to the perceived necessity to verify the falsification of the historical presence and position of African people in relation to Europeans. Cultural antimony, understandably, complicates the comprehension of the problem. With the continued uncritical use of psychometric methods and theories one can, in effect, make the phenomena equal to what the test is capable of measuring about the phenomena. By this is meant, that without knowing the meaning given to mental functioning which is consistent with the cultural laws of African and African-American reality, one can mistakenly settle for or accept a meaning of African-American mental functioning which is only that which is taped or measured by the existing psychometric instrumentation and/or techniques. Hence, or accordingly, the tools of psychometrics can become the ultimate instrument for delimiting the meaning and definition of African and African-American mental functioning.

It will be critical for the field of mental measurement that as African-American scholars as well as the better trained Euro-American scholars engage in the continued debate surrounding psychometry and African-American reality that we understand that the real source of the problem is to be found in the historical "clash of minds" and confrontation between African and European cultures. If, in effect, psychometry is to become a tool of mental measurement which assesses the universality of mental functioning (which parenthetically, given the centrality of culture in determining human meaning may be an impossibility) then the field psychometry must free itself from the legacy of the subtle and sublime as well as the overt and intentional European obsession with justifying its own superiority.

Notes

1. Grossman, H. J. (ed.). *Manual on Terminology and Classification in Mental Retardation.* American Association on Mental Deficiency, (Special Publication No. 2) Washington, D.C. 1977.
2. Hilliard, Asa G., III. "Alternatives to I.Q. Testing: An Approach to the Identification of 'Gifted' Minority Children." *Final Report.* California State Department of Education, Special Education Support Unit. Eric Clearinghouse of Early Childhood Education, 146-009, 1976.
3. Kamin, Leon J. *The Science of Politics of I.Q.* Potomac, Maryland: Lawrence Erlbaum Associates, 1979.
4. Bay Area Association of Black Psychologists. "Position Statement on the Use of I.Q. and Ability Tests" in Reginald Jones (ed) *Black Psychology.* Harper & Row Publishers, New York, 1972.
5. Putnam's Monthly, "Uncle Tom at Home" (anonymous contributor) Vol. VIII, No. XLIII, July, 1956, pp. 4–5.
6. Putnam, Carleton, *Race and Reason: A Yankee View.* Washington, D.C.: Public Affairs Press, 1961.
7. Deutsch, M., I. Katz and A. R. Jensen (eds.). *Social Class, Race and Psychological Development.* New York: Holt, Rhinehart and Winston, Inc. 1968.
8. Jensen, Arthur. "How Much Can We Boost I.Q. and Scholastic Achievement", *Harvard Educational Review,* 39 (1), 1969.
9. Jensen, Arthur. *Educability and Group Differences.* New York: Harper & Row, 1973.
10. Shuey, Audrey M. *The Testing of Negro Intelligence.* 2nd ed.; New York: Social Science Press, 1966.
11. Chase, Allan. *The Legacy of Malthus: The Social Cost of The New Scientific Racism.* University of Illinois Press, Chicago, 1980.
12. Hilliard, Asa G. III. "I.Q. Thinking as the Emperor's New Clothes: A Critique of Jensen's Bias in Mental Testing" in Cecil Reynolds (ed). *Perspectives on Bias in Mental Testing.* Plenum Press, 1982.
13. Nobles, Wade W., et al. "Critical Analysis of Scholarship on Black Family Life," United Church of Christ Commission for Racial Justice, *Final Report,* Washington, D.C. 1983.
14. Guthrie, Robert V. *Even the Rat was White.* Harper & Row Publishers, New York, 1976.
15. Banks, Curtis W. "Deconstructive Falsification: Foundations of Critical Method in Black Psychology" in Enrico Jones & Sheldon Korchin (eds.), *Minority Mental Health,* New York; Peneger Press, 1982.
16. Issac, Stephen and Michael B. William. *Handbook in Research and Evaluation,* Edits Publishers, San Diego, 1971.
17. Nobles, Wade W. "Paradym, Paradox and Power: The Dilemma of States in Racial and Comparative Research," Paper presented to the Institute for Urban Affairs and Research, Conference on Racial and Comparative Research, Howard University, Washington, D.C., Oct. 17 & 18, 1985.

REPLICATION: A DESIGN PRINCIPLE FOR FIELD RESEARCH

WILLIAM D. SCHAFER

University of Maryland

This article suggests the routine use of replications in field studies. Since replications are generally independent, it is usually possible to synthesize them quantitatively using meta-analysis, a technique heretofore associated primarily with amalgamating prior work. It is argued that the use of replication as a feature in data collection and quantitative synthesis for data analysis is especially attractive for those investigators whose research paradigm choices are limited because they are working in field environments. Two examples are described briefly.

Control of extraneous variables is a fundamental condition to causal interpretations of research (Johnson, 2001). Randomization of participants to treatment conditions has long been considered a powerful method of control, so much so that this is the distinguishing characteristic between true experimental and other types of research (Campbell & Stanley, 1963). When a researcher uses randomization, it is clear that the basis upon which participants receive treatment conditions is unrelated except by chance to any variable that can be confounded with the treatments.

A great deal of research is done in field settings in education. State-level or district-based researchers, for example, are often interested in practical interventions that can occur naturally in schools. However, randomization is typically unavailable to those who work in field settings because the investigator is not able to manipulate treatment conditions at the level of the individual participant. This often arises because institutions such as schools are reluctant to move participants (e.g., students) from group to group (e.g., class to class) or otherwise assign them to groups according to researcher needs. Similarly, it may not be possible even to determine randomly which group receives which treatment condition, that being decided through other means, such as teacher choice.

Failing randomization, one approach used in the field is to measure extraneous variables and employ statistical control (e.g., analysis of covariance). Pedhazur (1997) describes three common contexts for statistical control with intact groups: attempting to equate them on the outcome variable(s) using one or more pretest(s), attempting to control for other variable(s) in looking at mean differences, and attempting to control for other variable(s) in looking at differences in regressions. He points out that these are usually invalid uses of analysis of covariance.

Because statistical procedures are generally less effective than experimental control, theoretical inferences about relationships observed in field settings are often subject to multiple reasonable internal validity threats. And in many cases it is not even possible to measure extraneous variables effectively, such as when limited time is available, when the number of participants in the research is limited, or when the measurement is too intrusive. Johnson (2001) has recently concluded that there is little that can be gained from a single, non-experimental research study. A feasible alternative that can enhance the ability of field investigators to draw causal inferences in field settings clearly would be an advantage.

In field contexts, there are typically many opportunities available to investigators that are not open to researchers in more controlled settings. Laboratory researchers commonly have small pools of potential participants to select from and may need to expend nontrivial resources to obtain their cooperation. On the other hand, in applied settings such as classrooms and schools, and especially for employees of the institution, students or other participants are often generously available as long as the intrusion of the research is minimal. Many investigators in the field thus have broad feasible research opportunities that laboratory researchers do not enjoy. It is therefore possible in common applied research settings to be able to repeat, or replicate, a study design more than once.

It is argued here that careful planning of replications can enhance the interpretability of applied research. When results are consistent across several studies, there is a stronger basis for observed relationship(s) than the support that is available within each study by itself, since results that have been replicated are considered more likely to generalize (continue to be observed). It is also possible to compare the studies with each other to identify constructs that interact with, or moderate, relationships. Although these advantages exist whether or not the research includes experimental control, the opportunity to replicate a basic study design in multiple field contexts is more likely to be available to the applied researcher and is a technique that can lead to stronger inferences in any setting. Thus, it is recommended that persons who conduct field research try to include replication as a fundamental feature in their studies.

The analysis of the several studies' results should also be addressed. Meta-analysis is an attractive vehicle for combining, or synthesizing, a series of research replications. Although meta-analysis is generally thought of as a means for studying an existing research literature quantitatively, it also may be used to analyze a series of related studies generated within a single project.

In the remainder of this article, pertinent features of meta-analysis are discussed briefly and then two examples are described in which multiple replications of a basic field design have been analyzed using meta-analysis to strengthen the evidence available. The basic designs differ markedly in the two examples. Finally, some design approaches for applied researchers thinking about using replications are discussed.

Meta-Analysis

Meta-analysis is commonly used to synthesize the findings of multiple, but related, research studies. Those who are unfamiliar with meta-analysis can find a brief overview along with a completely analyzed example in Schafer (1999). More extensive discussions on a broad array of topics pertinent to meta-analysis are widely available in Hedges & Olkin (1985) and Cooper & Hedges (1994).

Fundamental to meta-analysis is an effect-size measure calculated within a study. An effect-size measure may be used to compare two groups or to relate two variables. For example, the difference between two group means divided by the pooled standard deviation of the two groups in a study might be the effect-size measure [when adjusted for bias, this is Hedges & Olkin's (1985) d index]. Another might be the correlation between two variables in a study. In general, to be used in a meta-analysis, an effect-size measure must be capable of transformation to a normally distributed statistic with a known variance. Under reasonable assumptions, both the examples here are appropriate.

Techniques are described in the cited sources that allow a researcher to model the size of the effect (the effect-size index) as a result of study characteristics. That is, equations may be written, as in multiple regression, for relationships between study characteristics as predictors and an effect-size index as the criterion. These study characteristics may be descriptive of the participants, of the settings, of the treatment implementations, or of the outcome variables; in other words, virtually anything that can differentiate studies from each other can be used in the analysis as study characteristics.

In one typical approach to meta-analysis, an effect-size index is calculated for each study. The suitably weighted average of the effect sizes is tested against a null hypothesis of zero. Variation of the studies' effect sizes about the average is tested to determine whether it is at a greater-than-chance level and, if it is, then a study characteristic may be entered into a model (equation), so that effect size is then predicted as the sum of a constant (intercept) and a study characteristic scaled with (multiplied by) a slope estimate. The slope estimate is tested against the null hypothesis of zero. The variance of the effect sizes about the model (the residuals) is compared with the chance level. If homogeneity (chance-level variance) is achieved, modeling ceases; otherwise further study characteristics are added to the model. Of course, variations exist, some as solutions to special problems that may arise; only a very (over) simplified treatment is described here.

Example 1: Descriptive Gains for Schools

A descriptive, or non-experimental, design is one in which there is no manipulation of treatments. The research problem studied in Guthrie, Schafer, Von Secker, & Alban (2000) was the relationships between instructional characteristics of schools and the variation they showed in their degrees of gain or loss in student achievement over a year's time (growth). The effect-size index was the bias-corrected difference between school means at a target grade level between year one and year two on a statewide, standardized test, divided by the pooled standard deviation for the two years. The indexes were scaled so a positive difference showed improvement. The study was replicated in all six tested content areas at both tested grade levels in all 33 schools in three volunteer districts for a total of 396 effect sizes.

The independent variables in the meta-analysis were school means for teacher-reports of emphasis devoted to different approaches in reading instruction. All teachers in each school were surveyed on a questionnaire with six subscales that had been developed through factor analysis using data from a fourth volunteer district in an earlier study.

The meta-analyses were used to evaluate the association of the set of six instructional variables to achievement growth, of each variable individually to growth, and of each variable as a unique predictor of growth in a six-predictor model. The six content areas at each of the grade levels were analyzed separately. The results of the syntheses were interpretable and generally consistent with an extensive literature review for these variables.

Although it is statistically possible to compare the two years of data for any one school, that single finding by itself would not have been remarkable. While the school might have developed instructional hypotheses for the direction and degree of growth observed, there would have been far too many plausible competing explanations for the difference, such as teacher turnover, test form calibrations, and student aptitude, for example. While the replicated study cannot entirely substitute for experimental control through randomization, the plausibility of at least some of the rival explanations is decreased if instructional explanations can be observed across replications, as they were in this example study. Indeed, only by replicating the fundamental growth-study design was it possible to study the instructional characteristics of the schools as variables used to explain differences among gains across schools.

Example 2: Static Group Comparisons

A static group comparison design is one in which intact groups are randomly assigned to treatments (Campbell & Stanley, 1963). Schafer, Swanson, Bené, & Newberry (2001) studied the effects on student achievement of a treatment consisting of a workshop for high school teachers centering on an instructional method (use of rubrics). Districts nominated teacher pairs within content areas, with the classes for the two members of a given pair chosen to consist of students with similar abilities. There were 46 teacher pairs who provided complete data, evenly divided among four instructional content areas (92 teachers and 3,191 students supplied useable data in the study).

The two teachers in each pair were randomly assigned by coin flip to treatment or control conditions. The treatment, attended by one teacher from each pair, was the experimental manipulation. At the end of the study's duration, each student received a test consisting of two parts, a selected-response section and a constructed-response section. The nature of the study suggested that these two parts might yield different results and so effect sizes were calculated separately for each of the item formats. Each effect size was the difference between the means of the two classes divided by the pooled standard deviation and scaled such that a positive effect size favored the treatment.

This study was part of a larger study that required more than one form of the test. Accordingly, there were three forms in each content area. They were distributed randomly in each classroom, yielding six effect sizes (two formats on each of three forms) for each of the 46 teacher pairs, or 276 effect sizes across the four content areas.

Although there were six non-equated test forms in each of four distinct content areas, it was possible to synthesize the results of these disparate conditions in one analysis and to differentiate the findings in a planned way by contents and by forms. An interpretable pattern of outcomes was obtained and related to prior literature.

In general, there are too many competing plausible rival explanations for observed achievement differences between the two intact groups for this study's single-replicate design, in isolation, to be interesting as evidence for a difference between the instructional methods. But by using replications it was possible to synthesize findings from multiple parallel studies and thus to enhance the ability to draw inferences from the overall results.

Discussion

Consistent with Johnson's (2001) suggestions for strengthening interpretations of causality from non-experimental research, this article has recommended planning replications in field settings. The examples illustrate ways in which these replicated field designs can be synthesized to enhance the inferences that can be drawn from them. Further, when planned replications are used, it is possible also to plan for the measurement of variables that should prove useful to model effect sizes in a meta-analysis (e.g., the instructional variables in example 1). Fortunately for the researcher, a meta-analysis based on planned replications is far more straightforward to implement than a traditional synthesis of a disparate literature since fewer challenges, such as design differences, inadequate information, and inconsistent reporting of results across studies, exist.

An investigator planning to use replications in field research must make several decisions. Some of these are discussed below.

The basic design. The stronger the basic design, the stronger the inferences that may be made from any one replicate, and thus from the overall meta-analysis. The strongest feasible design should be chosen. Cook and Campbell (1979) provide an overview of designs that are particularly suitable in applied research contexts and discuss their strengths and weaknesses. It is important to be very clear what variable is independent and what is dependent in the basic design. In the two examples here, the independent variable was time (year 1 vs. year 2) in the first and presence or absence of the instruction workshop in the second. In both, the dependent variable was achievement. While year could not be manipulated in the first (the basic design was non-experimental), it was possible to manipulate the workshop in the second. Random assignment of instructors to workshop conditions strengthened that study [the basic design was pre-experimental (Campbell & Stanley, 1963)].

The effect-size measure. Magnitude of effect should be capable of coding as a standardized measure indicating direction and strength of relationship between the independent and dependent variables. Its quantification should yield an index that is normally distributed and has a known or estimatable variance. Rosenthal (1994) provides a menu of possibilities. Three common examples that differ depending on the scaling of the two variables are: both continuous (the correlation coefficient, r); both dichotomous (the log-odds ratio, L); or, as in the two examples here, the independent variable a dichotomy but the dependent variable continuous (bias-corrected d, discussed above).

Maintaining effect-size independence. The effect sizes are assumed to be independent in a meta-analysis. That is generally the case across studies, but is not always true within studies. In our two examples, each study produced several dependent effect-size indices. Dependencies created by the measurement of six content areas in each school were ignored in the first study by analyzing each grade level and content area separately; in the second study, the six tests were analyzed together at first and a Bonferroni-like correction was applied throughout the analyses (Gleser & Olkin, 1994). Of course, care should be taken in field studies that the sites at which the replications occur maintain separation; sharing of information by participants across replications can threaten effect-size independence.

The variables to be measured. Besides the independent and dependent variables, it is advantageous to capitalize on the opportunity to measure variables that could be related to effect size (study characteristics). To generate a list of these, the researcher might consider how he or she might explain any observed differences that could appear among effect sizes across replicates. Whether substantive or artifactual, those explanations virtually always will be based on variables that should, if possible, be measured. These could be different contexts and dependent variables as in our second example in which effect sizes yielded by four different content areas and two test formats were combined into one meta-analysis. Or they may be descriptive of persons, such as demographics or aptitudes, or settings such as physical features in schools or classrooms. Coding characteristics of the replications that produced the different effect sizes provides data that are analyzed through relating these characteristics as independent variables to the effect sizes as dependent variables in the meta-analysis. The potential for assessing study differences that may be related to magnitude of effect represents an opportunity for creativity in designing robust multiple-study investigations through replication.

Meta-analysis is a relatively new approach to data analysis and the field is changing rapidly. One recent advance has been development of effective methods to conduct random-effects model analyses. Hedges & Vivea (1998) present a straightforward and relatively simple modification that is consistent with the techniques used in the two examples cited here. They also provide a worked example. An advantage of using a random model is that the results generalize to a population of studies not included in the present analysis, whereas in the two examples described here, the conclusions were restricted to the specific replications themselves. Hedges & Vivea (1998) discuss the conditions under which each type of analysis, fixed or random, is more appropriate.

References

Campbell, D. T., & Stanley, J. C. (1963). Experimental and quasi-experimental designs for research on teaching. In N.L. Gage (Ed.), *Handbook of research on teaching* (pp. 171–246). Chicago: Rand McNally.

Cook, T. D., & Campbell, D. T. (1979). *Quasi-experimentation: Design & analysis issues for field settings.* Chicago: Rand McNally.

Cooper, H., & Hedges, L. V. (1994). *The handbook of research synthesis.* New York: Sage.

Gleser, L. J., & Olkin, I. (1994). Stochastically dependent effect sizes. In H. Cooper & L. V. Hedges (Eds.), *The handbook of research synthesis* (pp. 339–355). New York: Sage.

Guthrie, J. T., Schafer, W. D., Von Secker, C., & Alban, T. (2000). Contributions of instructional practices to reading achievement in a statewide improvement program. *Journal of Educational Research, 93,* 211–225.

Hedges, L. V., & Olkin, I. (1985). *Statistical methods for meta-analysis.* Orlando, FL: Academic Press.

Hedges, L. V., & Vivea, J. (1998). Fixed-and random-effects models in meta-analysis. *Psychological Methods, 3,* 486–504.

Johnson, B. (2001). Toward a new classification of nonexperimental quantitative research. *Educational Researcher, 30*(2), 3–13.

Pedhazur, E. J. (1997). *Multiple regression in behavioral research: Explanation and prediction* (3rd Ed.). Orlando, FL: Harcourt Brace.

Rosenthal, R. (1994). Parametric measures of effect size. In H. Cooper & L. V. Hedges (Eds.), *The handbook of research synthesis* (pp. 231–244). New York: Sage.

Schafer, W. D. (1999). An overview of meta-analysis. *Measurement and Evaluation in Counseling and Development, 32,* 43–61.

Schafer, W. D., Swanson, G., Bené, N., & Newberry, G. (2001). Effects of teacher knowledge of rubrics on student achievement in four content areas. *Applied Measurement in Education, 14,* 151–170.

RECOMMENDED READINGS

Bickman, Leonard and Rog, Debra J. eds. (1998). *Handbook of Applied Social Research Methods.* Sage: Thousand Oaks.

Costello, Ronald W. and Cox, Marge (2000). Putting scholastic aptitude test results on an even playing field. ED447151.

Dey, Eric L. (1997). Working with low survey response rates: the efficacy of weighting adjustments. Research in Higher Education. v38 n2 pp. 215-217.

Dillman, Don A. (2000). Mail and Internet Surveys: The Tailored Design Method. Second Edition. John Wiley & Sons, Inc.: New York.

Ewell, Peter (2001). Statewide testing in higher education. *Change,* v. 33 n2 pp. 20-27. Mar-Apr.

Hambleton, Ronald and Rodgers, Jane H. (1995). Item bias review. *Practical Assessment, Research & Evaluation.* 4(6). Available online: http://ericae.net/pare/getvn.asp?v=4&n=6.

Hilliard, Asa G. (ed. 1995). *Testing African American Students. Special Issue of the Negro Educational Review.* Third World Press: Chicago.

Hood, Stafford and Johnson, Sylvia T. (eds. 1998). *The Journal of Negro Education,* v.67, n3. Summer 1998.

House, J. Daniel (1998). Gender differences in prediction of graduate course performance from admissions test scores: an empirical example of statistical methods for investigating prediction bias. Paper presented at AIE Annual Forum. ED424810.

Jalomo, Romero, Jr. (2000). Assessing minority student performance. *New Directions for Community Colleges.* v28 n4, pp. 7-18.

Kobayashi, Miyoko (2002). Method effects on Reading comprehension Test Performance: Text organization and response format. *Language Testing* v19, n2. pp.193-220.

Mark, Melvin M. Feller, Irwin and Button, Scott B. (1997). Integrating qualitative methods in a predominantly quantitative evaluation: A case study and some reflections. *New Directions for Evaluation* n74 pp. 47-59.

Messick, Samuel J. (ed. 1999). Assessment in *Higher Education: Issues of Access, Quality, Student Development and Public Policy.* Lawrence Erlbaum: Nahwah, New Jersey.

Miller, Allen H., Bradford, W. Imrie and Cox, Kevin (1998). Evaluation of assessment procedures. In Miller, Allen H., Bradford, W. Imrie and Cox, Kevin (1998). *Student Assessment in Higher Education.* Kogan Page: London, England. (pages 225-240/282)

Morgan, George A. and Gliner, Jeffrey A. (1997). Helping students to evaluate the validity of a research study. Paper presented at the annual meeting of the American Educational research Association. Chicago, IL ED408349

Rossi, Peter H. (1997). Advances in quantitative evaluation, 1987-1996. *New Directions for Evaluation* n76 pp. 57-68.

Wang, Huiming, Grimes, Judith Wilson (2001). A systematic approach to assessing retention programs: identifying critical points for meaningful interventions and validating outcomes assessment. *Journal of College Student Retention,* v2 n1 pp. 59-68.

Willingham, Warren W. (1999). A systemic view of test fairness. In Messick, Samuel J. (ed. 1999). *Assessment in Higher Education: Issues of Access, Quality, Student Development and Public Policy*. Lawrence Erlbaum: Nahwah, New Jersey. (pages 213-242/261).

Willingham, Warren W, and Cole, Nancy (1997). Gender and fair assessment. ED416293.